Richard
Schmidt

Introduction to Psychology

Introduction to
Psychology
Second Edition

Rod Plotnik
San Diego State University

RANDOM HOUSE
NEW YORK

Second Edition
987654321
Copyright © 1986, 1989 by Newbery Award Records, Inc.

Library of Congress Cataloging-in-Publication Data

Plotnik, Rod.
    Introduction to psychology / Rod Plotnik.
      —2nd ed.
      p.   cm.
    Bibliography: p.
    Includes indexes.
    ISBN 0-394-38336-2
    1. Psychology.   I. Title.
BF121.P626   1989
150—dc   19   88-32175 CIP

Manufactured in the United States of America

Book design: John Lennard
Cover design: John Lennard
Cover illustration: Jerry McDaniel
Cartoon drawings, Chapters 7, 8, 16: Dick Maccabe

To the Instructor

When I began to supervise a group of student teachers, I began to think about writing an introductory psychology text. Every two weeks we would meet to discuss problems we were having with the introductory psychology course. These discussions ranged from specific questions like "What is the clearest way to distinguish operant from classical conditioning?" to broad issues like "How can we motivate, challenge, and involve students?" Years of biweekly meetings made clear that some of our problems came from our teaching techniques and some came from the textbooks we were using. We developed a videotape feedback program to help us improve our teaching techniques. And we tried various textbooks, hoping to find one that would have all the features we were looking for.

We wanted a text that would provide a solid, up-to-date survey of the major theories, research, and findings in the field of psychology. We also wanted a text that would present the material in a way that was challenging and motivating to the student. Finally, the text had to help students master the material, not just learn it existed. After much discussion, we agreed upon four basic features:

What features would an ideal introductory text have?

- The material should be divided into small units for easy mastery.

- Major theories, findings, and concepts should be highlighted and tested.

- Cases, examples, and applications should be used throughout just like text, not considered separate in any way, to keep student interest, involvement, and motivation high.

- Challenging tasks should show the student how well he or she has mastered the material.

We were convinced that a text with these features would make it much easier for us to teach, and much easier for our students to learn. When we tried to translate our ideas into an actual book, the result was this text, which we have refined even more in this second edition, and which we hope comes even closer to our ideal than the first.

As you examine this edition, you will notice that each of the features serves a specific function, and that together they produce an integrated learning experience.

WHAT'S SO SPECIAL: FEATURES OF THE TEXT

The Modular Approach

Students made it very clear that they preferred short chapters; they reported that short chapters made the material more manageable, helped retain interest, and gave them a feeling of accomplishment. Research on the Personalized System of Instruction (PSI) also indicates that material is best presented in small, cohesive units. So each chapter of this text is divided

What's the advantage of the modular approach?

into two, three, and occasionally four *Modules* of about ten book pages each. Each module is a self-contained unit, with a full complement of teaching aids. Students will therefore feel a real sense of mastery when they finish a unit.

The modular approach also means that the instructor has unique flexibility in planning and personalizing a course. You have the option of assigning or deleting material by using a selection of modules or following the traditional chapter headings and sequence. For example, if you wanted to cover a traditional topic, such as biological bases of behavior, you could assign Chapter 2. If you wanted to cover only the basic structure and function of the nervous system, you could assign just Module 5. If you wanted to cover the topic of perception in the traditional way, you would assign Chapter 4. If you wanted to cover just basic perceptual processes, you could assign Module 10.

Major Concepts

How do students know what's important?

Within the text of each module, a short self-test on the material follows a discussion of major ideas or psychological principles. This feature, called *Major Concept*, consists of true-false, multiple-choice, matching, or fill-in-the blank questions that help students identify and learn main points. Each module contains two to four such self-tests.

Current Research Directions

Why are important research findings so hard to understand?

Like most instructors, we wanted students to have a basic understanding of how psychologists use research to answer questions, and how they decide what questions to answer. Most students are discouraged by detailed research reports. Our solution was a feature we call *Exploring Psychology*. It presents a short, interesting summary of major research findings. Almost every module contains an Exploring Psychology section.

Psychology in Everyday Life

Can anything be done for my insomnia?
What are some good ways to handle stress?

Students also want answers to their own real life problems. We realized that another way to maintain interest and motivation was to provide answers to practical questions using the results of research in a simple, interesting way. We called this feature *Applying Psychology*, and we provide one or two in most modules, integrated with the text.

Margin Questions, Vignettes, Case Studies

Why do real life examples work so well?

Student interest and motivation always seem to increase when the instructor uses examples, describes cases, or asks interesting questions. We decided to take advantage of these interest boosters by including them as features of the text. *Vignettes* and *cases* throughout each module introduce a psychological principle or concept in a real context and through a focus on the actual experiences of an individual. *Margin Questions* pique interest or signal important points.

Glossary and Review

I underlined all the important points; so why didn't I get a good grade on the exam?

Key terms are highlighted by boldface throughout the text and are listed again, with the pages on which they appear, at the end of each module. (Definitions appear again in the *Glossary* at the end of the book.) This aid to mastery follows a fill-in-the blank self-test section, the *Review*, which takes the place of the traditional summary. The Review tests for recall of important concepts in the module and allows students to see how well they have learned these concepts. Just as important, the Review encourages students to think by having them generalize the newly learned concepts to new situations.

WHAT'S NEW: SPECIAL FEATURES OF THE SECOND EDITION

A Bright New Four-Color Design

Text and features have been given a new look: a new design helps make concepts in the text easier to grasp, and new four-color art and photographs make learning from these features not only easier, but much more pleasant. Color is used throughout to set off the features and make them more accessible to the student. And chapter openings feature a chapter Contents, divided by Module, so the student gets an immediate preview/overview of the material.

Reorganization

The first edition's 60 modules have been reorganized in this edition into 53 modules to provide more continuity in the material. For example, Chapter 6, Learning, and Chapter 7, Remembering and Forgetting, were changed from three modules each in the first edition to two modules each in the second. Chapter 9, Motivation and Emotion, and Chapter 10, Human Sexual Behavior, were changed from four modules each to three.

The Latest Research

The references have been thoroughly revised and updated to give students access to the best and latest research results: 350 references have been added to this edition, and over 120 of them have been published since 1987.

New and Rewritten Modules

Many modules have been rewritten, and new material has been added. Here are some examples:

Module 25: Emotion. Includes new research on classifying emotions, the sequence for expression of emotions, as well as the functions emotions serve.

Module 35: Trait Approach. Presents the latest findings on identifying and classifying personality traits, plus the most recent information on the contributions of heredity and environment from the Minnesota studies comparing identical and fraternal twins.

Module 36: Freud's Psychodynamic Approach. Presents Freud's theory and concepts in great detail and depth.

Module 37: Social-Cognitive and Humanistic Approaches. Martin Luther King's life is used to illustrate the concepts in this module, and the humanistic approach is expanded by new material on Abraham Maslow.

Module 41: Coping. Presents the latest information on ways of coping, such as managing emotions and managing the task; includes as well a revised Stress Management Program.

Module 51: Aggression. Includes new research on the stability of aggression, a section on sexual aggression and a program to control aggressive behavior.

New/More Applying and Exploring Psychology Sections

Each Exploring Psychology section gives students an in-depth look at new and exciting areas of research. In this edition, there are 18 new Exploring Psychology sections:

Module 4   Effects of Alzheimer's Disease
Module 6   Recovery from Stroke
Module 7   Neurons Recognize Faces
Module 10   Making Movies Move
Module 12   Experimenting with Psi
Module 13   Control of Sleep
Module 15   Risk Factors for Alcoholism
Module 20   Intelligence and IQ Scores
Module 22   Chimpanzees Speaking
Module 24   Causes of Overeating, Overweight, and Obesity
Module 25   Which Comes First, Feeling or Thinking?
Module 26   Prenatal Hormones, Sex Role, and Sexual Orientation
Module 27   AIDS
Module 33   Getting Married
Module 35   Twins and Traits, Heredity and Environment
Module 40   Personality and Illness
Module 43   Causes of Depression
Module 44   Causes of Schizophrenia

The Applying Psychology feature shows students how psychological principles are applied in real-life situations. Here is a list of the 20 new *Applying Psychology* sections in the second edition:

Module 1   Careers in Psychology
Module 3   How to Study
Module 4   Use of Brain Transplants
Module 6   Psychological Treatment for Brain Damage
Module 9   Treatment of Pain
Module 11   Recognizing Faces
Module 12   Understanding Backward Messages
Module 14   Hypnosis as Therapy
Module 15   Treatment for Drug Abuse
Module 16   Conditioned Nausea and Treatment
Module 17   Treatment of Autistic Children
Module 18   Mood Affects Memory
Module 21   How We Make Decisions
Module 25   Staying Happy
Module 27   What Is Love?
Module 37   Dealing with Loneliness
Module 41   Stress Management Program
Module 42   Treatment of Agoraphobia
Module 43   Dealing with Mild Depression
Module 51   Programs to Control Aggressive Behavior

WHAT ELSE DOES THIS BOOK HAVE? ANCILLARIES

In this edition, I have been involved in writing the major supplements.

The STUDENT ORGANIZER AND SELF TESTING BOOK, written with Gary Poole of Simon Fraser University, helps students get the most out of the text by creating a study program based on SQ3R. It includes chapter summaries, checklists, exercises, and multiple choice questions. New to this edition are sections for the ESL student.

The INSTRUCTOR'S RESOURCE MANUAL AND TEST BANK, by Rod Plotnik, Gary Poole of Simon Fraser University, Marie Thomas of the College of Mount St. Vincent, and Paul Rosenfeld of the Navy Personnel Research and Development Center, is organized separately by chapter and module. These supplements allow instructors to create a personal arrangement of teaching materials. The INSTRUCTOR'S RESOURCE MANUAL features a new step-by-step system of presenting course material that is fully integrated with lectures, classroom demonstrations, transparencies, slides, self-test, handouts, films, and videos. A special feature is essays that discuss ways to teach introductory psychology and use PSI. This is a system that will help you easily bring the most to your teaching environment. For this edition, an entirely new TEST BANK has been prepared. There are over 1,500 multiple choice questions and more than 400 true-false questions, fill-ins, and matching items that test both factual and applied knowledge. Every item is referenced to a learning objective, correct answer, and text page. Multiple choice questions are grouped by level of difficulty. The TEST BANK includes a unique system of test analysis, along with the forms used to do the actual analysis.

INSTRUCTOR'S HANDBOOK OF LECTURE LAUNCHERS AND TRANSPARENCY/REPRO MASTERS contains more than 50 lecture launchers to stimulate class discussion or help apply key psychological principles. It includes self-tests, charts, and graphs for transparency masters or handouts.

COMPUTER ITEMS
The New Random House Testmaker (Apple, MAC, IBM) is packed with features that let you view questions; scramble, edit, and add items; sort and select questions by category; view the test; and save it. For those who would rather have us prepare the test, a customized testing service is available. Computerized Activities in Psychology (CAPS IV) (Apple, IBM) and Experiments and Personal Applications in Psychology are also available. All these software programs can be used to enhance student learning and promote mastery of basic concepts.

VIDEO/FILM ITEMS
Transparency and slide sets that illustrate key concepts are also available.

ACKNOWLEDGMENTS

Things Change. Because of other research and writing interests, my co-author of the first edition, Sandra Mollenauer, decided not to continue her active involvement in the second edition. However, without her continued encouragement and support, the manuscript of the second edition would still be a two-foot-high pile in the corner of my office.

More Things Change. Just as work on the new edition began, I was assigned a new editor. I am not particularly fond of changing editors and, if pushed, I would admit that I hate changing. However, my new editor, Rochelle Diogenes, turned out to have such good ideas, so much energy and enthusiasm, that she won me over. What I especially like about Rochelle is that she has promised to remain my editor for the next 100 years or so.

My support staff at Random House, which included a copy editor, project editor, and photo researcher, were all new for the second edition. They took care of all the details and were a joy to work with. When I would lose patience, I had only to call Jeannine Ciliotta and hear her wonderful laugh and know the world was right.

My new research assistant at SDSU, Anna Olson, worked so long and hard in the library that she has a room and xerox machine named for her. She also found absolutely all the errors in the manuscript and the galley and page proofs. Many, many thanks to Anna.

Things Remain. My current group of teaching assistants has provided me with a constant source of ideas and support. In no particular order, I wish to thank Margaret, Sue, Jim, Ken, Virginia, Marilyn, Lorri, Larry, Mitch, Stephanie, Kris, Patti, Rebecca, Tanis, Tricia, and Wendy. Great teachers one and all.

More Things Remain. As the many users of the first edition discovered, Gary Poole of Simon Fraser University, Vancouver, author of the *Student Organizer and Self-Testing Book* as well as the *Instructor's Resource Manual*, has an endless number of creative ideas. Gary agreed to continue his authorship and pour some more of his ideas into these two supplements to the second edition.

Yet More Things Change. As a user of the second edition, you will find a new test bank written by Marie Thomas of the College of Mount Saint Vincent and Paul Rosenfeld of the Navy Personnel Research and Development Center. Their collective experience with writing test banks will be obvious when you read their great questions for the second edition.

New Reviewers. Each time I received a batch of reviews I knew that I was in for a yin-yang, negative-positive experience. It is wonderful reading the praises and awful reading the criticisms. I did discover that no matter what I felt initially, their comments, criticisms, and suggestions were very useful and greatly improved the new edition. I wish to thank the following reviewers for their time and effort:

David Bernstein
Grand Valley State College

Larry Brandstein
Berkshire Community College

Lynn Brokaw
Portland Community College

Robert C. Brown, Jr.
Georgia State University

Samuel Clarke
North Adams State College

Lorry Cology
Owens College

Tom Eckle
Modesto Junior College

Julie Felender
San Diego State University

John Foust
Parkland College

Grace Galliano
Kennesaw College

Mike Garzo
Brookhaven College

Marvin Goldstein
Rider College

Albert Gorman
Suffolk Community College

Arthur Gutman
Florida Institute of Technology

William Hills
Coastal Carolina College

Bruce Jaeger
USAF Academy

Judy Keith
Tarrant County Junior College

Elinor MacDonald
Quinebaug Valley Community
College

Roger Mellgren
University of Oklahoma

Steve Mewaldt
Marshall University

William Owen
Virginia Western Community
College

Alan Schultz
Prince George's Community College

Janet Shaban
California State University

Jim Smrtic
Mohawk Valley Community College

Adolf Streng
Eastfield College

Marilynn Thomas
Prince George's Community College

Michael Zeller
Mankato State University

One Final Word.   Although I am certainly biased, I must admit that I really liked the first edition. However, we so greatly improved the content, layout, and design of the second edition that I now feel a little guilty admitting how much better in fact it is. I hope you'll agree.

Rod Plotnik

To the Student

You are about to begin a course that is one of the most popular on campus. The introductory psychology course is so popular because it discusses so many aspects of your life. It discusses how your brain functions, what happens when you sleep, how you learned to be anxious during exams, what an IQ score means, why you develop psychosomatic symptoms, how your personality changes, what are abnormal behaviors, why your social perception of others is probably inaccurate, and many more questions that affect your life. This course also discusses many of the techniques that help you overcome such common problems as how to reduce stress, stay on a diet, overcome insomnia, relieve mild depression, improve your memory, and reduce anger. As you can see, you will learn a lot about yourself in this course.

What am I in for?

Many people think that psychology is just common sense. We'll guarantee that if you used just common sense, you would never pass this course. That's because much of our common sense about human behavior is either inaccurate or just wrong. For example, using just your common sense, decide whether the following statements are True (T) or False (F).

Is this course going to be hard?

T F You only use about 50 percent of your brain.
T F IQ tests measure natural intelligence.
T F The first five years of your life are critical for the development of your personality.
T F Eyewitness testimony is always accurate.
T F You can learn a foreign language by listening to a recording during sleep.
T F Psychosomatic problems are imaginary.
T F The best way to get over an intense fear is to always avoid the feared thing.

Based on common sense, you may decide that some of these statements are true. Based on what psychologists have discovered, all of these statements are false. Psychologists were able to discover the falsity of these statements by analyzing and studying behavior systematically. This course will not only introduce you to this system of discovery, but also tell you about all the things that psychologists have discovered. Learning all the terms, concepts, and theories will be hard, but it will also be challenging, interesting, and rewarding. Learning all these things will also improve your common sense.

As you begin reading this text, you will immediately notice that it is unlike any other. Every chapter is divided into 3 or 4 **Modules** that are only about 10 pages long. This means that the material is broken down into small, manageable units. You will notice that each module begins with a real-life example and that each page has questions in the margins. The examples and **Marginal Questions** will spark your interest and introduce you to the material. As you continue reading, you will discover that there are short tests after major theories and concepts. These brief tests, called **Major Concept** exercises, signal the important concepts and test your

What's different about this textbook?

memory and understanding of them. Each module ends with an interesting and challenging test, the **Review.** By completing the review, you can determine how well you remember and understand the material as well as discover which material needs extra studying. You will notice that upon completing a Review you will also have a list of important terms, which are also defined in the **Glossary** at the end of the book. We suggest that you work on a module until you have mastered the Review. Only then should you go on to read and master a new module. If you would like additional help in mastering a module, you can use the separate *Student Organizer and Self-Testing Book*, which gives you step-by-step help in how to study as well as a chance to test your mastery by answering multiple-choice questions.

Now that we've told you about the course and the textbook, you're ready to begin. Here's your chance to use 100 percent of your brain.

Contents in Brief

Contents

7 Remembering and Forgetting 197

8 Intelligence, Thought, and Language 227

9 Motivation and Emotion 265

10 Human Sexual Behavior 303

11 Conception Through Childhood 339

12 Adolescence, Adulthood, and Old Age 371

13 *Personality* 403

14 *Stress and Coping* 435

Appendix: Statistics in Psychology 591

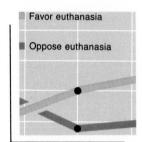

Discovering Psychology

Module 1 Approaches to Understanding Behavior

He didn't begin talking until he was almost 3. During most of his early schooling, his teachers said he seemed dull and uninteresting, had a poor memory, and could not express himself clearly. His grades in history, biology, and language were barely passing. It was not until his middle teens that Einstein began solving math problems that stumped most adults.

In college, Einstein angered his math professors by asking questions that they couldn't answer, and he surprised his friends by mastering an entire math course in just two weeks. Perhaps the best example of his genius is his theory of relativity, represented by the famous equation $E = mc^2$. This equation, which describes the relationship between states of energy, laid the groundwork for the atomic bomb. In 1921, at age 42, Einstein received the Nobel Prize for physics.

But what of his parents? Were they geniuses too? The answer, apparently, is no. Albert's father, kind and happy-go-lucky, was a moderately successful plant manager. His mother, quiet and plain, was a homemaker and music lover. They were not particularly creative or intellectual, and they did not have college degrees.

Although Einstein's genius was extraordinary, he was a mediocre teacher and had a number of problems in his personal life. He spent most of his energy thinking about and solving problems in physics and devoted little time to developing friendships. At one point, he commented: "It is strange to be known so universally and yet to be so lonely." He often forgot his children's birthdays, the first of his two marriages failed, and he confided to friends that he had married "disgracefully" both times, choosing women who mothered him (adapted from Ferris, 1983: Quasha, 1980).

Was there anything unusual about Albert Einstein?

Albert Einstein's life was full of contradictions: He was a mathematical genius but a lonely person, the winner of a Nobel Prize but a mediocre teacher, a world-renowned figure but a poor husband and father. (© 1986, Sylvia Gilbin)

Which of the seeming contradictions in Einstein's life makes you curious? Do you wonder how people of average intelligence could be the parents of a genius? Or why Einstein could formulate the spectacularly original theory of relativity but not be able to remember his children's birthdays? Or how Einstein could be recognized as one of the greatest scientists of the twentieth century yet not be able to overcome his loneliness? When psychologists examine Einstein's genius, they too emphasize different factors, depending on their perspectives. As we take you into the world of psychologists, notice how each different perspective offers a very different view of Einstein's genius and personal life.

3

MAJOR VIEWS ON THINKING AND BEHAVING

The Biological Perspective

Did Einstein have an unusual brain?

"Perhaps Einstein's genetic instructions resulted in the unique development and function of his nervous system. These biological factors influenced his mood, learning, and memory." Psychologists who explain behavior in this way have a **biological perspective** and are called physiological psychologists.

In 1985, physiological psychologist Marian Diamond of the University of California at Berkeley was able to examine Einstein's brain, which had been preserved. Professor Diamond reported that, compared to eleven other human brains, Einstein's brain had 73 percent more cells in certain areas, including one area involved in processing information (Bower, 1985). This remarkable difference may partially explain Einstein's mathematical genius.

Through research, physiological psychologists have provided answers to many questions. For example, they now know that a severed arm can be reattached and regain its functions, that healthy cells can be transplanted to help a damaged brain, and that only one side of the brain is involved in producing speech.

After his death, Einstein's brain was preserved for researchers like physiological psychologist Marian Diamond of the University of California Berkeley to study. Check the text to see what she discovered. (Doug Menuez/Picture Group)

The Cognitive Perspective

Did Einstein have an unusual way of thinking?

"Perhaps Einstein had a special ability to think in abstract symbols. If he did, he might more easily process, remember, and solve complex mathematical problems." Psychologists who explain behavior in this way have a **cognitive perspective.** They search for explanations in how you process, store, and use information and how this information affects your perceptions and behaviors.

If Albert Einstein were alive today, cognitive psychologists would surely want to study how he solved "what if" problems. For example, what if someone drops a quarter in an elevator that is moving downward. Will the quarter fall to the floor, rise to the ceiling, or remain where it was released? Answering this question is enormously complex because you must take into account whether you are watching the quarter from in the elevator or on the ground, whether the elevator's descent is subject to gravity or whether it is controlled, and so on. Einstein excelled at solving such problems, often spending years on particularly difficult ones.

Interest in the cognitive perspective increased dramatically in the 1970s and continues into the present. Cognitive psychologists study how you learn and remember, make decisions, develop stereotypes, and experience emotions.

The Behavioral Perspective

Why did Einstein do math problems?

"Perhaps Einstein learned to solve math problems because doing so resulted in so much attention and praise." Psychologists who empathize this possibility have a **behavioral perspective.** Behaviorists would search for factors in Einstein's environment that encouraged him to excel at mathematics and physics. For example, as a teenager, Einstein had an adult friend who brought him mathematical puzzles. As Einstein solved more difficult problems, his friend, parents, and teachers rewarded him with attention and praise. Unknowingly, the people around Einstein were using behavioral principles to encourage his interest in mathematics and pursuit of a career in that field.

The principles of behavioral psychology have been used in helping people to overcome extreme fears, in teaching severely retarded people to feed and dress themselves, and toilet training young children. If you were to begin a self-improvement program, such as one aimed at becoming more assertive, overcoming depression, or stopping smoking, you would be using behavioral principles.

Originally, behavioral psychologists studied only what they could observe. For example, a behaviorist who was studying your eating patterns would record such things as when and where you ate, the number of calories you consumed, the foods you selected, and the factors in your external environment that influenced your eating (for example, if you ate pizza because that was what your friends ate). Today, some behavioral psychologists would also study internal behaviors, such as your beliefs, thoughts, and feelings about food and eating. That is, how is your eating influenced by what you say to yourself and what you believe? With this in mind, behaviorists might attempt to alter unhealthy eating habits by modifying how you think about food, as well as what you actually eat. In later Modules, you will discover many examples of how to use behavioral principles to modify both your thought processes and your observable behaviors.

The Psychoanalytic Perspective

"Perhaps Einstein was driven to excel by an unconscious repression of his sexual desires." Those who emphasize this possibility are using the **psychoanalytic perspective.** According to this viewpoint, much of our motivation, behavior, and concerns have a basis in hidden or unconscious feelings. Sigmund Freud, a physician who began to practice in Vienna in the 1880s, developed this perspective. He argued that you repress, or push into your unconscious, those thoughts and feelings that threaten your self-esteem or make you feel fearful or guilty. Although you are not aware of these unconscious thoughts, they make you feel anxious or cause psychological problems. In Freud's treatment approach, which he called *psychoanalysis,* he encouraged troubled patients to confront and work through their unconscious thoughts and feelings.

According to Freud, many of the thoughts that you bury in your unconscious result from unresolved sexual conflicts. For example, Freud might have suggested that Albert Einstein never satisfactorily dealt with his sexual feelings toward his mother. As evidence, Freud would point to Einstein's two marriages to "mothering" women. Freud might also have wondered whether Einstein's great accomplishments were not a case of what he called **sublimation,** an unconscious effort to redirect forbidden impulses toward the pursuit of socially acceptable goals.

In the United States today, there are relatively few traditional psychoanalysts who follow Freud's original theories and methods of treatment. Contemporary psychotherapists who have been influenced by Freud adopt a modified viewpoint called the **psychodynamic perspective.** Psychodynamic psychologists place less stress on forbidden sexual urges than Freud did, and they are also more interested in motivations that stem from a person's conscious self.

The Humanistic Perspective

"Perhaps Einstein was lonely and had so few friends because he was not able to develop his full potential." Psychologists who emphasize this possibility are using the **humanistic perspective.** They believe that each individual has intrinsic worth, personal freedom, and the potential to strive for self-fulfillment. Unlike behaviorists and psychoanalysts, who believe that your behavior is determined by your environment or your unconscious

Was Einstein motivated by inner forces that he was unaware of?

Did Einstein find fulfillment in his personal life?

needs, humanists believe that you have control of your fate and are free to become whatever you are capable of being. The humanistic perspective emphasizes the positive side of human nature. It stresses your creative and constructive tendencies and your inclination to build caring relationships with others.

Humanistic psychologists would praise Einstein's remarkable achievements in mathematics and add that he reached his full potential in his professional life and career. However, they would note that the demands of his professional life interfered with his personal life, and denied him the fulfillment that comes with a happy marriage, lasting friendships, and freedom from loneliness.

One Question, Many Views

If you saw a rat pressing a lever to obtain food, a behaviorist would explain that the rat's lever pressing occurred because the action resulted in food. If you spoke with a stroke victim who had difficulty understanding language, a physiological psychologist would explain that the stroke had destroyed brain cells necessary for using language. If you were at a party and found it impossible to listen to two simultaneous conversations, a cognitive psychologist would explain that this problem results from the way we process auditory information. These examples tell us that psychologists may be able to answer relatively simple questions about behavior by using only one perspective.

However, in explaining complex behaviors such as Einstein's genius, loneliness, and forgetfulness, psychologists must examine his life and work from several different perspectives. This means examining his genetic

---

MAJOR CONCEPT   Psychological Perspectives

Different psychologists adopt different perspectives in trying to understand behavior.

Match each of the five major perspectives with its description.

1. Biological perspective

2. Cognitive perspective

3. Behavioral perspective

4. Psychoanalytic perspective

5. Humanistic perspective

a. __4__ Emphasizes the role of unconscious conflicts in motivating human thoughts and actions.

b. __1__ Studies how genetic influences and the structure and function of the nervous system affect learning, emotions, and memory.

c. __5__ Emphasizes personal growth and freedom and a person's striving for self-fulfillment.

d. __3__ Studies how behavior is influenced by the environment, especially by rewards and punishments.

e. __2__ Seeks to understand how we process, store, and use information and how this information affects our perceptions and behaviors.

Answers: a (4); b (1); c (5); d (3); e (2)

makeup and how it affected his brain, how he was rewarded and punished by his environment, whether he was driven by unconscious motivations, how he processed information, and what prevented him from finding fulfillment in his personal life.

DEFINING PSYCHOLOGY

Psychology's Past and Present

If you attended Wilhelm Wundt's psychology class in Germany in 1879, you would be told that psychology is the study of the conscious elements (sensations, images, and feelings) of the normal human mind. Because Wundt and his followers were interested in the structure of consciousness, they came to be called **structuralists.** Over the next fifty years, psychologists found that the structuralists' definition of psychology was too narrow.

If you attended Freud's series of lectures at Clark University in Massachusetts in 1909, you would be told that psychology is the study of unconscious processes. Freud would discuss the importance of analyzing dreams and free-flowing thoughts to find clues about unconscious feelings and repressed wishes. As evidence of Freud's lasting influence on the development of psychology, many of his concepts—such as id, ego, and superego—still occupy a central place in the practice of psychology.

If you attended John Watson's psychology class at Harvard University in the early 1940s, you would be told that psychology is the study of observable responses an organism makes to environmental stimuli. Since they were interested only in how an individual behaved, Watson's followers were called **behaviorists.** Behaviorists argued that, despite the structuralists' claim to the contrary, the workings of the human mind could not be studied scientifically.

Our present definition of psychology developed from the views of the structuralists, psychoanalyists, and behaviorists (Figure 1.1). Because this definition must be broad enough to explain an enormous range of behaviors—such as why Einstein was a genius, how a rat learns to press a lever, why a person becomes depressed, or how you learn to memorize the terms in this chapter—**psychology** is currently defined as the systematic, scientific study of behavior, both animal and human. The term *behavior* refers to observable actions, such as eating, speaking, and laughing, as well as to mental activities, such as planning, thinking, and imagining.

Psychology's Goals

Besides learning the definition of psychology, you also need to know its goals. Psychology wants to *explain*, or understand, why an organism behaves a certain way and to *predict* how an organism will behave in the future. For example, psychologists would like to understand why you performed well in high school and to predict how you will perform in college. Some psychologists would add another goal, to *control* behavior. This goal has both a comforting and frightening side. It is comforting to think that we can learn how to control anger, depression, overeating, smoking, and poor study habits. But it is frightening to think that certain of our behaviors may be controlled without our knowledge or intention. Although psychologists have developed techniques for controlling behaviors, they have also established guidelines for the subject's rights so that control is not misused (Module 52).

Figure 1.1
A Brief Early History of Psychology

Wilhelm Wundt

William James

Margaret F. Washburn

Sigmund Freud

Max Wertheimer

John Watson

1879

Considered the father of psychology, **Wilhelm Wundt** established the first psychology laboratory at the University of Leipzig in Germany. He defined psychology as the study of the elements (sensations, images, and feelings) of the conscious mind. Because he was studying the structure of the mind, this viewpoint became known as structuralism. Wundt's work established the foundation for the cognitive perspective.

1890

William James, one of the first important American psychologists, published his famous *Principles of Psychology*. Unlike Wundt, who felt that the mind could be divided into distinct elements, James viewed thought as a continuous flow that he termed *stream of consciousness*. Unlike Wundt, James was interested in the usefulness of our mental processes. This viewpoint was the historical basis for the applied focus of much of modern American psychology.

1906

The first edition of the *American Men of Science* listed three women psychologists: **Mary Whiton Calkins, Christine Ladd-Franklin, and Margaret Floy Washburn,** all of whom were subjected to considerable sexual discrimination during their studies and in the pursuit of careers. After obtaining their doctorates, the only positions open to them were teaching jobs at women's colleges or normal schools (Furumoto & Scarborough, 1986). Not surprisingly, in light of the difficulties that these women encountered, early experimental and academic psychology was dominated by men.

1909

Sigmund Freud was invited to give a series of lectures at Clark University, where he presented his revolutionary ideas on how sexual and other unconscious motivations contribute to the development of personality and psychological problems. These now-famous talks signified the official introduction of psychoanalysis to America. (Evans & Koelsch, 1985).

1912

Max Wertheimer, Wolfgang Köhler, and Kurt Koffka published a paper that reported a curious discovery. Imagine two light bulbs placed a few inches apart. The room is dark. First the bulb on the left blinks on, followed immediately by the one on the right. Although the bulbs are fixed in place, the light appears to move from left to right, a phenomenon that they called *apparent movement*. Notice that the apparent movement results from the pattern of flashing bulbs, rather than perceiving each individual bulb. Based on these kind of experiments, Gestalt psychologists said that our perceptual experiences depended more on total pattern than on individual stimuli. In the early 1900s, the phenomenon of apparent motion marked the beginning of Gestalt psychology, which is concerned with how sensations are organized into meaningful perceptional experiences, such as apparent motion. The concept of apparent motion is used today to produce the perception of dancing lights in theater and business signs.

1913

In a paper titled "Psychology as a Behaviorist Views It," **John B. Watson** rejected the structuralism of Wundt, who recommended looking inward to discover the structure of the human mind. In contrast, Watson stated that psychology should be considered an objective, experimental science whose goal was the prediction and control of behavior. He rejected introspection as a psychological technique because it could not be scientifically verified by other psychologists. This paper, which marked the birth of the school of psychology known as behaviorism, could be considered the beginning of modern psychology.

Careers in Psychology **APPLYING PSYCHOLOGY**

A career in psychology usually requires four to five years of postgraduate study and a Ph.D. degree. Most psychology students intend to become clinical psychologists or counselors, and some ultimately set up their own private practices. Work settings for psychologists include colleges and schools, hospitals, clinics, and industry.

How Good is Eyewitness Testimony? (Discussed in Module 19)

This question would interest **experimental psychologists,** who are primarily concerned with how we remember, think, and process information. In their research regarding sensation, perception, learning, motivation, and emotion, experimental psychologists have discovered principles that form the basis for teaching retarded children, developing weight-loss programs, and helping people overcome phobias.

Why Does Rubbing a Bruised Finger Make it Hurt Less? (Discussed in Module 9)

Physiological psychologists are concerned with questions about the structure and function of the human brain and nervous system. They study how drugs affect learning and memory, what deficits appear when the brain is damaged, and how your body responds to stress.

How Does Day Care Affect a Young Child? (Discussed in Module 30)

Developmental psychologists would answer this question, as well as study how a person develops morally, personally, intellectually, and emotionally. They are concerned with the entire developmental process, beginning with fetal development in the womb and ending with old age.

Are First Impressions Very Important? (Discussed in Module 50)

Social psychologists and **personality psychologists** want to know how you interact with others, how you explain your behaviors, and how your personality is formed. They do research on stereotypes, prejudice, aggression, helping, loneliness, assertiveness, and if personality changes.

This gruesome-looking scene was staged to convince people to stay in their cars as they drive through a wild animal park. Experimental and physiological psychologists can explain how when you looked at it, you felt a certain emotion and perceived the mannequins as real people. (AP/Wide World Photos)

You are right to be concerned about making a good impression: Social and personality psychologists can show that people do form definite opinions based on appearance and manner. (Dan McCoy/Rainbow)

Clinical psychologists can provide support, advice, and therapy to help people overcome the depression. (Richard Hutchings/Photo Researchers)

If you wanted to send your infant or child to a day care center, developmental psychologists could tell you how the experience might affect your child's social, emotional, and cognitive development. (Yada Claassen/Jeroboam)

What Can I Do If I'm Depressed? (Discussed in Module 45)

Clinical psychologists are concerned with determining the causes of emotional problems, assessing personality, and developing treatment programs. As part of the requirements for a Ph.D. in psychology, apprentice clinicians, under the guidance of an experienced psychologist, deal with people who have mental problems. Unlike **psychiatrists,** who are physicians with several years of residency in a clinical setting, clinical psychologists do not assess physical causes of mental problems or prescribe drugs.

Will I Fit Into This Job? (Discussed in Module 39)

Industrial psychologists, who work as consultants to business, industry, and government, develop tests to screen applicants for jobs. They also evaluate the employee's performance on the job and study working conditions to find ways to decrease accidents, increase production, and improve employer-employee relations. In addition, they try to make machines "user friendly" by analyzing how people respond to various machines.

Industrial and organizational psychologists can give you tests to determine whether you have the skills necessary for a particular job. (Joel Gordon/Design Conceptions)

REVIEW

Suppose psychologists want to know why certain people become alcoholics and how alcohol affects their behavior. Some psychologists would look for differences in the structure and function of the alcoholic's brain and nervous system. These researchers are taking the (1) _biological_ perspective. Other psychologists might seek to discover how alcoholism hinders a person's ability to process, store, and recall information. The approach that they are taking is called the (2) _Cognitive_ perspective. A third group of psychologists would search for answers in the way environmental factors, particularly rewards and punishments, control the alcoholic's drinking. These psychologists are adopting the (3) _Behavioral_ perspective. A fourth group of psychologists would want to discover any unconscious motivations that might be encouraging heavy drinking. These psychologists are taking the (4) _psychoanalytic_ perspective. A fifth group would focus on events in an alcoholic's life that somehow blocked the natural striving toward personal growth and self-fulfillment. Their viewpoint is known as the (5) _humanistic_ perspective.

When trying to understand a complex behavior like this one, psychologists find it useful to combine insights from many approaches. In the late 1890s, Wundt defined psychology as the study of the elements of consciousness. He and his followers became known as (6) _Structuralists_. In the early 1900s, Freud theorized that psychology should be concerned with hidden or (7) _uncon._ feelings. In the 1940s, John Watson objected to studying mental processes and redefined psychology as the study of observable (8) _behavior_. Today, psychology is defined as the systematic, (9) _Scientific_ study of human and animal behavior. One goal of psychology is to discover why organisms behave as they do—why, for example, certain people become alcoholics. This is the goal of (10) _explaining_ behavior. A second goal of psychology is to be able to say how particular organisms are likely to act in the future, for instance, which members of a population are apt to become alcoholics and which are not. This is the goal of (11) _predicting_ behavior. A third goal of psychology, which is more controversial, involves (12) _Controlling_ behavior. When psychologists develop programs to help alcoholics stop drinking, they are engaged in this goal. Along with the techniques for controlling behavior that psychologists have developed, they have also developed guidelines so that psychologists will not abuse these techniques.

Answers: (1) biological; (2) cognitive; (3) behavioral; (4) psychoanalytic or psychodynamic; (5) humanistic; (6) structuralists; (7) unconscious; (8) behavior; (9) scientific; (10) explaining; (11) predicting; (12) controlling

GLOSSARY TERMS

behavioral perspective (p. 4)
behaviorists (p. 7)
biological perspective (p. 4)
clinical psychologists (p. 10)
cognitive perspective (p. 4)

developmental psychologists (p. 9)
experimental psychologists (p. 9)
humanistic perspective (p. 5)
industrial psychologists (p. 10)

personality psychologists (p. 9)
physiological psychologists (p. 9)
psychiatrists (p. 10)
psychoanalytic perspective (p. 5)

psychodynamic perspective (p. 5)
psychology (p. 7)
social psychologists (p. 9)
structuralists (p. 7)
sublimation (p. 5)

Module 2: Asking, Observing, and Correlating

SURVEYS

How honest are most people?

More people (45 percent) say they have cheated on their marriage partners than on their tax returns (38 percent) or expense accounts (28 percent). Eighty-four percent of those who cheated on their spouse feel guilty about their infidelities; 59 percent feel guilty about falsifying their tax statements.

Nearly half of those surveyed predicted that if they were driving a car and scratched another car in a parking lot, they would drive away without leaving a note—although the vast majority (89 percent) agree it would be immoral.

Nearly a third admitted to deceiving a best friend about something important within the last year; 96 percent of them feel guilty about it (adapted from Hassett, 1981).

From this survey, it appears that if your car were damaged in a parking lot, there is little hope that a note would be left saying who did it. One of the many techniques psychologists use to study behavior is to question a representative group of people. This technique, called a **survey**, tells us what people believe, think or say they would do. As useful as surveys are, you must be aware of three potential problems. First, people may fail to answer a survey accurately, may not remember their behaviors and feelings, may wish to depict themselves in a more favorable light, or may not really know how they would behave in a situation they have never encountered. For example, how would you answer the following questions?

Would you put a healthy pet to sleep for $50,000?
Would you be content with a sexless but otherwise perfect marriage?
Would you reduce your life expectancy to be extremely attractive?

These questions were asked during a two-day phone-in poll by the newspaper *USA Today*. Of the over 6,000 people who phoned in, 81 percent said they would not put a healthy pet to sleep, 52 percent said they would not be content with a sexless marriage, and 73 percent said they would not reduce their life expectancy to be very attractive (*USA Today*, April 30, 1987). Since these people have probably never been in these situations, we have no way of knowing whether they would behave as they say they would.

A second potential problem with surveys is that those who answer a survey may not represent the majority of people. In the survey on honesty, for instance, 69 percent—or almost three-fourths—of those responding were young, well-educated women. Since this group comprises only a small percentage of the American population as a whole, we cannot be sure how representative members' actions are.

A third problem with surveys is that many people assume that what the majority believes must be "right." But opinions and beliefs change over time, and we have no way of knowing whether the majority is right or wrong, moral or immoral. For instance, in 1973, 61 percent of Americans surveyed answered "no" to the question, *"Do you think that a patient suffering from a terminal disease should be allowed to die?"* In 1985, about 61 percent of Americans surveyed answered "yes" to the same question

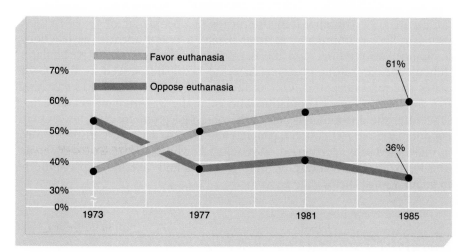

Figure 1.2
One of the biggest shifts in public opinion in recent years is the dramatic change in the American public's attitude toward euthanasia, the right of a terminally ill patient to die. The fact that a large majority approve of euthanasia doesn't tell us whether euthanasia is right or moral. (Louis Harris and Associates)

(Figure 1.2). These surveys tell us that values and feelings have changed over time—not that what was "wrong" in the past is now "right." Despite these potential problems, psychologists find that surveys are useful for finding out what large numbers of people believe.

Bias in Observation **APPLYING PSYCHOLOGY**

After years of observing young people on the Pacific island of Samoa, the anthropologist Margaret Mead reached a startling conclusion. In her 1928 best seller, *Coming of Age in Samoa*, she said that Samoan youths enjoyed premarital sex, easygoing relations with their parents, and an adolescence free of the anxiety and guilt that was characteristic of American teenagers. Mead said that compared with American youths, young Samoans grow up in a culture that is very amiable and peaceful and lacks violence and competitiveness (Harris, 1983).

Over fifty years after Mead wrote *Coming of Age in Samoa*, her views of Samoan youth were challenged by another anthropologist, Derek Freeman, who claimed that Samoan adolescents, far from being carefree, easygoing, and sexually liberated, had high rates of delinquency, suicide, and sexual offenses, including rape. Freeman claimed that Samoans had lied to Mead about their behavior and that Mead had believed these lies because they matched her own preconceptions. Freeman insisted that Mead had allowed her beliefs in the importance of social influences on behavior to bias her observations (Freeman, 1983).

Margaret Mead had been observing people in their own environments, which is called **naturalistic observations**. To reduce the risk of personal bias in observational research of any kind, data must be carefully and systematically collected, and researchers must take extensive notes, make tape and video recordings of what people say and do, and fill out various evaluation forms. You can be sure that Margaret Mead took many notes of what she saw and heard in Samoa. But even with the most painstaking care, it now appears that bias may have affected her observations.

The story of Margaret Mead and her critic Derek Freeman illustrates the pros and cons of naturalistic observation. On the positive side, naturalistic observation allows researchers to see actual behavior as it happens, which is far superior to asking people what they have done or are likely to

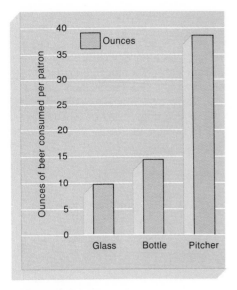

Figure 1.3
Do college males drink more beer if they order it by the glass, bottle or pitcher? To answer this question, researchers went to a bar and observed beer drinkers without their being aware. This is an example of naturalistic observation. (Adapted from Geller et al., 1986, p. 393)

do (Figure 1.3). This approach also means that people are observed in their own familiar environments, so their behavior is not affected by reactions to strange surroundings. On the negative side, however, it is particularly difficult for naturalistic observers to avoid being influenced by their own biases and preconceptions. One of the special dangers in Mead's case was that she lived among a population who *knew* she was studying them. Consequently, she encountered one of the potential problems that researchers conducting surveys encounter: people's tendency to distort the truth in order to make themselves look good. Psychologists who use naturalistic observation today are highly aware of these problems and take many precautions to guard against them.

OBSERVING

Naturalistic Observation

6 November 1960 By the termite hill were two chimps, both male. . . . I could see a little better the use of the piece of straw. It was held in the left hand, poked into the mound, and then removed coated with termites. The straw was raised to the mouth and the insects picked off with the lips along the length of the straw, starting in the middle (Goodall, 1986, p. 535).

This is one of a series of amazing observations of wild chimpanzees made by anthropologist Jane Goodall. She was one of the first to spend years observing and recording the behavior of animals in the wild. When she began her observations, Goodall had to remain far away from the wild chimps in order to avoid alarming them and disrupting their normal behaviors. It took her a year and a half before she could approach within 50 meters of the wild chimps without seriously disrupting their behaviors. As detailed above, Goodall's naturalistic observations paid off with many important discoveries. She learned that chimpanzees make and use rudimentary tools to fish for termites and observed important differences between the social behaviors of chimps in the wild and in captivity (Goodall, 1986).

Since 1960 Jane Goodall has been observing the behavior of chimpanzees in their natural setting in Gombe Stream National Park, Tanzania. She has found that, like us, chimps manufacture and use tools, form cohesive groups, cooperate in hunting, and communicate with one another. (Hugo van Lawick, © National Geographic Society)

Laboratory Observation

You're in a sleep laboratory and there are a dozen tiny wires attached to your head. One pair of wires indicates when your eyes move from side to side. The researcher tells you to have a good sleep and leaves the room, shutting off the light. The next thing you know, someone is softly telling you to wake up. As soon as you are awake, the experimenter asks, "What were you doing?" With only a slight hesitation, you answer "I was dreaming." (author's files)

What do your eyes do when you dream?

While you were sleeping, the researcher had been recording and observing your eye movements. When your eyes began moving rapidly from side to side, the researcher had awoken you and discovered that you were dreaming. This is an example of a **laboratory observation** in which the researcher creates a special setting to answer a specific question, such as, "Is there any way to tell if someone is dreaming?" In this case, researchers have learned that rapid movement of the eyes from side to side very often indicates that a person is dreaming (Dement & Kleitman, 1957). Laboratory observations can be conducted in anything from a room with a few toys for observing the play of children, to one equipped with sophisticated computers and equipment for recording brain waves and eye movements.

Laboratory observations have been very useful to psychologists in studying sleep and dreaming patterns, in finding out what happens after stroke or brain damage, as well as in studying all kinds of social behaviors, such as group decision making, conformity, aggression, prejudice, and interpersonal attraction.

One potential problem with such research is that the laboratory setting may be so artificial it prompts people to behave in ways they would not

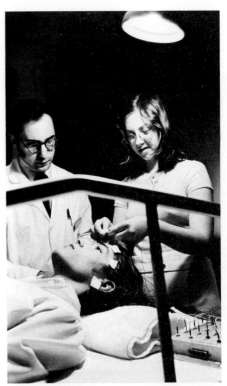

A subject's brain waves being monitored by electrodes attached to the scalp. With studies and tests like these, sleep researchers have discovered that each stage of sleep is associated with a unique brain wave pattern. (James H. Karales/Peter Arnold Inc.)

MAJOR CONCEPT   Surveys and Observations

Some of the techniques psychologists use to study behavior are surveys, naturalistic observations, and observations in laboratory settings.

Indicate which pros and cons best apply to each technique.

a. Survey

b. Naturalistic observation

c. Laboratory observation

___B___ 1. Researchers have the advantage of observing how subjects act in their real-life environments.

___a___ 2. A large number of people can be questioned about what they believe or think or how they act.

___c___ 3. Researchers create special situations or use special equipment to answer specific questions about behavior.

___a___ 4. Respondents may not tell the truth, may try to make themselves look good, or may simply guess how they would act in a particular situation.

___c___ 5. Subjects may behave differently than they normally do because the setting is artificial.

___b or c___ 6. Researchers' biases and preconceptions may distort their results.

Answers: 1 (b); 2 (a); 3 (c); 4 (a); 5 (c); 6 (b or c)

normally. Another problem is that laboratory observation, like naturalistic observation, is particularly susceptible to being influenced by the researcher's expectations. Most psychologists who conduct laboratory observations are very much aware of these problems and take steps to avoid them. Despite its potential problems, the method of conducting research through laboratory observations continues to be one of the more valuable methods psychologists use.

THE DRAWBACKS OF TESTIMONIALS

What cured this man's disease?

Olympic skater Tiffany Chin sprained her ankle and had an acupuncture treatment. Her doctor, Dr. K. C. Chan, gave this testimonial: "... After the 20-minute treatment she walked out with only minor discomfort." (Both, Union-Tribune Publishing Co.)

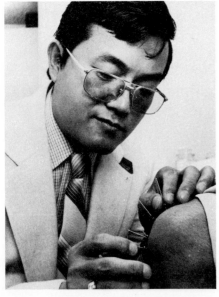

At the age of 49, Norman Cousins, former editor of the Saturday Review, *came down with a supposedly incurable illness. He had a general achiness, stiffness in his limbs and neck, and small lumps or nodules on his neck and hands. Cousins's symptoms were difficult to fit into a precise diagnosis, but it was generally agreed that he had a serious disease. A specialist gave him one chance in five hundred of complete recovery. Because he found himself very allergic to the drugs that were prescribed for him, Cousins developed his own treatment program. He began taking massive doses of vitamin C and worked on having a positive attitude by reading humorous books and watching funny TV programs. After a time, his achiness gradually lessened and his nodules disappeared. Cousins claimed that, against incredible odds, he had cured himself of a serious disease with vitamin C and laughter (adapted from* Discover, *1982).*

Cousins's claim to have cured himself is an example of a **testimonial**—a statement in support of a particular viewpoint based on personal experience. Psychologists distrust testimonials for several very good reasons. For one thing, it is hard for people to be objective about their own experiences. Often we have a personal stake in seeing things one way or another. In Norman Cousins's case, for instance, doctors at first gave him little hope for a cure, and this feeling of hopelessness could easily have biased his perceptions. Psychologists also distrust testimonials because they don't allow other possible explanations to be ruled out. Perhaps Cousins's disease would have cured itself *without* vitamins and laughter. We have no way of knowing, whether or not this would have happened; all we have is Cousins's testimony that the cure was due to his program.

Like many testimonials, Cousins's claim was based on a relationship in time between two events: his self-treatment program and his cure. Cousins was perfectly correct in noting that these two events had occurred close together in time. He was not necessarily correct in drawing the conclusion that one event had therefore *caused* the other. Psychologists would say that Cousins did not fully understand the concept of correlation.

CORRELATION IS NOT CAUSATION

In a Louis Harris poll, people who said they watched television for many hours each day reported more severe headaches, backaches, and joint pains than did less devoted television viewers (*Los Angeles Times*, Nov. 11, 1985). Is this poll saying that watching a lot of television causes people to develop aches and pains? Before jumping to that conclusion, you need to understand the meaning of correlation.

A **correlation** means that a change in one event (such as increasing the amount of television one watches) tends to be accompanied by a proportional change in another (such as the onset of headaches). The degree to which two events change together is indicated by a number called the **correlation coefficient**.

If twenty people watched many hours of television and all reported severe aches and pains, the correlation between heavy television viewing and aches and pains is said to be positive and perfect. A perfect positive correlation is indicated by $+1$. A correlation coefficient less than $+1$, such as $+0.5$, tells us that the relationship is still positive (both events tend to change in the same direction) but it is no longer perfect (change in the same direction doesn't occur in every case). If the correlation between number of hours of watching television and reports of aches and pains were $+0.5$, it would mean that a large number of viewers watch many hours of television and report aches and pains, while a smaller number of viewers watch many hours of television but report few if any aches and pains.

In contrast, if twenty people who had severe headaches watched many hours of television and all reported that their headaches disappeared, the correlation coefficient is said to be negative and perfect and indicated by -1. A negative correlation coefficient indicates that two events are associated inversely (that is, when one rises the other falls, and vice versa). A correlation coefficient between -1 and 0, such as -0.5, indicates a relationship that is still negative (the events tend to change in opposite directions) but it is no longer perfect (change in opposite directions doesn't occur all the time). As you may have guessed, a correlation coefficient of 0 tells us that there is *no* relationship (neither positive nor negative) between the two events being studied. Remember that a correlation coefficient can range from $+1$, which is perfect and positive, to -1, which is perfect and negative.

It is relatively easy to understand that a correlation means two events are associated, such as watching television and reporting headaches. What is harder to grasp is that a correlation does *not* necessarily prove that one event is *causing* the other. Can you think of a really good reason, that has nothing to do with watching television, that explains why heavy television watchers reported more aches and pains? A good possibility is that people who have bothersome physical problems tend to pass the time watching television.

Here is a strange association to help you remember that correlation doesn't imply causation. From the years 1972 to 1985, there was a perfect positive correlation $(+1)$ between which league won the Super Bowl (NFL or AFL) and whether stock market prices rose or fell. Now no one would say that the Super Bowl winner *caused* stock market trends. Instead, these two variables were simply correlated, with no implication of cause and effect.

Although correlation does not imply causation, correlations can be useful in helping researchers find the cause of an event. That is what happened in the search for the cause of premenstrual syndrome or PMS.

Correlation Provides Clues **APPLYING PSYCHOLOGY**

What is causing Roberta's powerful mood swings?

Roberta was one week short of earning her college degree when she almost dropped out. "I was having mood swings from rage to depression to paranoia," she recalled. "Then, after my period started, I could look back calmly and see what happened." Roberta might be said to have premenstrual syndrome, or PMS, although there is some disagreement about exactly which symptoms characterize PMS. Current estimates are that 3 to 10 percent of menstruating women experience severe symptoms which can be both physical, including headaches, backaches, extreme fatigue, and bloating, and psychological, including depression, lethargy, tension, and irritability. PMS is so disabling that their lives are disrupted for a week or two every month.

Usually, symptoms occur in the days just before menstruation begins, when there is a specific sequence of major hormonal changes. With the start of menstrual bleeding, which marks the end of those hormonal changes, the symptoms usually subside (adapted from Heneson, 1984; Hopson & Rosenfield, 1984).

Clearly, there is a negative correlation between the decrease in the levels of female hormones (estrogen and progesterone) and the increase in symptoms associated with PMS (Rubinow et al., 1984; Sanders et al., 1983). Since this is a correlation, we should not conclude that the hormonal changes are the *cause* of the PMS symptoms, but Katharina Dalton, a British physician, appears to have assumed just that. Dalton treated her PMS patients with doses of the female hormone progesterone, and she claimed that this treatment was very successful in relieving PMS symptoms.

It is true that Dalton's patients showed reduced symptoms with her hormone treatment. However, other researchers report that several non-hormone treatments also relieve the symptoms. For example, 60 to 70 percent of PMS patients report a significant improvement whether given doses of hormones, vitamin E, or even placebos (sugar pills), and the same number report relief with a change in diet or by simply being given general information and support (Herbert, 1982; Hopson & Rosenfeld, 1984). The fact that different treatments reduce PMS symptoms suggests that PMS may be caused by a combination of hormonal and psychological factors. The search for the causes of PMS provides an example of researchers using a correlation to tell them where to look for clues and answers.

Correlations Point to Causes

Does every cigarette smoker get cancer?

If correlations cannot identify causes, why have we spent so much time discussing them? As the premenstrual syndrome example showed, correlations often provide important clues about cause and effect. Some very important discoveries began with correlations that strongly suggested where to look for the cause. For a long time, cigarette smoking was positively correlated with lung cancer, but the exact cause of the cancer was unknown. Then, on the theory that some ingredient of cigarette smoke might trigger the development of lung cancer, researchers rubbed tar, an ingredient of cigarette smoke, on the skin of animals. After repeated rubbing, the animals developed cancerous growths. This example shows you that correlations are useful in pinpointing potential causes.

REVIEW

You have noticed that identical twins not only look exactly alike but seem to behave alike. To find out just how much alike their behaviors really are, you might decide to ask twenty sets of identical twins a long list of questions about how they would behave in many different situations. For example, you might ask, "How do you act when you're upset?" By doing this, you would be taking a (1) _Survey_. You should be aware of three potential problems with this method. First, the twins may not answer all the questions

(2) _honorently_. This is because they may not remember their behaviors, may want to appear different than they really are, or simply misjudged their own reactions.

To discover how the twins really act when they are upset, you would need to observe each one separately in upsetting situations. In this case, you would be using (3) _Natural_ observation. This kind of observation has the advantage of seeing how people behave in their own environments. But if you have a strong preconception that identical twins nearly always act alike, there is a good chance that your preconception could (4) _bias_ your observations.

If you want to test the twins' reactions to being upset under more controlled conditions, you could observe their reactions to a stress test in the (5) _lab_. In this case, you would be using

MAJOR CONCEPT   Correlations

A correlation means that a change in one event tends to be accompanied by a proportional change in another.

Mark true (T) or false (F) for each of the following statements about correlation.

1. T/F If your grades *decrease* as you spend *less* time studying, your grade point average and your hours spent on schoolwork are negatively correlated.

2. T/F You read in the paper that as temperature *rises* from the 70s into the 90s, people become *more* aggressive. This is an example of a positive correlation.

3. T/F The correlation coefficient +0.2 shows a much stronger relationship than the correlation coefficient −0.8.

4. T/F Suppose psychologists find that in the majority of families with a delinquent child the parents are very permissive. Psychologists have reasonable proof that parental permissiveness causes juvenile delinquency.

5. T/F Although a correlation doesn't demonstrate cause and effect, it can often provide valuable clues about possible causes.

Answers: 1 (F); 2 (T); 3 (F); 4 (F); 5 (T)

(6) __lab__ observation. One potential problem with this type of research is that the setting is sometimes so (7) __different__ that it causes people to act in ways they might not normally act. Despite this drawback, laboratory research has contributed a great many valuable insights to our knowledge of behavior. In your research, one set of twins claims that since taking vitamin B they feel less upset and stressed. This claim, which is based on the twins' personal experiences, is called a (8) __testimony__. You should be skeptical of testimonials because they are easily

(9) __biased__ by a person's beliefs, expectations, and feelings. The twins' testimonial is based on the association of two events occurring at the same time: taking vitamin B and feeling less stressed. Such an association is called a (10) __correlation__. The degree to which two events are associated across many instances is measured by a statistic known as correlation

(11) __coefficient__. If twenty sets of twins took vitamin B and all reported *more* stress, we would have a perfect (12) __positive__ correlation with a correlation coefficient of +1. In contrast, if twenty sets of twins took vitamin B and all reported *less* stress, we would have a perfect (13) __negative__ correlation with a correlation coefficient of −1. Correlations alone cannot demonstrate that one event (14) __caused__ another. However, in searching for and pointing to possible causes, (15) __correlation__ can be very useful.

Answers: (1) survey; (2) truthfully, accurately; (3) naturalistic; (4) bias, distort, color; (5) color, distort; (6) laboratory; (7) artificial, different; (8) testimonial; (9) biased, distorted, colored; (10) correlation; (11) coefficient; (12) positive; (13) negative; (14) caused; (15) correlations

GLOSSARY TERMS

correlation (p. 16)
correlation coefficient (p. 16)

laboratory observations (p. 15)

naturalistic observations (p. 13)

survey (p. 12)
testimonial (p. 16)

Module 3: Determining What Causes Behavior

USING THE EXPERIMENTAL METHOD

After being hypnotized, two subjects were told to reach into a box and pick up a rattlesnake. Without any hesitation, both subjects reached for the snake. They were prevented from touching it by invisible glass.

After being hypnotized, two other subjects were shown a bottle of sulfuric acid, which they were told was very dangerous to the eyes. When instructed to throw the acid at the researcher's face, they both did so. They did not know that the researcher's face was protected by invisible glass.

Next, the researcher asked 42 other people, none of whom was hypnotized, to pick up the rattlesnake. Of these, only one attempted to do so, believing that the snake was artificial (Rowland, 1939). When similar experiments were independently conducted by two other researchers, they obtained almost identical results (adapted from Young, 1954; Barber, 1961).

Can hypnosis make you reckless?

Based on these findings, you would have to conclude that hypnosis seems to cause people to do things they would not normally do. Before we tell you about later findings that qualify this conclusion, let's outline the steps you would follow in conducting an experiment on hypnosis. These steps are collectively called the **experimental method.**

Steps in Conducting an Experiment

You have a snake, two groups of subjects, and a procedure called hypnosis. You have a question "Would someone perform strange behaviors under hypnosis?" Researchers could answer this question by using the experimental method. This method consists of comparing subjects who are treated identically except for one condition. That one condition is the presence or absence or different degrees of some treatment. In your case, the treatment is hypnosis. The condition that the researcher varies is called the **inde-**

Would you pick up a poisonous snake? Would you pick it up if you had been hypnotized? The answers, which may surprise you, are given in the text. (Pamela Price/The Picture Cube)

pendent variable. To see if your treatment, hypnosis, has an effect, you will measure some aspect of behavior, such as picking up a snake. The behavior you measure, the willingness to pick up a snake, is called the **dependent variable.** It's important to remember the difference between the independent and dependent variables. The independent variable is the treatment conditions you assign to the subjects. The dependent variable is what you measure the subjects doing when they receive your treatment. Suppose you find that hypnotized subjects pick up the snake and nonhypnotized subjects do not. You can conclude that the willingness to pick up a snake was *caused* by hypnosis since that is the only apparent difference between the subjects. Now that you know the purpose of an experiment, we can tell you the steps that researchers actually use in conducting experiments.

Step 1: You first define all of the terms in the question very precisely by stating them in very concrete terms or operations. In your experiment on hypnosis, it is too vague to ask, "Will hypnosis make people do things they would not normally do?" Instead, you must ask a very specific question, "Will hypnosis make people willing to pick up a poisonous snake?" You should further define your independent variable, hypnosis, by describing the specific operations or procedures you will use for inducing hypnosis. Similarly, you should further define the dependent variable, willingness to pick up a snake, by describing the specific procedures or operations you will use to measure that behavior. For example, willingness is defined by whether the subject's hand touches the glass around the snake.

Step 2: You conduct the experiment by treating all the subjects alike except that one group is given a treatment, such as being hypnotized, and one group is not given the treatment. The group of subjects that is given the treatment, being hypnotized, is called the **experimental group.** The group that undergoes everything the experimental group does, except for receiving the treatment, is called the **control group.** In your experiment, the control group would not be hypnotized. By comparing the behavior of the subjects in the experimental and control groups, you can determine whether hypnosis causes unusual behavior. If most of the subjects in the experimental group reach for the snake and most of the control subjects don't, you conclude that hypnosis has an effect.

Suppose ten out of fifteen subjects in the experimental group reach for the snake but only five out of fifteen subjects in the control group reach for the snake. How can you determine whether relative differences like these are due to hypnosis or merely to chance? The answer brings us to the final step in conducting an experiment.

Step 3: You analyze the results of an experiment by using a statistical test that tells you the likelihood of whether your results were due to the treatment or to chance. Statistical tests are procedures for calculating the likelihood that any given outcome was due to chance alone. If your calculations indicate that the differences you found were too great to be explained by chance, you have good reason to conclude that your results were caused by the independent variable. Statistical procedures are discussed further in the Appendix.

Let's reconsider the study that we described earlier—the one in which hypnotized subjects were willing to reach for a poisonous snake. On the basis of this experiment you may have concluded that only under hypnotism will people perform apparently dangerous acts. If so, we would like you to reconsider that conclusion after seeing the results of a later study (Orne & Evans, 1965).

Like the initial experiment, this later study had a group whose members were hypnotized and asked to perform seemingly dangerous acts. Also like the initial study, the later study had a group whose members were *not* hypnotized but were asked to perform the same acts. So far the two studies are virtually the same. Here, however, is the critical difference. The later

Would you pick up a rattlesnake?

study had a third group whose members were asked to *pretend* they were hypnotized—pretend to the point of actually fooling the experimenter. You may be surprised to learn that the subjects in the third group were as willing to perform the "dangerous" acts as hypnotized subjects.

What a difference this third condition made in interpreting the results of your experiment! If people who are simply pretending to be hypnotized are as willing to follow instructions as are hypnotized people, we have to conclude that other instructions besides hypnosis can motivate people to perform seemingly dangerous acts. Apparently, hypnosis is just one of several strong motivational techniques. We will discuss hypnosis further in Module 14. The point here is that it is very hard to design the "perfect" experiment—one that overlooks nothing. That is why researchers must often redo a study, adding one or more new conditions to correct something that may have been left out in the original study.

Now that you know about the experimental method, let's look at how it has been used to answer questions about studying, note-taking, and procrastination.

APPLYING PSYCHOLOGY   How to Study

What should I do to improve my study skills?

Getting Specific Feedback. Have I studied enough to pass the exam? You have probably asked this question a hundred times. To determine how accurate your answer is, study Chapter 1 until you think you know the material well enough to pass a multiple-choice test. Before you take the test, answer this question: "How confident am I that I learned the material?" Suppose you answer, "I'm fairly confident."

How well will your confidence that you know the material correlate with the number of exam questions you answered correctly? Surprisingly, researchers have found that there is almost no correlation between how well you *think* you know the material and how well you *perform* on a test (Glenberg & Epstein, 1985; Glenberg et al., 1987; Pressley et al., 1987).

Why are students such poor judges of how prepared they are to take a test? The primary reason is that students tend to base their judgments on what they generally remember about new material rather than what they specifically remember (Glenberg et al., 1987). For example, you might be confident about knowing the material in Module 3 because you generally remember that it is about the experimental method. However, when you take an exam on Module 3, you will be required to know the specifics, such as definitions of independent and dependent variables, differences between experimental and control groups, and steps in the experimental method. When you ask yourself the question, "How well do I know the material?" you can improve the accuracy of your judgment by getting *feedback* on your knowledge of specific information (Glenberg et al., 1987). In this textbook, feedback on how much information you have absorbed is available in two different ways: first, by testing yourself on the Major Concept questions, and second, by completing the Review questions. For additional feedback on how well you have learned specific material, you can use the *Student Organizer and Self-Testing Book*, which accompanies this text. Remember, your performance on pretests, rather than your feeling of knowing, is a more accurate indicator of how well you have learned the material.

Setting Specific Goals. Which of the following is the best way to improve the effectiveness of your study time?

Set a time goal, such as studying 10 hours a week or more, and then keep track of your study time during the semester.

Set a general goal, such as trying to study hard and stay on schedule, and then try to reach this goal during the semester.

Set a specific performance goal, such as answering at least 75 percent of pretest questions correctly for each Module, and then keep track of how well you reach this specific goal.

Researchers told three different groups of students to set and follow either time goals, general goals, or specific performance goals when they studied on their own. To determine which of the goals led to more effective studying, students' performances on the final exam were compared. The researchers found that students who set *specific performance goals* did significantly better on the final exam than students who set either time or general goals (Morgan, 1985).

These findings indicate that if you want to study more effectively, you should set a specific performance goal every week. For example, the first week your goal might be to answer correctly 75 percent of the Major Concept questions and 75 percent of the Review questions. Keep track of and keep trying to reach your performance goal. Once you have reached it, you can aim higher and try to answer 80 percent of the questions correctly. Remember, there are two rules to follow to make your study time more effective. First, set specific performance goals rather than a general or time goal. Second, keep track of your progress.

Self-reinforcement. When you reach your specific goal, such as answering 75 percent of the Major Concept questions correctly, you might give yourself a reward, called a self-reinforcement. The use of some form of self-reinforcement has been shown to improve performance on a variety of tasks, including studying (Hayes et al., 1986). You can buy yourself a special treat, such as a record or clothes, or you can allow yourself the time to go to a movie or a party. Statements such as "I'm doing really well" or "I'm going to get a good grade on the test" are also forms of self-reinforcement. Remember, self-reinforcements work best if they occur fairly soon after you reach a specific performance goal.

Taking Notes. You may already have discovered what researchers have found: Taking lecture notes and reviewing them improves recall of information and test performance (Einstein et al., 1985; Knight & McKelvie, 1986). Researchers have several suggestions for taking good notes. First, write down the information in your own words. This will ensure that you understand the material and will increase your chances of remembering it. Second, use headings and an outline format because this will help you better organize and remember your notes. Third, try to associate new lecture or text material with material that you already know, because new information is more easily absorbed if it can be related to existing knowledge (Slater et al., 1985).

Procrastination. Some students find the task of learning five chapters or writing a 15-page paper so daunting that they cannot bring themselves to begin. If this is the reason you procrastinate, there are three things you can do to get started. First, stop worrying about the final goal. Instead, break the task down into a number of smaller, less overwhelming goals, such as reading 15 pages a day. Then, write down a realistic schedule for reaching each of your smaller goals. This schedule should detail what you will accomplish each day leading up to the final deadline. Last, use a variety of self-reinforcements to encourage yourself to stay on your daily schedule.

SOURCES OF BIAS IN EXPERIMENTS

Bias in Assignment to Groups

The advertisement claims, "Improve your grades by learning to use your Natural Memory." According to the ad, a study showed that subjects who learned to use their natural memories remembered more and did better on exams than those who did not. Before you enroll in a natural memory development course, however, you should determine how the study was designed and conducted.

First, suppose that researchers asked for volunteers to learn the natural memory method and assigned them to the experimental group—and these volunteers all happened to be highly motivated students who were getting good grades. Then, suppose that the control group (those who would not be taught the natural memory method) was made up of poorly motivated students who were not getting good grades. Under these conditions, it would come as no surprise if the experimental group performs better in school than the control group, but it is unlikely that this can be attributed to natural memory training.

Most researchers believe their treatments will have some effect. As a result, they may unintentionally choose people for their experimental group who are likely to respond in the "right" way. Unintentional bias that affects the makeup of experimental groups is called **self-selection bias.** Experienced researchers combat self-selection bias through **random assignment,** whereby every subject has an equal chance of being placed in the experimental or the control group. Drawing the names of experimental and control subjects out of a hat is one way of randomly assigning them. Random assignment greatly reduces potential error associated with self-selection bias.

Bias by the Experimenter

Could you make a rat act stupid?

How much can researchers' beliefs affect the results of experiments? The answer will probably surprise you. In one study, students were asked to test the ability of rats to find their way through a maze. Half the students were told that their rats had been specially bred for brightness at mastering mazes. The others were told that their rats had been specially bred for dullness at this task. After five days, rats handled by students who believed they were bright were making significantly fewer errors than rats handled by students who believed they were dull.

Actually, the two groups of rats were no different in intelligence. It was the students' expectations that caused the differences in performance. Students who expected their rats to be bright apparently treated them in a more relaxed and gentle manner, which resulted in fewer mistakes on the part of the rats (Rosenthal & Fode, 1963). The students were not deliberately trying to bias the results. Their beliefs and expectations had this effect without their knowledge.

If researchers' expectations can affect the behavior of rats, can they also affect the behavior of humans? To find out, psychologists gave elementary schoolchildren an IQ test (Rosenthal & Jacobson, 1968). They then told the children's teachers that the test results indicated certain youngsters would show "intellectual blooming" in the coming year—that is, they would make remarkable progress in their studies. Unknown to the teachers, of course, the children who were labeled "intellectual bloomers" were selected completely at random. They were no brighter or duller than children in the control group. Nevertheless, when the students were all given another IQ test at the end of the school year, the "bloomers" showed larger gains than the controls. The reason was that the teachers' expectations had affected their own behavior, which in turn encouraged the children to perform as predicted. This unintentional effect is called a **self-fulfilling prophecy.**

The Importance of Self-Fulfilling Prophecies. You can think of self-fulfilling prophecies as having two components. The first is developing very

MAJOR CONCEPT   Experimental Method

Match the term with its correct definition.

1. Independent variable

a. _3_ The subject's behavior in an experiment that is measured.

2. Experimental group

b. _1_ The condition in an experiment that will be varied.

3. Dependent variable

c. _4_ The group of subjects who do not receive a designated treatment.

4. Control group

d. _6_ A technique that reduces the effects of experimenter's and subject's expectations.

5. Statistical tests

e. _7_ A technique that reduces self-selection bias in forming experimental and control groups.

6. Double blind

f. _5_ A way to determine the likelihood that the results of an experiment were due to chance.

7. Random assignment

g. _2_ The group of subjects who receive a designated treatment.

Answers: a (3); b (1); c (4); d (6); e (7); f (5); g (2)

---

strong expectations about what is likely to happen in a given situation. The second is unintentionally changing your behavior in order to make those expectations come true. You will understand why this phenomenon is called a self-fulfilling prophecy if you think of making a prophecy about what will happen and then acting to fulfill it.

Self-fulfilling prophecies are so important because they can affect anyone. In the studies we have just described, students testing the "bright" and "dull" rats and teachers interacting with elementary schoolchildren fell into this bias. In Figure 1.4, you will see that the expectations of army instructors affected the performances of their trainees. Many other examples of self-fulfilling prophecies have been observed (Rosenthal & Rubin, 1978; Rosenthal, 1983).

Just like teachers and army instructors, researchers can create self-fulfilling prophecies. One way to prevent them from distorting a study's results is to withhold from both researchers and subjects all information about who belongs to the experimental group and who belongs to the control group. Only after the experiment is completed is this information revealed. With this procedure, called a **double-blind technique,** the participants have less opportunity to act on their expectations.

As you can see, psychologists have developed special procedures for reducing bias in experiments. When psychologists say a particular study was "well conducted," they mean that the researchers who performed it carefully followed the experimental method and all the techniques for minimizing bias.

Figure 1.4
Two groups of soldiers were matched for aptitude before training. The only difference between the groups was that the instructor of the high expectancy group had been led to believe that his trainees would perform at a high level. The figure shows that the instructor's expectancy level affected the trainee's performance. Those trainees who were expected to perform better did, in fact, do so according to objective measures of combat knowledge and practical skills.
(Adapted from Eden & Shani, 1982)

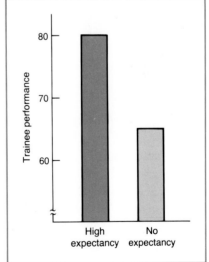

Expectations Influence Behavior **EXPLORING PSYCHOLOGY**

As you read about the "intellectual bloomers," you may have wondered how teachers could actually raise or lower IQ scores just through their beliefs about particular students. This is a question psychologists have wondered about too. For over ten years, researchers H.M. Cooper and T.L. Good (1983) have studied the effects of teacher expectations. Along with their assistants, they have gone into classrooms and recorded teacher-student interactions. Their findings reveal the many ways that teachers send signals regarding how well they *expect* students to do. These signals, in turn, influence the students' self-concepts, their levels of aspiration, and ultimately their actual performance. Here are some examples of teachers' behavior toward youngsters they consider "slow":

- Seating these students farther away from the teacher, making it more difficult to monitor them or treat them as individuals

- Paying less attention to them by smiling and making eye contact less often

- Calling on them less frequently to answer classroom questions

- Giving them less time to answer questions

- Failing to provide clues or ask follow-up questions in problem situations with these students

- Criticizing such students more frequently for incorrect answers

- Praising them less often for correct or marginal answers

- Demanding less effort and less work from these students (Cooper & Good, 1983)

This research tells us several things. First, without realizing it, teachers may behave differently toward students for whom they have high and low expectations. Second, these differences may affect students' willingness to volunteer answers, seek help, and try harder. As a result, the teachers' expectations eventually influence actual performance in the classroom. Fortunately, however, this is not inevitable. If teachers are made aware of the power of expectations, they can guard against unintentionally discouraging some students.

THEORY CONSTRUCTION AND TESTING

The Theory of Biorhythms

Can you predict your "bad days"?

In the early 1900s, a doctor and a psychologist noticed that people's performance on all kinds of tasks tends to undergo cycles, from excellent on some days to very poor on others. Based on this observation, they constructed the theory of biorhythms, which holds that these cycles, or rhythms, are biological in origin. A **theory** is an organized set of assumptions about why things happen the way they do. There are two parts to developing a scientific theory: construction and testing. Based on initial observations of some event, scientists make an educated guess to explain what they have observed. Such an educated guess is called a **hypothesis**. As scientists form a number of hypotheses and organize them in a formal way, they are *constructing a theory*.

The next step is *testing the theory*. Researchers do this by making specific *predictions* on the basis of their hypotheses and then conducting studies to see if those predictions hold true.

Let's examine how the theory of biorhythms was constructed and then how it was tested. According to the theory of biorhythms, at the moment of birth three cycles that continue over and over throughout life are set in motion. A health-related cycle takes 23 days to complete; a physical cycle takes 29 days; and a mental cycle runs its course in 33 days. The theorists predicted that performance in a particular area would be at its best when the associated cycle peaked, and at its worst when that cycle reached its low point. Whenever the lows of all three cycles coincided, a person was in a critical period when disaster was most likely to strike.

At first, hundreds of testimonials seemed to confirm biorhythmic predictions. For instance, former heavyweight boxing champion Muhammad Ali successfully defended his title on a day when two of his cycles were rising. On two of his critical days, the famous actor Clark Gable suffered two separate heart attacks. In Japan, taxi drivers claimed to have more accidents during their critical days.

As noted in Module 2, researchers are wary of testimonials. Researchers determine the accuracy of a theory by making specific predictions, which are then tested in carefully designed studies. The study on biorhythms involved computing a person's high- and low-performance days and observing actual behavior on them. The outcomes of numerous such studies were quite consistent: they failed to support the theory. For example, on a so-called critical day, a person is no more likely to perform poorly on an examination, a chess match, or a game of golf. Nor are critical days associated with poorer recovery from major surgery or with a greater likelihood of dying. Likewise, people are no more apt to perform well on a day when their cycles are rising than on any other day (Bradshaw, 1982; Floody, 1981). If a theory's predictions are not supported, scientists either modify or reject the theory. Based on their research, most scientists have rejected the theory of biorhythms.

Bernard Gittelson holds the book he wrote on how to compute your biorhythms. According to this theory, you can identify the days on which your performance will be good or bad. (The Honolulu Advertiser)

The Theory of Consolidation

If a blow on the head knocked you unconscious in a car accident, you might never remember the events just before and during the collision. At one time psychologists were puzzled by this fact. They wondered why a blow on the head would destroy memories. Working from thousands of observations, they eventually developed a theory to explain why. According to this theory, a certain amount of time is needed for the chemical or structural changes that form permanent memories to become firmly fixed, or consolidated, in the brain. If something happens during this time to disrupt the consolidation process, the memories will be lost.

What happens when you're knocked out?

MAJOR CONCEPT   Theory

Indicate whether each statement is true (T) or false (F).

1. T/F A theory is an organized set of assumptions about why things happen the way they do.

2. T/F If you wanted to test a theory, you would make specific predictions and then test those predictions.

3. T/F If a theory were supported by hundreds of testimonials, that theory would be said to be well tested and well supported.

4. T/F If a theory's predictions are not supported, that theory must be modified or rejected.

Answers: 1 (T); 2 (T); 3 (F); 4 (T).

Based on the theory of consolidation, a number of predictions have been made. For example, a blow to the head should destroy recollection of events immediately preceding it because such a blow disrupts the process of consolidation. However, the blow should *not* destroy recollection of much earlier events because the structural or chemical changes that formed these earlier memories have long since been consolidated.

Physiological psychologists have conducted thousands of experiments to test whether these predictions hold true. In most cases, the predictions have been supported. This gives us reason to believe that consolidation is a useful theory for helping us understand how permanent memories are created.

Notice, however, that we do not say that the theory of consolidation has been proved. In science, few theories are ever considered to be established with absolute certainty. We still need to know more about what goes on in the brain during consolidation. We can say that Einstein was a great consolidator, and that psychologists are slowly discovering why.

REVIEW

Dr. Nathan Pritikin claimed in his best-selling book that the following study showed that his diet was the healthiest in the world. For this study, Pritikin placed volunteer subjects on his special diet, which is low in fat and high in carbohydrates, for twenty-six days. Before, during, and after the designated period, subjects were checked to determine their cholesterol level and blood pressure, which were presumed to measure health. As Pritikin predicted, after twenty-six days the people on his special diet showed a lowered cholesterol count, and those with high blood pressure also showed a drop in blood pressure.

Let's see if you can identify the various steps of the experimental method in Pritikin's study. Pritikin's special low-fat, high-carbohydrate diet represents the experimental treatments and is called the

(1) _____ variable. Measures of the subjects' healthiness were cholesterol count and blood pressure. These two measures, which are used to assess the effectiveness of the treatment, are called the

(2) _____ variables. Usually there are at least two groups of subjects in an experiment. One group is exposed to the treatment and one group is not. In this study, the group of subjects who were exposed to the special diet for twenty-six days comprised the

(3) _____ group. To determine if the treatment is effective, researchers normally would compare the results of the experimental group with those of the

(4) _____ group, who do not receive the treatment. If you examine this study closely, you will discover that there is no control group. Without an experimental and control group, it is impossible to determine if the differences between the groups were due

to the treatment in question or to (5) _____. To determine if any difference between experimental and control conditions is due to the treatment or to

chance, we use (6) _____ tests.

If Dr. Pritikin wanted to guard against the self-selection bias in assigning subjects to groups, he would

use a procedure called (7) _____ assignment. If he had strong expectations that his diet would lower blood pressure, he might be biased in how he gauged his subjects' responses to his diet. If a person with a preconceived belief unintentionally acts in ways that makes that belief come true, that person is creating

what is called a (8) _____ prophecy. One way that these prophecies can be avoided is to use a procedure in which neither the researchers nor the subjects know who has been assigned to the experimental and control groups. This technique is called the

(9) _____. procedure.

Dr. Pritikin made an organized set of guesses or hypotheses about the effects of a low-fat, high-carbohydrate diet. His organized set of guesses, which explains why his diet lowers cholesterol and blood pres-

sure, might be called a (10) _____. To be considered useful and valuable, a theory must lead to

a number of specific (11) _____ that can be subjected to scientific tests. If the predictions prove untrue, researchers would reject or modify the theory.

If you wanted to improve your ability to study the material in this Module, you should set a specific

(12) _____ goal rather than a general or

time goal. A specific performance goal might be answering correctly 75 percent of the Major Concept or Review questions. When you reached your specific performance goal, you might reward yourself with a form of (13) _____, which might be the purchase of a desired item or a statement such as "I'm doing well in this course." Taking notes during lectures and when reading texts will improve your recall of material as well as your test performance. To take good notes, write them down in your own (14) _____,

use headings and an (15) _____ format, and try to make connections or (16) _____ between new material and material you already know. If you have problems with procrastination, break down the final goal into a number of smaller (17) _____ that will not feel as overwhelming. Develop a realistic (18) _____ for accomplishing your smaller goals and use self-reinforcements when you reach your goals.

Answers: (1) independent; (2) dependent; (3) experimental; (4) control; (5) chance; (6) statistical; (7) random; (8) self-fulfilling; (9) double-blind; (10) theory; (11) predictions; (12) performance; (13) self-reinforcement; (14) words; (15) outline; (16) associations; (17) goals; (18) schedule

GLOSSARY TERMS

control group (p. 21)
dependent variable
    (p. 21)
double-blind technique
    (p. 25)

experimental group
    (p. 21)
experimental method
    (p. 20)
hypothesis (p. 26)

independent variable
    (p. 20–21)
random assignment
    (p. 24)

self-fulfilling prophecy
    (p. 24)
self-selection bias
    (p. 24)
theory (p. 26)

PERSONAL NOTE

Sometimes we all behave like scientists: We make observations and construct our own personal theories. My favorite theory is that chocolate improves memory. For example, I can still remember my favorite chocolate bar when I was a child, even though I can't remember a single favorite vegetable. I can also remember the exact location of the best homemade fudge stores in six different states, even though I've forgotten the addresses of places I used to live. I can go on and on with hundreds of pieces of evidence showing that whenever I eat chocolate, my memory is superb. After reading this chapter, you should be able to point out the errors in my thinking. But before you do, I just want to add that fudge improves my memory the most. —R.P.

2

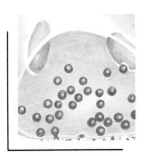
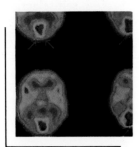
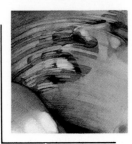

Biological Bases of Behavior

Module 4 Neurons

Janet, a forty-year-old woman, almost never drank. But one day, as she was crossing the street, a policeman stopped her and said, "Aren't you ashamed to be drunk so early in the morning!"

Janet was terrified. She remembered her father and her three older brothers walking like they were drunk. They walked that way because of a frightening hereditary condition called Huntington's disease. It made them lose their balance, twitch uncontrollably, and eventually lose their minds. When Janet was examined by her doctor, he confirmed her worst fears: she too had Huntington's disease and would become totally incapacitated and die within ten to twenty years. The doctor said that, at present, there was no cure for this disease (adapted from Pines, 1984).

What made Janet walk like a drunk?

Huntington's disease is a cruel disorder that will slowly destroy Janet's brain cells, called neurons. As this disease destroys her brain, what will happen to her mind? The mind is a mental thing, defined as an awareness of what you are thinking, feeling, or doing. The brain is a physical thing, defined as a structure that contains billions of cells and weighs about three pounds. In the case of diseases like Huntington's, it is clear that the brain and the mind are closely connected. As the brain is destroyed—as it is in a disease like Huntington's—so too is the person's mind.

If you looked inside a human skull, you would see one of the most powerful and sophisticated computers in the world. You would be looking at the human brain, a pinkish, jellylike mass that weighs about 1,450 grams (approximately 3 pounds), uses very little energy, and operates mainly on sugar. Its 100 billion cells can process and store enough information to fill 20 million books, and retrieve much of this information in a millionth of a second. At birth your brain had only a minimal set of programmed instructions, including those for crying, sucking, and grasping. From that point on, new programs were written daily. By now, your brain has acquired a set of programmed capacities that surpasses by far any machine's ability to think, solve problems, be creative, or understand and express ideas. Indeed, in the mid-1980s a human defeated the world's most powerful computer at chess, a game that requires thought, creativity, and intuition (Module 21). It is true that computers are being developed with larger and larger memories and programs that can perform increasingly difficult tasks. But no machine can match the human brain's ability to comprehend a dozen spoken languages and to make jokes in each one.

BASIC STRUCTURE AND FUNCTION OF NEURONS

What does a miniature message system look like?

To understand how your brain performs these remarkable feats, let's start with its smallest unit, the neuron, a cell that comes in all shapes and sizes and has a special structure that allows it to receive and transmit information. Each neuron is made of dendrites, a cell body (or soma), and an axon. As shown in Figure 2.1, **dendrites** are tubelike extensions that resemble a bushy tree. Dendrites receive information from the environment or from other neurons and carry it *to* the soma. The **soma,** often circular in shape, furnishes the cell with nutrients and manufactures chemicals used in transmitting information. Extending from the soma is a relatively long, single fiber called the **axon,** which carries information *away from* the soma to a neighboring neuron, a muscle, or a gland.

To understand how the dendrites, soma, and axon relay information, imagine reaching out for a glass of water. As you touch the glass, the stimulation of your fingers is received by **sensory neurons,** which carry information to your spinal cord. This information travels from each sensory neuron's dendrites, to its soma, and then along its axon. After reaching the spinal cord, which itself contains neurons, the information is relayed up to a certain area of the brain. It is here in the brain that the sensation of "touching a glass" occurs.

But before you can move your fingers to pick up the glass, another brain region must be activated. This second area sends instructions first down your spinal cord and then out your arm via **motor neurons** that control the muscles in your fingers. When the instructions reach the tips of these motor neurons' axons, they cause the muscle surrounding the axons to contract and move the fingers. Remember that axons carry instructions *away* from the soma to initiate some response in a neighboring cell, causing a muscle to move, a gland to secrete hormones, or another neuron to be excited or inhibited. Dendrites, in contrast, receive information from other cells and carry it *to* the soma.

As you think about how neurons function in the body, you can easily understand why people with Huntington's disease have the symptoms they do. This disease slowly destroys neurons in the brain that are involved in sending instructions to control muscle activity. The disease also destroys neurons involved in regulating emotions, causing its victims to suffer severe depression. Neurons, in short, direct virtually all of human behavior. It is through their actions that we see, hear, think, feel, and move.

Figure 2.1
Although they come in many sizes and shapes, all neurons have three parts: dendrites, soma, and axon. Dendrites receive information from the environment, skin, muscles, glands, or other neurons. The soma maintains the neuron and manufactures neurotransmitters. The axon carries information to neighboring neurons, muscles, or glands. Some neurons are covered with an insulating membrane called myelin.

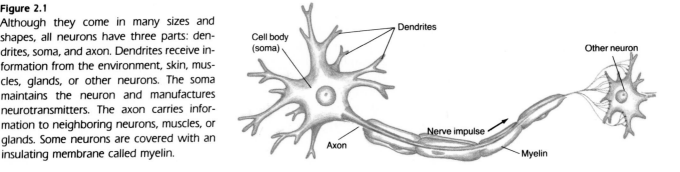

MAJOR CONCEPT   Neuron

Brain cells that are specialized to receive and transmit information are called neurons.

Label the parts of the neuron and match each part with its function. (a) dendrite, (b) axon, (c) soma

DRAWING OF NEURON

1. Receives information from the environment or from another neuron.

2. Provides nutrients and manufactures chemicals used in transmitting information.

3. Carries information from the soma to a neighboring neuron, muscle, or gland.

Answers: 1 (a); 2 (d); 3 (b)

WHY NEURONS CAN COMMUNICATE SO QUICKLY

Remember the last time you touched something very hot. Your hand jerked back before you were consciously aware of any pain. This is because you were born with a number of neural circuits that perform certain responses quickly and automatically. These circuits contain chains of neurons, called **reflex arcs,** that are programmed to react automatically to certain stimuli, such as pain, noise, or a tap on the knee. As Figure 2.2 illustrates, reflex arcs involve sensory neurons, which travel to the spinal cord, and from there link up with motor neurons, which travel to the appropriate muscles (or glands). Since reflexive responses do not require conscious thought or decision, your hand jerks quickly and automatically off a hot stove.

Can you move your hand without thinking?

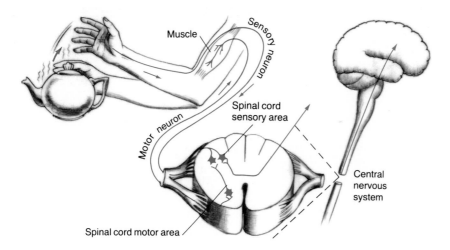

Figure 2.2
When you touch a hot pot, the pain receptors in your finger are activated. These receptors send their information on a sensory neuron to the spinal cord. Inside the spinal cord, the sensory neuron connects with several other neurons, one of them a motor neuron. The motor neuron sends a message to contract the muscles in your arm, which immediately contract and withdraw your finger. Other neurons carry information to the brain, which would result in your feeling pain.

Another reason is that reflexes involve motor neurons that share an important feature: their axons are wrapped with many layers of a coating called *myelin* (Stevens, 1979). Myelin insulates axons and permits faster transmission of instructions. As a result, messages can travel along these motor neuron axons at speeds as high as 100 meters per second, or over 200 miles per hour.

THE LANGUAGE OF NEURONS

There is a science fiction story about a tiny person who explores the human body by traveling through the blood vessels. If you could make a similar journey along a network of neurons, you would encounter a world of charged particles, electrical forces, and sudden bursts of chemicals. Most of the reactions you would see would take place in the blink of an eye. To make this journey, let's shrink you down to microscopic size and place you outside a neuron. The first thing you will notice is what is called an action potential.

Action Potentials

What happens when a neuron is activated?

In your role as tiny sightseer, you observe that neurons are surrounded by fluid that contains *ions*—chemicals that carry electrical charges, either positive or negative (see Figure 2.3). The neuron you are viewing is in its **resting state,** which means that it is not receiving or transmitting information. During the resting state most of the ions outside the neuron are positively charged sodium ions. However, this is not the case inside the neuron. As you peer through one of the tiny openings in the neuron's thin membrane, you see that in the neuron's interior there are mostly positive

Figure 2.3
During the resting state, most of the positively charged sodium ions, symbolized by Na$^+$, are outside the axon's membrane. Most of the negative chloride ions, symbolized by Cl$^-$, are inside the membrane, together with some positive potassium ions (K$^+$). Because of this distribution of ions, the outside of the axon has a more positive electrical charge than the inside. When some stimulus opens the axon's channels, all the Na$^+$ ions rush inside. This is called an action potential, or impulse. During an action potential, the inside of the axon has a more positive electrical charge than the outside.
(From Plotnik & Mollenauer, 1978)

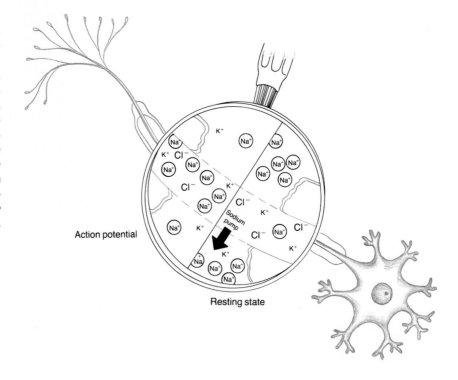

Action potential

Resting state

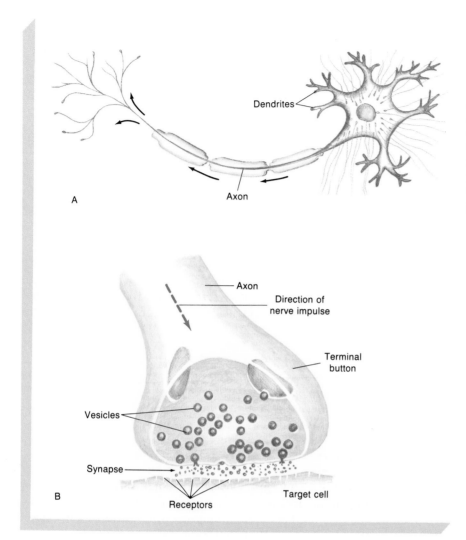

A

B

Dendrites

Axon

Axon

Direction of
nerve impulse

Terminal
button

Vesicles

Synapse

Receptors

Target cell

Figure 2.4

(A) Thousands of axons synapse, or make connections, with a single neuron. (B) This closeup of an axon's terminal button shows that it contains many tiny globules of vesicles, which store neurotransmitters. When an impulse arrives at the terminal button, it causes the vesicles to release their neurotransmitters into the synapse. Once released, the neurotransmitters bind to the receptors on the target cell. Depending upon the kind of neurotransmitters released, target cells may be excited or inhibited.

potassium ions and negative chloride ions. In fact, the cell membrane actively blocks sodium ions from entering; any stray sodium ions that manage to squeeze inside are quickly pushed back out by what is called a **sodium pump.** As you observe sodium ions being pushed to the outside, you notice that there are always fewer positive charges on the inside of the neuron. If you could actually measure the charges, you would find the inside is negatively charged and the outside is positively charged. Because of this difference in charges inside and out, the membrane is said to be **polarized:** the inside is negatively charged relative to the outside.

Seeing what happens next is like watching a dam being opened. When a neuron is stimulated, its cell membrane becomes temporarily open to sodium ions. Sodium ions by the thousand rush inside the neuron, making the inside of the membrane positively charged relative to the outside. This sudden reversal in polarity is called an **action potential.** It is also illustrated in Figure 2.3. As the action potential moves down the axon from point to point, it is known as a **nerve impulse.**

The axon, then, functions somewhat like the fuse of a firecracker. Once lit, a fuse continues to burn until the flame reaches the powder and causes an explosion. Because the fuse requires a certain amount of heat before it begins to burn, you can think of it as having an ignition threshold. If enough heat is applied, the threshold is reached and the fuse burns. The axon also has a certain threshold, but its threshold is for the opening of the sodium channels. With enough activation, the threshold is reached, the sodium channels open, sodium ions rush inside, and a nerve impulse is started.

Once started, that impulse continues down the entire length of the axon, no matter how long the axon is. This phenomenon is known as the **all-or-none law**. The law says that if activation is strong enough to reach the axon's threshold, an impulse will begin and, like a burning fuse, continue all the way to the end. If activation is too weak to reach the axon's threshold, nothing will happen. It is important to remember that the all-or-none law applies only to axons, not to dendrites or cell bodies.

When the flame of a burning fuse reaches the firecracker, it causes a loud explosion. Something similar happens when a nerve impulse reaches the end of an axon: it causes something of a miniature explosion of chemicals.

Synapses and Neurotransmitters

Normally, thousands of axons converge on a single neuron (see Figure 2.4A). At the very end of each axon are **terminal buttons**, swellings filled with tiny packets, or **vesicles** (VEH-sicklz), that store chemicals. Figure 2.4B shows what a terminal button looks like. When a nerve impulse reaches the terminal button, it causes the vesicles to open and secrete their chemicals. These chemicals, called **neurotransmitters**, are emptied into the **synapse** (SIN-aps), which is simply the separation or space between the neuron's terminal button and a neighboring neuron, muscle, or gland. You can move your fingers because terminal buttons secrete their neurotransmitters into synapses that border on the finger muscles. These neurotransmitters flow across the synapses and act on the muscles that cause the fingers to move. Neurotransmitters are said to be *excitatory* if they activate muscles, glands, or other neurons. They are said to be *inhibitory* if they relax muscles, or decrease the activities of glands or other neurons. Whatever you do—thinking, dreaming, walking, eating, riding a bicycle, and the like— is directed by neurotransmitters. When neurons die and their neurotransmitters dry up, the results are devastating, as we will now see.

MAJOR CONCEPT   How Neurons Communicate

Neurons communicate by a series of electrical and chemical reactions.

Match the term on the left with the correct statement on the right.

1. sodium ions

2. action potential or nerve impulse

3. neurotransmitters

4. resting state

5. polarized

a. ____ Secreted by the terminal buttons, these chemicals cross the synapse and excite or inhibit neighboring neurons, muscles, or glands.

b. ____ Positively charged chemicals that rush inside the neuron's membrane causing an action potential.

c. ____ The condition of the membrane when the outside is positively charged and the inside is negatively charged.

d. ____ Travels down the length of the axon and obeys the all-or-none law.

e. ____ The condition of an axon when it is not conducting an impulse.

Answers: a (3); b (1); c (5); d (2); e (4)

Effects of Alzheimer's Disease **EXPLORING PSYCHOLOGY**

Something was wrong with Tommy's memory. The first signs were when he forgot to put his tools away or forgot that he had put the kettle on the stove, or where he was going when he left his house. One night he went outside the house in his pajamas and tried to direct traffic on the street. Most terrifying of all was the time Tommy turned on his wife of forty years and demanded, "Who are you and what are you doing here? This is my house." His wife answered, "Honey, I'm your wife, and I have a right to be here." Tommy said "No, you are not my wife." As Tommy's condition worsened, he had to be hospitalized. Now, at age seventy-three, he lies on his back in a hospital bed, not recognizing his wife or his doctor and unaware of who he is (adapted from the *San Diego Union*, August 9, 1981).

Why did Tommy forget who he was?

Tommy's symptoms are not the result of aging or growing old but of a severe dementia. While dementia may have many causes, such as brain tumors, alcoholism or hardening of the brain's blood vessels, Tommy's dementia is caused by Alzheimer's disease. This disease affects 5 percent to 15 percent of people over the age of 65, including half of all nursing home residents, and is now the nation's fourth largest killer (about 100,000 deaths per year). Like all dementias, which result from the progressive destruction of brain cells, Alzheimer's disease slowly destroys a person's memory, cognitions, and personality.

Researchers do not know exactly what causes Alzheimer's disease. One of the things they do know is that Alzheimer's patients, like Tommy, have an abnormally low level of a neurotransmitter called acetylcholine. Without this neurotransmitter, communication between certain neurons becomes impossible. As the disease progresses, many of the neurons themselves are destroyed, and patients lose the ability to process information, perform tasks, recognize familiar people, and behave appropriately. In searching for the causes of Alzheimer's disease, researchers are focusing on six areas for clues: heredity, since there are families in which there is a high incidence of Alzheimer's; production of abnormal proteins, which interfere with the functioning of neurons and cause deficits in cognition; a decrease in acetylcholine levels, which interferes with memory and cognition; infectious agents, such as a virus, which cause destruction of neurons; toxic agents, such as salts of aluminum, which are found in drinking water and in foods contained in aluminum cans, or cooked in aluminum utensils; and decreases in blood flow in the brain (Davies & Wolozin, 1987; Selkoe, 1987; Wurtman, 1985).

One of the problems in diagnosing Alzheimer's in its early stages is that there has been no reliable laboratory test for the disease. Researchers Peter Davies and Benjamin Wolozin from New York City's Albert Einstein College of Medicine reported a possible laboratory test for Alzheimer's at the 1986 Annual Society for Neuroscience meeting. If this test proves reliable, it would mean that Alzheimer's could be diagnosed in its early stages and in the future, it might increase clinicians' chances of halting the destruction of neurons in Alzheimer's victims. At present, though, there is no cure for Alzheimer's. Although researchers have tried several different drugs to increase levels of acetylcholine in the brain, most treatments have met with limited success (Kopelman, 1986).

Psychologists have had some success in helping mildly impaired Alzheimer's patients to remain active by using memory aids and techniques, such as calendars, lists of "things to do today," and other such devices.

Because of the massive destruction of brain cells, a patient in the advanced stages of Alzheimer's disease may not know the day, place, or season. (Ira Wyman/Sygma)

Further, psychologists are trying to develop effective coping strategies, such as group support, management techniques, and psychotherapeutic intervention, to help family members deal with their own depression, anxiety, and feelings of being burdened, all of which are emotional states that Alzheimer's disease victims suffer from (Crook & Miller, 1985). Additional information on Alzheimer's disease and ways to cope with an Alzheimer's patient can be obtained from your local branch of the Alzheimer's Disease and Related Disorders Association.

In early 1987, medical researchers reported a new procedure that may lead to a treatment for diseases such as Alzheimer's. This revolutionary technique—transplanting tissue into the human brain—is already being used to treat another neurological disorder, Parkinson's disease (Lewin, 1987).

APPLYING PSYCHOLOGY   Use of Brain Transplants

Old rats are not very good at balancing themselves on a wooden pole suspended between two platforms. "They slip off the pole and then cannot correct themselves when they start to lose their balance," says Anders Bjorklund of the University of Lund. Old rats lose their ability to run along the bar because their brains lose some of the ability to make a neurotransmitter called dopamine. When Bjorklund gave these old rats transplanted dopamine-producing brain tissue from younger rats, the old rats were able to run along the bar once again (adapted from Kolata, 1983, p. 1277).

A number of researchers have reported this startling finding: brain tissue that was removed and transplanted from younger rats to older ones began to produce dopamine within days and to improve the older rats' motor abilities (Gage et al., 1983; Labbe et al., 1983; Perlow et al., 1979). Based on these findings, medical researchers have begun experimental treatments in which healthy tissue is transplanted into the brains of people suffering from the neurological disorder known as Parkinson's disease.

During the previous year, Joseluis was not able to speak clearly, walk, dress, bathe, or feed himself without help. He has Parkinson's disease, which is caused by damage to a part of his brain called the substantia nigra. As a result, his brain no longer produces sufficient dopamine, a neurotransmitter that helps regulate voluntary actions such as walking, talking, and writing. After experimental surgery to treat his Parkinson's disease, Joseluis can do all these things plus kick a soccer ball with his young son (adapted from the *Los Angeles Times*, December 8, 1986).

Fortunately for Joseluis, the inner core of the adrenal glands, located near the kidneys, also produce substantial amounts of dopamine. Dr. Ignacio Madrazo and his colleagues at La Raza Hospital, Mexico City, removed the walnut-sized right adrenal gland from 35-year-old Joseluis and transplanted part of the gland into his brain (Figure 2.5). Based on experiments with animals, Dr. Madrazo hoped that once the adrenal gland was transplanted, it would continue to make the neurotransmitter dopamine and relieve Joseluis's symptoms. A year after surgery, Joseluis and seven other Parkinson's patients who also received adrenal gland transplants continued to show remarkable improvement. They lost 60 to 90 percent of their hand trembling and 60 to 80 percent of their rigidity, enabling them to walk and speak clearly (Madrazo et al., 1987). The success of Madrazo and his surgical team has led to other surgeons performing similar operations on Parkinson's patients. In a recent workshop, Dr. Harold Klawans (1988) of Rush University said that 85 American transplant patients had shown some beneficial effects. However, none of the Americans had been cured, all still required medication, and none had shown the dramatic improvements reported by Madrazo. Because of these results, American researchers urged caution in using transplants until current patients have been thoroughly evaluated (Lewin, 1988). Researchers hope that transplants will eventually be used to treat many brain disorders.

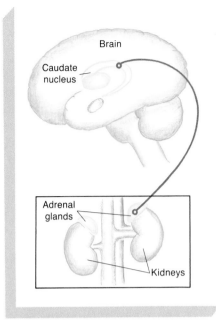

Figure 2.5

In Parkinson's disease, patients suffer from a decrease in the neurotransmitter, dopamine. Because of this decrease, the functioning of the caudate nucleus is disrupted and the result is a number of symptoms, such as uncontrollable trembling and shaking. Neurosurgeons take cells from the adrenal gland, which also make dopamine, and transplant them into or near the caudate nucleus. Following this surgery, some patients have had reductions in symptoms.

REVIEW

Alan puts on his roller skates and stands up. He's watched other skaters. They move their feet from side to side and glide down the sidewalk. Should be easy. He starts off, wobbles from side to side, leans forward, jerks backward, and falls to the concrete. Alan's 20 seconds of roller-skating involved billions of cells in his nervous system. Cells that are specialized to receive and transmit information are called (1) _____. Although these cells come in many sizes and shapes, they all have three parts. The part that receives information from the environment and other cells is called the (2) _____; the part that maintains and nourishes the cell is called the (3) _____; and the part that transmits information from the soma to other muscles, glands, or neurons is called the

(4) _____. As Alan tries to maintain his balance, he is activating a chain of neurons programmed to respond automatically to a stimulus such as falling. This chain of neurons is called a (5) _____ arc. In this particular arc, nerve signals travel to Alan's spinal cord via (6) _____ neurons, and then back out to the muscles of his arm via (7) _____ neurons.

When Alan was roller-skating, different neurons were activated than when he was sitting on the concrete. When a neuron is inactive it is said to be in the (8) _____ state. Because of the distribution of ions inside and outside the cell membrane during the resting state, the inside of the membrane is nega-

tively charged relative to the outside. The cell membrane is therefore said to be (9) _____.
When the neuron is activated by some stimulus, sodium channels in the membrane open up and positively charged sodium ions rush inside. This inrush of sodium ions causes a temporary reversal in the polarity of the membrane, a reversal called an (10) _____ potential. As this potential moves down the axon from point to point it is called a nerve (11) _____.
Once it begins in the axon, a nerve impulse will travel to the very end of the axon because it obeys the (12) _____ - _____ - _____ law. Everything Alan does, whether roller-skating, falling down, or sleeping, is made possible because of nerve impulses.

When a nerve impulse reaches the end of an axon it causes the terminal buttons to release chemicals called (13) _____. These chemicals are secreted into a tiny space called a (14) _____, which separates the axon from its neighboring muscle, gland, or other neuron. Alan is able to perform complicated motor acts, such as standing up on roller skates, because billions of neurons are secreting neurotransmitters on neighboring neurons or muscles.

Certain diseases, such as Parkinson's, Huntington's and Alzheimer's, result from a large decrease in the level of (15) _____. A new treatment for Parkinson's disease involves (16) _____ tissue into the brain. The transplanted tissue manufactures neurotransmitters and this results in restoring some of the lost functions.

Answers: (1) neurons; (2) dendrite; (3) soma; (4) axon; (5) reflex; (6) sensory; (7) motor; (8) resting; (9) polarized; (10) action; (11) impulse; (12) all-or-none; (13) neurotransmitters; (14) synapse; (15) neurotransmitters; (16) transplanting.

GLOSSARY TERMS

action potential (p. 35)
all-or-none law (p. 36)
axon (p. 32)
dendrites (p. 32)
motor neurons (p. 32)

nerve impulse (p. 35)
neurotransmitters
  (p. 36)
polarized (p. 35)

reflex arcs (p. 33)
resting state (p. 34)
sensory neurons (p. 32)
sodium pump (p. 35)

soma (p. 32)
synapse (p. 36)
terminal buttons (p. 36)
vesicles (p. 36)

Module 5 The Nervous System

**Can severed fingers be
reconnected?**

A young man named Michael Bates lost eight fingers in an industrial accident. Because the fingers were not badly damaged, surgeons were able to reattach seven of them (Figure 2.6). Within two or three weeks, Michael experienced limited sensation and movement in his fingers. His sensory and motor function returned almost completely in about a year. Now compare the story of Michael with that of Katie.

It was Katie's eighteenth birthday and she was having a great party. She and her best friends were spending the afternoon around a keg of beer. After drinking for several hours, they all agreed to go for a pizza. Katie said that she would drive and they all got into her car. They were talking about the kind of pizza they would get when a child ran out into the road. Katie's reactions were dulled by the alcohol, so instead of swerving quickly she made a slow turn and smashed into a parked car. Her last sensation was the snap of her neck as it broke and severed her spinal cord. Katie would be paralyzed from the neck down for the rest of her life. Her spinal cord could not be rejoined (author's files).

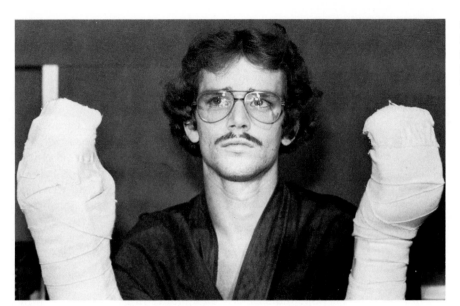

Figure 2.6
Michael Bates, shown here, had his fingers surgically reattached after an accident. The text explains why this was possible. (UPI/Bettmann Newsphotos)

The ability of Michael's severed fingers to be reattached but not Katie's severed spinal cord marks a primary difference between what are called the peripheral and central nervous systems.

BASIC ORGANIZATION OF THE NERVOUS SYSTEM

Michael's **peripheral nervous system** is made up of the nerves outside the brain and spinal cord, such as the nerves in his arms and fingers. Nerves are simply bundles of dendrite and axon fibers held together by connective tissue. Sensory nerves are composed of sensory neurons, which carry information to the spinal cord, while motor nerves are composed of motor neurons, which carry information from the spinal cord to the body's limbs and organs. When nerves in the peripheral nervous system are severed, they can be rejoined and will regain their sensory or motor function. That is why Michael's fingers could be reattached. The nerves in the peripheral nervous system have the capacity to **regenerate**.

Katie's **central nervous system** is made up of the brain and spinal cord. Until recently, it was assumed that damage to neurons or nerves in the central nervous system could never be repaired. One of the most intensive scientific searches of the 1980s has been for ways to stimulate regeneration in the central nervous system. Some of the developments have been very promising, as the following findings show.

Making Neurons Grow **EXPLORING PSYCHOLOGY**

"It's not only exciting, it's wonderful," said Dr. Fred H. Gage of the University of California at San Diego Medical School. "We've gone from zero, from a dead field, to a field that is just exploding with new knowledge all the time" (*San Diego Tribune*, May 30, 1987, p. A-1). What Dr. Gage is excited about is the possibility of regenerating nerves in the central nervous system.

One of the major reasons why nerves in Katie's spinal cord did not regenerate is because other cells grew over the damaged area, sealing it off from bacteria and toxins. Because of this barrier, nerve-promoting chemi-

Can Katie's broken spinal cord be repaired?

cals are prevented from reaching the damaged nerves, and axons cannot grow through the site of the injury.

What Dr. Gage and his associates have done is to bridge the damaged areas with an amnion membrane that is made from human placenta. The organ that nourishes a developing embryo in the womb, the placenta is expelled soon after birth and is usually discarded by hospitals. Now, however, placentas are being salvaged to make amnion membranes because the placentas have been found to be powerful stimulators of nerve growth. To test the success of this "bridge," researchers surgically separated the septum and hippocampus in a rat's brain. Next they inserted a piece of amnion membrane, which was rolled up like a soda straw, between the separated parts. They found that the amnion membrane released a chemical that stimulated the axons to grow as much as an eighth of an inch across the damaged area (Davis et al., 1987). Other researchers also have reported nerve growth in the central nervous system following treatment with various "bridges" and nerve-promoting chemicals (Freed et al., 1985; Korsching, 1986; Kromer, 1987). Although these techniques have not yet been tried on humans, there is hope that amnion membranes might be used to stimulate nerve growth in people who have damaged brains or spinal cords (Freed et al., 1985). It is unlikely that these procedures would help Katie, because treatment must be begun immediately after the damage has occurred.

Nonetheless, the development of methods to regenerate severed nerve fibers in the central nervous system—while still experimental—represents an important medical advance.

PERIPHERAL NERVOUS SYSTEM

Somatic Division

The razzle-dazzle of the Harlem Globetrotters basketball team is something to see. They can dribble balls every which way. They can spin balls on their fingers and make shots that border on impossible. At times it seems that the ball is attached to their fingers by a long string (author's files).

The Globetrotters can dribble a ball one inch off the ground by using their peripheral muscles, which are controlled by the **somatic division** of the peripheral nervous system (see Figure 2.7). Somatic pathways generally connect to the skeletal muscles, which are the muscles that move the bones of the body, such as those in the arms and legs. Because the Globetrotters can dribble and shoot at will, the somatic pathways are said to be "voluntary." This means that, to a large extent, the Globetrotters—and other healthy people—have conscious control over somatic pathways or at least they are aware of when they are activated. As the next example shows, some of our muscles and pathways are not under voluntary control.

Autonomic Division

Maybe it was the several drinks she consumed on top of some aspirin and a mild tranquilizer. For reasons that have never been determined, Karen Ann Quinlan lapsed into a coma in April 1975. After extensive tests, her doctors concluded that she would never recover any of her cognitive functions. Based on this information, her parents asked and received permission from the State Supreme Court of New Jersey to

When he was 15, Greg Framer dove into a shallow pool and broke his neck. Because nerve fibers in the spinal cord and brain do not usually regenerate, his legs are permanently paralyzed. In this photo he is trying a new technique. The muscles in his legs are being electrically stimulated by wires attached to a computer which has been programmed to move his leg muscles in the correct sequence to pedal the bike. This is the first step in a long-term program using the computer to stimulate muscles whose neural control has been lost through nerve damage or disease. (Enrico Ferorelli)

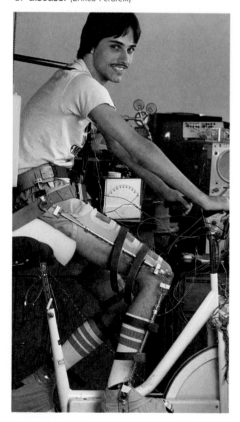

What keeps a person in a coma alive?

disconnect her from the respirator that was thought to be keeping her alive. Although the respirator was turned off in May 1976, Karen continued breathing on her own. She remained in a coma, described as a persistent vegetative state, until she died of respiratory failure in June 1985 (adapted from Time, *June 24, 1985).*

What kept Karen Ann Quinlan alive for ten years was the autonomic division of her peripheral nervous system (see Figure 2.7). Because she was unconscious, Karen's somatic nervous system was not functioning, but her autonomic nervous system continued to function. In fact, most of us are seldom aware that these pathways are working at all. For this reason, autonomic pathways are called "involuntary."

The **autonomic nervous system,** which is abbreviated ANS, is a network of nerve fibers and cell bodies that control your heart rate, blood pressure, digestive and eliminative systems, sweat glands, and many other internal organs. The autonomic nerves have connections with the central nervous system, but like somatic nerves they are located primarily outside the brain and spinal cord. You are about to discover that the ANS has two divisions.

Sympathetic and Parasympathetic Divisions

Martha Weiss, a 44-year-old woman who was five foot three inches tall and weighed about 120 pounds, watched as a small girl was hit and pinned beneath a large Cadillac. She rushed over, grabbed the corner of the 4,500 pound car, and was able to lift one corner enough to free the child (adapted from the San Diego Tribune, *December 6, 1979).*

Could anyone lift a 4,500 pound car?

Martha Weiss got her strength from one of the two divisions of her autonomic nervous system. The two divisions of the ANS have two generally different functions.

The **sympathetic division** increases heart rate, respiration, blood pressure and blood flow, release of sugar, and secretion of hormones, all of which cause physiological arousal, as Figure 2.8 shows. Martha Weiss was able to respond in an emergency because her sympathetic division aroused

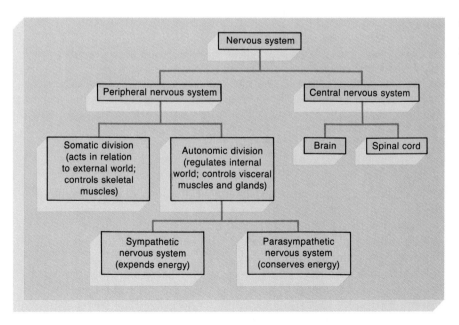

Figure 2.7
Diagram of the organization of your nervous system. (From Wortman & Loftus, 1985)

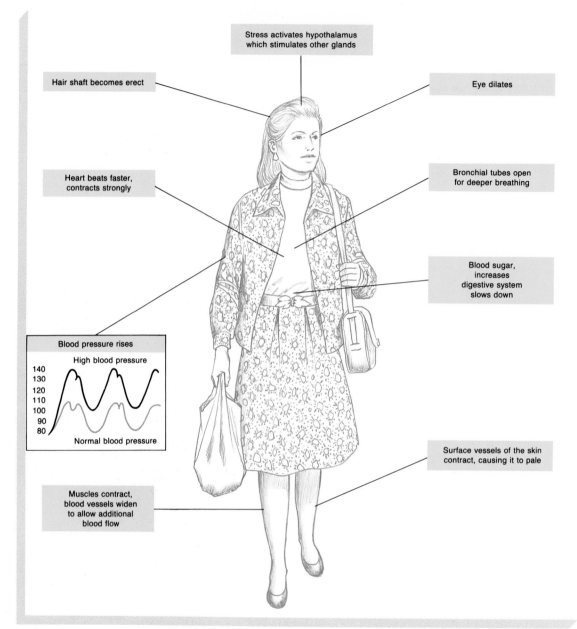

Stress activates hypothalamus
which stimulates other glands

Hair shaft becomes erect

Eye dilates

Heart beats faster,
contracts strongly

Bronchial tubes open
for deeper breathing

Blood sugar,
increases
digestive system
slows down

Blood pressure rises

High blood pressure

140
130
120
110
100
90
80

Normal blood pressure

Surface vessels of the skin
contract, causing it to pale

Muscles contract,
blood vessels widen
to allow additional
blood flow

Figure 2.8
If you were in a stressful or frightening situation, such as walking down a dark alley, one part of your autonomic nervous system, the sympathetic division, would automatically increase physiological arousal. You would have increased heart rate, blood pressure, blood flow, respiration, release of blood sugar, and secretion of several hormones. As external evidence of these internal changes, your hair might stand on end, your eyes dilate, and your skin pale. Some time later, when you were no longer frightened, another part of your autonomic nervous system, the parasympathetic division, would automatically return your body to a calm state

her body and gave her increased energy. Situations that are frightening, stressful, or annoying trigger the sympathetic division. In contrast, the **parasympathetic division** slows heart rate, decreases blood pressure, and stimulates digestion, all of which calm the body and return it to a normal level of physiological functioning.

Throughout the day, whether we are awake or sleeping, the sympathetic and parasympathetic divisions interact to keep internal organs working at optimum levels. This tendency of the body to regulate its own internal environment is called **homeostasis** (ho-me-oh-STAY-sis). The sympathetic and parasympathetic divisions continued to maintain Karen Quinlan's body in a state of homeostasis even though she remained in a deep coma.

When Martha Weiss saw the young girl pinned by the car, she did not have to think about activating her sympathetic division. Instead, her hypothalamus activated it for her without any conscious effort. This activation of the sympathetic division is often called the *fight or flight response* because it enables people to cope with threatening situations. Later, after the crisis was over, another part of Martha's hypothalamus activated her parasympathetic division to calm her body and help her return to a state of homeostasis. Additional functions of the ANS will be discussed in Module 39.

MASTER CONTROL CENTER: THE BRAIN

In the snake, it's the size of a grape. In the cat, it's the size of an apple. In the chimpanzee, it's the size of a grapefruit. In the human, it's the size of a melon. We're talking about the forebrain, or cerebrum, which is shown in Figure 2.9. One reason why a snake cannot add, a cat cannot divide, and a chimpanzee cannot multiply is that they do not have well-developed forebrains. It is your relatively huge forebrain that allows you to add, divide, and multiply, as well as perform countless other cognitive functions. The forebrain, one of the three major divisions of the brain, is what distinguishes humans from other species.

To give you a firsthand view of the human forebrain, as well as the hindbrain and midbrain, we are going to take you on a unique journey. You will be reduced to microscopic size and placed just at the point where the spinal cord enters the skull.

The Hindbrain

You'll notice that as it enters the skull, the spinal cord swells outward to form what is called the **hindbrain.** A look at Figure 2.10 will show you where that structure is. One area of the hindbrain, the **medulla,** controls vital reflexes such as heart rate, respiration, and blood pressure. Many famous rock stars have died from an overdose of drugs that depress the activities of neurons in the medulla. When these neurons are depressed, the result can be suffocation or heart stoppage. In some coma victims, one of the few parts of the brain that continues to function is the medulla. Because of damage elsewhere in the brain, such persons may not be able to move, sense, speak, think, or feel. Still, the medulla keeps the body

Why can't a snake add?

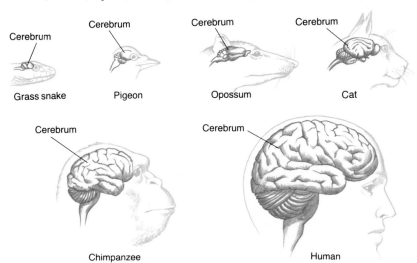

Figure 2.9
Comparison of the size and shape of the brains of various animals. Note the evolutionary trend toward an enlarged forebrain. (From Hubel, 1979)

Cerebrum — Grass snake
Cerebrum — Pigeon
Cerebrum — Opossum
Cerebrum — Cat
Cerebrum — Chimpanzee
Cerebrum — Human

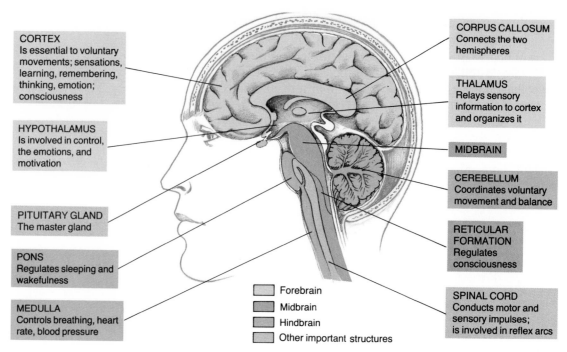

Figure 2.10
Major areas and structures of your brain.

alive by maintaining vital reflexes. That is what happened to Karen Quinlan.

The next stop on your tour of the hindbrain lies a few centimeters above the medulla, in a structure called the **pons.** If you were to spend many hours in the pons, you would discover that it is very active at night. The reason is that one of the many functions of the pons is the manufacture

---

MAJOR CONCEPT   Divisions of the Nervous System

The nervous system can be thought of as divided into a number of different parts.

Match each of the parts listed here with its description.

1. Central nervous system

2. Peripheral nervous system

3. Autonomic nervous system

4. Somatic nervous system

5. Sympathetic division

6. Parasympathetic division

a. ____ The part of the autonomic nervous system that triggers physiological arousal

b. ____ The part of the autonomic nervous system that returns the body to a state of calm

c. ____ The division of the peripheral nervous system that controls largely voluntary movements of muscles attached to bones

d. ____ The division of the peripheral nervous system that controls largely involuntary reactions in internal organs

e. ____ The brain and spinal cord

f. ____ All the neurons in the body outside the brain and spinal cord

Answers: a (5); b (6); c (4); d (3); e (1); f (2)

---

and distribution of chemicals that regulate sleep. If certain areas of the pons are damaged, an animal has difficulty going to sleep or waking up.

From the pons you travel toward the back of the skull into one of the brain's most beautiful structures, the **cerebellum.** It is like entering an enchanted forest. The neurons of the cerebellum have dendrites that curve and arch to form what look like delicate branches of miniature trees. Row after row of these neurons make millions of connections not only within the cerebellum itself, but to the rest of the brain. The cerebellum, you learn, serves as a kind of coordination center for voluntary movements and balance.

When you ride a bike, for example, nerve impulses from your forebrain mingle with those from your cerebellum as they travel down your spinal cord to your feet. The instructions from your cerebellum help you to pedal in a smooth, fluid fashion. As you might guess, injury to the cerebellum can result in jerky, uncoordinated movements. The peculiar shuffling step that long-time alcoholics sometimes develop is due to the damage heavy drinking has done to the cerebellum over the years. These people have trouble keeping their balance and so hold their feet wide apart when they walk.

The Midbrain

Your tour continues back to the pons and up a few centimeters to the **midbrain.** As you look down into the midbrain's center, you see a long column of neurons that extends down into the hindbrain. Some of these send fibers down into the spinal cord, while others send fibers up into the forebrain. This column of neurons is called the **reticular formation,** and it plays a vitally important role in regulating consciousness. Part of it sends impulses that arouse the neurons of the forebrain. Once aroused, the forebrain is able to receive and process information coming from the senses. A general anesthetic works by suppressing the neurons of the reticular formation and causing loss of consciousness. In fact, if the neurons were seriously damaged, you would lapse into a coma. Scientists think that other brain regions suppress the activity of the reticular formation on a regular cycle, permitting the forebrain to sleep.

Why do you lose consciousness when given a general anesthetic?

The Forebrain

You are now ready to move up to the **forebrain,** an area that has evolved through millions of years into its present large size. As you move through the forebrain, you will encounter a neural "wiring" plan of incredible complexity. This region contains billions of neurons, which in turn make billions of connections. The relatively large cell bodies are grayish-pink in color, while the long, thin axons are whitish. This difference in color is seen in other brain areas too, but it is most apparent in the forebrain.

If you were to view the forebrain from above you would notice that it is divided into two halves or *hemispheres.* You are going to wander primarily through the left hemisphere, but bear in mind that most of the major structures you explore are also found in the right hemisphere. The areas you will explore in the forebrain, the thalamus, the hypothalamus, and the limbic system, are very old from an evolutionary point of view.

The Thalamus. If you traveled toward the center and lower part of the forebrain, you would enter a walnut-shaped structure known as the **thalamus.** You are immediately dazzled by all the activity since the thalamus is made of millions of nerve fibers and it has separate areas that receive information from all of the body's senses except smell. This information is processed and relayed to the cortex, or surface of the forebrain. For example, if you followed nerve impulses from the eye into the brain, you would see that they are routed to one specific area of the thalamus. Once in the thalamus, the impulses would activate neurons that would receive and modify the information. Finally, neurons in the thalamus would send the information to a number of higher brain centers. By watching this chain of events you would learn that the thalamus is not just a relay station; it is also a critical center for processing incoming information.

What happens when you get a fever?

The Hypothalamus.   If you moved immediately below the thalamus, you would enter one of the important structures of the forebrain, the **hypothalamus.** You would notice that it contains dozens of separate nerve centers involved in many different processes. Some centers help control body temperature, others are involved in emotions, and still others are implicated in motivations such as hunger, thirst, and sex. Damage to these centers can cause dramatic changes in behavior such as voracious eating, hyperirritability, and inability to maintain a normal body temperature. When you get a fever, it may be because some virus or toxin temporarily disrupted your hypothalamus.

If you stand in the hypothalamus and look down, you'll spot a small pea-shaped structure hanging directly below it. What you are seeing is the **pituitary gland,** which is often called the master gland of the body's endocrine or glandular system. The pituitary is not considered part of the brain, itself. However, the hypothalamus regulates the secretion of hormones from the pituitary, and these pituitary hormones in turn affect secretions from other glands. In this way the nervous system, via the hypothalamus, · is involved in controlling the activities of hormones throughout the body. Some of the effects these hormones have are described in Figure 2.11.

The Limbic System.   Connecting with the hypothalamus are a number of other structures that form a ring in the forebrain. These interconnected structures, called the **limbic system,** are involved in memory and emotions. For example, one limbic system area, the hippocampus, is necessary for placing memories into long-term storage. Without it, you would not remember what you read two hours earlier. Another limbic system structure, the amygdala, is involved in emotional expression. All these limbic system structures are connected with and send their information to the top of the forebrain, the cortex, which is your next stop.

The Cortex

Your walk across the surface or **cortex** of the forebrain is a journey through valleys and ridges. That's because the cortex, a thin layer of cells, has a very wrinkled appearance. It is easy to see the adaptive value of this wrinkled surface: it allows a large, flat area to fit into a small, curved space, much as a large sheet of paper can be crumpled to fit into a small bowl. If the wrinkled cortex could be ironed flat, it would measure about 50 × 40 cm, or approximately 2⅔ square feet. This substantial area of human cortex has allowed us to develop our impressive powers of thought and reason.

As Figure 2.12 shows, the cortex is divided into four sections, or **lobes.** The front is called the **frontal lobe,** the middle is called the **parietal** (pa-RYE-eh-tull) **lobe,** the back is called the **occipital** (ahk-SIH-pih-tull) **lobe,** and the side is called the **temporal lobe.** You can begin your tour of the cortex by exploring the most forward region of the frontal lobe, the *prefrontal area.* But first, consider the amazing story of Phineas P. Gage.

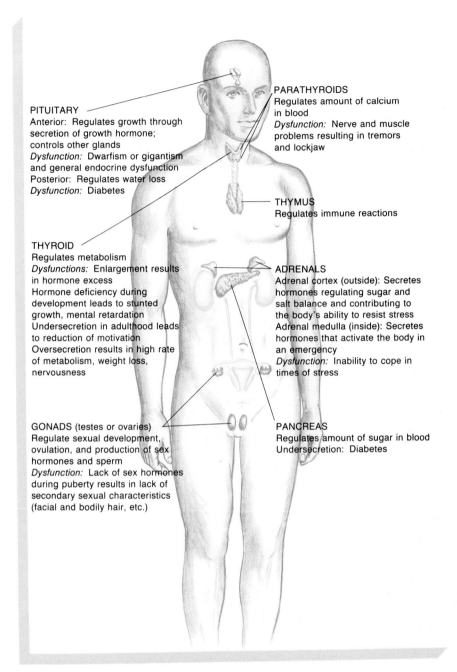

PITUITARY
Anterior: Regulates growth through secretion of growth hormone; controls other glands
Dysfunction: Dwarfism or gigantism and general endocrine dysfunction
Posterior: Regulates water loss
Dysfunction: Diabetes

THYROID
Regulates metabolism
Dysfunctions: Enlargement results in hormone excess
Hormone deficiency during development leads to stunted growth, mental retardation
Undersecretion in adulthood leads to reduction of motivation
Oversecretion results in high rate of metabolism, weight loss, nervousness

GONADS (testes or ovaries)
Regulate sexual development, ovulation, and production of sex hormones and sperm
Dysfunction: Lack of sex hormones during puberty results in lack of secondary sexual characteristics (facial and bodily hair, etc.)

PARATHYROIDS
Regulates amount of calcium in blood
Dysfunction: Nerve and muscle problems resulting in tremors and lockjaw

THYMUS
Regulates immune reactions

ADRENALS
Adrenal cortex (outside): Secretes hormones regulating sugar and salt balance and contributing to the body's ability to resist stress
Adrenal medulla (inside): Secretes hormones that activate the body in an emergency
Dysfunction: Inability to cope in times of stress

PANCREAS
Regulates amount of sugar in blood
Undersecretion: Diabetes

Figure 2.11
A number of glands secrete chemicals called hormones. Unlike the nervous system, which uses nerve impulses and neurotransmitters to control body functions, the endocrine system uses hormones that circulate in your bloodstream. These hormones regulate many physiological responses, such as release of blood sugar, production of sperm, and ovulation. The glands and their hormones make up the endocrine system.

The Frontal Lobe

The accident occurred at about half past four on the afternoon of September 13, 1848, near the small town of Cavendish, Vermont. The railroad crewmen were about to blast a rock that blocked their way. Foreman Phineas Gage himself took charge of the delicate business of pouring gunpowder into a deep narrow hole drilled in the stone. The powder in place, he rammed in a long iron rod to tamp down the charge before covering it with sand. But the tamping iron rubbed against the side of the shaft and a spark ignited the powder. The massive rod, 3½ feet long, 1¼ inches in diameter, weighing 13 pounds, shot from the hole under the force of the explosion. The rod struck Phineas just beneath his left eye and tore through his skull. It shot out the top of his head and landed some 50 yards away (adapted from Blakemore, 1977).

Can someone's personality be changed in an instant?

Figure 2.12
This is your brain's left hemisphere, which is divided into four different lobes: frontal, parietal, occipital, and temporal. Along the side of the frontal lobe, the narrow strip of cortex called the motor area controls all your voluntary muscle movements. The motor area and the body parts it controls are shown in the upper left corner. The size of the body parts illustrates how much space each area has. Body areas that have muscles capable of complex movement, such as your face, have more space in the motor area. Immediately in back of the motor strip in the parietal lobe is the somatosensory area, which receives sensory information from your body. That area and the body parts it controls are shown in the upper right corner. The more sensitive a body part is, the more space it has in the somatosensory area.

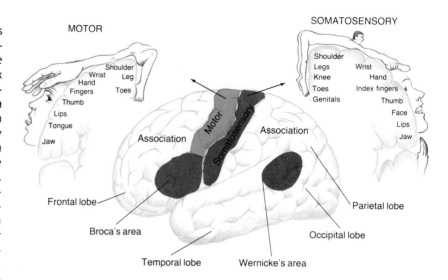

Do lobotomies turn people into vegetables?

The Phineas who miraculously recovered from this terrible accident was not the same man his friends had known. The old Phineas was a considerate, efficient, and capable foreman. The new Phineas was capricious, impatient, incapable of completing a project, given to cursing his workers, and unconcerned about the social propriety of his actions. The iron rod had extensively damaged the prefrontal region of Phineas's brain and changed his personality dramatically.

Phineas had suffered a crude and massive form of *prefrontal lobotomy*, an operation in which part of the frontal lobe is separated from the rest of the brain. In the 1930s and 1940s, neurosurgeons performed about 18,000 prefrontal lobotomies. The procedure was used to curb uncontrollable behavior in mental patients, although lobotomies were also performed on people who had less severe mental problems. The patient—who was often awake—was placed in a chair. His or her eyelids were anesthesized and rolled back. A tool resembling an ice pick was inserted above the eyes and pushed into the prefrontal region. When the tool was moved back and forth, it severed a large part of the frontal lobe. Some patients who underwent the operation did become less violent, but improvements in this area of behavior were often accompanied by serious problems in other areas.

A prefrontal lobotomy did not necessarily turn people into vegetables, as some movies and novels suggest. In fact, it often had little effect on performance in memory or intelligence tests. But the operation did interfere with the abilities to make plans and carry them out, to adjust to new social demands, or to know when it was appropriate to laugh or cry or make other emotional responses. Few prefrontal lobotomies have been performed since the early 1950s, primarily because their success in relieving symptoms was little better than chance, and because of the advent of antipsychotic drugs, which improve behavior with fewer side effects (Valenstein, 1986). From these unfortunate operations, we learned that the prefrontal area of the brain directs some of our most human qualities, including the ability to think ahead and to behave normally in social and emotional situations.

How does the brain move your feet?

Continuing your journey across the cortex, walk to the very back of the frontal lobe, where you will discover a region called the **motor area.** For your examination of this part of the brain, let us give you a small probe with which you can deliver a mild electrical current and activate neurons. As you stimulate neurons of the motor area, the person whose brain you are observing begins to move about. First, you stimulate neurons at the top of the left motor region and then move systematically down. As with a remote-controlled puppet, the person's right shoulder, arm, and wrist move first, then the right hand, the right thumb, the right side of the face, the lips, the tongue, and the jaw. Each set of muscles in the body is apparently controlled by a specific place in the motor area. You conclude that the motor area is the part of the brain that regulates voluntary movements.

As you continue to stimulate the motor area, you make another discovery: the more complicated the muscle movements, the larger the portion of the motor area devoted to controlling them. The fingers, for instance, are controlled by a sizable part of the motor area, the trunk of the body by a much smaller one. Figure 2.12 shows a map of the motor area, indicating the parts of the body that each segment of it governs.

The Parietal Lobe.   You would not be very good at pedaling a bike, walking upstairs, or driving a car if you did not know exactly where your feet were at all times. To provide you with this information, neural messages concerning pressure and touch to the skin and joints travel up your legs and spinal cord to the **somatosensory area** of your parietal lobe. Figure 2.12 shows that this region lies directly behind the motor area of the frontal lobe. Once again let us give you the stimulation probe. As you activate neurons beginning at the top and moving down along the somatosensory region, the person whose brain you are stimulating feels tingling sensations in a succession of places: the trunk, the arm, the hand, the forehead, the face, the nose, the tongue.

You notice that the more sensitive the body part is, the larger the portion of the somatosensory area devoted to it. You also observe, as you did in the motor area, that the *left* side of the brain governs the *right* side of the body, while the *right* side of the brain controls the body's *left* side.

Moving back from the somatosensory area, you come to an **association area** in the parietal lobe. The human cortex has many association areas; researchers are not yet certain what functions all of them serve. It is known that this particular association area is involved in the ability to recognize objects by touch. As you reach for your keys in the dark, for instance, you can usually tell with your fingers alone which one opens your front door. The association area adjacent to the somatosensory area enables you to do this. If this area were damaged, you could still feel an object, but you could not tell exactly what it was unless you looked.

How can you find the right key in the dark?

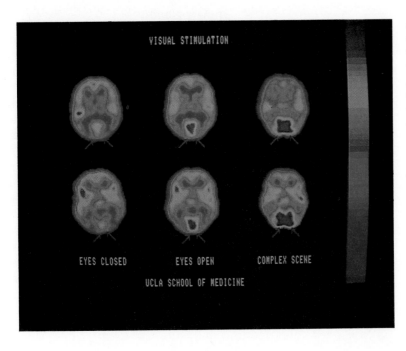

VISUAL STIMULATION

EYES CLOSED   EYES OPEN   COMPLEX SCENE

UCLA SCHOOL OF MEDICINE

In an imaging technique called PET (positron emission tomography), subjects are injected with harmless, radioactive glucose, which is taken up and used as fuel by the brain. Brain areas that are more active use more fuel and thus take up more radioactive glucose than those that are less active. The greater uptake of radioactive glucose is measured and displayed in red (subject with eyes and ears open), with decreasing amounts shown in yellow, green, blue, and violet (subject with eyes and ears closed). In medicine, PET scans help doctors identify brain tumors, which show very active areas, or brain damage, which would show inactive cells. (Dr. M. Phelps, Dr. J. Mazziotta et al./Science Photo Library/Photo Researchers)

Why do you see stars when hit hard on the head?

The Occipital Lobe. As you move to the very back of the brain, you arrive at the occipital lobe, an area involved in vision. If you stimulate the neurons in this area, the person whose brain you are exploring will see flashes of light. This is exactly what happens when you suffer a hard blow to the head: you see "stars" because the neurons in your occipital lobe are stimulated.

You may wonder why you do not see people or rabbits when you are hit on the head. The reason is that the primary visual area at the back of the occipital lobe processes only textures, contours, and light and dark shadows. In order to recognize these visual sensations as some object, the nerve impulses must be processed by neighboring association areas. Association areas, then, are the parts of the brain where higher-order perception and "thought" occurs.

How about the tarripoi?

The Temporal Lobe. Traveling from the occipital lobe to the left side of the brain brings you to the left temporal lobe. Although both right and left temporal lobes are involved in hearing, for most people it is primarily the left lobe that is involved in producing and understanding language. When

---

MAJOR CONCEPT   Brain Structures and Functions

Different regions of the brain perform different functions.

Match each region listed here with its major role.

1. Medulla
2. Pons
3. Cerebellum
4. Reticular formation
5. Hypothalamus
6. Thalamus
7. Limbic system
8. Frontal lobe
9. Parietal lobe
10. Occipital lobe
11. Temporal lobe

a. ____ Helps coordinate voluntary movements and balance.

b. ____ Receives information from all the senses except smell

c. ____ Plays an important role in regulating consciousness

d. ____ Involved in regulating eating, drinking, body temperature, emotions, and control of the pituitary gland

e. ____ Manufactures chemicals that regulate sleep

f. ____ Controls vital reflexes such as heart rate and respiration

g. ____ The front part of this lobe is involved in planning and social behaviors and the back part is involved in the control of voluntary movements

h. ____ Contains areas important to hearing and understanding speech

i. ____ Contains areas important to vision

j. ____ Critically involved in emotions and memory

k. ____ Contains an area where feeling sensations such as touch are perceived

Answers: a(3); b (6); c (4); d (5); e (2); f (1); g (8); h (11); i (10); j (7); k (9)

you arrive at the temporal lobe, the person whose brain you are examining is in the process of talking on the phone. As he listens, receptors in his ears send signals to his thalamus, which in turn relays the data to the primary auditory areas in his temporal lobes.

If these nerve impulses stopped at the primary auditory regions, your host would hear only general sounds such as clicks, buzzes, and hums. For him to identify these sounds as words, the information must be passed on to association areas in the left temporal lobe. And for the meaning of the words and sentences to be grasped, they must be processed by a part of the left temporal lobe called **Wernicke's area**, which is involved in the ability to produce meaningful speech. Damage to this part of the brain causes *aphasia*, which is a loss of the ability to use or understand words. For example, a person with Wernicke's aphasia, which is characterized by difficulty in understanding spoken or written words as well as putting words into meaningful sentences, might say something like: "I'm awful nervous, you know, once in a while I get caught up, I mention the tarripoi, a month ago, quite a little, I've done a lot well, I impose a lot, while, on the other hand, you know what I mean" (Gardner, 1976, p. 68).

There is another kind of aphasia that makes a person speak like this: "Yes, sure. Me go, er, uh, P.T. non o'cot. speech . . . two times . . . read . . . wr . . . ripe, er, rike, er, write . . . practice . . . get-ting better (Gardner, 1976, p. 61). This was the patient's answer to the question "What have you been doing in the hospital?" The patient is trying to say "I go to P.T. (physical therapy) at one o'clock to practice speaking, reading, and writing and I'm getting better." This person has Broca's aphasia, which is a difficulty in the production of speech that is caused by damage to a nearby part of the frontal lobe called **Broca's area**. Unlike a victim of Wernicke's aphasia, a person with Broca's aphasia is able to understand speech.

REVIEW

As you're walking home, you see a terrible accident. A construction crane falls on top of a worker, injuring his neck and his left arm. As you watch the ambulance arrive and take the worker away, you wonder how the doctors will treat the injuries. You remember that neurons and nerves in the brain and spinal cord make up

the (1) _____ nervous system, while nerves outside the brain and spinal cord compose the

(2) _____ nervous system. If the nerves in the worker's arm were crushed, there would be a return of feeling and movement because nerves in the periph-

eral nervous system have the ability to (3) _____. However, without special treatment, nerve fibers in his central nervous system, such as his spinal cord, have little ability to regenerate.

You are able to walk away from the accident because you can voluntarily control your skeletal muscles

through the (4) _____ division of your peripheral nervous system. However, you have great dif-

ficulty in calming yourself. This is because many of your physiological responses are not under conscious or voluntary control. They are regulated by part of your

peripheral nervous system called the (5) _____ nervous system. Because seeing the accident frightened you, your hypothalamus automatically triggered the

(6) _____ division of your ANS. Once triggered, the sympathetic division automatically increased your heart rate, blood pressure, and the release of key hormones, all of which raised your physiological arousal and prepared you for flight. Once you get home

and forget about the accident, the (7) _____ division of your ANS will calm your body and return it to a normal state. The interactions of the sympathetic and parasympathetic divisions enable your body to maintain an optimum internal state of functioning

called (8) _____.

After the injured worker is taken to the emergency room, one of the doctors begins her examination. She checks for functioning of the lowermost division of the brain, the areas right above the spinal cord, which together are called the (9) _____. Since the worker's vital reflexes, such as breathing, are functioning, the doctor concludes that an area in the hindbrain called the (10) _____ has not been damaged. If the worker had damage to another hindbrain region called the (11) _____, he might have trouble falling asleep or waking up, since this area manufactures chemicals that regulate sleep. At this point the worker regains consciousness and looks around the room. The doctor asks the worker to move rapidly the fingers of his undamaged right hand. He moves his fingers in a smooth, coordinated way indicating that a part of the hindbrain called the (12) _____ is undamaged.

Above the hindbrain lies a division of the brain called the (13) _____. Since the worker is not in a coma, it means that a column of fibers called the (14) _____ formation is undamaged. The reticular formation, which begins in the midbrain and continues down the center of the hindbrain, plays a vital role in regulating (15) _____.

The doctor now asks the worker a series of questions, such as "What day is this and where are you?" The worker answers "It's Tuesday and I'm in the hospital." By asking these questions, the doctor is testing the functions of the wrinkled covering of the forebrain called the (16) _____. Near the center and lower part of the forebrain is a structure called the (17) _____, which receives and processes information from most of the body's senses and relays it on to the cortex. Right below the thalamus is a structure with many separate nerve centers that are involved in regulating hunger, thirst, sexual arousal, emotions, and body temperature. The structure involved in all these functions is called the (18) _____.

This structure also controls the (19) _____ gland, which secretes hormones that affect many other glands and organs. The hypothalamus, along with the hippocampus and amygdala, form a ring of interconnected structures in the forebrain called the (20) _____ _____. This system is involved in memory and regulating emotional responses.

The doctor asks the worker to move various parts of his body. This is to check for damage to the (21) _____ area, which controls voluntary movements and is located in the (22) _____ lobe. If the worker has difficulty in planning, expressing his emotions, or dealing with new social situations, he would have damage to his (23) _____ area, which is part of the frontal lobe.

The doctor places a key in the worker's right hand and asks him to identify it. The worker knows there is something in his right hand because sensory information from his fingers travels up the spinal cord and reaches the (24) _____ area of his left (25) _____ lobe. The worker knows the object is a key when the neural information reaches the (26) _____ area of the parietal lobe. If the worker could not see well, he might have damage to his (27) _____ lobe, where the primary visual area lies. If he could not hear well, he might have damage to his (28) _____ lobe, where the primary auditory area lies. If the worker could understand speech, but had difficulty in putting words into fluent sentences, he would have (29) _____ aphasia, which results from damage to the left frontal lobe. If he could not understand speech and had difficulty speaking in coherent sentences, he would have (30) _____ aphasia, which also results from damage to the left frontal lobe. If the worker had difficulty in perceiving and thinking, the doctor would suspect damage to one or more of his (31) _____ areas, which are located in each of the four lobes.

GLOSSARY TERMS

association area (p. 51)   homeostasis (p. 44)   parietal lobe (p. 48)   somatosensory area
autonomic nervous   hypothalamus (p. 48)   peripheral nervous system   (p. 51)
  system (p. 42)   limbic system (p. 48)   (p. 41)   sympathetic division
Broca's area (p. 52)   lobes (p. 48)   pituitary gland (p. 48)   (p. 43)
central nervous system   medulla (p. 45)   pons (p. 46)   temporal lobe (p. 48)
  (p. 41)   midbrain (p. 47)   regenerate (p. 41)   thalamus (p. 47)
cerebellum (p. 47)   motor area (p. 50)   reticular formation   Wernicke's area (p. 52)
forebrain (p. 47)   occipital lobe (p. 48)   (p. 47)
frontal lobe (p. 48)   parasympathetic division   somatic division (p. 42)
hindbrain (p. 45)   (p. 44)

Module 6 Brain Function, Damage, and Recovery

Victoria had measles and scarlet fever when she was 6. Shortly thereafter she had recurring seizures, periods when she would lose consciousness and her muscles would twitch. She took anticonvulsant medicine and had no more seizures until she was 18, when the seizures returned with greater intensity and anticonvulsant medication no longer had any effect. Finally, at age 27, she had to make a frightening decision. The only chance she had of reducing her terrible, uncontrollable seizures was to have a very risky operation that would sever the major connection between her right and left hemispheres, leaving her with a split-brain. Victoria chose the operation (adapted from Sidtis et al., 1981).

STUDYING "SPLIT-BRAIN" HUMANS

Besides Victoria (identified as V.P. in published reports), about 30 people have had what is called a **split-brain** operation for treatment of severe, uncontrollable seizures. In this operation, doctors open the top of the skull, expose the brain, and then carefully cut the corpus callosum. This structure contains about 200 million nerve fibers, which connect and allow information to flow between the left and right hemispheres. Severing the corpus callosum disrupts the major pathway between the hemispheres and, to a large extent, leaves each hemisphere functioning on its own. In some patients, severing the corpus callosum prevents the spread of seizures from one hemisphere to another and therefore reduces the frequency and occurrence of seizures.

    Four months after her operation, Victoria was alert, talked easily about past and present events, could read, write, reason, and perform everyday functions such as eating, dressing, and walking. In fact, her neurological exam gave no indication that she had a split-brain. Occasionally, however, there are reports of split-brain people exhibiting conflicting behaviors. A patient claimed that one morning his left hand was trying to put his pants on while his right was trying to take them off. The same patient also reported being angry and forcibly reaching for his wife with his left hand while his right hand grabbed the left hand in an attempt to stop it (Gazzaniga, 1970). However, reports of conflicts between the right and left hemispheres are relatively rare.

One of the major reasons Victoria appears normal in everyday conversation is because only one of her hemispheres is involved in speech. The speech and language areas of about 95 percent of right-handed and 70 percent of left-handed people are located in the brain's left hemisphere. In about 5 percent of right-handed and 15 percent of left-handed people these areas are located in the right hemisphere. The remaining 15 percent of left-handed people show signs of speech and language activity in both hemispheres. Most of us, therefore, whether we have a split-brain or not, are most likely to speak with our left hemisphere (Springer & Deutsch, 1985). Although your right hemisphere has many other abilities, it usually lacks the capacity to speak. Thus, one reason a split-brain person appears normal in casual conversation is that only one hemisphere is directing this behavior.

What is Victoria's right hemisphere doing?

Victoria can tell you what her left hemisphere is doing because it can speak. Since her right hemisphere cannot speak, it takes special procedures to find out what it is doing. This procedure is shown schematically in Figure 2.13.

Victoria is seated before a screen upon which pictures are flashed. She is told to stare straight ahead at a black dot in the screen's center. As Victoria does so, a picture of a horse is flashed very quickly slightly to the *right* of the dot. Because of the way nerves lead from her eyes, the information "horse" reaches only her *left* hemisphere. When asked "What did you see?" Victoria can answer with the word "horse" because her left hemisphere, which saw the horse, also has the ability to speak. This procedure is then repeated with one critical difference. As Victoria stares straight ahead, a picture of a spoon is flashed very quickly to the *left* of the dot. Because of the way nerves lead from Victoria's eyes, the information "spoon" reaches only her *right* hemisphere. When she is asked "What did you see?" she cannot answer "spoon" because her right hemisphere, which saw the picture, lacks the ability to speak. To make matters worse, her speaking left hemisphere may offer the answer "nothing" because nothing is what the left hemisphere saw.

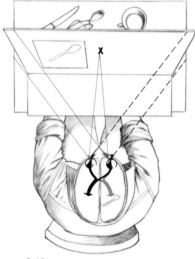

Figure 2.13
The man seated here has a severed corpus callosum. He stares straight ahead while pictures are flashed very briefly to the left of his visual field. These pictures are seen only by his right hemisphere. When his right hemisphere records the pictures, he is unable to identify what he sees, because speech is controlled by his left hemisphere. But when he is given objects and told to select the one he sees with his left hand, he makes a correct selection because touch information is controlled by his right hemisphere.

To find out if Victoria's right hemisphere saw the spoon, researchers asked her to identify the object by touch. She was given a bag containing a number of different objects. With her *left* hand (controlled by the *right* hemisphere) she reached in the bag, felt each object, and easily picked out a spoon. These results tell us that in split-brain patients, the two hemispheres really do function separately.

SPECIALIZATIONS OF THE TWO HEMISPHERES

Not too long ago the left hemisphere was thought to be dominant because it directs speech. But data from split-brain subjects clearly indicate that this belief is incorrect. We now know that each hemisphere is specialized for certain functions, excels at certain tasks, and appears to process information in its own unique way. Figure 2.14 outlines the major capacities of the two sides of the brain. Here are some of the more important research findings on specialization in the hemispheres.

For most of us, the left hemisphere is the side of the brain that controls speech (Sperry, 1974). The left hemisphere is also superior in other language abilities, including reading, writing, and spelling. Debate continues, however, over just how poor the right hemisphere is at these and other language tasks (Gazzaniga, 1983; Zaidel, 1983). When spoken to, the right hemisphere can understand simple sentences; it can also read simple words and spell them with cut-out letters. These findings suggest that the right hemisphere has some reading, writing, and speech comprehension capacities. But these capacities are at the level of a child rather than at the level of an adult (Sperry, 1982; Zaidel, 1983).

Which hand should you use to write an essay exam? Since you do not have a split-brain, you could use either hand to write an essay exam since information will be transferred across your corpus callosum. However, you would write much more quickly and legibly if you wrote with your preferred hand. Of course, if you had a split-brain and speech was in your left hemisphere, you would do best to write a language exam with your right hand since that is controlled by your language-smart left hemisphere.

The left hemisphere also excels at mathematics. When you solve complex problems in calculus or physics, you are primarily using your left hemisphere. The right hemisphere, in contrast, is more limited in math ability. Generally, the right hemisphere can perform simple addition and subtraction (Sperry, 1974).

But the right hemisphere is far from inferior at everything. For instance, the right brain is better than the left at recognizing and identifying faces (see Figure 2.15). This idea has been supported in tests of split-brain subjects (Levy et al., 1972). It has also been demonstrated in people with damage to the right hemisphere. In one study, such people made significantly more errors in recognizing famous faces than did people with damage to the left hemisphere (Van Lancker & Canter, 1982). There is also evidence that the right hemisphere is involved in both recognizing emotional expressions and producing them (Springer & Deutsch, 1985).

Which hand should you use to write an essay test?

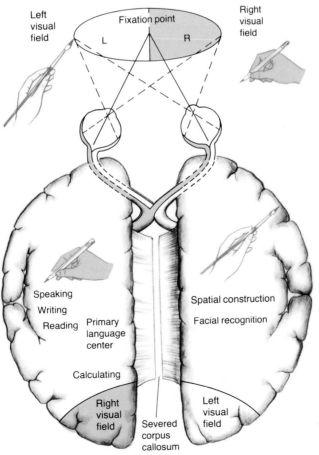

Figure 2.14
Your left hemisphere specializes in tasks that require analysis, such as reading, writing, speaking, and doing math. Your right hemisphere is better at tasks that require synthesizing wholes, such as recognizing faces and making designs. (Adapted from Wortman & Loftus, 1985)

Figure 2.15

A woman with a split-brain is told that she will see a picture. In A, she is instructed to stare at the center of the screen on which a composite picture is flashed. Her left hemisphere will see only the picture on the right, "the child," while her right hemisphere will see only the picture on the left, "the woman with glasses." In B, she is asked to identify the picture *verbally*. She says "It was the child," because only her left hemisphere, which saw that picture, can speak. In C, she is asked to identify the picture by *pointing*. She points to the "woman with glasses" because that is the picture her right hemisphere, which cannot speak, saw. (Adapted from Levy, J., Treverthen, C., and Sperry, R.W. 1972. Perception of bilateral chimeric figures following hemispheric disconnection. *Brain*, 95, p. 68)

"Whom did you see?"

"It was the child."

"Point to the person you saw."

In addition, the right hemisphere is superior at solving spatial problems, such as arranging blocks to match a geometric design. One of the most dramatic demonstrations of this superiority was recorded on film in a test of a split-brain patient. W.J. is given a number of blocks, each containing two red sides, two white sides, and two sides divided diagonally into half red and half white. He is asked to arrange the blocks to match a red and white pattern shown in a picture. W.J. easily does this with his left hand. His skill is due to the fact that the left hand is controlled by the right hemisphere, which is very good at solving this kind of problem. Then W.J. is asked to use his right hand, controlled by his left hemisphere, which has little ability at spatial tasks. The right hand has great trouble arranging the blocks to match the picture. At one point, W.J.'s left hand reaches up to help the fumbling right hand out. Apparently, this help is not appreciated. W.J.'s right hand firmly grasps the left one and removes it from the table. Oddly enough, W.J. does not seem disturbed by this conflict between his two hands (adapted from Springer & Deutsch, 1985).

The left hemisphere may excel at language tasks and the right hemisphere at visual-spatial problems because of differences in the way the two sides of the brain process information. After testing a number of split-brain patients, Jerre Levy and her colleagues concluded that the left hemisphere seems to process *analytically* (that is, piece by piece) while the right hemisphere seems to use a more *holistic* style (Levy & Trevarthen, 1976). According to this view, the left hemisphere is better at language because its approach is to analyze structure (how sentences are composed of phrases, phrases are composed of words, and words are composed of speech sounds). In contrast, the right hemisphere is better at recognizing faces because it tends to focus on the whole of an overall pattern.

These findings have given us a very different view of hemispheric function. We no longer assume that the left hemisphere is superior and the right hemisphere is inferior. We now know that the right hemisphere has its own area of intelligence or expertise (Levy, 1983). The idea of dominance has given way to the idea of specialization: the hemisphere that is more active at any given moment will be the hemisphere specialized for the task at hand.

ONE MIND OR TWO?

There is a popular notion that some of us primarily use our right brains while others primarily use their left brains. According to Jerre Levy, who has spent her whole career studying how the hemispheres interact, this is much too simple a distinction. In fact, she believes that the opposite is true. Since each hemisphere is specialized for processing certain kinds of information, they must work together to accomplish their goals. For example, you might think that while reading this paragraph, you are primarily using your left language-smart hemisphere. However, Levy suggests that you are using both hemispheres. It is true that the left hemisphere has a special role in translating written words into appropriate sounds and deriving meaning from words and understanding sentences. But, at the same time, the right hemisphere may play a special role in maintaining a coherent story line, appreciating humor and emotional content, and decoding visual information. Levy concludes that there is no activity in which only one hemisphere is involved (Levy, 1985). We now have a very different view of how the hemispheres function. It is not a question of dominance but one of specialization and working together.

A split-brain person was asked "What job would you pick?" His left hemisphere responded verbally, "a draftsman." His right hemisphere responded by arranging block letters with his left hand to spell "automobile race" (Gazzaniga & LeDoux, 1978). Based on this and other observations, Roger Sperry (1974, 1982), who received the Nobel Prize in 1982 for his work in this field, argues that each hemisphere may indeed have its own thoughts, motivations, goals, and mind of its own. Michael Gazzaniga (1985), in his latest book on split-brain patients, is in general agreement with Sperry. Gazzaniga states that having a corpus callosum does not necessarily mean that the two hemispheres are completely aware of each other's thoughts. He believes that the brain has hundreds of modules that store information in both language and nonlanguage form. Information that is stored in nonlanguage form, such as mood or emotion, may not always be available for recall by the left hemisphere. In these cases, the left hemisphere makes a guess or develops a theory about why you feel the way you do. According to Gazzaniga, there are times that you may feel depressed but can't say why. In these cases, the information about your mood is stored in a nonlanguage module that is not accessible to the left hemisphere. However, since one of the main functions of the left hemisphere is to explain your behavior, the left hemisphere makes up a reason for your

Are you right brained or left brained?

MAJOR CONCEPT   Hemispheric Specialization

For each of the functions listed below, indicate whether it is primarily controlled by the left (L) or the right (R) hemisphere.

——— 1. Speaking

——— 2. Visual-spatial ability, such as recognizing faces

——— 3. Solving algebra problems

——— 4. Reading and writing

——— 5. Visual-spatial ability, such as arranging blocks to match a pattern

——— 6. Thinking analytically

——— 7. Recognizing and producing emotional expressions

——— 8. Thinking in a holistic fashion

1 (L); 2 (R); 3 (L); 4 (L); 5 (R); 6 (L); 7 (R); 8 (R)

depression. The result is that the left hemisphere's explanation of your mood or emotional state may or may not be true!

Sperry and Gazzaniga's theories may also explain one of our most puzzling and frustrating experiences: saying that we will do one thing, and finding ourselves doing something else.

Now that you know some of the functions of the hemispheres, let's see what happens when some part of them is damaged.

DAMAGE TO THE BRAIN

What is a stroke?

She had been admired for her acting, especially her ability to portray a wide range of emotions. Suddenly, in a short period of time, she found that she could not utter a single word or move a single muscle on the right side of her body. Patricia Neal, a well-known actress, had suffered a series of three near-fatal strokes in her left hemisphere. With great effort that lasted almost a year, she relearned how to talk, much like the way a young child might learn. Gradually, she regained control over many of the muscles on her right side. Patricia Neal's recovery from the devastating effects of these strokes is often regarded as something of a miracle. She was even able to make TV commercials. However, few stroke victims show as complete a recovery as Neal did (author's files).

Strokes like the ones suffered by Patricia Neal usually result from a blockage of arteries that supply nutrients and oxygen to brain cells. Deprived of oxygen for even a short period of time, neurons in the affected area die and are not replaced. If these damaged neurons are involved in moving an arm, that arm will be paralyzed; if they are involved in receiving sensory information from a leg, that leg will be without feeling; if they are involved in the process of producing speech, the person will be mute. Patricia Neal lost both movement on her right side and the ability to speak, called aphasia, because strokes in her left hemisphere destroyed some of the neurons involved in these functions. For the effects of temporary brain damage, please see Figure 2.16.

One clue to Patricia Neal's remarkable recovery comes from research on animals. When neurons are destroyed by a stroke, the axons of healthy neighboring neurons may show new growth, called **sprouting,** which helps compensate for the lost neurons. Research on animals has shown that sprouting actually promotes new connections among neurons. In one experiment, researchers destroyed a small area in the brains of different-aged rats and then assessed the amount of sprouting 15 days later. The immature rats (only 35 days old when the experiment began) had significantly more sprouting than did the adult rats (those 180 days old at the start of the study). Still, sprouting did occur in the brains of the older rats (Bregman & Goldberger, 1982; Chen & Hillman, 1982; McWilliams & Lynch, 1983). Scientists do not yet have direct evidence that sprouting occurs in humans, for obtaining such evidence requires that the brain be removed and examined. But because human neurons share so many features with neurons in other animals, it is reasonable to assume that sprouting takes place in the human brain as well.

One of the results of brain damage, such as a stroke, is an accumulation of fluid, which in turn causes brain tissue swelling and a depression of neural activity in cells that have survived the injury. It has been found that when this swelling is treated with appropriate drugs, the survival rate of the victims dramatically increases (Cragoe et al., 1982). Apparently, a rapid reduction of swelling prevents damage to the neurons involved. It is likely that some of Patricia Neal's recovery was due to a reduction in the swelling of her brain.

Finally, Patricia Neal's recovery was undoubtedly aided by an exhaustive retraining program. Day after day, she spent hours in physical therapy and in relearning how to speak. One researcher who has developed a recovery program for the victims of stroke believes that such a program may both promote and take advantage of the new neural connections associated with sprouting (Grady, 1981).

Now that you know what happens to brain cells after they are damaged, let's look at how victims of brain damage are taught to cope with their problems.

How did Patricia Neal learn to speak again?

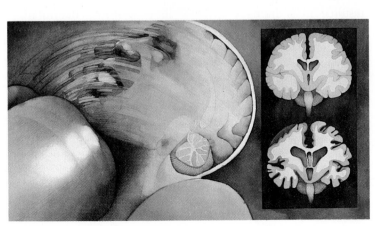

Figure 2.16
On the left, you can see that when a boxer takes a blow to his jaw, his head snaps back and causes the brain to smash against the skull. This quick movement of the brain puts pressure on the hindbrain (medulla, pons) and midbrain and especially on the reticular formation of the midbrain. Pressure here may interfere with the normal function of keeping the brain alert. The diagram on the right shows a second blow twisting the head and interfering further with the reticular formation's functions. If its functioning is seriously disrupted, the result is unconsciousness or, in boxing terminology, a knockout. After years of fighting and knockouts, boxers may sustain permanent brain damage. In fact, about one-third of professional boxers have symptoms of slowed motor reactions, clumsiness, tremors, memory deficits, and personality changes, apparently due to the punishment their brain takes during a fight. (Adapted from *Discover,* 1983)

APPLYING PSYCHOLOGY   Psychological Treatment for Brain Damage

How can Steven stop his mind from wandering?

Steven had spent a lot of time climbing up and down ladders and walking across scaffolds in his job as a construction worker. On the day that he had the accident, he was working on a scaffold that was two stories off the ground. Perhaps he was thinking of the coming weekend or how he was going to spend his paycheck when he missed a step and fell. He had some cuts and bruises but otherwise he didn't seem to be seriously injured. Some time later, when the doctors said it was all right for him to return to work, Steven didn't. As it turned out, keeping his feet on the ground as opposed to returning to work probably saved Steven's life (adapted from Chance, 1986).

Each year, about 300,000 people like Steven survive injuries that cause significant brain damage. The real problem is that because only a few of these individuals are aware of the true nature of their problem, as few as 15,000 or 5 percent of them will enter a good rehabilitation program.

Similar to most brain-damaged people, Steven had problems with concentrating and remembering things, and complained of not being able to think quickly enough. In this condition, he might not have survived working on scaffolds and it was lucky he decided not to return to work. He also had a number of other problems that are characteristic of brain damage. For instance, he had difficulty solving problems. Although he could read the manual for his new camera, he could not seem to apply the instructions to operating the camera. He also had difficulty in relating to his friends, partly because his face showed little emotion and partly because he had trouble following a conversation, which made it no fun for his friends to be around him. All of these symptoms are typical of brain injury and in most cases, including Steven's, lead eventually to withdrawal and depression. Finally, almost two years after Steven's injury, a neuropsychological evaluation indicated that his problems were due to mild brain damage.

Steven's story has a happy ending. After eight months in a good rehabilitation program, he is capable of living on his own, goes to movies, dates, dresses well, has just completed a trade school program, and is looking for a job repairing office machines. Steven's bright future was made possible by the pioneering studies of two clinical neuropsychologists, Yehuda Ben-Yishay and Leonard Diller. Instead of the wait-and-see attitude toward brain-damaged people that prevailed into the 1970s, these clinicians developed an intensive treatment program that requires many months of systematic training in social and intellectual skills. The Ben-Yishay–Diller approach has proven so successful that it has been widely imitated and resulted in a dramatic increase in head-injury treatment centers—from about 55 in 1980 to over 400 today.

Here is an outline of the rehabilitation program that Steven went through. It is characteristic of current head-injury treatment center programs (Chance, 1986).

To help Steven with his attention, memory, and problem-solving deficits, he was given *cognitive* training. A therapist taught Steven ways to improve his memory and helped him master one skill at a time, starting with a simple skill and going on to more difficult ones. Throughout the cognitive training, the therapist drilled Steven and gave him much encouragement and reinforcement. More recently, computers are being used in cognitive training. For example, a program called City Map teaches brain-injured people how to find their way around their city using a map.

Other computer programs are available to teach memory, attention, and problem-solving skills.

To help Steven function on his own, he was given *functional-skills* training. This involved teaching him to perform various everyday routines that were once second nature. For example, he learned that when. interacting with others he should say hello, make eye contact, smile, ask questions, listen to answers, and initiate conversation. Also, with the help, guidance, and encouragement of a therapist, he was taught routines concerning self-care, housekeeping, leisure, business and finance, community affairs, school, and work. As Steven struggled to relearn these skills, other brain-injured people were sometimes present to add support.

To help Steven minimize the effects of his limitations, such as attention wandering, he received *environmental management* training. He was advised not to play his radio or television when working on a project or conversing with someone, thereby reducing environmental distractions and stimulation, and he learned to set an alarm to go off every few minutes to remind him to keep his mind on one thing.

Although cognitive, functional-skills, and environmental management training increase the chances of a brain-injured person overcoming his or her injuries, the entire process is slow, painful and expensive. In Steven's case, the rehabilitation took eight months and cost $20,000—and his injuries were relatively mild. However, in terms of increasing the quality of human life, the time, effort and money seem a small price to pay. If you want to find out more about rehabilitation programs for head injury, you can call the National Head Injury Foundation at 1-800-262-9500.

MAJOR CONCEPT   Brain Damage

Brain damage and recovery involve a number of complex processes.

Indicate which of the following statements are true (T) or false (F).

1. ____ When brain cells are deprived of oxygen for a short period of time, they usually die and are not replaced.

2. ____ After brain cells die, the axons of healthy neighboring neurons may actually show new growth, which is called sprouting.

3. ____ After brain damage, there is an accumulation of fluid that promotes sprouting and cushions the brain from further damage.

4. ____ In treating brain damage, it is important to wait and see how the patient does before beginning an intensive and comprehensive treatment program.

Answers: 1 (T); 2 (T); 3 (F); 4 (F)

REVIEW

John (J.W. in published report) had a problem in grade school. Every so often he would stare off into space, oblivious to all around him. Much later, he began to have severe seizures that could not be controlled by medicine. As a last resort, he agreed to a radical treatment for his seizures. The major nerve connection between his right and left hemisphere, called the

(1) _____, was cut, resulting in what is called a split-brain (Gazzaniga & Smylie, 1983).

About four to six months after recovering from split-brain surgery, John appeared normal in most ways. He was able to carry on a normal conversation because the hemisphere that controlled his speech before surgery, namely, his (2) _____ hemisphere, continued to control speech after the surgery. However, if John reached into a bag full of objects and selected a banana without looking at it, he would not be able to say verbally what was in his hand because

his (3) _____ hemisphere is mute.

For John and virtually all right-handed and most left-handed people, the areas of the brain that primarily

control (4) _____ and (5) _____ abilities are located in the left hemisphere. The right hemisphere does have the ability to understand language and spell simple words by arranging letters. This ability appears to be at the level of a child rather than an adult.

In solving a visual-spatial problem, such as arranging blocks to match a pattern, John should use his

(6) _____ hand because it is controlled by

his (7) _____ hemisphere, which is better at visual-spatial tasks. When John looks through his high school yearbook, the hemisphere that is best at

recognizing the (8) _____ of his old classmates is his right. When John makes a face to show fear at diving off a high board, the hemisphere most

involved in producing and recognizing (9) _____ expressions is his right.

According to Jerre Levy, each side of John's brain

seems to have a characteristic way of processing information. If John were to write a computer program bit by bit, he is probably relying mainly on the left hemisphere, which tends to process information in a more

(10) _____ manner. When John is asked how much he likes a certain sculpture, he is probably relying mainly on the right hemisphere, which tends

to process information in a more (11) _____ way.

According to Roger Sperry, each hemisphere has

the ability to function (12) _____ and has its own goals and motivation. According to Michael Gazzaniga, information that is stored in a nonlanguage form, such as mood or emotion, may not be available to the left hemisphere. However, the left hemisphere

may guess or invent an (13) _____ for the way we feel and it will be difficult to know how true this explanation is.

If John were to have a stroke, there are a number of reasons why he might recover some of his lost functions. One reason is that some of his undamaged neurons might show new growth, a process called

(14) _____. Based on animal data, researchers guess that this process occurs in the human brain and contributes to recovery after stroke.

People who survive injury to their brains usually have concentration and memory problems. To help brain-injured people, head-injury treatment centers use three different training programs. To deal with problems of attention and memory, clients are given

(15) _____ training. To deal with problems of learning or managing a routine, such as self-care or personal events, clients are given

(16) _____ _____ training. To deal with problems caused by the limitations from

the injury, clients are given (17) _____ management training. Although training is slow, painful, and costly, it does greatly improve the quality of the brain-injured person's life.

Answers: (1) corpus callosum; (2) left; (3) right; (4) speech, language; (5) mathematics; (6) left; (7) right; (8) faces; (9) emotional, facial; (10) analytical; (11) holistic; (12) independently, separately; (13) explanation, reason; (14) s...; (15) cognitive; (16) functional-skills; (17) environmental

GLOSSARY TERMS

split-brain (p. 55)   sprouting (p. 61)

PERSONAL NOTE

There was a time when I worried about my brain. I had learned from my anatomy professor that a blow to the head could cause brain damage. So I made a list of all my blows. When I was 7 years old, I fell down an entire flight of stairs, alternating between bouncing on my butt and my head. When I was 12, I got hit in the head with a baseball. When I was 18, I banged my head on a car door. When I was 23, I fell on my head while attempting to roller skate. When I was 31, I took a dangerous fall on an icy ski slope and remember the terrible sound of my head striking the ice. After that particular fall, I shook my head from side to side, listening for any unusual noises. All this makes me think that if someone were to look inside my skull, they would probably find that it was only half full. Someday I may have my head X rayed just to find out. Until then, I have decided to stop worrying. I'm doing all right with however much I have left.   —R.P.

3

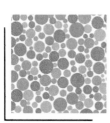

Sensation

Module 7 Seeing

It was the kind of accident that changes one's life forever. Craig remembered the gunshot, the searing pain as the bullet passed through his skull, and then darkness. The bullet had destroyed the nerves that send visual information from Craig's eyes to his brain, leaving him totally blind. Until recently, this story would have ended here. But today, with the help of an experimental surgical procedure, Craig is able to see flashes of light.

This medical miracle was accomplished by doctors who implanted a plate with 64 tiny wires on top of the visual area in the occipital lobe of Craig's brain. Electrical currents passing through these wires activate brain cells and enable Craig to see flashes of light. Craig has learned a kind of visual Braille in which flashes at different locations stand for different letters of the alphabet. After considerable practice, Craig is now able to identify a flash of light on the far left as the letter A, while a flash in a different location stands for the letter B, and so on. Craig learned the entire alphabet by associating each letter with a differently placed light flash. Craig is even able to read simple words, such as "cat," by using his flash alphabet (author's files).

In a limited but very real sense, Craig is seeing through direct stimulation of the visual area of his brain. As Craig's experience shows, you do not really see with your eyes. You see something when information from your eyes reaches your brain. Seeing is a form of **sensation**, the process by which information about the world is registered by your senses and transmitted to your brain. Let's take a closer look at how you see things.

LIGHT WAVES: THE INPUT FOR SIGHT

When you watch the sun setting in the evening, you see an orange-red circle of light. What you see as light is a form of electromagnetic energy, in this case, **light waves**. The sun, as well as an electric bulb or any other source of light, generates light waves that radiate out and strike your eyes and other surfaces. Your eyes begin the process of seeing because they have receptors that can absorb these light waves. There are other forms of electromagnetic energy, such as X rays and radar waves, that the receptors in your eyes cannot absorb. For example, you do not see the waves emitted by the machine the dentist uses to X ray your teeth, or those emitted by the radar gun the state trooper uses to check your car's speed on the highway. To learn more about the various kinds of electromagnetic waves, look at Figure 3.1. Some waves are very short; others are quite long. The re-

Why can't you see X rays?

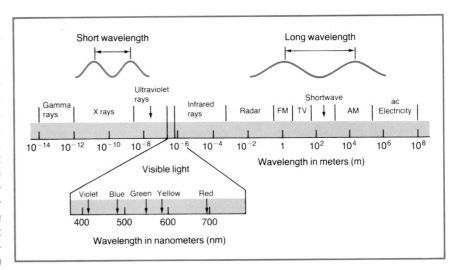

Figure 3.1
Light is only one of a number of forms of electromagnetic energy, which comes in an enormous range of wavelengths. AM radio waves and alternating current electricity have the longest wavelengths, some measuring many miles. All radio, TV, and radar waves are invisible because the receptors in your eye are not sensitive to (that is, cannot absorb) them. Some of the shortest waves are X rays, which are measured in trillionths of a centimeter. These waves are not visible because they are too short to be absorbed by the eye. Between the very long and very short waves are light waves. Light waves measure only about 400 to 700 nanometers (a nanometer is one-billionth of a meter) and are visible because the receptors in your eyes can absorb these medium-length waves.

ceptors in your eyes are sensitive to only a small portion of the middle of the electromagnetic spectrum. This small middle portion is called the **visible spectrum**. You can see the dazzling orange-red ball of sun setting in the west because some of the light waves it generates are in the visible spectrum.

STRUCTURE AND FUNCTION OF THE EYE

Although the eyes cannot actually see, they are beautifully structured to gather, focus, absorb, and transform light waves into nerve impulses. To help you understand these first steps, let's follow some light rays from a sunset as they travel into your eyes.

Through the Cornea and Pupil

As light waves from the setting sun travel through space, they tend to scatter. Your eyes gather these scattered waves and focus them onto the receptors at the back of the eyeball. The first structure that helps to do this is the **cornea**, the transparent shield that covers the very front of the eye. If you look at Figure 3.2A, you will see a cross-section of a cornea. Its rounded shape is ideally suited to bending incoming light waves into a more narrow beam.

Figure 3.2B shows that beyond the cornea, light waves pass through the **pupil**, an opening surrounded by a circular muscle called the **iris**. It is the pigment of the iris that determines the color of your eyes. The iris controls the amount of light that enters the eye. In dim light, the iris relaxes, allowing more light to enter; in bright light, it constricts, allowing less light to enter. If you look in the mirror in bright light, you will see that the iris is constricted and your pupil—the black dot in the center of your eye—is very small.

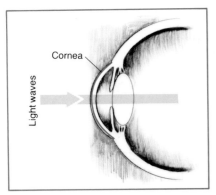

Figure 3.2A
The cornea.

Through the Eye's Lens

A short distance beyond the pupil, light passes through an almost transparent structure known as the **lens**. If you look at Figure 3.2C, you will see that the lens has a rounded surface. This rounded surface serves to further bend incoming light waves into a narrow ray. Muscles attached to the lens can change the lens's shape slightly, depending on the distance between the eye and the object being viewed. When something is far away, like a ship on the horizon, the light waves reflected off it need *less* bending,

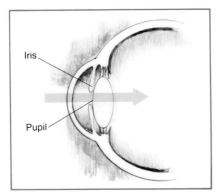

Figure 3.2B
The pupil and iris.

and the lens automatically flattens. When an object is close, like a word on this page, light reflected from it needs *more* bending, so the lens becomes rounder. These adjustments help focus incoming light waves directly onto the surface at the back of the eye called the **retina**. If all goes well, the result is a clear, sharp image. Figure 3.2D reviews all the major structures of the eye that contribute to converting light waves into this sharp image.

However, images are blurry to those of us who take off our glasses or contacts. A blurry image means that the incoming light is *not* being focused directly onto the retina. If, for example, you can see your wristwatch clearly but a distant billboard appears blurry, it may be because you are near-sighted. This condition is often caused by an eyeball that is too long, so that light from distant objects focuses at a point slightly in front of the retina. In traveling somewhat further to reach the retina, light scatters a little and the image of the distant billboard appears blurry. On the other hand, if your wristwatch looks blurry and you can see the distant billboard clearly, you are probably farsighted, a condition that is often caused by the eyeball being too short. This means that light from nearby objects focuses at a point slightly behind the retina, and again the light that strikes the retina is scattered. These common problems are illustrated in Figure 3.3. Glasses or contact lenses help your eyes to bend and focus incoming light directly on the retina. The thicker the glasses, the more help your eyes need.

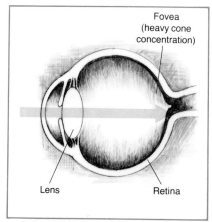

Figure 3.2C
The lens, retina, and fovea.

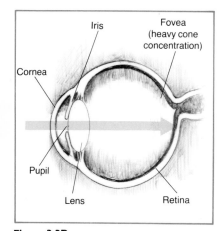

Figure 3.2D
The major structures of the eye.

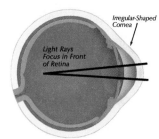

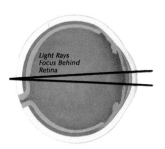

Figure 3.3
Normal (top), nearsighted (middle), and far-sighted (bottom) vision. If you are near-sighted, your eyeball is too long. The image is focused in front of the retina and you can see objects clearly up close but not at a distance. If you are farsighted, your eyeball is too short. The image is focused in back of the retina and you can see objects clearly at a distance but not up close. Glasses or contacts correct for the shape of your eyeball and help to focus the image on the retina. If you had cataracts, there would be an opaque film inside or on the surface of the lens. In this case, no image would be focused on the retina and you would be blind.
(Courtesy Robert Meyers studios)

In the elderly, increasing nearsightedness may signal the development of *cataracts*, in which an opaque film grows slowly over the lens, preventing light from reaching the retina. This once devastating condition—which can result in blindness—can now be successfully treated by surgery that replaces the damaged lens with a plastic one.

Onto the Retina

Why do bulls charge at a red cape?

Now you are ready to watch what happens as light waves from the sunset actually strike the retina at the back of the eye. The retina contains **photoreceptors** that are called rods and cones because of their shapes. The rods and cones absorb light waves and begin the process that will result in your seeing the sunset.

The **rods** are concentrated primarily around the outer edges of the retina and are highly sensitive to small amounts of light. For this reason, you depend on the rods for vision in dim light. But because of the way the rods connect to neighboring cells in the visual system, you cannot perceive fine details when only the rods are stimulated. If you were to look at a piece of the retina under a powerful microscope, you would see that many rods often connect to a single neighboring cell. This means that as information is passed from those rods to the neighboring cell, much of that information gets blurred or lost. Reading in dim light is difficult because you are using only your rods. You have probably also noticed that it is hard to see colors in dim light. The reason is that rods are not sensitive to the differences in light waves associated with different colors. When only the rods are operating, therefore, you see in shades of black, white, and gray.

When you read in bright light, the **cones** operate, which allows you to see both color and fine detail. Cones are concentrated in the center of the retina in an area called the **fovea** (FOH-vee-ah; see Figure 3.2C). Cones can reproduce fine details because fewer of them converge on each neighboring cell in the visual system. They allow you to see colors because they are specialized to respond to the differences in light waves associated with the color spectrum. The disadvantage of the cones is that they are activated only by fairly bright light. Consequently, you can see colors and fine detail only when enough light is present to stimulate your cones. Not every creature has cones in their retinas. Birds, dogs, and cats have few, if any. And despite popular belief, bulls cannot distinguish color. What makes bulls charge at a red cape is not the color, but the movement as the matador waves the cape around.

ADJUSTING TO DIFFERENT LIGHT INTENSITIES

When you first enter a darkened theater in which the movie has already begun, you sometimes find that you cannot see the seats. Why does this happen? Part of the reason is that chemicals in your rods and cones have been affected by the bright daylight and need some time to become sensitive to lower light intensities. After about 5 minutes, the chemicals in your cones will have become sensitive, and you will be able to see better. Further improvement in your vision will depend on increased sensitivity of your rods. The rods take up to 30 minutes to become as sensitive as possible. At this point you will be able to see the inside of the theater quite well. The process of adapting from bright light to dim is called *dark adaptation*.

When you leave a darkened theater in the middle of the day, you have

As this man comes out of a lighted subway station and starts down a dark street, he will gradually be able to see because of a process called dark adaptation. (Jack Prelutsky/Stock, Boston)

the opposite problem. Your rods and cones are now extremely sensitive, and they will take some time to adapt to brightness. If the day is particularly sunny, the bright light may seem blinding. But soon the chemicals in your eyes readjust, and you can see very well.

HOW LIGHT BECOMES SIGHT

Transforming Light into Nerve Impulses

Your retina contains photoreceptors, the rods and cones, which contain chemicals that absorb light waves. When they absorb light waves, these chemicals break down, and this breakdown generates a tiny electrical force. If a large enough force is generated, the threshold of neighboring cells is reached and nerve impulses are triggered. These impulses then begin their journey to the brain.

Rods contain a single light-sensitive chemical, called **rhodopsin** (row-DOP-sin). One of the chemicals needed to make rhodopsin is Vitamin A. If your diet were lacking in this vitamin, your body would not be able to manufacture sufficient rhodopsin. This causes a condition known as *night blindness,* in which the rods become less efficient at transforming light into nerve impulses. As a result, the person has difficulty seeing in dim light.

Cones contain three different chemicals, called **iodopsins** (eye-oh-DOP-sins), which will prove to be the basis for color vision.

From the Retina to the Primary Visual Cortex

The impulses triggered from the reddish-orange glow of the sunset leave the eye via the **optic nerve,** a bundle of neural fibers that exits out the back

What becomes of the nerve impulses?

Figure 3.4
Rods, cones, and the optic nerve.

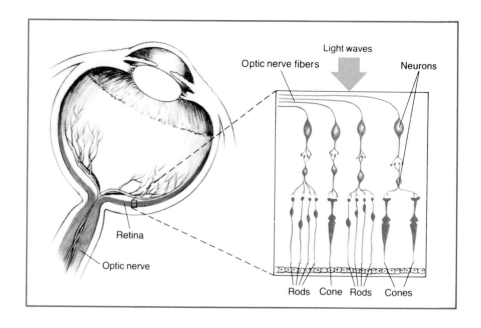

of the eye. If you look at Figure 3.4, you will be able to see how rods and cones connect to neighboring neurons, which in turn connect to other neurons, the fibers of which form the optic nerve. The optic nerve carries the impulses, among other places, to a part of the thalamus. The thalamus processes this information and then relays it to the **primary visual area** in the occipital lobe at the back of the brain. Figure 3.5 shows you the pathway these impulses follow.

It is in the primary visual area of the occipital lobe that the sensation of "seeing" begins. This area, you may remember, was the part of the brain that doctors stimulated to give Craig his limited sensations of sight. But unlike Craig with his sixty-four implanted wires, a normal primary visual area has a huge number of circuits connecting over 100 million cells. Much of our knowledge about these cells has come from the research of David Hubel and Torsten Wiesel, two psychologists who won the Nobel prize in 1981. Hubel and Wiesel (1962, 1979) discovered that cells in the primary visual area respond to very specific stimuli. For instance, some respond best to a line of a particular width, oriented at a particular angle; others respond best to a line that is moving, often in a particular direction. But neural activity in this region is not enough to produce the experience we call sight. If neural information were to stop at the primary visual area, you would see only spots and lines of light, textures and contours, not the full beauty of a setting sun. Craig sees only flashes of light when neurons in his primary visual area are being stimulated because neurons in this area can only produce simple visual sensations.

Damage to parts of the primary visual area of the cortex can cause blind spots in the visual field. In fact, if the entire primary visual area is destroyed, a person cannot see at all, except perhaps to distinguish day from night. Although we tend to think of blindness as an all-or-nothing phenomenon, there are degrees of blindness, depending on the extent of damage to the visual system.

Beyond the Primary Visual Cortex

To understand how you manage to see a sunset, we must follow nerve impulses beyond the primary visual cortex into the *visual association areas.*

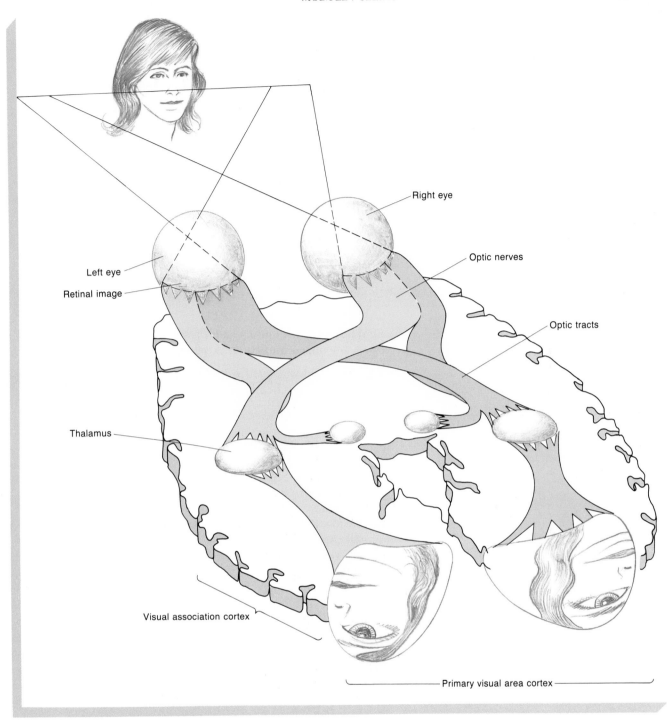

Right eye

Optic nerves

Left eye

Retinal image

Optic tracts

Thalamus

Visual association cortex

Primary visual area cortex

Figure 3.5
Imagine that your right and left eyes are staring straight ahead, looking at the young woman. We know that neural impulses leave each eye on the optic nerve, travel via the optic tracts to the thalamus, which processes and relays the visual information to the primary visual area in the cortex. Not until the visual information reaches the nearby visual association cortex, would you know that you were looking at a young woman. (Adapted from Frisby, 1980)

MAJOR CONCEPT   Vision

The eyes are just the beginning of a complex visual system that extends into various parts of the brain, where "seeing" ultimately occurs.

Below are the principal stages in transforming light waves into sight. Number them in the order in which they occur.

_____ Impulses signaling visual stimuli travel along the optic nerve to the part of the brain called the thalamus; from there they are routed to the primary visual cortex, where simple forms such as lines and contours are processed.

_____ Light is bent and focused as it passes through the lens, a structure that becomes flatter or rounder, depending on how far away or how close the object being viewed is.

_____ Light waves are bent into a narrower beam as they pass through the cornea.

_____ When nerve impulses reach association areas, simple visual stimuli are organized into complex perceptual images.

_____ When light waves strike receptor cells in the retina, they break down light-sensitive chemicals and nerve impulses are triggered.

Answers: 4, 2, 1, 5, 3

In the association areas, lines, contours, spots, and colors are turned into the visual experience of a red-orange fireball settling beyond the horizon. There are visual association areas in both the occipital lobe and the temporal lobe.

What has two circles and a crossbar?

"I'm doing pretty good," said Tony. And he was, considering his problem. The doctor gave Tony a picture and asked him to identify it. Tony took the picture and turned it this way and that, all the time trying to figure out what it was. Tony started to guess. "There is a circle," he said, "and another circle, and a crossbar. Of course, it must be a bicycle." Tony was wrong. It was a picture of a pair of glasses (adapted from Coren et al., 1984, p. 502).

Tony can identify pieces of objects but has difficulty determining what the whole object is. His condition, which is called *visual agnosia*, may be caused by damage to an association area located in the temporal lobe. Normally, this association area is involved in recognizing visual information, so that when you see an object, such as a pair of glasses, you can correctly identify it. If your association area were damaged, you would have the very strange experience of seeing objects but being unable to say what they are. Studies of brain-damaged people show the importance of association areas in giving visual experiences complexity and meaning. The following experiment with animals provides a clue to how association areas work.

Neurons Recognize Faces **EXPLORING PSYCHOLOGY**

A horned sheep was suspended in a comfortable hammock to prevent any movement. Then a microelectrode, which is a glass tube whose tip is so fine that it is visible only under a microscope, was lowered into the sheep's brain. Since neither animal nor human brains have pain receptors, the sheep would not experience pain when the microelectrode is lowered into its brain. Researchers use a microelectrode when they want to record the electrical activity from a single neuron, which, in this case, is located in the association area of the temporal lobe. Although most visual association areas are located in the occipital lobe, the temporal lobe has association areas involved in processing and identifying visual information.

Researchers showed the sheep a series of slides, including faces of sheep of the same breed (with horns) and of different breeds (with and without horns), and faces of a goat, pig, sheepdog and human (Figure 3.6). As the sheep looked at one face after another, microelectrodes recorded electrical activity from single neurons. The researchers wondered if some neurons would respond more to certain faces than to others. Their findings indicated that some neurons responded with more electrical activity when the sheep was looking at faces of sheep or goats with horns than at faces of a dog, man, or pig. A second group of neurons responded more when the sheep was looking at pictures of familiar faces, such as sheep of the same flock. A third group of neurons responded more when the sheep was looking at faces of a sheepdog or human, and less when the sheep was viewing a pig or a goat (Kendrick & Baldwin, 1987).

In similar experiments on monkeys, researchers reported finding neurons in the monkey's temporal association area that responded more to faces, monkey or human, than to other objects. Even more interesting, some neurons responded more to specific faces or facial expressions, such as the face of a young monkey, or a facial stare (which represents a threat) (Baylis et al., 1985; Perrett et al., 1982). Taken together, these results mean that sheep and monkeys have neurons in their association areas that are involved in recognizing faces. This may also be true for humans. Following brain damage to certain association areas, humans lose their ability to recognize faces but have no difficulty recognizing other objects (Springer & Deutsch, 1985). You can begin to appreciate how much processing must take place before neural information from your eyes results in seeing a face or a sunset.

Was that the face of a sheep, pig, dog, or man?

Familiar Dalesbred   Man   Pig   Sheepdog

COURTESY K. M. KENDRICK

Small-horned sheep   Hornless sheep   Large-horned sheep

Figure 3.6
When recording the activity from single neurons in a sheep's brain, researchers found that some neurons responded most to photos of similar horned sheep; other neurons responded most to photos of a sheepdog or human and very little to a photo of a pig. Single neurons also responded most to drawings of large horned sheep, which are more similar to the sheep being tested and less so to small horned or hornless sheep. (Reprinted with permission of Science, courtesy of Discover Publications, Inc. Photos by K. M. Kendrick)

Figure 3.7
The light from the sun is white light, since it is a mixture of all wavelengths. As white light passes through a glass prism, or through raindrops, the light waves are bent. The amount of bending differs, depending on the lengths of the waves. This bending results in our experiencing wavelengths separately as different colors. The shorter lengths (400–500 nanometers) are bent more and are seen as shades of violet, blue, blue-green, and green. The longer lengths (600–700 nanometers) are bent less and are seen as shades of yellow and red.

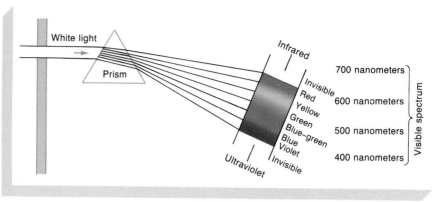

COLOR VISION

What color is red?

There was a problem with her eyes when she was born. She had congenital cataracts that made her almost totally blind. For the first 28 years of her life, she could tell if it were night or day, but see little else. Then she underwent a newly developed operation in the hope that, for the first time in her life, she would be able to see. When the bandages were removed from her eyes, she cried with delight as she looked around her room and saw things she had only imagined. "Colors were a real surprise to me," Debra said. "They were so bright. You can't conceive what colors are until you've seen them. They are my favorite things in the world, and red is my very favorite color" (adapted from the San Diego Tribune, *April 3, 1984).*

Wavelengths and the Color Spectrum

Unlike Debra, most of us have always seen the world in brilliant colors and find it hard to imagine a world without them. Colors and rainbows may also be among your favorite things. If you have ever seen a rainbow, you will remember seeing a range of beautiful colors. A rainbow is caused by sunlight bending as it passes through raindrops, just as light bends when it passes through a prism. Figure 3.7 shows that the amount of bending depends on the *lengths* of the light waves involved. As a result, the various wavelengths (which mixed together produce white light) are separated. We experience these separate wavelengths as different colors. The shorter wavelengths we see as shades of violet, blue, and green, the longer wavelengths as shades of yellow, orange, and red.

You see sunlight reflected off a sail as white because a mixture of all wavelengths is reflected. You see an apple as red because its surface absorbs most wavelengths of light and reflects back to your eyes only those wavelengths associated with red. But what is it about a particular wavelength that causes your visual system to give you the experience "red"? To answer this question, we must reenter the human eye and brain.

Theories of Color Vision

An article published in 1986 confirmed an idea proposed almost 200 years ago by an American chemist named John Young. He said there are three *primary colors*, blue, green, and red, which can be mixed to form *all* other colors. His idea became known as the **trichromatic** (TRI-crow-MAA-tic) **theory** of color vision. Since then, researchers have been searching for the receptors for the three primary colors. Now, just as Young thought, researchers have found three light-sensitive chemicals or pigments that respond to the three primary colors, red, green and blue. They found three different light-sensitive pigments located in different cones in the retina. Each cone contains only one of the three pigments. The same research team has also identified the genes responsible for producing the three light-sensitive pigments (Nathans et al., 1986a). One of the main, but not the only reason, you see the rainbow in brilliant colors is because there are three light-sensitive pigments in the cones which match the three primary colors.

Types of Color Blindness

Probably not unless he has *color blindness*, which is the inability to distinguish two or more shades in the color spectrum. Total color blindness, in which the world looks like a black and white movie, is very rare. It occurs not just in people who have only rods, but also in people who are born with one kind of functioning cone (instead of three). Such people are called **monochromats** (MOH-no-crow-MATS). A more common form occurs in people who have just two kinds of cones. These people, who are mostly males, are called **dichromats** (DIE-crow-MATs) and inherit this condition (Nathans et al., 1986b). Dichromats usually have trouble distinguishing red from green; they cannot tell whether a traffic signal is red or green except by the position of the light. You might think that color-blind people would quickly discover that they have a problem. In fact, many do not find out until quite late in life; they assume that others see the world exactly as they do (Coren et al., 1984). You may want to test yourself for certain kinds of color blindness using the chart in Figure 3.8A. Figure 3.8B offers you an opportunity to experience a colored afterimage.

Would a bank president wear yellow pants and a green plaid shirt?

Figure 3.8A
To test for color blindness, try to read the numbers contained in the circles. People with red-green deficiencies read 70 rather than 29, and the number 7 is illegible or hard to read for people with red-green deficiencies. (Ishihara Color Blindness Test Charts reprinted with the permission of Graham-Field, Inc., New Hyde Park, N.Y.)

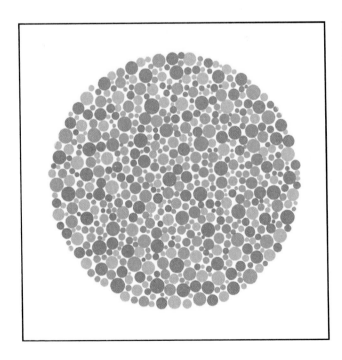

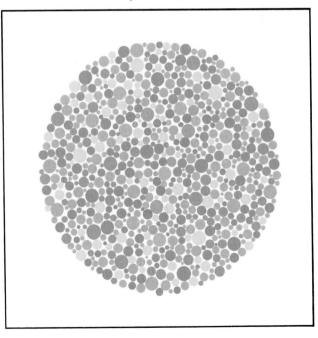

Figure 3.8B
To experience a colored afterimage or sensory impression that persists after removal of a stimulus, rest your eyes for a moment or two and then stare at the lower right-hand star of the flag for forty-five seconds. Then gaze at a white area, a blank sheet of paper, for example. You should see the flag in red, white, and blue, which are the complements of the colors shown in the figure.

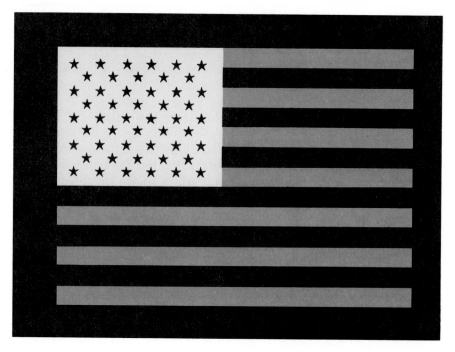

REVIEW

Suppose one day you open your door to find a peacock standing there. You see the peacock partly because receptors in your eyes absorb (1) _____, one form of electromagnetic energy. The small portion of the electromagnetic spectrum to which your eyes are sensitive is called the (2) _____ spectrum. This spectrum consists of light waves of different (3) _____.

Light waves reflected off the peacock scatter as they travel toward your eye. The first part of the eye they strike is the curved outer surface called the (4) _____. This surface helps to gather and bend the light into a narrow beam. Next, the light waves pass through an opening called the (5) _____. The size of the pupil is controlled by a muscle called the (6) _____, which surrounds the pupil. This muscle relaxes or constricts, depending on the amount of (7) _____ present. After passing through the pupil, light waves are further bent and focused by a clear structure called the (8) _____, which has the ability to change its shape. This clear structure projects a narrow light beam directly onto the (9) _____ at the back of the eye.

Light-sensitive cells called (10) _____ are embedded in the retina. The periphery of the retina primarily contains a type of photoreceptor that is known as a (11) _____. These receptors can function in dim light, but when you use only your rods you cannot discriminate colors, nor can you see fine detail. This is why, on a dark night, a peacock would look like nothing more than a vague, grayish-black object in the shape of a huge fan. Your ability to perceive the brilliant colors of a peacock and the details of its feathers is dependent upon a second kind of photoreceptor, called a (12) _____. Unlike rods, cones function only in fairly bright light. Cones are concentrated in an area at the center of the retina known as the (13) _____.

Rods contain a light-sensitive chemical called (14) _____, and cones contain chemicals called (15) _____. As the light-sensitive chemicals absorb light waves, the absorption generates a small electrical charge. If the electrical charge is strong enough, it triggers a nerve (16) _____ in neighboring cells. If light reflected from the peacock is intense enough to start nerve impulses firing in your retina, these nerve impulses will leave the eyes via a bundle of neural fibers called the (17) _____ nerve. After leaving the eye impulses will travel, among other places, to your thalamus and from there to the

(18) _____ _____ area in your occipital lobe. Stimulation of the primary visual area gives you the experience of seeing angles, lines of lights, textures, and contours. To recognize the object on your doorstep as a peacock, impulses must reach one or

more of your (19) _____ areas, which for vision are located in both the occipital and temporal lobes. In animals, researchers have found specific neurons in the temporal association areas that respond dif-

ferently to different types of (20) _____. If you had damage to your visual association areas, you might have difficulty recognizing objects or faces, a

problem called visual (21) _____.
    You see the peacock's tail as a combination of blue and green because these feathers are reflecting certain

(22) _____. The idea that there are three different types of receptors (cones) that match the three

primary colors is called the (23) _____ theory of color vision. Researchers have found three different kinds of cones, each containing a different light-sensitive pigment that matches the three primary colors

of (24) _____, _____,

and _____.
    Absence of one or more of the three kinds of cones in the retina gives rise to various types of color blindness. If you had only one kind of functioning cone,

you would be called a (25) _____, and you would see a peacock in shades of black, white, and gray. If you had two kinds of functioning cones, you would

be called a (26) _____. The most common type of dichromat is the person who has trouble distinguishing between red and green.

Answers: (1) light waves; (2) visible; (3) lengths; (4) cornea; (5) pupil; (6) iris; (7) light; (8) lens; (9) retina; (10) photoreceptors; (11) rod; (12) cone; (13) fovea; (14) rhodopsin; (15) iodopsins; (16) impulse; (17) optic; (18) primary visual; (19) association; (20) faces; (21) agnosia; (22) wavelengths; (23) trichromatic; (24) blue, red, green; (25) monochromat; (26) dichromat

GLOSSARY TERMS

cones (p. 70)
cornea (p. 68)
dichromats (p. 77)
fovea (p. 70)
iodopsins (p. 71)
iris (p. 68)

lens (p. 68)
light waves (p. 67)
monochromats (p. 77)
optic nerve (p. 71)
photoreceptors (p. 70)

primary visual area
  (p. 72)
pupil (p. 68)
retina (p. 69)
rhodopsin (p. 71)

rods (p. 70)
sensation (p. 67)
trichromatic theory
  (p. 77)
visible spectrum (p. 68)

Module 8 Hearing

One morning Dave was in his kitchen, where his wife was talking to him. He looked at her in a puzzled way. "I could see her talking to me, but I couldn't hear anything." Dave pointed to his ears and shook his head back and forth. His wife walked over and almost yelled "What's wrong?" Her yell sounded like a faint whisper to him. Only months before Dave's hearing had been normal. Now his world was growing silent. At age 32, he was almost totally deaf (adapted from the Los Angeles Times, *May 14, 1984).*

Why did Dave's world grow silent?

SOUND WAVES: THE INPUT FOR HEARING

Later on we will tell you why Dave went deaf and how some of his hearing was restored. At the moment, let's try to understand the ability to hear

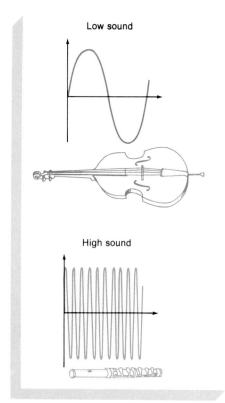

Figure 3.9
Low and high sound frequencies.

normally. If you snap your fingers, you will hear a crack. This sound comes from waves of air that were compressed and expanded by the quick movement of your fingers. If you could see sound waves, you might compare them to the ripples on a lake. Each ripple—that is, each time air is compressed and expanded—is called a cycle. You can tell the difference between low and high sounds by their **pitch**, which is determined by the number of cycles that occur per second. Figure 3.9 shows that the low-pitched tone of a bass has fewer cycles per second than the high-pitched tone of a piccolo. The term **frequency** is used to express the number of cycles per second.

Most college students can hear frequencies from 20 to 20,000 cycles per second. With normal aging, we lose the ability to detect the very highest of these frequencies, so that by the age of seventy, many people have trouble hearing sounds above 6,000 cycles. At age thirty-two, Dave had lost most of his hearing, which means that he could only hear a tiny range of frequencies.

Before he lost his hearing, Dave loved to listen to Beatles records, which he played loudly. Loudness is determined by the height or **amplitude** of the sound wave and is measured in units called *decibels*. Table 3.1 gives you an idea of how loud certain sounds are. For example, a whisper is about 30 decibels and a live rock band is about 110 decibels. The higher the decibel level, the more intense the sound and the greater the danger of damaging the organs of hearing. This is why people who work around jet engines wear protective covers over their ears. Rock bands, especially those that use powerful amplification equipment, can generate decibel levels that may cause pain and possible hearing loss.

STRUCTURE AND FUNCTION OF THE EAR

The Outer Ear

The odd-shaped projection on the side of your head that you think of as your ear is not really your whole ear at all. This is just the visible part of what is called the **outer ear**. Its funnel-like shape gathers sound waves and channels them down a short tunnel known as the **ear canal**. At the end of the ear canal the sound waves strike a thin membrane called the **eardrum**, which moves in and out in response to the sound waves' patterns. These major parts of the outer ear are shown in Figure 3.10A.

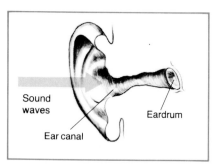

Figure 3.10A
The outer ear.

The Middle Ear

Using a special instrument, a doctor can look down the ear canal and see your eardrum, which marks the beginning of the **middle ear**, an area that serves to amplify the pressure exerted by sound (see Figure 3.10B). When sound waves strike the eardrum and cause it to vibrate, they set in motion three tiny bones, the first of which is attached to the eardrum's inner side. These bones are called the **hammer**, the **anvil**, and the **stirrup** because of their shapes. Each one acts as a lever increasing the pressure on the next, until the pressure exerted by the stirrup is many times greater than what the hammer exerts. The stirrup presses against a membrane called the **oval window**, which lies at the end of the middle ear. Because the oval window is much smaller than the eardrum, and because of the lever effects that the three tiny bones create, the oval window receives much more pressure per square millimeter than the eardrum does. This increased pressure is needed to move the fluid in the next chamber of the ear.

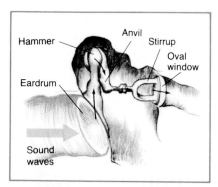

Figure 3.10B
The middle ear.

The Inner Ear

If you could see into your **inner ear**, you would notice that it looks like two straws that are joined side by side, rolled up and filled with fluid, with their ends affixed to the oval window (see Figure 3.10C). This set of straws

TABLE 3.1   Comparison of Sound Levels

Level	Amplitude (in decibels)	Source of Sound
Harmful to hearing	140	Jet engine (25 meter distance)
	130	Jet takeoff (100 meters away) Threshold of pain
	120	Propeller aircraft
Risk hearing loss	110	Live rock band
	100	Jackhammer/Pneumatic chipper
	90	Heavy-duty truck Los Angeles, 3rd-floor apartment next to freeway Average street traffic
Very noisy	80	Harlem, 2nd-floor apartment
Urban	70	Private car Boston row house on major avenue Business office
	60	Conversational speech or old residential area in Los Angeles
Suburban & small town	50	San Diego—wooded residential area California tomato field
	40	Soft music from radio
Very quiet	30	Quiet whisper
	20	Quiet urban dwelling
	10	Rustle of leaf
	0	Threshold of hearing

Source: *Science News*, June 5, 1982, p. 377.

Figure 3.10C
The inner ear.

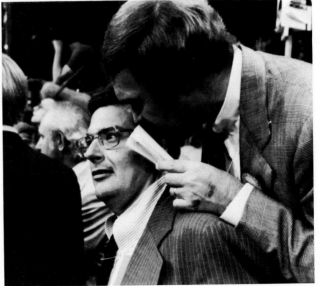

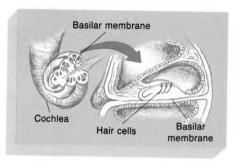

Figure 3.10D
The interior of the cochlea.

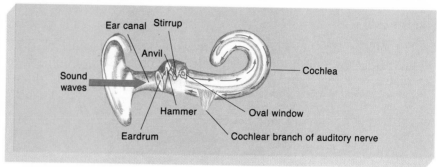

Figure 3.10E
The major structures of the ear.

or tubes is called the **cochlea** (KOCK-lee-ah). When the stirrup causes the oval window to vibrate, the fluid in the cochlea moves back and forth, matching the vibrations.

To understand the inner workings of the cochlea, look now at Figure 3.10D. Separating the fluid-filled canals of the cochlea are various membranes, one of which is called the **basilar** (BAZ-i-lahr) **membrane**. The left of the drawing shows that the basilar membrane contains cells known as **hair cells** because they resemble tiny hairs. These hair cells are the auditory receptors. Like the rods and cones in the retina of the eye, the hair cells of the inner ear can generate nerve impulses. These nerve impulses begin when movement of the cochlear fluid causes movement of the basilar membrane, which in turn causes the hair cells to bend, creating a small electrical charge. If enough hair cells are bent and the charge is great enough, nerve impulses are triggered.

The path of sound waves from the outer through the middle to the inner ear is shown in Figure 3.10E.

FROM THE INNER EAR TO THE EXPERIENCE OF HEARING

Neural Pathways to the Brain

How did Dave know that he was hearing a Beatles song? Remember that sound waves generated by playing a record are changed into nerve impulses by the hair cells in his inner ear. Nerve impulses leave the cochlea via the **auditory nerve** (see Figure 3.10E). From there they travel to the thalamus and then to the **primary auditory area** located in the temporal lobe of the cortex. If nerve impulses stopped at Dave's primary auditory area, he would have heard tones of different pitches and different degrees of loudness, but not the familiar melody of the Beatles. Neural information from the primary auditory region had to be processed by surrounding association areas for Dave to know he was hearing the Beatles. Hearing the Beatles brought back many memories for Dave and made him feel a little sad. His memories and feelings also came from various association areas in the cortex.

Perceiving Loudness

How can you tell if someone is shouting?

A whisper is about 30 decibels and a shout is about 90. But decibels are only a measure of physical intensity, not of loudness as you experience it. *Loudness* is a subjective experience. To measure perceived loudness, psychologists present sounds of different decibel levels and ask listeners how

MAJOR CONCEPT   How We Hear

Hearing is a complex process in which sound waves are transformed into nerve impulses that travel to the brain.

Below are the major structures involved in the auditory system. Match each one with its description.

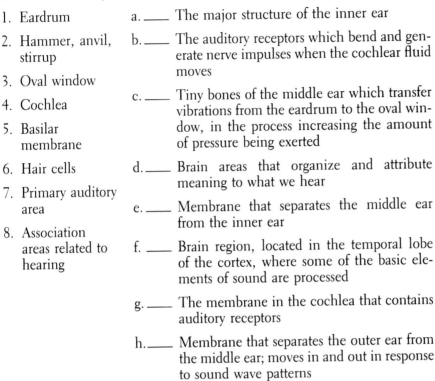

1. Eardrum

2. Hammer, anvil, stirrup

3. Oval window

4. Cochlea

5. Basilar membrane

6. Hair cells

7. Primary auditory area

8. Association areas related to hearing

a. ____ The major structure of the inner ear

b. ____ The auditory receptors which bend and generate nerve impulses when the cochlear fluid moves

c. ____ Tiny bones of the middle ear which transfer vibrations from the eardrum to the oval window, in the process increasing the amount of pressure being exerted

d. ____ Brain areas that organize and attribute meaning to what we hear

e. ____ Membrane that separates the middle ear from the inner ear

f. ____ Brain region, located in the temporal lobe of the cortex, where some of the basic elements of sound are processed

g. ____ The membrane in the cochlea that contains auditory receptors

h. ____ Membrane that separates the outer ear from the middle ear; moves in and out in response to sound wave patterns

Answers: a (4); b (6); c (2); d (8); e (3); f (7); g (5); h (1)

loud or soft they sound relative to each other. It may surprise you to learn that when the intensity of a sound is increased threefold, it usually sounds only twice as loud. This tells us that the human auditory system is not just reproducing physical stimuli in the environment. It is processing and interpreting those stimuli in its own special way.

How does your auditory system interpret the loudness of a sound? The secret lies in the cochlea. Near the hair cells of the basilar membrane are thousands of neurons, all with slightly different thresholds. A whisper causes little movement of the cochlear fluid and basilar membrane, bending few hair cells and reaching the thresholds of few neurons, thus triggering few impulses. A jet engine, in contrast, causes great movement of the cochlear fluid and basilar membrane, affecting many hair cells and reaching the thresholds of even more neurons, thus triggering a great many impulses. Basically, then, the perceived loudness of a sound is determined by how many neurons are firing.

Perceiving Pitch

Try making a very high-pitched squeak and then a very low growl. One of the ways your brain tells the difference between these two sounds is by which part of the basilar membrane vibrates the most.

As a wave moves across a pond, it will reach a high point at a certain place. So too does the wave inside the fluid-filled cochlea. If a sound caused the wave to be highest near the oval window, your brain would interpret the sound as high. If a sound caused the wave to be highest near the far end of the cochlea, your brain would interpret the sound as medium-high.

Georg von Bekesy won a Nobel Prize a number of years ago for his careful study of these wave patterns. According to von Bekesy's theory, one way the brain knows the pitch of a sound is by receiving information about where on the basilar membrane the maximum wave occurs. This is known as the **place theory** of pitch, and explains how your brain can distinguish between high and medium-high sounds.

The brain uses different information to distinguish between medium-low and low sounds. The brain perceives the pitch of these lower sounds by analyzing how fast groups of neurons are firing. Researchers suspect that low-pitched tones cause groups of neurons to fire at roughly the same number of cycles per second as the original sounds. This process is called the **frequency theory** of pitch and explains how your brain can distinguish between medium-low and low sounds.

Locating the Direction of Sound

Where do you look when someone yells "Hey you"?

You don't need to think. Hearing "Hey you!" causes you to turn your head toward the source of the shout. If both your ears were on the same side of your head, you would not only look peculiar, you would also lose the ability to tell the direction of a sound. You are able to locate sounds in space only because your ears are separated. A sound coming from the right reaches your right ear a split second before it reaches your left. Your brain automatically interprets this difference in timing as an indication that the source of the sound is to the right.

Whenever you have difficulty telling where a sound is coming from, it usually means that the sound is arriving at both ears simultaneously. In such cases, you probably turn your head from side to side to locate the direction. When you do this, you are causing the sound to reach one ear before the other.

Like these children, you can locate the direction from which a sound is coming because your ears are separated. Sound reaches one ear a little before the other, and your brain compares the difference in time and then locates the sound. This is also how you know where to look when someone calls your name. (Therese Frare/The Picture Cube)

HEARING PROBLEMS

After his last medical checkup Michael, age fifty-three, was told what he already knew. He had almost normal hearing in his right ear, but poor hearing in the left. Michael had been an active hunter most of his life, and the doctor told him that the loud sound of gunshots may have caused his hearing loss. Like most of us, Michael's first impulse was to get a hearing aid. But the doctor told him this would not help. What Michael did not realize is that there are two kinds of deafness (author's files).

Should I get a hearing aid?

Two Types of Deafness

If Michael's hearing loss is caused by wax in the ear canal, or by injury to the eardrum or the bones of the middle ear, it is called **conduction deafness.** The basic problem is that vibrations from the original sound wave die out before they reach the oval window. If simple cleaning of the ear canal is not enough to restore normal hearing, this kind of deafness can usually be helped with a hearing aid, which essentially replaces the function of the middle ear. It changes sound waves into mechanical vibrations and sends these vibrations through the skull bones to the inner ear.

If Michael's hearing loss is caused by injury to the hair cells or to the auditory nerve, it is called **neural deafness.** In this case vibrations of the basilar membrane are never converted into nerve impulses, or nerve impulses, once started, never reach the brain. Since hair cells and auditory nerve fibers do not regenerate, neural deafness is generally irreversible. Michael suffered this type of hearing loss. His long-term exposure to gunshots damaged some of the hair cells in his left inner ear. As a result, sound vibrations reaching his left cochlea triggered fewer nerve impulses than normal.

Prolonged exposure to loud music can cause similar damage. Rock musicians who were tested were found to have hearing loss compared with others their age (Rice et al., 1968). Even orchestra musicians are not without risk. In one study 42 percent of them were discovered to have poorer hearing than a control group (Axelsson & Lindgren, 1982). Presumably, repeated exposure to loud music irreversibly injures the delicate hair cells of the inner ear.

You may have been troubled by a temporary loss of hearing after attending a rock concert. After the experience, sounds may have seemed fainter than normal for a while. This condition, called **auditory fatigue,** is caused by a drop in the sensitivity of your auditory system after significant exposure to loud noise. The longer the exposure, the more persistent the auditory fatigue, which can last anywhere from minutes to hours (Postman & Egan, 1949).

Rock musicians run a special risk of hearing loss: Long, continuous exposure to loud sound can cause irreversible injury to the delicate hearing mechanisms of the inner ear. (Dennis Stock/Magnum)

Can Hearing Be Restored? **APPLYING PSYCHOLOGY**

At the beginning of this Module we told you about Dave, who started to go deaf when he was thirty-two. For the next 20 years, Dave lived in a world of muffled, garbled noises. He didn't enjoy talking with others, since he couldn't hear the conversations. Gradually, he withdrew into himself. Dave had neural deafness, caused by damage to his cochlea. Finally, when Dave was fifty-two, doctors implanted a plug with eight tiny electrodes inside his cochlea. This device allows

Figure 3.11
Cochlear implants can help people with certain kinds of deafness. Recipients must wear a device that converts sound waves to electronic impulses. At the heart of the device is an implanted plug with attached wires leading into the cochlea. The wires take the place of the damaged hair cells in the cochlea, sending electrical impulses to the auditory nerve. Because it is not possible to replace all of the ear's hair cells by wires, hearing is never sharp, though it is improved. (Adapted from *Time,* March 12, 1984, p. 60)

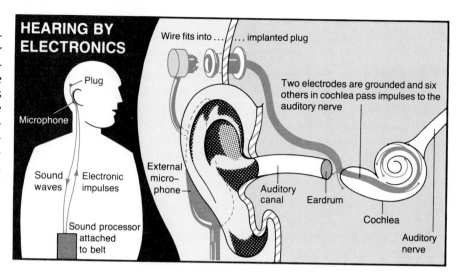

Dave to hear sounds and understand a little conversation. Although his hearing is not even close to normal, it has made Dave's life happier (adapted from the *Los Angeles Times,* May 14, 1984).

The most likely cause of Dave's hearing loss is that his auditory receptors were destroyed by some disease. Before the early 1970s, nothing could have been done about his condition. That was before scientists began developing a miniature electronic device to take the place of damaged hair cells. To understand how this device works, look at Figure 3.11. As you can see, a tiny microphone worn behind the ear picks up sound waves and turns them into electrical impulses. These impulses, in turn, are sent to a plug implanted in the skull. From the plug, a number of thin wires extend into the cochlea. The impulses travel along these wires and trigger impulses in the auditory nerve, thus bypassing the need for the hair cells. From the auditory nerve the impulses take their normal route to the brain, where they are then processed and interpreted (*Time,* March 12, 1984).

Although Dave's artificial hearing device, called a **cochlear implant,** has improved his life greatly, it cannot duplicate normal hearing. Only a small number of wires extend from the skull into his cochlea. In a normal ear, thousands of hair cells trigger impulses in thousands of neighboring neurons, the axons of which form the fibers of the auditory nerve. Normal hearing is therefore far richer and more detailed. When only one person is speaking, Dave can understand about 70 percent of the words in a conversation, but he cannot decipher more than one voice at a time. Similarly, he can hear the music of a single instrument, but a full orchestra sounds garbled to him.

In 1984, the U.S. Food and Drug Administration approved the use of cochlear implants in treating neural deafness, which is the problem for about 90 percent of those who are hearing impaired. Doctors estimate that about 200,000 of the roughly 2 million people who suffer from neural deafness in the United States could be helped by this device.

Besides the cochlea, there are two other structures in the inner ear. Under certain conditions, these structures are involved in a rather common and dreaded problem.

Motion Sickness **EXPLORING PSYCHOLOGY**

Max broke out in a cold sweat and turned pale. He could feel the saliva building up in his mouth and had to swallow every few seconds. Then came the familiar feeling of nausea and dizziness. Perhaps closing his eyes would help. That only made his nausea worse. Max loved to fish for the big ones, which meant long ocean trips. When the wind and waves came up and the boat started to rock back and forth, Max knew he was doomed. As Max made his way to the restroom, he wished he had never heard of motion sickness (author's files).

Max, along with about 25 percent of the population, experiences moderate to severe signs of motion sickness. In contrast, about 20 percent rarely experience motion sickness and the remaining 55 percent experience only mild symptoms (Dobie et al., 1987).

Oh, no, where is that sick feeling coming from?

Although the exact cause is unknown, researchers know that motion sickness involves structures in the inner ear. Besides the cochlea, the inner ear contains two other structures, called **vestibular** (ves-TIH-bew-lar) **organs.** Normally, these organs provide information about body motion, but under certain conditions they are involved in producing motion sickness.

Max can walk across a rocking boat deck because the vestibular organs, which sense movement and the position of his head and body, send that information to his brain. If he stood on his head, Max's vestibular organs would send information about the position and movement of his body in relation to gravity, that is, which way was up and which way was down. Max's brain uses vestibular information to determine his position with respect to gravity, help maintain his balance, or initiate movements to correct his balance. The problem arises when information from Max's vestibular organs conflicts with the information sent to his brain from his eyes. In a rough sea or bumpy air voyage, Max's vestibular organs register sharp motions, while his eyes report that things in the distance look fairly steady. Or, if you are watching a movie of a car speeding through city streets, your vestibular organs send information that you are not moving while your eyes send information that you are moving and turning fast and furiously. Researchers believe that if your vestibular organs send information that conflicts with what your eyes are telling you, the resulting sensory mismatch can result in motion sickness. Studies have shown that vestibular information is more important than visual information in causing motion sickness (Matsnev et al., 1987), but no one knows how the vestibular systems of 25 percent of the population who are susceptible to motion sickness differ from those who are not.

Earthbound people are not the only ones who are bothered by motion sickness; astronauts in space have a related problem. About four out of every ten astronauts experience space motion sickness, usually within 24 hours after lift-off. This condition, which is a persistent problem for both American and Soviet astronauts, lasts three to four days and is usually gone by the fifth day. The cause of space motion sickness is slightly different from that caused by motion sickness on earth. Researchers believe that space motion sickness results when an individual must move about in gravity that is less than that on earth. The astronauts' adaptive movements that were learned under earth gravity are no longer appropriate for controlling movement and position in the weightless conditions of outer space. Until the astronauts learn to adjust their movements—a process that takes about three or four days—they experience the nausea and discomfort associated with motion sickness (Lackner & Graybiel, 1986).

If you suffer from motion sickness, you have several treatment options. A number of over-the-counter drugs, such as dramamine, decrease motion sickness, but these preparations may cause drowsiness, blurred vision, and other unwanted side effects. A new prescription drug called transdermal scopolamine has been found to be effective in reducing motion sickness and has few side effects (Attias et al., 1987). As an alternative to drugs, a number of studies have reported a successful reduction in motion sickness after a behavioral training program in which individuals learned to perform relaxation responses, think positive thoughts, or use calming images at the first sign of symptoms. Out of a total of 53 fliers who were grounded because of chronic, severe motion sickness, 49 were able to overcome their problem and start flying again after completing the behavioral program (Jones et al., 1985).

REVIEW

When a police siren is turned on it produces

(1) _____ _____ by causing air molecules to alternately compress and expand. The high-pitched wail of the siren tells you that its sound waves have many cycles of compression and expansion per second. These sound waves are therefore said to

have a high (2) _____.

As the police car comes nearer and the siren sounds louder, the sound waves your ears are receiving

are increasing in (3) _____. This refers to the height of a sound wave and is related to loudness.

In order for you to hear the siren, sound waves

from it must first be gathered by your (4) _____ ear. This structure consists of more than just the external part you can see on the side of the head. Beyond the external ear is a short passageway, called the

(5) _____ _____. When sound waves reach the end of the ear canal they strike

a thin membrane known as the (6) _____. As a result of the sound waves' pressure, the eardrum begins to vibrate.

Attached to the inner side of the eardrum is a series of three tiny bones, called because of their shapes the

(7) _____, _____ and _____. These bones are located in the part of the ear known

as the (8) _____ ear. These bones act as levers, increasing the pressure originally exerted on the eardrum. They also amplify this pressure because they

transfer vibrations from the relatively large area of the eardrum to the relatively small area of a second mem-

brane called the (9) _____ _____. This membrane marks the beginning of a part of the

ear known as the (10) _____ ear.

The major organ in the inner ear is called the

(11) _____. This structure consists of rolled-up, fluid-filled tubes that are separated by membranes. The most important of these membranes for

the sensation of hearing is the (12) _____ membrane. This membrane contains the auditory re-

ceptors, also known as (13) _____ cells. When these cells are bent, a tiny electrical charge is generated and nerve impulses are triggered.

These impulses travel to the brain via the

(14) _____ nerve. In the temporal lobe of the cortex, the nerve impulses are first processed in the

(15) _____ _____ area. Processing by this area gives you the sensation of clicks, clangs, and tones. But in order to have the experience of hearing a meaningful police siren, the nerve impulses from your ear must be further processed by

(16) _____ areas in your cortex.

Your brain has a way to determine how loud the siren is. As the intensity of the sound waves increases, there is greater movement of the fluid within your cochlea. As a result, more hair cells are bent and more nerve impulses are triggered and sent to your brain.

Perceived loudness, therefore, is directly related to the (17) _____ of auditory neurons that are firing.

Your brain can tell the difference between the high-pitched wailing of a siren and the low-pitched rumble of a bus. This is because sound waves of high and medium-high frequencies cause maximum movement along different parts of the basilar membrane.

This is called the (18) _____ theory of pitch. For medium-low and low frequency sounds, a second factor contributes to pitch perception: the frequencies at which groups of auditory neurons fire. This is known as the (19) _____ theory of pitch.

Your brain can tell the direction of the siren. It does this by analyzing the slight difference between the (20) _____ it takes for sound waves to reach your two different ears.

You would have difficulty hearing the siren if you had damage to your eardrum or to the bones of your middle ear. This condition is called (21) _____ deafness. A hearing aid may be useful in treating conduction deafness. If you had damage to the hair cells of your cochlea you would suffer what is called (22) _____ deafness, and a hearing aid would be of no help. A new technique for partially restoring hearing in cases of neural deafness is called a (23) _____ implant.

If you took a wild ride in a police car, you would keep your balance and not fall off the seat because of signals coming from two structures, called (24) _____ organs. Along with the cochlea, these organs are located in the inner ear. Motion sickness is thought to occur when the brain receives information from the vestibular organs that is in (25) _____ with information from the visual system.

Answers: (1) sound waves; (2) frequency; (3) amplitude; (4) outer; (5) ear canal; (6) eardrum; (7) hammer, anvil, stirrup; (8) middle; (9) oval window; (10) inner; (11) cochlea; (12) basilar; (13) hair; (14) auditory; (15) primary auditory; (16) association; (17) number; (18) place; (19) frequency; (20) times; (21) conduction; (22) neural; (23) cochlear; (24) vestibular; (25) conflict

GLOSSARY TERMS

amplitude (p. 80)
anvil (p. 80)
auditory fatigue (p. 85)
auditory nerve (p. 82)
basilar membrane (p. 82)
cochlea (p. 82)

cochlear implant (p. 86)
conduction deafness
  (p. 85)
ear canal (p. 80)
eardrum (p. 80)
frequency (p. 80)

frequency theory (p. 84)
hair cells (p. 82)
hammer (p. 80)
inner ear (p. 81)
middle ear (p. 80)
neural deafness (p. 85)
outer ear (p. 80)

oval window (p. 80)
pitch (p. 80)
place theory (p. 84)
primary auditory area
  (p. 82)
stirrup (p. 80)
vestibular organs (p. 87)

Module 9 Other Senses

TOUCH SENSATIONS

Lightly touch your index fingers together. Try to concentrate on experiencing where the sensations of touch are felt, that is, on which of the two fingers. Most people report sensations of about equal intensity from both fingertips. Now touch your fingertip (either one) repeatedly to your lower lip with light, quick touches. When asked to say where the sensation is, most people report that they feel it most on the lip and little or not at all on the fingertip, even though both are of about equal sensitivity and are being stimulated approximately equally. Now use

How do you know where you are touched?

the same finger to touch, with the same light, quick touches, your little toe or your ankle. Most people now report that the sensation seems to be located mostly in the finger, rather than in the toe or ankle, even though both are being equally stimulated.

The explanation of how you localize touch is quite simple. It takes somewhat more than one-thousandth of a second longer for nerve impulses to travel from the fingertip to the brain than from the lip to the brain. Similarly, it takes more than one-thousandth of a second longer for impulses to travel from the foot to the brain than from the finger to the brain. The impulses that arrive at the brain first (providing the difference is more than one thousandth of a second) seem to dictate where the sensation will be experienced, even though the two places on the skin are being stimulated equally (adapted from Coren et al., 1984).

Touch and the Skin Receptors

Was that an ice cube or a coffee cup?

If you lightly pressed one of your fingers to a coffee cup, you would feel pressure and warmth. If you touched a hot iron, you would feel pain. If you held your finger against an ice cube, you would feel cold. If you touched a tuning fork, you would feel vibration. What you have discovered is that the sense of touch is a mixture of a number of different skin senses, namely, warmth, cold, pain, vibration, and pressure. As your finger touched the cup, you were activating receptors located in the skin of your fingertips. Most of the sensations from our skin begin in receptors that look structurally alike. These receptors are called **free nerve endings** because they have no capsules, or small swellings, around their dendrites. At one time it was thought that there was a different receptor for each skin sensation. Now we know that most skin receptors respond to a number of different kinds of stimulation.

After the free nerve endings convert pressure, warmth, cold, and pain into nerve impulses, these impulses ultimately reach the somatosensory area of the cortex. At this point, you would experience the sensation of touching the coffee cup.

What is very puzzling is how stimulation of the same receptor, a free

This child knows the watermelon is cold because receptors in the skin of her fingertips flash messages to her brain as her fingers touch the melon. (Michael Weisbrot/Stock, Boston)

MAJOR CONCEPT   Sense of Touch

Indicate whether the following statements are true (T) or false (F).

1. ____ The sense of touch actually includes a mixture of different senses: pressure, pain, warmth, cold, and vibration.

2. ____ Your skin contains five different kinds of receptors that respond to the five different senses of pressure, pain, vibration, warmth, and cold.

3. ____ The kind of sensation you experience depends in part on the kind of sensory nerve being activated and on where exactly in the brain nerve impulses are received.

Answers: 1 (T); 2 (F); 3 (T).

nerve ending, results in the different sensations of pressure, warmth, cold, pain, or vibration. There are several answers to this question:

Answer #1: the same receptor may carry information about different sensations by having different patterns of neural activity. For example, a warm stimulus might trigger a pattern with slow bursts of activity, which results in the sensation of warmth. A cold stimulus might trigger the opposite neural pattern, fast bursts of activity, which results in the sensation of cold.

Answer #2: receptors in the skin use different sensory nerves to send information to the brain. For example, one group of sensory nerves carries information about touch, pressure, and limb movement; another group carries information about heat, cold, warmth, light touch, and tissue damage.

Answer #3: information carried by different sensory nerves is processed in different areas of the cortex, especially the somatosensory area, resulting in your experiencing different sensations. Answers 1, 2, and 3 tell us how different kinds of stimulation of the same free nerve endings can result in different kinds of sensations.

The Sensation of Pain

Charles had a serious problem with his right leg. The doctors told him that the circulation in the leg was getting worse and gangrene had set in. His only choice was amputation. A day after surgery, Charles began to have a severe pain. It felt like an explosion inside his leg and it kept him awake at night. The terrible pain bothered Charles. What bothered him even more was that the pain was coming from his right leg, the very leg that had been amputated the day before (adapted from Catchlove, 1983).

Charles was experiencing a sensation in a limb that had been removed, a phenomenon called **phantom limb.** At first he thought the pain was coming from the nerves in the stump of his leg. But this could not have been possible. Charles had a severed spinal cord and had no sensations from his waist down. His feeling of pain could only be coming from his brain. Researchers think that pain of this type may be triggered, among other things, by the patient's thoughts and emotions about the amputation (Shukla et al., 1982). The phenomenon of phantom limb shows that the experience of pain, like all the other sensations, occurs when information reaches the brain.

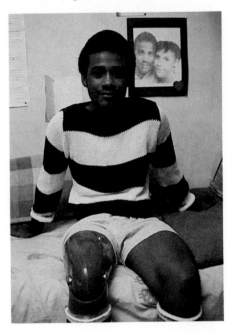

For days and maybe weeks after a limb is amputated, the person may feel pain in the "phantom limb." This phenomenon shows that sensation is controlled by what information reaches the brain, rather than by the physical event. The person may think about the lost limb and then feel pain where it once was. (Eugene Richards/Magnum)

APPLYING PSYCHOLOGY   Treatment of Pain

Why does it help to rub a stubbed toe?

Gate Control Theory.   Stubbing a toe is guaranteed to produce a sharp pain. Gently rubbing the stubbed toe often lessens the pain. The theory that explains why rubbing helps is called the **gate control theory** (Melzack & Wall, 1965). According to this theory, your experience of pain depends upon the relative difference in activity between large-diameter sensory nerves, which carry pressure sensations, and small-diameter sensory nerves, which carry pain sensations. Presumably, when you stub your toe you feel pain because the small-diameter sensory nerves are primarily active. If you rub your toe, however, you activate the large-diameter nerves which inhibit or "close the gate" on the small-diameter ones. As a result, pain impulses are prevented from reaching the brain and your toe seems to feel better. The next time you experience pain from a mild bump or bruise, try gently rubbing the area to reduce the pain.

Attention and Emotion.   One of the coauthors of the gate control theory, Ronald Melzack, explains why football players sometimes play for hours with a broken bone (Warga, 1987). The football player's intense attentional and emotional state causes the brain to send impulses to the spinal cord. These impulses close the gate at the spinal cord so that incoming messages about the broken bone do not reach the brain. When the game is over, the player's attention is no longer on football and his emotional state calms down. This decreases some of the brain's impulses to the spinal cord. The result is that the gate is opened, messages about the broken bone reach his brain, and he feels pain.

Besides attentional and emotional factors, the gate in the spinal cord can be closed by a number of conscious behaviors, thoughts, and images. For example, it is well documented that a person's perception of mild pain can be reduced if he or she focuses on some pleasant image (McCaul & Malott, 1984). This means that the next time you stub a toe, imagining a scene from your favorite movie will help decrease your pain.

This baseball player is trying to reduce the pain in his hand by following the gate control theory: Rubbing the affected area to "close the gate" on small-diameter nerves that carry pain sensations. (AP/Wide World Photos)

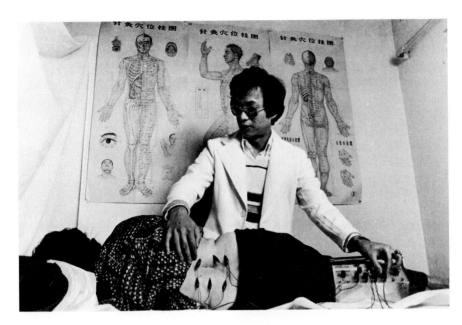

One of the reasons acupuncture may relieve pain is that it causes the release of painkilling chemicals called endorphins. (Charles Kennard/Stock, Boston)

Endorphins. In 1975, neuroscientists made a stunning discovery: the human body naturally produces chemicals with the same properties as morphine, the powerful pain-killing drug. These chemicals, called **endorphins** (en-DOOR-fins), are secreted by the pituitary gland in response to situations that evoke great fear and anxiety. In the laboratory, subjects showed increased secretion of endorphins when fear and anxiety were maximized, such as when receiving painful electric shock or holding their hands in ice water (Millan, 1986). In real life, patients showed increases in endorphins when having their tooth pulp touched, which is very painful, or when having their bandages removed from badly burned areas of the body (Szyfelbein et al., 1985). These and other studies indicate that one of the major functions of endorphins is to reduce pain.

Acupuncture. One kind of treatment for pain is **acupuncture.** During this procedure, the therapist inserts thin needles into various points on the body's surface, points often far removed from the site of pain. The needles are manually twirled or electrically stimulated. Ten to 20 minutes later, patients report an average of 50–80 percent reduction in pain. In comparison, patients reported an average of 30–35 percent reduction in pain produced by placebo conditions, such as having needles inserted without any stimulation.

There is considerable evidence that acupuncture may relieve acute or short-lived pain and, in some cases, chronic or long-lasting pain (Richardson & Vincent, 1986; Kreitler et al., 1987). One way that acupuncture works is by increasing the secretion of endorphins, which we know can reduce pain (Chen et al., 1986).

Behavioral and Cognitive Programs. Some people who suffer from chronic pain, such as that produced by a back injury, may get only limited or temporary relief from drugs or acupuncture. In these cases, psychologists have developed a number of behavioral and cognitive programs to help reduce pain. One behavioral program teaches the patient to monitor his or her muscle tension. As muscle tension increases, so does pain. Patients are taught relaxation techniques that reduce tension and thus reduce pain. Some chronic pain sufferers have learned that their complaints often result in attention, administration of a drug, or avoidance of some unwanted social, family, or occupational responsibility. These kinds of complaints are called *pain behaviors*. Pain behaviors focus the patient's attention on his or her pain. A behavioral program can decrease the patient's pain behaviors by increasing the performance of *well behaviors*. Well behaviors, which include taking walks, exercising, relaxing, and doing hobbies, directs the patient's attention away from feelings of pain.

Besides encouraging well behaviors, therapists explain to chronic pain sufferers how stress can increase bodily arousal and thus increase their pain. Patients learn how to identify or monitor stressors in their environment. Once a stressor is identified, the patient learns behavioral or cognitive methods to cope with it rather than getting upset. Behavioral methods might include practicing relaxation techniques, which calm the body. Cognitive methods might include substituting positive self-statements, such as "I can do something about my pain," for negative ones, such as "Nothing I do helps my pain." A combination of behavioral and cognitive programs have proved very successful in reducing pain in chronic sufferers (Corey et al., 1987; Keefe & Gil, 1986; Shaw & Ehrlich, 1987).

THE CHEMICAL SENSES

If you want to win a bet, here is a sure thing. Bet people that they cannot consistently tell the difference between cola and 7-Up when blindfolded and holding their noses. Let's see why this is a sure bet.

Taste

If your sense of taste depended solely on your tongue, your taste experiences would be quite dull. Humans can respond to only four basic tastes: *sweet*, *salty*, *sour*, and *bitter*. Taste begins when foods or other substances are placed on the tongue. The tongue is covered with approximately 10,000 *taste buds*. These tiny projections contain *taste receptors* sensitive to molecules that become dissolved in saliva. Taste, then, is a **chemical sense**: taste receptors respond to the chemical structure of substances. As with the other senses, you actually experience a taste sensation when information reaches your cortex. If an area in your somatosensory cortex were stimulated, you might experience a sensation of sweet, salty, sour, or bitter.

Figure 3.12 shows that specific parts of the tongue are more sensitive

Figure 3.12
The tongue contains taste cells or receptors that are sensitive to various chemicals dissolved in saliva. Four basic tastes—sweet, salty, sour, and bitter—form the basis for all other tastes. Each of these four tastes results from a different group of chemicals. Different areas of the tongue appear to be more sensitive to one of the four tastes.

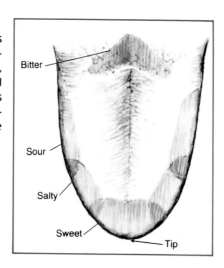

to one of the four tastes than to the others. The front edge of the tongue, for instance, is particularly sensitive to sweet. That is why, if you burn the tip of your tongue, you lose some of your ability to perceive sweetness until the taste receptors there have a chance to be replaced. Usually this automatic replacement takes just a few days.

If your taste receptors are sensitive to only four basic tastes, how can you tell the difference between two sweet tastes (a brownie and vanilla ice cream, for example), or between two sour ones (lemon juice and vinegar)? This takes us back to the sure bet. A person holding his or her nose usually cannot tell the difference between the tastes of cola and 7-Up. The reason is that taste receptors on the tongue are only partly responsible for what we experience as taste. As you have probably guessed by now, some of our "taste" experiences come from a second chemical sense, the sense of smell. That is why, when you have a bad cold, foods taste very bland. Your nasal passages are so swollen that your sense of smell is partially blocked, which is exactly what happens when you hold your nose.

Smell

Just when everyone said that they were full of Thanksgiving dinner, Frances brought out her warm pumpkin pie. One smell and everyone had to have at least one piece. Most had seconds. Frances had none. The pleasant aroma did not entice her because she can't smell anything. Her sense of smell, which once was as sharp as her other senses, had slowly faded away. Now, with her eyes closed, she can't tell warm pumpkin pie from mashed potatoes (adapted from the Los Angeles Times, *March 29, 1987).*

Why can't Frances smell her pumpkin pie?

At one time Frances could smell chocolate, onions, pine trees, and perfume, and hundreds of other substances because these things release molecules into the air. When Frances sniffed, these molecules were drawn

---

MAJOR CONCEPT   Chemical Senses

Taste and smell are both called chemical senses because they respond to the chemical makeup of stimuli.

For each statement below, indicate whether it relates to taste (T), smell (S), or both (B).

1. _____ This sense is quite limited in the number of different sensations it can detect.

2. _____ This sense is called olfaction.

3. _____ This sense is responsible for some of the flavors you experience when eating pizza.

4. _____ This sense is ultimately experienced in the brain.

5. _____ This sense is the one that is the most responsible for the "taste" of food.

Answers: 1 (T-taste); 2 (S-smell); 3 (B-both); 4 (B-both); 5 (S-smell)

Figure 3.13
The basic steps in the process of smelling. Substances such as chocolate release molecules into the air that may be drawn into your nose by sniffing. The molecules are then dissolved in mucus and stimulate olfactory cells. Those cells next produce nerve impulses that travel to olfactory bulbs located at the base of the brain. From there, the nerve impulses travel to other areas of the brain.

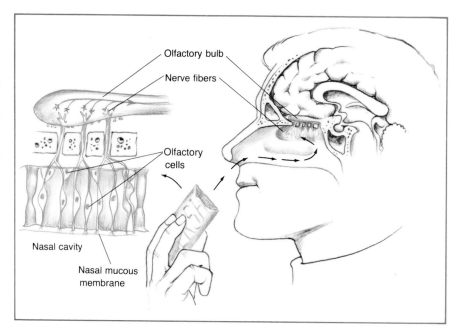

into her nose. Inside her nose, the molecules were dissolved in mucus and stimulated smell receptors, called olfactory cells. The **olfactory cells**, in turn, produced nerve impulses, which traveled to the olfactory bulbs at the base of the brain, and from there to other brain regions. These basic steps in the process of smelling are outlined in Figure 3.13. In contrast to taste, which is limited to four basic sensations, people can identify hundreds of different odors. Still, researchers do not yet fully understand why certain molecules produce the odors they do. The reason Frances lost her sense of smell is that something—perhaps a virus or an inflammation—destroyed her olfactory cells. About a half dozen centers in the United States treat people who have lost their sense of smell. Some one-third to one-half of these people are successfully treated and regain their sense of smell (Davidson et al., 1987).

Why is a dog's sense of smell better than yours?

One reason why smell is so important for the experience of taste is that the sense of smell is ten thousand times more sensitive than taste (Reyneri, 1984). Although you may have the impression that your sense of smell is not very good, studies indicate it may be just as acute as your senses of vision and hearing (Cain, 1977). This fact may explain why people who work with perfumes and wines develop such incredible abilities to detect subtle differences in odors. Although humans may learn to increase their smell sensitivity, however, they can never match that of a good hound dog. The dog has an olfactory receptor area the size of a small handkerchief, while the human olfactory receptor region is the size of a postage stamp.

SENSORY ADAPTATION

- Why can't you smell your own breath?

- Why is the first taste of a brownie more delicious than the last?

- Why can't you feel your sock a few minutes after you put it on your foot?

After a few minutes, the student wearing this strange hat will not feel it on top of his head and may even forget he is wearing it. One reason for this "lack of feeling" is sensory adaptation. (Barbara Alper/Stock, Boston)

These questions all ask about the same phenomenon: sensory adaptation.

Sensory adaptation refers to a decrease in your sensitivity to a constant stimulus after steady exposure to it. Adaptation occurs in all our sensory systems, with the possible exception of pain. It takes place because our senses are designed to be most sensitive to *changing* stimuli, not to constant ones. Your touch receptors, for example, are most sensitive to objects brushing across the skin. Articles of clothing, such as a watchband, a sock, or a hat, apply steady pressure, and so we adapt to them. Adaptation can involve all levels of our sensory systems, from the receptor cells that trigger the original nerve impulses to the neurons in the cortex that analyze incoming data.

If adaptation ceased at 4 o'clock this afternoon, you would suddenly find yourself aware of hundreds of stimuli: the pressure of eyeglasses on your nose, the hum of street traffic, the smell of a coffeepot you forgot to empty, the taste of what you had for lunch. Being aware of all these stimuli would be terribly distracting. How could you study or even read a novel? Adaptation allows you to ignore many of the constant aspects of the environment and focus instead on what you find important.

Why doesn't the hum of a fan keep you awake at night?

REVIEW

The stranger gave Claire's hand a good shake as they met in the doctor's office, waiting for their check-ups. Claire had noticed the stranger's firm grip and how cold his hand was. These sensations came primarily from sensory receptors, called (1) _____ endings, which are located in her skin. The sense of (2) _____ is actually a mixture of at least four discrete senses, pressure, pain, warmth, and cold. You can distinguish among different stimuli received by a free nerve ending because of several factors: the nature of the original stimulus, the particular sensory nerves that carry the information, the pattern of nerve impulses activated, and the exact destination of those impulses in the brain. One part of the cortex that is primarily involved in the experience of

touch is the (3) _____ area in the parietal lobe.

The stranger told of the car accident that damaged his left leg and his back. His leg was so bad that it had to be amputated. What really scared him was the searing pain he felt after his leg was gone. His doctor told him that this strange phenomenon was called

(4) _____ limb and resulted when neurons involved in body sensations were activated in his brain.

The stranger says that ever since the accident he's had chronic back pain. At first, he engaged in many behaviors, called pain behaviors, which focused his attention on his pain. Therapists helped him with a behavioral program that decreased his pain behaviors by

encouraging his performance of (5) _____ behaviors, such as relaxing and doing hobbies. Because getting upset increased his pain, he learned ways to identify and reduce things that caused him

(6) _____. A combination of behavioral and cognitive programs have proved effective in helping

people reduce chronic (7) _____.

The stranger remembers that right after his accident he felt very little pain. One reason is that his attentional and emotional states may have activated large-diameter nerves in his spinal cord, which stopped the passage of pain messages. This idea is the basis for

the (8) _____ _____ theory of pain. Another reason he felt less pain immediately after the accident is that his pituitary gland secreted pain-

reducing chemicals called (9) _____.

For a time the stranger said that he got some pain relief from having needles, which were electrically stimulated, put into his skin. This procedure, called

(10) _____, may produce a 50–80 percent reduction in both acute and chronic pain. One of the ways that acupuncture lessens pain is by triggering the

release of (11) _____.

The stranger apologizes for doing all the talking and asks Claire about herself. Claire begins telling how, about a year ago, she suddenly lost all sense of smell. Her doctor explained that smell occurs when molecules

in the air reached receptors, called (12) _____ cells, in her nose. These cells triggered nerve impulses

that traveled to the (13) _____ bulbs at the base of her brain and then to other areas. In her case, something destroyed her olfactory cells. All she has now is memories of what pizza smelled like.

The stranger asks her if pizza still tastes good. Claire replies that it tastes hardly at all since much of what we label as "taste" is actually due to the sense of

(14) _____. Her tongue still has receptors

that can respond to the four basic tastes: (15) _____,

_____, _____, and _____.

But foods seem rather (16) _____ now that she has to depend solely on the sense of taste. Claire

has lost one of her two (17) _____ senses.

The stranger wonders if his nose is failing him. When he first walks into a pizza place it smells wonderful but after a few minutes, he hardly notices the smell at all. The reason for this decrease in odor is because his system of smell has undergone sensory

(18) _____. In this case, sensory adaptation probably involves both olfactory receptors and olfactory neurons becoming less responsive to the constant "pizza" stimulus. All of the stranger's sensory systems are designed to be most responsive to stimuli

that are (19) _____ rather than stimuli that are continuous or steady.

Answers: (1) free nerve; (2) touch; (3) somatosensory; (4) phantom; (5) well; (6) stress; (7) pain; (8) gate control; (9) endorphins; (10) acupuncture; (11) endorphins; (12) olfactory; (13) olfactory; (14) smell; (15) sweet, salty, sour, bitter; (16) bland, tasteless; (17) chemical; (18) adaptation; (19) changing

GLOSSARY TERMS

acupuncture (p. 93)   endorphins (p. 93)   gate-control theory   phantom limb (p. 91)
chemical sense   free nerve endings (p. 90)   (p. 92)   sensory adaptation
  (p. 94)   olfactory cells (p. 96)   (p. 97)

PERSONAL NOTE

The elevator takes me to the top of the world's highest building. I leave the elevator and walk around the viewing area. When I look down, I see tiny cars and tiny people. I carefully avoid walking too close to the outside wall, fearing that a sudden gust of wind might blow me over the edge. In one corner there is a platform you can climb up on and look through a telescope. I hesitate and then climb the platform, which is several feet up. I don't think I should be there, but I look through the telescope anyway. Someone bumps me and I hear the words "Excuse me." I lose my balance and fall into space. I am tumbling head over heels, faster and faster, screaming and yelling. The moment before I hit the street, I wake up. I am sweating. I look around and see that I am safe in bed. It's quite amazing how my brain just gave me this very vivid and scary experience. It takes me two bowls of popcorn to get back to sleep. —R.P.

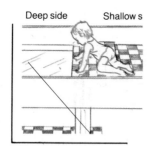
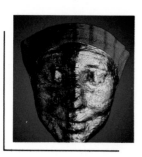
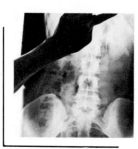

Perception

Module 10 Perceiving the World Around Us

Look at Figure 4.1. At first glance, this figure may appear to be nothing more than black spots arranged randomly on a white background. If that is what you see, it means that you do not have enough cues to organize these spots into a meaningful pattern. Later in this chapter we will provide cues to help you do just that. Once you interpret this drawing as a meaningful pattern, you will never again be able to see it as random spots.

The spots in Figure 4.1 introduce you to the difference between a sensation and a perception. A *sensation* is the experience you have when some outside stimulus, such as light, sound, or physical pressure, reaches one of your sensory organs and is then relayed to your brain. If you close your eyes and gently rub your lids, the splashes of color you see are sensations, not perceptions. When your visual system first recorded the spots in Figure 4.1, they were little more than sensations. But your brain immediately added meaning. Perhaps the spots appeared messy, beautiful, or just strangely shaped. However you interpreted the spots, they were more than flashes of light. Almost instantaneously your brain organized your sensations and added meaning. **Perception,** then, refers to the experience you have when you organize sensations into some meaningful pattern.

Look now at Figure 4.2. There is something unusual about this body builder besides his physique. It is his height. You probably assumed he is tall. In fact, he is only 5 feet 6 inches tall. Your initial impression of his height was probably inaccurate because you based it on past experiences with muscled men, namely, that they are big and tall. This picture introduces you to the idea that perception is an active process in which past experiences influence and even distort reality. Those experiences involve learning, memory, beliefs, and motivational factors.

For an unusual perceptual experience, look at Figure 4.3. As the gold-painted mask in the upper left photo begins to turn, you begin to see another face painted on its concave back surface. After you watch the mask turn 180°, you see the complete face in the bottom photo. Although you have just seen and know that this face is painted on the back of a concave surface, you suddenly see it as being painted on a convex surface. You have automatically transformed the face onto a convex surface and perceived it as you think the face should be rather than as it is. Your visual system has created an *illusion*, a distortion of reality. Figure 4.3 introduces you to the idea that your active perceptual processes may dramatically change and even distort reality.

When is a spot more than a spot?

Figure 4.1
What do you see in this picture? Turn to p. 104 for an explanation. (From Wortman, p. 117)

Can you stop yourself from being fooled?

Figure 4.2
How tall do you think this body builder is?
For the answer, see the text. (All Sport/Vandy-
stadt/West Light)

Generally, your perceptions are relatively accurate reflections of reality. However, in some cases, your perceptual process may alter reality to match your experiences. For example, if you do not approve of body builders, you may perceive the man in Figure 4.3 as ugly or misshapen. If you like body builders or happen to be one, you may perceive this man as being perfectly formed. Let's see how your perceptual processes actually work either to reflect, change, or distort reality.

FORM AND PATTERN PERCEPTION

If you look closely at Figure 4.4, you will see that it is composed of hundreds of individual lines and dots. Does the scene simply emerge from adding all these lines and dots together? Or is the perception of the scene something more than the many separate pieces that compose it?

These questions were the basis for a serious debate between two groups of early psychologists, the structuralists and the Gestalt psychologists. The structuralists believed that perceptions could be dissected into many individual elements. By studying the elements, they argued, we could understand the perceptions. Gestalt psychologists took the opposite view: they maintained that perceptions could *not* be understood by dividing them into individual elements, because perceptions are often *more* than the sum of the elements that make them up. This something more is a meaningful pattern that the brain actively constructs. In German the word for "pattern" or "whole form" is *Gestalt*, which is how the Gestalt psychologists got their name.

Figure 4.3
This sequence of photos demonstrates how your perceptual process distorts reality. As the gold-painted mask in the upper left photo begins to turn, you begin to see another face painted on its concave back surface. After you watch the mask turn 180°, you see the complete face in the bottom photo. Although you know the face is painted on the back of the mask and should be concave, you suddenly see it as painted on a convex surface. You have distorted reality by perceiving the face as you think it should be rather than as it is. (Walter Wick)

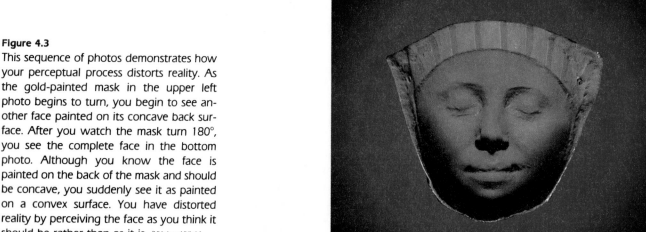

Figure 4.4
Why do you see a scene rather than a collection of lines and dots?

Principles of Perceptual Organization

In a remarkable series of studies in the early 1900s, Gestalt psychologists discovered many of the rules that govern how we organize elements into meaningful perceptions. We will demonstrate these principles with a series of pictures.

How do you see an airplane in the sky?

Look first for about 10 seconds at Figure 4.5. As you look at this picture, you will probably have two perceptual experiences. The first is of a white figure, a vase, with a black area surrounding it. This is one of the simplest kinds of perceptual organization: seeing objects in terms of **figure and ground**. The figure tends to dominate or be the center of attention, and the ground tends to recede into the background. You automatically differentiate something with more detail into figure and something with less detail into background (Chen, 1982). Your ability to separate figure from ground is probably innate. People who become blind at an early age and regain their sight as adults are able to distinguish between figure and ground with little or no training (Hebb, 1949).

Figure 4.5
A reversible figure. Do you see a vase or two faces?

You will also experience something else when looking at Figure 4.5. If you stare at this picture long enough, you will see the figure and ground reverse. The white vase on a black background becomes two faces looking at one another (the figure), and the white recedes into the background. After you have had both these perceptions, you will find that you can switch from one to the other at will.

Figure and ground is not the only principle by which we organize elements into perceptions. Look, for example, at drawing A of Figure 4.6.

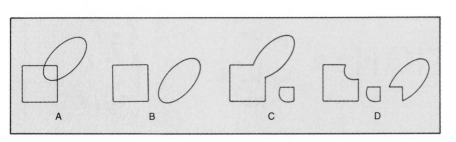

Figure 4.6
The principle of simplicity. Is A composed of B, C, or D?

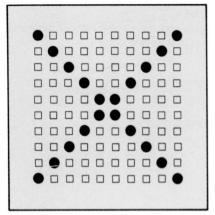

Figure 4.7
The principle of similarity. Why do you see an X?

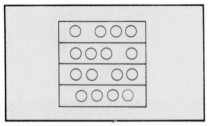

Figure 4.8
The principle of proximity. Why do you see groups of dots?

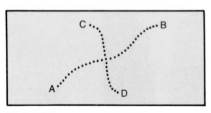

Figure 4.9
The principle of continuity. Does the line beginning at A go to B, C, or D?

Figure 4.10
The principle of closure. What forms do you see here?

Almost everyone sees this drawing as a square with an oval overlapping the upper right-hand corner, as shown in drawing B. This perception illustrates the principle of **simplicity**: we tend to organize stimuli in the simplest way possible. No one sees this pattern as the complicated figures in drawings C and D.

Now look at Figure 4.7. You probably see it as a black X through a field of white squares. You see the black X because of the principle of **similarity**: you tend to group together elements that appear similar. The principle of similarity is so powerful here that it is almost impossible to see the figure as just occasional circles, interrupting a row of squares.

Next, look at Figure 4.8. Each rectangular segment contains four identical objects, and yet you do not perceive these segments as being alike. You see the objects in groups depending on how they are spaced. This illustrates the principle of **proximity**: we tend to see as groups those objects that are physically close together.

Look this time at Figure 4.9. As you scan the drawing, beginning at A, notice what path your eyes follow. If you are like most people, your eyes will move from left to right in a continuous line. You probably see a continuous wavy line running to point B rather than a line turning abruptly to point C or D. This illustrates the principle of **continuity**: we tend to perceive a series of points or lines along a smooth or continuous path.

Finally, please look at Figure 4.10. You can easily read the letters PERCEPTION at the far left, even though they are not fully formed. You can probably also perceive the dog at the far right, despite the fact that the lines that compose it are also incomplete. These perceptions illustrate the principle of **closure** (KLO-zur), the tendency to fill in missing parts of a figure and see the figure as complete. You may have a little more difficulty with the form in the center of Figure 4.10. In this case, you may have to make a deliberate effort to fill in the missing parts of the "elephant."

Using Several Principles to Perceive a Form

Now let's return to the figure that began this module and use the principles of perceptual organization to see it differently. As you look at Figure 4.11, can you see a Dalmatian dog? The animal is in the center, facing left and sniffing the ground. How are you able to form this perception from a series of black blotches?

Using the principle of proximity, you group tightly spaced blotches together, such as those that form the dog's head and belly. Using the principle of similarity, you group together the spots on the dog's body because they are rounder than most of the others. Using the principle of continuity, you take the line that begins at the head and mentally extend it across the back and down the right hind leg. Using the principle of closure, you fill in the missing parts, such as the rear leg on the left. With the principles of perceptual organization, your brain has grouped the black

MAJOR CONCEPT   Principles of Pattern Organization

You see a world of forms and patterns because your brain automatically organizes the mass of sensations you receive.

Here are some of the principles your brain uses to carry out this task. Match each one with its description.

Figure 4.11

1. Figure and ground
2. Simplicity
3. Similarity
4. Proximity
5. Continuity
6. Closure

a. ____ Grouping together elements that look alike

b. ____ Perceiving elements as smooth, continuous lines

c. ____ Organizing sensations in the easiest way possible

d. ____ Filling in details to complete a pattern

e. ____ Grouping together elements that are physically close

f. ____ Distinguishing objects from what surrounds them

Answers: a (3); b (5); c (2); d (6); e (4); f (1)

blotches into the figure of a dog sniffing the ground. Once you have seen the dog, the figure will never again appear to be a group of black blotches. Your brain organizes the sensations so quickly and automatically that it is virtually impossible *not* to perceive the dog's form. Throughout the day, your brain organizes and gives meaning to the millions of sensations that you receive and process. In fact, at this very moment you are using the same principles to organize the marks on this page into words.

DEPTH AND DISTANCE PERCEPTION

How far away is 12 inches?

Try holding this book about 12 inches away. Your ability to estimate 12 inches is based on your ability to perceive depth, which is related to distance. What you don't realize is that the visual images projected onto your retinas have only two dimensions: height and width. Where does the third dimension, depth, come from? To answer this question, we will look at two different kinds of cues: those that are built into the visual system (*bodily depth cues*), and those that arise from how objects are arranged in space (*environmental depth cues*). Let's consider the bodily cues first.

Bodily Depth Cues

Can you see your own nose?

Hold an arm straight out in front of you and raise your index finger. Now watch the end of your finger as you slowly bring it forward and touch your nose. You have just done a test for **convergence,** the ability of the eyes to converge or turn inward in order to focus on a near object, in this case your finger (see Figure 4.12).

The muscles that turn your eyes inward provide cues to your brain about how far away the object you are viewing is. The more your eyes turn inward, the nearer the object, as illustrated by the photo of the woman with the fly on her nose. Convergence cues are *binocular*, meaning that they depend on the movement of both eyes. If you had only one eye, you would not have convergence cues for depth.

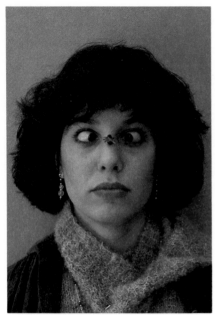

Figure 4.12
In order for this woman to see the fly on her nose, her eyes must turn inward, an example of convergence. The amount of convergence is one cue as to how distant objects are. (Random House photo by Charlotte Green)

A person with only one eye would see the fly on her nose as being very near. When an object is near, muscles that control the shape of the lens contract, and the lens becomes rounder. As the object moves away, the muscles relax and the lens becomes flatter. This process is called **accommodation.** This cue, however, provides meaningful information only over a limited range. Your lenses obtain their roundest shape when you are viewing an object about eight inches away and are at their flattest when that object is ten feet away. Accommodation, therefore, is useful only within these distances. Since accommodation occurs separately within each eye, it is a *monocular* depth cue. The limited range of accommodation means that a person with one eye would be able to use this process only to judge the distance of relatively near objects.

Probably the most important bodily cue for depth arises from the fact that your two eyes are several inches apart. This separation means that the eyes look at the world from slightly different angles and receive slightly different images. The closer the object, the greater the difference between the images. The difference in image is called **retinal disparity.** As retinal disparity decreases, your brain perceives the object to be more distant.

A 3-D movie works on the principle of retinal disparity: two slightly different images are projected onto the screen. The special glasses you wear allow one of these images to be seen by your right eye and the other to be seen by your left. When your brain processes the disparate images, you experience the illusion that the shark in the movie is swimming right into your seat. Retinal disparity is obviously a binocular depth cue and would not be experienced by someone with only one eye.

Environmental Depth Cues

The way objects are arranged in the environment also provides cues for depth and distance. Here are some of the most important of these cues.

Linear Perspective. If you look down a long stretch of highway, as in Figure 4.13, the sides of the road form parallel lines that seem to come together in the distance. This convergence of parallel lines is called **linear perspective,** and it creates the perception of depth.

Atmospheric Perspective. The presence of dust, smog, or water vapor gives distant objects a hazy look and makes them appear farther away. This is called **atmospheric perspective,** and it is illustrated in Figure 4.14.

Relative Size and Closeness to the Horizon. When you look at the two figures in Figure 4.15, the one on the right appears farther away because her image is smaller and is closer to the horizon. These two factors—**relative size** and **relative closeness to the horizon**—give the perception of distance.

Interposition. In Figure 4.16, the triangle overlaps the square and therefore appears closer. This partial overlap of objects is called **interposition** and provides another depth cue.

Light and Shadow. Although the object in Figure 4.17 is really just a circle, it appears to be a distinctly three-dimensional object: a sphere. This perception of a third dimension is due to the way that **light and shadows** are cast.

Texture Gradient. Look at the flowers in Figure 4.18 and notice how their textures differ from near to far. The near flowers are extremely clear and sharp, while the far flowers are more grainy and much less detailed.

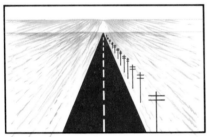

Figure 4.13
Linear perspective.

Figure 4.14
Atmospheric perspective.

The far flowers also appear more densely packed than the near ones. These gradual changes in texture, called a **texture gradient,** help give the impression that the field of flowers is receding into the distance.

Motion Parallax.   Look out your window and focus on two objects: a very near one (such as a vertical piece of window frame) and one several hundred feet away (say, a telephone pole). Now rock your body slowly from side to side. Both the window frame and the telephone pole will appear to be moving back and forth, but the frame will look as if it is moving a greater distance. As you go about your daily activities, you use such differences in the apparent motion of objects to judge their relative distances from you. This cue to distance is called **motion parallax.**

Figure 4.15
Relative size and closeness to the horizon.

MAJOR CONCEPT   Perceiving Depth and Distance

You see the world in three dimensions even though the images your eyes receive are in two dimensions only.

Imagine you are watching a fleet of sailboats sailing off toward the horizon. Match each of the following cues to depth and distance with its proper term.

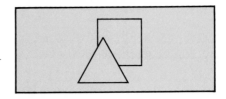

Figure 4.16
Interposition.

1. As you look from the boats in the distance to the dock you are standing on, your brain detects that each eye has turned slightly more inward.

2. As you look toward the distance, your brain detects that the muscles controlling your lenses have now relaxed.

3. Each of your eyes receives a slightly different image of this scene, and when the two images are processed in your brain you have the impression of depth.

4. Boats in the distance are shrouded in mist and therefore look farther away.

5. The fact that boats farther away appear smaller and nearer the horizon also gives a sense of distance.

6. As one boat crosses behind another, the one overlapped looks more distant.

7. Shadows on the edges of a sail and sunlight on the rest of it help make the sail appear three-dimensional and full.

8. Boats toward the horizon look closer together and much less detailed than near boats.

9. As you move from side to side, near boats seem to move back and forth more than distant boats do.

a. _____ Retinal disparity

b. _____ Relative size and closeness to the horizon

c. _____ Atmospheric perspective·

d. _____ Convergence

e. _____ Texture gradient

f. _____ Light and shadow

g. _____ Accommodation

h. _____ Motion parallax

i. _____ Interposition

Figure 4.17
Light and shadow.

Figure 4.18
Texture gradient.

Answers: a (3); b (5); c (4); d (1); e (8); f (7); g (2); h (9); i (6)

Why Isn't a One-Eyed Person Depth Blind?

Does it surprise you that a one-eyed person can land an airplane or hit a baseball speeding over home plate? If you think about what you have just learned about depth perception, these facts should not be so surprising. Although people with one eye lack binocular depth cues, such as convergence and retinal disparity, they have the monocular cue of accommodation, as well as all the environmental depth cues. Such people learn to use the cues available to them in order to perceive depth and distance accurately. They can even perform tasks requiring very precise depth judgments, such as landing an airplane or hitting a home run.

PERCEPTUAL CONSTANCIES

Why don't cars shrink as they drive away?

As the car in front of you speeds away, its image on your retina grows smaller and smaller, until it becomes similar in size to a toy auto. Still you know that the car is not actually shrinking. From your experience with objects, you have learned that things do not shrink just because they move farther away and appear smaller. You have developed what is called **size constancy**: the tendency to perceive objects as the same size even when the images they project on the retina are continually growing and shrinking. Size constancy is one kind of perceptual constancy; others have to do with shape, color, and brightness.

Size, Shape, Brightness, and Color Constancies

In Figure 4.19, the image of the woman in the red sweater is the very same size in both the photos. Why, then, does she seem of normal height in photo A and the size of a doll in photo B? The reason has to do with *size constancy* adjustments that your brain automatically makes. Photo B is an example of what happens when the distance cue of being close to the

Figure 4.19
Size constancy. Which of these photos is a trick photo? *(Random House photos by Charlotte Green)*

horizon is removed. The woman in the red sweater seems to be standing next to the man, so you see her as incredibly tiny. This, of course, is a trick photograph. In the real world, the depth cues we receive are accurate, and we are able to perceive the actual size of objects even though they are far away and look small.

The Allies took advantage of size constancy during their invasion of Germany in World War II. In the dim light of early morning, they dropped two-foot-tall dummies of paratroopers onto fields away from the planned landing site. When the dummies hit the ground, the impact set off small explosions, simulating rifle fire. In the poor light and general confusion, German observers thought the dummies were real soldiers attacking from quite far away. Only when the Germans moved closer did they realize that their expectations based on the size of the dummies had misled them about distance. In the meantime, the Allies had gained extra time for their invasion.

We are also able to perceive the actual shape of an object even though the image it projects on our retinas changes drastically. For instance, if you were to hold a book in front of you and then put it down, it would undergo the changes in shape shown in Figure 4.20. The actual image cast on the retinas goes from a rectangle to a trapezoid. Despite these changes, you continue to see a rectangular-shaped cover. The reason is that you possess what is called **shape constancy,** the tendency to see an object as retaining its actual shape no matter what angle it is viewed from.

We make adjustments for shape and size constancy so automatically that it is hard *not* to make them. Look at Figure 4.21. Most people assume that a dime will fit inside the top of this box. Try placing a dime (flat on one side) into the box. Does it fit? The reason the top surface of the box appeared large enough to accommodate the dime is that we tend to perceive constancies. Even though the top of this box is a parallelogram, we make a shape constancy adjustment and see it as a square with the back end receding. We also make a related size constancy adjustment: we see the sides of the top as being equal. Because of these constancies we perceive that a dime, which fits widthwise, will fit lengthwise as well—but this perception is wrong.

In addition to size and shape constancy, we experience several other constancies, including those of brightness and color. When you read this book in dim light, you see the page as having roughly the same brightness as it does in full sun. This is an example of **brightness constancy,** the perception of stable brightness even though actual brightness changes substantially. You also tend to see a red shirt as red even though you are looking for it in a dimly lit closet where its actual color is more grayish. This is an example of **color constancy,** the perception of stable colors despite color changes due to differences in lighting. Apparently, the brain takes differences in lighting into account when perceiving brightness and color. As a result, things seem to retain the brightness and color we expect them to have.

The Importance of Constancies

Imagine what it would be like if you lacked perceptual constancies. You would have the impression that your house was shrinking as you drove away from it. When the car ahead of you turned a corner, you would see it as actually changing shape. As you passed through a dimly lit tunnel, your white car would suddenly seem to turn gray. Without perceptual constancies, in short, life would be much more chaotic. Perceptual constancies give your world a very reassuring stability.

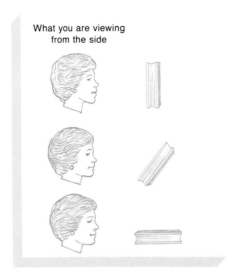

What you are viewing from the side

Figure 4.20
Shape constancy. Why is the book cover always perceived as a rectangle? (Adapted from Lindsay & Norman, 1977)

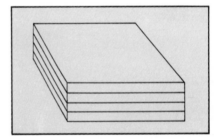

Figure 4.21
Will a dime fit in this box?

MAJOR CONCEPT   Perceptual Constancies

Your brain tends to ignore many moment-to-moment changes in sensory information in favor of a view of the world that is constant and predictable.

For each of the examples listed below, indicate what kind of perceptual constancy is involved.

<table>
<tr><td></td><td>Type of
Perceptual Constancy</td></tr>
<tr><td>1. When you put a record on a turntable, you always see it as round no matter what angle you view it from.</td><td>_____</td></tr>
<tr><td>2. When you are wearing a white shirt and the sky clouds over, you do not perceive the shirt as suddenly becoming dimmer.</td><td>_____</td></tr>
<tr><td>3. When you put on a pair of rose-tinted glasses, the world looks no rosier than before.</td><td>_____</td></tr>
<tr><td>4. When you are driving on a highway and see a tunnel in the distance, you do not have a moment of panic that it is too small for your car.</td><td>_____</td></tr>
</table>

Answers: 1 shape constancy; 2 brightness constancy; 3 color constancy; 4 size constancy

---

FOOLING OUR PERCEPTIONS: ILLUSIONS

Can a warning help you see straight?

Warning: This section contains *illusions* that will fool your senses. Most of the time, your perceptions are reasonably accurate reflections of reality. But here conditions are purposely distorted so you see things differently than they actually are.

Look, for example, at Figure 4.22A. These children appear to be of different heights although they all are actually about the same height. Their distorted heights are caused by the strange shape of this room, called the *Ames room* after its inventor, Adelbert Ames. In Figure 4.22B you see that the room's back wall is sharply angled. The result is that a child in the near right corner of the room will appear relatively tall and a child in the far left corner will appear relatively short. You see the children's heights as distorted because you rely more on your assumptions about shape constancy, what a room looks like, than about size constancy, how tall children should be. To obtain the greatest illusion, subjects view the Ames room with one eye through a peephole, which greatly reduces cues about size and depth. If subjects are allowed to view the Ames room with two eyes and to move their heads, the illusion is greatly reduced but still remains (Gehringer & Engel, 1986).

Another powerful illusion is called the *Margaret Thatcher illusion* (Figure 4.23). When you look at Thatcher's face upside down, she appears to have a fairly normal expression. For a surprise, turn the face right side up and notice how grotesque the facial expression becomes. Researchers found that subjects have great difficulty evaluating a mouth when it is upside down. They suggest that it is this difficulty in interpreting an upside-down mouth that creates the Thatcher illusion (Parks & Coss, 1986).

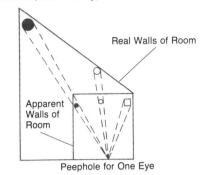

Figure 4.22A,B
Have you ever wanted to be taller or shorter than you are? Visit the Ames room (A, left). Its odd construction (B, below) helps explain how the illusion of tallness or shortness arises. (Arthur Sirdofsky)

● Real place and size of "smallest" child
• Apparent place and size of "smallest" child
○ Real place and size of "medium" child
○ Apparent place and size of "medium" child
□ "Largest" child

Your experience with rooms and corners may be the basis for the illusion shown in Figure 4.24, known as the *Muller-Lyer illusion*. Although line A appears to be shorter than line B, your ruler will tell you that the two are equal. One explanation is that your experience with rooms has resulted in your interpreting corner C to be closer and therefore shorter and corner D to be farther away and therefore longer. Similarly, it is suggested that you interpret line B as longer than line A because line B is seen as "farther away" (Eijkman et al., 1981).

They call it the devil's tuning fork. Study Figure 4.25 for half a minute and then try to draw it from memory. After you have tried for a while, read the next paragraph.

You probably found this task frustratingly difficult. The reason is that your experience with line drawings causes you to interpret the figure as a three-dimensional object. Unfortunately, it is almost impossible to draw this figure as a three-dimensional object because the depth cues are ambiguous. If you look at the right of the figure, the shading gives the impression that this is a solid, U-shaped object with two square-cornered prongs. But as you move your eye left, the perception of square edges vanishes.

What makes you see the impossible?

Figure 4.23
After looking at this face upside down, look at it right side up. The reason for the startling change in the expression is discussed in the text. (Dr. Peter Thompson, Department of Psychology, University of York, England)

Figure 4.24
Which line, A or B, is longer? Check the text. If you were wrong, the reason may be that you were fooled by your everyday experience of corners, shown in C and D.

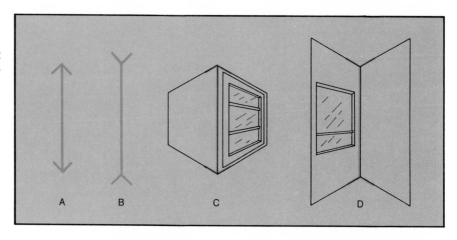

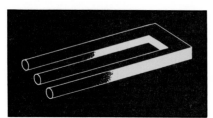

Figure 4.25
The devil's tuning fork.

Suddenly you see three rounded prongs. The middle prong in particular causes a problem because it seems to emerge out of nowhere.

It is interesting that Africans with no formal education have no difficulty drawing this figure from memory. Since they have not spent years looking at three-dimensional representations in books, they do not interpret the figure as having three dimensions, but see it as a pattern of flat lines. Such a pattern is very easy to draw (Coren et al., 1984).

All the illusions we have talked about so far have been created to deceive. But illusions also occur naturally. One such illusion that has intrigued people for centuries is a rising full moon (Figure 4.26). Why does the moon look as much as 50 percent larger when it is near the horizon than when it is overhead? One explanation involves depth cues from the horizon. As you know, the closer an object is to the horizon, the farther away we perceive it. We therefore interpret a rising moon as more distant than one overhead, and our brain automatically makes a size correction.

Illusions are more than fun. They remind us that perception is an active process and that we are constantly making assumptions about the size, shape, and color of objects in our environment. Illusions show us that once we have become perceptually experienced, our experiences affect our perceptions without our even being aware, and often in spite of our awareness (Hoffman, 1983). For example, does knowing that things do not really move in movies make any difference to your perception?

Figure 4.26
Is this rising harvest moon actually bigger than a moon high in the sky? (Bob Waterman/West Light)

Making Movies Move **EXPLORING PSYCHOLOGY**

You're watching a stunt-bike contest. Carol, one of the contestants, is twirling in circles, jumping over objects, and riding her bike on one wheel. As you watch Carol, you are seeing real, continuous motion. If you watched a movie of Carol flying through the air on her bike, you would be seeing **apparent motion,** which is created by presenting a rapid series of *still* images of Carol's movements. This illusion of motion is called apparent motion to distinguish it from the actual motion that you observe in real life. How does your visual system create apparent motion from rapidly presented still pictures?

How is your brain tricked into seeing movies move?

The basis for apparent motion is deceptively simple. Each successive movie frame shows Carol to be in a slightly different posture or position. When you view these frames one after the other, your brain fills in the blanks and creates the illusion of Carol performing on her bike. The principle for creating apparent motion is the same whether it is used in movies, television, or flip-through comic books. You can see this for yourself if you examine the still pictures that make up a flip-through Superman comic book. Look at each page one by one, and you will find that each picture of Superman differs only slightly from the preceding one. Then flip through the pages rapidly, and Superman swings into action. If successive pages showed Superman to be in very different postures, the illusion of movement could not be created. This brings us to the next question: how does the visual system detect the slight difference in an object's posture or position between still picture frames?

In a series of ingenious and complex experiments, researchers Vilayanur Ramachandran and Stuart Anstis (1986) found that the visual system has several mechanisms to detect apparent motion. One such mechanism is the visual system's ability to pick out salient or relevant features from the environment. For example, their studies indicate that our visual systems are more likely to pick out a dark blur moving through a forest before identifying the outline of an individual tree blowing in the wind. The researchers think that this ability helped early humans detect unfriendly creatures who might do them harm. Ramachandran and Anstis also found that the visual system operates as if things have predictable physical properties. For example, their research shows that if the visual system is given a choice, it will choose to follow an object moving in a linear direction rather than one moving in a path that constantly changes direction. They conclude that in perceiving apparent motion in movies, television, and flip-through comic books, your visual system quickly picks out the salient features and then applies built-in laws of motion when processing these features.

REVIEW

Driving home at twilight, you see a billboard with a huge hand holding a glass of milk. Below the picture, several letters are missing in the sign's slogan. The top line reads "Be nice to your bo y," and the bottom line reads "Drink three gla es of milk." What you are seeing is more than just a set of sensations. Your brain has organized sensations from the billboard into a meaningful experience. This meaningful experience is called a (1) _____.

Without being aware of it, you have automatically used a number of perceptual principles to organize this perception. For example, when you differentiate the figure of the hand and the glass from its background, you are demonstrating a principle of organization called

(2) _____. and _____. You

see the fingers as all part of the same object partly because they look alike in form and color. This illustrates

the principle of (3) _____. You also see the fingers as composing a whole hand, because this is by far the easiest way to perceive the stimulus. This is

an example of the principle of (4) _____. On the basis of their closeness and spacing, you organize the letters "benicetoyour" into four words: "be nice to your." This demonstrates the principle

of (5) _____. Your eye naturally follows the line of the glass, illustrating the principle of

(6) _____. When you provide the missing letters for the words "bo y" and "gla es," you are us-

ing the principle of (7) _____.

You see the billboard in three dimensions and a substantial distance away because you interpret a number of bodily and environmental depth cues. For instance, as your gaze moves from the dashboard to the milk ad, the muscles in your eyes automatically relax and cause your lenses to become flatter. This small

adjustment in muscle tension is called (8) _____. Your brain detects accommodation and uses it as a cue to distance. Another cue to distance is the degree to

which your eyes turn inward, called (9) _____. The fact that each eye receives a slightly different view of the billboard is probably your most important bodily cue to depth. These two different images are called

(10) _____ _____, and they are processed in the brain to give the sense of a third dimension.

As you view the billboard, you are also using a number of environmental cues to judge distance. For instance, the billboard looks relatively smaller than a sign in the foreground, and so you conclude that it must be farther away. This depth cue is called

(11) _____. The billboard also looks closer to the (12) _____, which makes you assume it is farther away. The fact that there is a telephone pole in front of the billboard also tells you that the billboard must be farther away. This overlap of objects is a cue to distance known as

(13) _____. Other environmental cues for

depth come from the convergence of parallel lines, called (14) _____ _____, from the haze that surrounds objects in the distance, called (15) _____ _____, from the presence of different lighting effects, called (16) _____ and _____ , from the change in the texture of objects, called (17) _____ _____, and from the fact that far objects appear to move less than near ones as you turn your head, called (18) _____ _____.

As you drive closer and closer to the billboard, its image on your retina gets larger and larger. But despite this increase in retinal image, you do not see the billboard as expanding. The fact that your perception of the sign's size remains constant is an example of

(19) _____ _____. As you drive past the billboard and view its edge, it changes from an oblong rectangle to a thin vertical line. Despite these changes, you do not see the billboard as actually

changing shape. This is an example of (20) _____ _____. Although it is twilight, the white glass of milk appears bright to you, and you recognize the flesh color of the hand. The first of these percep-

tions shows (21) _____ _____, while the second shows (22) _____ _____. These various perceptual constancies add greatly to the impression of a stable world.

Although your perceptions of the billboard were accurate, this is not always the case. Sometimes we see objects differently than they really are. Such distortions

in perceptions are called (23) _____. In order for us to have the illusion of motion when viewing movies and television, our visual system uses a number of different mechanisms to create

(24) _____ motion. The study of illusions tells us that perception is an active process of inferring what the world is like.

Answers: (1) perception; (2) figure, ground; (3) similarity; (4) simplicity; (5) proximity; (6) continuity; (7) closure; (8) accommodation; (9) convergence; (10) retinal disparity; (11) relative size; (12) horizon; (13) interposition; (14) linear perspective; (15) atmospheric perspective; (16) light, shadow; (17) texture gradient; (18) motion parallax; (19) size constancy; (20) shape constancy; (21) brightness constancy; (22) color constancy; (23) illusions; (24) apparent

GLOSSARY TERMS

accommodation (p. 106)
apparent motion (p. 113)
atmospheric perspective
  (p. 106)
brightness constancy
  (p. 109)
closure (p. 104)
color constancy (p. 109)

continuity (p. 104)
convergence (p. 105)
figure and ground
  (p. 103)
interposition (p. 106)
light and shadows
  (p. 106)

linear perspective
  (p. 106)
motion parallax (p. 107)
perception (p. 101)
proximity (p. 104)
relative closeness to the
  horizon (p. 106)

relative size (p. 106)
retinal disparity (p. 106)
shape constancy (p. 109)
similarity (p. 104)
simplicity (p. 104)
size constancy (p. 108)
texture gradient (p. 107)

Module 11 Interaction of Heredity and Learning

Sam's window ledge was four stories up, but he assumed it was only a few feet above the ground. He crawled out on the window ledge to get a better look at the tiny objects on the street below. Those tiny objects turned out to be cars.

Sam had trouble keeping track of the hospital staff because he had trouble recognizing faces. He had no idea if his doctor was smiling or frowning when she entered his room because Sam was unaware of facial expressions. The doctor held out two objects and asked Sam if they differed. Sam could see the objects, but he had to count the sides to tell a square from a triangle.

Sam had been blind since he was ten months old. Now, at age fifty-three, his vision had been restored with a corneal transplant. When he first regained his sight, Sam made many visual errors. Within six months, however, he could recognize faces, safely cross a busy street, and draw detailed pictures of triangles and squares (adapted from Gregory, 1974).

What Sam saw when his bandages were first removed provides some answers to the question: how much of perception is inherited and how much requires learning and experience? Let's look at how psychologists have answered this question.

THE CONTRIBUTIONS OF HEREDITY AND LEARNING

Immediately after his vision was restored, Sam had no trouble distinguishing figure and ground, suggesting that this ability was *innate*—that is, it existed from birth. In contrast, he had trouble recognizing faces and facial expressions, telling a triangle from a square, and judging distance and depth. These aspects of perception seem to require *experience*. There is a problem, though, in drawing conclusions from Sam's case because he was never totally blind; even before his operation, he could tell the difference between night and day. To avoid this type of problem, which might bias the findings, psychologists have designed a number of laboratory experiments to determine which of our perceptual abilities are innate and which develop as a result of learning and experience.

Would a baby creep off a cliff?

If depth perception depends partly on visual experience and learning, how long does it take a baby to develop this ability? Psychologists have spent quite some time trying to answer this question. One clever apparatus designed to help reveal whether infants perceive depth is the *visual cliff* (Gibson & Walk, 1960). Figure 4.27A shows that a visual cliff is basically a table with two different sides. On one side, the surface of the table is painted with a checkerboard pattern. On the other side, the surface is glass and the checkerboard pattern is several feet below, creating the impression of a clifflike drop to the floor (see Figure 4.27B).

Once they can crawl, babies are placed on the solid checkerboard surface and encouraged to cross the "cliff." If they hesitate when they reach the glass and peer warily over the "edge," they are showing signs of depth perception. The significant finding from the visual cliff is that at least by the age of 9 months or so, babies can see depth. In fact, even babies only

Figure 4.27A,B
The glass table, shown in drawing A, has a checkerboard pattern on one side and clear glass on the other, which looks down on a checkerboard pattern below. An infant placed on the table would have the illusion of a visual cliff, shown in B. How old does an infant have to be to perceive this cliff? (B, courtesy of Richard Walk)

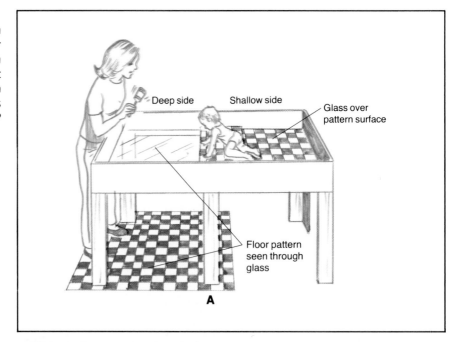

3 months old (too young to crawl) who are placed face down on the glass surface show an accelerated heartbeat, which indicates that they too see the cliff. This evidence suggests that the visual experience needed for depth perception to develop begins very early in life.

Figure 4.28 shows a kitten exposed to a world consisting only of vertical stripes. After a number of weeks in this strange setting, activity in the kitten's visual cortex is examined. How do you think the cortical cells react to visual stimuli? The neurons respond mostly to vertical stimuli and hardly at all to horizontal ones (Hirsch & Spinelli, 1970; Mitchell, 1980). Not surprisingly, kittens raised in a vertically striped world may have trouble seeing horizontal objects when placed in a normal environment. This and similar studies show that particular *sensory experiences* early in life can actually change the way the brain functions.

Are neurons in the visual cortex already functioning at birth? When researchers measured the electrical readings taken from the visual cortex of newborn animals, they found that the cells responded in much the same way as they do in the brains of adults (Hubel & Wiesel, 1979). This suggests that heredity plays a key role in the development of the visual cortex prior to birth. After birth, however, the presence or absence of visual experience can alter greatly neural activity. If a newborn animal is kept in total darkness for many weeks, the cells in its visual cortex become much less responsive than normal. Apparently, cortical cells require early exposure to visual stimuli in order to function normally (Mower et al., 1983). From studies of the brains of developing animals, psychologists now emphasize that both *heredity* and *experience* play vitally important roles in the development of perceptual abilities.

Figure 4.28
Does upbringing affect what we perceive? A kitten prevented from seeing itself by a large collar and raised in an environment where it saw only stripes has difficulty seeing horizontal patterns once removed from this environment. (Adapted from Blakemore & Cooper, 1970)

How might a baby's brain differ from an adult's?

Recognizing Faces   **APPLYING PSYCHOLOGY**

Why can't I recognize your face?

Gary, who had a brain injury, was talking to his physical therapist about his rehabilitation program. Suddenly, Gary realized that he could no longer recognize his therapist's face. He knew she was sitting there, could hear her voice and see her, but could not recognize her face. In fear and puzzlement he blurted out, "What is happening to me? I can no longer recognize you!" (adapted from Lhermitte et al., 1972).

As Gary was talking to his therapist, he had a small stroke. This stroke, combined with previous brain damage, resulted in a sudden inability to recognize familiar faces, called **prosopagnosia** (pro-soe-pag-NOE-see-ah). However, the rest of Gary's basic visual perception of his world has not altered. He could see many objects around him and they made sense. He could tell the relationships of objects in space. He retained his sense of identity, ability to use language, and general memory for past and present events. What was missing was his ability to look at a familiar face and know who he was seeing. Gary could only recognize his physical therapist from the sound of her voice.

Gary's problem is a form of agnosia, which means that although sensation is intact and Gary can see objects, his perception is disrupted and he has trouble in recognizing or naming objects. With prosopagnosia, patients have the greatest difficulty recognizing and naming familiar faces but may also have varying degrees of difficulty in recognizing and naming

---

MAJOR CONCEPT Heredity, Experience, and Perception

Your perceptual abilities develop through the interaction of heredity and experience.

For each of the following pieces of evidence, indicate what it primarily shows: a contribution of heredity (H) or a contribution of experience (E).

1. H/E A woman who has been blind since birth is given sight through surgery and is immediately able to differentiate a vase of flowers from the wall behind it.

2. H/E A man who likewise receives sight as an adult through surgery cannot at first identify his wife's face, even though he knows it by touch.

3. H/E A kitten that has been exposed since birth only to horizontal stripes is less sensitive than normal to vertically oriented lines.

4. H/E Certain cells in the brain of a newborn cat respond to visual stimuli much as they do in the brain of an adult cat.

Answers: 1 heredity; 2 experience; 3 experience; 4 heredity

---

common objects in their environment. Researchers know that prosopagnosia is caused by specific damage to both hemispheres of the brain. They think that this damage interferes with the retrieval of visual memories that are necessary for visual recognition (Damasio et al., 1982). These memories are still present, since Gary can recognize his therapist by her voice. However, he can no longer retrieve memories of her face from visual cues alone.

Gary's problem illustrates how perceptual experiences result from the interaction of inherited structures and learned experiences. To recognize a familiar face, Gary needs certain areas of his brain, which he inherited, and certain memories, which he formed through learning. When these brain areas are destroyed, even though Gary's memories remain, he can no longer recognize familiar faces with visual cues.

EXPECTATIONS AND PERCEPTUAL SET

Imagine that you have just completed police training, part of which has prepared you to recognize and deal with violence. Is it possible that this training has made you more likely to focus on violent activity? One researcher tried to answer this question by showing students two pictures simultaneously, one to each eye.

Drawing A in Figure 4.29 (a violent scene) was presented to one eye, while drawing B (a peaceful scene) was presented to the other. When two different pictures are displayed in this manner, the brain usually copes with the conflict by suppressing conscious awareness of one picture and focusing on the other. The viewer therefore remembers seeing just one of the two drawings. In this particular experiment, students who had just completed police training focused on and recalled the violent picture more than twice as often as did students who hadn't been trained for police work (Toch & Schulte, 1961). These findings suggest that our past experiences produce an organized network of information that influences how we perceive and react to people and events. This organized network of information is called

Figure 4.29
(A) A violent scene. (B) A peaceful scene.
(Adapted from Toch & Schulte, 1961)

a **perceptual set.** Perceptual sets may unknowingly influence what we perceive, how we perceive, and how we react and behave. To give you an example of how perceptual sets might work, let's look at how people perceive their weight.

Influence of Perceptual Set

When college women were asked "How important is your weight," a moderate percentage said that weight was important to their self-concept and some admitted to being overweight. When college men were asked this same question, almost none said that weight was important to their self-concept and very few admitted to being overweight (Markus et al., 1987).

In a similar study, college women who were overweight made fairly accurate estimates of their weight. They underestimated by an average of six pounds. In contrast, college men who were overweight made very inaccurate estimates of their weight. They underestimated by an average of 23 pounds (Klesges, 1983). These two studies suggest that men and women have different perceptual sets regarding the importance of their own weight. As a result of their perceptual sets, women are much more conscious of and accurate in estimating their weight than are men.

When normal-weight college females (normal group) were asked "What is your ideal body size?" most of them chose an ideal weight very close to their current, normal weight. When normal-weight college females who had a history of eating problems (problem group) were asked this question, most of them chose an ideal weight much lower than their current, normal weight. The researchers concluded that the normal group perceived themselves to be about the same size as their desired body size. In contrast, the problem group, which did not differ in weight from the normal group, wished to be much smaller (Williamson et al., 1985). In this example, women of approximately the same weight probably perceived their bodies differently because of their different perceptual sets.

What is your ideal body size?

These studies indicate that men and women develop different perceptual sets about weight and body size. Once developed, perceptual sets greatly influence how we perceive ourselves.

HOW CULTURE AFFECTS PERCEPTION

The anthropologist showed the African natives a black and white picture of an ox and a dog, animals they were familiar with. The natives looked puzzled and their looks suggested the anthropologist was lying. The anthropologist then took out a color photograph of the same animals, and the natives began to smile and nod in recognition (adapted from Deregowski, 1980).

Does the world look different in black and white?

Because the people of this tribe had never seen black and white photos, they could not immediately identify objects in them. But when they were shown color photographs, they had no trouble seeing in them what you and I see. Presumably, they drew on their everyday experiences with colored objects and related what they saw in the pictures to what they saw in the real world (Hagan & Jones, 1978). Psychologists say that our *cultural* experiences, the experiences typical in our particular society, affect what we perceive.

Another example of cultural influence on perception can be seen in Figure 4.30. When you look at what is portrayed there, you perceive that things are moving: the fire engine is speeding toward the mother, who is wagging her finger at her little boy. Of course, no real motion is involved.

Figure 4.30
How do you know that these drawings are portraying motion?

It is just that through cultural experience with drawings of this sort, we have learned a set of conventions to depict movement. We are so accustomed to seeing these conventions that the fire engine and the mother's finger really do seem to be in motion. From what you learned in the previous example, it may no longer surprise you that people from non-Western cultures who have never seen such drawings see no movement in Figure 4.30. Instead, they perceive our indicators of motion for exactly what they are—nothing more than lines on a page (Friedman & Stevenson, 1980).

Are those insects or buffalo?

This is a story told by a researcher who was studying a tribe of African pygmies that lived in a dense jungle. The jungle restricted the pygmies' visual experiences to relatively short distances. One day the researcher took Kenge, one of the pygmies, out of the forest for the first time. As they were driving across a broad plain, they spotted a herd of buffalo. Here is how the researcher tells what happened:

Kenge looked over the plains and down to where a herd of about a hundred buffalo were grazing some miles away. He asked me what kind of insects they were and I told him they were buffalo, twice as big as the forest buffalo known to him. He laughed loudly and told me not to tell such stupid stories. . . . We got into the car and drove down to where the animals were grazing. He watched them getting larger and larger . . . and muttered that it was witchcraft. . . . Finally, when he realized that they were real buffalo he was no longer afraid, but what puzzled him still is why they had been so small and suddenly grown larger, or whether it had been some kind of trickery (Turnbull, 1961, p. 305).

This story clearly tells us how important learning is to perception. Kenge's visual system is virtually identical to yours and mine. The reason we can see buffalo of a stable size gradually approaching, whereas Kenge sees magical changes, is that we have learned through experience the effect that great distance has on what we see. If you had spent your entire life in a dense jungle, where vision is limited to distances measured in feet, you too would be perplexed by your first sight of objects miles away. Where you are born and raised, in other words, and what you learn in your culture greatly influence the kinds of perceptions you have—whether you are gazing at far-off buffalo, black and white photos, or cartoons depicting movement.

REVIEW

According to the newspaper article, Anna Mae Pennica had been blind since birth. Now at age 62, an operation has restored her vision (*Los Angeles Times*, February 3, 1981). Following her operation, we know that her visual perception will be influenced by two factors, namely, (1) _____ and (2) _____.

After the doctor removes Anna's bandages, she will immediately see objects against their backgrounds. This would suggest that distinguishing figure from ground is largely an (3) _____ process. The doctor hands Anna a quarter and a postage stamp and asks her if these objects have different shapes. Because Anna cannot see the difference, it suggests that ability to identify shapes by sight requires some prior (4) _____.

Contemporary psychologists stress that heredity and experience (5) _____ to produce our perceptual abilities. This can be seen by studying the activities of cells in the primary visual cortex. In most newborn animals these cells are genetically programmed to respond to visual stimuli much as do cells in an adult. But if you were to eliminate or restrict a newborn's sensory (6) _____, you would change the way that cells in its visual cortex function. This shows that the workings of inherited brain structures can be modified by experiences.

In the hospital room next to Anna is a woman who has damage to certain areas in both hemispheres of her brain. She can see objects, recall things from her past, and tell how things are oriented in space. What she cannot do is recognize the face of her family doctor, whom she has known for 15 years. This woman has a type of visual agnosia, called (7) _____.

George says that he would like to have a giant pizza before the movie. Sara would rather have a salad because she is trying to lose a few pounds. Sara's concern about her weight and George's lack of concern about his probably indicate two different kinds of (8) _____ sets about weight. This set is based on our experiences and refers to certain expectations that (9) _____ what we see. Because of his perceptual set, it is unlikely that George will realize that he is 15 pounds overweight.

Anthropologists have noticed that people with different cultural experiences may see things differently than Americans. For example, you have learned how motion is depicted in cartoons and you have no trouble recognizing objects in black and white photos. People in other cultures may have difficulty with both of these tasks. This difficulty indicates that part of what you see is influenced by the particular world or (10) _____ that you were raised in.

Answers: (1) heredity; (2) experience, learning; (3) innate or inherited; (4) experience, learning; (5) interact; (6) experiences; (7) prosopagnosia; (8) perceptual; (9) influence; (10) culture

---

GLOSSARY TERMS

perceptual set (p. 119)   prosopagnosia (p. 117)

Module 12 Thresholds, Subliminal Perception, and ESP

PERCEPTUAL THRESHOLDS

Helen's family had a history of breast cancer. Her mother had died of this disease, and her older sister had had a mastectomy at the age of 36. Helen's gynecologist recommended that she have a mammogram (a diagnostic X ray of the breasts) once a year. The doctor explained that this technique would help detect a possible tumor much earlier than external examination. She also explained that it was important to be able to compare mammograms over the years to detect any changes in the tissue that might be early signs of cancer (author's files).

How could a doctor make a mistake reading an X ray?

When the doctor recommended a mammogram, Helen assumed there would be no question about what the X ray showed. She was therefore shocked to learn that the radiologist might fail to spot an early sign of cancer. Helen was learning something about perceptual thresholds.

The Concept of Absolute Threshold

Like Helen, you have probably assumed that whenever a stimulus is present, it is automatically perceived. However, one of the fundamental questions considered by psychologists who study perception is that of **perceptual threshold**: how intense a stimulus must be before it will be perceived. If you have ever had your hearing checked, you know that as the tone becomes fainter and fainter, it finally reaches a point where you no longer hear it. You have probably assumed that this is an absolute point, that you stop hearing the sound when it reaches a specific intensity.

In making this assumption you are agreeing with Gustav Fechner, an important figure in the history of perceptual research. Fechner developed **classical threshold theory**, which assumes that for any type of stimulus, such as light or sound, there is an *absolute threshold*, defined as the smallest amount of stimulus energy needed in order for a stimulus to be observed. Thus, if measurements could always be made under exactly the same conditions, you would always have a sensation of light, sound, or touch above a certain level but never below it. Fechner recognized that thresholds differ for different people, depending, among other things, on how acute their individual senses are. But he assumed that each person has a specific absolute threshold for each of the five senses.

Fechner introduced various methods for identifying an absolute threshold. One is the method used in hearing tests. Stimuli are presented in ascending or descending order of intensity until the person first detects or first fails to detect one. Averaging the threshold level over a number of trials gives the overall threshold. Another method for measuring the same thing is to present stimuli of various intensities in random order. The intensity level that the person detects 50 percent of the time is defined as that person's **absolute threshold**. This definition of threshold continues to be one of the most commonly used in perceptual research.

The Concept of Just Noticeable Difference

Why don't you hear that strange noise in your old car?

The answer to this question comes from the work of E. H. Weber, who lived over 150 years ago. To understand the answer, you first need to understand Weber's concept of **just noticeable difference**. This is defined as the increase or decrease in the intensity of a stimulus a person can just manage to detect.

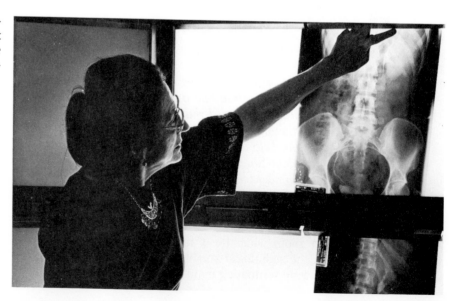

As the doctor examines an X ray, she is looking for signs of abnormal tissue. The text describes three factors that influence the doctor's success in detecting abnormal tissue. (Richard Sobol/Stock, Boston)

Weber asked people to compare stimuli of different intensities, such as two different weights, and say when they could detect the difference between them. He found that if the two stimuli presented had very low intensities (a weight of 2 ounces, for instance, versus one of 3 ounces), people could detect very small differences between them. However, if the stimuli involved had high intensities (a 50-pound weight versus one of 50½ pounds), small differences between them would go unnoticed. In this case, a much larger absolute difference was needed in order for the difference to be detected.

From these experiments came what is called **Weber's law.** It states that the amount of increase in intensity of a stimulus needed to produce a just noticeable difference grows in proportion to the intensity of the initial stimulus. This means that if you are playing your stereo very softly, you must increase the volume only slightly in order to detect a just noticeable difference in loudness. However, if you are playing your stereo very loudly, a sizable increase in volume is needed in order for it to be detected.

Now you can understand why you may fail to hear the engine start to knock in an old rattletrap car. The car is making so much noise to begin with that the addition of an engine knock is not enough to produce a just noticeable difference. The same knock in a new car, however, would be easy to notice because the overall noise level is much lower.

Signal Detection Theory

The question of a doctor misreading X rays is very different from the classic question of what stimulus intensity is detected 50 percent of the time. Now we must consider other factors. For example, how would the doctor's training or motivation affect her detecting cancer on the X ray? Researchers interested in questions like this have radically changed our thinking about perception, particularly about our ability to detect thresholds (Tanner & Swets, 1954). Their approach is called signal detection theory.

Signal detection theory assumes that perceptual threshold is relative and varies, depending on the interaction of three sets of factors: (1) the properties of the stimulus, or *signal*; (2) the characteristics of the subject, called the receiver; and (3) the presence of other stimuli, called noise, in the environment. For example, if you are alert, highly motivated, and tested in a soundproof room, your threshold for a faint click will be quite different than it is when you are exhausted and driving home in the noise of heavy traffic. In both cases, the intensity of the click has remained the same. What has changed is your own psychological condition and the level of distracting environmental noise.

Signal detection theory assumes that when you report "yes" or "no" to a stimulus in a hearing test, you are actually making a decision. Suppose we alter the conditions of your hearing test: we are going to present very faint tones, and each time you correctly specify when a tone occurs, you will receive five dollars. If you give a false alarm, there will be no penalty. Under these conditions, you will probably decide that the tone has occurred on nearly every trial, even though you will be mistaken a good portion of the time.

Now suppose we change the rules. Each time you detect the sound correctly you receive nothing, but for every false alarm you must pay 5 dollars. Under these conditions, you will probably decide to be very conservative about saying you have heard the signal. In this case, it pays to answer "no." By changing factors other than the stimulus (in this case, consequences), we can greatly alter the probability that the stimulus will be detected. Of course, these examples exaggerate the role of payoff, but signal detection theory assumes that similar processes occur more subtly in everyday life.

MAJOR CONCEPT   Perceptual Thresholds

Please match the term with the appropriate statement on the right.

1. just noticeable difference

2. Weber's law

3. perceptual threshold

4. classical threshold theory

5. signal detection theory

a. ____ Developed by Fechner, this theory assumes that a stimulus has an absolute threshold.

b. ____ This theory assumes that a stimulus has a relative threshold, which depends upon three factors: signal, receiver, and noise.

c. ____ Defined as the increase or decrease in the intensity of a stimulus a person can just manage to detect.

d. ____ Stimulus intensity needed to produce a just noticeable difference must increase in proportion to the initial stimulus.

e. ____ How intense a stimulus must be before it will be perceived.

Answers: a (4); b (5); c (1); d (2); e (3)

Now let's return to our earlier example of interpreting Helen's mammogram. Imagine that you are the radiologist examining her X ray for signs of breast cancer. You will probably be highly motivated to detect the slightest signs of cancer because you know that early detection greatly increases the probability of cure. A false alarm, on the other hand, while emotionally upsetting to the patient, does not carry the penalty of endangering life. As a result, in interpreting Helen's X rays, you will be more likely to report early signs of cancer than conclude that no such signs are present. Helen's case is just one of many situations where the principles of signal detection theory can be applied in real life.

SUBLIMINAL PERCEPTION

In the middle of bland background music, some stores insert "inaudible" sentences: "I will not steal. If I steal, I will go to jail." Stores that are playing these so-called subliminal messages are hoping to decrease shoplifting (adapted from the San Diego Tribune, January 26, 1981).

The store's anti-shoplifting message is called subliminal because it is presented below the threshold for conscious awareness. Psychologists explain subliminal messages by drawing a distinction between a person's physiological and perceptual thresholds. A stimulus is said to reach the **physiological threshold** when it is sufficiently strong to excite the appropriate sensory receptors and send nerve impulses to the brain. But even though nerve impulses are triggered by a stimulus, you may not be consciously aware of what that stimulus is. In order for conscious awareness to happen, the stimulus must be able to reach a higher perceptual threshold. In most of this research, threshold is defined according to classical threshold theory: the intensity at which a stimulus is perceived 50 percent of the time. Any stimulus below this intensity is assumed to be subliminal. Knowing what you do about signal detection theory, you can probably think of a number of problems with this assumption. For example, depending on the alertness,

Would people be less likely to shoplift if they heard subliminal messages such as "Shoplifters go to jail?" See text for answer. (Sepp Seitz/Woodfin Camp and Associates)

tiredness, or attentiveness of the shoppers, the store's anti-shoplifting message may or may not be subliminal. That is, some of the shoppers some of the time may be aware of hearing the anti-shoplifting message. What have psychologists discovered about subliminal messages?

The Evidence for Subliminal Messages

Although it seems strange that people can actually perceive subliminal messages, a sizable amount of evidence suggests that under the right conditions they can. For instance, in several studies words were presented so quickly that subjects reported seeing nothing at all. Recordings of their brain waves indicated that visual information had in fact been processed (Shevrin, 1975; Shevrin & Fritzler, 1968; Shevrin et al., 1971).

In other studies, subjects were first sensitized to certain words by pairing them with electric shock. When these particular "shock words" were later shown to them, they became physiologically aroused. Next, the shock words, along with other words, were played to the subjects using a procedure called *masking*. The procedure involves presenting one set of words to one ear and another set of words to the other ear, while the listener is asked to attend to one ear only.

As a result of masking, the words played into the unattended ear are not consciously processed. On some level, however, the unattended ear processes information. When words previously paired with electric shock were played into the unattended ear, subjects were more physiologically aroused than they were with neutral words (Corteen & Wood, 1972; Corteen & Dunn, 1974). These studies suggest that our brains may respond to emotionally meaningful subliminal messages without our awareness.

Based on these and other findings, some researchers believe that our brains can process general sensory information presented to us subliminally (Dixon, 1981; Fowler, 1986; Merikle & Cheesman, 1986). On the other hand, the author of a critical review of subliminal perception argues that

What proof is there that we can detect subliminal messages?

it is very difficult to prove that messages can be processed without conscious awareness (Holender, 1986). In any case, there is very little evidence that you can process complex messages presented subliminally or that such messages will influence you to perform specific behaviors, such as buy a particular product (McConnell et al., 1958; George & Jennings, 1975; Moore, 1985; Vokey & Read, 1985).

APPLYING PSYCHOLOGY   Understanding Backward Messages

Are there secret messages on rock and roll records?

Played forward, the witness told the legislative committee, the record is the Beatles' "Revolution." Played backward, the record croaks an eerie but audible message: "Turn me on, dead man. Let me out." The witness claimed that the recording process is a way of presenting subliminal, or subconscious, messages to the listener because the human brain can "unscramble" the backward message as a record is played in normal fashion (adapted from the *Los Angeles Times*, April 28, 1982).

This press clipping raises two basic questions. If you played a record backward, could you hear audible, recognizable messages? If you played a record forward, could you process the backward messages and would they affect your behavior? Backward messages would be considered a form of subliminal perception, since the listener is unaware of hearing them. Two psychologists, John Vokey and Don Read (1985), set out to answer these questions with a series of experiments. Here's what they found.

First, can listeners hear messages when they are played backward? Instead of using rock and roll records, Vokey and Read used sentences from a variety of sources, including the 23rd Psalm and part of Lewis Carroll's *Jabberwocky*. When these sentences were played backward, listeners could pick out particular words or phrases if they had been told what they would hear. That is, these phrases were not clear cut, rather they were ambiguous sounds that had to be interpreted by the listener. If, for instance, you were told to listen for the phrase "I saw Satan," you might hear it provided the sounds could be so interpreted. However, if you were not told what to listen for, it is unlikely that you would hear this particular message. The researchers concluded that if a backward message is heard, this is most likely due to an active interpretation on the part of the listener.

Second, can backward messages influence behavior? Vokey and Read found no evidence on any of their tasks that backward messages influenced subjects' behaviors. In one task, backward messages suggested spelling the word "read" as "reed" and the word "feat" as "feet." If the subjects were comprehending the backward message, either consciously or unconsciously, they would be expected to spell the words accordingly. The fact that this did not happen led the researchers to conclude that backward messages had no influence on the subjects' behavior. Applying these findings to real life, we can assume that backward messages on rock and roll records, if such messages do exist, are not likely to influence behavior. This study provides an excellent example of how psychologists can answer real-life questions in the laboratory.

MAJOR CONCEPT   Subliminal Perception

Subliminal perception involves processing sensory data you are not consciously aware of.

Indicate whether the following statements about subliminal perception are true (T) or false (F).

1. T/F If the word "Coke" was flashed so rapidly on your TV screen that you had no idea what the message said, you might still be able to pick "Coke" out when given several words to choose from.

2. T/F If the word "Coke" was flashed so rapidly on your TV screen that you had no idea what the message said, you would nevertheless be unable to resist the urge to get up and get a Coke.

Answers: 1 (T); 2 (F)

EXTRASENSORY PERCEPTION

Is there in all the world a single psychic who can discern the contents of a sealed envelope, move remote objects, or read minds? If so, magician James Randi will be surprised—and poorer. For nearly 20 years, he has been offering $10,000 to anyone who can perform just one such feat. Nearly 600 have inquired, and 57 have taken the test. All so far have failed (adapted from Science Digest, *August 1981).*

One of the reasons why James Randi is not $10,000 poorer is that he requires all challengers to perform their feats under his observation. Since Randi has done all the feats mentioned above using trickery, he knows what to look for when someone is trying to fool him. According to Randi and others acquainted with magic, much of what passes for extrasensory perception is actually done through tricks (Gardner, 1981).

Extrasensory perception or ESP can be defined as any perception that is paranormal, meaning that it is outside the realm of normal sensory processes. More recently, such experiences are referred to as **psi** (SIGH, for psychic) **phenomena** and include claims of having one or more of the following abilities: foretelling the future, called *precognition*; transferring thoughts from one person to another or reading the thoughts of others, called *telepathy*; perceiving events or objects for which there is no sensory stimulation, called *clairvoyance*; and mentally influencing the movement of objects, called *psychokinesis*. Out-of-body experiences, another psi phenomenon, have been claimed by some people who have been near-death. In out-of-body experiences, people claim to be awake and to perceive the world from a location outside of their physical body (Blackmore, 1987a; Moody, 1976).

Psi Testimonials

According to a recent Gallup poll, about 15 percent of the population reported having had a very close brush with death and about 34 percent of these people reported out-of-body experiences (Zaleski, 1987). Other polls

Would you like to win $10,000?

The Amazing Randi (with the beard) believes that the general public, as well as many scientists, often mistake clever tricks for psychic abilities. He demonstrated this point when he sent the two young magicians shown here to a lab that studies psychic phenomena. Instead of admitting they were magicians, the pair claimed to have psychic powers and proceeded to perform "psychic feats," such as mentally bending keys and making images on film. After 120 hours of testing, the lab's researchers reported that the two did indeed have genuine psychic abilities. (Dana Fineman/Sygma) indicate that 58 percent of the adults in the United States claim to have had a psychic experience or to possess psi abilities (Marks & Kammann, 1980; Myers, 1981). Because it is difficult to evaluate the accuracy of personal experiences reported in polls and surveys, scientists prefer to use experimental methods to study psi phenomena.

EXPLORING PSYCHOLOGY Experimenting with Psi

Where did that image come from?

I sat in a reclining chair. I had half of a Ping-Pong ball over each eye so that all of my visual input was restricted to gross changes in light. I wore headphones through which I heard only white noise so that all of my auditory input was restricted to a hissing sound. During this time, my brother was in a neighboring room, without any means of physically contacting me. I reported all the images that I experienced. One of the images involved lakes, mountains, Swiss chalets, and people fishing. Later, I was shown a number of pictures and told to select the one that I thought my brother had been concentrating on. I selected a picture that resembled the image of lakes, mountains, and people fishing. This image happened to be similar to the one that my brother had been concentrating on (adapted from Blackmore, 1987b).

This particular procedure is called a ganzfeld psi experiment and is representative of experiments in the area of psi research. In this case, the subject had correctly identified a picture that was similar to the one that her brother was concentrating on in a neighboring room. Is this an example of a psi experience or just a coincidence?

One way to answer this question is to repeat the procedure many times. Thus, the researcher, who was also the subject, repeatedly tried to select the picture that she thought her brother had been concentrating on. Except for her first correct pick, her overall success rate was no better than chance (Blackmore, 1987b). From this single study, the researcher concluded that her initial success was due to coincidence. But what if dozens of ganzfeld studies are done?

Between 1974 and 1981, approximately 42 separate ganzfeld studies were reported. Charles Honorton (1985), a respected researcher and believer in psi phenomena, and Ray Hyman (1985), a respected critic of psi phenomena, analyzed and argued about the meaning of these studies. Finally, in a joint report, they concluded that positive findings were reported significantly more often than would be predicted by chance (Hyman & Honorton, 1986). They did not agree, however, on whether the positive findings could be attributed to psi experiences. Hyman, the respected critic of psi phenomena, concluded that many ganzfeld studies contained flaws in either their design, their execution, or their analysis. For example, some studies had not randomized the procedure for the choice and selection of the image that the sender was concentrating on. Hyman concluded there was no way to rule out the possibility that these flaws, and not psi phenomena, had produced the positive findings. Honorton, the respected researcher and believer in psi experiences, acknowledged that some studies had flaws, but he maintained that overall the positive findings were produced by psi phenomena. Both researchers agreed that future ganzfeld experiments must follow strict guidelines to control potential flaws. Until better controlled ganzfeld experiments are completed, serious questions remain about whether chance or psi was operating in the ganzfeld experiments.

MAJOR CONCEPT   Extrasensory Perception

Extrasensory perception is perception that supposedly occurs outside the realm of normal sensory processes.

Is each of the following statements about extrasensory perception true (T) or false (F)?

1. T/F   The majority of Americans claim to have had a psychic experience at some time.

2. T/F   An intelligent person can easily tell when a psychic is performing feats through trickery.

3. T/F   Most scientists believe that psychic phenomena have *not* been adequately demonstrated.

Answers: 1 (T); 2 (F); 3 (T).

One Hundred Years of Psi Research

Begun in 1886, the American Society for Psychical Research has been studying psi phenomena for over 100 years. Throughout this long history, some basic problems have remained.

There are many reports of people experiencing things that cannot readily be explained in terms of normal perception. For example, Susan Blackmore (1987a), a researcher of psi experiences for 10 years, and Ernst Rodin (1980), a respected neurologist, both reported the feeling of perceiving the world from outside their bodies. Although some researchers would claim that these out-of-body experiences are examples of psi phenomena (Moody, 1977; Ring, 1980; Sabom, 1982), neither Rodin nor Blackmore are convinced that they really left their bodies. Rodin thinks his experience resulted from an anesthetic-induced delusional state and Blackmore thinks she experienced an illusion, similar to visual illusions discussed in Module 10. These differing views highlight a major difficulty in demonstrating and understanding psi: what one person considers a psi experience may be seen as something entirely different by another. It is very difficult, if not impossible, to determine which interpretation is correct.

Perhaps the most serious problem with psi research has been that many of its positive findings, those that indicate the existence of psi, cannot be replicated by the same or by a different researcher (Blackmore, 1985; Gardner, 1981; Girden, 1978). After 10 years of doing psi research and finding difficulty in repeating her own results, Susan Blackmore suggested that perhaps the best policy is to keep an open mind about psi. Indeed, although no series of studies has demonstrated the occurrence of psi to the satisfaction of most researchers, we should not rule out the possibility that psi phenomena may exist (Blackmore, 1987b).

REVIEW

Suppose you turn on your TV set, but the volume is so low you cannot hear it. As you turn the knob that controls the sound, the voice becomes audible. If you assume that some fixed point exists above which you will hear the sound and below which you will not, you are agreeing with Gustav Fechner, a pioneer in research on perceptual thresholds. Fechner developed the theory called (1) _____ _____ theory. According to classical threshold theory, the lowest intensity of sound detected 50 percent of the time is called your (2) _____ _____ for sound.

When your TV volume is turned down to the point where you can barely hear it, just a small increase in intensity is needed for you to detect an increase in loudness, also called a (3) _____

_____ _____. In contrast, when your TV is blaring loudly, a large increase in volume is necessary to create a just noticeable difference. This relationship between the initial intensity of a stimulus and the increase in intensity needed to produce a just noticeable difference is described in

(4) _____ law.

Contemporary psychologists have criticized classical threshold theory because it tends to focus on the intensity of the stimulus, while ignoring other factors that can also influence whether someone detects that particular stimulus. For example, what other factors would influence an air traffic controller's perception of seeing a new blip on his radar screen? One factor would be the properties of the blip, which is called the

(5) _____, such as how bright or movable it is. Another are characteristics of the subject, who is

called the (6) _____, such as how tired or motivated he is. A third characteristic is the presence of other blips on the screen, which is called the

(7) _____. The theory that takes these three factors into account when determining a person's

perceptual threshold is known as (8) _____

_____ theory.

Suppose you buy a device that flashes slogans like "Study harder" for a fraction of a second as you are watching your favorite TV programs. In order for these messages to trigger nerve impulses that travel to your

brain, they must be above your (9) _____ threshold. However, if the messages are so rapid that

they are below your (10) _____ threshold,

you will not be aware of seeing them. In this case, the

messages are called (11) _____ messages. Although there is evidence that your brain may process

general (12) _____ information at a subliminal level, it is doubtful that you can process complex subliminal information or that subliminal infor-

mation influences your (13) _____. A backward message is one kind of subliminal message. The kind of words or phrases that people detect in backward messages depends primarily on how the listener

(14) _____ the sounds rather than on the sounds themselves. Researchers found no evidence that

backward messages had any (15) _____ on the listener's behaviors.

If you tried by means of thought processes alone to send an image of a panda to a person in the next room, you would be trying to get that person to have perceptions that are outside of normal senses. Paranormal perceptions, such as precognition, telepathy, clairvoyance, psychokinesis, and out-of-body experiences,

are called (16) _____ phenomena. In analyzing 42 ganzfeld psi experiments, a critic of psi concluded that there were significant positive results but that these results may have been caused by

(17) _____ that could have biased the results. In analyzing the same studies, a researcher and believer in psi concluded that the significant positive results in the ganzfeld experiments were not due to

flaws but rather to (18) _____ phenomena. At this point, we must wait for more controlled studies in order to determine if flaws or psi produced the positive results.

One of the most serious criticisms of psi phenomena is that positive results cannot always be

(19) _____. One long-time researcher in this area suggests that we should keep an open mind regarding either the too-quick belief that certain experiences were produced by psi or the too-quick rejection of studies showing the possibility of psi.

Answers: (1) classical threshold; (2) absolute threshold; (3) just noticeable difference; (4) Weber's; (5) stimulus, signal; (6) receiver; (7) noise; (8) signal detection; (9) physiological; (10) perceptual; (11) subliminal; (12) sensory; (13) behavior; (14) interprets; (15) influences; (16) psi; (17) flaws, problems, errors; (18) psi; (19) replicated, repeated

GLOSSARY TERMS

absolute threshold
    (p. 122)
classical threshold theory
    (p. 122)

extrasensory perception
    (ESP) (p. 127)
just noticeable difference
    (p. 122)

perceptual threshold
    (p. 122)
physiological threshold
    (p. 124)

psi phenomena (p. 127)
signal detection theory
    (p. 123)
Weber's law (p. 123)

PERSONAL NOTE

When I was young, I could read my dog's mind. There was never any question about it. I knew when my dog wanted to play or sleep, and when he was feeling sad or happy. My dog could also read my mind. He knew when I was sad, and he knew when to come over and lick my face and wag his tail to cheer me up. My dog and I had special abilities to read each other's minds. We both showed the form of extrasensory perception called telepathy. I know that this is a testimonial and that one should be careful of believing testimonials. But this one is true.   —R.P.

5

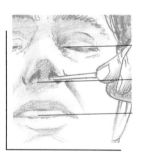

States of Awareness

Module 13 Consciousness, Sleep, and Dreams

Steven Beck wasn't there any more, and it was strange for his parents not to have to listen for his breathing, wondering if he was in trouble. Ten years after the traffic accident that sent him into a coma, Beck died when a blood vessel ruptured in his throat. Ten years earlier, at the age of eighteen, Steven had moved into his own apartment and was helping a friend move his belongings to it when the truck he was driving hit a car and crashed into a tree. Steven lapsed into a coma from which he never recovered. "For five years, he lay on the bed in his room practically lifeless," said the father. Then he seemed to improve. "He got to a stage where he'd move his arms and legs around him. He'd turn his head when you walked through the room. He'd hold your hand when you talked to him. He could pretty well 'talk' with the family through his expressions. He'd smile if he was feeling good or frown if he didn't like what you said," the father explained. Steven Beck did all these things, yet he never once "woke up." "All we've got are questions," said Steven's father. "Why did he survive so long but not come to?" (adapted from the Los Angeles Times, *February 9, 1983).*

One likely cause of Steven's coma was damage to his reticular formation, a region at the base of the brain. You may remember from Module 5 that one function of this region is to arouse the cortex and alert it to incoming information. When the reticular formation is injured, a person may become unconscious (Miller, 1982).

DEFINING STATES OF AWARENESS

There is little doubt that Steven was unconscious for the first five years after his accident. In the second five years, however, he began to be somewhat responsive to his environment (turning his head in the direction of a sound or grasping a hand that held his). But these behaviors do not prove that Steven had regained consciousness. They could have been reflex movements that occurred without his awareness. In order for Steven to be considered conscious, he would have had to show clear-cut evidence that he was experiencing thoughts and perceptions, no matter how vague and disjointed. *Consciousness*, then, refers to an *awareness* of one's own mental processes. It can be thought of as ranging along a continuum from total

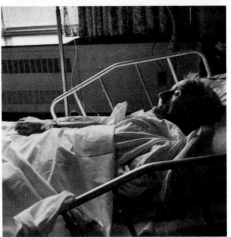

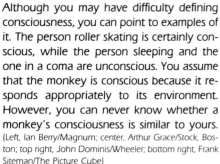

Although you may have difficulty defining consciousness, you can point to examples of it. The person roller skating is certainly conscious, while the person sleeping and the one in a coma are unconscious. You assume that the monkey is conscious because it responds appropriately to its environment. However, you can never know whether a monkey's consciousness is similar to yours. (Left, Ian Berry/Magnum; center, Arthur Grace/Stock, Boston; top right, John Dominis/Wheeler; bottom right, Frank Siteman/The Picture Cube)

unconsciousness on the one hand to high mental alertness on the other. The more aware we are of our thoughts, feelings, and reactions, the greater our level of consciousness.

When we refer in this chapter to **states of consciousness,** we are talking about noticeable variations in patterns and styles of awareness. If these patterns diverge from what we experience when wide awake and highly alert, we say that we are in an **altered state of consciousness.** Let's look at one altered state of consciousness that most of us spend a third of our lives in: sleep.

SLEEP

What time would you go to sleep if the world had no clocks?

Imagine living in a world without clocks—being able to do whatever you wanted, whenever you wanted. Imagine having no one to tell you it is time to work, eat, sleep, or play. A number of people had a chance to live in just such an environment for months at a time. As with most good things, there were catches. They could not listen to the radio, watch television, have visitors, or leave their rooms, which were windowless to prevent looking outside. The reason for asking people to live under these conditions was to see when they would fall asleep and wake up if they had no cues about time (Weitzman et al., 1982). Do you think that in this situation people would continue to sleep and wake on a fairly regular cycle?

If you say "yes," you are right. People *did* continue on a fairly regular sleep-wake cycle even though they could not tell what time of day it was. The reason is that the sleep-wake cycle is an example of a **circadian** (sir-KAY-dee-un) **rhythm,** a naturally occurring daily cycle in the body. But the internal clock that regulates your sleep-wake cycle is set for 25 hours, not 24 (Moore-Ede & Czeisler, 1984). If you were placed in a "timeless" experimental room, you would tend to go to bed about an hour later each day. Normally, of course, your sleep-wake clock is "reset" daily, keeping you in tune with the 24-hour day on earth (Anders, 1982; Przewlocki et al., 1983). This relatively small adjustment is easy to make. Larger adjustments, however, can be more difficult. Consider what happens when you fly across time zones.

Suppose on your vacation you fly from New York City to Los Angeles. Your friends meet you at the airport and are ready to show you the town. Although you are excited to see them, you must admit you are feeling tired. The reason is that your circadian sleep-wake rhythm is set three hours later. Although the clock in Los Angeles says 9 P.M., your biological clock reads midnight. Several days may be needed for your body to reset its clock and eliminate this *jet lag*. The length of the resetting process depends in part on how far out of sync with local time you are. It also depends in part on your age; as we grow older, the adjustment takes longer.

The Stages of Sleep

Researchers who have studied sleep know when their experimental subjects are sleeping because during sleep the body shows great changes in physiological arousal, and the brain undergoes a remarkable series of changes in electrical activity. These changes show that sleep occurs in several distinct stages. In fact, just by looking at tracings of brain waves, a psychologist could tell whether someone was awake or asleep, how deep or light the sleep was, and whether or not the person was dreaming. What are these tracings that tell so much about sleep?

The tool sleep researchers use to monitor brain waves is called an **electroencephalogram** (ih-LECK-troh-en-SEF-ul-la-gram) or **EEG**, a printout made on a machine called an electroencephalograph. An EEG is made by placing small metal disks, called electrodes, on certain areas of a person's skull (Figure 5.1). The electrodes are connected to a machine that detects and magnifies the activity of nerve cells located primarily in the cortex. These patterns of electrical activity are then traced on graph paper. The result is the EEG, which shows a number of squiggly lines. Each of these lines has a certain height, called *amplitude*, and a certain number of ups and downs or cycles per second, called *frequency*. As you enter different stages of sleep, the amplitude and frequency of your EEG waves change.

Most of the stages of sleep you pass through belong to a general category called **Non-Rapid-Eye-Movement**, or **NREM sleep**. NREM sleep consumes about 80 percent of your sleep time, especially the first half of the night. The remaining 20 percent is taken up by **Rapid-Eye-Movement**, or **REM, sleep**. It is called REM sleep because during it, your eyes move rapidly back and forth beneath your closed eyelids. When you fall asleep, you first pass into NREM stages. After about an hour to an hour and a half, however, you enter a REM period, which is when your most vivid dreams occur. This REM period then ends and you reenter NREM. The alternation between REM and NREM sleep is repeated throughout the night.

So that you can literally see the changes in brain activity as someone goes to sleep, you are going to watch as a college student named Tom spends the night in a sleep laboratory. With a number of electrodes in place, you can see Tom's brain waves being traced on the rolling graph paper. Because Tom is still wide awake, with his eyes open, his EEG shows mostly **beta waves**—waves with a low amplitude but a fast frequency (12 to 30 cycles per second). Figure 5.2 shows beta waves.

As Tom becomes relaxed and drowsy, his EEG shows **alpha waves.** These are low in amplitude, just like beta waves, but they have a slightly

Why does jet lag occur?

What is a sleeping brain doing?

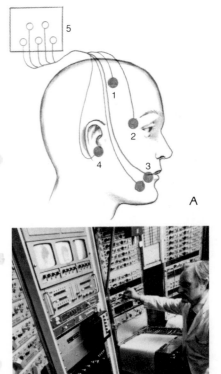

Figure 5.1
Drawing A shows the placement of electrodes in sleep studies. Electrode 1, which measures EEG waves, is placed on the skull. Although only one electrode is shown here, a dozen or more may be positioned around the skull. Electrode 2 measures eye movement, and electrode 3 measures muscle tension in the jaw. Electrode 4, called a *neutral electrode*, is used for comparison. All the electrodes go to a box labeled 5, which is connected to an EEG recording machine, shown in B. (B. Dan McCoy/Rainbow)

After flying across the Atlantic, this woman is about to experience jet lag. (Mark Antman/ The Image Works)

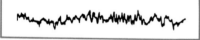

Figure 5.2
Beta waves: low-amplitude and fast-frequency waves. (From Hauri, 1982, p. 7)

Figure 5.3
Alpha waves: low-amplitude but slower frequency waves. (From Hauri, 1982, p. 7)

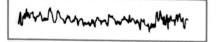

Figure 5.4
Theta waves: low-amplitude, still slower frequency waves. (From Hauri, 1982)

slower frequency (8 to 12 cycles per second) than beta waves. Alpha waves are shown in Figure 5.3. They tend to occur when you are generally relaxed, usually with your eyes closed. In Tom's case, they signal that he is ready to fall asleep.

NREM Stage 1. Tom is now entering *NREM stage 1*, which will last from 1 to 7 minutes. During stage 1, Tom will lose his responsiveness to most stimuli around him, and his thoughts will begin to drift. Although this period is usually labeled a stage of sleep, some people who are aroused from it feel subjectively that they have been awake. Thus, stage 1 is probably better described as the transition from wakefulness to sleep. Stage 1 is marked by the presence of **theta waves,** which are lower in amplitude and slower in frequency (3 to 7 cycles per second) than alpha waves. The theta waves in Tom's stage 1 brain recordings can be seen in Figure 5.4.

NREM Stage 2. When Tom enters what is called *NREM stage 2*, he is undeniably asleep. If you were to awaken him now, he would tell you that he had been sleeping. Whatever thoughts he had been having would be very short and fragmented. NREM stage 2 is defined by the presence of both fast-frequency bursts of brain activity (12 to 14 cycles per second, forming *sleep spindles* in the EEG) and giant amplitude waves called *K complexes.* Figure 5.5 shows what Tom's stage 2 recordings look like.

NREM Delta Sleep. Within 30 to 45 minutes after drifting off, Tom enters his deepest sleep, called *NREM* **delta sleep,** after the delta waves that characterize this phase. Figure 5.6 shows that delta brain waves are very slow in frequency and very high in amplitude. Delta sleep is the stage during which it is most difficult to awaken someone. A buzzer, for instance, would have to be much louder to awaken Tom from delta sleep than from stage 2. After spending a few minutes to an hour in delta, Tom will return to stage 2 sleep and from there he may enter a REM period.

Figure 5.7 shows that the average person has several periods of delta sleep during a night, most often in the first half of the night. Total amount of delta sleep is related to age: the younger a person is, the more time spent in delta. During delta sleep, there is a marked secretion of growth hormone from the pituitary gland. Growth hormone controls many aspects of metabolism, physical growth, and brain development (Shapiro, 1981).

REM Sleep. About every 30 to 90 minutes throughout the night, Tom passes from stage 2 into REM sleep. He remains in REM for an average of 15 minutes at a time, although some REM periods last up to an hour. As the night progresses REM periods often become longer, especially in the second half of the night. During REM sleep, Tom's brain waves are fast in frequency and low in amplitude, as shown in Figure 5.8. Notice that these REM waves are very similar to the beta waves that we saw when Tom was awake, and yet he is now sound asleep. To add to the puzzle, Tom's body is now in a state of physiological arousal: his heart rate, breathing, and oxygen consumption have all increased, and his eyes are moving rapidly beneath his closed eyelids. But paradoxically Tom, like other REM sleepers, is incapable of thrashing about. This is because REM sleep is accompanied by a loss of muscle tonus in the neck and limbs.

REM sleep is also the stage of sleep during which dreams are most vivid and most easily recalled. About 80 percent of the time he is awakened from a REM period, Tom will report that he was dreaming. Dreams that occur during REM are vivid, well organized, and relatively long.

In the late 1950s, many psychologists believed that if people were not allowed to enter REM sleep and therefore not allowed to dream, they might suffer harmful effects to their personalities and behaviors. Since that time, many volunteer subjects have been deprived of REM sleep and dreaming by being awakened whenever their physiological signs showed they were starting a REM period. Such subjects have shown no obvious ill effects (Cohen, 1979). However, suppression of REM does produce a *REM rebound*: on the night that REM-deprived people were once again allowed to sleep as usual, they spent a larger than normal percentage of the night in REM periods.

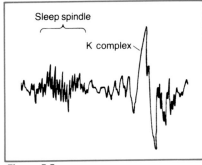

Figure 5.5
NREM stage 2: some fast bursts and high-amplitude waves. *(From Hauri, 1982)*

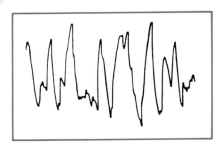

Figure 5.6
Delta sleep: high-amplitude slow waves.
(From Hauri, 1982)

Figure 5.8
REM sleep: low amplitude, fast frequency.

Figure 5.7
This is a diagram of the typical sleep pattern of a young human adult. You read the diagram from left to right. Beginning at the very left, the person goes successively from awake to Stage 1, from Stage 1 to Stage 2, and then into delta. Next the person goes from delta back to Stage 2 and then into the first of six REM periods. *(From Hauri, 1982)*

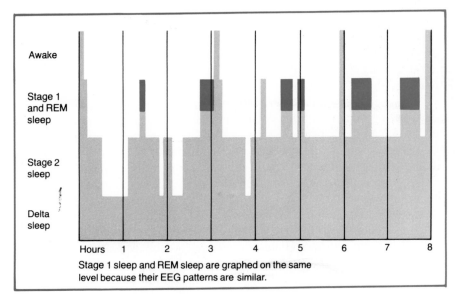

Awake

Stage 1 and REM sleep

Stage 2 sleep

Delta sleep

Hours 1 2 3 4 5 6 7 8

Stage 1 sleep and REM sleep are graphed on the same level because their EEG patterns are similar.

MAJOR CONCEPT   The Stages of Sleep

Although we tend to think of sleep as a single state of consciousness, in fact it has several distinct stages. During the night you alternate between REM and NREM sleep.

For each of the following statements, indicate whether it describes REM (R) or NREM (N).

1. R/N About 80 percent of our time is spent in this sleep.

2. R/N The remaining 20 percent of sleep time is this.

3. R/N This is the stage during which your body is physiologically aroused and your eyes move rapidly back and forth beneath closed eyelids.

4. R/N This is the sleep from which it is hardest to be awakened.

5. R/N This is the kind of sleep during which your most vivid dreams occur.

Answers: 1 NREM; 2 REM; 3 REM; 4 NREM; 5 REM

THE HUMAN NEED FOR SLEEP

Mrs. C felt unconcerned about her sleeping habits, but she agreed to a sleep evaluation at the urging of her husband and her physician. Mrs. C was 71 years old and, for as long as she could remember, she had never slept more than three hours a night. She felt well during the day and was physically fit, still cross-country skiing every day in the winter and hiking frequently during the summer. An extensive medical workup revealed that there was nothing wrong with Mrs. C. Getting only three hours of sleep daily had apparently done her no harm. When she left the doctor's office, Mrs. C seemed pleased and satisfied with the news (adapted from Meddis et al., 1973).

Short and Long Sleepers

Although documented cases are rare, there are people like Mrs. C who sleep no more than a few hours nightly, rarely nap, and yet seem to lead normal, healthy, productive lives. Compared to 8-hour sleepers they show the same percentage of REM and NREM. They just spend less time in each stage (Jones & Oswald, 1968).

The average number of hours that a healthy young adult sleeps nightly is 7½. About 95 percent of us sleep somewhere between 6½ and 8½ hours. For the remaining 5 percent, some are short sleepers, requiring less than 6½ hours, and some are long sleepers, requiring more than 8½ hours.

Is there any difference in personality traits or intelligence between short and long sleepers? Early studies reported a few such differences. For example, short sleepers were said to be generally more "energetic," while long sleepers were more prone to be "worriers" (Webb & Friel, 1971; Hartmann, 1973). But these findings were not confirmed by later studies, and it now seems that there are few reliable differences (Webb & Cartwright, 1978; Hume, 1983). To the question of how much sleep a particular person should get, researchers answer that it is more important to satisfy the body's need for sleep than it is to conform to any group average.

Sleep Deprivation Studies

As his science project, Randy wanted to be the first person to stay awake for 264 hours, 11 straight days. By the end of the first day, Randy felt he could last for 12 or even 15 days. By the second day, he had some trouble focusing his eyes. By the third day, he felt nauseous and could no longer read to stay awake. By the fourth day, he sometimes forgot what he was saying and occasionally what he was doing. By the fifth day, Randy's motivation almost failed. By the sixth day, he wanted to sleep as much as a drowning person wants to breathe. By the seventh day, his speech had become slurred. By the ninth day, Randy was not always able to finish his sentences, and he was becoming very irritable.

By the tenth day, the sleep record seemed unimportant compared to the terrible drudgery and pain of trying to keep his eyes open. On the eleventh and last night, Randy stayed awake by playing 100 games on a baseball machine with one of the researchers. He beat the researcher every game. The researcher's excuse was that he was tired. Finally a few minutes past 11 sleepless days, Randy closed his eyes and went to sleep (adapted from Gulevich et al., 1966; Johnson et al., 1965).

People who have been deprived of sleep for one or more days have been studied carefully for physical and behavioral changes. Their heart rate, blood pressure, and hormone secretions appear normal, as do their reflexes, such as the knee-jerk response. They rarely experience hallucinations or illusions, and never do so before 60 hours of deprivation. When confronted with boring tasks that require vigilance (such as picking out a certain kind of blip on a radar screen), they do less well than usual. But when confronted with complex and interesting tasks (such as playing a mechanical baseball game), they may show remarkably little drop in performance (Goleman, 1982; Gulevich et al., 1966; Naitoh, 1976).

It is also remarkable how quickly sleep-deprived people recover from the experience. In Randy's case, his first sleep after he set the new record lasted for 15 hours and showed REM rebound. When he awoke the next morning, however, he seemed normal in mood and behavior. His second night's sleep also showed REM rebound but lasted only 8 hours. Given that Randy experienced so few ill effects, we might well ask what sleep does for human beings that makes the urge to sleep so strong.

Why We Sleep

Psychologists have actually found this a difficult question to answer, but you will probably feel that the answer is very obvious. After missing sleep for 1 or 2 nights you feel tired, and your tiredness disappears after a night's sleep. Your experience supports the **restorative theory** of sleep, which holds that your activities during the day somehow deplete key factors in your body which then require sleep to be replenished. But as logical as the theory may seem, scientists have not yet been able to identify exactly what is being replenished or repaired during sleep. The possible list includes neurotransmitters, hormones, cells in the body, and metabolic functions (Webb, 1983). Researchers are still trying to determine the critical factor or factors (Rechtschaffen et al., 1983).

According to the **behavioral theory** of sleep it was dangerous for early humans to be active at night since they might be attacked by nocturnal predators. The behavioral view held that sleep is a behavioral trait that evolved and endured because it helped our ancestors survive (Webb, 1983). By lying still until daybreak they were protected to a great extent from roving nighttime predators. Similarly, some animals have evolved a daytime sleep pattern which removed them from daytime predators. The particular sleep

Could anyone stay awake for 11 straight days?

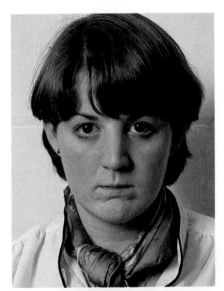

As part of a science project, this woman agreed to go without sleep for 72 hours. Although you can see obvious changes in her face, she was able to perform reasoning and logic problems provided the problems were interesting and of short duration. However, she was not able to perform tasks that were boring. After one night's sleep, she reported feeling restored. (Patrick Ward © Discover Magazine 2/83, Time Inc.)

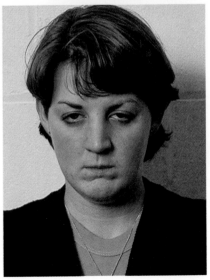

Does sleep keep you out of trouble?

pattern evolved depends on the characteristics of the animal and its environment. The behavioral theory, you will notice, is not incompatible with the restorative view. One focuses on the biological factors underlying sleep, while the other focuses on how sleep once had survival value.

EXPLORING PSYCHOLOGY Control of Sleep

Most of us fall asleep within 15 to 30 minutes after going to bed and sleep an average of 8 hours. Research on why and how this happens has focused primarily on two structures, the hypothalamus, which is located in the forebrain, and the pons, which is in the midbrain.

In one study, researchers placed a number of ultrafine tubes of glass, called microelectrodes, into individual cells in an animal's hypothalamus. This way, the researchers could measure the activity of cells in the hypothalamus during the animal's regular sleep-wake pattern. They found that the hypothalamus was involved in controlling going to sleep, which is called sleep onset. The hypothalamus may do this by secreting chemicals and/or lowering the temperature of the body. We know that temperature is important because we usually go to sleep several hours after our body temperature drops and get up many hours later as our body temperature starts to rise (Lewy et al., 1980; Moore-Ede & Czeisler, 1984; Sewitch, 1987).

The hypothalamus may also secrete chemicals that affect the pons, which, researchers believe, produces neurotransmitters that are involved in the control of REM and NREM sleep. Researchers who destroyed parts of the pons and observed changes in animals' sleep patterns noticed that cats did not go into REM sleep if one part of their pons was destroyed, and did not go into NREM sleep if a different part was destroyed. When the researchers analyzed these two sections of the pons, they discovered that one section produced a neurotransmitter, norepinephrine, which was involved in triggering REM sleep, and the other section produced a different neurotransmitter, serotonin, which was involved in triggering NREM sleep (Hobson et al, 1986).

There are still some missing pieces to the puzzle of sleep. For example, if you withdrew blood from sleeping animals and injected it into awake animals, you would notice that many of the awake animals went to sleep. Researchers who did this concluded that there are sleep-inducing chemicals in the blood that are involved in the onset of both NREM and REM sleep (Krueger et al., 1982; Maugh, 1982).

From all these data, we see that the control of sleep involves at least two areas of the brain, two neurotransmitters, and a substance in the blood. Researchers are now trying to identify the substance in the blood as well as specify the order in which these mechanisms come into play as we drift off to sleep, stay asleep, and wake up.

THE PROBLEM OF INSOMNIA

For the vast majority of us, the sleep-wake cycle operates reliably day after day, without our giving it thought. An unfortunate minority, however, suffer sleep disorders (see photo). One of the most common disorders is called **insomnia,** which involves difficulty going to sleep or staying asleep for the night. About 10 to 20 percent of Americans report having bouts of insomnia, and they spend more than half a billion dollars yearly on medications for it (Hopson, 1986). Insomnia is very often caused more by psychological problems than physical ones. The story of Mrs. S is a case in point.

The Causes of Insomnia

Mrs. S had been a poor sleeper all her life. However, four years ago her 19-year-old son became involved in drug trafficking. Mrs. S was distraught and became "almost totally sleepless for at least two months." She never recovered and still reported extremely poor sleep when she entered the Sleep Disorders Center three years after the scandal. By then her son had become rehabilitated and had made a good adjustment.

Nine months after being treated, Mrs. S had returned to the "adequate" sleep that she had shown before the drug scandal. Although she still suffered a few poor nights each month, she took them in stride. Anxiety and agitation were no longer chronic but developed only when she was put under serious stress. She felt "cured" (adapted from Hauri, 1982).

Insomnia can be caused by unusual stress and anxiety arising from personal, financial, or marital problems or from difficulties at work or at school. This was apparently the origin of Mrs. S's insomnia: she felt worry, shame, and guilt over her son's drug involvement. In many such cases, the insomnia disappears when the crisis is over or the personal problem solved. In Mrs. S's case, however, the insomnia persisted even after her son was rehabilitated. Another frequent cause of insomnia is change in sleep schedule. If you stay up late Saturday night and sleep late Sunday morning, you will probably not be ready for sleep if you go to bed at your usual time Sunday night. This kind of sleeplessness, often called "Sunday night insomnia," is very common. A third cause of insomnia is excessive use of drugs, including tranquilizers, sedatives, and alcohol at bedtime. Heavy use of these drugs disrupts the organization of sleep stages and results in poor sleep. Finally, insomnia may be caused by sleep-induced respiratory problems. One of the most common and serious of these is *sleep apnea*, in which a sleeping person literally stops breathing and then wakes up to start breathing again. Sleep apnea has been found to occur in about 40 percent of elderly people, but is less common in younger adults (Coleman

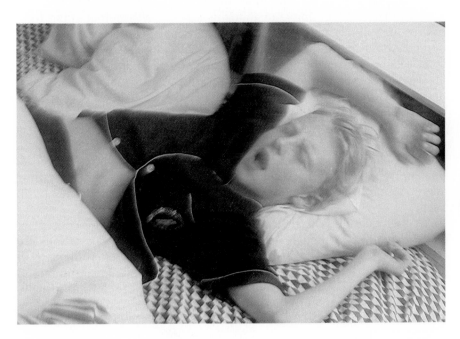

Children are sometimes subject to **night terrors,** which take place during delta sleep and involve sudden waking, screaming, and behaving in a frightened manner, with no memory of the experience next morning. Some adults, during REM sleep, experience *nightmares*, which involve emotionally charged images that provoke fear and anxiety, all of which may be vividly remembered. Both children and adults may have episodes of **sleepwalking** during delta sleep, which involve either sitting up or leaving the bed and walking around without becoming conscious. (Dan McCoy/Rainbow)

et al., 1981). In severe cases, sleep apnea can be treated successfully by different surgical procedures, one of which is enlarging the upper airway passages in the nose (Klonoff et al., 1987).

People with insomnia may feel very sleepy during the daytime; many of them consider this the most serious aspect of the problem (Coleman et al., 1982). In order to get the rest they need at night, millions turn to nonprescription sleep medications, such as Sominex, Sleepeze, and Nytol. The main ingredient in these drugs is an antihistamine that produces drowsiness as a side effect. There is no evidence, however, that antihistamines are effective in treating insomnia (Kales & Kales, 1973). Whatever benefits they have are due primarily to the **placebo** (pluh-SEE-bo) **effect**: the reaction occurs merely because the person *expects* the pill to cause that reaction. In this case, if you are firmly convinced that Sominex, Sleepeze, or Nytol will work, these beliefs are likely to help you get to sleep after taking one of these medications.

At one time, many doctors prescribed drugs called *barbiturates* for insomnia, but few reputable physicians do so today. Barbiturates have been found to be addictive and to cause additional sleep problems after prolonged use. Today, the most commonly used prescription drugs for insomnia are benzodiazepines or minor tranquilizers (such as Dalmane). These drugs have been shown to be effective in treating insomnia, but they are recommended only for short-term use, usually no longer than two weeks. Longer use poses the risk of drug dependence. Even when used on a short-term basis, tranquilizers can have undesirable side effects, such as daytime drowsiness and mild depression.

APPLYING PSYCHOLOGY   Treating Insomnia

How can you get to sleep without using drugs?

Because insomnia is often caused by excessive worrying, thinking, and restlessness, psychologists have developed behavioral programs to help people overcome these problems (Lichstein & Rosenthal, 1980; Borkovec, 1982). One is called **progressive relaxation.** It is designed, as the name implies, to get insomniacs to relax all the muscles of the body and thus to eliminate the physical tension that often contributes to sleeplessness.

Learning progressive relaxation involves sitting or lying in a comfortable position and focusing your thoughts on the feelings that come from contracting and relaxing the major muscle groups in your body. You would normally begin by contracting and relaxing the muscles in your toes, and then working up your body until you reach your face and forehead. With this technique, you can learn to distinguish between a tense and a relaxed muscle anywhere in your body, and you are better able to relax your muscles at will.

Insomniacs who practiced progressive relaxation once during the day and once in bed before bedtime fell asleep significantly faster than those who just scheduled a time to relax, not necessarily at bedtime (Nicassio & Bootzin, 1974). This finding suggests that people who have trouble falling asleep can profit from using progressive relaxation right before they try to sleep.

Other techniques have also helped. One is based on the concept of **stimulus control.** Although we do not like to think that our actions are controlled by environmental cues around us, this is very often the case. If you suffer from insomnia, getting into bed may be a cue for beginning to worry that you are about to spend another sleepless night. Not surprisingly, this worrying contributes to the insomnia you wish to overcome.

The idea behind stimulus control applied to insomnia is to make sure that "going to bed" is a stimulus for sleeping, not for worrying. Presumably, if going to bed and sleeping are repeatedly paired with one another, getting into bed will automatically elicit the sleep response. The trick is to make sure that going to bed is never associated with thoughts and behaviors that can prevent sleep. Here is a program two researchers created to accomplish this goal:

1. Engage in some relaxing activity, such as reading, before bed and make it a point not to think about the next day's activities.

2. Go to bed only when you are relaxed or sleepy. Do not use your bed for anything except sleep; that is, do not read, watch television, eat, or worry in bed. Sexual activity is the only exception to this rule.

3. If you find yourself unable to fall sleep once you have gone to bed, get up and go into another room. Stay up as long as you wish, and engage in some activity that will be relaxing and stop your worrying. Return to the bedroom only when you feel sleepy. Although clock watching is undesirable, you should get out of bed if you do not fall asleep immediately. The goal is to associate your bed with falling asleep quickly. If you are in bed more than about 10 minutes without falling asleep and have not gotten up, you are not following this instruction.

4. Repeat step 3 as often as necessary throughout the night.

5. Set your alarm and get up at the same time every morning regardless of how much sleep you got during the night. This will help you acquire a consistent sleep rhythm. Continue to get up at the same time each morning until you have established a regular sleep-wake pattern.

6. Do not nap during the day. Daytime naps will tend to interfere with establishing a regular sleep-wake pattern (adapted from Bootzin & Nicassio, 1978).

The researchers who developed this program tested it on a group of chronic insomniacs. Before the treatment began, these subjects required an average of 85 minutes to fall asleep at night. After the treatment, they averaged only 36 minutes (Bootzin & Nicassio, 1978). Researchers also found that the stimulus control program helped people who suffered from sleep-maintenance insomnia, which is having trouble staying asleep. After four weekly one-hour training sessions on stimulus control, subjects reported significantly fewer awakenings during the night (Morin & Azrin, 1987).

But suppose you are the type of person who likes to read or watch TV in bed before you go to sleep. If you suffer from insomnia, the stimulus-control approach might not be right for you. Instead, you might try a form of treatment that uses **visual imagery**. In one study, researchers compared the effectiveness of visual imagery with that of relaxation.

The researchers trained one group of insomniacs in a visual-imagery technique. First, they showed these subjects color drawings of six common objects: a candle, an hourglass, a blackboard, a kite, a lightbulb, and a bowl of fruit. Once the subjects were familiar with the objects, they were asked to imagine each of them in great detail for two minutes. To help the subjects along, the researchers prompted them in this manner:

Picture the general outline of the candle itself. Once this is clear let your focus move downward to the candle holder. Notice how round the holder is. Just to the right of the candle is the handle of the candle

What does imagining a candle have to do with getting to sleep?

holder. Notice how it curves around. Let your focus move up the candle to the top. See how uneven the top of the candle is compared to the smooth sides . . . Slightly above this, picture the wick and then observe the shape of the flame (adapted from Woolfolk & McNulty, 1983, p. 496).

These subjects were then told to practice visual imagery twice daily, once during the daytime and once in bed before trying to go to sleep. Other insomniacs were instructed to practice relaxation, or a combination of relaxation and visual imagery. After four weeks of treatment, *all* groups of subjects required less time to get to sleep at night. Six weeks later, however, those trained in visual imagery continued to show the most improvement (Figure 5.9). Apparently, visual imagery combats sleeplessness by giving people a method of stopping worrisome thoughts at bedtime.

DREAMS

Does everyone dream every night?

Some people insist that they never *dream*. But research suggests that such people are probably mistaken. Apparently, everyone dreams during the night, even though many have forgotten their dreams by morning. When people in sleep laboratories are awakened from REM periods, they report dreaming on average 80 percent of the time, and in some cases the percentage is closer to 100 (Foulkes, 1983).

Researchers have collected hundreds of dream descriptions from people who have just been aroused from REM sleep. They have found that dreams usually have several characters, involve motion such as running or walking, are more likely to take place indoors than out, and are more often unpleasant than pleasant. Oddly enough, although most dreams are filled with visual sensations, very few involve the sensations of taste, smell, or pain.

Figure 5.9
Before treatment, three groups of insomniacs needed an average of 105 minutes to fall asleep. Following four weeks of treatment, and follow-up at six weeks, those in the control group not subject to treatment needed about the same amount of time to get to sleep. But those who had been trained in progressive relaxation needed about 25 minutes less time to fall asleep, and those who had been trained in imagery needed the least time—almost a full hour less than previously. (Data from Woolfolk & McNulty, 1983)

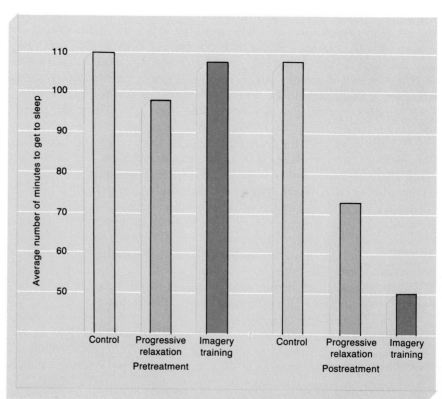

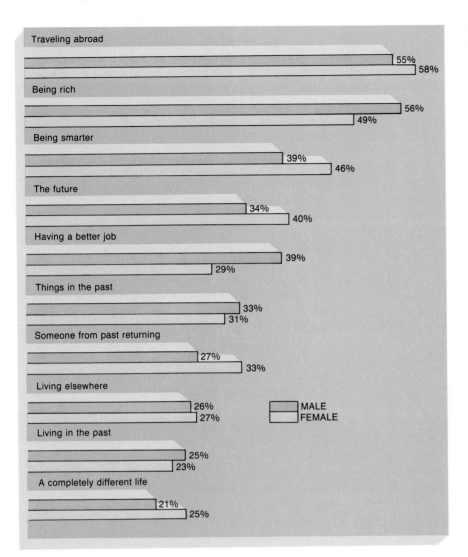

Figure 5.10
Popular daydreams. (From The Roper Organizaton © Info-Graphics, 1984)

Dreams often seem bizarre because they disregard physical laws and the ways we normally behave. Less frequently we have dreams of experiences we would never have in real life, experiences such as flying or jumping to the top of a building. Also, if dream reports can be believed, we rarely dream about sexual encounters and almost never about sexual intercourse (Hall & Van de Castle, 1966; Kiester, 1980).

When college students were asked whether they had recurrent dreams, 60 percent said that they did. The recurrent dream most frequently mentioned was one in which the dreamer was being threatened or pursued and was trying to hide. Anxiety dreams like this one, however, may be reported relatively often simply because they are so disturbing and therefore more likely to be remembered (Robbins & Houshi, 1983).

To see what people "dream" about during the day, look at Figure 5.10.

Interpretation of Dreams

I am in an elevator sitting by myself against the wall. Now this girl comes in, and I say "Come sit by me," and she sits by me (I didn't even know her), and I lean over and try to kiss her, and she says "No, don't do that." I say, "How come?" and she said something about her acne, and I said it didn't matter and she laughed and we ended up kissing and stuff on the elevator, and then these parents got on . . . and the elevator was real shaky, and I was thinking that the elevator would crash or get stuck. . . . I asked her "Is the elevator always like this?" and she said "Yes" . . . so we finally got off at number 2—I was trying to get off at number 11—but we finally got off at 2. It was weird; I was scared of riding it (Cohen, 1979, p. 228).

Let's look at three different theories about what this dream might mean.

According to **Freudian theory,** we experience many unacceptable desires that we cannot deal with because they cause us too much anxiety. Our defense is to repress these guilt-provoking wishes—to push them back into the unconscious. Freud (1900) believed that dreams are full of symbols that represent the thoughts and desires we have locked away in the unconscious, and interpreting these symbols is one way of discovering submerged ideas and feelings. Thus, Freud might say that the elevator in the young man's dream is a symbol for the female's genital organs and riding in an elevator symbolizes sexual intercourse. The man's statement that he was "scared of riding" suggests that he is fearful of sex. Although Freudian dream interpretation can be fascinating, no one has yet devised a method to test the hypothesis that dreams express forbidden urges or to determine whether any given dream analysis is correct (Webb & Cartwright, 1978).

According to Hobson and McClarley's (1977) **activation-synthesis theory,** dreaming is caused by nothing more than random activity in the brain. Their theory holds that certain neurons in the pons are activated during REM sleep. The pons then sends millions of random nerve impulses up to the cortex. The cortex tries to make sense of these incoming signals, just as it would of signals from the body and sense organs. The result is a series of often disjointed feelings, perceptions, imagined movements, and changing scenes that we define as dreams. According to this view, there is no reason to interpret dreams because they arise simply from the random activation of neurons, not from desires hidden in some unconscious part of the mind.

Most present-day dream researchers argue that dreams are mainly a continuation of our waking thoughts and concerns rather than symbols of unconscious desires (Webb & Cartwright, 1978; Cohen, 1979). According to this view, our young man's dream may simply mean he is worried about his difficulty in meeting women or he is nervous about bringing someone home to meet his parents. The next time you wonder about the meaning of your dreams, you might try considering the dream's relationship to things that are currently on your mind.

She walked down the steps of the public library, wearing her nightgown and cradling a bowl of raspberry Jell-O in her arms. At the foot of the long staircase she could distinguish the dim figure of her high school algebra teacher. His right arm was upraised and he seemed to be shouting at her, but she could not make out the words. She hurried toward him, straining to hear *(Kiester, 1980)*

According to Freudian theory, this dream is full of symbols that have hidden meanings. According to the activation-synthesis theory, this dream is simply the result of random neural impulses. According to many sleep researchers, this dream is a continuation of waking thoughts and reflects current concerns and worries. *(Ron Miller)*

REVIEW

Astronaut Arnie is being sent on a long space voyage to the planet Venus. Ground control can both affect and monitor Arnie's states of (1) _____ because they have implanted one electrode in his reticular formation and fastened many more to the outside of his skull. The scientists on earth can tell that Arnie is conscious by analyzing the readout of his brain waves, a readout that is called an (2) _____ or _____. From Arnie's viewpoint his own consciousness entails (3) _____ of the many thoughts, feelings, and perceptions that occupy his mind. Loss or diminution of that awareness would result in an altered state of consciousness.

If Arnie lost contact with ground control and his space ship's chronometer malfunctioned, his sleep-wake cycle would probably span (4) _____ hours rather than the 24 on earth. The sleep-wake cycle is an example of a daily biological rhythm known as a (5) _____ _____. Psycholo-

MAJOR CONCEPT   Sleeping and Dreaming

Virtually everyone sleeps at least part of each day and virtually everyone dreams. Yet as common as these two phenomena are, researchers do not yet fully understand why they occur.

Below is a list of some of the theories psychologists have proposed. Match each one with its proper description.

1. Restorative theory
2. Behavioral theory
3. Freudian theory
4. Activation-synthesis theory
5. Extension-of-waking-life theory

a. _3_ The theory that dreams are the result of thoughts and conflicts, often sexual ones, which have been pushed into the unconscious

b. _1_ The theory that activities during the day deplete key factors in the body, which are then replenished during sleep

c. _4_ The theory that dreams are caused by nothing more than the brain's effort to interpret random neural impulses initiated by the pons

d. _5_ The theory that dreams reflect a person's current experiences and concerns

e. _2_ The theory that sleep once had survival value because it kept our early ancestors safe from nighttime predators

Answers: a (3); b (1); c (4); d (5); e (2)

---

gists are interested in studying Arnie's sleep-wake cycle while he is in space.

When Arnie is fully awake, the psychologists notice that his brain waves exhibit a low-amplitude, high-frequency pattern characteristic of (6) _Beta_ waves. These waves are replaced by (7) _alpha_ waves as Arnie initially drifts off to sleep. He then enters the first stage of what is generally called (8) _N_ - _R_ - _E_ - _M_ sleep, abbreviated _NREM_. NREM stage 1 is marked by brain waves, called (9) _theta_ waves, that are slower in frequency and higher in amplitude than those Arnie shows when he is awake. After a few minutes Arnie enters NREM stage 2, and half an hour later he slips into the deepest of NREM stages, called Stage 4 or (10) _Delta_ sleep. If ground control tried to awaken Arnie from delta sleep just by speaking to him,

they would probably find it quite hard to do. Another half hour passes, and Arnie reenters NREM stage 2. Soon the researchers notice that his brain waves are showing what resembles a waking pattern, while his eyes are moving rapidly beneath his closed eyelids.

These signs tell them that Arnie is now experiencing (11) _Rapid_ - _Eye_ - _Movement_ sleep, abbreviated _REM_. If ground control were to stimulate Arnie's reticular formation and awaken him from REM sleep, he would probably report that he had been (12) _asleep_. During the night Arnie will alternate between REM and NREM periods, spending about 20 percent of his sleep time in REM and 80 percent in NREM.

Arnie wonders why he needs to sleep at all. One reason is that sleep may restore important biological processes, an idea that is called the (13) _restorative_ theory of sleep. The other is that the sleep-wake cycle evolved long ago and endured because it helped to keep early humans relatively safe from predators at night.

This idea is called the (14) _behavioral_ theory of sleep.

Sometimes Arnie worries about being lost in space and cannot get to sleep. He is suffering a form of the

sleep disorder generally called (15) _insomnia_. Fortunately, the sleep researchers on earth can give him good advice on how to overcome his sleeplessness. They suggest he follow one of three treatments: systematically relaxing the muscles in his body, called pro-

gressive (16) _relaxation_; making sure that he associates his bunk only with sleeping, called stimulus

(17) _control_; or imagining common objects

in great detail, called visual (18) _imagery_. Soon Arnie's insomnia is cured. If Arnie's insomnia had become severe, he might be advised to take a pre-

scription drug, called (19) _Dalmane_. One

possible side effect of this drug is daytime drowsiness or mild depression.

Arnie has the same dream over and over and asks the sleep researchers at ground control what they think it means. He dreams that he takes off all his clothes and walks through a hotel lobby to take a shower. The

researchers answer that (20) _Freud_ would say the dream expresses an unconscious urge, very likely a sexual one. On the other hand, the researchers tell Arnie, the dream may have *no* particular meaning because it is caused by nothing more than random nerve impulses. This perspective on Arnie's dream is

based on the (21) _____ - _____ theory. Many present-day sleep researchers believe that Arnie's dream is an extension of things he is thinking

about during (22) _____ hours. In short, Arnie may simply be expressing his desire to take off his space suit and have a long, hot shower.

Answers: (1) consciousness; (2) electroencephalogram, EEG; (3) awareness; (4) 25; (5) circadian rhythm; (6) beta; (7) alpha; (8) Non-Rapid-Eye-Movement, NREM; (9) theta; (10) delta; (11) Rapid-Eye-Movement, REM; (12) dreaming; (13) restorative; (14) behavioral; (15) insomnia; (16) relaxation; (17) control; (18) imagery; (19) Dalmane; (20) Freud; (21) activation-synthesis; (22) waking

GLOSSARY TERMS

activation-synthesis theory (p. 146)
alpha waves (p. 135)
altered states of consciousness (p. 134)
behavioral theory (p. 139)
beta waves (p. 135)

circadian rhythm (p. 134)
delta sleep (p. 136)
electroencephalogram (EEG) (p. 135)
Freudian theory (p. 146)
insomnia (p. 140)
night terrors (p. 141)

Non-Rapid-Eye-Movement (NREM) sleep (p. 135)
placebo effect (p. 142)
progressive relaxation (p. 142)
Rapid-Eye-Movement (REM) sleep (p. 135)

restorative theory (p. 139)
sleepwalking (p. 141)
states of consciousness (p. 134)
stimulus control (p. 142)
theta waves (p. 136)
visual imagery (p. 143)

Module 14 Hypnosis

Pamela, a gifted actress, had been plagued by insomnia since childhood. Recently, however, because of the natural anxiety of any performer who goes from audition to audition seeking a part in a play, her sleeplessness was worse than ever. "I was in a state of desperation," she remembers. "I was literally shaking from complete tiredness when I went to Dr. Spiegel" [a well-known hypnotist].

Dr. Spiegel guided Pamela into a hypnotic state and taught her the "screen technique." She was asked to visualize "a movie screen, a TV screen, or, if you wish, a clear blue sky that acts like a screen." She was encouraged to see it as a split screen so that she could put her problems on one side: "on your worry screen." Other thoughts and images could be placed on the other side. Thus, if there were troubles in her life that were causing her tension and anxieties, those troubles could be put on the worry screen instead of being inflicted on her body. The worries would still be there, available for examination, but the body could relax. While she was still in a trance, Dr. Spiegel told her that she would be able, by herself, to go into hypnosis at any time and use the screen.

Pamela headed home that evening feeling euphoric. After a brief self-hypnosis exercise, she got into bed and fell asleep. She has since been able to sleep well (adapted from Connery, 1982).

Could hypnosis help break you of your worst habit?

DEFINITION

One reason Pamela reduced her insomnia was because she was highly motivated to enter a treatment program. Another reason was that she responded very well to **hypnosis,** a centuries-old procedure that is currently defined in two very different ways.

Some researchers maintain that being hypnotized involves being put into a *trance state* that is qualitatively different from any other conscious state. While in a trance state, people perform suggested behaviors that are no longer under conscious or voluntary control (Hilgard, 1979). According to this view, Pamela, while in a trance state, learned a relaxation technique that enabled her to fall asleep easily.

Other researchers disagree that hypnosis involves a trance state. Instead, they argue that being hypnotized involves nothing more than a researcher or therapist creating pressures so that a subject will conform and perform suggested behaviors. In this view, actions performed as a result of hypnosis are similar to other forms of *social behavior*, such as conformity and obedience (Sarbin & Coe, 1972; Spanos, 1986). Researchers who hold this view would say that the therapist's suggestions encouraged or motivated Pamela into visualizing her "worry" screen and relaxing her body, which helped her overcome her insomnia.

Is Hypnosis a Unique State? **EXPLORING PSYCHOLOGY**

Case for a Unique State

Imagine yourself a subject in the following experiment.

You are highly susceptible to hypnosis and have been put into a deep trance. The hypnotist tells you that you now have both a "hypnotized part" and a "hidden part." Your hypnotized part will follow the hypnotist's suggestions and experience related changes in sensation. Your hypnotized part will also be able to answer any questions verbally. Your hidden part, in contrast, will be aware of normal sensations, which often will contradict the hypnotist's suggestions. Although your hidden part cannot answer questions verbally, it can answer by tapping a finger—once for "yes" and twice for "no." Now the hypnotist asks you to plunge one hand in icy cold water with the suggestion that you will not feel pain. When asked "Do you feel great pain?" your voice answers "no," but the finger of your free hand taps "yes."

In this experiment, one part of a person is said to respond to the environment and answer questions verbally. At the same time, another "hidden part" responds and answers questions by tapping a finger (Hilgard, 1979). This finding, called the **hidden observer phenomenon,** suggests that a hypnotized person may be in a unique state of divided consciousness.

Figure 5.11
Would you follow these suggestions? They are similar to those on hypnotic susceptibility scales. (1) Your right arm is heavy and moving down. (2) Your right arm is weightless and moving up. (3) Your hands are welded together and cannot be separated. (4) You are becoming very thirsty. (5) Your throat and jaw muscles are rigid and you cannot speak your name. (6) Your body is heavy and you cannot stand up. (7) After the entire procedure is over, you will cough automatically when you hear a click. (8) After the entire procedure is over, you will not remember any specific suggestion. (Ken Robert Buck/The Picture Cube)

Researchers cite other evidence to support the idea that hypnosis is a unique state. For example, hypnotized subjects seem able to suspend logic and see things that are not there, such as two images of the same person, which are examples of hallucinations (Orne, 1959). Based on these kinds of data, some researchers hold to the idea that hypnosis is a unique state.

Case Against a Unique State

You are going to watch the behaviors of three groups of subjects given different instructions. Group A subjects are simply told that they will be given a test of imagination that involves following suggestions. Group B subjects are hypnotized and informed that they will be having some unusual experiences. Group C subjects are also told that they are about to be tested for the ability to imagine, but in addition they are asked to try to score as high as possible so that the experiment will be successful.

Following these initial procedures and sets of instructions, subjects in each group are given eight different suggestions and rated on how well they follow them. These suggestions are similar to those listed in Figure 5.11. Researchers wanted to know which group would follow the most suggestions. Subjects in group A, who were simply told they were being tested for imagination, complied with the fewest requests. As you probably guessed, group B subjects, the hypnotized ones, carried out significantly more suggestions. But here is something that may surprise you. Group C subjects, who had been urged to do their best, carried out as many suggestions as the hypnotized subjects. In both group B *and* group C, over 50 percent of the subjects complied with six or more of the researcher's requests (Barber, 1965, 1979). This study shows that behaviors performed under hypnosis are very similar to those performed under nonhypnotic, motivational instructions.

Nicholas Spanos and his associates agree that hypnotic phenomena such as analgesia (insensitivity to pain), posthypnotic amnesia (inability to remember what happened while under hypnosis), and disturbances in seeing the real world, need not involve a trance state explanation. For example, Spanos has shown that just by providing strong motivation, unhypnotized subjects can be induced to act as if part of them were hypnotized and part were a hidden observer. In fact, with motivational instructions alone, Spanos reports that subjects will perform most of the same behaviors that are observed in hypnotized subjects. For this reason, he explains these hypnotic phenomena as being another form of social behavior, in which a subject performs suggested behaviors in response to the pressures of the situation (Spanos, 1986).

Is hypnosis a unique state? As you can see, leading researchers in the field disagree.

BEHAVIORS UNDER HYPNOSIS

Although entertainers who present hypnotism demonstrations claim that they routinely hypnotize large groups of people, only about 15 percent of the population can be easily and deeply hypnotized. About 75 percent can be hypnotized to some extent, and the remaining 10 percent show little if any susceptibility to hypnosis. However, recent research indicates that individuals who showed little susceptibility to hypnosis initially showed significantly more susceptibility after receiving positive information about hypnosis and training sessions in producing images (Gfeller et al., 1987; Spanos et al., 1987). Apparently susceptibility to hypnosis can be increased with training.

Now, let's look at some of the behaviors that people perform under hypnosis.

Imagined Perceptions

If you were highly susceptible to hypnosis or were hypnotized, you might be led to experience strange sensations or perceive stimuli that do not exist. If the hypnotist suggests "Your left arm is becoming rigid," you may be unable to bend your arm. If the hypnotist says "You see a fly buzzing around your head," the fly might indeed seem to be there.

Insensitivity to Pain

People under hypnosis have been observed to hold one hand in a bucket of icy cold water and yet say they feel no discomfort (Hilgard et al., 1978). They have even been known to stick needles through their hands and still report no pain. This effect is called **analgesia** (ah-nahl-GEEZ-ee-ah), or pain insensitivity. Studies have shown that hypnosis can produce this phenomenon.

Age or Previous Life Regression

What would you do if you were hypnotized and asked to return to the age of 2? If you stuck a thumb in your mouth and began talking like a baby, you would be showing **age regression**—acting and thinking as if you were much younger than you are. During age regression, hypnotized subjects may act out early life experiences, such as playing with a favorite toy or attending a birthday party. But the fact that they sometimes do things that only an adult could do (reading difficult words, for example) shows that they have not *really* become a child again. Instead, it appears that age regression involves both acting out past memories and behaving as one thinks a child should behave (Foenander & Burrows, 1980).

Occasionally, people who have been hypnotized are asked to regress beyond their childhood to a previous life. Critics of **previous-life regression** point out that the kind of instruction given before hypnosis affects the reports of hypnotized subjects (see Figure 5.12). Those who are told to be skeptical of previous-life experiences report fewer such experiences under

Figure 5.12
Subjects in three different groups were hypnotized and asked to regress to previous lifetimes. Before hypnosis, those in the encouraged group were told that regression was a positive experience and that they should try to comply; those in the neutral group were given neutral instructions; those in the discouraged group were told the experience would be negative, and they should be skeptical about returning to past lives. The kind of prior instruction had a very strong influence on whether the hypnotized subjects reported experiencing another life. (Data from Baker, 1982)

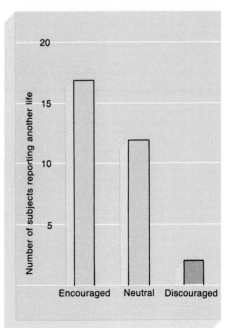

hypnosis than those who are told to expect such experiences. In addition, when claims of hypnosis-induced previous-life regression were thoroughly examined, many proved to be unsubstantiated (Venn, 1986).

Posthypnotic Amnesia

During hypnosis, subjects may be told that once they leave hypnosis they will not remember all or part of what happened. If they follow this suggestion and cannot remember what went on under hypnosis, they are displaying **posthypnotic amnesia.** A common explanation for posthypnotic amnesia is that the person forgets because the experiences have been repressed and made unavailable to normal consciousness. A different explanation, based on a number of studies, is that the subjects can remember what happened but that they inhibit verbally reporting these suggestions because they have been "forbidden" to report them (Huesmann et al., 1987; Spanos, 1982, 1986). According to this theory, the subjects do not have amnesia. Instead, they have a problem with reporting verbally what occurred when they were under hypnosis.

Posthypnotic Suggestions

Under hypnosis, a person may be told that after "waking up," he or she will perform a certain behavior, such as cough, when he or she hears the word "warm." If the person does indeed cough upon hearing "warm," he or she is following a simple **posthypnotic suggestion.** Some researchers contend that subjects who follow posthypnotic suggestions are acting automatically in response to the predetermined cue, and may even respond the same way outside the situation in which the hypnosis took place. Other researchers disagree that the subject is responding automatically. They believe that the subject is performing a certain goal-directed behavior in response to the demands and pressures of the hypnotist and the situation. This latter view is supported by recent findings which indicate that subjects may not perform the posthypnotically suggested behavior outside of the situation associated with hypnosis (Spanos et al., 1987).

As you can see, hypnotic phenomena, such as imagined perceptions, analgesia, regression, and posthypnotic suggestions, can be attributed to both hypnosis and motivational instructions. At this point, researchers disagree as to which interpretation is better.

APPLYING PSYCHOLOGY   Hypnosis as Therapy

How effective is hypnosis in treating behavioral problems, such as smoking, overeating, and drinking?

Posthypnosis suggestion is sometimes used to try to get people to break undesirable habits. By itself, however, hypnosis does not appear to be very effective in eliminating habits we have mixed feelings about giving up. The reason, according to one researcher, is that we are unlikely to perform behaviors we do not want to perform simply because we have been hypnotized and given motivational instructions (Orne, 1980). In one study, for example, alcoholics were hypnotized on six different days and given suggestions to attend Alcoholics Anonymous. They were also told that they would not like the taste of alcohol after coming out of hypnosis. Yet when the behavior of these subjects was later compared with that of other alcoholics who had *not* been hypnotized, the two groups showed no difference in drinking patterns (Wadden & Penrod, 1981).

MAJOR CONCEPT   Hypnosis

Psychologists are still debating what hypnosis is and whether it represents a unique state of consciousness.

Here are some statements about hypnosis; indicate whether each is true (T) or false (F).

1. T/F A hypnotist could get you to stick to a program of vigorous exercise even though you hate the very thought of jogging around the block.

2. T/F Scientists have discovered several physiological changes that are sure signs a person is hypnotized.

3. T/F When people under hypnosis regress to a much earlier age, they recall events from real childhood with flawless accuracy.

4. T/F About three-fourths of the general population can be hypnotized to some extent.

5. T/F Experiments have been performed in which people under hypnosis seem to experience a "split" in consciousness.

6. T/F Many of the feats performed under hypnosis—such as reporting no pain in a painful situation—have also been performed by people who are simply urged to try their hardest.

Answers: 1 (F); 2 (F); 3 (F); 4 (T); 5 (T); 6 (T).

As seen in Figure 5.13, hypnosis was significantly better than no treatment in helping smokers stop smoking, but it did not work significantly better than other therapies. Hypnosis has also been reported to help overweight subjects lose weight (Cochrane & Friesen, 1986), and in rare cases

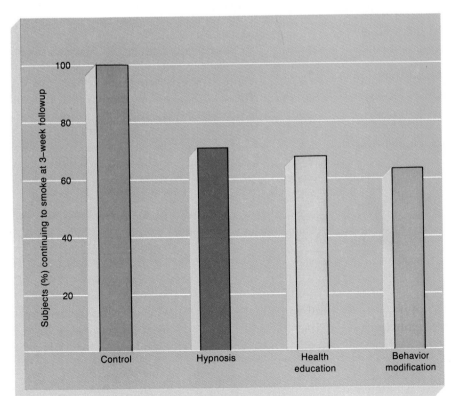

Figure 5.13

If hypnosis is a powerful motivator, how much would hypnosis help people change a behavior, such as to stop smoking? Researchers compared hypnosis with two other treatments. One group of subjects was hypnotized and given suggestions to stop smoking. Subjects in the second group were given health education—they were told about the adverse health effects of smoking. Behavior modification techniques were used on the third group of subjects, who were asked to record when and where they smoked and to substitute deep breathing or relaxation for smoking. The data indicate that hypnosis was no more or less effective in motivating people to stop smoking than was health education or behavior modification. (Data from Rabkin et al., 1984) hypnosis has been used as a primary anesthetic during general surgery (Silberner, 1986).

If we look at the studies of hypnosis and its effects on behavior, we can see that hypnosis is not a miracle treatment for unwanted habits, but it is useful if subjects are highly motivated to change their behaviors *prior* to hypnosis (Lazar & Dempster, 1981; Wadden & Anderton, 1982; Wadden & Penrod, 1981).

REVIEW

Terry, who wants to stop her two-pack-a-day smoking habit, goes to a therapist who uses hypnosis. Terry is a little worried and asks the therapist what hypnosis does.

The therapist explains that researchers have two very different definitions of hypnosis. Some say that hypnosis is different from other states of consciousness and will put a person into a special state, called a

(1) _____. While in this state, a person may perform suggested behaviors automatically. Others say that hypnotic phenomena are similar to other forms

of (2) _____ behaviors, such as conformity. According to this view, a person will perform suggested behaviors because of pressures created by the situation.

Evidence for a trance—or unique—state comes from data interpreted as showing divided consciousness,

such as from (3) _____ observer phenomenon. Additional data that hypnosis is a unique state come from reports of subjects experiencing hallucinations.

Evidence against hypnosis being a trance state comes from data that show that people who are given

instructions to increase their (4) _____ will perform behaviors similar to those reported under hypnosis.

The therapist explains that people perform a number of behaviors under hypnosis. For example, if you imagined a bee on your nose, that would be an example

of an imagined (5) _____. If you thought and acted as if you were 4 years old, that would be an

example of age (6) _____. If you recalled a former life, that would be an example of reincarna-

tion or (7) _____ - _____ regression. However, many cases of this kind of regression have not been substantiated. If you felt *no* pain when holding your hand in ice water, that would be

an example of hypnotic (8) _____. Finally, if the hypnotist tells you that upon awakening, you will act in a certain manner, that would be an

example of posthypnotic (9) _____.

Terry really wants to stop smoking. The therapist

says that (10) _____ has been shown to help people change unwanted behaviors. However, he adds that hypnosis may be no more or less effective than other types of therapies and is often used in combination with other therapies. In addition, hypnosis appears to be most effective if the client initially is highly

(11) _____ to change his or her unwanted behaviors.

Answers: (1) trance; (2) social; (3) hidden; (4) motivation; (5) perception; (6) regression; (7) previous-life; (8) analgesia; (9) suggestion; (10) hypnosis; (11) motivated

GLOSSARY TERMS

age regression (p. 151)
analgesia (p. 151)
hidden observer
    phenomenon (p. 149)

hypnosis (p. 149)
posthypnotic amnesia
    (p. 152)

posthypnotic suggestion
    (p. 152)

previous-life regression
    (p. 151)

Module 15 Drugs and Awareness

KINDS OF DRUGS

My name is Jeff. I am a student like you. I always intend to study more than I really do and wish I got better grades. I enjoy partying, seeing my friends, and going camping. I don't know about you, but some of the time I feel really insecure about myself. I thought that I had found a solution to my insecurity. I would use drugs. I first experimented with drugs in the sixth grade. From there I just continued using drugs in high school and when I started college.

When my friends came over, the first thing we all did was smoke some marijuana. After a few hits, I laughed and talked and felt accepted. When we went camping, I took plenty of beer and mushrooms. I would sit under the stars and drink beer and eat mushrooms and feel that some wonderful experience was filling my soul. After class I would smoke a little dope to help me relax. When I used drugs I didn't worry about studying or exams or what I was doing with my life.

Besides alcohol, marijuana, and mushrooms, I smoke cigarettes and I've experimented with cocaine. I know a lot of students who have. But I think it was different for me. Something had changed without my really noticing. I had begun to run my life around drugs (adapted from the Daily Aztec, *April 2, 1987).*

Like millions of people, Jeff used drugs to change his awareness, mood, and feelings. But for Jeff things got out of hand, and he developed a drug habit that he could not control.

Jeff used three different classes of drugs: depressants, stimulants, and hallucinogens. **Depressants,** such as alcohol, heroin, or morphine, depress the activity of the central nervous system and result in feelings of relaxation, apathy, and decreased attention. **Stimulants,** such as cocaine, amphetamines, caffeine, and nicotine, increase the activity of the central and peripheral nervous system and result in feelings of alertness, arousal, and euphoria. **Hallucinogens,** such as psilocybin (mushrooms) and LSD, produce visions or imaginary perceptions by acting on chemicals in the brain. Because high doses of marijuana sometimes produce hallucinations, we will include it under hallucinogens.

Jeff noticed that when he used cocaine regularly, he had to use a little more each time to get the same feeling. This is because he had developed a tolerance to cocaine. **Tolerance** means that the body builds up a resistance to the drug so that larger and larger doses are needed to produce the same behavioral effects.

A chronic smoker who stops smoking will probably get headaches and feel irritable. This is because the nicotine in the tobacco, like many other drugs, results in a physical addiction to the drug. **Addiction** means that the drug is now needed for normal functioning and stopping the drug leads to *withdrawal* symptoms. Depending upon the drug, withdrawal symptoms may include headaches, irritability, nausea, body pains, and delusions. Addiction, which is defined by the presence of withdrawal symptoms, is different from psychological dependency. **Dependency** refers to the strong psychological need or desire to use a drug. For example, Jeff might become psychologically dependent upon alcohol or cocaine if he used these substances in moderate amounts. If he frequently used large amounts of either drug, he would probably become physically addicted.

How might using drugs cause problems?

Figure 5.14
Drug usage in the United States. (From Psychology Today, 1984, p. 76)

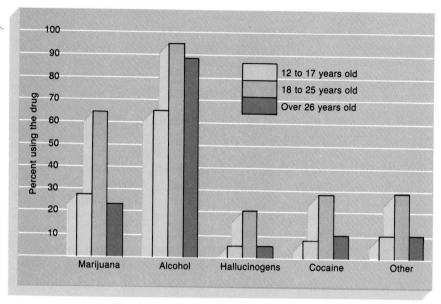

For all age groups, alcohol is the most popular mind-altering drug. Among those aged 18 to 25, marijuana is the second most popular drug, followed by cocaine and hallucinogens (Figure 5.14). In addition, a little more than 50 percent of adult Americans drink coffee for the stimulating effects of caffeine and a little more than 30 percent smoke cigarettes for the arousing properties of nicotine. Why are drugs used so frequently to change mood, feeling, or awareness? The reason is simple: Many drugs are easy to obtain and produce their effect quickly, effortlessly, and reliably. For a list of frequently used drugs and their effects, please see Table 5.1.

NEUROTRANSMITTERS AND EXPECTATIONS

It took four strong men to bring Mike into the emergency room. The day before he started to suspect that people were staring at him and whispering about him. Perhaps planning to kill him. This afternoon he began hearing voices (adapted from Snyder, 1972).

Mike had been using very high doses of amphetamine, a powerful stimulant. One of the ways that high doses of amphetamine produce paranoid symptoms is by acting on certain chemicals, called *neurotransmitters*, that carry messages between brain cells. For a detailed explanation of how neurotransmitters work, please see Module 4. Some stimulants, such as amphetamine and cocaine, increase the amount of neurotransmitters. This increase results in more messages, more stimulation, and feelings of arousal and alertness. Some depressants, such as heroin and morphine, replace the naturally occurring neurotransmitters with an enormous amount of similar acting chemicals. The result of this dramatic chemical replacement is to inhibit functioning of the brain cells that produce relaxation and apathy. One of the primary ways that drugs produce physiological and behavioral changes is by affecting neurotransmitters that control the number of messages flowing between brain cells.

A group of men were served drinks and then asked to rate their sexual arousal while watching erotic movies. Some of the men were given tonic water and were told that this is what they would be drinking; others were given vodka and tonic and were so informed. A third group of men, however, was served exactly the opposite of what they expected. They were told they would be drinking vodka and tonic, but were actually given tonic water with only two drops of vodka floating on the top. This mixture mimics the smell and taste of real vodka and tonic. The results showed that subjects drinking vodka and tonic rated their sexual arousal higher than those who drank only tonic. Here's the curious result. Subjects who *believed* that they were drinking vodka and tonic but were actually given tonic with only two drops of vodka rated their arousal as high as those drinking real vodka and tonic (Abrams & Wilson, 1983). It was the men's *expectations* about alcohol that made them feel aroused even though they had drunk only two drops of vodka. This study shows that a change in awareness, mood, or feeling can result from a person's expectations as well as how the drug affects neurotransmitters.

Can you feel drunk from drinking nonalcoholic beer?

DEPRESSANTS

Alcohol

Alice orders a drink at her favorite "happy hour" place. It doesn't matter if she orders a 12-ounce can of beer, either regular or lite, a 5-ounce glass of wine, or a mixed drink with 1½ ounces of 80-proof whiskey. All contain the same amount of pure ethyl alcohol. If Alice drinks only one drink per hour, she will feel very little of the alcohol's effects. That is because in the average person, alcohol is broken down or metabolized by the liver at the rate of about one ounce per hour. If Alice drinks several drinks per hour there will be more alcohol in her bloodstream than can be metabolized and she will feel the alcohol's effect. The relative amount of alcohol in a person's blood, called the *blood alcohol level* or BAL, is expressed in percentages. For example, after two drinks per hour, Alice will probably feel less inhibited, more relaxed and talkative, and have a BAL of about .04 percent. After 4 or 5 drinks per hour, she will probably have problems with coordination, talk loudly, feel intoxicated, and have a BAL of about 0.1. In most states, a person with a BAL of 0.1 percent is considered legally drunk. How quickly your BAL reaches 0.1 depends upon a number of

In moderate doses, PCP (phencyclidine), commonly called angel dust, produces euphoria, hallucinations, and feelings of being overwhelmed by sensory stimuli. At higher doses, PCP may cause feelings of sensory overload, agitation, inability to test reality, and emotional disorganization. According to Hall and Popkin (1981), PCP is the most dangerous hallucinogen because of its tendency to produce a severe psychotic state that may include violence and aggression. (Alan Carey/The Image Works)

TABLE 5.1   Major Substances Used for Mind Alteration

Drug	Slang Name	Source	Effects	Withdrawal Symptoms	Adverse/ Overdose Reactions	Physical Addiction Potential	Psychological Dependence Potential
DEPRESSANTS Morphine	Drugstore dope, cube, first line, mud, white, stuff, M	Natural (from opium)	Apathy, difficulty in concentration, slowed speech, decreased physical activity, drooling, itching, euphoria, nausea	Anxiety, vomiting, sneezing, diarrhea, lower back pain, watery eyes, runny nose, yawning, irritability, tremors, panic, chills and sweating, cramps	Depressed levels of consciousness, low blood pressure, rapid heart rate, shallow breathing, convulsions, coma, possible death	Yes	Yes
Heroin	H, hombre, junk, smack, dope, horse, crap, scat	Semisynthetic (from morphine)				Yes	Yes
Codeine	Schoolboy	Natural (from opium), semisynthetic (from morphine)				Yes	Yes
Methadone	Meth, dolly	Synthetic (morphine-like)				Yes	Yes
Barbiturates	Barbs, red devils, yellow jackets, phennies, peanuts, blue heavens, candy	Synthetic	Impulsiveness, dramatic mood swings, bizarre thoughts, suicidal behavior, slurred speech, disorientation, slowed mental and physical functioning, limited attention span	Weakness, restlessness, nausea and vomiting, headache, nightmares, irritability, depression, acute anxiety, hallucinations, seizures, possible death	Confusion, decreased response to pain, shallow respiration, dilated pupils, weak and rapid pulse, coma, possible death	Yes	Yes
Alcohol	Booze, juice, sauce	Natural (from fruits, grains)	Drowsiness, decreased alertness and inhibitions	Delirium tremens (hallucinations, disorientation, convulsions, nausea, anxiety)	Toxic psychosis, addiction, neurologic damage, stupor, liver damage, obesity, violence, death	Yes	Yes
STIMULANTS Amphetamines	Bennies, dexies, hearts, pep pills, speed, lip proppers, wake-ups	Synthetic	Increased confidence, mood elevation, sense of energy and alertness, decreased appetite, anxiety, irritability, insomnia, transient drowsiness, delayed orgasm	Apathy, general fatigue, prolonged sleep, depression, disorientation, suicidal thoughts, agitated motor activity, irritability, bizarre dreams	Elevated blood pressure, increase in body temperature, face-picking, suspiciousness, bizarre and repetitious behavior, vivid hallucination, convulsions, possible death	Yes	Yes
Cocaine	Coke, blow, toot, snow, lady, gold dust, crack, rock	Natural (from coca leaves)				Yes	Yes
Caffeine (coffee, tea, colas)	Java, coke	Natural	Mood elevation, irritability, increased metabolism rate, in some cases irregular heartbeat, hallucinations, convulsions	Severe headache, drowsiness	Jitteriness, insomnia	Possible	Yes

factors, such as your weight, amount of fat tissue, the time since your last meal, and how quickly you down your drinks.

Although its precise action is unknown, alcohol is thought to affect various chemicals that regulate the functioning of the brain (Loomis, 1982). The net result is that alcohol is a depressant; it acts to depress the central nervous system. People have the feeling of being more relaxed, talkative, or social after several drinks because alcohol is inhibiting brain cells, not stimulating them.

In moderate amounts, there is presently no evidence that alcohol destroys brain cells. However, after prolonged (many years) and heavy drinking, both humans and research animals were found to have significantly fewer brain cells (Golden et al., 1981; Walker et al., 1980). In addition,

TABLE 5.1   Major Substances Used for Mind Alteration (*continued*)

Drug	Slang Name	Source	Effects	Withdrawal Symptoms	Adverse/Overdose Reactions	Physical Addiction Potential	Psychological Dependence Potential
Tobacco	Fag, coffin nail	Natural	Mood elevation, increased heart rate and blood pressure	Irritability	Heart disease, lung disease	Possible	Yes
HALLUCINOGENS LSD	Electricity, acid, quasey, blotter acid, microdot, white lightning, purple barrels, big D, sugar, trips, cubes, windowpane	Semisynthetic (from ergot alkaloids)	Fascination with ordinary objects; heightened esthetic responses; vision and depth distortion; hear colors, see music; slowing of time; heightened sensitivity to faces, gestures; heightened emotions; paranoia, panic, euphoria, bliss, impairment of short-term memory, projection of self into dreamlike images	Not reported	Nausea, chills; increased pulse, temperature, and blood pressure; trembling, slow, deep breathing, loss of appetite, insomnia, longer, more intense "trips"; bizarre, dangerous behavior possibly leading to injury or death	No	Possible
Mescaline	Peyote buttons, mesc	Natural (from peyote cactus)	Similar to LSD but more sensual and perceptual; fewer changes in thought, mood and sense of self; vomiting	Not reported	Resemble LSD, but more bodily sensations, vomiting	No	Possible
Psilocybin	Mushrooms, shrooms, rooms	Natural (from fungus on a type of mushroom)	Similar to LSD but more visual and less intense; more euphoria, fewer panic reactions	Not reported	Resemble LSD, but less severe	No	Possible
Marijuana/ Hashish	Bhang, kif, ganja, dope, grass, pot, smoke, hemp, joint, weed, bone, Mary Jane, herb, tea, hash	*Cannabis sativa*	Euphoria, relaxed inhibitions, increased appetite, disoriented behavior	Hyperactivity, insomnia, decreased appetite, anxiety	Severe reactions are rare, but include panic, paranoia, fatigue, bizarre and dangerous behavior	No	Possible
Phencyclidine	PCP, angel dust, hog, rocket fuel, superweed, peace pill, elephant tranquilizer, dust, bad pizza	Synthetic	Increased blood pressure and heart rate; sweating, nausea, numbness, floating sensation, slowed reflexes, altered body image; altered perception of time and space; impaired short-term memory, decreased concentration, paranoid thoughts and delusions.	Not reported	Highly variable and possibly dose-related; disorientation, loss of recent memory, lethargy/stupor; bizarre and violent behavior, rigidity and immobility; mutism, staring, hallucinations and delusions, coma	No	Possible

Source: Compiled from J. Kaufman, H. Schaffer, and M. E. Burglass. 1983. The clinical assessment and diagnosis of addiction. II: The biological basics—drugs and their effects. In T. Bratter and G. Forrest, eds., *Current Treatment of Substance Abuse and Alcoholism.* New York: Macmillan; and *Teaching About Drugs: A Curriculum Guide, K–12,* by the American School Health Association and the Pharmaceutical Manufacturers Association.

prolonged and heavy drinking causes severe deficits in reasoning, memory, and motor skills (Grant, 1987).

When college students were asked, "What is the most dangerous drug?" they ranked heroin #1 and alcohol as #3 or #4. However, as Figure 5.15 shows, alcohol in many ways is far more dangerous (Saxe et al., 1983).

About 30 percent of college students reported that drinking caused them problems in some areas of their lives. Sometimes people with drinking problems go on to become alcoholics. About 10 to 15 percent of the 100 million Americans who use alcohol are alcoholics (Chafetz, 1979). An **alcoholic** is usually defined as someone who has drunk heavily for a long period of time and has had problems in two or three major life areas, such

How does a person get to be an alcoholic?

as in social, personal, financial, medical, legal, or business matters. What kind of factors increase the chances or make a person prone to becoming an alcoholic?

EXPLORING PSYCHOLOGY Risk Factors for Alcoholism

Should I worry if my mother or father was an alcoholic?

Figure 5.15
Because it is associated with a number of serious problems, alcohol is one of our most dangerous drugs. In many cities, alcohol-related health problems are one of the five major causes of deaths, and are a leading cause of mental retardation as a result of fetal alcohol syndrome. The graph shows the contribution of alcohol to rates of violent and sudden death.

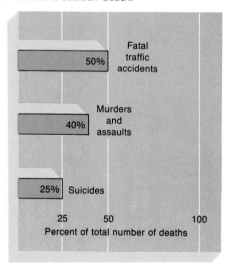

We have known for some time that a person's risk for becoming an alcoholic is increased 3 to 4 times if members of his or her family are alcoholics. Researchers have identified both genetic and environmental factors that explain why alcoholism runs in families. **Environmental factors** might include difficulties that children of alcoholic parents have in showing too much or too little trust and dependency in their relationships and careers. In turn, these psychological problems may lead to substance abuse by the adult children of alcoholic parents. Recently, researchers have identified a number of **genetic factors** that affect the physiological, neurological, and psychological functioning of children of alcoholics.

When researchers compared sons of alcoholic fathers to sons of non-alcoholic fathers, none of the sons was an alcoholic at the time of the study. With the same level of alcohol in their bloodstreams, the sons of alcoholic fathers reported less intoxication than the sons without alcoholic fathers. This suggests a *physiological* difference in metabolism of alcohol in sons of alcoholic fathers (Schuckit, 1987). In addition, when their brain waves were compared, sons of alcoholic fathers had a different pattern than sons of nonalcoholic fathers. This suggests a *neurological* difference in how information is processed and remembered (Begleiter et al., 1984).

Dr. Robert Cloninger (1987) and his associates have found that certain genetic predispositions increase the risk for alcoholism. They identified these predispositions by studying the contributions of heredity and environment in babies who were adopted at birth. Some of the babies had biological parents who were alcoholics and some had biological parents who were not alcoholics. In most cases, the babies were adopted by parents who were not or did not become alcoholics.

The researchers wanted to learn if babies of alcoholic parents would still be at risk for developing alcoholism if they were adopted and raised by nonalcoholics. They discovered that babies of alcoholic parents, even when adopted by nonalcoholics, were 3 or 4 times more likely to become alcoholics than babies born to nonalcoholics. Cloninger also found evidence for two different subgroups of potential alcoholics, which were called alcoholic-seeking types and loss-of-control types. Each type had different personality traits and courses of development.

Alcohol-seeking behavior, which contributes to developing alcoholism, begins in adolescence and early adulthood. An alcohol-seeking person tends to act impulsively, take risks, and engage in antisocial acts, such as fighting in bars. **Loss-of-control behavior,** which also contributes to developing alcoholism, begins in late adulthood. The personality associated with this behavior includes a tendency to be emotionally dependent, rigid, and introverted, and to feel fearful and guilty about developing a dependency on alcohol. Having a loss-of-control personality, which is more characteristic of women alcoholics, increased the risk 3 to 4 times for becoming an alcoholic.

Cloninger and his associates concluded that a predisposition for either alcohol-seeking or loss-of-control behavior might indeed be inherited. They believe that these two different personality types may reflect different brain systems that activate, modify, inhibit, or maintain a person's response to alcohol and the environment. The result is that these personality types increase the risk for developing alcoholism (Cloninger, 1987; Cloninger et al., 1981).

What Does "At Risk" Mean?

The first thing to note is that the term being at risk for alcoholism only means an increased chance of developing the problem. Being at risk does not mean that a person will develop the problem. A child with alcoholic parents runs the risk of developing alcoholism in the same way that children with diabetic parents run the risk of developing diabetes.

The second thing to note is that knowing one is at risk for developing alcoholism is likely to induce a person to take extra steps to avoid the problem. In the latter case, children of alcoholics need to be especially careful in their use of alcohol, just as children of diabetic parents need to be especially alert in watching their weight and diet.

Finally, it is important to note that not every child of an alcoholic parent becomes an alcoholic. Environmental variables, such as childhood experiences, quality of home life, and various other stress factors, interact with inherited dispositions in the development of alcoholism (Zucker & Gomberg, 1986). From the data above, it should be clear that there is a relationship between heredity and environment in the development of complex behaviors.

STIMULANTS

Cocaine

Approximately 4 to 5 million Americans use cocaine monthly, and about 1 million experience problems with cocaine usage. About 130,000 metric tons of cocaine were imported into the United States in 1985, with a street value of about $25 billion.

The major reason for the popularity of cocaine, which is often snorted through the nose, is its ability to produce bursts of energy, arousal, and alertness. Users tend to feel euphoric, self-confident, and certain that they are thinking more clearly than ever before. People who are on cocaine usually overestimate their own capacities or the quality of their work. In moderate doses, the main difference between cocaine and amphetamine is that cocaine is short acting (the high lasts 10 to 30 minutes), while the effects of amphetamine usually last for several hours.

Regular use of cocaine in purified form, such as by smoking, can result in addiction and serious health problems (Figure 5.16). In addition, high doses may trigger profound depression when the cocaine wears off. The user may smoke more cocaine to escape the depression, and begin a vicious circle. If cocaine is causing the user problems, he or she may have to seek professional help to stop the habit and treat the problems.

Caffeine and Nicotine

One cup of regular coffee, two cups of regular tea, one No Doz pill, two diet Cokes, and about four chocolate bars all contain about the same amount of caffeine, 100 milligrams. Far less powerful than cocaine, caffeine is a mild stimulant that affects the autonomic nervous system and produces such symptoms as increased heart rate and a mild feeling of alertness or arousal (Zahn & Rapoport, 1987). Drinking 2 to 3 cups of coffee a day will not cause addiction, but 5 to 6 cups might cause addiction as

Figure 5.16
What cocaine can do to the body. From G. Maranto (1985). Coke: The random killer. *Discovery*, March, p. 18.

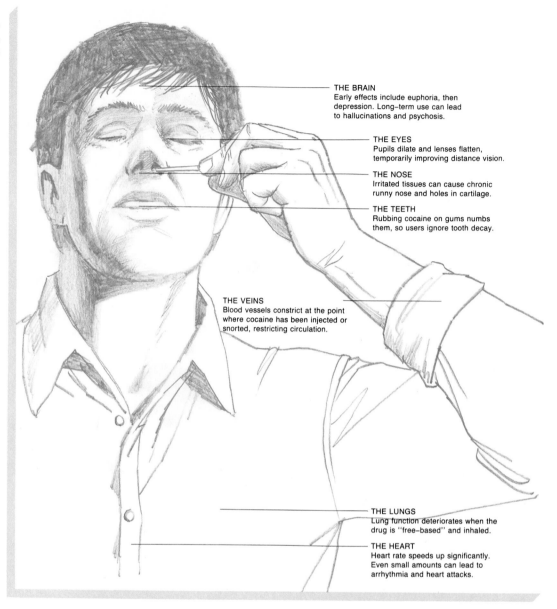

THE BRAIN
Early effects include euphoria, then depression. Long–term use can lead to hallucinations and psychosis.

THE EYES
Pupils dilate and lenses flatten, temporarily improving distance vision.

THE NOSE
Irritated tissues can cause chronic runny nose and holes in cartilage.

THE TEETH
Rubbing cocaine on gums numbs them, so users ignore tooth decay.

THE VEINS
Blood vessels constrict at the point where cocaine has been injected or snorted, restricting circulation.

THE LUNGS
Lung function deteriorates when the drug is "free–based" and inhaled.

THE HEART
Heart rate speeds up significantly. Even small amounts can lead to arrhythmia and heart attacks.

well as sleeplessness, periods of depression when the caffeine wears off, and heart problems. Now that the potential health hazards of caffeine have become public knowledge, the percentage of coffee drinkers in the United States has declined from 75 percent in 1962 to 52 percent in 1985.

Similar to caffeine, nicotine, which is present in tobacco, is a mild stimulant. Among its primary physiological effects, nicotine causes a smoker's average heart rate throughout the day to be 8 to 10 times faster than a nonsmoker's. Among its psychological effects, nicotine had been reported to improve concentration, short-term memory, and other cognitive skills (Edwards, 1986). However, the regular use of nicotine results in addiction and this makes stopping smoking more difficult. In 1985, nicotine caused 60 times more deaths from lung and heart diseases than cocaine and far more deaths than any other drug (Figure 5.17). In addition, recent evidence indicates that nonsmokers who are exposed to smoke have increased respiratory problems and chances of getting lung cancer (Holden, 1986). Because of the well-publicized health threats of nicotine, cigarette smoking among American adults in 1986 dropped to 31 percent, the lowest since the survey was begun in 1944.

HALLUCINOGENS

These drugs are so named because they produce hallucinations that may be so vivid the user believes they are real. Common hallucinogens include LSD, mescaline (derived from peyote cactus), psilocybin (found in certain mushrooms), and PCP (commonly called angel dust). Of these, PCP is the most dangerous. Moderate and high doses may produce feelings of sensory overload, agitation, violence, aggression, and psychotic reactions. The most serious problem with all hallucinogens is having panic attacks or bad trips and flashbacks. Flashbacks, which may or may not be pleasant, occur weeks or months after drug usage.

Marijuana

The most widely used illegal drug in the United States is marijuana. In a 1985 survey, 18 million said they had used marijuana in the month before the survey. Approximately 10 million tons of marijuana were used in 1985 with a street value of $45 billion. However, the monthly use of marijuana among high school seniors has declined from 37 percent in 1978 to 26 percent in 1985 (Kozel & Adams, 1986).

People who use marijuana report getting a "high," which includes some of the following experiences. Users report that marijuana intensifies sensations, such as making music sound fuller and foods taste better. It also may change perceptions so that ordinary events seem more interesting or funnier, or events that normally last seconds seem to last minutes. But marijuana may also heighten or distort unpleasant experiences, moods, or feelings. For instance, if a person is anxious, tense, or frightened to begin with, marijuana may dramatically increase these negative feelings. Thus, the experience produced by marijuana seems to depend upon and vary with the user's initial feelings and mood.

Researchers know that the experience of getting high is caused by marijuana's active ingredient, tetrahydrocannabinol, or THC, but it has

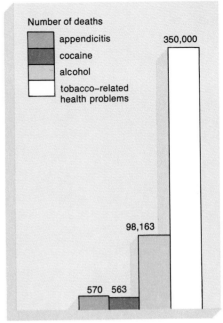

Figure 5.17

The number of deaths caused by drugs in 1985, compared with the number of deaths caused by appendicitis. As is clear from the graph, tobacco- and alcohol-related health problems are significant causes of death in our society.

MAJOR CONCEPT   Drugs and Awareness

Millions of people use drugs to alter their awareness, mood, or feelings.

Match each drug or class of drugs with its appropriate description.

1. Alcohol
2. Marijuana
3. Hallucinogens
4. Stimulants
5. Nicotine

a. _3_ LSD, psilocybin, and PCP are examples; they cause vivid perceptual distortions

b. _5_ This drug is responsible for more deaths than any other drug.

c. _4_ Amphetamine, cocaine, caffeine, and nicotine are examples; they cause arousal and alertness.

d. _1_ If a person's blood level of this is 0.1, he or she is legally drunk in most states.

e. _2_ Its active ingredient is THC; it heightens sensations but also impairs short-term memory and physical coordination.

Answers: a (3); b (5); c (4); d (1); e (2)

not yet been determined how marijuana affects the brain to produce these effects. We also know that recent street samples of marijuana are 10 times more potent than samples taken 10 years ago (Cohen, 1986). This means that present-day marijuana may produce experiences and problems that are more intense and last longer.

The National Institutes of Mental Health asked a panel of 22 scientists to evaluate hundreds of marijuana studies (Relman, 1982). As we tell you the panel's conclusions, remember that the effects are related to dosage, with stronger effects at higher doses. Marijuana causes the same kinds of respiratory problems as smoking tobacco. Indeed, marijuana smoke contains 50 percent more cancer-causing substances than tobacco smoke. Marijuana also causes a modest decrease in male hormones and sperm, but these effects are reversible. The panel found no conclusive evidence that prolonged marijuana use causes permanent changes to the brain or nervous system. Marijuana temporarily impairs learning ability, short-term memory, physical coordination, and attention span. For these reasons, a person who is under the influence of marijuana should not be at the controls of a car, plane, or boat.

Unlike what was believed in the 1970s, marijuana is not a safe drug. Continuing research leaves little doubt that regular marijuana use has the potential for many physical and psychological problems.

APPLYING PSYCHOLOGY   Treatment of Drug Abuse

Can I solve my drug problem on my own?

We began this Module with a description of Jeff's drug problems. We would like to continue his story because it illustrates some of the steps involved in drug treatment.

For a long time, Jeff believed that he was using drugs for recreation and he could cut down any time he wished. After continued problems, he was forced to admit that it was impossible for him to stop; he was addicted.

The first step in treatment is to admit that you have a drug problem. The next step is to get help. Jeff sought help from a local Narcotics Anonymous (N.A.) center. Because Jeff had sufficient motivation, personal resources, and skills, he was able to live at home while being treated on an outpatient basis. During the course of his treatment, Jeff learned that he needed to change his friends, habits, and desires.

In other cases, because of the seriousness of the problem, need for intensive treatment, or lack of motivation on the part of the drug user, it may be best for a person to enter an inpatient treatment center. Here is an example of what happens at one such facility. Although this center is for alcoholics, its approach is typical of many drug treatment programs.

After being admitted, the alcoholic undergoes a complete medical checkup and a two-week period of detoxification. The client then discusses his or her treatment program with members of the treatment team, which usually consists of a physician, psychologist, counselor, and nurse. One part of this program involves aversive conditioning, in which drinking alcohol is associated with nausea and vomiting so that these unpleasant sensations are evoked whenever the client takes a drink. Not all programs use aversive conditioning. By itself, aversive conditioning is only moderately effective once the client leaves the treatment program. For this reason, the client is counseled on how to replace alcohol with relaxation training and other activities. Group discussions enable clients to share their experiences, make plans for the future, and encourage each other to stay sober. Family workshops help both the client and his or her family members to work out their problems and learn to alter behavior patterns that trigger the client's alcohol abuse.

A psychologist helps the client to deal with psychosocial problems that might contribute to or intensify alcohol or drug abuse, such as shyness, unassertiveness, or poor social skills. Finally, an aftercare plan is set up to provide the client with continued support. Aftercare might include referrals to Alcoholics Anonymous (AA) or family therapy. For a year after inpatient treatment is completed, the client must return at least seven times for additional sessions of aversive conditioning, counseling, and evaluation. Additional appointments can be made as needed. Of the clients who completed the treatment program discussed here, 54 percent remained abstinent (did not drink) for at least 12 months (Neubuerger et al., 1982). This compares with an abstinence rate of about 33 percent for 12 months for most treatment programs (Holden, 1987). The goal of alcohol treatment programs is total abstinence, because most alcoholics are unable to drink socially or in moderate amounts (Helzer et al., 1985; Nathan & Skinstad, 1987; Nordstrom & Berglund, 1987).

REVIEW

Millions of people use drugs to change their awareness, mood, and feelings. Alcohol, morphine, and heroin, which depress the activity of the central nervous system and cause relaxation, decreased attention, and apathy, are called (1) _____. Cocaine, amphetamine, caffeine, and nicotine, which increase the activity of the peripheral and central nervous systems and cause arousal, alertness, and euphoria, are called (2) _____. Psilocybin (mushrooms), LSD, and marijuana, which act on chemicals in the brain and cause hallucinations and altered perceptions, are called (3) _____.

When Judy began smoking, she felt alert after a couple of cigarettes. After smoking for a couple of weeks, she had to smoke 10 to 15 cigarettes to get the same feeling. The fact that Judy had to smoke more cigarettes to get the same behavioral effect means that she had built up a (4) _____ to nicotine. Her constant intake of nicotine has caused her body to need nicotine for normal functioning. If she were to stop smoking, she would probably have headaches and feel irritable, both (5) _____ symptoms. Because Judy needs nicotine for normal functioning and would experience withdrawal symptoms if she stopped, we can say that she is physically (6) _____ to nicotine. When Judy cut her smoking down to three cigarettes a day, she was no longer addicted, but she still looked forward to and craved smoking her three cigarettes. Her strong desire indicates that she has developed a psychological (7) _____ on cigarettes.

When Judy goes to a party, she likes to have a few drinks to help her relax. One of the reasons that alcohol makes her feel more relaxed is because alcohol affects the amount of chemicals that carry messages between brain cells. These chemicals are called (8) _____. Another reason drinking helps her feel relaxed is that she has developed certain (9) _____ about what alcohol will make her feel.

If Judy drank four or five drinks in an hour, her blood alcohol level, which is abbreviated (10) _____, might reach 0.1 percent. At this level, she would feel intoxicated, probably talk loudly, have problems with coordination, and be considered legally (11) _____ in most states. It takes years of heavy drinking before alcohol destroys cells in the (12) _____ and causes severe deficits in reasoning and memory.

Of the millions of people who drink alcohol, some may develop drinking problems, which may lead to alcoholism. If a person has drunk heavily for long periods of time and has had problems in two or three major life areas, he or she would be called an (13) _____.

Researchers have identified a number of inherited

or (14) _____ components which make becoming an alcoholic 3 to 4 times more likely for children of alcoholic parents. Adolescents and young adults who act impulsively, take risks, and engage in anti-

social behaviors are said to have (15) _____ -

_____ behavior. Middle aged adults who are emotionally dependent, rigid, and introverted and feel guilty about depending on alcohol, are said to have

(16) _____ - _____ - _____ behavior. People who inherit predispositions for either of these behavior types are at an increased risk for becoming an alcoholic. However, being at risk for alco-

holism does not mean that one will (17) _____ become an alcoholic. This is because there is always an interaction between heredity and environment.

People use stimulants such as amphetamines or

(18) _____ to produce arousal, alertness, and feelings of euphoria. At high doses of cocaine, it

is likely that the user will become (19) _____ to the drug. Between feelings of euphoria, the chronic user of cocaine will experience severe periods of

(20) _____. The heavy cocaine user may need outside help to treat his or her problem.

A mild stimulant found in coffee, tea, and chocolate is (21) _____. Drinking 5 to 6 cups of coffee a day may result in addiction, sleeplessness,

mild depression, and heart problems. A mild stimulant found in cigarette tobacco and smoke is (22) _____. Daily cigarette smoking boosts heart rate, the risk for respiratory and throat problems, and results in addiction.

Drugs such as LSD, mescaline, psilocybin, PCP, and higher doses of marijuana produce vivid experi-

ences called (23) _____. The major problems with these drugs is the occurrence of flashbacks and bad trips.

The most widely used illegal drug in the United

States is (24) _____. This drug heightens sensations, distorts perceptions, and enhances the user's initial mood and feelings, either positive or negative. Regular use of marijuana can cause respiratory problems and impair learning ability and short-term memory. Because marijuana distorts time and impairs motor

coordination, it (25) _____ the user's ability to operate a motor vehicle.

If Judy had a serious drug problem, the first thing

she would have to do is to (26) _____ the problem. The second thing would be to seek treatment on either an outpatient or inpatient basis. Treatment programs use many different approaches, including

aversive (27) _____, individual and group counseling, family sessions, and therapy for psychosocial problems. When the person leaves the program, it is important that he or she continues to receive help and support.

Answers: (1) depressants; (2) stimulants; (3) hallucinogens; (4) tolerance; (5) withdrawal; (6) addicted; (7) dependency; (8) neurotransmitters; (9) expectations; (10) BAL; (11) drunk; (12) brain; (13) alcoholic; (14) genetic; (15) alcohol-seeking; (16) loss-of-control; (17) automatically, necessarily; (18) cocaine; (19) addicted; (20) depression; (21) caffeine; (22) nicotine; (23) hallucinations; (24) marijuana; (25) impedes, lessens, decreases; (26) admit, recognize; (27) conditioning

GLOSSARY TERMS

addiction (p. 155)
alcoholic (p. 159)
alcohol-seeking behavior
  (p. 160)

dependency (p. 155)
depressants (p. 155)
environmental factors
  (p. 160)

genetic factors (p. 160)
hallucinogens (p. 155)
loss-of-control behavior
  (p. 160)

stimulants (p. 155)
tolerance (p. 155)

PERSONAL NOTE

Research on sugar pills or placebos indicates that their effectiveness depends on the strength of your expectations and beliefs. Your expectations will be stronger and make the placebos more effective if you take two because you believe that two pills are stronger than one, if they taste slightly bitter because you believe that medicine should have a slightly unpleasant taste, and if they are colored because you believe that medicine should come in colored capsules (Moerman, 1981). These findings help solve a very important problem. If you eat M&Ms, you will discover a certain color that you like least. You can either throw these away, save them for last, or try to trade them. Now there is another possibility. Put them into a medicine bottle and use them as placebos. I have a whole bottle of brown ones and they are very effective for insomnia.   —R.P.

6

Learning

Module 16 Classical Conditioning

From the time he was about 5, Rod's favorite food was peanut butter. Some days he would eat it right out of the jar. Other days he would make elaborate sandwiches with layers of peanut butter, jelly, and bananas. His mother would allow him to eat only two of these at any one time. There were days when Rod waited for hours to have his peanut butter at night, on top of ice cream. He would keep eating the peanut butter off the top and piling more on until his mother finally said, "That's enough, Rod." Rod's favorite times were when he and his dog ate peanut butter together. They would sit on the back steps, and Rod would take one spoonful for himself and give one to his dog. The only thing that stopped them from eating a whole jar was Mother's stern warning: "It will make the dog sick."

Then came a day that began like all others but ended sadly. Rod's mother was suddenly called to help a neighbor. When she left, she said: "I'll be back in an hour. You be good." Rod knew exactly what he would do. He got out a full jar of peanut butter and a spoon and sat on the steps with his dog. They ate peanut butter spoonful by spoonful until the jar was empty. When Rod's mother returned, she found him lying on the couch. He said he felt sick. The dog looked sick too. Rod became more and more nauseated and finally had to vomit. For the first time in his entire life, he hated the taste of peanut butter. He couldn't even stand the thought of eating it. Ten years passed before he tried to eat peanut butter again. Although he can eat it now, his passion for it has never returned (author's files).

What caused Rod to give up peanut butter for ten years is technically called a *taste aversion*. After a taste is associated with nausea, vomiting, or illness, a person or animal will avoid that taste in the future. Taste aversions to distinctive or novel substances appear to be acquired more easily. A majority of college students reported having at least one taste aversion, usually involving alcohol, that they acquired after a single association and that lasted an average of 4 to 5 years. (Logue et al., 1981; Rozin, 1986).

If you have acquired a taste aversion, you have had an unpleasant learning experience. **Learning** is defined as a relatively permanent change in *behavior* resulting from experience. The term **behavior** is defined very broadly to include reflexes, voluntary behaviors, verbal behaviors, unobservable behaviors, such as thinking, or even neural activities in the brain.

Taste aversions also occur in animals. Farmers have discovered that poisoned baits used to eliminate rats may gradually lose their effectiveness. The reason: rats that eat a small amount of the bait and manage to survive

On the left, a bluejay is eating a poisonous monarch butterfly. On the right, the bird is trying to cough up the butterfly. The monarch butterfly contains poisons that make the bluejay sick. Through classical conditioning, the bluejay will learn to associate monarch butterflies with being sick and to avoid eating them. (Left and right, Lincoln P. Brower)

have learned a taste aversion. They avoid the bait in the future because it has been associated with sickness. Ingenious researchers have put this finding to practical use. They have baited sheep ranges with pieces of sheep flesh laced with chemicals that make coyotes very ill. The coyotes that eat this bait thereafter tend to avoid attacking sheep (Garcia et al., 1974). Without realizing it, Rod, the rats, and the coyotes have acquired their taste aversions through a process called classical conditioning.

WHAT IS CLASSICAL CONDITIONING?

You can think of **classical conditioning** as arranging two events so that a person or animal forms an association between them. For example, when Rod tasted peanut butter and then became sick, he formed an association between the taste of peanut butter and nausea. Such an association is the basis of classical conditioning.

Psychologists once believed that classical conditioning could take place only when the two events to be associated occurred very close together—usually with one following just seconds after the other. The example of learned taste aversions shows, however, that this initial assumption was not entirely correct. Rod's nausea occurred some time after his peanut butter binge, yet he still learned to hate peanut butter. Apparently, in some cases one event need not follow another *immediately* in order for classical conditioning to occur. What is important is that one event *predicts* the occurrence of another (Mackintosh, 1983; Rescorla, 1966). For Rod, eating peanut butter predicted his becoming sick, and so he became susceptible to classical conditioning. With this basic requirement in mind, let's see how some other classically conditioned responses are acquired.

ACQUIRING A CLASSICALLY CONDITIONED RESPONSE

Why do you grow tense at the sound of the dentist's drill?

As you waited in the dentist's chair for your first tooth filling, the various sights, sounds, and odors meant very little to you. Your reactions to them were probably quite neutral. But then the drilling started. Because of the general discomfort and occasional pain you experienced, your muscles automatically grew tense and your palms sweaty. When you left the office, you were no longer the naive child who had entered. The next time you sat in the dentist's chair and heard the whine of the drill, your muscles tensed and your palms perspired even before the drill touched your tooth.

What you acquired here was a classically conditioned reaction to a certain sound (the dentist's drill) because that sound had been associated previously with pain. For you, the drill had come to *predict* the onset of pain, and you reacted to it as if pain were actually occurring. The dentist's office is such an effective setting for classical conditioning that approximately 6 percent of the population avoids dental treatment out of fear arising from the very thought of someone working on their teeth (Bernstein & Kleinknecht, 1982).

Sam was a subject in a classical conditioning experiment. Now whenever someone whistles, his right eye blinks. As we describe how Sam's eyeblink was conditioned, we will introduce you to the procedures used to study classical conditioning and to the special vocabulary used in these procedures.

In Sam's experiment, there were two important stimuli. **A stimulus** is any change of energy to which someone is capable of reacting (sight, sound, smell, taste, or touch). One of the stimuli was the sound of a whistle; the other was a puff of air blown through a small tube near Sam's eye. Sam's physical reactions are called his **responses.** In this case, as in all classical conditioning studies, the researchers are interested in an innate, automatic response that requires no conscious effort. These automatic responses are called reflexes.

Not surprisingly, when a small puff of air is directed at Sam's eye, he blinks reflexively. The eyeblink in this case is called the **unconditioned response** because it is not learned; instead, it is built right into Sam's nervous system. The puff of air is similarly called the **unconditioned stimulus** because this stimulus elicits a response that is automatic and unlearned. The word "elicit" here is carefully chosen: the unconditioned stimulus automatically produces the reflex response without any effort or thinking on Sam's part.

In contrast to the puff of air, the sound of the whistle does not at first cause an eyeblink response. The whistle is called a **neutral stimulus** because it does not elicit the eyeblink. This neutrality, however, does not last long. Immediately after the researchers sound the whistle, they direct a puff of air at Sam's eye. Sam, of course, blinks. This procedure is repeated several times. Notice that it is fulfilling the basic requirement for classical conditioning: two events are being paired close together in time, so that the whistle comes to *predict* the occurrence of the puff. Now when the re-

Why would a whistle cause an eyeblink?

While studying salivation in dogs, Russian scientist Ivan Pavlov discovered the basic principles of classical conditioning. These principles explain why the person sitting in the dentist's chair will develop a fear of various stimuli associated with painful drilling.
(Left, The Bettman Archive; right, Joel Gordon)

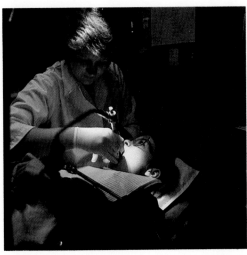

searchers sound the whistle and do not follow it by the puff, Sam's eye blinks anyway.

At this point, we can say that the sound of the whistle has become a **conditioned stimulus** eliciting a **conditioned response,** an eyeblink. The term "conditioned" in both cases means that the connection between the stimulus and the response has been learned through a prior association. Compared with the unconditioned response, the conditioned response is usually similar in appearance but smaller in magnitude. Sam's eye blinks at the sound of the whistle presented alone, but the blink is not as strong as that elicited by a puff of air.

Now let's apply the terminology of classical conditioning to the learning that occurs in the dentist's chair. On your very first trip to the dentist, the whining sound of the drill is a neutral stimulus; it means nothing to you. But then this sound is immediately followed by the discomfort of having a tooth drilled. The drilling is an unconditioned stimulus that elicits the unconditioned response of discomfort and anxiety, tensed muscles and sweaty palms. The next time you go to the dentist, the sound of the drill alone produces physiological signs of discomfort and anxiety. The drill sound, in other words, has become a conditioned stimulus for the conditioned response of anxiety.

You can apply this knowledge of classical conditioning to many everyday situations. Why do some of us feel a knot in the stomach when we sit at a desk to take a final exam? Why do some of us feel our hearts skip a beat when we see a doctor with a hypodermic needle? Why do some of us

---

MAJOR CONCEPT   Classical Conditioning

Ivan Pavlov was studying salivary functions when he noticed that his dogs showed the salivary reflex *before* food was placed in their mouths. They salivated at the sight and smell of food and even at the appearance of the assistant who normally brought food. This led Pavlov to conclude that salivating in anticipation of food is a learned response. To find out how this learning takes place, he designed his famous experiments with dogs.

In one experiment, Pavlov measured how much saliva was secreted into a tube placed in a dog's cheek when food entered the animal's mouth. Next, Pavlov rang a bell just before the food was given. After several pairings of the bell and the food, the previously neutral bell began to elicit salivation. Eventually, the bell alone was enough to produce the response.

Now see if you can answer the following questions about this experiment:

1. The unconditioned stimulus was: _food in mouth_.
2. The unconditioned response was: _salivation reflex_.
3. The conditioned stimulus was: _Bell sound_.
4. The conditioned response was: _salivation at the sound of the bell_
5. Classical conditioning occurred because the conditioned stimulus repeatedly occurred _before_ the unconditioned stimulus.
6. Pavlov knew that classical conditioning had been accomplished when: _Bell alone elicited salivation_

salivation at the sound of the bell; 5 before; 6 the bell alone elicited salivation
Answers: 1 food in the mouth; 2 the salivation reflex; 3 the sound of a bell; 4

smile when we hear a song associated with a special person? Why do some of us salivate when we imagine a brownie topped with two scoops of ice cream and hot fudge sauce? The answer offered by classical conditioning is that these sights, sounds, and thoughts have become conditioned stimuli that elicit conditioned responses. For instance, after repeatedly being with someone who makes us happy while we hear a certain song, the song alone can make us smile even though the person is not there. We have acquired a learned association between two stimuli, so that one which was previously neutral elicits the emotional reaction automatically produced by the other. This is the essence of classical conditioning. Because classical conditioning was discovered by the famous Russian scientist Ivan Pavlov, it is sometimes called *Pavlovian conditioning.* Pavlov's procedure for conditioning dogs to salivate at the sound of a bell is described in the Major Concept box.

OTHER CONDITIONING CONCEPTS

Generalization and Discrimination

If a certain song makes you smile because it has been paired with a special person, might a similar song by the same performers also make you smile? If you think the answer to this question could be "yes," you already have an intuitive grasp of **stimulus generalization.** When a stimulus that is similar to, but not identical with, the conditioned stimulus elicits a conditioned response, this is called stimulus generalization. When Sam leaves the laboratory and hears a traffic cop's whistle, his eye may blink because the sound is very similar to the one he was conditioned to. In the study of learned taste aversions mentioned earlier, 29 percent of those surveyed reported that their aversions had generalized to similar-tasting foods. An aversion to fried chicken, for example, might spread to fried fish, while an aversion to Southern Comfort might generalize to most strong-tasting liquors (Logue et al., 1981). As you might expect, the response elicited by these generalized stimuli is not as strong as that elicited by the original conditioned stimulus. Still, some response does occur.

But Sam's eye does not blink in response to every sound he hears. Nor do people with learned taste aversions give up eating. The reason is that people learn to discriminate between stimuli. **Stimulus discrimination** means that we learn to make a particular response only to one of several similar stimuli. For example, hearing the sound of a dentist's drill was followed by your feeling pain, but hearing the sound of a carpenter's drill was not followed by an unpleasant sensation. Because the sound of the dentist's drill was followed by an unconditioned stimulus, pain, and the sound of the carpenter's drill was not followed by an unconditioned stimulus, you have learned to discriminate between these two sounds. Stimulus discrimination explains why only the sound of the dentist's drill elicits sweating and heart pounding.

Extinction and Spontaneous Recovery

The reason the dentist's chair continues to elicit anxiety responses from you is that the unconditioned stimulus, painful drilling, continues to be paired with it. If on your next visit to the dentist your cavities could be treated with a painless miracle drug, the dentist's chair would lose some of its ability to elicit nervous sweating in you. After many visits without pain, you might eventually stop sweating altogether. Psychologists would say that your classically conditioned fear had undergone **extinction.**

Extinction occurs when a conditioned stimulus is repeatedly presented *without* the unconditioned stimulus. As a result, the conditioned stimulus

If you're scared of snakes, are you scared of lizards?

Figure 6.1
Why would seven young geese follow Konrad Lorenz? Because they were exposed to Lorenz, rather than their mother, soon after birth. This early exposure resulted in a special form of learning, called *imprinting*, which results in the young geese responding to Lorenz as if he were their mother.
(Thomas McAvoy/Life Magazine)

no longer predicts the occurrence of the unconditioned stimulus. Because sitting in the dentist's chair no longer signals that painful drilling is about to start, the chair loses its power to evoke the reflex. After this conditioned response has undergone extinction, however, something strange may happen on one of your trips to the dentist. Sitting in the chair may once again elicit the old tensed muscles and sweaty palms. This phenomenon is called **spontaneous recovery**. It is as if the memory of the old association is unexpectedly revived. Spontaneous recovery, of course, probably will not last very long. If the conditioned stimulus is still not paired with the unconditioned stimulus, the recovered response will quickly undergo extinction.

If you want to get over a learned taste aversion, you can do so by using the principle of extinction. Shortly after you have acquired the aversion, force yourself to eat a small amount of the food. The first time you do this you may feel somewhat queasy, but you will not vomit. If you repeat the process, you will find you are less queasy the next time. By repeatedly tasting the food without becoming ill, you are extinguishing the conditioned response. Research has shown that people who follow this simple procedure overcome a taste aversion faster than those who simply try to forget the association between the food and nausea (Logue et al., 1981).

Prepared Learning

Why is it that rats can easily learn by taste, but not by sight, to avoid foods that made them ill? The answer is that rats have evolved very complex taste systems and not very good visual systems.

Why is it that soon after birth, goslings will follow almost any receding object that emits a certain "kum-kum" call and thereafter will treat that object like a parent? The answer is that goslings, chickens, and ducks have inherited tendencies to follow the first moving object that they encounter soon after birth. This tendency-to-follow is one of the primary ways that a young chick, duck, or gosling establishes a social attachment with a member of its species. The set of responses by which an animal establishes social attachments early in life is called **imprinting**. Figure 6.1 shows an example of goslings which have imprinted on a human.

James Gould and Peter Marler (1987) explain that some responses are learned more easily than others because animals, and perhaps humans, are *preprogrammed* to learn particular things in particular ways. They believe that animals are innately equipped to recognize, attend, and store certain cues over others, and this innate tendency is called **prepared learning**. For example, a chickadee, with its tiny bird brain, can remember the location of hundreds of hidden seeds while humans forget after hiding about a dozen. This means that animals are very smart in ways that are favored by natural selection and very stupid in other ways. For example, a cat required three weeks of training to learn to dunk its foot into a fishbowl, but it needed very little training to learn to hunt and capture prey, a response favored by natural selection (Figure 6.2). Contrary to what early behaviorists believed, not all responses can be conditioned with equal likelihood. Preprogramming, which is due to innate or inherited processes, may also occur in humans. For instance, many psychologists believe that human children may be preprogrammed to learn language (Module 22).

Importance of Ivan Pavlov

As we saw in the Major Concept, Ivan Pavlov clarified many of the principles of classical conditioning in his early experiments on the salivary response in dogs. Who would have guessed that something as unusual as conditioning salivation would have proved to be so important? As it has turned out, Pavlov's principles of classical conditioning underlie our un-

Figure 6.2
Why did Speedy the cat need three weeks of training before he learned to perform the relatively simple task of dunking his paw in a fishbowl? Check the text for the answer. (Moser, P. W., "Are cats smart? yes, at being cats." *Discover*, May 1987. Photo by Mark S. Wexler)

derstanding of so many different concepts, including taste aversion, sweating in the dentist's office, conditioned nausea, and the procedure of systematic desensitization.

| Conditioned Nausea and Treatment | **APPLYING PSYCHOLOGY** |

An hour earlier, Michelle had received her second chemotherapy treatment for breast cancer. Now she was feeling very nauseous, a side effect of the powerful anticancer drugs. Her nausea, accompanied by intense vomiting, would last for 6 to 12 hours. The medication that she had been given to control the terrible nausea was not working.

When Michelle arrived at the clinic for her third treatment, she began to feel nauseous while she was sitting in the waiting room. Michelle, like 25 to 35 percent of patients receiving chemotherapy, had developed nausea and vomiting in *anticipation* of the actual treatment.

Many researchers believe the nausea and vomiting that Michelle experienced in anticipation of her third chemotherapy treatment was established through classical conditioning (Andrykowski & Redd, 1987; Burish & Carey, 1986). When Michelle's treatments first began, the unconditioned stimulus, the chemotherapy, elicited the unconditioned response, nausea and vomiting. Various stimuli in the chemotherapy setting, such as sights, smells, and thoughts, were the conditioned stimuli. Then these sights, smells, and thoughts were paired with chemotherapy (unconditioned stimulus), which elicited Michelle's intense nausea and vomiting (unconditioned response). After several pairings, the conditioned stimuli begin to elicit the conditioned response, nausea and vomiting, before the actual chemotherapy even begins. Once established, conditioned nausea is very difficult to treat or control with medication.

The development of conditioned nausea is very similar to taste aversion (Bernstein, 1978). In both cases, the nausea develops after a few trials and several hours may elapse between the administration of the unconditioned stimulus (the chemotherapy) and the unconditioned response (nausea). However, in taste aversion, the nauseating substance can simply be avoided. In conditioned nausea that results from chemotherapy, the patient cannot avoid anticancer drugs because his or her life may depend upon them.

Michelle, who developed her conditioned nausea through classical conditioning, may be treated with a three-part procedure called **systematic desensitization,** also based on the principles of classical conditioning. First, Michelle is taught to relax by tensing and then relaxing sets of muscles, beginning with her toes and proceeding up to her head. Then, after practicing to relax for several weeks, she begins the second part by making up a list of 7 to 12 stressful situations associated with chemotherapy treatment. She arranges her list in a hierarchy from the least stressful situation, such as thinking about chemotherapy the next day, to the most stressful situation, such as driving to the clinic and entering the waiting room.

In the third part of the procedure, Michelle puts herself into a deeply relaxed state and then imagines the least stressful situation, such as the night before she has chemotherapy. She is told to remain in a relaxed state while imagining the situation. If she becomes stressed, she stops imagining the situation and returns to a relaxed state. Once she is sufficiently relaxed, she imagines the situation again. She proceeds up her hierarchy of stressful situations, trying to remain in a relaxed state. By imagining stressful situations while remaining in a relaxed state, Michelle is using classical conditioning to make new associations. She is trying to associate stressful situations with feelings of relaxation. Systematic desensitization was found to be significantly more effective than psychotherapy or relaxation alone in reducing conditioned nausea (Morrow, 1986). Notice that both the cause and treatment of conditioned nausea are based on the principles of classical conditioning.

REVIEW

George, a 34-year-old man was intensely fearful of the inside of automobiles. The fear had started four years previously. While waiting for a red light to change, his car was suddenly hit from behind. The impact thrust him forward so that his head struck the windshield. Although he was only slightly injured, he had panicked; he thought his last moment had come. Thereafter he was fearful not only of driving, but even of sitting in a parked car (adapted from Wolpe, 1981). George's fear of cars developed because he came to associate being in a car with a serious threat to his personal safety. The learning process through which this happened is called

(1) _Classical Conditioning_. Researchers who study classical conditioning are concerned with people's reflex responses to sights, sounds, and other

changes in energy, called (2) _Stimuli_.

In order for classical conditioning to occur, the two events that come to be associated usually must occur close together in time. Because one event rapidly

follows the other, the first is viewed as (3) _predicting_ the occurrence of the second. Usually the two events must be paired repeatedly for conditioning to occur. In the case of traumatic experiences, however, one pairing may be enough to establish a classically conditioned

fear. The same is true of taste aversions: once is enough. Some psychologists believe that aversions to tastes paired with nausea are established so quickly be-

cause this is a form of (4) _prepared_ learning, which helps organisms survive.

Before the accident, George had no aversion to cars. Driving a car at this stage was for him a

(5) _Natural_ stimulus. But when his car was hit from behind, George experienced a reflex response that included tensed muscles, a pounding heart, and rapidly increased breathing, which we will call a panic response. In the terminology of classical conditioning, the act of being hit and thrust against the glass is called

the (6) _Unc_ _Stim._, while the panic response that resulted is called the

(7) _Unc._ _resp._. Now George feels panic simply sitting in a car. The reason is that the sight of a car's interior has become a

(8) _Cont._ _Stim_ eliciting a

(9) _Cont_ _response_ of fear.

Even though the accident happened in his own

car, George has developed a fear of being in *any* automobile. In other words, he is showing stimulus

(10) _Generalization_. The fact that he does not feel panic when he rides on a bus is an example of stimulus

(11) _disc._.

If George could somehow be encouraged to drive a car again, and no more accidents happened to him, he would gradually lose his panic response because the conditioned stimulus and the unconditioned stimulus would no longer be paired. When the conditioned stimulus no longer elicits the conditioned response, we

say that the response has undergone (12) _extinction_.

Following extinction, however, there may come a time when being in a car unexpectedly produces the old feeling of fear. This phenomenon is known as

(13) _spont. recovery_.

The principles of classical conditioning are used

to explain how a person might develop (14) _conditioned_ nausea in anticipation of chemotherapy. This problem

can be treated with a procedure, called (15) _systematic desensitization_, which is based on the principles of classical conditioning.

Answers: (1) classical conditioning; (2) stimuli; (3) predicting; (4) prepared; (5) neutral; (6) unconditioned stimulus; (7) unconditioned response; (8) conditioned stimulus; (9) conditioned response; (10) generalization; (11) discrimination; (12) extinction; (13) spontaneous recovery; (14) conditioned; (15) systematic desensitization

GLOSSARY TERMS

behavior (p. 169)
classical conditioning
   (p. 170)
conditioned response
   (p. 172)
conditioned stimulus
   (p. 172)

extinction (p. 173)
imprinting (p. 174)
learning (p. 169)
neutral stimulus (p. 171)
prepared learning
   (p. 174)
responses (p. 171)

spontaneous recovery
   (p. 174)
stimulus (p. 171)
stimulus discrimination
   (p. 173)
stimulus generalization
   (p. 173)

systematic desensitization
   (p. 176)
unconditioned response
   (p. 171)
unconditioned stimulus
   (p. 171)

Module 17 Operant Conditioning and Observational Learning

John's favorite snack was a chocolate chip cookie. Or sometimes a butter cookie. But never an apple. For 15 straight days in preschool, his teacher offered him a choice between a cookie snack and an apple snack. Each day he chose the cookie.

Something happened to John on day 16 that made a great change in his choice of snack. On day 17 and for the next 15 days, John chose the apple over the cookie when the teacher offered him a choice. You are about to learn what happened to John on day 16 (adapted from Stark et al., 1986).

WHAT IS OPERANT CONDITIONING?

On Day 16, John was told that if he chose a healthy snack, such as an apple, he would get a toy and praise from the teacher. If he chose an

Figure 6.3
On days 1–15, when offered a choice between a cookie and an apple, John always picked the cookie. The text explains why on day 16 and thereafter, John picked the apple. (Adapted from Stark et al., 1986)

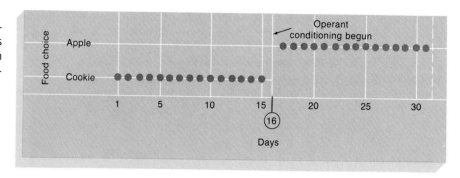

What made 4-year-old John turn down his favorite cookie?

unhealthy snack, such as a cookie, he would receive neither a toy nor praise. This procedure, which is called **operant conditioning,** is a kind of learning in which the consequences of a behavior influence whether a person or animal will perform the same behavior in the future. As you can see in Figure 6.3, operant conditioning produced a rapid and dramatic change in John's behavior. John learned that the choice of an apple would also bring him a toy and praise. These consequences influenced him to continue to make healthy snack choices in the future.

Operant and Classical Conditioning Compared.   Remember that in classical conditioning the responses to be learned were reflexes, such as blinking, sweating, salivating, or becoming nauseous. These responses are *elicited* automatically by stimuli such as a puff of air or the sound of a dentist's drill. The elicited behavior occurs whether the subject wants it to or not. In operant conditioning, in contrast, the behaviors to be learned are *voluntary*. Notice that in taking the apple snack offered by the teacher, John is performing a behavior on his own accord, or "operating" on his environment. Neither the teacher nor the sight of the snacks elicits John to do anything. Rather, John is purposely *emitting* a certain behavior because he has learned that it is advantageous for him to do so.

Although operant behaviors are voluntary, they are greatly influenced by the environment. In operant conditioning, the event that comes *after* the behavior—the consequences—may serve to increase or decrease the behavior. Receiving the teacher's praise and a toy after taking the apple increased the probability of John's choosing the apple in the future. In other words, it reinforced John's desire to select a healthy snack. Any stimulus that increases the probability of a behavior occurring again is called a **reinforcer.** On the other hand, any stimulus that decreases the probability of a behavior occurring again is called a **punisher.** If the teacher had reacted to John's snack choice by rebuking him or telling him that he would not be allowed to play with a favorite toy, John would be less likely to select that snack again. In classical conditioning, what happens *after* a person performs a conditioned response is not crucial. It is what happens *before* the conditioned response—the action of the unconditioned stimulus—that leads to the classically conditioned behavior.

To operantly condition John's snack-selection behavior, two events are necessary. First, John must voluntarily emit some behavior, such as take a piece of apple. Second, John's behavior must be followed immediately by a reinforcer. If we were trying to decrease the probability of John's taking a piece of apple, his behavior would be followed by a punisher. As these two conditions are repeated over and over, John learns a connection between his own behavior and certain consequences.

Importance of Edward Thorndike and B. F. Skinner.   In a laboratory experiment, American psychologist Edward Thorndike placed a hungry cat in a puzzle box that contained an escape latch. When the cat accidentally hit the latch, the door opened and the cat could escape and get a piece of fish. With repeated trials, the cat took less and less time to hit the latch, indicating that the cat had learned something through trial and error. B. F. Skinner, perhaps the best-known American psychologist of the twentieth century, followed up on Thorndike's studies of trial and error learning. Thorndike's and Skinner's work formed the basis for explaining many kinds of behaviors and led to the development of several therapeutic procedures. Let's see how Skinner might operantly condition a rat to press a lever and obtain food.

ESTABLISHING AN OPERANTLY CONDITIONED RESPONSE

Suppose it is 1930 and you are watching Skinner train a rat to press a lever. Skinner explains that since there are no levers in a rat's natural environment, it rarely presses them. However, since rats have a tendency to explore objects with their paws, it is relatively easy to train this behavior. He places a white rat in a small rectangular chamber that is empty except for a lever with a food cup below it. The chamber is bare to make it more likely that the rat will find and explore the lever. Forever after, and to Skinner's dismay, this kind of chamber will be called a Skinner box.

To ensure that the rat is active and susceptible to a food reward, Skinner has not fed it for many hours. A hungry rat tends to roam restlessly about, sniffing at whatever it finds. Skinner explains that as soon as the rat makes some move toward the lever, he will deliver a pellet of food. At that moment, the rat turns and faces the lever, and Skinner delivers a food pellet into the food cup. The rat approaches the food cup, discovers the pellet, and eats it. The rat now moves to the opposite side of the chamber, and Skinner watches it. When the rat once again faces the lever, Skinner does not deliver more food. Instead, he waits for the rat to perform some behavior that is slightly closer to the one ultimately desired.

Skinner's patience pays off, because the rat soon walks two steps toward the lever. Only now does Skinner release another pellet into the food cup. After eating the pellet, the rat wanders a bit but soon returns to the lever and actually sniffs it. A third pellet immediately drops into the cup, and the rat once again eats. When the rat places one paw on the lever, a fourth pellet drops into the cup. The final reward comes when the animal presses the lever downward. This process of gradually reinforcing behaviors leading up to a **target behavior** is called **shaping**.

Skinner explains that in shaping the reinforcer should follow *immediately* after the desired behavior. In this way, the rewarding consequence will come to be associated with the desired behavior and not with some other behavior that just happens to intervene. Skinner tells how he once delivered the food too late; by then, the rat was facing *away* from the lever, and it took quite a while to get the rat to give up this "wrong" behavior. Depending on the experience of the trainer and the rat, it usually takes from five minutes to an hour to get a rat to press a lever. As you might expect, Skinner accomplished the task in less than four minutes.

The key to operant conditioning, then, is selecting an observable target behavior and shaping the organism's behaviors toward it in small, incremental steps. After each closer approximation of the target behavior, the organism is immediately reinforced. You can apply your knowledge of operant conditioning to a real-life human example by reading and completing the Major Concept section on page 182.

How would you get a rat to press a lever?

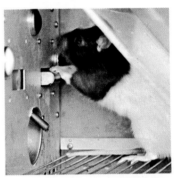

In a special compartment, called a Skinner box, a rat has learned to press a bar to obtain a drink of water. The Skinner box is an environment in which lights, sounds, rewards, and punishments can be controlled and in which the animal's behaviors, such as bar pressing, can be recorded. (Steve McCarroll)

Operant conditioning may be used to train a killer whale to perform routines and also to train a child to use a potty. (Left, Cheryl A. Traendly; right, Erika Stone)

GENERALIZATION, DISCRIMINATION, AND EXTINCTION

When John's regular teacher offered him a choice between an apple and a cookie, John took the apple because this behavior had been reinforced. When a substitute teacher offered John the same choice, he also took the apple. When John performed his taking-an-apple behavior in the presence of a new stimulus, the substitute teacher, he was showing *generalization*. In operant conditioning, generalization means that the person *emits* the behavior in the presence of a stimulus similar to the original stimulus that was present at the time the behavior was first reinforced.

At home, John's mother offers him a choice of an apple or cookie snack. As it turns out, John chooses the cookie snack about 50 percent of the time (Stark et al., 1986). This means that John has only partially generalized performing his take-the-apple behavior when in the presence of his mother. This means that the stimulus Mother is seen by John as generally similar to the stimulus Teacher.

When John visits his Aunt Martha, she offers him a choice between a cookie or an apple. John takes the cookie. In this case, John shows discrimination. *Discrimination* means that John usually performs his operantly conditioned behavior only in the presence of particular stimuli, such as his teacher and his mother, and not in the presence of different stimuli, such as Aunt Martha. After John takes the cookie, Aunt Martha says, "What a good boy!" This praise is certainly a reinforcer and will strengthen John's discrimination, making him more likely to take a cookie from his aunt but not from his teacher or mother.

If the teacher stops reinforcing John's taking-an-apple behavior, John will gradually stop taking the apple. When John's taking-an-apple behavior wanes because it is no longer reinforced, the process is called *extinction*. During extinction, John's taking-an-apple behavior will decline in frequency and eventually stop altogether. However, John may one day suddenly show the conditioned behavior and select an apple instead of a cookie. The recurrence of John's extinguished behavior is called *spontaneous recovery*. If John's taking-an-apple behavior is still not reinforced, it will undergo extinction once again, and it might not recover a second time. Remember that the terms generalization, discrimination, extinction, and spontaneous recovery are also used to describe similar phases of classical conditioning. But in classical conditioning, the terms refer to changes in *elicited* behaviors—that is, behaviors that occurred automatically in the presence of certain stimuli.

A CLOSER LOOK AT REINFORCERS

Positive and Negative Reinforcers

We know that John began to select an apple regularly when this behavior was followed by the teacher's praise and a toy. If a stimulus is presented immediately after a behavior and it increases the probability that the behavior will occur again, the stimulus is called a **positive reinforcer.** In John's case, the teacher's praise and receiving a toy are examples of positive reinforcers because they increased the likelihood of John's choosing an apple snack in the future.

Sometimes taking care of 10 little children is too much for John's nursery school teacher and she gets a headache. She takes two aspirin and the headache goes away. Now the teacher is likely to take aspirin for future headaches because the behavior of taking aspirin is followed by the removal of the headache, an unpleasant stimulus. In this case, the removal of the headache is called a **negative reinforcer.** As with positive reinforcement, negative reinforcement increases the likelihood that the behavior associated with it—such as taking an aspirin—will be continued. The concept of a negative reinforcer is difficult to get at first, so let's go over it again. First, the performance of some behavior is followed by the removal or avoidance of an unpleasant event. In our example, the performance of some behavior, taking aspirin, is followed by the removal of an unpleasant event, a headache. Therefore, taking aspirin is negatively reinforced by the removal of the headache. The negative reinforcer is the removal of the headache because it increases the probability that the teacher will take aspirin in the future.

Primary and Secondary Reinforcement

Suppose that, on average, you study two hours a day. If we want to increase your study time to four hours daily, how might we go about it? One way would be to provide you with food and water only when you had met the four-hour goal. In this case we would be using what psychologists call **primary reinforcers,** stimuli such as food, water, shelter, and sex that satisfy basic needs. But such an approach would not be very practical, and if we actually forced you to go hungry or thirsty, it would also be unethical.

If you were not wealthy and if you valued money, we could try another tactic. We could present you with $40 after you finished studying for four hours in any one day. In this case, we would be using what psychologists call a **secondary reinforcer**—some stimulus that has become associated with a primary reinforcer. Money, for instance, can buy food, clothing, shelter, and anything else required to satisfy basic needs.

For humans, stimuli may also become secondary reinforcers by being associated with positive personal experiences such as attention and affection from others. It is actually a process of classical conditioning that causes neutral stimuli to become secondary reinforcers. Money, praise, and high grades are all secondary reinforcers because they have been associated with primary reinforcers or positive experiences.

How often should you reinforce yourself for studying?

Schedules of Reinforcement

Suppose a rat is given a food pellet whenever it presses a lever, a boy is given a bag of M&Ms each time he cleans his room, and you are given $40 after every four-hour period you study. In these cases, you, the boy, and the rat have been placed on schedules of continuous reinforcement. A **continuous reinforcement schedule** is one in which every target behavior is followed by a reinforcer. Continuous reinforcement is often used in the initial stages of operant conditioning because it produces rapid learning of the behavior.

Now suppose the rat is given a pellet after every ten lever presses, the boy is presented with M&Ms every third time he cleans his room, and you are given $50 after a week of studying. In these cases, you, the boy, and the rat are on schedules of partial reinforcement. A **partial reinforcement**

MAJOR CONCEPT   Operant Conditioning

Two-year-old Johnny's mother has just acquired a book called *Toilet Training in Less Than a Day* (Azrin & Foxx, 1974). She plans to toilet train her son according to the operant conditioning techniques the book recommends. Before training begins, she puts away all Johnny's toys so he will not be distracted and then gives him a glass of apple juice so he will have to urinate soon. Every time Johnny performs a behavior that is closer to the desired behavior, he is given M&M candies or verbal praise and a hug. For instance, when Johnny enters the bathroom, his mother tells him, "That's a good boy," and when he lowers his pants by himself he is given a candy to eat. Soon Johnny is urinating into the toilet. His mother gives him a big hug.

1. Urinating in the toilet in this case is the _target behavior_.

2. Hugs, praise, and candies are providing _reinforcement_.

3. More specifically, a word of praise is an example of a _secondary reinforcement_
   while an M&M candy is an example of a _primary reinforcer_.

4. A reinforcer is any stimulus that _likelihood preceding behavior being repeated_

5. Johnny's mother has actually shaped his behavior, which means that she has _____.

6. Once Johnny learns to use the toilet consistently, his mother will begin to cut down on the number of reinforcers she gives him for doing so.
   In other words, she will place Johnny on a _____.

7. With intermittent rewards, Johnny's newly learned behaviors will be more _____.

Answers: 1 target behavior; 2 reinforcement; 3 secondary reinforcer, primary reinforcer; 4 increases the likelihood of the preceding behavior being repeated; 5 systematically rewarded behaviors closer and closer to the target behavior; 6 partial schedule of reinforcement; 7 resistant to extinction

schedule is one in which only some of the target behaviors are followed by reinforcers. After an operantly conditioned response has been established, it is not necessary to reinforce it continuously. In fact, a partial reinforcement schedule seems to be more effective in maintaining the behavior in the long run. Partial reinforcement schedules usually make behaviors more resistant to extinction because people expect that the next time will bring the payoff.

There are two basic procedures for partial reinforcement. With *ratio schedules*, reinforcement occurs after a certain *number* of target behaviors. With *interval schedules*, reinforcement follows the first target behavior that occurs after a certain period of *time* has elapsed. Either type of schedule can be *fixed* or *variable*.

Fixed-Ratio Schedule.   Suppose you were a factory worker who got paid or received a reinforcer after you had assembled 12 circuit boards. You would be on a fixed-ratio schedule, in which the reinforcement occurs after a fixed number of target behaviors, in this case, assembling 12 units. Since you know that the more sets of 12 units you assemble, the more payoffs you get, you tend to work as fast as possible (Figure 6.4). The reason this schedule is used in assembly plants is that people tend to maximize their effort on fixed-ratio schedules—the more work completed, the more the worker is paid.

Fixed-Interval Schedule.   Suppose that in five days you have an exam, which we will call a reinforcer. The first two days, you perform very little of the target behavior, studying. During the next two days, you study more and more and finally cram all morning before the exam. On a fixed-interval schedule, you receive a reinforcer (such as an exam) after performing a target behavior (such as studying) for a fixed-time interval, in this case, five days (Houston, 1976). What is characteristic of a fixed-interval schedule is its shape: a person or animal begins responding slowly, but as the time for the reinforcer draws near, the response rate accelerates markedly. This pattern of responding is called the scallop effect (Figure 6.4).

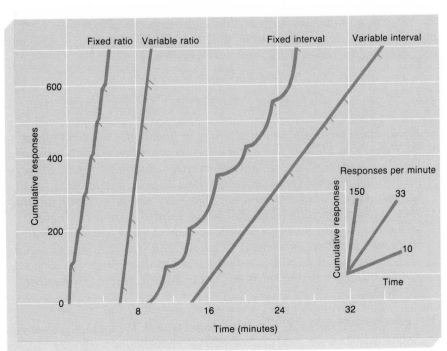

Figure 6.4
Each of these "lines" represents the behavior of a pigeon on a key. Each of the "blips" in the lines represents the occurrence of a reinforcer. The steepness of the line indicates the rate or speed of the pigeon's pecking ratio schedules, the reinforcer occurs after the performance of a certain number of target behaviors. In interval schedules, the reinforcer occurs after a certain amount of time has passed. (From J. L. Williams, 1973. *Operant Learning.* Monterey, CA: Brooks/Cole. Copyright © 1973 by Wadsworth Publishing Company, Inc. Used by permission of Brooks/Cole Publishing Company, Monterey, California 93940)

If you watch people play slot machines, you will notice that they do so in a speedy fashion. This is because slot machines have been programmed to reward the player on a schedule, called variable ratio, that promotes the fast responding. (Leif Skoogfors/Woodfin Camp and Associates)

Variable-Ratio Schedule. Suppose you are playing a slot machine that pays off after a certain number of pulls. As you play, you discover that the number of pulls to a payoff—the reinforcer—varies quite widely. For example, the slot machine may be set to pay off after 10, 83, 4, and 57 pulls. You conclude that the slot machine is on a variable-ratio schedule, which means that reinforcement occurs after an *average number* of target behaviors. Since you never know how many pulls will be needed to produce a payoff, this schedule generates a high rate of performance (Figure 6.4).

Variable-Interval Schedule. Suppose you are dialing a radio station's telephone number to see if you are the lucky caller to win $1,000. The target behavior is your dialing the number and the reinforcer is hearing the announcer's voice. Since you do not know when the line will be free, the best bet is to keep dialing the number at regular intervals. On a variable-interval schedule, the reinforcer occurs after an average amount of time has elapsed, with the actual time differing at intervals of, say, 60, 10, 23, and 42 seconds. A variable-interval schedule results in a more regular rate of responding than does a fixed-interval schedule (Figure 6.4).

PUNISHMENT AND ITS EFFECTIVENESS

A year-long crackdown on illegal drug use apparently has paid off for the Navy. The Atlantic fleet's crackdown began when officials estimated that 28.5 percent of its 250,000 sailors were using illicit drugs. Surveys in 1980 showed that the number may have been as high as 48.5 percent. As part of its war on drugs, the Navy has been stern with drug abusers, dismissing all officers and senior enlisted personnel caught with drugs, levying heavy fines on lower-ranking first offenders, and booting them out for subsequent violations. Since the crackdown began, urine analysis tests have shown that the use of illicit drugs has dropped to only 3.7 percent (adapted from the Los Angeles Times, *November 28, 1983).*

Judy, who is 5 years old, is grocery shopping with her mother. While her mother is looking for a salad dressing, Judy breaks open a bag of

*cookies and begins to eat them. Her mother finds the dressing and also
sees Judy eating her third cookie. She snatches the bag of cookies
away and grabs Judy by the arm, saying: "I've told you a thousand
times not to do that!" Judy throws a colossal temper tantrum. The
mother is embarrassed and warns Judy that when she gets home, her
father will punish her. The mother then goes to the checkout line with
Judy, who is now in the shopping cart, still crying loudly. As the
mother is placing items on the counter, Judy reaches through the bars of
the cart and takes a pack of chewing gum from the adjacent stand.
She opens the pack and puts a stick of gum in her mouth, trying to be
careful so that her mother doesn't see her (author's files).*

*Pete and Susan, both 6 years old, are playing in the sandbox at their
day school. Without warning, Susan grabs a handful of sand and
throws it in Pete's face. Pete's crying brings the teacher. In a sobbing
voice, Pete explains that Susan threw sand in his face and eyes and
mouth. The teacher tells Susan that she will have to spend 6 minutes
in the time-out room. She takes her to a small room containing only a
single chair and leaves the child there alone. Six minutes later, Susan
returns to play in the sandbox. The teacher reminds Susan that any
more sand throwing will result in a return to the time-out room. Susan
nods her head and begins to play with Pete. She doesn't throw sand at
Pete any more that day (adapted from Goldstein et al., 1981).*

These three examples illustrate the use of **punishment,** a consequence
that follow a particular behavior and decreases the likelihood of that behavior being repeated. In the first example, the threat of unannounced
tests, heavy fines, and immediate dismissals greatly suppressed illegal drug
use in the U.S. Navy. Although these results are impressive, it would be
interesting to know whether this crackdown increased the use of another
drug, such as alcohol. In the second example, the mother's use of punishment was clearly not effective. It did not prevent Judy from taking things
off the shelves. In the third example, however, punishment seemed to work
quite well. It suppressed Susan's sand throwing and had few undesirable
side effects. Why does punishment seem to work on some occasions and
not on others? Can we make any generalizations about when it will be most
effective?

For one thing, punishment is most effective when it *immediately* follows the unwanted behavior. Immediately after Susan threw sand, she was
sent to the time-out room. Judy's mother threatened future punishment.
Even if Judy's father *did* punish her when she got home, a great deal of
time would have elapsed before that punishment took place. Such a long
delay between an unwanted behavior and a negative consequence makes
the consequence ineffective.

One common misconception about punishment has to do with its
intensity. We often think we should start with a mild punishment and
increase the intensity only if necessary. The problem with this approach,
however, is that the person being punished may learn to tolerate the gradual
increases, making even quite strong punishments ineffective by the time
they are reached. That is why psychologists recommend using a consequence negative enough to suppress the unwanted behavior the *first* time
punishment is administered. The Navy clearly followed this advice in setting severe penalties for first-time offenders. California legislators failed to
do this, however, when they passed a drunk-driving law. As Figure 6.5
illustrates, their efforts failed to suppress this behavior significantly.

If a level of punishment turns out to be ineffective, even though you
thought it would be strong enough, what should you do next? Should you

When will punishment work best?

Figure 6.5
The passage on January 1, 1982, of a stiffer law for driving under the influence (DUI) of alcohol resulted in a sharp drop in drunk-driving arrests in February. This decline resulted from a fear of stiffer fines and jail sentences and confirms that punishment can be used to suppress behavior. However, as people discovered that the new law was not as punishing as they thought, they returned to their previous habits of drinking and driving. As a result, the number of drunk-driving arrests increased. What would happen to drunk-driving arrests if the laws were made five times as stiff as the present ones? (From the *San Diego Tribune*, November 29, 1982)

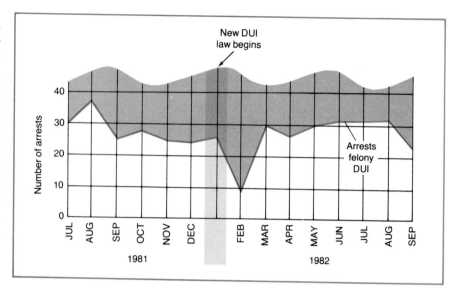

escalate? According to some researchers, the answer is "probably not." A better tactic may be to reinforce behaviors that are incompatible with the unwanted one (Yulevich & Axelrod, 1983). Judy's mother, for example, upon discovering that a scolding did not work, might have tried encouraging the child to help her find the groceries on her list.

One factor closely related to the intensity of punishment is the form punishment takes. A poorly chosen punishment can often make a behavior problem worse. For example, a spanking is not very effective for controlling undesirable aggression in children because the punishment itself provides a model of aggressive behavior that the child may later imitate.

A better form of punishment in this case is the type Susan experienced, a procedure called **time-out.** The child is sent to a room without any games, books, or other amusements that could serve as rewards. A child's own bedroom, for instance, would not be a very effective time-out place, because it is usually filled with toys. On the other hand, a time-out room should not be dark or frightening to a child. Experts recommend 1 minute of time-out for each year of the child's age (6 minutes of time-out for a 6-year-old child).

The adult should be careful not to give the youngster too much attention while the punishment is being administered. For some children, even negative attention such as a scolding can be a form of reward. As you may have noticed, time-out is not just a form of punishment; it is also a form of extinction because it eliminates any reinforcement of an unwanted behavior. The removal of reinforcers is key to time-out's success (Brantner & Doherty, 1983).

Time-out is most effective when combined with efforts to teach a child alternative desired behaviors. For example, if Susan threw sand at Pete because he had started to play with her favorite toy, she should be taught other ways to deal with this situation. Otherwise, Susan will probably respond aggressively again, especially when adults are not around to see. Not providing alternative ways to cope with boredom and stress may be one shortcoming in the Navy's crackdown on illicit drug use. The oversight might inadvertently encourage a simple substitution of alcohol for illegal drugs. Psychologists who have studied punishment say that when alternative behaviors are suitably encouraged, and when punishment itself is properly administered, most negative side effects of punishment can be controlled or avoided (Newsom et al., 1983; Rimm & Masters, 1979; Van Houten, 1983).

Let's look at what might happen when an animal or person is punished over and over and cannot escape the punishment.

Learned Helplessness **EXPLORING PSYCHOLOGY**

What began as a study of shock avoidance in dogs resulted in a theory of why people fail. Researchers studying the effects of unavoidable shock made a new discovery. They had restrained dogs in harnesses, and then given them electric shocks. The shocks were unavoidable: no matter what the dogs did, they could not turn off or escape the shock. In the next step, the dogs were placed in a situation in which they could avoid shock. Each dog was placed in one part of a box divided in the middle by a barrier. By jumping over the barrier into the other side of the box, the dog could escape an electric shock delivered through the floor. But when the floor was electrified, the dogs did not jump the barrier and escape. The puzzled researchers repeated the experiment, this time with naive dogs—dogs that had not previously been given unavoidable shocks. When a naive dog was placed in one side of the box and the floor was electrified, it soon learned to jump over the barrier to escape the shock. Later it learned to jump at a signal that preceded the shock and thus avoid the shock altogether. Why this difference between the two groups? The researchers concluded that the dogs which had initially received unavoidable shock had learned that there was no way they could stop the shock. Because of this experience, they gave up trying to escape shock and behaved helplessly. A repetition of this experiment on rats produced similar results (See Figure 6.6). The researchers called this phenomenon **learned helplessness** (adapted from Overmier & Seligman, 1967; Maier & Seligman, 1976).

This finding in animals was significant in itself. Even more significant was the possibility that it might explain certain human behaviors. For ex-

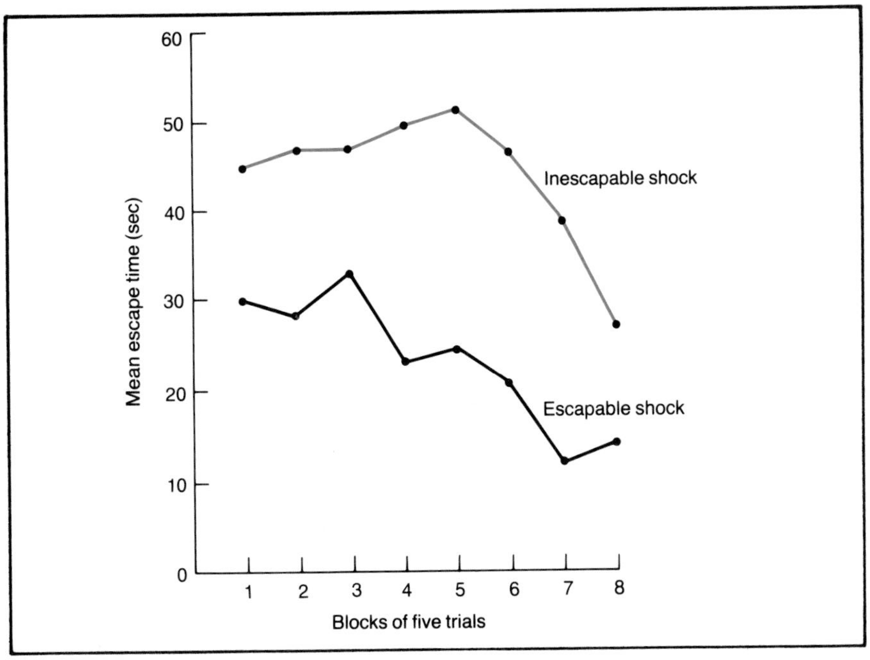

What encourages giving up?

Figure 6.6
This graph illustrates learned helplessness. The top line shows that rats exposed previously to inescapable shock have difficulty learning to escape shock when they have the chance. The bottom line shows that rats previously exposed to escapable shock have no difficulty learning to escape shock when they have the chance. (Adapted from Minor & LoLordo, 1984)

ample, why do humans sometimes stop trying to get good grades, lose weight, stay in shape, or achieve countless other goals? Researchers hypothesized that humans might stop trying in these and many other situations because they too have acquired learned helplessness (Abramson et al., 1978; Seligman, 1975; Seligman et al., 1971).

Consider the case of Carla:

Carla had never studied hard in high school but seemed to be able to get Bs anyway. In her first semester of college, however, she was having serious doubts about her abilities. She found herself behind in her work, always struggling to finish at the last minute, and then doing poorly on the exam. She tried studying longer, but didn't seem able to concentrate. She hired a tutor but found that her attention wandered. As the semester came to an end, she was very worried about her finals. Then she received her grades, and her worst fears were realized: she had gotten mostly Ds. As a result of her experience, Carla now believes that no matter what she does nothing will help, that getting good grades is beyond her control (adapted from Abramson et al., 1978).

According to learned helplessness theory, Carla observed that all her efforts had meant nothing and concluded that she had no control over the outcome of her college career. The central point of learned helplessness theory is that repeated exposure to failure results in a belief that one cannot control events in one's life. A strong sense of helplessness and a tendency to give up are then natural outgrowths of this belief.

Many studies have confirmed the basic finding that the experience of not being reinforced or of feeling powerless results in deficits on subsequent tasks. In one study, for example, students who were exposed to loud and unavoidable noises made significantly more errors on later tests of mental abilities (Tennen et al., 1982a). But it is not clear exactly why this happened. Let's look at two possible explanations.

The first is, of course, learned helplessness theory. This theory holds that helplessness occurs because people think their failure results from an inability to control events in their own lives. This explanation involves a cognitive factor, a belief that one's behaviors have no effect on events. Having come to this conclusion, the person stops making any effort.

What do you learn from failing?

Not all psychologists agree with this explanation. Another explanation is that people give up trying simply because they have the experience of not being reinforced. Carla, for instance, tried studying longer and then got a tutor, but neither effort was rewarded. Psychologists who take this view say that these behaviors gradually underwent *extinction* because no reinforcement followed them. At the same time, Carla's efforts were also followed by a painful consequence—failure and the drop in self-esteem it brings. Her efforts, in short, were actually being punished, and so they naturally decreased in frequency. Note that according to this view, no conscious interpretation of why she is failing occurs to Carla. Her behaviors simply result from her experience of unavoidable failure.

The story of learned helplessness is a good example of how psychologists search for the causes of human behavior and often come up with different answers. What began with an accidental discovery evolved into an explanation of why people sometimes give up trying. The theory of learned helplessness proposes a cognitive reason: people stop trying because they come to believe that they cannot control events in their lives. Although this view is widely accepted and has received experimental support, some evidence suggests that people may stop trying simply as a result of extinction and punishment, without any self-perceptions of helplessness. Both views, in other words, add to our understanding of why people behave as they do (Alloy, 1982; Oakes, 1982; Oakes & Curtis, 1982; Tennen et al., 1982a, 1982b). They remind us that a single explanation is seldom enough for something as complex as human behavior.

Now let's see how operant procedures have been applied to treat a very serious behavioral problem, autism.

Treatment of Autistic Children   **APPLYING PSYCHOLOGY**

When Susan was about a year old, her parents began to notice that she was different. When she was picked up and held, she sometimes struggled and rarely cuddled. When her parents made friendly noises and talked to her, Susan rarely made eye contact and never responded with sounds of her own. When she was two, she would often sit on the floor and rock back and forth for long periods of time, totally wrapped up in her inner world. When other two-year-olds in the neighborhood were beginning to speak, Susan rarely made any sounds, much less said a word. When she had a chance to play with other children her own age, Susan made no attempt to interact with her peers and showed no interest in toys. At the age of three, Susan continued to rock back and forth for hours, did not speak or make any sounds, avoided eye contact, was unresponsive to her parents, and did not play with toys or her peers. After an extensive series of medical and psychological tests, Susan was diagnosed as being autistic (adapted from Lovaas, 1987).

The cause of autism is unknown, but mental health experts do know that, without treatment Susan and others like her will probably continue to be unresponsive and uncommunicative and will remain severely retarded for the rest of their lives. Since the early 1970s, Dr. Ivar Lovaas of the University of California at Los Angeles has treated autistic children using procedures based on operant conditioning. When operant conditioning is used to change human behavior, it is referred to as behavior modification or, more colloquially, as "behavior mod."

Why does Susan just sit and rock?

Specially trained therapists and parents used behavior modification procedures in an attempt to get Susan and 18 other autistic children, all under four years old, to substitute normal behaviors for autistic ones. The program involved adults working with children on a one-to-one basis for 40 hours each week, every week, for two years. Dr. Lovaas reasoned that the earlier the training was begun, the longer it lasted, and the more intense it was, the better the chance that the children would learn appropriate behavior patterns.

Dr. Lovaas and his colleagues (1981) have written a detailed manual for parents and teachers on using behavior modification to train developmentally disabled children. Here is one of the procedures they recommend (adapted from Lovaas, 1981, pp. 49–50).

First a *target behavior* is selected, such as getting the child to make eye contact following the command, "Look at me."

Step 1: Have the child sit in a chair facing you.

Step 2: Give the command "Look at me" every 5 to 10 seconds.

An autistic child may sit and rock for extended periods of time. By using behavior modification techniques, counselors can decrease time spent in rocking behavior and increase time spent in learning new skills and interacting with others. *(Costa Manos/ Magnum)*

Step 3: Reward the child with praise and food for correctly looking at your face. In the beginning, a correct response is when the child looks in your eyes within two seconds after the command is given and continues looking for at least one second. In general, if you have a clear idea of what you are rewarding, the child will catch on. When a correct response occurs, say "Good looking," and simultaneously reward the child with food.

Steps 4–7: Repeat Step 3 until the child is repeatedly following the command "Look at me." Gradually increase the duration of the child's eye contact from one second to periods of two to three seconds. Do this by giving praise throughout the two to three seconds and then reward the child with food only after the requisite amount of time has passed.

In training a child to make eye contact, notice that the parent or therapist selects a specific target behavior, which is maintaining eye contact for one second after the command, "Look at me." Next the adult shapes the target behavior by using positive reinforcers of praise and food, which are given immediately after the child emits the target behavior. The parent continues the shaping until the child is making the target behavior after each command. The adult trains the child to make eye contact for longer and longer periods by giving continuous praise but delaying the food reinforcer. After the child learns to make eye contact while sitting in a chair facing the adult, the behavior should be generalized to other situations, such as when the child is standing or is in another room. To do this, the parent or therapist takes the child into different situations, uses the command "Look at me," and then rewards correct behavior with praise and food.

Intensive behavior modification therapy enabled Susan to make eye contact, and she learned to stop the incessant rocking that had characterized her behavior. She also learned to respond to verbal requests, such as "wash your hands," and gradually she began to play with toys, interact with peers, speak, and engage in preschool tasks such as reading and writing. After two years in this special program, Susan was able to enter and successfully complete first grade in public school. To avoid any possible biases, neither the school nor the teacher was told that Susan was originally diagnosed as autistic. In Susan's group of 19 autistic children, 9, or 47 percent, achieved normal intellectual and educational functioning as shown by their normal-range IQ scores and successful performances in the first grade. None of these 9 children was recognized by teachers as being autistic. However, even with such intensive training, 8 of the children (40 percent) remained mildly retarded and 2 (10 percent) remained profoundly retarded and were assigned to classes for retarded children. In contrast, only 2 percent of a control group of autistic children, who received only minimal treatment, were able to achieve normal intellectual and educational functioning. Of the remaining children in the control group, 45 percent remained mildly retarded and 53 percent were severely retarded. Dr. Lovaas concluded that without intensive behavioral modification treatment, autistic children will continue to show severe behavioral deficits (Lovaas, 1987).

Later in this book you will learn how behavior modification has been used to control weight (Module 24), reduce stress (Module 41), treat phobias (Module 47), and stop annoying thoughts (Module 47).

OBSERVATIONAL LEARNING

An informal survey of college students revealed that some hate and fear bugs while others do not. Those who feared bugs often remembered watching a parent, sibling, or friend react with horror upon noticing a bug. If you have a fear and hatred of bugs from watching someone's reaction, psychologists would say that you acquired the fear through **observational learning**. In observational learning you do not perform any behavior or receive any external reinforcers. Rather, you learn a new association by simply watching or hearing a model. The model might be seen live or on film, or it could be a verbal set of instructions. If you actually perform the observed behavior, such as scream when the model screams, it is called *overt rehearsal*. If you only think about performing the behavior, it is called *covert rehearsal*.

Are you afraid of bugs?

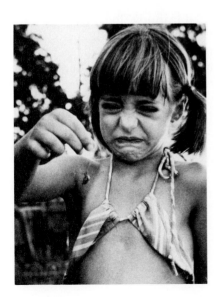 

One child here has developed a fear of bugs from watching and imitating adults' fearful reaction to bugs. The other shows no fear of bugs because she too is imitating the reaction of adults she has observed. In these cases, the children's reactions occurred through observational learning. (Both, Erika Stone)

How Do We Learn Through Observation?

If you watched your mother panic when she saw a bug, you would be responding in a *selective fashion* to her behavior. You would see her fearful facial expression, her hands thrown up in the air, and her quick retreat from the bug, and you would hear her raised voice. Through your own words, thoughts, and images, which are called *cognitive representations*, you store the "bug" reaction in your brain. The next time you see a bug, you may imitate your mother's "bug" reaction by using your cognitive representations.

Notice that your learning the "bug" reaction was strictly observational. You may or may not have engaged in covert or overt rehearsal. Unlike classical and operant conditioning, observational learning does not involve any paired sequence of stimulus and response, and it is not followed by a reinforcer or a punisher. However, observational learning may involve **self-reinforcers**, which are thoughts or statements that you make to yourself. For example, a self-reinforcer might be the thought, "I'm behaving like mother." But no one other than you is deliberately controlling or reinforcing the learning process.

New Associations

How many ways can you learn to fear a bug?

You can develop a new association, such as a fear of bugs, in several different ways. You might learn through classical conditioning if someone paired a conditioned stimulus, a bug, with an unconditioned stimulus, a shock, so that you would come to associate bugs with feelings of pain and fear. For you to learn to loathe bugs through observational learning, you might watch someone show a fear of bugs, and then adopt and show this fearful behavior in your next encounter with a bug. To show the effectiveness of observational learning, Albert Bandura (1974, 1986) conducted a number of ingenious experiments. Here is one of his classics.

In Bandura's study, preschool children were involved in their own art projects. In another part of the room, an adult got up and, for the next 10 minutes, hit, kicked, and yelled ("hit him, kick him") at a large, inflated Bobo doll. Some children watched the model's aggressive behaviors. Later, each child was subjected to a mildly frustrating situation and placed in a room with toys and the Bobo doll. Without the child knowing, researchers observed the child's behaviors. Children who had observed the model's aggressive attacks on the Bobo doll also kicked, hit, and yelled ("hit him, kick him") at the doll. Through observational learning, these children had internalized the aggressive behaviors and were now performing them. Children who had not observed the model's aggressive behaviors did not hit or kick the Bobo doll after they had been mildly frustrated (Bandura et al., 1961). In related studies, psychologists are trying to determine how much aggressive behavior children learn from watching television (Module 51).

Of course, not all observational learning is negative. Children may, for example, learn to perform helpful behaviors by watching their teachers help other students with school problems. Bandura believes that much of our learning takes place through observation: we learn by watching others perform, and then we imitate what we observe. Bandura's ideas on how observational learning affects personality development are discussed in Module 37.

REVIEW

Jim notices that his six-year-old son, Kenny, often gets angry and kicks things, doesn't pick up his toys no matter how many times he is asked, and doesn't go to bed on time. Jim is going to use operant conditioning procedures to change Kenny's behavior.

Jim thinks that Kenny gets angry and kicks things to get attention. Jim tells Kenny that every time he kicks things, he is going to sit alone for six minutes in a small guest room with no toys or television. Jim is using a procedure called (1) _____ - _____. Because this procedure decreases the likelihood of Kenny kicking things, it is a form of mild (2) _____. For this procedure to be effective, the punishment should be administered (3) _____ after the behavior and it should be aversive enough to suppress the unwanted behavior. Jim also decides to reward Kenny with attention when he is playing quietly. In this case, attention would be considered a positive (4) _____ because it increases the likelihood that Kenny will continue to play quietly. When the *presentation* of a stimulus increases the probability that the behavior preceding it will be repeated, it is a (5) _____ reinforcer. When the *removal* of a stimulus increases the probability that the behavior preceding it will be repeated, it is a (6) _____ reinforcer.

By not giving Kenny attention for kicking things, Jim is withholding reinforcement, a procedure called (7) _____. During this procedure, the frequency and duration of Kenny's kicking things should decrease.

Jim tells Kenny that each time he picks up a toy he will get a cookie. In this case, the cookie is serving as a (8) _____ reinforcer. Each time Kenny goes to bed on time he will receive a bright red chip. On weekends, Kenny can exchange the chips for treats. In this case, the chips are serving as (9) _____ reinforcers because they are associated with primary reinforcers.

Jim finds that Kenny picks up his toys but instead of taking them to his room, he puts them on chairs, tables, and anything handy. Jim first reinforces Kenny's behavior of just picking up toys. Next, he reinforces Kenny's picking up toys and carrying them to his room. Finally, he reinforces Kenny's picking up toys, carrying them to his room, and putting them away. In this case, putting the toys away in his room would be considered the goal or (10) _____ behavior. To get Kenny to perform the target behavior, Jim reinforced behaviors leading to the target behavior, a process called (11) _____. After a few days of shaping, Kenny is not only picking up his toys and putting them away, but he is also picking up his dirty clothes and putting them in the closet. This is an example of (12) _____, in which Kenny is emitting the target behavior in the presence of stimuli slightly different from those present during previous reinforcement. However, Kenny does not pick up books, newspapers, or magazines lying around the house. In this case, Kenny is showing (13) _____, in which he shows the target behavior in the presence of some stimuli but not others.

When Jim first began shaping Kenny's behavior, he gave Kenny a red chip every time. This is an example of a (14) _____ schedule of reinforcement, which leads to rapid learning of the target behavior. After a week, Jim reinforces Kenny's behavior every other time, an example of a (15) _____ schedule of reinforcement. One of the reasons that Jim is changing Kenny to a partial reinforcement schedule is that behaviors on this schedule are more resistant to (16) _____. Partial reinforcement schedules that are based on a time dimension are called (17) _____ schedules. Partial reinforcement schedules that are based on the performance of behaviors are called (18) _____ schedules.

Sherry, a neighborhood friend, watches Kenny pick up and put away his toys. When she goes home, she picks up and puts away her toys. This is an example of (19) _____ learning in which Sherry learned the behavior by simply observing it without having to perform the behavior or get an external reinforcer. Sherry is able to perform the observed behavior in her own home because she has a (20) _____ representation, which may be stored in words, images, or thoughts. Although Sherry does not receive any external reinforcer, she may give herself a (21) _____ - _____ for putting away her toys.

    Kenny has one big disappointment. No matter how hard he tries, he seems to have little success in learning to read. As a result, his teacher criticizes his efforts and the other children laugh when he reads aloud in class. If Kenny gives up trying to learn to read, some would say that he is showing a pattern called learned (22) _____. One explanation for this pattern is that the teacher's criticisms and the chil-

dren's laughter serve to (23) _____ Kenny's efforts to learn to read. As a result, his efforts at reading will be suppressed. The cognitive explanation for learned helplessness is that Kenny's experience of repeated failure has resulted in a (24) _____ that he has no control over his reading skills, no matter how hard he tries. Perhaps his father could use operant conditioning procedures to help Kenny overcome his learned helplessness.

    When operant conditioning procedures are applied to changing human behavior, it is called (25) _____ modification. After intensive behavior modification training, about 40 percent of a group of (26) _____ children were able to enter and successfully complete the first grade in a public school. This study showed that behavior modification is a very effective procedure for eliminating unwanted behaviors and training new ones.

Answers: (1) time-out; (2) punishment; (3) immediately; (4) reinforcer; (5) positive; (6) negative; (7) extinction; (8) primary; (9) secondary; (10) target; (11) shaping; (12) generalization; (13) discrimination; (14) continuous; (15) partial; (16) extinction; (17) interval; (18) ratio; (19) observational; (20) cognitive; (21) self-reinforcer; (22) helplessness; (23) punish; (24) belief; (25) behavior; (26) autistic

GLOSSARY TERMS

continuous reinforcement schedule (p. 182)
fixed-interval schedule of reinforcement (p. 183)
fixed-ratio schedule of reinforcement (p. 183)
learned helplessness (p. 187)

negative reinforcer (p. 181)
observational learning (p. 191)
operant conditioning (p. 178)
partial reinforcement schedule (p. 182)

positive reinforcer (p. 181)
primary reinforcer (p. 181)
punisher (p. 178)
punishment (p. 185)
reinforcer (p. 178)
secondary reinforcer (p. 181)

self-reinforcer (p. 192)
shaping (p. 179)
target behavior (p. 179)
time-out (p. 186)
variable-interval schedule of reinforcement (p. 184)
variable-ratio schedule of reinforcement (p. 184)

PERSONAL NOTE

One baseball player has been wearing the same pair of pants for two years. His reason? "I've been very successful with these pants. These pants give me an edge mentally." We can explain this baseball player's behavior with one of the principles of operant conditioning. When he is hitting well, it's not just his batting style that's being reinforced but also other things that just happen to coincide with his hitting, such as wearing a particular pair of pants. Psychologists call these coincidences superstitious behaviors. Ball players maintain that these superstitious behaviors really affect their performance. From my own personal experience, I think they may have a point. When I played Little League baseball, I developed the superstitious behavior of pounding my bat three times on the ground before stepping up to the plate. And what do you know—every time I did so, I struck out. —R.P.

7

Remembering and Forgetting

Module 18 Three Kinds of Memory

Norman, in his mid forties, is an impressive six feet one inch tall and weighs 240 pounds. Although you spent two hours visiting with him yesterday, Norman remembers neither your visit nor your name. If you ask him what he did yesterday, he will remember almost nothing. If you ask him about events before his accident, however, he can remember them quite well. Norman is very friendly and can carry on a simple conversation. But if he has to answer the phone in the middle of a conversation, when he returns he will not remember what you were talking about. He doesn't watch television too often because the commercial interruptions cause him to forget what the show is about. Although he has attended an outpatient treatment center for many years, he does not remember the names of the other patients. He can only carry out those routines that he has learned through years of constant practice. For example, after four years of traveling the same route, Norman can drive to the hospital, although he doesn't remember the names of any of the streets. Norman lives with his mother, who notices that he is constantly misplacing things and losing money. Norman's mother does all the cooking because if Norman puts something on the stove to cook, he usually forgets about it. Norman's memory deficit has caused problems in almost every area of his life (adapted from Kaushall et al., 1982).

How does Norman live without remembering?

In 1960, at age 22, Norman had a one in a million accident. A fencing sword entered his nose, penetrated his brain, and destroyed an important area involved in memory. Since that day, Norman has lost much of his ability to store permanent memories—that is, to remember events from day to day. If you carried on a conversation with Norman, you might not notice his problem. He can register sensory information and remember *immediate* events well enough to do simple chores and talk with others. He can also remember events that happened over twenty years ago, *before* his accident. Why, then, will he not remember your conversation tomorrow? To answer this question, you must understand the difference between three kinds of memory: sensory memory, short-term memory, and long-term memory.

SENSORY MEMORY

To demonstrate sensory memory to yourself, have someone make a rapid circular motion with a lighted cigarette in a totally dark room. As the glowing tip moves, you will have the sensation of seeing a continuous circle of light. This sensation occurs because the image of the tip in each of its various positions is being held briefly in **sensory memory,** the momentary lingering of sensory information after a stimulus has been removed. In this case, new images are being registered before the old ones fade, and so you see the outline of a circle.

Researchers have established the existence of sensory memory for vision and hearing, and they assume that it exists for the other senses as well. You have no voluntary control over the information that enters sensory memory, and its capacity seems unlimited. Any stimulation processed by your senses is held briefly in sensory memory. Why, then, aren't you overwhelmed by incoming data? The answer is that you do not attend to everything that enters sensory memory. If you fail to attend to the information, it simply fades away in a matter of a second or so.

Despite its very brief duration, sensory memory allows you to do several things. For example, sensory memory makes your visual world seem smooth and continuous despite frequent blinks of your eyes. Whenever you blink, your vision is momentarily interrupted. Sensory memory maintains the visual images so that you are not aware of these interruptions.

Sensory memory also gives you the moment or two that you need to determine if incoming data should be processed further. Have you ever been engrossed in reading a book or watching a movie when a friend suddenly asks you a question? Just as you are about to ask, "What did you say?" you realize that you did hear after all. In this case your friend's speech sounds were held in sensory memory long enough for you to shift your attention to them. In addition, by momentarily holding the string of speech sounds in sensory memory, you are able to group related ones together and recognize them as words. This is an example of how you use sensory memory to recognize complex patterns (Norman, 1982). Similarly, you can group facial features into the complex pattern of a face. Without sensory memory, the world would be a jumble of unrelated elements.

You see a pattern of light from a moving flashlight because, for 1 to 2 seconds, the light stimulus is stored in your sensory memory. In this photograph the pattern of a moving flashlight is captured as the artist Pablo Picasso traces a wild beast in the air in a darkened room. (Gjon Mili, *Life* Magazine © 1950 Time, Inc.)

Returning to the case of Norman, you can clearly see that nothing is wrong with his sensory memory. Since he can recognize words, we know he is able to retain information in sensory memory and recognize patterns. In fact, Norman must be able to retain information for longer than just the fleeting duration of sensory memory, or he would not be able to carry on a conversation. When Norman attends to the words that are spoken during a conversation, he is processing them into what is called short-term memory.

SHORT-TERM MEMORY

Norman lives in Southern California, an area inhabited by thousands of runners. It is not unusual for five or six runners to go by his home on any given day. What is unusual is for a naked runner to jog past Norman's house. But that is exactly what happened one warm summer night. As Norman looked out his window he saw a runner approaching, and just for a moment the visual image was stored in his sensory memory. This brief sensory storage allowed Norman to notice something strange about the runner: the man was wearing nothing except his running shoes and socks. Ordinarily, Norman would not pay much attention to a jogger, and the image would fade quickly from his sensory memory. In this case, however, Norman paid attention, and the image was processed into **short-term memory**. Short-term memory refers to the process of attending to information in sensory memory or attending to your conscious thoughts and perceptions at any given moment. Like everyone else, Norman has some conscious control over what he holds in short-term memory: he can to some extent ignore the information, or he can selectively attend to it and think about it. In this case, Norman might have wondered about the runner's motivation.

What kind of memory are you using right now as you remember the words in this question?

Characteristics of Short-Term Memory

Researchers have found that short-term memory has two characteristics. First, information that enters it is available for only a very limited time unless it is actively processed. This processing can take the form of **maintenance rehearsal**, as when you repeat a telephone number over and over to yourself. It can also take the form, as in Norman's case, of manipulating information—of wondering about the subject and its implications. Without some kind of active mental effort, however, information that enters short-term memory will fade in about 20 to 30 seconds.

Short-term memory also has a limited capacity. Most people can hold only about seven bits in it at any one time (Miller, 1956). For instance, if you were given a string of random numbers to remember and you came to the seventh one, you would be approaching the limits of your short-term memory. Given a short-term memory this limited in size, you may well be asking how we manage to process as much information as we do. For example, how can you remember the phrase "Do not chew bubble gum during examinations," which contains thirty-six individual letters, far more separate items than working memory can possibly hold? The answer is through a process called **chunking**. By chunking individual letters into seven meaningful words, you can easily keep this information active. In fact, you may actually store the "idea" of this phrase as a single chunk, leaving room for still more information in short-term memory.

Why is it so easy to forget a
phone number?

Forgetting from Short-Term Memory

Just before Norman saw the naked runner, he was searching for a pencil
in a desk drawer. When the runner jogged past the window his attention
was diverted, and soon he had completely forgotten about the pencil. This
experience of losing something from short-term memory because other
information interferes is not unique to Norman. You have the same experience when something distracts you before you can write down a phone
number or before you learn the definition you just read. Some researchers
believe that *interference* is the primary reason why information is forgotten
from short-term memory (Zechmeister & Nyberg, 1982).

Although we often forget things from short-term memory, we very
seldom have the experience that Norman repeatedly has. He loses all trace
of what just happened before a brief distraction occurred. For instance, you
may forget a phone number if the doorbell suddenly diverts your attention,
but you usually do not lose all recollection that you wanted to make a call.
This, however, is what happens to Norman. After the naked runner passed
and captured Norman's attention, the prior search for a pencil was entirely
lost from his memory. Even if Norman later noticed that the desk drawer
was open, he would not remember how it got that way. In fact, if tomorrow
you reminded Norman of the naked runner, he would not know what you
were talking about. This is because Norman is totally unable to transfer
new information to what is called long-term memory.

LONG-TERM MEMORY

Norman's case demonstrates the existence of a long-term memory separate
from short-term memory. In contrast to short-term memory, **long-term
memory** stores information with relative permanence and has an almost
unlimited capacity. Norman clearly has long-term memory stores, as evi-
denced by his recall of events from before his accident. He also has short-
term memory, as shown by his ability to carry on simple conversations.
What Norman lacks is the ability to enter new information into long-term
storage.

Information is normally transferred into long-term memory through
an attention-related process. One such process is rehearsal, which itself can
take several forms. In *maintenance rehearsal*, you repeat information silently over and over, without giving it any real thought. Maintenance rehearsal is usually not enough to transfer information into long-term storage.
If you are planning to use a number only once, and so merely say it to
yourself as you are reaching for the phone, the number probably will not
be stored in your long-term memory. This mechanical sort of repetition
will retain the number in short-term memory long enough for you to place
the call, but very soon thereafter the number will be lost. Much more
effective at getting information into long-term memory are attention-related
processes that involve making associations between aspects of the new information and things you already know (Howard, 1983). For instance, if
you can associate a phone number with someone's date of birth, or with a
year in which some famous event happened, you are much more apt to
enter the number into long-term storage. We will say more about this later.

How Long-Term and Short-Term Memory Work Together

Suppose you read a list of thirty-one flavors of ice cream and are then asked
to recall as many as you can. For each one you remember, you receive a
coupon for a free quart. This is an example of a *free recall test*, in which

After reading a long list of ice cream flavors, this girl may remember only six or seven new flavors, which is about the capacity of her short-term memory. (Joel Gordon)

you are asked to remember a string of previously presented items in any order you wish. You would probably remember common flavors like vanilla and chocolate regardless of where they appeared on the list, and you might also have a good recall of your own favorite flavors. But aside from these, which flavors would you remember best?

Tests like these show that you have the best recall for items presented at the beginning of a list, which is known as the *primacy effect*, and for items presented at the end, which is known as the *recency effect*. Psychologists explain these effects by pointing to the different functions of short-term and long-term memory. On the one hand, you show good recall of items at the end of the list because these items are still in short-term memory when the free recall test begins. On the other hand, you also have good recall of items at the beginning of the list because you have had more time to rehearse them and transfer them into long-term memory. Your poorest recall would be for items in the middle of the list. These items were not yet placed in long-term storage, and at the same time new items have displaced them from short-term memory.

Can you remember the thirty-first flavor of ice cream?

Kinds of Long-Term Memory

Why can you so easily perform a number of skills, such as drive a car, ride a bike, rollerskate, ski, or play tennis? It is because you have stored the necessary knowledge to perform skills in one type of long-term memory that is called **procedural memory**. You can perform a skill, even if you have not engaged in it for many months or years, by recalling the knowledge from procedural memory.

Why can you so easily remember hundreds of daily events, such as getting up late, spilling cola on your shirt, ordering a tuna sandwich, and seeing a particular movie? It is because you have stored distinct episodes you personally experienced in a type of long-term memory that is called **episodic** (EP-ih-SAH-dik) **memory**. You can answer the question, "How was your day?" by recalling this information from episodic memory.

Why can you remember the definition of classical conditioning, the first president of the United States, and the reason that you must study to get good grades? It is because you have stored knowledge of facts or relationships between things in a type of long-term memory that is called

The fact that this grandmother can tell her grandchild about people and events from 25 or 50 years ago points to the durability of items stored in long-term memory. (Michal Heron/Woodfin Camp and Associates)

semantic memory (Tulving, 1972, 1984). When you take an exam, you recall information about mental representations of objects, facts, and relationships from semantic memory.

You are able to transfer information from short-term memory into various kinds of long-term memory by using a number of attention-related processes. The general act of attending to new information, perhaps using old information to analyze or manipulate the new, and then placing the result in long-term memory, is called **encoding** (Klatzky, 1984). Let's see why you encoded certain information today but not everything you wished.

Types of Encoding

"I remember that I ate five times today (including snacks) and I can tell you everything I ate."

"I can't remember the difference between operant and classical conditioning, which I studied this morning."

Most of the personal episodes in your life are encoded automatically in long-term memory. When you store information very quickly and without deliberate effort, such as how many times you ate and what you ate, it is called **automatic encoding**. If you were to read a list of words, you would be able to recall how many times you saw a certain word on that list because information about frequency is encoded automatically (Sanders et al., 1987). You can recall how often you heard your name today for the same reason. Your ability to recall dozens of events at the end of each day indicates that recent memories that are automatically encoded are often very easy to recall.

Other information, such as the differences between operant and classical conditioning, must be encoded through **attentional processing**: you deliberately attend to and make an effort to put something into long-term memory. Let's look at why efforts at attentional encoding may or may not be successful.

Attentional processing of the differences between conditioning proce-

Figure 7.1
How words are processed was shown to affect later recognition. Before viewing a list of words, subjects were given three different sets of instructions. The first group was told to look at the words and make up associations, such as which words are related to cars. The second group was told to notice some feature of the words, such as all those containing the letter "g." The third group was told to look at the words while performing a secondary task. When tested later, subjects who made up associations recognized most words (top line). Subjects who noticed some feature of the words had poor recognition (middle line). Subjects who only noticed the words had no recognition (bottom line). (Adapted from Fisk & Schneider, 1984)

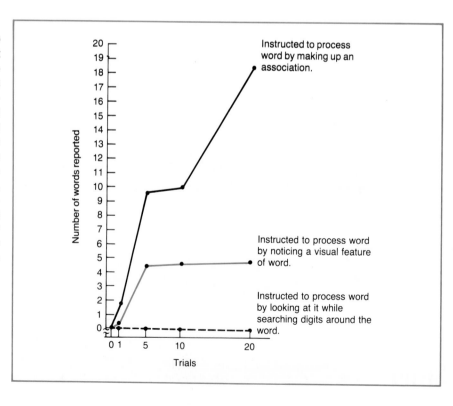

dures can involve a number of different encoding strategies. One common strategy is rehearsal, in which you repeat something to be learned either out loud or to yourself. There are two kinds of rehearsal and only one kind is likely to encode information in long-term memory. If you were to repeat the differences between conditioning procedures so that you could write them down in your notes, you are probably engaging in *maintenance rehearsal*. This type of rehearsal, which involves little thought or effort, is very useful for maintaining information in short-term memory. However, maintenance rehearsal is not very effective for encoding information into long-term memory. To encode information into long-term memory, you would want to repeat the information in a way that will make new associations. Repeating and making new associations is called **elaborative rehearsal** and will likely result in encoding the information into long-term memory (Stein et al., 1984). For example, students who used elaborative rehearsal to make new associations were significantly better at word recognition than those who did not (Figure 7.1). Besides using words to encode information, we also use images. Researchers found that our earliest childhood memories, usually from age 3 or 4, are often visual (Kihlstrom & Harackiewicz, 1985). We will tell you about ways to improve encoding in Module 19. First, let's look at an interesting form of visual imagery found in children.

Special Memory Abilities EXPLORING PSYCHOLOGY

RESEARCHER: Do you see anything?

YOUNG SUBJECT: Ground is dark greenish brown, then there's a mama and a little leopard and there's a native sitting against him. Then there's a pool with a crab coming out . . . with a fish in it, and I think there are turtles walking in front and a porcupine down near the right. There's a tree that separates a cow in half. The cow's brown and white, and there's something up in the tree—I can't see the bottom right-hand corner. There's a sun with a lot of rays on it near

Can you hold the details of this picture from Rudyard Kipling's *The Jungle Book* before your mind's eye for several minutes? If so, you may have the capacity for eidetic imagery. (From Haber, 1980)

the top on the right . . . eight rays . . . the porcupine has a lot of bristles on it . . . the right is disappearing. I can still see that cow that's divided by the tree . . . . Oh, there's a crocodile or alligator in the right-hand corner . . . . It's very faint . . . . It's gone (Haber, 1980, p. 72).

Can you form an exact picture in your mind?

The subject in this study, an 11-year-old girl, had been shown the picture on the next page a few minutes before and then the picture was removed. Now she is describing the picture to the researcher. What is unusual about her description is not so much its amount of detail but the fact that she seems to be examining a visual image of the drawing that still lingers before her eyes. This is not an example of normal sensory memory, because the image lasts for several minutes before it fades away. As you probably remember, sensory memories disappear almost instantaneously.

Research suggests that about 5 percent of children between the ages of 6 and 12 have this distinctive visual memory capacity, called **eidetic imagery** (eye-DET-ik IM-ij-ree). After examining a complex picture for 10 to 30 seconds, these children appear to retain the image for at least a few more minutes. Some skeptics have wondered if perhaps the children are simply recalling the pictures from normal long-term memory but using active descriptive words such as "I see." This does not appear to be the case, however. In recent studies, children with eidetic capabilities have been presented with two separate images—images that when superimposed form a third image, different from the others. These youngsters seem able to retain the first of the images in eidetic storage long enough to super-impose it mentally on the second even when presentation of the second image is delayed. As a result, they are able to see the "hidden" image, something that could not be done with long-term memory alone (Haber, 1980).

In the small percentage of children who can form eidetic images, the ability almost always disappears as the child enters adolescence. Adults who can form eidetic images are very rare indeed (Stromeyer, 1970). However, a few researchers have reported adults who possess what is commonly called a **photographic memory**. These individuals seem able to form very sharp and detailed visual images that they can recall at will, even after substantial time has passed since the image was first encoded (Neisser, 1976). For example, a woman could view a pattern of dots in her right eye and fuse them with a pattern of dots in her left eye, which resulted in her seeing a new image, in this case the letter T (Stromeyer, 1970). There are also cases of people who probably do not have photographic memories but who never-theless can perform amazing memory feats. One man had memorized an entire book and could tell you the exact word that appeared four lines down, next to the right-hand margin of every page (Stratton, 1917). Although most of us do not have photographic memories and many people complain of having poor memories, we can all improve our ability to recall what we have learned by practicing some of the memory techniques discussed in Module 19.

Besides eidetic imagery, another kind of unusual encoding exists. In this case, the encoding is associated with very vivid events.

Explaining Flashbulb Memories

The motorcycle driver who walked away with minor cuts and bruises from the spectacular accident (Figure 7.2) will probably remember every detail. He will be able to recall the sensation as he started to lose control and the feeling of flying through the air and hitting the dirt.

Figure 7.2
The driver of this motorcycle will probably remember this crash in great detail, a kind of memory called flashbulb memory. (Abram G. Schoenfeld/Photo Researchers)

The very vivid recollections we sometimes form of dramatic incidents are often called **flashbulb memories** (Brown & Kulik, 1977). Flashbulb memories usually deal with events that are extremely surprising, emotionally arousing, or very important in their consequences (Figure 7.3). You may have experienced something similar to a flashbulb memory yourself. For example, when people were questioned about what they were doing

Why do you easily remember terrifying events?

MAKING MEMORY'S FLASHBULBS POP

Cues	Percent*
A car accident you were in or witnessed	85
When you first met your roommate at Duke	82
The night of your high school graduation	81
The night of your senior prom (if you went or not)	78
An early romantic experience	77
A time you had to speak in front of an audience	72
When you got your admissions letter from Duke	65
Your first date–the moment you met him/her	57
President Reagan was shot in Washington	52
The night President Nixon resigned	41
The first time you flew in an airplane	40
The moment you opened your SAT scores	33
Your 17th birthday	30
The day of the first space shuttle flight	24
The last time you ate a holiday dinner at home	23
Your first class at Duke	21
You heard that President Sadat of Egypt was shot	21
When you heard that the Pope had been shot	21
The first time your parents left you alone for some time	19
Your 13th birthday	12

*Percent of Duke students in memory experiment who reported events on experimenter's list were of "flashbulb" quality

Figure 7.3
Memories that are complete in every detail are called flashbulb memories, since they seem to resemble a flash-photo. Notice that students were more likely to form flashbulb memories in emotionally charged situations. (Rubin, 1985)

when they heard President Reagan had been shot, 94 percent could recall the exact details even seven months later (Pillemer, 1984). Events involving deaths, accidents, sports, and sex are among those people say they remember most vividly (Rubin & Kozin, 1984). These are all very emotional experiences that people are apt to dwell on long after the actual occurrence.

MAIN CONCEPT   Three Kinds of Memory

There are three basic kinds of memory: sensory memory, short-term memory, and long-term memory.

Below are some statements about these memory types. Indicate in each case which type is being described.

	Sensory Memory	Short-Term Memory	Long-Term Memory
1. Stores information with relative permanence, often over a lifetime.	—	—	X
2. The kind of memory you are using when you repeat the number 2485 over and over to yourself.	—	X	—
3. Allows the second or so that is needed to determine if incoming information deserves further processing.	X	—	—
4. Involves attending to information in sensory memory or attending to conscious thoughts and perceptions.	—	X	—
5. Is thought to have unlimited capacity.	X	—	X
6. Information can be placed in it by automatic encoding or by attentional processing.	—	—	X
7. One way to hold things here for as long as you want is to engage in maintenance rehearsal.	—	X	—
8. Is the repository of numerous episodic, semantic, perceptual, and procedural memories.	—	—	X
9. Is responsible for the primary effect in a free recall test.	—	—	X
10. Is responsible for the recency effect in a free recall test.	—	X	—
11. One way to encode things here is to use elaborative rehearsal.	—	—	X

Answers: 1 long-term; 2 short-term; 3 sensory; 4 short-term; 5 sensory and long-term; 6 long-term; 7 short-term; 8 long-term; 9 long-term; 10 short-term; 11 long-term

What happens in your body when a flashbulb memory is formed? The answer comes partly from research on animals. When rats are placed on an elevated, well-lighted platform, their natural response is to step down and go to a dark corner. However, if the rats receive a shock to their feet whenever they step down, they learn within one or two trials to remain on the platform. Since this experience involves being shocked, it produces physiological arousal, which in turn triggers the release of several *hormones* (epinephrine, ACTH, and vasopressin). Apparently, these hormones are important for rapid learning. When the hormones are eliminated by removal of the glands that produce them, the rats require significantly more trials to learn to remain on the platform (Burbach et al., 1983; McGaugh, 1983a, 1983b). This finding suggests that secretion of the hormones somehow facilitates memory formation. Like rats, humans also secrete hormones when physiological arousal occurs, and these hormones may contribute to the formation of flashbulb memories.

Mood Affects Memory   **APPLYING PSYCHOLOGY**

Jeremy was unhappy because he had received a low grade on his math exam. When the math class ended at 11:00 A.M., Jeremy discussed his grade with the other students standing around the corridor. Some complained of getting low grades and of disliking the class and the teacher. Others said that they were happy with their grades and liked the class and the teacher. Later, Jeremy met his friends for lunch in the cafeteria. They talked about the fun of going to a Saturday football game, the high cost of textbooks, a great party the night before, the pain of writing papers, the excitement of an upcoming rock concert, and the number of exams coming up. After his two afternoon classes, Jeremy stopped at the library for a minute. He talked to a friendly librarian about how to find a book he needed. The book was out but the librarian said it could be recalled in a few days. Jeremy left the library, walked to the bus stop, and sat down and waited. Not far away, a person was playing frisbee with his dog. Some of the dog's catches were amazing. On Jeremy's bus-trip home, the bus passed a funny-looking 50-foot balloon shaped like a gorilla, which was advertising a new shopping center. The bus ride took almost twice as long because the traffic was very heavy.

When Jeremy got home he studied for a while and then watched a movie on television. The movie had a sad ending. At the end of the movie, his roommate came home and asked, "How was your day?" Jeremy said, "Most of the students in my math class got low grades and hate that class. I wish I could drop it. All my friends are mad about how much they had to spend on textbooks. I've got two exams coming up and another paper due and the book I need isn't in the library. I don't know what I'll do. Besides, I'm tired of waiting for that stupid bus. The traffic was so bad today I thought I'd never get home. I've had an awful day" (author's file).

One reason that Jeremy especially noticed and encoded unpleasant events was that he was in a sad mood that day. You can understand why this happens if you look at the research on mood and memory by Alice Isen and her associates (1982), John Teasdale and Louise Russell (1983), and Paul Blaney (1986). For example, Teasdale and Russell asked college students to read a list containing negative words (dishonest, unfriendly,

When you're sad, what kind of things do you remember?

This woman is obviously very angry. Being in a certain mood or experiencing a particular emotion such as anger can trigger the memory of other events that occurred during that same mood or emotion. This phenomenon is called mood-dependent memory. (AP/Wide World Photos)

heartless), positive words (friendly, pleasant, likable), and neutral words (cautious, shy, excitable). Next a depressed mood or a happy mood was induced by having the students read either a list of depressed statements (I feel unhappy, I feel sad and blue) or happy statements (I feel happy, I feel cheerful and confident). When the students were then asked to recall as many words as they could, the "depressed" students recalled more negative words, while the "happy" students recalled more positive ones. This phenomenon, which is called **mood convergence,** means that you are more likely to attend to, encode, and recall information and events that are consistent with your present mood (Blaney, 1986). If, for instance, you are in a sad mood, you will especially notice, encode, and recall unpleasant things; if you are in a happy mood, your memories will likewise be pleasant. According to the concept of mood convergence, Jeremy especially noticed and encoded unpleasant events because these events matched his negative mood.

Later that night, when Jeremy watched a sad movie, his unpleasant memories of that day came flooding back. To further explore this phenomenon, experimental psychologist Gordon Bower used hypnosis to create a happy or sad mood in the laboratory. After hypnotizing subjects, Bower asked them to image a happy scene, which resulted in a happy mood, or to imagine a sad scene, which resulted in a sad mood. The hypnotized subjects then were asked to write down as many childhood incidents as they could recall in a 10-minute period. The next day, when the subjects were not hypnotized, they were asked to rate the childhood incidents as being pleasant, unpleasant, or neutral. Not surprisingly, the hypnotized subjects who were in a happy mood remembered more pleasant childhood incidents, while those in a sad mood remembered more unpleasant incidents. Bower (1981) concluded that what subjects recalled at a later time was enormously dependent upon what mood they were in.

Let's apply Bower's results to our example. As Jeremy watched a sad movie, he began thinking about the unpleasant incidents of the day because the movie had put him in a sad mood. This phenomenon, which is called **mood-state-dependent memory,** means that while you are in a certain mood-state, you are most likely to remember events that were learned previously in that particular mood-state.

Researchers on mood and memory tell us that being in a particular mood will influence what events you notice, encode, and recall and what events you will remember at a later date when you are in that same mood again.

REVIEW

As you are walking to the drugstore you pass an apartment with a "For Rent" sign in the window. The first type of memory this stimulus enters is known as

(1) _Sensory_ memory. This kind of memory involves a momentary lingering of sensory information, even after a stimulus is removed. It gives you the second or so you need to determine if a particular stimulus deserves further processing. In this case, your attention is captured by the sign in the window, since you happen to be looking for an apartment to rent.

As you focus your attention on the sign, you are putting its information into what is called

(2) _short_ - _term_ memory. This memory refers to the process of attending to information in sensory memory or of attending to your conscious thoughts and perceptions at any given moment. You read the sign and notice that underneath the words "For Rent" is a handwritten telephone number. You search your pockets for a paper and pencil to copy the number but discover you have neither. You know that if you want to remember the number later that day, you must transfer it to (3) _long_ - _term_ memory. The process of attend-

ing to new information, using old information to analyze or manipulate it in some fashion, and then storing the result in long-term memory is called

(4) *Encoding*

As you walk on down the street, still repeating the numbers to yourself, a man rushes out of a liquor store and nearly knocks you down. As you turn around to get a better look at him, he jumps into a waiting car. All you noticed clearly was that he was carrying a gun and a large wad of money. It flashes through your mind that you must be witnessing a holdup and you rivet your eyes on the car's license plate.

You realize that the license plate will not stay in short-term memory for very long, so you begin to repeat the numbers to yourself, a process called (5) *maintenance* rehearsal.

Your experiences of the last few minutes illustrate several of the different kinds of long-term memories a person can form. First, your memories of the events that happened to you are called (6) *Episodic* memories because they pertain to distinct episodes in your life. Episodic memories are usually encoded quickly and with little conscious effort, a process known as (7) *Automatic* encoding. Forming long-term memories of the phone number and the license plate, in contrast, requires more deliberate thought and attention. This type of encoding involves what is generally called (8) *attentional* processing. The numbers, moreover, are pieces of factual information that fall into the category of (9) *Semantic* memories. You would be able to write down the numbers on a piece of paper as well as perform other skills because

you have (10) *procedural* memories.

One way to keep the license number in short-term memory is by using maintenance rehearsal. One way to encode the license number into long-term memory is to form an (11) *association* between the number and something you already know. You can form new associations by using (12) *elaborative* rehearsal.

Looking for an apartment has put you into a sad mood. Being in a sad mood means that you will especially notice things that are unpleasant and match your mood. This phenomenon is referred to as mood (13) *Convergence*. Later that day or week, when you are again in a sad mood, you are likely to remember the unpleasant things that you experienced in a sad mood. This phenomenon is referred to as (14) *mood* - *state* -dependent memory.

If several months later your recollection of the holdup is extremely vivid, psychologists might say that you are experiencing something similar to a (15) *flashbulb* memory. A flashbulb memory typically involves events that are surprising, emotionally arousing, or very important in their consequences. One reason for the vivid recall may be that you hold thoughts of the incident in short-term memory for a long time. This repeated "replay" is a form of rehearsal.

In addition, the release of certain (16) *hormones* associated with physiological arousal may help to make flashbulb memories unusually strong.

Answers: (1) sensory; (2) short-term; (3) long-term; (4) encoding; (5) maintenance; (6) episodic; (7) automatic; (8) attentional; (9) semantic; (10) procedural; (11) association; (12) elaborative; (13) convergence; (14) mood-state; (15) flashbulb; (16) hormones

GLOSSARY TERMS

attentional processing
(p. 202)
automatic encoding
(p. 202)
chunking (p. 199)
eidetic imagery (p. 204)
elaborative rehearsal
(p. 203)

encoding memory
(p. 202)
episodic memory (p. 201)
flashbulb memory
(p. 205)
long-term memory
(p. 200)

maintenance rehearsal
(p. 199)
mood convergence
(p. 208)
mood-state-dependent
memory (p. 208)
photographic memory
(p. 204)

procedural memory
(p. 201)
semantic memory
(p. 202)
sensory memory (p. 198)
short-term memory
(p. 199)

Module 19 Retrieving and Forgetting

RETRIEVAL FROM LONG-TERM MEMORY

A television station showed a short film of a young woman walking down a hallway. Suddenly, a man in a brown leather jacket jumped out of a doorway, ran toward the woman, grabbed her purse, and knocked her down. As the assailant ran away, his face was visible for several seconds. The entire film lasted 12 seconds. TV viewers were asked to look at a lineup of six men to decide if the assailant was among them, and if so to pick him out and call in the correct choice to the station. Of the more than 2,000 viewers who called in to identify the assailant, only a small proportion (14 percent) were correct. The remaining 1,800 viewers identified the wrong man (adapted from Buckout, 1980).

Should you always believe an eyewitness?

Why did so many people identify the wrong man as the assailant? Before we answer this question, let's see how many details you can recall. Without looking back at the description above, answer the following questions:

1. What was the color of the mugger's coat.?
2. Where had the mugger been hiding?
3. The mugger knocked the woman down. (yes/no)
4. The film lasted for 30 seconds. (yes/no)

Questions 3 and 4 ask you to retrieve information from long-term memory through a process called **recognition**. In recognition, you basically decide whether a particular stimulus "matches" what you have in memory. Is knocking the woman down part of the original memory you formed of this mugging? If so, you will recognize this statement as correct. Picking an assailant out of a police lineup also involves recognition because the witness simply has to match one of the faces that are presented with the face stored in long-term memory.

Questions 1 and 2, in contrast, do not present you with stimuli you may have seen before. Instead, these questions require you to search

These customers may be unable to *recall* what their waiter looked like the next day. However, if several waiters were placed in a lineup the following day, the customers might be able to pick out, or *recognize*, the correct one. Compared with recall, recognition is easier because more cues are present. If the waiter spilled the contents of a plate on a customer, recall and recognition would both be made easier, since the waiter's face would now be associated with many more cues. (Charles Harbutt/Archive)

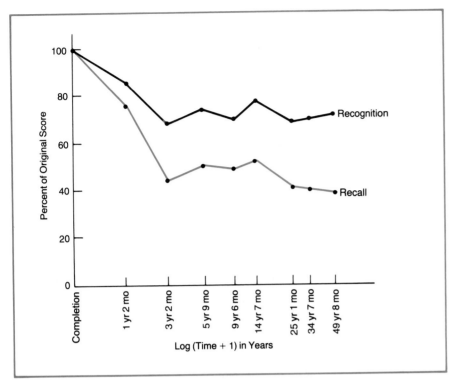

Figure 7.4
The top line indicates that subjects were able to recognize the correct definition of a relatively high percentage of Spanish words after having taken a Spanish class 1 to 50 years earlier. Notice that subjects had amazingly good recognition even after 50 years. The bottom line indicates that when subjects were asked to provide a definition of a word, a measure of recall, their performance was much poorer than their recognition performance. (Adapted from Bahrick, 1984)

through long-term memory and find specific pieces of information. This process is called **recall.** Recall is generally more difficult than recognition because it entails an extra step. Before you can decide whether an answer "matches" the correct one, you must first retrieve a possible answer of some kind. What color was the mugger's coat? Was it black? . . . No. Brown? . . . Yes. You may have noticed this difference between recall and recognition yourself. Most students find that fill-in-the-blank tests (recall) are harder than true-false or multiple choice (recognition). Figure 7.4 shows the results of one experiment which confirms that for semantic memories, recognition is easier than recall.

HOW IS MEMORY ORGANIZED?

Donald Norman, a cognitive psychologist, was taking a shower in a motel room in Champaign, Illinois. In the middle of his shower, he remembered the name of the store in his hometown city of San Diego where he could buy trays to hold his slides. How is his memory organized so that he could go from taking a shower in Illinois to recalling a particular store in San Diego? If we asked this question in a more general way, it would be "How did Norman recall things from long-term memory?" By examining Norman's recall process, you will get a glimpse into one way that long-term memory might be organized (adapted from Norman, 1982).

In Figure 7.5, notice that Norman's recall process began with his taking a shower. As his thoughts wander, he thinks of a *party* he was at in a *house* he visited during a *tour* and the house contained a *smoke detector* which needed *batteries* which he had searched for in San Diego in a *department store* which also sells *trays* for slides. Notice how he jumps from one concept—which can be a thought, image, or idea—to another concept.

Figure 7.5
While taking a shower in Champaign, Illinois, Norman remembered one event (a party) that triggered another (house) and another until the chain of memories ended with his remembering the name of a department store in San Diego where he had purchased slide trays. The text explains how this chain of memories was probably triggered. (Adapted from Norman, 1982)

Each concept in this chain is referred to as a **node.** At first, his jumping from one node to another seems haphazard. However, as Norman explained in his book, he jumped from *party*-node to *house*-node to *tour*-node, and so forth, because he has personal associations between these particular nodes. By following his personal associations between a series of different but related nodes, Norman was able to recall a particular store in San Diego while taking a shower in Champaign, Illinois.

Norman's example illustrates one of the more popular theories of how long-term memory is organized. According to this theory, called the **semantic network model,** concepts are represented by nodes and there are connections or associations between the related but different nodes. Although experts are still not sure exactly how information is organized in long-term memory, many psychologists believe that some type of semantic network is involved (Anderson, 1983; Norman, 1982).

If you have difficulty retrieving items from long-term memory, the semantic network model has some good advice. You will be more likely to retrieve information if you have encoded the information with many associations. That is, you will be more likely to recall a particular concept, such as mood convergence, if you encoded this concept by associating it with an old concept. For example, you might recall a particular time you were in a bad mood and associate this experience with the term mood convergence. Or, you can make up new associations. You might imagine a moving van called "mood convergence" which carries emotional experiences. By encoding the term mood convergence with many associations, you will have many **retrieval cues** to recall the term from long-term memory. On the other hand, if you just write the term down in your notes, or repeat it to yourself without any other associations, you will have very few retrieval cues and may find the term difficult to recall.

If you want to be able to retrieve information efficiently, you should encode it with as many associations as possible, thereby linking it to many nodes. Forming associations between new and old information is exactly what happens when you create visual images, wonder about implications, think up concrete examples, and rephrase or outline information. Let's look at some very practical suggestions about how to encode information with many retrieval cues.

Mnemonic Techniques   **APPLYING PSYCHOLOGY**

Improving Recall of Individual Facts

Like most people, you have probably found it difficult, at one time or another, to remember phone numbers or people's names. If you were to take a memory course, you would probably learn one of several proven methods for remembering such things. These methods, called **mnemonic** (nee-MON-ik) **devices,** help you store and retrieve facts better by providing organization for your encoding.

One of the easiest ways to encode fairly long numbers is through chunking. As you may recall, **chunking** involves grouping a number of items into a unit that is then processed as a whole. For instance, if you wanted to remember the number 6524518, you could divide it into three chunks: 65, 245, 18. These three chunks would be easier to encode than seven separate digits. In addition, you could try to think of an association for each of the chunks you had created. For example, you might think to yourself "65, the year I was born; 2:45, the middle of the night; 18, my age at graduating from high school." These associated thoughts will later serve as retrieval cues when you want to recall the numbers.

If you think this technique sounds too simple to be very effective, consider a study in which memory researchers worked for several years with a college student of average intelligence (Ericsson et al., 1980). They gave him repeated practice in the recall of random numbers until after 20 months he was able to remember a string of up to eighty digits presented at the rate of one every second! How did he do it? By means of clever chunking and association. The student was an accomplished long-distance runner, and he hit upon the scheme of categorizing digits whenever possible according to running times. Thus, he would encode the sequence 3492 as "3 minutes and 49.2 seconds, near the world record mile time." Several additional similar strategies give him his remarkable powers of recall.

Memory experts have also devised a number of techniques to help people memorize lists of terms. One of these, called the **method of loci,** allows you to encode and retrieve information in a certain order. First, you must memorize a series of places (*loci* in Latin means "places"), such as buildings along a certain street or places you encounter on a walk through your apartment. It is important to visualize and learn these locations in a specific order. Second, you must develop a vivid image for each of the items to be memorized. Suppose, for example, that you were memorizing the American presidents in order of their terms in office. You would have to associate each one with a vivid mental image of some kind. George Washington, for instance, might be pictured with his necktie caught in a washing machine. Once this series of images was formed, you would mentally place the image of each president in one of your memorized places, working from first to last. If the first location on your list was the front door of your apartment, you would place George Washington, straining to free his tie from the washer, at the door. The forty other presidents would be placed in your other locations in the correct order. Later, to recall the presidents, you would simply take an imaginary stroll through your apartment and note the image stored in each of your special places.

A mnemonic device that serves much the same purpose as the method of loci is the **pegword system.** It requires that you memorize a set of number-word rhymes, which act like pegs on which other ideas can be hung. Commonly used pegwords are: one is a bun; two is a shoe; three is a tree; four is a door; five is a hive; six is sticks; seven is heaven; eight is a gate;

How can you improve your recall of numbers?

This young person is trying to spell a difficult word. She is searching her memory not only for the word itself but for rules of spelling. She may be able to increase her chances of winning the spelling contest if she uses some of the mnemonic techniques described in this chapter. (Sylvia Plachy/Archive)

What will help you remember lists of facts?

nine is a line; and ten is a hen. Your next step would be to associate each of the terms you wanted to memorize with one of the pegwords. For instance, if you wanted to remember to pick up coffee, bread, potatoes, milk, eggs, and breakfast cereal at the store, you might picture a bun being dunked in a steaming cup of coffee, a loaf of French bread protruding from the inside of a shoe, clusters of potatoes growing on a tree, and so forth. When you get to the store, you would then retrieve your list of pegwords and the associated images.

Both the method of loci and the pegword system are time-consuming to learn, but each is very effective for retrieving lists in a specific order. One individual, using the method of loci, could remember a list of fifty words backward and forward even fifteen years after he first stored it in long-term memory (Luria, 1968). There have also been many cases of "ordinary" people developing impressive memory skills using these mnemonic devices (Neisser, 1982). Apparently, most of us could improve our memories greatly if we took the time to improve our methods of encoding information.

The Use of Visual Imagery

Why would you visualize a woman with a price tag hanging from her ear?

You probably noticed that both the method of loci and the pegword system depend not just on forming associations but also on creating visual images. Research shows that people can remember verbal material better if they can relate the words to be learned to visual images of some kind. When two or more words must be remembered together, interactive images appear to be most effective. By **interactive images,** psychologists mean mental pictures where the key elements involved are somehow actively related. In one study, for instance, some students were asked to remember pairs of nouns

---

MAJOR CONCEPT   Effective Encoding and Retrieval

Successful recall of facts from long-term memory depends greatly on the quality of your initial encoding, as well as on the availability of good retrieval cues.

Here is a list of techniques designed to improve encoding and retrieval. Match each one with its description.

1. Chunking

2. Method of loci

3. Pegword system

4. Interactive imagery

5. Associations

a. _3_ Associating an image of each item to be remembered with a set of number-word rhymes

b. _1_ Grouping a number of items into a unit, which is then processed as a whole

c. _5_ Forming a visual image of two things to be remembered so that the two elements are actively involved with one another

d. _4_ Creating mental relationships between new information to be learned and old information that is already firmly fixed in long-term memory

e. _2_ Associating an image of each item to be remembered with one of the places in a previously memorized set of places

Answers: a (3); b (1); c (5); d (4); e (2)

"No pain, no gain."

To unlock your body's potential, we proudly offer Soloflex. Twenty-four traditional iron pumping exercises, each correct in form and balance. All on a simple machine that fits in a corner of your home.
For a free Soloflex brochure, call anytime 1·800·453·9000. In Canada, 1·800·543·1005.
VHS Video Brochure™ available upon request.

BODY BY SOLOFLEX®
©1984, SOLOFLEX, INC. HILLSBORO, OREGON 97124

One of the primary reasons advertising uses strong visual images is that you tend to remember them better than messages containing words. The chances are very good that a week from now you will be able to recall the visual image of this ad, but not the name of the company. (Courtesy of Soloflex, Inc.)

by creating interactive images. If given the noun pair apple-clock, for example, they might imagine a large red apple with the hands of a clock extending from it. Other students were asked to remember the same noun pairs, but without forming interactive images. At the end of the learning session, those who had employed interactive images recalled about 50 percent of the noun pairs, compared with a recall rate of only about 10 percent among those who had not used such imagery (Begg & Sikich, 1984).

These findings suggest that a good way to remember a name and the face that goes with it is to make up an interactive image between the two. If you are trying to remember a woman named Price, for example, you might picture her with a price tag attached to one ear. Or if you are trying to remember a man by the name of Barber, you might visualize him leaning against an old-fashioned barber pole.

One reason that visual images serve as such good memory aids is because they create distinctive associations. Researchers Mark McDaniel and Gilles Einstein (1986) asked students to remember three words—dog, bicycle, and street—using bizarre associations, like "The *dog* rode the *bicycle* down the *street*," or common associations, like "The *dog* chased the *bicycle* down the *street*." They found that bizarre associations made the words more distinctive, and thus easier to remember. McDaniel, Einstein, and other researchers have concluded that it is the *distinctiveness* of associations, rather than their bizarreness, that leads to better recall of information (Kroll et al., 1986).

REASONS FOR FORGETTING

Selective Attention

Do you remember exactly what a penny looks like?

Look at the pennies in Figure 7.6 and decide which is the correct one. Most people find this task quite difficult. Although they have looked at pennies thousands of times, they have never paid attention to the details of the coin and so cannot remember precisely how a penny is designed. The process of attending actively to only some of the information received by one of our senses is called **selective attention**. Without selective attention, we would soon be overwhelmed by sensory data. But as we attend selectively to some details, others are forgotten. Selective attention probably explains much of the forgetting of the mugger's face in the TV film we mentioned earlier. The viewers' attention was probably captured by the dramatic actions of the attacker, making it unlikely that they would process his features well enough to remember them later.

Interference

When Marigold Linton (1978, 1982) regularly tried to remember her personal experiences, she found that she slowly but steadily forgot almost a third of the events she had considered memorable enough to record in a file six years earlier. One reason for her forgetting was a kind of confusion called **interference,** in which old memories become blended with new ones similar in content. For example, after Linton ate at a new restaurant, she was unable to remember a restaurant she ate at three weeks before. When new information interferes with previously learned information, it is called *retroactive interference.*

In addition, the more professional conventions Linton attended and the more colleagues she met, the more difficulty she had in remembering the names of new colleagues. When old information interferes with the learning of new information, it is called *proactive interference.* Psychologists think that proactive and retroactive interference are common causes of forgetting.

Inadequate Retrieval Cues

We have all had this problem. Where do you hide something valuable so that it will be in a safe location but one that you will certainly remember? I remember hiding the key to my safety deposit box in a very unlikely location, but one I was sure I would remember. Six months later, when I needed the key, I could not remember the unlikely location that I thought I would never forget. A study by Winograd and Soloway (1986) reports that

Figure 7.6
Which penny is the real one? Find a penny and find out.

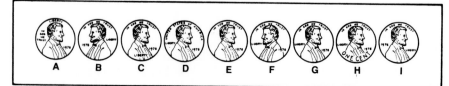

I made a common mistake. One group of students was asked to hide objects by putting them in common places. A second group was asked to hide objects by putting them in unusual places. When asked, the students reported that they would surely remember the unusual places. However, when they were asked later to recall where the objects were, students remembered the locations of more objects hidden in common places than in unusual places. One of the reasons that we forget unusual hiding places is that we do not have enough retrieval cues, which, as we noted earlier, are associations between new and old information.

Just as lack of retrieval cues keeps us from remembering where we hid something, a similar lack of cues may interfere with our remembering a name or some information that we are sure we know. This frustrating experience, which is called the **tip-of-the-tongue phenomenon,** is thought to result from having too few retrieval cues. In many cases, it is our lack of retrieval cues that causes us to forget terms, formulas, concepts, dates, and other information. Remember that you can increase retrieval cues by using visual images, concrete examples, mnemonic devices, or by rephrasing and outlining.

Why is it that we sometimes forget where we carefully hid something valuable? Check the text for the answer. (Mark Antman/The Image Works)

Repression

Suppose your grades were suffering and you decided to keep track of how much time you actually spend studying. Unknown to you, a psychologist was secretly observing and keeping track of your study time. At the end of a week, your record showed that you studied an average of four hours a day. The psychologist's record showed a much lower daily average of only two hours. One reason for this discrepancy might be a process called repression. According to Sigmund Freud, **repression** occurs when feelings or information that is threatening to our self-concept is prevented from reaching consciousness. Because these threatening occurrences do not reach consciousness, they are not remembered. In our example, you may want to protect your self-concept of being a good student by repressing the knowledge that you are often either watching television or partying when you should be studying.

Test Anxiety

For some students, taking an exam creates so much distress that they are unable to remember material that they have studied. This problem, known as **test anxiety,** can be so severe that the student's mind "goes blank" during an exam. Researchers have found that a combination of treatments, rather than a single treatment, decreases test anxiety and improves test performance. Students with text anxiety need one program to decrease their feelings of physiological arousal (heart pounding, dry mouth, sweaty palms), a second program to improve their study skills, and a third program to decrease negative self-statements that increase worrying.

To decrease physiological arousal, psychologists taught students to relax their muscle groups, beginning with their toes and working up to their heads. This technique, called *progressive relaxation,* must be practiced about 20 to 30 minutes a day for a week or two. Students were then taught study strategies, such as setting study goals, managing time, taking notes, studying for and taking tests. The last program, aimed at eliminating negative self-statements, presented students with examples of irrational beliefs—such as "I'm a failure for doing poorly on an exam"—that might lead to feelings of worthlessness and heightened anxiety. The students were encouraged to substitute rational beliefs, like "If I don't study enough, I probably won't do well." Students who completed only one of these programs reported less anxiety but did not necessarily perform better on exams. Those who completed all three programs, however, reported less anxiety and, more important, performed significantly better on exams (Crowley et al., 1986; Dendato & Diener, 1986).

Let's next look at a situation in which forgetting may have very important social consequences.

EXPLORING PSYCHOLOGY Eyewitness Testimony

Why did people identify the wrong man?

How reliable is eyewitness testimony? Several eyewitnesses identified Father Bernard Pagano (top) as the man who had committed a series of robberies, when it was really Ronald Clouser (bottom) who was responsible. (Both, UPI/Bettmann Newsphotos)

Several years ago a series of armed robberies occurred in the Wilmington, Delaware, area. The robber was dubbed the "gentleman bandit" because of his very polite manners and well-groomed appearance. The police had few leads on the gentleman bandit until a local citizen informed them that a Roman Catholic priest, Father Bernard Pagano, looked remarkably like the sketch of the robber being circulated in the media. Seven eyewitnesses positively identified Father Pagano as the culprit. At his trial, the case against him seemed airtight. But at the last minute another man, Ronald Clouser, stepped forward and confessed to the robberies. He knew details about them that only the true gentleman bandit could have known. The case against Father Pagano was dropped immediately and Clouser was charged with the crimes (adapted from Rodgers, 1982).

If you look at the photos to the left, you will wonder how this case of mistaken identity could possibly have happened. Ronald Clouser is shorter than Father Pagano, fourteen years younger, and not nearly as bald. Their facial features are dissimilar. Why, then, did seven eyewitnesses say with certainty that Father Pagano was the robber they had seen?

The explanation has to do with how the witnesses were questioned. Before showing pictures of suspects to witnesses, the police apparently had suggested the possibility that the robber was a priest. Since Father Pagano was the only suspect wearing a clerical collar, the witnesses concluded that he must be the robber. As a result, their recall was influenced, and they began to focus on the few similarities Father Pagano had to the real robber. Soon they were remembering him as the person who had committed the holdups.

In a series of clever experiments, Elizabeth Loftus and her colleagues have shown that we are all susceptible to the same kinds of memory distortions. In one experiment, for instance, subjects watched a film of an automobile accident and then were asked questions about it. One of the questions the experimental subjects were asked contained a false piece of information: "How fast was the white sports car going when it passed the barn while traveling along the country road?" In fact, no barn was shown in the movie. But for many of the experimental subjects, this very plausible suggestion was enough to cause them to infer the existence of one. When asked a week later about the film, over 17 percent of them answered "yes" to the question "Did you see a barn?" In contrast, only about 3 percent of control subjects answered "yes" to the same question (Loftus, 1975).

In another series of experiments, Loftus asked subjects to estimate the speed of two cars involved in an accident. The wording of the question differed in only one verb. Some of the subjects were asked, "How fast were the cars going when they contacted?" For others, the verb "contacted" was replaced with "hit," "bumped," "collided," or "smashed." Estimates of the speed of the cars increased with each verb, "contacted" producing the lowest estimates and "smashed" the highest. Based on many such studies, Loftus and others have concluded that information introduced at the time of questioning a witness can prompt inferences that actually alter the original memories (Loftus, 1979, 1984; Weinberg et al., 1983). Furthermore, a person's confidence about the accuracy of a recollection is *not* a good barometer of how correct the memory actually is. As the case of Father Pagano illustrates, eyewitnesses can be absolutely confident and yet be absolutely wrong.

Not only can witnesses be influenced by misleading questions, they can also be swayed by misleading visual information. Felicity Jenkins and Graham Davies (1985) showed subjects a film of a staged shoplifting crime and asked them to remember the face of the shoplifter. Next, one group of subjects saw a police artist's composite drawing of the shoplifter on which a mustache had been added. A different group saw a composite drawing on which the shoplifter's hairstyle had been changed. Finally, subjects were asked to pick out the composite drawing of the shoplifter they saw in the film. Subjects who had been shown a "doctored" drawing of the shoplifter made significantly more errors than a group that was not shown the misleading visual information. The implications of this study are clear: misleading visual information may distort eyewitness testimony in the same way that misleading questions do.

Are children more susceptible to misleading information than adults? Stephen Ceci and his colleagues (1987) found that 3- and 4-year-old children were more susceptible than older children (Figure 7.7), and that children were more easily misled if the questions were asked by adults rather than other children. Other researchers have also found that children's eyewitness testimony may be less reliable than adults' (List, 1986; Parker et al., 1986).

Psychologists have studied ways to make the interrogation of eyewitnesses more reliable. As the studies above indicate, the police should avoid asking misleading questions or showing misleading photos. Police should refrain from pressuring witnesses to make "yes/no" decisions. Witnesses under pressure may be even more susceptible to misleading cues (Warnick & Sanders, 1980). Researchers also recommend that the standard police procedure of asking open-ended questions be replaced with a cognitive interview method. In the cognitive interview, witnesses are told to go back in their memory and reconstruct the environment in which the crime occurred. After asking the witnesses to report everything they can remember, the interrogators then ask them to recall the events in a different order

Could you be influenced by misleading information?

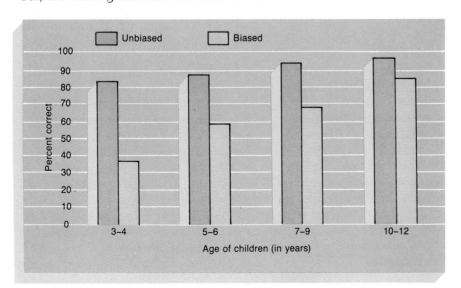

Figure 7.7

When adults asked children of different ages to answer misleading or biased questions, the younger the age, the more likely the child was to answer incorrectly. In contrast, younger children were able to respond correctly to unbiased questions. (Ceci et al., 1987)

and to envision the crime from a different perspective, such as adopting the role of a prominent character at the scene of the crime. According to researchers, the cognitive interview resulted in significantly more correct information than the standard police interview (Geiselman et al., 1985).

THE PUZZLE OF AMNESIA

A middle-aged man of normal intelligence has undergone radical brain surgery in an effort to control his frequent and severe epileptic seizures. After the surgery, he is given a number of psychological tests, including a game called the Tower of Hanoi. The game consists of three pegs plus five wooden blocks of different sizes, each with a hole in the center. At the start, the blocks are stacked in a pyramid on the left-hand peg. The object is to move all five blocks to the peg on the right. Only one block at a time can be moved, and it must be placed on one of the three pegs. In addition, no block can ever be put on a block smaller than itself. This man, who is known in medical journals as H.M., makes a few hesitant moves and announces: "I'm stuck. It can't be done."

"Yes, it can," says a watching scientist. "Just guess." H.M. makes a few more moves and then stops again. "I can't do it," he says. "Of course you can," answers the scientist. "You've done this many times before." H.M. is incredulous. "I have?" he says (McKean, 1983b, p. 19).

Kinds of Amnesia

Can someone really remember almost nothing?

H.M. is suffering from **amnesia,** a persistent total or partial forgetting of past experiences often due to some kind of brain disorder, but occasionally caused simply by severe psychological stress. The form of amnesia H.M. has is called **anterograde amnesia** because he has lost the ability to recall events occurring *after* his operation. In this respect, H.M. is very much like Norman, the brain-damaged man we discussed at the beginning of this chapter. Neither H.M. nor Norman seems to be able to transfer information from working memory into long-term storage.

From brain-damaged patients like H.M. and Norman, we have learned about some of the brain structures involved in organically caused amnesia. One of these is the hippocampus, a part of the brain that lies below the temporal lobes of the cortex (Woods et al., 1982). H.M., for instance, had part of his temporal lobes removed, along with the hippocampus beneath them. From alcoholics who have engaged in years of heavy drinking, we have learned that brain structures linked to the hippocampus are also important for memory. Such people often suffer damage to these hippocampus-related regions. The damage causes them to display *Korsakoff's syndrome,* a disorder that includes the inability to learn new information (Butters & Albert, 1982; Jacoby, 1982). From people who suffer from the form of senility called *Alzheimer's disease* we have discovered the importance to memory of the neurotransmitter acetylcholine. Alzheimer's patients show a loss of acetylcholine, and as the disease progresses, they lose all ability to form new memories (Bartus et al., 1982). Finally, from people who have suffered severe blows to the head or concussions, we have learned that temporary injury to the brain may result in loss of memories immediately preceding the accident. This type of amnesia is called **retrograde amnesia.** Some scientists suspect that in cases of severe concussion, the blow disrupts the brain processes needed to consolidate memories into long-term storage. In cases of milder concussion, in contrast, retrograde amnesia may be only temporary (Grady, 1983).

Where Are Memories Stored and How Are They Formed?

"I hear my mother and father talking and singing." And after a pause, *"Christmas carols."*

    "Oh, gee, gosh. Robbers coming at me with guns. Oh gosh, there they are. He is aiming an air rifle at me."

    "My mother is telling my brother that he has his coat on backward."
(Penfield & Perot, 1963, pp. 617, 645).

Patients reported these memories when certain areas of their brains were electrically stimulated during brain surgery. If these areas were removed, would the patients lose the memories? Maybe not, according to Mortimer Mishkin and his colleagues, who have been studying the location of memories in the brain for over 20 years. To understand where memories might be stored, the researchers removed different brain areas from monkeys and then tested the monkeys for memory deficits. Based on this study, Mishkin and Appenzeller (1987) reported that memories are formed and stored in at least six major and different structures in the brain (Figure 7.8).

Knowing that six different brain areas are involved in forming and storing memories helps us explain some of the behaviors of H.M., who lost

What do patients remember when their brains are electrically stimulated?

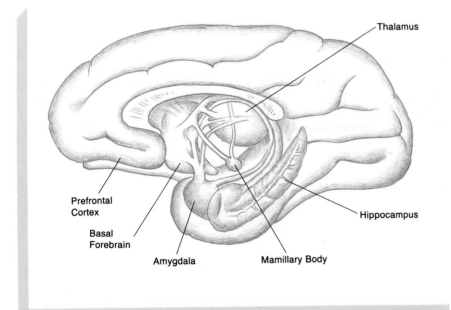

Figure 7.8
In this side view of the brain, you can see some of the structures that are involved in the formation and storage of memories. In the graph below the brain, you can compare the percent correct responses made by normal monkeys on a visual recognition task with monkeys who had one or more of these areas damaged. For example, normal monkeys make about 95 percent correct responses, while monkeys with damage to the prefrontal cortex make about 65 percent correct responses. (Adapted from Mishkin & Appenzeller, 1987)

the ability to transfer short-term semantic memories into long-term memories after his hippocampus was removed. According to Mishkin and Appenzeller, the hippocampus is one of the major areas involved in forming and storing semantic memories. However, H.M. retained the ability to remember events that happened before his surgery, and he also was able to form and store procedural or skill memories. This is because previously formed long-term memories, as well as skill memories, are located in areas other than the hippocampus. Besides tracking down the brain areas responsible for storing and forming memories, researchers are studying exactly how memories are formed. One of the ways they study the formation of memories is by looking at how memories are formed in a very simple nervous system. This brings us to the sea slug.

MAJOR CONCEPT   Forgetting

Here is a list of some of the factors that can cause forgetting. Match each one with its description.

1. Retrograde amnesia

2. Selective attention

3. Proactive interference

4. Anterograde amnesia

5. Test anxiety

6. Repression

7. Retroactive interference

8. Misleading questions

a. _8_ The eyewitness is being questioned by the police about a crime. The police have a suspect in mind and ask questions that fit their suspect. The eyewitness looks at a lineup and picks out the police's suspect, who later turns out to be innocent.

b. _3_ Your previous course in biology makes it difficult for you to learn the terms in the physiological psychology class you are presently studying.

c. _2_ You go to the large parking lot where you left a rented car and realize that all you remember was that the car was red.

d. _1_ A woman is in a car crash and, after recovering from the accident, she cannot remember events right before the crash.

e. _7_ After studying for a psychology test, you realize that you have forgotten many of the terms you learned previously for a history test.

f. _5_ When taking an exam you become so worried, aroused, and upset that you have difficulty remembering the material.

g. _4_ Because of a tumor, a person has a part of her brain removed. After the surgery, she had great difficulty forming new long-term memories.

h. _6_ You see yourself as a very friendly, considerate person. However, your friend notices that when you meet someone new, you tend to be unfriendly. When your friend asks you about your unfriendliness to strangers, you can't remember being that way.

Answers: a (8); b (3); c (2); d (1); e (6); f (5); g (4); h (6)

The sea slug is an ideal subject for studying the formation of memory because, even though it has only about 20,000 cells compared to our billions, it can form and store simple memories. For example, slugs can form and store the memory that a touch is associated with a shock, an example of classical conditioning. After being classically conditioned, the slug's nervous system is explored for any chemical or structural changes that might accompany the formation and storage of memories. Researchers have also explored the nervous system of snails as well as tiny pieces of rat brain tissue which are removed and kept alive in petri dishes. From these studies, researchers have discovered that the formation of memories involves *structural* changes in the neuron, including changes in the amount of neurotransmitter secreted, as well as *chemical* changes, including changes in the amount of enzymes needed to make neurotransmitters (Barnes, 1987; Kandel & Schwartz, 1982; Larson & Lynch, 1986; Thompson, 1986). Scientists assume that since snail, slug, and rat neurons are similar in structure and function to human neurons, human memories are formed through similar structural and chemical changes. As you studied this Module, memories were probably being formed and stored through structural and chemical changes in your brain.

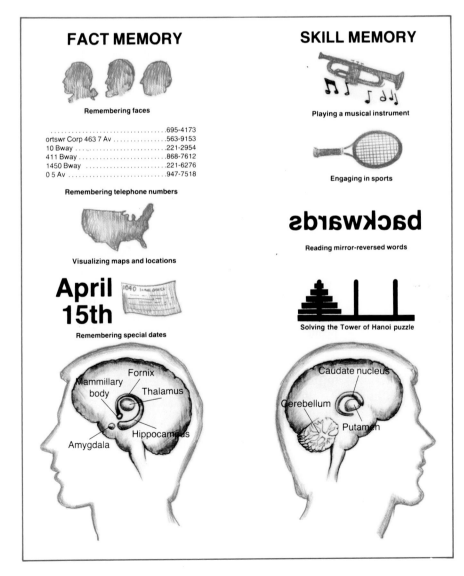

FACT MEMORY

Remembering faces

```
...........................695-4173
ortswr Corp 463 7 Av ..............563-9153
10 Bway .....................221-2954
411 Bway .....................868-7612
1450 Bway ....................221-6276
0 5 Av .......................947-7518
```

Remembering telephone numbers

Visualizing maps and locations

April 15th

Remembering special dates

Mammillary body · Fornix · Thalamus · Hippocampus · Amygdala

SKILL MEMORY

Playing a musical instrument

Engaging in sports

backwards

Reading mirror-reversed words

Solving the Tower of Hanoi puzzle

Caudate nucleus · Cerebellum · Putamen

Figure 7.9
New research shows there are at least two broad types of memory circuits in the brain. One is devoted to fact memories—explicit information such as telephone numbers, dates, and faces—that can be rapidly learned and rapidly forgotten. The other, skill memory, is concerned with less conscious learning, ranging from simple motor skills to certain types of problem solving. Skill memories are learned by repetition and are hard to unlearn. They are not "remembered" except in the doing of them. The brain structures associated with each of these types of memory are shown here. *(Adapted from McKean, 1983)*

Kinds of Memory

A few paragraphs ago you read about H.M. as he struggled with a puzzle he had solved many times but had no recollection of. The scientist working with him encourages him simply to guess, and minutes later H.M. has solved the puzzle once again—in the minimum number of moves! Initially, H.M. may have needed twice as many moves in order to win the game. After weeks of practice, however, he is quite good at solving it. His behavior suggests that he has learned the solution and is recalling the proper procedures. Yet consciously he has no memory of ever having seen this puzzle, much less worked on it before. What could possibly explain these contradictory facts?

Larry Squire (1986) believes that we may have two stores of knowledge: one for facts, such as terms and faces, and one for skills or procedures, such as solving a puzzle. Researchers further suspect that each store of knowledge may involve different areas of the brain, as Figure 7.9 shows (Cohen & Square, 1980; Graf et al., 1984; Square, 1982; Weingartner et al., 1983). Thus, H.M. cannot remember that for the last several days he has played the Tower of Hanoi game because this is factual knowledge. But without conscious awareness, he can apparently store and retrieve new procedural information, including how to solve this puzzle. This theory also explains why persons with Alzheimer's disease can remember how to swing a golf club and play the game of golf (procedural knowledge), even though they may not remember where they hit the ball or how many strokes they have taken (factual knowledge). These two kinds of knowledge seem to be processed and stored in different ways (Schacter, 1983). Let's look at where memories are stored in the brain.

REVIEW

As you stand in line to deposit your money at the bank a man runs past holding a gun and a bag of money. You were one of a dozen people who had witnessed a bank robbery. Later, police will ask you questions about the robbery.

When you search for and retrieve a specific piece of information about the robbery, it is called

(1) _____. When you retrieve information by matching the robber's gun with ones the police show

you, it is called (2) _____.

In describing what you saw, your memory jumps from going to the bank, standing in line, thinking about an exam, seeing a man running, being afraid of a gun, and wishing you had put off going to the bank until tomorrow. According to one theory of how memory is organized, each of these concepts would be considered

a (3) _____ among which you have personal associations. This theory is called the

(4) _____ network model of memory. You will be better at retrieving information from long-term memory if you have many associations between the nodes.

If you have difficulty recalling exactly how the robber looked it may be because this information was

stored with very few associations or (5) _____ cues. Perhaps your attention was captured by the sight of a gun and you did not notice his face. This tendency to attend only to some of the information available to

your senses is called (6) _____ attention. If being taken downtown and questioned by the police disrupts your memory of how much money you deposited in the bank, this would be an example of

(7) _____ interference, in which new information interferes with the recall of old information. If watching many police shows and robberies on television disrupted your memory of this particular rob-

bery, this would be an example of (8) _____ interference, in which old information interferes with the learning of new information.

You forget that you tried to leave the bank before you answered questions about the robbery. Freud would say that your action of not helping may threaten your self-concept of being a responsible citizen and therefore this information is kept from consciousness through a process called (9) _____.

You are having trouble describing the robber to the police. The questioner keeps asking whether the robber had a beard. After a while you think the robber did have a beard, when in fact the robber was clean shaven. This would be an example of your eyewitness

testimony being distorted by (10) _____ questions.

Later you hear that the robber's car crashed after a high-speed chase and the robber was knocked unconscious. When the robber woke up in the hospital later that day, he had no memory of the car crash. This is

called (11) _____ amnesia, in which a blow or damage to the brain disrupts previously learned information.

In the bed next to the robber, there is a woman who had part of her brain removed because of a tumor. The woman was told about the bank robber and the high-speed chase. However, the next day she did not remember any of this information. This is an example

of (12) _____ amnesia, in which some form of brain damage interferes with the learning of new information. Although this woman could not remember new information about the robber, she had no difficulty learning how to operate the switches to con-

trol her hospital bed. Data like this suggest there are several kinds of long-term memories that are stored in

at least six different areas of the (13) _____. The actual formation of memories involves both struc-

tural and chemical changes in (14) _____ in the brain.

Some students become so worried and physiologically aroused when they take a test that they cannot remember or think clearly. This problem, called test

(15) _____, can be helped through a combination of programs that teach relaxation, study skills, and elimination of negative self-statements.

Techniques that help people store and retrieve facts by providing strategies for organizing and encoding

information are called (16) _____ devices. For example, if you memorized the number 16411543 by forming two groups of 1641 and 1543, you would

be using a technique called (17) _____. If you had to learn a list of items in a specific order, you

might use the method of (18) _____ or the

(19) _____ system.

Answers: (1) recall; (2) recognition; (3) node; (4) semantic; (5) retrieval; (6) selective; (7) retroactive; (8) proactive; (9) repression; (10) misleading; (11) retrograde; (12) anterograde; (13) brain; (14) neurons; (15) anxiety; (16) mnemonic; (17) chunking; (18) loci; (19) pegword

GLOSSARY TERMS

amnesia (p. 220)
anterograde amnesia
 (p. 220)
chunking (p. 213)
interactive images
 (p. 214)
interference (p. 216)

method of loci (p. 213)
mnemonic devices
 (p. 213)
node (p. 212)
pegword system
 (p. 213)
recall (p. 210)

recognition (p. 210)
repression (p. 217)
retrieval cues (p. 212)
retrograde amnesia
 (p. 220)
selective attention
 (p. 216)

semantic network model
 (p. 212)
test anxiety (p. 217)
tip-of-the-tongue
 phenomenon (p. 217)

Intelligence, Thought, and Language

Module 20 Intelligence

When at the age of four Charlie was in a store with his father, the clerk thought it quite funny to see him looking through a "grown-up" book. "I'll give you that book if you can read it," the clerk teased. To his surprise, Charlie began to read fluently. When Charlie started school at the age of six, he was far ahead of his class. By age nine he had decided to become a doctor instead of an astronomer or a Standard Oil executive, two professions he had also considered. Astronomers, Charlie reasoned, didn't earn enough money, and corporate executives led lives that were too dull. At this young age most of Charlie's peers were still dreaming about becoming cowboys, baseball players, and firefighters. In high school, Charlie was placed in a special class for very bright students. His classmates admired Charlie's intelligence and agreed that he seemed to know everything. But they also agreed that Charlie was not very likable. He was tactless, unsympathetic, and very impatient when other people made any kind of error (adapted from Hollingsworth, 1942).

Michael is 19. He has never spoken an intelligible word in his life, yet he seems to know what is going on around him. His eyes are both penetrating and strangely preoccupied. It is as if he is thinking about something profoundly important that he can't convey to others. Michael has a habit of rocking his muscular body back and forth in his chair, often with grunting sounds or quick, nervous gestures. Michael suffers from autism, a mysterious and disabling disorder that affects communication, concentration, learning, and emotions. Its cause is unknown. While Michael is in many ways typical of autistic young adults, he has some extraordinary talents most of them don't have. For example, on his first try, Michael managed to solve a scrambled Rubik's cube in less than 40 seconds! This puzzle is so difficult that many people work on it for days without success. An entire book is needed to describe the steps involved in the solution. No one knows how Michael solved the Rubik's cube as quickly as he did because Michael does not speak. He is among the 10 percent of autistic persons who exhibit genius in one tiny area (adapted from Restak, 1982).

Charlie is very unusual. He has an IQ of over 180, a score obtained by less than 1 percent of the population. His extremely high IQ predicted that he would do very well in academic settings, which he does. But his high IQ could not predict whether he would be likable, which he is not. Michael too is unusual. He can solve a puzzle that very few people with high IQs can solve. In this one area, Michael is a genius. In almost every

Who do you consider exceptionally smart?

227

Is someone who has the skills to play pro football or climb dangerous mountains more or less intelligent than someone who is a great chess player? The text explains that there are different kinds of intelligence. (Right, Peter Southwick/Stock, Boston; bottom right, Bernard Giani/Photo Researchers; bottom left, courtesy of MENSA, photo by John Schmidt)

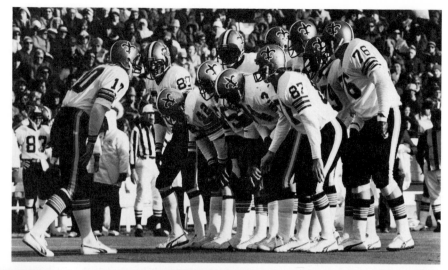

other area, however, he is retarded. What Charlie and Michael illustrate is that many different factors are involved in what we call intelligence. As you will see, IQ tests measure only certain aspects of intelligence.

HOW WOULD YOU DEFINE INTELLIGENCE?

You probably use the term *intelligent* to mean something different than psychologists do. When most people are asked to name the qualities of an intelligent person, they tend to list first *practical* problem-solving skills. Next they list verbal ability (speaking clearly, having a good vocabulary, reading widely), and then social competence (getting along with others and having a social conscience). When psychologists were asked the same question, they placed these skills and abilities in a different order: they listed verbal ability first.

What would happen if we compared your self-rating of how intelligent you think you are with your IQ score? Researchers found a low correlation (0.23) between people's self-ratings and their actual IQ scores (Sternberg & Davidson, 1982). This study indicates that IQ scores are not measuring what most people consider intelligence. In trying to define intelligence, psychologists have used two different approaches.

The Psychometric Approach

You have a number of cognitive abilities that are different from someone else's and that influence your intellectual performance. The exact number of cognitive factors has been debated; estimates range from 2 to 120. These cognitive factors might include verbal comprehension, memory ability, perceptual speed, and reasoning. Psychologists who take the **psychometric approach** decide on a list of such factors and then develop tests to measure each of them. By combining scores on the various tests, they determine overall IQ. According to the psychometric approach, then, intelligence is defined as performance on intelligence tests; it does not claim to measure natural intelligence or to explain intelligence. The major advantage of this approach is that it measures individual differences in cognitive abilities, and these differences have proved useful in predicting performance in school. The major disadvantage is that the psychometric approach does not really explain what differences in IQ scores mean (Mayer, 1983).

The Cognitive Components Approach

Try to solve the analogy problem in Figure 8.1. As you work, think about how you arrived at your answers. Typically, the solutions involve breaking down each question into smaller cognitive components. For example, in the picture analogies, you had to perceive the figures, find the rule that underlies the relationship between the first two small figures, apply that rule to the next three large figures, and then make your response. Psychologists who take a **cognitive components approach** focus on just such underlying mental processes (Sternberg, 1977, 1983, 1985). They believe it is not so much your answer that is important, but the process you use to arrive at the answer. According to this approach, differences in intelligence are reflected in differences in the cognitive components involved in solving problems. A person with high verbal ability, for example, would probably spend a great deal of time encoding and analyzing problems with words. A person with excellent visual-perceptual ability, in contrast, would be more inclined to process problems through mental imagery. In this way, the cognitive components view can begin to *explain* how people differ in their thinking. Unfortunately, however, no standardized tests yet exist to identify various cognitive components. Until such tests are developed, the cognitive components approach will not be widely used to measure intelligence. That is why in the rest of this module we will focus on tests of intelligence that come from the psychometric tradition.

CONTEMPORARY IQ TESTS

The time is the early 1900s, and you are hired as an assistant to a gifted French psychologist named Alfred Binet. Unlike many of his predecessors,

Do the smartest people have the largest brains?

Figure 8.1
To solve these analogies, you must figure out the relationship between the first two elements and then use this information to select the correct answer. Studying the cognitive processes involved in making analogies is one way to define intelligence.

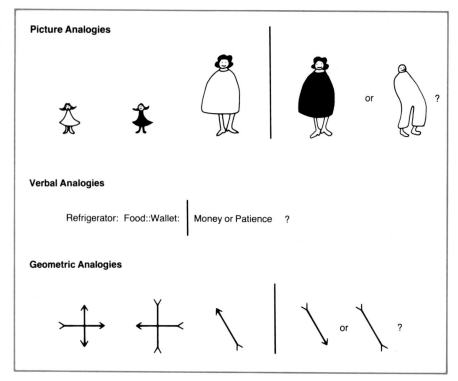

Binet does not believe intelligence can be assessed by measuring skull size, which in turn reflects the size of the brain (Yeo et al., 1987). There is simply too much evidence that the size of the brain is not closely related to powers of intellect. Instead, Binet suspects that intelligence can best be measured by assessing a person's ability to perform certain cognitive tasks, such as understanding the meaning of words or being able to follow directions.

The Beginnings of Modern Intelligence Testing

The Paris public schools have commissioned Binet and a psychiatrist named Theodore Simon to develop a test that can differentiate children of normal intelligence from those who need special help. In 1905 they succeed in introducing the world's first standardized intelligence test.

Binet's test consists of items arranged in order of increasing difficulty, with different items designed to measure different cognitive abilities. For each item, Binet has determined whether an average child of a certain age can answer the question correctly. For example, at age 2 the average child can name certain parts of the body, while at age 10 the average youngster can define abstract words such as "quickly." Suppose a particular child passed all the items that can be answered by an average 3-year-old, but none of the items deemed appropriate for older children. That child would be said to have a *mental level* of 3. In Binet's view, the concept of mental level is a means of estimating a youngster's intellectual progress relative to the average child of his or her age. For example, if a child is 6 years old but has a mental level of only 3, that child would be considered retarded in intellectual development.

It is still the early 1900s, but now you are at Stanford University in California. Professor Lewis Terman and his associates are revising Binet's test and have devised a formula to calculate the now famous **Intelligence Quotient**, or **IQ**, score (Terman, 1916). What they have done is to change mental level to mental age. A child's **mental age** is determined by the

Where did the concept of IQ come from?

number of test items passed. For example, if a 4-year-old girl passes the test items appropriate for a 5-year-old, she is said to have a mental age of 5. Terman's formula for IQ uses the terms MA, meaning mental age, and CA, meaning **chronological age** or the child's age in months and years. The formula is:

$$MA/CA \times 100 = IQ$$

To figure out the IQ of the child in our example, substitute 5 for MA, 4 for CA, and multiply by 100. You would get:

$$5/4 = 1.25 \times 100 = 125$$

An IQ of 125 is relatively high. Only a little over 2 percent of the population have IQs above 130, and only about 1 percent have IQs above 145. Charlie, whom we described earlier, has an IQ of 180. Michael, the autistic young man who is a whiz at Rubik's cube, has an IQ well below 100, which is considered the average IQ. An IQ below 40 is considered a sign of severe mental retardation.

Although Binet saw the benefits of identifying children in need of special educational classes, he realized that his intelligence tests were potentially dangerous. He warned that they did not measure innate abilities and that they should not be used to label people. History shows that neither of his warnings was heeded. In the early 1900s it became common practice to treat IQ scores as measures of inborn intelligence and to label people from moron to genius (Gould, 1981). Later in this module we will consider whether IQ tests are still being misused.

Some Widely Used IQ Tests

One of the most widely used IQ tests in America today is the **Stanford-Binet.** Developed by Terman and his associates from the original Binet test, it has since been revised several times. It can be given to children and young adults aged 2 through 18. A trained examiner administers the test on an individual basis. It consists of a number of test items, some *verbal* such as naming things and understanding instructions, and some *performance*, such as completing a picture or using colored blocks to reproduce a pattern. The test items are arranged in order of increasing difficulty and are designated appropriate for certain age levels. A child continues through the series until he or she reaches the age level at which he or she can answer none of the questions.

Another widely used series of IQ tests are the **Wechsler scales,** which are also administered individually by trained examiners. The Wechsler scales consist of separate tests for preschool children aged 4 to 6, for school-age youngsters from 6 to 16, and for adults 16 and older. Unlike those in the Stanford-Binet tests, items on the Wechsler scales are organized into various subtests. In the verbal section, for instance, there is a subtest of general information, a subtest of vocabulary, a subtest of verbal comprehension, and so forth. In the performance section, there is a subtest that involves arranging pictures in a meaningful order, a subtest that requires assembling objects, and a subtest that involves using codes, among others. The test taker receives a separate score for each of the subtests, which are then combined to yield overall scores for verbal and performance abilities. Finally, the verbal and performance scores are combined to produce a general IQ. Figure 8.2 (page 232) shows some of the items on the Wechsler Intelligence Scale for Children and the scores one child received.

If you took the Wechsler Adult Intelligence Scale as a senior in high

What IQ test have you taken?

Figure 8.2

(A) When a child takes the Wechsler Intelligence Scale for Children (WISC), she or he is asked, among other things, to arrange pictures in a correct sequence, such as for a birthday party; complete a picture, such as notice that a cup's handle is missing; assemble an object, such as putting the parts of a cat together; and code numbers into symbols. (B) To arrive at an IQ score, scores on all performance and verbal tests are totaled to yield a full-scale score. The scaled score is then converted to an IQ score—in this case, 103, which is about average. (From WISC record from © 1971, 1974, The Psychological Corporation)

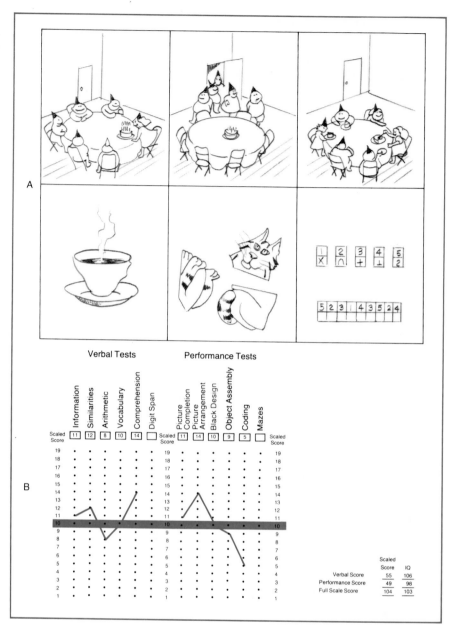

school and then took the test again as a freshman in college, you would find that your score would probably be much the same. This is another way of saying that the Wechsler scales, like other standardized IQ tests, are *reliable*. A test is reliable if it produces reasonably consistent results for any given person. *Inconsistent test scores*, in contrast, are a sign of *unreliability*. If your IQ were to fluctuate widely (high one month, low the next, and somewhere in the middle the third), psychologists would suspect that the test was not reliable. They have found that a person's scores on both verbal and performance sections of standardized IQ tests tend to remain quite stable over many years, even into old age (Denney, 1982).

INTERPRETING IQ SCORES

What does an IQ score predict?

An IQ score, of course, is nothing more than a number that tells if you scored average, above average, or below. So why do educators in this country and others devote so much effort to IQ testing? The answer is that scores on IQ tests have been found to be quite good predictors of success in school.

Predictions Based on IQ

The correlation between IQ score and performance in academic settings is as high as 0.60–0.70. If you read our discussion of correlation in Chapter 1, you may recall that 0.70 is a very high correlation coefficient. It tells us that in most cases, the higher the IQ, the higher the grades a student earns. Nevertheless, the cognitive abilities that IQ measures account for only about half of a person's performance in school, according to some estimates. The other half is attributed to personality factors and to motivation. Thus, if a person lacks persistence, is unable to concentrate, or for some reason simply does not care about schoolwork, that person's academic grades may be very poor despite a high IQ.

Although IQ is in general quite a good predictor of success in academic settings, it is *not* a good predictor of success in other areas of life. Based on IQ alone, it would be difficult to predict whether a person will have a successful career after graduating from college. Based on IQ alone, it would also be difficult to predict someone's personality or how effective that person will be in adjusting to life's problems (Zigler & Seitz, 1982). How then does a high IQ affect an individual's life?

This question was answered in a classic study begun in the early 1920s by Lewis Terman. He selected a sample of almost 1,500 children with IQs ranging from 135 to 200. (The average IQ for the group was 151.) Over the next 35 years, he followed these people to see how they did in life. He found that *in general* they enjoyed health, adjustment, and achievement above that of people with average IQs. But not all Terman's subjects were success stories. Although 80 percent of those who finished college earned an average grade of B or better, 30 percent of the total never earned a college degree, and 2 percent actually flunked out of school. And, although 85 percent of the men became professionals or managers, about 10 percent of them were dissatisfied with their work. In keeping with the times, only about 50 percent of the women sought careers outside the home, and they were generally limited to secretarial and teaching posts. Finally, although 91 percent of the Terman sample reported satisfactory mental health, the remaining 9 percent had serious emotional problems and in some cases had to be hospitalized. Of these, about 1 percent committed suicide, and 1 percent became alcoholic. A high IQ, in other words, helps but is no guarantee against academic, career, and mental health problems (Terman & Oden, 1959).

This child is taking the Stanford-Binet IQ test. For many children, IQ scores predict relatively well how they will perform in academic settings. (Mimi Forsyth/Monkmeyer)

Does a high IQ guarantee wealth and happiness?

The Misuse of IQ Tests

Larry, a black child, was assigned to special classes for the educable mentally retarded. His assignment was based on his having scored below 85 on an IQ test. However, several years later, a black psychologist retested Larry and found that his IQ score was higher than originally thought. Larry was taken out of the special classes, considered a dead end, and placed in regular classes that allow for more advancement (adapted from Kaplan & Saccuzzo, 1982).

On the basis of Larry's experience, a class action suit was brought against the San Francisco school system on behalf of all black schoolchildren in the district. The suit was based on the finding that while black youngsters made up 27 percent of all the students enrolled in classes for the mentally retarded, they comprised only 4 percent of the entire school population. Black parents wanted to know why their children were so overrepresented in these special classes. They felt there must be a bias against black children in the selection process. The federal court of appeals agreed with them. It argued that the IQ test the schools were using to determine mental retardation was biased against ethnic minorities. The court ruled

Figure 8.3

If you are white and middle class, you will probably have difficulty answering these questions because they are based on experiences in a black culture. These questions demonstrate that cultural bias can influence test performance.

Please answer the following questions:
1. A "handkerchief head" is (a) a cool cat, (b) a porter, (c) an Uncle Tom, (d) an oddi, (e) a preacher.
2. Which word is most out of place here? (a) splib, (b) blood, (c) gray, (d) spook, (e) Black.
3. A "gas head" is a person who has a (a) fast-moving car, (b) stable of "lace," (c) "process," (d) habit of stealing cars, (e) long jail record for arson.
4. "Bo Diddley" is a (a) game for children, (b) down-home cheap wine, (c) down-home singer, (d) new dance, (e) Moejoe call.
5. If a man is called a "blood," then he is a (a) fighter, (b) Mexican-American, (c) Negro, (d) hungry hemophine, (e) Redman or Indian.

(All the answers are "c.")

that California schools could not place minority children in classes for the mentally retarded on the basis of this test alone. The schools must come up with an intelligence test that does not favor whites or refrain from using a standardized test to identify slow learners (*San Diego Union*, January 24, 1984).

In order to experience cultural bias yourself, take the brief "IQ" test in Figure 8.3 Do not begin the next paragraph until you have finished it.

If you are a white, middle-class student, you probably missed most of the questions in Figure 8.3. However, if you are a black student who grew up in a ghetto, most of the answers were probably easy for you. The differences in scores between whites and blacks is due not to intelligence, but to cultural bias in the test. **Cultural bias** means that the wording of the questions and the experiences on which they are based are more common for members of some social groups than for others. Many psychologists believe that current IQ tests are significantly biased in favor of the white middle class.

Cultural bias is seldom as obvious as in Figure 8.3, but it is no less unfair. Consider the following question from the Wechsler Intelligence Scale for Children: "What would you do if you were sent to buy a loaf of bread and the grocer said he did not have any more?" If you think the answer is "Go to another store," you are correct according to the developers of the Wechsler scale. However, when 200 minority children were asked this same question, 61 said they would go home. When asked to explain their answers, they gave reasonable explanations. Some children answered "Go home" because in their neighborhood there were no other stores. Yet the answer "Go home" would be scored "incorrect," even though it was correct from the child's experience (Hardy et al., 1976). Because minority children often lack the experiences that white, middle-class test developers take for granted, they are often penalized on standardized tests of intelligence.

What can be done about cultural bias in IQ tests? One answer is to develop a **culture-free test**. Although psychologists have attempted to do this, to date they have not been successful (Anastasi, 1982). Another possibility is to use other measures to assess intellectual skills. For instance, suppose a minority student scored low on an IQ test, but showed the ability to function well in his or her environment. Based on ability to function, the child might be placed in regular school classes, rather than in a special program for the mentally retarded. This approach is likely to be hard on the child unless he or she is given remedial help to "catch up" on the cognitive skills that are needed to earn a higher IQ score and to perform well in the classroom.

Do IQ tests measure what they're supposed to measure?

If IQ tests are culturally biased, are they nevertheless valid? Surprisingly, the answer is "yes." **Valid** means that a test measures what its users want it to measure. Remember that psychologists do not think IQ tests measure innate intelligence. Rather, they measure how you perform on a number of cognitive abilities. Since your performance on IQ tests can predict future academic performance, those tests are said to be valid.

In the past, some have mistakenly interpreted IQ score as a measure of innate potential. In fact, though, an IQ score reflects both inherited potential *and* learning experiences. If a child comes from a disadvantaged environment, with few opportunities for acquiring the cognitive skills important on such tests, that child's IQ score will be low. However, placing the child in special classes for the mentally retarded is clearly not the solution. That practice merely continues the youngster's history of environmental disadvantage. The solution is to counteract the restricted opportunities for learning that have led to both low IQ and poor academic performance. We will explore some of the efforts to do just that a little later in this Module.

Now that you know something about intelligence and IQ tests, let's take a closer look at how intelligence is defined and how it is related to IQ tests.

Intelligence and IQ Scores **EXPLORING PSYCHOLOGY**

Redefining Intelligence

Alice had almost a 4.0 average as an undergraduate, scored high on the Graduate Record Exam (GRE), and was supported by excellent letters of recommendation. She seemed to have everything that smart graduate students need and was admitted to graduate school as a top pick. During her first year or two in graduate school, which involved mostly taking classes and exams, she was at the top of her class. This outstanding performance would be predicted from her proven ability to think critically and logically. However, by the time she finished, she was in the bottom half of her class. What happened to Alice? During her last two years of graduate school, she was involved in doing research, which demanded that she think creatively. Although Alice was a logical and critical thinker, she was not a creative or innovative thinker. As a result, she did not perform as well doing research as she did taking exams.

Unlike Alice, Barbara rarely did well on tests. She barely passed most of her undergraduate courses, and her GRE scores were quite low. But Barbara had superlative letters of recommendation that said she was extremely creative, had good ideas, and was a top-notch researcher. Because of her weak academic performance, Barbara was not admitted to graduate school, but one of the professors on the admissions committee was so impressed with Barbara's letters of recommendation that he hired her as a research associate. As it turned out, she proved to be a very creative and innovative thinker who helped the professor do some of his best work. As the professor said, "Alice had academic smarts, but Barbara had creativity." Then there was Celia.

Celia's grades, GRE scores, and letters of recommendation were good but not great. She was admitted to graduate school, where her performance was no more than satisfactory. When it came time to look for a job, however, Celia was the easiest to place. Although she didn't have Alice's superb logical thinking ability or Barbara's creativity, Celia had what might be called "academic street smarts." Her research projects dealt with topical issues and impressed others in her field,

Who is more intelligent, Alice, Barbara, or Celia?

and she was able to get her results published in prominent journals. So who would you say is more intelligent, Alice, Barbara, or Celia (adapted from Trotter, 1986)?

Robert Sternberg (1985), who created these examples, points out that traditional IQ tests primarily measure Alice's kind of intelligence, which is described as logical or analytical thinking. IQ tests do not indicate whether these abilities will result in her being a creative researcher or enable her to get a good job. For this reason, Sternberg and others believe that the traditional psychometric model of intelligence—which focuses on describing thinking processes or mental structures—should be revised to reflect how this structure relates to the real world (Frederiksen, 1986). That is, future models should take into consideration the intelligence shown by Barbara's creativity, Celia's practicality, and, of course, Alice's analytical thinking. Sternberg, who has developed such a model of intelligence, would conclude that Alice, Barbara, and Celia are all intelligent, but in different ways.

The question asked by Sternberg, "How are IQ scores related to real-world intelligence?" was partially answered by Stephen Ceci and Jeffrey Liker (1986). They studied the thinking and computational skills of race-track handicappers, who show an amazing kind of real-world intelligence. First, handicappers analyze an incredible amount of factual information about horses, tracks, and jockeys. Second, they combine all this information into a sophisticated model that will be used to predict how racehorses will finish. When the handicapper's success at picking winning horses was correlated with IQ score, the correlations turned out to be very low (.04–.07). This means that IQ scores would not predict the computational abilities of handicappers. The researchers concluded that there are many kinds of cognitive functions, not all of which are measured by IQ tests—and IQ tests are limited in predicting how people will react to life's challenges.

Because of this discrepancy between IQ scores and real world intelligence, Sternberg has redefined intelligence. He says **intelligence** consists of those mental functions that you use intentionally when you adapt to, shape, and select the environment in which you live and function (Sternberg, 1985). Notice that Sternberg's definition includes but goes beyond the traditional, psychometric model's definition of intelligence, which focuses on describing thinking processes or mental structures. Sternberg and others believe that it is time for a new model of intelligence, one that includes how a person functions in the real world (Sternberg & Wagner, 1986).

One of the problems with the traditional, psychometric view of intelligence is interpreting IQ scores. For example, do increases in IQ scores mean that people have become more intelligent? To answer this, we need to look closely at what IQ tests measure.

What Do IQ Tests Measure?

In the Netherlands, almost all 18-year-old men are tested by the military. When James Flynn (1987) compared the IQ scores of the men tested in 1952 with those tested in 1962, 1972, and 1982, what he found was an event that he says is unique in the literature. He reported that in the 30-year period between 1952 and 1982, IQ scores rose a whopping 21 points. In addition, Flynn reported that similar large gains in IQ scores (15–20 points) also occurred in France, Australia, Japan, West Germany, and to a lesser extent in the United States (12 points between 1932 and 1972).

Flynn described what such large gains in IQ scores mean in practical terms. Individuals with IQs above 130 should find school easy and have the potential to succeed at virtually any occupation; those with IQs above 140 have the potential to make the kinds of contributions that are internationally recognized; an IQ above 150 indicates the potential to become the kind of creative genius who makes an important contribution to civilization. With the increase in IQ scores in the Netherlands alone, there would be over 300,000 people who qualify as potential geniuses.

In spite of the dramatic increase in IQ scores in the Netherlands and other countries, there has not been an equivalent rise in the performance of schoolchildren, in the incidence of geniuses, or in mathematical or scientific discoveries.

Because the massive increase in IQ scores was not accompanied by other evidence of increases in intelligence, Flynn reached two important conclusions. First, based on the best available data, he estimated that about 5 points of the 20-point rise in IQs resulted from a combination of genetic and environmental factors, such as higher levels of education, social and economic gains, and increased sophistication at taking tests; the remaining 15 points of the gain were attributed to unknown environmental factors. Second, Flynn cast doubt on the widely held assumption that IQ tests measure general intelligence. According to Flynn, these tests only measure something that is weakly linked to intelligence, such as the ability to solve abstract problems. This conclusion is contrary to the belief that IQ tests measure general intelligence, which is held by some psychologists (Eysenck, 1971; Jensen, 1978). Flynn points out that the data on huge increases in IQ scores clearly indicate that IQ tests do not measure general intelligence but only something weakly related to it, such as abstract problem-solving ability.

Although psychologists have not identified the environmental factors that caused the 15–20 point increase in IQ scores in many parts of the world, they have identified some of the factors that contribute to an individual's IQ score.

CONTRIBUTIONS OF HEREDITY AND ENVIRONMENT TO IQ

Psychologists have long been curious about the relative contributions of heredity and environment to individual differences in IQ. If you have ever wondered why one friend has a high IQ and another an IQ around average, you are asking a question many psychologists have tried to answer. What they have done is to study people whose genetic and environmental similarities can be reasonably estimated. Studies of twins have been particularly useful for this purpose. Such studies show that when considering members of the white middle class, heredity makes a relatively large contribution to IQ differences. This makes sense when you stop to think that one white middle-class environment is often very much like another. Therefore, IQ differences *within* this social group are bound to be rather heavily influenced by genes.

However, the causes of differences *within* a social group tell us nothing whatever about the causes of differences *between* groups. Although the difference in IQ between two middle-class white children may be explained to a large extent by heredity, this is not to say that the IQ difference between the average black and average white American child is equally attributable to genes. The reason is that the average black and the average white have very different environments, which are also contributing to their test scores.

Why might blacks on average have lower IQ scores than whites?

To do well on IQ tests, a child must have acquired certain cognitive skills and information that are more available in a white, middle-class environment than in a minority environment. (Left, Joel Gordon; right, Alice Kandell/ Photo Researchers)

Many psychologists believe these environmental differences alone are enough to account for any IQ gap between the two groups.

What would happen if lower-class children were given the same advantages as upper-class children? To answer this question, a group of French researchers studied children who had been abandoned as babies by their lower-class parents and adopted during the first 6 months of life into upper-middle-class families. The IQs of these children were compared with those of other lower-class youngsters who had been raised by their natural parents. Any average differences between the two groups could be assumed to be caused by differences in environment. The researchers found that the mean IQ of the adopted children was 14 points higher than that of the children born and raised in lower-class settings. The adopted children also failed in school four times less often. Apparently, changes in environment can go a long way toward boosting both IQ scores and performance in the classroom (Schiff et al., 1982).

Knowing this, what would you guess would happen if black children from disadvantaged families were adopted and raised by white, middle-class parents? Researchers who studied just such children found that their IQs were as much as 20 points higher than those of black children raised in disadvantaged homes (Scarr & Weinberg, 1976). Once again, we see how strongly environment can affect IQ level. It has been estimated that, depending on environment, IQ can vary as much as 20 to 25 points (Zigler & Seitz, 1982).

Based on these findings, many developmental psychologists now believe that the debate over the relative importance of heredity and environment in determining intelligence is no longer useful or meaningful. Instead, they recommend that psychology focus on measuring what they call the reaction range for intelligence (Zigler & Seitz, 1982). **Reaction range** refers to the degree IQ scores may vary as a result of environment. Since the reaction range may be as much as 20 to 25 points, heredity establishes a very broad range for intellectual development. Within that range, a child's IQ may vary greatly depending on his or her environment. Thus, instead of asking whether heredity or environment is more important, we should ask, "How much does the environment raise or lower IQ scores?" Let's look at how a change in environment affects IQ scores.

Which is more important, heredity or environment?

Intervention Programs   **APPLYING PSYCHOLOGY**

Nancy, in her mid-twenties, is pregnant. She lives in a lower-class black neighborhood and earns less than $1,500 a year. She has completed only two years of high school, and her IQ is 85. Given this background, psychologists would predict that Nancy's child is unlikely to acquire the kind of cognitive skills needed to do well in school. The youngster is a good candidate for an intervention program (adapted from Ramey et al., 1982).

Can preschool programs boost IQ?

The **intervention** program in which Nancy enrolled her child was called the Abecedarian Project (Ramey et al., 1982). After birth, the baby spent 6 or more hours daily, 5 days a week, in a carefully supervised day-care center. The day care continued until the child entered public school. The goal of the program was to teach youngsters from disadvantaged environments the cognitive and social skills needed for success in academic settings. Stress was placed on language skills, including the use of daily routines to help master concepts. For example, as a child helped to set the table for lunch, he or she might be encouraged to count the utensils or name the shapes of the dishes.

At the end of the fourth year, children in the intervention program had IQ scores that were 12 points higher than control children from disadvantaged environments. This difference clearly showed that intervention programs could raise IQ scores. However, by the end of the fifth year the difference in IQ scores was reduced to 7 points. Apparently the disadvantaged children who were not in the intervention program were benefiting from having started public schooling. Herman Spitz (1986) reviewed a number of intervention programs and concluded that, in most of the programs, IQ increases were transitory and difficult to maintain (Figure 8.4). The reason for the transitory increase in IQ scores is not clear. Some believe that when the child leaves the intervention program and is no longer provided with the proper environment, the IQs start to decline. Others believe that young children do learn skills that lead to IQ gains but that these skills do not generalize to different IQ tests and thus scores decline.

At the same time, no one denies that intervention programs, such as the Abecedarian Project or the well-known Head Start program, can be positive experiences for the child and parents. For example, adolescents who had been in the Head Start program were more likely to be in classes appropriate for their ages rather than to have had to repeat a class, were less likely to show antisocial or delinquent behavior, and were more likely

Figure 8.4
Children from disadvantaged homes may score low on IQ tests, partly because they have not been exposed to the kinds of skills assessed by IQ tests. With 100 considered the average IQ, one group of disadvantaged children scored below 80. Some of these children, called the experimental group, were placed in a special program, which gave them many kinds of educational experiences. Others, called the control group, were given no additional training and remained in their home environments. The children in the experimental group showed a significant increase in IQ scores for the first 5 years. However, the difference in IQ scores between the groups disappeared by age 8, when those in the control group finished the first grade of regular school. Studies such as this suggest that gains in IQ scores due to early educational programs are not very long lasting. (Adapted from Schweinhart & Weikart, 1980)

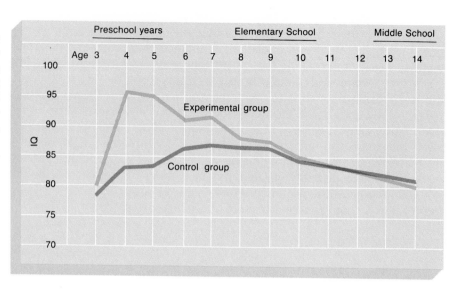

to hold jobs (Zigler & Seitz, 1982). Mothers who had been in the Head Start program reported fewer psychological symptoms, greater feelings of mastery, and greater current life satisfaction (Parker et al., 1987). These data indicate that although IQ increases may be transitory, there are long-term positive benefits to both the participating children and mothers in terms of social and personal well-being.

MAJOR CONCEPT Intelligence and IQ Testing

A great many misunderstandings surround the subject of IQ testing.

Below are several statements about this topic. Are they true (T) or false (F)?

1. T/F IQ tests measure innate intelligence.

2. T/F If a child receives a score of 65 on an IQ test, it definitely means that the child is retarded.

3. T/F IQ tests are good predictors of success in school.

4. T/F People with high IQs are virtually guaranteed to earn a lot of money.

5. T/F Many psychologists believe that almost all the currently available IQ tests are to some extent culturally biased.

6. T/F If an IQ test is reliable, it will provide reasonably consistent results for any given person.

7. T/F An IQ test can still be valid even if it fails to measure the cognitive abilities it is intended to measure.

8. T/F A person's scores on IQ tests usually change quite dramatically from one stage of life to another.

9. T/F Heredity seems to establish a broad range within which IQ can vary, depending on the environment.

10. T/F Most psychologists believe that the average difference in IQ scores between white and black Americans can be taken as evidence of genetic differences.

Answers: 1 (F); 2 (F); 3 (T); 4 (F); 5 (T); 6 (T); 7 (F); 8 (F); 9 (T); 10 (F)

REVIEW

A time machine takes you back to the early 1900s, to the office of the Minister of Public Education in Paris. He is talking to a psychologist who has just produced for the Paris schools the world's first standardized intelligence test. The psychologist's name is Alfred

(1) _____. The minister is listening to Binet tell how the new test will allow the schools to assess each child's ability to perform certain cognitive tasks, such as understanding the meaning of words and following directions. For each question, Binet has determined whether the average child of a certain age can get that item right. By seeing which age-level questions a particular youngster can answer, Binet has a yardstick for identifying students who lag behind their peers.

You recognize Binet's name because it appears in a test you took in grade school called the

(2) _____ - _____. On this test, the number of questions you answered right determined what is called your (3) _____ age. Then your mental age was divided by your

(4) _____ age to yield your (5) _____

_____, or IQ.

Having seen the great optimism with which Binet's new test is greeted, you are anxious to move into the future and see how intelligence testing develops. You reenter your time machine and set the dial for the year 1950. This time you emerge in the United States, in the office of a psychologist named David Wechsler. He and his colleagues have just introduced an intelligence test for adults, and they are now working on a similar test for school-age children. The series of IQ tests they

are designing is collectively called the (6) _____

_____. These scales illustrate the

(7) _____ approach to measuring IQ. Another approach, which measures IQ by assessing underlying mental processes, is called the (8) _____

_____ approach.

As you enter Wechsler's office, he and his associates are discussing the extent to which their IQ test for children has so far yielded consistent results. When the test is given to the same group of youngsters on two separate occasions, the scores they receive are very similar. This finding shows that the preliminary Wechsler Intelligence Scale for Children looks to be very

(9) _____. Wechsler and his colleagues are

also concerned that the test they are developing will in fact measure the cognitive abilities they want it to measure. In other words, they want to be sure that the

test is also (10) _____.

As you move through the 1950s and 1960s, you can see how popular intelligence testing has become in American schools. You set your dial for the year 1970 and touch down in the middle of a U.S. Senate hearing on a federally funded project called Head Start. A psychologist is giving the senators on the committee a progress report on Head Start's efforts to teach cognitive skills to preschool children from underprivileged homes. The psychologist explains that heredity alone does not determine a child's IQ. Instead, heredity gives a child a range of developmental possibilities that may then be fulfilled or thwarted, depending on the child's learning experiences. This range through which

IQ may vary is called the (11) _____

_____. According to the psychologist, studies show that the reaction range for intellectual development is usually quite broad. A person's IQ can vary by as much as 20 or 25 points, depending on environment.

You enter the time machine once again and move on to the year 1980. This time you are in a federal courtroom in the state of California. You eavesdrop on a suit being brought against a school system for placing black children in classes for the mentally retarded solely on the basis of IQ scores. You hear psychologists testify that IQ tests contain questions which favor the knowledge and experience of children from the white middle class. Standardized IQ tests, they say, are to some ex-

tent culturally (12) _____. In the opinion of many experts, it is very hard to produce a totally (13)

_____ - _____ test.

At the present time, some psychologists believe that IQ tests measure general intelligence. However, in a number of countries, there have been huge increases in IQ scores without evidence of increases in general intelligence. From these data, Flynn concluded that

IQ scores do not measure general (14) _____ but rather something that is weakly associated with it,

such as the ability to solve (15) _____ problems.

Sternberg noted that traditional, psychometric IQ

tests primarily measure (16) _____ thinking and do not relate this thinking to the real world. In light of this problem, he suggests a new model of intelligence. This new model takes into account analytical thinking, as well as innovative or (17) _____ thinking and how one functions in the real (18) _____.

GLOSSARY TERMS

chronological age
   (p. 231)
cognitive components
   approach (p. 229)
cultural bias (p. 234)

culture-free text (p. 234)
intelligence (p. 236)
Intelligence Quotient
   (IQ) (p. 230)

intervention (p. 239)
mental age (p. 230)
psychometric approach
   (p. 229)

reaction range (p. 239)
Stanford-Binet (p. 231)
valid (p. 234)
Wechsler scales (p. 231)

Module 21 Thought
FORMING CONCEPTS

How do you know a dog when you see one?

Look at the dogs in Figure 8.5. Notice that some of the animals are tiny, others huge; some are big-eared, others small-eared; some are fuzzy, and others smooth-haired. Despite all these differences and without the slightest hesitation, you classify each one as a dog. What has puzzled psychologists is exactly how you learn to place things into such categories or **concepts.**

Theories of Concept Formation

As you were growing up, you encountered a four-legged animal and were told that it was a *dog.* You began calling any four-legged creature, including

Figure 8.5

The text explains how you decide which of these animals best fits your concept of "dog." (Chuck Fishman/Woodfin Camp & Associates)

cats, sheep, and pigs a "dog." With help from your parents, you learned to identify animals that were certainly dogs. Several major theories explain how you developed the concept of "dog."

According to the **classical theory,** an animal is a "dog" because it has certain **defining characteristics,** such as four legs, a tail, a nose, and hair. You learned that these features or characteristics had to be present for an animal to be called a "dog." For many years, most psychologists favored the classical theory. However, the theory poses a serious problem. Think again of the defining characteristics of a dog. You will discover that these characteristics also apply to other animals, such as bears, wild pigs, and certain monkeys. From this example, you can see that for some concepts, it is very difficult to specify the defining characteristics that distinguish that concept from all others (Rey, 1983; Smith & Medin, 1981).

As a child, you noticed that animals called "dogs" have certain traits in common, such as a tail and a nose. You also noticed that these traits vary within certain limits. Some dogs have very short noses and others have very long ones, but no dog had a nose as long as an elephant's. After observing the most frequently occurring characteristics of many animals called "dogs," you formed a general concept of what a dog looks like. This general concept is called a **prototype.** For example, your prototype of a dog might include the following: an animal that is about 2 feet high, since this is the average height of dogs, has a relatively short nose (midway between the flat nose of a bulldog and the long thin nose of a collie), and makes a barking sound. Your prototype of a dog is not of any particular dog; it is an abstract idea of what an average dog looks and sounds like. Once you have developed a prototype of "dog," you can use it to decide whether a small animal you see is close enough to that prototype to be labeled a dog rather than a large cat (Cohen & Murphy, 1984; Rosch, 1978).

Classical theory suggests that you reject the idea that a large cat is a dog because it does not possess a dog's defining characteristics, but the theory has difficulty specifying what these defining characteristics are. In contrast, **prototype theory** says that a large cat does not fit your prototype of a dog. As shown in Figure 8.6, some examples do not always fit our prototypes.

The Importance of Concepts

Take a walk around your neighborhood and notice all the individual objects, including cats, dogs, birds, people, bikes, and cars. As you encounter each object, you do not have to stop and think about what it is. Your prototypes allow you to determine whether a four-legged animal with a tail is a dog or an alligator, whether a two-legged animal is a bird or a person. One advantage of concepts is that they allow you to process information more effectively by grouping objects into categories (Rosch, 1978). Another advantage of concepts is that they provide clues as to how you should behave in different situations (Tversky & Hemenway, 1984). Your behavior would be very different if you placed a four-legged animal into the category "alligator" instead of the category "dog." In much the same way, you know how to use a new telephone, drive a stranger's car, or register for a new class. You are able to draw on the knowledge of concepts that you have learned.

Knowledge of one concept may help you to understand another concept. For example, you may find it easier to understand the concept one trillion by drawing on your knowledge of time. Figure 8.7 shows how long it would take to count to one trillion.

Why isn't a small dog called a large cat?

Figure 8.6
Although they are birds, turkeys look strange perched on a windowsill. That's because turkeys do not completely fit your prototype of a "bird." (From Allman, W.F. (1986). Mindworks. *Science 86,* May, p. 26)

Figure 8.7

Most of us have a very difficult time grasping the concept, one trillion. By translating it into something we already know, such as time, we get an idea of how big one trillion really is. For example, the 32,000 years it takes to count to one trillion is longer than there has been civilization on earth. *(From Parade magazine, May 31, 1987, p. 9)*

BIG NUMBERS

Name (U.S.)	Number (written out)	Number (scientific notation)	How long it would take to count to this number from 0 (one count per second, night and day)
One	1	10^0	1 second
Thousand	1,000	10^3	17 minutes
Million	1,000,000	10^6	12 days
Million	1,000,000,000	10^9	32 years
Trillion	1,000,000,000,000	10^{12}	32,000 years

MAJOR CONCEPT   FORMING CONCEPTS

Concepts simplify and order our surroundings, helping us to predict events and plan our own responses. Most psychologists today favor the prototype theory of concept formation.

Decide whether each of the statements below is consistent with the prototype theory (P), with the classical theory of concept formation (C), or with both (B).

1. P C B   Although you know full well what the concept "game" means, you find it hard to define precisely.

2. P C B   You learn in your biology course that reptiles are egg-laying, cold-blooded animals with lungs.

3. P C B   You think an apple is a better example of the concept "fruit" than a pea pod.

4. P C B   You decide that a penguin is a bird because it has feathers and lays eggs just as all birds do.

Answers: 1 (P-prototype theory); 2 (B-both); 3 (P-prototype theory); 4 (B-both)

SOLVING PROBLEMS

In 1968, when computers were just beginning to be programmed to solve complex problems, David Levy, a British international chess master, wagered $1,000 that no machine would beat him at chess in the next ten years. When that deadline came and went and he was still undefeated, Levy was persuaded to renew the challenge until 1984. Additional backers were found, and a total of $6,000 was offered to any computer that could beat Levy. Recently, a four-game match was held in London. The result: human 4, computer 0. The failure of the best computer chess program to defeat the brain of a chess master underlines the difficulty in programming machines to think and solve problems as effectively as people (adapted from the Los Angeles Times, *June 12, 1984).*

Can a human defeat the world's fastest computer in chess?

Understanding why a computer loses a chess match to a human will help you understand something of what is involved when you try to solve a problem. A chess match between a human and a computer is essentially a match between cleverness and speed. Human chess masters disregard most of the moves and identify only those that have the most potential for winning. Once they have identified these moves, experts examine them in great depth. In contrast, a computer is programmed to examine *all* the positions on the board for about the next four moves. To do this, the computer must search through about 30 million possibilities (Peterson, 1983). The obvious question is, "Why doesn't the computer use a problem-solving strategy similar to that of humans?" The answer is that no one has been able to specify the exact steps that chess masters use in determining which moves to make. But psychologists have identified some of the general elements involved in solving complex problems. Let's look at some of these elements.

What's Involved in Problem Solving?

There are two main requirements for effective problem solving. The first is having ample knowledge of the subject area involved. Chess masters, for instance, can beat a computer because they have thousands of hours of playing experience. With experience comes a knowledge of what to look for and how to respond in various situations. In the same way, a trained mechanic is much better than the average person at solving a problem with a car. From many hours of experience with engines, the mechanic has detailed knowledge of them that enables him to diagnose most problems quite quickly.

The second requirement for effective problem solving is a thoughtful solution strategy of some kind. If you approach a difficult problem in a random hit-or-miss fashion, it is not very likely that your efforts will be successful. Far more effective are problem-solving strategies that give order and direction to the task.

A number of psychologists have tried to develop computer models that incorporate some of the general problem-solving strategies people use in approaching problems of all kinds. One of these models is called the **general problem solver** (Newell & Simon, 1972). It is based on verbal reports collected from people who were in the process of solving a problem and who were asked to describe their thinking. The general problem solver includes a number of commonly used strategies. One is **subgoal analysis,** in which the overall problem is broken down into a series of smaller, more manageable subproblems, each involving a goal of its own. For example,

How would you solve the problem of a car that won't start?

Figure 8.8
Following the general problem-solver model, you would break these problems down into a series of smaller, more manageable steps.

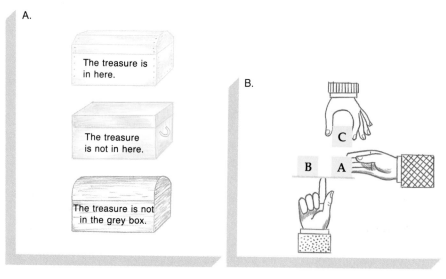

A. If one—and only one—of the inscriptions on the boxes is true, which box should you open to find the treasure?

Answer: If the treasure is in the grey box, then the first inscription is true but so is the second. Since only one inscription can be true, the treasure cannot be in the grey box. If the treasure is in the green box, the second and third inscriptions are true. The only case in which just one of the three statements is true is when the treasure is in the yellow box.

B. Computers are powerful because many tasks can be reduced to a set of rules and symbols. But if the rules are in the wrong order, computers are helpless. How would you rearrange these rules so the computer can find the heaviest block?
a. Weigh A against B. b. Weigh B against C. c. Weigh A against C. d. If A is heavier, skip the next 3 statements. e. If A is heavier, skip the next 4 statements. f. If B is heavier, skip the next 5 statements. g. Mark A "heaviest." h. Mark B "heaviest." i. Mark C "heaviest." j. Skip the next statement. k. Skip the next two statements. l. Skip the next three statements. m. End.

Answer: a, d, b, f, k, c, e, i, l, h, j, g, m.

if your car will not start, you might check the fuel supply, the spark plugs, and the carburetor, in that order. Your subgoal is to make sure nothing is wrong in these areas. If you find something wrong, a second strategy would come into play, one called **means-end analysis.** It involves trying to find a way to close the gap between your current situation and one of your subgoals. For example, if you discovered you were out of gas, you would try to think of a way to get a few gallons to put into your tank. In using means-end analysis, you are constantly asking yourself three questions: (1) What is my subgoal? (2) What obstacles are in my way? (3) How can I overcome those obstacles? (Mayer, 1983). Both subgoal and means-end analyses are central to the general problem solver.

To test your problem-solving skills, try solving the problems in Figure 8.8 a and b. Another kind of problem solving involves making decisions. How would you make the following decision?

APPLYING PSYCHOLOGY   How We Make Decisions

In which situation would you buy another $30 ticket to a rock concert?

You have decided to see a rock concert and have bought a $30 ticket. As you approach the ticket-taker, you discover that you've lost your ticket. You can't remember your seat and can't prove to the ticket-taker that you have lost your ticket. Would you spend $30 to buy a new ticket?

You have decided to see a rock concert and have reserved a $30 ticket at the ticket booth. As you approach the booth to pay for your ticket, you discover that you've lost the $30 you put in your back pocket for the ticket. You still have $30 in your wallet. Would you use this money to pay for the ticket (adapted from McKean, 1985)?

Framing

In both examples, you have lost $30. If you are like most people, you would be more likely to buy a ticket after losing the cash, but not after losing the ticket. Since you lose $30 either way, are you being illogical or irrational in deciding to spend the money in one case and not in the other? Amos Tversky and Daniel Kahneman (1974, 1980, 1983), two very creative thinkers and problem solvers, have determined that our decision making is greatly determined by how a decision is presented, which Tversky and Kahneman call **framing**. According to Tversky and Kahneman, you would probably decide to buy another ticket only after losing the cash because, in the first instance, the $30 loss is presented or framed as if you are buying another ticket. This means spending a total of $60 on tickets, which may be more than you wanted to spend. If you lose the cash, however, the loss is presented or framed as if you are simply replacing the $30 you lost; the cost of the ticket remains at a manageable $30.

The importance of framing in decision making was illustrated by researchers who asked subjects whether they would choose surgery or radiation as a treatment for cancer. Many more subjects choose radiation treatment over surgery if the choice was framed in terms of how many people survive after radiation treatment, rather than if the choice was framed in terms of how many people die from radiation treatment.

Availability

In my late afternoon class I often ask students, "Did more good things or bad things happen to you today?" Their most common answer is, "More bad things." But if I press them, they can often come up with as many good things as bad things. If they had experienced about an equal number of good and bad things, why did they decide that more bad things had happened? According to Tversky and Kahneman, the judgment that "more bad things" had happened was based on a decision-making rule called heuristic. **Heuristics** (hyoo-RIS-tiks) are rules of thumb or cognitive strategies that serve as shortcuts in making decisions. One such rule, the *availability* heuristic, explains why students decided that more bad things had happened to them. According to the availability heuristic, we will decide that certain events occurred more frequently if we can more easily recall other, similar events. This means students will decide that more bad things happened provided they can more easily recall other, similar bad things.

However, if students are given an assignment to pay attention to good things for the next few days, they will often answer that "more good things" happened to them on those days. Try this yourself, and you will experience the availability heuristic.

Representativeness

Linda is 31, single, outspoken, and very bright. She majored in philosophy in college. As a student, she was deeply concerned with discrimination and other social issues, and participated in antinuclear demonstrations. Which of these two statements is more likely to be true?
  (a) Linda is a bank teller.
  (b) Linda is a bank teller and active in the feminist movement.
    (McKean, 1985)

If you are like most people, you picked "b" because being a bank teller and a feminist seems more representative of Linda than just being a bank teller. That is, you compared the description of Linda to your mental image of someone who would be involved in social issues. You look for a match between your mental representation of a socially involved person and either someone who is a bank teller, or a bank teller and feminist. The best match between your mental representation of a socially involved person is alternative "b," which is the one that is most often chosen. But as you will see, it is the wrong answer. This choice is based on the *representative heuristic,* which means that you make an intuitive judgment about how likely some event is by comparing that event with your mental image or representation of that event.

Very often the representative heuristic results in a reasonably accurate conclusion. Suppose you had to answer this question: If you had an accident with a truck, is the truckdriver more likely to be a man or a woman? Using the representative heuristic, you would probably answer "man," because "man" matches better your mental representation of a truckdriver. And because a much higher percentage of truckdrivers are in fact male, your answer would be correct. But in using the representative heuristic in answering the question about Linda, you would be wrong because you overlooked a basic law of probability. This law says that the likelihood of two independent events happening together, such as Linda's being *both* a bank teller and a feminist, is always less than the odds of either event happening alone, such as Linda being *either* a bank teller or a feminist. According to this law, Linda is more likely to be just a bank teller. In some cases, using the representative heuristic may lead to making the wrong decision because we overlook other considerations, such as the laws of probability.

Although some of our decisions may seem irrational, Tversky and Kahneman have pointed out that there is an underlying logic, as exemplified by framing and the use of heuristics. Being aware of these underlying conditons and rules may help us make better decisions.

MAJOR CONCEPT   Problem Solving and Decision Making

Match each term with the description that fits it best.

a. Subgoal analysis

b. Means-end

c. Framing

d. Availability heuristic

e. Representative heuristic

1. __C__ How you make a decision will be affected by how a question or statement is stated or presented.

2. __C__ You decide how likely a situation is by matching the situation to your mental image.

3. __a__ You break down the problem of studying for a final exam into a list of facts and concepts that must be mastered.

4. __B__ You think of ways to close the gap between your current situation and what you want to achieve.

5. __d__ You decide that certain events occurred more frequently because you can more easily recall other, similar events.

Answers: 1(c); 2(e); 3(a); 4(b); 5(d)

THINKING CREATIVELY

Can you answer these puzzles?

1. Two men play five games of checkers. There are no ties, yet each man wins the same number of games. How could this happen?
2. The barber of Seville shaves all those men and only those men of Seville who do not shave themselves. If the barber is also a resident of Seville, who shaves the barber?
3. A gardener is asked to plant five rows of four trees each, but the nursery delivers only ten trees. "Never mind," the gardener says, "I can do the job with ten trees." How does he manage?

The answers to these questions are given in Figure 8.11. But before you look, try thinking of different, unusual, or imaginative solutions to these puzzles. Solving them is different from answering multiple-choice questions. Their solution requires that you suspend logic and make an intuitive or creative leap. Who says, for example, that your five rows of trees cannot cross one another? Now think of a simple geometric form that involves five criss-crossing lines. When you break free of traditional ways of thinking, you are displaying one form of creativity.

What Is Creativity?

How creative is Dr. Seuss?

Michelangelo's paintings, Einstein's and Freud's theories, and Dr. Seuss's books would all be considered creative according to one definition of creativity. That definition says that creativity involves cognitive activity that results in socially valuable products. Creativity is thus measured by inventions, discoveries, paintings, and other recognized novel products (Simonton, 1984).

A second definition of creativity ignores the social value of an outcome and requires only a shift of viewpoint that will result in as many answers as possible to a single question. According to this definition, creativity may be measured by **divergent thinking**—that is, thinking that involves many possible solutions. Some of the traits assumed to be related to divergent

Figure 8.9
Water lilies double in area every 24 hours. At the beginning of the summer, there is one water lily on a lake. It takes 60 days for the lake to become covered with water lilies. On what day is the lake half covered? *Hint:* If you try to work forward from one water lily to the next, you will have little success. Instead, begin on the sixtieth day and work backward. (Answer in Figure 8.11.) (After Sternberg and Davidson, 1982)

thinking include language fluency, flexibility, originality, and the abilities to change approaches and produce unusual solutions (Guilford, 1967; McCrae, 1987). People who can name many possible uses for a paper clip are said to be high in creativity because of their divergent thinking ability. The opposite of divergent thinking is **convergent thinking,** which refers to starting with a problem and thinking of a single solution. If someone asked you how long it would take to drive across the United States at 55 mph using the shortest route, you would need to use convergent thinking to answer this question.

You might naturally assume that IQ and creativity are closely related, but are they? The answer to this question is not simple. Compared with the general population, creative scientists, writers, and artists generally score above average on intelligence tests. However, when creative individuals are compared among themselves, there is at best only a modest correlation between creativity and IQ. In other words, those who are generally recognized as creative do tend to have above-average IQ scores, but those with the highest IQs are not necessarily those who are the most creative (Barron & Harrington, 1981).

Increasing and Decreasing Creativity

Based on her research, Teresa Amabile (1983) described the characteristics of creative work: knowledge and expertise in a particular area, the ability to concentrate and persist, a thinking style that generates new ideas, and, most important, intrinsic motivation and a love of what you are doing.

In Amabile's studies, the importance of intrinsic motivation was highlighted when subjects wrote less creative stories or made less inventive art pieces if they were told to make them for an external or extrinsic reward (Amabile, 1985; Amabile et al., 1986). Of course, many people who receive fame and money as a result of their creativity continue to be creative. The reason is that these individuals maintain their intrinsic motivation *in spite of* the external rewards (Kohn, 1987). In light of her studies, Amabile has said that creativity will be discouraged if parents, educators, and managers promote competition and reward certain behaviors. To stimulate creativity, Amabile suggests that parents, educators, and managers encourage creativity for is own sake, which in turn will increase intrinsic motivation.

Amabile (1983) has outlined a comprehensive program for encouraging creativity in children and adults. Her program includes providing a stimulating environment, teaching children how to identify creative thinking, advising parents, educators, and managers to encourage certain nonconforming and unpredictable behaviors that may lead to creative performances, allowing as much freedom as possible in working and completing tasks and, of course, decreasing competition and increasing intrinsic motivation. She believes that the efforts needed to develop and implement this program in a school or a workplace would be more than justified by the accompanying increase in creativity.

Other approaches to encouraging creativity involve training in divergent thinking (Figure 8.10). One of the best known, called **brainstorming,** involves a group of people trying to solve a specific problem (Osborn, 1963). Group members must follow four rules:

1. Do not criticize the suggestions of others.
2. Generate as many ideas as possible.
3. Attempt to be original.
4. Build on others' suggestions.

Figure 8.10

What can you make with a paper plate, a cup, a plastic spoon, a piece of yarn, a napkin, and 4 toothpicks? *(Courtesy of IBM)*

Great minds don't think alike.

What can you make with a paper plate, a cup, a plastic spoon, a piece of yarn, a napkin and 4 toothpicks? That's the sort of problem students will face May 29 and 30 in Mt. Pleasant, Michigan, in the finals of a creative problem-solving competition called Odyssey of the Mind.

Odyssey of the Mind encourages young people to expand their imaginations. They are challenged to come up with creative solutions to problems in areas such as art, science, history and literature. Finalists include over 500 teams of students from all age groups. They are among 250,000 young people who participated in the program during the school year. Although awards are given, the real satisfaction is being part of a creative venture.

As corporate sponsor, IBM salutes every participant, because we believe that great ideas come in all shapes and sizes. **IBM**

The answer to the problem in Figure 8.9

The most important fact for this problem is that the lilies double in number every 24 hours. If the lake is to be completely covered on the sixtieth day, it has to be half covered on the fifty-ninth day.

Answers to problems on p. 249:

Checkers problem: Two men can play five games of checkers and each win the same number of games without ties by not playing each other.

Barber problem: The barber is a woman.

Planting: 10 trees can be planted in five rows of four trees each in this manner.

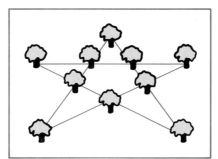

Figure 8.11
Answers to problems.

Brainstorming, which is very popular in industry, does result in new and useful ideas, but these ideas are not necessarily more effective than those generated by individuals (Stein, 1975). In creativity training programs, such as Synectics, Creative Problem Solving, and the Purdue Creativity Training Program, participants refrain from making judgments during the problem-solving task and learn rules of thumb that can be used in generating new ideas. Rules of thumb include using analogies, following five stages of problem solving, and making positive self-instructional statements while solving problems.

REVIEW

You are very excited about having invented a gadget you are sure every student will want. It's a book holder that attaches to the shoulders and supports a text about 15 inches from the face while the reader lies beneath it, never having to raise an arm. Pages can be turned by means of a wire within easy reach of one hand. The holder even comes equipped with small trays for snacks so students do not have to interrupt their studying for occasional food.

With great enthusiasm, you unveil your new creation to a group of your closest friends. You are shocked when they stare at it and ask: "What is it?" In asking this question, your friends are searching for a

(1) _____ by which to classify this strange device.

After some consideration, one friend asks if it is a bird cage. You answer indignantly that your new invention looks nothing like a bird cage at all. To come to this conclusion, you compared your invention with the mental image you have of what a typical bird cage looks like. This example of the average bird cage that

you have stored in memory is your (2) _____ of the concept. Encoding concepts largely in terms of prototypes is central to what is known as the prototype theory of concept formation.

Your friend explains it was the food trays that made him think of a bird cage. They reminded him of the little cups in which you put seed for a bird. You answer with some impatience that your invention lacks most of the features all bird cages must have. It has no totally enclosed area for a bird to live in, nor does it have a door to allow an animal to get in and out. In making these observations, you are focusing on the

(3) _____ characteristics of a bird cage. According to what is called the (4) _____ theory of concept formation, concepts like "bird cage" are formed and encoded in terms of such defining features.

You feel you face a difficult problem in marketing your new invention. Judging from your friends' reactions, you fear the public may dismiss your invention without giving it a fair chance. You decide that the first step in your marketing campaign must be to get a sizable number of students to try your device. Now all you have to do is figure out how to accomplish this subgoal. You come up with the idea of running a raffle that only people who have evaluated your product will be allowed to enter. In breaking down the overall problem of marketing your invention into smaller, more manageable subproblems, you are engaging in a problem-solving strategy called (5) _____

_____. This analysis is closely tied to another strategy you are also using—trying to find means of closing the gaps between your current situation and the ends you want to achieve. This problem-solving

strategy is known as (6) _____ - _____ analysis. Both subgoal analysis and means-end analysis are part of a computer model of problem solving called

the (7) _____ _____ solver.

You reassemble your friends to help you decide on a name for your new product. You explain that you want them to generate as many ideas as possible, to try to be original, to build on each other's suggestions, and to avoid being critical. These instructions are the four

basic rules of a technique known as (8) _____. This technique is one way of trying to foster a mode of

thought called (9) _____ thinking. Divergent thinking is the ability to shift one's viewpoint and come up with many different answers to a single question. It is considered one measure of the cognitive trait

called (10) _____. In contrast, when people select and focus their ideas and perceptions on one solution, they are engaging in what is called

(11) _____ thinking.

In selling your product, you decide to emphasize how much it will improve reading rather than how much it costs. In making decisions about buying products, consumers cannot help but respond to how the information is presented. Presenting information in

certain ways, which is called (12) _____, is known to influence decision making. Rules of thumb or cognitive strategies that are shortcuts to making de-

cisions are called (13) _____. You decide to advertise your product only to students who get good grades because they are more likely to buy it. If you determine the likelihood of a certain event—good students are more likely to buy your product—on the basis of your mental image—good students read a lot—you

are using the (14) _____ heuristic. You decide that students who get good grades read more than students on athletic scholarships because you can recall many instances of students who get good grades reading in the library. In this case, your decision is

based on the (15) _____ heuristic, which means that you decide that events occur more frequently if you can easily remember other, similar events.

In designing your product, you used a certain amount of creativity. According to Amabile, the attributes that characterize a creative act are having exper-

tise or (16) _____ in the area, being able to concentrate and persist in your work, having a

(17) _____ style that generates new ideas, and having a love of what you are doing, called

(18) _____ motivation. There is a chance that if you start coming up with ideas solely to make money, some of your future ideas may be less

(19) _____.

Answers: (1) concept; (2) prototype; (3) defining; (4) classical; (5) subgoal analysis; (6) means-end; (7) general problem; (8) brainstorming; (9) divergent; (10) creativity; (11) convergent; (12) framing; (13) heuristics; (14) representative; (15) availability; (16) knowledge; (17) thinking; (18) intrinsic; (19) creative

GLOSSARY TERMS

Module 22 Language

During a trial, the judge, attorneys, plaintiffs, defendants, and witnesses may all be using different styles of speech, each with its own psychological force. Consider, for example, the trial of Dr. Kenneth Edelin, a Boston physician accused of manslaughter. He had performed a late abortion and allowed the fetus to die. During the trial, the defense used a very different set of words than the prosecution did. The defense said that Dr. Edelin had "aborted" a "fetus." The prosecution said that Dr. Edelin had "murdered" a "baby boy." The judge agreed that certain words have connotations above and beyond their meanings. Accordingly, the judge barred the use of the words "murdered" and "baby boy" from this case.

As another example, consider the way witnesses answer questions during a trial. Some answer in a very direct, confident manner; others answer in a hesitant and qualified way. One researcher has called these different styles of speech "powerful" versus "powerless." Here are some examples:

QUESTION: *What was the nature of your acquaintance with her?*
POWERLESS ANSWER: *We were, uh, very close friends. Uh, she was even sort of a mother to me.*
POWERFUL ANSWER: *We were close friends. She was like a mother to me.*

Subjects playing the part of jurors in a mock trial listened to tapes of both kinds of answers. They rated the "powerful" answers, whether made by men or women, as being more convincing, competent, intelligent, and trustworthy than the "powerless" ones. These findings have applications to other areas of life, including college classrooms. The next time you listen to yourself and others answering questions in class, take note of the different speech styles being used (adapted from Andrews, 1984, pp. 28, 30, 31).

These examples illustrate the power of language in expressing ideas, communicating information about the self, and influencing others' attitudes and behaviors. With language, people can convey far more meaning than the dictionary definitions of the words they use. What enables human language to communicate so richly? Part of the answer lies in the fact that language is built up from a series of components (sounds, root words, prefixes, and suffixes) that can be combined in an enormous variety of ways. Our first step in exploring human language, therefore, is to look at these components and how they are put together in everyday speech.

THE STRUCTURE OF LANGUAGE

Why does what you say make sense?

As you speak, others can make sense of what you are saying because you automatically follow three sets of rules. The first set consists of the **rules of phonology.** Phonological rules specify what speech sounds are acceptable in a particular language and how those sounds can be combined to form meaningful units of speech (Figure 8.12).

The distinctive categories of sounds used in a given language are called **phonemes.** English has about 40 phonemes, depending on the regional dialect spoken. For instance, the sound of the *c* and the *k* in *cake* is one phoneme, while the sound of the *a* is a second phoneme (also heard in the word *weigh*). These examples show that phonemes are not the same as the letters of the alphabet; the same phoneme may be represented by different letters or different groups of letters. What is important in identifying phonemes are the *sounds* made.

To convey ideas, the sounds of a language must be combined in some fashion, and phonological rules limit which combinations are permissible. If you were presented with the series of sounds *ctrpllr*, for instance, you would know right away that this is not an acceptable word in English. This is because one of the phonological rules for forming English words is that the speech sounds cannot be all consonants. Instead, they must be some mix of consonants and vowels. By adding the vowels *a*, *e*, *i*, and *a*, we solve this problem and form the legitimate English word "caterpillar."

Because this combination of sounds has meaning in English, it is considered an English **morpheme.** Morphemes are the smallest combinations of speech sounds in a given language that convey meaning. Many morphemes, like *caterpillar*, are words that can stand alone. *Book*, *break*, *blunder*, and *brilliant*, for example, are all English morphemes. Other morphemes, however, cannot stand alone, but must be attached to the beginning or end of a root word. In the word *unbreakable*, for instance, there are three morphemes: *un-* meaning "not," the root word *break*, and *-able* meaning "capable of being done." Likewise, the word "books" has two morphemes: *book*, which can stand alone, and the suffix *-s*, which indicates "more than one."

Besides the above phonological rules, speakers of a language also follow **rules of syntax.** These rules specify the order in which words can be combined to form meaningful sentences. The sentence "Caterpillars many fuzzy are," for instance, violates rules of English syntax. In English, an adjective should precede the noun it modifies, unless it is part of the predicate, in which case it should follow the verb. Using these rules, we can do some rearranging and make the perfectly meaningful sentence: "Many caterpillars are fuzzy." The syntactic rules of any language are so numerous and complex that most speakers have trouble stating them in abstract terms. We seem to follow these rules automatically—following them seems to be the only right way to speak.

We also adhere quite automatically to **rules of semantics**—that is, to rules that specify the meaning of words in various contexts. When you look at the cartoon in Figure 8.13, for instance, you laugh because the words in this particular context do not really make any sense. This is because they represent a semantic self-contradiction. If you did in fact disregard the notice on the fence, you would actually be doing what it tells you to do! Note that there is nothing wrong with the phonology or syntax of this particular sentence. What is wrong is the impossible meaning the sentence conveys. You know implicitly not to write such a sign yourself because it violates the rules of semantics.

Figure 8.12
We normally comprehend only about 70 percent of the words we hear. Our minds fill in the rest according to the context of the conversation. This explains why it is so difficult to understand a stranger's last name over the telephone. An unfamiliar name in a telephone message has no context and usually must be spelled. (Adapted from Allman, 1986)

Figure 8.13
You can read and understand the "notice" because you have learned three different sets of language rules. The reason this cartoon makes you smile is because the "notice" violates one of these rules. To decide which one, check the text. (Drawing by Chon Day; © 1975 The New Yorker Magazine, Inc.)

INTERPRETING LANGUAGE

"Sam dropped the ice cream cone."

"The ice cream cone was dropped by Sam."

In the first of these two sentences, Sam is the subject; in the second, the ice cream cone is. Yet you have no trouble making a decision about who is doing the dropping and what is being dropped. How can you interpret most sentences so quickly and accurately? One of the people who has helped to provide an answer is the linguist Noam Chomsky.

Chomsky (1957) considered the question, "How can an idea be expressed in several different ways, with different grammatical structures, yet mean the same thing?" He answers by making a distinction between a sentence's surface structure and its deep structure. By **surface structure,** Chomsky means a sentence's actual words. "Sam dropped the ice cream cone" and "The ice cream cone was dropped by Sam" are two different surface structures. But Chomsky believes a single, deeper meaning underlies both wordings. That underlying meaning, which is represented in memory, is the sentence's **deep structure.** Chomsky argues that in learning a language we acquire certain **transformational rules** which allow us to convert surface structures into deep structures, and deep structures back into surface ones.

When you hear the sentences about Sam and his ice cream cone, you transform the words into their deep structure, which you then store in memory. Later, when someone asks you what happened to Sam, you transform the deep structure into a surface structure, which can take any number of forms. Chomsky's theory is widely considered an important first step in explaining how we produce and understand speech. Figure 8.14 illustrates the difference between surface and deep structure.

Of course, Chomsky and other linguists are still faced with the question of how we learn the transformational rules in the first place. How did you

Figure 8.14
The chickens are ready to eat could have two different meanings. It could mean "the chickens are cooked enough to be eaten" or "the chickens are ready to eat their food." According to Chomsky, the sentence's actual words are called the surface structure. The sentence's two different meanings are called the deeper structure. (Fisher, 1986)

MAJOR CONCEPT   Using Language

The ability to communicate through a complex system of language is widely considered the crowning achievement of human intelligence.

For each of the questions about human language asked below, select the correct answer from among this list of terms:

morphemes	semantics	deep structure
phonemes	phonology	surface structure
	syntax	

1. Each language has its own distinctive categories of sounds from which words can be built. These categories of sounds are called _phonemes_.

2. The smallest combinations of speech sounds that have meaning in a language are called _morphemes_.

3. The English word "weigh" has two of these: _phonemes_.

4. The prefix *anti-* and the root word *freeze* in *antifreeze* are two examples of _morphemes_.

5. The combination of speech sounds *tzumlp* violates the English rules of _syntax phonology_

6. The sentence "Elm trees make wonderful house pets" violates the English rules of _syntax semantics_

7. The sentence "Your text don't use doorstop for a" violates the English rules of _syntax_.

8. Sentences with exactly the same wording have the same _surface structure_.

9. Sentences with the same meaning have the same _deep structure_

10. When you store a statement that you hear in your long-term memory, you seldom remember the statement verbatim. Instead, you remember the sentence's _deep   structure_.

Answers: 1 (phonemes); 2 (morphemes); 3 (phonemes); 4 (morphemes); 5 (phonology); 6 (semantics); 7 (syntax); 8 (surface structure); 9 (deep structure); 10 (deep structure)

become a fluent user of English, able to take any idea and express it in a sentence, able to listen to other people's words and extract the underlying meaning? Such questions bring us to another major area in the study of language: acquiring language.

LANGUAGE ACQUISITION

Steps in Acquiring Language

Whether learning to speak English, French, Japanese, Spanish, or any other language, all the children of the world seem to learn language in the same sequence. The following timetable is only approximate, since individual children vary in how rapidly they develop language ability.

Babbling. Beginning at about the age of 6 months, babies begin to make sounds or one-syllable utterances called **babbling.** By 9 months, the baby's babbling sounds usually become more like the sounds used in the child's own language. The baby begins making sounds that resemble the vowels and consonants that will be used later in speech.

First Words. By about 1 year of age, the child utters **first words.** First words usually refer to what can be seen, heard, and felt. The child may refer to concrete objects, such as "milk" or "cat," or simple actions, such as "eat" or "go." The child may also say a word in a certain way so that it means much more. For instance, he or she may point to an unfamiliar drink and say "milk" with a rising pitch at the end, indicating "Is that milk?"

Two-Word Utterances. At about 2 years of age, the child combines words into two-word utterances, such as "Where doggie?" or "Me play." Starting with these two-word sentences, a child learns to make longer and longer sentences, but the sentences still differ from an adult's. An adult will say "There is a cat"; the child will say, "There cat." Because the child leaves out articles, prepositions, and parts of verbs, this pattern is called **telegraphic speech.** At this stage, a child may have a vocabulary of more than 50 words.

Rules of Grammar. By about 4 to 5 years of age, a child has learned the basic rules of grammar. These include both the rules for combining various morphemes into more complex words and the rules for combining nouns, verbs, and adjectives into meaningful sentences. In learning grammar, children sometimes commit **errors of overgeneralization**—that is, they overgeneralize a grammatical rule to instances where it does not apply. For example, having learned that the past tense of many verbs is formed by adding a *d* sound to the end, the child may add a *d* to the wrong verbs and come up with a sentence like "I goed to the zoo." By the time children enter school, they usually have a good grasp of the general rules of their language as well as the exceptions. Besides learning words and sentences, children also learn to recognize facial and bodily cues that also express meaning (Figure 8.15).

Is There a Critical Period for Learning Language?

From the age of 1 to 13, Genie was raised in near total isolation from other human beings. Her mentally disturbed father insisted that she remain in a back room either strapped to her potty chair or bound in a cagelike crib. Genie's mother and brother were forbidden to talk with her. She never heard the sound of a radio or television. If Genie made any noise her father would threaten her. When discovered by a social worker, Genie could not speak one word (adapted from Curtiss, 1977).

Genie's case illustrates that children learn language by interacting with others who know how to speak. This interaction gives children the oppor-

What do all the children of the world have in common?

Can a person learn a first language at age 13?

Figure 8.15
What do these nonverbal expressions mean to you? In talking with another person, you have learned to listen to the person's spoken words, as well as to "read" nonverbal cues, such as facial and body movements. For example, the cues in the lefthand photo indicate confidence; those in the righthand photo indicate disagreement. (Rusk, 1987. Photos, Union-Tribune Publishing Co.)

tunity to imitate, practice, and get feedback and encouragement for making sounds and words (Rice, 1982). It also enables children to begin making simple guesses about the meaning of what they hear and then to revise their guesses when they are wrong (Weisberg, 1980).

Some researchers believe there is a **critical period** from age 2 until puberty, during which it is much easier for a person to acquire language. Genie's case offers evidence both for and against a critical period. On the one hand, although Genie did eventually learn to speak, she had trouble grasping some of the complex rules of syntax. This suggests that age 13 may be late to learn language easily, just as the critical period predicts. On the other hand, Genie's experience shows that even after thirteen years of severe intellectual and emotional deprivation, a human is still able to learn to speak reasonably well (Reynolds & Flagg, 1983).

Explaining How Language Is Learned

How does a child learn the rules of grammar?

CHILD: *Nobody don't like me.*
MOTHER: *No, say, "nobody likes me."*
CHILD: *Nobody don't like me.*

(8 repetitions of this dialogue)

MOTHER: *No, now listen carefully; say* nobody likes me."
CHILD: *Oh! Nobody don't* likes *me. (McNeill, 1966)*

This mother is trying to teach her child one of the finer points of forming negative statements—with frustrating results. In just a few more years, however, the child will be very skilled at using language. Psychologists have wondered how children around the world manage to master language at such an early age. Basically, there have been two different kinds of answers: Chomsky's theories, which emphasize genetic factors, and learning theories, which emphasize environmental factors.

The Genetic Position.   According to Chomsky (1957, 1980), a child learns the rules of grammar because the brain is genetically programmed to learn these rules. This does not mean that a child's brain is programmed to learn a specific language, such as English or Chinese. Rather, it means that the child's brain is programmed to learn the basic, underlying grammatical rules of a language. Chomsky maintains that it is because of this genetic programming that children are able to acquire the rules of grammar as readily as they do. Chomsky's position, however, does not tell us how language is actually learned.

The Environmental Position. The environmental position has been stated in different ways by Piaget (1980), Skinner (1957), and social learning theorists (Rosenthal & Zimmerman, 1978). According to Piaget, the brain is not preprogrammed for language. Rather, a child acquires language and its grammatical rules through interaction with the environment. Like Piaget, Skinner also believes that a child acquires language by interacting with the environment, but Skinner focuses specifically on the principles of operant conditioning. According to Skinner, a child learns to speak in exactly the same way that a rat learns to press a bar—by being systematically rewarded for behaviors that come increasingly closer to the desired response. However, as the earlier conversation between mother and child illustrates, it is doubtful that children learn to speak simply through *shaping* and *reinforcement*.

Social learning theorists have added to the list of environmental factors involved in acquiring language the concepts of *observational learning* and imitation. By listening to the speech of older children and adults, preschoolers can try as best they can to fashion their own speech accordingly.

The environmental position has been helpful in trying to understand how language is acquired. It explains, for example, why language is learned more slowly by children who are deprived of opportunities to observe and imitate. On the other hand, environmental theories have difficulty explain-

Learning a language is one thing; learning to talk to someone else is another. When males talk to females, males make from 75 to 96 percent of the interruptions and generally choose what to talk about. When males talk to males or females talk to females, the number of interruptions is about equal for each partner. (Mark Antman/The Image Works)

ing how children can understand and compose sentences never before heard.

It was hoped that a debate between Chomsky and Piaget would help resolve the differences between the genetic and environmental views of how language is acquired. However, this debate was little more than a restatement of established positions (Piatelli-Palmarini, 1980). While there is little question that both genetic and environmental factors are involved in language acquisition, psychologists tend to study the environmental influences (Berman, 1983; Rice, 1982). Like Piaget, most contemporary psychologists view children as active thinkers who take in information, organize it mentally, and fashion simple theories about how things in their world seem to work.

EXPLORING PSYCHOLOGY Chimpanzees Speaking

Could you have a conversation with a chimp?

"What do you want to do?"
"Tickle me."
"What do you want to eat?"
"Banana."
"What color is this fruit?"
"Apple red."

This conversation is between a human and a chimp. The human is asking these questions using American Sign Language, in which a hand gesture represents a word. The chimp is replying by making appropriate hand gestures, which it has learned. Because chimps lack the vocal apparatus necessary for speech, researchers have tried to teach chimps nonverbal forms of language, such as American Sign Language. Beatrice and Allen Gardner (1975) began teaching sign language to a 1-year-old chimp named Washoe. After four years of training, Washoe had learned about 160 signs. The Gardners noticed a number of similarities between the progress of Washoe and that of a young child. For instance, Washoe was observed to generalize words she learned in one situation, such as to request "more" tickles, to other situations, such as to request "more" apple. The Gardners believed that, in many ways, 5-year-old Washoe's language ability seemed like that of a 3-year-old child. This research generated great interest and a very big question: How similar was Washoe's language ability to that of a human?

There followed a series of long, painstaking studies on the language abilities of chimpanzees and gorillas. David Premack (1972) taught a chimp named Sarah to use small, meaningless plastic symbols to stand for words. Sarah asked and answered questions by moving the symbols. Duane Rumbaugh and his colleagues (1977) taught a chimp named Lana to type on a special keyboard that had 50 keys. When a key was pushed, a geometric symbol appeared on a screen. Each symbol stood for a word. Lana asked and answered questions by typing on her keyboard. Similar to the Gardners, Herbert Terrace (1981) spent four years teaching a chimp named Nim Chimpsky to use sign language. Nim learned 125 hand gestures that stood for words, enabling him to ask and answer questions. In studying the language ability of Washoe, Sarah, Lana, Nim, and other chimps, researchers have discovered both similarities and differences between language in chimps and humans.

The chimp and its trainer are communicating through sign language. (Dr. H. S. Terrace, Columbia University)

The Gardners believe that like humans, chimps use language to refer to things that are not present, such as juice in the refrigerator. Likewise, Terrace asserts that in using signs, chimps are employing symbols to stand for real objects or actions, just as words are symbols for real things. When Nim signed "more tickle," he used the sign for "tickle" to represent actual tickling, and the sign for "more" to represent an additional amount. Indeed, all of the researchers found that the chimps were able to form two-word sentences, such as "more tickle," "apple red," and "more sweet."

More recently, Sue Savage-Rumbaugh (1986) and her associates reported several new similarities between language in chimps and humans. All previous researchers used common chimps (Pan troglodytes), while for the first time Savage-Rumbaugh used pygmy chimps (Pan paniscus). She discovered that pygmy chimps, without any explicit training, learned to associate an object, such as an apple, with a symbol. The chimps learned this association primarily through the same kind of observational learning that is observed in young children. In contrast, common chimps learned object-symbol associations only after considerable training. Also, pygmy chimps showed that they could understand English words spoken by humans and match the spoken word with its appropriate symbol. Common chimps have been unable to do this. Finally, pygmy chimps have begun to make requests that are much more complicated than those made by common chimps. Savage-Rumbaugh concluded that pygmy chimps show a greater potential for language and more similarities to human beings than any of the apes studied so far. This finding is particularly interesting because the pygmy chimp is thought to be the best living prototype of the ancestor of humans (Lowenstein & Zihlman, 1985).

But there are also differences between how chimps and humans use language. Chimpanzees acquire language skill much more slowly than humans. By the age of 2, most human children know the meaning of approximately 50 words, and by the age of 3 their vocabularies have grown to roughly 1,000 words. After four years of training, common chimps had acquired about 160 words. Compared to human children, chimps did not initiate or make many signs spontaneously and were less likely to expand on statements. Finally, compared to human children, chimps show less evidence of learning the rules of syntax, which govern how words are combined into sentences. By the age of 5, children have learned complex rules that allow them to create four-, five-, and six-word sentences, far beyond anything that chimps have learned to date (Benderly, 1980; Sugarman, 1983; Terrace, 1981).

If we look at the similarities between chimps and humans, we see that chimps, especially pygmy chimps, have the ability to learn and use basic language to communicate. If we look at the differences, we see that chimps have great difficulty acquiring a large vocabulary and learning the complex rules of syntax. It is because of our large vocabularies and knowledge of syntax that we can create long, meaningful sentences, discuss politics, write poetry, and tell jokes, however bad they may be.

REVIEW

A spaceship lands on Earth one day, and when its door opens out steps a large yellow thing with a transparent head and a big friendly smile. Earthlings quickly nickname the yellow thing Smiley. Soon a group of American psychologists is urging Smiley to learn more about human languages. Smiley obliges by enrolling in a course taught by the noted linguist Noam Chomsky.

Smiley discovers that all human languages can be described by three sets of rules. Those rules that specify acceptable speech sounds and how they can be combined are known as a language's rules of

(1) _____. Every human language has distinctive categories of speech sounds its speakers use to form words. These categories of speech sounds are

called (2) _____. Smiley calculates that his own native language contains about 200 phonemes, far more than people use in any Earth language.

Smiley also learns that the smallest combination of speech sounds that has meaning in a given language

is called a (3) _____. He is pleased to discover that his own name consists of (4) _____ morphemes: *smile*, which means "to spread the lips and bare the teeth in a sign of happiness," and *-y*, which means "characterized by or inclined to." Smiley thinks this is a wonderful name for himself.

Smiley next learns that languages also have rules that specify how words can be combined to form sentences. These rules designating proper word order are

called rules of (5) _____. In addition, languages also have rules that specify the meaning of words

in various contexts. These are known as rules of

(6) _____.

One day Professor Chomsky describes his own theory about why speakers of a language can express ideas in different ways and yet be understood as saying the same thing. Chomsky argues that this is because the particular words of a sentence are merely its

(7) _____ structure. For instance, the sentences "You must wear shoes to be served" and "No service will be given unless shoes are worn" have different surface structures. But because their underlying meaning is the same, they are said to have the same

(8) _____ structure. Professor Chomsky says that when we use language, we convert deep structure into surface structure and vice versa by means of

(9) _____ rules.

In another lecture, Smiley learns that human children all pass through much the same sequence in acquiring their native language. At about the age of 6 months they begin to chant single-syllable sounds,

which is known as (10) _____. At a somewhat older age, infants tend to babble selectively the speech sounds heard in the home. This sets the stage for putting those sounds together into meaningful first

(11) _____. When children begin to combine several words together, they at first leave out nonessential parts of speech. This form of language is aptly

called (12) _____ speech. Gradually children learn more about the rules of syntax, and as they do they sometimes apply them more consistently than they actually should. When this happens, they make

mistakes of (13) _____. By school age, however, most chidren know the rules of their language quite well.

Professor Chomsky tells the class his own ideas about why human children acquire language so easily at an age when they are still quite immature cognitively. He says it is because the human brain is genetically programmed to grasp certain basic grammatical principles. Some other theorists believe that human children may have a special facility for learning language between the ages of 2 and puberty. If this were true, there would be a (14) _____

_____ for language acquisition.

Several learning mechanisms are involved in acquiring language. When parents applaud their child's first words, they are providing the child with

(15) _____. When a child listens to the speech of adults and tries to imitate what they say,

(16) _____ learning is coming into play. Most contemporary psychologists believe that children form their own hypotheses about the rules of language, filtering what they hear and say through them. Smiley did not learn to speak human languages in the same manner as children. He took a series of classes. Smiley's great skill at using language sets him apart from any other nonhuman creature on Earth. Chimpanzees, for example, do not seem able to master the complexities of grammar as a human child can.

Answers: (1) phonology; (2) phonemes; (3) morpheme; (4) two; (5) syntax; (6) semantics; (7) surface; (8) deep; (9) transformational; (10) babbling; (11) words; (12) telegraphic; (13) overgeneralization; (14) critical period; (15) reinforcement; (16) observational

GLOSSARY TERMS

babbling (p. 257)
critical period (p. 258)
deep structure (p. 255)
errors of
    overgeneralization
    (p. 257)

first words (p. 257)
morpheme (p. 254)
phonemes (p. 254)
rules of phonology
    (p. 254)

rules of semantics
    (p. 254)
rules of syntax (p. 254)
surface structure (p. 255)

telegraphic speech
    (p. 257)
transformational rules
    (p. 255)

PERSONAL NOTE

Sometimes what appears intelligent to us may appear dumb to someone else. Once when I was very young, my brother offered me a choice between a dime and a nickel as a reward for doing him a favor. I chose the nickel because it was larger and I assumed it was more valuable. My brother told his friends about the incident, and soon they were offering me the same choice. They thought it was very funny when I picked the nickel. I didn't like people laughing at me, but I did like getting the nickels, so I didn't let on that I knew the joke. I thought I was acting very intelligently, while my brother and his friends thought I was acting very dumb. I made a lot of nickels that summer.   —R.P.

9

Motivation and Emotion

Module 23 Theories of Motivation

As the youngest child, Annette was very pleasant, intelligent, and cheerful and never caused any trouble. Her parents praised her for always being cooperative, patient, and understanding. She grew up in an upper-middle-class home in a large western city. Her father was a very successful businessman, and her family played a prominent role in the community. Annette had all the advantages that social status and money can bring. Both her parents were tall and slim, and so were most of her brothers and sisters. One of her sisters had gained extra weight in boarding school but had returned to her ideal weight through dieting. Thereafter she maintained this ideal weight by continually watching what she ate. During that period, Annette became impressed by the importance of being slender. When she was 15, she was 5' 6½" tall and reached her highest weight of 106. At this weight, she was very slim. But for some reason Annette began to restrict her eating. When brought in for treatment she weighed a mere 70 pounds and looked like a skeleton. Every bone was showing. Despite having every possible social and financial advantage, Annette had spent the last months literally starving herself. Her condition of self-inflicted starvation is called anorexia nervosa (adapted from Bruch, 1981).

Why Annette starved herself is just one of hundreds of questions you might ask about human motivation. **Motivation** refers to a set of physiological and psychological forces that influence your behavior in three different ways: by changing your level of *activity*, by directing your actions toward particular *goals*, and by making you responsive to certain goal-related *stimuli*. A motivated person shows an organized, directed pattern of behavior that includes these three characteristics (Pervin, 1983). For example, we would say that you were motivated to eat if you became restless (a change in activity level), if you purposefully got up and went to the refrigerator (a goal-directed behavior), and if the sight of a piece of chocolate cake made your mouth water (a high responsiveness to food stimuli). Annette's reaction to chocolate cake is just as strong as yours, but is approximately the opposite. We would say that she is motivated to starve herself: she is very responsive to food cues and shows increased activity that is specifically directed to avoiding eating.

Why did Annette starve herself?

INSTINCT THEORIES

In the early 1900s motivation was explained by the concept of instinct. Human instincts were thought to be similar to animal instincts, such as the spider's instinct to weave a web or the salmon's instinct to return from the sea to the stream where it was born. **Instinct** is defined as an innate biological force that predisposes someone to behave in a certain way when specific environmental conditions are present. Psychologists at the time, such as William McDougall (1908) and Sigmund Freud (1920), proposed lists of human instincts. McDougall's list included acquisition, curiosity, flight, and self-abasement. Freud's list included life instincts, expressed in sexual behaviors, and death instincts, expressed in aggressive urges. According to instinct theories, human behavior was controlled by these innate forces, rather than by rational goal setting and decision making.

But instinct theories of motivation failed to explain the cause of behavior. Instincts were labels, not explanations. If you were jealous, curious, clean, or cruel, it was because a jealousy, curiosity, cleanliness, or cruelty instinct made you do it. In the case of Annette, McDougall might have said that she starved herself because of a strong self-abasement instinct (the urge to degrade herself), while Freud might have said that the cause lay in a powerful death instinct. But neither view really explains Annette's condition. Today it is generally agreed that the concept of instinct should be reserved for lower animals, where complex behaviors are programmed genetically. Human behaviors are thought to be much more influenced by learning than the concept of instinct allows.

DRIVE-REDUCTION THEORY

Beginning in the 1930s and lasting into the 1960s, the concepts of drive and drive reduction replaced the theory of instincts. Drive-reduction theory has three components. First, a person has a biological *need*, such as a need for food, water, oxygen, or avoidance of pain. Second, the biological need causes an aroused state or **drive.** Third, the person engages in some behavior to reduce the drive and return the body to a more balanced state. For instance, not eating for a long time causes a biological need for food, which in turn causes arousal or drive. As a result, the person is motivated to eat and reduce the drive, returning the body to a normal condition.

Although drive-reduction theory applies best to physiological states such as hunger and thirst, it has also been applied to psychological ones, such as anxiety. To explain Annette's self-starvation, for instance, drive-reduction theorists might say that she feels very anxious about the possibility of being overweight. As a result, she develops a powerful drive to reduce that anxiety by eating very little. You will see, however, that this is not a very good explanation: it overlooks many cognitive factors involved in human motivation, such as Annette's perceptions of herself and her expectations about being thin.

Drive-reduction theory has declined in popularity since the 1960s because of two major criticisms. First, it cannot explain why we continue to engage in certain behaviors after our "needs" are met. Why do you eat a brownie at the end of lunch when you feel full? Why do you buy a new sweater even though you already have a dozen in your closet? Such behaviors are better explained by the concept of positive *incentives* (a delicious taste, the thought of looking good) than they are by the drive reduction. Second, drive-reduction theory cannot explain why we sometimes seek ways to *increase* our states of tension. People who take up hang-gliding or mountain climbing describe these activities as increasing levels of arousal (Zuckerman, 1979). Clearly, some other theory is needed to explain why people enjoy such activities.

Why does a spider weave a web, or a leopard and baboon display such ferocity? Many complex behavior patterns of animals are controlled primarily by instinct. (Lawrence Cameron/Jeroboam) (John Dominis/Wheeler Pictures)

COGNITIVE THEORIES

Because Annette's behavior, as well as other human motivations, cannot easily be explained by drive-reduction theories, they have declined in popularity. In their place, Albert Bandura, Bernard Weiner and others have used cognitive theories to explain human motivation. **Cognitive theories** refer to what is taking place in your head, such as your beliefs, expectations and explanations. Let's look at how cognitive theories would explain Annette's behavior.

Annette may believe that she looks better being very thin. She may expect that by controlling her eating, she is controlling her life. Notice how these particular **expectations** and **beliefs** increase her motivation for starving herself. According to Albert Bandura's social cognitive theory (1986), beliefs and expectations greatly influence motivation.

Richard deCharms (1980) believes that motivation is influenced by one particular belief, a sense of personal control or self-determination. **Self-determination** refers to a person's belief that he or she is in control of what happens. The fact that Annette is able to strictly control her eating increases her self-determination to continue starving herself. The concept of self-determination is an example of a motivating belief.

Annette may explain that she controls her eating so completely because she must remain very thin. According to Bernard Weiner (1986), Annette is motivated by her own explanations for her behaviors. When you give explanations for your behaviors, psychologists refer to these explanations as **attributions.** Weiner's attributional theory (1986) holds that people who attribute successes to their own abilities and failures to their lack of effort are motivated to work toward goals. On the other hand, people who attribute success to nothing more than luck and attribute failure to personal

What motivates Annette to starve herself?

MAJOR CONCEPT   Theories of Motivation

Match each of the statements below with the theory it is describing.

	Instinct Theories	Drive-Reduction Theory	Cognitive Theories
1. When you are thirsty, your physiological need motivates you to seek something to drink.	—	X	—
2. Freud was one of those who supported this view.	X	—	—
3. When you see a delicious strawberry tart, you expect that eating it will give you great pleasure.	—	—	X
4. This theoretical perspective fell out of favor because it never provided a real explanation of human behavior.	X	—	—
5. This theoretical perspective replaced drive-reduction theory in explaining human motivation.	—	—	X
6. Major problems with this perspective include overlooking the role of incentives and not being able to explain why we sometimes seek to raise our levels of arousal.	—	X	—

Answers: (1) drive-reduction theory; (2) instinct theories; (3) cognitive theories, (4) instinct theories; (5) cognitive theories; (6) drive-reduction theories

shortcomings lose their motivation and give up trying to reach their goals. More than likely, Annette attributes her success at not becoming fat to her own extraordinary self-control. She therefore takes pride in this accomplishment and is motivated to stick to her life-threatening diet.

To show the usefulness of cognitive concepts, let's apply them to another example, explaining your motivation to study. You would be motivated to study hard if you believed that you were a responsible student, expected to master the material, thought that you controlled your grades, and attributed your success to your efforts and abilities, not to chance or luck. You would be motivated to study less if you believed in mixing studying and partying, expected to miss some of the material, thought that you could only do so much to control your grades, and attributed your success to chance lucky guesses and your failure to some personal failing. According to cognitive theorists, your motivation to study would increase if you changed your expectations, beliefs, and attributions.

REVIEW

You want to know why Barry is the best car salesman in his city. You watch him at work and discover that he is highly motivated. Barry's high level of motivation affects his behavior in three ways: by raising his

(1) _____ level (he works 60 hours a week), by increasing his responsiveness to sales-related stimuli (Barry is more attentive to customers than any other salesman in the showroom), and by directing his be-

havior toward specific (2) _____ (he strives to beat the deals of every competitor).

If you asked a psychologist in the early 1900s why Barry is such a super salesman, the answer would prob-

ably involve the concept of (3) _____. This concept is defined as an innate biological force that predisposes an organism to behave in certain ways under certain environmental conditions. The instinct theory of motivation fell out of favor because it did little to explain behavior and because it downplayed the extent to which human behavior is influenced by learning.

If you asked a psychologist in the 1950s to explain Barry's behavior, the answer would probably involve

the concept of (4) _____ reduction. According to this concept, a physiological or psychological

(5) _____ gives rise to a drive or state of arousal, which motivates the person to engage in some behavior that will reduce the drive. Drive-reduction theory is best at explaining behaviors with a physiological basis, such as drinking water when you are thirsty. It is not very good at explaining behaviors with a psychological basis, such as striving to be a top salesman. Drive-reduction theory is also poor at explaining why people sometimes seek to increase their levels of arousal, and why they are often drawn to positive

(6) _____ when no drive state exists. For explaining many aspects of human behavior, drive-reduction theory has been replaced by

(7) _____ theories of motivation. These theories would say that Barry is a super salesman partly

because he has developed the (8) _____ that making many sales will earn him respect and a high income. According to cognitive theories, Barry is also motivated because he believes he has the ability to control his own success; in other words, he has a strong

sense of (9) self- _____ . In addition, he

(10) _____ his successes to his own abilities rather than to luck.

(1) activity; (2) goals; (3) instinct; (4) drive; (5) need; (6) incentives; (7) cognitive; (8) expectations; (9) determination; (10) attributes

GLOSSARY TERMS

attributions (p. 267)
beliefs (p. 267)
cognitive theories
  (p. 267)

drive (p. 266)
expectations (p. 267)

instinct (p. 266)
motivation (p. 265)

self-determination
  (p. 267)

Module 24 Hunger, Achievement, and Intrinsic Motivation

Psychologists can tell you about the combination of learned and physiological factors that make you feel hungry or tell you when you are full. They can also suggest why 30 to 40 percent of Americans have a problem with overeating and being overweight. Psychologists can tell you which weight-reduction programs are most effective and why losing weight and keeping it off is often so difficult. They can tell you that a small percentage

What can psychologists tell you about eating?

Your motivation to eat comes from a combination of physiological factors, such as sensations from the stomach, and psychological cues, such as always having a nighttime snack. (Michael Melford/Wheeler Pictures)

of people use eating to cope with various psychological problems. They can describe the most serious eating disorders and suggest possible causes and treatments. We begin with what makes you hungry.

WHAT CAUSES HUNGER AND EATING?

Physiological Mechanisms

Because people often report feeling hungry when the stomach is empty and "growling," scientists once thought that the stomach might be the major source of hunger cues. This idea was abandoned when it was found that people who had the stomach removed still reported feeling hungry and satiated or "full" (Lytle, 1977). Apparently, only some of our cues about when it is time to begin and stop eating come from the stomach, from receptors in the intestines, and from intestinal hormones (Houpt, 1982).

Would you still feel hungry if your stomach were removed?

It is difficult to say whether you could still feel hunger if you no longer had a liver, since a person cannot live without this organ. However, we do know that the liver is involved in providing important hunger cues. As you digest food, your liver monitors the *glucose* (sugars), *fats*, and proteins in your blood and sends this information to your brain, specifically to the region called the **hypothalamus.** It is thought that the hypothalamus processes this information from the liver and sends out signals to start or stop eating (Friedman & Stricker, 1976). We would guess that if your liver were removed and you were somehow kept alive, you would have difficulty knowing when your body needed food and when it did not.

You might think that when your blood sugar is low you become hungry, and when your blood sugar rises you lose the desire to eat. Although this is a very popular idea, there is relatively little relationship between blood sugar level and hunger sensations. What seems to matter in providing cues for hunger is the body's *utilization* of blood sugar (Mayer, 1972). You can understand the difference between absolute level of blood sugar and utilization of blood sugar if you think about what happens to diabetics. Without insulin injections, a diabetic's muscle cells are unable to absorb sugar from the blood. As a result, the level of blood sugar often rises very high, but these cells are actually starving because they cannot utilize the sugar. Many studies have shown that as glucose utilization declines, animals begin eating and humans report feeling hungry. Cells that monitor glucose utilization, so-called *glucose receptors*, have been found in the hypothalamus and more recently in the hindbrain (Ritter et al., 1981).

According to another major theory, your body's fat stores also contribute to feelings of hunger and satiation. Many experiments with rats have shown that these animals tend to eat more when fat stores are low and less when fat stores are high. There is some question, however, about the extent to which fat stores provide eating cues in humans; people with large fat stores do not necessarily decrease their eating.

Learned Cues

The sight of a fudge cake may be a cue to eat more, even though you have just finished dinner. Or you may notice that it is almost noon and begin to think about what you will have for lunch. Rather than eating only when biological need arises, we often eat because of learned cues. The time of day, the sight or smell of something tasty, engaging in some activity you associate with eating, feeling a negative emotion and turning to food to relieve it are all common *learned* cues for eating.

Why do you eat when you're not really hungry?

It is easier than you think to condition humans and other animals to eat in response to an arbitrary signal. For example, each time rats were given food, researcher Herbert Weingarten (1983) sounded a buzzer and turned on a light. After many pairings of the light and the buzzer with the arrival of food, Weingarten waited until the rats stopped eating and presumably were full. Then they turned the buzzer and the light back on. The animals began to eat once again, and they consumed 20 percent more food than they had eaten before. Apparently, the light and the buzzer had become powerful signals that eating should begin (see Figure 9.1). Similar behavior has been observed in humans. For instance, some people eat more food when extra food is on their plates or when they think it is time for a

Can you be conditioned to eat?

Margaret Thatcher, Prime Minister of England, weighs about 140 pounds, which would be considered normal for her occupation. Takamiyama, a sumo wrestler, weighs about 430 pounds, which would be considered normal for his. Notice how situation, career, and culture influence what is considered an acceptable weight and body size. (AP/Wide World Photos)

Figure 9.1

In this experiment, researchers wanted to know if the sound of the buzzer would eventually cause rats to eat. Each time animals were given food, a buzzer was sounded. On trial 1, the first time the buzzer and food were paired, the buzzer sounded for more than 60 seconds before rats began to eat. However, on trial 10 and most trials thereafter, the buzzer sounded for an average of only 6 seconds before the rats began to eat. The rats had learned to eat when the buzzer came on and ate even if they were already full; in other words, the rats had been conditioned to eat at the sound of the buzzer. (Based on Weingarten, 1983)

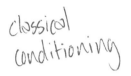

classical conditioning

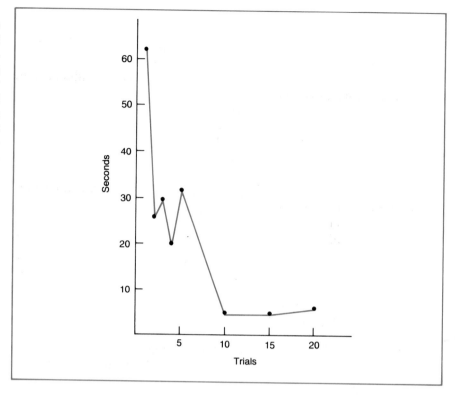

meal (Schachter & Rodin, 1974). Here we have two converging sets of data: both rats and humans often respond to learned eating cues.

These findings suggest how important learned cues are in controlling eating. In fact, studies indicate that learned cues may be more important than physiological ones in regulating eating in humans. This is why one of the first steps in any weight-reduction program is to become aware of how common and powerful learned cues are. Later in this chapter you will discover that learned cues are also very important in eating disorders.

EXPLORING PSYCHOLOGY Causes of Overeating, Overweight, and Obesity

"I was a little overweight as a child. But so was my mother. She told me not to worry, that I would lose weight as I got older. Well, I didn't lose weight, I just kept right on gaining. I don't think that I eat that much. Oh sure, there are days when I snack a lot but I try to watch my eating. No matter what I do, I seem to gain weight. I know that I should exercise more but I never seem to have the time. What makes me really mad is that my friend Jane seems to eat all she wants and never exercises and she never gains weight. It's not fair" (author's files).

Know 6 reasons & italicized words

Because Theresa, the narrator of the above story, is 20 percent heavier than her recommended weight, she is considered overweight. Individuals who exceed their recommended weight by 30 percent are considered obese. Approximately 80 million Americans are overweight and 40 million are obese (Langone, 1981). Let's look at six important factors in overeating, overweight, and obesity.

First: Theresa may have inherited a tendency to be overweight. Albert

Stunkard and his associates (1986) studied 540 adults who had been adopted as infants. They found a strong relationship between the adults' weights and the weights of their biological parents, especially their biological mothers. No relationship was found between the weights of.the adopted adults and their adopted parents. Stunkard concluded that *genetic* influences are important determinants of body fatness. Genetic information might regulate the level of a chemical (adipsin) which is produced by fat cells and involved in certain kinds of obesity (Flier et al., 1987). Genetics might also influence how much fat cells can expand to hold more fat. Adults have from 30 to 40 billion fat cells, which shrink with dieting but do not disappear and expand with overeating.

Second: Theresa may not be subjected to enough *social* and *environmental pressures* to compel her to watch her weight. As evidence for this, Albert Stunkard and associates (1986) cite the fact that about 30 percent of lower-class women, 18 percent of middle-class women but only 5 percent of upper-class women are obese. Apparently, social-environmental pressures to be thin are greater in the middle and upper classes. In addition, George Bray (1986) reports that identical twins are remarkably close in weight until early puberty. After that their weights may deviate, apparently because they are subjected to different environmental pressures.

Third: Theresa might have been a fat child, which means that her weight problem could be *developmental* in nature. Leonard Epstein (1986) reported that 40 percent of American children who were obese at age 7 become obese adults. In addition, William Dietz (1986) reported that the incidence of obesity among 6- to 11-year-old American children increased by 54 percent in recent years. This result predicts an increasing number of overweight adults.

Fourth: Theresa's overweight involves *calories, metabolism,* and *exercise.* Theresa gains weight because she consumes more calories (units of energy) per day than her body needs to maintain its functions. For example, if she drank just one more soft drink (about 100 calories) per day than her body needed, she would gain about 10 pounds a year. How many calories Theresa's body needs per day depends on her metabolic rate, which is the rate that her body consumes energy. Metabolic rates vary greatly among people. Theresa may eat no more than her friend Jane, but because Theresa has a lower metabolic rate than Jane, she needs fewer calories. All the extra calories she consumes are stored as fat. Indeed, Brownell and Venditti (1982) found that overweight adults do not necessarily eat much more than normal-weight adults. Instead, their lower metabolic rates may be responsible for their weight gain.

Besides differences in metabolism, researchers commonly find that overweight individuals, both children and adults, are less active than people of normal weight (Kolata, 1986; Stern, 1984). If Theresa were to exercise more, she would burn off more calories and raise her metabolic rate for an hour or two after stopping. If she were to exercise vigorously, she would raise her resting metabolic rate (the rate at which her body consumes energy when she is idle) for many hours and even days. Researchers Claude Bouchard and Angelo Tremblay (1987) found that 10 moderately obese women who spend five hours a week doing aerobic exercises (dancing, running, swimming) increased their resting metabolic rate by 6.6 percent. They concluded that exercise can raise one's resting metabolic rate if the exercise is very intense or continues for a long period of time. In contrast, brief periods of exercise, such as a 15-minute walk or workout, raises resting metabolic rate for only an hour or two.

Fifth: Theresa may be overweight due to her ratio of body fat to lean, called her *setpoint.* According to setpoint theory, Theresa's body will try to maintain a certain ratio of fat to lean. The evidence for setpoint came

One of the few ways to increase your rate of metabolism is through intense or long periods of exercise. (Ken Levinson/Monkmeyer)

originally from animal research. Rats were forced to lose weight because they were given less food. When the rats were then given all the food they wanted, they ate enough extra food to return to their original weight and then maintained that weight. Presumably, the rats increased their food intake only until they reached their setpoint and restored the original ratio of fat to lean. In Theresa's case, her setpoint may be set at a larger ratio of fat to lean than someone like Jane, and this contributes to Theresa's being overweight. Some researchers favor the idea of a setpoint that once established is difficult to change, but others believe the concept of a setpoint has been overstated (Brownell & Venditti, 1982; Grinker, 1982).

→ Sixth: Theresa may be overweight due to a number of *psychological* factors. She might, for example, be extra-responsive to external food cues. Judith Rodin (1984) found that someone who is extra-responsive to external food cues will eat an entire bowl of potato chips at one sitting, while a less responsive person will not. Although extra-responsiveness to food cues may

---

MAJOR CONCEPT   Eating, Overeating, Overweight, and Obesity

Match the term with its correct description.

1. hypothalamus

2. learned cues

3. liver

4. genetic factor

5. setpoint

6. psychological factor

7. metabolic rate

8. developmental factor

9. environmental pressures

a. _3_ A body organ that monitors glucose, fats, and protein and sends this information to the brain.

b. _5_ A mechanism that is thought to keep track of the body's ratio of fat to lean.

c. _6_ This is an example of a factor that contributes to overeating by making a person extra-responsive to external food cues.

d. _1_ An area in the brain that receives and processes information from the body and sends out signals involved in starting or stopping eating.

e. _2_ An example of this is eating because you see or smell food or because of the time of day.

f. _4_ This was demonstrated by showing that the weights of adults who were adopted as infants more closely resembled their biological parents than their adopted parents.

g. _9_ This was demonstrated by showing that 30 percent of lower-class women are obese while only 5 percent of upper-class women are.

h. _7_ This determines how many calories your body uses each day. One way to increase the number of calories used is through exercise.

i. _8_ Becoming overweight as a child, continuing to be overweight as a teenager, and maintaining this pattern into adulthood is an example of this factor.

Answers: a (3); b (5); c (6); d (1); e (2); f (4); g (9); h (7); i (8)

contribute to overweight, it is not a primary cause, since not all people who eat a great deal become overweight. Other psychological factors that contribute to weight gain include the tendency to eat to cope with stress and to eat when unhappy.

As recently as the late 1970s, researchers thought a single primary factor accounted for most cases of obesity. Now, based on years of studying the differences between obese and normal-weight individuals, Rodin (1984) has concluded that overeating, overweight, and obesity result from the interaction of biological factors (genes, metabolic rate, setpoint), psychological factors (extra-responsiveness to food cues, unhappiness), and social-environmental factors (advertising pressures and social norms).

Like many overweight people, Theresa would like to lose weight—not only because slimness is greatly admired in our society, but because obesity is associated with a number of health problems, such as high blood pressure and diabetes. Let's look at a proven weight control program Theresa might try.

Weight Control Program **APPLYING PSYCHOLOGY**

Please look at Table 9.1. If you are overweight (20 percent heavier than the recommended weight range for your height and build) and especially if you are obese (30 percent above the recommended range), you might want to consider a weight-reduction program. Before you do, however, check with a doctor to see if you have any health problems that might rule out a vigorous exercise and diet program.

How do I go about losing weight?

TABLE 9.1 **Metropolitan Life Insurance Height-Weight Tables**

Men*					Women†				
Height		Small Frame	Medium Frame	Large Frame	Height		Small Frame	Medium Frame	Large Frame
Feet	Inches				Feet	Inches			
5	2	128–134	131–141	138–150	4	10	102–111	109–121	118–131
5	3	130–136	133–143	140–153	4	11	103–113	111–123	120–134
5	4	132–138	135–145	142–156	5	0	104–115	113–126	122–137
5	5	134–140	137–148	144–160	5	1	106–118	115–129	125–140
5	6	136–142	139–151	146–164	5	2	108–121	118–132	128–143
5	7	138–145	142–154	149–168	5	3	111–124	121–135	131–147
5	8	140–148	145–157	152–172	5	4	114–127	124–138	134–151
5	9	142–151	148–160	155–176	5	5	117–130	127–141	137–155
5	10	144–154	151–163	158–180	5	6	120–133	130–144	140–159
5	11	146–157	154–166	161–184	5	7	123–136	133–147	143–163
6	0	149–160	157–170	164–188	5	8	126–139	136–150	146–167
6	1	152–164	160–174	168–192	5	9	129–142	139–153	149–170
6	2	155–168	164–178	172–197	5	10	132–145	142–156	152–173
6	3	158–172	167–182	176–202	5	11	135–148	145–159	155–176
6	4	162–176	171–187	181–207	6	0	138–151	148–162	158–179

*Weights at ages 25–59 based on lowest mortality. Weight in pounds according to frame (in indoor clothing weighing 5 lbs, shoes with 1″ heels).
†Weights at ages 25–59 based on lowest mortality. Weight in pounds according to frame (in indoor clothing weighing 3 lbs, shoes with 1″ heels).
Source: Basic data from *1979 Build Study* Society of Actuaries and Association of Life Insurance Medical Directors of America, 1980. Courtesy *Statistical Bulletin*, Metropolitan Life Insurance Company.

One of the more successful programs for weight reduction is a combination of **cognitive-behavior modification** plus exercise. This program teaches new ways of eating and new ways of thinking about eating plus asks the participants to exercise (Collins et al., 1986; Epstein & Wing, 1987; Rodin, 1978; Stunkard & Penick, 1979). In these programs, subjects lose weight without using any drugs. You might be thinking: Wouldn't it be easier to take a couple of diet pills each day to lose weight rather than having to work at changing my thoughts and behaviors about eating?

Researchers compared weight loss in subjects using a cognitive-behavior modification program with those using over-the-counter diet drugs. Initially, both groups lost an average of 20 to 30 pounds. However, a year later the diet-drug group had gained back far more of the lost pounds than had the cognitive-behavior modification group (Craighead et al., 1981). Apparently, people need to learn new eating habits and new ways of thinking about eating to be successful in keeping off lost weight.

Here is a six-step cognitive-behavior modification program used by many researchers. The "cognitive" part refers to identifying and changing specific *thoughts* that may contribute to overeating. The "behavior" part refers to identifying and changing specific *behaviors* associated with overeating. Lorraine Collins and her associates (1986) found that subjects using a combined cognitive-behavioral approach lost more weight than subjects who used only a cognitive or a behavioral approach.

Step 1: Monitoring Your Thoughts and Behaviors

Step 1 is to keep a careful written record of what, when, and where you eat, how much you exercise, and the kinds of thoughts or self-statements you make about eating, especially when you reach for a snack or for a second helping. The purpose of this record is to make you more aware of your eating and exercise habits. It is not uncommon for overweight people to have little idea of how often they eat and how may calories they consume in a day. After keeping this record for a week or two, you would be ready for the second step in the program.

Step 2: Identifying Stimuli Associated with Eating

This can be done by looking over the diary you have just completed. For example, you may discover a pattern of overeating when you feel stressed and anxious. Eating in these instances may reduce your tension, and so it is reinforced. Or you may find that you snack heavily when watching television not because you are hungry, but because it has become a habit. Your diary may also reveal self-defeating thoughts associated with overeating. When taking a second helping, you may say to yourself, "A few more bites won't make a difference," or "I'll be more careful tomorrow." These kinds of self-statements tend to encourage overeating.

Step 3: Changing Self-statements and Eating Behaviors

This step might include learning to eat more slowly and to take smaller bites, and restricting your eating to certain rooms or situations. For instance, you would try to cut out eating in front of the television set, eating just because others are doing so, and having snacks when you are anxious. Or you might try eliminating a morning, afternoon, or evening sugar snack. Robert Thayer (1987) found that subjects reported more energy and less tension after taking a brisk 10-minute walk rather than eating a sugar snack (Figure 9.2). You would also try to eliminate self-statements that justify overeating and replace them with ones that help control your appetite. For

Figure 9.2
If you felt tired, would you feel more energetic after eating a sugar snack or taking a brisk walk? Subjects reported feeling more energetic after taking a brisk 10-minute walk. *(Adapted from Thayer, 1987, p. 122)*

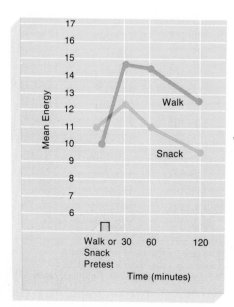

example, instead of thinking, "Another bite won't matter," you might say to yourself, "If I stop now, I'll look and feel better tomorrow." Or instead of thinking, "I have no will power," substitute the self-statement "If I try, I can control how much I eat."

Step 4: Reinforcing New Behaviors

Next, you need a system for reinforcing your new eating patterns. As reinforcers, you could use points, money, or simple self-praise. For example, you might give yourself a certain number of points for eating more slowly, avoiding snacks, and going for walks. You might find the accumulation of points itself rewarding, or you might convert the points into some more tangible pleasure (buying yourself something special when you reach a certain number). Since significant weight loss usually takes time, it can help to use self-praise and self-approval to reinforce each small improvement. In addition, you could ask friends or relatives to encourage you with social approval after you accomplish various goals.

Step 5: Exercise

One of the difficulties with dieting is that after several weeks of eating less, you may stop losing weight. This is because your body automatically compensates for the reduction in calories by reducing its metabolic rate by 20 to 40 percent. At this point, you may need to further reduce your calories to lose additional weight, or you could combine your diet program with an exercise program. Michael Perri and his colleagues (1986) found that overweight people who combined a diet program with exercise lost significantly more weight than those on a diet program alone. In this study, the exercise consisted of 80 minutes a week of either walking briskly or riding a stationary bike. Remember that exercise is one of the few known ways to raise your metabolic rate.

Step 6: Maintenance

Some people find it difficult to stay in a weight-reduction program that lasts from three to six months. In fact, the dropout rate ranges from 20 to 60 percent (Bennett & Jones, 1986; Brownell & Venditti, 1982; Stunkard, 1981). Others find it difficult to keep off the pounds they lost once they leave a program. For example, in a five-year follow-up, people reported that since they left a behavior modification program they had gained back all but about seven of their lost pounds, had tried about three other programs in the interim, and wished to lose an additional 55 pounds (Graham et al., 1983). One way for dieters to stay on their program, as well as maintain their weight loss, is to form a buddy system. That is, find others who are following a similar program and encourage and support each other to stay on the diet and keep exercising (Perri et al., 1986).

EATING DISORDERS

Anorexia Nervosa

At the beginning of the chapter, we described Annette's eating problem. It is called **anorexia nervosa,** (AN-uh-REX-see-ah ner-VOH-sah). This is an intense fear of fatness and a persistent pursuit of thinness, most often through willful starvation and excessive exercising and less often by vom-

Why did Annette starve herself?

iting and using laxatives (purging). Anorexics usually have a cessation of their menstrual cycle (amenorrhea) and sometimes have a disturbance in body image. No matter how skinny they become, they do not see themselves as wasted or emaciated (Hsu, 1986). Anorexics are almost exclusively female (90 percent) and white (99 percent). They are between the ages of 15 and 24 (60 percent) and come from the two highest socioeconomic classes (75 percent) (Jones et al., 1980; Murray, 1986). Contrary to reports in the popular press, anorexia nervosa, as defined by the above symptoms, is a relatively rare eating disorder, occurring in about .001 percent of the female population (Szmukler, 1985).

According to Hilde Bruch (1981, 1982), anorexia nervosa arises from a number of psychological problems, such as increased feelings of dependency and decreased feelings of identity and self-assertion. Bruch believes that anorexics engage in willful starvation to obtain a sense of control, independence, and assertiveness. Other researchers have found that anorexics often show obsessive-compulsive symptoms (Murray, 1986). Family dynamics may contribute to the problem. Laura Humphrey and her associates (1986) observed the interactions of anorexics with their mothers and fathers. They reported that mothers and fathers gave many more negative messages and less positive messages to their anorexic daughters than did control parents. Although physical changes, such as changes in hormone levels, have been reported in anorexics, it is difficult to determine whether these changes contributed to or resulted from the self-starvation (Gwirtsman et al., 1983).

Treatment for anorexics like Annette involves two phases. The first is to encourage weight gain. This is often accomplished through behavior modification, in which new eating habits are systematically rewarded. But even if the patient returns to near normal weight, the disorder has not been cured. To prevent relapse, the anorexic must usually enter phase 2 of

This woman is considering using one of the many over-the-counter drugs for weight reduction. If she uses a drug for weight reduction, she may lose weight in the short run but not learn how to keep the weight off in the long run. (Courtesy of Schick Laboratories, Inc.)

Both photos show Karen Carpenter of the Carpenters, a brother and sister singing team. In one she appears smiling and happy, in the other, sad and depressed. In an attempt to deal with a number of personal problems, Karen developed an eating pattern in which she literally starved herself. She died of a heart attack, apparently brought on by the anorexia nervosa. (Left, Memory Shop; right, Schiffmann/Gamma-Liaison)

treatment, a psychotherapy program. The goal of this program is to instill the feelings of independence, self-assurance, and assertiveness that the anorexic lacks. A four-year follow-up period is the minimum recommended to evaluate the success of treatment. Follow-up studies show that approximately 40 percent of anorexics had good outcomes (normal body weight and only mild psychological symptoms), 30 percent had fair outcomes, 27 percent had poor outcomes, and 3 percent died (Hsu, 1980, 1986). These findings indicate that anorexia nervosa is a long-term problem that is sometimes resistant to treatment.

Bulimia

Carol, 23, is a good student and has many friends. Although her life seemed perfect when she was growing up, something was terribly wrong. "It was like I had to live in this fantasy world where everything was sweet and good and I got straight As," Carol explains. "I started work when I was really young and I would do anything for anyone there and everyone thought I was so nice and so sweet. And I was just dying inside, literally." While her 5-foot-7, 127-pound frame shows no sign of an eating disorder, Carol began binge eating at the age of 15. She would eat large numbers of calories in one brief period and then force herself to vomit as a way of avoiding weight gain. In addition to her already low self-esteem, Carol had to cope with the turmoil of a family move. The resulting loneliness led her to eat more, and in response she increased the purging. Before she realized it, her occasional purging had become a serious problem. "I was 16 and it wasn't long before it was like an obsession, eating all the time, throwing up," she says. "It got so that it was automatic" (adapted from the Daily Aztec, *March 22, 1984).*

Why would someone go on eating binges?

Carol's eating disorder, which is called **bulimia,** (boo-LEE-me-ah), is characterized by a minimum of two binge-eating episodes per week for at least three months, fear of not being able to stop eating, and regularly engaging in vomiting, use of laxatives, or rigorous dieting and fasting. Ruth Striegel-Moore and her associates (1986) report that, like Carol, 90 percent of bulimics are women and that the incidence of bulimia is greater than it was several years ago. However, despite a pervasive attitude among today's women that they are too fat and that fat is bad and thin is good, only a very small percentage of women (2 to 5 percent) become bulimic.

Striegel-Moore has identified four factors that make a woman at risk for bulimia. First, women who live in a culture where the dominant sentiment is "fat is bad and thin is good" are more likely to take desperate measures to stay slim. Such a culture is the college campus; the incidence of bulimia is reported to be higher among college students than among working women (Hart & Ollendick , 1985). Second, women are also at risk for bulimia if they have an occupation or seriously engage in a sport that requires thinness, such as dancing, modeling, gymnastics, or figure skating. A third risk factor is the acceptance of the traditional feminine sex role that equates attractiveness with thinness. Fourth, certain personality traits are associated with bulimia. For example, in one experiment bulimics reported more depression, anxiety, mood swings, and impulsiveness than did controls (Johnson et al., 1982; Ruderman, 1986). This brings us to how bulimics, such as Carol, are treated.

Terence Wilson and his associates (1986) described a cognitive-behavioral program for bulimics that uses many of the steps involved in the weight-reduction program described earlier. This program caused a significant reduction in binging and purging, and increased healthy eating habits and positive thoughts and feelings associated with eating.

Eating Disorders and Motivation

Although both anorexia nervosa and bulimia involve eating, neither seems to be related to the biological mechanisms of hunger and satiation. Rather, these disorders appear to be caused by cognitive and personality factors that interfere with normal biological controls. These two disorders also show the influence of social and cultural factors in motivation.

ACHIEVEMENT

Do you see college as a challenge or a threat?

In some ways Rich and Jan, brother and sister, were very similar. Rich seemed to be as smart as Jan, since they both received similar scores on the college entrance exams. Jan seemed to be as sociable as Rich, since both were well liked and had many friends. In other ways, however, the two were very different. Rich, a junior, spent most of his time socializing and partying; he was barely passing his classes. Jan, a sophomore, spent most of her time studying and planning for graduate school; she got very good grades. Rich had many reasons why he studied so little: he thought the tests were unfair, he wasn't sure he could do well even if he tried, and deep down he was fearful of trying hard and failing. Jan, on the other hand, had many reasons for working as diligently as she did: she expected to succeed in college, she attributed that success to her own abilities and efforts, and she wanted to prove her competence to herself and others. Notice that Jan and Rich, despite their similar intelligence, respond very differently to the same demanding situation (author's files).

Need for Achievement and Fear of Failure

Since Rich and Jan scored about the same on their college entrance exams, let's assume that they were equally likely to do well in college. Then how do we explain the fact that Jan is getting good grades and Rich is not? According to David McClelland and John Atkinson, one reason might be their differing **need for achievement,** which refers to their motivation to set challenging goals and persist in meeting those goals, despite obstacles or setbacks.

Why might a brother and sister get such different grades?

In a series of experiments, McClelland and Atkinson measured need for achievement by showing subjects ambiguous pictures and asking them to make up stories about the pictures. For example, one such picture shows a young man gazing off into space, apparently daydreaming. Jan might say that the young man is daydreaming about going on to graduate school, while Rich might say that he is thinking about just getting through college. By analyzing a series of such stories, McClelland and Atkinson distinguished between people who had a high need for achievement, such as Jan, and people who had a low need for achievement, such as Rich (Atkinson, 1958; McClelland et al., 1953). They found that compared with people who have a low need for achievement, people with a high need for achievement persist longer, show better performance on exams, set challenging but realistic goals, and are attracted to jobs that require initiative (Atkinson & Raynor, 1974; McClelland, 1955; 1985).

Besides having a low need for achievement, Rich may be less successful in college because he has a high **fear of failure,** which is characterized by avoiding challenges and failing to persist at difficult tasks. His fear of failure pushes him to study just enough to keep from flunking out of college but not enough to set higher goals and get better grades. In contrast, Atkinson (1964) observed that people like Jan seek and meet challenging goals because their need to achieve is stronger than their fear of failure. One of the reasons that Jan and Rich perform so differently in college is because Jan's need for achievement drives her to succeed while Rich's fear of failure keeps him from testing his own abilities.

Cognitive Factors

Jan and Rich differ in how they think about college. If you recall our earlier discussion of cognitive theories (Module 23), you will remember that three factors seem to be especially important: expectations, attributions, and sense of self-determination. Let's look at each of these in more detail.

According to Albert Bandura (1986), level of achievement depends on a person's *expectations* about performance on a given task. If Jan expects to master the material in her courses while Rich expects never to understand much of what he is taught, Jan is likely to get better grades. In the same way, if you enter this course with the expectation that you can learn the information, you are more likely to achieve that goal than a person of equal ability who expects failure.

According to Bernard Weiner (1986), the *attributions* you make about your successes and failures also influence your level of achievement. For example, if you, like Jan, attribute high grades to your own conscientious efforts, you are apt to expect that future efforts will bring the same rewards and so continue to study hard. On the other hand, if you, like Rich, attribute low grades to tricky test questions, you are apt to expect unfair tests in the future and so lose much of your motivation to work toward getting good grades.

Finally, according to Richard deCharms (1980), your level of achievement is greatly influenced by the degree to which you feel in control of a

know bold & italics

situation—that is, your *sense of competence and self-determination*. In general, your level of achievement will be higher in situations where you think you possess the abilities and skills needed to take charge of what happens and determine the outcomes. If you, like Jan, feel competent and in control of your study habits, you will be more likely to do what is needed to earn high grades. On the other hand, if like Rich you have doubts about your abilities, you are more likely to give up trying before you even give yourself a chance.

Do you think that feelings of competence and self-determination can be taught? Some psychologists who wondered about this tried to increase these feelings in grade-school children. The children were taught how to set goals for themselves, make realistic choices, determine their own actions, and take personal responsibility for what they did. Soon their academic performance had improved significantly compared with that of students who had not been taught these skills (deCharms, 1980). This study is important for two reasons. First, it shows that people can learn to be more confident and self-determined. Second, it shows that once people develop a sense of competence, their levels of achievement are likely to rise.

What can we conclude about achievement?

In the 1920s, level of achievement was thought to result from instincts. In the 1950s, level of achievement was explained by drive-reduction theory. Currently, level of achievement or failure is explained in terms of cognitive processes. Compared with earlier theories of achievement, cognitive explanations appear to be much more useful (Clifford, 1980). Cognitive explanations identify specific thought processes and point out how these might be changed to increase achievement level. For example, cognitive theory would suggest that Rich could become more successful in college by changing his negative expectations into positive ones, by changing his attributions about success and failure, and by realizing that he can gain control over his study habits. As you will now see, Rich may also have to change his explanations for failure.

EXPLORING PSYCHOLOGY Failure and Self-Handicapping

How do you expect to do on your next exam?

"All of you who think you'll do well on Friday's exam, raise your hands." Most of the students raised their hands. After taking the exam on Friday and seeing their grade the following Monday, the students were asked to indicate whether they did as well as they thought. Typical responses were, "I did worse than I thought," and "I'm disappointed with my grade" (author's files).

When students are asked how they expect to do on their next exam, they usually say they expect to do well. Their high expectations are based primarily on the belief that they will study hard when the time comes. If actual performance turns out to be consistent with these high expectations, students will usually attribute their success to ability. But if actual performance turns out to be disappointing, they attribute the failure to the difficulty of the test. In this way the students maintain a positive self-image: the failure wasn't their fault; it was due to the professor's "toughness" (Davis & Stephan, 1980). Given this attribution, students are unlikely to consider their own shortcomings, such as poor study habits. As a result, they may continue to study as they have in the past and so fail again. In this case a "false" attribution may preserve self-esteem, but it is also perpetuating a serious problem.

Making up excuses or false attributions for *potential* failures is espe-

While looking over grade sheets, these students may make up excuses, which is called self-handicapping, if they had expected to do poorly on exams. (Howard Dratch/The Image Works)

cially common when we think we might fail at something. For example, a student fails to get enough sleep before an exam, an employee drinks too much at lunch with his boss, an investor says that he never has any luck in the stock market. According to Edward Jones and Steven Berglas (1978), these individuals are making up excuses so that they can blame some external thing if they fail. The student can blame lack of sleep if she does poorly on the exam, the employee can blame drinking too much if he does not get his raise, and the investor can blame a run of bad luck if he loses money on the stock market. Researchers Jones and Berglas (1978) call this tendency to make up an excuse for one's potential failure the use of a self-handicapping strategy. By attributing to yourself all kinds of handicaps (missing sleep, drinking, bad luck), you can fail without it seeming your own fault.

Mark Leary and James Shepperd (1986) point out that people use two different kinds of self-handicaps. The student who misses sleep or the employee who drinks too much is engaging in an actual behavior, which they call a *behavioral self-handicap*. The investor who says he has poor luck in the stock market is only claiming or reporting an event, which they call a *self-report handicap*. Other examples of self-reported handicaps are blaming failure on feeling ill or tired, being anxious, or being angry. We blame failure on a behavioral or self-reported handicap to preserve our self-esteem.

An example of self-handicapping is a study by Timothy Smith and his colleagues (1983), who compared excuses made by normal and hypochondriacal students. Hypochondriacal students commonly worry about and experience many physical symptoms, such as headaches, upset stomachs, congestion, and the like. As shown in Figure 9.3, when hypochondriacal students believed they were being evaluated, they reported significantly more physical symptoms than when they were told that their performance could not be affected by poor health. In other words, hypochondriacal students reported more symptoms when aches and pains provided a reasonable excuse for failure and fewer symptoms when they did not provide a very good excuse. In a related study, Smith and his colleagues (1982) found that students who tended to become very anxious when taking exams reported more anxiety when nervousness was a reasonable excuse for poor performance on an intelligence test and less anxiety when nervousness was

Figure 9.3

Self-handicapping strategies. Students who reported being very worried about their health and having experienced many physical symptoms, such as headaches, upset stomachs, congested nose, and so on, were called hypochondriacal. When these students believed they were being evaluated, they reported many more symptoms or made many more excuses than did nonhypochondriacal students. Hypochondriacal students reported the fewest symptoms or made the fewest excuses when they were told specifically that their performance could not be explained by poor health. These data illustrate self-handicapping, that is, using symptoms as excuses for poor performance. (Adapted from Smith et al., 1983)

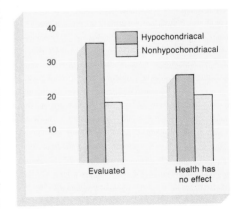

not a very good excuse. Finally, Robert Harris and C. R. Snyder (1986) discovered that students who were uncertain about how to rate their self-esteem (low to high) were more likely to engage in self-handicapping than students who rated themselves high in self-esteem.

What all these studies tell us is that when we think that we may experience failure, we use a strategy of self-handicapping. This strategy allows us to blame some external thing for our failure and thus protect our internal self-esteem. The less sure we are about our level of self-esteem, the more likely we are to use a self-handicapping strategy.

INTRINSIC MOTIVATION

Would you give blood?

You must admit that it takes a certain kind of motivation to walk into a blood bank, fill out the forms, lie on a couch, have a needle put in your vein, and then wait for many minutes as your blood fills up the bag. Do people give blood because of some external reward, such as social approval? Or do they give in expectation of an internal reward, such as the feeling of doing good? First-time donors are mainly motivated by external rewards, such as social approval, while people who donate a second and third time are motivated mainly by internal (intrinsic) rewards (Callero & Piliavin, 1983). Many of the behaviors for which we receive no pay—doing volunteer work, engaging in hobbies—also involve **intrinsic motivation.**

According to Edward Deci and Richard Ryan (1980), intrinsic motivation comes from an underlying need to demonstrate competence and the ability to master situations. When behaviors are intrinsically motivated, they are performed in the absence of any apparent external rewards. Intrinsic motivation causes us to seek out or create challenging situations which we then attempt to meet. For example, many people recognize the need for blood and meet this challenge by making blood donations. This gives them an inner sense of satisfaction and accomplishment that motivates future donations.

What do you think would happen if people were suddenly paid for doing something they are intrinsically motivated to do? Surprisingly, the introduction of this external reward usually *decreases* interest in and enjoyment of the activity. This phenomenon is called the **overjustification effect,** because the decreased interest seems to result from an unnecessary justification (money) for doing something the person already liked to do (Deci & Ryan, 1980). The overjustification effect predicts that blood donors motivated by intrinsic rewards would get less enjoyment out of giving blood if they were paid to do so. They might even end up donating less often.

What affects intrinsic motivation?

The extent to which external rewards decrease intrinsic motivation depends in part on the nature of the task. For example, when subjects were given money for working on interesting tasks, such as challenging puzzles, their intrinsic motivation dropped. But when subjects were given money for working on much less interesting puzzles, there was little effect on intrinsic motivation (Daniel & Esser, 1980). Apparently, if a task is boring and unchallenging, intrinsic motivation is very low to begin with, and providing an external reward does not cause a decrease. You can easily apply these principles to your own behavior. For instance, if you find jogging very boring, you may increase your motivation to jog by giving yourself some external reward. On the other hand, if you think that jogging is challenging and fun, introducing an external reward may only serve to decrease your intrinsic motivation and enjoyment.

Sometimes, however, external rewards do not have this dampening effect on intrinsic motivation. For instance, when subjects were given verbal feedback saying they had performed a task competently, their intrinsic mo-

MAJOR CONCEPT   Explaining Human Motivation

Amy wants to be a world champion gymnast. Below are some of her ways of thinking that could help her reach this goal.

Match each one with the words psychologists would use to describe it.

1. Amy's strong desire to excel at gymnastics keeps her practicing long hours despite sacrifices.

2. When Amy performs a move poorly she assumes the reason is just insufficient concentration.

3. Amy is convinced that she is in control of her own future.

4. When Amy does poorly at a routine, she seldom makes up excuses in order to save face.

5. Amy experiences great inner satisfaction from gymnastics and needs no external reward to keep her working hard.

a. ____ She has a strong sense of self-determination.

b. ____ She has a high intrinsic motivation.

c. ____ She avoids self-handi-capping.

d. ____ She has a high need for achievement.

e. ____ Her attributions encourage practice.

Answers: a (3); b (5); c (4); d (1); e (2)

---

tivation actually increased (Deci & Ryan, 1980). Why in this case did verbal feedback, an external reward, increase rather than decrease intrinsic motivation? It seems that what is critical is how the person who receives the reward interprets what it means. If people interpret an external reward to mean that they are working mainly for this payoff, their sense of intrinsic satisfaction from the task is likely to decline. But if people interpret an external reward merely as a sign of competence (not as their major source of motivation), their intrinsic enjoyment should not drop. In fact, it may actually increase (Earn, 1982). These findings make an important point about intrinsic motivation. External rewards in themselves do not necessarily decrease intrinsic motivation. Rather, the effects they have depend on the meaning people give to them.

Many Kinds of Motivation

Although we have only discussed hunger, achievement, and intrinsic motivation, you know from your own experiences that there are many other kinds of motivation. We have used these three examples to make a number of important points. First, many of the behaviors you engage in are unrelated to biological needs. It is true that eating is a biological necessity, but often you eat because of learned cues, and behavior such as overeating and eating disorders cannot be explained in terms of biological need. Second, psychologists explain many human motivations in terms of cognitive concepts, such as expectations and attributions. These concepts not only describe why a person is motivated but, in many cases, point to how motivation levels can be changed.

Other major motivational systems are discussed in future modules: sexual behavior in Module 28, aggression in Module 51, and helping in Module 53.

REVIEW

When Kim's 11 o'clock class is over, she is hungry. Cues for her to start and stop eating come from a variety

of sources, such as her stomach and her (1) _____, which monitors glucose, fats, and proteins in her blood. This information is sent to an area of her brain,

called the (2) _____, which also sends out cues to start and stop eating.

Kim thinks that she feels hungry when her level of blood sugar drops. However, according to one the-

ory, it is not the level but rather the (3) _____ of blood sugar that provides cues for hunger. Cues for starting and stopping eating may also come from how

much (4) _____ her body has stored. As she enters the cafeteria, she smells pizza and gets very hungry. Cues for feeling hungry which come from the environment, such as time and smell, are examples of

(5) _____ cues.

Because Kim is more than 20 percent over her recommended weight, she would be considered

(6) _____. If she were 30 percent over her recommended weight, she would be considered

(7) _____. There are a number of factors that may contribute to Kim's being overweight. If she inherited this tendency from her parents, it is called a

(8) _____ factor. If she came from a lower-

class background, it would be called an (9) _____ factor. If she were fat as a child, it would be a

(10) _____ factor. If she eats very little but

still gains weight, it would be a (11) _____ factor. If her body is trying to keep a higher ratio of fat to lean, it is a factor involving the concept of

(12) _____. If she eats when she is un-happy or if she is extraresponsive to external food cues,

it would be an example of a (13) _____ factor.

One successful weight-reduction program that

Kim could go on is called a (14) _____ - _____ modification program. People who followed this six-step program were better able to main-

tain their weight loss than people who used diet drugs.

In rare cases, women develop an eating problem that is characterized by an intense fear of fatness, self-starvation, and body wasting. This condition, which is

called (15) _____ _____, is treated by encouraging eating through a program of behavior modification, followed by a program of psy-chotherapy to prevent relapse.

About 2 to 5 percent of females have recurrent episodes of binge eating and purging and fear of not being able to stop eating. This problem, called

(16) _____, has been treated successfully with a cognitive-behavior modification program.

Both anorexia and bulimia are examples of be-haviors that are motivated by cognitive, personality, so-cial, and cultural factors, rather than biological ones.

Sharon is very concerned that her new job as a computer programmer might be too demanding. If she persists despite her initial reservations, meets the chal-lenge, and succeeds at her work, she would be said to

have a high level of (17) _____ motivation. The level of achievement Sharon attains depends not just on her inner desire for success. Also important is the degree to which Sharon anticipates that she can do

well at the job—that is, her (18) _____ of success. Sharon's achievement is also influenced by how she explains what happens to her, known as her

(19) _____. If she attributes her success to her own efforts rather than to luck, her level of achieve-ment will probably rise. Her achievement is also apt to increase if she feels she is in control of the situation, known as a sense of (20) self-_____.

After her first week on the job, Sharon attributes the difficulties she is having to her supervisor's attitude rather than to the real reason, her own insecurity. If Sharon continues to attribute her failures falsely to fac-tors beyond her control, she will be engaging in what

is called a (21) self-_____ strategy. Al-though self-handicapping may allow Sharon to keep her self-esteem intact, it may prevent her from facing things about herself in need of change.

On weekends, Sharon has volunteered to act as a "Big Sister" to a little girl who has no mother. Because Sharon does this for no apparent external reward, her

efforts are said to be (22) _____ motivated. If Sharon were suddenly paid for her volunteer work and she began to think she was doing it for the money, her interest in and enjoyment of the Big Sister program might very well decline. This phenomenon is referred

to as the (23) _____ effect.

GLOSSARY TERMS

anorexia nervosa
    (p. 277)
bulimia (p. 280)
cognitive-behavioral
    modification (p. 276)

fear of failure (p. 281)
hypothalamus (p. 270)

intrinsic motivation
    (p. 284)
need for achievement
    (p. 281)

self-handicapping strategy
    (p. 283)
overjustification effect
    (p. 284)

Module 25 Emotion

THEORIES OF EMOTION

As Steve walked across campus, he was hopeful about his chances. But as he entered the building, he worried about not studying enough. He walked into the large classroom, found his favorite seat, and sat down. "If only I could stay calm," he thought as his foot tapped out a constant beat, his heart pounded, and his hands sweated. Some of the students next to him were flipping desperately through their notes. Before Steve knew it, 50 minutes had passed and he was handing in the exam. As he left the classroom, he felt a strange combination of relief and fear. Then somebody bumped into him and spilled cola all over his shirt. Suddenly angry, Steve spun around, ready to yell. To his surprise, the person with the soda was his girlfriend, who had promised to meet him after the exam. She started to laugh at his wet shirt and his fierce expression, and soon Steve was laughing too. She said jokingly, "I like to make an impression on people." Steve smiled and replied, "You certainly did. I'm happy to see you."

What is exam day like?

How Many Emotions Are There?

Steve spent his day on an emotional roller coaster, going from hope to nervousness, relief, fear, sadness, surprise, anger, and then joy, love and happiness. Before you read any further, guess which of these are considered the major pleasant and unpleasant emotions. Philip Shaver and his colleagues (1987) asked students to do something very similar. They asked students to rate 213 words according to whether or not they could be labeled as emotions. At one extreme, all said that love, anger, and hate were definitely emotions and, at the other extreme, all said that intelligence, carefulness, and practicality were not. By analyzing the students' ratings of the emotion words, Shaver found six clusters which he labeled primary emotions. Three are considered pleasant—love, joy, and surprise—and three are considered unpleasant—anger, sadness, and fear.

Figure 9.4

How many different kinds of emotions are there? Under pleasant emotions, subjects rated love, joy, and surprise as the three main emotions, with related emotions listed under each of the three. Similarly, under unpleasant emotions, subjects rated anger, sadness, and fear as the three main emotions, with related emotions listed under each of these three. (Adapted from Shaver et al., 1987, p. 1067)

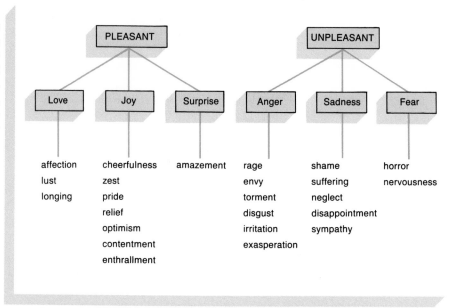

You can see Shaver's emotion hierarchy pictured in Figure 9.4. He categorized emotions as either pleasant or unpleasant with three primary emotions under each category. Shaver has noted that the six primary emotions identified in his study are similar to lists of basic emotions reported by other researchers (Izard, 1977). Shaver further subdivided the six primary emotions into 24 other emotions. For example, love includes affection, lust, and longing. At this point, you may ask, "What good is this emotion hierarchy?" Shaver and his colleagues explain that the hierarchy in Figure 9.4 represents an attempt to organize our emotional experiences. It illustrates how you might think about, talk about, and identify your emotional experiences.

Shaver's study also describes the most likely scenario for each of the six primary emotions. The scenario includes (1) situations or thoughts that are most likely to result in an emotion, and (2) the most likely subjective, physiological, and behavioral responses that accompany that emotion. Let's look at a scenario for one emotion: fear. In the situation described at the beginning of this module, Steve feared that he would do poorly on his exam, which would cause him to experience feelings of failure, loss, and personal rejection. Steve might also feel fearful in environmental settings that he perceives as dangerous, such as walking down a dark alley. Steve's fear arises from his thoughts about the terrible things that might happen in these situations, such as failing the course or being physically harmed. His most likely behavioral responses are darting eyes, trembling voice, being jumpy and jittery, yelling, running, or crying. His most likely physiological responses are sweating, dry mouth, heart pounding, and quick, rapid breathing. Of course, not all of these responses occur, and in the case of the exam Steven's behavioral responses are limited by his being in a classroom. From Shaver's study, we know that when Steve feels fear, he experiences three different components. First are his thoughts and personal or subjective experiences, second are his physiological responses, and third are his observed behaviors. We can define an **emotion** as an affective experience that includes a cognitive, behavioral, and physiological component.

Why Get Emotional?

Have you ever wondered why you become angry, fearful, or happy? Part of the answer lies in our distant past. In prehistoric times, when our ancestors hunted for food and struggled to survive, their anger helped to protect themselves from threatening animals or hostile tribes, their fear helped them escape from dangerous situations, and their happiness helped them relax and recuperate after a successful hunt. These examples point to a general *adaptive* function of emotions (Smith & Ellsworth, 1987). However, in our complex, highly structured environment, the same emotion may be adaptive in one situation and maladaptive in another. For example, being angry is clearly adaptive if it helps you defend yourself against an assailant. Being angry is clearly maladaptive if it motivates you to assault a professor over a grade disagreement. Being fearful is clearly adaptive if it helps you escape from a burning building. Feeling fearful is maladaptive if it motivates you to escape from a classroom during an exam. These examples indicate that in many present-day situations, personal, societal, or cultural values dictate that we must not perform the "adaptive" responses that the emotion has prepared us for.

Besides motivating Steve's *ongoing* behaviors, such as fighting or escaping, emotions may have three other functions. If Steve is angry about a grade, the anger may prod him to study harder for the next exam rather than pick a fight with his professor. In this case, emotions *motivate new* behaviors. If Steve is worried during an exam, the worry may interfere with his ability to concentrate and think clearly. In this case, emotions *disrupt* ongoing behaviors. Or the worry may remind him to read the exam questions with greater care. In this case, emotions may help Steve *attend* to other, relevant cues. Depending upon the situation, emotions may motivate ongoing behaviors, motivate new behaviors, disrupt a particular action or train of thought, or help you focus your attention on a specific problem.

Where Do Emotions Come From?

Suppose you feel very happy after getting a high grade on a test. Where does this feeling come from? In the examples below, choose the factor you think is the major cause of your emotional experience.

_____ You feel happy primarily because of sensations arising from the movement of your facial muscles and skin as you smile and laugh. Your brain interprets these sensations and you experience the subjective feeling of happiness.

_____ You feel happy primarily because you experience specific physiological changes in heart rate, breathing, blood pressure, and secretion of hormones. Your brain interprets these specific physiological changes and the result is your feeling of happiness.

_____ You feel happy primarily because of the way you have learned to interpret or think about a given situation, in this case, getting a good grade. Your cognitive interpretation results in your subjective feeling of happiness.

Now that you have decided which of these three theories you think is best, read on to discover what psychologists have discovered.

#1: Facial Feedback Hypothesis

A particular situation, waiting for an exam to begin, triggers a neural network in Steve's brain, which in turn elicits a certain pattern of facial movement. Steve pulled his lips back toward his ears, raised his eyebrows slightly, and opened his eyes. This facial expression is commonly interpreted as fear.

What does your face tell you?

Notice the changes in Judy's facial muscles as she experiences different emotions while auditioning for a television game show. The sensations or feedback from her facial muscles contribute to the intensity of her emotional feeling. (Union-Tribune Publishing Co.)

Charles Darwin, best known for his famous theory of evolution, was the first to claim that making a particular facial expression actually resulted in feeling the emotion, in this case fear. Darwin also claimed that each emotion has its own innate pattern of muscle movement in the facial muscle and skin. Today, Darwin's idea is called the **facial feedback hypothesis.** Two prominent supporters of this hypothesis, Carroll Izard (1981) and Silvan Tomkins (1981), believe that under certain conditions, feedback from facial muscles and skin can result in feeling distinct emotions. We will discuss the evidence for this hypothesis later in this Module.

What does a pounding heart tell you?

#2: James/Lange Theory

As Steve waits for an exam to begin, his hands sweat, his heart pounds, and certain hormones are secreted. In the late 1800s, two psychologists, William James and Carl Lange, suggested that stimuli in the environment affected the autonomic nervous system to produce different patterns of physiological arousal, and these patterns are interpreted as different emotions. The idea that it is the experience of physiological arousal that causes emotions came to be known as the **James/Lange theory** of emotions. James/Lange would explain that, in Steve's case, he notices that his hands are sweating and his heart is pounding; his brain then interprets this pattern of physiological arousal and he feels the emotion of fear.

The James/Lange theory ran into two major difficulties. First, different emotions do not necessarily have distinct physiological patterns. Anger, fear, and sadness, for example, seem to share similar physiological patterns of arousal (Ekman et al., 1983). Second, people whose spinal cords have been severed at the neck are deprived of most of the feedback from their autonomic systems, yet these people experience emotions. However, without autonomic feedback, people often report that emotions often are reduced in intensity (Hohmann, 1966; Linton & Hirt, 1979). Apparently, feedback from the autonomic nervous system does not cause distinct emotions, but rather increases the *intensity* of emotions.

#3: Cognitive Theory

What do your thoughts tell you?

A situation, waiting for an exam to begin, causes physiological arousal in Steve. In his aroused state, he worries about doing poorly, thinks about failing the exam, and sees other students looking worried. These thoughts, worries, and observations result in his labeling his arousal as fear. This illustrates the **cognitive theory** of emotions, which holds that after you are physiologically aroused by a situation, you identify the emotion according to your thoughts and environmental cues. Stanley Schachter and Jerome Singer (1962) were the first to demonstrate the importance of cognitive factors in emotions. Here's how they did their now famous experiment.

Schachter and Singer injected some of their subjects with a hormone, epinephrine, which causes physiological arousal (increased heart rate and blood pressure). They told these subjects that the injections were vitamins and did not warn them about the physiological effects they were about to experience. After the injection, subjects were placed in different situations. In one situation, an accomplice in the study was laughing and throwing paper airplanes, creating a happy atmosphere. In another situation, an accomplice was acting very annoyed over filling out a long questionnaire, creating an angry atmosphere. Subjects who had been physiologically aroused by the injections but did not know how to explain that arousal tended to use situational cues to label their arousal as a specific emotion. Those in the happy situation often reported being happy, while those in the angry situation often reported being angry.

Why did some subjects report feeling happy while others reported feeling angry? Schachter and Singer reasoned that these different emotional reactions resulted primarily because the subjects noticed and thought about the situational cues. The epinephrine alone produced nothing more than a *general* state of physiological arousal. Perceptions and thoughts were the critical factors in labeling this arousal as a specific emotion. According to Schachter and Singer's cognitive theory, then, a stimulus causes physiological arousal, which the aroused person notices. The arousal itself does not cause any particular emotion, but it does create the need for an explanation of some kind. The person then searches the environment for some likely cause of the arousal. When a cause is found, the perception of that cause results in subjective feelings of an emotion.

Because of later criticisms, Schachter and Singer's cognitive theory has undergone two general revisions. First, Schachter and Singer originally proposed that some kind of physiological arousal was needed to start a person searching for an emotional explanation. Today, some researchers argue that arousal is not always necessary to experience an emotion (Clarke & Fiske, 1982; Lazarus, 1984). For example, if a friend walks up to you and says, "I just saw somebody back into your car and drive away," you might feel angry even before you have time to be physiologically aroused. Indeed, psychologists Richard Lazarus (1984) and Robert Zajonc (1984) have been debating whether arousal or thinking comes first when you experience an emotion. We'll tell you about their debate a little later.

A second revision in Schachter and Singer's theory concerns their emphasis on the importance of environmental cues in labeling emotions. Today, some researchers argue that, in addition to environmental cues, you use your own thoughts and interpretations to label an emotion (Lazarus, 1984).

Emotional Components and Emotional Theories

We began this Module by describing the three components of Steve's fear. Notice how each one of the three components formed the basis of one of the three major theories. Supporters of the James/Lange theory emphasized the *physiological* component and believed that discrete patterns of physiological arousal created emotions. Supporters of the facial feedback hypothesis emphasized the *behavioral* component and believed that facial

MAJOR CONCEPT   Theories of Emotions

Three major perspectives proposed to help explain emotions are the facial-feedback hypothesis, the James/Lange theory, and various cognitive views.

Decide which of these perspectives is being expressed in each statement below.

1. This perspective focuses on the physiological component of emotions.   _____

2. When Linda tells George he would have a more pleasant time with his in-laws if he just tried smiling once in a while, she is subscribing to this perspective.   _____

3. When Ted tries to cure his sadness over breaking up with Lynn by thinking about all the times she was thoughtless and self-centered, he is acting on this perspective.   _____

4. This perspective focuses on the behavioral component of emotions.   _____

5. The person who suggests you can stop feeling angry by closing your eyes and taking deep breaths until your heart stops pounding is a believer in this perspective.   _____

Answers: (1) James/Lange theory; (2) facial-feedback hypothesis; (3) cognitive views; (4) facial-feedback hypothesis; (5) James/Lange theory

expressions activate emotions. Supporters of the cognitive theory emphasized the *cognitive* component and believed that thoughts or cues from the environment are used to identify emotions. Researchers agree that all three components—physiological arousal, facial expressions, and cognitions—are involved in an emotional experience. But researchers disagree on the importance of each component in triggering an emotional experience. To get to the heart of an emotional experience, we will examine the behavioral and cognitive components in more detail. Then we will discuss how all three components interact.

THE BEHAVIORAL COMPONENT

Did you learn how to smile?

Please look closely at the faces in Figure 9.5. Match each face with the emotion that you think it portrays. Then continue reading the text below.

Facial expressions (such as smiling, crying, etc.) present us with two interesting questions: First, "Did you have to learn how to cry or smile or make other facial expressions?" Second, "Of what use are smiling and crying?"

Since you cried immediately after birth, it means that the neural patterns necessary to make this facial expression were already in place. Thus, crying is an unlearned, innate response. Although smiling does not occur in babies until one to two months after birth, there is evidence that it too is an innate response. Eibl-Eibesfeldt (1973) found that children who were born blind and so were unable to imitate their parents' facial expressions began smiling at about the same time as sighted children. These findings

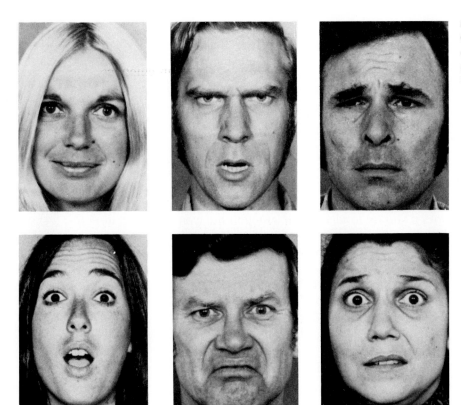

Figure 9.5
Can you label the emotion each of these expressions is showing? The answers are given in the text. *(Courtesy of Paul Ekman, Human Interaction Laboratory U. of California)*

tell us that we did not have to learn to smile or cry. Rather, we inherited the ability to make the facial expressions involved in smiling or crying.

"Of what use are smiling and crying?" is one of the questions that Paul Ekman and Wallace Friesen (1975) along with Carroll Izard (1977) set out to answer. They showed pictures of emotional expressions, similar to those in Figure 9.5, to people in many different cultures, including the United States, Borneo, Brazil, and Japan. They were trying to determine whether people throughout the world agree on which facial expression indicated which emotion. They found that, regardless of the culture, people agreed 50 to 90 percent of the time that an open mouth, widened eyes, and raised eyebrows indicate surprise, a scowl indicates anger, and so on. In other words, most people would identify the emotional expressions in Figure 9.5, beginning with the upper left face and moving clockwise, as happiness, anger, sadness, fear, disgust, and surprise. Based on this remarkable agreement between facial expression and specific emotion, these researchers answered our second question "of what use are smiling and crying?" They concluded that facial expressions function to express feelings and serve as social signals. You would probably have fewer reservations about walking up to a smiling stranger in a foreign country to ask for directions than you would about approaching a frowning stranger for the same thing. You are often accurate in judging how someone is feeling from his or her facial expression, and this information guides your interactions with that person. However, the next study tells us that if we used facial expressions alone, we might make mistakes in judging emotional experiences.

Recognizing Everyday Expressions

You were probably very accurate in identifying the emotions depicted in Figure 9.5. One reason for your accuracy is that these faces were chosen because they best expressed a specific emotion. But in everyday social interactions, people may not make such obvious facial expressions. H. L. Wagner and associates (1986) asked students to identify emotional expressions that were not posed but occurred naturally as people viewed emotionally loaded slides. The students were generally accurate in identifying these emotional expressions, but the level of accuracy was far below that attained in research using posed expressions. The lower level of accuracy suggests that we may misidentify an emotion when using only ordinary facial expressions. However, we do not make many mistakes because, besides using facial expressions to identify an emotion, we also use nonverbal or bodily cues as well as vocal and situational cues (Gallois & Callan, 1986; Russell & Bullock, 1986). You can see the importance of these additional cues if you try to identify the emotion the woman in Figure 9.6 is feeling. Is it disgust, sadness, fear, or some other emotion? If you consider only her facial expression, you may misidentify her emotion. But if you are told that the woman has just received a painful electrical shock, you easily identify her emotional expression as one of hurt or discomfort. The more situational, facial, and nonverbal cues you have, the more accurate you will be in recognizing other people's emotional expressions. This brings us to a very important question: How important is your face in emotions?

Facial Feedback and Emotions

What does your face make you feel?

Please relax your facial muscles and try not to think of any particular emotion. Now turn the corners of your mouth up and back toward your ears and hold that pose for 10 seconds.

As you made and held that pose, you were creating a pattern of movement in your facial muscles similar to the one you make when you smile. Did holding that "smile" pose make you *feel* happy? Paul Ekman (1984), Carroll Izard (1977), and Silvan Tomkins (1981) hypothesized that feedback from facial muscles, and perhaps facial skin, contribute to your feeling specific emotional states, such as anger, happiness, fear, or sadness. This interesting idea has received close study in the laboratory.

James Laird and his colleagues reported that subjects who held a "smile" pose later reported being in a better mood than those who held a "frown" pose. And compared with control subjects, people who held a "smile" pose while watching cartoons reported that the cartoons were fun-

Figure 9.6
Compare the face on the left, which has a neutral expression, with the face on the right. Why is it so difficult to decide if the face on the right has an expression of sadness, disgust, fear, or discomfort? Check the text for the answer. (Patrick et al., 1986, p. 1297)

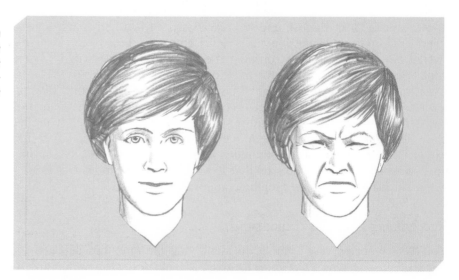

nier, that pleasant scenes produced more positive feelings (Laird, 1974; Zuckerman et al., 1981), or that electric shocks were less painful (Lanzetta et al., 1976). In a similar study, however, Robert Tourangeau and Phoebe Ellsworth (1979) found that facial expressions had no effect on mood. In this study, subjects who posed and held a "fear" expression did not report feelings more fearful while watching a scary movie or report any fear while watching a neutral movie.

To help us interpret these studies, Ward Winton (1986) pointed out that there are two questions here. First, does facial feedback *cause* you to experience a specific emotion, such as happiness, sadness, or anger? Second, rather than causing an emotion, does facial feedback contribute to a general mood? Winton concluded that a number of studies provide evidence that facial feedback can influence one's general mood. However, he added that there is very little evidence that facial feedback actually causes a specific emotion, which was what Ekman, Izard, and Tomkins had hypothesized originally. When David Matsumoto (1987) analyzed the studies on facial feedback and mood change, he concluded that facial feedback does affect mood, but that the effect is very small.

If facial feedback does not initiate specific emotional experiences, what does? In many cases, psychologists think that your thoughts or cognitions do. Here's a study that explores thoughts and emotions in a situation that you have been in many times yourself.

THE COGNITIVE COMPONENT

We introduced this Module with a hypothetical description of what Steve might have thought and felt before and after an exam. Craig Smith and Phoebe Ellsworth (1987) have actually done such a study. They compared students' thoughts and feelings before an exam with what went through their heads and how they felt after getting grades back. One of the questions Smith and Ellsworth asked was, "How accurately do certain thoughts reflect your emotions?"

Let's imagine that you were one of the subjects in Smith and Ellsworth's study. After taking your seat and before beginning your midterm psychology exam, you are asked to describe how you interpret or appraise this situation. You respond by expressing your thoughts, which are the cognitive components of your emotions. You are also asked to read a list of adjectives that describe certain emotions and indicate to what extent you feel each emotion. About two weeks later, immediately after receiving your grade, you are again asked to appraise the situation and check off the adjectives and describe your emotional state. Here's what Smith and Ellsworth found.

Before the exam, most students appraised the situation as one that required great attention and effort, and they were optimistic about their chances of doing well. They reported feeling a combination of hope and challenge, which was often combined with fear. After getting their grades back, the students' appraisals and emotions were more varied. Those who performed well appraised the situation as pleasant and fair and reported strong feelings of happiness, which were often combined with hope and challenge. In contrast, those who performed poorly appraised the situation as unpleasant and unfair and reported feelings of anger mixed with various combinations of guilt, fear, and apathy. Finally, they found that the kind of appraisal the student made about the situation was a very accurate predictor of the emotion that the student felt. Smith and Ellsworth concluded that the students' appraisals were very closely associated with their emotional experiences.

Does what you think match what you feel?

Now that we know that appraisals are closely associated with emotions, our next question is, "Do appraisals cause emotions?" Smith and Ellsworth acknowledge that since their study reports correlations between appraisal and emotions, they cannot determine cause and effect. However, they hypothesize that appraisals do cause emotions and are now testing this hypothesis. Not everyone agrees that appraisals always cause emotions, especially not Robert Zajonc.

EXPLORING PSYCHOLOGY Which Comes First, Feeling or Thinking?

Can you experience an emotion without thinking about it?

For several weeks you have been noticing someone in your class whom you find very attractive. One day, as you are leaving class, the person walks up to you and says "Hi." Immediately you feel a rush of happiness and excitement.

Robert Zajonc (1980, 1984) explains that in this example, the happiness you experience occurs very quickly, with a minimum of conscious thought or appraisal. He believes that in cases like this, cognitions and emotions are separate, parallel, and practically independent processes. Although Zajonc does not deny that cognition may sometimes precede emotion, he emphasizes the separateness of the two. Being separate, he believes that emotions may occur without conscious thought or appraisal. Now, consider the next example.

As you drive toward the only available parking place in the lot, another car appears from nowhere and takes the spot. You immediately become very angry, just as Zajonc says. The person gets out of the car, looks around, sees your car and comes over. As you think about how long you waited and how inconsiderate this person was, your anger builds.

By the time the person reaches your open car window, you are steaming. The person says, "I didn't see you waiting and I'm really sorry. Look, I know you must be really angry. I'll pull out and give you the spot. Wait right behind me." As the person walks away, you think about what the person said. Your anger fades and you feel good about how nice this person is.

Sometimes we may feel sad or cry after thinking about some situation rather than being in it. (John Ficara/Woodfin Camp and Associates)

It is true, Richard Lazarus (1984) explains, that your initial burst of anger required little conscious thought. But at some level, perhaps subconscious, your brain had to process information so that you could respond with anger. As you thought more and more about what an awful thing the person had done, your thoughts made you angrier. But after the person apologized and offered to make amends, your appraisal of the situation changed, your anger disappeared, and you began to feel happy. Lazarus points out that in some cases, subconscious thoughts and appraisals precede emotions. In other cases, conscious thoughts and appraisal obviously precede or may change entirely our emotional experience.

Notice that the Lazarus-Zajonc debate is almost entirely about instantaneously elicited emotions. The question comes down to whether the information that your brain processes and responds to in a split-second is considered true thought and appraisal. Zajonc seems to discount subconscious thoughts while Lazarus considers subconscious thoughts to be another form of appraisals.

Putting aside the debate over instantaneously elicited emotions, we are left with emotions, such as jealousy, pride, and guilt, in which we often think ourselves into the emotion. Beginning with the initial study of Schachter and Singer and continuing into the present, a large body of research indicates that, for these emotions, thoughts and appraisals often precede the emotional experience (Clark & Fiske, 1982; Weiner, 1986).

Now that we have discussed the separate components of an emotion, let's see how they interact to produce a complete emotional experience, such as feeling happy.

Staying Happy   APPLYING PSYCHOLOGY

Tony said, "You pick three numbers and I'll pick three. We'll split the five buck fee." His friend nodded OK and added, "And we'll split the winnings." Each one filled in three numbers on the ticket. A few days later their lottery ticket won. Tony and his friend split over $10 million. Tony said, "I am very happy, very, very, happy (adapted from the *Los Angeles Times*, October 10, 1987).

How happy would you be six months after winning a lottery?

According to our definition of an emotion, Tony's happiness has three components. The cognitive component is his appraisal and thoughts about winning $10 million. The behavioral component is his smiling, laughing, and jumping around. The physiological component is his increased heart rate, blood pressure, respiration, and hormone secretions.

But how does Tony's emotion of happiness arise from these three components? Phillip Shaver and his colleagues (1987) have developed a model of how the emotion process probably occurs. According to their model (Figure 9.7), the first step in an emotional experience involves mak-

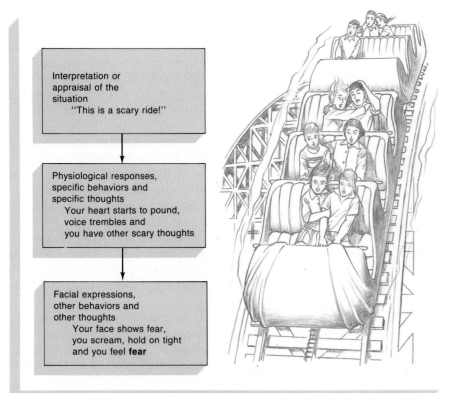

Figure 9.7
Interaction of separate components of an emotion to produce the complete emotional experience. (Adapted from: Shaver, P., Schwartz, J., Kirson, D., & O'Connor, C. (1987). Emotion knowledge: Further exploration of a prototype approach. *Journal of Personality and Social Psychology*, 52, 1061–1086, p. 1080)

Tony and Keith were extremely happy after winning over $10 million in a state lottery game. How long will their happiness last? Studies of previous winners found that after 12 months, lottery winners reported being no happier than nonwinners. The text explains why the winners' happiness declines over time. *(Wide World Photos)*

ing an appraisal of the situation (the cognitive component). This is immediately followed by physiological and behavioral responses, as well as other related thoughts. Finally, the three components interact to produce a complete emotional experience. In Tony's case, Shaver points out that during any part of the emotional experience he can change the appraisal ("How much will taxes take?"), show different behavioral tendencies (cry for joy), act differently (give away $20 bills), as well as deny, distort, or not attend to subjective feelings (he might insist that his new-found wealth will not change his life-style). Some of the previous models of an emotion, such as the facial feedback hypothesis, were based primarily on a single component rather than on the interaction of all three. The advantage of Shaver's model is that it shows how all three components interact to produce an emotional experience.

How long will Tony's happiness last? Philip Brickman and his associates (1978) interviewed lottery winners 1 to 12 months after they had won large sums of money. The researchers wanted to know how this significant event affected their level of happiness. First, they asked the winners to rate winning the lottery, with 0 meaning that it was the worst thing that ever happened to them and 5 meaning that it was the best thing that ever happened. Asking the winners to rate the event is another way of asking them to appraise it. The average rating was 3.78, probably not as high as you might have expected. The majority of winners did report positive changes, such as financial security, more leisure time, and earlier retirement. But when asked to rate how happy they were now, lottery winners, on average, turned out to be no more happy than nonwinners. There is one more interesting finding. Brickman asked lottery winners and nonwinners to rate how pleasant they found seven everyday activities, such as talking with a friend, watching television, buying clothes, and reading a magazine. Winners rated their pleasure in these pursuits significantly lower than nonwinners.

There are two curious findings here: in spite of winning enormous sums of money, lottery winners were no happier than nonwinners and took less pleasure in doing ordinary things. Brickman says these findings make perfect sense. His explanation is based on his **adaptation level theory,** which has two principles, contrast and habituation. According to the *contrast principle*, the thrill of winning the lottery became a reference point for winners to judge other, ordinary experiences. As a result, when ordinary experiences were compared to the emotional high of winning the lottery, the ordinary experiences were judged to be less pleasurable.

But why was the level of happiness reported by winners no different from that of nonwinners? The answer to this question lies in the *habituation principle*, which says that winners became accustomed or habituated to the pleasures of having a great deal of money. As time passes, these pleasures are taken for granted, are not appreciated as much, and thus contribute less to the winners' level of happiness. The habituation principle explains why Brickman found that the winners' level of happiness was no greater than the nonwinners'. Brickman concluded that because of the contrast principle, an exceedingly good fortune makes ordinary things seem less pleasurable and thus takes away some of the happiness of a good fortune. And because of the habituation principle, we eventually take new pleasures for granted, and thus they contribute less and less to our level of happiness.

Brickman's adaptation level theory explains why wonderful events such as getting an A in a course, buying a new car, landing a much-wanted job, or starting a new relationship makes you initially very happy. But after some time, you take for granted the pleasures associated with these situations and thus they do not contribute as much to your current happiness. This raises our next question: "What does it take to be in a good mood?"

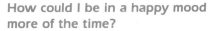

How could I be in a happy mood more of the time?

Cope with Daily Stressors.   What if you kept a diary of what happened to you throughout the day, and at the end of the day you rated your mood from extremely bad to extremely good? When John Eckenrode (1984) asked a group of women to do just that, he discovered that their daily mood was more related to the number of ordinary stressors, such as children misbehaving or the car breaking down, rather than to long-lasting major stressors, such as having an unemployed husband. The fewer daily stressors they encountered, the better their moods; the more daily stressors, the worse their moods.

Applying Eckenrode's findings to your own life, you can see that if you want to feel happy more of the time you must first become more aware of your daily stressors and how much they affect your mood. Then you must learn effective ways to cope with these stressors, whether they be waiting in line, getting up in the morning, traffic, a difficult roommate, or some other problem.

As you cope better with these daily stressors, your mood and level of happiness will rise. We will explain effective ways to cope with daily stressors in Module 41.

Focus on Positive Events.   Suppose you are wearing a beeper, and each time it goes off you are to write down what you are thinking and how you are feeling. This is what Mihaly Csikszentmihalyi and Thomas Figurski (1982) asked 100 people to do in order to determine how their thoughts affected their feelings. The researchers found that the more the subjects thought about or focused on themselves, the lower was their mood. Apparently, when people focus on themselves, they tend to focus on the negative aspects and this depresses their mood. In a similar study, Irwin Sarason and his colleagues (1986) asked students to recall positive or negative things that had happened to them the past week. Then, the students were asked to describe themselves. Students who recalled more positive things made twice as many positive self-statements, such as, "I'm a good student" or "I'm easy to get along with," while those who recalled more negative events tended to have a poorer self-image. These studies suggest that if you make a conscious effort to think about and focus on the positive aspects of your daily life, you will feel better about yourself and improve your mood.

✱ *Create a Positive Mood.*   By now you can see that your daily happiness depends more on your ability to notice and remember positive events than it does on something wonderful happening to you. In fact, researchers have discovered that you can improve your mood simply by reading and thinking about a list of positive self-statements, such as "I feel really good," "I feel energetic," "I like myself," "I'm happy about things," "I'm looking good today," "I'm in a good mood." Conversely, you will probably feel more gloomy if you read and reflect on a list of negative self-statements (Bower, 1981; Lichter et al., 1980; Velten, 1968).

All of these studies tell us that day in and day out we can take an active role in raising our level of happiness. Or, we can wait patiently until we win a lottery.

REVIEW

Hank and Marge got into the front seat, sat down, and put on their safety harness. As the roller coaster started its climb, Hank felt scared and Marge felt excited. For six very long minutes, Hank was in the grips of fear. According to our component definition of emotion, Hank's screams and yells would be part of the

(1) _____ component, his sweaty palms and increased heart rate would be part of the

(2) _____ component, and his thoughts about being hurled off into space would be part of the

(3) _____ component. After the ride, Hank felt very relieved and Marge felt exhilarated. "I hate roller coasters," Hank said. "I love them," Marge said.

If we were to follow Hank and Marge around the amusement park, we could divide their emotions into

three pleasant ones, (4) _____, _____,

and possibly _____ and three unpleasant

ones, (5) _____, _____, and

_____. One function of Hank's fearful feelings is to help him escape from dangerous situa-

tions, which is referred to as the (6) _____ function of emotions. However, with Marge's encouragement, Hank knowingly puts himself into a situation that not only elicits fear but prevents his escape from the fear-inducing ride. This is an example of how per-

sonal, cultural, or societal (7) _____ may override the adaptive functions of emotions. The adaptive functions of emotions may change Hank's behavior in three different ways. During the ride, Hank's fear makes it difficult for him to carry on a normal conversation. This is an example of an emotion

(8) _____ an ongoing behavior. During the ride, Hank's fear makes him especially notice when to lean or hold on extra tight. This is an example of an

emotion causing us to (9) _____ to relevant cues. After the roller coaster ride, Hank's fear may make him want to relax by playing some games. This

is an example of an emotion (10) _____ a new behavior.

How does riding a roller coaster produce emotions in Hank and Marge? There are three theories about what causes emotions. If you believed that feedback from the muscles and skin in Marge's face were primarily responsible for an emotion, this would be the

(11) _____ feedback hypothesis, first suggested by Charles Darwin. If you believed that there are separate physiological patterns for each emotion,

this would be the (12) _____ theory. If you believed that Marge used cues from the environment to label her emotion, this would be the

(13) _____ theory, which was first suggested by Schachter and Singer. All of these original theories have been modified by subsequent research. There is little evidence that each emotion has its own physiological pattern. Instead of causing an emotion, physiological responses are believed to contribute to the

(14) _____ of an emotion. Evidence suggests that feedback from facial muscles and skin does not actually cause separate emotions but rather affects

Marge's (15) _____.

How does the same situation, a roller coaster ride, produce different emotions: fear in Hank and excitement in Marge? Shaver's model for the emotion process suggests that Hank and Marge go through three steps. In the first step, Hank and Marge interpret or

(16) _____ the roller coaster ride very differently. Their difference in appraisal initiates two different emotional processes. For some human emotions, such as jealousy, the appraisal may be an active, conscious process. For emotions that occur instantaneously, the appraisal may also be instantaneous or perhaps subconscious. In the second step, Hank and Marge experience immediately increased heart rate and

blood pressure, which is part of the (17) _____ component, and increased screaming and yelling,

which is part of the (18) _____ component, as well as other emotion-related thoughts. In the

third step, the interaction of all three (19) _____ results in Hank's feeling fear and Marge's feeling excitement.

Hank says, "Mondays make me unhappy." Marge says, "There's three things you can do about it. First, your daily stressors have a great effect on your mood,

so if you learn to (20) _____ more effectively your mood will be better. Second, if you complain and focus on Monday's problems throughout the day, it will make you unhappy. Instead, if throughout

the day you focus on Monday's (21) _____ events you will improve your mood. Third, if you repeat negative mood statements throughout the day, such as, "Nothing goes right, I hate Mondays," you will induce a more negative mood. Instead, if you repeat positive mood statements, such as, "I'm doing really well today," you will induce a more positive

(22) _____.

Answers: 1) behavioral; (2) physiological; (3) cognitive; (4) love, joy, surprise; (5) fear, sadness, anger; (6) adaptive; (7) values, norms; (8) disrupting; (9) attend; (10) motivating; (11) facial; (12) James/Lange; (13) cognitive; (14) intensity; (15) mood; (16) appraise; (17) physiological; (18) behavioral; (19) components; (20) cope; (21) positive; (22) mood

GLOSSARY TERMS

adaptation level theory
  (p. 298)

cognitive theory (p. 291)
emotion (p. 288)

facial feedback hypothesis
  (p. 290)

James/Lange theory
  (p. 290)

PERSONAL NOTE

Many parents strongly believe that breakfast is a very important meal. If you do not eat breakfast, so parents say, your body will be off to a bad start and your entire day will be ruined. My parents' warning had a profound influence on my emotional reaction to breakfast. I hated breakfast, but felt very guilty whenever I skipped it. I could not wait to grow up and stop eating breakfast with no one there to tell me what harm I was doing to my body. I thought there must be hundreds of others who, like me, do not eat breakfast, have not ruined their bodies, and lead happy lives. As it turns out, about 25 percent of the population skips breakfast with few, if any, deficits in performance (Dickie & Bender, 1982). I feel much better knowing that there are other people who do not eat breakfast and are still alive and well. —R.P.

10

Human Sexual Behavior

Module 26 Gender Identity, Sexual Anatomy, and Arousal

"He's my brother. I don't understand what's going on. All my friends are asking about Greg." Nancy tried not to get angry as she waited for her mother to answer. "Does it mean that I will have a problem too? That's all I need." Her mother spoke slowly. "When Greg was born, the doctor told us that he was a boy. So we raised him as a boy. You know how much your father likes sports and, well, he got Greg going on football and loves to take him fishing. And it seemed perfectly normal when Greg wanted to date and have girlfriends. Now the doctor tells us that a mistake had been made when Greg was born. That Greg has the genes of a girl. That Greg has ovaries like a girl, and that is why his breasts are starting to grow. But the doctor says that he can give Greg hormones and he will develop like a boy. We've talked to Greg and he wants to stay a boy." As her mother was talking, Nancy's face turned from anger to sympathy. Her mother added gently, "There's nothing for you to worry about. You're perfectly normal. You've got girl genes and your breasts are developing and you're going to be very pretty." Nancy looked into her mother's eyes and asked, "But what's going to happen to Greg?" (adapted from Money & Ehrhardt, 1972).

What happens if a boy is really a girl?

Sometimes an unusual case like Greg's can best illustrate how our anatomy develops and how we develop our gender identity and sex role. What we are about to discover is that sexual behavior is a blend of genetic, hormonal, and environmental influences.

Greg was mislabeled a boy because his external sexual organs or genitalia were abnormally formed at birth. Although his external sexual anatomy appeared to be that of a male, his penis, which was very small, was actually an enlarged clitoris. In the past, a female infant with an enlarged clitoris might be labeled a boy, while a male infant with an underdeveloped penis and undescended testes might be labeled a girl. Mislabeling a newborn's sex is less likely to occur today because an infant's genetic sex can easily be checked, a task that was technically very difficult to do in the 1940s and 1950s.

What makes you think of yourself as male or female?

We can use Greg's case to show the many steps you go through in acquiring both your gender identity and your sex role. **Gender identity** refers to your private or subjective feelings that you are a male or a female. When you think "I am a woman" or "I am a man," you are expressing this basic perception about yourself. Greg thought of himself as a male and preferred to remain a male, indicating a male gender identity. Not only did Greg have a male gender identity, he also had a male sex role. **Sex role** refers to the combination of attitudes and behaviors considered appropriate for a particular sex in a given culture. In Greg's case, he behaved in the stereotypic ways of an American male, such as playing football, going fishing with his father, and dating a girlfriend. In contrast, Nancy was behaving in ways that were stereotypically female.

At this point, notice two things: (1) As happens in most cases, Nancy's female sex role matched her gender identity and Greg's male sex role matched his gender identity; but (2) because Greg was mislabeled a boy when he was born, his chromosomes and hormones did not match his male sex role and gender identity. To understand how this mismatch occurred, we need to follow Greg's and Nancy's development from conception through sexual development.

Effects of Genetic Instructions

The tiny egg or ovum from which you were formed contributed half your **chromosomes** (CROW-ma-zomes)—microscopic structures within the cell that carried the **genes** or blueprints for your development. One of the chromosomes in every egg is called the **X chromosome.** Some of its genes affect sexual development. Every sperm also contains a sex chromosome, an X or a **Y chromosome.** If an egg is fertilized by a sperm with an X chromosome, the result is an XX combination that contains instructions for the development of ovaries, vagina, and clitoris. Greg and Nancy had XX or female chromosomal patterns. If an ovum is fertilized by a sperm with a Y chromosome, the result is an XY combination that contains instructions for the development of testes and formation of a penis.

In the formation of a penis, the critical factor is presence of male hormones in the blood, especially **testosterone** (tes-TAHS-ter-own), which is normally secreted by the testes. Since fetuses with an XX chromosome pattern do not develop testes, they are usually not exposed to significant amounts of testosterone. The result is the normal development of female sex organs, as happened to Nancy. But if large amounts of testosterone or a hormone like it somehow do enter the bloodstream of an XX chromosome fetus, that fetus may develop masculine-looking external genitals. This is what happened to Greg. His XX chromosome pattern resulted in the development of normal ovaries. Once his external sex organs began to develop, however, their growth was modified by the abnormal presence of male-like hormones. Because these hormones had their effects before Greg was born, they are referred to as *prenatal hormones.*

Although this man and woman may take being male and female for granted, in fact a number of steps lead to the formation of sexual identity. (Carol Lee/The Picture Cube)

PRENATAL HORMONES AND THE BRAIN

The case of Greg comes from the research of John Money (1987) who has spent 30 years studying the effects of prenatal hormones. Money and Anke Ehrhardt (1972) and others have gathered data by studying humans who had been accidentally exposed to abnormal levels of sex hormone because of naturally occurring "mistakes." Some of Money's data come from mothers who took hormones during pregnancy to prevent miscarriages. Although this practice was stopped, a number of male and female fetuses were exposed to unusually high levels of female and male-like hormones. Other data come from cases involving a naturally occurring hormonal abnormality. For example, one of the fetal glands may malfunction and produce testosterone, which affects the fetal brain. If the female fetus is exposed to testosterone, sex organs can be masculinized, which is what happened to Greg.

Besides affecting the development of sex organs, prenatal hormones are also assumed to program the brain.

There is considerable evidence from laboratory studies on animals that the presence or absence of prenatal hormones program the brain for specific reproductive responses. If no prenatal male hormones are present, fetal rats have genetic instructions to develop a brain programmed for female reproductive functions and responses. Having a female programmed brain means that one part of the rat's brain, the *hypothalamus*, will trigger the *cyclic* secretion of hormones at puberty, and the rat will perform characteristically female sexual behaviors, such as assuming a certain posture when the male rat makes sexual advances. However, if testosterone is present during critical periods, rats will develop a brain programmed for male reproductive responses. Having a male programmed brain means that the rat's hypothalamus will trigger male reproductive functions and behaviors, which include the *continuous* secretion of hormones and performance of certain sexual behaviors, such as mounting. Researchers conclude that with no prenatal testosterone present, the rat's brain has genetic instructions to develop a brain programmed for female reproductive responses. However, if prenatal testosterone is present, the rat's brain, especially the hypothalamus, develops a brain reprogrammed for male reproductive responses (MacLusky & Naftolin, 1981). Does a similar kind of programming occur in human brains?

Researchers assume that if no testosterone is present, the human brain, like the rat's brain, has genetic instructions to develop a brain programmed for female reproductive responses. Having a female programmed brain means that at puberty, the hypothalamus triggers hormones to be secreted in a *cyclic* pattern, which is known as the menstrual cycle. Researchers also assume that the presence of prenatal testosterone makes the human brain, like the rat's brain, develop a program for male reproductive responses. Having a male programmed brain means that, at puberty, the hypothalamus triggers hormones to be secreted in a *continuous* pattern (Figure 10.1). These assumptions about how prenatal hormones program the human brain are based on similarities between the functions of hormones in animals and humans and on clinical observations of individuals with hormonal abnormalities.

But what about the finding that prenatal hormones also programmed the rat brain to trigger the performance of reproductive behaviors in the sexually mature animal. Does the same thing happen to the human brain?

In many animals, including lions, sexual behavior is almost totally controlled by hormones. (George B. Schaller/Bruce Coleman)

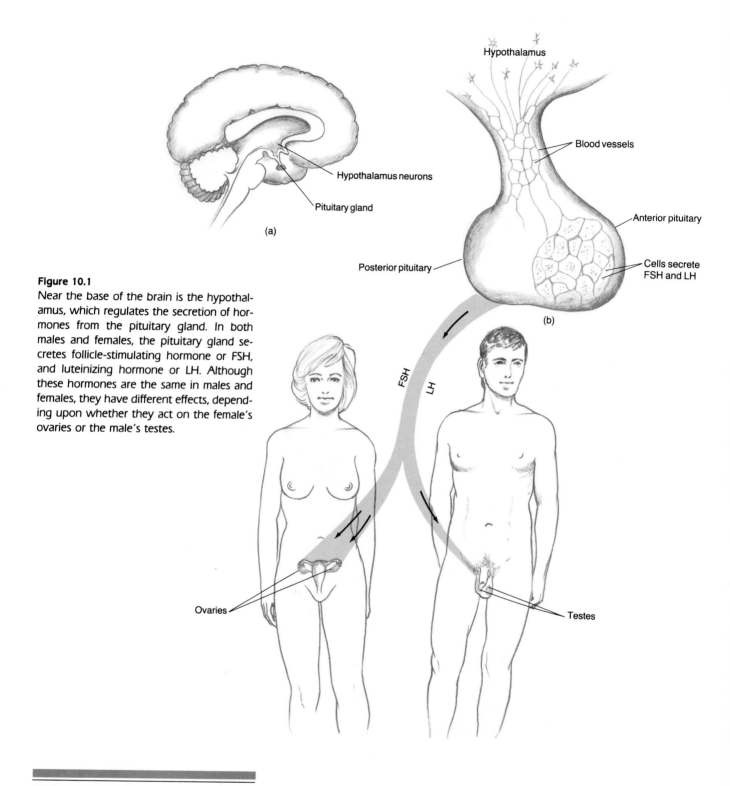

Figure 10.1
Near the base of the brain is the hypothalamus, which regulates the secretion of hormones from the pituitary gland. In both males and females, the pituitary gland secretes follicle-stimulating hormone or FSH, and luteinizing hormone or LH. Although these hormones are the same in males and females, they have different effects, depending upon whether they act on the female's ovaries or the male's testes.

EXPLORING PSYCHOLOGY   Prenatal Hormones, Sex Role, and Sexual Orientation

How powerful are prenatal hormones?

Do prenatal hormones program the human brain and predispose us to have a certain sex role, gender identity or sexual orientation? To answer this question, we again turn to Money's studies.

Money and Matthews (1982) followed twelve female infants who were exposed to male-like hormones, which their mothers had taken to prevent miscarriages. At birth, their genitalia showed various degrees of masculinization, but all were correctly labeled and raised as girls. Follow-up on these females, now aged 16 to 27, indicated that during childhood they showed more rough-and-tumble play, and during high school more interest in sports. However, all appeared to develop female gender identities. From studies like this, Money and others have concluded that prenatal hormones may affect the development of sex role behaviors, such as rough-and-tumble play. However, prenatal hormones do not seem to have a major effect on the development of gender identity (Ehrhardt & Meyer-Bahlburg, 1981). Now we must turn to a more difficult question: Do prenatal hormones affect sexual orientation—that is, whether one is bisexual, heterosexual, or homosexual?

Money and his colleagues (1984) studied individuals who had female chromosomes (XX pattern), but because of a malfunction of one of their glands were exposed to testosterone during fetal development. This exposure resulted in the masculinization of their sex organs so that, at birth, some had an enlarged clitoris. Depending on the extent that their sex organs were masculinized, some were labeled and raised as boys and others were labeled and raised as girls. Upon reaching sexual maturity, 100 percent of those who were labeled and socialized as boys indicated a heterosexual preference; that is, they were sexually attracted to women. Money explains that these "boys" were predisposed by the presence of prenatal male hormones, which are thought to affect the brain, to prefer female sexual partners. The development of a heterosexual preference was facilitated by their being socialized as boys.

In contrast, of those who were labeled and socialized as girls, 52 percent indicated a heterosexual preference and 48 percent indicated a bisexual or homosexual preference. Money says that these individuals were predisposed by the presence of prenatal male hormones to prefer female sexual partners. However, their socialization as females, which encouraged a heterosexual orientation, worked against this predisposition. Money concluded that in about half of these cases, socialization overcame the predisposing effects of prenatal hormones. In the other half, the predisposing effects of prenatal hormones overcame the effect of socialization.

"How strongly is a person predisposed by prenatal hormones to become bisexual, heterosexual or homosexual?" Money's (1987) answer is clear. Developing a sexual orientation occurs in two steps. The first step is predisposition produced by prenatal hormones. However, Money believes that this predisposition influences sexual orientation, but does not cause an automatic response. Rather, prenatal hormones are assumed to program the brain, and this program facilitates the development of a bisexual, heterosexual, or homosexual orientation. The second step in acquiring a sexual orientation is the contribution of, and facilitation by, postnatal socialization. A person would be more likely to follow his or her predisposition depending on how much the socialization process helps or hinders.

EFFECTS OF HORMONES AT PUBERTY

Sally is almost 16 years old, but her body looks more like a boy's than a girl's. She has no signs of breast development or widening of the hips. She will not experience these physical changes or begin menstruating because she was born without ovaries. Unlike the normal female chromosome pattern of XX, Sally has a single X chromosome. Without

What is the connection between hormones and puberty?

the second X chromosome, there is no development of ovaries and no secretion of female hormones at puberty. Sally does not date and shows no interest in sex (adapted from Bekker, 1974).

Sally's condition is known as Turner's syndrome and is like that of a boy who is castrated before puberty. The lack of functional ovaries or testes means that, at puberty, there is no increase in sexual hormones, no development of **secondary sexual characteristics,** such as breasts, and little interest in dating or sexual behavior. A normal adolescent, in contrast, undergoes many sex-related changes. If you are a normal male, at puberty you experienced a great increase in secretion of the male hormone testosterone, the development of facial and pubic hair, a lower voice, and the production of sperm in the testes. If you are a normal female, at puberty you experienced a great increase in secretion of the female hormones **estrogen** and **progesterone** (pro-JEST-er-own); ovulation, which is signaled by the beginning of the menstrual cycle; and the development of breasts, pubic hair, and wider hips. These hormonal changes during puberty were actually programmed during fetal development. If Sally were to be injected with female hormones, she would develop secondary sexual characteristics, as well as interest in dating and sex.

From cases such as Sally's, researchers conclude that increased secretion of sexual hormones at puberty is necessary for the development of normal secondary sexual characteristics, as well as the development of normal sexual interest and *motivation* (Money & Ehrhardt, 1972). At puberty, Greg experienced a great increase in female hormones from his ovaries, and so his breasts began developing. When he decided to remain a boy, his ovaries were removed and he was given the male hormone testosterone, which resulted in the development of male secondary sexual characteristics.

Notice that it is an *increased secretion* of sexual hormones at puberty, not whether these hormones are male or female, that influences feelings of sexual interest and motivation. Sexual hormones may have this effect by acting directly on the brain and/or by triggering the development of secondary sexual characteristics, which in turn lead people to think of themselves as sexually mature and active.

EFFECTS OF SOCIALIZATION

What makes Nancy so interested in Tom?

"I've gotta get some new makeup and I'm tired of my same old hairstyle." Nancy, Greg's sister, was talking on the phone. "Tom's taking me out tonight and I can't decide what to wear. He's picking me up in an hour. Gotta get going. Bye." Nancy put the phone down and looked into her closet for the hundredth time. She started to try on clothes, throwing things everywhere. Her mother walked in and noticed the mess. "Mom, I might be home late tonight." Nancy was asking more than telling and kept right on talking. "Is dating always so much bother and so much fun? I really like Tom. This time it's really serious." Her mother smiled and wondered what "serious" really meant (author's file).

To understand Nancy's interest in Tom, we need to go back in time to her conception. Nancy began with an XX chromosomal pattern, which resulted in her developing ovaries and female sex organs. Since Nancy was not exposed to prenatal testosterone her genetic instructions resulted in a female programmed brain which triggered a cyclical pattern of hormone secretion at puberty. John Money would theorize that the lack of prenatal testosterone also predisposed Nancy to develop a heterosexual orientation. However, Money would add that, from the moment the doctor said, "It's a girl," a powerful and long-lasting socialization process began. This means that from her moment of birth, Nancy was rewarded by her parents, peers, and society for adopting a female sex role and either subtly or openly punished for behaving in ways that were not appropriate for her sex role (see Module 31). As Nancy adopts a female sex role, she will begin to think of herself as a female and thus develop a female gender identity. As Nancy enters adolescence and begins to develop female secondary sexual characteristics, she will experience increased interest in sexual things and, most probably, increased interest in male sexual partners. As she begins to date, the socialization process will continue to reward and punish her for appropriate sex role behavior, such as encouraging heterosexual dating. Here is how John Money would explain Nancy's interest in Tom. Nancy's prenatal hormones gave her a heterosexual predisposition, her socialization process facilitated and encouraged this predisposition and her increased level of hormones at puberty increased her interest in things sexual. It is the interaction of all these elements that now finds Nancy getting ready for her date with Tom.

As Nancy thinks about becoming sexually active, she may have a number of questions about male and female anatomy and function of sexual organs. That is what the next section is all about.

MAJOR CONCEPT Sexual Anatomy and Gender Identity

Sexual anatomy refers to the structure of a person's genital organs, while gender identity refers to a person's subjective feelings of being male or female. Sexual anatomy and gender identity are influenced by four basic factors: chromosomal patterns, prenatal hormones, hormones at puberty, and socialization.

For each of the cases described below, decide which of these four factors is the major influence.

Major Influence

1. A human embryo with an XY chromosome pattern begins to form a structure that resembles a penis. ___

2. At about six weeks after conception, part of a male embryo begins developing into the male sex glands or testes. ___

3. A child with an XY chromosome pattern is insensitive to testosterone. At birth, the child was labeled a girl and she now has a female gender identity. ___

4. A 13-year-old girl begins to develop breasts, wider hips, and other secondary sexual characteristics. ___

James Morris began life with the male XY chromosomal pattern, developed male sexual organs, secreted male hormones, and developed male secondary sexual characteristics. In spite of all these male factors, James developed a female gender identity. He chose to undergo a sex change operation, became Jan Morris, and described the experience in the book *Conundrum.* (Above, Jerry Bauer; below, Jerry Bauer for *Last Letters from Hav* by Jan Morris, Random House, 1985)

Answers: 1 prenatal hormones; 2 chromosomal pattern; 3 socialization; 4 hormones at puberty

SEXUAL ANATOMY
AND SEXUAL RESPONSE

In 1899, all the papers presented at the annual meeting of the American Medical Association were published, except one. That one, titled "The gynecologic consideration of the sexual act," was not published because it had a discussion of how the female genitalia respond during sexual activity. One of the doctors who opposed publication said that the discussion of sex "is attended with more or less filth and we besmirch ourselves by discussing it in public" (quoted in Hollender, 1983, p. 28).

The paper was finally published in 1983 and is now considered a landmark in the study of sexual behavior (Lewis, 1983). Its history illustrates the prejudices that scientists, in this case medical doctors, had against the study of sexual responses, prejudices that continued until fairly recently.

In the 1950s two researchers, William Masters and Virginia Johnson, finally defied the prejudice and undertook a thorough observational study of the physiology of human sexual behavior. Over a twelve-year period they observed hundreds of volunteer subjects engaging in thousands of sexual acts. In 1966 they published their findings in a book called *Human Sexual Response*. Some criticized Masters and Johnson for conducting research on sexual behavior in the laboratory. Today, however, Masters' and Johnson's research is recognized as the first comprehensive and scientific study of the physiological changes during arousal and orgasm. It was their research that led to an understanding of human sexual physiology and provided a basis for developing techniques to treat sexual problems.

THE GENERAL STAGES
OF SEXUAL RESPONSE

What happens when you are sexually aroused?

If you were to close your eyes and think about an erotic scene or begin to touch and kiss your partner, it is very likely that within 3 to 10 seconds your body would show signs of physiological arousal. Based on laboratory research, Masters and Johnson (1966) have divided the sexual response pattern into four stages: **excitement, plateau, orgasm,** and **resolution.** We will describe Masters' and Johnson's four-stage model here, since it is a good introduction to the sexual response pattern. As you read, it may be helpful to look periodically at Figures 10.2 and 10.3, which show the various parts of the male and female sex organs. It is important to remember, however, that there is much variability in sexual response among individuals.

Excitement

Whether you are male or female, arousing stimuli cause your body to have increased muscle tension (or myotonia) and a moderate increase in heart rate and blood pressure. You also experience increased blood flow in the genital organs, resulting in engorgement and swelling. If you are a female, your clitoris swells, your labia minora increase in size, and vaginal lubrication occurs. If you are a male, your penis becomes erect or partially so, and your testes increase in size and become elevated or drawn up closer to the body.

Plateau

With continued arousal, you experience increased muscle tension and further increases in heart rate and blood pressure. If you are a female, your

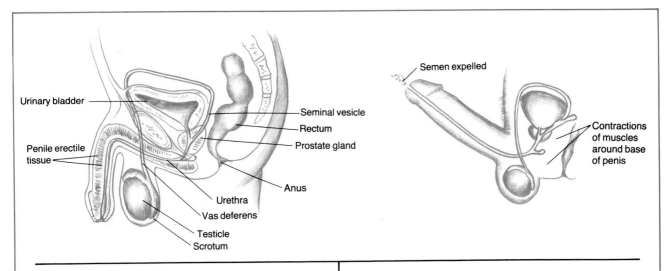

Penis. The head of the penis is called the *glans* and the rest is called the *shaft*. The shaft contains three chambers that fill with blood and produce an erection. The shaft does not contain a bone or muscle. At birth the glans is covered with foreskin, which may be removed by circumcision. The glans is very sensitive to touch because it contains a large number of nerve endings. A number of commonly held ideas about the penis have now been shown to be myths. For example, there is no evidence that an uncircumcised penis is less sensitive than one that is circumcised. There is no evidence that a woman has an increased risk of cervical cancer if her partner has an uncircumcised penis. Except for surgical implants, there is no method to enlarge an adult penis. There is no relationship between body build and penis size. There is no relationship between size of penis and ability to perform sexually.

Testes. The testes are enclosed in a sac of skin called the scrotum. The scrotum is highly innervated so that touching this area may result in very pleasurable sensations. The two main functions of the testes are the production of sperm and the secretion of male sex hormones, especially testosterone.

Vas deferens. This is a tube that transports sperm from the testes to a storage area called the seminal vesicles.

Urethra. This is a tube that extends the length of the penis. During urination, urine passes down and exits from the urethra. During ejaculation, semen passes down and exits from the urethra.

Prostate gland. Located beneath the bladder, the prostate produces a milky and alkaline fluid that makes up some of the fluid ejaculated. The fluid's alkaline content helps to counteract the acidity of the vaginal tube. As a man grows older, chances of prostate cancer increase. In its early stages, this cancer is relatively easy to treat and cure.

Seminal vesicles. Not only are sperm stored here, but these glands provide fluids that are rich in fructose (a sugar) which nourishes the sperm.

Erection. An erection results when blood fills the three chambers in the shaft of the penis. An erection is an involuntary process under the control of the autonomic nervous system. During sexual excitement, the autonomic nervous system allows more blood to enter than leave the penis, and this results in an erection. Although the erection process is under involuntary control, psychological factors can trigger or interfere with it.

Ejaculation. This is the process by which semen is expelled from the penis. Semen is composed of both sperm and fluid from the prostate. Ejaculation is a reflex that is controlled by the autonomic nervous system. During ejaculation, semen is expelled from the penis by strong, rhythmic muscle contractions in the urethra lasting 3 to 10 seconds. Sensations during ejaculation give rise to the experience of orgasm. During puberty, young males may experience orgasm without ejaculation.

Figure 10.2
Structure and functions of the male sex organs.

clitoris withdraws under its hood and the outer one-third of your vagina becomes markedly engorged. If you are a male, your erection continues and your testes increase greatly in size. No single response marks this phase, which may last for only a few seconds or continue for much longer. Some persons report that the experience of continued arousal during the plateau phase results in a more intense orgasmic experience.

Orgasm

Continued sexual stimulation during the plateau phase may cause you to experience an orgasm. Whether you are male or female, the experience of orgasm is one of intense pleasure. Written descriptions of the orgasmic experience are often difficult to label as having been done by men or by women. Whether you are male or female, you experience involuntary muscle spasms, great increases in heart rate (up to 180 beats per minute), blood pressure, and breathing, and rhythmic contractions of the muscles in the anal-genital area (Bohlen et al., 1982). If you are a male, your orgasm is accompanied by ejaculation, in which semen is expelled by strong

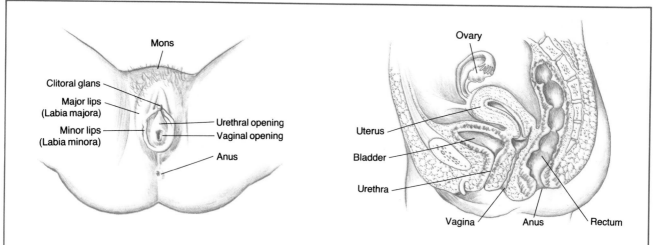

Mons. This is a pad of fatty tissue covering the pubic bone. The skin over the mons is covered with pubic hair. Because of its many nerve endings, touching this area may result in pleasurable sensations.

Labia majora. These are the outer lips, which are covered with pubic hair and extend down from the mons. Because of their many nerve endings, touch to the labia majora can result in pleasurable sensations.

Labia minora. These are the inner lips, which are not covered with hair and are often visible between the labia majora. The labia minora form a covering over the clitoris called the clitorial hood. Like the mons and labia majora, the labia minora have many nerve endings and are very sensitive to touch. The labia majora and minora vary in size, shape, and color from woman to woman.

Clitoris. This tiny structure, usually covered by the clitoral hood, is the most sentisitive of the female's sexual organs. It has about the same number of nerve endings as does the penis. The head of the clitoris, called the glans, is so sensitive that many women prefer to stimulate this area indirectly by touching the hood which covers it. It is now well accepted that stimulation of the clitoris is essential for triggering orgasm.

Urethral opening. Urine flows from the bladder down the urethra, which is a short tube, and out the urethral opening. A common problem in women is bladder infections or cystitis. This condition can be caused by irritation of the urethra during intercourse or by infection from a partner's sexual organs, but it can also occur in women who are sexually inactive. Prevention of cystitis is aided by hygienic practices. Medical treatment often involves antibiotics.

Hymen. A fold of tissue, the hymen, may partially cover the entrance to the vagina. The structure of the hymen varies greatly from being virtually nonexistent to covering the vaginal opening almost completely. The idea that the presence or absence of the hymen can indicate whether a woman is a virgin is a myth. Other than protecting the vaginal tissues early in life, the hymen has no other function. By manually stretching her hymen beforehand, a woman can minimize the discomfort of first intercourse.

Vagina. In the nonaroused state, the vagina is a flat, hollow tube, approximately 3 to 5 inches long. During intercourse, the walls of the vagina can expand or contract to accommodate the penis. During sexual excitement the walls of the vagina produce a clear, slippery fluid. This lubrication is the first sign of sexual arousal and is analogous to erection in the male. Lubrication has two functions. It reduces the normal acidity of the vagina, which allows sperm to travel faster and survive longer. It also increases the pleasure from touching and facilitates the entry of the penis during intercourse. Just as psychological factors (anxiety) can inhibit an erection in the male, they can also inhibit lubrication in the female.

Grafenberg spot. This is a dime-sized area that may be located one-third to one-half the distance into the vagina, on the upper wall. Also called the G-spot, it can be located by applying deep pressure to the upper wall of the vagina. Although initial pressure may be unpleasant, some women report that continued stimulation is arousing and pleasurable, while others report few sensations.

Figure 10.3
Structure and functions of the female sex organs.

rhythmic muscle contractions. If you are a female, you may experience increased lubrication during orgasm.

Resolution

Following orgasm, you experience a gradual release of muscle tension and a return to normal heart rate, blood pressure, and breathing. If you are a female, your clitoris descends and your labia minora return to unaroused size. If you are a male, loss of erection occurs in two stages. There is a 50 percent decrease within the first minute, with the remaining decrease occurring over a longer period of time. If you are a male, you experience a *refractory* period following orgasm during which additional stimulation cannot produce orgasm. According to Masters and Johnson, if you are a female there is no refractory period, and continued stimulation may result in another orgasm. However, Masters' and Johnson's conclusions about women obtaining repeated orgasms with continued stimulation may or may not apply to most women. This is because Masters and Johnson studied women who had volunteered to perform sexual acts and therefore might have a more relaxed attitude toward sexual behavior.

Since Masters' and Johnson's original description of the sexual response pattern, other researchers have noted considerable variability in this pattern (Kaplan, 1974; Zilbergeld, 1978; Steinman et al., 1981). For this reason, you should view their four-stage sequence as a general description, rather than as a standard for the "right way" to respond.

A Closer Look at Orgasm

The heart races, blood pressure soars, breath comes in gasps. The skin flushes and tissues swell with blood, changing the size, shape, color, and position of the organs. As the nervous system is electrified, the face contorts, muscles tense and convulse. Sensations of vibration and pulsation, expansion and contraction, heat and cold, herald a loss of contact with the environment, a hallucinatory immersion in the moment, often accompanied by fragments of speech, sighs, groans. This "brief clouding of consciousness," as one sex researcher describes orgasm, makes time seem to stand still, exalts emotions, alters perceptions. Yet after it's over, few can describe it accurately or even truly remember it (adapted from Gallagher, 1986, p. 51).

What does an orgasm really feel like?

Where do all these feelings come from? William Masters and Virginia Johnson (1966) and Joseph Bohlen and his associates (1982) have measured the physiological changes that accompany orgasm, such as muscle contractions, heart rate and blood pressure increases, elevated oxygen consumption, and many others. After many years of research, Bohlen (1986) has found very little association between physiological responses and duration or intensity of orgasmic feelings. He concluded that physiological responses are the *basis* for the orgasmic experience but the perception of these responses, which takes place in the brain, is the *actual* orgasmic experience. Agreeing with Bohlen, Helen Singer Kaplan (1986) adds that physiological responses to sexual stimulation are similar for much of the population, but people perceive these responses in very different ways and thus report different kinds of orgasms. Since our perceptions depend upon our thoughts, memories, and associations, what goes on in our brains is probably more important to having a good orgasm than what goes on in our genitals.

In the early 1980s, the first reports appeared of some women who reported reaching orgasm from stimulation of the Grafenberg or **G-spot** alone (see Figure 10.3). Some of these women were also reported to show ejaculation analogous to male ejaculation during orgasm from G-spot stimulation. These claims were repeated in a popular book (Ladas et al., 1982), but the data supporting them are very limited and at times contradictory. For these reasons, we can draw only the following tentative conclusions: A certain percentage of women can locate the G-spot, but it is not clear whether stimulation of the G-spot alone can result in orgasm for most women. During G-spot stimulation, a very small percentage of women may secrete a fluid similar to that produced by the male prostate gland, but this secretion has not been confirmed (Addiego et al., 1981; Alzate & Hoch, 1986; Belzer, 1981; Goldberg et al., 1983; Perry & Whipple, 1981). One of the reasons for interest in the G-spot is that it suggests an additional way to trigger orgasm in women.

Is there a new way for women to reach orgasm?

Hormones and Sexual Motivation

Do sex hormones trigger sexual behavior?

You might assume that the male hormone testosterone triggers sexual drive in men. You might also assume that the female hormones estrogen and progesterone trigger sexual behavior in women. However, the normal range of sex hormone secretions is very wide. Within this normal range, human sexual *motivation* has a low correlation with the levels of sex hormones in the blood (Harvey, 1987; Knussmann & Christiansen, 1986; Morris et al., 1987). For example, the level of testosterone normally rises and falls throughout the day. These variations in testosterone level are poorly associated with variations in sex drive. Rather, in people with normal levels of sex hormones, sexual motivation seems to depend primarily on psychological factors.

What happens when there are no sex hormones?

What about people with abnormally low levels of sex hormones? Do they still experience sex drive? In women, the answer is very often "yes." After menopause, women experience a virtually complete loss of female sex hormones unless they choose to use hormone replacement therapy. Yet many women continue to experience normal sexual drive and to lead active sex lives (Arlington-Mackinnon & Troll, 1981).

The loss of sex hormones in males has somewhat more variable effects. One source of data comes from men who have been castrated and so experience a virtually complete loss. A small percentage of these men report that they continued to have erections and engage in sexual behavior. The majority, however, report both difficulty in having erections and a lowered

---

MAJOR CONCEPT   Human Sexual Response and Motivation

Many people are misinformed about human sexual responses and motivations for sex.

Indicate which of the following statements are true (T) or false (F).

1. T/F The vagina has about the same number of nerve endings as the penis.

2. T/F During the excitement stage, a person feels psychologically aroused but not physiologically aroused.

3. T/F During the orgasm stage, both males and females experience an increase in a number of physiological responses, including rhythmic contractions of the muscles in the anal-genital area.

4. T/F There is very little association between the intensity and duration of the physiological responses that occur during orgasm and the intensity and duration of the orgasmic experience.

5. T/F The primary reason for a person's increase or decrease in sexual desire and behavior is the increase or decrease in sexual hormones.

6. T/F The primary reason our orgasmic experiences differ is due to our differing perceptions of the physiological responses rather than to the physiological responses themselves.

7. T/F Certain physiological responses, such as erection in the male and lubrication in the female, are associated with having a normal level of sex hormones.

Answers: 1 (F); 2 (F); 3 (T); 4 (T); 5 (F); 6 (T); 7 (T).

sex drive (Hein & Hursch, 1979). It is difficult to know whether this lowered sex drive results directly from the loss of hormones or indirectly from the effects on erection.

What can we conclude about sex hormones and sexual motivation? In the normal adult, the presence of sex hormones is associated with certain *physiological* responses, such as erection in the male and vaginal lubrication in the female. These physiological responses provide sensations that contribute to sexual motivation. For males in particular, the alteration of these physiological responses can have an impact on sexual motivation. For both males and females, however, human sexual behavior and motivation often continue when there has been a virtually complete end to production of all sex hormones. These data suggest that in adult humans with normal levels of sex hormones, *psychological* factors, such as beliefs, expectancies, and worries and anxieties about sexual functioning, exert a major influence on sexual motivation.

Everyday Questions about Sex   **APPLYING PSYCHOLOGY**

After teaching a course in human sexual behavior for many years, we have noticed that the following questions are asked repeatedly. If you read Module 28, you will discover that some of these questions stem from common problems sex therapists often treat. Others arise from difficulties in communication, and still others from incomplete knowledge about the physiology of sex. Here we want to give you some straightforward answers to four of the questions we are asked most frequently.

What do students almost always ask about sex?

Question: "I (female) have never experienced an orgasm while engaging in sexual intercourse. Will I ever?" The same question is very often asked by males: "Why doesn't," or "How can I help my partner reach orgasm during intercourse?"

Answer: You may find it helpful to use a position in which the female is on top. In this way, you (the female) are better able to control the stimulation of your clitoris. After you have achieved orgasm several times in this position, you and your partner will have a better understanding of the kind of stimulation you need to reach orgasm. You will probably find that positions that provide a fairly continuous rubbing stimulation, as opposed to thrusting, are more effective in triggering your orgasm. When you are experimenting with positions, it would be best not to require yourself to reach orgasm. Just enjoy the position and concentrate on the good feelings it gives you. As you become more relaxed and learn not to worry about your partner, the orgasm is more likely to occur. Incidentally, after experimenting with positions you may still find that you are more likely to achieve orgasm if you or your partner stimulates your clitoris manually during intercourse. This would not be at all abnormal.

Question: "My partner really wants to please me and he tries to last long enough (during intercourse) for me to reach orgasm, but most of the time I'm too worried or he comes too quickly. How can I learn to reach orgasm faster?" The same question is very often asked by males: "How can I get my partner to come faster?"

Answer: Learning to achieve orgasm faster is not the solution to this problem. As you have already discovered, worrying about the situation interferes with your ability to become aroused and reach orgasm. And worse, in your partner's case, worrying about the situation is likely to make his ejaculation occur even *more* rapidly. Both of you need to stop worrying, and there are a number of things you can do to bring this about. If you feel comfortable about discussing the situation, you could suggest working with the stop-start or squeeze technique (described in Module 28), which will help your partner achieve better control over the ejaculatory reflex. As you both become confident that he can control this reflex, he will be less likely to "come too quickly," and you will be less likely to be distracted by worry. Another approach is for you to become much more aroused before your partner begins the movements that trigger his orgasm. You could ask your partner deliberately to try to increase your arousal, or you could just try to bring it about naturally in the lovemaking process. One way is to tell your partner while you are making love just what arouses you the most. You can be sure that your partner will be very pleased to learn about your wishes. When you try this, you may find that you achieve orgasm before intercourse or before your partner is close to orgasm, but do not be concerned. You will probably find that you continue to be as excited if not more excited after this orgasm. Finally, the common problem you have described is less likely to occur if you and your partner are having sex when you are both well rested.

Question: "Sometimes if we have been making love for a long time, I will lose my erection briefly and my partner gets upset about it. Why does this happen?"

Answer: It is a very normal physiological reaction for the erection to come and go during long periods of lovemaking. You should explain to your partner that even sex organs need a rest now and then, and it doesn't mean that you have lost interest. It might be helpful for you and your partner to read Bernie Zilbergeld's *Male Sexuality* (1978). Zilbergeld explains that we often have very unreasonable expectations of the penis.

Question: "How can I get my partner to tell me what pleases her (him)?"

Answer: Part of the problem here may be that your partner doesn't really know what is most pleasing. To find out, you might try experimenting. For example, play a game of "warm or cold," in which you touch your partner in various ways, and she or he responds with "warm" or "cold." Avoid asking open-ended questions like "How would you like me to touch you?" since these can be very difficult to answer. You may have better luck if you use an either-or question: "Would you like me to use a lighter touch or a heavier touch?" Robert Crooks and Karla Baur (1983) have an excellent chapter on such communication in their book *Our Sexuality.*

REVIEW

Although Charles seems like a normal infant, he has an abnormal chromosome pattern. Instead of having the normal XY male pattern, Charles has an XXY pattern, called Klinefelter's syndrome. Charles's sexual development will be normal until he reaches puberty. This means that as a fetus, he developed testes according to instructions carried on the (1) _____ chromosome. Once developed, the fetal testes secreted the male hormone, (2) _____. The presence of prenatal testosterone caused the growth and development of his (3) _____, so that at birth the doctor said, "It's a boy." The presence of testosterone also affected a part of his brain, called the (4) _____, which became programmed for male reproductive functions, such as (5) _____ secretion of hormones. If testosterone were not present, Charles's hypothalamus would be programmed for female reproductive functions, such as cyclic secretion of hormones.

If a female human fetus were accidentally exposed to large amounts of male hormones, her sexual organs would be masculinized and she might show behaviors, such as rough-and-tumble play, that are more stereotypic of the male sex (6) _____. However, there is no evidence that the presence of prenatal male hormones will directly affect whether she thinks of herself as a male or female; in other words, it will not affect her gender (7) _____. At puberty, a female's hypothalamus would trigger a tremendous increase in the secretion of two female hormones, (8) _____ and _____, which in turn promote development of female (9) _____ sexual characteristics.

When Charles reaches puberty, his XXY pattern will result in little or no development of his testes. This means that he will not develop secondary sexual characteristics because his testes cannot produce testosterone. Without the production of sex hormones at puberty, Charles may not have any sexual (10) _____ or interest in dating. If Charles is injected with testosterone during puberty, he will develop secondary sexual characteristics and will show an interest in dating. According to Money, the development of Charles's sexual orientation takes place in two steps. In the first step, a predisposition is laid down by the presence or absence of (11) _____

hormones, which are presumed to affect the brain. In the second step, the carrying out of the predisposition is facilitated or inhibited by (12) _____.

A man and woman are making love. According to Masters and Johnson, people experience four general stages of sexual responsiveness. As sexual partners begin to kiss and fondle, they enter the first stage, called (13) _____. A man has an erection and a woman experiences vaginal lubrication. With continued arousal, the couple enter Masters' and Johnson's second stage, called (14) _____. A man's penis generally remains erect and a woman's clitoris withdraws under its hood. Eventually, the partners become extremely excited and experience the third stage, called (15) _____. During orgasm, both men and women experience rhythmic muscle contractions in the genital and anal areas. These contractions are accompanied by extremely pleasurable sensations and feelings. A number of years ago it was reported that some women could reach orgasm by stimulation of the (16) _____ spot alone. Whether this is true has not yet been established. According to Masters and Johnson, female orgasm during intercourse results instead from indirect stimulation of the clitoris. Orgasm is followed by a fourth stage of sexual responsiveness, called (17) _____, in which physiological responses return to normal. During the resolution phase, a man experiences a period of time, called the (18) _____ period, during which he cannot have another orgasm. A woman does not go through a refractory period and may be capable of another orgasm with continued stimulation. These four sexual response stages should be considered a general description, rather than the "correct" way to respond.

If a person's secretions of sexual hormones are within the normal range, there is little relationship between the levels of these hormones and sexual (19) _____. For people in general, sexual motivation is primarily a function of (20) _____ factors rather than physiological ones.

Answers: (1) Y; (2) testosterone; (3) penis; (4) hypothalamus; (5) continuous; (6) role; (7) identity; (8) estrogen, progesterone; (9) secondary; (10) motivation; (11) prenatal; (12) socialization; (13) excitement; (14) plateau; (15) orgasm; (16) Grafenberg or G; (17) resolution; (18) refractory; (19) motivation or behavior; (20) psychological

GLOSSARY TERMS

chromosomes (p. 304)   genes (p. 304)   progesterone (p. 308)   sex role (p. 304)
estrogen (p. 308)   G-spot (p. 313)   resolution (p. 310)   testosterone (p. 304)
excitement (p. 310)   orgasm (p. 310)   secondary sexual   X-chromosome (p. 304)
gender identity (p. 303) plateau (p. 310)   characteristics (p. 308) Y-chromosome (p. 304)

Module 27 Sexual Behavior

SEXUAL BEHAVIOR YESTERDAY AND TODAY

What did you do on your date?

If you were told that the person on the left was the one who drove the car to the sporting event, paid for the tickets, and would later initiate sexual advances, you would most likely guess that that person was male.
(Arnold J. Saxe/Jeroboam)

Sandy and Pat had been dating for about six months. That night, Sandy picked Pat up at 8:00. They had agreed earlier to go to a movie and Sandy paid for the tickets. During the movie, Sandy embraced Pat and they kissed several times. After the movie, they went back to Pat's house. Pat put some music on and Sandy suggested they get comfortable on the couch. Once on the couch, Sandy initiated the kissing and touching, and finally Pat said that they had gone far enough. Sandy agreed reluctantly. Sandy gave Pat one last kiss, smiled, and said, "Good night" (author's files).

After reading only a line or two of this dating scenario, you assume that Sandy is the male and Pat is the female. What has not changed very much through the years is the male and female's role in dating. When Marcia LaPlante and others (1980) asked college students to read different strategies for initiating or avoiding sexual behavior, they rated all strategies for initiating as being used primarily by males and all strategies for avoiding as being used predominantly by females.

What has changed significantly is the frequency of sexual behaviors engaged in, especially by females. For example, John Earle and Philip Perricone (1986) found that in 1970, 1975, and 1981, the percentage of nonvirgins among women at a small university was 35, 45, and 52 percent. The corresponding percentages for male nonvirgins were 40, 61, and 62. Although the percentage of sexually active women has increased, their percentage was lower than that of men. This difference was also true for other sexual behaviors, such as masturbation. In their survey of college students, Carol Darling and Kenneth Davidson (1986) found that 58 percent of women reported masturbating, compared with 80 percent of men. Although these percentages indicate an increase in sexual behavior among college students, these percentages should not be viewed as the norm or as pressure to behave sexually in a certain way. These two surveys also found that 38 percent of college men and 47 percent of college women reported being virgins and that 42 percent of women and 20 percent of men reported not masturbating (Darling & Davidson, 1986; Earle & Perricone, 1986). That is, one-fifth to almost one-half of these college students were not sexually active. Surveys tell us only what people say they are doing, and not whether it is better to be sexually active or celibate.

There is no question that throughout the 1970s, surveys reported that men and especially women showed a significant increase in many sexual behaviors. Because of this increase, the 1970s have been referred to as the "sexual revolution." By the mid-1980s, two things have slowed and maybe stopped the revolution. One is fear of the life-threatening disease AIDS, which can be transmitted through sexual contact. We will discuss AIDS later in this Module. The second development is the return of more conservative attitudes toward sex. This trend is reflected in Meg Gerrard's (1987) study. She found that in the early 1970s, 35 percent of college women reported having sexual intercourse at least once a month. That figure rose to 51 percent in the late 1970s, but by the mid-1980s it has dropped to 37 percent, which was almost identical to the frequency reported in the early 1970s. Gerrard concluded that the sexually permissive attitudes of the early 1970s encouraged women to become more sexually active. But as the sexual attitudes became more conservative in the mid-1980s, the frequency of sexual intercourse decreased among college females. What should be clear from surveys of sexual behavior through the years is that sexual practices do change. In every survey, men reported higher frequencies of almost all sexual behaviors than did women. However, women have reported an increased frequency of sexual activity through the 1970s, followed by a decrease in the mid-1980s. No one is predicting what the 1990s will bring.

COMMITMENT AND SATISFACTION

When do college students believe that it is all right to become sexually active—in this case, engage in intercourse? Two different surveys found that about 30 percent of the college women compared with 56 percent of the college men considered sexual intercourse acceptable if the couple was dating regularly; 73 percent of the women and 75 percent of the men considered it acceptable if the couple was engaged (Earle & Perricone, 1986; Roche, 1986). The major difference is that more college women than men

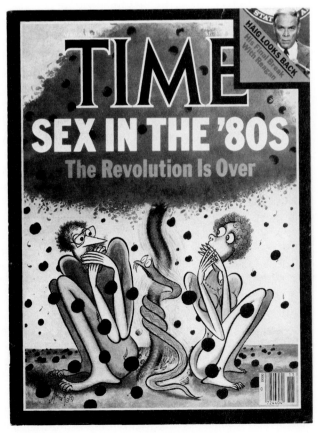

Beginning in the 1970s, American attitudes and sexual practices changed so radically that the phenomenon was called the "sexual revolution." Some of the revolutionary ideas included beginning sexual activity during adolescence, making more sexual behaviors acceptable, having sex for fun, and weakening the double standard, which means that women are allowed greater freedom in sexual behavior. According to *Time* magazine, the sexual revolution may be over. Surveys indicate that people are looking beyond sex for fun and seeking sex with love and commitment. (© 1984 Time Inc. All rights reserved. Reprinted by permission from *TIME.*)

This young couple has probably been exposed to much more liberal sexual standards than were their parents. For example, the percentage of women engaging in premarital sex was about 20 percent when the parents were married; this percentage is now about 30–40 percent. *(Hazel Hankin)*

reported the need for greater commitment and deeper feelings when engaging in intercourse.

If college couples do become sexually active, including engaging in intercourse, how psychologically satisfied are they with their sexual experiences? Carol Darling and J. Kenneth Davidson (1986) reported that among those students who were engaging in sexual intercourse, 28 percent of the college women compared with 80 percent of college men reported being psychologically satisfied with their sexual experiences. Some of the reasons that 72 percent of college women reported being psychologically dissatisfied were lack of orgasm during intercourse and having feelings of guilt and fear. Some of the reasons that 20 percent of the college men reported being psychologically dissatisfied were infrequent opportunities for sexual intercourse or not enough variety in partners. Darling and Davidson concluded that although there has been an increase in the frequency of sexual behaviors among college students, that increase has not been matched with increased psychological satisfaction, especially among women. These findings indicate a need to focus less on the frequency of sexual acts and more on attitudes, feelings, and concerns that people have about sexual behavior. One of the feelings critical to a relationship is love, our next topic.

APPLYING PSYCHOLOGY   What Is Love?

How will I know if it's really love?

"Is there love at first sight?" "Why doesn't a summer love last?" "Why do some people get married after being in love for just one month?" "Can you be in love and not have sex?" "What's the best kind of love?" are but a sample of the questions students ask. Robert Sternberg (1986) answers these questions with his *triangular theory of love*, which has three components: passion, intimacy, and commitment (Figure 10.4).

If you feel physically attracted to someone, you are experiencing *passion*, which leads to feelings of arousal and romance and the motivation to be physically involved. Passion arises very quickly and has strong influence on our judgments. For example, people rate their satisfaction with a first date almost entirely on the basis of physical attraction. That is, people tend to use the passion component to make initial judgments about their feelings for the person.

If you feel close or connected to someone, you are experiencing the *intimacy* component, which gives rise to your feelings of warmth. One of the primary ways that intimacy develops is through attempts to communicate with another person, usually by discussing one's inner feelings. (Sternberg & Grajek, 1984). We will discuss effective and ineffective communication patterns in Module 33. Other ways of promoting intimacy include sharing one's time, self, and possessions, promoting the other person's well-being, offering emotional and material support, touching, hugging, and engaging in what you would consider appropriate sexual behaviors.

If you think that you are in love and you wish to maintain that love, you are experiencing the *commitment* component, which leads to thoughts and feelings of commitment. Some of the ways of expressing commitment include making promises, agreeing to be sexually faithful to each other, staying in the relationship through hard times, becoming engaged, and getting married.

Here is how Sternberg uses his triangular theory of love, with its components of intimacy, passion, and commitment, to answer our questions.

"Is there love at first sight?" Love at first sight occurs when you are overwhelmed by passion, without any intimacy or commitment. Sternberg calls this *infatuated love* and adds that it can arise in an instant, involves a great deal of physiological arousal, and lasts varying lengths of time. Most often, friends recognize the infatuation before the person does. Since there is no intimacy or commitment, infatuated love is destined to die away.

"Why doesn't a summer love last?" One reason may be that a summer affair is *romantic love*, which is a combination of intimacy and passion, but no commitment. As soon as the summer is over, you both go your separate ways, and so does your summer love.

"Why do some people get married after being in love for just one month?" Sternberg calls this *Hollywood love* and explains that it is a combination of passion and commitment without any intimacy. In Hollywood love, two people make a commitment based on their passion for each other, but because this couple does not have intimacy, which takes time to develop, the relationship is likely to fail.

"Can you be in love but not have sex?" Sternberg answers "Yes" and calls this *companionate love*, which is a combination of intimacy and commitment without any passion. An example of companionate love is a married couple who are committed to each other and share their lives, but whose physical attraction has waned.

"What is the best kind of love?" If all three components, intimacy, passion, and commitment, are combined, the result is what Sternberg calls *complete love*, the kind of love most of us strive toward. Sternberg describes reaching complete love as being analogous to reaching a goal in an exercise program. Once you reach your exercise goal, you may feel very happy and enormously satisfied but there is no guarantee that you will maintain it. Once you reach complete love, there is no guarantee that it will last.

Sternberg offers a number of suggestions for maintaining complete love. To maintain intimacy, he suggests fostering change and growth by taking vacations together, developing new mutual interests, or learning new behavioral patterns, such as new ways of communicating. It is important that the change be individualized to the couple. To preserve passion, which may be the most difficult component to sustain, Sternberg suggests that the

Figure 10.4

What is love? According to Robert Sternberg, love is composed of three components, passion, commitment, and intimacy. If you visualize love as a triangle, the more commitment, intimacy, and passion you have, the larger the triangle and the greater the love. (Sternberg, *Psychology Today*, September, 1986, p. 46)

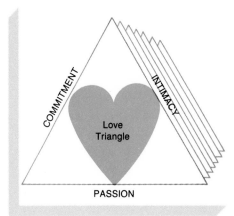

couple discuss what their sexual needs are and how they can satisfy each other's needs. For example, in one survey a majority of college women said that sexual experiences were more satisfying if they felt more intimacy, while males reported more satisfaction if they could engage in sexual behaviors more frequently. The couple must recognize these differences and work out solutions that please both partners. To maintain the commitment component, Sternberg recommends working together and doing things to maintain passion and intimacy. By working on these components, the couple will demonstrate their commitment to each other.

But just who should one fall in love with? Someone of the opposite sex, the same sex, or either sex?

SEXUAL PREFERENCE

Where did my sexual preference come from?

Tony looked at Lori and wished it were so simple and easy for him. Lori had asked Tony why he was gay and Tony had replied by asking Lori why she was straight. "I never thought much about it." said Lori. "I just am. Who knows why? You're the first person to ever ask me that." Tony had been asked about his sexual preference many times, and for him there was no simple answer. "No one cares if you're straight. But just tell one person that you're gay and everything changes. People stare at you, avoid you, and constantly try to put you down." Tony stopped talking. Lori was staring at him. She was like all the straights. She didn't understand either (author's files).

Since about 90 percent of the population is straight, there is a very good chance that you are straight and, like Lori, have not wondered why or been asked to defend your choice. If you are straight, or **heterosexual**, it means that you have developed a sexual preference opposite that of your gender identity. Since about 10 percent of the population is gay, there is a smaller chance that you are gay and, like Tony, have wondered why and been asked to defend your choice many times. If you are gay, or **homosexual**, it means that you have developed a sexual preference that is the same as your gender identity. Of this 10 percent, a very small percentage consider themselves bisexual. If you are **bisexual**, it means that you have developed a sexual preference for both sexes.

How do you know if you are heterosexual, homosexual, or bisexual? One way is to answer the Kinsey scale of sexual orientation. Your answer is rated on a continuum from 0 to 6, with 0 meaning that you are exclusively heterosexual, 1 meaning that you are predominantly heterosexual, with occasional or incidental homosexual activity, and so on through 5, which means that you are predominantly homosexual, with occasional or incidental heterosexual activity, to 6, which means that you are exclusively homosexual. On Kinsey's scale, people with rankings of 0 to 2 are considered heterosexual even though they have occasional homosexual thoughts, fantasies, or activities. And people with rankings of 4 to 6 are considered homosexual even though they have occasional heterosexual thoughts, fantasies, or activities.

There are two important points to remember about the Kinsey scale. First, it is a continuum that ranges from exclusively heterosexual (rating of 0) to bisexual (rating of 3) to exclusively homosexual (rating of 6). Second, because the scale is a continuum, individuals who consider themselves either heterosexual or homosexual may experience occasional thoughts and fantasies about or even occasional activities with the opposite sex. Your sexual preference, however, is not determined by occasional thoughts, fantasies, or activities; it is determined by the sex partner upon whom you *consistently* focus your sexual thoughts, fantasies, and activities.

Although most of us have developed a heterosexual preference, most of us are also not aware of how this occurred. By looking at how someone developed a homosexual preference, it may be possible to better understand the process of developing a sexual preference.

HOMOSEXUALITY

Deep down, Richard Failla knew he was different. At the age of 11, while his friends whispered about their grade-school sweethearts, he remained silent. "I didn't feel that excitement," he recalls. Worse yet, he found himself physically attracted to boys. Terrified, Richard began sneaking into a public library, where he read whatever he could find on homosexuality. "Everything was negative," he says. "Homosexuality was defined as an illness, a deviation, or a perversion." Richard repressed his feelings and dated women. Much later, Richard realized that he wanted to be a homosexual and that the only way he could have a normal life was to come out of the closet. He went through the painful process of telling his parents and friends and suffering the contempt of some of his colleagues. Richard is now New York City's chief administrative law judge (adapted from Newsweek, *August 8, 1983).*

How does it feel to be different sexually?

In the early 1980s, two books appeared that greatly increased our knowledge of homosexual behavior. One is *Sexual Preference* by Alan Bell and his associates (1981) of the Kinsey Institute for Sex Research. This book is one of the few for which the authors surveyed and interviewed a large sample of homosexual males (686), homosexual females (293), heterosexual males (337), and heterosexual females (140). The second book is *Homosexuality*, edited by William Paul and others (1982). This book is a report to the Society for the Psychological Study of Social Issues, a division of the American Psychological Association. It attempts to summarize accurately our current knowledge on homosexuality. We have used these and other sources to answer questions about homosexuality.

As he was growing up, Richard did not conform to the stereotypical male sex role. While his male peers engaged in such behaviors as playing baseball, Richard tended to engage in more stereotypic female behaviors, such as playing games with girls. A major predictor of homosexual preference is how much a child or teenager engages in opposite-sex behaviors, called **cross-gender behaviors.** Researchers found that adult male homosexuals engaged in significantly more opposite-sex or cross-gender behaviors as children than did heterosexuals (Green, 1987; Grellert et al., 1982; Harry, 1983; Whitam, 1980). These researchers concluded that the more people conform to the stereotypic roles of the opposite sex, the more likely they are to experience homosexual feelings and engage in homosexual behavior. However, it is impossible to say whether nonconformity to the male sex role is the cause or the result of Richard's homosexual feelings.

Richard was aware of his homosexual feelings before adolescence and before he began behaving as a homosexual. Researchers have found that homosexual feelings in childhood are generally associated with homosexual activities in adolescence, which in turn are closely related to adult sexual preference. Researchers have also found that individuals may report having

For many gays or lesbians, the most important stage of building self-acceptance is coming out: making their sexual preference public. (Kit Nedman/Jeroboam)

homosexual feelings for an average of three years before they engage in homosexual activities (Bell et al., 1981).

The evidence is now overwhelming that homosexuality itself is not a sign of psychological problems (Paul et al., 1982). Differences between homosexuals and heterosexuals are often found on psychological tests, but they tend to be within the normal range. There are disturbed homosexuals just as there are disturbed heterosexuals, but as a group homosexuals show no greater incidence of maladjustment (Gonsiorek, 1982).

Why is Richard a homosexual?

Now we come to a question that has scientific, social, and political overtones: "What caused Richard's homosexual preference?" Some of the answers were discussed in Module 26 and will just be stated briefly here.

John Money (1987), who studied the effects of prenatal hormones on sexual preference, believes that Richard has a homosexual preference because of a two-step process. First, prenatal hormones create a predisposition for either a male or female sexual preference, and second, socialization facilitates or inhibits the carrying out of this predisposition. Money's theory, which we discussed in Module 26, stresses the interaction between biology and socialization in the development of sexual orientation.

Allan Bell and his associates (1981) at the Kinsey Institute for Sex Research, who surveyed, interviewed, and compared a large sample of homosexuals and heterosexuals, believe that Richard has a homosexual preference less because of genes and biology than because of complex learning and socialization forces. Among these forces were Richard's relationship with his parents, his degree of conformity to a stereotypic sex role in childhood, and his personal sexual experiences. According to Bell and his associates, learning and socialization are more important than biology in the development of a sexual preference.

John Gagnon (1987) believes that much of the interest in what causes homosexuality is based less on scientific interest than on social and political debate over whether homosexuality is morally right or wrong. Gagnon is suggesting that even if the cause of homosexuality were determined, people would still find social, political, or religious reasons to discriminate against homosexuals.

Changing Views on Homosexuality

Is homosexuality "sick"?

Until the early 1970s, the majority of psychologists and psychiatrists considered homosexuality to be abnormal because it seemed to interfere with a person's psychological functioning and well-being. However, in 1973 and 1975, the American Psychiatric and Psychological Associations, respectively, declared that homosexuality was not an abnormal behavior. They made this change because many studies showed that homosexuality was not necessarily maladaptive and that there were homosexuals who were as happy and well adjusted as their heterosexual counterparts (Paul et al., 1982). Because of these findings, homosexuality is now regarded as a normal variant of human sexual behavior by both mental health organizations.

There has also been a steady increase in the acceptance of homosexuality by Americans. Ten years ago, well over 50 percent of Americans considered homosexuality abnormal. Today Americans are about equally divided, half believing that it is normal and half believing that it is abnormal. Reasons for the growing acceptance of homosexuality include the actions of the American Psychological and Psychiatric Associations, changes in the policies of some religious organizations, publication of data showing that homosexuals are as mentally healthy as heterosexuals, and the gay movement, which has actively campaigned for legal, economic, and social acceptance.

Although homosexuality is more accepted today than in the past, some fear that the spread of AIDS may erase many of the gains that homosexuals have made in recent years. To prevent increased discrimination, we need to know the facts about AIDS.

AIDS **EXPLORING PSYCHOLOGY**

As of late 1987, researchers estimate that between one and two million people in the United States have been infected with the virus that causes **Acquired Immune Deficiency Syndrome** or **AIDS** (Silberner, 1987). This virus, called the human immunodeficiency virus or HIV, attacks the immune system, which normally *protects* us from disease. HIV not only destroys many components of the immune system, but it actually takes over cells of the immune system and uses them for its own reproduction (Gallo, 1987). The result is that infections that stimulate an immune response also stimulate more production of HIV (Zagury et al., 1986). As HIV destroys the immune system, the AIDS patient becomes vulnerable to many life-threatening infections, such as pneumonia. At the present time there is no known cure for AIDS. As of this writing, only 23 persons were known to be living five years after being diagnosed as having AIDS. Against these few were over 20,000 who had died from AIDS in the United States alone. The average time from diagnosis to death was 18 months.

One reason that the AIDS epidemic has grown so enormously is that persons who are infected typically experience an *incubation* period of two to five years (Goedert et al., 1986). During this time, the individual has no symptoms but is capable of transmitting the virus to others. Thus, in the early years of the epidemic, many persons unknowingly infected others.

Despite the terrifying statistics, investigators believe that the AIDS epidemic can be contained. We now know that the AIDS virus is not transmitted easily. Although many thousands of persons ill with AIDS have been in close daily contact with family members, roommates, and health care workers, there are no known cases in which AIDS was transmitted by casual contact. Casual contact includes touching or hugging, or coming in contact with the saliva, sweat, or tears of someone who is infected. Infection is known to occur when the AIDS virus reaches a person's blood supply through intimate contact with the blood or semen of an infected person or through the perinatal fluid to an unborn child. The majority of those who have been infected in the United States have been homosexual or bisexual men, intravenous drug users, and prostitutes, but this does not mean that persons outside these groups are protected. Heterosexual intercourse has been a major mode of transmission in Africa, and there is evidence that intercourse with an infected partner poses greater risk to females than to males (Quinn et al., 1986; Barnes, 1987b).

Researchers have recommended a number of ways to avoid sexual transmission of AIDS, beginning with celibacy—that is, avoidance of sexual contact. Another way is for two people who have tested negative for the AIDS virus (meaning that their blood contains no HIV antibodies) agree to be sexually faithful. If there is any question about sexual fidelity, or if either partner is an intravenous drug user, couples should practice only *protective* sex. This means that no semen, vaginal fluid, or blood is exchanged between partners. Examples of protective sex include hugging, kissing (if no oral lesions are present that might allow the virus to enter the blood supply), and caressing the genitals and other parts of the body (if no skin lesions are present). Vaginal or rectal intercourse is considered safe only if a *latex* condom is worn at all times. Over-the-counter spermicides that contain nonoxynol-9 are thought to provide additional protection against the virus (Francis & Chin, 1987).

As of 1988, tests for AIDS identify only the presence of antibodies that are formed when a person is exposed to HIV, the AIDS virus. These tests cannot determine whether an individual actually has—or will develop—AIDS. However, a seemingly healthy person who tests positive is capable of transmitting the virus to others.

It is important to understand that HIV antibodies may not appear in the bloodstream for several weeks—or as long as six months—after infection. As a result, negative test results may give a false sense of security to people who should be practicing protective sex (Francis & Chin, 1987). Experts recommend that even people who do not use drugs and who have agreed to be faithful to each other practice protective sex for at least six months after a negative test. Then both people should be retested. Voluntary testing can play a role in our fight against AIDS, but the emphasis needs to be on practicing protective sexual behaviors.

ABNORMAL SEXUAL BEHAVIOR

Defining Abnormality

What do you consider abnormal sexual behavior?

Using your personal standards, decide which of the following sexual behaviors are normal (N) or abnormal (A).

N   A   1. *Oral sex:* Stimulating sexual organs with mouth, lips, and tongue.

N   A   2. *Prostitution:* Paying money for sexual favors.

N   A   3. *Voyeurism:* Becoming sexually aroused by secretly watching others engaged in sexual activity.

N   A   4. *Exhibitionism:* Exposing one's sexual organs to strangers, usually in public places.

N   A   5. *Homosexuality:* Engaging in sexual behavior with a person of one's own sex.

N   A   6. *Extramarital affairs:* A married person engaging in sexual activity with someone other than his or her spouse, usually without the spouse's knowledge.

N   A   7. *Orgies:* Sexual parties where nudity is often the rule and sexual activities take place between any of the consenting adults.

N   A   8. *Golden shower:* Being aroused by activities involving urination.

N   A   9. *Anal intercourse:* Penetrating the anus with a penis.

N   A   10. *Buggery:* Stimulating a partner's anal area with tongue, mouth, or lips.

N   A   11. *Masturbation:* Self-stimulation to orgasm by manual or mechanical means.

N   A   12. *Pedophilia:* Being sexually aroused by engaging in sexual activities with young children.

N   A   13. *Pornography:* Being sexually aroused by viewing sexual activities in pictures or movies.

N   A   14. *Bondage:* Enjoying and being aroused by being tied up by your partner during sexual play.

N A 15. *Sadism:* Receiving sexual pleasure from inflicting pain on someone during sexual activities.

N A 16. *Masochism:* Deriving sexual pleasure from the experience of pain during sexual activities.

N A 17. *Transvestism:* Habitually dressing and acting as a member of the opposite sex.

N A 18. *Rape:* Using force to engage in sexual activity with a nonconsenting person.

N A 19. *Bestiality:* Engaging in sexual activity with animals.

N A 20. *Necrophilia:* Being aroused by sexual activity with a dead person.

N A 21. *Open-ended marriage:* Both spouses agreeing to develop close relationships with persons of either sex, outside the marriage.

N A 22. *Bisexuality:* Enjoying sexual interactions with persons of the same or opposite sex.

N A 23. *Fetishism:* Needing an object or piece of clothing to produce arousal during sexual play.

Here are the ratings 160 college students gave to these sexual practices, arranged in descending order of "normalcy" (data from authors' files).

Behavior	Percentage Considering Behavior Normal	Behavior	Percentage Considering Behavior Normal
1. Oral sex	97%	3. Voyeurism	36%
11. Masturbation	96	14. Bondage	33
13. Pornography	78	17. Transvestism	18
9. Anal intercourse	61	8. Golden shower	7
6. Extramarital affairs	58	15. Sadism	6
10. Buggery	58	16. Masochism	4
2. Prostitution	53	4. Exhibitionism	3
5. Homosexuality	46	12. Pedophilia	3
21. Open-ended marriage	45	19. Bestiality	2
22. Bisexuality	44	20. Necrophilia	0
23. Fetishism	38	18. Rape	0
7. Orgy	36		

If you were similar to these college students, you considered oral sex normal and rape abnormal. How did you decide what was abnormal? You could have used a number of different ways to define abnormal behavior. According to a **statistical definition,** abnormal behavior is that which the minority does and normal behavior is that which the majority does. This is not a very useful definition, since many behaviors we consider normal, such as going to college, are engaged in by a minority of people. According to a **social norms definition,** abnormal behavior is that which falls outside the agreed upon social norms or standards of the society. The problem with this definition is that the same behavior, such as homosexuality, is considered normal by some sectors of society and abnormal by others. According to a **maladaptive behavior definition,** abnormal behavior is that which interferes with a person's *functioning* or that which is a threat to the person or society. This is the definition of abnormality most mental health professionals use.

The American Psychiatric Association used the maladaptive behavior definition to define abnormality in its *Diagnostic and Statistical Manual*

MAJOR CONCEPT   Sexual Behavior

Please indicate which of the following statements about sexual behavior are true (T) or false (F).

1. T/F In dating situations, college students usually identify the male role as initiating sexual behaviors and the female role as avoiding sex.

2. T/F In the 1970s, the frequency and number of sexual behaviors engaged in by females was higher than that engaged in by males.

3. T/F In the 1980s, about one-fifth of college males and one-half of college females reported that they were not sexually active.

4. T/F About 70 percent of college women and 20 percent of college men reported that they were presently satisfied with their sexual experiences.

5. T/F According to Sternberg's triangular theory, the three components of love are passion, warmth, and commitment.

6. T/F Since the early 1970s, the American Psychiatric Association and American Psychological Association have considered homosexuality to be part of the normal range of human sexual behavior.

7. T/F The definition of abnormality that most mental health professionals use is the statistical definition.

8. T/F Most researchers believe that homosexuality results from both prenatal factors and later socialization.

9. T/F A person is equally likely to get AIDS from exposure to the blood, semen, or saliva of someone with AIDS, or from casual touching.

10. T/F AIDS is caused by a virus and is primarily a threat to the homosexual population. If you are a heterosexual, you have no need to worry about getting AIDS.

Answers: 1 (T); 2 (F); 3 (T); 4 (F); 5 (F); 6 (T); 7 (F); 8 (T); 9 (F); 10 (F)

---

of Mental Disorders (1980). Here are some of the abnormal sexual behaviors described in that manual.

Gender-identity disorders, which are rare, are characterized by feelings of discomfort about one's anatomical sex and a persistent desire to be and live like the other sex. An example of this disorder is transsexualism.

Paraphilias (pah-rah-FEEL-yahs) involve being aroused by objects or situations that are not usually associated with sexual arousal and that interfere with the capacity for affectionate sexual activity. Examples of paraphilias include exhibitionism, fetishism, and sado-masochism. These behaviors become abnormal only when they become necessary for sexual arousal. For example, someone with a fetish for women's panties would become sexually aroused only by the panties and not by sexual activity with a person. There is nothing abnormal about being sexually aroused by imagined or real articles of clothing. This reaction would be considered abnormal only if these articles become necessary and preferred for sexual excitement. Similarly, if consenting partners periodically used mild forms of bondage in their sexual play, it would not be considered abnormal. Sado-masochistic behaviors, such as being whipped or administering whipping, are considered abnormal only if they become the primary and exclusive means of sexual arousal, or if they involve physical or psychological harm to one of the partners.

Psychosexual dysfunctions are characterized by inhibitions in sexual desire or inability to complete the sexual response cycle. Examples include the inability to have an erection or an orgasm. We will discuss the more common psychosexual dysfunctions and their treatments in Module 28.

REVIEW

Harriet, who is 19, is talking to her mother about dating and sex. Harriet says that most of her dates end up the same. She wants to go at a comfortable sexual pace while her male date is constantly trying to

(1) _____ sexual activity. Her mother agrees that dating was like that in her time too. Harriet says that in the 1970s, all the surveys reported that

college women engaged in more (2) _____ behaviors than in her mother's time. Even though women reported more sexual activity, college men always reported a (3) _____ frequency of sexual behavior. Harriet says that what bothers her most is a big difference between how college men and women think about sex. College women who were sexually active reported being dissatisfied with their current sexual experiences because of feeling fear or guilt or

not having (4) _____ while college men reported being dissatisfied because of not having more

sexual (5) _____. Another difference was that college women wanted their sexual activity to take place in a relationship that involved more

(6) _____ than was required by college men. Her mother agreed that these male-female differences were also true in her time.

What Harriet really wants to talk about is Danny, whom she has been dating for three weeks. Harriet thinks that it is really serious and that she is in love with Danny. According to Sternberg's triangular theory, love has three components of (7) _____,

_____, and _____. In Harriet's case, her kind of love seems to have passion and commitment but there is not enough time for intimacy to develop. Harriet's love would be an example of

(8) _____ love.

Harriet says that she has been reading about homosexuality for a paper due next week. So far she has discovered that there is a relationship between chil-

dren or teenagers engaging in (9) _____

- _____ behaviors and developing a homosexual preference. Also, that homosexuals were as

(10) _____ healthy as were heterosexuals. She just finished reading how sexual preferences, such as homosexuality, develop. The major theories point

to both the influence of prenatal (11) _____ as well as the later influence of learning and

(12) _____. Her mother wonders whether people are as prejudiced against gays as they were in her day. Harriet says that it is better today with about

(13) _____ percent of the American population considering homosexuality normal.

Mother asks Harriet what she knows about AIDS.

Harriet says that gays are in the high (14) _____ group because of their sexual practices, followed by intravenous drug users and prostitutes. However, a small percentage of American heterosexuals have

AIDS. AIDS is caused by a (15) _____ that as of now has no cure. It is important to remember that AIDS is not spread or acquired through casual contact, such as touching or drinking from the same glass as a person with AIDS. Rather, one gets AIDS when the blood or semen of someone with AIDS reaches another's blood supply. At present, the recommended ways to avoid AIDS is to avoid having sex, which is called

being (16) _____, being sure that your partner does not have AIDS, or practicing protective sex, which includes avoiding exposure to semen by us-

ing (17) _____.

After reading the article on homosexuality, Harriet says that a lot of her friends are talking about whether homosexuality is normal or abnormal. Harriet says that she learned three different definitions of abnormal. If you believe that homosexuality is abnormal because very few people engage in it, you are using the

(19) _____ definition of abnormality. If you believe that homosexuality is abnormal because it is outside the standards of society, you are using the

(20) _____ norm definition. Most mental health professionals define a behavior as abnormal if it

interferes with the person's (21) _____ or is a threat to self or society. Because surveys of the homosexual population indicate that being homosexual does not necessarily interfere with a person's functioning, the American Psychiatric Association and the American Psychological Association have stated that

homosexuality should be considered a (22) _____ part of human sexual behavior.

Some of the sexual behaviors that the American Psychiatric Association's manual defines as abnormal

include transsexualism, which is a (23) _____ identity disorder; exhibitionism and fetishism, which

are (24) _____; and the inability to have

an erection or orgasm, which are (25) _____ dysfunctions.

Answers: (1) initiate, start; (2) sexual; (3) greater, higher; (4) orgasms; (5) partners; (6) love, commitment; (7) passion, intimacy, commitment; (8) romantic; (9) cross-gender; (10) psychologically, mentally; (12) hormones; (13) socialization; (14) 50; (15) risk; (16) virus; (17) celibate; (18) condoms; (19) statistical; (20) social; (21) functioning, well-being; (22) normal; (23) gender; (24) paraphilias; (25) psychosexual

GLOSSARY TERMS

acquired immune deficiency syndrome (AIDS) (p. 325)
bisexual (p. 322)
cross-gender behaviors (p. 323)

gender-identity disorders (p. 328)
heterosexual (p. 322)
homosexual (p. 322)

maladaptive behavior definition (p. 327)
paraphilias (p. 328)
psychosexual dysfunctions (p. 329)

social norms definition (p. 327)
statistical definition (p. 327)

Module 28 Sexual Dysfunction and Treatment

PROBLEMS

"I have difficulties having an orgasm."
"I have difficulty maintaining my erection."
"I would like to delay my orgasm."
"I don't get aroused by my partner."

These are some of the more common sexual difficulties or dysfunctions often expressed by Americans. The causes include poor sexual techniques, such as ineffective stimulation of the clitoris; psychological factors, such as fear or anxiety; and medical problems, such as the side effects of prescription drugs. **Sexual dysfunction** is defined as **primary** if the person has never functioned successfully—for example, has never had an erection or orgasm. Sexual dysfunction is defined as **secondary** if the person previously functioned successfully but no longer does or is able to function successfully in one situation and not in another. An example of the latter is a woman who reaches orgasm through manual or oral stimulation, but not during intercourse. It is estimated that about 80 to 90 percent of sexual dysfunctions are caused by psychological factors and 10 to 20 percent are caused by organic or physiological factors.

Masters and Johnson revolutionized the treatment of sexual problems with the publication of their book *Human Sexual Inadequacy* (1970). Previously, sexual problems were treated with long-term therapy that had uncertain results. In *Human Sexual Inadequacy*, Masters and Johnson described a rapid-treatment program that took only two weeks and produced dramatic results. This unique program required both partners to participate actively and to spend two weeks in full-time therapy. A major feature of the program was the development of **sensate focus**, a procedure designed to help couples overcome demand pressures. We will describe sensate focus at the end of this Module.

Critics have questioned whether Masters' and Johnson's cure rates are really as high as reported and whether these rates can be replicated by others (Zilbergeld & Evans, 1980). In a careful reply to this criticism, Robert Kolodny (1981), associate director of the Masters and Johnson Institute, presented additional data to support their high success rates. From this dispute, it has become clear that their success rates cannot be generalized to programs other than the rapid-treatment program. Still, many features of the rapid-treatment program have been adapted and used to treat a number of sexual dysfunctions (Marks, 1981b).

Sex therapists would generally agree that psychotherapy alone is ineffective in treating most sexual problems. Even if the initial cause is a relationship problem, such as anger or resentment, resolution of the relationship problem does not necessarily solve the sexual problem. One reason is that the sexual problem itself can create a condition of performance anxiety that lingers when other problems have been solved. Thus, most current treatment methods have in common the assignment of "homework" in which the person actually practices sexual responses.

How effective is the treatment of sexual problems?

ORGASMIC DYSFUNCTIONS

She does not have any difficulty having orgasms when he stimulates her with his hand. However, during intercourse she has great difficulty and rarely has an orgasm. She doesn't know what is wrong. Her partner feels disappointed, and this puts a strain on their relationship. The technical name for her difficulty is secondary orgasmic dysfunction (author's files).

Secondary orgasmic dysfunction is a condition in which a woman who previously had orgasms no longer has them or fails to have them in certain situations. Survey data indicate that a large percentage of women, 20 to 40 percent, have difficulty experiencing orgasms during one particular situation—namely, intercourse without simultaneous clitoral stimulation. The positions used in intercourse may fail to provide adequate stimulation, and the woman's anxiety about pleasing her partner may worsen the situation. Often this problem can be corrected with the partner's cooperation in adjusting stimulation techniques. The problem has been successfully treated with sensate focus, directed masturbation, and group education programs (Barbach & Flaherty, 1980; Kilmann et al., 1983; LoPiccolo & Stock, 1986; Masters and Johnson, 1970; Sotile & Kilmann, 1977; Springer, 1981).

Primary orgasmic dysfunction is the condition in which a woman has never experienced an orgasm. Survey data indicate that as many as 1 out of 10 adult women have never experienced orgasm. Several different treat-

A number of self-help books offer programs for dealing with common sexual problems, such as difficulties in achieving orgasm or experiencing rapid ejaculation. (Random House photo by K. Bendo)

ment programs have been shown to be effective (Andersen, 1983; Clement, 1980). Directed masturbation involves a program of homework exercises in which the woman learns to experience arousal and orgasm through masturbation (LoPiccolo, 1978). For this problem particularly, much of the success of treatment depends upon performing various homework assignments (Van Wyk, 1982). After a women experiences orgasm by herself, she and her partner practice sensate focus exercises. These exercises begin with nongenital touching and proceed to genital touching and finally orgasm. The exercises help the couple relax and feel less pressure about having an orgasm.

ERECTILE DYSFUNCTIONS

Very often she enjoys taking the initiative in their sexual activity. When she does, he feels threatened, unsure of his sexual performance, and has difficulty maintaining his erection. The more she tries to excite him, the more threatened he feels and the less able he is to maintain his erection. The technical name for his problem is secondary erectile dysfunction, previously called impotence (author's files).

Secondary erectile dysfunction—psychological is an inability to have or maintain an erection because of psychological factors such as tension, anxiety, stress, or depression (Munjack et al., 1981). One way to distinguish between physically and psychologically caused erectile (ee-REK-tile) dysfunction is to measure erection activity during Rapid Eye Movement (REM) sleep. Since men normally experience erections during periods of REM sleep, the absence of such erections is an indication of some organic problem. In contrast, if a male experiences erectile dysfunction but has erections during REM sleep, the cause of the problem is assumed to be psychological

(Karacan et al., 1983). The initial episode of dysfunction may have been caused by fatigue or alcohol, and later episodes may actually be caused by the male's fear of a recurrence.

Treatment for erectile dysfunction combines therapy for stress or anxiety reduction with homework-type programs, such as sensate focus. In this case, an important stage of sensate focus is allowing the erection to come and go without proceeding to intercourse. This helps to establish a pattern in which loss of erection is not threatening.

During early adolescence, he was attracted to females and enjoyed kissing and touching, but he never experienced an erection. As time passed, he continued to be attracted to females, but took care to avoid sexual situations where he would be embarrassed by his inability to have an erection. The technical name for his difficulty is primary erectile dysfunction, previously called primary impotence (author's files).

Erectile dysfunction—organic is an inability to have or maintain an erection because of some organic or physical problem. The disorder can result from alcoholism, diseases such as diabetes, and in rare cases, abnormally low levels of testosterone; it is also a side effect of some prescription drugs. Treatment takes different forms, depending on the particular cause. If the cause is a medication, another drug may be substituted. If the cause is abnormally low levels of testosterone, the person may be given doses of this hormone. In two recent studies, men with very low testosterone levels who reported erectile and ejaculatory problems showed increased frequency of erections and ejaculations when given testosterone (Davidson et al., 1979; Skakkebaek et al., 1981).

Treatment for organically caused erectile dysfunction is much the same whether the condition is primary or secondary, but the probability of success is not as great if the male has never had an erection (a primary erectile disorder). If the condition is one that cannot be corrected, a rodlike device or inflatable tube may be implanted in the penis. These devices, called penile prostheses, provide an erection and permit intercourse (Sotile, 1979).

There is a very good possibility that if this couple's problem is sexual, it can be treated successfully by a mental health professional.
(Louis Fernandez/Black Star)

MAJOR CONCEPT   Sexual Dysfunctions

It is not uncommon for people to experience problems in sexual performance. Here are descriptions of some of the most frequent sexual dysfunctions.

Match each one with its technical term.

1. Erectile dysfunction— psychological

2. Primary orgasmic dysfunction

3. Premature ejaculation

4. Erectile dysfunction— organic

5. Inhibited sexual desire

6. Secondary orgasmic dysfunction

a. ＿＿＿ A man who is under a great deal of stress at the office finds that he has lost much of his interest in sex. His wife feels hurt and rejected when he tells her repeatedly that he is "too tired" to make love.

b. ＿＿＿ A woman, age 30, has never had an orgasm during sexual intercourse. Her only way of achieving orgasm is through masturbation.

c. ＿＿＿ A mother tells her daughter that all these "how-to" books on sex greatly exaggerate what women experience. She bets that many women, like herself, have never had an orgasm.

d. ＿＿＿ A young man has erections during his sleep, but in sexual encounters with women he is almost totally impotent.

e. ＿＿＿ A man who is taking a prescription drug for hypertension finds that he cannot sustain an erection long enough to have intercourse.

f. ＿＿＿ A college student complains to his girlfriend that she has unrealistic expectations. Men, he says, have no control over how soon they "come."

Answers: a (5); b (6); c (2); d (1); e (4); f (3)

RAPID EJACULATION

She becomes excited during intercourse but finds that he does not go on long enough for her to have an orgasm. He says that he becomes so excited that he cannot delay his orgasm. The technical name for his problem is rapid or premature ejaculation (author's files).

Rapid or **premature ejaculation** can be a problem if the male reaches orgasm so quickly that it interferes with the enjoyment and gratification of his partner. Masters and Johnson think that this is the most frequent male sexual problem. An effective treatment for it is the **squeeze** or **stop-start** technique. Both techniques make the male aware of the sensations that immediately precede ejaculation and orgasm. Once he recognizes these sensations, he can learn to postpone them.

In the stop-start procedure, the partner stimulates the man's penis, either manually or orally, just to the point of impending orgasm, being careful to stop before the ejaculation has begun. At this point stimulation stops until the feelings of impending ejaculation decrease. In the squeeze procedure, the partner squeezes either the tip or base of the penis from back to front for a few seconds, until the feelings of impending ejaculation subside. Both techniques have been shown to be very effective in treating rapid ejaculation (Kilmann & Auerbach, 1979).

INHIBITED SEXUAL DESIRE

She finds that she is not excited or aroused by sexual activities. Although she tries to get excited during petting and genital touching, she finds that she enjoys these activities less and less. Because of her lack of arousal, she has developed all kinds of excuses to avoid sexual activities with her partner. The technical name for her difficulty is inhibited sexual desire (author's files).

Inhibited sexual desire is characterized by an overall lack of interest in initiating or participating in sexual activity. In a 1983 poll of *Psychology Today* readers, over 30 percent of the men and 40 percent of the women replied that lack of desire was one of the major reasons for their lack of sexual expression. Common psychological and physiological factors associated with inhibited sexual desire include depression, severe stress, very low testosterone levels, and certain drugs and illnesses. The treatment for this dysfunction depends on the particular cause.

For example, if anxiety over sexual expression is involved, treatment would focus on the anxiety. If the person lacks awareness of the body's sexual arousal cues, the treatment program would include helping the person become aware of these cues. One of the most commonly used programs is sensate focus, developed by Masters and Johnson. In this program, a couple progresses through a series of homework exercises that teach them first to enjoy touching nongenital areas, and then gradually, after several sessions, to enjoy genital touching. Let's look now at what sensate focus involves.

Sensate Focus **APPLYING PSYCHOLOGY**

An important part of Masters' and Johnson's sex therapy program is sensate focus. Its goals are to help each partner become aware of and appreciate bodily sensations, overcome any fears of performance pressures, and learn to indicate what kind of touching feels good. In addition to its use in sex therapy, sensate focus is a wonderful exercise to help a couple learn about each other's bodies. Although written as an exercise for a heterosexual couple, it could easily be adapted for a homosexual couple.

How to use sensate focus:

In the first stage of sensate focus exercises, the couple is told to have two sessions in which they will each have a turn touching their partner's body—with the breasts and genitals "off limits." The purpose of the touching is not to be sexual but to establish an awareness of touch sensations by noticing textures, contours, temperatures, and contrasts (while doing the touching) or to simply be aware of the sensations of being touched by their partner. The person doing the touching is told to do so on the basis of what interests him or her, not on any guesses about what their partner likes or doesn't like. It is emphasized that this touching should not be a massage or an attempt to arouse their partner sexually. The initial sensate focus periods should be as silent as possible, since words can detract from the awareness of physical sensations. However, the person being touched must let his or her partner know—either nonverbally (by body language) or in words—if any touch is uncomfortable. . . .

In the next stage of sensate focus, touching is expanded to include the breasts and genitals. . . . The person doing the touching is instructed to begin with general body touching and to not "dive" for the genitals. Again, the emphasis is on awareness of physical sensations and not on the expectation of a particular sexual response. At this stage, the couple is usually asked to try a "hand-riding" technique as a more direct means of nonverbal communication. The couple takes turns with this exercise. By placing one hand on top of her partner's hand while he touches her, the woman can indicate if she would like more pressure, a lighter touch, a faster or slower type of stroking or a change to a different spot. The male indicates his preferences when the situation is reversed. . . .

In the next phase of sensate focus, instead of taking turns touching each other, the couple is asked to try some mutual touching. The purpose of this is twofold: first, it provides a more natural form of physical interaction (in "real life" situations, people don't usually take turns touching and being touched); and second, it doubles the potential sources of sensual input. This is a very important step in overcoming spectatoring, which is watching what is happening without being aware of and appreciating the sensations. To avoid spectatoring, one can try to shift attention to a portion of his or her partner's body (getting "lost" in the touch) and away from watching his or her own response. Couples are reminded that no matter how sexually aroused they may feel, intercourse is still "off limits."

The next stages of sensate focus are to continue the same activities but at some point to shift into the female-on-top position without attempting insertion. . . . If there is an erection, and she feels like it, she can engage in intercourse, all the while focusing on the physical sensations and stopping the action or moving back to simple nongenital touching or cuddling if she or her partner becomes goal-oriented or anxious. When comfort is developed at this level, full intercourse can usually occur without difficulty (Masters et al., 1982, pp. 386–387).

Although the procedure of sensate focus was originally developed for couples with sexual problems, it could easily be used to enhance any sexual interaction.

REVIEW

Organic sexual dysfunctions, which account for about 10 to 20 percent of sexual problems, are caused by physical factors, such as disease or prescription drugs. Approximately 80 to 90 percent of sexual problems are

thought to be caused by (1) _____ factors. A person who has very little interest in sexual activities

is said to have (2) _____ sexual desire. Treatment for this difficulty may involve treating psychological problems, as well as helping the person become more aware of and responsive to the physiological cues of arousal. A woman who has never experienced

orgasm is said to have (3) _____ orgasmic

dysfunction. A woman who has experienced orgasms at one time but has now stopped or does not have them

in certain situations is said to have (4) _____ orgasmic dysfunction. Effective treatments for both primary and secondary orgasmic dysfunctions may include learning to reach orgasm through directed masturbation and learning to focus on bodily sensations with a pro-

gram called (5) _____ focus. Erectile dysfunction is usually treated by identifying and eliminat-

ing (6) _____ problems, such as anxiety, followed by a program of homework. Organic erectile

dysfunction may be treated by a penile implant, by changing medications, or by injections of testosterone if the level is abnormally low. Effective treatments for rapid ejaculation are either the stop-start or squeeze techniques, which help the male become aware of the

sensations that signal (7) _____. Once aware of these sensations, the male can learn to delay ejaculation. Masters and Johnson developed a tech-

nique called (8) _____ _____, which helps a couple learn how to touch each others' bodies and to decrease performance pressure.

Answers: (1) psychological; (2) inhibited; (3) primary; (4) secondary; (5) sensate; (6) psychological; (7) ejaculation; (8) sensate focus

GLOSSARY TERMS

erectile dysfunction—
  organic (p. 333)
inhibited sexual desire
  (p. 335)
premature ejaculation
  (p. 334)
primary orgasmic
  dysfunction (p. 331)

primary sexual
  dysfunction (p. 331)
rapid ejaculation (p. 334)
secondary erectile
  dysfunction—
  psychological (p. 332)

secondary orgasmic
  dysfunction (p. 331)
secondary sexual
  dysfunction
  (p. 330)
sensate focus (p. 331)

sexual dysfunction
  (p. 330)
squeeze technique
  (p. 334)
stop-start technique
  (p. 334)

PERSONAL NOTE

When I was growing up, I heard a lot of talk about the "birds and bees." I had the impression that if I understood how they did it, I would understand how I should do it. To this day, I do not know how birds and bees do it. When I recently asked some of my very educated friends, "How do birds and bees do it?" they gave me puzzled looks. When I pressed them further, it was clear that they did not know either. They had guesses and assumptions and hypotheses, but none of them had actually observed two bees or two birds (chickens do not count because they cannot fly) or some combination of birds and bees engaging in sexual activity. I don't know where that expression came from. However, I do know that almost no one has ever seen birds and bees do it.   —R.P.

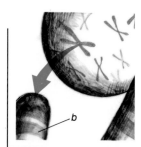

Conception Through Childhood

Module 29 Pre- and Postnatal Influences

Afton Blake, a psychologist interested in child development, chose her baby's father from a catalog. "It was time to have a child," she says. "I was secure emotionally and not in a steady relationship with a man." From the Repository for Germinal Choice in Escondido, California, she chose male donor #28. The catalog describes #28 as 6' tall, 170 lbs., hazel eyes, blond hair, handsome, excellent health, highly creative, plays classical music, very friendly, interested in swimming, bicycle riding, and hiking, a very bright scientist who has won many prizes and fellowships. After being artificially inseminated with sperm from donor #28, Blake gave birth to a male infant whom she named Doran. Blake believes that intelligence is both inherited and acquired. She hopes that some of the traits of donor #28 were passed on to Doran. Since 1960, more than 300,000 children have been conceived through artificial insemination (adapted from Mother Jones, *August 1983).*

What are the chances that Doran has inherited the good looks, creativity, interests, and intelligence of his father? To answer this question, you will need a basic understanding of genetics and the kinds of traits that are likely to be passed on through genes.

Would you want to pick your child's father from a catalog?

GENETICS

Each month, an ovum or egg cell is released from one of a woman's ovaries in a process called *ovulation*. After being released, the ovum travels through the fallopian tube to the uterus. If no sperm are present, no fertilization will occur. The ovum, together with the lining of the uterus, will be sloughed off in the process called *menstruation*. However, if a woman has had sexual intercourse or, as in Afton's case, if she has been artificially inseminated, approximately 100 to 500 million sperm will make their way from the vagina to the uterus and into the fallopian tubes. If one of the sperm penetrates the ovum's outside membrane, *fertilization* occurs. After penetration, the ovum's outside membrane changes and becomes impenetrable to the millions of remaining sperm. The fertilized ovum attaches itself to the wall of the uterus and continues dividing and developing, slowly taking on the physical characteristics of a human body.

In most cases, only a single ovum is released during ovulation. Sometimes, however, two ova are released. If both are fertilized, the result is the development of two individuals, called *fraternal twins*. Since fraternal twins develop from two different ova, they are no more alike genetically than any other two children of the same parents. Even less frequently, an ovum that

During ejaculation, 100 to 500 million sperm are released. Many will die before reaching the egg, but as this picture shows, many reach the egg and attach themselves to its surface. The sperm release enzymes that break down the egg membrane. When enough enzyme has been released, the cell membrane breaks down, and a single sperm enters and fertilizes the egg. As soon as this happens, the cell membrane is sealed off to all other sperm. (Dr. Sundstroem/Gamma-Liaison)

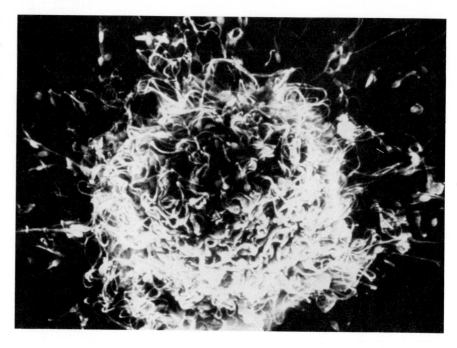

Why are some infants born with defects?

has already been fertilized splits into two parts and results in the development of two individuals. Since these two individuals developed from a single fertilized ovum, they share the same genetic makeup and are called *identical twins*.

If you looked inside an ovum or sperm, you would discover 23 miniature hairlike structures called **chromosomes.** Located on the chromosomes are thousands of **genes,** which are composed of deoxyribonucleic acid, abbreviated **DNA.** DNA has a structure like a spiral staircase, with each step in the staircase forming one "letter" of a chemical code. The sequence of the "letters" determines the meaning of the code (see Figure 11.1). A fertilized ovum contains the equivalent of 600,000 pages of instructions for the development of all the body's parts. During fertilization, the ovum's 23 chromosomes are joined with the sperm's 23 chromosomes to produce a total of 23 pairs of chromosomes.

During the millions of cell divisions required to form a human infant, chromosomes may be broken and genes mispositioned, resulting in developmental errors. One example is **Down's syndrome,** which occurs when the mother's ovum (or sometimes the father's sperm) contains not one twenty-first chromosome, but two. The fertilized egg therefore has a total of three twenty-first chromosomes, and this causes abnormal development. A child with Down's syndrome has both abnormal physical traits (a fold of skin at the corner of each eye, a wide tongue, heart defects) and abnormal brain development, resulting in mental retardation. Developmental abnormalities may also occur when DNA is affected by X rays, various drugs such as thalidomide, viruses such as German measles, and toxic chemicals. Depending upon how much these agents affect DNA and the genetic code, a fetus's development will be more or less affected. Doran was born without any obvious genetic birth defects because his genetic instructions remained intact.

GENOTYPE AND PHENOTYPE

How is eye color determined?

A single gene contains the instructions for certain physical traits, such as eye color. Doran inherited one gene for eye color from his mother and one from his donor father. If both genes contained instructions for brown eyes, his eyes will be brown; if both were for blue eyes, his eyes will be blue. However, if one gene has the instructions for brown and the other for blue eyes, Doran's eyes will be brown. This is because the gene for brown eyes is overriding or *dominant*, while the gene for blue eyes is *recessive*, or overridden by the dominant gene.

Observable physical traits, such as eye color, bone structure, height, and hair texture, are called **phenotypes.** In contrast, genetic patterns carried inside cells, patterns that cannot normally be seen, are called **genotypes.** Because Doran's eyes are brown, he is said to have a brown-eyed phenotype. Within his cells, however, he may have one dominant gene for brown eyes and one recessive gene for blue. If so, this brown-blue genetic combination would be his genotype. Note that you cannot always tell Doran's genotype just by looking at his phenotype. Often a genotype can be determined only by looking at the children a person produces. For instance, if both your parents have brown eyes and you were born with blue eyes, it would mean that your parents' genotypes included genes for blue eyes (see the illustration in Figure 11.2).

There are times when it is useful to know your genotype before you become a parent. If you are Jewish, with an Eastern European background, there is a possibility that you may be a carrier of certain genes that result in severe mental retardation (Tay-Sachs disease). If you are black, there is a possibility that you may be a carrier of certain genes that result in defective

Why are genotypes important?

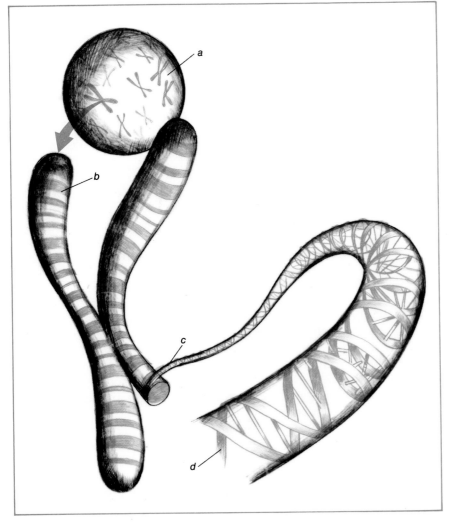

Figure 11.1

(a) A human cell has a nucleus with 46 chromosomes that contain about 100,000 genes. The genes are made up of DNA. (b) The chromosomes, 23 of them contributed by the mother, 23 by the father, consist of DNA and protein. (C) The tightly coiled DNA can be released from the chromosome with a chemical wash and unraveled to form a long strand. (d) The DNA strand is arranged like a spiral ladder, and the rungs in the ladder are made up of four bases or chemicals. (Adapted from *Discover*, March, 1984, pp. 84–85)

Figure 11.2

Transmission of dominant and recessive genes. In this case, the mother has brown eyes and the father has blue eyes. Eye color is controlled by a single gene. The gene for BROWN color, represented by B, is dominant and the gene for blue color, represented by b, is recessive. Since each parent contributes half of the genes, their children will receive a dominant gene for BROWN from the mother and a recessive gene for blue from the father. This combination is represented by the symbols Bb. Because the gene for BROWN is dominant over the recessive gene for blue, they will all have brown eyes. Since eye color is an observable trait, we say that the children have a phenotype for BROWN eyes. Since the children also have a recessive gene for blue, which is not observable, we say that they have a genotype for blue eyes.

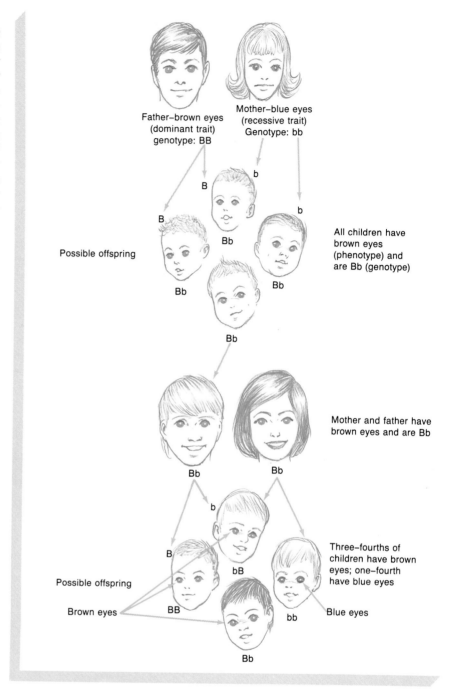

red cells (sickle-cell anemia). Although you may not have these problems yourself, you may still possess recessive genes for these or other harmful conditions as part of your genotype. If so, these harmful genes could be passed on to your children. For some inherited disorders, such as Tay-Sachs disease or sickle-cell anemia, parents can be tested to determine if one or both are carriers and to calculate the probability that their children might inherit the disorder.

After conception, it is also possible to test for genetic abnormalities. Between 14 and 20 weeks of pregnancy, a long needle is inserted through the mother's abdominal muscles into the fluid surrounding the fetus, and a sample of that fluid is collected. The fluid contains cells from the fetus that can be analyzed to determine if the fetus has some genetic disorder.

In addition to Down's syndrome, 100 other inherited biochemical disorders can now be identified. This process of obtaining fetal cells is called **amniocentesis** (AM-nee-oh-sen-TEE-sis) and is an example of fetal screening. For women over 35, amniocentesis may be especially relevant, since this age group has a higher percentage of infants born with Down's syndrome.

At birth, an infant may be tested for other genetic problems. For example, some newborns inherit an enzyme deficiency that prevents them from breaking down a protein found in certain foods, including milk. The result is a buildup of the protein called phenylalanine, which acts as a toxic chemical on the brain and causes mental retardation. To prevent this problem, known as *phenylketonuria* or *PKU*, a newborn is placed on a diet low in phenylalanine. Through newborn screening, PKU can be identified and treated so that mental retardation is prevented. One researcher suggests that basic genetic mechanisms be taught in public schools so that prospective parents will be more aware of avoidable genetic disorders (Rowley, 1984).

GENETIC ENGINEERING

An embryo develops human physical characteristics because of the instructions contained in over 100,000 genes (see Figure 11.3). In the early 1970s, scientists knew the exact location of only 3 human genes; today that number has grown to over 600. The knowledge of where genes are located on the chromosomes often makes it possible to pinpoint the causes of inherited

Could you make a mouse double in size?

Figure 11.3
Development of the embryo, 29 days to 16 weeks. Beginning with a single cell the size of a pinhead, the human embryo shows incredible growth as it develops human physical characteristics.

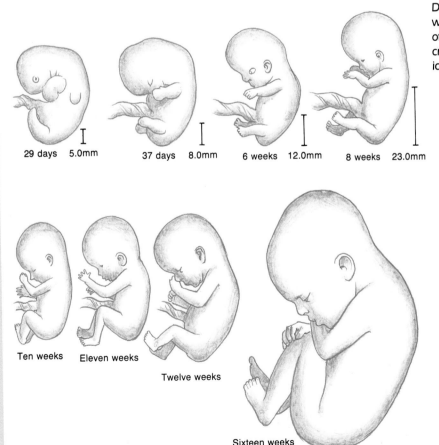

29 days   5.0mm   37 days   8.0mm   6 weeks   12.0mm   8 weeks   23.0mm

Ten weeks   Eleven weeks

Twelve weeks

Sixteen weeks

On the left is a normal size mouse and on the right is a supermouse, created through genetic engineering: The genes that regulate growth in the mouse were altered by adding genes that control human growth, so the mouse's genes produced more growth hormone and caused the mouse to grow twice as big. (Culliton, 1985). *(Photo courtesy of Gerald S. Williams)*

problems. It is now possible to remove a gene and actually replace it with another, a process called **genetic engineering.** As the photo of the two mice shows, researchers were able to double the size of a mouse by adding genes that control growth. Through this process, simple organisms have been given the capacity to produce human insulin. In these organisms, certain genes have been removed and replaced with different genes that carry instructions for the production of human insulin, which can be used in the treatment of diabetes. It is hoped that genetic engineering may someday make possible the correction of genetic defects such as PKU in the fertilized ovum or after birth. Dwarfs, for example, may be treated by replacement of their defective "growth" gene with one that produces growth hormone and allows them to reach a normal size.

APPLYING PSYCHOLOGY   What Interferes with Development?

Alcohol

After studying several hundred children over three years, Dr. Sally Shaywitz of Yale's Mental Health Clinical Research Center found that significantly more mothers of children with learning disabilities regularly drank alcohol. Learning disabilities include a short attention span, poor language skills, and perceptual problems. Shaywitz's studies suggest that even small amounts of alcohol, such as two drinks per day, may have a harmful effect on the development of a fetus (adapted from the *San Diego Union,* July 13, 1982).

The blood supply of the mother and the blood supply of the fetus are connected by an organ called the **placenta.** In many cases the placenta acts like a filter, allowing oxygen and nutrients to pass and keeping out toxic or harmful substances. But many drugs (including nicotine, caffeine, marijuana, and heroin) and certain viruses, as well as the mother's own hormones can pass from the placenta into the fetus's blood vessels. Alcohol is one of the potentially harmful drugs that crosses the placenta and can affect fetal development.

We now know that as few as one to three drinks per day during pregnancy can result in newborns who show lower levels of arousal and who later show learning problems (Streissguth et al., 1980; 1984). We also know that heavy drinking during pregnancy results in a combination of physical and psychological symptoms called the **fetal alcohol syndrome (FAS).** FAS is the third leading cause of mental retardation in the United States (Streissguth et al., 1980). Michael Miller (1986) found that when pregnant female rats were given the human equivalent of two six packs of beer daily, their offspring had abnormal brain development. He believes that this is how alcohol produces the Fetal Alcohol Syndrome in humans. Because of the potential risk to the fetus, no one is sure what is a "safe" level of alcoholic consumption during pregnancy; abstinence is recommended for that reason (Kolata, 1981b).

Nicotine

Smoking can also have harmful effects on fetal development. We know that two of the effects of nicotine are to decrease blood flow through the umbilical cord and to increase carbon dioxide in the blood. These may be the reasons why babies born to mothers who smoke during pregnancy weigh an average of 200 grams less at birth than babies born to nonsmokers. Mothers who smoke also have a higher rate of stillbirths and premature births, with rates increasing as smoking increases. Prenatal exposure to nicotine even appears to affect a child's later development. Four-year-olds who had been exposed to nicotine in their mothers' wombs had significantly poorer attention spans than children of nonsmoking mothers (Streissguth et al., 1984).

Malnutrition, Disease, and Stress

Besides being concerned over consumption of alcohol and intake of nicotine, a mother-to-be must be careful of her diet. If a mother suffers from malnutrition during much of pregnancy, the result can be retarded development of the fetal brain, reduced brain weight, and various degrees of mental retardation (Stechler & Halton, 1982). An expectant mother should also be concerned about exposure to certain viruses that may interfere with fetal development, such as the virus that causes German measles. Finally, if an expectant mother is continually stressed during pregnancy, she will release a number of hormones that may result in her infant being more fussy and colicky (Bee, 1980). The mother's diet, drug intake, exposure to disease, and level of stress can directly affect fetal development, in some instances adversely.

What should a woman be concerned about during pregnancy?

Anesthesia

During the birth of her first child, a mother may be in labor an average of 14 hours; for her second child, the labor averages 8 hours. Because of the anxiety and pain associated with giving birth, it is common for laboring mothers to receive anesthetics or analgesics. These drugs pose a potential danger, especially at higher doses, since they depress the baby's nervous system and decrease oxygen supply to the brain. Because of this concern, methods have been developed to reduce anxiety and pain during childbirth without the use of drugs.

Several methods involve the mother in the birth process instead of treating her like a passive patient. One of the best known, the **Lamaze method,** requires the mother to take a series of classes to prepare for childbirth. In these classes, the mother is informed about the birth process to relieve some of her anxiety, worry, and stress. She is also taught how to control her breathing as one way to divert her attention from the pain of labor, and she is taught how to use her muscles to aid in the delivery process. There is some evidence that mothers who are trained in childbirth techniques require less medication and have a better attitude toward childbirth, especially if the father is present during delivery (Vander Zanden, 1981).

Protein Deficiency

A newborn's brain has most of its neurons, but lacks many of the connections between neurons and many of the supporting cells that contribute to neural functioning. In order for the brain to develop properly, the infant's diet must contain an adequate supply of protein. If an infant's diet is very low in protein and this condition persists over a long period of time, physical growth and brain development will be retarded. If a child suffering from protein deficiency is placed in a program of good nutrition, health care, and education, the retardation in physical growth and cognitive skills may be partially reversed (Herrera et al., 1980; McKay et al., 1978).

Toxins

The development of the baby's brain can also be harmed by exposure to toxic substances. For example, there is evidence that certain children, especially in lower social classes, have much higher than normal levels of lead in their blood, as Figure 11.4 shows. This lead comes primarily from breathing air with a high concentration of auto exhaust fumes and from eating chips of old paint that have peeled off walls. High levels of lead can

Figure 11.4
Lead in gasoline and lead in the bloodstream. The top two lines of the graph indicate the amount of lead in black and Hispanic children's bloodstreams. The bottom line indicates the lead in gasoline. These three lines show an incredibly high correlation between lead in gasoline and lead in blood of New York City children. Since such concentrations of lead in the bloodstream can have adverse effects on health and psychological functioning, the Environmental Protection Agency has taken steps to reduce lead in gasoline by 91 percent. (Adapted from *Science News*, August 4, 1984, p. 71)

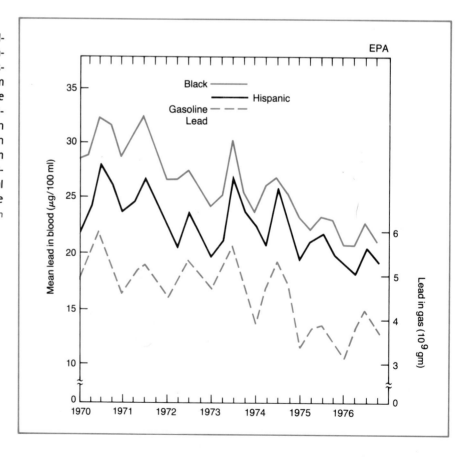

result in retarded brain development, as well as in behavioral and cognitive deficits (Raloff, 1982; Shaheen, 1984).

In all of these examples, we see how many elements in the fetus's or child's environment, such as alcohol or lead, interact with the genetic instructions to impede development. Indeed, it is the *interaction* between genetic instructions and the environment—not the genes or the environment alone—that is critical to the normal or abnormal development of the fetus and the child.

MAJOR CONCEPT   Prenatal Influences on Development

To understand human development in the nine months following conception, you must understand the interaction of genes and environment.

Test your understanding of this important process by indicating whether the following statements are true (T) or false (F).

1. T/F If a person's genes carry instructions for growing unusually tall, nothing can stop this hereditary plan from being carried out.

2. T/F Doctors can treat the genetic abnormality known as PKU by controlling the newborn's internal environment through diet.

3. T/F Through genetic engineering (a form of environmental intervention) scientists are now able to insert new genes into organisms.

4. T/F The abnormal brain development of a fetus with Down's syndrome is caused by the presence of an extra chromosome.

5. T/F Just one or two alcoholic drinks a day during pregnancy is not enough to affect how a fetus's genes are expressed.

6. T/F A woman's malnutrition throughout pregnancy will not affect her fetus. A fetus is always capable of extracting the nutrients it needs from stores within the mother's body.

Answers: 1 (F); 2 (T); 3 (T); 4 (T); 5 (F); 6 (F)

REVIEW

As a genetic counselor, you are telling Dave and Helen, an infertile couple, about how they might have a child. You explain that a donor ovum can be fertilized in a test tube by donor sperm. After fertilization, the ovum will be placed in Helen's uterus. In nine months, if all goes well, Helen will give birth to an infant boy or girl. Dave wants to know what happens during fertilization. You explain that during fertilization, an ovum and a sperm combine to form a single cell that contains 23 pairs of (1) _____. On each of the chromosomes are thousands of (2) _____, which are made up of deoxyribonucleic acid, abbreviated (3) _____. The DNA forms a chem-

ical code that contains the instructions for the development of the human body.

Helen tells you that if possible, she would like the child to have a physical resemblance to herself and Dave. You explain that observable traits, such as dark hair and brown eyes, are called a person's (4) _____. If donor parents were selected on the basis of phenotypes, there is no guarantee that the child will have these traits. This is because donor parents also carry recessive genes and other genetic patterns, called their (5) _____. Genotypes are not observable and must usually be inferred from seeing what traits a person's children inherit.

Dave wants to know if they can be sure that the

infant will be born without any birth defects. You explain that birth defects sometimes occur because of an error in the number of chromosomes, as happens in

(6) _____ syndrome. Other defects occur

because of a defect in (7) _____, as in infants with PKU. It would be possible to determine if the developing fetus has certain genetic problems

through a procedure called (8) _____. In amniocentesis, some of the fluid surrounding the fetus is drawn out with a needle and the fetal cells contained in it are examined. Helen wonders if it is possible to correct genetic problems, such as PKU, by actually replacing the defective gene, a process known as

(9) _____ engineering. You tell her that although genetic engineering has produced remarkable changes in simple plants and animals, using this technique on humans is only in the initial stages.

Both Dave and Helen would like their child to be creative and intelligent, and have a good sense of humor. You smile and tell them that behavioral traits are the result of interaction between genes and

(10) _____. Helen asks about the things she should not do when she is pregnant. You strongly advise her not to drink alcohol or smoke cigarettes, since both drugs have been linked to later learning problems. For instance, the alcohol a pregnant woman drinks flows in her bloodsream to the organ that transfers oxygen and nutrients to the bloodstream of her

fetus, an organ called the (11) _____. Repeated heavy drinking during pregnancy results in a combination of physical and psychological symptoms

called the (12) _____ _____ syndrome. You also tell Helen about the importance of maintaining a proper diet and avoiding environments that contain industrial chemicals. Finally, you advise Helen and Dave to consider some form of childbirth

training, such as the (13) _____ method. With this method, the mother generally needs fewer pain-killing drugs during labor, which in turn benefits her baby.

Answers: (1) chromosomes; (2) genes; (3) DNA; (4) phenotype; (5) genotype; (6) Down's; (7) genes; (8) amniocentesis; (9) genetic; (10) environment; (11) placenta; (12) fetal alcohol; (13) Lamaze

GLOSSARY TERMS

amniocentesis (p. 343)
chromosomes (p. 340)
DNA (p. 340)

Down's syndrome
 (p. 340)
fetal alcohol syndrome
 (p. 345)

genes (p. 340)
genetic engineering
 (p. 344)
genotypes (p. 341)

Lamaze method (p. 345)
phenotypes (p. 341)
placenta (p. 344)

Module 30 Social and Emotional Development

DEVELOPMENT OF SOCIAL ATTACHMENTS

Does a baby have a mind of its own?

"I don't believe you. I know that a baby can't do much more than cry, eat, and sleep. You're saying that your baby recognizes your face. A baby's brain isn't big enough to do that." The neighbor had finished talking and stood there with her arms crossed, looking down at the 10-week-old infant. The mother smiled, *"OK, I'll show you. You stand on the left side of the crib and I'll stand on the right. Then we'll play peek-a-boo. If the baby spends more time looking at me, it means that*

she recognizes my face. If she spends more time looking at you, it means that she doesn't." The mother took her place on the right and the neighbor walked over and stood on the left side of the crib. The neighbor and the mother alternately played peek-a-boo. There was little doubt about the results. The baby spent more time looking at her mother's face. The neighbor was shaking her head from side to side. "Could be a coincidence. I still don't believe that tiny Kim really recognizes your face."

Whom would you believe, the mother or the neighbor? In a study similar to the peek-a-boo game played by the mother and the neighbor, Tiffany Field and her associates (1986, 1987) reported that 4-day-old infants initially spent more time looking at their mother's face than a stranger's. Field concluded that even newborns can learn some distinctive features of their mother's face.

Lewis Lipsitt (1987) says that until recently, parents were told that their infants were mostly blind at birth and could not taste, smell, feel pain, learn, or remember. Now we know that newborns can see, taste, feel pain, detect their mother's odor, and show taste and flavor preferences. Even more remarkable, Lipsitt (1982) has shown that infants can learn and remember. The first time Kim hears a new sound, her heart accelerates briefly. But after the sound is presented a number of times, her heart no longer accelerates. This indicates that she "remembers" or recognizes the sound, a process called *habituation.* Lipsitt has also shown that newborn Kim can learn to turn her head at the sound of a tone but not a buzzer to get a taste of sugar water. This is an example of *associative learning.* All these studies indicate that newborn Kim's senses and brain are functioning to a remarkable degree. One way that researchers could assess normal brain development is by analyzing Kim's crying to see whether it fits a normal or abnormal pattern (Figure 11.5). If her brain development is normal, within months she will develop further sensory and cognitive functions and form attachments to her parents.

Forming Attachments

Between 4 and 6 weeks, rhythmically moving stimuli, such as the nodding head of a puppet or a rotating mobile, will cause Kim to smile. Then gradually, between the ages of 2 and 3 months, a human face becomes the most effective stimulus for eliciting a smile. Because this smile is directed toward another person, it is called **social smiling.** Psychologists believe that Kim's social smiling may be increased by parental reinforcement. But her social smiling also serves a very important social function, that of communication. The emergence of social smiling is thought to mark the beginning of a period during which the infant forms social attachments with caretakers (Lamb, 1984).

By 6 months, Kim will recognize her parents' faces. Soon she will begin to give them happy greetings when they reappear after a short absence. When Kim's father comes home from work, she may smile and gurgle, bounce up and down in her highchair, and hold out her arms to him. In a few more months, when Kim is able to crawl, she will begin to follow her parents wherever they go. At the same time, Kim will begin to show distress whenever her mother and father temporarily leave her in the care of someone else. This reaction, called **separation anxiety,** may include loud protests, crying, and agitation, as well as despair and depression when the separation is very long. Both separation anxiety and joyous greetings on reunion are signs that Kim is developing strong affectional bonds toward

When will a baby begin to smile?

Figure 11.5

Analyzing a baby's cries. (a) Dr. Barry Lester is recording a baby's cries, which are analyzed for possible irregularities. (b) The bottom graph compares differences in pitch between the crying of four abnormal babies, numbers 1 to 4, with that of seven normal babies, numbers 5 to 11. Abnormal crying may indicate abnormal brain development or an impaired respiratory system. (a, Richard Howard/*Discover Magazine* ©1984 Time Inc.; b, adapted from Angier, 1984)

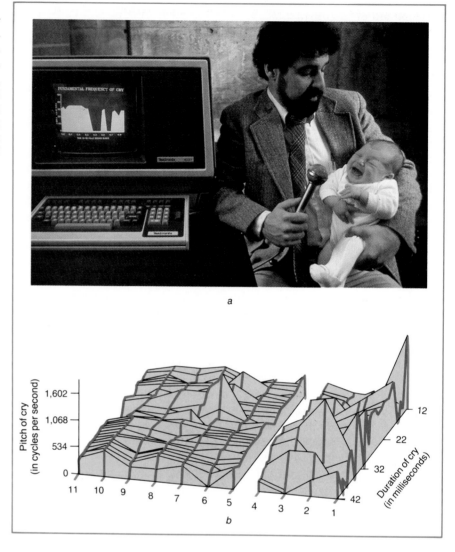

Do infants form different kinds of attachments?

her parents, bonds called **social attachments.** A social attachment will form toward whoever is a child's primary caretaker—whether mother, father, grandparent, or any other caring adult.

By studying the reactions of infants to being separated from and reunited with their mothers, Mary Ainsworth (1983) found that infant-mother attachments vary greatly in quality. When placed in an unfamiliar room containing many interesting toys, a **securely attached** infant tends to explore freely as long as the mother looks on. If the mother leaves, most of these babies cry and become upset. But when mother returns, they greet her happily and are very easily soothed. In contrast, an **anxiously attached** infant does not respond positively when the mother comes back to the room. Some show great ambivalence toward her, one minute clinging and wanting to be held, and the next minute squirming and pushing away. Other anxiously attached infants simply avoid the mother upon her return; they turn their heads in another direction or move away from her.

There is some relationship between the security of the infant-caretaker attachment and the child's later behaviors. For example, the more secure the infant-caretaker attachment, the less dependence the child later shows and the better he or she copes with the stress of attending kindergarten, as Figure 11.6 shows (Jacobson & Wille, 1984; Sroufe et al., 1983). The development of the infant-caretaker attachment is important because it establishes an initial pattern of trust and understanding in the infant's life.

Why does the quality of infant-caretaker attachments vary so greatly? The answer lies in a complex interaction between traits of the parent, traits of the baby, and the kind of environment in which they both live. For instance, researchers have found that mothers of securely attached infants tend to be more sensitive to their baby's needs than mothers of anxiously attached infants. When the child is crying and upset, these mothers usually respond quickly and offer comfort until the baby is soothed. This style of mothering is called *sensitive care.* Mothers of anxiously attached infants, in contrast, are less likely to respond right away when their baby is distressed and are more apt to let the infant "cry it out." These women may also have more negative feelings toward motherhood and are more tense and irritable toward their child.

At the same time, many infants who become insecurely attached start life with certain characteristics that make them harder for an adult to respond to. For example, anxiously attached infants in general have been found to be less active, less alert, and less socially engaging as newborns. Outside conditions may also enter into the development of an insecure attachment. When a woman with a difficult baby has many additional stresses in her life and little emotional support from others, the relationship between mother and child may get off to a bad start. The development of attachments is a very complex process that involves many interacting factors (Belsky et al., 1984b, Egeland & Farber, 1984).

Although psychologists have long studied the infant-mother attachment, they have only recently studied the infant-father attachment. Researchers found that mothers were more likely to interact with their infants during routine caretaking, such as feeding or bathing, and to pick up their infants at these times. In contrast, fathers were more likely to interact with their infants for the sole purpose of play. The researchers concluded that infants become attached to their fathers as well as to their mothers, and that fathers provide different kinds of stimulation and activities than do mothers (Belsky et al., 1984a).

As you can see, the kind of attachment a child develops with a mother, father, or other adult depends on a complex interaction among a host of factors. When this interaction goes very badly, the result can be tragic, as in the development of child abuse.

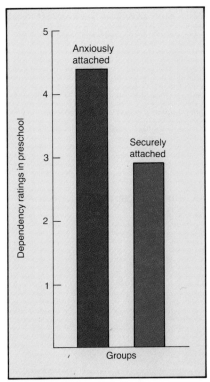

Figure 11.6

As 1-year-olds, infants were rated as anxiously or securely attached to their mothers. When these same children were about 4, teachers rated them on dependency in preschool. One-year-olds rated as anxiously attached were found to be significantly more dependent as 4-year-olds. (Data based on Sroufe et al., 1983)

When separated from their mothers, some young children may fuss and cry while others may play. Which reaction the child shows depends, to some extent, on how the mother interacts with her infant. (Both, Erika Stone)

EXPLORING PSYCHOLOGY Child Abuse

What I remember most about my mother was that she was always beating me. She'd beat me with her high-heeled shoes, with my father's belt, with a potato masher. When I was eight, she black-and-blued my legs so badly I told her I'd go tell the police. She said, "Go, they'll just put you into the darkest prison" (*Time*, Sept. 5, 1983, p. 20).

What kinds of parents abuse their children?

In the United States, between 500,000 and a million children suffer physical abuse each year. Even more children are thought to suffer from emotional or psychological abuse (Hart & Brassard, 1987). Psychologists have identified a number of personal and environmental factors that place parents at risk for abusing their children. Parents are at risk if they were abused as children, if they have few parenting skills, and if they show high rates of marital problems and divorce. Parents who abuse are also more likely to be young, poorly educated, and socially isolated. Because they have little contact with others, they lack the help and emotional support from friends and family that can be very important in dealing successfully with stress. And because abusing parents tend to be poor and from lower social classes, stress is very common in their lives. Sometimes child abuse is only one symptom of a violent family pattern, which may also include abusive interactions between husband and wife (Parke & Salby, 1983).

What kinds of children are likely to be abused?

Just as certain social, economic, and psychological conditions place parents at risk to be abusers, certain characteristics of children place them at risk to be abused. Infants and children are at risk if they have a difficult temperament, a serious illness during the first year, or a mental or physical handicap. Some children are at risk if they behave in a complaining, aggressive, crying, teasing, or destructive manner.

What is clear from these findings is that to understand child abuse, it is necessary to take into account the traits of the child as well as those of the parents. Researchers now realize that child abuse is a function of the *interaction* between child and parent, rather than a function solely of the parent (Isaacs, 1982). Child abuse is also a function of the family's environment, particularly the stresses family members face. Poverty, unemployment, and isolation from others who care and want to help can all put enormous strain on the parent-child interaction.

Since many abusing parents have personal problems, one form of treatment involves long-term therapy to help them deal with their problems and learn self-control (Kempe & Kempe, 1978). In addition, abusing parents need to learn more positive ways of interacting with their children. Researchers have found that abusing parents are less likely to use behaviors such as smiling, praising, and touching, and more likely to use behaviors such as threatening, disapproving, and showing anger (Reid at al., 1981).

Behavior modification techniques, discussed in Chapter 6, can help parents learn to reduce the negative interactions. This form of treatment includes helping the parent identify specific situations that trigger abuse, modeling how to reward appropriate behaviors, using time-out periods instead of physical punishment and threats, and learning how to settle problems and arguments through negotiation rather than violence. Using a combination of long-term therapy and behavior modification, intervention programs have been relatively successful in decreasing child abuse (Isaacs, 1982; Kempe & Kempe, 1978; Patterson, 1982).

EMOTIONAL DEVELOPMENT

Since infants cannot talk, they need another way to express their emotions. Carroll Izard (1987) and his colleagues videotaped the expressions of infants as they were exposed to emotion-producing stimuli, such as seeing an approaching stranger, hearing a balloon pop, tasting lemon juice, and receiving a regularly scheduled shot. Izard found that shortly after birth, infants showed signs of interest, distress, and disgust. Within three to eight months, infants showed signs of joy, anger, surprise, sadness, shyness, and fear (Figure 11.7). Not only did infants show emotions very early, but the magnitude of their initial emotional responses predicted later emotionality. For example, the amount of anger a 2-month-old child showed when getting a shot predicted how much anger, in general, the child showed at 19 months of age (Izard et al., 1987).

To find out how soon infants could imitate emotional expressions, Andrew Meltzoff spent much of his time smiling, opening his mouth wide,

How many words is a baby's expression worth?

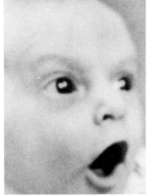

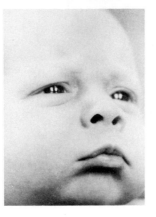

Figure 11.7
Emotional development in infants. (a) During their first three days after birth, babies were able to imitate human facial expressions of emotions—happy, sad, and surprised. By measuring how long the infants stared at the faces, researchers concluded that newborns were able to discriminate between emotional expressions (Field et al., 1982). These data indicate that infants are born with the ability to make certain emotional expressions. (b) The table indicates when infants begin to show emotional behaviors. (From Trotter, 1983)

Infant Emotions: Arrival Times

Expression of Fundamental Emotions	Approximate Time of Emergence
Interest Neonatal Smile (a sort of half smile that appears spontaneously for no apparent reason) Startled response Distress (in response to pain) Disgust	Present at birth
Social Smile	4–6 weeks
Anger Surprise Sadness	3–4 months
Fear Shame/Shyness/Self-awareness	5–7 months 6–8 months
Contempt Guilt	2nd year of life

and sticking out his tongue at 2-week-old babies. To his surprise, he and his colleagues as well as researcher Tiffany Field found that infants as young as 12 days could imitate an adult's facial expression. (Field et al., 1982; Meltzoff & Moore, 1977). As Figure 11.7 shows, a baby's face is worth at least a thousand words.

If infants can imitate emotional expressions, does it also mean that they "know" the expressions stand for different emotions? Jeannette Haviland and Mary Lelwica (1987) found that when mothers expressed joy, their infants' movements increased to show their excitement and the babies looked more at their mothers' smiling faces to show their interest. In contrast, when mothers expressed anger, their infants moved less to show fear, looked less to show disinterest, and many of them cried and had to be removed from the testing room to be soothed. The researchers reached a startling conclusion: 10-week-old infants were able to discriminate between their mothers' facial and vocal emotional expressions of joy, sadness, and anger. This conclusion is startling because no one suspected that very young infants could process and respond to complex emotional information.

Based on his many years of studying emotions, Carroll Izard (1987) hypothesizes that *emotional development* in infants is a two-step process. The first step is the infants' biological capacity to produce, imitate, and discriminate between emotional expressions. The second step is the infants' responsiveness to the parents' emotion or mood. Thus infants imitated their mothers' emotional expressions and then altered their behavior, more or less playing and exploring, depending upon their mothers' happy or sad expressions and moods. According to Izard, infants develop emotionally because of an interaction between their biological capacity to express emotions and their responsiveness to the environment.

STABILITY OF EARLY EMOTIONAL BEHAVIOR

Parents sometimes wonder if their infant's early emotional behaviors, which are referred to as an infant's *temperament*, will persist into childhood and beyond. The answer is "yes" and "no." Researchers have discovered that a fretful temperament, such as crying and being irritable and fussy, sometimes does not persist as the child grows older (Rothbart & Derryberry, 1981). Similarly, children who were often fearful, angry, and had temper tantrums during their first three years did not necessarily show these behaviors when they reached adolescence. The researchers found much more correlation between emotional behaviors children showed between ages 6 to 10 and their adult temperament (Kagan, 1980). We can conclude, therefore, that a difficult temperament in infancy does not always persist into adolescence or adulthood. Then we come across cases like David's:

David, who is almost 2, is sitting on his mother's lap. Around him are other mothers with their toddlers. All of the toddlers are playing with the toys, making noises, and having a wonderful time. Except David. He sits on his mother's lap, glances at the other toddlers, and refuses to play. When David finally leaves his mother's lap to pick up a toy, he is very cautious and tentative and does not go too far from her side.

Jerome Kagan (1984) and his associates studied 21-month-old toddlers and discovered that about 10 percent, like David, were very cautious, tentative, and shy in new situations. Besides showing what Kagan called a very *inhibited* behavioral pattern, these toddlers also had significantly higher heart rates compared to uninhibited toddlers. To determine if this inhibited behavior and increased heart rate persisted as the toddlers got older, the researchers retested them when they reached age 5½. Many of the toddlers who had shown inhibited behaviors and increased heart rates at 21 months, showed similar patterns at 5½ years, demonstrating the stability of these responses. The researchers speculated that the increased heart rates found in inhibited children reflected nervous systems that had lower thresholds for arousal. In turn, lowered thresholds for arousal mean that inhibited children would have increased heart rates in many new or stressful situations and would be more likely to behave in a tentative, cautious, or shy manner (Reznick et al., 1986).

Can inhibited children overcome their shyness? To answer this question, imagine two different sets of parents. One set is impatient and pushes the child to be more outgoing. As a result of the parents' pushiness, the already inhibited child becomes more tentative and shy and this makes the parents even more impatient and pushy. In this kind of parent-child interaction, the inhibited child is unlikely to become more outgoing. A second set of parents is patient and helps and encourages their inhibited child to deal with new or stressful situations. As a result of the parents' help, the child becomes a little more outgoing and this encourages the parents to be even more patient and supportive. In this parent-child interaction, the inhibited child is likely to become more outgoing.

These different kinds of parent-child interactions illustrate the **principle of bidirectionality.** According to this principle, a child's behaviors influence how the parents respond and, in turn, the parents' behaviors influence how the child responds. In Kagan's study of inhibited children, a majority of the mothers said that they were worried about their child's shy and inhibited behaviors. However, many of the mothers had taken special steps, such as being more patient and teaching the inhibited child how to cope with new, stressful situations. These remedial practices proved successful. Some children who were very inhibited and shy at 21 months behaved less so when observed at 5½ years (Kagan, 1987; Reznick et al., 1986). One of the leading researchers in child development, Eleanor Maccoby (1984, 1987), points to the principle of bidirectionality as the key to understanding and explaining children's emotional development.

We have examined the biological factors and learning experiences that contribute to a normal child's social-emotional development. But what happens to a child who goes through a potentially very stressful social-emotional experience, such as being abandoned by his or her mother or having a chronic health problem? The case of Delia will help answer our question.

Easy babies are happy, cheerful, and adapt quickly to new situations. Difficult babies are fussy, fearful of new situations, and more intense in their reactions. (Above, Charles Harbutt/ Archive; below, H. Gritscher/Peter Arnold)

The Effects of Early Emotional Experiences

Delia was born to an unwed 17-year-old mother who was described during the infant's early years as indifferent, withdrawn, childlike, and discontented. Shortly after her first birthday, Delia went to live with her grandparents and was eventually adopted by them at age 7, along with her younger brother. Before and after her adoption, Delia had only fleeting contacts with her mother. Her father had died when she was 5. The environment provided by the grandparents would be considered below average in both socioeconomic status and educational stimulation (adapted from Werner & Smith, 1982).

Does a bad early experience always cause problems later?

Delia was one of over 600 children researchers followed from birth to the age of almost 20. Like Delia, all the children in this study were from a small rural community on the Hawaiian island of Kuaui. Like Delia, all the children were exposed to increased risks during their early years, such as problems during pregnancy, family instability, and lower-class environments. In some cases, the parents had serious mental health problems. About 200 of these children developed serious behavioral or learning problems at some time during their first 20 years. However, the most remarkable part of this study is that over 400 of the children developed into competent and autonomous young adults (Werner et al., 1971; Werner & Smith, 1977; 1982). Why did 200 children develop serious problems while 400 children did not? We will give you two answers, each from a slightly different perspective.

Psychosocial Stages

How was Delia's personality affected by life's problems?

As Delia develops from an infant to an elderly person, imagine her experiencing a series of eight challenges or life crises, which include how she interacts with her caretaker, learns self-control, and finds her identity. Erik Erikson hypothesized that each of us goes through eight different life crises, which he calls **psychosocial stages.** Erikson believed that if we cope successfully with the potential problems inherent in each psychosocial stage, then we develop positive personality traits and are better able to cope with the next stage. However, if we do not cope successfully, we may become anxious, worried, or troubled and develop personality problems. We'll look at the first two stages here and describe the later stages in the next Module.

Look at Figure 12.1, p. 372. You will notice that Erikson's first psychosocial stage, which is called *trust* versus *mistrust*, centers on Delia's interactions with her caretaker. If her caretaker is responsive to her needs, Delia may develop a positive view of her world and learn to trust others. If her caretaker is neglectful of her needs, Delia may view her world as uncaring and learn to become mistrustful. Delia's failure to develop what Erikson calls *basic trust* during her first year may result in her having difficulty dealing with the second psychosocial stage as well as learning to trust people later in life.

The second psychosocial stage, which Erikson called *autonomy* versus *shame*, centers around Delia using her newly developed abilities, such as walking, exploring, or speaking. If her caretakers encourage and support her efforts, Delia may develop a sense of independence or autonomy. If her caretakers disapprove of or punish her behaviors, Delia may develop instead a feeling that independence is bad and may feel shame. With regard to the 600 children in the Kuaui study, Erikson might explain that 200 developed serious problems as adults because they did not resolve successfully their psychosocial crises and developed mistrust, guilt, and other personality problems.

Many psychologists agree with Erikson that psychosocial conflicts, which are based on interpersonal and environmental interactions, are important and contribute to later social-emotional development.

Besides Erikson's psychosocial stages, Sigmund Freud proposed that we go through a series of psychosexual stages that influence personality development. We will discuss Freud's psychosexual stages in Module 36.

Concept of Resilience

Remember that Delia was born to a 17-year-old unwed mother who was withdrawn and indifferent to Delia. When Delia was 1 year old, her mother abandoned her, and when she was 5, her father died. Delia was raised and

Few experiments have had more dramatic impact on developmental psychology than Harry Harlow's studies with infant monkeys. Harlow and his associates removed infant monkeys from their mothers at birth and raised them in isolation or by surrogate mothers. One surrogate was made from wire, and one from cloth. Harlow found that infants preferred the cloth mother even if they had been raised and fed on the wire surrogate. Prior to Harlow's studies, many psychologists had maintained that touching and affection were not as important as food. Harlow showed that in fact touching and affection were just as important. (Martin Rogers/Stock, Boston)

MAJOR CONCEPT   Early Social and Emotional Development

To help explain how children develop socially and emotionally, psychologists have proposed a number of concepts.

Match each of the concepts listed below with its correct description.

1. Social attachment

2. Secure attachment

3. Anxious attachment

4. Development of basic trust

5. Resilient children

6. Principle of bidirectionality

a. __6__ The idea that while parents are affecting the behavior of their child, the child is also affecting the parents' behavior.

b. __5__ Studies on this subject demonstrate that negative early life experiences need not result in emotional problems that persist into adulthood.

c. __3__ The kind of attachment that tends to form when a baby's principal caregiver fails to respond fully and reliably to the child's needs.

d. __2__ The kind of attachment that tends to be related to more independence and better adjustment during the preschool years.

e. __1__ A strong affectional bond, usually toward both mother and father, that begins to be evident in the second half of the first year.

f. __4__ According to Erik Erikson, this is the major challenge a child faces in the first year of life.

Answers: a(6); b(5); c(3); d(2); e(1); f(4)

---

adopted at age 7 by her grandparents. Nonetheless, according to the latest evaluation of Delia at age 20, she has a fair degree of insight into her life, adequate self-esteem, high achievement motivation, and realistic plans for the future. Why was Delia able to overcome such serious social-emotional problems and develop into a reasonably normal, healthy adult?

After following the 600 subjects of the Kuauai study across 20 years, Emmy Werner and Ruth Smith (1982) have identified a number of factors that characterize **resilient children,** those who cope successfully with stresses. Resilient children, from birth to 2 years old, are perceived by their caretakers as more active and socially responsive, such as being cuddly and affectionate. Because of these characteristics, these infants elicit and receive a great deal of attention, which in turn leads to an affectionate bond between infant and caretaker. This affectionate bond helps the children show a healthy independence at age 2, with a good balance between attempting things on their own and asking for support when they need it. The mother's employment outside the household during childhood has no negative effects on resilient children.

In contrast to the 400 resilient children in the study that included Delia, some 200 children faced with similar early experiences of poverty and family instability developed a serious learning or emotional problem. Some of the factors that contributed to later problems were: being perceived as fussy, irritable infants, experiencing prolonged separations from their mothers, having serious health problems, and being exposed to more family discord and to a larger number of stressful events during their first two years.

How might a child overcome early difficulties?

This study on resilient children makes three important points. First, the occurrence of a traumatic emotional event in childhood, such as Delia's loss of her parents, does not necessarily lead to later social-emotional problems. However, some children do have problems later in life because of early stressful emotional experiences. Second, the occurrence of an emotional trauma in childhood, such as loss of one's parents, may be offset by some other positive experience, such as the presence of a loving and supportive caretaker. Third, the early years of childhood are not necessarily the most important, since most children develop into healthy adults provided that positive experiences offset the effects of early emotional stress.

One early and potentially stressful experience that is becoming more common in our society of working parents is the placement of an infant or child in a day care center. Let's look at that issue next.

APPLYING PSYCHOLOGY   Day Care and Development

What should a working parent do?

Herb strokes his beard as he explains his problem. "I'm recently divorced, have a good 9 to 5 job, and best of all I have a terrific 7-month-old daughter named Sarah." His eyes narrow. "I guess I don't have a choice. Unless I find a day care center for Sarah I'll lose my job and her too." He stops stroking his beard. "Got any good advice?"

Like Herb, an increasing number of working and single parents must find day care for their children. In fact, about 500,000 children under the age of 6 and about 5 million children under the age of 10 are in need of day care facilities (*Newsweek*, September 1984).

For six years, Sandra Scarr and her associates have been studying day care in Bermuda, where about 90 percent of the children are placed in day care centers before they are 2 years old. The following findings come from these studies.

What happens to a child in day care?

In general, until they are 2 years old, children need a lot of warm, loving care from adults. Babies do not need other babies; they need adults. This kind of care can be provided in the baby's home by a sitter, in a small neighborhood day care home, or in a larger day care center that keeps babies and toddlers separate from older children and provides a consistent adult relationship. For any of these settings to provide quality day care, there should be no more than four babies to each adult. When children were placed in quality day care centers or left with sitters before they were 2 years old, they did just as well in intellectual and emotional development as children who were at home with their mothers.

When 2-year-olds in day care do not do as well intellectually or emotionally as children who stay at home, the most important factor seems to be a less than optimal ratio of staff to children. Three- and 4-year-olds who are placed in day care centers actually do better than children who stay at home with their mothers. The most likely reason for this is that the centers provide these older children with more peer contact and better educational programs.

We used to think that placing a child in day care would result in a great reduction in the parent-child interaction. However, studies show that mothers who stay home all day spend very little time in direct interaction with their preschoolers. Compared with mothers who stay home all day, working mothers spend about the same amount of time in direct interaction with children, reading to them or playing with them (Scarr, 1984).

This research paints a relatively positive picture of good-quality day

Present research indicates that a good day care center does not interfere with a child's intellectual, social, or emotional development. (Larry Voigt/Photo Researchers)

care. Two psychologists who have reviewed the findings in this area have generally agreed and have reached three conclusions. (These conclusions apply only to *quality* day care centers.) First, children placed in day care centers continue to be attached to their mothers. At the same time, they show more independence than children who remain at home with their mothers. Second, after attending day care centers, children's interactions with their peers are more socially competent or mature. That is, day care children are more self-confident, self-assured and outgoing, and less timid. However, their social competence is not always in a positive direction; they may be less polite, agreeable, and respectful of others' rights. Third, children in day care show intellectual, language, and perceptual development either equal to or surpassing that of children who remain at home with their mothers. (Clarke-Stewart & Fein, 1983).

It is reassuring to know that *quality* day care centers do not retard the social-emotional or intellectual development of a child. However, Edward Zigler (1986), a prominent researcher in this area, cautions against generalizing the results from *quality* day care centers to centers that may have an untrained staff and a larger ratio of staff to children. Zigler says that preliminary research from lower quality centers indicates that infants and children may not do as well as those who attend quality centers. For example, Kathleen McCartney and her associates (1985) found that children in quality centers were more considerate and sociable than children in other centers.

If experts were to give Herb some advice about day care centers, here is what they might say. First, try to find a quality center, which is determined primarily by the presence of a trained staff and an appropriate child to staff ratio. If the child is under 2 years old, the child to staff ratio should be no higher than four infants for every one staff member. This low ratio is necessary because infants need to develop a warm, consistent, nurturing relationship with their caretakers or sitters. If the child is over 2 years old, a quality child to staff ratio increases to eight to one because these children are beginning to socialize and interact with their peers. Thus, parents of children over 2 years old have more leeway when selecting a day care center than do parents of infants (Meredith, 1986).

REVIEW

Sam, only 2 weeks old, has his parents worried by his constant fussing and crying. Sam may have a fussy or difficult (1) _____, and this will influence his parents' responses to him. If the parents understand the principle of (2) _____, they will take special care to react toward Sam with patience and sensitivity, thus making sure that they do not contribute to his fussy behavior. Sam's parents would be pleased to learn that generally a newborn's temperament is not very predictive of later emotional behaviors.

After several months, Sam's parents are especially happy to see that Sam (3) _____ when he sees their faces. Around the age of 6 months, Sam can recognize his parents' faces partly because his sensory systems are almost as well developed as an adult's. This marks the beginning of a period when Sam will develop a social (4) _____ to his mother and father. If his parents are sensitive and responsive to his needs, Sam will develop what is called a (5) _____ attachment; if they are not, he will develop what is called an (6) _____ attachment. Sam becomes very upset when his parents leave him with a new babysitter, a sign of stranger anxiety as well as (7) _____ anxiety.

During his first six years, Sam suffers a number of traumatic experiences, including his parents' divorce and a long hospitalization. Whether these early traumatic experiences cause Sam later emotional problems depends on many factors. Children who cope well with early setbacks, called (8) _____ children, are more likely to have easy temperaments, secure attachments, well-developed social skills, and the ability to act independently.

Freud's theory of (9) _____ stages and Erikson's theory of (10) _____ stages are different ways of viewing Sam's early experiences. The study of resilient children has shown that positive experiences help many children survive early traumatic experiences.

Although Sam's early life has been far from perfect, we can predict that he will probably not be a candidate for child abuse. Both his parents are well educated and well employed, and we know that these conditions are not usually associated with child abuse. Researchers now know that child abuse results from a complex interaction among three factors: traits of (11) _____, traits of the (12) _____, and environmental conditions in which the family lives. Since both of Sam's parents do work, they are concerned about placing him in a day care center. Research indicates that good-quality day care does not retard a child's emotional, social, or intellectual development. The critical factor in good day care seems to be the ratio of (13) _____ to children.

Answer: (1) temperament or disposition; (2) bidirectionality; (3) smiles; (4) attachment; (5) secure; (6) anxious; (7) separation; (8) resilient; (9) psychosexual; (10) psychosocial; (11) parent; (12) child; (13) staff.

GLOSSARY TERMS

anxiously attached (p. 350)

principle of bidirectionality (p. 355)

psychosocial stages (p. 356)

resilient children (p. 357)

securely attached (p. 350)

separation anxiety (p. 349)

social attachments (p. 350)

social smiling (p. 349)

Module 31 Cognitive and Sex-Role Development

PIAGET'S DEVELOPMENTAL STAGES

Tim, 7 months old, is sitting on the floor, playing with a ball. He brings the ball toward his mouth and tries to bite it, but the ball drops to the floor and rolls under the sofa. Although Tim saw the ball roll under the sofa, he neither points at the sofa nor tries to creep over and look for the ball. Tim's sister Sally, who is 3 years old, also saw what happened. Without any hesitation, she walks over to the sofa, looks underneath it, and gets the ball. Kate, who is 10 years old, walks into the room and sees Tim crying and Sally holding the ball. She tells Sally to give the ball back to Tim so that he will stop crying (author's files).

Does a rolling ball just disappear?

Jean Piaget spent much of his life studying the cognitive differences between children like Tim, Sally, and Kate. He observed the behaviors of hundreds of children in their natural settings—in their cribs, sandboxes, and playgrounds. After years of such observations, Piaget found that 7-month-old Tim perceives, thinks, and interacts with his world in a very different way than does 3-year-old Sally, and both differ greatly from 10-year-old Kate.

Here is how Piaget might describe his theory: I think that at whatever age—infant, child, adolescent, or adult—you try to understand and make sense of your world. Your understanding has occurred primarily through an interactive process between you and the environment. For example, your interactions with objects helped you develop the ability to figure out in your head where a ball had rolled. I call this **operations,** which is the ability to perform actions mentally or to rehearse some sequence of events in your head. I am convinced that your ability to perform operations was basic to your cognitive development. As illustrated by Tim, Sally, and Kate, I propose that your understanding of the world underwent several major changes or reorganizations. I divide these major changes into four cognitive stages. You proceeded from one stage to another through the processes of assimilation and accommodation.

Assimilation means that you incorporate some object or experience into your present strategies or concepts. For example, if you were given a stuffed cat when you were a year old, you would try to put part of it into your mouth. You incorporate or assimilate the stuffed cat into one of your existing strategies for dealing with the world—putting things into your mouth. **Accommodation** means that you modify your actions in response to some new environmental demand. If you happened to encounter a live cat, you might try to put some part of it into your mouth. You would then discover that the cat hisses and scratches and does not fit into your idea of a toy. You would have to change your behaviors and accommodate to the new object by petting it instead of putting it into your mouth. As you learn to make accommodations, such as how to treat a live cat, you reach a state of *equilibrium* or of cognitive harmony with your environment. I believe that you and all humans go through the same four stages in learning to understand your environment, but you pass through these four stages at different speeds (Ginsburg & Opper, 1979).

Piaget is best known for his four stages of cognitive development. However, one writer suggests that Piaget's most important contribution was not his idea of stages; rather, it was his observation that you come to understand your world by interacting with it, by seeking out challenges and making your own interpretations of events (Kuhn, 1984).

The Sensorimotor Stage

What is a baby "thinking" when a ball rolls out of sight?

As a newborn, Tim shows responses that are primarily reflexive, such as sucking and grasping. At 7 months, he can reach out and grasp a ball and bring it to his mouth. However, if the ball rolls out of sight, Tim does not search for it. His lack of searching indicates that Tim thinks that an out-of-sight object no longer exists. At the end of his first year, Tim will search for a ball that rolls under the sofa.

According to Piaget, Tim has learned the concept of **object permanence,** that objects are permanent and do not cease to exist if hidden from view. By the time he is 2 years old, Tim has learned to perform *mental actions* to solve problems, such as how to get a cookie from the shelf. He can also imitate the actions of others, such as using a chair to reach the shelf, as he saw his sister Kate do. According to Piaget, Tim's cognitive abilities, especially learning object permanence and how to perform mental actions, are characteristic of infants at the end of the *sensorimotor stage.*

The sensorimotor stage is the first of four stages and lasts from birth to about 2 years old. (The ages Piaget gives for each stage serve as approximate guidelines, since children vary greatly in their acquisition of cognitive abilities.) During the sensorimotor period, Tim's cognitive development occurs mainly through sensory experiences and motor actions. It is not until the end of this stage that he is able to think about things that are not present and form simple plans for solving problems.

According to Piaget, Tim develops from an infant who simply senses and behaves into a problem-solving child by using the processes of assimilation and accommodation. Through assimilation, Tim incorporates a new object into one of his existing strategies, such as putting it into his mouth. Through accommodation, Tim changes his behavior because of some new demand, such as learning to throw and catch a ball. As time passes, he will be required to make more complex accommodations. Next he will learn not to throw and catch balls in the house.

This young child saw a toy duck, then a blanket was placed over it. This child has learned the concept of object permanence as he lifted the blanket to retrieve the toy. (Hazel Hankin)

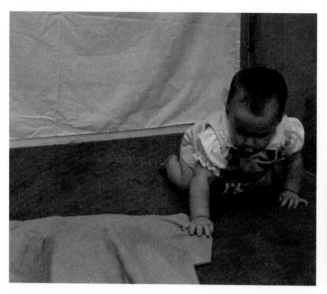
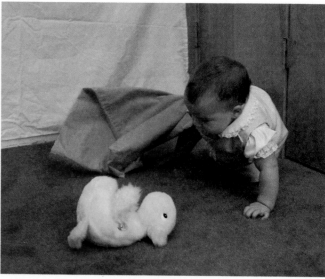

The Preoperational Stage

Sally, 3 years old, is playing with her toy animals. She gets a shoebox and puts all the animals inside. While making loud truck sounds, she moves the box around the floor, pretending it is a truck. When asked what she is doing, she explains that she is taking her favorite animals to the park.

When does a child learn to pretend?

Sally's ability to pretend that a box is a truck and to use words to communicate indicates that she can use *symbols*. This marks her entrance into Piaget's preoperational stage. Her ability to use symbols opens up a whole new way to understand and interact with her world. Whenever she wants, she can use symbols to pretend or to talk about things that are not physically present. Although Sally can use and manipulate symbols in speech and play, her thinking differs in several ways from that of adults.

One of the characteristics of preoperational thought is that Sally tends to see the world from a very self-centered or **egocentric** (ee-goh-SEN-trik) viewpoint and has difficulty seeing something from another's viewpoint. When she wants a cookie, she tries to get one without considering her mother's rule about no cookies between meals. When she wants a toy, she may take it from her younger brother without considering that it will make Tim cry. Because she is alive, Sally believes that the sun and moon are alive also and that they follow her around. According to Piaget, Sally's use of symbols and her egocentric thinking are characteristic of behaviors during the **preoperational stage.** This second of Piaget's four stages lasts from approximately 2 to 7 years of age.

Concrete Operations

Three-year-old Sally watches as Kate takes two identical bottles of soda out of the refrigerator. One Kate keeps for herself, and the other she pours into a short, wide glass for Sally. The soda fills the glass only two-thirds of the way. Sally becomes upset when she sees what she is getting. She says she wants the same amount of soda as Kate has in her bottle. Kate tells her that the two amounts are equal, but Sally refuses to believe her (author's files).

What happens if you pour soda from a tall skinny bottle into a short wide glass?

Sally thinks that there is less soda in the glass because the glass is only two-thirds full. Sally, at the preoperational stage, has difficulty understanding that quantities can remain the same even though they take on different shapes and arrangements.

Kate, who is 10, knows that the amount of soda in the glass is the same as in the bottle. She has learned the principle of *conservation,* which means that things remain the same although their shape or arrangement is changed. She recognizes that a change in one dimension, such as height, can be compensated for by a change in another dimension, such as width. She has also learned how to arrange objects according to some dimension, such as arranging all her pencils according to length. She has learned to think about relationships between objects. She knows that a baseball is larger than a marble but smaller than a basketball.

Sally, in the preoperational stage, thinks in more absolute terms. She would have a difficult time thinking that a baseball can be both larger and smaller than other objects. In addition, Kate has learned how to classify objects according to categories, and she understands that objects may fit into more than one category. For example, suppose Kate were shown four black puppies and two brown ones. If she were asked, "Are there more black puppies or more puppies?" Kate would answer "more puppies." If Sally were asked the same question, she would answer "more black puppies." Unlike Sally, Kate has learned that the object "black puppy" belongs

John looks at the short, wide beaker of water and watches as it is poured into a tall, thin beaker. When he is asked whether there is more or less water in the tall beaker, he replies that there is more. John has not yet learned the principle of conservation. (Mimi Forsyth/Monkmeyer)

to two categories (color and animal) at the same time. In contrast, Sally pays attention only to color and classifies the animals only according to this trait.

According to Piaget, Kate's cognitive abilities, such as arranging, classifying, and figuring out relationships, indicate that she is in the stage of **concrete operations.** This is the third of Piaget's four stages and lasts from approximately 7 to 11 years. Piaget calls this stage "concrete" because even though Kate can easily think about relationships among real objects, she has difficulty thinking about relationships among imaginary or hypothetical objects and situations.

Formal Operations

When asked if yellow grass would still have to be cut, Sally, in the preoperational stage, would reply that grass cannot be yellow. Kate, in the concrete operations stage, would reply that you cut only green grass. She would have difficulty thinking about a hypothetical situation in which grass was yellow. In contrast, 14-year-old Andy would reply that if yellow grass had the same properties as green grass, then you would have to cut it. If yellow grass was artificial or was dead grass, you would not have to cut it.

Notice that Andy can think about hypothetical problems and can use logic to solve them. Andy's ability to use logic allows him to solve a whole range of problems that Kate cannot solve. For example, Andy could solve the following kind of problem.

> Bill is shorter than John.
> John is shorter than Mike.
> Mike is _____ than Bill?
>   shorter/taller

Andy would reason that Mike is taller than Bill. His solution indicates that he has learned to solve abstract problems in a systematic manner. Andy has the ability to pass high school chemistry and physics classes, while Kate does not. According to Piaget, Andy's ability to solve abstract problems in a logical manner is characteristic of the stage of **formal operations,** which begins at about age 12 and continues through adulthood. Formal operations is the fourth and last stage in Piaget's theory.

BEYOND PIAGET

Almost singlehandedly, Piaget changed the way psychologists view cognitive development. Most psychologists would agree with Piaget that, as children develop, there are major qualitative differences in their cognitive abilities, in the way they think and reason. They would also agree that many of these changes occur through interactions with the environment, and that children are active rather than passive participants in their cognitive development (Gelman & Baillargeon, 1983).

However, many psychologists now question Piaget's explanation of what happens during his proposed stages. Researchers have found that changing the way in which a task is presented changes the ability of children to solve the problem. For example, preoperational children solved hypothetical problems about who is taller or shorter than whom, provided the problems were repeated many times (Kuhn, 1984). Piaget had held that only children in later stages would be able to solve these kinds of problems. Thus, Piaget's stages of cognitive development may not be as rigid as he proposed.

MAJOR CONCEPT   Piaget's Theory of Cognitive Development

The famous developmental psychologist Jean Piaget helped to create the current view of children as active participants in their own cognitive development. By this Piaget meant that children are constantly striving to understand what they encounter, and in the process they form their own hypotheses about how the world works.

Below are some of the major concepts in Piaget's theory. Match each one with the appropriate description.

1. Assimilation

2. Accommodation

3. Preoperational stage

4. Stage of concrete operations

5. Sensorimotor stage

6. Stage of formal operations

a. **5** When a child does not yet understand that an object that disappears from sight still exists somewhere, he or she is in this cognitive stage.

b. **4** The child who knows that as a coiled piece of string is pulled out it does not actually grow longer is in this stage of development.

c. **6** The child who is able to think abstractly, reason systematically, and solve "what-if" problems has reached this cognitive stage.

d. **3** A child who is able to use language but who still has trouble seeing the world from another person's viewpoint is in this stage of development.

e. **1** A 6-month-old baby is displaying this concept when she puts the corner of a book in her mouth and tries to suck on it because mouthing things is one of her major strategies for exploring the world.

f. **2** A baby is displaying this concept when he discovers that sucking is not effective for getting milk out of a cup, and so gradually learns a new strategy for drinking.

Answers: a(5); b(4); c(6); d(3); e(1); f(2)

Today, psychologists are dividing cognitive development into separate areas of memory, problem solving, creativity, and social interactions. For each of these areas, there is a flexible schedule for change and growth which is affected both by a person's age and the quality of his or her environment (Chance & Fischman, 1987).

SEX-ROLE DEVELOPMENT

Karen likes for me to wipe her face. She doesn't like to be dirty and yet my son, Bob, is quite different. I can't wash his face for anything. I have noticed that Karen seems to be daintier. Maybe it's because I encourage it. One thing that really amazes me is that Karen is so feminine. I've never seen a little girl so neat and tidy as she can be when she wants to be. She just loves to try on a new dress and have her hair set (adapted from Money, 1975).

When does a child start to act like a boy or girl?

This seems to be nothing more than a mother's description of her young son and daughter. But it is much more because Karen began life as a male, as one of a pair of identical male twins. During circumcision, one twin's penis was accidentally damaged and destroyed. When the twins were 17 months of age, the family decided to raise the infant boy as a girl, and reconstructive surgery was performed to make the child's genitals appear more like those of a female. After the family's decision to change the gender identity of the injured twin, the parents and remaining twin boy began to think of and react to her as a girl. The powerful influence of parents and peers on a child's sex role is dramatically illustrated by this case. Although both identical twins are genetically male, one has been socialized to be a boy, the other to be a girl.

Your sex role has had an incredible impact on almost every aspect of your life, including your emotional reactions, attitudes, sexual behavior, and psychological and social adjustment. **Sex role** refers to your culture's expectations about the different behaviors, attitudes, status, and traits of males and females. What is amazing is how early in life you began to accept a sex role. By the age of 2 or 3, you probably already showed a preference for "boy" toys, such as trucks and building blocks, or "girl" toys, such as dolls and dress-up clothes. What causes these *stereotypes* to emerge at such a young age?

The Process of Learning a Sex Role

How did you learn to behave like a boy or girl?

Within 24 hours after birth, your parents already had certain expectations about you. Fathers and mothers are significantly more likely to describe their newborn daughters as little, beautiful, pretty, and cute, when in fact infant girls do not differ from infant boys in size, weight, or general appearance (Rubin et al., 1974). Although parents often report that they treat an infant boy the same as an infant girl, careful observations of parent-infant interactions reveal a different picture. In one study, adults were more likely to offer a doll to a child they thought was a girl and a stereotypical male toy, such as a truck, to a child they thought was a boy. They were also more likely to talk differently to an infant they thought was a girl than to one they thought was a boy. One of the most interesting results of this study was that the adults, eight married couples, were generally unaware of treating boys and girls differently (Culp et al., 1983). Yet psychologists have found over and over that from birth on, parents subtly and not so subtly tell their children what sex-role behaviors are expected of them (Ruble, 1984).

Karen, who is now 6 years old, shows many stereotypic female behaviors and personality traits, such as wearing dresses, playing with dolls, being less assertive and more dependent. There is no doubt that sex roles are learned in the process of growing up. The question psychologists ask is how much of this learning is imposed by others and how much arises from the child's own motivations. To answer this question, let's look at how two theories would explain why Karen, genetically identical to her twin brother, came to act like a little girl instead of a little boy.

Social Learning Theory. According to social learning theory, Karen acquired her sex role because her parents and peers reinforced or punished certain behaviors and because she observed and imitated adult sex-role behaviors. This means that Karen acquires her sex role, such as a tendency toward dependency and a preference for dolls, through continuing experiences of reinforcement, observation, and imitation. Social learning theory is supported by the findings that parents do have expectations about how boys and girls should act and do reinforce stereotypical sex-role behaviors. However, social learning theory does not take into account the importance of the child's cognitive development and abilities.

Cognitive-Developmental Theory. According to cognitive-developmental theory, children are internally motivated to master their environments. One of the forms this mastery takes is learning social rules. Karen learns rules, such as male and female sex roles, by interacting with her environment, especially with other people. At the same time, she comes to realize that she is a girl and that certain behaviors are "correct" for girls and "wrong" for boys. Based on this knowledge, she develops an image of how girls should act and then acts according to her image (Maccoby, 1980).

Notice that these two theories are not contradictory. Rather, they differ in emphasis. Social learning theory emphasizes how the child learns sex roles through environmental processes such as reinforcement, observation, and imitation. Cognitive-developmental theory emphasizes how the child learns sex roles through internal processes, such as learning rules and forming images (Ruble, 1984).

Sex Differences in Abilities **EXPLORING PSYCHOLOGY**

In the 1870s, the United States Supreme Court based one of its rulings on an assumed innate difference between the sexes. The Court decided that it was not unconstitutional to deny a woman a lawyer's license on the grounds that her "natural timidity" made her unfit for this profession. This legal ruling was based on anecdotal rather than scientific evidence.

Based on thousands of studies, only four reliable sex differences have been found: (1) Girls tend to perform better on tasks involving *verbal* skills; (2) boys tend to score higher on tasks involving *mathematical* abilities; (3) boys also tend to do better on tasks involving *perceptual-spacial* skills; and (4) boys tend to show more rough-and-tumble play and more *aggressive* behavior than girls (Maccoby & Jaklin, 1974).

Generally, these sex differences tend to be relatively minor, and they do not necessarily hold true for individual males or females (Hyde, 1981, 1984). This means that if you know only someone's sex, you cannot accurately predict his or her verbal, spatial, or mathematical skills, or how aggressively he or she might behave. This conclusion is important, because it means that our present stereotypes of men as strong and intellectual and women as weak and emotional are not based on proved sex differences. Rather, these stereotypes are based on what people imagine sex differences to be.

Despite the fact that these differences are quite small, many people still want to know if they are genetic in origin. For example, in the late 1970s a heated debate erupted over whether the generally higher scores of boys on mathematical tests were innate or environmental in origin (Benbow & Stanley, 1980; Tobias, 1982). Researchers discovered that during elementary school, girls generally have higher grades than boys. Beginning in high school and continuing into college, females showed less interest and achievement in math and science compared to males. At the end of high school, researchers reported a consistent sex difference in math scores, especially at the extreme end of the achievement range. For example, for

Do boys and girls inherit different traits?

MAJOR CONCEPT   Sex-Role Development

Many people are misinformed about how sex roles develop.

Check what you have learned from this chapter by marking the following statements true (T) or false (F).

1. T/F Although parents often report that they do not treat sons and daughters differently, psychologists have observed subtle ways in which parents reinforce expected sex-role behaviors.

2. T/F Many psychologists believe that the motivation to act in accordance with socially expected sex roles may come in part from children's own desire to be competent in what they do—including competence at the various behaviors considered appropriate to their sex.

3. T/F The common stereotypes of men as active, aggressive, independent, dominant, and competitive, and women as tactful, quiet, sensitive to others, tender, and emotional have more basis in reality than many people would like to think.

4. T/F Even if the behavioral differences observed between the sexes are partly genetic in origin, these differences can be made even smaller than they already are by appropriate changes in the environment.

Answers: 1 (T); 2 (T); 3 (F); 4 (T).

---

every female who scored above 700 on the mathematical portion of the Scholastic Aptitude Test, there were almost 13 males (Stanley, 1987).

Why does this difference show up in high school and college, and what is it based on? Frank Besag (1987) reported that males and females in grades 9 through 11 did not differ on measures of overall grades, dropout rates, self-esteem, or math anxiety. He concluded that sex differences in math scores were probably not caused by math anxiety. One contributing factor toward sex differences in math scores appears to be that females receive less pressure and encouragement from parents and peers to choose a career in math or science. Camilla Benbow (1987) reported that of 2,000 mathematically gifted students, 63 percent of the males and only 35 percent of the females chose to major in math or science.

At this point, researchers have not identified which of many possibilities is responsible for the small but consistent difference in math scores between the sexes. Unfortunately, the one difference that the popular press focused on was a possible genetic or inherited difference. Whatever the reason, Susan Chipman (1987) believes that the interest in this discrepancy has been blown all out of proportion to its possible meaning and might be used to discourage girls from careers in math and science or to block the appointment of women to important governmental, business, or academic positions in these fields.

In general, studies of sex differences tell us that few exist and that those that have been identified are relatively minor (Hogrebe, 1987). More important, these studies provide little justification for our existing stereotypes that boys and girls, men and women, have large inherited differences in abilities (Ruble, 1984).

REVIEW

Robo the robot has no cognitive abilities. You are going to program Robo according to Piaget's stages of cognitive development. One of the first things you must do is program Robo to interact with its environment. You program Robo to sense objects in its path and when it encounters a new object, to move around it. Once this programming is completed, you watch with satisfaction as Robo smoothly navigates around chairs and tables. Upon encountering any new object Robo moves around it, using the behavioral strategy you have just created. What Robo is doing is similar to Piaget's process of (1) _assimilation_, in which children incorporate new objects and experiences into their current strategies and concepts. What would Robo do if it encountered an object it could not move around, such as a dog that kept getting in its way? Robo must be programmed to change its behavior and make a new response, such as making a scary noise. What Robo is doing in this case is similar to Piaget's process of (2) _accommodation_, in which children change their responses because of some new environmental demand.

If you programmed Robo to behave like a child during the late sensorimotor stage, Robo would know that objects are (3) _permanent_. Robo would also know how to perform simple mental actions to solve problems, such as figuring out how to plug its own battery into the charger. If Robo were able to pretend that it was a person and learned to respond to symbols such as verbal commands, you would say that Robo was behaving like a child in the (4) _preoperational_ stage. If Robo insisted on making scary noises whenever it chose, it would be demonstrating a very self-centered or (5) _egocentric_ way of thinking typical of children at this stage. If Robo knew the principle of conservation and could classify and arrange objects according to size, you would say that it was programmed according to the stage of (6) _concrete_ operations. If Robo were enrolled in a high school chemistry class, it would have to be programmed according to the stage of (7) _formal_ operations. At this stage, Robo could solve hypothetical problems, such as imagining how its structure would have to be changed to run on solar power. Of course, programming Robo to display such complex cognitive abilities would be very difficult, because no one yet knows exactly how humans accomplish these feats.

Robo the robot also needs a sex role. If Robo has no sex role, people will not know what social and emotional reactions to expect of it. You decide to give Robo a female sex role. According to social learning theory, Robo would acquire a female sex role primarily through environmental factors, such as being (8) _reinforced_ or punished for certain behaviors, or by observing and imitating how females behave. According to (9) _cognitive_-developmental theory, Robo would acquire a female sex role primarily through an internal desire to understand and master its world. Part of this understanding involves learning the behaviors expected of females and recognizing that these behaviors apply to oneself. According to research on sex differences, you might program Robo with slightly less rough-and-tumble play and slightly poorer mathematical and spatial skills than you would a male, but also with slightly better (10) _verbal_ skills. You also know that if you want to make Robo a mathematics whiz, this would not be incompatible with a female sex role, since sex differences refer to averages rather than descriptions of individuals. In any case, Robo will discover that the relatively few and minor sex differences do not justify the sex (11) _stereotypes_ that people have.

Answers: (1) assimilation; (2) accommodation; (3) permanent; (4) preoperational; (5) egocentric; (6) concrete; (7) formal; (8) reinforced; (9) cognitive; (10) verbal; (11) stereotypes.

GLOSSARY TERMS

accommodation (p. 361)
assimilation (p. 361)
concrete operations (p. 364)

egocentric (p. 363)
formal operations (p. 364)

object permanence (p. 362)
operations (p. 361)

preoperational stage (p. 363)
sex role (p. 366)

12

Adolescence, Adulthood, and Old Age

Module 32 Adolescence

THE SEARCH FOR IDENTITY

The high point for Warren was a high school graduation party. He and his friend picked up their dates and went to a pre-dance cocktail party. After drinking some punch, Warren loosened up. He took off his coat and tie and began drinking beer. Warren remembered liking the party and feeling full of energy. Everyone took off for the dance, which seemed like most other dances except for the fight in the men's room. After the dance, Warren and his friends stopped at a restaurant and had some more beer and wine with their meal. Warren remembers being "drunker than hell" and was glad his friend was driving. He could hardly wait to tell everyone about his wild, drunken time.

Lilly, a classmate of Warren's, spent some of her weekend at home, helping her mother clean closets and listening to Barbra Streisand records. She spent some of Saturday working as a clerk in a drugstore. Working as a clerk is very dull, but Lilly likes to have spending money. In fact, during her noon break, she bought an outfit for working out. Except for that, most of her weekend was dull. She thinks about what it will be like when she goes away to college.

Andy, also a classmate of Warren's, spent his weekend making a movie for film class. Throughout the weekend, he and his collaborators were involved in picking out locations, filming scenes, splicing, joking, and listening to sound tracks. From Friday to Saturday, Andy was completely absorbed in the filming, feeling more challenged and motivated than he had in a long time. At times he was so involved that he paid no attention to the feelings of others. He created havoc in his neighborhood and had a fight with his mother, who he thinks is an "incompetent bitch" (adapted from Csikszentimihalyi & Larson, 1984).

Although Warren, Lilly, and Andy seem to have very different problems, thoughts, and interests, Erik Erikson (1968, 1982) would say that they have one very important problem in common. In their own ways, all three are searching for who they are, for their identities. How do Warren, Lilly, and Andy find their identities as well as show personal growth throughout their lives? Erikson's answer is that they will progress through eight stages, with each stage focusing on a different **psychosocial** or interpersonal conflict. Please look at Figure 12.1 and notice that Erikson's stages begin at birth and continue into old age. As adolescents, Warren, Lilly, and Andy would be at Stage 5, which focuses on a conflict of *identity* versus

What are these three teenagers looking for?

371

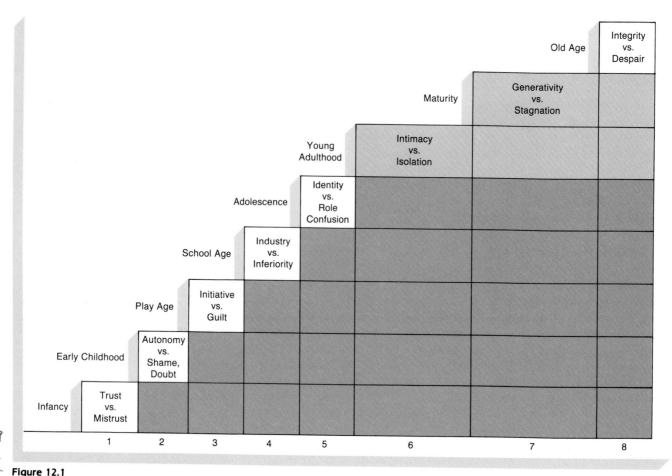

							Old Age	Integrity vs. Despair
						Maturity	Generativity vs. Stagnation	
					Young Adulthood	Intimacy vs. Isolation		
				Adolescence	Identity vs. Role Confusion			
			School Age	Industry vs. Inferiority				
		Play Age	Initiative vs. Guilt					
	Early Childhood	Autonomy vs. Shame, Doubt						
Infancy	Trust vs. Mistrust							
	1	2	3	4	5	6	7	8

Figure 12.1

According to Erik Erikson, each of us goes through a series of conflicts, called psychosocial stages, which begin in infancy and end in old age. Erikson believed that our personality development is greatly influenced by how we resolve the conflict at each stage. (Adapted from "Reflection on Dr. Borg's life cycle": Erikson, Daedalus, Spring, 1974)

Erik Erikson in a recent photograph. Erikson continues to work on his theories and to focus more now on the later stages of life. (Bonnie Schiffman/Onyx)

role confusion. In part, this conflict is brought on by noticeable physical changes which signal that Warren, Lilly, and Andy are no longer children and that childish behaviors are no longer appropriate.

But which adult behaviors, roles, and goals should they pursue? They find their answers by trying different roles, questioning their behaviors, and resolving their self-doubts. Erikson says that Warren, Lilly, and Andy's chief self-doubt is "who am I?" How they resolve this self-doubt will depend upon how successfully they resolve the conflict of Stage 5. Erikson believed that if Warren, Lilly, and Andy successfully resolve this conflict, they will achieve a sense of *confidence*, of knowing who they are. If they are unsuccessful, they might have low self-esteem and less confidence. In Andy's case, he must resolve his lack of concern about other people's feelings and his fighting with his mother to develop a sense of confidence.

As Andy becomes a young adult, Erikson says that he enters Stage 6, which focuses on a conflict of *intimacy* versus *isolation.* That is, will Andy establish close, meaningful relationships or end up feeling isolated from other people? If successful in resolving this conflict, Andy will continue to develop intimate relationships in the future. If unsuccessful, he may develop relationships but not intimate ones.

In middle adulthood, Andy enters Stage 7 and faces another crisis. Will he become productive, creative, and be a good example for others or will he develop a feeling that he is going nowhere and hang onto the past? Erikson calls this conflict between productivity and going nowhere a conflict of *generativity* versus *stagnation.*

In old age, Andy enters Stage 8 and faces his final conflict. Erikson calls this a conflict of *integrity* versus *despair.* Integrity means that Andy is satisfied with his life and feels that it has meaning. Despair means that Andy is dissatisfied with his life and has mostly regrets.

The advantage of Erikson's stage theory is that it alerts us to major crises that arise across the life span. The disadvantage is that we cannot be sure we will experience these stages in the order he specified or how we should deal with the crises when they do arise. Psychologists view Erikson's stages more as general descriptions, rather than as challenges everyone confronts in a certain order (Miller, 1983).

Nevertheless, psychologists do believe that the search for identity, which Erikson associated with the teenage years, often takes on unusual importance during that time of life. To understand how difficult and painful this search for identity can be, let's consider what American adolescents think about and feel during a "normal" week.

Imagine you are wearing a beeper. When it goes off at random times throughout the day, you are to write down your thoughts, feelings, and behaviors. For one week, 75 high school students did just that. Based on almost 5,000 reports from 13- to 19-year olds, researchers were able to put together a picture of adolescent feelings, thoughts, and behaviors. About 71 percent of the times they were beeped, the students in this study wished they were doing something else. The activities they liked best and what were the most rewarding to them were leisure pursuits such as art, hobbies, and sports. When asked who they wished to be with, they ranked, in order of preference, friends, family, alone, and classmates. In contrast to adolescents who were 13 to 14, those who were 18 to 19 spent 10 hours a week more with their friends than with their families, and more time with opposite-sex friends. One of the reasons adolescents often have poor interactions with family members is that adolescents have ten times more negative thoughts than positive ones when with their families. Examples of negative thoughts include "how pigheaded Mom and Dad are," "the bullshit exiting from my sister's mouth," and "how ugly Mom's taste is."

Compared with adults, adolescents have greater but shorter-lasting mood swings, alternating between extreme highs and lows. Compared with adults, adolescents are also more likely to perceive the world as filled with things that can go wrong, from family relations, to friendships, to dealings with teachers. Problems in these areas often cause much conflict in the adolescent's life, as the data in Figure 12.2 show. (Csikszentimihayli & Larson, 1984).

What emerges from this study is a portrait of an adolescent as someone who prefers the company of friends, thinks primarily negative thoughts when with family, finds each day filled with real conflicts, and experiences wide but brief mood swings. You can begin to understand the factors contributing to this often difficult stage of life by considering the great physical changes experienced at puberty.

What would adolescents rather be doing?

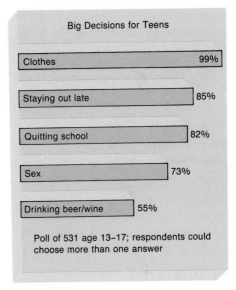

Figure 12.2
The majority of adolescents surveyed felt that they should decide these things for themselves. Because of their strong feelings about these issues, adolescents are likely to have serious disagreements with their parents. (Data from *Public Opinion*, May–June 1987)

PHYSICAL CHANGES AT PUBERTY ✱

Warren looks at his classmates taking showers and notices that many of them are taller, more muscular, and have more pubic hair than he does. He wonders why he is developing so slowly (author's files).

Between 9 and 14, usually around 11 and 12, an area of the brain, the hypothalamus, triggers the male pituitary gland to secrete certain hormones. These hormones circulate in the bloodstream and stimulate the testes to produce *testosterone*. Testosterone and other hormones from the pituitary cause growth of the sexual organs, penis and testes, and growth of secondary sexual characteristics, including pubic hair, increased muscle

What happened to your body during puberty?

mass, and a lower-pitched voice. Warren's personality and adjustment may be different, depending upon whether his puberty occurs early or late.

For girls, puberty may begin anytime between the ages of 7 and 13, usually around 10 or 11. This is when a girl's hypothalamus begins secreting hormones which, in turn, trigger her pituitary to produce other hormones that travel throughout the bloodstream. These hormones stimulate her ovaries to produce female hormones, one of which is estrogen. _Estrogen_ and other hormones cause further development of the external sexual organs, the vagina, and the ovaries, and the appearance of secondary sexual characteristics, such as pubic hair, breasts, and a widening of the hips. In addition, puberty marks a girl's **menarche** or beginning of the menstrual cycle. Whether Lilly experiences puberty early or late may also influence her personality and adjustment.

Besides the changes in sexual organs and the development of secondary sexual characteristics, Warren and Lilly will experience an enormous spurt in physical growth. The result of these physical changes is that Warren and Lilly will have an increased awareness of their bodies, be very concerned about physical appearance, report dissatisfaction with some part of their physical development or appearance, and experience more acceptance the more physically attractive they are (Siegel, 1982).

PERSONALITY AND SOCIAL DEVELOPMENT

Early and Late Maturers

Does it matter how early you reach puberty?

Warren was one of the last in his class to mature. As a result, many of his friends had an advantage over him in physical development, athletic ability, and social interactions. Generally, late maturing boys are found to be lacking in self-confidence and self-esteem and to be anxious, tense, more dependent on their parents, and less highly regarded by peers. Early maturing boys are found to be almost the opposite. They are more confident, relaxed, and socially responsible, and they are more popular and highly regarded by their peers. However, when early and late maturing boys were followed into their thirties, researchers found that many of these earlier differences had disappeared (Siegel, 1982). Although early maturing boys have advantages over later maturing boys during adolescence, the differences tend to disappear across years.

During adolescence, girls generally mature physically and sexually several years before boys. Early maturing boys have a social and athletic advantage, whereas early maturing girls usually do not. (Donald Dietz/Stock, Boston)

Lilly was one of the first of her class to mature. By the time she was 12, she had well-developed secondary sexual characteristics and was taller than most girls and boys in her class. In contrast to boys, early maturing girls do not have a psychological or social advantage. Psychologically, they may be more shy and introverted. Socially, they may be rated lower on social skills and poise and be less involved in social activities then their late maturing classmates (Siegel, 1982). However, the differences between early and late maturing girls also decrease with age.

Self-Esteem and Self-Concept

Lilly writes in her diary almost every day. "Tuesday was just awful. Mary and Sue are having a party and I was not invited. I'm sure it's because they don't like how I dress. I almost died in history class when the teacher caught me staring out the window. I was thinking about going to the dance with John, but he hasn't asked me yet. What should I do? What if my face doesn't clear up by Friday? Maybe Mary and Sue just forgot to invite me" (author's files).

Taken together, Lilly's thoughts, worries, feelings, and physical appearance are referred to as her <u>self</u>. You might consider the development of her self as a major part of her search for identity. Throughout much of her adolescence, Lilly will be self-conscious, self-admiring, and self-critical, all indications of how much she is focused on what is called self.

At the beginning of adolescence, Lilly may show a decrease in self-esteem. Compared to boys, girls show a greater decrease in self-esteem in early adolescence because they are more concerned with personal appearance. One study showed that females who eventually developed psychologically healthy adult selves went through several reversals. For example, as a preadolescent, Lilly might have been independent, with high self-esteem; as an adolescent, she might have been dependent, with low self-esteem; and as an adult, more independent, with high self-esteem. Males may go through similar reversals. As a preadolescent, Warren might have been passive; as an adolescent, active and irritable; as an adult, settled into a more stable pattern (Livson & Peskin, 1980). These data tell us that during adolescence self-esteem may undergo dramatic changes which are finally resolved in adulthood (McCarthy & Hoge, 1982).

COGNITIVE CHANGES

Thursday's entry from Lilly's diary: "I'm sure that everyone can see that my mouth is too wide and my lips are too narrow. I asked Mary and Sue about my mouth and they said that it might be, but that I shouldn't worry. That's easy to say. How can I not worry? Every time I look in the mirror, I see that it is too wide. If I know, then everyone must know. Everytime I talk to someone I know that they are staring at my mouth. I'm going to put tape over it" (author's files).

One characteristic of adolescence is **self-centered thinking**, the inability to separate one's thoughts and feelings from those of others. One result of self-centered thinking is that adolescents feel as if they are constantly on stage, performing before an audience (Elkind, 1974). For example, Lilly believes that everyone she meets sees that her mouth is too wide. Because of self-centered thinking, Lilly may feel uncomfortable in many social situations; she believes that others will evaluate her negatively, just as she does herself. Self-centered thinking may make Lilly especially sensitive to criticism, since she cannot separate others' thoughts from her own. Lilly may feel a special need for privacy so that she can find relief from her feelings of being constantly observed by others.

Why does Lilly feel that no one understands her?

Saturday's diary: "My mother just doesn't understand why I want to date Kevin. What if he is four years older than me? He's so much more mature. How can my mother be so dense?" (author's files).

In this case, Lilly's thinking is the opposite of self-centered. She is exaggerating the differences between her thoughts and feelings and those of others. This is an example of what is called a **personal fable**, a subjective explanation that is not based in reality (Elkind, 1974). Personal fables, such as "my parents cannot understand me," help adolescents think they are unique. In some cases, the use of personal fables can prompt adolescents to do unwise things, such as not using contraceptives because they believe they are unique and cannot get pregnant, or drinking and driving because they believe they will not get into accidents. Lilly's self-centered thinking and her use of personal fables are characteristics of adolescent thinking. Around the age of 15 or 16, both these kinds of thinking will decrease.

As you may remember from Module 31, the age of 11 or 12 is the beginning of Piaget's fourth and last stage of cognitive development, the stage of formal operations. During this stage, which lasts into adulthood, Lilly will learn to solve abstract problems and answer hypothetical questions. In the view of some psychologists, entry into the stage of formal operations will also affect how she reasons about moral issues.

MORAL DEVELOPMENT

Would you steal a drug to save your best friend's life?

Suppose your best friend is dying of cancer. You hear of a chemist who has just discovered a new wonder drug that could save her life. The chemist is selling the drug for $20,000, many times more than it cost him to make. You try to borrow the full amount, but can get only $10,000. You ask the chemist to sell you the drug for $10,000 and he refuses. Later that night, you break into the chemist's laboratory and steal the drug. Should you have done that? (adapted from Kohlberg, 1969).

Did you decide that it would be right to steal the drug for your dying friend? If you did, what did you base your moral decision on? Lawrence Kohlberg (1981, 1984) asked males of different ages to make decisions about similar kinds of moral dilemmas. Based on their responses, Kohlberg formulated a theory of how moral reasoning develops. His theory of moral development has three levels, with two stages at each level.

Preconventional Level. Most children under the age of 9 are at this level.

Not what you do, but why.

Stage 1: Focus is on obedience and punishment. Children make moral decisions based on avoiding being caught, getting into trouble, and punished. They do not consider the interests of others.

Stage 2: Focus is on making a good deal. Children continue to make moral decisions based on avoiding punishment but also want to further their own self-interests. In satisfying their own interests, they may make deals with other people, something they do not do at Stage 1.

Conventional Level: Many adolescents are at this level.

Stage 3: Focus is on conforming to expectations of those close to us. Individuals make moral decisions based on their feelings of loyalty to peers, parents, teachers, or groups and their desire to live up to what these people expect. Decisions are based primarily on the philosophy "do to others as you wish them to do to you."

— to gain acceptance

Stage 4: Focus is on laws, social conscience, and duties. Individuals make moral decisions based on their desire to maintain social institutions, such as the family, community, or country.

Postconventional Level: Many but not all adults reach this level.

Stage 5: Focus is on relativity of values, but there is a belief that some values, such as life and liberty, should be upheld in any society. Adults make decisions based on the idea that they are bound by a social contract. Under this contract, they are required to weigh and balance the rights, values, and legal principles of one person against those of a larger group, such as the community or society.

— to promote society's welfare

Stage 6: Moral decisions are based on universal principles, such as the right to life and respect for the dignity of others. Very few adults reach this stage. Examples of individuals using Stage 6 moral reasoning might include the civil rights leader Martin Luther King, Jr., the social reformer and pacifist Mahatma Gandhi, and the social worker and Nobel Prize winner Mother Theresa. The most recent system to determine an individual's level of moral reasoning does not make a distinction between Stage 5 and Stage 6. The result is that researchers now refer to five stages of moral development instead of Kohlberg's original six.

— transcends social norms

Once he had described the stages of moral reasoning, Kohlberg made two important claims. First, he claimed that you go through the stages in exact order. For example, you could not jump from Stage 1 to Stage 4. Second, the stages are arranged in a developmental hierarchy, with Stage 1 being the lowest level of moral reasoning and Stage 5 being the highest. Kohlberg added that we are either *at* one of the stages—that is, we show moral reasoning typical of Stage 4—or we are *between* stages—that is, we

According to Kohlberg's theory of moral reasoning, the juvenile delinquent obeys laws primarily because of fear of being caught and punished. The Boy Scout obeys laws because he wants to be a good person in his own eyes and in the eyes of others. (Left, Susan Lapides/Design Conceptions; right, Mimi Forsyth, Monkmeyer)

show some moral reasoning typical of Stage 4 and some typical of Stage 5, which is shown as Stage 4/5. Let's see if evidence supports Kohlberg.

Claim #1: Everyone goes through the stages in exact order (but not everyone reaches the higher stages). John Snarey (1987) reviewed 45 studies that had been conducted in 27 different cultures around the world. The studies used moral dilemmas similar to the one about stealing the drug, but the dilemmas were adapted to the particular culture. Snarey concluded that individuals around the world progressed through the stages in exact order but not everyone reached the higher stages. For example, there was evidence that people in all cultures used moral reasoning typical of Stages 1 through 4. However, people in communistic and communal societies did not show evidence of moral reasoning typical of Stage 5. According to Snarey's review, there is strong support for Kohlberg's first claim, which says that people in various cultures pass through the stages in exact order, but not everyone in every culture reaches the higher stages.

Claim #2: The stages represent a development hierarchy with Stage 1 being the lowest stage of moral reasoning and Stage 5 being the highest. Kohlberg believed that one did not reach the higher stages until about the age of 18 and that continuing education facilitated reaching the higher stages. One way to investigate Kohlberg's second claim is to compare the moral reasoning of individuals who are in different age groups, have different educational levels, or display different behavior patterns. For example, at what stage would you rank the following groups: college students, teenage delinquents, social activists, and convicted adult felons?

As might be predicted from their young age and limited educational experience, teenage delinquents were found to use moral reasoning typical of Stages 1 and 2 (Niles, 1986). Convicted felons who were on parole primarily used moral reasoning typical of Stage 3, but none of them used moral reasoning typical of Stage 5 (Van Voorhis, 1985). Since discussion and role playing are encouraged and facilitated in college, college students should reach higher stages of moral reasoning. Indeed, researchers found that no college students were at Stage 2. The majority of college students showed moral reasoning typical of either Stage 3/4 or Stage 4/5 (Colby et al., 1983). Finally, college students who might be considered social activists because they participated in sit-ins during the 1960s were reported to use primarily Stage 4/5 reasoning (Candee & Kohlberg, 1987).

These studies generally support Kohlberg's second claim, which says that the five stages are arranged in a hierarchy from low to high stages of moral reasoning and development. Reaching the higher stages of moral development is related to cognitive development, which in turn, is facilitated by a continuing educational experience.

Although Kohlberg's stages are useful ways to analyze moral reasoning, researchers have made several criticisms. First, being at a higher stage of moral reasoning or being able to describe higher moral principles does not guarantee that the person will actually behave according to those principles (Kurtines & Greif, 1974). For example, many college students are at the higher levels, yet repeated surveys of college students indicated that a high percentage of them engage in various kinds of cheating. In addition, Kohlberg's stages do not reflect possible sex differences, since his data were gathered from males. Let's look at this criticism more closely.

Are There Sex Differences in Moral Reasoning?

Janice said, "I didn't want to. I hadn't planned to. I was in shock when I found out." Two weeks earlier, Janice had been told that she was pregnant. Now she was talking to a counselor about whether to have the baby or have an abortion.

Carol Gilligan (1977) asked women in Janice's situation how they reached their moral decisions whether to continue their pregnancy or have an abortion. Gilligan discovered that women talked about issues of selfishness, responsibility, care, avoiding hurt, and their relationships with others in making their moral decisions, which she called a _care orientation_. In contrast, Kohlberg had found when talking about making moral decisions, men focused on issues of law, equality, and reciprocity, which is called a _justice orientation_. Is it true that men use more of a justice orientation and women use more of a care orientation in making moral decisions? In studying this possible difference, Maureen Ford and Carol Lowery (1986) asked college students to fill out a questionnaire on moral dilemmas they had recently experienced. The researchers reported a small difference in moral reasoning between men and women and that both men and women used care and justice orientations. However, there was evidence that women were more consistent in their use of a care orientation and that men were more consistent in their use of a justice orientation in making moral decisions. We can conclude that the sex differences in moral reasoning are small but that there is a consistent difference in the kind of orientation that men and women use.

One of the most serious moral decisions that one makes concerns the taking of one's own life. Let's examine some of the events and psychological factors that contribute to the relatively high rates of suicide among America's youth.

APPLYING PSYCHOLOGY

Adolescents and Suicide

Dear Mom, Dad, Chuck, Family and Friends,
    I am sorry I had to go and do this. I know I am running from a problem that is nobody's fault but mine. I know I'm letting a lot of people down. I just can't take the pain and hurt I have brought upon myself. I could never be happy again without Kathy. . . . I am really sorry for letting everybody down. Mom and Dad, I really love you a lot and I'm really sorry. Thanks for putting up with all my shit for so long.

All my love forever,
Scott (Breskin, 1984, p. 26)

The suicide rate for young Americans ages 15–24 peaked in 1977 with 5,565 deaths. Since 1977, the suicide rate has continued to drop slightly each year except for a slight increase in 1984 (_Los Angeles Times_, November 19, 1986). Among young Americans, suicide is currently the fourth leading cause of death, accounting for approximately 5,000 deaths per year. Approximately four or five more males than females commit suicide.

Could Scott's suicide have been prevented?

Scott's suicide note points to one of the major traumatic events that triggers suicide in young people, namely, the breakup of a relationship. Robert Litman (1986) of the Los Angeles Suicide Prevention Center has identified events that cause shame, guilt, or humiliation as being especially difficult for young people's immature self-concepts to handle. That is the reason that the breakup of a relationship, a serious family fight, or getting into trouble can become such powerful impetuses for suicide.

In an attempt to understand the causes of suicide, David Shaffer (1986) analyzed the lives of 160 youths who killed themselves between 1984 and 1986 in the greater New York area. He found that 80 percent of the suicide victims were male. The most common event to push someone to suicide was getting into trouble; often the victims had used drugs or had a drug problem. Shaffer also found that strife and psychological abuse was significantly higher in families of the suicide victims. In a similar study, Mohammad Shaffi (1986) studied the lives of 21 suicide victims, 19 males and 2 females, by interviewing their families, friends, teachers, and other contacts. Shaffi found that about 70 percent were drug or alcohol abusers, 76 percent were depressed, 70 percent had been in trouble with the law or involved in impulsive or antisocial behaviors. He reported that 85 percent of the victims had talked about their intent in one way or another and 40 percent had made a prior attempt. As a result of his study, Shaffi believes that completed suicides are the end result of serious emotional problems that, in most cases, are not recognized or not treated.

With this background on suicide, let's return to our original question, "Could Scott's suicide have been prevented?" In answering this question, Mary Rotheram (1987) proposed a model to identify those youths who may be at risk for suicide. The *at risk* factors for suicide include being male, having a history of antisocial behavior, having a close friend or family member who committed suicide, frequently using drugs and alcohol, feeling depressed, and previously attempting suicide. She considers a youth to not only be at risk but to be in *imminent danger* of committing suicide if the youth has current thoughts about or plans for suicide or is characterized by five or more of the at risk factors.

If a youth is judged to be in imminent danger of committing suicide, Rotheram recommends that a counselor take the following four steps. First, the youth is requested to make a written promise that he or she will not engage in suicidal behavior for a specified period of time, such as two weeks. Rather than agreeing, many youths in imminent danger refuse to make a written promise which confirms the seriousness of their situation. Second, youths in imminent danger are typically unable to see anything good or positive about themselves. The counselor needs to help the youth recognize and praise his or her strengths, and focus on the good things in the envi-

---

MAJOR CONCEPT   Adolescence

Adolescence is an often misunderstood stage of the life cycle. Below are some statements about adolescence discussed in this chapter.

Indicate which you think are true (T) and which you think are false (F).

T/F 1. According to Erik Erikson, the major challenge a person faces during adolescence is to develop a sense of autonomy and to learn to be self-sufficient.

T/F 2. Although we hear a lot about conflict between teenagers and their parents, studies show that adolescents in general think as positively about their parents as they do about their friends.

T/F 3. The insecurity and lack of self-confidence that late maturing boys experience usually stays with them throughout life.

T/F 4. By adolescence, a person's moral development has usually progressed as far as it is likely to go.

T/F 5. Suicide is the fourth leading cause of death among adolescents in this country.

Answers: 1 (F); 2 (F); 3 (F); 4 (F); 5 (T)

ronment as opposed to the unpleasant things. Third, although suicide attempts frequently follow arguments or breakups, youths typically deny how upset they are at the time. The counselor should help the youth recognize and assess the intensity of his or her feelings. If the youth can identify the point at which negative feelings are becoming intense, he or she will know when to seek help and support. Fourth, the counselor should help the youth make a detailed plan for what kind of help and support to seek when negative feelings intensify. A plan for getting help and support gives the youth an alternative to thinking about or committing suicide. From her experience in suicide counseling and prevention, Rotheram adds that if youths cannot carry out all four steps, it is another sign of their being in imminent danger of commiting suicide.

Scott's suicide might have been prevented if some family member, teacher, counselor, coach, or friend had recognized the presence of the at risk or imminent danger signs. If this had happened, Rotheram's four preventive steps might have been taken and Scott might have chosen to live.

REVIEW

"I want to go to the party. All my friends are going and staying out late too. I'm not a child. I know how to behave." Karen, age 12, finished talking and stared at her mother. Her mother was shaking her head "No."

According to Erikson, Karen's argument with her mother is typical of the problems encountered at one of his eight (1) _____ stages of development. As an adolescent, Karen is at Stage 5, which involves a conflict of (2) _____ versus role confusion. If this conflict is successfully resolved, Erikson believed that Karen would achieve a sense of (3) _____. When she becomes a young adult, Karen will enter Erikson's Stage 6, which involves a conflict of (4) _____ versus isolation. If successfully resolved, Erikson believed that in the future, Karen will be able to develop intimate (5) _____. When she reaches middle adulthood, Karen enters Erikson's Stage 7, which involves a conflict of generativity versus (6) _____. And finally, in old age, Karen will enter Erikson's Stage 8, which involves a conflict of (7) _____ versus despair.

As an adolescent, Karen is going through puberty, which is signaled by her first menstrual period, called the (8) _____, and by the increased secretion of the hormone (9) _____, which contributes to ovulation and the development of secondary (10) _____ characteristics. In boys, puberty is signaled by the increased secretion of the hormone (11) _____, which contributes to the development of secondary sexual characteristics. As Karen goes through puberty, her increased growth and sexual maturity results in an increased awareness and concern about her body and physical appearance; these and other worries relate to her developing concept of (12) _____. For girls, there is little social advantage to being an early maturer, while for boys the opposite is true. However, the differences between early and late maturers decrease through adulthood. Karen assumes that everyone is as concerned about her physical appearance as she is; this reflects an adolescents's (13) _____ - _____ thinking. Karen also believes that no one else understands her, an example of the use of personal (14) _____.

Karen's best friend asked her to attend a party, even though her mother has forbidden her to go. According to Kohlberg, many adolescents would use a (15) _____ level of moral reasoning, while younger children would use a (16) _____ level. As Karen develops into an adult, she may develop a (17) _____ level of moral reasoning. Kohlberg made two claims about Karen's development of moral reasoning. First, Karen would not skip stages but would progress through the stages of moral

reasoning in a definite (18) _____. However, depending upon her cognitive development, Karen may or may not reach the higher stages of moral reasoning. Second, Kohlberg claimed that the stages

are arranged in a developmental (19) _____, with Stage 1 being the lowest level and Stage 5 being the highest level of moral reasoning. Researchers have found evidence to support both of Kohlberg's claims.

Researchers found a small but consistent difference between the moral reasoning of males and females. For example, if we compared the moral reasoning of Karen's mother with that of her father, we might find that her mother was more consistent in the use of

a (20) _____ orientation while her father

was more consistent in the use of a (21) _____ orientation.

Simply being a female means that Karen is at a

lower (22) _____ for committing suicide since the ratio of males to females is 4 or 5 to 1. Some of the more common triggers for suicide in young Americans include getting into trouble or breaking up

a (23) _____. If a youth had five or more at risk factors or thought or talked about committing suicide, the youth would be considered to be in

(24) _____ danger of committing suicide. Suicide prevention depends upon the early recognition of the at risk and imminent dangers factors.

Answers: (1) psychosocial; (2) identity; (3) confidence; (4) intimacy; (5) relationships; (6) stagnation; (7) integrity; (8) menarche; (9) estrogen; (10) sexual; (11) testosterone; (12) self; (13) self-centered; (14) fables; (15) conventional; (16) preconventional; (17) postconventional; (18) order; (19) hierarchy; (20) care; (21) justice; (22) risk; (23) relationship; (24) imminent

GLOSSARY TERMS

conventional level
   (p. 376)
menarche (p. 374)
personal fable (p. 376)

postconventional level
   (p. 377)
preconventional level
   (p. 376)

psychosocial stages
   (p. 371)
self (p. 375)

self-centered thinking
   (p. 375)

Module 33 Adulthood
CONSISTENCY VERSUS CHANGE

What can happen to a high school prom queen?

I remember standing on stage in front of all the students. I was thinking "Can this really happen to me?" The next minute everyone was applauding and shouting my name, "Susan, Susan." It was my junior year of high school and I had been elected prom queen. It was like being in a fairy tale.

I cried at my high school graduation. I felt sad about leaving all my friends. At the same time I was excited about going away to college and being on my own. I considered myself a very sensible, logical, and level-headed person. So what did I do? I began seriously dating a guy who was my opposite. He was a fun-loving, kidding-around, cocky-type person. I met him in January, got engaged in February, and was married in September. Was that sensible and level-headed?

As I look back over my five years of marriage, I now realize that it was okay but not great. It was great to have two wonderful children. It wasn't great to have to move a lot because of my husband's job. The worst thing was that when I was pregnant the second time, I found out that my husband was having an affair. We got divorced soon after my daughter was born. It was hard being single again. Here I was with two children and no job. How many times can you start over? Thank God my parents helped me.

And then everything got worse. My 12-year-old son developed a brain tumor. He was in and out of the hospital, suffering through surgery, chemotherapy, recovery, and relapse. Several years later, he died. How does one prepare for the death of one's child? Without help from my parents and friends, I would never have survived. But survive I did.

I'm now almost 40. My daughter and I are doing pretty well. I think about getting married again. I don't know if I will. You see, I also like my independence. Come back and see me when I'm 70 and I'll tell you what happened (adapted from Wallechinsky, 1986).

Like Susan, most of you are beginning your adult years by going to college. No doubt you have an idea or dream of what you would like to achieve in the next 20 years. Susan dreamed of finishing college, getting married, and having a family. She did not figure on a divorce, having to support herself and her children, and her son's dying of a brain tumor, all before she was 40 years old. Susan's story brings up the two major questions of this Module: 1) How much will you change as you go through adulthood? and 2) What kinds of problems are in store for you?

Let's begin with the first question, "How much will you change between adolescence and middle age?" One way researchers answer this question is by studying the same group of people across many years. Suppose, for example, Susan's high school class was studied when they were 15, 30, 45, and 50 years old. This would be an example of a **longitudinal study**, meaning that the *same* group of individuals is studied repeatedly across many years. In contrast, a **cross-sectional study** means that groups of *different*-aged individuals, such as a group of 15-year-olds, a group of 30-year-olds, a group of 40-year-olds, and so forth, are all studied at the *same* time. The advantage of the cross-sectional study is that it allows us to immediately compare any developmental differences between the groups. However, the cross-sectional study does not allow us to draw conclusions about how the development of certain traits, such as being shy at age 15, will affect these same individuals at age 45. The advantage of the longitudinal study, which focuses on the same subjects as they grow older, is that it allows us to chart developmental patterns and determine how specific characteristics, such as being shy as a teenager, will affect later development. The disadvantage of the longitudinal study is that researchers must actually wait many years for their subjects to age. And, for any number of reasons, some of the subjects may drop out of the study. Despite these difficulties, researchers prefer longitudinal studies because they can study the developmental progress of the same individuals across time.

A Longitudinal Study

Psychologist D. Eichorn (1981) and his associates answered this question, "What kind of adult will I be?" by studying a group of 248 individuals from birth until they were in their fifties. We are only interested here in part of their findings: the continuity and change between adolescence, ages 14–18, and middle adulthood, ages 36–48. Eichorn found that the correlation between adolescent and adult IQ scores was about .80. This high correlation means that IQ scores were relatively stable across 30 years. Still, half the subjects showed as much as a 10-point increase or decrease. Besides IQ

What kind of adult will I be?

John Wideman, on the left, was a very good student and athlete. His younger brother Robby, on the right, was very concerned about black rights and led strikes at his high school to convince administrators to authorize black history courses. John became a Rhodes scholar, college professor, and novelist. Robby became involved in hard drugs and in murder, and was sent to prison. John's adolescent behaviors might have predicted that he would become a successful and responsible adult. Robby's adolescent behaviors gave little indication of what kind of adult he would become. (Both, Christopher Little/PEOPLE Weekly © 1985 Time Inc.)

scores, subjects showed considerable consistency in certain personality traits, such as impulse control and introversion-extroversion. For example, adolescents who acted impulsively or were extroverted during adolescence tended to behave that way as adults.

In predicting which adolescents would grow up to be mentally healthy middle-aged adults, Eichorn found that there were differences between males and females. If adolescent boys were responsible and intellectually competent, they were likely to become mentally healthy adults. If adolescent girls were intellectually competent and did not have stereotypic feminine traits, such as dependency and nonassertiveness, they were likely to become mentally healthy adults. However, the correlations between mental health in adolescence and adulthood were only moderate, which indicates that this time period involves considerable change and growth.

Eichorn did find a major difference between the concerns and stresses experienced by adolescents and middle-aged adults. Adolescents were primarily concerned about their physical appearances, issues relating to finding their identities, and questions about sex. Middle-aged adults were primarily concerned about forming an intimate relationship or building a marriage, establishing or maintaining a career, and reaching their set goals.

Eichorn's study makes several important points. First, you would have considerable success in predicting a middle-aged person's IQ score and certain personality traits based on measures taken in adolescence. Second, you would have limited success in predicting how mentally healthy a middle-aged person would be based on measures taken during adolescence. Third, you would have little success in predicting the kinds of concerns and stresses a middle-aged person would experience based on measures taken during adolescence. Eichorn's study presents us with an interesting conclusion. As we pass from adolescence through middle age, we will experience an interesting combination of consistency and change. Is it possible to list beforehand the kinds of changes and problems that we might experience throughout adulthood? One researcher has drawn up just such a list.

STAGES OF ADULTHOOD

Would you like to know your future?

Susan's story showed us that progressing through adulthood means facing a continuing series of problems, such as leaving home, getting married, and finding a job. Daniel Levinson (1978, 1986) believes that during your adult years you will face a series of problems that you may or may not solve. Levinson's theory is not about personality development but about the kinds of problems adulthood brings. After conducting a series of in-depth interviews with 40 men between the ages of 35 and 45, Levinson and his colleagues concluded that adults pass through a series of five stages, encountering a different kind of problem at each stage.

- Early Adult Transition (Ages 17–22)
  When should I move away from home? The problem at this stage is to develop a sense of *independence* by separating from your family and trying out different life-styles. The majority of Levinson's subjects moved away from home during this period of life, and about 70 percent of them went to college. Generally this was the time they began to develop some grand idea or dream about what they wanted to achieve.

- Entering the Adult World (Ages 22–28)
  Should I be serious about my career, or should I enjoy life? The problem at this stage is to explore and acquire the many different adult *roles* you will need in a career, in romantic relationships, and in other situations. If you spend too much time exploring all the possibilities and not acquiring any stable roles, life may seem to be meaningless. But if you choose stable roles very early, you may feel you have not explored enough.

- Age Thirty Transition (Ages 28–33)
  Should I stick with my present career? The problem at this stage is to reevaluate earlier choices and make decisions about them. For example, should you commit yourself more firmly to your earlier decision to build a career in business, or should you think about changing to a career in law? It is during this period that you decide what to do with your temperament and talents and what your goals should be. If you make the right decisions, you lay the groundwork for many productive and satisfying future years. If you make the wrong decisions, you may have many problems in the coming years. It was during this period that Levinson's subjects were most likely to change careers or seek a divorce.

- Settling down (Ages 33–40)
  How successful do I feel about my life? The problem at this stage is to be *successful* in the major areas of life, including career, intimate relationships, and personal dreams. Your sense of worth and accomplishment is tied to your perception of your success. For example, if you wanted to have your own business by the time you were 35 and do, you will feel successful. If you have not reached your goal, you may feel less successful and less happy.

- The Midlife Transition (Early Forties)
  Can I accomplish all that I wanted to? The problem at this stage is to evaluate life *goals* and *commitments*, keeping in mind that there is only a limited amount of time left. A feeling that time is running out contributes to what is often called the midlife crisis. At this stage, many people must face the prospect of not reaching some of their goals and not having enough time to make major changes in their careers. Eighty percent of Levinson's subjects in this age bracket reported serious emotional struggles.

- Entering Middle Adulthood (Middle Forties)
  What do I do now that it's too late to change? The problem at this stage is to learn to live with previous *decisions*. Some of Levinson's subjects solved this problem by showing more commitment to fami-

lies and careers. Others, because of decisions they had made during the previous period, had changed their commitments and life-styles.

What makes Levinson's stage theory different from Freud's theory of psychosexual stages (Module 36) or Erikson's theory of psychosocial stages (Module 32) is that Levinson does not focus on personality development. Rather, his theory centers on the *timing* and *type* of tasks we face throughout adulthood. His theory is concerned with our success or failure at these tasks, which depends upon how much we remain the same or struggle to change and grow.

Because Levinson's theory is based entirely on data from men, does it also apply to women? Priscilla Roberts and Peter Newton (1987) reviewed similar studies on women and reported that the timing and nature of the tasks were roughly the same for men and women. For example, during Early Adult Transition (ages 17–22), both men and women developed a dream or a grand idea about what they wanted to achieve. However, there were significant differences in these grand ideas: men dreamed of their careers while women focused on careers *and* on establishing close, long-lasting relationships. There were several other important differences between the problems faced by men and women. Women who were pursuing both a career and a relationship reported difficulty in achieving success in both. If the career goals of a husband and a wife conflicted, it was almost always the wife who sacrificed her goal. Further, husbands often discouraged their wives from pursuing interests outside the home. Compared to men, Roberts and Newton concluded that women attached more importance to and had additional concerns about relationships. Women were also far more likely than men to try to balance the dual goals of building a relationship and a career.

You will probably experience many of the problems described in Levinson's stages. For example, as a young adult you may have problems deciding to what extent you should follow sex-role stereotypes, problems forming a stable intimate relationship, and problems building a successful marriage. Let's look at each of these areas more closely.

ADULT SEX ROLES

What traits are desirable for a man and for a woman?

Write down the traits you think are desirable for a woman to possess and those you think are desirable for a man.

A woman should be

1. _____

2. _____

3. _____

4. _____

5. _____

A man should be

1. _____

2. _____

3. _____

4. _____

5. _____

What you have just done is similar to how researchers discover the stereotypes people have about men and women. You can compare the traits you listed with those 128 college students gave most frequently when asked the same question (Ruble, 1983).

A desirable woman is	*A desirable man is*
1. kind	1. aggressive
2. gentle	2. dominant
3. cries easily	3. less excitable
4. helpful	4. competitive
5. neat	5. acts as leader

The fact that today's college students describe men and women so differently shows that sex-role stereotypes are still very much with us.

What is wrong with sex-role stereotypes? For one thing, stereotypes encourage you to attribute to others traits they do not really possess. This is not so detrimental when a man is being viewed in a stereotyped fashion, for in our society the male stereotype is perceived very positively. Women, however, are less fortunate. When psychologists, psychiatrists, social workers, and college students were asked to specify the traits of a mentally healthy adult, the traits they rated as healthy corresponded very closely to those of the male sex role and were different from those of the female sex role (Broverman et al., 1970; Wise and Rafferty, 1982). Apparently, most people think that the stereotyped female sex role is not a very healthy one, primarily because it involves a passive rather than an active attitude toward dealing with life's problems.

When college students were asked to judge the advantages and disadvantages of being a member of the other sex, both sexes judged the male's sex role to have significantly more advantages and significantly fewer disadvantages than the female's (Fabes & Laner, 1986). One major advantage was the perception of the male's sex role as being more powerful and domineering than that of the female's. This perception of the male's sex role may lead to more career opportunities for men. However, most women pointed out that the male's stereotypic sex role had one serious disadvantage. Men who behave in stereotypic ways are required to be assertive, aggressive, or unemotional—all behaviors that may interfere with forming close relationships with other people.

One way to avoid the disadvantages of rigid, stereotypic sex roles is for each sex to adopt desirable "masculine" and "feminine" traits. Individuals who have taken on the desirable traits of both sexes are said to be androgynous.

In the past, having a particular sex role was associated with having certain kinds of jobs. Now sex roles are changing, as indicated by the increasing number of women who hold nontraditional jobs like this one. (Owen Franken/Stock, Boston)

Which sex role is considered healthier?

The Concept of Androgyny

Read the following list of adjectives and check those that you would like to think of yourself as being.

Adjectives		*Adjectives*	
1. ____	helpful	4. ____	confident
2. ____	dominant	5. ____	empathetic
3. ____	expressive	6. ____	assertive

The odd-numbered adjectives are associated with femininity and the even-numbered ones with masculinity. An androgynous person would be more likely to check all six. **Androgyny** (an-DROJ-ih-nee) refers to the idea that a person may possess traits characteristic of both males and females. Initially it was thought that a continuum existed, with masculinity at one end and femininity at the other, and each person located somewhere along this continuum.

The concept of androgyny assumes that there is no continuum, but that masculinity is independent of femininity. Because these traits are in-

Is there any advantage to being androgynous?

dependent, it is possible for someone to possess traits associated with masculinity, femininity, or both. Individuals who score high on stereotypic masculine traits are labeled "masculine," those who score high on stereotypic feminine traits are labeled "feminine," and those who score high on a combination of masculine and feminine traits are called "androgynous."

Sandra Bem (1974, 1976), the psychologist who introduced the concept of androgyny to the study of personality, originally assumed that being androgynous would allow a person to be more flexible in sex role. For example, an androgynous woman might function more effectively in the business world because she possessed both the stereotypic male trait of assertiveness and the stereotypic female trait of empathy. Similarly, an androgynous man might function more effectively in a personal relationship because he possessed both the stereotypic female trait of empathy and the stereotypic male trait of assertiveness. Although this idea seems very logical, it has received relatively limited experimental support.

What has received support is the finding that, in general, indicators of healthy psychological functioning are consistently related to masculinity, somewhat related to androgyny, and poorly related to femininity (Bem, 1979; Lubinski et al., 1983; Spence, 1983, 1984; Long, 1986). Here is how researchers explained this finding. Stereotypic masculine traits, which include taking the initiative and being in control, should result in a high level of success and this should contribute to healthy psychological functioning. On the other hand, stereotypic feminine traits, which include passivity and having less control, should result in a lower level of success and be less related to healthy psychological functioning (Frank et al., 1984; Long, 1986).

The success that a young adult will have in carrying out his or her grand idea of a career, relationship, or both may very well depend upon his or her sex role. Now let's look next at the kind of relationship that the vast majority of men and women choose, marriage.

EXPLORING PSYCHOLOGY Getting Married

Who was Susan searching for?

"I'd guess you would say I was a very sensible, logical, and level-headed person. That's probably why the first person I dated was very much like me. We had serious talks and read poetry together. After we broke up, a friend of mine said that she knew someone who wanted to date me. Can you imagine serious me agreeing to date Charlie, a fun-loving, arrogant, cocky, abrasive basketball player? Well I dated Charlie, got engaged, and about a year later we were married. I knew we were different, but I thought that was a good thing. Our marriage lasted five years" (adapted from Wallechinsky, 1986).

 ## Selecting a Mate

Susan spent considerable time and effort dating and selecting Charlie. In fact, for about 90 percent of the population, selecting a mate is one of the important decisions an adult makes. Psychologists have formulated a number of interesting theories about how adults select their mates (Figure 12.3).

David Buss and Michael Barnes (1986) believe that in seeking a life partner we form a mental list of ideal characteristics and then look for someone who matches this description. To determine the typical list of ideal characteristics, Buss and Barnes asked unmarried college students to rank traits for a potential mate in terms of desirability. The students' top 10 rankings are shown in the margin.

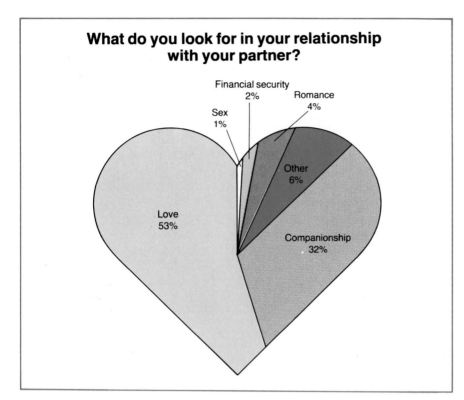

What do you look for in your relationship with your partner?

Financial security
2%

Romance
4%

Sex
1%

Other
6%

Love
53%

Companionship
32%

Figure 12.3
What people look for in a relationship. *Psychology Today* readers were asked, "What do you look for in your relationship with your partner?" The majority of those responding ranked love first and sex last. (From *Psychology Today*, July 1983, p. 46)

Men and women differed on their rankings of the three characteristics in italics. Compared to women's rankings, men ranked physical attractiveness as significantly more important in selecting potential mates. Compared to men's rankings, women were more concerned that their potential mate be a college graduate and have a good earning capacity. When married couples were asked to rate characteristics they considered important in their mates, their ratings were generally similar to the college students'. The researchers concluded that men and women do have somewhat similar mental lists of characteristics that they search for in potential mates. However, there were significant differences between men and women in their rankings of several of these characteristics.

After how many dates would Susan and Charlie mutually agree that each had many of the characteristics on the other's ideal list? That is, how long would it take for them to develop a lasting attachment? Although part of forming an attachment involves "falling in love," we have omitted a discussion of love here, since it was covered in Module 27.

1. Kind and understanding
2. Exciting personality
3. Intelligent
4. *Physically attractive*
5. Healthy
6. Easygoing
7. Creative
8. Wants children
9. *College graduate*
10. *Good earning capacity*

Forming an Attachment

How committed to each other were Susan and Charlie after only five dates? Would their feelings at such an early point in their relationship indicate whether they would be together four months later? John Berg and Ronald McQuinn (1986) answered this question by having college couples assess their relationship after five dates and again four months later. The students were asked how much they liked one another, how well they communicated, how satisfied they were, and related questions. Using these measures, researchers found that after five dates they could predict with about 85 percent accuracy which couples would still be together four months later. Compared with couples who had broken up, the intact couples had demonstrated more love, more behaviors that maintained the relationship, and had evaluated their relationship more favorably. Although previous studies indicated that the development of attachments is a slow, gradual process,

In 1983, Reverend Sun Myung Moon conducted the largest wedding ceremony in human history by marrying 2,075 couples. Some of the couples had not met before the ceremony, and some did not speak the same language. Under these conditions it would be difficult to establish a good communication pattern, which is one of the best predictors of a happy marriage. This may explain why 40 percent of these couples were divorced two years later. (Ethan Hoffman/Archive)

Berg and McQuinn's data suggest that attachments may form more quickly than once was thought.

Personality Characteristics and Long-Term Success

If Susan and Charlie had taken a number of personality tests, could a marriage counselor have used these tests to predict that their marriage would fail? In three large longitudinal studies, researchers correlated the personality characteristics of newlyweds with the success or failure of the marriage. Lowell Kelly and James Conley (1987), who followed 278 couples from the 1930s until 1980, reported a moderate correlation of about .5 to .6 between personality variables of the newlyweds and the success or failure of their marriages. This finding was consistent with the results of the other two large studies. In practical terms, a moderate correlation of .5 to .6 means that a marriage counselor would have had only limited success in using personality assessments of Susan and Charlie to predict whether their marriage would succeed or fail.

There are a number of reasons why psychologists have considerable difficulty in predicting marital success or failure based on personality assessments (Figure 12.4). Psychologists have no way of knowing, for example, whether couples who seem incompatible as newlyweds will recognize and work on solving their problems. Suppose a newly married couple has difficulty in communicating. If the couple is aware of this problem and tries to improve communication, the marriage will be more likely to succeed. However, if a communications problem is neither identified nor resolved, the marriage will be more likely to fail. In fact, one of the main reasons for trouble in relationships involves faulty communication patterns. Let's see how that happens, and what can be done to improve communication.

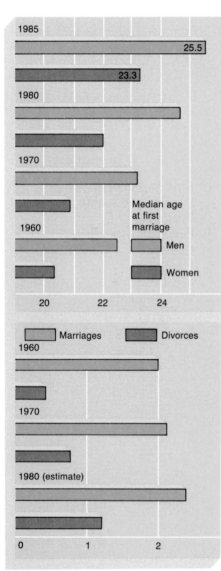

Figure 12.4
Marriage and divorce rates, 1960–1980. Along with the steady increase in marriage rates has come a steady increase in divorce rates: the divorce rate has more than doubled in the last twenty years. (From *Newsweek*, January 10, 1983, p. 45; *Time*, December 2, 1985, p. 41)

Communication in Marriage   APPLYING PSYCHOLOGY

As you read this conversation between an unhappily married couple, see if you can pick out their problem.

Bob: The thing that really gets me is that you are always running around and spending all your time with the kids and never have two minutes to sit down and talk to me. I'm just tired of having to spend all of my evenings alone, with you always so busy and always having a million other things to do and not having any time to spend with me.

Alice: How can I sit in front of the television all night with all the things I'm stuck doing and the work I have to do? If you would lift a finger and help out a little bit around the house, maybe I wouldn't be so busy.

Bob: You're just like your mother; you make work for yourself around the house. And another thing, you're always on the kids. You drive them crazy with all your picking and nagging.

Alice: You expect me to just be able to drop whatever I'm doing whenever you want and spend the whole evening with you. You don't appreciate all the time that it takes to take care of the children and just do the normal chores around the house, which you don't help out with. And you, you just ignore the kids (adapted from Broderick et al., 1981).

Psychologists have found that couples who report their relationships to be unhappy, called distressed couples, have a characteristic pattern of *communication*. Generally, distressed couples are more critical of each other's efforts, focus more on unpleasant events, and use punishment more than positive reinforcement in their interactions (Jacobson et al., 1982; Koren et al., 1980; Robinson & Price, 1980; Wieder & Weiss, 1980). If distressed couples do not change their communication pattern, we can predict that they will continue to experience a low level of marital happiness. In fact, a communication pattern that is low in positive reinforcements and high in punishment is one of the best predictors of future marital unhappiness (Markman, 1981).

How can distressed couples change their negative pattern of communication? To do so, they may have to seek professional help. If Bob and Alice consult a therapist who specializes in family problems, the first step will be to observe and record their interactions for a period of time. This baseline data will then be used to identify the situations most likely to create punishing interactions. Once they have identified problem situations, such as discussions of how to spend their time, the therapist will help them learn how to make requests and propose solutions to their grievances without accusing or punishing each other. For example, Bob would learn to say to Alice "I would like you to spend more time with me," rather than "You never spend enough time with me." Distressed couples who learned new communication skills, such as making requests without punishing their spouses, reported an increase in marital happiness and less distress (Jacobson, 1979; Jacobson & Anderson, 1980; Stuart & Roper, 1979).

Can anything be done to help Bob and Alice?

MAJOR CONCEPT   Adulthood

Please indicate which of the following statements are true (T) or false (F).

1. T/F   IQ score is one of the many things that changes greatly between adolescence and adulthood.

2. T/F   If someone is judged to be mentally healthy as an adolescent, he or she is almost certain to be mentally healthy as an adult.

3. T/F   Levinson's stage theory focuses on the timing and type of tasks that one faces throughout adulthood.

4. T/F   Men's grand idea of what they would like to achieve is focused primarily on relationships and careers while women's grand idea is focused primarily on their careers.

5. T/F   Androgyny refers to the idea that a person may possess traits characteristic of both males and females.

6. T/F   In selecting a potential mate, males are more concerned with physical appearance and females are more concerned with earning capacity.

7. T/F   Couples with communication problems are often too critical of each other and use punishment more than reward in their interactions.

Answers: 1(F); 2(F); 3(T); 4(F); 5(T); 6(T); 7(T)

REVIEW

Tim, who is 15, is talking with his father, who is 45. Tim wonders what he will be like in 30 years when he is his father's age. Tim's father replies that no one can really predict, because people change in some ways and remain the same in others. For example, one study found that IQ scores and some personality traits were relatively (1) _____Stable_____ between adolescence and adulthood. However, there was only a modest relationship between being mentally (2) _____healthy_____ as an adolescent and as an adult.

Tim wants to know what kind of problems he will run into as an adult. His father tells him about Levinson's five stages and how each stage involves a particular challenge and way of approaching life. For example, in the first stage, the early adult transition, you will think about moving away from home and developing a certain degree of (3) _____independence.___ In your mid-twenties, you will be entering the adult world and exploring a number of different (4) _____roles_____ that you will need for your career and personal life. At about age 30, you will be settling down, evaluating your notion of how (5) _____successful___ you are. In your late thirties, you will be in midlife transition, and will be evaluating your life's (6) _____goals_____. In your middle forties, you will be entering middle adulthood and will learn to live with the (7) _____decisions___ you have made.

Tim wonders if the problems his father faced were similar to those of his mother. Researchers have found that men and women experience roughly the same kind of (8) _____problems_____ at the same (9) _____times_____ as they progress through adulthood. However, men and women differ in their grand ideas of what they want to achieve. Men focus primarily on their (10) _____careers_____ while women focus both on their careers and on their (11) _____relationships.___

Tim has noticed that teenage boys are supposed to act very cool, while the girls are allowed to be more emotional. He asks why this is so. His father explains that this is an example of society's stereotypic male and female (12) _____sex_____ _____roles_____. He says that some people seem to grow up with a combination of both roles and are said to be (13) _androgyny_. Whether androgyny is advantageous is currently being questioned, but we do know that those who learn to adopt an active role, which is more similar to the stereotypic male role, are judged to be more mentally (14) _healthy_.

Tims squirms and asks about getting married. His father smiles and says that Tim will develop a list of ideal (15) _men_ and will search for these in a potential mate. Tim's father adds that men seem to consider (16) _physical attractive_ more important in a potential mate than do women. However, women consider being a college graduate and having a good (17) _earning_ capacity to be more important in a potential mate than do men.

Tim wonders how his father and mother have managed to stay married while some of his friends' parents are divorced. His father answers that it is very difficult to predict the success or failure of a marriage based on the (18) _personality_ characteristics of the newlyweds. In fact, the father admits that there were a few personality differences that gave him and his wife problems initially and sometimes still do.

This is a lot of serious conversation for Tim and he has only one more question. He wonders if there is a secret to being happily married. His father says that the secret lies in the couple having a good pattern of (19) _communication_. Couples who communicate well use more rewards than (20) _punishments_, focus more on (21) _positive_ than negative events, and aren't too (22) _critical_ of one another. Tim decides that he will watch his father and mother more closely and learn how to do that.

Answers: (1) stable, consistent; (2) healthy; (3) independence; (4) roles; (5) successful; (6) goals; commitments; (7) decisions; (8) problems; (9) times; (10) careers; (11) relationships; (12) sex roles; (13) androgynous; (14) healthy; (15) characteristics; (16) physical attractiveness; (17) earning; (18) personality; (19) communication; (20) punishments; (21) positive; (22) critical

GLOSSARY TERMS

androgyny (p. 387)

cross-sectional study (p. 383)

longitudinal study (p. 383)

Module 34 Old Age

AGING

"I'm 84 years old," Herman said proudly. "And I'll tell you the secret to my living so long." Herman sat forward in his chair and said in a clear voice, "Never retire. Never get fat. Never give up." Herman smiled and continued, "I've got this neighbor, Eileen. Well, Eileen's only 69 years old. There's really nothing wrong with her. But what does she do all day long? Sits around and complains about being old and how she can't do as much as she once could. Says she's afraid to take the bus and do her shopping and needs help around the house. I say she's just acting like a old person. Says she's too tired to take walks and old people shouldn't exercise. I say she's behaving like someone who's given up. Says she can't concentrate enough to read or have a hobby. I say she just won't make any effort to keep her mind sharp." Herman furled his brow and spoke in a very serious tone. "You be the judge. At 84, I'm 15 years older than Eileen. I'm also 15 times more active, healthy, and happy. I've tried to talk to Eileen. Tried to get her to stop acting old. She always gives the same dumb reply. She says

How's an old person supposed to act?

Although Fransie Geringer was only 8 years old in this photo, he was already totally bald and had facial wrinkles of someone many times his age. A rare and incurable disease (progeria) causes him to age at ten times the normal rate. His life span is about 13 years, and he will probably die from a disease of old age. (AP/Wide World Photos)

she's getting old and old people can't do as much and need more help. Well, that's nothing but crap. Just because you're getting old doesn't mean that you have to act old" (adapted from Fries & Crapo, 1981).

Is Herman correct in believing that Eileen is "acting old" rather than suffering from some psychological problems that inevitably occur with aging? When we talk about growing old, it is important to distinguish between normal aging and pathological aging. Both Herman and Eileen are experiencing **normal aging,** which is a gradual slowing of some of their physical and psychological processes. We will describe these processes a little later. In **pathological aging,** an illness, such as Alzheimer's disease (Module 4), destroys some part of the brain or body and results in serious physical and psychological deficits.

If normal aging is only a gradual slowing down of functions, why is 84-year-old Herman so much more active, happy, and healthy than 69-year-old Eileen? According to John Rowe and Robert Kahn (1987), the effects of normal aging can be overcome if individuals eat the right foods, exercise, and involve themselves in personal and social activities. For example, there are three communities—the district of Abkhazia in the Caucasus Mountains of the USSR, the province of Hunza in the Karakoram Mountains of northwest Pakistan, and the isolated village of Vilcabamba in the Andes Mountains of Ecuador—in which many of the inhabitants claimed to be between 120 and 170 years old. Although these claims were shown to be greatly exaggerated, these people *were* between 80 and 100 years old. What is the secret of their longevity? According to experts, the elderly inhabitants of Abkhazia, Hunza, and Vilcabamba eat a diet that is low in calories and animal fats, rarely become obese, use alcohol and tobacco in moderation, maintain a high level of physical activity and fitness, and feel actively involved and useful in their communities (Fries & Crapo, 1981). As you can see, this regimen describes Herman's life-style and is helping him overcome the effects of normal aging. Eileen, on the other hand, does not exercise, has few hobbies or outside interests, and exaggerates the effects of normal aging by "acting old."

Rowe and Kahn concluded that research on aging needs to focus more on how individuals such as Herman age successfully and happily. As researchers identify more variables that modify and overcome the effects of aging, such as diet, exercise, and involvement, they can develop programs to help people such as Eileen continue to enjoy life during their later years. The need for such programs is stressed by the information in Figure 12.5, which shows that the percentage of Americans 65 or older will continue to increase.

Let's look in more detail at the potential physical and cognitive changes Herman's and Eileen's bodies and minds might undergo as they reach their sixties, seventies, and eighties.

PHYSICAL CHANGES

How long can Herman expect to live?

Without getting a disease, Herman may live to be 100. Biology appears to set 100 as the normal limit to one's life span. The average life expectancy for male infants born in the United States in 1986 is 71.5 years and for female infants it is 78.5 years. One of the primary reasons that average life expectancy increases every year is that modern medicine develops new ways to treat health problems and control diseases. But why is it that our bodies age in the first place?

The National Institute on Aging sponsored a meeting of 140 scientists to provide current answers to the question of why we age and die (Schimke

& Agniel, 1983). According to their report, the body ages for a number of reasons. It ages because of inherited _genetic mechanisms_ that lead to age-related problems, such as hardening of the arteries, bone disorders, or brain changes resulting in senility. The body also ages because of changes in _DNA programming_ that lead to changes and errors in how cells function—for example, causing growth of tumors. The body ages because of changes in _protein synthesis_ that lead to a gradual decrease in skeletal muscle, brain cells, and other tissues. The body ages because of changes in the _immune system_ that lead to increased susceptibility to infection, tumors, and disease.

The body ages because of a combination of all these factors rather than any one of them (Burch, 1983). The age-related changes that occur in the body's internal organs, muscles, and brain can be observed in a number of external changes, as well as in behavioral ones.

Between the ages of 50 and 60, as Figure 12.6 shows, you may experience a gradual decline in height because of loss of bone, an increase in skin wrinkles, and a tendency for deterioration in joints. Lung and respiratory functions will decline with age, but this decrease can be slowed by a regular exercise program. _Sensory_ organs will become less sensitive with age, resulting in decreased vision, hearing, and taste. The heart, which is a muscle, will become less effective at pumping blood, and this may result in as much as a 35 percent decrease in blood flow through the coronary arteries. You will experience a general decrease in both number and diameter of muscle fibers, which may explain some of the slowing in motor functions that usually accompanies old age (La Rue & Jarvik, 1982, Stevens-Long, 1984).

How much these physical changes affect a person's quality of life depends upon many factors, including exercise, smoking, diet, and attitude. For example, two researchers studied a group of men with a mean age of 65 (ranging from 60 to 88) who had been running for the past ten years, currently ran about 37 miles per week, and regularly ran marathons (26 miles). Despite their age, these men reported about the same number of injuries as would be expected in younger runners (Hogan & Cape, 1984). Apparently, for some individuals the physical changes that occur with aging may be reduced by regular exercise.

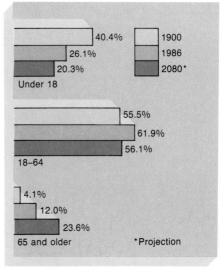

Figure 12.5
How we're aging: The dramatic change in the age composition of the U.S. population—the "graying of America"—is expected to continue through the next century. (Source: U.S. Bureau of the Census)

COGNITIVE CHANGES

A famous psychologist, Donald Hebb, noticed three particular changes that occurred as he entered his seventies. He had difficulty stopping himself from thinking the same thoughts over and over, keeping up his motivation, and recalling familiar words. "To put it simply, I no longer have the arrogant confidence that I can master the new ideas and developments in the field. . . . However, I'm not quite senile, not yet. I can still keep up appearances and there are points on which I can still out-talk younger colleagues. But—between you and me, privately—the picture is one of a slow, inevitable loss of cognitive capacity. For one of my theoretical persuasion, it's fascinating to watch" (Hebb, 1978, p. 18).

Why can't I think of that word?

What you should note here is that even though Hebb complains of decreasing cognitive abilities at age 74, he remains mentally alert and active and probably the equal of most individuals who are 30 or 40 years younger. Is Hebb right that intellectual powers inevitably decline with aging, or is his view too pessimistic? What answers do we have from psychologists who have studied cognition over the life span?

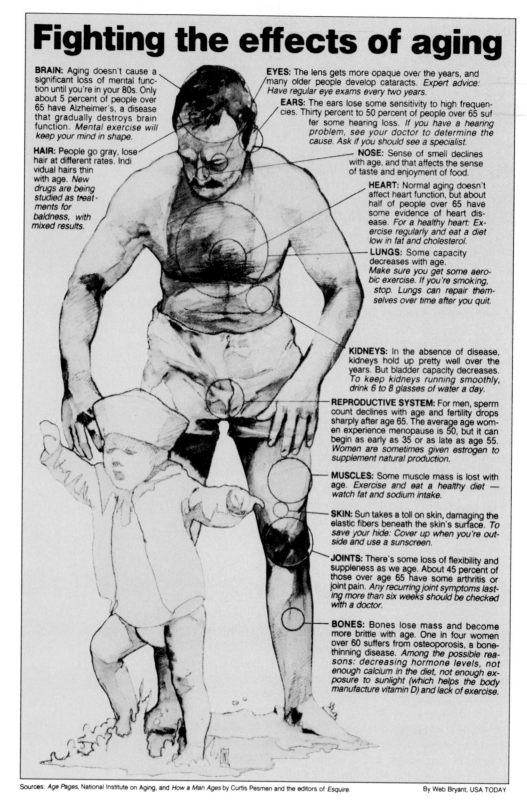

Fighting the effects of aging

BRAIN: Aging doesn't cause a significant loss of mental function until you're in your 80s. Only about 5 percent of people over 65 have Alzheimer's, a disease that gradually destroys brain function. *Mental exercise will keep your mind in shape.*

HAIR: People go gray, lose hair at different rates. Individual hairs thin with age. *New drugs are being studied as treatments for baldness, with mixed results.*

EYES: The lens gets more opaque over the years, and many older people develop cataracts. *Expert advice: Have regular eye exams every two years.*

EARS: The ears lose some sensitivity to high frequencies. Thirty percent to 50 percent of people over 65 suffer some hearing loss. *If you have a hearing problem, see your doctor to determine the cause. Ask if you should see a specialist.*

NOSE: Sense of smell declines with age, and that affects the sense of taste and enjoyment of food.

HEART: Normal aging doesn't affect heart function, but about half of people over 65 have some evidence of heart disease. *For a healthy heart: Exercise regularly and eat a diet low in fat and cholesterol.*

LUNGS: Some capacity decreases with age. *Make sure you get some aerobic exercise. If you're smoking, stop. Lungs can repair themselves over time after you quit.*

KIDNEYS: In the absence of disease, kidneys hold up pretty well over the years. But bladder capacity decreases. *To keep kidneys running smoothly, drink 6 to 8 glasses of water a day.*

REPRODUCTIVE SYSTEM: For men, sperm count declines with age and fertility drops sharply after age 65. The average age women experience menopause is 50, but it can begin as early as 35 or as late as age 55. *Women are sometimes given estrogen to supplement natural production.*

MUSCLES: Some muscle mass is lost with age. *Exercise and eat a healthy diet — watch fat and sodium intake.*

SKIN: Sun takes a toll on skin, damaging the elastic fibers beneath the skin's surface. *To save your hide: Cover up when you're outside and use a sunscreen.*

JOINTS: There's some loss of flexibility and suppleness as we age. About 45 percent of those over age 65 have some arthritis or joint pain. *Any recurring joint symptoms lasting more than six weeks should be checked with a doctor.*

BONES: Bones lose mass and become more brittle with age. One in four women over 60 suffers from osteoporosis, a bone-thinning disease. *Among the possible reasons: decreasing hormone levels, not enough calcium in the diet, not enough exposure to sunlight (which helps the body manufacture vitamin D) and lack of exercise.*

Sources: *Age Pages,* National Institute on Aging, and *How a Man Ages* by Curtis Pesmen and the editors of *Esquire.*   By Web Bryant, USA TODAY

Figure 12.6
Some ways to moderate the physical effects of aging. (From *USA Today,* May 20, 1987, p. 4D)

The dress and behavior of these adolescents seem very puzzling and humorous to the two older women. The differences in behavior and attitude of young and old is often referred to as the generation gap. (AP/Wide World Photos)

People in their sixties reported having significantly more problems with memory than people in their twenties. People in their sixties and seventies were consistently found to have some memory deficits, as in remembering a list of words, but these deficits tended to be relatively small (Cornelius, 1984; McCarty et al., 1982; Perlmutter, 1978). These data partially confirm Hebb's complaint of not being able to recall words as easily as he once did. However, when older adults were asked to practice a strategy for recalling words they performed at a higher level, indicating that some of their deficits can be reduced through training (Schmitt et al., 1981). In addition, older people showed no deficits in remembering facts or daily routines (Light & Anderson, 1983). Researchers have concluded that older individuals do not have difficulty retrieving information from short-term memory, but they need more time to retrieve information from *long-term* memory (Lorsbach & Simpson, 1984).

Another way to compensate for memory loss with aging is to continue to be involved in the educational process, such as taking college courses. Individuals in their seventies who were taking college courses showed no significant differences in memory or reasoning abilities compared with college students in their twenties (Blackburn, 1984). All these data indicate that although people may complain of memory loss as they enter their sixties and seventies, the loss tends to be mainly for verbal information, tends to be relatively small, and may be compensated for by practicing mnemonic strategies or by keeping mentally active.

How often do you forget words and names?
How often do you forget facts?
How often do you misplace things?

SEXUAL BEHAVIOR IN LATE ADULTHOOD

Among the common stereotypes about sex and "old people" is that the elderly do not have any interest in sexual activity or that it is inappropriate for them to engage in it. Masters and Johnson (1981) point out that the field of aging, called *geriatrics*, is one of the strongholds for the prejudicial stereotype of older people being asexual. There is a decrease in sexual responsiveness with aging, but this decrease need not interfere with sexual activity, provided the individual is in good health.

Older men and women may experience physiological changes that influence sexual behavior. Older men may require more time and stimulation to have an erection and reach orgasm. Upon ejaculation, there may be a reduction in force and amount of fluid. Older women may require more time and stimulation for vaginal lubrication, and there may be a

How does sexual responsiveness change after 60?

reduction in the amount of lubrication. The vagina loses some of its elasticity, which may lead to some discomfort during intercourse. With minor adjustments, such as using a lubricant, the elderly couple can usually compensate for these changes. They can also compensate for reduced responsiveness by longer periods of stimulation.

Older individuals may also experience a number of psychological changes related to sexual behavior. They may worry about their decreased physical responsiveness or interpret that decrease as an end to their sexuality. They may acquire the stereotype that sex is inappropriate for older people. If their partner dies, they may have difficulty finding another (Masters & Johnson, 1981). For many older males, sexuality plays a crucial role in maintaining self-esteem. For older females, feeling attractive, rather than sexual behavior, appears to be crucial to maintaining self-esteem. Generally, the more sexually active people were in their thirties and forties, the more sexually active they are in their sixties and seventies (Masters & Johnson, 1981; Stimson et al., 1981).

APPLYING PSYCHOLOGY   Nursing Homes

Residents can be observed sitting close to one another in the lobby or dining room, yet they rarely speak to one another. They may sit in a group facing a television screen, yet may not attend to or discuss the program. They frequently sit alone in their bedrooms, merely looking into space. When engaged in conversations, they often show a lack of interest. When told about some new event, they may show apathy. When asked to engage in some activity, they may show little or no creativity (adapted from Feier & Leight, 1981).

How can nursing homes be made more stimulating?

This is a description of residents in a typical nursing home. Because of serious health problems, about 5 percent of older people live in nursing homes. How can we explain their withdrawn behavior? One important factor is the *unstimulating* environment of the nursing home. Many homes offer their residents very little opportunity to be involved in their own care or in social or recreational activities. Another factor contributing to withdrawn behavior is the fact that nursing home residents often have serious physical and mental disabilities. For example, elderly patients often have deficits in memory or in understanding language. Because much of staff time is spent in meeting residents' basic physical needs, there may be little time given to developing programs to meet their psychological needs (Feier & Leight, 1981). As a result, an elderly person may show a further decline in physical and psychological funtioning after entering a nursing home. Several studies have found decreases in cognitive and physical functioning, increased feelings of social isolation, and higher mortality rates with increased time spent in a nursing home (Langer & Rodin, 1976; Weinstock & Bennett, 1971).

Nursing home residents were more alert and sociable when they were given pets to play with. This is one example of how researchers are making nursing home environments more stimulating. (Bill Foley/Time Magazine)

Judith Rodin (1986), one of the researchers studying ways to help nursing home patients overcome the feelings of dependency, depression, and social isolation that are common in unstimulating environments, believes that patients should be given some *control* over their lives. In one experiment, E. J. Langer and Rodin (1976) found that a group of nursing home residents who were encouraged to make choices about daily activities were more alert and active and reported being happier than a group of residents who did not receive such encouragement. In a related study, Rodin (1983) discovered that telling older patients how to cope with daily stressors increased their feelings of control and the percentage of time they spent in energetic activities. Finally, Helen Hendy (1984) found that when nursing home patients were given the chance to play with pets, their feelings of control increased and they smiled more readily and were more sociable and alert. In a review of studies in this area, Rodin (1986) concluded that, for nursing home residents, greater feelings of control are accompanied by increased physical and psychological well-being.

DEATH AND DYING

"You have six months left to live. There is nothing more we can do for you." Most young adults would react with fear and disbelief on hearing these words from a doctor. For young adults, fear of *death* arises from three sources: a fear of losing self-fulfillment, a fear of the consequences to one's family, and a fear of the unknown or of punishment in the hereafter (Florian & Kravetz, 1983). Middle-aged people try to avoid thinking about or making any preparations for dying, apparently because they have more fear of death than do older people. People who have already grown old, such as residents in nursing homes, are much more open and willing to talk about death than people of middle age. Still, contrary to what many people believe, research suggests that neither the fear of death nor concern about dying dominates the thoughts of the elderly (Bengtson et al., 1977).

Until the early 1970s, research on dying was taboo. At that time,

MAJOR CONCEPT Growing Old and Dying

Please indicate which of the following statements are true (T) or false (F).

1. T/F The major difference between normal and pathological aging is that normal aging occurs between ages 60 and 70 and pathological aging occurs between ages 70 and 80.

2. T/F The major physical and psychological effects of normal aging can be slowed greatly by a program combining diet, exercise, and involvement.

3. T/F Some of the reasons that our bodies age is because of inherited genetic mechanisms, errors in DNA programming, and changes in protein synthesis and the immune system.

4. T/F As a person grows old, memory for faces, events, and daily activities gets worse and worse and, at present, there is no way to slow this age-related memory loss.

5. T/F If a person is physically and psychologically healthy, there is no reason why he or she cannot continue to be sexually active even after age 80.

6. T/F Nursing homes promote feelings of dependency, depression, and social isolation because patients are given more control over their lives than they are capable of dealing with.

7. T/F Elisabeth Kübler-Ross has identified a series of emotional reactions that a dying person passes through, such as denial, anger, bargaining, depression, and acceptance. However, not everyone experiences all these emotional reactions or goes through them in a certain order.

Answers: 1 (F); 2 (T); 3 (T); 4 (F); 5 (T); 6 (F); 7 (T)

What emotions can we experience in facing death?

Elisabeth Kübler-Ross (1969, 1970) interviewed patients who were dying and asked them to describe their feelings. She identified a number of psychological reactions that many dying people experience. One of the first responses to news of impending death is: "There must be some mistake; it can't be me." A person may seek other doctors' opinions or additional tests to prove the verdict wrong. The use of *denial,* "it can't be me," is one way of coping with the stress of dying. If you deny that you are about to die, then you free yourself from having to face this crisis and prepare for it.

As the illness grows more serious, however, denial becomes increasingly difficult. A person may next become *angry* and ask "Why does it have to be me?" He or she may also come to resent those who are healthy. This reaction may be difficult for family and hospital staff to deal with, since the anger is directed at them. Kübler-Ross suggests dealing with anger by making the dying person feel especially cared for and by providing as much understanding as possible. A person may attempt to cope with dying by *bargaining* with the staff or with God. He or she may ask for just another year or a few more months in return for a pledge of doing something good or constructive with the extra time. But soon the increasing severity of the illness may make such bargaining unrealistic.

The impending loss of loved ones and all things in life that the dying person loves and wants to keep may result in *depression.* Kübler-Ross suggests allowing depressed dying persons the chance to express their sorrow without constantly being told not to be so sad. If a dying person works through the feelings of denial, anger, and depression, that person may come to accept and acknowledge impending death. *Acceptance* does not mean a person is happy about dying, but rather that the person acknowledges death's inevitability. In some cases, a dying person may be more accepting of death than the family (Kübler-Ross, 1969, 1974).

Initially, Kübler-Ross regarded these emotional reactions to dying as a series of stages through which a person passed. Her stages were criticized, however, because they were too rigid and fixed. Not everyone who is dying displays all these responses, and those who do do not necessarily experience them in a certain order. Many dying people have varied emotions, fluctuating between denial, depression, anger, and acceptance (Kastenbaum, 1981). Kübler-Ross has since acknowledged that a person may experience more than one reaction at the same time and may not progress through these reactions in a set order. But Kübler-Ross's work is recognized as important because it brought to our attention the kinds of feelings a dying person and the family must deal with.

REVIEW

Herman and Eileen are having one of their weekly arguments about growing old. Eileen, who is 69, is complaining about all the things that aging prevents her from doing. Herman, who is 84, says that there are two kinds of aging. The first, which involves the gradual slowing of some physical and psychological processes, is called (1) _____ aging. The second, which involves some disease that causes physical and psychological problems, is called (2) _____ aging. Eileen says that the effects of normal aging can't be overcome and that's why she has problems. Herman tells her about three communities in which inhabitants have apparently overcome many of the problems of normal aging. In these communities, a high percentage of individuals are between 80 and 100 years old. Some of the reasons that these individuals are physically and psychologically healthy include (3) _____,

_____, and _____.

Eileen says that her parents both died before they were 65 years old and she has already outlived them. Herman adds that people would probably live to be

(4) _____ if there were no diseases. Herman explains that our bodies have a number of mechanisms that contribute to aging. These include inherited (5) _____ mechanisms, changes in

(6) _____ programming that can lead to errors in cell functioning, changes in protein synthesis, and changes in the body's (7) _____ system that leads to increased susceptibility to infection, tumors, and disease.

Eileen gets angry and says that she really can't do as much as she did 30 years ago. Herman admits that there may be a gradual decline in the sensitivity of her (8) _____, such as vision, hearing, and taste. She can also expect a decreased blood flow and decline in muscle functioning, but she can reduce these changes with an (9) _____ program. She may experience some decline in memory because of more time needed to retrieve information from (10) _____ - _____ memory. However, this memory loss may be slight and she could compensate for it by learning memory techniques or taking classes to keep her mind active.

Herman and Eileen are a little embarrassed to talk about sex. Many older people acquire the belief that sex is inappropriate for them or they worry that their sexual performance at 60 or 70 doesn't match their performance at 30 or 40. It is true that with aging, men may need more stimulation to have an (11) _____ and women may experience a decrease in vaginal (12) _____. However both changes can be dealt with and need not interfere with sexual functioning in older people.

Unlike Eileen and Herman, about 5 percent of the population have serious health problems and live in nursing homes. Generally, the unstimulating environment of nursing homes promotes feelings of (13) _____, _____, and social _____. However, these negative feelings can be overcome if nursing home residents are given a sense of (14) _____ over their activities.

According to Elisabeth Kübler-Ross, if Herman or Eileen were to discover that they had cancer and had only a short time to live, they would experience a number of emotional reactions, such as (15) _____, _____, and _____. However, not everyone experiences all of these emotional reactions or experiences them in an exact order.

Answers: (1) normal; (2) pathological; (3) diet, exercise, involvement, lack of obesity, moderate use of alcohol and tobacco; (4) 100; (5) genetic; (6) DNA; (7) immune; (8) senses; (9) exercise; (10) long-term; (11) erection; (12) lubrication; (13) dependency, depression, isolation; (14) control; (15) denial, anger, depression, bargaining, acceptance

---

GLOSSARY TERMS

normal aging (p. 394)   pathological aging (p. 394)

PERSONAL NOTE

I have a great fear of seeing my own blood. During minor surgery, I watched my doctor remove a small mole. For some reason, there was a lot of bleeding. I remember watching the bleeding and feeling faint, and the next thing I knew I was floating through space. I very clearly remember standing in front of someone dressed entirely in white. I could not see the person clearly, but I knew that it must be God. I knew that I had died and was at this very moment standing before God, waiting for judgment. I heard my name being called over and over. I slowly regained consciousness. I found myself staring at a person dressed in white. It was my doctor, standing in front of me, calling my name. He explained that I had only fainted. I said I was very happy that I had not died. He laughed and said no one ever died from removal of a mole. I said I almost had. —R. P.

13

Personality

Module 35 Trait Approach

ISSUES IN PERSONALITY

It was all over in eight days.

> *On day one, an anonymous tipster told the* Miami Herald *that Gary Hart, the front runner in the race for the 1988 Democratic nomination for president, was spending the weekend with a Miami model while his wife was in Colorado. On day two, a team of Herald reporters staked out Hart's Washington, D.C. town house. The reporters observed that Hart and the model remained inside until Hart became aware of the reporters' presence. On day three, a front-page story appeared in the* Herald *with the headline "Miami Woman Is Linked to Hart." On day four, other newspapers picked up the story. On day five, Hart issued a statement in which he denied having had a sexual affair, as the* Herald *story implied. On days six and seven, the press raised serious questions about Hart's truthfulness, character, and judgment. For example, it emerged that, in the past, Hart had gone on an overnight boat trip with the same model. On day eight, after endless questions, criticisms, and accusations, Hart announced that he was withdrawing from the presidential race. He said, "I've made some mistakes. Maybe big mistakes, but not bad mistakes."*

> *According to a writer for* Time *magazine, the American people do not like leaders who evade the truth and pretend to be one thing while being another (adapted from* Time, *May 18, 1987).*

What do you expect from a presidential candidate?

Why did Gary Hart drop out of the 1988 presidential primaries? (Ira Wyman/Sygma)

Definition

To understand why Gary Hart behaved as he did, we must look at his personality. **Personality** refers to a combination of relatively stable and distinctive traits and how these traits influence thinking, behaving, and feeling in response to other people and situations. Psychologists would use a number of different approaches to understanding Hart's personality. In this Module, we will discuss the **trait approach,** which focuses on measuring personality characteristics or traits and studying how these traits influence behavior. In Module 36, we will discuss Freud's psychodynamic approach, which emphasizes early experiences and unconscious motivations. In Module 37, we will examine the social-cognitive approach, which emphasizes cognitive and social influences, and the humanistic approach, which emphasizes personal growth and fulfillment. In Module 38, we will explore the various ways that personality traits are assessed.

In trying to understand Gary Hart's personality, the trait approach makes three basic assumptions. First, it assumes that Hart's personality, as

403

well as your own, could be described completely by listing all his traits. Second, that his traits are relatively consistent and stable and influence his behavior. Third, that we can use our knowledge of his personality traits to explain and predict his behavior. Let's see how well these three assumptions have stood up.

Beginning with the first assumption, psychologists might use several different methods to identify Gary Hart's personality traits. For example, they might ask him to read a list of statements and check off those that apply to him; they might ask people who know him to describe his characteristics; or he might be given a series of psychological tests, such as those described in Module 38. At this point we would like to give you the experience of answering questions about your own personality traits.

APPLYING PSYCHOLOGY   Identifying Traits

How outgoing would you say you are?

Answer the following questions as honestly as you can

		yes	no
1A.	Do you often long for excitement?	yes	no
2A.	Are you usually carefree?	yes	no
3B.	Do you stop and think things over before doing anything?	yes	no
4A.	Would you do almost anything for a dare?	yes	no
5A.	Do you often do things on the spur of the moment?	yes	no
6B.	Generally, do you prefer reading to meeting people?	yes	no
7B.	Do you prefer to have few but special friends?	yes	no
8A.	When people shout at you, do you shout back?	yes	no
9A.	Do other people think of you as very lively?	yes	no
10B.	Are you mostly quiet when you are with people?	yes	no
11B.	If there is something you want to know about, would you rather look it up in a book than talk to someone about it?	yes	no
12B.	Do you like the kind of work you need to pay close attention to?	yes	no
13B.	Do you hate being with a crowd in which people play jokes on one another?	yes	no
14A.	Do you like doing things that require you to act quickly?	yes	no
15B.	Are you slow and unhurried in the way you move?	yes	no
16A.	Do you like talking to people so much that you never miss a chance to talk to a stranger?	yes	no
17A.	Would you be unhappy if you could not see lots of people most of the time?	yes	no
18B.	Do you find it hard to enjoy yourself at a lively party?	yes	no
19A.	Would you say that you are fairly self-confident?	yes	no
20A.	Do you like playing pranks on others? (Adapted from Wilson, 1978.)	yes	no

Scoring:

Count up each question followed by an A to which you answered "yes."

Count up each question followed by a B to which you answered "no."

Add these two numbers

You have just completed a personality questionnaire that measures two traits, **introversion** and **extroversion**. A high score indicates that you tend to be outgoing or extroverted. You spend much energy in social activities, have many social and interpersonal skills, like to take some risks and have some adventures, and prefer to take action rather than think about what you might do. A low score indicates that you tend to be private or introverted. You are usually quiet and reserved, shun excitement, prefer books to people, act on thought rather than impulse, and remain distant except to close friends (Wilson, 1978). Rather than being typical introverts or extroverts, most of us are on a continuum between introversion and extroversion. This is true of all dimensions of personality.

Once you have determined whether Gary Hart is an extrovert or an introvert, how many other traits would you have to list to describe his personality? Early trait researchers, such as Raymond Cattell (1947), Gordon Allport (1937), and Hans Eysenck (1953), made important contributions by identifying traits that they believed essential to describing personality. However, these researchers disagreed as to the exact number of traits or factors, such as 3, 16, or many more, that would adequately describe all of one's personality. Recently, two researchers have suggested that the number may be closer to 5.

Robert McCrae and Paul Costa, Jr. (1987) found that all the personality traits we use to describe ourselves and others can be divided into five groups. They called these five groups of traits a *five-factor model* of personality and gave each group or factor a name. One factor, called *neuroticism*, includes such traits as secure–insecure. A second factor, called *extroversion*, includes such traits as sober–fun loving. A third factor, called *openness*, includes such traits as down-to-earth–imaginative. A fourth factor, called *agreeableness vs. antagonism*, includes such traits as irritable–good-natured. A fifth factor, called *conscientiousness vs. undirectedness*, includes such traits as undependable–reliable.

McCrae and Costa, as well as other researchers, believe that these five factors can be used to represent, describe, and assess all of human personality and serve as the basic model for future research in personality (Buss & Finn, 1987; Digman & Inouye, 1986; Digman & Takemoto-Chock, 1981).

CONSISTENCY IN TRAITS AND BEHAVIOR

Why did Gary Hart behave so differently in public and private?

This question brings us to the second assumption of trait theory: traits are relatively consistent and stable and influence behavior. If this assumption is true, how do we explain the apparent inconsistency between Hart's pretending to be one thing and being another? His inconsistency fits in very well with what psychologists have known for some time. In a series of critical papers, Walter Mischel (1968) pointed out that a person who is perceived as having a certain personality trait, such as honesty, cannot be expected to behave honestly in all situations. Since an essentially honest person will occasionally behave dishonestly, we have reason to doubt the third assumption: that we can use our knowledge of personality traits to predict accurately a person's behaviors in different situations.

Because Mischel clearly pointed out that traits are not always consistent with behaviors, psychologists made two major revisions in their thinking about traits. First, traits were redefined as being enduring and consistent characteristics that are often but *not always* evident in particular situations (Magnusson & Endler, 1977). Second, psychologists agree that our behavior is influenced by how our personality traits interact with the different situations in which we find ourselves (Funder & Ozer, 1983). For example, Hart's behavior changed depending upon whether he was in the public eye or in the privacy of his home, even though his personality traits remained the same. Let's look at a study on the interaction between traits and situations in college students.

Traits and Situations

Would you behave the same way in 19 different situations?

If college students said that they were "highly conscientious," would they behave this way consistently—attending more classes and study sessions, getting their homework in on time, keeping themselves and their rooms neat, and so forth? To answer this question, Walter Mischel and Philip Peake (1982) observed students' conscientiousness in 19 different situations.

The researchers found that students who rated themselves as highly conscientious behaved that way day after day in *some* situations, but not in all 19 situations. For example, students who were considered by themselves and others to be highly conscientious might clean their rooms daily, but not get their homework in on time. These results confirm Mischel's earlier suggestion that certain situations have as much influence on behavior as do traits. But why were these students seen as behaving in a consistently conscientious manner when, in fact, they were not? According to Mischel and Peake, the answer is that we judge a person's consistency by observing the *same* behavior in the *same* situation, day after day. In doing so, we fail to consider that the behavior might not carry over to other situations.

How can we predict behavior?

If behavior is sometimes inconsistent across situations, how can we hope to predict it with any accuracy? If you score high on the trait of honesty, for example, does it mean that you will never hide your feelings, cheat a little on your income tax, or lie about your accomplishments? How can we make predictions about how you will behave in different situations?

Psychologists have increased the accuracy of their predictions by observing behavior in real-life situations. For example, researchers observed a group of adolescents on a two-week camping trip. Without their knowing, the adolescents were rated on how often they helped or dominated a fellow camper. The researchers concluded that in this real-life setting, the adolescents could be rated from low to high on the traits of helpfulness and dominance and that those who were helpful in one situation tended to be helpful in others (Small et al., 1983). These and other findings suggest that

In a romantic situation, this woman may behave in a traditional, passive way. In a work situation, the same woman may behave in a nontraditional, assertive way, showing that situations greatly influence behavior. (Dan McCoy/Rainbow)

predictions about behavior can be made more accurate if the measurements are taken in real-life situations or taken over a period of time (Epstein and O'Brien, 1985; West, 1983).

Traits Across Time

If you are 20 or 25 now, what will your personality be like at 45 and 75? In a longitudinal study, Paul Costa and his colleagues (1983) followed men from their early twenties to their early seventies. They found that on a number of traits, such as general activity level, sociability, emotional stability, friendliness, and thoughtfulness, individuals showed a very high degree of stability across the years. This means that some of the personality traits you have now may persist throughout the rest of your life. On the other hand, some traits, such as the tendency to be anxious or neurotic, were not as stable across the years. These researchers believe that stressful situations play a large role in anxiety or neurotic tendencies and account for the fact that these traits are less stable.

How much will your personality change between now and age 70?

Since some personality traits do change, are there periods when change is more likely to occur? Norma Haan (1986) and her colleagues, who studied a group of individuals at seven different points over a 50-year period, found that personality changed the least during childhood and adolescence and the most during the transition period between adolescence and early adulthood. Moderate amounts of personality change occurred during middle and late adulthood. The personality traits that showed the most stability across 50 years were achievement orientation or the lack of it, dependability or rebelliousness, and sociability or aloofness. The least stable personality traits were self-confidence or its opposite, self-doubt. This study tells us that even though our personality is most likely to change between adolescence and early adulthood, we may continue to experience change in certain traits, such as self-assurance, throughout middle and late adulthood.

Twins and Traits, Heredity and Environment   EXPLORING PSYCHOLOGY

Jim Lewis and Jim Springer drove the same model blue Chevrolet, chain-smoked the same brand of cigarettes, owned dogs named Toy, held the same jobs of deputy sheriff, enjoyed the same woodworking hobby, and had vacationed on the same beach in Florida. When they were given personality tests, they scored almost alike on traits of flexibility, self-control, and sociability. The two Jims are identical twins who were separated four weeks after birth and raised separately. When reunited at age 39, they were flabbergasted at how many things they had in common (adapted from *Time*, January 12, 1987).

How similar are twins in personality?

The two Jims are part of a multiyear University of Minnesota study on the significance of genetic and environmental factors in the development of personality. Before this study, many psychologists believed that a shared family environment was the major influence on personality development. The Minnesota results suggest something a little different.

According to Auke Tellegen (1988) and his colleagues at the University of Minnesota, their study was the first to compare simultaneously the personality traits of the following four groups: identical twins reared together, identical twins reared apart, fraternal twins reared together, and fraternal twins reared apart. Remember that identical twins have the same genetic

Jim Lewis (left) and Jim Springer (right) are identical twins who were raised separately. When reunited, they were found to have many traits in common, as well as many habits and preferences. (Bob Sacha/Discover Magazine)

makeup, while fraternal twins are no more genetically alike than any other siblings.

When the researchers administered the same personality tests to all of their subjects, they found that the correlations for identical twins, whether reared apart or together, were about twice as large as those for fraternal twins. Based on these data, the researchers concluded that about 50 percent of personality similarities are due to *genetic influences* and the remaining 50 percent are due to *environmental influences*. The researchers also found that whether twins were identical or fraternal, the correlations for those reared together were very similar to those reared apart. Based on these data, the researchers stated that sharing a common environment generally has only a modest influence on determining many personality traits. They concluded that a shared family environment had less effect and that genetic factors had more effect on personality development than had been believed previously. As they noted, this later conclusion runs counter to the popular conception that personality is profoundly shaped by a shared family environment. Although the Minnesota twin study found that genetic factors may influence personality development by as much as 50 percent, this does not mean that personality is biologically determined. Rather, it means that one's personality develops from an interaction between approximately equal percentages of genetic and environmental factors.

Thomas Bouchard, Jr. (1984), one of the participants in the Minnesota twin study, has pointed out that while identical twins, reared together or apart, share remarkable similarities, this finding should not overshadow the fact that each member of the pair is a unique human being. For instance, while the two Jims have remarkable similarities, they also have differences. Jim Lewis says that he is more easygoing and worries less than his identical twin, Jim Springer. When the twins get on a plane, Jim Springer worries about the plane being late, while Jim Lewis says that there is no use worrying (*San Diego Tribune*, November 12, 1987). Bouchard added that no matter how similar twins were found to be, each twin's fundamental uniqueness has always come through.

EVALUATION OF THE TRAIT APPROACH

Remember that the trait approach makes three assumptions. First, it assumes that one's personality can be described completely by a list of traits. Although researchers have had difficulty in agreeing on a list, recent studies by McCrae and Costa suggest that all traits can be grouped under a five-factor model. It remains to be seen whether future research will confirm McCrae and Costa's claims. Second, the trait approach assumes that one's traits greatly influence one's behavior. We now know that this assumption is only partly true. Since behavior is also influenced by particular situations, we must study how traits interact with situations and how this interaction affects behavior. Third, the trait approach assumes that knowledge about traits can be used to explain and/or predict behaviors. This too is only partly true: Researchers find that traits may indeed be used to predict behaviors in the same situation. However, traits are not as useful for predicting behavior across many different situations.

On a practical level, personality traits help us make quick judgments about people and provide consistency in our social interactions. However, we may overlook the fact that someone may behave differently in different situations and that some traits may continue to change throughout life.

If we consider traits to be building blocks, then by assembling and combining traits we could construct an individual's personality. But how are these building blocks combined and assembled? Researchers suggest that genetic factors may influence how traits are combined and assembled by as much as 50 percent, and environmental factors are responsible for the other 50 percent.

MAJOR CONCEPT   Traits

Please indicate which of the following statements are true (T) or false (F).

1. T/F Personality is defined as a combination of one's relatively stable and distinctive traits as well as how they influence one's thinking, behaving, and feeling in response to other people and situations.

2. T/F If you knew that someone scored very high on an assertiveness test, you could predict accurately how assertively they would behave in almost every situation.

3. T/F Although some personality traits are stable and consistent across time, personality traits are likely to change the most during childhood and adolescence.

4. T/F According to the five-factor model, all personality traits can be grouped under the following five factors: neuroticism, extraversion, openness, agreeableness vs. antagonism, and conscientiousness vs. undirectedness.

5. T/F The Minnesota study of identical and fraternal twins concluded that a shared family environment had a much greater influence on personality development than did genetic factors.

6. T/F In predicting how someone would behave, you need only consider a person's traits because traits rarely interact with situations.

Answers: 1 (T); 2 (F); 3 (F); 4 (T); 5 (F); 6 (F)

REVIEW

You are looking for a new roommate with a great personality. Personality refers to a combination of one's relatively stable and distinctive (1) _____ as well as how they influence one's (2) _____, _____, and _____ in response to other people and (3) _____. In order to find the right personality, you decide to run a newspaper ad. But how many traits should your ad list to describe completely a particular personality? According to McCrae and Costa, you could group all personality traits under five general factors, which they named (4) _____, _____, _____, _____, and _____.

Your ad reads: "Roommate wanted who is responsible, cheerful, neat, and outgoing." What your ad is asking for is enduring and relatively consistent characteristics called (5) _____. One of the reasons that you list these particular characteristics is because you think that they will influence how your roommate will (6) _____. You prefer a roommate who is sociable and outgoing, a trait called (7) _____, rather than one who is private and withdrawn, a trait called (8) _____. However, you must remember that all personality traits are on a continuum.

After many interviews, you select Danny because he seems to be neat, responsible, outgoing, and cheerful. However, you soon discover that Danny is a real grouch in the morning and is messy in the kitchen. Psychologists have two explanations for why Danny's behavior is sometimes inconsistent with his basic traits. First, although traits are considered to be relatively consistent, they may not affect behavior in every (9) _____. Second, although traits influence behavior, so too does the situation, and this means that Danny's behavior results from an (10) _____

between his traits and the situation. If you wanted to increase your accuracy in predicting Danny's behavior, you should observe his behavior in different (11) _____ - _____ situations.

If Danny is 20 years old now, what will he be like at 50? Researchers have found that on a number of traits, such as sociability, friendliness, and thoughtfulness, individuals show a high degree of (12) _____ across time. The least amount of personality change occurs during (13) _____ and _____, and the most occurs during the transition between (14) _____ and _____.

Danny tells you that he has an identical twin. If you met his twin, you would notice a considerable similarity in their personalities. This is because the correlation between identical twins on personality tests is about (15) _____ as large as that for fraternal twins. Researchers estimate that about (16) _____ percent of the similarities in traits is due to environmental factors and the remaining percentage is due to (17) _____ factors. One of the environmental factors that was shown to be less influential than once thought was the effect of a shared (18) _____ environment.

Some of the advantages to knowing Danny's traits include helping you predict how he will (19) _____ in some but not all situations and helping you know what to expect and how to (20) _____ socially with him. Some of the disadvantages of relying too heavily on your knowledge of Danny's traits include being wrong in predicting how he will behave in certain (21) _____ and forgetting that traits are often descriptions of what Danny does rather than (22) _____ of why he behaves that way.

Answers: (1) traits, (2) thinking, behaving, and feeling; (3) situations, (4) neuroticism, extroversion, openness, agreeableness vs. antagonism, conscientiousness vs. undirectedness; (5) traits; (6) behave; (7) extroversion; (8) introversion; (9) situation; (10) interaction; (11) real-life; (12) stability; (13) childhood, adolescence, early adulthood; (14) adolescence, early adulthood; (15) twice; (16) 50; (17) genetic; (18) family; (19) behave; (20) interact; (21) situations; (22) explanations.

GLOSSARY TERMS

extroversion (p. 405)   introversion (p. 405)   personality (p. 403)   trait approach (p. 403)

Module 36 Freud's Psychodynamic Approach

Martin Luther King, Jr., was engaged in a civil rights struggle that would put him in constant danger. Over a period of a dozen years, the FBI would record over 50 assassination plots against him.

King was in danger when he helped organize a year-long strike against the segregation policies of the Montgomery bus company. Although tempers raged on both sides, King had insisted on using nonviolent tactics. King and the blacks of Montgomery won their case, and the buses were desegregated. King's leadership in the civil rights movement was recognized by his selection for the cover of Time *magazine when he was only 27 years old. From then on, he devoted most of his time and energy to achieving civil rights for all.*

What kind of forces drove Martin Luther King?

How might Freud explain why Martin Luther King, Jr., risked his life in the struggle for civil rights? (Bruce Davidson/Magnum Photos)

King was in danger when he was arrested and jailed during civil rights marches in Birmingham, Alabama, and throughout the South. He was perhaps in greatest danger when he led a march toward the Selma, Alabama, courthouse, protesting voting discrimination policies. Like so many times before, he was arrested and jailed. When he was released, he demanded that the United States Congress pass stronger laws against voter discrimination.

King was in danger when he helped organize a massive civil rights march on Washington, D.C., in August 1963. The march was attended by over 250,000 people, and King's speech was so moving and so full of hope that it made people weep. In 1964, when King was 35 years old, he was awarded the Nobel Prize for Peace.

King's efforts took him throughout the South. This particular night he was speaking to a congregation in Memphis, Tennessee. He said he had no fear of dying. "I'm not worried about anything. I'm not fearing any man. Mine eyes have seen the glory of the coming of the Lord."

The next day, April 4, 1968, King left his motel room to join his friends for dinner. As he walked out onto the second-floor balcony, a rifle cracked. The bullet ripped through his neck and jaw. About an hour later, Martin Luther King, Jr., was dead. He was 39 years old. What had he done to make someone want to kill him? He had waged a nonviolent fight for the civil rights of everyone (adapted from Downing, 1986; Lewis, 1978).

What kind of forces shaped King's personality and made him risk his life for his beliefs? Psychologists use a number of different approaches to answer this question. We discussed the trait approach in Module 35. In this Module, we will examine Sigmund Freud's **psychodynamic approach,** which in King's case would emphasize his early childhood experiences as well as his unconscious drives and motives.

STRUCTURE OF THE MIND

Three Mental Systems

Sigmund Freud's approach, which was the first complete theory of personality, had a major impact on psychology. In fact, three of Freud's terms—id, ego, and superego—have become part of our everyday conversation. Freud used these terms to help us understand the structure of the mind rather than to refer to something concrete and observable.

Had he been asked to describe the personality development of Martin Luther King, Freud might have said that, like all people, King was born with two biological drives, sex and aggression, which were the source of all his mental energy. Freud named this energy source the **id,** and said that it provides the energy for the development of the ego and superego. As a very young child, King's behavior was essentially controlled by the id. Freud said that the id follows the **pleasure principle,** which means that the id operates in a totally selfish, pleasure-seeking fashion, without regard for reason, logic, or morality.

However, King soon learned that his needs cannot always be met immediately and that he must find another way to relieve his tension. A new system develops, drawing its energy from the id. This new system, called the **ego,** tries to find safe and socially acceptable ways of satisfying the biological desires of the id. Unlike the id, which operates according to the pleasure principle, the ego operates according to the **reality principle.**

Following the reality principle means that the ego searches for safe and socially acceptable ways to fulfill the id's desires. For example, suppose the young King saw a candy bar at the supermarket. His id, following the pleasure principle, wants to take a candy bar off the shelf and eat it. His ego knows from experience that his father will punish this behavior. Instead, his ego suggests a safer solution, such as asking his father for a candy bar that he can eat later. King's ego functions like an executive, which considers the id's wishes and then checks with reality to determine how, when, and where these wishes can be fulfilled.

King's father was a Baptist preacher who enforced very strict moral principles, values, and standards in bringing up his son. As young Martin accepted or internalized his father's standards, his third system, the superego, was developing. The **superego** contains the moral values and standards of one's parents and one's society. King's superego strove for the ideal or perfect way of behaving and functioned much like what we would call a conscience. His superego created feelings of guilt if he engaged in behaviors or thoughts that were contrary to his parents' and society's standards. For example, King's superego might try to deal with racial anger by expressing it in a nonviolent way, according to ideal moral standards. If he were to express his feelings in a violent way, his superego might arouse guilt feelings.

Usually, the three interacting systems—the id, ego, and superego—worked together to satisfy King's needs. However, there will be times when id, ego, and superego are in conflict over how a need should be satisfied. The result of such a conflict is that the person feels anxious. If he cannot identify the exact cause of his anxiety, it may be because the cause lies in his unconscious.

Is there a part of you that you don't know about?

Levels of Consciousness

Why might a woman with no apparent neurological problems lose all sensations in her hand? As a medical doctor who specialized in nervous diseases, Freud treated a number of patients who had problems like this. Since he could find no physical cause for the complaints, Freud began to look for psychological causes. In his search, Freud developed the concept of the *unconscious,* which he believed might explain symptoms for which there was no apparent physical cause.

Freud's distinction between conscious and unconscious events is one of the keys to understanding his approach. According to Freud, *conscious events* include only a limited amount of mental activities, including the thoughts, fears, and desires we are aware of at any given moment. *Unconscious events* include an enormous amount of mental activity that we are not aware of but that is stored in memory. There are two additional points to remember about Freud's concept of the unconscious. First, when we encounter some thought, memory, or situation that is disturbing to us, we actively force it into our unconscious. This active forcing of disturbing material into our unconscious is called **repression.** Under certain conditions, such as under hypnosis or in dreams, unconscious material may be made conscious, but during most of our waking lives we are unaware of the disturbing material that is locked away in our unconscious. Second, the disturbing thoughts, fears, or memories are locked away in our unconscious. These locked-away fears cause anxiety that may be revealed in various symptoms, such as the woman's loss of sensations in her hand, or in other types of personality problems. According to Freud, many personality problems arise from what happens to us very early in life.

In his autobiography, star rock performer Michael Jackson says, "I'm one of the loneliest people in the world" (Moonwalk, 1988). How might Freud have interpreted this statement? (Ethan Hoffman/Archive)

MAJOR CONCEPT   Freud's Psychodynamic Approach

Indicate whether the following statements apply to the id (I), ego (E), or superego (S).

1. I (E) S This force tries to express one's needs in safe, socially acceptable ways.

2. (I) E S This force is present at birth.

3. I (E) S This force tries to mediate between the other two forces.

4. I (E) S This force operates according to the reality principle.

5. (I) E S This force operates according to the pleasure principle.

6. I E (S) This force functions like a conscience and makes one feel guilty if one's behavior does not match ideal standards.

7. I E (S) This force develops when one begins to adopt the values and standards of one's parents.

Answers: 1 E—ego; 2 I—id; 3 E—ego; 4 E—ego; 5 I—id; 6 S—superego; 7 S—superego

PERSONALITY DEVELOPMENT

Psychosexual Stages

What is an oral personality?

From treating his patients, Freud became convinced that the first five years were the most important in personality development. He saw the child as going through a series of **psychosexual stages** in which the child's primary goal is to satisfy, in order, the desires associated with the mouth, anus, and genitals. Each stage is a source of potential conflict between the id, which seeks immediate satisfaction, and the parents, who place restrictions of when, where, and how. Freud believed that personality is shaped by how the desires of the id are dealt with at each of the following stages.

The first stage, called the **oral stage,** is when the infant's pleasure-seeking is centered on the mouth. During his first 18 months, the infant's id seeks gratification in sucking, chewing, and biting.

The second stage, called the **anal stage,** lasts from about 18 months to 3 years. During this stage, the infant's primary source of satisfaction involves the elimination or retention of material from the bladder or bowels.

The third stage, called the **phallic (FAL-ik) stage,** lasts from the third to the sixth year. During this stage, the child's primary source of satisfaction involves stimulation of his genitals. In addition, the child feels unconscious sexual desires for his opposite-sex parent and hatred and jealousy for his same-sex parent, whom he views as a competitor. At the same time, he feels fearful and guilty about his same-sex parent discovering his feelings and punishing him. This combination of unconscious sexual desires and feelings of hatred and jealousy is called the **Oedipus (ED-ih-pus) complex.** Children resolve this complex by repressing the sexual feelings toward the opposite-sex parent and trying to become like the same-sex parent, a process called **identification.** For example, through identification, Martin Luther King, Jr., adopted many of his father's values, standards, and behaviors.

Between the ages of 6 and 12, the child enters the fourth stage, called the **latency stage.** His sexual desires are on hold and he plays mostly with children of his same sex. Finally, beginning at puberty and lasting until sexual maturity, the adolescent enters the fifth and last stage, the **genital stage.** Now the adolescent experiences sexual feelings toward others.

According to Freud's theory, King's personality was shaped primarily by how the conflicts at each of the psychosexual stages were resolved. If a strong conflict between the young Martin and his parents developed and was not resolved, he may have been locked in or *fixated* to seek the pleasures associated with that particular psychosexual stage. For example, if King had become fixated at the oral stage, as an adult he might have been very passive and dependent, like a nursing infant. Or he might have been very vocal about denying his dependence, such as by using biting sarcasm. He might also have continued to seek oral gratification through excessive eating and smoking. If fixated at the anal stage, King might have been either very messy and disorganized or highly compulsive and neat.

Anxiety and Defense Mechanisms

When King was treated badly by whites, he probably felt a conflict between acting out the id's aggressive tendencies and following his superego's moral directives to be nonviolent. Because his ego is caught in the middle of this conflict, the result is a general feeling of anxiety.

Aren't you being a little too defensive?

This general feeling of anxiety is very difficult to deal with because we cannot easily pinpoint the cause. To protect itself from these general feelings of anxiety, Freud theorized that the ego uses **defense mechanisms.** These mechanisms, such as repression, denial, and rationalization—which will be discussed in Module 41—reduce anxiety by unconsciously changing and distorting reality. At this point, just note that if King does not relieve his anxiety, he may develop personality problems, such as feeling guilty or anxious much of the time.

POST-FREUDIAN PERSPECTIVES

Initially, Freud's psychodynamic theory attracted a number of followers. Later, those who came to disagree with various aspects of Freud's theory were called neo-Freudians.

Carl Gustav Jung, initially a student and friend of Freud, later objected to Freud's excessive emphasis on the sexual drive. Jung also believed that the unconscious holds more than the personal experiences that Freud had described. According to Jung, there is a *collective unconscious* which contains images and symbols inherited from our early ancestors. Jung believed that the symbols contained in the collective unconscious explain why people in different cultures share certain images and myths.

Karen Horney and Alfred Adler believed that Freud placed too much emphasis on early childhood sexual experiences. They argued that social experiences in childhood are more important to personality development. Freud considered women to be dependent, vain, and submissive, and believed that these characteristics were based on basic biological forces. Horney disagreed and argued that women's characteristics were not dependent upon biological forces, but rather on social and cultural forces.

As discussed in Module 30, Erik Erikson believed that everyone goes through a series of stages, but not psychosexual ones. Erikson hypothesized that we go through a series of psychosocial stages that involve conflicts between our ego and society. Erikson also did not agree with Freud's contention that failure at one stage significantly affects later stages of personality development.

The neo-Freudians generally agreed with Freud's basic ideas, such as the importance of the unconscious, the division of mental energy into the id, ego, and superego, the development of anxiety, and the use of defense mechanisms to protect the ego. But they disagreed with Freud's emphasis on sexual drives and the importance of the psychosexual stages. Their criticisms changed the emphasis of psychodynamic theory from one of biological drives and the importance of the id's desires to one of psychosocial and cultural processes and the importance of the ego's development.

EVALUATION OF THE PSYCHODYNAMIC APPROACH

Since Freud formulated his theory well over 50 years ago, it stands to reason that some of his concepts may need revision. Let's see how present-day researchers regard Freud's key ideas.

Are the first five years the most important in shaping one's personality, as Freud maintained? Research on resilient children shows that in spite of experiencing serious psychological and physical problems during their first five years, many developed into healthy, mature adults (Module 30). Longitudinal studies indicate that personality development is not completed in the first five years, but continues well into middle adulthood (Module 33). Research does not confirm Freud's hypothesis that personality is determined during the first five years.

Is our behavior influenced by mental activity, much of which occurs at an unconscious level? Current researchers would substitute the term *unaware* for Freud's term *unconscious*. They would agree with Freud's idea that our behavior may be influenced by information of which we are unaware. For example, evidence from split-brain patients suggests that the right and left hemispheres may have separate goals and motivations (Module 6). Researchers have shown that we can process general information without always being aware of the information (Module 12); that perceptual sets may influence our behavior, often without our awareness (Module 11); and that organized networks of information, called schemas, may influence our behaviors without our awareness (Module 48). Instead of viewing the unconscious as a battleground between the id's desires and the superego's moral directives, present-day researchers see the unconscious as part of an information processing system whose content we may not always be aware of.

Is Freud's theory correct in its explanations and predictions about our behaviors? The first problem in testing Freud's theory is that many of his concepts, such as the id, ego, and superego, the Oedipal complex, and others cannot be defined operationally and thus are almost impossible to test (Module 3). The second problem is that Freud's theory is so comprehensive it can explain every possible behavior. For example, Freud would say that being very neat is caused by fixation at the anal stage, just as being very messy is. Since Freud's theory can explain every behavior after it occurs but cannot predict which specific behavior will occur, many researchers have questioned the usefulness of Freudian personality theory (Mischel, 1981; Pervin, 1980). However, some of Freud's ideas, such as the importance of the unconscious, continue to have an influence in clinical psychology and psychiatry (Module 46).

REVIEW

To help you understand the psychodynamic approach, let's apply it to your personality.

According to Freud's psychodynamic approach, the source of your mental energy comes from two biological drives, (1) _____ and _____. As an infant, your behavior was under control of your (2) _____, which seeks immediate fulfillment of its needs by following the (3) _____ principle. As you grow older, you learn that all of your needs cannot be met immediately. Drawing energy from the id, a second force develops, called the (4) _____, which seeks socially acceptable ways to meet your needs. Because this second force seeks acceptable ways to meet your needs, it is said to follow the (5) _____ principle. As you grow older still and adopt the values and standards of your parents, a third force develops, called the (6) _____, which functions very much like a conscience. This third force wants you to behave in an ideal way and creates feelings of (7) _____ if you do not live up to its idealized standards.

If the id, ego, and superego are in conflict over how a need should be satisfied, you may feel anxious. Your anxious feeling is a symptom of some conflict that is going on in your (8) _____, which is mental activity of which you are not aware. If you force into your unconscious an idea that is disturbing to you, it is called (9) _____. Your ego tries to protect itself from anxiety by using repression and other (10) _____ mechanisms. These mechanisms reduce anxiety by unconsciously distorting (11) _____.

According to Freud, during your early years you went through a series of five (12) _____ stages. At each stage, there is a potential conflict between the id and the parents over how your needs will be satisfied. The five stages are, in order, the (13) _____, _____, _____, _____, and _____ stages. During the phallic stage, Freud said that you felt sexual feelings toward your opposite-sex parent and hatred and jealousy toward your same-sex parent. Together these feelings are called the (14) _____ complex. You resolved these feelings by trying to become like your same-sex parent, a process called (15) _____. Freud believed that if you did not resolve the conflict at one of the five stages, you were locked in or (16) _____ at that stage.

In light of current research, we would say that Freud placed too much emphasis on what happened during the first (17) _____ years of life. Most modern researchers agree with Freud that there is information that we are unaware of and may influence our (18) _____. One of the major weaknesses of Freud's theory is that researchers have been unable to prove or disprove its major (19) _____.

Answers: (1) sex, aggression; (2) id; (3) pleasure; (4) ego; (5) reality; (6) superego; (7) guilt; (8) unconscious; (9) repression; (10) defense; (11) reality; (12) psychosexual; (13) oral, anal, phallic, latency, genital; (14) Oedipal; (15) identification; (16) fixated; (17) five; (18) behavior; (19) concepts

GLOSSARY TERMS

anal stage (p. 414)
defense mechanisms (p. 415)
ego (p. 412)
genital stage (p. 415)
id (p. 412)

identification (p. 414)
latency stage (p. 414)
Oedipus complex (p. 414)
oral stage (p. 414)

phallic stage (p. 414)
pleasure principle (p. 412)
psychodynamic approach (p. 412)

psychosexual stages (p. 414)
reality principle (p. 412)
repression (p. 413)
superego (p. 413)

Module 37 Social–Cognitive and Humanistic Approaches

What did King learn from watching?

When Martin Luther King, Jr., was 6 years old, he experienced the cruel effects of segregation. King was told by his best friend's parents that he could no longer come over and play with their son. The reason King was given was that he was black and his best friend was white. Now that they were both of school age, it was not right for a white and black child to play together. King never forgot the hurt he felt when he was forced to give up his childhood friend.

When King was 11, a white woman he had never seen before walked up to him in a department store and slapped him in the face. She said, "That little nigger stepped on my foot." He had not. Because he was black, he could not protest being unjustly accused or being slapped.

When he was 14, he and a friend were returning by bus to Atlanta. King was proud and happy after winning a speech contest in a neighboring city. When the bus stopped to pick up additional passengers, the driver made King and his friend get up and give their seats to two white passengers. When King and his friend did not move quickly enough, the bus driver called them "black sons of bitches." Many years later King recalled, "It was the angriest I have ever been in my life."

King often watched and listened to his father, who was pastor of a large church, preach stirring sermons. His father preached and worked for justice, civil rights, and the welfare of the black community. In observing his father, young Martin could not help but be impressed. Besides going to his father's church, King was often taken by his mother to services at the neighboring churches. After listening to a spellbinding preacher, King promised his mother, "Someday, I'm going to have me some big words like that."

Let's see how these many experiences affected King's personality development. (adapted from Downing, 1986; Lewis, 1978).

SOCIAL-COGNITIVE APPROACH

According to the previous Module, Freud's psychodynamic approach would explain King's personality development by analyzing his progress through the psychosexual stages and examining his feelings of anxiety caused by hidden conflicts among the id, ego, and superego. Freud's psychodynamic approach suggests that inner forces and unconscious processes are the major influences on personality development. In contrast, a number of researchers, including Albert Bandura (1986), Walter Mischel (1984), and Nancy Cantor (1981) suggest something very different with their social-cognitive approach. According to Bandura, the **social-cognitive approach** views personality development as arising from the *interaction* among three factors—cognitive and personality factors, behavior, and the environment. In explaining King's personality development and behavior, Bandura would focus on the interaction among King's thoughts and memories, his personality traits, his past behaviors, and the pressures of his environment.

Cognitive and Personality Factors

King told his mother, "Someday, I'm going to have me some big words like that."

For the last 10 years, Angela Davis has been active in civil rights and related political causes. She was the vice-presidential candidate for the U. S. Communist Party in the 1984 elections. In contrast, a winner of the Miss America Pageant probably holds more conservative political and social views of the world. (Left, Steve Smith/Liaison Agency; right, AP/Wide World Photos)

According to Bandura, this example of King setting a goal for himself indicates how cognitive factors can influence behavior. Thoughts or cognitions include King's goals, self-standards, self-evaluations, self-estimates, and expectations. Bandura explains that, like King, many of us base our actions on our *thoughts* or *cognitions*.

However, our thoughts may not always be logical or rational. There are times when our course of action is based on faulty information, on bad reasoning, or on our misreading or misinterpreting the world around us. The result is that we may have false beliefs about ourselves or our environment. Whether accurate or not, Bandura believes that our thoughts and cognitions influence our behaviors and help us set goals and plan for the future.

When King set a goal, such as "using big words," he did so based on his cognitions as well as on his *personal traits*, such as being smart and determined. In King's case, his cognitions, goals, and personal traits all worked together to influence his behavior and help him achieve his goal of becoming a great preacher. Bandura believes that cognitions and personal factors make up one's *internal standards*. King used his internal standards to motivate himself to struggle for civil rights, as well as to evaluate his behaviors in terms of how much he was doing and how much more needed to be done.

Behaviors and Environmental Pressures

From early on, King acquired the cognitions and skills that were needed for becoming an outstanding preacher and leader. Because his initial attempts at public speaking were received with great enthusiasm, he became increasingly determined to set higher and higher goals. To explain the acquisition and development of cognitions and skills, social-cognitive researchers draw heavily on learning principles that were described in Module 17. From classical and operant research, we know that learning takes place if we perform responses and experience reinforcement. However, Bandura emphasizes that besides learning from direct experience, we also learn through observation, which he calls *vicarious* learning. The advantage of vicarious learning is that we can learn rules and standards without having to go through an endless process of trial and error. This means that King acquired his cognitions, preaching abilities, and leadership skills, as well as many of his internal standards, through both direct and vicarious learning.

> King's father was morally strict and King usually obeyed his father. However, there were times when young Martin sneaked off to a local dance place even though his father had forbidden him to dance.

Notice how the differences in environments interacted with King's personal factors and cognitions. King followed his father's moral values in the home but showed a different side of his personality at the local dance hall. The differences in King's behavior between the home and the dance hall emphasize Bandura's point that human functioning is a result of the *interaction* between cognitions and personal factors, behavior, and the environment.

EVALUATION OF THE SOCIAL-COGNITIVE APPROACH

In the 1960s it was called the social learning approach. In the early 1980s the term "cognitive" was added to stress the importance of cognitive processes in human behavior. The present social-cognitive approach borrows ideas from many areas of psychology, including learning, information processing, and social psychology. The advantages of the social-cognitive approach are its emphasis on the role of vicarious learning, on the interaction between cognitions, behavior, and the environment, and on developing programs for personality and behavioral change. The disadvantages of the theory are that almost any behavior can be explained, after the fact, by pointing to complex interactions among cognitions, behavior, and the environment. Finally, the social-cognitive approach will have to recognize that genetic factors contribute as much as 50 percent to the development of certain personality traits.

We mentioned that one of the advantages of the social-cognitive approach was developing programs for personality change. Here is one such program for a relatively common personality problem.

MAJOR CONCEPT   Social-Cognitive Approach

Please indicate which of the following statements are true (T) or false (F).

1. T/F Human functioning is primarily the result of our cognitions and is less influenced by our environment.

2. T/F We can learn cognitions, behaviors, and skills through direct learning as well as through observation, which is called vicarious learning.

3. T/F Our internal standards, which motivate our behaviors, are acquired primarily through direct learning.

4. T/F Bandura believes that our behaviors result from an interaction of three processes, namely, our emotions, beliefs, and experiences.

5. T/F Our thoughts or cognitions include a number of things, including our standards, goals, and expectations.

Answers: 1 (F); 2 (T); 3 (F); 4 (F); 5 (T).

Dealing with Loneliness   **APPLYING PSYCHOLOGY**

Sarah's first three weeks were very lonely. She had transferred to a college where she didn't know a single person. She spent most of the time by herself, waiting to make some friends. Sam has been attending the same college for three years now. During the day he goes to class and talks to some of the students. Most nights and weekends he spends by himself.

Jeffrey Young (1985) would say that Sarah is experiencing *situational* loneliness, which results from an important event, such as a geographic move, a divorce, or death. He would say that Sam is experiencing *chronic* loneliness, which is a long-lasting problem in making social contact and achieving intimacy. On one college campus, Carolyn Cutrona and colleagues (1985) found that about 52 percent of freshmen reported situational loneliness and about 13 percent reported chronic loneliness. Young adds that chronically lonely people can become convinced that there is nothing they can do to overcome their loneliness.

According to the social-cognitive approach, chronically lonely people may have certain personal factors and cognitions that contribute to their problem. Studying personal factors, Letitia Peplau and Daniel Perlman (1982) found that lonely individuals are generally more shy, introverted, and less willing to take risks, traits that interfere with being socially sought after as a friend. Studying cognitions, Warren Jones and his colleagues (1981) found that lonely college students make more negative self-evaluations, have lower self-esteem, and assume that others share this negative view of them. Because of these negative cognitions and self-images, lonely students are less likely to initiate social interactions, and if they do they report the interactions to be less intimate (Williams & Solano, 1983).

Finally, lonely individuals may have less developed social skills. For example, Richard Bootzin (1982) found that lonely people may not reveal themselves to others, may not be good listeners, may not be assertive, and may not know how to initiate social interactions.

Do you feel lonely much of the time?

Shyness can be overcome—see, for example, the program described in the text. (Alan Carey/ The Image Works)

∿How Does One Learn to Be Less Lonely?

—*Changing Cognitions.*   A social-cognitive learning program to combat loneliness would focus on personal factors and cognitions. Carolyn Cutrona (1982) found that students who overcome loneliness do not differ much in their behaviors from students who remain lonely. Both engage with equal frequency in various activities, such as joining clubs, playing sports, going to parties, and initiating conversations with strangers. However, these two groups of students do differ in their *styles of thinking.* Those who overcome their loneliness keep thinking that they will eventually find someone to be close to, while those who do not overcome their loneliness think more and more about the prospect of remaining lonely. These findings fit in perfectly with Bandura's point that our self-expectations greatly influence our goals. Obviously, lonely people need to reset their goals in the direction of thinking that they will meet someone and get over their loneliness.

One way for lonely people to reset their goals is by changing their cognitions. Specifically, by eliminating negative self-statements and substituting positive ones. For example, instead of repeating negative self-statements, such as, "No one likes me, finds me attractive, or is interested in me," lonely people need to substitute positive self-statements, such as "I can be very likable, I can be humorous, I can be a good friend."

—*Changing Behaviors.*   Perhaps lonely people remain that way because they either have poor social skills or have adopted a passive role in social interactions. To help lonely students learn better social skills, Warren Jones and his colleagues (1982) trained lonely people to show more interest in others by asking questions and making statements about their partners. As a result of this training, lonely people reported feeling less lonely and their self-ratings improved on a number of personal measures. To study the effect of social role, John Vitkus and Leonard Horowitz (1987) asked lonely students to play one of two social roles. In role #1, they were to describe a personal problem to another student. In role #2, they were to listen and offer suggestions as a student described a personal problem to them. When lonely students·played role #2, in which they were the active listener, they paid more attention to their partners, asked more questions, and talked longer than when they played role #1. The researchers concluded that some lonely people have the necessary social skills but have adopted a passive role which keeps them from using their skills. If this is so, lonely people may need to practice playing a more active social role.

In some cases, a social-cognitive learning program can be initiated and carried out on one's own, or with the support of friends. In other cases, one may need the encouragement and guidance of a trained therapist.

HUMANISTIC APPROACH

Why were they crying, shouting, and applauding?

They came to Washington to send their message to those in government. They were 250,000 strong. They were of every color, from every part of the United States.

Many civil rights leaders had already spoken to the crowd. It was King's turn to speak. He walked to the podium and began to speak in a voice that made everyone listen.

"I have a dream. . . ."

The immense crowd grew silent.

"I have a dream that my four little children will one day live in a nation where they will not be judged by the color of their skin but by the content of their character. . . ."

Washington, DC, August 1963: Martin Luther King's "I Have a Dream" speech epitomizes the humanistic approach. (Bob Adelman/Magnum)

All eyes were on King.

"This is our hope. This is the faith that I go back to the South with. With this faith we will be able to hew out of the mountain of despair a stone of hope. With this faith we will be able to transform the jangling discords of our nation into a beautiful symphony of brotherhood. With this faith we will be able to work together, to pray together, to struggle together, to go to jail together, to stand up for freedom together, knowing that we will be free one day. . . ."

King had just made the most famous speech of his lifetime (adapted from Garrow, 1986, p. 284).

The Washington speech of Martin Luther King, Jr., was a rousing statement of what one should dream about, work toward, and try to achieve. These beliefs personify the humanistic approach, which emphasizes developing one's potential or working toward self-fulfillment.

The humanistic approach began from two different sources. One founder of this approach began as a behaviorist who studied animals. One began as a psychotherapist who studied Freud's psychodynamic approach. Both became dissatisfied with the limits of these approaches. Abraham Maslow (1968) felt that behaviorism, with its emphasis on rewards and punishments, left out feelings and subjective experiences. Carl Rogers (1959, 1980) felt that Freud's approach, with its emphasis on unconscious forces and neurotic problems, left out the potential for self-fulfillment. In the 1960s, Abraham Maslow, Carl Rogers, and several others developed an approach different in concept from that of Freud or the behaviorists. Their approach, which stresses the achievement of self-fulfillment, came to be known as the **humanistic approach.**

ABRAHAM MASLOW: SELF-ACTUALIZATION

Maslow attempted to do something that no one had done. He arranged all human needs in a sequence, which he called the **hierarchy of needs** (Figure 13.1). According to Maslow's theory, we satisfy our needs in a certain order.

Figure 13.1

Maslow's hierarchy of needs. (After Abraham H
Maslow. 1970. Self-actualizing people. In Motivation and
Personality, 2nd ed. New York: Harper & Row. Reprinted
by permission of Harper & Row, Publishers, Inc.)

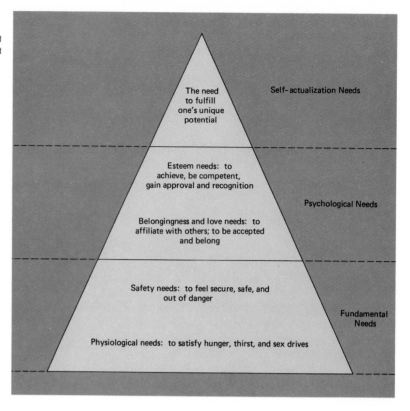

Furthermore, we cannot advance up the hierarchy of needs until we satisfy first the needs lower in the hierarchy. For instance, we are motivated to satisfy first our *fundamental needs*, which include physiological needs such as hunger and thirst, and safety needs such as feeling secure. Once satisfied, the fundamental needs no longer motivate us. At this point, we move up the hierarchy to the next set of needs, the *psychological needs*. These include belongingness and love needs, such as seeking friendships and being accepted, and esteem needs, which include wanting to achieve and be competent. If these psychological needs remain unsatisfied, we remain at this level. If satisfied, we move up to the final need, self-actualization. **Self-actualization** means fulfilling one's unique human potential. Maslow believed that very few individuals reach the highest level in the hierarchy, that of self-actualization. He would certainly say that Martin Luther King, Jr., had achieved self-actualization. Although many may not reach this highest level, Maslow said that everyone had a self-actualizing tendency. This tendency motivates us to become the best kind of person we are capable of becoming. In Martin Luther King's case, this tendency motivated him to become one of the outstanding civil rights leaders of all time.

Unlike Freud, who arrived at his theory after treating psychologically disturbed patients, Maslow developed his ideas after studying very productive, exceptional people, such as Abraham Lincoln, Albert Einstein, and Eleanor Roosevelt. Maslow considered these exceptional individuals to be examples of people who had reached the highest level in his hierarchy of needs, the level of self-actualization.

What was it that these self-actualized people shared in common? Maslow identified a number of common characteristics. For example, self-actualized people perceive reality in a very accurate fashion, while most of us allow our defenses and biases to distort reality and thereby skew our perceptions. In addition, self-actualized people are very independent and prefer to have a deep, loving relationship with only a few people. Unlike many of us, they accept themselves, others, and their environments instead of becoming upset with themselves and the world around them. Because of their self-acceptance, self-actualized individuals are able to focus on and accomplish their goals, rather than having to worry about doing something to build their self-images. Finally, Maslow discovered that these individuals report moments of great joy and satisfaction, which he called *peak experiences*. Maslow's approach differed from Freud's or the behaviorists' in his belief that everyone has a tendency or has felt a push toward self-actualization, toward fulfilling one's own unique capabilities. There is no doubt that Maslow would have considered Martin Luther King, Jr., an example of a self-actualized person.

CARL ROGERS: SELF THEORY

Like Maslow, Rogers believes that everyone has an inherent self-actualizing tendency or a push for reaching a healthy psychological state and self-fulfillment. How much each of us self-actualizes and reaches self-fulfillment depends upon our being in a psychological climate that stimulates growth and is free of unreasonable environmental constraints. As you will see, Rogers has very definite ideas on what kind of psychological climate stimulates growth and promotes self-actualization. But first, let's look at some of the key concepts of Rogers' **self theory.**

"Who are you?" Your answer to this deceptively simple question defines one of Rogers' key concepts, the self. According to Rogers, the **self** includes characteristics that you see yourself as having and that you reveal in your interactions with others. The self is important because it influences your behaviors and perceptions of your environment. Rogers believes that the self develops from your experiences, thoughts, and feelings. Whether or not you develop a positive self-concept depends on your psychological climate.

As you develop from child to teenager to adult, you have a need for being shown **positive regard,** which includes receiving love, sympathy, acceptance, and respect from your family, friends, and people important to you. Although many of us receive positive regard, it might be dependent or conditional on our behaving in certain ways, in living up to the standards of our parents or friends. For instance, our parents may not give as much support and approval if we do poorly in school. In this case, positive regard is conditional on good academic performance.

Through the years, well-known rock star David Bowie has changed his appearance, clothes, and personality. According to Carl Rogers' theory of personality, these changes might reflect Bowie's attempts to reach his potential. (First and second, Steve Schapiro/Gamma-Liaison; third, Joe Traver/Gamma-Liaison; fourth, "Merry Christmas Mr. Lawrence"/Sygma; fifth, Francois Lochon/Gamma-Liaison)

Rogers believes that our self or self-concept develops best if we are given unconditional positive regard. **Unconditional positive regard** means that others show us love and acceptance despite the fact that sometimes we behave in ways that are different from what they think or value. For example, unconditional positive regard means that our parents show their love and respect even if we do not always get high grades in school or college. If we have a psychological climate in which we receive unconditional positive regard, Rogers believes that we will develop a positive self-concept. As a result, not only will we feel good about ourselves, but we will perceive and interact with our environment in a positive way. On the other hand, if we have a psychological climate in which we receive primarily *conditional* positive regard, we will develop a negative self concept. As a result, we may compare ourselves to the ideal standards of our friends or parents and feel unsatisfied or unhappy with our lives. Rogers' ideas about personal growth had a far greater impact on psychotherapy, discussed in Module 47, than on personality development.

In contrast to Freud's psychodynamic approach and the social-cognitive approach, Maslow and Rogers' humanistic approach stresses that we are basically good and have an inherent human potential for self-fulfillment.

EVALUATION OF THE HUMANISTIC APPROACH

The advantages of Maslow and Rogers' humanistic approach is that it emphasizes the importance of developing a positive self concept, it focuses on our inherent potential for self-actualization, self-fulfillment, and self-improvement. In fact, the self-actualization concept has made its way into many areas of psychology as well as business and industry.

Some of the features that set apart the humanistic approach are the ones most often criticized. First, the humanistic approach assumes that we are inherently good and that each of us has an inherent potential for self-

---

MAJOR CONCEPT   Humanistic Approach

Please match the term with the correct statement.

1. hierarchy of needs

2. self-actualization

3. self

4. unconditional positive regard

a. _2_ An inherent tendency to achieve one's unique potential.

b. _1_ Lowest level is fundamental needs, middle level is psychological needs, and highest level is self-actualization.

c. _4_ Receiving love and acceptance even when we behave in ways that are different from what others value.

d. _3_ Includes characteristics that you recognize in yourself and that you reveal in interacting with others.

Answers: a (2); b (1); c (4); d (3)

actualization and positive growth. Because these ideas are very difficult to study scientifically, these assumptions remain unproven. Second, Maslow cites Abraham Lincoln, Eleanor Roosevelt, and Albert Einstein as examples of individuals who reached the highest need level of self-actualization. However, we have no way of deciding if these individuals' personality traits are examples of self-actualization or simply represent Maslow's personal champions. Third, Maslow's hierarchy of needs represents his personal view of how human needs should be organized. There is very little research to support his hierarchy of needs.

The next time someone says, "I'm trying to develop my true potential," you will recognize the humanistic approach's pervasive influence.

REVIEW

To help you understand the social-cognitive and humanistic approaches, let's apply them to your personality.

According to the social-cognitive approach, your personality and behavior result from an interaction of three factors—namely, (1) _____ and _____, _____. and _____. Albert Bandura believes that cognitions and personal factors combine to form your internal (2) _____, which motivate much of your behavior.

Although you may base many of your actions on your thoughts or (3) _____, these may not always be logical or rational. When our thoughts are based on bad reasoning or misinterpretations, we end up with false (4) _____ about ourselves or our environment. Whether accurate or false, Bandura believes that our beliefs or cognitions influence our (5) _____ and help us set goals.

Besides learning cognitions, skills, and behaviors through direct experience, you may have also learned them through observational or (6) _____ learning.

Advantages of the social-cognitive approach include its emphasis on the (7) _____ between cognitions, behavior, and environment and its focus on vicarious learning. One criticism of this approach is that it can explain any behavior after the fact but has difficulty (8) _____ behaviors.

If you were lonely, the social-cognitive approach would suggest a program of behavioral change that would include substituting positive for negative self-statements, which is an example of changing your (9) _____. This program would also include having you play a more active social role, which is an example of changing your (10) _____.

Abraham Maslow's and Carl Rogers' ideas are part of the (11) _____ approach. According to Maslow, all human needs can be arranged in a hierarchy. At the bottom of the hierarchy are the (12) _____ needs, which include (13) _____ needs, such as hunger and thirst.

Above these needs are the (14) _____ needs, such as seeking friendships and being accepted. At the top of the hierarchy is the need for (15) _____ - _____. This need is defined as a tendency for you to achieve your unique potential or reach self-fulfillment. Both Maslow and Rogers believed that everyone has an inherent tendency for self-actualization.

For Rogers, the characteristics that you see yourself as having make up your (16) _____. You are more likely to have a positive self-concept and a positive outlook on life if you received (17) _____ _____ regard when you were growing up. You are more likely to have a negative self-concept and have a negative outlook on life if you received (18) _____ _____ regard.

Advantages of the humanistic approach include its

focus on your inherent potential for (19) _____

-_____. However, critics say that it is very

difficult to define and study self-actualization in a scientific way or to know whether Maslow's hierarchy of needs is valid.

Answers: (1) cognitions and personality factors, behavior, environment; (2) standards; (3) cognitions; (4) beliefs; (5) behavior; (6) vicarious; (7) interaction; (8) predicting; (9) cognitions; (10) behaviors; (11) humanistic; (12) fundamental; (13) physiological; (14) psychological; (15) self-actualization; (16) self, self-concept; (17) unconditional positive; (18) conditional positive; (19) self-actualization

GLOSSARY TERMS

hierarchy of needs
   (p. 423)
humanistic approach
   (p. 423)

positive regard (p. 425)
self (p. 425)
self-actualization (p. 424)

self theory (p. 425)
social-cognitive approach
   (p. 418)

unconditional positive
   regard (p. 426)

Module 38 Personality Assessment

EXPLORING PSYCHOLOGY The Barnum Principle

Is this horoscope true for you?

You are bright, sincere, likable, and have a good sense of humor. At times you are too critical of yourself and take the negative comments of others too seriously. You should be careful of acting on impulse and remember to stop and think before making decisions. You tend to trust people and see their good side. You should select a career that will allow you to interact with people and make use of your trusting nature (author's files).

If you are like the majority of horoscope readers, you will find that this horoscope is very accurate (Saklofske et al., 1982; Snyder, 1974). By using what is called the **Barnum principle,** you too could write very "accurate" horoscopes. The Barnum principle is named after the famous circus owner P. T. Barnum, who knew how to phrase things so they would appeal to the widest possible audience. Writing a horoscope according to the Barnum principle involves focusing on traits that almost everyone considers to be true of themselves (Snyder et al., 1977). For example, the statement "You are likable and sincere," is one that most people feel is true for them. Horoscopes appear to be accurate because what they say would be accepted by almost everyone. This means that you and thousands of other people would all believe that the statements above were a picture of you.

Astrologists claim that your career and personality are influenced by the sign under which you were born. However, researchers who have studied these claims scientifically have found no relationship between the twelve signs of the zodiac and either personality traits or career choices (Gauguelin, 1982; Jackson & Fiebert, 1980; Saklofske et al., 1982). The researchers concluded that the star under which you were born has no influence on the personality you develop or the career you select. Why, then, do so many people continue to believe in astrology and horoscopes? One reason is the Barnum principle we just mentioned; a second is the belief in fate (Sosis et al., 1980). Both factors keep horoscopes very popular as a form of personality assessment, despite the clear-cut evidence against them. Let's see how psychologists assess personality.

Assessment Approaches

Ruth, a college junior, wonders if she needs to be more assertive in her personal relationships, if she has the personality to be a good salesperson, and if she has some problems of which she may be unaware. **Personality assessment** involves describing Ruth's personality, making predictions about how she might behave (Will she be a successful salesperson?), and identifying any psychological disorders she may have (Is her lack of assertiveness really a way to compensate for her very low self-esteem?).

Why are there different ways to assess personality?

In the previous Modules, we discussed a number of different approaches to understanding personality. Since each of these approaches emphasizes a different way to understand personality, each uses a different way to assess personality. For instance, the trait approach, which identifies specific traits, uses tests that ask you to answer a list of specific questions. These question-and-answer tests are called personality inventories. The psychodynamic approach, which examines hidden or unconscious motivation, uses tests that ask you to describe what you see in an inkblot or make up a story about a scene in a picture. Since these tests require you to project your feelings or thoughts, they are called projective tests. The humanistic approach, which explores self-fulfillment and self-concept, asks people to rate how they see themselves. These tests are called self-rating scales. The cognitive-social approach, which looks at the interaction of cognitions, behaviors, and environment, may use personality inventories or may observe how people behave in specific situations. Although these methods represent different forms of personality assessment, they must have two common features to be useful: they must be both reliable and valid.

RELIABILITY AND VALIDITY

You want to know if Ruth is honest and responsible and can be trusted to work in a jewelry store. Ruth takes a personality test on Monday and scores very high on honesty, trustworthiness, and responsibility. If she takes the same test four weeks later and scores very high on the same traits, we would have evidence that the test is reliable. **Reliability** means that you will receive approximately the same score on a test if you take it on a number of different occasions. In Ruth's case, if she scored very high on three traits at the beginning of the month and very low on these traits at the end of the month, we would have evidence that the test is not reliable.

Would you steal from your employer?

Even though a test is very reliable, it may still not be useful. Suppose you gave a test to all your employees, and among those who scored high on honesty and trustworthiness were people you knew often padded their expense reports. In this case you would have reason to believe that your test was not very good at assessing honesty and trustworthiness. As a measure of these two traits, the test is invalid. **Validity** means that a test measures what it was constructed to measure and that we can use the results to predict behavior. A valid test of honesty and trustworthiness, for example, should be able to predict with reasonable accuracy which employees would be likely to steal from a jewelry store. Psychological tests vary widely in validity. Horoscopes have little validity because they have been shown to be no better than chance at predicting behavior or career choices.

TYPES OF PERSONALITY TESTS

How well do you know your own personality?

You are given a long list of adjectives, such as "honest," "friendly," "sincere," "happy," and "temperamental," and asked to rate yourself in terms of each one. Researchers have found that such **self-ratings** of personality traits are equal to or slightly better in validity than standard personality tests (Burisch, 1984). The fact that the validity of self-ratings matches that of standard personality tests means that many people have a fairly good understanding of their own traits. Asking people to rate themselves can therefore be a useful way to assess personality. Another way is to administer a standard personality test.

Personality Inventories

What kind of personality do you have?

Ruth goes to the counseling center to find out more about herself. The counselor gives her a number of personality tests which contain the following questions:

True	False	I like to set my goals very high.
True	False	I rarely work harder than I have to.
True	False	Sometimes I cheat on exams.
True	False	I prefer having many friends.
True	False	Sometimes I worry too much.

These kinds of very specific or structured questions, which require very specific responses, are typical of questions used in **personality inventories.** Personality inventories are used to assess the personalities of normal people, to research the structure of personality, or to identify personality problems. Depending on which of these goals the psychologist is pursuing, he or she will use different inventories. In Ruth's case, she would be given tests designed to identify personality traits in normal people. From her answers, the counselor or psychologist would provide Ruth with a personality profile, which is a description of her personality traits. However, from her personality profile, the psychologist would have only moderate success in predicting how Ruth would behave in specific situations, such as being a jewelry salesperson. This is because personality inventories usually identify general traits and do not take into account how a person's traits will interact with particular situations (Mischel, 1983).

The principal advantages of personality inventories are that they are easily administered, have relatively good reliability, and can identify major traits, such as introversion or extroversion. Their major disadvantages are that they are not very effective at predicting behavior in specific *situations* and that people may introduce *bias* by giving socially desirable answers to make themselves look good.

If the psychologist thought that Ruth might have a serious personality problem, he or she might give her an inventory with these kinds of questions. She is to answer "true," "false," or "cannot say."

I do not tire quickly.
I am worried about sex matters.
When I get bored, I like to stir up some excitement.
I believe I am being plotted against.
Most people will use somewhat unfair means to gain profit or an advantage rather than to lose it.

These questions come from one of the widely used personality inventories, the **Minnesota Multiphasic Personality Inventory,** or **MMPI.** The

MMPI contains over 500 such statements and is used to identify abnormal patterns of behaviors, such as paranoia or depression. The MMPI has standardized scoring and reasonably good reliability and validity (Anastasi, 1982).

Projective Tests

After working for a year at a jewelry store, Ruth began to steal small pieces of jewelry from the store. When she was caught, she said that she did not know why she stole the jewelry, since she neither wore it nor sold it. We want to know what makes Ruth steal. In her case, it will do little good to ask her outright, because she apparently does not know the reason or simply will not tell us. Some psychologists believe that secret or guarded feelings may be revealed by **projective tests.** In a projective test, the person is presented with ambiguous or unstructured stimuli, such as inkblots or pictures, and asked to report what each stimulus looks like or to compose a story about it. The underlying assumption behind projective tests is that Ruth will project her feelings, needs, motives, and personality traits onto the ambiguous stimuli. In doing so, she may reveal things about herself that she is not aware of.

The best-known examples of projective tests are the **Rorschach Inkblot Test,** usually called the Rorschach, and the **Thematic Apperception Test,** usually called the **TAT.** The Rorschach consists of 10 cards with pictures of inkblots (see Figure 13.2). The test is used primarily to identify behavior problems, such as not knowing why one steals. The TAT consists of a series of 20 cards that depict people in ambiguous situations. For example, one card shows a man standing next to a woman in bed. The TAT is used to identify behavior problems as well as to study normal personality structure. Because they use ambiguous stimuli, projective tests are difficult to fake or bias in your favor. No one response on projective tests is important; rather, it is the overall pattern of responses that is significant. The main assumption of projective tests is that they may reveal secret, hidden, or guarded aspects of your personality (Anastasi, 1982).

Suppose Ruth makes up stories about people doing things they are ashamed of. The person giving Ruth the TAT must interpret her responses, and different test administrators may interpret her answers differently. One of the disadvantages of projective tests is that they have low reliability and validity because the subject's responses change from time to time and the

What does your description of an inkblot tell?

How useful are projective tests?

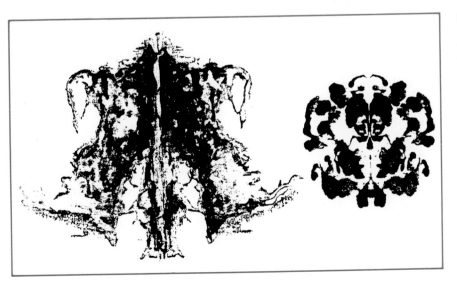

Figure 13.2
Inkblots like those used in the Rorschach test. The Rorschach inkblot test assumes that as you describe what you see in inkblots, you will reveal your needs, desires, wishes, and personality traits. Although the Rorschach test is widely used in clinical settings, its basic assumption is still questioned.
(From Lanyon & Goodstein, 1971)

MAJOR CONCEPT   Personality Assessment

Psychologists have developed many tools to assess personality.

Match each of the following concepts related to personality assessment with its proper description.

1. Personality inventories

2. Validity

3. Barnum principle

4. Projective tests

5. Reliability

6. MMPI

7. Rorschach test

a. __2__ What a test possesses when it measures what it was designed to measure.

b. __7__ A commonly used projective personality test.

c. __1__ Personality tests that use structured questions and require very specific answers.

d. __5__ What a test possesses when most people who take it more than once receive approximately the same score each time.

e. __6__ A personality inventory used to test for serious personality problems.

f. __4__ Personality tests that use unstructured stimuli and that have no clear-cut answers.

g. __3__ The idea that people tend to believe a statement about them is true if the statement is so generally worded it applies virtually to everyone.

Answers: a (2); b (7); c (1), d (5); e (6); f (4); g (3)

responses are open to interpretation. After 60 years of use and over 5,000 articles on the Rorschach, one of the major figures in psychological testing concludes that the reliability and validity of the Rorschach continue to be generally low (Anastasi, 1988).

In addition, there is not much supporting evidence for the assumption that a person taking the Rorschach will project or reveal hidden needs, motives, and personality traits. In spite of their disadvantages, however, projective tests are widely used because clinicians feel that they provide worthwhile information (Lanyon, 1984). Most often projective tests are used in combination with other personality tests.

Choosing the Best Assessment Method

Which kind of personality test is best?

If Ruth were a normal student who wished to find out more about herself, a psychologist would give her a self-rating scale or a personality inventory. If Ruth were a compulsive thief, a psychologist might give her a combination of personality inventories and projective tests. Some psychologists believe projective tests can provide much more information about the person because they are unstructured and the answers cannot be faked. Other psychologists prefer personality inventories because they are easy to score and have higher validity and reliability. Because projective tests and personality inventories have different strengths and weaknesses, they are often used together, especially in assessing personality problems.

REVIEW

As a psychologist, you are going to use personality assessment techniques to select a new roommate. You know that selecting a roommate by horoscopes would not be very useful, because horoscopes lack two important characteristics that any good assessment tool must have, (1) _____ and _____. Since a horoscope does not predict behavior better than chance, it lacks (2) _____, meaning that it does not measure what it is supposed to be measuring. Also, if you asked three different people to do a horoscope for you, you would probably find many differences in the three reports you got. This suggests that horoscopes are often inconsistent, or lacking in (3) _____. You could learn to write "accurate" horoscopes by using the (4) _____ principle—that is, using statements that are almost certain to seem true because they are true for virtually everyone.

If you asked potential roommates to rate themselves in terms of a list of traits, this would be an example of (5) _____ - _____. The validity of self-ratings is about equal to that of standard personality tests. If you asked potential roommates to answer either true or false to very specific questions about personality traits, this would be an example of a personality (6) _____. One such test that is used to identify behavioral problems is abbreviated the (7) _____. One advantage of personality inventories is that their validity and reliability are relatively high because they use very structured questions and scoring techniques. However, you would have only modest success in predicting a roommate's behaviors from a personality inventory because it does not take into account how traits interact with (8) _____. One disadvantage of personality inventories is that the test-takers may (9) _____ their answers in a socially desirable direction.

If potential roommates were asked to look at ambiguous stimuli and describe what they saw, they would be taking (10) _____ tests. If they were asked to describe what they saw in inkblots, they would probably be taking the (11) _____ inkblot test; if they were asked to make up stories about people in pictures, they would be taking the (12) _____. The main assumption of projective tests is that people will (13) _____ needs, motives, and desires which they may be unaware of. This assumption is held by many who use projective tests, but researchers have been unable to find strong support for it. The main advantage of projective tests is that they are difficult to (14) _____. The main disadvantage of projective tests is that they generally have low validity and reliability because people may respond differently on different occasions and because the scoring is open to interpretation.

Answers: (1) reliability, validity; (2) validity; (3) reliability; (4) Barnum; (5) self-rating; (6) inventory; (7) MMPI; (8) situations; (9) bias or fake; (10) projective; (11) Rorschach; (12) TAT; (13) reveal or project; (14) bias or fake

GLOSSARY TERMS

Barnum principle (p. 428)
Minnesota Multiphasic Personality Inventory (MMPI) (p. 430)

personality assessment (p. 429)
personality inventories (p. 430)

projective tests (p. 431)
reliability (p. 429)
Rorschach Inkblot Test (p. 431)

self-ratings (p. 430)
Thematic Apperception Test (TAT) (p. 431)
validity (p. 429)

14

Stress and Coping

Module 39 Cognitive and Physiological Responses to Stress

Waiting for the national anthem to end, Tim Flannery of the San Diego Padres was pumped up with emotion. He hated waiting. No sooner had the song ended than Tim was running to his position at second base. For the next two and a half hours, he prowled the infield, caught impossible balls, shouted at the opposing team, got two hits, and made a head-first dive to score a run at home plate. Tim's life was playing professional baseball.

He loved it when his team won. He worried when they lost. He worried about striking out, making an error, pulling a muscle, and on and on. Sometimes, upon waking up in the middle of the night, he could see himself striking out with two men on base, missing an infield ball, or being thrown out stealing. Worrying made his emotions flow and he would be awake all night.

His team was in New York for a big series with the Mets. Tim was on the sidelines, stretching and getting ready for the game. There was a sharp pain in his head. "It's nothing," he thought. They played hard but lost by one run. On the bus trip back to the hotel, Tim had the feeling that someone was tightening a belt around his chest. "Probably gas or something I ate," he reassured himself. During the next couple of weeks, the headaches came almost every day and the chest pains grew sharper and lasted longer. He kept on playing.

The team arrived in San Francisco to play the Giants. Several hours before the game, Tim took a morning walk along the docks. He wanted some peace and quiet and time to relax. Suddenly his head was really hurting. He began to get dizzy. His chest pains started. He felt himself blacking out. He sat down and held his head. He was really scared. He made it to the ballpark, but he sat out the game. Immediately after the game, the coach made him fly home.

The next day he entered a clinic for a complete medical checkup. The doctor was shaking his head as he looked over Tim's records. "You know, there's nothing wrong with you. Nothing physical." Tim was surprised. "What about the headaches and the chest pains. Do you think I'm imagining them? Well, I'm not. They're real and scare the hell out of me." The doctor was firm. "No, you're not imagining the pain. It's real. But there's no physical cause. I hate to say this, but you're the cause. All your worrying. You're pushing yourself too hard." The doctor paused. "If you don't start relaxing, you're in for a lot more headaches and chest pains" (adapted from the San Diego Tribune, September 11, 1986).

Is it dangerous to worry too much?

Why did Tim Flannery, second baseman for the San Diego Padres, develop severe chest pains? (San Diego Padres Baseball Club)

435

Like Tim, many of us know the feeling of being stressed and the accompanying physical symptoms. In this Module, we will look at how Tim's thoughts contributed to his stress and physical symptoms. In Module 40, we will discuss how personality factors and social environments either increase or decrease feelings of stress. Finally, in Module 41, we will examine some of the methods used to cope more effectively with stress.

APPRAISAL

Why has baseball become so stressful for Tim, while for the rest of us it may be fun, boring, or exciting—but never headache-producing? No one can better answer this question than Richard Lazarus and Susan Folkman (1984), who have developed a very useful theory of how stress develops. According to Lazarus and Folkman, **stress** is the feeling we have when we interpret or appraise a situation as being threatening or challenging and when our personal resources are strained or outstripped by our dealing with this situation. Our personal resources include our personality traits, social supports, and coping skills.

To demonstrate the importance of appraisal, Lazarus and his colleagues asked subjects to watch a film of a man who had a bloody accident with a power saw. One group of subjects was instructed to identify with the man who had the accident and imagine themselves in his place; another group was instructed to watch the movie from a detached viewpoint by remembering that it was only a movie. Would the difference in the subjects' appraisals of the film affect their physiological arousal and stress levels? In several such experiments, Lazarus found that subjects who were told to appraise the situation by identifying with the severely injured man had significantly higher levels of physiological arousal and stress levels than subjects who were asked to use an objective appraisal (Lazarus & Alfert, 1964; Lazarus et al., 1965). Lazarus concluded that when we feel stressed, our feelings arise more from our appraisal and our dealing with the situation than the situation itself. However, when you ask people to identify the cause of their stressful feelings, they usually point to a particular situation and rarely to their appraisals (Figure 14.1).

To explain why Tim developed severe head and chest pains, Lazarus would examine changes in Tim's appraisal. Apparently, when Tim first began playing professional baseball, he felt challenged to make the team and become a good player. After playing for many years, he may have begun to feel threatened by the intense competition from younger players and his growing list of physical injuries. Tim's appraisal of playing baseball has changed from seeing it as more of a challenge to seeing it as more of a threat.

Lazarus and Folkman argue that if Tim appraises playing baseball as a threat, he will feel more stress. This is because a threat appraisal focuses his attention on potential harm and this brings out negative emotions, such as fear, anger, or anxiety. On the other hand, if Tim appraises playing baseball as a challenge, he will feel decreased stress. This is because a challenge appraisal focuses his attention on developing and maintaining his skills and this brings out positive emotions, such as excitement and eagerness.

Appraisal and Coping

When asked to appraise an upcoming exam, students said it was both threatening and challenging. Most potentially disturbing situations have both threatening and challenging aspects. However, we usually focus more on one than the other. For instance, Krantz (1983) found that students who use more of a challenge appraisal, such as striving to get a good grade,

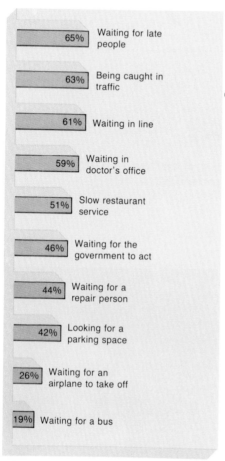

65%	Waiting for late people
63%	Being caught in traffic
61%	Waiting in line
59%	Waiting in doctor's office
51%	Slow restaurant service
46%	Waiting for the government to act
44%	Waiting for a repair person
42%	Looking for a parking space
26%	Waiting for an airplane to take off
19%	Waiting for a bus

Figure 14.1

In one survey, Americans rated these situations as major causes of anger or impatience. But in fact, psychologists think it is our appraisal of the situation that causes feelings of stress. (Data from *USA Today*, August 19, 1987, p. 4D, from a poll entitled "What Ticks You Off, What Makes You Angry or Impatient." Respondents could choose more than one response)

How do you feel about an upcoming exam?

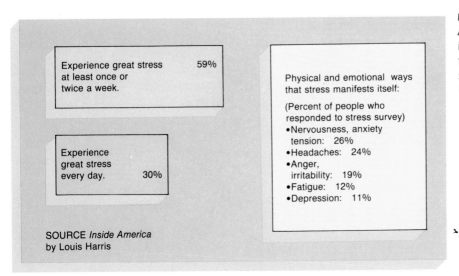

Figure 14.2
A Louis Harris poll shows that many Americans frequently experience stress, and that the feelings frequently result in physical symptoms. (From *Inside America* by Louis Harris, *San Diego Union*, September 12, 1987, p. C-1)

are more likely to take some direct action to deal with the situation itself, such as developing a study program or organizing a review session. Students who use more of a threat appraisal, such as doing poorly or feeling their self-esteem jeopardized, are more likely to focus on negative emotions like anxiety and fear instead of studying. Responses to these negative emotions may take the form of complaining, using drugs, or seeking pleasurable escape activities.

In some situations, we may need to take direct action to deal with both the challenging and the threatening aspects of a situation. Students who have test anxiety can deal with the threat to their self-esteem by participating in a relaxation program, and they can deal with the situation itself by developing an effective study program. When explaining the importance of appraisal, Lazarus and Folkman ask us to remember two critical points. First, since our appraisals of situations usually contain both threatening and challenging aspects, we can reduce our feelings of stress by focusing more on the challenge than on the threat. Second, there are times when we may need to take direct action to deal with both challenges and threats. For example, if we are faced with the loss of a loved one, we would need to deal with the threat to our feelings of security, as well as take direct action to meet the challenge of going on with our own lives.

Tim has come to view baseball more as a threat than a challenge, and this appraisal has brought out several negative emotions, especially anxiety and worry. Trying to deal with these negative emotions as well as continue to play has apparently overwhelmed his personal resources. The result is his feeling of constant stress, which has led to his developing the severe headaches and chest pains. We'll review some coping skills that Tim might use in Module 41. At this point, just notice the close relationship among our appraisals, our feelings of stress, and the kinds of action we take.

Tim is not alone in experiencing physical symptoms when stressed. Figure 14.2 shows that 59 percent of the American population experience *great* stress at least once or twice a week, and many of these people develop physical symptoms. Let's see what feeling stressed does to the body.

PHYSIOLOGICAL AROUSAL

You walk to the front of the classroom, turn around, face 35 students, and get ready to give your speech. As you stand there, your face turns red, your heart pounds, your mouth becomes dry, your hands sweat, your stomach knots, and your muscles become tense (author's files).

Have you ever felt tense when giving a speech?

If you interpret giving a speech as threatening to your self-esteem, you will activate a group of physiological responses known as the flight-fight response. (Allen Green/Photo Researchers)

What is interesting about your physiological response to giving a speech is that it is similar to the response you might experience in a traffic accident. Having an accident is a real threat to your physical survival. Giving a speech is interpreted by you as a real threat to your psychological well-being. Stimuli that cause a threat to your physical or psychological well-being elicit what is commonly called the **flight-fight response.** This response is so named because in many situations it prepares people to flee from the threat they are facing or to try to defend themselves against it. The flight-fight response, in other words, provides the body with increased energy to deal with threatening situations.

One important point to remember about the flight-fight response is that many different kinds of stimuli can elicit it. For example, getting angry over waiting in line triggers the flight-fight response, just as running from a mugger does. In Tim's case, his constant worrying activates his flight-fight response, which keeps his body in a state of physiological arousal. This constant arousal contributes to his recurring headaches, as well as to his chest pains.

What exactly is involved in the flight-fight response? Imagine walking to the front of the room, turning around, facing the class, and starting your speech. If you interpret this situation as threatening to your self-esteem, your appraisal would activate a part of your brain, called the *hypothalamus*, which initiates the fight-flight response. In turn, the hypothalamus triggers the *sympathetic division* of your *autonomic nervous system*, which causes the many physiological changes that function to arouse your body.

These changes include increases in heart rate, blood pressure, and sweat gland secretions. At the same time, your liver releases sugar into the bloodstream, providing your muscles with a source of energy. Blood is also diverted from skin and digestive organs to skeletal muscles (such as arms and legs) and to vital organs (heart, lungs, and kidneys). One part of a tiny gland above the kidneys, the *adrenal medulla*, releases two hormones, *epinephrine* (formerly called adrenalin) and *norepinephrine* (formerly called noradrenalin). These hormones are involved in the release of blood sugar and in further increases in heart rate and blood pressure.

Your appraisal of giving a speech as threatening causes your hypothalamus to activate not only your sympathetic division, but also a neighboring gland, the *pituitary*. One part of the pituitary secretes a hormone called ACTH (*adrenocorticotropic hormone*) directly into the bloodstream.

know italicized stuff

ACTH soon reaches the adrenal gland and acts on its outside layer, called the *adrenal cortex*. In response to ACTH, the adrenal cortex secretes over 50 different hormones, called *corticoids*. Some of the corticoids increase metabolism and cause more blood sugar to become available to meet increased energy needs. Others affect mineral balance (sodium and potassium) to prevent loss of vital body fluids. Still others affect the immune system, which fights off infections. In some cases, corticoids suppress the immune system and make you more susceptible to infections, colds, or flus. Some days after giving your speech, you would probably get a cold.

Besides ACTH, the pituitary also secretes hormones called *endorphins*. One function of these hormones is similar to that of morphine, the reduction of pain. It is thought that in times of extreme stress, such as a serious car accident, the pituitary secretes endorphins, which circulate in the bloodstream and reduce pain from possible injury.

What is curious about the flight-fight response is that it can be activated by many strong emotions, both positive and negative. For instance, the flight-fight response may be triggered by Tim's feeling happy after winning a baseball game, or by your feeling fear when giving a speech. However, the exact pattern of physiological responses may differ for different emotions. Researchers found that although emotions such as anxiety, fear, or excitement all trigger the same general fight-flight response, different emotions trigger different patterns of hormone secretions (Mason, 1975; Veith-Flanigan & Sandman, 1985). Nonetheless, the overall result is the same: both positive and negative emotions cause physiological arousal. The fact that emotions affect the body is the basis for a much-feared and mislabeled procedure, the lie detector test.

Why does Tim's heart pound after winning a baseball game?

APPLYING PSYCHOLOGY

Lie Detector Tests

Floyd Fay was arrested for the shooting and death of a liquor store employee during a robbery. All the evidence was circumstantial. Soon after Fay's arrest, the Wood County prosecutor offered to drop all charges if Fay agreed to take, and pass, a polygraph (lie detector) exam. He readily agreed—and promptly failed the exam. He took a second test and failed again (adapted from the *Los Angeles Times*, December 22, 1980).

Floyd Fay was connected to a *polygraph* machine, commonly called a lie detector. The polygraph is used to record changes in heart rate, blood pressure, and respiration, as well as changes in the skin (electrodermal response) caused by action of the sweat glands. An examiner asked Floyd a number of questions, some of which were neutral, such as "What is your name?" Others were critical because they were related to the crime, such as "Did you rob a liquor store on 5th Street?" Floyd's physiological responses were recorded as he answered the questions.

If Floyd is like most people, answering a critical question with a lie might make him feel guilty about lying or fearful about being caught, and these feelings are stressful. The stress of lying, in turn, would cause his hypothalamus to trigger the sympathetic division of his autonomic nervous system, which automatically causes increased heart rate, blood pressure, and changes in sweat gland activity. The examiner then compares Floyd's physiological responses when answering the critical questions with his responses when answering the neutral questions. Based on the difference between physiological reactions in these two situations, the examiner de-

Can you be telling the truth and fail two lie detector tests?

know italics

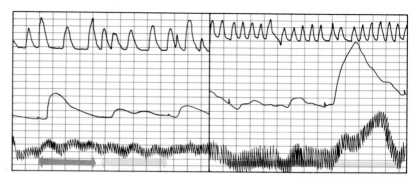

Figure 14.3

Responses to polygraph tests. In the top left panel, you see the responses of an alibi witness for an accused murderer. The witness reacted more strongly to the control question "Up to age 18, did you ever deceive anyone?" (indicated by the dark blue arrow) than she did to the relevant question "Was the accused at another location at the time of the murder?" (the light blue arrow). Based on this difference, the examiner judged this person to be telling the truth. In the top right panel, you see the responses of an accused murderer who pleaded self-defense. He reacted less strongly to the control question "Up to age 18, did you ever physically harm someone?" (indicated by the dark blue arrow) than to the relevant question "Did the deceased threaten to harm you in any way?" (the light blue arrow). Based on this difference, the examiner judged the person to be deceptive. (Diagram from David Raskin, University of Utah, in Meyer, 1982; photo, Bruce Roberts/Photo Researchers)

cides whether Floyd is lying about his involvement in the crime (see Figure 14.3).

After Floyd had served several years behind bars, his lawyer tracked down the real killers, and Floyd was released from prison. But if he was innocent, why did he fail two lie detector exams? The answer is that stressful feelings can be caused not only by guilt from lying, but by nervousness over answering questions. Many different kinds of stressful or emotional situations result in very similar physiological reactions. The polygraph or lie detector measures physiological changes that occur automatically during stressful or emotional situations; it does not measure lying itself.

There is much debate about how often polygraph examiners make correct decisions; estimates range from 65 to 95 percent of the time. This means that, depending upon the ability of the examiner, from 5 to 35 percent of the time he or she will fail to detect a lie or will accuse an innocent person of lying (Joyce, 1984; Lykken, 1979, 1980; Podlesny & Raskin, 1977; Waid & Orne, 1981). Because of this possibility of error, lie detector results are not permitted as evidence in most trials.

SELYE'S GENERAL ADAPTATION SYNDROME

At the end of each semester, Joan finds herself in a terrible fix. She has put off writing several papers, hasn't studied at all for two exams, and must take them both on the same day. Usually she stays up and crams all night, snacks constantly, and gets stomach pains. A day or two after final exams are over, she always gets a cold (author's files).

Joan's stomach pains and colds, as well as the earlier example of Tim's headaches and chest pains, are examples of how stressful situations can directly affect the body. Hans Selye (1956), the first researcher to study the physiological effects of stress, saw these symptoms as direct outcomes of what he called the general adaptation syndrome.

According to Selye, when Joan or Tim is under stress, their bodies go through three stages, which he called alarm, resistance, and exhaustion. These three stages make up the **general adaptation syndrome** and explain why psychosomatic problems develop. Let's use Selye's general adaptation syndrome to explain why Joan gets a cold.

As Joan realizes the semester is almost over, she feels threatened by all she has to do. This threatening appraisal activates her fight-flight response and puts her body in a state of physiological arousal. This is the **alarm stage.** During the alarm stage, you may experience any number of psychosomatic problems. In Joan's case, she has stomach pains. As the semester ends and Joan is in an almost continual state of stress, many of

What can stress do to the body?

her physiological responses apparently return to normal, but her body's energy stores continue to be depleted. This the **resistance stage,** a period when Joan may think her body is functioning normally. Her stomach pains may disappear, and she believes she is dealing effectively with her stress. However, as the stress of final exams continues across days or weeks, her body may enter the **exhaustion stage.** It is during this period that her internal organs may break down and she will become more susceptible to infection because her immune response is suppressed. This is why Joan gets a cold after exams are over.

Selye's general adaptation syndrome is considered important because it provided one of the first explanations of how psychosomatic symptoms could develop.

PSYCHOSOMATIC SYMPTOMS

In one study, over 1,200 subjects were asked to list their most frequent **psychosomatic (SY-ko-sew-MAH-tik) symptoms**—those physical symptoms that occur primarily because of stressful feelings. Their lists included stomach problems, heart irregularities, breathing difficulties, feeling fatigued, headaches, backaches, muscle tension, skin problems, and elimination difficulties (Smith & Seidel, 1982). Besides these relatively common psychosomatic symptoms, others include hypertension or high blood pressure, ulcers, allergy and asthma attacks, insomnia, colds, and flu. Some symptoms, such as headaches, may develop after several hours of stress. Other symptoms, such as stomach problems, may develop after days or months of stress.

Why does Tim get headaches while Joan has stomach problems?

If you get psychosomatic stomach cramps, rashes, colds, or headaches, you know that the symptoms and the accompanying pain are real. Psychosomatic symptoms occur when thoughts and emotional reactions maintain the body in a state of physiological arousal. If that arousal is prolonged, it can lead to pain, infection, or organ breakdown. Psychosomatic symptoms illustrate the close connection between your thoughts and the body's physiological responses.

The link between stress and psychosomatic symptoms is well established. In one study, researchers exposed young male college students to a stressful situation in which they had to recognize and respond to a target faster than a competitor. At the time of testing, all these males had normal blood pressure. However, some of them had a family history of hypertension (high blood pressure) and were therefore considered to be at risk for developing this problem. The researchers asked what would happen to the males at risk for hypertension when they were psychologically stressed. Compared with males who were not at risk, those at risk retained more sodium, which caused more fluid retention, which in turn caused higher blood pressure and heart rates. These authors conclude that psychological stress affects kidney function (retention of sodium), which may play a critical role in the development of hypertension in those who have a predisposition for this condition (Light et al., 1983).

Besides studies on humans, numerous studies on animals clearly show the negative effects stress can have on health. Researchers have found that a single session of inescapable shock, which is very stressful, causes a significantly more rapid growth of tumors in rats than does escapable shock (Sklar & Anisman, 1979). Apparently, the stress of inescapable shock suppresses the rats' immune systems. Other researchers have found that when adult male monkeys are stressed by constantly changing the social makeup of their groups, they tend to develop atherosclerosis, or fatty buildup in the arteries (Kaplan et al., 1983). Notice that these findings share one common

Why might grief increase the chances of dying?

theme: psychological stress can directly affect physiological responses. In other words, it is clear that stress can directly affect your body.

Why do different people develop different kinds of psychosomatic symptoms? According to several studies, the answer is that each of us has inherited a predisposition to develop a particular psychosomatic problem when under stress. For example, in one study, healthy college males were exposed to stressful situations that involved completing a series of mental tasks to avoid shock (Figure 14.4). Some of these males had parents who had hypertension; others had parents who had normal blood pressure. During the stressful mental tasks, those students who had parents with normal blood pressure showed minimal increases in blood pressure and heart rate. Those students who had parents with hypertension showed significantly higher increases in blood pressure and heart rate. The latter students were identified as having overresponsive vascular systems, probably inherited from their parents (Light, 1981; Light & Obrist, 1980). Although you may have inherited a predisposition for developing a particular psychosomatic disease, there are things you can do to decrease your risk. For example, if you inherited a predisposition for hypertension, you might decrease your risk with proper diet, exercise, and a stress management program.

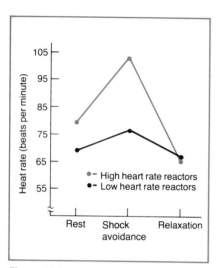

Figure 14.4
Why are some people more likely to develop high blood pressure? One reason is that their heart rate is much more reactive, especially under stress. Some students, labeled high heart rate reactors, were found to have a big increase in heart rate during mild psychological stress; others, labeled low heart rate reactors, were found to have a small or moderate increase. Notice that at rest, there is no significant difference between the two groups. However, when tested on a shock avoidance task, which is a moderate stressor, the high heart rate reactors showed a significantly higher increase. This indicates that the high heart rate reactors were much more responsive to stress and are at risk for developing cardiovascular problems such as high blood pressure. (Adapted from Light & Obrist, 1980)

How can final exams suppress your immune system?

STRESS AND THE IMMUNE SYSTEM

Why are a husband's chances of dying significantly increased after his wife's death? After studying 15 men whose wives had died, researchers found that these men had a significant decline in the activity of their lymphocytes, which are white blood cells that fight off disease. This means that after their wives' deaths, the men became more susceptible to disease and thus more likely to die (Schleifer et al., 1983).

This finding is an example of *psychoneuroimmunology*, a new field of research that began in the late 1970s. Psychoneuroimmunology is the study of how psychosocial factors affect the brain and alter the body's *immune* system, making the person more or less susceptible to disease. In the example above, the death of a spouse resulted in feeling stress that caused a suppression of the immune system and increased the likelihood of contracting some disease. What is important about this research is that it demonstrates a direct connection between psychosocial factors, the brain, and the immune system (Jemmott & Locke, 1984). The fact that the brain can affect the immune system explains why a hay fever victim may sneeze when smelling a plastic flower or why you are more likely to get a cold after final exams.

It was long suspected that stress, such as final exams or grief over someone's death, affected the brain, which in turn influenced the immune system. However, only recently has direct evidence for such a connection appeared. In a very clever series of experiments, Robert Ader and Nicholas Cohen (1975, 1981) classically conditioned animals' immune responses. Drug injections that suppressed immune responses were repeatedly paired with saccharin. After a number of pairings, injections of saccharin alone suppressed the animals' immune responses.

The ability of the immune responses to be conditioned has several important implications. First, it demonstrates a mechanism by which purely psychological or cognitive stressors can affect immune function. For example, through conditioning of the immune system, some stimulus, such as taking final exams or receiving inescapable shock, could suppress the immune system and increase susceptibility to disease, such as colds or cancerous tumors (Laudenslager et al., 1983). Figure 14.5 shows that con-

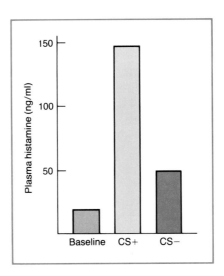

Figure 14.5
Why is it that people with allergies often report that their allergies worsen under stress? One of the substances released by the immune system during stress is histamine, which contributes to the allergic response. Researchers wanted to know if the release of histamine could be learned. Using animals, researchers paired an odor, labeled CS+, with a chemical that elicits the release of histamine. After repeated pairings, the CS+ alone elicited a significant increase in histamine. Another odor, labeled CS−, did not elicit histamine release. This showed that it was the conditioning and not just the odor that caused the release. If these data are generalized to allergic humans, it means that repeated stressful situations themselves may come to elicit the release of histamine and bring on or worsen allergic reactions. *(Adapted from Russell et al., 1984; photo, Mimi Forsyth/Monkmeyer)*

ditioning of the immune system can also result in release of a chemical that may worsen allergic reactions (Russell et al., 1984). Second, the ability to condition immune responses raises the possibility that conditioning procedures can be used to *increase* immune reactions and help fight off disease (Ader, 1981; Anderson, 1982; Gottschalk et al., 1983; Wingerson, 1982). Research on procedures to increase the immune response are now just beginning.

MAJOR CONCEPT   Stress

Please match the term with the correct concept.

1. appraisal

2. Lazarus's definition of stress

3. Selye's general adaptation syndrome

4. psychoneuro-immunology

5. psychosomatic symptoms

6. lie detection test

7. hypothalamus

a. _6_ This procedure is based on the fact that many different kinds of emotions cause physiological arousal which can be measured.

b. _7_ When this part of the brain is activated, it triggers the sympathetic division of the autonomic nervous system to cause physiological arousal.

c. _1_ The way we interpret a particular situation.

d. _2_ The feeling we have when we appraise a situation as being either threatening or challenging and when our personal resources are strained or exceeded by our dealing with the situation.

e. _3_ Our bodies go through three stages: alarm, resistance, and exhaustion. During the alarm and exhaustion stages, we may experience psychosomatic symptoms.

f. _5_ These are real physical symptoms, such as headaches, chest pains, or stomach problems, which result from periods of feeling stressed.

g. _4_ A relatively new field that studies how psychosocial factors affect the brain and the body's immune system.

Answers: a (6); b (7); c (1); d (2); e (3); f (5); g (4)

REVIEW

Several hours' drive from the city brings you to the start of your favorite hiking trail. You put on your hiking boots, make your backpack comfortable, and start off. After about a mile, you sit down on a stone, take off your pack, and get out your water jug. As you begin to drink, your eye catches the movement of something on the ground. Not far away is the largest rattlesnake you ever saw. You get out of there as fast as you can. Your ability to escape or avoid threatening situations is enhanced by physiological changes, which together are called the (1) _fight_ - _flight_ response. These changes began when your fear of the snake activates an area of your brain, called the (2) _hypothalamus_. In turn, this brain area triggers the (3) _sympathetic_ division of your autonomic nervous system as well as your (4) _pituitary_ gland. The sympathetic division causes physiological arousal by increasing (5) _heart_ - _rate_ and _blood_ _pressure_; releasing blood (6) _sugar_ from the liver, diverting blood to (7) _vital_ organs, and causing the adrenal (8) _medulla_ to release two hormones, (9) _epinephrine_ and (10) _norepinephrine_. The hypothalamus also stimulates the (11) _pituitary_ gland to secrete the hormone ACTH, which flows through the bloodstream and causes the adrenal cortex to secrete numerous hormones, called (12) _corticoids_. These hormones help regulate your blood sugar and mineral levels but they may also suppress your (13) _immune_ system. If this system is suppressed, you may get more colds, flus, or infections.

Your fight-flight response is activated by two different kinds of situations: situations that you interpret as threatening to your physical well-being or survival, and situations that you interpret as threatening to your self-esteem or (14) _____ well-being.

After your encounter with the snake, you decide to skip the rest of the hike and head back home. As you approach the city, you get stuck in a traffic jam. How you interpret the traffic jam will determine whether you will feel stressed. According to Lazarus and Folkman, stress is the feeling you have when you interpret or (15) _____ a situation as being threatening or challenging and when your personal (16) _____ are strained or outstripped by your dealing with the situation. Your personality traits, social supports, and coping skills make up your personal resources.

Because you appraise the traffic jam as threatening to your getting-where-you-want-when-you-want, your fight-flight response is activated. By the time you reach your apartment, the physiological arousal caused by the activation of your fight-flight response has resulted in your getting a headache. Painful physical symptoms, such as a headache, that result from feelings of stress are called (17) _____ symptoms.

To explain how psychosomatic symptoms develop, we can use Selye's (18) _____ _____ syndrome, which has three stages. If you appraised the traffic jam as threatening or frustrating, your body would enter into the first stage, called (19) _____. During this first stage, you may develop any number of psychosomatic symptoms. If, during the next week, you appraised studying for and taking midterms as very threatening, your body might enter the second stage, called (20) _____. During the second stage, your body might seem to be dealing with your feeling of stress and you may not have any psychosomatic symptoms. However, if your feelings of stress continued for a period of time, your body might go into the third stage, called (21) _____. During the third stage, you might develop a more serious psychosomatic symptom, such as a cold, a long-lasting headache, or ulcers.

If you developed a cold or got the flu, it might be because your feelings of stress suppressed your immune system. A new field of research, called (22) _____, studies how psychosocial factors affect the brain and the immune system. For example, if a person were to develop an allergy to flowers, and then sneeze in the presence of flowers that proved to be artificial, we would guess that this immune system response has been (23) _____ to the sight of flowers. Evidence such as this indicates that purely (24) _____ factors can affect the immune system.

You receive a notice to take a lie detector test in

order to get a job at a national chain store. You know that a lie detector or polygraph test measures physiological arousal that results from the activation of the

(25) _____ division of the autonomic nervous system. This division may be activated by any

number of (26) _____ feelings, including guilt from telling a lie as well as feelings of nervousness, fear, or anxiety. You pass the test, get the job, and live happily ever after. Except for the daily traffic jams.

Answers: (1) fight-flight; (2) hypothalamus; (3) sympathetic; (4) pituitary; (5) heart rate; blood pressure; (6) sugar, glucose; (7) vital; (8) medulla; (9) epinephrine; (10) norepinephrine; (11) pituitary; (12) corticoids; (13) immune; (14) psychological; (15) appraise; (16) resources; (17) psychosomatic; (18) general adaptation; (19) alarm; (20) resistance; (21) exhaustion; (22) psychoneuroimmunology; (23) conditioned; (24) psychological; (25) sympathetic; (26) emotional

---

GLOSSARY TERMS

alarm stage (p. 440)
exhaustion stage (p. 441)
flight-fight response
  (p. 438)

general adaptation
  syndrome (p. 440)

psychosomatic symptoms
  (p. 441)

resistance stage (p. 441)
stress (p. 436)

Module 40 Personality, Social, and Situational Factors in Stress

PERSONALITY FACTORS

The door opened. Dr. Michael DeBakey entered and walked quickly to the operating table. His assistants had already opened the patient's chest and removed the diseased heart. With the skill and precision of a master, Dr. DeBakey transplanted a healthy donor heart into the patient's chest. It took about an hour. When Dr. DeBakey finished, he left the operating suite and went to the scrub room. He took off his operating clothes, scrubbed down, and put on clean, sterilized clothes. In a matter of minutes, he entered another operating suite, and the whole process started over. In a normal working day, Dr. DeBakey operates on between five and nine patients. He follows a work schedule that begins in the early morning hours and continues well past midnight. He normally spends 15 hours a day, 7 days a week in the hospital and performs as many heart operations in one month as most surgeons do in a year. Dr. DeBakey spends every day making life and death decisions about his patients.

In the surgical suite Dr. DeBakey is in absolute control. His standards are incredibly high, and anyone not measuring up is sternly admonished. There is one more thing you should know about Dr. DeBakey. As of this writing, he is 79 years old (adapted from the San Diego Tribune, November 27, 1987).

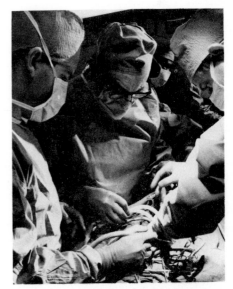

Dr. Michael Debakey, well-known heart surgeon, has three personality traits—challenge, commitment, and control—that help him meet the demands of working 15-hour days. (UPI/Bettmann Newsphotos)

Why has Dr. DeBakey been able to function so successfully for so many years in such a potentially disturbing environment? Richard Lazarus and Susan Folkman (1984) gave us one answer in Module 39. They said that if you appraise a situation more as a threat, your feelings of stress may increase. This is because a threat appraisal focuses your attention more on the potential harm and this brings out negative emotions, such as fear, anger, or anxiety. On the other hand, if you appraise a situation more as a challenge, your feelings of stress may decrease. This is because a challenge appraisal focuses your attention more on solving the problem and this brings out positive emotions, such as excitement and eagerness. There is no doubt that Dr. DeBakey appraises his heart operations more as a challenge than a threat. His use of a challenge appraisal is one of the reasons he functions so well in such a potentially disturbing environment.

You also learned in Module 39 that feelings of stress increase when the demands of the situation strain or exceed our personal resources. A second reason that Dr. DeBakey has functioned so well is that he has a unique combination of personal resources that rarely seem strained or exceeded. Not only has he demonstrated incredible motivation, drive, and surgical skill, but he has three personality traits that are known to protect people from stress. Let's examine these traits.

Hardiness

In a series of experiments, Suzanne Kobasa, Salvatore Maddi, and their associates asked why certain people handled potentially stressful situations much better than others. In a study of the personality characteristics of middle- and upper-level executives and lawyers who had experienced considerable stress in the previous three years, they discovered that some of the executives and lawyers became ill while others stayed healthy. Kobasa and Maddi found that those who stayed healthy in spite of stressful life situations had three personality traits—control, commitment, and challenge—which together they called **hardiness.** Kobasa suggested that the three hardiness traits protect or buffer us from the potentially harmful effects of stressful situations and reduce our chances of developing psychosomatic illnesses (Kobasa, 1979, 1982; Kobasa et al., 1982a; Kobasa et al., 1982b). Kobasa and Maddi's research on hardiness explains why some individuals develop psychosomatic problems in potentially stressful situations and others do not.

From what we know of Dr. DeBakey, he appears to be the perfect example of a hardy person. His medical reputation shows he has *commitment*, which means he knows and pursues his goals and values. His pursuit of open-heart surgery shows he likes a *challenge*, which means he actively confronts and solves problem situations. His role as head of surgery indicates his desire to be in *control*, which means he believes that his actions directly affect how situations turn out.

Dr. DeBakey's life clearly illustrates what researchers have discovered about reducing stress. You can lower your stress level by using a challenge appraisal instead of a threat appraisal and by developing the trio of personality traits—commitment, challenge, and control—which make up hardiness.

One of the hardiness traits has been studied more than the other two. Let's see what researchers have discovered about the importance of control.

Locus of Control

For each of the following numbered choices, select the alternative (a or b) that you think is more true (adapted from Rotter, 1966).

1. ____ a. Many of the unhappy things in people's lives are partly due to bad luck.
   ____ b. People's misfortunes result from the mistakes they make.

Why doesn't his schedule kill him?

Do you make things happen, or do things happen to you?

2. ____ a. No matter how hard you try, some people just don't like you.
   ____ b. People who can't get others to like them don't understand how to get along with others.
3. ____ a. It is not always wise to plan too far ahead, because many things just turn out to be a matter of good or bad fortune.
   ____ b. When I make plans, I am almost certain I can make them work.
4. ____ a. Often exam questions tend to be so unrelated to course work that studying is really useless.
   ____ b. In the case of a well-prepared student, there is rarely such a thing as an unfair test.

This brief test comes from a longer one that assesses how much control you believe you have over what happens to you. In each case, alternate (a) indicates a belief that you do not have much control over life's events, while alternate (b) indicates a belief that you do have such control. Beliefs about whether you control the situation or the situation controls you determine your **locus of control**. If you believe you are basically in control of life's events and that what you do influences what happens, you are said to have an *internal locus of control*. If you believe chance and luck are major factors and that you do not have much influence over what happens, you are said to have an *external locus of control*. Locus of control should be thought of as a continuum, with internal on one end and external on the other. Most of us lie somewhere along this continuum, generally being more or less internal or external, rather than totally one or the other (Lefcourt, 1982).

Locus of Control and Stress

"No matter how much I study, it never seems to help." This statement is more characteristic of a student with an external locus of control. A student with an external locus of control will tend to believe that there is nothing he can do when things go badly. This belief leads to his appraising situations, such as exams, as being more of a threat than a challenge. A threat appraisal results in his feeling increasing levels of stress during exams. In contrast, a student with an internal locus of control will tend to believe that her actions can overcome potentially unsettling situations, such as exams. This belief leads to her appraising exams as more of a challenge than a threat. The result is that she feels lower levels of stress during exams.

An example of the interaction between locus of control and appraisal is shown in Figure 14.6. Subjects who perceived situations as uncontrollable felt increased levels of stress and were more likely to develop physical and psychological problems (Grant et al., 1982; Stern et al., 1982; Suls & Mullen, 1981). On the other hand, subjects with an internal locus of control have been found to appraise situations as less stressful and were better able to cope. For instance, cardiac patients with an internal locus of control were more cooperative, less depressed, and had shorter stays in intensive care than patients with an external locus of control (Cromwell et al., 1977).

From research on locus of control and hardiness, we see that personality traits influence our appraisals, which in turn may increase or decrease feelings of stress and chances of developing psychosomatic illnesses. Let's look next at one particular combination of personality traits that has received much scientific and popular attention.

Figure 14.6
How onset of illness is influenced by perceptions of control. Individuals who thought of themselves as being in control of their lives, labeled high controllability, were found to have significantly fewer illnesses than people who thought they had little control over their lives, labeled low controllability. (Data adapted from Stern et al., 1982)

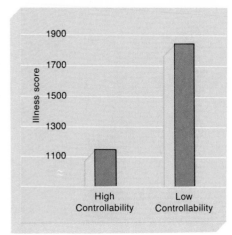

EXPLORING PSYCHOLOGY Personality and Illness

What does it mean to be called a "Type A"?

In 1974, Meyer Friedman and Ray Rosenman published a book that startled the medical community. They reported that besides the known risk factors associated with coronary heart disease, such as diet, exercise, and smoking, there was a psychological risk factor, which they called **Type A behavior.** According to Friedman and Rosenman, a person with Type A behavior had a combination of personality traits, including an excessive, competitive, and aggressive drive to achieve, a hostile attitude when frustrated, a habitual sense of time urgency, and a very rapid and explosive pattern of speaking. In contrast, **Type B behavior** was characterized by being easygoing, calm, relaxed, and patient. Compared to Type Bs, Type As were found to have two to three times as many heart attacks (Rosenman & Chesney, 1985). By 1978, Type A behavior was officially recognized as an independent risk factor for heart disease by a National Institutes of Health panel. However, at about this same time, data began coming in that raised two questions about Type A behavior. First, is Type A behavior really a risk factor as earlier research had suggested? Second, which personality traits make up Type A behavior?

In answer to our first question, Stephanie Booth-Kewley and Howard Friedman (1987) analyzed 83 studies on Type A behavior. They concluded that there was a modest but reliable association between Type A personality variables and cardiovascular disease. For reasons not fully understood, a number of studies since 1977 had failed to find an association between Type A behavior and coronary heart disease. The reason might be that the overall rate of heart attacks was dropping during this time, or there were problems in identifying Type As. One of the strongest cases to be made for Type A behavior being a risk factor comes from a study on changing this behavior. Figure 14.7 shows that a program using psychological techniques (described in Module 41) was successful in decreasing Type A behaviors. More important, this program also reduced subsequent heart attacks by one-half compared with a control group (Friedman et al., 1984). These studies suggest that Type A behavior is about the same magnitude as smoking as a risk factor for coronary disease.

Everyone faces difficult days and unhappy situations, but not everyone responds to events in the same way. See the text for one explanation. (Gregg Mancuso/Jeroboam, Inc.)

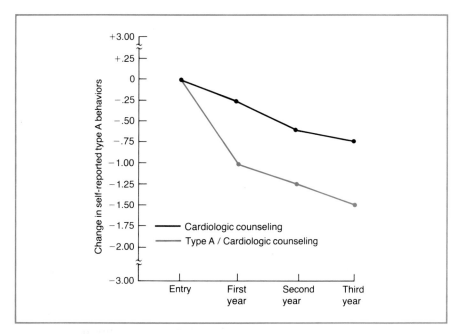

Figure 14.7
Over the course of three years, cardiac patients who received counseling in how to reduce Type A behaviors showed a much greater reduction in their reported Type A behaviors than cardiac patients who did not receive this counseling. In addition, the percentage of subjects who experienced another heart attack during the three years of counseling was much lower in the Type A counseling group (8.9%) than in the cardiac counseling only group (18.9%). (Adapted from Friedman et al., 1984)

"What kind of personality traits make up Type A behavior?" The popular conception of the Type A person is someone who is hurried, impatient, and a workaholic. According to Booth-Kewley and Friedman's analysis, a truer picture of a Type A behavior person is someone who frequently expresses one or more negative emotions, such as anger, hostility, or aggression. In a new finding, Booth-Kewley and Friedman associated depression with coronary disease, and they suggested that the description of Type A behavior be broadened to include this psychological disorder. In a related review, Karen Matthews and Suzzane Haynes (1986) also suggested that negative emotions, such as anger, hostility, or mistrust, should be considered the distinguishing features of Type A behavior. These researchers now describe a Type A person as someone who may be depressed, aggressively competitive, easily frustrated, anxious, angry, or some combination. Interestingly, Booth-Kewley and Friedman found that coronary disease was not associated with a workaholic attitude and recommended that this trait be dropped from the Type A behavior pattern. Besides Type A behavior, is there a single trait or combination of traits that make one at risk for headaches, ulcers, asthma, or rheumatoid arthritis?

The Disease-Prone Personality

"Do worriers get ulcers and anxious types get headaches?" Although the exact cause of headaches, ulcers, asthma, and rheumatoid arthritis is unknown, doctors estimate that between 30 to 50 percent of these symptoms are caused by psychological factors. Is it possible that certain personality traits, such as anxiety, depression, and anger, contribute to developing these symptoms? Howard Friedman and Stephanie Booth-Kewley (1987) analyzed 101 studies to answer this question. They found that the relationship between a personality trait, such as anxiety, depression, anger, or hostility, and one of the diseases is low but comparable to that reported for other medical risk factors. For example, the correlation between anxiety and ulcers is about .15, which is very similar to that reported between smoking and coronary heart disease.

Contrary to the popular notion that worriers get ulcers and anxious types get headaches, the researchers found that many different personality traits are associated with a particular disease. For example, higher levels of anxiety and depression are associated with a greater likelihood of developing headaches. Because a combination of traits rather than a single trait is associated with disease, Friedman and Booth-Kewley concluded that there is a **disease-prone personality** rather than a "headache-prone personality" or an "ulcer-prone personality." What surprised them was the finding that besides anxiety, anger, hostility, and aggression being related to a disease, so too is depression. The importance of depression in disease was also suggested by Victoria Persky (1987) and her colleagues. In a 20-year follow-up study, Persky found that men who had scored high on a depression scale had a higher incidence of cancer and death from cancer than men who had scored low. This means that the frequent expression of certain personality traits, such as depression, anger, aggression, anxiety, or hostility, puts one at risk for developing a number of disorders, just as being a smoker puts one at risk for developing coronary heart disease.

Besides the frequent expression of certain personality traits, being in certain kinds of situations may also increase our stressful feelings. Which situations do you think are most likely to increase your stressful feelings?

SITUATIONAL FACTORS

Life Events and Hassles

How many of the following situations have you found yourself in during the last six months?

- Entered, dropped out, or changed colleges.

- Were engaged, married, or divorced.

- Failed a course or were put on academic probation.

- Experienced the death of a close family member or friend.

- Had financial problems.

- Changed your major field of study.

- Had an outstanding personal achievement.

- Had a major car accident.

- Took a trip or vacation.

When is one more thing one too many?

By asking subjects similar questions, researchers Thomas Holmes and Richard Rahe (1967) studied the effects of potentially disturbing situations, which they called *major life events*. They reasoned that if we faced a large number of major life events, we would have to make major adjustments and, in turn, feel increasing levels of stress. Since we know that increased stress levels often lead to psychosomatic problems, perhaps facing many life events would be associated with increased illness. Holmes and Rahe and many others did find a modest correlation (0.2–0.3) between number of major life events and a subsequent physical or psychological illness (Brown, 1981; Maddi et al., 1987; Minter & Kimball, 1980; Schroeder & Costa, 1984).

In their initial scale, Holmes and Rahe made no distinction between desirable events (entering college) and undesirable events (failing a course). They assumed that it was the accumulation of life events, whether desirable or undesirable, that increased a person's chances of becoming ill. Irwin Sarason (1979) and his colleagues argued that it is not the accumulation of

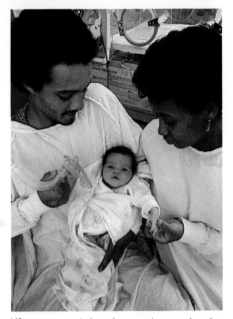

life events, but rather our appraisal of events as desirable or undesirable that is important. They and others found that undesirable life events are more important predictors of developing an illness than are desirable events (Sarason et al., 1985; Vossel & Froehlich, 1979). These studies tell us that experiencing many major life events, especially undesirable ones, may ultimately contribute to our becoming ill.

Suppose you have not faced many major life events in the past six months or year but have had a number of illnesses. Besides medical reasons, what other kinds of situational factors could have contributed to these illnesses? Surprisingly, one source turns out to be **hassles,** which are those small, irritating, frustrating events of everyday life. Hassles include getting stuck in traffic, noise, running out of time, looking for a parking spot, having too many things to do, car problems, waiting, and on and on. Researchers found that the number of hassles we face is a better predictor of our daily mood than are major life events (Eckenrode, 1984; Kanner et al., 1981). If we combine these studies, we arrive at the following possible sequence: daily hassles affect our overall mood, which affects our level of stress, which affects our subsequent development of psychosomatic problems. One of the reasons that daily hassles so greatly affect our mood is that they are frustrating.

Life events and situations such as registering for classes, having to move, or having a baby may all be stressful. Experiencing a large number of stressful events within a short time, especially those that are aversive, may contribute to developing an illness in the future. (Michael Kagan/Monkmeyer, Liane Enkelis/Stock, Boston, Dan McCoy/Rainbow)

Frustration and Conflict

• After leaving home early to be on time, you are caught in a traffic jam.

• You miss getting a good grade on an exam because you made several dumb mistakes.

• Your boss insists that you work on a weekend that you were planning to take off.

Frustration is the feeling you have when your attempts to reach some goal are blocked. You may not be able to reach a goal because of personal limitations, such as making dumb mistakes on an exam. Or a goal might slip beyond your grasp because of social or environmental limitations, such as your boss changing your work schedule. No matter what the cause, how you respond when frustrated will affect your stress level.

If you respond to frustrating situations with anger, complaints, or hostility, you may feel increased stress. This is because emotional responses tend to cause physiological arousal, thereby intensifying your feelings, including feelings of stress. If you respond to frustrating situations with helplessness or the belief that nothing can be done—in other words, if you view a situation as being uncontrollable—you may also feel more stressed (Grant et al., 1982). Notice that many of our common responses to frustrating situations tend to increase stressful feelings. In Module 41, you will find a section on how to manage frustration. Now let's look at what we feel when we must choose between two conflicting goals.

Conflict

Does having to make choices cause you stress?

When faced with a choice between studying for an exam and enjoying yourself on the weekend, you will probably experience conflict. "Yes," you may want to study to get a good grade, but "no," you want to avoid the effort of studying. In this case, the conflict is called **approach-avoidance.** The approach part involves wanting to get a good grade; the avoidance part involves wanting to avoid hard work. If you are in a situation where you must choose between two options, *both* of which are desirable (such as going to a movie *or* to a party), it is called an **approach-approach** conflict. If you are in a situation where you must choose between two *un*desirable options (such as studying or writing a paper), it is called an **avoidance-avoidance** conflict.

Your attempts to resolve a conflict, such as whether to study or not, usually result in feelings of stress. You feel ambivalent, wanting both to get good grades and to avoid studying. As the time to make the decision approaches, you will change your mind many times, alternating between deciding to study and deciding not to study. Each time you decide not to study, you will imagine the awful consequences and your stress level will continue to rise.

Why is it that situations involving conflict trigger feelings of stress? One reason is that no matter which decision you make, you must deal with giving up one of your choices or goals. The longer it takes you to resolve the conflict, the more your feelings of stress may increase and the greater your chances of developing psychosomatic problems. According to Lazarus

Frustrated by the umpire's call, a baseball manager responds with rage. Situations like these have great potential for causing stress. (AP/Wide World Photos)

"If I buy this new car I'll really enjoy driving it, but I'll also have to go into debt." This is an example of an approach-avoidance conflict, which often results in stressful feelings. (Peter Menzel/Stock, Boston)

and Folkman (1984), you are more likely to resolve your conflict early if you appraise the situation more as a challenge than a threat. This is because appraising the situation as a challenge is more likely to motivate you to work on a solution.

Situation and Appraisal

"That situation drives me up the wall." Most of us have experienced situations that we cannot avoid and that increased our stress levels and chances of developing psychosomatic symptoms. In unavoidable situations, people often say, "There's nothing I can do about it." According to Lazarus and Folkman, there are a number of things we *can* do about disturbing, unavoidable situations. Since we cannot change or avoid the situation, we must work instead on changing our appraisal of it. Remember that subjects who watched a film of a bloody accident were able to alter their levels of stress and physiological arousal by changing their appraisal from one of involved participant to one of objective observer. We will discuss other ways to change appraisals in Module 41. Another thing we can do to deal with a disturbing or unavoidable situation is to do something that a whole town did.

SOCIAL SUPPORT

There was something curious about the town of Roseto, Pa. Only one Rosetan man in 1,000 died of a heart attack, compared with a national rate of 3.5 per 1,000; the rates for women were even lower. Rosetans also had lower rates for ulcers and emotional problems compared with the rest of the United States and their neighboring towns. This was very puzzling, because the men and women of Roseto were relatively obese. They also ate as much animal fat, smoked as much, and exercised as little as residents of the other towns. "One striking feature did set Roseto apart from its neighbors," says Stewart Wolf, vice president for medical affairs at St. Luke's Hospital in Bethlehem, Pa., and a principal investigator of the Roseto phenomenon. . . . "We found that family relationships were extremely close and mutually supportive. This cohesive quality extended to neighbors and to the community as a whole" (adapted from Greenberg, 1978, p. 378).

Why did this community have so few heart attacks?

As Rosetan families prospered, they moved into the surburbs and their social support system began to break down. With its breakdown came an increase in heart attacks, especially in younger men. The study therefore suggests the importance of social support in dealing with stress.

Social support refers to all the human relationships that have a lasting and positive impact on an individual's life. Social support systems help you

---

MAJOR CONCEPT   Personality, Situational, and Social Factors in Stress

Please match the term with its correct statement.

1. hardiness
2. frustration
3. Type A behavior
4. conflict
5. disease-prone personality
6. social support
7. locus of control
8. major life event
9. hassles

a. __4__ The feeling that results when we have to choose between two goals, such as in an approach-avoidance or approach-approach situation.

b. __6__ Refers to human relationships that protect or buffer us from the potentially harmful effects of disturbing situations.

c. __9__ These are small, irritating, frustrating daily events that greatly influence our mood, which in turn, affects our stress level.

d. __1__ A combination of personality traits, including control, commitment, and challenge, which protect or buffer us from the harmful effects of potentially disturbing situations.

e. __2__ The feeling we have when our goals are blocked.

f. __8__ Facing a large number of these situations, especially if they are undesirable, may contribute to our developing illnesses.

g. __3__ A combination of personality traits that represent a risk factor for developing coronary heart disease. These traits may include one or more negative emotions, such as anger, hostility, or aggression, as well as depression.

h. __7__ A belief about how much influence you think you have over a situation. If you believe you have very little influence over situations, you have an external one and if you believe you have great influence, you have an internal one.

i. __5__ A combination of personality traits that makes one at risk for developing ulcers, asthma, headaches, or rheumatoid arthritis. These traits may include anxiety, anger, hostility, aggression, and depression, or some combination.

Answers: a (4); b (6); c (9); d (1); e (2); f (8); g (3); h (7); i (5)

mobilize resources to gain control of emotional and stressful situations. Such help may include helping with a task, lending money, solving problems, talking, and giving love and affection. Social support systems help raise self-esteem, self-confidence, and feelings of self-worth, which in turn promote and maintain psychological adjustment (Caplan, 1974). Apparently, it is not the quantity of friends you have that matters in coping with stress. Rather, it is the quality of your friendships that is important in receiving social support (Gove et al., 1983).

People with a strong social support network report fewer neurotic and depressive symptoms than people in control groups (Aneshensel & Stone, 1982, Caplan, 1981; Greenblatt et al., 1982; Henderson, 1981). These findings suggest that family and friends help you to deal with stressful situations. These findings also suggest that one goal of a stress management program is the development of a social support system. After reviewing a decade of literature on social support, Sheldon Cohen and Thomas Wills (1985) concluded that social support contributes to our well-being, both physically and psychologically. Among other things, they found that social support protects or buffers us from potentially harmful situations by changing our appraisal, improving our self-esteem, providing us with information, and changing our coping patterns. Now we have another reason to be thankful for good friends.

What do your best friends do for you?

REVIEW

Laura is both excited and concerned about doing well her first semester in college. She will feel less stress if she appraises "doing well in college" as more of a

(1) _____ than a threat. Laura will be better able to deal with her feelings of stress if she has the

following three personality traits: (2) _____,

_____, and _____, which together are called (3) _____. This trio of traits will help protect or buffer Laura from the potentially harmful effects of stressful situations and will re-

duce her chances of developing (4) _____ illnesses.

Laura believes that how much she studies and how she applies herself will directly affect her academic performance. This attitude means that Laura has a more

(5) _____ locus of control. In contrast, her roommate believes that she can only study so hard and that much of how she performs on exams is due to chance. This attitude means that Laura's roommate has

a more (6) _____ locus of control. Because of her internal locus of control, Laura will be more

likely to appraise situations as (7) _____ stressful and be better able to cope than will her roommate.

Besides being concerned about college, Laura is worried about her father. After his last checkup, he was warned about the potential dangers of having Type A behaviors. According to the most recent definition, Type A behavior includes one or more negative emo-

tions, such as (8) _____, _____,

and _____. Besides these three personality

traits, an additional trait, (9) _____, was shown to be associated with coronary heart diseases. Because Laura's father shows Type A behaviors, it

means that he has twice the (10) _____ for developing coronary heart diseases compared with Type B individuals. Unlike the original definition of Type A

behavior, being a (11) _____ is no longer considered a risk factor or part of Type A behavior.

Laura thinks she gets headaches because she worries so much. Although worry may be a factor, it is not associated only with headaches. Researchers found that

a combination of (12) _____ traits, including anxiety, depression, anger, aggression, and hostility, made people at risk for developing headaches, ulcers, asthma, and rheumatoid arthritis. This combi-

nation of traits is called the (13) _____-

_____ personality and is known to be a risk factor in developing illnesses.

During the past year, Laura broke up with her boyfriend, had to work part time at a boring job, went away to college, was involved in a car accident, and worried over her father's heart condition. These kinds of major, undesirable life events may increase the likelihood of Laura's getting some (14) _____. However, Laura's daily mood is more influenced by how she deals with regular, irritating events called (15) _____.

When Laura went to pick up her car, she was told the car would not be ready for at least two more days. Because her goal of getting her car was blocked, she had a feeling of (16) _____. If she reacts to this situation with anger, complaining, or hostility, she may increase her level of stress because these responses increase physiological (17) _____ which, in turn, will intensify her feelings.

Laura wants to have an apartment of her own but knows that she would have to borrow money from her parents to do so. This is an example of an (18) _____ - _____ conflict.

If she were deciding between two things that were both desirable, such as living by herself or with her best friend, she would experience an (19) _____ - _____ conflict. If she were deciding between two things she did not like, such as living in a crowded dorm or finding a stranger to share an apartment with, she would experience an (20) _____ - _____ conflict. Although Laura may not be able to change potentially frustrating or conflicting situations, she can reduce her feelings of stress by working on changing her (21) _____ of the situation.

Being away from home, Laura misses her family and friends, which is part of her (22) _____ _____ system. In a number of ways, this system helps to protect or (23) _____ her from potentially disturbing situations. Her mother advises Laura to make a few really good friends at college because it is not the number of relationships that is important, but rather their quality.

Answers: (1) challenge; (2) control, commitment, challenge; (3) hardiness; (4) psychosomatic; (5) internal; (6) external; (7) less; (8) anger, hostility, aggression; (9) depression; (10) risk, chance; (11) workaholic; (12) personality; (13) disease-prone; (14) illness, disease; (15) hassles; (16) frustration; (17) arousal; (18) approach-avoidance; (19) approach-approach; (20) avoidance-avoidance; (21) appraisal; (22) social support; (23) buffer

GLOSSARY TERMS

approach-approach (p. 452)
approach-avoidance (p. 452)

avoidance-avoidance (p. 452)
disease-prone personality (p. 450)

frustration (p. 451)
hardiness (p. 446)
hassles (p. 451)
locus of control (p. 447)

social support (p. 454)
Type A behavior (p. 448)
Type B behavior (p. 448)

Module 41 Coping

KINDS OF COPING

Who is to blame when you have a bad day?

"I did the best I could."

Robert was explaining what happened.

"I had to wait 30 minutes. You know how much I hate waiting. All the time I kept worrying about the questions. By the time it was my turn, I was really anxious."

The father waited for Robert to continue.

"I walked into the room. As soon as the interviewer said "Hello" I knew I didn't like her. She was the pushy kind. She asked questions I hadn't planned on. I got defensive. I didn't think about what I was saying. I gave some really dumb answers."

The father asked, *"Why didn't you stop yourself?"*

"Well, by then I was getting mad. What would you have done? I mean, this interviewer was awful."

The father answered, *"I think I might have thought about how much I wanted that job. I think I might have tried to relax so I could think straight."*

"Sure, easy for you to say. You weren't the one feeling pushed around. There's no way I could have stayed calm."

The father noticed that Robert was tapping his foot, something Robert did when he was feeling anxious.

"After the interview, I had to go to the bank because there was a problem with my account. After ten minutes of checking, they found the problem. The teller said it would have been quicker if I had brought in my bank statement as I had been asked to do. Can you imagine that? They make a mistake and then blame me. I had a few choice words for the teller."

The father asked, *"Was it the teller's fault?"*

"No. But I felt I should have been treated better."

The father tried once more. *"Is it possible you got upset so easily because you take things too personally?"*

"I can't help it. That's the way I am. Mom does it too."

The father thought it best to change the subject. *"How about going out for a pizza?"*

"I had a quick snack just before I came home. I know I shouldn't have eaten that greasy burger. Now my stomach hurts."

The father knew what might help. *"Let's rent a movie. It will take your mind off your bad day"* (author's files).

The coping style we use can affect how well we manage stress and deal with life situations. (Alex Webb/Magnum)

Robert had to cope with three potentially disturbing situations. One was major, having a job interview, and two were relatively minor, having to wait for 30 minutes and clearing up a problem at the bank. According to Richard Lazarus and Susan Folkman (1984), **coping** refers to the cognitive and behavioral efforts we use in managing a situation that we have appraised as taxing or exceeding our personal resources. Situations may be external, such as events in our environment, or internal, such as our thoughts or beliefs. One of the main reasons that Robert had a "bad day" was because his coping methods were not effective. Let's figure out what Robert did wrong.

Coping with Emotions vs. Coping with Problems

If you examine Robert's coping methods closely, you will find that he spent most of his time and energy dealing with his negative emotions and not with what causes those emotions. Lazarus and Folkman would say that Robert is using emotion-focused coping rather than problem-focused coping. *Emotion-focused coping* means that Robert is managing his emotional responses to the problem rather than doing something about the cause of his negative emotions. *Problem-focused coping* means that Robert is working on solving the problem itself.

To see the difference in these two kinds of coping, look at how Robert dealt with a relatively minor problem at his bank. Before even arriving at the bank, Robert allowed himself to get angry. Once at the bank, Robert remained angry and uncooperative. He used emotion-focused coping to deal with his anger by telling off the teller. This was not a very effective way of coping with the bank problem, since he left the bank feeling increased levels of stress. His increased stress no doubt contributed to his stomach problem. Although Robert thought otherwise, his stomach problem was probably a psychosomatic symptom of the increased stress he felt all day long. Since his emotion-focused coping did not remove the causes of his problems, Robert had a "bad day" and felt greatly stressed.

If Robert had used problem-focused coping, he would have told himself on the way to the bank that this was a minor problem and would soon be solved. He would have brought in his bank statement, been cooperative, solved the problem, and left the bank feeling decreased levels of stress.

Lazarus and Folkman warn against taking an all-or-none approach when discussing the two kinds of coping. There are many situations, especially those that are uncontrollable, frustrating, or involve conflict, that require the use of both emotion-focused and problem-focused coping. For instance, you probably need both kinds of coping to deal with your midterm and final exams. Let's look at how we might use both kinds of coping to deal with an uncomfortable feeling we all have from time to time.

Causes of Anxiety

"Taking exams always causes me a lot of anxiety."

"Just walking into the library makes me feel anxious."

"Making decisions creates terrible anxiety."

"I feel anxious but I don't know why."

As these statements indicate, sometimes we can point to the cause of our anxieties and other times we cannot. **Anxiety** is an unpleasant state which we associate with feelings of uneasiness and apprehension. Anxiety is usually accompanied by heightened physiological activity, such as increased heart rate and blood pressure. As we discussed in Module 39, you are likely to feel anxious when your goal is blocked, when you must choose between two goals, or when you have little control over a situation. There are several more causes.

Why is it that simply walking into the library might make a student feel anxious? The answer is classical conditioning. When the student goes to the library, she worries about studying and failing exams. The stimulus, "walking into the library," is associated with the student's worry and anxiety

If you feel anxious or tense when facing any situation that involves waiting, it is probably because you have developed a conditioned emotional response to waiting. (Freda Leinwand/Monkmeyer)

over studying and exams. After repeated pairings, the stimulus, "walking into the library," elicits the emotional response, feeling anxious. When an emotional response is classically conditioned to a neutral stimulus, it is called a **conditioned emotional response**. Once acquired, these responses, such as anxiety, anger, or sadness, will manifest themselves quickly and automatically upon presentation of the stimulus.

In addition to being acquired through classical conditioning, Albert Bandura (1986) has shown that emotional responses may develop through observational or vicarious learning. As explained in Module 17, **vicarious** (vy-CARE-ee-us) **learning** takes place if you acquire a behavior by observing other people. Feelings of anxiety from entering the library may come from walking into the library and observing other students' anxiety. Bandura would say that our feelings of fear and anxiety are learned through either direct or vicarious learning.

Unlike Bandura's belief that anxious feelings are learned, Sigmund Freud suggested a very different cause. As we discussed in Module 36, Freud theorized that we feel anxious when the more primitive desires of the id are in conflict with the moral directives of the superego. The ego is caught in the middle of this *unconscious* conflict and the result is a general feeling of anxiety. Although it is difficult to establish how much anxiety comes from unconscious conflicts, clinical psychologists find that clients do report feeling anxious without being able to identify the cause. Whether our feelings of anxiety arise from direct or vicarious learning or from unconscious causes, we still need to cope with these feelings.

COPING WITH ANXIETY

Since Bandura believed that our anxious feelings are acquired through either direct or vicarious learning, he suggested we cope by *unlearning*.

Methods to unlearn anxiety or other negative emotions might include some combination of behavior modification, systematic desensitization, role playing, or thought substitution. These methods, which were discussed in Modules 16, 24, and 36, require that we actively work to change certain thoughts and behaviors that may be the cause of our anxious feelings. These "unlearning" techniques might be characterized as being primarily problem-focused coping, since they represent attempts to deal with the problem itself. But how do we cope if we cannot identify the cause of our anxiety or negative emotions?

"I feel anxious but I don't know why?" According to Freud, unconscious conflicts between the id and superego can result in anxiety. Freud theorized that to reduce this anxiety, the ego used a number of **defense mechanisms**, which operate at an unconscious level and which reduce anxiety by changing or distorting our perceptions of reality. According to Lazarus and Folkman, defense mechanisms are a form of self-deception and are effective only if we are unaware of their operation. Defense mechanisms can best be characterized as emotion-focused coping since they manage our emotions rather than the causes of our emotions.

USING DEFENSE MECHANISMS

What kind of things do we say or think to protect our true feelings?

know list of defense mechanisms.

- A baseball pitcher rationalizes his poor performance by blaming the umpires, crowd noises, the weather—everything and everybody but himself.

- A smoker denies the health risks of smoking.

- A brother represses envy of his sister's abilities.

- An employee attributes her own quick temper to her boss.

These people are reducing their anxiety by using defense mechanisms. According to Freud, defense mechanisms can be helpful or harmful, depending on how much people rely on them. The occasional use of defense mechanisms helps reduce our anxieties so we can continue to function while developing the skills to deal with the real causes of our negative emotions. However, the frequent use of defense mechanisms prevents us from recognizing, confronting, and dealing with these disturbing feelings. Here are some of the defense mechanisms Freud identified.

Rationalization.   A baseball pitcher blames his poor performance on the umpire's unfair calls. This is an example of **rationalization**, making up acceptable excuses for behaviors that cause us to feel anxious. Rationalization may have beneficial effects if it reduces the pitcher's anxiety over losing the game and motivates him to practice for the next game. It would have harmful effects if the pitcher maintained his poor throwing habits because he convinced himself that none of the blame for failure is his.

Denial.   A heavy smoker may refuse to believe the scientific finding that smoking increases the risk of lung cancer. This is **denial**, the refusal to recognize some anxiety-provoking event or piece of information. If the truth of a situation is too painful or stressful, we may cope by denying the seriousness of it. In some cases, denial is helpful. If the smoker does not intend to quit, he reduces his stress by denying the serious effects of smoking. Denial can also be harmful, however. A heavy smoker may, in fact, get lung cancer by denying the link between smoking and cancer.

How can a student cope with a critical analysis? Freud suggests that we all use a number of defense mechanisms, such as rationalization, to cope with thoughts that threaten our self-esteem. (Susan Lapides/Design Conceptions)

Repression. You are envious of your sister's academic abilities, and so you put these thoughts out of your conscious thinking. This is **repression**, a pushing of unacceptable feelings or impulses into the unconscious. While denial is a way of dealing with a threat that arises from some external situation, repression is a way of dealing with a threat that arises from our own thoughts or beliefs. Repression is different from suppression, which is a voluntary and conscious attempt to remove some threatening thought or desire. Repression is assumed to occur at an unconscious level. Repression may have positive effects if it helps you maintain a good relationship with your sister and eventually work out your envious feelings toward her. Repression may have negative effects if it prevents you from resolving your feelings of envy.

Projection. You get angry very quickly. Not wanting to admit that you cannot control your temper, you blame others for having a quick temper and making you angry. **Projection** is the assignment of our own undesirable traits to others. Projection may have positive effects if it allows you time to develop other ways to deal with your quick temper. Projection may have negative effects if it prevents you from realizing that you have a quick temper which needs to be controlled.

Reaction formation. A person who feels guilty about premarital sexual activity joins a group that has very strict beliefs against it. **Reaction formation** is the repression of an unacceptable motive by enthusiastically endorsing the opposite one. But you should be careful about labeling another person's enthusiastic efforts in some cause as a reaction formation. In many cases, people's motives are precisely what they seem to be.

Displacement. If you were angry at your boss for her severe criticism, you might be afraid to express your anger directly to her. Instead, you might pick an argument with a friend or co-worker. This is **displacement**, the redirecting of an emotion toward a safer, more acceptable target. One kind of displacement is sublimation.

Sublimation.   A good friend works all the time and has no personal or sexual life. **Sublimation,** a kind of displacement, is the redirection of threatening or forbidden desires to socially acceptable goals. Since displacement is an unconscious process, there is no way to know whether someone's intense working is due to displacement of threatening sexual desires.

At the beginning of this Module, Robert explained that he did not get the job because the interviewer was pushy. Suppose we had secretly videotaped Robert's performance during the interview. Now, as we watch the tape, we see that the interviewer was not pushy. Instead, we notice that Robert is giving very jumbled answers, apparently because he had not taken the time to prepare for the interview. As his answers become more disorganized, he is the one who becomes pushy. Using Freud's terminology, we would say that Robert is reducing his anxiety over not getting the job by using the defense mechanisms of projection and rationalization. Psychologists generally agree that we use defense mechanisms to reduce anxious and stressful feelings (Holmes, 1981; Sherwood, 1981).

Defense mechanisms are unconscious processes that we would characterize as emotion-focused coping. There are many potentially upsetting situations that require both emotion- and problem-focused coping. Here is a stress management program that uses both kinds of coping.

How would you know if you used a defense mechanism?

APPLYING PSYCHOLOGY   Stress Management Program

whole section

What might you do to cope better with the problems of being a college student?

Two clinical psychologists, Ethel Roskies and Jacqueline Avard (1982), developed a stress management program that helped Type A individuals change their maladaptive coping patterns. We can use their program, which combines emotion- and problem-focused coping, to help students tackle potentially upsetting situations.

Self-observation

The stress management program begins with you observing and recording your behaviors, self-statements, and psychosomatic symptoms for two weeks. This can be done easily by keeping a daily diary. Your goal is to identify your daily hassles, negative self-statements, and psychosomatic symptoms. Before you dismiss the importance of observing yourself, consider a study by Harvey Featherstone and Bernard Beitman (1983). They found that migraine sufferers were far more likely to improve with treatment if they were aware of how much their own thoughts and behaviors contributed to their problem. Migraine sufferers who denied the impact of their thoughts and behaviors rarely improved, even though they were receiving treatment. This means that becoming aware of your thoughts and behaviors is a necessary first step in successful coping. After several weeks of self-observation, you should have identified and become aware of your hassles, negative self-statements, and psychosomatic symptoms. Now you are ready to do something about these three things.

Appraisal and Coping

You know that a threat appraisal will increase your feelings of stress and a challenge appraisal will decrease these feelings. Since most situations include threat and challenge appraisals, your goal is to emphasize the challenge over the threat. The key to changing your appraisal from less of a threat to more of a challenge is to substitute positive self-statements for negative ones. Write down the negative self-statements that you have identified on one side of a piece of paper, and positive ones that you can substitute on the other. For example, on one side you might have the negative self-statements, "I'll never do well on the exam." "There's no time to study." "I'm not smart enough." "I'm not very popular." "No one likes me." These negative self-statements are examples of emphasizing a threat appraisal. You need to catch yourself saying them and substitute positive self-statements, such as "I'll do OK on the exam." "I'll make time to study." "I've got plenty of ability." "I'm very likable." "I'm a nice person." These positive self-statements are examples of emphasizing a challenge appraisal.

It is important to remember that your appraisal of a situation influences your kind of coping. For example, Susan Folkman, Richard Lazarus, and their colleagues (1986) studied the kinds of appraisals and the coping patterns of married couples. They reported that challenge appraisals were related to using more problem-focused coping, which means that people who use challenge appraisals are more likely to deal with the causes of their problems.

After appraising a situation, you need to balance your time and energy between emotion-focused and problem-focused coping. Suppose you appraise going to a party where you know very few people as being both threatening and challenging. Problem-focused coping might include finding out if people who you know will be there, asking a friend to go with you, and thinking up interesting stories or jokes you might tell. Emotion-focused coping might include reappraising the party as "no big deal," or thinking, "It doesn't really matter," or "I'll do just fine." Emotion-focused coping might also include using a relaxation technique, which is an effective way to reduce negative emotions.

Biofeedback, Progressive Relaxation, and Meditation

When told to "calm down," most of us are unable to do so. The ability to calm down or *relax on cue* comes only after weeks of practicing. Trying to relax on cue without first practicing is like expecting to play a decent game of tennis the first time you step onto a tennis court. Let's look at three different techniques that will teach you to calm down.

What is the best way for me to calm down?

Biofeedback. Nancy suffers from tension headaches, which are thought to be caused by muscle tension. As part of her treatment, she learns to relax her muscles through biofeedback. Several small metal disks are placed on her forehead. The metal disks are connected to a machine that measures tiny changes in electrical activity. Each time Nancy tenses the muscles in her forehead, the machine senses the increased electrical activity and makes a high tone. When she relaxes the muscles in her forehead, the machine senses the decreased electrical activity and makes a low tone. Through her thoughts and/or mental images, Nancy tries to keep the tone low, which means the muscles in her forehead are relaxed. **Biofeedback** is a process of making Nancy aware of one of her body's physiological responses and then helping her to increase or decrease that response. Nancy will have to search through her thoughts and mental images to find ones that help her decrease her muscle tension. After several weeks of regular biofeedback training, Nancy would be able to calm down on cue. But she could also learn to relax with several other techniques.

Progressive Relaxation and Meditation. Nancy could learn to calm down by using **progressive relaxation,** an exercise of tensing and relaxing the major muscle groups of the body. She would start by tensing and relaxing her toes and then continue up her body, tensing and relaxing the muscles

Connected to a machine that measures muscle tension in her forehead, this woman "hears" a high tone when she tenses her forehead and a low tone when she relaxes her forehead. This technique, called biofeedback, will help her learn to use images or thoughts to relax her muscles. (Joel Gordon)

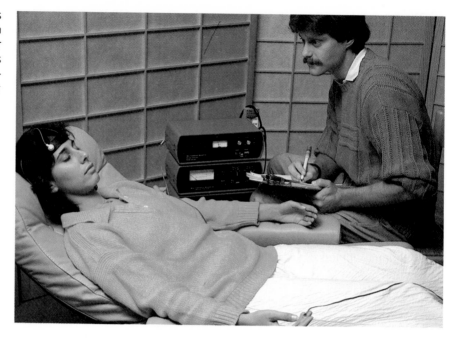

of her legs, torso, arms, neck, and head. She would repeat the tensing and relaxing exercise for about 20 minutes. After several weeks of regular practice, she would be able to use this exercise to calm down. With continued practice, she would learn to relax within minutes.

Nancy could learn to relax through several different kinds of meditation. If she used **Transcendental Meditation (TM)**, she would begin by assuming a comfortable position. With eyes closed, she would repeat a meaningless sound over and over, concentrating on the sound so as to clear her head of all thoughts. By doing this for about 20 minutes a day for several weeks, she would learn to clear her mind of all upsetting thoughts and allow her body to calm down.

Comparing Techniques.   Which relaxation technique is best for calming down, decreasing anxiety, or reducing psychosomatic problems? Edward Blanchard and his associates (1987) found that progressive relaxation and biofeedback were equally effective in reducing headaches. After comparing many studies, Deane Shapiro (1985) concluded that Transcendental Meditation, biofeedback, and progressive relaxation were about equally effective in reducing anxiety and high blood pressure. There is now sufficient evidence to show that all three techniques are about equally effective and valuable in helping a person calm down and reduce mild anxiety. In treating more serious anxiety or psychosomatic problems, these relaxation techniques are usually combined with other forms of therapy (Module 47). At this point, remember that any one of these techniques would be an extremely effective way to reduce bodily arousal and negative emotions that arise from daily hassles and other upsetting situations. Because the three techniques generally produce similar results, which one you choose is not as important as how often you use it.

Success.   A stress management program works best if you follow all its steps. Remember that a stress management program similar to the one just described helped Type A individuals reduce their Type A behaviors and lower their risk of heart attacks (Friedman et al., 1984; Nunes et al., 1987; Roskies & Avard, 1982).

MAJOR CONCEPT   Coping

Please match the term with its correct statement.

1. coping

2. conditioned emotional response

3. emotion-focused coping

4. defense mechanisms

5. anxiety

6. relaxation techniques

7. problem-focused coping

a. _5_ A feeling of uneasiness and apprehension that is usually accompanied by increased physiological arousal.

b. _7_ You deal with a problem by directing most of your time and energy toward managing and solving the problem itself.

c. _6_ These methods, which include biofeedback, progressive relaxation, and Transcendental Meditation, are ways to decrease physiological arousal and feelings of anxiety and stress.

d. _1_ Refers to cognitive and behavioral efforts that you would use to manage a situation that you have appraised as taxing or exceeding your personal resources.

e. _2_ When an emotional response is classically conditioned to a neutral stimulus.

f. _3_ You deal with a problem by focusing on the emotional responses caused by the problem rather than solving the problem itself.

g. _4_ Unconscious processes, such as denial, rationalization, and repression, that decrease feelings of anxiety by distorting or changing your perceptions of reality.

Answers: a (5); b (7); c (6); d (1); e (2); f (3); g (4)

REVIEW

Roberta is in the process of getting divorced. Each time she thinks about it, she feels apprehensive and notices that her heart pounds and her palms sweat. We would say that Roberta is feeling (1) _____. There are several explanations of what causes anxiety. Freud would say that anxiety arises from the unconscious (2) _____ between the impulses of the id and the social directives of the superego.

   Roberta now feels anxious each time she drives by a restaurant that was a favorite of hers and her ex-husband's. This is due to classical conditioning, and Roberta's anxiety in this instance is an example of a (3) _____ _____ response. Bandura would say that Roberta acquired her anxious feelings through direct as well as through (4) _____ learning.

Freud believed that a person like Roberta might deal with her anxiety by unconsciously distorting reality through a number of (5) _____ _____. For example, if she really thought that her divorce was unacceptable but made up an acceptable reason for it, she would be using (6) _____. Other examples of defense mechanisms include refusing to recognize some anxiety-provoking event, called (7) _____; assigning our own undesirable traits to others, called (8) _____; and repressing one motive by emphasizing the opposite, called (9) _____ _____. The occasional use of defense mechanisms may reduce Roberta's anxiety so that she may continue to function and work on the real causes of her problems. However,

Roberta's frequent use of defense mechanisms may prevent her from confronting the real causes of her anxiety.

Roberta is said to be (10) _____ when she is using behavioral and cognitive efforts to manage her divorce, a situation that she has appraised as threatening and that exceeds her personal resources. If she were to devote most of her time and energy to dealing with her feelings resulting from the divorce rather than dealing with getting her life back to normal, she would be using primarily (11) _____ - _____ coping. If she were to devote most of her time and energy to dealing with getting her life back to normal, she would be using primarily (12) _____ - _____ coping. Freud's defense mechanisms are examples of using (13) _____ - _____ coping. In most cases, we need to use both kinds of coping.

To cope with her divorce and reduce feelings of stress, Roberta begins a stress management program. She starts by spending two weeks observing and keeping track of her (14) _____ - _____, _____, and _____ _____. The purpose of self-observation is to make Roberta (15) _____ of her hassles, negative self-statements, and psychosomatic symptoms. By changing her negative self-statements, she will try to make more (16) _____ than (17) _____ appraisals. In trying to get her life back to normal, she should use (18) _____ - _____ coping. In managing the negative feeling caused by her divorce, she should use (19) _____ - _____ coping. To help her remain calm, reduce her anxiety, and decrease her insomnia, she may use any one of three (20) _____ techniques. Roberta will have more success in reducing her stress, anxiety, and insomnia if she follows all the steps in the stress management program.

Answers: (1) anxiety; (2) conflict; (3) conditioned emotional; (4) observational, vicarious; (5) defense mechanisms; (6) rationalization; (7) denial; (8) projection; (9) reaction formation; (10) coping; (11) emotion-focused; (12) problem-focused; (13) emotion-focused; (14) self-statements, behaviors, psychosomatic symptoms; (15) aware; (16) challenge; (17) threat; (18) problem-focused; (19) emotion-focused; (20) relaxation

---

GLOSSARY TERMS

anxiety (p. 458)
biofeedback
   (p. 463)
conditioned emotional
   response (p. 459)
coping (p. 457)

defense mechanisms
   (p. 460)
denial (p. 460)
displacement (p. 461)
progressive relaxation
   (p. 463)

projection (p. 461)
rationalization
   (p. 460)
reaction formation
   (p. 461)
repression (p. 461)

sublimation (p. 462)
Transcendental
   Meditation (TM)
   (p. 464)
vicarious learning
   (p. 459)

PERSONAL NOTE

Getting up in the morning is one of my great hassles. And if I am not careful, I find that a bad start in the morning can ruin much of my day. Knowing that, I have tried very hard to develop a stress management program to cope with getting up. There are a number of reasons why my program has been only moderately successful. In the morning I am just too tired to cope with anything. I know what I should say and do but somehow nothing much gets said or done. Thanks to technology, I may soon be experiencing greater success. I now listen to a tape cassette that tells me positive things to say and do and I simply follow the good advice of my tape recorder. If you are interested in starting such a program, I must warn you about one problem. Some mornings you will be tempted to relapse and not turn on your tape recorder. These temptations can be very strong. I still don't love getting up, but at least I don't hate it as much. I don't use my tape recorder on weekends because then I don't have to get up in the morning.   —R. P.

15

Abnormal Behavior

Module 42 Abnormality, Anxiety, and Related Disorders

As a teenager, John Hinckley was withdrawn and had no friends. He liked music and listened to it alone in his room. He had an above-average IQ (113) and received mostly As and Bs in college. While in college, he made up a story about having a girlfriend so he could get more money from his parents. A turning point in his life came when he saw the movie Taxi Driver. After that, he began collecting guns and became obsessed with Jodie Foster, an actress who played a teenage prostitute in that movie. He spent the summer of 1980 feeling very depressed until he conceived of a plan to meet Jodie Foster. After getting money from his parents for summer school, he went to New Haven, where Foster was attending Yale University. He called her several times, but she refused to meet him. After this, he said that he went through a period of unparalleled emotional exhaustion. His mind was at the breaking point the whole time. A relationship he had dreamed about went absolutely nowhere. He felt totally disillusioned with everything. He wrote a number of notes to Foster. A final love letter indicated he was going to do something to impress her and make her understand how much he loved her (Figure 15.1). Several days later, Hinckley waited in a Washington crowd for President Reagan to appear. As Reagan emerged from a building, Hinckley opened fire, wounding the president and three other men (adapted from the Los Angeles Times, May 14, May 15, June 22, July 10, 1982, February 14, 1983).

John Hinckley (Phil Huber/Black Star)

ASSESSING ABNORMAL BEHAVIOR

Psychiatrists examined Hinckley soon after his arrest. If Hinckley was found to be legally sane, meaning that he understood right from wrong, he would be held responsible for the shootings. If convicted, he would be sent to prison. If Hinckley was found to be legally insane, he would not be held responsible for the shootings and instead would be sent to a mental hospital for treatment. The procedures psychiatrists used to determine Hinckley's condition illustrate the major methods of assessing abnormal behavior: clinical interviews, psychological tests, and neurological exams.

A number of psychiatrists conducted **clinical interviews** of Hinckley that lasted for many hours. In these interviews they tried to establish a good

How did psychiatrists assess John Hinckley?

469

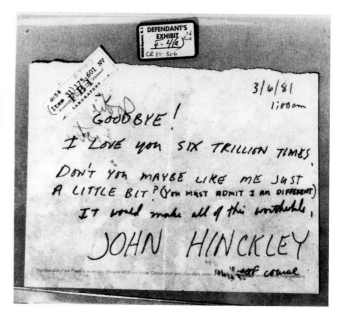

Figure 15.1
Left: President Reagan at the moment he is shot. Right: John Hinckley's note to Jodie Foster. (Left, AP/Wide World Photos; right, AP/Wide World Photos)

rapport and create a trusting environment so that Hinckley would reveal very private and, at times, stressful information. The advantages of the clinical interview include providing an enormous amount of information about a person's background and current problems (Sundberg et al., 1983). The disadvantages include the likelihood that the person will give different information to different psychiatrists. For example, Hinckley apparently revealed certain of his fantasies to some psychiatrists and not to others. In addition, the psychiatrists' biases might result in their interpreting his answers in different ways. In spite of these potential problems, the clinical interview is perhaps the primary technique mental health professionals use to assess abnormal behavior (Leckman et al., 1982).

Hinckley was also given a number of *psychological* tests, including projective tests such as the *Rorschach inkblot test*, and personality inventories such as the *MMPI*. The advantages and disadvantages of these tests were discussed in Module 38.

In addition, Hinckley was given a number of *neurological* tests to check for possible brain damage. These tests include evaluation of reflexes, motor coordination, EEG waves, and brain structures. A recent procedure, called the CAT (computerized axial tomograph) scan, combines X rays of the brain from different angles with computer analysis. As discussed later in this chapter, CAT scans may show structural changes in the brain, such as would occur with tumors or degenerative brain damage. According to one radiologist, Hinckley's CAT scans indicated possible brain abnormality (enlarged fissures) (McKean, 1982). Because some abnormal behaviors may be caused by tumors, diseases, or infections of the brain, neurological tests are necessary before these causes can be ruled out.

DEFINING ABNORMAL BEHAVIOR

How abnormal was John Hinckley?

After their assessments, all the psychiatrists agreed that the following behaviors displayed by Hinckley were abnormal: he had long periods of great anxiety, was very socially withdrawn, lived in a fantasy world, felt obsessed with Jodie Foster, and attempted murder to demonstrate his devotion. What kind of criteria do mental health professionals use to decide that these behaviors are abnormal?

Statistical Frequency

Very few people are as socially withdrawn as Hinckley. A behavior may be defined as abnormal on the basis of **statistical frequency,** or how often that behavior occurs in the general population. A behavior that occurs infrequently is abnormal in a statistical sense. By this definition, extreme social withdrawal would be considered abnormal, but so would behaviors such as getting a Ph.D. or raising orchids, since relatively few people do them. As these last examples indicate, the statistical frequency definition of abnormality has limited usefulness.

Deviation from Social Norms

Hinckley violated one of society's norms when he shot another human being. According to a second definition of abnormality, a behavior is considered abnormal if it deviates greatly from accepted **social norms.** In Hinckley's case, this definition seems valid. However, definitions of abnormality based solely on deviations from social norms may encounter a problem when social norms change with time. For example, thirty years ago a divorced woman almost always retained custody of her children, and those who did not were considered in some ways abnormal. Today this social norm is rapidly breaking down. Should our ideas about what is abnormal be so flexible that they change with each generation? Many mental health professionals think not.

Maladaptive Behavior

For months, Hinckley was obsessed with winning Jodie Foster's attention, in spite of the fact that she rebuffed his approaches. He finally decided that he would prove his love by shooting the president. A behavior may be defined as abnormal if it is **maladaptive**—that is, if it has adverse consequences for the person or society. For example, being terrified to go out in public, hearing voices that dictate dangerous acts, having to wash one's hands for hours on end, drinking so much alcohol that it interferes with personal and family interactions, starving oneself to the point of death, and committing a violent act to get someone's attention would all be considered maladaptive and, in that sense, abnormal.

There is no absolute definition of abnormal behavior. However, of the three definitions given here, most mental health professionals would agree that the maladaptive definition is probably the most useful.

CLASSIFYING ABNORMAL BEHAVIOR

I was flying with a friend in a private plane when we had to make an emergency landing. Now whenever I think about an airplane, I feel a pressure in my chest and have difficulty breathing. I feel like I am going to lose control, and I usually get a bad headache and upset stomach. I cannot even bring myself to go to an airport to pick up a friend (author's files).

Why do psychiatrists sometimes agree and sometimes disagree?

This person's symptoms are so clear-cut that everyone would diagnose the problem as an irrational fear. John Hinckley's symptoms, in contrast, were much harder to classify. In a widely publicized trial, psychiatrists for the prosecution maintained that Hinckley had problems but was not suf-

In many cases, nonviolent patients from mental hospitals have been sent back into society without adequate support and follow-up care. Many of these homeless people wander the streets as derelicts or bag ladies. (Paul Solomon/Wheeler Pictures)

What do professionals use to make a diagnosis?

fering from a serious mental illness. Psychiatrists for the defense presented evidence that Hinckley did not know right from wrong at the time of the shootings because he was suffering from a very serious mental disorder—namely, schizophrenia. Here are the opinions of four of these expert witnesses.

Dr. John J. Hopper, a psychiatrist in private practice, had treated John Hinckley for four months before the shooting. Hopper said he saw no evidence that would have predicted Hinckley's later violent act. Hopper described Hinckley as a typical socially underdeveloped young man who had anxiety spells, but not serious psychotic behaviors, such as thought disorders, which occur in schizophrenia.

Dr. William T. Carpenter, a University of Maryland psychiatrist, disagreed. He interviewed Hinckley for 45 hours after the shooting and felt Hinckley was driven by an inner world of fantasies. According to Carpenter, Hinckley believed that by shooting Reagan, he could achieve a magical union with Jodie Foster. Carpenter diagnosed Hinckley as suffering from schizophrenia.

Dr. Sally Johnson, a staff psychiatrist at the federal corrections institution at Butner, North Carolina, interviewed Hinckley 57 times after the shooting. She said that Hinckley had an adolescent admiration, not an obsession, for Jodie Foster. She diagnosed Hinckley as having a personality disorder, but said that he functioned too well to have schizophrenia.

Dr. David M. Baer, a professor of psychiatry at Harvard, spent 30 hours talking to Hinckley after the shooting. Baer testified that Hinckley's delusions about winning Foster's love were a major factor in his attack on Reagan. In disagreement with Drs. Johnson and Hopper, Baer agreed with Carpenter. He too maintained that Hinckley was suffering from the severe mental illness called schizophrenia.

After literally hundreds of hours of assessment, psychiatrists agreed that Hinckley had displayed abnormal behaviors, but they disagreed on the exact nature of his disorder. Two psychiatrists diagnosed Hinckley as having schizophrenia, a serious mental disorder. Two other psychiatrists diagnosed him as having a personality disorder, but not a serious mental illness. The diagnosis of schizophrenia, like the diagnosis of a phobia or any other mental problem, depends upon the presence of certain symptoms. However, an individual may, as in Hinckley's case, show some of the symptoms usually associated with a condition but not others. When this happens, the diagnosis is difficult to make and mental health professionals may disagree.

In most cases, people who display abnormal behaviors have not committed a crime, and so diagnosing their problems has no legal implications. Their diagnoses do, however, have important implications for therapy. Different kinds of abnormal behaviors are treated with different kinds of psychotherapy and different kinds of drugs. Before mental health professionals begin treating someone with a psychological disorder, they try to classify the person's problem into a certain category of abnormal behavior.

To know which symptoms are characteristic of which mental disorders, most mental health professionals use the revised third edition of the *Diagnostic and Statistical Manual of Mental Disorders* (1987), abbreviated **DSM-III-R**. It is published by the American Psychiatric Association. DSM-III-R defines a mental *disorder* by assessing symptoms on five different *dimensions* or axes, such as the severity of the condition, the presence of other health problems, and the amount of environmental stress. Because DSM-III-R lists very specific behavioral criteria for a diagnosis, it is expected to be more reliable than previous diagnostic systems.

TABLE 15.1 Classification of Abnormal Behaviors According to the *Diagnostic and Statistical Manual of Mental Disorders,* revised third edition.

1. *Disorders usually first evident in infancy, childhood, or adolescence.* Within this broad category are a variety of intellectual, emotional, physical, and developmental disorders. They include mental retardation, hyperactivity, eating disorders (such as anorexia nervosa), and childhood anxieties.

2. *Organic mental disorders.* In organic mental disorders, the functioning of the brain is known to be impaired, either permanently or temporarily. The primary symptoms are delirium (wandering attention, incoherent stream of thought), dementia (deterioration of intellectual capabilities and memory), and disturbed emotions.

3. *Psychoactive substance use disorders.* In substance use disorders the ingestion of various substances—alcohol, opiates, cocaine, amphetamines, and so on—changes behavior enough to impair social or occupational functioning.

4. *Schizophrenic disorders.* The major symptoms of this group of disorders include delusions (such as believing that thoughts not your own have been placed in your head), hallucinations (in particular, hearing voices that no one else hears), blunted or inappropriate emotions, and loss of contact with the world and others.

5. *Delusional (paranoid) disorders.* The most obvious symptoms of people with paranoid disorders are delusions of being persecuted.

6. *Mood disorders.* These disorders are disturbances of mood, which may include extreme depression, marked elation (mania), or a cycle of depression and mania.

7. *Anxiety disorders.* In these disorders, some form of anxiety is the central disturbance. Individuals who are phobic have an irrationally intense fear of some object or situation. Individuals with obsessive-compulsive disorders have uncontrollable recurrent thoughts (obsessions) that dominate their consciousness and strong urges to perform rituals (compulsions) intended to ward off an anxiety-arousing situation.

8. *Somatoform disorders.* Although the symptoms are physical, somatoform disorders have no known physiological cause. The symptoms seem to serve a psychological purpose. These disorders include hypochondriasis or the misinterpretation of minor physical sensations as serious illness, and conversion disorder, in which the person suddenly loses some motor or sensory function, such as movement of a limb or the ability to see.

9. *Dissociative disorders.* Psychological dissociation is a sudden alteration in consciousness that affects memory and identity. These disorders include amnesia, or forgetting of one's past, and multiple personality, in which the individual possesses two or more distinct personalities.

10. *Sexual disorders.* Included in this category are problems with gender identity or feeling uncomfortable with one's anatomical sex. Also included are a broad classification of behaviors known as paraphilias: sexual patterns in which arousal is caused by some unusual stimulus, such as animals or inanimate objects. These patterns are considered abnormal if they occur persistently, are necessary for sexual excitement, and interfere with the development of affectionate relationships. Other sexual disorders involve forcing sexual behaviors on children, or requiring pain or humiliation for sexual arousal. Psychosexual dysfunctions also include erectile, arousal, or orgasmic difficulties. These disorders were discussed in Module 28.

11. *Personality disorders.* These disorders involve inflexible and maladaptive patterns of behavior. Examples include persons who are aloof, have few friends, and are indifferent to praise or criticism (schizoid personality); persons who have an overblown sense of self-importance, require constant attention, and are likely to exploit others (narcissistic personality); and persons who show chronic irresponsibility, lack of concern for others, and no remorse after wrongdoing (antisocial personality).

12. *Conditions not attributable to a mental disorder.* These include grief over the death of a loved one, moderately antisocial behaviors, academic and occupational problems, and problems among family members.

Several categories that are relatively rare have been omitted from this table. (Adapted from American Psychiatric Association, 1987, Davison & Neale, 1982.)

If you look at Table 15.1, you will see the major diagnostic categories of DSM-III-R. You may be surprised to see that the term "neurosis" does not appear. In recent years, psychiatrists and psychologists have moved away from the psychoanalytic or Freudian idea of neuroses, which were defined as problems that were assumed to be related to underlying conflicts. DSM-III-R has abandoned the term neurosis and instead focuses on defining problems according to specific, observable symptoms. Before we discuss some of the specific symptoms, let's consider how prevalent psychological problems are.

How many Americans suffer from the mental disorders listed in Table 15.1? As part of a $15 million study, researchers conducted 17,000 door-to-door interviews to determine what percentage of the American population had mental disorders. Using the DSM-III-R system, researchers asked people about their symptoms and then used these symptoms to make diagnoses. Although this study is not yet complete, preliminary data indicate that about 20 percent of all adults suffer from at least one mental disorder.

The breakdown of mental disorders is shown in Figure 15.2. The overall rate is approximately the same for men and women. However, women report many more problems with depression and phobias, while men report more problems with "antisocial personality" and drug abuse, especially alcohol. About 1 percent of those interviewed were found to have symptoms of schizophrenia. Researchers also found that people under 45

What kinds of psychological problems do men and women report?

MAJOR CONCEPT   Defining Abnormal Behavior

It is not always easy to specify which behaviors are abnormal. Much depends on the definition of abnormality used. In this module we have presented three definitions—statistical infrequency, deviation from social norms, and maladaptive behavior.

For each of the cases below, decide by which of these definitions the person would be classified abnormal.

	Statistical Infrequency	Deviation from Social Norms	Maladaptive Behavior
1. During the first few months at a new school, a transfer student feels lonely and becomes withdrawn.			X
2. A woman suddenly decides to give up her high-paying job and live by herself in a remote mountain cabin where she thinks she can find peace of mind.	X	X	
3. A man arrested for setting fire to a bookstore that sells pornography tells police that voices instructed him to rid the world of filth.	X	X	X
4. Most mental health professionals would say that this definition of abnormality is probably the most useful.			X

Answers: 1 maladaptive behavior; 2 statistical infrequency and deviation from social norms; 3 all three definitions; 4 maladaptive behavior

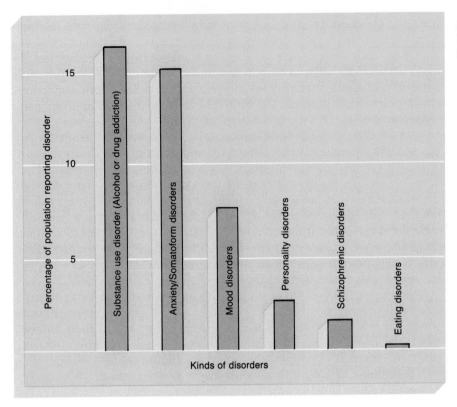

Figure 15.2
Frequency of mental disorders reported by the general population. (Data from Robins et al., 1984)

have twice as many mental disorders as people over 45 and that only a small percentage of those with mental disorders (7 percent) actually sought or received treatment. This study is important because, for the first time, we have an accurate report on the prevalence of mental disorders in America (Freedman, 1984, Myers et al., 1984; Robins et al., 1984). Let's look at one of the more common mental disorders, anxiety.

ANXIETY DISORDERS

Fred was quite visibly distressed during the entire initial interview, gulping before he spoke, sweating, and continually fidgeting in his chair. His repeated requests for water to quench a never-ending thirst were another indication of his extreme nervousness. At first, Fred spoke only of his dizziness and problems with sleeping. However, it soon became clear that he had nearly always felt tense. He admitted to a long history of having difficulties interacting with others, difficulties that led to his being fired from two jobs. He constantly worried about all kinds of possible disasters that might happen to him (adapted from Davison & Neale, 1982).

What is it like to be so nervous you can no longer function?

Anxiety disorders are divided into generalized anxiety disorders, panic attacks, phobias, and obsessive-compulsive disorders. We will tell you about each of these. Let's begin with Fred's problem.

Generalized Anxiety Disorder

Fred is suffering from what is called a **generalized anxiety disorder.** This disorder is characterized by a chronic and pervasive feeling of anxiety in many life situations, a feeling of general apprehension, worry about impending disasters, and extreme sensitivity to criticism. Physical symptoms may include sweating, flushing, pounding heart, diarrhea, cold, clammy hands, headaches, muscle tension, and muscle aches. Psychological symptoms frequently include attacks of nervousness, persistent nervousness, fatigue, restlessness, irritability, and insomnia (Noyes et al., 1980). It is estimated that about 5 percent of the population suffers from generalized anxiety disorder. Some people with this disorder also suffer from panic attacks.

Generalized anxiety disorder is commonly treated with some form of psychotherapy (discussed in Chapter 16) and/or drug. The drugs most frequently prescribed are tranquilizers, such as Valium and Librium. These drugs belong to a group known as the *benzodiazepines*. In moderate doses, the benzodiazepines are usually not physically addicting. In higher doses, however, these drugs are addicting, which means that a person would suffer withdrawal symptoms if the drug were stopped. In severe cases, withdrawal symptoms may include seizures. In addition, there is the danger that a person may become psychologically dependent on a tranquilizer and find it difficult to function without the drug.

In a six-year follow-up of people who had been treated for generalized anxiety disorder with drugs and psychotherapy, 68 percent were either recovered or less impaired than untreated controls. But despite their improvement, the treated subjects continued to show social impairment and experience periods of depression (Noyes et al., 1980).

Sometimes people with a generalized anxiety disorder have a very frightening experience, known as a panic attack.

Panic Disorder

Why might someone panic for no apparent reason?

Karen went down the street to Antoine's Beauty Shop to have her hair set. As she was sitting under the dryer, a sudden feeling swept over her. She thought she was losing her mind. Her heart started beating fast. Her legs felt weak. Her body trembled. It was the most incredible feeling of fear. She wanted to scream, to run out of there. Karen got up with all the pins in her hair, slapped a $5 bill on the counter and ran all the way home (adapted from the Los Angeles Times, *December 13, 1981).*

Like Karen, 4 to 10 million Americans, the vast majority of them women, suffer from a number of symptoms known as panic disorder (Fishman & Sheehan, 1985). During a **panic disorder,** a person usually has a combination of physiological symptoms, such as a pounding heart, labored breathing, dizziness, and sweating, and psychological symptoms, such as great apprehension, terror, and feelings of impending doom. Panic attacks may occur in generalized anxiety disorder as well as in some phobias.

Phobias

Can you imagine feeling terror just from stepping outside your door?

Fear trapped Rose in her house for years. If she thought about going outside to do her shopping, pain raced through her arms and chest. She grew hot and perspired. Her heart beat rapidly and her legs felt like rubber. She said that thinking about leaving her house caused stark terror, sometimes lasting for days. This 39-year-old mother of two is one of millions of Americans suffering from an intense fear of public places called agoraphobia (adapted from the Los Angeles Times, *October 19, 1980).*

Another kind of anxiety disorder is a **phobia** (FOE-bee-ah), an intense and irrational fear out of all proportion to the danger posed by the object

John Madden, CBS Football commentator, has such a fear of flying that he must travel around the United States by motor home or train rather than by airplane. *(AP/Wide World Photos)*

or situation. DSM-III-R divides phobias into three categories: *simple, social,* and *agoraphobia.* Simple phobias are usually triggered by common objects, situations, or animals, such as a fear of heights or bugs. Social phobias are brought on by the presence of other people. Someone with a social phobia may not be able to make public speeches or eat in a restaurant. Agoraphobia is a fear of open or public places, such as being out on a public street or in a shopping center; it is much more common in women than men. Persons who have phobias usually go to great lengths to avoid the object or situation that triggers the intense fear.

Some phobias may be learned through classical conditioning. If you were in a car accident, you might associate riding in cars with pain and develop an irrational fear of riding in cars. Other phobias may be learned through operant conditioning. Suppose that on the one or two occasions you tried to give a speech and the result was embarrassment and ridicule. Because of this punishment, you might develop an intense fear of ever giving a speech again. Still other phobias may be learned through observation or modeling. A child watches her mother overreact to the sight of a spider. The next time she sees a spider, she models her mother's fearful reaction. In some instances, people report the occurrence of a frightening experience preceding the development of a phobia. This finding supports the assumption that phobias are learned. In other cases, however, people cannot recall any frightening event preceding the phobia's development (Emmelkamp, 1979). In these cases, it is more difficult to discover the phobia's origin.

After a phobia is established, it is extremely persistent and will continue for years unless treated. For example, agoraphobics may avoid leaving their home for years at a time. It appears that their agoraphobia is maintained by one of the principles of operant conditioning—specifically, negative reinforcement. *Negative reinforcement* means that a behavior is reinforced by the removal or avoidance of an aversive stimulus. The agoraphobic is able to avoid the aversive stimulus, going out in public, by staying at home. When phobic persons continue to avoid the situation they fear, they never have the opportunity to learn that nothing terrible happens. In other words, their fear is never permitted to extinguish. Support for this idea comes from research on the treatment of phobias. One of the most effective treatments involves *exposure* to the feared stimulus. Here is how a therapist treated a woman with agoraphobia who had not left her home in 30 years.

APPLYING PSYCHOLOGY   Treatment of Agoraphobia

"I began visiting Marge at her home," Ross (the therapist) said. "At the first session, she was terrified that I'd try to drag her out. She sat there in tears, saying over and over again, 'Are you going to make me go out? Are you going to make me go out?' I kept saying no. Finally, at the end of the session, I asked her if she would like to walk me to my car, which was parked right out front. For 20 minutes she put her foot out the apartment door, then back in again. Finally, she broke down, cried and ran out to my car." During the next session, Ross was able to coax Marge into walking to the mailbox on the corner. Gradually, the territory was expanded to two blocks. Then a store. Ross would walk down the street—first side by side with Marge, then in front of her, then behind. . . . Today, Marjorie Goff is training to be a paralegal at the George Washington University Institute of Law and Aging. . . . But there are still shaky moments, fading tinges of the old fear. One day she was walking down the street to work and started having a panic attack, but she knows now that the surge of fear lasts only 20 seconds. "Any other time, I would have run back home," she said. "But I didn't turn round. I just kept going. I kept going. I kept going" (*Los Angeles Times*, December 13, 1981, p. C3).

It is most unlikely that Marge's agoraphobia would have extinguished without treatment. The treatment she received has proven very effective because it involves *live* or *in vivo* exposure to the feared situation. In Marge's case, the therapist actually accompanied her as she gradually confronted the feared situations. In other cases, clients learn how to confront their feared situations on their own. Researchers A. Ghosh and Isaac Marks (1987) compared the reduction in fear among agoraphobics who received their in vivo exposure instructions from a psychiatrist, a self-help book, or a computer program. In all three situations, the agoraphobics were not simply told to confront their feared situation. Rather, they were instructed to do *all* the following: identify each of several feared situations; confront each target situation one by one; practice each confrontation regularly for hours at a time; record panic level in special diaries; anticipate and deal with setbacks; and, if possible, get mates or close friends to help and provide support. The participants in this study had been agoraphobics for an average of nine years. They had complained of it being a handicap in their everyday lives and reported nearly always avoiding certain situations and experiencing strong fear if they could not. After 10 weeks of treatment, all three groups showed a significant improvement. All reported no longer avoiding the situations that once caused them to panic, and they felt only slight anxiety when involved in these situations. When evaluated six months later, subjects reported increased reductions in avoidance and fear. The researchers concluded that agoraphobia can be treated successfully with in vivo exposure, even when the instructions are given by a self-help book or computer program. Besides in vivo exposure, there are other behavioral techniques for treating phobias, which we will discuss in Module 47.

The Ghosh and Marks study, as well as many others, have found that the behavioral treatment of agoraphobia results in a success rate similar to that reported for drug treatment. A program using drugs, such as an antidepressant (imipramine), is often used in combination with a behavioral treatment (Marks et al., 1983; Zitrin et al., 1983). One problem with drug treatment programs is the high dropout rate due to the unpleasant side effects of the medication (Noyes et al., 1986).

Today, individuals have the choice of a behavioral treatment, drug treatment, or combination behavioral/drug treatment, all of which have proved successful in reducing the fear and anxiety of agoraphobia.

Obsessive-Compulsive Disorders

Bernice was obsessed with a fear of being dirty. She tried to reduce her anxiety about being dirty by spending almost all her waking hours in a variety of compulsive cleaning rituals. In the morning she spent three to four hours in the bathroom, washing and rewashing herself. She was afraid that eating food would contaminate her, so she followed a ritual that would "magically" clean the food. She ate three bites of food at a time and chewed each mouthful 300 times (adapted from Davison & Neale, 1982).

Why would a person spend hours washing her hands?

Bernice would be diagnosed as having an obsessive-compulsive disorder. **Obsessions** are persistent and recurring thoughts that a person is unable to control. For example, Bernice is obsessed with the idea that food makes her dirty. This kind of irrational thought interferes with normal functioning. **Compulsions** are irresistible impulses to perform some act or ritual over and over. The ritual's occurrence is clearly excessive and serves no rational purpose. Bernice's compulsions were her excessive washing and chewing. Obsessive-compulsive behaviors make normal functioning and social interactions very difficult. This disorder is relatively rare, affecting less than 5 percent of psychiatric patients.

Bernice's compulsive behaviors are thought to be one way that she reduces or avoids anxiety—in this case, the anxiety about being dirty (Salzman & Thaler, 1981). Based on this idea, many successful treatment programs involve exposing the person to the very situations or objects he or she is attempting to avoid, just as treatment of phobias involves exposure to the feared stimulus (Murray, 1986b). In many cases, persons with compulsions are given homework assignments that require exposing themselves to whatever situation the compulsion is intended to avoid. In a three-year follow-up, those treated with this self-exposure therapy maintained their improved status. Treatment failure was most often associated with failure to complete the homework sessions (Marks, 1981a).

Treatment programs involving self-exposure showed higher success rates than conventional psychotherapy that did not involve self-exposure (Steketee et al., 1982). Obsessive-compulsive persons with the highest probability of successful treatment are those who are not markedly depressed and who have a relatively low level of anxiety. Those who are markedly depressed benefit less from treatment and tend to relapse more frequently (Foa et al., 1983).

SOMATOFORM DISORDERS

One hundred and twenty-six people were taken to eight area hospitals Friday night after they complained of stomach pains, nausea, dizziness, numbness, and chills. Most of the people were treated and released, but five were hospitalized overnight. All five were released Saturday, but one victim returned to the hospital briefly after fainting at home. Most of the people believed they had become sick after consuming a soft drink sold at a high school football game. It is much more likely that their symptoms were caused by anxiety (adapted from the Los Angeles Times, *October 24, 1982).*

Can thoughts make you sick?

After complaining of dizziness, nausea and numbness, this person is being taken to a hospital. She thought she had drunk a poisoned soft drink at a local high school football game. In fact, the drink was not poisoned. The physical symptoms did not have a physical cause. (Donald Dietz/Stock, Boston)

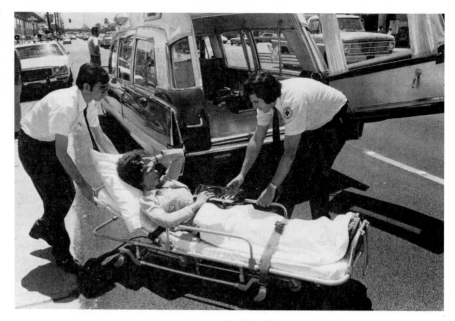

These 126 individuals were probably suffering from a *somatoform disorder*, in which there is some physical symptom caused by psychological distress. More specifically, these people probably had one kind of somatoform disorder called a conversion disorder. In a **conversion disorder,** the bodily organs are healthy but the person reports physical problems. For example, a person may report paralysis or blindness when, in fact, the limb or eye has no structural damage.

Conversion symptoms, whether paralysis, blindness, nausea, or dizziness, are associated with psychological factors and are usually brought on by stressful situations. The conditions for *mass conversion* disorder include being in a relatively confined area; being under some stress; watching someone, usually a leader, become sick; and hearing rumors of impending disaster (Herbert, 1982). Most of these conditions were met at the football game. Another example of mass conversion disorder occurred when 224 grade school students, most of them female, complained of dizziness, headaches, nausea, and abdominal pains after seeing their class leader fall from a stage. Within four hours of beginning, these conversion symptoms had totally disappeared (Small & Nicholi, 1982).

In conversion disorders it is assumed that the physical symptoms have no physiological basis. If some physiological cause of the symptoms is later found, the diagnosis of conversion disorder was incorrect. In one study, organic brain disease was found in about 40 percent of cases initially thought to be conversion disorders (Roy, 1980). However, in the remaining 60 percent, no organic causes could be found for the symptoms.

Conversion disorders, though relatively rare, are exceedingly interesting. Why is it that a person with no organ damage becomes nauseous, dizzy, or blind? These individuals, almost always women, do not seem to be faking. Apparently, they develop conversion symptoms to help them cope with a stressful situation or to obtain wanted attention.

DISSOCIATIVE DISORDERS

Can several minds share one body?

Nancy was alone in her kitchen smoking a cigarette. "Go ahead and finish it," she heard Alice say. "It'll be the last one you'll have." Nancy

MAJOR CONCEPT Anxiety and Related Disorders

A number of psychological disorders involve anxiety or are frequently related to it.

Match each of the disorders listed here with its correct description.

1. Generalized anxiety disorder

2. Panic disorder

3. Phobia

4. Obsessive-compulsive disorder

5. Conversion disorder

6. Dissociative disorder

a. _3_ A woman experiences intense fear in high places. She cannot even sit near a closed window in the twelfth-floor office where she works.

b. _4_ A man complains to his doctor that he is not sleeping well because he feels a need to get up every hour to make sure the doors and windows are locked.

c. _6_ A woman is talking to you. Suddenly, she begins talking and acting like a young girl. When you ask her about the woman you were talking to a moment ago, she replies that she doesn't know that person.

d. _2_ A woman riding home from work on a crowded bus suddenly experiences faintness, a pounding heart, and difficulty breathing, but the feelings subside after several minutes.

e. _1_ A man comes to a clinic complaining of persistent worrisome thoughts and nervousness that interfere with his work.

f. _5_ A promising young pianist awakes the morning before his first major concert and discovers that one of his hands has become paralyzed.

Answers: a (3); b (4); c (6); d (2); e (1); f (5)

---

withdrew as if behind a curtain. When she returned, she was standing on a bench with a telephone cord wrapped around her neck. Shocked, she suddenly realized that what her therapist had been telling her must be true. She was sharing her body with someone else. In fact, Nancy eventually learned she was living with an "inner family" of 13 personalities, each with a name and a purpose. They included the Actress, a promiscuous flirt; the Nun, a righteous moralist; the Kid, a mischievous 5-year-old; Marsha, who faints under stress; and Richard, the gatekeeper who directs their comings and goings. There was also Alice, a suicidal personality who didn't care that if she killed herself Nancy would die too (adapted from the Los Angeles Times, January 29, 1985).

Nancy has a *dissociative disorder*, in which part of her memory or personality is split off or dissociated. There are a number of different dissociative disorders. In Nancy's case, her disorder is called multiple personality. A

multiple personality is the presence of two or more distinct personalities within a single individual. Usually the personalities are quite different and quite complex. The original personality is seldom aware of the existence of the others, and each personality takes its turn at being in control.

Multiple personality is an extremely rare phenomenon, with only 93 cases reported between 1944 and 1981. Females with this disorder outnumber males eight to one. In virtually every case of multiple personality, the individual had experienced severe psychological or physical *abuse* and/or sexual trauma during early childhood. Apparently, other personalities arose as a defense against or way to cope with this trauma (Boor, 1982; Putnam et al., 1986).

Different brain wave patterns have been recorded in individuals who suffer from multiple personality. Researchers initially thought that these patterns were indicative of which personality was in control at the moment (Putnam, 1982). But it was later found that the patterns were most probably caused by differences in emotional states. Different brain wave patterns also occur in normal individuals who simply vary their mood, concentration, and muscle tension (Coons et al., 1982). (Multiple personality disorder should not be confused with schizophrenia, which we discuss in Module 44.)

REVIEW

Helen roams the neighborhood with all her possessions in several shopping bags. During the day, she sorts through trash containers and sells the cans, bottles, and newspapers she finds. At night, she tries to find a warm, dry place to sleep. Helen is called a bag lady. Would Helen's behavior be considered abnormal?

Because only a very small percentage of the population behaves as Helen does, her behavior would be defined as abnormal according to the (1) _____ definition. Because Helen does not follow many of society's guidelines, her behavior would be defined as abnormal according to the social (2) _____ definition. On the surface, it appears that Helen is not a threat to herself or society; she seems to have adapted very well to her homeless environment. Without further testing, we do not know if she has any

(3) _____ behaviors, which might indicate the presence of a mental disorder.

One day Helen appears at the mental health clinic, complaining that people follow her and that she hears voices. The clinical psychologist assesses Helen's symptoms by asking her questions during a

(4) _____ interview. Helen may also be given a number of (5) _____ tests, which might include personality and projective tests. In addition, she might be examined for (6) _____ problems, such as tumors, diseases, or infections of the brain.

Based on Helen's symptoms, the clinical psychologist makes a diagnosis about whether Helen has a mental disorder and if she does, what kind. The psychologist consults DSM-III-R, an abbreviation for the

(7) _____ and _____ _____ *of Mental Disorders* published by the American Psychiatric Association. DSM-III-R lists the symptoms for various mental (8) _____. Unlike previous systems, DSM-III-R classifies symptoms according to

five (9) _____ and is very specific regarding behavioral symptoms.

The family members were discussing some of their relatives. It seemed that many of them had anxiety disorders. First there was Aunt Jule, who for most of her life felt apprehensive and anxious, with a general feeling that some disaster would strike. She would be diagnosed as having a (10) _____ _____ disorder. Every so often, without warning, she had the feeling that she was out of control and noticed her heart pounding and her hands sweating. She was probably

experiencing a (11) _____ _____. After going into psychotherapy and being placed on

drugs called (12) _____, she functioned much better and reported fewer symptoms.

Then there was Uncle Hank, who had a terrible fear of being in small closed spaces, called claustrophobia. For about 10 years, he could not get into an elevator or use the small bathrooms on airplanes. He would be diagnosed as having a simple (13) _____, which is an irrational fear of some object or situation. Besides simple phobias, there are phobias brought on

by the presence of others, called (14) _____ phobias, and fear of open or public places, called (15)

_____. Psychologists believe that most phobias are learned. In Uncle Hank's case, his phobia developed after he was trapped in an elevator as a small child. One of the reasons his phobia persisted for many years was that his fearful avoidance of elevators resulted

in reduced anxiety, a form of (16) _____ reinforcement. When Hank got a job in a 12-story building, he decided he needed psychotherapy for his phobia. He was successfully treated through a gradual

(17) _____ to the very stimulus, an elevator, that had caused his fear.

Uncle Bob was obsessed with the idea that germs would get on his skin and make him sick. He developed a ritual of taking four showers a day and putting on clean clothes after each shower. Bob would be diag-

nosed as having an (18) _____ - _____ disorder. It is thought that this disorder is an attempt

to reduce (19) _____ by avoiding a situation that provokes abnormal uneasiness. Successful treatment of this disorder includes gradual exposure to the anxiety-arousing situation.

One day Aunt Helen went deaf and could no longer hear her husband, with whom she constantly

argued. A medical examination revealed that her auditory system was not damaged. Helen would be diag-

nosed as having a (20) _____ disorder. Her conversion symptom, deafness, is thought to be her way

of coping with (21) _____, caused perhaps by her husband's persistent badgering. Under certain conditions, a large group of people may report physical symptoms in the absence of any physical causes. This

is an example of (22) _____ _____ disorder. Most of the victims of conversion disorders are women.

The family could never understand Uncle Al. He seemed to be different people at different times. Most often he was a responsible person, but periodically, and without his awareness, he would become a little boy, a stand-up comic, a hostile bully, or a minister. Al

would be diagnosed as having a (23) _____ personality. This disorder may arise in childhood after severe physical, psychological, or sexual

(24) _____. Apparently, a person copes with the resulting great anxiety by developing a multiple personality. In Al's case, his father had a terrible temper and beat him so badly as a child that he needed hospitalization. Al's different personalities usually take turns exercising control over his thoughts and behaviors. Multiple personality disorder should not be confused with another serious disorder called schizophrenia.

Answers: (1) statistical; (2) norms; (3) maladaptive; (4) clinical; (5) psychological; (6) neurological; (7) *Diagnostic and Statistical Manual*; (8) disorders; (9) axes or dimensions; (10) generalized anxiety; (11) panic attack; (12) tranquilizers or benzodiazepines; (13) phobia; (14) social; (15) agoraphobia; (16) negative; (17) exposure; (18) obsessive-compulsive; (19) anxiety; (20) conversion; (21) anxiety; (22) mass conversion; (23) multiple; (24) abuse.

GLOSSARY TERMS

clinical interviews
   (p. 469)
compulsions (p. 479)
conversion disorder
   (p. 480)

DSM-III-R (p. 473)
generalized anxiety
   disorder (p. 475)
maladaptive (p. 471)

multiple personality
   (p. 482)
obsessions (p. 479)
panic disorder (p. 476)

phobia (p. 476)
social norms (p. 471)
statistical frequency
   (p. 471)

Module 43 Mood and Personality Disorders

MOOD DISORDERS

Why would someone lose all interest in life?

Joe's wife had died in an automobile accident during a shopping trip. Joe was supposed to have gone with her, but because of business pressures he had canceled at the last minute. He blamed himself for her death. During the following weeks and months, Joe seemed to lose all capacity for enjoying life. His friends couldn't remember the last time he had smiled. During the next five years, Joe suffered from continuing bouts of depression. He had occasional thoughts of suicide and at times withdrew from any social interaction with friends. After he had spent a week closeted in his home, his physician referred him for psychotherapy. With continued treatment, Joe seemed to emerge from his despair and began to feel his old self again (adapted from Davison & Neale, 1982).

Joe was diagnosed as having major depression, one of the most common of the *mood disorders*. Mood disorders always involve disturbances in mood or affect. The symptoms of **major depression** include a sad or dejected mood. In addition, there may be poor appetite, difficulties in sleeping, a change in activity level (becoming either lethargic or agitated), loss of interest and pleasure in usual activities, and negative self-concepts. People diagnosed as having major depression seldom have all these symptoms, but they do invariably have a dejected mood, together with some of the other symptoms. Although depressive episodes may recur and last for months, they often dissipate with time. Major depression affects about 5 to 10 percent of men and 10 to 20 percent of women during their lifetimes.

Another mood disorder is **bipolar disorder,** in which a person suffering from periods of depression may suddenly have periods of exaggerated elation, called *mania*. Manic individuals are enthusiastic and full of energy,

Compared with men, women report two to three times the amount of depression. (Joel Gordon)

making hundreds of plans that can never be carried out. Symptoms of mania include a hyperelevated mood, greatly increased activity, rapid speech suggesting an extremely active thought process, inflated self-esteem, and involvement in activities that may have undesirable consequences, such as reckless spending of money. Mania unaccompanied by depression is very rare; it is much more common for periods of mania to alternate with periods of depression, including sad mood, loss of interest, and negative self-concept. This was formerly called manic-depressive disorder, but following DMS-III-R, we use the term bipolar disorder. Bipolar disorder affects less than 1 percent of the population.

Let's review some of the recent findings on the causes of depression.

Causes of Depression **EXPLORING PSYCHOLOGY**

Most of the 12,500 residents of the Amish community in Lancaster County, Pennsylvania, were quiet, peaceful, gentle folks. Their community had very little unemployment, alcohol or drug abuse, divorce or violence. It was easy to notice when someone talked all the time, and bragged and showed off. It was also easy to notice when the same person did a 180-degree turn and acted depressed or suicidal. We would call this pattern of behavior bipolar disorder (manic-depression). The Amish believed that it was caused by something "in the blood." Combining the Amish's handwritten ancestral records with modern methods for exploring genetic makeup, Janice Egeland (1987) and her associates set out to discover if something "in the blood" did, in fact, give rise to this abnormal behavior pattern.

Why were they acting so strangely?

Working as scientific detectives, Egeland and her research group made what has now been recognized as a landmark discovery. They found a dominant gene on chromosome 11 that gives a person a *predisposition* for developing bipolar disorder (manic-depression). Her research group found that children of parents with this particular gene have a 50 percent chance of inheriting it. The reason that some of the Amish behaved in a peculiar way was because they had inherited a gene that gave them a predisposition for developing bipolar disorder and had ultimately developed the disorder.

But there are two important qualifications about Egeland's finding. First, about 63 percent of those carrying the gene actually show signs of bipolar disorder. This means that inheriting this particular gene results in a predisposition but does not necessarily mean that the individual will develop the disorder. Behavioral geneticist Robert Plomin (1987) believes that the genetic predisposition may be "turned on or off" by social-environmental factors. These factors may include: a tendency of depressed individuals to perceive more situations as potentially upsetting, to experience higher levels of stress, to have fewer social supports, and to deal with their problems more by expressing negative emotions than by seeking solutions (Billings et al., 1983; Hammen & Cochran, 1981; Hirschfeld & Cross, 1982; Warren & McEachren, 1983).

The second qualification of Egeland's study is that the gene on chromosome 11 identified in the Amish is only one of several causes of bipolar disorder. Studies on six different non-Amish families with a history of bipolar disorder failed to implicate this particular gene (Detera-Wadleigh et al., 1987; Hodgkinson et al., 1987). There apparently are other genes that result in a predisposition for bipolar disorder.

The importance of Egeland's finding is that it offers the strongest support yet for an interactive model of mental disorders. According to this model, the development of a mental disorder results from the interaction of genetic and environmental factors. Egeland's finding provides direct evidence for the genetic factor. Since not all of the individuals with a predisposition for bipolar disorder develop the illness, it appears that social-environmental factors either trigger or suppress the genetic predisposition. The advantage of the interactive model is that it sheds light on two puzzles about mental disorders. The genetic component explains why mental disorders may run in families; and the social-environmental component explains why not everyone with a predisposition develops the disorder. Researchers believe that other mental disorders, such as depression and schizophrenia, may also result from an interaction of genetic and social-environmental factors (Andreasen et al., 1987; Holden, 1986).

Egeland's group is now trying to locate the exact position of the "bipolar disorder" gene on chromosome 11. Once located, they hope that information about what the gene does will provide clues for new, more effective treatments for bipolar disorder. A genetic or physiological factor that occurs *only* when a specific disorder is present is called a **biological marker**. Researchers believe that such markers, when found, will lead to more accurate diagnosis and treatment of mental disorders. Individuals who are found to have a biological marker for a mental disorder can be counseled about prevention and treatment programs. Let's see how major depression and bipolar disorder are now treated.

TREATMENT OF MAJOR MOOD DISORDERS

What does one do to escape major depression?

Cathy's first complaints were physical. She couldn't sleep, lost her appetite as well as 15 pounds. She moved slowly and talked in a monotone. She lost all sexual interest in her husband. After this went on for three months, she made herself see a therapist. As she talked to the therapist, all her depressed feelings poured out. "I look successful. Like I've got it all. But I feel like a sham, a failure. I'm a third-rate lawyer, wife, mother, and lover and I'm doomed to stay that way. No matter what I do, there's no joy, no pleasure. Just a treadmill of duty and guilt. I'm exhausted. What's the point of continuing?" (adapted from Rosenfeld, 1985).

Psychotherapy and Drug Treatment

The question of how depressions such as Cathy's should be treated was the subject of a six-year, $10 million research program conducted by the National Institute of Mental Health. The clients, 70 percent of whom were women, suffered from varying degrees of major depression. None had bipolar disorder.

To answer the question, "Is psychotherapy as effective as drug therapy?" clients were assigned randomly to one of four groups. The first group received *cognitive-behavior* therapy, which attempts to correct a person's distorted views and beliefs about the self and the world, such as Cathy's belief that "I'm a failure and I'm doomed to stay that way." The second group received *interpersonal therapy*, which operates on the assumption that some depression is caused by role conflicts, grief, and deficient interpersonal relationships. For example, Cathy may have a conflict in trying to be a perfect lawyer, wife, mother, and lover.

The third group received a commonly used *antidepressant* drug, imipramine. Imipramine is from a group of drugs known as **tricyclics,** which raise the level of certain neurotransmitters, called catecholamines. According to the *catecholamine theory*, depression results when levels of catecholamines are extremely low and mania results when the levels are extremely high (Snyder, 1980). This theory has been generally supported but many of the newer antidepressant drugs do not affect catecholamines (Mendels, 1987). The fourth group received a placebo (a sugar pill with no medicinal value). The drug and placebo groups received minimal supportive therapy.

Preliminary results showed that after an average of 16 weeks, about 50 percent of the clients in the first three groups got better while only 29 percent in the placebo group improved (Holden, 1986). Although the quickest improvement occurred with drug therapy, by the end of treatment there were no significant differences between the two psychotherapy groups and the drug group. This study suggests that people who suffer from major depression, such as Cathy, would show about equal improvement from either cognitive-behavior therapy, interpersonal therapy, or antidepressant drug treatment.

If Cathy had been suffering from the mood swings characteristic of bipolar depression, especially the periods of mania, she might have been successfully treated with a natural mineral salt called **lithium.** Studies in four different countries, including the United States, have shown that lithium is effective in preventing mood swings in about 64 percent of patients with bipolar depression, while only 21 percent of those treated with placebos showed significant improvement (Murray, 1986). Lithium has also been found to be about equally effective in treating individuals who have **mania** (MAY-nee-ah)—that is, manic episodes without the depression. Exactly how lithium affects the brain's neurotransmitter systems to reduce manic episodes in mania and mood swings in bipolar disorder is unclear.

If all drug and behavioral treatments have failed to help an individual with severe depression, there is a treatment of last resort—electroconvulsive shock therapy.

Electroconvulsive Shock Therapy

One of the most controversial treatments for depression involves the use of **electroconvulsive shock therapy** or **ECT.** ECT involves placing electrodes on the skull and passing a mild electrical current through them. As the current passes through the brain, it causes a seizure. Although it is not known exactly why ECT is effective in the treatment of depression, it is known that the seizures are essential for producing a reduction in depressive symptoms. Over a period of several weeks, a series of approximately ten ECT treatments is administered. Figure 15.3 shows that eight of nine seriously depressed patients showed a rather dramatic reduction in depressive symptoms after ECT and remained symptom-free after one year (Paul et al., 1981). ECT is usually used only in cases of serious depression and only after antidepressant drugs have been tried and have failed (Fink, 1981). In these cases, ECT has been shown to reduce depressive symptoms (Davis & Janicak, 1982).

There is no evidence that using present ECT techniques causes damage to the brain. However, it should be kept in mind that it may be very difficult to measure slight or moderate brain damage. One serious side effect is possible *memory* impairment; there may be a persistent loss of memory for events experienced during the weeks of treatment. Following ECT treatment, there is a gradual improvement in memory functions. Although 50 percent of patients given ECT reported poor memory three years after treat-

When might someone be given electroconvulsive shock?

Figure 15.3
Left: Protesters against electroconvulsive shock therapy, or ECT, are presenting only one side of the issue. As the graph shows, ECT reduced depressive symptoms in nine patients who were suffering from major depression. The red line indicates the extent of the ECT treatment. (Photo, Ken Stein: graph, adapted from Paul et al., 1981)

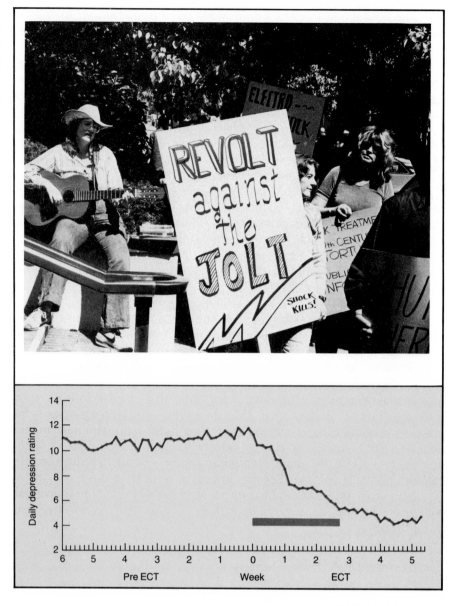

ment, it is not known whether this was caused by the ECT or by the long-standing depression (Squire & Slater, 1983; Squire et al., 1981).

In 1985, a National Institute of Mental Health panel of experts gave a cautious endorsement to the use of ECT as a treatment of last resort for some types of severe depression. The panel added that the patient should be informed as fully as possible of the potential risks (Holden, 1985).

APPLYING PSYCHOLOGY　　　Dealing with Mild Depression

What can you do when complaining doesn't help?

"I've got the sophomore blues," says Harold. "At first I was excited about going off to college and being on my own. Now all I feel is the pressure to study, get good grades and scrape up enough bucks to pay my rent. It's just sheer luck that I'm passing my classes. From what I can see, I don't have the drive to make it through college. To make matters worse I find myself complaining about every little thing. I want to get out of this hole but I don't know how." (author's files)

Harold is suffering from mild depression. Although programs to overcome depression are often supervised by a trained therapist, psychologists have a number of suggestions to help people overcome mild depression.

Focus on Positive Events

Harold is stuck in a rut of noticing and remembering primarily negative things and few if any positive things. Of course, his remembering unpleasant events will increase his depression. According to Paul Derry and Nicholas Kuiper (1981), a depressed individual such as Harold has a tendency to select and remember unhappy or depressing thoughts and events. For example, when asked to remember a list containing both depressed and nondepressed words, depressed individuals better remembered more depressed words, while nondepressed individuals better remembered more nondepressed ones. Along the same lines, Rick Ingram and colleagues (1983) reported that depressed individuals had more difficulty remembering good things about themselves than bad things. These studies suggest that unless Harold takes some action, he will continue to focus on the negative aspects of his life and have a harder time overcoming his depression. Psychologist Lynn Rehm (1982) would suggest that Harold get out of his remembering-depressing-things rut by making a daily list of positive events, conversations, and self-statements. Rehm found that depressed individuals who make, read, and remember a daily list of pleasant events begin to focus more on the positive and improve their daily mood.

Give Yourself Credit

Harold is not taking any credit for passing his classes and thinks he lacks the drive to make it through college. In other words, he thinks his failures are due to his personal deficiencies, while at the same time he does not credit himself for his successes. After reviewing many studies, Paul Sweeney and associates (1986) concluded that people who were depressed were more likely to credit themselves for their failures and more likely to explain their successes by pointing to luck or chance. Like Harold, depressed people are caught in a vicious circle. The more they blame themselves for their failures and credit their successes to luck or chance, the more depressed they will feel. Psychologist Rehm (1982) would suggest that Harold blame himself less for his failures and credit himself more for his successes. He could do this by monitoring and writing down negative self-statements, such as "I'm passing my classes through luck." Then he would make up a list of positive self-statements, such as "I wouldn't be here unless I was smart." By substituting positive for negative self-statements, he would learn to feel better about himself.

Take Some Action

Harold said, "I want to get out of this hole but I don't know how." He can follow the two suggestions described above—and he can also start an exercise program. Lisa McCann and David Holmes (1984) compared the effects of aerobic exercise, relaxation training, and no treatment on a group of depressed college women. After 10 weeks, the exercise group showed significantly less depression than the other two groups. In a related study, Jeffrey Fremont and Linda Craighead (1987) found that mildly depressed subjects showed a significant improvement whether they took part in 10

MAJOR CONCEPT   Mood Disorders

Please indicate whether the statement is true (T) or false (F).

1. T/F Major depression involves a very sad and dejected mood that persists for weeks.

2. T/F A person suffering from bipolar disorder experiences sudden swings in mood from being very depressed to very elated or manic.

3. T/F The evidence that a predisposition for bipolar disorder can be genetically transmitted is very weak.

4. T/F The catecholamine theory of depression states that when levels of catecholamines are very high a person feels depressed and when levels are very low a person feels manic.

5. T/F When drug therapy was compared with two different kinds of psychotherapy, drug therapy proved to be significantly better in treating major depression.

6. T/F The natural mineral salt *lithium* is effective in treating bipolar disorder as well as mania.

7. T/F A panel of experts from the National Institute of Mental Health recommends that electroconvulsive shock therapy (ECT) be only used as a last resort in treating severe depression.

8. T/F Although ECT may produce memory deficits, patients show no deficits in memory three months after treatment.

9. T/F Researchers have discovered a genetic predisposition for certain kinds of bipolar disorder. However, not everyone who has the genetic predisposition actually gets the disorder.

10. T/F In overcoming mild depression, researchers have found that exercise may be an effective treatment.

Answers: 1 (T); 2 (T); 3 (F); 4 (F); 5 (F); 6 (T); 7 (T); 8 (T); 9 (T); 10 (T).

weeks of cognitive therapy, 10 weeks of running, or 10 weeks of both cognitive therapy and running. In reviewing studies on exercise and depression, Anne Simons and her colleagues (1985) concluded that there is now reason for cautious optimism on the potentially helpful effects of exercise in overcoming depression.

PERSONALITY DISORDERS

What is different about this person?

As an adolescent, Jim had committed many petty antisocial acts, including stealing money from his mother's pocketbook. Jim's first serious trouble with the law occurred when he was charged with raping a young woman he had picked up at the local skating rink. He was sentenced to five years at a reform school, but received an immediate parole on the condition that his sentence would be activated if he violated parole. After several parole violations, such as petty theft and speeding, he was sentenced to one year at the reform school. When he returned to his hometown a year later, he continued to get into trouble with the law (adapted from Davison & Neale, 1982).

Jim was diagnosed as having a personality disorder—specifically, antisocial personality or sociopathy. Although many sociopaths have criminal records, some do not.

DMS-III-R lists ten other personality disorders, including paranoid (being excessively suspicious), schizoid (being very self-absorbed and socially withdrawn), narcissistic (having an exaggerated sense of self-importance), and passive-aggressive (always indirectly resisting what others ask or expect). A *personality disorder* exists when someone has traits that are inflexible and maladaptive, resulting in significantly impaired functioning or in personal distress. As in Jim's case, the signs usually appear in adolescence and continue throughout most of the person's life.

Jim, as we said, has an **antisocial personality disorder.** Some of its symptoms include flagrant disregard for obligations, unabashed lying, total lack of guilt or remorse, very impulsive, often reckless behavior, and failure to learn from experience. On the surface, antisocial or sociopathic individuals may be quite charming and above average in intelligence, but they seem to lack any concern for others. Sociopaths are found in all walks of life.

Parents who brought their child to a clinic because of serious behavior problems were asked to describe the child's earlier behaviors. Some parents reported that the child had always had problems. For example, from infancy on the youngster displayed temper tantrums, became furious when frustrated, bullied other children, did not respond to punishment, and was generally unmanageable. Because of this aggressive and unsociable manner, the child created negative and hostile reactions in others, including the parents. In turn, the parents became rejecting and hostile toward the child. Thus, a vicious circle is set in motion that reinforces the child's antisocial behaviors (Millon, 1981).

A number of childhood problems seem to be associated with becoming a sociopath. One researcher followed up over 500 cases of children who had been referred to a clinic for behavior problems (Robins, 1966). When the former problem children were adults, aged 30 to 40, the researcher again interviewed them. Those who became sociopaths had been brought

What would cause a person to lie and feel no guilt?

Writing graffiti on walls and subway cars is a common form of adolescent antisocial behavior in urban areas. (Mitchell Bleier/Peter Arnold)

to the clinic as children because of aggressive and antisocial behaviors, such as truancy, theft, disobeying their parents, and frequent lying with no signs of remorse. In addition, some children had fathers who were role models for antisocial behaviors. These data suggest that antisocial behavior patterns observed in young children persist into adulthood, that sociopathic children become sociopathic adults.

The treatment outcome for sociopaths is not very promising. They are mistrusting, irresponsible, guiltless, and learn little from past mistakes. They may challenge and provoke their therapists. Most therapists are pessimistic about modifying delinquent and sociopathetic behavior, whether it occurs in teenagers or adults (Millon, 1981).

REVIEW

Family members were having a serious discussion about their relatives who had suffered mental disorders. They all felt sorry for Aunt Sally, who had become very sad after she lost an arm in a car accident. For many months she could not sleep, had no appetite, and thought badly of herself. Sally would be diagnosed as

having (1) _____ _____, one of the mood disorders. If Sally were to have alternating periods of depression and mania, she would be said to

have (2) _____ disorder. In some cases,

people may inherit a genetic (3) _____ for bipolar disorder. However, not everyone who inherits a predisposition for bipolar disorder will develop this illness. This finding suggests that the genetic predisposition for bipolar disorder may be turned on or off

by (4) _____ - _____ factors. In the treatment of bipolar disorder as well as mania,

the natural salt (5) _____ has been shown to be effective.

What kind of treatment would be best for Sally's depression? A lengthy study on the treatment of major depression compared two kinds of psychotherapy,

(6) _____ - _____ and

(7) _____, with drug therapy. The antidepressant drug was imipramine, which comes from a

drug group known as the (8) _____. Because these drugs treat depression by raising the level of certain neurotransmitters, these drugs support the

(9) _____ theory of depression. According to this theory, a person may feel depressed when the levels of this neurotransmitter are very low and may feel manic when the levels are very high. This study found that compared to a placebo group, the patients

in the two psychotherapy groups showed about the same level of improvement as did the patients in the

(10) _____ therapy group.

If Sally's depression cannot be treated with psychotherapy or drugs, she might consider a controversial treatment. A panel of experts from the National Institute of Mental Health gave a cautious recommendation

for the use of (11) _____ _____ therapy. However, the panel recommended that this treatment be used only as a last resort and only after the patient is fully informed about possible risks. One of the major risks following ECT is that Sally might

experience (12) _____ problems.

The family members are trying to help Uncle Fred deal with a period of mild depression. They notice that when Fred is mildly depressed, he is more likely to

focus on and remember (13) _____ events

and is likely to take more personal (14) _____ for his failures and less for his successes. To learn to focus on positive events, Fred is making a daily list of

(15) _____ thoughts and events. To learn to take more credit for his successes, Fred is learning

to substitute positive for negative (16) _____

- _____. Finally, Fred has started to run because there is encouraging evidence that

(17) _____ helps overcome depression.

The family remembers only one relative, Uncle Jake, who seemed to have social problems most of his life. As a child and adolescent he was very difficult to discipline. As a young adult he was arrested three times and spent six years in jail. The family could not understand why Jake never felt any guilt for any of the terrible things he did. Jake would be diagnosed as having an (18) _____ personality. For many

reasons, treating this personality disorder has proved very difficult.

Answers: (1) major depression; (2) bipolar; (3) predisposition; (4) social-environmental; (5) lithium; (6) cognitive-behavior; (7) interpersonal; (8) tricyclics; (9) catecholamine; (10) drug; (11) electroconvulsive shock; (12) memory; (13) negative; (14) credit, responsibility; (15) pleasant, happy; (16) self-statements; (17) exercise; (18) antisocial, sociopathic

GLOSSARY TERMS

antisocial personality disorder (p. 491)
biological marker (p. 486)

bipolar disorder (p. 484)
electroconvulsive shock therapy (ECT) (p. 487)

lithium (p. 487)
major depression (p. 484)

mania (p. 487)
tricyclics (p. 487)

Module 44 Schizophrenia

A fire-drill alarm went off in school. Jeanette Keil, 29 years old, was taking classes in how to do remedial tutoring. She knew that the alarm was a message from God and became excited. This message was the key to solving her own personal problems as well as having worldwide implications. She came home and told her husband that God had sent her a message. She talked wildly of writing a book, of changing the world, of ridding lives everywhere of problems and handicaps. When her husband asked her questions about the message, her answers made very little sense. She woke in the middle of the night. She went to the family room, where she lit candles and filled wine glasses with grape juice. She was conducting her own private communion service. That morning Jeanette was admitted to a hospital for treatment. She remained in the hospital for 13 days, receiving antipsychotic medication. After her symptoms decreased, she was released. For the next six years, she continued to take antipsychotic medication and received psychotherapy as an outpatient. Presently she is symptom-free, writing a book about her experience, and serving on two mental health boards (adapted from the Los Angeles Times, *June 21, 1984).*

What if a fire alarm becomes a message from God?

Jeanette was diagnosed as having a **psychosis,** which is a loss of contact with reality. The type of psychosis affecting Jeanette is called acute **schizophrenia,** "acute" meaning that her problems developed suddenly, without any previous history of mental disorder. People with acute schizophrenia, like Jeanette, have a relatively good chance for recovery. This is not true of all schizophrenics. Consider this patient being interviewed by a therapist:

"How old are you?"
"Why I am centuries old, sir."
"How long have you been here?"
"I've been now on this property on and off for a long time. I cannot say the exact time because we are absorbed by the air at night, and they bring back people. They kill up everything; they can make you lie; they can talk through your throat."
"Who is this?"

"Why, the air."
"What is the name of this place?"
"This place is called a star."
"Who is the doctor in charge of your ward?"
"A body just like yours, sir. They can make you black and white.
I say good morning, but he just comes through there. At first it was a
colony. They said it was heaven. These buildings were not solid at the
time, and I am positive that this is the same place. They have others
just like it. People die, and all the microbes talk over there, and
prestigitis you know is sending you from here to another world. . . . I
was sent by the government to the United States to Washington to
some star, and they had a pretty nice country there. Now you have a
body like a young man who says he is of the prestigitis?"
"Who was this prestigitis?"
"Why, you are yourself. You can be prestigitis. They make you say
bad things; they can read you; they bring back Negroes from the dead
(White, 1932, p. 228).

Bary, the person answering the questions, is psychotic. He was diagnosed as having chronic schizophrenia, "chronic" meaning that he has a
long history of the disorder. Although Jeanette may have sounded initially
as confused as Bary, the main difference between them is that Jeanette's
problem occurred suddenly and her treatment was successful. Bary's problems developed over the years and his treatment was not successful. Individuals with chronic schizophrenia have a much poorer chance of recovery.

SYMPTOMS OF SCHIZOPHRENIA

Jeanette's and Bary's cases illustrate that schizophrenia is a serious mental
disorder. Its symptoms include disorders of thought, attention, perception,
motor behavior, and emotion. *Thought disorders* are characterized by incoherent patterns, formation of new words (called neologisms), inability to
stick to one topic, and irrational beliefs or delusions—for example, the
belief that a fire alarm is a message from God. *Problems of attention* or
concentration include difficulty in focusing on a single chain of events.

Schizophrenia is the most frequently diagnosed psychotic disorder; in mental hospitals, approximately half the patients are
diagnosed as schizophrenics. Patients with
acute schizophrenia have a relatively good
chance of recovery, but those with chronic
schizophrenia have little chance. (Eric A. Roth/
The Picture Cube)

Andy Wilf painted these three self-portraits across a period of years when he was having serious drug problems. He died at age 32 of an apparent drug overdose. (Courtesy of Ulrike Kantor, Ulrike Kantor Gallery)

Many schizophrenics report being overwhelmed by different thoughts and sensations and having no control over which thoughts enter and leave their minds. Disorders of *perception* include reporting strange bodily sensations and *hallucinations*, such as hearing voices. *Motor symptoms* may include making strange facial expressions, being extremely active, or the opposite, remaining immobile for long periods of time. *Emotional symptoms* may include having little or no emotional responsiveness or having emotional responses that are inappropriate to the situation—for example, laughing when told of the death of a close friend. According to DSM-III-R, a person must have a certain number of these symptoms for at least six months to be diagnosed a schizophrenic.

Schizophrenia is the most frequently diagnosed psychotic disorder in mental hospitals. Approximately half of the patients in mental hospitals are diagnosed as schizophrenics. The incidence of schizophrenia is approximately the same in women and men (Seeman, 1982).

Certain problems surround the diagnosis of schizophrenia. When 300 psychiatrists were asked to list the symptoms they used in diagnosing the disorder, the four symptoms most commonly mentioned were hallucinations, delusions, affective disturbances, and thought disorders. But no combination of any three of these symptoms was used by the majority of the psychiatrists (Lipkowitz & Idupuganti, 1983). The result is that patients may be diagnosed as schizophrenic by one psychiatrist and not by another, as happened in the case of John Hinckley. Another problem in diagnosis is that some medical problems can mimic schizophrenic symptoms. For example, in one medical-psychiatric hospital, 63 percent of those admitted with a diagnosis of schizophrenia were later found to have a treatable medical condition that was responsible for their symptoms (Hoffman, 1982). The DSM-III-R diagnostic system hopes to overcome this problem by specifying symptoms along five different dimensions, including physical and behavioral ones.

Suppose you believed that strangers were plotting to kidnap you?

If you believed that strangers were plotting against you, you might be suffering from a particular form of schizophrenia. Another complexity in diagnosing schizophrenia is that the symptoms vary somewhat depending on the type of schizophrenia involved. DSM-III-R lists several different types of schizophrenia, including paranoid, catatonic, and disorganized.

The most obvious symptoms of **paranoid schizophrenia,** which is a relatively common type, are delusions. These delusions often involve thoughts of being persecuted by others, sometimes in bizarre ways. For example, a paranoid schizophrenic may think that the crowd of people waiting in line at a movie theater is plotting to kidnap him. At the same time, many paranoid schizophrenics have delusions of grandeur. They may attribute to themselves all kinds of fantastic accomplishments that have no basis in reality. Some believe that they are actually a famous person. All these delusions may be accompanied by perceptual hallucinations. The symptoms of **disorganized schizophrenia** include bizarre ideas, often about one's body (bones melting), confused speech, very childish behavior (giggling for no apparent reason, making faces at people), great emotional swings (fits of laughing or crying), and often extreme neglect of personal appearance and hygiene. Symptoms of **catatonic schizophrenia** include periods of wild excitement and/or periods of rigid, prolonged immobility, sometimes assuming the same frozen posture for hours on end. One reaction will usually predominate. For unknown reasons, there has been a decrease in the number of cases of catatonic schizophrenia between 1900 and 1979 (Tempier & Veleber, 1981). It rarely occurs today.

Differentiating between types of schizophrenia can be very difficult since some symptoms, such as disordered thought processes and delusions, are shared by all types. In an attempt to deal with this problem, there has been a great research effort to try to differentiate among types of schizophrenia, using neurological or biological markers. So far, this effort has met with only limited success (McGuffin et al., 1987).

EXPLORING PSYCHOLOGY Causes of Schizophrenia

Is it possible to inherit schizophrenia?

The birth of four identical baby girls is a vary rare occurrence. Even rarer was the fact that by the time they had developed into young adults, all four were diagnosed as schizophrenic (Figure 15.4). Known as the Genain quadruplets, their shared disorders pointed to a genetic factor in schizophrenia.

Genetic Factor

The Genain quadruplets are a more dramatic example of what has been found in identical twins: If one member of a pair of identical twins has

Figure 15.4
Left: Born in 1930, the so-called Genain quadruplets received great publicity. However, by the time they reached high school, all four were labeled "different." They sometimes broke light bulbs, tore buttons off their clothes, complained of bones slipping out of place, and had periods of great confusion. For these and other reasons, all four were diagnosed as schizophrenic. Right: By the time of their 51st birthday party, the Genains had spent much of their adult lives in and out of hospitals. (Courtesy of the Genain quadruplets and Allan F. Mirsky, Ph.D.)

schizophrenia, there is about a 50 percent chance that the other twin will also develop schizophrenia. In comparison, Figure 15.5 shows that if one member of a pair of nonidentical twins has schizophrenia, there is only about a 10 percent chance that the other twin will develop the disorder (Gottesman & Shields, 1976). After reviewing many twin and adoption studies, Stephen Faraone and Ming Tsuang (1985) concluded that genetic factors play a greater role in developing schizophrenia than do cultural factors. These findings suggest that a person may inherit a *predisposition* for schizophrenia. Researchers are looking for a genetic or biological marker for schizophrenia, similar to the one researchers recently found for some cases of bipolar disorder (Module 43). However, Miron Baron (1986) reports that, at present, no genetic or biological markers have been found to differentiate schizophrenia from other mental disorders.

Brain Factors

At the beginning of this Module you were told about Jeanette Keil, who developed acute schizophrenic symptoms that were lessened with antipsychotic drugs. The majority of antipsychotic drugs work by decreasing

Is a schizophrenic's brain different?

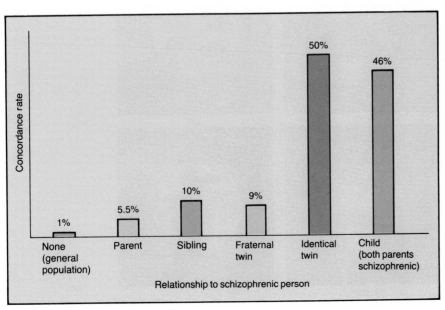

Figure 15.5
The genetic component in schizophrenia. In this example, concordance rate means the chances of being schizophrenic if another person is. For example, if a brother or sister (sibling or fraternal twin) is schizophrenic, the chances of other brothers or sisters being schizophrenic are between 9 and 10 percent. If one identical twin is schizophrenic, there is a 50 percent chance that the other twin will be schizophrenic. In the case of the Genain quadruplets the concordance rate was 100, meaning that if one was schizophrenic, so were all. (Adapted from Gottesman & Shields, 1976)

the activity of the dopamine system. This supports the **dopamine** (DOPE-ah-meen) **theory,** which says that abnormalities in the dopamine system may not cause schizophrenia but may be involved in the disease. Until very recently, it was difficult to decide whether changes in the dopamine systems of schizophrenics were due to the disease itself or were caused by the action of antipsychotic drugs. This question has now been answered by Dean Wong and his associates (1986). They used a process called positron emission tomography, usually referred to as PET scans. Here's how PET scans work. Brain cells get their fuel by taking glucose from the bloodstream. The more active certain parts of the brain are, the more glucose they take up and use. If researchers inject a short-lived radioactive glucose into the bloodstream, they can measure the activity level of different areas of the brain by recording how much radioactive glucose is being taken up and used (Figure 15.6). The advantage of PET scans is that the process can be done on living humans without causing any damage to the brain.

Dean Wong used PET scans to compare the dopamine activity of three different groups: a group of schizophrenics that had been given antipsychotics, a group of schizophrenics that had *never* been given antipsychotics, and a group of normal volunteers. Compared with the normal volunteers, Wong found a higher number of dopamine receptors in both groups of schizophrenics. Wong concluded that schizophrenia itself is associated with an increase in the number of dopamine receptors. This finding partly explains why antipsychotic drugs reduce schizophrenic symptoms. Many antipsychotic drugs block dopamine receptors. It is hoped that research on the dopamine system will lead to more effective drug treatments and clues as to what causes schizophrenia (Barnes, 1987c).

Environmental Factors

Did some particular stressor bring on Jeanette's symptoms?

So far we have focused on the biological side of schizophrenia. But there is clear evidence that psychological factors are also involved in the onset of this disorder. Remember that if one identical twin develops schizophrenia, the other twin has a 50 percent chance of also developing it. This suggests

Figure 15.6
By measuring how fast the brain's cells metabolize specially treated glucose, researchers obtain a colored picture or PET (positron emission tomography) scan. The amount of brain activity is indicated by different colors, with blue and green showing relatively little activity, while orange indicates increased activity. Researchers use PET scans to look for differences in brain functioning in individuals with mental disorders. (Courtesy of the Genain quadruplets and Allan F. Mirsky, Ph.D.)

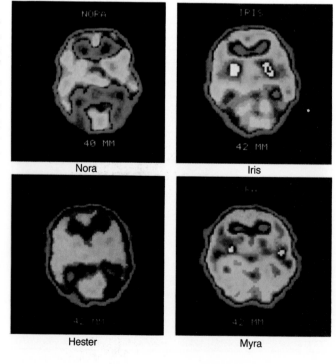

Nora

Iris

Hester

Myra

that the *environment* makes a substantial contribution. Particularly important are certain environmental stressors. For example, Jeanette remembers that for several weeks before her break with reality, when she suddenly thought that the fire alarm was a message from God, she had felt under stress, felt trapped and without direction. What are some of the specific stressors that can contribute to a breakdown like Jeanette's?

People who develop schizophrenia have often been found to have parents who are hostile and critical, and who communicated in a highly emotional way (Parker, 1982; Wynne, 1981). In addition to these family pressures, other life stressors may increase the likelihood of schizophrenia. These include weak social contacts, loss of a parent, difficulty in adjusting to school, and career or personal problems (Rosenthal, 1980). According to the current view, an inherited predisposition for schizophrenia may be triggered by stressful family relationships and other negative life experiences.

TREATMENT OF SCHIZOPHRENIA

As soon as Jeanette was admitted to the hospital, she was probably given chlorpromazine (trade name, Thorazine). As the drug took effect, her thinking became less confused. Chlorpromazine belongs to a family of drugs called *phenothiazines*. In addition to the phenothiazines, other drugs are also used to treat schizophrenia. As a group, these drugs are called *antipsychotics* because they reduce the bizarre hallucinations and delusions mental health professionals label "psychotic." We have already told you that one of the primary actions of many antipsychotic drugs is to reduce the level of dopamine in the brain. The fact that these drugs also decrease schizophrenic symptoms supports the dopamine theory of schizophrenia. On the other hand, the fact that some patients do not improve or relapse on these medications suggests that the dopamine hypothesis is not the entire answer.

As was true for Jeanette, a person may remain on antipsychotic drugs for a long period of time—in her case, six years. Individuals with chronic schizophrenia (as opposed to Jeanette's acute schizophrenia) often remain on antipsychotics for much of their lives. Do these drugs produce any undesirable side effects? Here is what one person who took Thorazine has to say:

> Thorazine has lots of unpleasant side effects. It makes you groggy, lowers your blood pressure, making you dizzy and faint when you stand up too quickly. If you go out in the sun your skin gets red and hurts like hell. It makes muscles rigid and twitchy. The side effects were bad enough, but, I liked what the drug was supposed to do even less. It's supposed to keep you calm, dull, uninterested and uninteresting. . . . What the drug is supposed to do is keep away hallucinations. What I think it does is just fog up your mind. . . . On Thorazine everything's a bore. . . . You can read comic books and *Reader's Digest* forever. . . . The weather is dull, the flowers are dull, nothing's very impressive (Vonnegut, 1976, pp. 252–253).

As this description indicates, antipsychotic drugs not only affect schizophrenic symptoms, they also have a number of side effects, such as depression and emotional dulling. One of their most serious side effects involves motor function. The longer a person remains on phenothiazines or related drugs, the higher the probability of developing slow, rhythmic movements of the mouth and lips, as well as unusual movements of the limbs. These uncontrollable movements, called **tardive dyskinesia** (TARD-

How can Jeanette be helped?

Does drug therapy make a schizophrenic feel normal?

MAJOR CONCEPTS   Schizophrenia

Please match each item with its correct description.

1. Acute schizophrenia

2. Chronic schizophrenia

3. Disorganized schizophrenia

4. Paranoid schizophrenia

5. Catatonic schizophrenia

6. Dopamine

7. Phenothiazines

a. _5_ A form of schizophrenia characterized by marked disturbance in body movements, sometimes alternating between complete immobility and extreme agitation.

b. _3_ A form of schizophrenia characterized by bizarre ideas, incoherent speech, and very childish behavior.

c. _2_ What schizophrenia is labeled when a person has a long history of the disorder.

d. _1_ What schizophrenia is labeled when the disorder comes on suddenly and previous behavior was relatively normal.

e. _4_ A form of schizophrenia characterized by delusions of persecution and often delusions of grandeur.

f. _7_ A group of drugs used widely in the treatment of schizophrenia.

g. _6_ A neurotransmitter believed to be involved in schizophrenic symptoms.

Answers: a (5); b (3); c (2); d (1); e (4); f (7); g (6)

Figure 15.7

Effectiveness of various therapies. In treating schizophrenia, psychotherapy alone was least effective while drugs alone or psychotherapy and drugs were more effective.

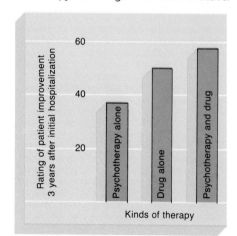

iv dis-cah-NEE-zee-yah), occur in approximately 26 percent of patients who have been maintained on antipsychotics (Jeste & Wyatt, 1982). About 37 percent of patients with tardive dyskinesia will have a reduction in these symptoms if taken off the antipsychotic drugs. In the remaining patients, tardive dyskinesia may persist even when the drug therapy is stopped. This suggests that the drugs have caused irreversible changes in the brain. At present, there is no cure for tardive dyskinesia.

As you see in Figure 15.7, the symptoms of schizophrenia can be reduced by several different kinds of drug treatment. While the symptoms are reduced, the person may benefit from psychotherapy and may begin to function at a more normal level. However, the schizophrenia may not have been cured and the symptoms may return. Follow-up studies of patients one to three years after treatment generally indicate the following: approximately 25 percent of schizophrenics have recovered; approximately 50 percent continue to suffer some behavior impairment and have to be rehospitalized; and approximately 25 percent do not recover at all (Tsuang, 1982). Even if patients are maintained on drugs when released from the hospital, approximately 50 percent still relapse during the next one to two years and have to be hospitalized again (Bland, 1982; Caton, 1982; May et al., 1981). One of the reasons we do not yet have a "cure" for schizophrenia is that we do not yet understand its causes.

REVIEW

At first the voices were difficult to understand, but little by little they fused into the single voice of his mother. James came to believe that the voice was trying to destroy him by taking over his life. The voice would tell James how much to eat, what to wear, even when to go to work. If James disobeyed, he experienced physical pain. The pain, the torment, and the fear were becoming unbearable. One day in early June, James visited his mother's house and killed her. He wanted to put an end to his voices. After the killing he went home and drank a bottle of vodka and went to sleep. He confessed the murder to a policeman who came to tell him of his mother's death (adapted from the *Los Angeles Times*, May 23, 1984).

James was diagnosed as suffering from paranoid (1) _____. Besides hearing voices, which is an example of (2) _____, other symptoms of schizophrenia include thinking incoherently, such as believing that killing his mother would end the voices, and having delusions, both of which are examples of (3) _____ disorders. Schizophrenics may also make strange facial expressions or become excessively active, examples of (4) _____ symptoms, and they may show inappropriate feelings, such as laughter at a friend's death, which is an example of (5) _____ symptoms. Because he showed a number of symptoms specified by DSM-III-R, James was diagnosed as a schizophrenic. More specifically, he was diagnosed a (6) _____ schizophrenic because he felt persecuted by his mother's voice. In a second type of schizophrenia, individuals have bizarre ideas about their bodies and experience great emotional swings; this is called (7) _____ schizophrenia. In a third type of schizophrenia, the individual may have periods of wild excitement and/or periods of prolonged rigidity; this is called (8) _____ schizophrenia.

In searching for the causes of James's schizophrenia, we might study his grandparents, parents, and other relatives for mental disorders, since James may have inherited a (9) _____ for schizophrenia. But even though he may have inherited a predisposition for this disorder, it is assumed that (10) _____ stressors triggered the appearance of his symptoms. For example, as a professional drummer for a number of well-known rock bands, James experienced many of the frustrations of having to compete for a hit record.

Researchers are currently searching for biological markers of schizophrenia. One theory is that schizophrenia may be caused in part by dysfunction of a particular neurotransmitter system in the brain, the (11) _____ system.

After his arrest, James was put on antipsychotic drugs, specifically chlorpromazine, which belongs to a group of drugs called the (12) _____. These particular drugs, which reduce some schizophrenic symptoms, apparently lower the level of dopamine activity in the brain. This finding supports the (13) _____ theory of schizophrenia. One of the effects of chlorpromazine is to dull the person's emotional reactions. In addition, the longer the person remains on chlorpromazine, the greater the chance he or she will develop uncontrollable muscle movements, called (14) _____ dyskinesia. Follow-up studies of schizophrenics after hospitalization and treatment indicate that approximately 25 percent recover completely. Of those who are treated and released, approximately (15) _____ percent will relapse within a year or two. About 25 percent do not recover with any therapy.

Answers: (1) schizophrenia; (2) hallucinations; (3) thought; (4) motor; (5) emotional; (6) paranoid; (7) disorganized; (8) catatonic; (9) predisposition; (10) environmental or life; (11) dopamine; (12) phenothiazines; (13) dopamine; (14) tardive; (15) 50

GLOSSARY TERMS

catatonic schizophrenia (p. 496)

disorganized schizophrenia (p. 496)

dopamine theory (p. 498)

paranoid schizophrenia (p. 496)

psychosis (p. 493)

schizophrenia (p. 496)

tardive dyskinesia (p. 499)

16

Psychotherapies

Module 45 Overview of Psychotherapies

Case 1: *George was a handsome, articulate young man. A junior in college, he mentioned several problems which, during the first therapy hour, he compressed into "school and my girlfriend." Regarding school, he stated with some depth of feeling that "school means absolutely nothing to me"; he had hated all classes since coming to college; and he considered the professors "creeps to screw you over." In contrast, during his high school years, "I looked up to my teachers." He was currently failing one of his classes, which troubled him. The second problem was stated as follows: "I have these bad personality traits. . . . I am super jealous." He specifically stated that he wanted help and came to therapy at the suggestion of his girlfriend (Strupp, 1980b, p. 596).*

Can psychotherapy help when things are just generally lousy?

The kind of help George receives will depend upon which particular approach his psychotherapist follows. A psychotherapist may focus on discovering unconscious conflicts, pointing out irrational beliefs, unlearning maladaptive behaviors, changing self-statements, or some combination of these (Figure 16.1). One question we want to answer in this module is which of these approaches would best help someone like George?

Case 2: *Jack, a 16-year-old boy in his final year of school, was seen because of a phobic reaction to the sight and mention of blood. . . . He had been afraid of blood for years. He had passed out about 20 times in science and biology classes in school. He felt very queasy when blood and operations were shown on television and had to look away. He worried that if he were to see someone at work cut himself, he would faint and this would jeopardize his chance of getting a job as an ambulance driver. Jack described himself as someone who takes things as they come. He was happy at school and rarely became depressed. His only problem was an intense anxiety reaction at the sight of blood (adapted from Yule & Fernando, 1980).*

Some therapies, such as psychoanalysis, might involve years of treatment as the therapist searches for unconscious conflicts. Other therapies, such as behavior modification, focus on the behavior that the client feels is a problem, in Jack's case fear of blood. A second question we want to answer is which approach is most effective for treating specific anxieties and phobias?

Figure 16.1
Some of the problems that are dealt with in psychotherapy.

I am super jealous

I'm terrified of blood

My relationships don't work out

I'll show my love by shooting the president

Does psychotherapy have to take years?

As a child, Johnny M was sent to an institution for the mentally retarded. Later, following a nervous breakdown, he was committed to a mental hospital, and after treatment, discharged. Johnny now lives on the streets. (J. Berndt)

Case 3: *Joan, a 29-year-old teacher, reported symptoms of depression, chronic anxiety, difficulties in her job, and disturbances in interpersonal relations, especially with men. None of her relationships with men had been satisfactory and they had all ended in disappointment. Her last relationship, in which marriage had been planned, had ended a few months prior to her coming for an initial interview. During the interview it became clear that at one time she had had a very close relationship with her father, but this relationship had changed to a disturbed and hostile one (adapted from Davanloo, 1980a).*

If Joan were in traditional psychoanalysis, the treatment would last for two or three years, or about 600 sessions. Recently, a new and shorter version of traditional psychoanalysis has been developed. Called short-term dynamic psychotherapy, this treatment lasts a maximum of several months, or 30 sessions. A third question we want to answer is how effective are short-term therapies?

Case 4: *A jury found John Hinckley, Jr., not guilty of shooting President Reagan by reason of insanity. Following this verdict, he was committed to St. Elizabeth's Hospital in Washington, D.C. During his first months there, he attempted suicide. At present, he remains in St. Elizabeth's.*

Patients with serious mental disorders, such as John Hinckley, Jr., are usually confined to mental hospitals for treatment. Serious disorders are usually treated with a combination of psychotherapy and drugs. Generally, psychotherapy alone is not very effective in treating serious disorders such as schizophrenia. Psychotherapy is most effective in treating milder disorders, such as those illustrated in the first three cases.

NONSPECIFIC FACTORS
IN PSYCHOTHERAPY

In case 3, Joan has a problem maintaining relationships with men. To solve this problem, she might try any one of over 100 different therapies, such as art, behavior, client-centered, cognitive, crisis management, ego-state, Gestalt, mainstreaming, multimodal, Plissit, psychoanalysis, primal, radical, rational emotive, rebirthing, social influence, structured learning, and verbal behavior therapy, to name just a few (Corsini, 1982). In spite of the differences among these approaches, they share many features that can be called *nonspecific factors* in psychotherapy (Goldfried, 1980).

Most forms of psychotherapy involve a relatively structured verbal interaction between at least two individuals, the *client* (in this case Joan) and the *therapist*. If Joan had entered group therapy, there would ordinarily be one therapist and a number of other clients in addition to herself. Through their *verbal* interactions, the therapist tries to help Joan identify and face her problems. Joan's emotional upset over her disappointing relationships provides the motivation to discuss, actively and willingly, highly personal and distressing matters and to work out solutions. The therapist has the role of a socially recognized healer who presumably has the training and personal resources to help Joan with her problems. Joan's interaction with her therapist leads to the formation of a *supportive relationship*, which increases the chances that she will follow her therapist's suggestions, interpretations, and directives (Garfield, 1980). If Joan were involved in group therapy, the

Is psychotherapy more than talking?

In the mid-1960s, Richard Brautigan's book, *Trout Fishing in America*, sold over 2 million copies. In the mid-1980s, Brautigan killed himself. His friends recalled him as someone who was very creative, impossible to live with, loved to shoot things, liked bondage, drank too much, and wanted unconditional love (Wright, 1985). (Baron Wolman)

verbal interactions and supportive relationship would involve other members of the group as well.

Although psychotherapies differ in the specific techniques they use to help people overcome their problems, virtually all involve these same nonspecific factors: (1) they provide a therapist who is recognized as a healer; (2) they attempt to establish a supportive relationship; (3) they use verbal interactions to solve the client's problem; and (4) they depend on the client's *motivation* to solve problems.

THE PSYCHOTHERAPIST

How does one become a psychotherapist?

A number of professionals conduct psychotherapy: psychiatrists, clinical psychologists, social workers, psychiatric nurses, counselors, teachers, ministers, and others. Some receive more training in psychotherapy techniques than others. Let's look at the kind of training psychiatrists and clinical psychologists receive.

If you wanted to be a **psychiatrist**, you would first be trained as a physician. After receiving an M.D. degree, you would go on to a psychiatric residency, which involves additional training in pharmacology, neurology, psychopathology, and psychotherapeutic techniques. Psychiatrists who receive additional training in psychoanalytic institutes are called **psychoanalysts**.

If you wanted to be a **clinical psychologist**, you would complete a Ph.D. program in psychology, which usually takes four to five years after graduation from college. Although there are similarities between the training of psychiatrists and clinical psychologists, there are many differences. For example, psychiatrists receive extensive training in medicine and drugs and less training in basic psychology and experimental method. Clinical psychologists receive less training in drugs and medicine and extensive training in basic psychology, psychotherapy techniques, and experimental method. Psychiatrists tend to view psychological disorders as diseases and to treat them with drugs. Clinical psychologists are more likely to view psychological disorders as learned problems and to treat them with psychotherapy. Psychiatrists tend to study the effects of drugs on mental disorders, while clinical psychologists tend to study the effects of psychotherapy. When psychiatrists do use therapy, they tend to use psychoanalytical and psychodynamic approaches. Clinical psychologists tend to use a wider variety of techniques, including behavior and cognitive therapies.

If you were to become a therapist, you would have a number of different approaches to choose from. In psychoanalysis, the therapist searches for unconscious causes of problems and interprets clients' verbal statements. In person-centered therapy, the therapist is supportive and accepting and assumes that clients have the potential to help themselves. In behavior therapy, the therapist is directive, making specific suggestions for change. When therapists were asked why they chose a certain approach, they answered that personal satisfaction was the primary reason (Garfield, 1980). Apparently, therapists choose a particular approach both because of its presumed effectiveness and because it suits their personalities.

APPROACHES TO PSYCHOTHERAPY

Which approaches are today's therapists using?

In one study, psychologists were asked, "Which approach do you use in therapy?" The answers are given in Figure 16.2. The majority of those surveyed agreed that the days of a single approach, or one school dominating the field, were drawing to a close (Prochaska & Norcross, 1983;

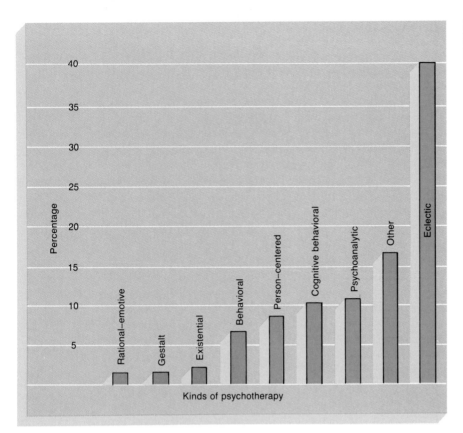

Figure 16.2
Preferences for different kinds of psychotherapy. (Adapted from Smith, 1982)

Smith, 1982). In fact, the most widely used approach is **eclectic** (ek-LEK-
tik), which means that the psychotherapist combines features from several
schools of thought. For example, a therapist might use elements of behavior
therapy, such as specifying behavioral goals, along with elements of cognitive therapy, such as changing irrational beliefs, and elements of person-
centered therapy, such as providing a very supportive environment.

This survey indicates a dramatic shift in the general methods of psychotherapy. In the 1940s and 1950s, most mental health professionals were
trained in the psychoanalytic approach, and in the general method of long-
term psychoanalysis. In more recent decades, however, with the discovery
of antipsychotic drugs and the rise of cognitive-behavior therapy, the popularity of psychoanalysis has declined in favor of *short-term* therapies (Garfield, 1981b; Neill & Ludwig, 1980). In Modules 46 and 47, we will discuss
how some of the more widely used contemporary psychotherapies are used
to help people with their problems. At this point, let's see how effective
psychotherapy is.

PSYCHOTHERAPY EVALUATED   **EXPLORING PSYCHOLOGY**

- George has emotional and school-related problems.

- Jack suffers an intense fear of blood.

- Joan has chronic anxiety, mild depression, and problems with personal relationships.

**Should George, Jack, and Joan go
into therapy?**

Effectiveness

Would George, Jack, and Joan be better off using psychotherapy to overcome their problems, or should they just wait for these problems to work themselves out?

Researchers Mary Smith and Gene Glass (1977) were the first to use a statistical procedure, called *meta-analysis,* to evaluate almost 400 studies on psychotherapy. Meta-analysis is a powerful procedure that determines the effectiveness of some treatment, in this case psychotherapy, across many studies. As shown in Figure 16.3, Smith and Glass found that psychotherapy was generally more effective in treating problems than was doing nothing or waiting for the problem to go away. Since Smith and Glass's first study using meta-analysis, there have been at least five more such studies on the effectiveness of psychotherapy (Smith et al., 1980; Landman & Dawes, 1982; Miller & Berman, 1983; Shapiro & Shapiro, 1982; Prioleau et al., 1983). Joseph Brown (1987), who reviewed all six studies that used meta-analysis, pointed out a number of methodological problems with all six studies. Brown noted, however, that all but one study (Prioleau et al., 1983) found that psychotherapy was more effective than waiting for the problem to go away. There are now a large number of studies showing that approximately 66 percent of clients who seek psychotherapy show improvement. However, of this 66 percent, only a small percentage of clients show great improvement while most show some type of positive results. The remaining 33 percent of the clients do not improve or, in a very small number of cases, actually get worse. If clients do not seek psychotherapy, there is about a 33 percent chance that they will report improvement with the passage of time or by working out the problem themselves (Garfield, 1981a).

Differences

If George, Jack, and Joan were to seek psychotherapy, which kind of therapy would help them the most? For example, a psychoanalyst would focus on their past and search for unconscious conflicts as the source of their problems. A person-centered therapist would provide an atmosphere of warmth

Figure 16.3
Effectiveness of different kinds of psychotherapy. [Adapted from Glass & Kliegl, 1983]

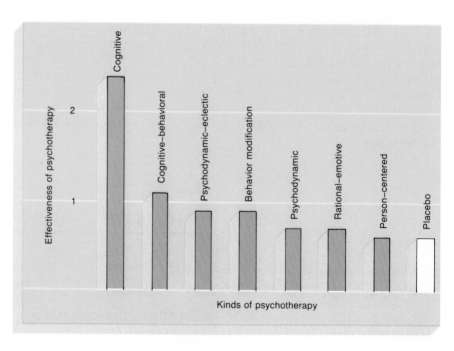

and unconditional acceptance to help them change. A behavior therapist would emphasize changing current target behaviors. A cognitive therapist would focus on changing maladaptive thoughts and irrational beliefs. Each of these therapists would agree that certain procedures are needed to treat problems, but they would disagree on what these procedures are or how they should be carried out.

In their first study, Smith and Glass (1977) compared the effectiveness of 10 different types of therapies, which they divided into two groups, behavioral and nonbehavioral. Among those included in the behavioral group were behavior modification and systematic desensitization. Among those included in the nonbehavioral group were psychoanalysis, person-centered therapy, and eclectic therapy. Although both behavioral and non-behavioral therapies proved to be effective, Smith and Glass found little difference among the 10 therapies in terms of effectiveness.

A slightly different finding was reported by researchers David A. Shapiro and Diana Shapiro (1982). In their meta-analysis of different kinds of psychotherapies, they primarily selected studies on clients, mostly students, who reported relatively specific problems, such as phobia, test anxiety, dating anxiety, and being unassertive. In treating these target behaviors, behavioral therapies were found to be more effective than nonbehavioral therapies.

"Are all psychotherapies equivalent?" was the title of an article by

Is one therapy better than another?

MAJOR CONCEPT   Psychotherapy

Most people have little knowledge of the kinds of psychotherapies available, the professionals who provide them, or the effectiveness of the treatments.

Below are some statements about psychotherapies. Indicate whether they are true (T) or false (F).

1. T/F Except for a few unusual forms of psychotherapy, most mental health professionals use basically the same form of therapy.

2. T/F Psychotherapy is most effective in treating relatively mild psychological problems. For serious mental disorders, psychotherapy is usually used in combination with drug treatment.

3. T/F Virtually all forms of psychotherapy have certain nonspecific factors in common which appear to be a major cause of their effectiveness.

4. T/F A psychiatrist is a medical doctor who specializes in treating mental disorders.

5. T/F Clinical psychologists are very similar to psychiatrists in the forms of treatment they use.

6. T/F Your chances of overcoming a psychological problem are improved if you enter some form of psychotherapy.

7. T/F For most relatively mild psychological problems, the various forms of psychotherapy do not seem to differ much in effectiveness.

8. T/F If you suffered from a phobia, you would probably be best off entering a behavior therapy program.

Answers: 1 (F); 2 (T); 3 (T); 4 (T); 5 (F); 6 (T); 7 (T); 8 (T).

William Stiles and his colleagues (1986). In agreement with the above studies, they found a great deal of evidence showing that different kinds of psychotherapies are equally effective. For those clients who seek help in overcoming certain target problems, such as phobia, test anxiety, or unassertiveness, the Stiles group agreed with Shapiro and Shapiro that behavioral therapies may have an advantage over nonbehavioral therapies. Stiles concluded that the primary reason for the effectiveness of most psychotherapies was the nonspecific factors that we discussed earlier in this Module, rather than their specific approaches. This means that George's emotional problems and Joan's anxiety and relationship problems can be treated effectively by either behavioral or nonbehavioral therapies. However, Jack's phobia of blood may be better treated by a behavioral than a nonbehavioral therapy.

REVIEW

During your sophomore year in college, you develop an emotional problem. After being in a relationship for three or four months, you begin to get very jealous, start accusing your partner of being interested in other people, and pick fights over tiny things.

Your problem with jealousy would be considered a relatively mild mental disorder and is one that could be helped by (1) _____.

You wonder if you should seek some form of psychotherapy, but are not sure what kind of treatment would be best. If you investigated the forms of psychotherapy available, you would discover that all share certain features, called (2) _____ factors. For example, all therapies involve yourself and a therapist taking part in a relatively structured (3) _____ interaction. Through your interaction with the therapist, you form a supportive (4) _____ which helps you accept and follow the therapist's suggestions. How successful you are in therapy will depend on how (5) _____ you are to overcome your problem no matter what form of therapy you enter. Although all forms of psychotherapy share these nonspecific factors, they differ in specific factors, such as the kinds of causes or solutions they focus on.

If you went to a therapist who was trained as a physician and then received additional training in pharmacology, neurology, and psychotherapy, he or she would be called a (6) _____. Only a small percentage of psychiatrists who had trained in psychoanalytic institutes would be called psychoanalysts. If you went to a therapist who had completed a doctoral program in psychology that emphasizes basic psychology, psychotherapeutic techniques, and experimental method, he or she would be called a (7) _____ psychologist. Generally, psychiatrists tend to view mental disorders as (8) _____ and to use drugs in their treatment. Clinical psychologists tend to view mental disorders as problems that have been (9) _____ and that can be treated with psychotherapy.

If you had lived during the 1940s and 1950s, the primary approach to treating your jealousy problem would have been (10) _____, which would have required two or three years of treatment. In the 1980s, you discover that the long-term psychoanalytic approach has declined in popularity. Today, more therapists are using (11) _____ - _____ approaches. You also discover that the most popular approach today is one that combines features from a number of different approaches, called an (12) _____ approach.

Will psychotherapy help you overcome your jealousy? Approximately (13) _____ percent of clients who receive psychotherapy improve to some extent. Will your problem go away without psychotherapy? Only about (14) _____ percent of people with problems who do not receive psychotherapy get better.

Which kind of approach would be the most effective for treating your problem? The general conclusion is that, for the treatment of many problems, there is little difference in effectiveness between specific psychotherapeutic approaches. This conclusion supports the idea that (15) _____ factors are primarily responsible for improvement in psychotherapy.

The one exception to this conclusion is the treatment of certain target behaviors, such as phobias. For phobias the (16) _____ approach appears more effective than others.

Answers: (1) psychotherapy; (2) nonspecific; (3) verbal; (4) relationship; (5) motivated; (6) psychiatrist; (7) clinical; (8) diseases; (9) learned; (10) psychoanalysis; (11) short-term; (12) eclectic; (13) 66; (14) 33; (15) nonspecific; (16) behavioral

GLOSSARY TERMS

clinical psychologist (p. 506)

psychiatrist (p. 506)

psychoanalyst (p. 506)

eclectic (p. 507)

Module 46 Psychoanalysis and Person-Centered Therapy

PSYCHOANALYSIS

Henry, a man in his mid-forties who was well advanced in treatment, casually mentioned his somewhat late arrival at the analyst's office (which might not otherwise have attracted attention). "You will think it is a resistance," Henry remarked sarcastically, "but it was nothing of the kind. I had hailed a taxi that would have gotten me to the office on time. However, the traffic light changed just before the cab reached me, and someone else got in instead. I was so annoyed that I yelled 'F___ you!' after the cab driver." A brief pause ensued, followed by laughter as Henry repeated "F___ you!"—this time clearly directed to the analyst. (The analyst assumed that the cabbie had been a displaced object in the first place and Henry's anger was relieved by the opportunity to "curse out" the analyst.) After another brief pause, it was the analyst who broke the silence and injected his first and only interpretation of the session. He asserted that Henry seemed to be angry about a previously canceled therapy session. Henry was furious over the interpretation. "Who are you that I should care about missing that session?" he stormed. Henry paused again, and then reflected more tranquilly, "My father, I suppose." This time it was the word "father" that served as the switch word to a new line of thought. "My father was distant, like you," he began. "We never really had a conversation" (adapted from Lipton, 1983).

What does a psychoanalyst do and say?

This very brief excerpt from a psychoanalytic session illustrates some of the basic features of **psychoanalysis.** Notice that the patient is encouraged to say anything he chooses and the analyst makes very few comments. When the analyst does comment, he interprets something the patient says, such as the meaning of the anger at the taxi driver (Figure 16.4). This may sound like a very indirect way of solving the patient's problems. How was the psychoanalytic approach originally developed?

Figure 16.4
A psychoanalytic session.

So what if I'm late…
I cussed out the cab driver…
You remind me of my father.

I will maintain a passive role,
interpret the patient's thoughts
and deal with his transference.

The Origins of Psychoanalysis

**Why did Freud develop
psychoanalysis?**

Here is how Sigmund Freud might explain why he developed psycho-analysis:

I came to believe that problem behaviors were actually symptoms of underlying conflicts the person had repressed. For example, in the opening cases you read in Module 45, I would say that George's jealousy, Jack's phobia, and Joan's difficulties with men are all symptoms of conflicts that were repressed because they were too threatening or painful to be faced. You see, Jack's real problem is not the fear of blood, but rather some unconscious conflict that shows up in this particular symptom. When I realized that behind every symptom was an unconscious conflict, I developed a technique to make these conflicts conscious and to help the patient resolve them.

One of Freud's most influential contributions was his development of psychoanalysis, a method for treating what he called **neurotic behaviors.** These are all the maladaptive thoughts and actions that indicate anxiety over some repressed conflict. Although some of Freud's original methods have been modified by his followers, psychoanalysts today continue to share a set of common assumptions about how to treat neurotic behaviors.

What Happens in Psychoanalysis?

**Why does a psychoanalyst let the
client talk so much?**

As you saw in the case of Henry, the client in a psychoanalytic session is allowed to talk about whatever he or she wishes. Why does the therapist not do more to guide the conversation toward a discussion of the client's specific worries and problems? Here is how Freud might answer that question:

On page 511 you read a very brief description of a psychoanalytic session that, perhaps to you, seemed to have no point. Why is the client allowed to ramble on and on and why does the psychoanalyst say so very little?

Remember that one of the keys to treating a problem is to discover the patient's unconscious *conflicts*. Since the patient is unaware of these conflicts, it was necessary to develop indirect ways to discover them. One such method I call **free association.** During free association, I encourage the patient to relax and say whatever comes to mind, to hold nothing back. If the patient lets thoughts flow freely, those thoughts will arouse certain associations, which in turn will give clues to the unconscious cause of the problem. For example, if you sat in on Henry's entire therapy session, you would discover that he talks about many things: enjoying parties and missing a taxi.

During this free association, the therapist interrupts very little so as not to stop the flow of ideas. When the therapist does interrupt, it is usually to make an interpretation, to suggest to the patient what the associations mean. For example, the client's story about missing the taxi is interpreted by the therapist to mean that the client is angry about the previous session being canceled. But notice how this interpretation serves as the springboard for more associations: links between anger, the patient's father, and negative personality traits the father possessed.

Freud lights his pipe and continues: Besides free association, there is a second way to discover a patient's unconscious conflicts. That method is **dream analysis**. I believe that your unconscious conflicts are reflected in your dreams. As you tell me your dreams, I will interpret their hidden meaning and, in so doing, discover clues to your unconscious conflicts.

You probably noticed that Henry projects onto the therapist certain negative traits of his father. The therapist, in effect, serves as a "substitute father," toward whom Henry can direct the anger and hostility he feels toward his real father. This process of feeling toward the therapist all the conflict-ridden emotions felt toward someone important in the patient's childhood is called **transference**. The patient develops a distorted view of the therapist and transfers certain feelings to the therapist. I believe that if the feelings involved in transference are not worked out, therapy will be stalled. Thus, at some point the analyst must help the patient deal with these feelings so that therapy may proceed.

Freud pauses briefly and then says: Many people ask me why psychoanalysis takes so long. I believe that one of the essential requirements for improvement is that the patient achieve *insight* into the causes of his or her problem. Achieving insight, however, is a very long and difficult process because the patient has so many defenses against admitting repressed thoughts and feelings into consciousness. The patient's reluctance to recognize these unconscious conflicts I call **resistance**. I think that one of the important functions of the analyst is to overcome the patient's resistance so that insight can be obtained. Once the patient develops insight into problems, he or she is on the way to finding solutions.

Why does psychoanalysis take so long?

Status of Psychoanalysis **EXPLORING PSYCHOLOGY**

You have just read how Freud might describe psychoanalysis. What do others think of this approach? Many critics have focused on the analyst's interpretations of dreams and free associations. These *interpretations* are critical in providing clues about unconscious conflicts. But how do we know whether an interpretation is accurate? For example, when Henry's session was reviewed by a second psychoanalyst, that second analyst interpreted many of his statements very differently than the original analyst had (Kanzer, 1983). It is impossible to know which analyst's interpretations were correct. The same problem arises over the interpretation of dreams, which we discussed in Module 13. Although Freud believed that unconscious conflicts could be uncovered through free association and dream analysis, there is very little evidence to support this belief.

Another criticism of psychoanalysis is that the development of insight does not necessarily lead to a change in behavior. For example, a patient may realize that he hated his father and that this had led to his problem in dealing with all people in authority. However, this understanding does not necessarily lead to better relations with his boss.

Until the late 1950s, psychoanalysis was the major psychotherapeutic approach. Although psychoanalysis has declined in popularity, some of its concepts have been incorporated into other approaches, such as the psychodynamic approach. Similar to traditional psychoanalysis, the **psychodynamic approach** assumes that symptoms are signs of more basic underlying problems, that transference needs to be worked out, and that the primary role of the therapist is to interpret and clarify the patient's behaviors. But unlike traditional psychoanalysts, psychodynamic therapists take a much more active role in interpreting, clarifying, and suggesting solutions. Let's look next at one of the newer psychodynamic approaches.

SHORT-TERM DYNAMIC PSYCHOTHERAPY

Is Joan's therapist acting as Freud would have done?

As described in case 3 in Module 45, Joan is a 29-year-old teacher with problems of depression, chronic anxiety, difficulties in her job, and disappointing relationships with men. Here is a conversation between her and her therapist:

THERAPIST: How do you feel about talking to me about yourself?
CLIENT: I feel uncomfortable. I have never done this before, so I don't really, you know . . . I feel I don't really know how to answer some of your questions.
THERAPIST: Um-hum. But have you noticed that in your relationship here with me you are passive, and I am the one who has to question you repeatedly?
CLIENT: I know.
THERAPIST: Um-hum. What do you think about this? Is this the way it is with other people, or is it only here with me? . . . this passivity, lack of spontaneity.
CLIENT: Yeah. To some extent. I mean I'm . . . there are a lot of things hidden, you know. Somebody once described me "like a hidden flower" or something. There are a lot of things about me that I don't think I have ever really . . . uh . . . explored that much.
THERAPIST: Do you see yourself as a passive person?
CLIENT: In certain situations where I don't feel . . . when I get involved with a man . . . I find I tend to take a passive role, and I don't like that.
THERAPIST: What specifically do you mean by not liking it?
CLIENT: I feel upset inside.
THERAPIST: You say you take a passive role in relation to men. Are you doing that here with me?
CLIENT: I would say so (adapted from Davanloo, 1980a).

Even in this brief excerpt, you can see that this therapist takes a very active role compared with the more traditional psychoanalyst (Figure 16.5).

Although there are several different versions of **short-term dynamic psychotherapy (STDP)**, they all have in common the following features: using a face-to-face setting; going over the client's feelings and fantasies; breaking down the client's defenses and resistances; focusing on interpretations that help the client resolve conflicts; building up the client's confidence and self-esteem, working through transference problems; and preparing the client for the termination of therapy (Malan, 1980; Pierloot, 1981). Like the traditional psychoanalyst, the STD psychotherapist places

Figure 16.5
A short-term dynamic session.

I think of myself as a passive person.

I will take an active role and treat her problem in 20 to 30 sessions.

great importance on interpreting behavior and working through transference. But unlike the traditional psychoanalyst, the STD psychotherapist takes a very *active* role, freely challenges the client's beliefs, and limits the length of treatment to a maximum of 25 to 30 sessions (compared with an average of 600 sessions spread over two years in traditional psychoanalysis).

For some problems, such as Joan's, short-term dynamic psychotherapy results in successful treatment. Consequently, STDP has challenged the validity of some of the basic concepts of psychoanalysis. For example, traditional psychoanalysts assumed that a limited number of sessions would result in a treatment that was superficial and temporary. Data from STDP indicate, however, that impressive and lasting psychological changes can be achieved in just 20 to 30 sessions (Davanloo, 1980a; Pierloot, 1981; Sifneos, 1981). A number of therapists believe that short-term dynamic psychotherapy will become even more popular and, in many cases, replace traditional psychoanalysis (Davanloo, 1980b; Kovacs, 1982; Strupp, 1980a).

Can Joan be successfully treated in just 30 sessions?

PERSON-CENTERED THERAPY

Edward is a 58-year-old man involved in a cardiac rehabilitation program. He suffered a major coronary two years prior to beginning his counseling.

COUNSELOR: How are things going?

CLIENT: It can't get any better. It's as good as can be expected. Life goes on with its little "ups and downs."

COUNSELOR: Tell me a little bit about the "downs."

CLIENT: Down is when I feel I should be able to do more than I'm doing. When I say to myself, "Ed, you can do more than that." I don't feel I'm doing what my body should be doing at its full capacity. But if I try—then I notice—well—I get tired but I don't know where to draw the line. Then I think possibly I get discouraged a bit—to a point. To a point where I say to myself, "How come you can go just this far?"

COUNSELOR: Uh huh.

CLIENT: There is so much to do. If I can't finish a job, I smile and say, "I'm tired."

COUNSELOR: So, I've improved but I'm also a little bit disappointed when I think I can do more and I find I really can't. (Notice that the counselor restates what Ed has said so that he can reflect on these feelings.)

CLIENT: Umm (now experiencing the feeling of discouragement and disappointment that he was not fully aware of in the beginning of the session). Down deep I think—there's a little jealousy in me about the human race. That is—I've got to come down and face facts and look at it that way. I've had a heart attack. I look at the other person. If I'm trying to walk and carry something—that's really difficult . . . I used to do it. I've lost all this. To me it's natural to feel the way I do. I had this strength and now it's gone.

COUNSELOR: Sounds to me like you realize you feel a lot of anger, disappointment, and jealousy about the fact that this had to happen to you. (Notice that again the counselor restates what Ed has said so that he can reflect on these feelings.)

CLIENT: Well, this is what I think "down days" are really about.

COUNSELOR: So, I can look at my heart attack and say—there are people who aren't as well off as I am, but still, there is always that feeling there are a lot of people better off physically than I am—they can carry bags and lift chairs and damn, I wish I were one of them

Why does the therapist restate what the client says?

again. (Again the counselor restates what Ed has said so that he can reflect on these feelings) (adapted from Boy & Pine, 1982).

What Happens in Person-Centered Therapy?

Notice in this excerpt from a **person-centered therapy** session that the therapist avoids giving any directions, advice, or disapproval. Instead, the therapist shows the client that she understands what the client is feeling (Figure 16.6). One technique for showing understanding is to restate or reflect the client's concerns. Reflection of the client's feelings is one of the basic techniques of the person-centered approach.

Sometimes I feel really down and don't know what to do.

I will show warmth, empathy and acceptance.

Figure 16.6
A person-centered session.

MAJOR CONCEPT   Psychoanalysis, STDP, and Person-Centered Therapy

Indicate to which of these forms of therapy the statements below apply

	Psychoanalysis	Short-Term Dynamic Psychotherapy	Person-Centered Therapy
1. Patients are encouraged to say anything they wish and the therapist makes very few comments.	X		
2. Was originated by Carl Rogers.			X
3. Assumes that problems arise from repressed conflicts.	X	X	
4. The length of treatment is limited to 25 to 30 sessions.		X	
5. The therapist carefully avoids giving directions or interpreting what the client says.			X
6. Free association and dream analysis are two of its major methods.	X		
7. The therapist takes a very active role, freely challenging the client's beliefs.		X	
8. Assumes that transference and resistance are two naturally occurring processes in psychotherapy.	X	X	
9. The therapist tries to reflect the client's feelings, showing empathy for them.			X

Answers: 1 psychoanalysis; 2 person-centered therapy; 3 psychoanalysis and STDP, 4 STDP; 5 person-centered therapy; 6 psychoanalysis; 7 STDP; 8 psychoanalysis and STDP; 9 person-centered therapy

The person-centered approach also assumes that each client has the capacity to change. Carl Rogers, the originator of this therapy, believed that the client's capacity for change could be facilitated by certain characteristics of the therapist: empathy, nonpossessive warmth, and genuineness. *Empathy* means the ability to feel the emotions that the client is feeling. *Nonpossessive warmth* means the ability to communicate caring, respect, and regard for the client. *Genuineness* means the ability to be real and nondefensive in interactions with the client. Rogers and his followers assumed that a therapist with these three characteristics would be able to help a client change and grow.

Are empathy, warmth, and genuineness critical to the success of therapy? One way to answer this question is to determine whether these characteristics tend to be associated with successful resolution of clients' problems. A number of studies have shown that these three characteristics are not always related to successful outcomes (Garfield, 1980; Lambert et al., 1979; Stiles, 1979). These studies indicate that Rogers and his followers were wrong in assuming that empathy, warmth, and genuineness were the keys to effective therapy. Person-centered therapy does result in successful treatment, but not necessarily for the reasons Rogers claimed. It appears that this therapy is successful in treating clients because of *nonspecific* factors it shares with other psychotherapeutic approaches (Garfield, 1980).

The Origins of Person-Centered Therapy

Why did Rogers and his followers develop person-centered therapy? Here's what Rogers might say:

In the 1930s I became very dissatisfied with the role of the therapist in traditional psychoanalysis and began to develop my own approach. I objected to the "expert" role the therapist played and the assumption that the psychoanalyst was responsible for the client's progress. I believe that clients themselves have the capacity for change and that the role of the therapist as an expert actually hinders the client's own natural striving toward self-improvement. Initially, I called my approach "nondirective" but later changed it to "client-centered" and finally to "person-centered."

What Rogers did was to develop an alternative to psychoanalysis. His person-centered therapy is often referred to as a *humanistic approach*, because so much emphasis is placed on the client's own potential and ability to change. In the 1940s and 1950s, Rogers' ideas had a great impact on psychotherapy. Today only about 9 percent of clinical psychologists, counselors, and psychotherapists indicate that they use an exclusively person-centered approach. However, many of Carl Rogers' techniques have been adopted by therapists who use an eclectic approach.

How does person-centered therapy differ from psychoanalysis?

REVIEW

How would Sigmund Freud, Carl Rogers, and Dr. Lopez, a short-term dynamic psychotherapist, treat your problem of jealousy?

Freud says that he has developed an approach called (1) _____ to treat your problem. Freud explains that your jealousy is simply a symptom of what he calls (2) _____ behavior. He believes that the real cause of this neurotic behavior is an unconscious (3) _____. To uncover your unconscious conflict, Freud asks you to say whatever comes to mind, called (4) _____ _____, and he then interprets your flow of ideas. Freud also interprets your dreams, called (5) _____ analysis. During the course of psychoanalysis, you will project feelings related to your conflicts onto your therapist in a process called

(6) _____. You may also be unwilling to accept his guidance or interpretations, called

(7) _____. Freud explains that you will be cured of your symptoms only if you develop

(8) _____ into the cause of your problem.
During one of your free associations, you tell Freud that there are two major criticisms of psychoanalysis. One is the difficulty in knowing whether an

analyst's (9) _____ of free associations and dreams are correct; the other is that even if you develop insight into the real cause of your jealousy, it does not necessarily mean that you will change your

(10) _____.
With no disrespect to Freud, you decide that you want a treatment that takes only 20 to 30 sessions. One such approach is abbreviated STDP, which stands for

(11) _____ - _____ _____ psychotherapy. Dr. Lopez explains that this is a

(12) _____ approach because it uses many psychoanalytic ideas, such as interpretation, transference, and resistance. However, unlike the psychoanalyst, the short-term dynamic psychotherapist will ask you questions, challenge your statements, and focus on a specific problem, such as jealousy. Dr. Lopez explains that for some clients, STDP results in successful treatment in such a short time because of the more (13)

_____ role of the therapist.
If you did not like the STDP approach, you could

see Carl Rogers, who developed (14) _____

- _____ therapy. Rogers explains that it is you, the client, who has the ability to change and that the therapist's role is to help you grow. He believes that a therapist should have three characteristics, warmth,

genuineness, and (15) _____ and that these are sufficient to produce a change in your behavior. However, studies indicate that person-centered

therapy is successful probably because of (16) _____ factors it shares with other approaches.

Answers: (1) psychoanalysis; (2) neurotic; (3) conflict; (4) free association; (5) dream; (6) transference; (7) resistance; (8) insight; (9) interpretations; (10) behavior (jealousy); (11) short-term dynamic; (12) psychodynamic; (13) active; (14) person-centered; (15) empathy; (16) nonspecific.

GLOSSARY TERMS

dream analysis (p. 513)
free association (p. 512)
neurotic behavior
   (p. 512)

person-centered therapy
   (p. 516)
psychoanalysis (p. 511)

psychodynamic approach
   (p. 514)
resistance (p. 513)

short-term dynamic
   psychotherapy (STDP)
   (p. 514)
transference (p. 513)

Module 47 Behavior and Cognitive-Behavior Therapies

BEHAVIOR THERAPY

Why doesn't this therapist ask about the client's childhood conflicts?

CLIENT: The basic problem is that I have the tendency to let people step all over me. I don't know why, but I just have difficulty in speaking my mind.
THERAPIST: So you find yourself in a number of different situations where you don't respond the way you would really like to. And if I understand correctly, you would like to learn how to behave differently.

CLIENT: Yes. But you know, I have tried to handle certain situations differently, but I just don't seem to be able to do so.

THERAPIST: Well, maybe you've tried to do too much too fast in the past, and consequently weren't very successful. Maybe a good way to look at the situation is to imagine yourself at the bottom of a staircase, wanting to get to the top. It's probably too much to ask to get there in one gigantic leap. Perhaps a better way to go about changing your reaction in these situations is to take it one step at a time.

CLIENT: That would seem to make sense, but I'm not sure if I see how it could be done.

THERAPIST: Well, there are probably certain situations in which it would be less difficult for you to assert yourself, such as telling your boss that he forgot to pay you for the past four weeks.

CLIENT: (Laughing) I guess in that situation, I would say something. Although I must admit, I would feel uneasy about it.

THERAPIST: But not as uneasy as if you went in and asked him for a raise.

CLIENT: No. Certainly not.

THERAPIST: So, the first situation would be low on the staircase, whereas the second would be higher up. If you can learn to handle easier situations, then the more difficult ones would present less of a problem. And the only way you can really learn to change your reactions is through practice.

CLIENT: In other words, I really have to go out and actually force myself to speak up more, but taking it a little bit at a time?

THERAPIST: Exactly. And as a way of helping you carry it off in the real-life situations, I think it would be helpful if we reviewed some of these situations and your reactions to them beforehand. In a sense, going through a dry run. It's safer to run through some of these situations here, in that it really doesn't "count" if you don't handle them exactly as you would like to. Also, it can provide you an excellent opportunity to practice different ways of reacting to these situations, until you finally hit on one which you think would be best.

CLIENT: That seems to make sense (adapted from Goldfried & Davison, 1976).

What Happens in Behavior Therapy?

Instead of searching for hidden conflicts or exploring the client's feelings, the behavior therapist moves very quickly to discussion of a program for behavior change (Figure 16.7). The emphasis in **behavior therapy** is on modifying observable behaviors, which is why this therapy is also called **behavior modification.** The therapist focuses on a specific problem—in this case, the client's unassertiveness. The therapist discusses *specific goals* with the client—in this case, learning to be assertive or to speak up. The client is helped to change the problem behaviors, first in less threatening situations and then in more threatening ones.

The therapist uses various techniques to modify the problem behaviors, such as having the client role-play being assertive. In contrast to the psychoanalyst or the short-term psychodynamic therapist, the behavior therapist does not search for hidden causes of problems. Instead, the therapist assumes that the client has *learned* maladaptive behaviors, such as being unassertive, and that a program can be developed to modify these behaviors. In contrast to the person-centered therapist, the behavior therapist offers much more direct instruction and guidance. The behavior therapist also encourages the client to see the cause of any improvement as a result of the client's increased skillfulness and not as a result of the therapist's role.

Figure 16.7
A behavior-modification session.

I will focus on her observable problem and show her ways to become more assertive.

I let people walk all over me.

Consequently, improvements provide the client with a great sense of accomplishment and are intrinsically rewarding (Lewisohn & Hoberman, 1984). Let's see how a behavior therapist might treat a phobia.

APPLYING PSYCHOLOGY   Treatment of Phobias

Desensitization

How would Jack's extreme fear of blood be treated?

As we described in case 2 in the previous module, Jack has a phobia about blood. Since he wants to get a job as an ambulance driver, he is motivated to get over his fear. Compared with psychoanalytic, psychodynamic, and person-centered therapies, behavior therapy is especially effective for the treatment of phobias (Wilson, 1982). Let's follow Jack through one particular technique, **desensitization,** which has three different phases.

Phase 1

Jack would practice some form of relaxation, such as **progressive relaxation.** This involves tensing and relaxing various muscle groups, beginning with the toes and working up to the head. For example, Jack might begin by bending his toes, holding them in that position for a few seconds, then relaxing them. Next, he would tense his calf muscles for a few seconds and then relax them. By tensing and relaxing various muscle groups, he would learn how to put himself into a relaxed state.

Phase 2

Next Jack would make up a list of feared stimuli, arranging them in order from least to most feared. This is called **hierarchy construction.** With the help of his therapist, Jack made a list of various situations associated with blood. A rating of 1 indicated that he felt "not at all scared" if confronted by this stimulus. A rating of 10 indicated that he would probably feel "about to pass out." The following is the actual hierarchy that Jack constructed, with "seeing the word blood" least feared and "needle drawing blood out" most feared. Notice that this hierarchy provides a gradual exposure to the feared stimulus, blood.

Situation	Rating
Seeing the word "blood"	1
Small cut on own finger	1
Bad cut on own finger	5
Watching heart operation on TV	5
Needle being put into arm	5
Seeing someone being cut in school	5 +
Blood from own finger dripping on floor	5–6
Unable to stop blood on own	9–10
Needle drawing blood out	9–10

Phase 3

Jack would then begin desensitization training. Following the instructions of his therapist, he would put himself into a relaxed state and then *imagine* the first or least-feared item in his hierarchy, which is seeing the word "blood." He would try to remain in a relaxed state while vividly imagining the word "blood." He would repeat this procedure until he felt no tension or anxiety in this situation. At this point, he would go on to the next item in his hierarchy. Jack would repeat the procedure of pairing relaxation with images of each feared item until he reached the last and most feared item.

If Jack became anxious and could not remain in a relaxed state while imagining or being exposed to one of his feared items, exposure to that item would stop. For example, suppose Jack could not remain relaxed while imagining a needle being put into his arm. In this case, he would go back to the immediately preceding item, watching a heart operation on TV, and repeat the procedure. If he remained relaxed while imagining watching a heart operation on TV, he would try the next item again, imagining a needle being put into his arm. If Jack can imagine the last item on his list while remaining relaxed, there is an excellent chance that his fear of blood will be cured.

Desensitization appears to be most effective if, instead of just imagining the items on his list, Jack is gradually exposed to the actual situations, such as drawing blood. If Jack is exposed to the feared situations themselves, the treatment is called *in vivo desensitization*. As we discussed in Module 42, an effective treatment for agoraphobia is gradual exposure to actually going out in public places. You will now recognize this procedure as in vivo desensitization.

Through a desensitization program, Jack's blood phobia was cured in five one-hour sessions. A follow-up two and a half months later indicated that Jack had not fainted at the sight of blood in science classes. A follow-up five years later indicated that Jack was in training to be an ambulance driver and, contrary to psychoanalytic theory, had not developed any substitute symptoms. He was well-adjusted, very happy, and had suffered no fainting attacks over this time period (Yule & Fernando, 1980).

Jack's fear of blood would be considered a simple phobia, and for these, desensitization has proved to be very effective. Social phobias, agoraphobia, and phobias that are accompanied by panic attacks are more difficult to treat and may require 20 to 30 sessions (Figure 16.8). However, even in these cases, desensitization has been shown to be an effective treatment (Wilson, 1982). But desensitization is not a guaranteed cure; a small percentage of people with phobias fail to benefit from the treatment or benefit

As part of the behavioral treatment for a phobia, such as the fear of heights, the therapist (right) gradually helps the client (left) confront the feared object or situation.
(Jaques M. Chenet/Woodfin Camp and Associates)

Figure 16.8

Changes following treatment. Clients with agoraphobia were treated with twelve hours of exposure (going out in public) over a two-week period. Twelve months after completing treatment, clients reported a significant reduction in agoraphobia, panic attacks, and anxiety. *(Adapted from Hafner, 1983)*

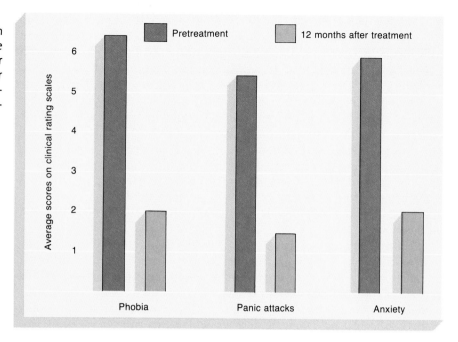

to only a small degree (Klein et al., 1983). Psychologists are not yet certain why desensitization works as often as it does. Some believe it is the exposure to the feared stimulus that is critical and that desensitization is simply one way of doing this (Boyd & Lewis, 1983; Marks et al., 1983).

Flooding

Is holding a container of blood a good way to overcome a fear of blood?

During desensitization, Jack was gradually exposed to his feared stimulus, blood. In another technique, called **flooding,** Jack would be *immediately* exposed to the thought or sight of blood.

During a flooding session, which may last several hours, Jack would be asked either to imagine a needle drawing blood from his arm or to hold an actual container of blood, called *in vivo flooding.* During flooding, Jack is encouraged to experience the fear and not to try to escape it. Because Jack will experience intense fear and anxiety during flooding, this procedure requires the guidance and support of a trained therapist. Flooding has been shown to be an effective treatment for phobias (Landl, 1982; Wilson, 1982).

Self-Help

Unlike flooding, which requires a trained therapist, Jack could carry out a desensitization program on his own (Rosen, 1976, 1982). Although many self-help books are available, there are several problems to consider when engaging in a self-help program. First is the need for adequate motivation. One of the main problems with self-help programs is that the dropout rate is 50 percent and higher. This suggests that you may need social support from friends, spouse, or therapist in order to complete a self-help program. Second, you should beware of any self-help program that promises a quick, painless, and easy solution to your problem (Rosen, 1987). There is no such program. As in Jack's case, unlearning or modifying a long-standing habit requires effort, some discomfort, and much perseverance (Karoly & Kanfer, 1982).

Evaluating Behavior Therapy

Depending upon a client's particular problem, a behavior therapy program could include other procedures besides desensitization and flooding. In previous chapters we described a variety of specific behavioral techniques, such as self-observation, setting specific goals, use of reinforcement, modeling, and role-playing. In many cases, these techniques may be used in self-help programs without the assistance of a therapist. For more serious problems, the aid and support of a therapist may be needed.

One of the early criticisms of behavior therapy was that it could be used for only a very narrow range of problems. However, behavior therapy has been found to be successful for a wide range of problems. These include overeating, lack of social skills, depression, negative emotions, sexual dysfunctions, and difficulties in managing stress (Deffenbacher & Suinn, 1982; Marlatt & Parks, 1982; Morokoff & LoPiccolo, 1982).

Some consider behavior therapy's emphasis on changing observable behaviors to be its major advantage over other approaches (Garfield, 1980; Krasner, 1982). Others have criticized this emphasis, arguing that unobservable cognitive behaviors, such as maladaptive thought patterns, must also be modified (Beck, 1976; Kendall & Hollon, 1979; Meichenbaum, 1977). These criticisms have resulted in a more recent approach, called cognitive-behavior modification, which we discuss later in this module.

Therapists who prefer a more psychodynamic approach also criticize behavior therapy for being too narrow in focus. For example, consider the problem of failing grades in college. Failing grades may simply indicate

How well does behavior therapy work?

The self-help smorgasbord: Self-help books are the second largest book market after cookbooks. *(John Lei/Omni-Photo Communications)*

lack of academic skills or excessive test anxiety, which is what a behavior therapist would concentrate on. In these cases, simply treating the symptoms may solve the problem. However, failing grades may also reflect the presence of some more basic conflict, such as dealing with achievement pressures from parents. In these cases, treating the symptoms may not solve the problem (Wachtel, 1982).

Behavior therapists are also criticized for not paying sufficient attention to the *therapist-client relationship* (Goldfried, 1982). For example, the fact that a client misses sessions, misunderstands instructions, or does not complete homework assignments might be interpreted by a psychodynamic therapist as a sign of resistance. Psychodynamic therapists argue that behavior therapists should be more aware of signs of resistance that may interfere with treatment.

COGNITIVE-BEHAVIOR MODIFICATION

What is the focus of this therapist's attention?

Frank is discussing his disturbing thoughts about being a homosexual.

THERAPIST: What's the main thing that's bothering you?
CLIENT: I have a fear of turning homosexual—a real fear of it!
THERAPIST: Because "if I became a homosexual," what?
CLIENT: I don't know. It really gets me down. It gets me to a point where I'm doubting every day. I do doubt everything, anyway.
THERAPIST: Yes. But let's get back to—answer the question: "If I were a homosexual, what would that make me?"
CLIENT: *(Pause)* I don't know.
THERAPIST: Yes, you do! Now, I can give you the answer to the question. But let's see if you can get it.
CLIENT: *(Pause)* Less than a person?
THERAPIST: Yes. Quite obviously, you're saying: "I'm bad enough. But if I were homosexual, that would make me a total shit!"
CLIENT: That's right.
THERAPIST: But the reason you're obsessed is the same reason you'd be obsessed with anything. I see people who are obsessed with five thousand different things. But in every single case, just about, I can track it down; and they're saying, "If I were so-and-so. . . ." For example, "If I went to school and failed, I'd be a shit!"—"If I tried for a better job and failed, I'd be a shit!" Now, you're doing the same thing about homosexuality: "If I ever did fail heterosexually and became a homosexual, I'd be an utter worm!" Now that will obsess you with homosexuality (adapted from Ellis, 1962).

Notice that the therapist is trying to identify irrational beliefs and maladaptive thought patterns, such as "If I'm a homosexual, I'm worthless" or "If I fail, no one will like me." **Cognitive-behavior modification** is the general name for a number of different approaches, such as rational emotive therapy, cognitive therapy, stress inoculation, or problem solving. All these approaches share the following common assumptions. First, behavior is mediated by Frank's cognitions or thought patterns. If these thought patterns are faulty, the result may be any number of symptoms, such as depression, anxiety or, in Frank's case, fear of being worthless. Second, treatment primarily involves changing these maladaptive thought patterns (Figure 16.9). Third, Frank's faulty cognitive patterns are modified with a combination of behavioral techniques (Bedrosian & Beck, 1980; Meichenbaum & Cameron, 1982).

In contrast to the psychoanalyst, the cognitive therapist does not think

Figure 16.9
A rational-emotive session.

Sometimes I think I'm worthless.

I will help him change his beliefs.

it important to explore a person's childhood for the causes of present problems. In contrast to the person-centered therapist, the cognitive therapist specifies a set of goals and techniques for solving a problem. In contrast to the behavior therapist, the cognitive therapist emphasizes the modification of thought patterns in treating problems.

How Thoughts Contribute to Disorders

Effects of Irrational Beliefs.   Read the following ways of thinking and feeling and indicate how true each one is of you. Try to think how you really feel about the particular topic, and not how you think you should feel. Fill in a number from 1 to 5, with 1 indicating that the statement has no application to you; 2, some application; 3, moderate application; 4, considerable application; 5, great application.

Do you have irrational beliefs?

Self-rating

_____ 1. It is very important to me to be loved or approved of by almost everyone I meet.
_____ 2. I believe I should be competent at everything I attempt.
_____ 3. I believe some people in the world are bad or wicked. They should be held responsible for their actions and punished.
_____ 4. I become more upset than I should when things are not the way I want them to be.
_____ 5. I believe that most human unhappiness is caused by external factors: that people have little ability to control their own sorrows and disturbances.
_____ 6. I become very concerned about things that are dangerous and dwell on the possibility of their occurrence.
_____ 7. I believe it is better in the long run to avoid some life difficulties and responsibilities than to face them.
_____ 8. I believe I need another person stronger than myself on whom to rely.
_____ 9. My past history is an important determinant of my present behavior. I believe that once something strongly affects my life, it will always affect my behavior.
_____ 10. I become more upset than I should about other people's problems and disturbances.
_____ 11. I believe there is one right solution to any given problem. If I do not find this solution, I feel I have failed (questions adapted from Ellis, 1970, in Alden & Safran, 1978, p. 361).

Here's what Albert Ellis, one of the earliest cognitive therapists, would say about these statements:

I use these statements to help you recognize some of the common *irrational beliefs* you may hold. The more of these statements to which you have given a high score, the more irrational beliefs you hold and the greater your chances of developing some emotional or behavioral problem. For example, people who are unassertive score significantly higher than assertive people on this list of irrational beliefs, especially high on item 2, "I believe I should be competent at everything I attempt," and item 10, "I become more upset than I should about other people's problems and disturbances" (Alden & Safran, 1978). This kind of finding suggests that irrational beliefs may contribute to behavioral problems, such as being unassertive or depressed (Smith, 1982).

Ellis continues: In my rational emotive therapy I use a number of different techniques to change irrational beliefs. Notice that in my interaction with Frank at the beginning of this section, I challenged his irrational beliefs. In other sessions, I had Frank model rational thinking and taught him better interpersonal skills through role-playing.

Although Ellis's approach contributed to the development of cognitive-behavior modification, less than 2 percent of clinical psychologists surveyed recently said they use his rational emotive therapy (Smith, 1982). However, many of Ellis's ideas about the effects of irrational beliefs have been incorporated into eclectic approaches.

Effects of Maladaptive Cognitive Patterns

"I'm a failure."
"Most people don't like me."
"Why do people always criticize me?"

Here's what another cognitive therapist, Aaron Beck, would say about these kinds of thoughts:

Based on my clinical practice and research, I have identified a number of specific maladaptive thought patterns that contribute to various symptoms, such as anxiety and depression. For example, thinking "I'm a failure" after doing poorly on one test is an example of *overgeneralization*, of making blanket judgments about yourself based on a single incident (Figure 16.10). Thinking "Most people don't like me" is an example of *polarized thinking*, which is sorting information into one of two categories, good and bad. Thinking "Why does everyone criticize me?" is an example of *selective attention*, which is focusing on one detail so much that you do not notice other events, such as being complimented. I believe these maladaptive thought patterns cause a very distorted view of yourself which, in turn, may result in emotional problems. The primary goals of my cognitive therapy are to identify and change maladaptive thoughts (Bedrosian & Beck, 1980).

What Happens in Cognitive-Behavior Modification?

In Module 42 you read about Rose, who felt terror at the very thought of leaving her house (agoraphobia). A behavior therapist would treat Rose using desensitization, or perhaps flooding. A cognitive therapist, however, would take a different approach.

A cognitive therapist would ask Rose a number of questions to identify her maladaptive thought patterns. For example, the therapist might ask: "When you begin to think about going out, what thoughts occur to you? Imagine you are standing at the door ready to leave; what are you thinking? If you did leave the house, what do you think would happen to you?" On the basis of these kinds of questions, the therapist identifies the maladaptive thought patterns that cause Rose anxiety about leaving the house. For example, she may overgeneralize and think "the last time I went out I was terrified; it's sure to happen again." Or Rose may engage in polarized thinking: "All my happiness is right here in this house; nothing outside could give me any pleasure."

In addition to providing information about her thought patterns, Rose may also be asked to keep track of her activities, a procedure called **self-monitoring**, and to rate in terms of pleasure activities outside the house that she once enjoyed. She will undoubtedly discover that there are pleasurable activities she has forgotten about because of selective attention—focusing only on unpleasant events.

As a first step in overcoming her fear, Rose might be asked to imagine going outside, a procedure called **behavioral rehearsal**. Through behavioral rehearsal, Rose becomes aware of her maladaptive thoughts and can begin

Why should you watch what you think?

Figure 16.10
A cognitive session.

to work at modifying them. One way to modify maladaptive thoughts is for the therapist to help Rose compose and rehearse rational responses. For example, a maladaptive thought might be "I am much safer if I stay at home." A rational response might be "That is not true, since rarely has anything bad happened when I have gone out." It is not uncommon for an entire session to be spent on rehearsing and writing down rational responses.

Rose will also be asked to perform activities that will gradually expose her to the feared stimulus. These activities, called **graded task assignments** might begin with going to the mailbox, then walking to the corner, and finally going downtown alone. During these graded task assignments, she would self-monitor her thoughts and become aware of how they may be interfering with her leaving the house. Rose would also practice her rational responses in stressful situations. Cognitive-behavior modification uses some of the techniques of behavior modification, plus additional techniques to change maladaptive cognitive patterns (Bedrosian & Beck, 1980).

Therapists who practice cognitive-behavior modification assume that irrational thoughts or maladaptive cognitive patterns are the primary causes of emotional and behavioral problems. Their emphasis on changing these negative cognitions distinguishes them from other kinds of therapists.

MAJOR CONCEPT   Behavior and Cognitive-Behavior Therapies

Decide to which form of treatment each of the statements below applies.

	Behavior Therapy	Cognitive Behavior Modification
1. Desensitization and flooding are two techniques widely used in this form of treatment to alleviate specific anxieties and fears.	X	
2. Treatment primarily involves changing maladaptive thought patterns.		X
3. One early form of this type of treatment is Albert Ellis's rational emotive therapy.		X
4. This form of treatment has been criticized because of its emphasis on observable behaviors.	X	
5. Identifying overgeneralizations and rehearsing rational responses would often be part of this kind of therapy.		X
6. Uses techniques such as self-observation and setting specific goals, as well as modeling and role-playing, to help overcome problems.	X	X

Answers: 1 behavior therapy; 2 cognitive-behavior modification; 3 cognitive-behavior modification; 4 behavior therapy; 5 cognitive-behavior modification; 6 both forms of therapy

Evaluating Cognitive-Behavior Modification

How successful is cognitive-
behavior modification?

In 16 different studies, the effectiveness of cognitive-behavior modification was compared with that of behavior modification. Problems that were treated included unassertiveness, smoking, overimpulsiveness, and speech anxiety. In 6 of these 16 studies, cognitive-behavior modification and behavior therapy resulted in similar success rates; in 5 of the studies, cognitive-behavior modification was more successful than behavior therapy; in 2 of the studies, the results were inconclusive; and in one study, the behavior therapy approach was more successful (Phillips, 1981). These results suggest that both approaches are effective, and that in some cases, cognitive-behavior modification is somewhat more effective. It should be noted that these 16 studies involved relatively mild problems—the need to learn social skills or to learn some form of self-control.

In treating more serious problems, such as major depression, cognitive-behavior modification was compared with an antidepressant drug. Clients in cognitive-behavior modification, which lasted 12 weeks, were told how their maladaptive thought patterns and irrational beliefs can result in feelings of depression. The clients were instructed in self-monitoring and asked to record their thoughts and beliefs. Therapists helped them to recognize maladaptive patterns, such as overgeneralization and polarized thinking, and to compose rational responses. Clients were also given homework assignments that involved practicing new thought patterns.

The results showed that depressive symptoms were significantly reduced by both antidepressant drugs and cognitive therapy, but that there were fewer dropouts in the cognitive therapy group. Dropouts in the drug group were often related to the drug's side effects. As you can see in Figure 16.11, a follow-up one year later found that clients who had been treated with cognitive therapy reported fewer depressive symptoms than clients who

Figure 16.11
Drug versus cognitive therapy. In this study, clients suffering from depression were treated with either cognitive therapy or drugs during a 12-week period. One year later, those who had received cognitive therapy rated their depressive symptoms as being significantly less than those who had received only drugs. (Adapted from Kovacs et al., 1981)

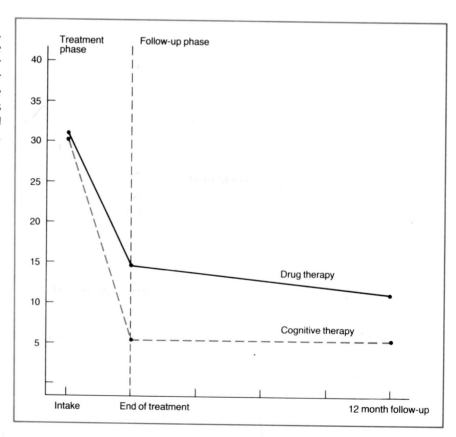

had been treated with drugs (Kovacs et al., 1981; Rush et al., 1982). These data indicate that cognitive therapy was as effective in the short run as antidepressant drugs and that cognitive therapy may have better long-term effectiveness.

In a survey of clinical and counseling psychologists, approximately 10 percent said they used a cognitive-behavior modification approach and another 8 percent said they used behavior therapy (Smith, 1982). In addition, many of the features of these two approaches have been adopted by clinicians who use eclectic approaches.

Thought Substitution   **APPLYING PSYCHOLOGY**

Carol was depressed because she could not stop thinking about her former boyfriend, Fred. She reported that she thought about Fred almost every day. Her thinking about Fred triggered a chain of other thoughts: "I feel that I am a failure. I feel ugly and useless. I keep thinking about not being able to 'keep a man,' and not being able to have a husband. I feel really depressed and I don't want to do anything. And then I start crying." Carol indicated that sometimes at work, when she started thinking about her boyfriend, she would go to the bathroom and cry and stay there for as long as an hour. Her boss realized that she was under some stress and had been very understanding. But her depression and crying had been going on for three months, and she was now in danger of losing her job (adapted from Martin, 1982).

How can Carol stop thinking about her ex-boyfriend?

Carol has a relatively common problem, the inability to stop thinking about something that bothers her. Let's look at one of several effective cognitive-behavior techniques for stopping troublesome thoughts.

As with all cognitive-behavior modification procedures, the first step is self-monitoring. For one week, Carol was asked to write down all depressing thoughts about Fred that lasted for more than a couple of minutes. In addition, she was asked to bring in pictures of herself that showed her in pleasurable activities. These pictures would provide cues for thinking desirable thoughts.

The treatment program had two main components. Each time Carol began to experience a disturbing thought, she would stop what she was doing, clasp her hands, close her eyes, silently yell "Stop" to herself, and silently count to 10. This was the **thought-stopping procedure**. After counting silently to 10, she would open her eyes and take five photographs out of her purse. She would look at each photograph and read what she had written on the back. For example, one photograph showed her about to board an airplane for a trip. On the back she had written, "I'm my own boss. My life is ahead of me. I can do what I want to do." Carol would then think about the trip and how much she liked to travel. She would do the same for all five photographs. This **thought-substituting procedure** took from one to two minutes. After that, she would return to whatever she had been doing.

During Carol's first week of self-monitoring, she thought about Fred constantly and spent from 15 minutes to one hour each day crying. However, after using the thought-stopping and thought-substituting procedures for eight weeks, Carol reduced the time thinking about Fred to the point that she rarely cried or was depressed. A follow-up interview four months after therapy revealed that Carol was no longer having problems thinking about Fred, was no longer depressed, had developed no new symptoms, and had a new boyfriend (Martin, 1982). This and other studies indicate that thought-stopping techniques are very effective in turning off annoying thoughts (Logan, 1985).

REVIEW

Let's return to a problem of feeling excessively jealous and insecure in a relationship that is very important to you. You decide to consult a behavior therapist who

will focus on treating specific (1) _____, such as feeling tremendously jealous when your partner walks to class with someone else, or picking fights with your partner over petty incidents. Unlike Freud, your behavior therapist believes that your problems are the

result of (2) _____ experiences, and that your maladaptive behaviors can be unlearned. To help you, the therapist uses a number of behavioral techniques. She asks you to spend the next week observing

or (3) _____ - _____ your behaviors. She then sets up specific treatment

(4) _____, such as identifying situations that make you jealous. Next she helps you learn to perform new behaviors, such as how to communicate with your partner in these problem situations. Finally, she helps you practice these skills through modeling and role-playing.

You tell the therapist that in addition to your intense jealousy, you have always had a problem with great anxiety when taking tests. She describes a three-phase method for treating specific fears, anxieties, and

phobias, called (5) _____, which gradually exposes you to the feared situation. In the first phase of desensitization you practice relaxing different muscle

groups, called (6) _____ relaxation. In the second phase, you construct a list of situations, called

a (7) _____, arranging the situations from least to most feared. In the third phase, which is the desensitization itself, you try to remain in a relaxed state

while (8) _____ the items in your hierarchy. The therapist explains that there is another treatment for phobias, called (9) _____, in which you are immediately exposed to the feared stimu-

lus itself. Both flooding and desensitization have been shown to be effective treatments for phobias.

When you ask your therapist whether this approach is the best one, she admits that there are several criticisms of behavior therapy. First, behavior therapy

has been criticized for treating specific (10) _____ without regard for their meaning. Second, it has been accused of neglecting certain aspects of the

(11) _____ - _____ relationship, such as transference and resistance.

Having noticed that there is a cognitive therapist in the same building, you decide to ask him how his approach differs from behavior therapy. He explains

that his approach, (12) _____ - _____ modification, includes a number of different approaches that share two beliefs. The first is that your problem of jealousy is primarily caused by maladaptive

(13) _____ patterns, such as overgenerali-

zation and polarized thinking, or by (14) _____ beliefs. The second assumption of cognitive-behavior modification is that the major focus of treatment should be on changing these maladaptive thoughts and irrational beliefs, even though a client may also be helped to change specific behaviors.

The cognitive therapist goes on to say that treatment for your problems would begin with identifying your maladaptive thought patterns through (15)

_____ - _____. Next you could begin changing these maladaptive patterns by substituting more positive and rational ones. In addition, you would work at changing some actual behaviors by learning new skills much as you would do in behavior therapy. In this part of the treatment you would use a number of behavioral techniques, such as modeling, role-playing, and completing homework assignments. You would imagine or actually practice new

behaviors, called (16) _____ _____ and gradually expose yourself to problem situations, called (17) _____ _____ assignments.

You ask, "Which is more effective, behavior therapy or cognitive-behavior modification?" The therapist replies that both have proved to be (18) _____ in treating many different kinds of problems. In addition, cognitive therapy seems to be as effective as an-

tidepressant drugs in treating major depression. One type of cognitive therapy can be used by everyone to rid themselves of disturbing thoughts or images. The techniques used in this therapy are called (19) thought-_____ and (20) thought-_____ procedures.

Answers: (1) behaviors; (2) learning; (3) self-monitoring; (4) goals; (5) desensitization; (6) progressive; (7) hierarchy; (8) imagining; (9) flooding; (10) behaviors; (11) client-therapist; (12) cognitive-behavior; (13) cognitive or thought; (14) irrational; (15) self-monitoring; (16) behavioral rehearsal; (17) graded task; (18) effective; (19) stopping; (20) substituting

GLOSSARY TERMS

behavioral rehearsal (p. 526)
behavior modification (p. 519)
behavior therapy (p. 519)

cognitive-behavior modification (p. 524)
desensitization (p. 520)
flooding (p. 522)

graded task assignments (p. 527)
hierarchy construction (p. 520)
progressive relaxation (p. 520)

self-monitoring (p. 526)
thought-stopping procedure (p. 529)
thought-substituting procedure (p. 529)

PERSONAL NOTE

Some people, including me, believe their pets help them get over everyday problems. When I was young, I had a fuzzy white dog. Sometimes when I was feeling lonely and unappreciated, he would wag his tail and lick my face and make me feel good and important. And there were things my dog understood that my parents didn't. For instance, my dog understood that there was nothing wrong with snacking between meals or making unnecessary noise or running when I was supposed to be walking. Now I have discovered that pets are being used in therapy because they have three very important characteristics (Angier, 1983): pets are always accepting, totally uncritical, and very understanding. In his way, my dog was a great therapist. —R. P.

17

Social Cognition

Module 48 Social Perception

As you read the following description of Cindy's dating experiences, try to form an impression of how moral and responsible you would judge her to be.

What influences first impressions?

> The most pleasant thing about my college is the sexually liberated attitude that everyone seems to have. I slept with six different guys last year and there were no problems at all. Nobody seems to have any hang-ups about it. After all, if you're attracted to someone, why shouldn't you have sex with him? All my girlfriends seem to feel pretty much the same way. I'm really looking forward to this next year. I've already met several guys that I'm attracted to, and I'm anxious to develop relationships with them (Janda et al., 1981, p. 192).

Based on this information, fill in the words you think best describe Cindy's behaviors:

I would judge Cindy to be _____ (not very, somewhat, very, extremely) responsible and (not very, somewhat, very, extremely) _____ moral.

Your social perception is influenced by beliefs, attitudes, and expectations. You would probably judge this woman to be moral and responsible because she is attractive. (Bob Daemmrich/The Image Works)

Cindy is an attractive woman. If you had seen Cindy's photograph before you read about her, would you have judged her differently? One study says that many of us would. In this study, college students read information about a female's dating experiences, such as the statement by Cindy. Using written information alone, students rated the woman in a relatively negative way regarding responsibility and morality. However, when the same information was accompanied by a photo of an attractive female, students rated the woman significantly more positively—that is, as being more moral and more responsible (Janda et al., 1981). In other words, students perceived and interpreted her dating experiences in a positive or negative way, depending upon whether they knew her to be attractive. This study suggests that your social *perception*, the way you perceive yourself and others, is significantly influenced by a number of cognitive processes, including beliefs, attitudes, and expectations.

Why is the same information about Cindy's dating practices interpreted differently, depending upon whether or not you think she is attractive? Part of the answer lies in the finding that you automatically attribute a number of positive personality characteristics, such as responsive, interesting, sociable, and intelligent, to an attractive person (Cunningham, 1987). Since you expect attractive people to have desirable traits, you assume that attractive Cindy must be reasonably moral and responsible in her dating practices.

Why do you think an attractive person is more moral?

533

Social perception is just one aspect of the field called *social psychology*, the study of how an individual's thoughts and actions are influenced by other people and the characteristics they have. A recent trend in social psychology is a renewed emphasis on cognitive processes. In Cindy's case, you employed a number of cognitive processes, including drawing on your expectations about attractive people and making inferences about the causes of her behavior. *Social cognition* is the study of how these and other cognitive processes influence the processing of social information (Isen & Hostorf, 1982). As we will see later in this chapter, understanding cognitive processes is the key to understanding many social behaviors: why attitudes are so difficult to change, why explanations for the same behavior may be very different, and why stereotypes are so persistent.

According to cognitive social psychology, your beliefs, expectations, and attitudes create a personal filter through which you see your world. We're going to examine your personal filter and show you how it changes your perceptions of yourself and others.

SCHEMAS

A woman and man are waiting in a checkout line at a supermarket. The woman notices that the man's basket contains a new brand of sweet rolls she has been meaning to try.
"Are those sweet rolls as good as the TV ad claims?" she asks.
"They're even better. I think I'm addicted to them. Would you like to try one?" He smiles and holds the package out to her.
"Oh, no thank you. I was just wondering about them. Thanks anyway. Next time I'll remember to buy a package" (author's files).

The woman may interpret this brief interaction very differently than the man. For her, it may simply be a way to find out about a new product. For him, it may be an indication that she is interested in him. Women frequently report that friendly interactions with males are often mistaken for signs of flirtation or sexual interest. How much truth is there to this observation?

Imagine watching and listening to a conversation between a male college student and a female college student who have just met. After the conversation, you are asked to decide how flirtatious each was. If you are a male observer, you will probably rate the female as being more flirtatious and seductive. If you are a female observer, you will probably rate the female as being less flirtatious. The researcher who conducted this study concluded that males do seem to misperceive female friendliness as a sign of sexual interest (Abbey, 1982). It is then easy to see how such a misinterpretation can lead to problems like inappropriate sexual advances.

Apparently, in our society men learn to interpret a female's friendliness as a sign of sexual interest. A social psychologist would say that men have formed a schema about how to interpret a woman's friendliness. A **schema** (SKEE-mah) is an organized network of information that develops from past experiences and influences the way you perceive people and events. Schemas help you gather relevant information, interpret, and explain that information, and recall the information when you need it. Schemas also provide guidelines for how you should behave.

Imagine that you are a male who has periodically been reinforced for interpreting a woman's friendly behaviors as a sign of flirting. Imagine you have now developed a schema that a woman's friendliness is a sign of sexual interest. Having developed such a schema, you will tend to *notice* a woman's friendly behaviors toward you rather than her reserved ones. You will

Why do males continue to see females in the same way?

Who is more likely to think that the other is flirting? (Donna Jernigan/Monkmeyer Press)

tend to *interpret* all her friendly behaviors as a sign of sexual interest, rather than as simple social interactions. You will tend to *behave* toward a friendly woman with sexual advances rather than with friendly interest. You will tend to *remember* the woman's appearance and friendly gestures rather than what you talked about. All this filtering of information is due to the particular schema you possess.

People have many different kinds of schemas. Here are some examples:

I am very intelligent.
I am generally good natured.
I am trustworthy.

These are examples of *self schemas*, which are about your own stable traits.

Professors are demanding.
Football players are macho.
Attractive people are exciting.

These are examples of *person schemas*, which are about traits of particular individuals or groups.

You drink at a happy hour.
You feel anxious when taking an exam.
You may sing in the shower, but not in an elevator.

These are examples of *event schemas*, which are about performing some well-practiced routines.

Why do people form schemas? Schemas help you organize complex stimuli, seek out relevant information, fill in missing information, and make predictions about how you and others should behave in various situations. But schemas also have a disadvantage. Because they restrict what you attend to, encode, and recall, they cause you to lose information (Fiske & Linville, 1980; Taylor & Crocker, 1981). Let's look more closely at the effects schemas have.

INFLUENCE OF SCHEMAS

Schemas Influence What You Notice

What kind of people do customs officials search?

Suppose you are a customs official whose job it is to prevent illegal items from entering this country. What kind of people would you search? After years of experience with all kinds of smugglers, customs officials develop a schema for a smuggler. The schema makes their job much easier, since it helps them identify who should be searched. In this case, the schema serves a very practical purpose: identification of possible smugglers. According to one study, the person schema of a smuggler is someone who hesitates before answering, gives short answers, avoids eye contact with the official, and shifts posture (Kraut & Poe, 1980).

A smuggler schema has the advantage of helping customs officials selectively attend to certain cues in order to identify possible smugglers. However, a smuggler schema has the disadvantage of focusing *attention* on individuals who fit this schema and thus allowing many others to avoid detection. This is a practical example of how schemas influence the processing of information in real-life situations.

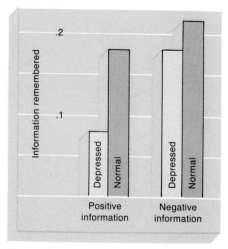

Figure 17.1
Positive and negative information remembered by normal and depressed students. When depressed and normal students were asked to recall negative information about themselves, both remembered about the same amount. However, the depressed students recalled significantly less positive information than the normal students. This is an example of how having a depressed self-schema influences the recall of positive information. (Adapted from Kuiper & MacDonald, 1982b)

Schemas Influence What You Remember

Suppose you have a feminine self schema—that is, you think of yourself as having feminine traits. As you read a list of adjectives, some masculine and some feminine, which are you more likely to remember? Researchers found that individuals with feminine self schemas recalled more feminine than masculine adjectives from a list of 60 they had previously read, responded more quickly to feminine than masculine adjectives, and remembered more examples of past feminine behaviors than masculine ones. Similar effects were found for persons having masculine self schemas (Crane & Markus, 1982; Markus et al., 1982). These data suggest that self schemas about masculinity and femininity influence how you process information—that is, which information you respond to and incorporate.

Suppose you are in a depressed mood and are asked to read a list containing both positive and negative adjectives. Later, you are more likely to recall many more negative adjectives, indicating that you were selectively attending to negative or depressing events. If you are not depressed, you recall primarily positive adjectives, indicating that you were selectively attending to positive events (Figure 17.1). Apparently, having a self schema such as "I am depressed" causes you to notice and process information which matches that schema (Kuiper et al., 1982a). These findings suggest that it may be difficult to overcome a negative emotional state, such as depression, because your self schema makes you focus on negative events.

Although we are very likely to process and incorporate events that agree with our self schemas, there is an exception to this rule. When events are *highly incongruent* with our self schemas we remember them very well. Suppose you consider yourself a very good student. On a recent term paper, you received twelve positive comments and three negative ones. A week later, you are asked to recall the comments. It is likely that you will remember the negative comments better than the positive ones. Apparently, your better recall of the negative comments has to do with your self schema. Since it is that of being a good student, receiving negative comments is unexpected. Such comments are incongruent with your self schema.

Many studies indicate that, in general, you will remember best those events that are highly incongruent with your self schema, next best those events that match your self schema, and least well those events that are irrelevant to your view of yourself (Crocker et al., 1983; Ferguson et al., 1983; Hastie, 1981; Wyer & Martin, 1986).

Schemas Persist

Although you may now be a relatively mature, responsible, and independent adult, your parents may still think of you as somewhat immature, not always responsible, and in some ways still dependent on their judgment and advice. Why has your parents' schema of you failed to change?

Once schemas are formed, they are very resistant to change. This is because we generally select and attend to information that supports our schemas and discount information that is inconsistent with them (Baron & Byrne, 1984). For example, if your parents think of you as sometimes irresponsible, they will attend to situations that support this schema, such as your failure to phone when you said you would. At the same time they may overlook events that show great responsibility, such as the fact that your professor trusts you enough to make you her research assistant.

STEREOTYPES

How powerful is stereotyping?

Woman President Elected in Close Vote

For the first time in the history of the United States, a woman was elected president. Joan Ann Walker, a former attorney and congresswoman, received just over 51 percent of the vote. The election was not decided until early Wednesday morning, when the West Coast states finished counting their votes. The election was hard fought, with charges and countercharges over whether or not a woman was capable of governing one of the most powerful nations in the world. Apparently, the stereotype of a woman as being too emotional and irrational to hold the nation's highest office is no longer held by a majority of the American people. When asked about the makeup of the cabinet, which has in the past been almost totally male, President-elect Walker suggested that there would certainly be more women in positions of power (author's files).

Tommie Faye Bateman, a pharmacy student in her final year at the University of Georgia, was dismissed by the owners of a local pharmacy because some customers had complained about her race. Although Tommie was competent and well-trained, these customers were apparently judging her on the basis of negative stereotypes rather than ability. (AP/Wide World Photos)

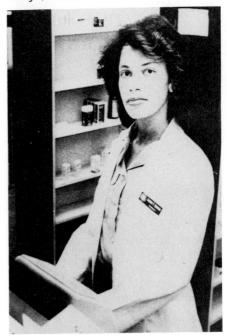

If you have no trouble deciding this article is fictitious, you may also have no trouble understanding stereotypes, prejudice, and discrimination—forces that keep some people in subordinate positions.

In 1984, Geraldine Ferraro was nominated as the first woman vice-presidential candidate of a major American political party. One of her tasks was to defeat some of the stereotypes we hold of women. A **stereotype** is a set of beliefs or traits that we attribute to a particular group of people, such as women or minorities. Stereotypes tend to be applied uniformly to all members of the group, tend to be extreme, and are most often negative. For example, common stereotypes of women are that they are less competent, assertive, and intelligent, and more emotional, moody, and irrational than men. Stereotypes can be considered a form of schema—specifically, a person schema.

Negative stereotypes are often accompanied by prejudice and discrimination. **Prejudice** refers to an unfair, biased, or intolerant *attitude* toward another group of people. An example of prejudice would be the attitude that women should not be in positions of power because they are not as

The men in the white robes are members of the Klu Klux Klan (KKK). This organization has consistently promoted negative stereotypes of blacks. (Ethan Hoffman/Archive)

logical or competent as men. **Discrimination** refers to specific unfair *behaviors* exhibited toward members of a group. There are countless examples of discrimination against women in government, such as the fact that very few women are appointed to the president's cabinet or to other positions of power.

Psychologists are not immune to having and furthering stereotypes of women. In the 1960s, an active area of research involved identifying the traits of leaders. Many of the questionnaires used in this research were constructed using only the pronoun "he," suggesting that only men could be or were leaders (Deaux & Wrightsman, 1984).

How Do Stereotypes Develop?

How are women portrayed on television?

Popular television characters, both black and white, have been evaluated in terms of intelligence, achievement, self-recognition, dominance, and nurturance in a study done some years ago. Although almost all the black characters appeared in comedies, there were very few differences between the ratings for black and white males. Black females, however, were rated especially low on achievement and self-recognition and high on dominance and nurturance, whereas white females were rated as submissive and helpless. In general, the black and white females in television roles matched their popular stereotypes (Reid, 1979). Viewers of these programs may therefore have their own racial and sexual stereotypes reinforced by seeing black and white females behaving in stereotypic ways.

Psychologists believe that we develop stereotypes when parents, peers, co-workers, teachers, and others reward us with social approval for holding certain attitudes and beliefs. Stereotypes, as we have said, are one kind of person schema. Once you have developed person schemas that black women are dominant and nurturant and white women are helpless, your future perceptions of these groups will be biased. For instance, you will notice and remember the black women on television who portray these roles. In turn, these selective observations will reinforce and maintain your original stereotypes. The cognitive approach to stereotypes, which is relatively new, looks at how stereotypes are maintained, why they are so persistent, and how they affect the processing of information (Hamilton, 1981).

Why Are Stereotypes So Difficult to Change?

How many times have you seen a black person who appeared to have no motivation?

How many times have you seen a woman who appeared to be helpless?

Researchers find that we *overestimate* the number of times we have observed a situation that matches one of our stereotypes. This means that if you hold a stereotype of blacks as lacking motivation, you will overestimate the number of times you have observed blacks not working. The result of the overestimation is that your stereotypes are repeatedly confirmed and will therefore persist. The opposite is also true: you *underestimate* the number of times you have observed a situation that does not match your stereotype. If you hold a stereotype of women as helpless, you will underestimate the number of times you have observed a woman effectively handling a difficult job. This underestimation also perpetuates the stereotype, because you are paying little attention to information that proves it wrong (Hamilton & Rose, 1980). These data indicate that stereotypes cause you to pay attention to and remember only information that reinforces your stereotypes (Hamilton, 1983).

Imagine watching an interaction between a white man and a black man. After a heated argument, one man shoves the other. How accurately would you perceive this interaction? White students were asked to watch two versions of a movie showing a heated argument between a black man and a white man. In one version, students saw the white man shove the black man; in the other, students saw the black man shove the white. Later they were asked to describe what happened. Would white students' perceptions of the same behavior, one person shoving another, differ depending upon whether a black or a white man did the shoving? Yes, their perceptions *did* differ. When a white man did the shoving, the students tended to judge it as simply aggressive; when a black man did the shoving, the students tended to judge it as violent (Duncan, 1976). Here is an example of the same behavior being judged differently depending upon the stereotypes of the observers. These findings demonstrate that stereotypes may distort perceptions so that events seem in agreement with those stereotypes. These

Do you think this is a very common sight? In fact, you are likely to overestimate the number of times you have observed a black man carrying a large radio. (Ken Robert Buck/The Picture Cube)

Can you make people behave the way you expect them to?

perceived "confirmations" in turn help to make stereotypes persist over time. Now let's see how stereotypes can actually affect others' behaviors.

Before making a telephone call to a young woman they had never met, male college students were shown a photograph said to be of the woman they would soon be talking with. Some of the males were shown a picture of an attractive young woman, and others were shown a picture of an unattractive one. In reality, the females in this study did not differ in attractiveness; only the males' *expectations* of them differed.

As the researchers expected, males who believed they were talking to attractive females were warm, humorous, and friendly on the telephone, presumably because they were behaving according to their stereotypes of attractive females. In turn, these females responded in a friendly and likable manner, matching the males' stereotypes of attractive females. Males who believed they were talking to unattractive females were uninteresting and reserved on the telephone, presumably because they were behaving according to their stereotypes of unattractive females. In turn, these females responded in a cool and aloof manner, matching the male's stereotypes of unattractive females (Snyder et al., 1977). These and similar findings further explain why stereotypes tend to persist: our own expectations cause us to encourage other people to behave in ways that confirm our stereotypes of them (Snyder, 1981, 1982a).

These studies indicate that you are much more responsive to information which confirms and maintains your stereotypes than you are to information which contradicts them (Hamilton, 1981). You also have a tendency, through your own perceptions and behaviors, to make your stereotypes self-fulfilling prophecies. For these reasons, stereotypes remain very difficult to change. It will take many women in government to change the stereotype that women are not suited for high government office.

APPLYING PSYCHOLOGY   *Reducing Prejudice*

Are children in desegregated schools less prejudiced?

In 1954, the Supreme Court decreed an end to segregated schools (*Brown v. Board of Education*). Since that time, social psychologists have studied desegregated schools to assess changes in racial prejudice. What they have found clearly shows that desegregation alone is only minimally successful in reducing prejudice.

Based on a review of over 80 studies on desegregated schools, one researcher drew the following conclusions (Stephan & Feagin, 1980, p. 217):

1. Desegregation generally does not reduce prejudices of whites toward blacks.
2. Desegregation leads to increases in black prejudice toward whites about as frequently as it leads to decreases.
3. The self-esteem of blacks rarely increases in desegregated schools.

Contrary to our hopes, simply putting white, black, and other minority students together in the same classroom does little to reduce their prejudice.

Why is desegregation by itself so ineffective in fighting prejudice? We know that in spite of progress, whites are still prejudiced against blacks, and they may show much more prejudice in real-life situations than they admit to on questionnaires (Crosby et al., 1980). We also know that prejudice is learned very early. Beginning about age 3, children develop prejudice, primarily from listening to and observing their parents' reactions (Milner, 1981). We know too that racial prejudice tends to persist over the years because it is reinforced by the members of a person's group. Given these facts, is it any wonder that simply placing prejudiced groups together in a classroom may have little effect on reducing their prejudice?

Are there any factors that can make desegregation more effective in lowering prejudice? One is the active support of community leaders. Desegregation has been least effective in reducing prejudice when community, school administration, and teachers were involved in a battle over desegregation. In other words, desegregation itself has little effect on prejudice unless various authority figures endorse it and provide appropriate role models for the students to follow (Stephan, 1983). The attitudes and behavior of the teacher in the desegregated classroom are particularly important (Miller, 1980). For example, if the *teacher* uses techniques that increase competition among whites and minority students, prejudice is likely to increase. If the teacher uses techniques that increase cooperation among students of different races, such as assigning joint projects, prejudice is likely to decrease.

Desegregation will also be more effective in reducing prejudice and will result in more interracial friendships if the percentage of minorities in the classroom is more than a token number. In addition, the more equal the socioeconomic status and level of academic achievement of whites and minorities, the more likely it is that interracial friendships will form (Rosenfield et al., 1981). These findings indicate that desegregation can be effective in reducing prejudice, but only under certain conditions (Stephan & Feagin, 1980).

Can teachers help reduce prejudice?

MAJOR CONCEPT   Social Perception

Below are some statements about the topic of social perceptions. Decide whether each is true (T) or false (F).

1. T/F If you saw a very attractive child and a very homely one throwing stones at a defenseless dog, you would be apt to judge the personality of the homely child more negatively.

2. T/F A schema is an organized network of information that develops from past experiences and influences how you perceive people and events.

3. T/F In perceiving attractive children as generally kind, responsible, and intelligent, you are screening what you see through a person schema.

4. T/F If your self schema includes the belief that you are shy and lacking in confidence, you are likely to focus selectively on all the times you feel awkward and uncomfortable in social situations.

5. T/F A stereotype is an extreme, usually negative form of person schema applied uniformly to all members of a particular group.

6. T/F When a husband makes all the important family financial decisions because he has a stereotype of women as less competent decision makers than men, he is acting in a way that may actually make this sex rule stereotype seem true.

7. T/F When black and white students are put together in desegregated classrooms, they automatically see how groundless their mutual stereotypes are.

Answers: 1 (T); 2 (T); 3 (T); 4 (T); 5 (T); 6 (T); 7 (F)

REVIEW

As a child, Pam can remember being called a dumb Polack. She lived in a town that was about half Polish and half German. Her family did all their shopping in Polish shops, went to the Polish church, and told jokes about the Germans. Against the wishes of her parents, Pam married Gus. He was wonderful in every way except his nationality. He was German.

Pam thinks of herself as bright, friendly, and cheerful. She has organized information about her stable traits into a network called a (1) self _____. She has also developed schemas about the traits and behaviors of Germans, called (2) _____ schemas, and about how to behave in well-practiced situations, called (3) _____ schemas, such as what to do in a supermarket. One of the advantages of schemas is that they help Pam organize a vast amount of information and provide clues as to how she should behave in different situations. One disadvantage is that Pam loses information because of selective (4) _____. For example, she may not notice Germans who are intelligent and flexible.

In elementary school and high school, Pam usually received good grades. One of the reasons she remembers being called a "dumb Polack" is that this information was very different from or (5) _____ with her self schema of "being bright." Pam's self schemas will influence which kinds of events she notices and recalls. She tended to recall the "dumb Polack" remark because it was so incongruent. She also recalls events that agree with her self schema. She is least likely to notice events that are irrelevant to her self schema.

As Pam was growing up, she listened to how her parents and peers talked about Germans as stubborn, stupid, and rigid. Her set of negative beliefs and traits about Germans is one kind of person schema, called a (6) _____. Pam and her friends usually avoided socializing with Germans, a sign of both (7) _____ (holding intolerant attitudes) and (8) _____ (acting unfairly toward members of a certain group). One of the reasons that Pam's stereotype of Germans will be very persistent is that she will tend to (9) _____ the frequency of events that match her stereotype of stubborn, rigid Germans. When Pam interacts with a German, her biased (10) _____ may elicit responses that seem to confirm her stereotypes. This is another reason stereotypes are so resistant to change.

Just before Pam entered high school, German and Polish students began attending the same school. In this school, desegregation was effective in slowly changing the German and Polish students' stereotypes. For desegregation to work and to change stereotypes, the community leaders and school administrators must provide appropriate role models for the students to follow. Further, the attitudes and behaviors of the (11) _____ in their classrooms greatly influence whether prejudice continues or declines.

Answers: (1) schema; (2) person; (3) event; (4) attention; (5) incongruent; (6) stereotype; (7) prejudice; (8) discrimination; (9) overestimate; (10) expectations or beliefs; (11) teachers

GLOSSARY TERMS

discrimination (p. 538)   prejudice (p. 537)   schema (p. 534)   stereotype (p. 537)

Module 49 Attribution

In the 1970s, one of the symbols gays most loved to hate was Chief Ed Davis and his Los Angeles Police Department. Under Chief Davis, the police department vigorously enforced laws in gay bars and was accused of spying on peaceful gay organizations. Davis went so far as to refuse to issue a permit for the first Los Angeles gay pride parade, saying that it would be like holding a parade for burglars or robbers. As late as 1977, Davis said and wrote that gays were mentally ill "fruits and fairies" and that gay groups "pose a serious threat to the welfare and safety of the citizens of Los Angeles." In 1980, Davis, a conservative Republican, was elected to the California senate. Early in 1984, Davis did something that baffled the entire state. He cast a decisive vote and made an impassioned speech to help pass a bill that would ban job discrimination against gays. Davis kidded, "My God, did you ever think you would see the day?" After the governor vetoed the bill, Davis went around the state urging gays to keep pressing for their rights (adapted from the Los Angeles Times, *September 29, 1984).*

DEFINITION

Following Davis's pro-gay actions, everyone wondered what had caused such a dramatic change of mind. Davis's explanation was that religious extremists have too much voice and power and need to become tolerant of others' rights. The media suggested a somewhat different explanation. Reporters pointed out that Davis had received about $10,000 from gay-oriented political groups and that these groups would support him in future elections.

How would you explain a dramatic change in attitude?

Social psychologists use the term **attribution** to refer to the explanations you give for someone's behavior or beliefs. You could attribute Davis's pro-gay actions to internal factors, such as a change in his beliefs or in his basic disposition. If you attribute his behavior to an internal factor, you are making a **dispositional attribution**. You could also attribute Davis's pro-gay behavior to external situations, such as political contributions and support. If you attribute his behavior to an external situation, you are making a **situational attribution**. You can now see that your social perception of Ed Davis involves two things. As you learned in the previous module, you form a person schema of Davis, such as "anti-gay police chief and aspiring politician." In addition, you also make dispositional or situational attributions for the ways he speaks and acts.

What motivates you to make attributions? You may make attributions to help understand or explain some event or behavior, such as Davis's pro-gay vote. You may also make attributions to defend or enhance your *self-image* or to justify your own actions. Davis, for example, maintains a much better image if he attributes his pro-gay vote to dispositional factors, such as a change in beliefs, rather than to situational factors, such as political contributions. In Davis's case, we would like to think that the dispositional attribution is more accurate.

Can you think of any instances in which you made an attribution to defend or enhance your self-image? As a college student, you probably have a self schema of being reasonably intelligent. If you do poorly on an exam, what kind of attributions do you make to explain your poor performance? In one study, students were asked to estimate their performance on an upcoming exam. After taking the exam and getting back their scores, they were asked to judge which of the following four factors was primarily re-

How do you explain your performance on exams?

sponsible for their performance: ability, effort, test difficulty, or luck? Students chose different factors depending on whether they had performed well or poorly.

If they expected to perform well on an exam and actually did, they attributed the good performance to ability, an internal factor. In other words, they used a dispositional attribution to explain good performance. If students expected to perform well on an exam but actually performed poorly, they attributed their poor performance to test difficulty, an external factor. In other words, they used a situational attribution to explain poor performance. Researchers Mark H. Davis and Walter G. Stephan (1980) suggest that students use situational attributions to explain poor performance because these explanations do not question their ability and therefore help maintain a positive self-image.

MISTAKES IN MAKING ATTRIBUTIONS

Why didn't you get the job?

You explain, "I didn't get the job because the interviewer disliked me."

The interviewer explains, "He didn't get the job because he seemed to have little motivation."

As you have just learned, numerous investigations have shown that whenever you make attributions about your own behaviors, you tend to protect or enhance your self-esteem (Kleinke et al., 1983). Specifically, you tend to attribute success or good events to internal factors and failure or bad events to situational ones. This attributional bias can sometimes lead to problems. For example, in attributing your failing to get a job to a situational factor (the interviewer disliked me), you ignore the real reason (poor interview skills). Although this attention may defend your self-esteem, it may also keep you from making necessary changes in your behavior (Kleinke et al., 1983). Let's examine a common error in attribution.

You explain, "That salesperson was rude because she is probably a rude person."

The salesperson explains, "I was rude because that customer treated me badly."

MAJOR CONCEPT   Attribution

Please match the term to its correct statement.

1. situational attribution

2. self-image

3. fundamental attribution error

4. dispositional attribution

a. ____ To explain why your mother worries about your riding a motorcycle without a helmet, you point to one of her personality traits.

b. ____ To explain why your professor gives a surprise quiz, you point to the professor's personality rather than to the fact that students are not reading the assigned material.

c. ____ To explain why your mother worries about your safety on the highway, you point to your riding a motorcycle without a helmet.

d. ____ One of the reasons we make errors in attribution is to protect this part of ourselves.

Answers: a (4); b (3); c (1); d (2)

Many studies have found that when people try to explain *another person's behavior*, they tend to overestimate the importance of dispositional factors and underestimate the importance of situational ones (Reeder, 1982). Because this tendency is so common, it has been labeled the <u>fundamental attribution error</u>. When you attribute a salesperson's rudeness to a personality trait rather than to the situation (dealing with an aggressive customer), you are committing the fundamental attribution error. In this case, the fundamental attribution error makes another person look bad because you attribute her behavior to a negative personality trait rather than to a difficult situation.

When you started reading this module, you probably believed you were objective in assessing the causes of your own and others' behaviors. You now know that your attributions are subject to various biases, such as a need to enhance your self-esteem and a tendency to make the fundamental attribution error. Attributional biases also explain how you sometimes maintain inaccurate explanations for others' behaviors. Consider the following example.

Suppose you are a man who had developed a person schema that women are generally less competent in business than men. Your boss hires a new employee, a woman. During her first week, you notice that she makes several serious mistakes. How would you explain her mistakes? According to the fundamental attribution error, you might attribute her mistakes to dispositional factors, such as incompetence or lack of ability, rather than to situational factors, such as the pressures of learning a new job. Attributing her mistakes to dispositional factors such as incompetence reinforces your person schema of women as incompetent. As this example illustrates, attributional biases both influence your social perceptions and perpetuate them (Hamilton, 1981).

Ruth, 92, gets a hug from her new husband, Kevin, who is 28. In explaining why he married Ruth, Kevin says he "loves her for herself" and is not interested in her property. How might Ruth's relatives and friends explain Kevin's motives? (Associated Press)

APPLYING PSYCHOLOGY

Attributions and Grades

If you are a college freshman, here is an example of how attributions may influence your grades.

How can freshmen get better grades?

> We chose as our target group college freshmen who were concerned about their academic performance. This group of people would seem to be particularly susceptible to damaging attributions about the permanence of their problems. Most freshmen enter college with fears about whether they can handle the work, and many are dismayed to discover the amount of studying required far exceeds that which was needed to do well in high school. When academic problems first occur, as they do with many freshmen, students may see this as confirming their worst fears about their inability to succeed at college. Such attributions may cause additional worrying and anxiety, making it even more difficult to study. Thus, convincing freshmen that their problems are caused by temporary rather than permanent factors may well have beneficial effects (Wilson & Linville, 1982, p. 368).

If freshmen attribute the causes of their academic problems to relatively permanent conditions, they have little expectation of improvement and therefore little motivation; as a result, their chances of doing better are low. However, if freshmen attribute the causes of their academic problems to temporary conditions, they can develop expectations of improvement, work harder, and actually do better (Figure 17.2). This important role of attributions is why, in this study, researchers tried to change the factors to which freshmen attributed academic problems from permanent to temporary ones.

Figure 17.2

Attributions and grades. In this study, beginning college students were told that their problems were due to temporary things and that they were likely to overcome these problems as the year progressed. Believing or attributing their problems to temporary factors resulted in their showing better academic performance and dropping out less than students who were not given this attribution. (Based on data from Wilson & Linville, 1982)

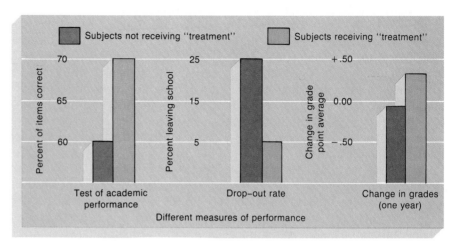

Freshmen who were having academic problems read a booklet about students who had similar academic problems as freshmen but who showed improvement later in college. In addition, these freshmen watched videotapes of these students, who described very convincingly how their grade-point averages had risen after their freshman year. After this, the freshmen were asked to write down all the reasons they could think of why grade-point averages might increase after the freshman year. Another group of freshmen, also with academic problems, did not receive any of this information and served as a control group.

Freshmen who were encouraged to attribute their problems to temporary conditions showed a significant improvement in grade-point averages one year after the completion of this study. In addition, only 5 percent of them dropped out of college, while 25 percent of those in the control group dropped out. These data suggest two things: first, it is possible to change students' attributions and, as a result, their expectations about performance; second, and more important, changing their attributions and expectations can actually improve grade-point averages. As this study illustrates, attributions play a very important role in influencing behaviors.

REVIEW

Pam, who was raised on the Polish side of town, married Gus, who was raised on the German side of town. Let's see what happens when Gus's German parents come for a weekend visit.

Gus's mother carefully looks over the house and notices that it is clean but not spotless. She tells her husband that the house will never be spotless because Polish people are messy. Gus's mother has explained Pam's failure to be a spotless housekeeper by making a

(1) _____ attribution. She remarks to Gus that the house is not as clean as it should be. Gus says that this is his week to do the cleaning and he hasn't had time. Gus's explanation of why he wasn't a spotless

cleaner is an example of a (2) _____ attribution.

Gus's father asks Pam about her job in advertising.

Pam says that she just got a raise because she came up with a great advertising idea. Pam is enhancing her

(3) _____ - _____ by making

a (4) _____ attribution for her success in getting a raise. However, she says that she was passed over for a promotion because all her bosses are males. She is defending her self-esteem by making a

(5) _____ attribution for her failure to be promoted. Pam may well be correct in her attributions, but if she is not correct, she may be failing to consider other factors that account for her successes and failures.

Gus, a college teacher, tells his father that students today all seem to major in business because they are mostly interested in making money. Because Gus is attributing other people's behavior primarily to dispositional rather than situational factors, he is making the

(6) _____ _____ error. Gus adds that some of his freshman students showed an improvement in their grades when they were told that their academic problems were temporary rather than permanent. This is a practical example of how chang-

ing people's (7) _____ can influence their behavior.

Gus's father says that he likes being retired, but some of his retired friends are always complaining about being short of money. He comments that these men are gripers by nature. His wife reminds him that he too was complaining about lack of money just the other day. Gus's father tells her that his complaints were different: he had been overcharged for those repairs on the house. Gus's father is attributing the com-

plaining of his friends to (8) _____ factors

and his own complaining to (9) _____ factors.

Answers: (1) dispositional; (2) situational; (3) self-esteem or self-image; (4) dispositional; (5) situational; (6) fundamental attribution; (7) attribution; (8) dispositional or internal; (9) situational or external.

GLOSSARY TERMS

attribution
  (p. 543)

dispositional attribution
  (p. 543)

fundamental attribution error (p. 545)

situational attribution
  (p. 543)

Module 50 Attitudes

People pictured with cigarettes were ranked by college students as being less sexy, less honest, and less mature than the same people pictured without cigarettes. These findings may indicate that smoking is no longer considered "cool" by the younger generation, said Marshall Dermer, an associate professor of psychology at the University of Wisconsin-Milwaukee who conducted the study. Dermer said that in the old days, smoking was cool. Friends who saw you smoke approved of it. But today, when it comes to younger, well-educated people, a smoker may be limiting his or her circle of friends and job opportunities by smoking. Among this segment of the population, smokers are stereotyped negatively, Dermer said. However, about 300 "older" people questioned in a similar manner failed to show any preference between individuals pictured with cigarettes and those pictured without them (adapted from Dermer & Jacobsen, 1986).

According to this study, college students today hold more negative schemas of smokers than did college students some years ago. Part of what makes up your schema of a smoker or a nonsmoker are your beliefs and attitudes. We're going to look at how beliefs and attitudes influence your behaviors as well as your social perceptions.

If you are a smoker, you probably believe that smoking relieves nervous tension, makes social interactions easier, helps you relax and concentrate, and keeps your weight down. Although you may know about the health hazards of smoking, you do not take them as seriously as a nonsmoker does. You continue to smoke because you concentrate on the beneficial aspects of smoking. If you are a nonsmoker, you probably take the health hazards of smoking very seriously, and you probably are less likely to believe that smoking has benefits, such as control of weight or reduction of tension (Loken, 1982).

What we want you to notice is that smokers' beliefs about the health hazards of smoking are inconsistent with their positive attitude toward smoking and their behavior of smoking. In contrast, nonsmokers' beliefs about the harmful effects of smoking are consistent with their negative attitudes and their behavior of not smoking. To understand the smoker's inconsistency and the nonsmoker's consistency, we need to examine the relationship between attitudes and behaviors.

ATTITUDES AND BEHAVIOR

What's your attitude toward smoking?

One reason that the concept of attitude has been studied so intensely for so long is that your attitudes influence how you behave. An **attitude** is a combination of feelings and beliefs that predispose you to respond in a certain way to people, objects, or events. Suppose you have a very negative attitude toward smoking and smokers. If you encountered a smoker, your *belief* that smoking causes lung cancer would make you *feel* uncomfortable about breathing smoke and you might *respond* by asking the smoker to put out the cigarette. Suppose however, you were being interviewed for an important job and the interviewer began to smoke. Despite your negative attitude toward smoking, in this particular situation you would probably not ask the interviewer to put out the cigarette. We want to know when attitudes affect behavior, how attitudes can be changed, and what we can predict from knowing a person's attitudes.

Fire chief Omar Fernandez has smoked two packs of cigarettes a day for 15 years. He says, "When I started, smoking was the big thing: you were a man if you smoked." Today, because of the serious health risks associated with smoking, attitudes have changed, and more and more men are stopping smoking. (Acey Harper/The Picture Group)

What Can We Predict from Attitudes?

If you know that Sam "really hates" smoking, you can predict that his perception of smokers will be greatly biased. For instance, while interviewing a smoker for a job, Sam's negative attitude toward smoking may result in his seeing the person as less mature and intelligent than other applicants. Attitudes, in other words, influence how people perceive and process information.

After learning that Sam hates smoking, you can use his attitude to predict that he does not smoke himself. One advantage of knowing a person's attitudes is that attitudes can often be used to predict behavior. However, you must be careful about using attitudes in this way. For example, we know that many teenagers have negative attitudes toward smoking, but still begin to smoke because of peer pressure. Although attitudes may generally be used to predict behavior, there are some cases in which those predictions will be wrong. Let's look at some of the reasons for this and at how the accuracy of predictions can be increased.

Increasing the Accuracy of Predictions

Would a straight student be likely to room with a gay?

Surveys indicate that most of us have positive attitudes toward maintaining our health. How is it possible for someone with a positive attitude toward health to smoke cigarettes? The explanation is that *general attitudes* seem to be only slightly related to specific behaviors. This means that your general attitude toward health is not a very good predictor of whether or not you smoke. Here's another example to show that general attitudes are not very predictive of specific behaviors.

Suppose a heterosexual student has a very positive attitude toward homosexuality in general. Based on this general attitude, we would not be very successful in predicting whether that student would be willing to have a gay roommate. The primary reason for this poor prediction is that we are trying to predict a very specific behavior, accepting a gay roommate, on the basis of a very general attitude, feelings toward homosexuality. A heterosexual student may have a positive attitude toward homosexuality in general, but may have a negative attitude toward one specific behavior, rooming with someone who is gay.

Measuring a general attitude does not predict very well whether a person would engage in a specific behavior (Ajzen et al., 1982). However, measuring a student's attitude toward the *target behavior* itself, accepting a gay roommate, does predict relatively well how he would respond if offered this choice. Studies indicate that attitudes are related to and generally predict behaviors, provided that the attitudes focus directly on the target behaviors we want to know about (Ajzen et al., 1982; Ajzen & Fishbein, 1977).

Dave has developed positive attitudes toward blacks primarily because of his job experience with a black co-worker. Mark has developed positive attitudes toward blacks primarily because of what he has observed and read. Both Dave and Mark become bosses and must hire workers. Although both have positive attitudes toward blacks, we would be more accurate in predicting that Dave would actually hire blacks. This is because attitudes that are developed through *direct behavioral experience* are much more predictive of subsequent behavior than attitudes developed from indirect experiences. Studies indicate that, as Figure 17.3 shows, direct experience with a particular behavior may result in attitudes, either positive or negative, that are good predictors of subsequent behavior (Fazio & Zanna, 1981).

Mary and Helen both have negative attitudes toward getting drunk. However, they differ in how much they think their behaviors should be influenced by personal beliefs versus the situation. Helen believes that her behaviors should be tailored to fit the situation. Individuals such as Helen, who adapt their beliefs and attitudes to the demands of social situations, are called *high self-monitors*. These individuals are constantly monitoring their behavior to bring it in line with the behavior of their peers. Mary believes that her public behaviors should be determined by her private beliefs and attitudes. Individuals such as Mary, who value a close relationship between their private attitudes and public behaviors, are called *low self-monitors*. These people are less likely to monitor their behavior; instead, they behave according to a consistent set of personal beliefs and attitudes (Snyder, 1974).

Who is more likely to get drunk in public, Mary or Helen? Based on attitudes alone, you would find it difficult to say. However, based on self-monitoring information, you could increase the accuracy of your prediction. Mary, a low self-monitor, would be less likely to get drunk because she values behavior consistent with her private beliefs and attitudes. Helen, a high self-monitor, would be more likely to get drunk because she places more value on situational cues, such as pressure from friends to drink. A number of studies have compared low self-monitors with high self-monitors. They have found that we can use the attitudes of low self-monitors to predict behaviors, such as voting in presidential elections or smoking marijuana (Ajzen et al., 1982; Snyder, 1982b). Apparently, self-monitoring is a personality variable that influences whether attitudes can be used to predict behavior.

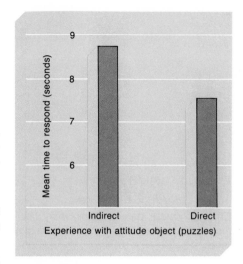

Figure 17.3
How direct experience affects attitudes. In the "direct" group, each subject spent time solving a puzzle. In the "indirect" group, none of the subjects spent time working on the puzzle. Next, both groups of subjects were told to answer questions about their attitude toward solving puzzles by pressing a key. "Direct" subjects responded more quickly than "indirect" subjects, indicating that attitudes formed during experience were stronger than those formed without such experience. (Based on data from Fazio et al., 1982)

FORMATION OF ATTITUDES

Parents who smoke provide their children with positive role models for smoking. Role modeling and imitation help explain why parents who smoke are more likely to have children who smoke (Oskamp, 1984). There are many other examples of how imitation and modeling influence the for-

Why did so many people once think smoking was smart?

Children whose parents smoke may later model this behavior and begin to smoke when they become teenagers. (Richard Hutchings/Photo Researchers)

mation of attitudes. For example, children develop attitudes toward minorities primarily through observing and imitating their parents' behavior toward minorities. Children also develop attitudes about male and female sex roles primarily through observing and imitating the behavior of their parents and other adults toward males and females. Thus, one way we develop attitudes is through *imitation* and *modeling*.

Besides forming attitudes through imitation and modeling, we also form attitudes based on our beliefs. For example, teenagers who smoke believe that smoking helps them relax, win friends, lose weight, and show their independence and fearlessness. Like adults, they know the general health risks of smoking, but do not believe that their own health will be affected (Study by the National Institute of Cancer, reported in the *Los Angeles Times*, April 19, 1982). Teenagers' beliefs about smoking are based on information from their peers, their parents and other adults, direct experience, the media, advertising, and various institutions such as schools and churches. From this example, you can see that *beliefs* form the basis for many attitudes.

ATTITUDE CHANGE

How would you change attitudes toward smoking?

The Surgeon General has determined that cigarette smoking is dangerous to your health.

Since 1966, health warnings have appeared on every pack of cigarettes. The idea behind this program is that attitudes can be changed by changing beliefs—in this case, by giving information about the health hazards of smoking. In 1954, before this campaign began, 57 percent of American males and 30 percent of females smoked. In the mid-1980s, after twenty years of the program, 40 percent of males and 36 percent of females smoked. These figures suggest only moderate success for a long campaign that emphasized changing people's attitudes by changing their beliefs about health risks. However, there has been a significant change in the attitudes of college students toward smoking, and one researcher has suggested that without this campaign, there would have been far more smokers today (Warner, 1981).

There have been many studies of the effectiveness of using information to change attitudes. In general, the use of *health threats* has been only moderately effective in changing attitudes and has not been very successful in changing behavior (Beck & Davis, 1980; Beck & Lund, 1981). For example, a health-threat campaign was found to have little effect on the smoking attitudes of sixth- to eighth-graders, apparently because they were not very concerned about the long-term dangers of smoking (Hurd et al., 1980). As you will see, more successful programs have usually gone beyond the simple presentation of information.

The Yale Communication Program on Persuasion

How can the attitudes of teenage smokers be changed?

One of the primary reasons that 12- to 13-year-old students begin smoking is because they imitate peers who smoke. With this in mind, an antismoking program was developed which used peer imitation to change behavior. For instance, students watched videotapes of their peers saying "No" to social pressure to smoke and videos of students stating why they were not going to smoke. Next, students role-played saying "No" to their peers and role-played stating why they were not going to smoke. In two different studies, this kind of program resulted in decreased smoking among sixth- to ninth-grade students (see Figure 17.4) (Evans et al., 1981; Hurd et al., 1980).

This is your brain,

this is drugs,

this is your brain on drugs.

Partnership For A Drug-Free America

How much of an effect will this dramatic *health-threat* message have on attitudes and behaviors toward drugs? Check the text for the answer. (Partnership for a Drug-Free America)

The approach was patterned after the *Yale communication program* on persuasion, so named because the researchers involved in it conducted their work at Yale University.

We can use the antismoking campaign for teenagers to illustrate the components of the Yale program. The first component is the *source* of the message. A change in attitude is more likely if the source is attractive, likable, familiar, and credible. *Credible* means that the person has expertise in an area and/or the person is trustworthy. In the antismoking program, peers were used as the source of the message because they would be perceived as being attractive, likable, familiar, and trustworthy.

The second component of the program is the *content of the message.* This component includes whether the message presents one or two sides of the argument and whether threat or fear is used. Generally, a *two-sided* message, one that presents both sides of an argument, has more impact if the audience is known to be initially opposed to the message. A one-sided message will have more impact if the audience is known to be already in favor of the message. The antismoking campaign for teenagers used a *one-sided* message because the vast majority of the students were nonsmokers. In contrast, a two-sided message would probably be more effective in an antismoking campaign for adults, since many of them would be smokers and would be initially opposed to an antismoking message. A message based

Figure 17.4
An antismoking campaign that had a significant effect on reducing the number of teenagers who smoked. (Adapted from Hurd et al., 1980)

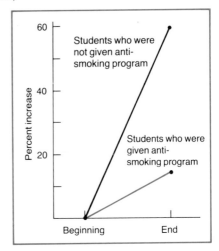

Students who were not given antismoking program

Students who were given antismoking program

just on fear will be only moderately effective in changing attitudes and behaviors.

The third component of the Yale program is the *type of audience*. Studies generally indicate that some individuals are more easily persuaded than others, but it is not clear why this is true. One suggestion is that some individuals are better able to remember the message and its implications for changing attitudes (Wood, 1982). For example, students who better remembered how the videotaped role models resisted peer pressure may have shown more attitude change.

The Yale program focuses primarily on the characteristics of the source, the message, and the audience to change attitudes. In addition, the antismoking program for teenagers used role modeling or behavioral experience, which is also an effective way to change attitudes.

Behavioral Experience and Attitude Change

Why do so few people wear seat belts?

Most drivers know that wearing seat belts reduces the risk of injury and death in accidents. Despite this knowledge, many drivers have negative attitudes toward wearing seat belts, and only 20 to 30 percent of drivers actually wear them. If you wanted to increase positive attitudes toward and actual use of seat belts, which would be more successful, an educational campaign or a mandatory seat belt law?

This was the question the Swedish government attempted to answer. In Sweden, about 30 percent of the drivers used seat belts. To increase the percentage of users, the government began an information campaign that showed how wearing seat belts reduced the risk of injury and death. Recalling our discussion of the effectiveness of the health-threat anti-smoking campaign in the United States, you can probably guess that this campaign had little effect on attitudes toward or use of seat belts. When the information campaign proved ineffective, the Swedish government passed a law requiring drivers to wear seat belts. A year after the law was passed, seat belt use had risen from 30 to 80 percent. And a curious thing happened to individuals who began to fasten their seat belts in accordance with the new law. Their use of seat belts resulted in the development of positive attitudes toward seat belts.

The same phenomenon occurred when Sweden changed from driving on the left side of the road to driving on the right side. Initially, drivers had negative attitudes toward driving on the right side. After the change, however, drivers reported positive attitudes toward driving on the right side (Fhaner & Hane, 1979). These data indicate that experience may result in attitude change.

Suppose you know it is safer to wear a seat belt, but do not bother to fasten yours. Suppose you know that smoking may cause cancer, but you smoke anyway. Suppose you know that women are as competent as men, but you still do not hire women for important jobs. How do you deal with these inconsistencies? We'll answer that next.

CONSISTENCY THEORY

According to Bill Maupin, on June 28, a trumpet would sound and all who had accepted the Lord would slowly rise from the ground and drift into the clouds. When asked about the possibility that his prophecy might not come true, Bill answered that there was no question in his mind. He was absolutely convinced that millions would ascend into heaven (adapted from the Los Angeles Times, *June 16, 1981).*

Bill Maupin is leader of the 50-member Lighthouse Gospel Tract Foundation. After his prediction, many of his followers quit their jobs and

Although bumper stickers may express in a clever way what you believe, they are probably an ineffective way to change someone else's beliefs or attitudes. (Philip John Bailey/The Picture Cube)

gave away their possessions to nonbelievers. They had two weeks to wait for the predicted "liftoff." During this two-week period, these followers were behaving according to **consistency theory.** That is, they were trying to maintain consistency among their beliefs, attitudes, and behaviors.

When the "liftoff" failed to occur, the followers were confronted with information that was inconsistent with their former beliefs. How did they resolve this problem and restore consistency? Their problem is similar to the inconsistencies you face in your own life. You may believe you are a good student, but behave inconsistently by not studying for an exam. You may believe people should be treated fairly, but behave inconsistently by discriminating against members of a minority group. One of the explanations of how you deal with inconsistencies is the theory of cognitive dissonance.

Cognitive Dissonance

On Sunday, June 28, Bill Maupin and his followers waited all day to be lifted to heaven. Bill conceded that he could have made an error about the date of departure. He added that even if it didn't happen on Sunday, it would happen shortly. Later, Bill said that he had miscalculated the liftoff and that it would now occur 40 days later, on August 7. He said that this time he was absolutely confident. The liftoff did not occur on August 7. Many members of the sect said that they had lost faith in Bill Maupin. Bill explained that he is not bothered by the failure of his liftoff prophecy. His prophecy allowed him to reach so many people (adapted from the Los Angeles Times, *June 29, 30, July 21, August 10, 1981).*

What would you do if your prophecy failed?

How is Bill Maupin dealing with the inconsistency between his beliefs and what actually happened? Here is how Leon Festinger (1957), who developed cognitive dissonance theory, would explain how Bill resolves this problem:

Based on his beliefs, Bill promised his followers that they would all be taken to heaven on June 28. But they were not. Bill's problem is that his promise is not consistent with what happened. I believe Bill needs to maintain consistency among his cognitions, attitudes, and behaviors. When something happens to produce inconsistency, such as failure of the promised liftoff, Bill finds himself in a state of mental discord or **cognitive**

dissonance. In this state, Bill feels an unpleasant psychological tension that motivates him to reduce the dissonance.

Festinger continues: I think Bill can reduce his cognitive dissonance in three different ways. First, he can change one of his cognitions to make it consistent with what happened. Bill did just that when he changed the date of the liftoff. By changing the date, he made his original belief in a liftoff consistent with the fact that no mass ascension to heaven had happened on June 28. Second, Bill can reduce his dissonance by adding new cognitions. If Bill had argued that God was simply testing believers' faith by postponing the liftoff, he would be adding a new cognition that would make his beliefs consistent with actual events. Third, Bill can reduce his dissonance by changing the importance of one of his cognitions. Bill did that when he said that failure of his prophecy was not really important, since the media coverage had given him the opportunity to reach so many people on earth. By making the liftoff no longer important, Bill has reduced his dissonance.

Because of his theory of cognitive dissonance, Festinger is considered an important figure in social psychology. We are going to focus next on one aspect of cognitive dissonance theory: how it can explain the effects of doing something in disagreement with your attitudes.

Explaining the Effects of Counterattitudinal Behavior

What happens when you do something you do not believe in?

Imagine having an antihomosexual attitude. As part of a class assignment, you are asked to give a speech sympathetic to the problems a homosexual faces in our society. What effect would giving a speech sympathetic to homosexuality have on your original antihomosexual attitude? Many studies have used this technique, which involves what is called **counterattitudinal behavior:** you take a public position (such as giving a sympathetic speech) that is counter to your private attitude (in this case, being antihomosexual). Many studies indicate that freely engaging in counterattitudinal behavior may result in a change in a person's original attitude (Deaux & Wrightsman, 1984). But note that for counterattitudinal behavior to be effective in changing attitudes, the person must feel that the public behavior is relatively freely performed. If you were paid $100 to write a paper sympathetic to homosexuality, this counterattitudinal behavior would have little effect on your attitudes because you would simply discount it, saying that it was done for money.

Although we know that attitudes frequently change following counterattitudinal behavior, there is a question about why this happens. One explanation is given by the theory of cognitive dissonance. According to this theory, you are motivated to reduce the dissonance between your public behavior (a speech sympathetic to homosexual problems) and your private attitude. You reduce the dissonance by changing your antihomosexual attitude to a more sympathetic one. Your new sympathetic attitude is now consistent with your sympathetic speech (Festinger & Carlsmith, 1959).

This cognitive dissonance explanation has recently been challenged. According to the *impression management* and *self-esteem* explanations, you might change your antihomosexual attitude after freely making a sympathetic speech because you want to make a good impression in front of others or want to maintain your self-esteem (Greenwald & Ronis, 1978; Tedeschi et al., 1971). Notice that these two explanations say nothing about maintaining consistency among your cognitions, as does cognitive dissonance theory. Rather, these explanations say that the motivation to change an attitude comes from a desire to make a good impression (to have people think you are honest and say what you really mean) or to maintain a favorable self-image. There is considerable support for both explanations over that of cognitive dissonance (Abelson, 1983; Baumeister, 1982).

MAJOR CONCEPT   Attitudes

For each of the statements about attitudes listed below, decide whether it is true (T) or false (F).

1. T/F If you believe that exercise is good for your health, you will have a positive attitude toward exercise and will very likely exercise regularly.

2. T/F Social psychologists have found that a general attitude (such as opposing the buildup of nuclear weapons) is a very good predictor of how you will act (such as writing letters to express your views to government officials).

3. T/F The more specifically an attitude is related to a particular behavior, the greater the correlation between the two.

4. T/F The best way to encourage adolescents not to use drugs is to lecture them on the health risks many drugs pose.

5. T/F If you were trying to convince a group of students that semester breaks should be shortened, you should probably present a one-sided argument.

6. T/F The theory of cognitive dissonance assumes that whenever your cognitions and behaviors are inconsistent, you are thrown into a state of psychological tension that you then seek to reduce.

7. T/F A desire to reduce cognitive dissonance is the only way to explain why someone would develop a positive attitude toward smoking after taking a job as an advertising executive for a tobacco company.

Answers: 1 (F); 2 (F); 3 (T); 4 (F); 5 (F); 6 (T); 7 (F)

Much research has shown that counterattitudinal behavior may cause attitude change. However, in any given situation it is not known whether this attitude change is caused by a motivation to reduce cognitive dissonance or by a desire to create a good impression or maintain self-esteem. It appears that these different explanations are not mutually exclusive, but rather operate in different situations (Abelson, 1983).

Attitudes Toward Contraceptives   **APPLYING PSYCHOLOGY**

Approximately 11 million American teenagers are sexually active, and approximately 1 million unplanned teenage pregnancies occur each year. It was previously assumed that teenagers fail to use contraceptives because of lack of knowledge. Now it has been found that even though knowledge may promote contraceptive use in some cases, knowledge itself does not ensure the use of contraceptives (Jaccard et al., 1981). Most of the studies on contraceptive use among teenagers have focused on females, primarily because most of the current contraceptive methods are for women. In the

Would you be more careful if it was you that got pregnant?

See your pharmacist for more information on family planning, responsible use and other community services.

For the Clinic near you call Health Department or (800) 952-5750

Sponsored by Pharmacists Planning Service, Inc.
In conjunction with California Venereal Disease Advisory Council

Having sexually active male teenagers discuss the problem of unwanted pregnancies may help change their attitudes and result in more responsible use of contraceptives. (Courtesy of Pharmacists Planning Services, Inc.)

very near future, however, a contraceptive pill will probably be available for males. Would teenage males be willing to use such a pill?

Almost 500 male and female teenagers were asked this question. They read reports about four new male contraceptives that are being developed. The reports were written in a believable fashion, but were hypothetical. After reading the reports, the teenagers were asked to underline information that was important to them. They were also asked whether they found the method acceptable and whether they would use it themselves or encourage others to use it. The results showed that females rated the male oral contraceptives as more acceptable than did the males. Females were more likely to urge their male partners to use a male oral contraceptive than were males to urge other males.

Males reported that their major concerns about using male oral contraceptives were first the possible health risks, and second the question of effectiveness (Jaccard et al., 1981). The issue of health risks is, of course, a valid concern about birth control pills, whether for males or females. However, some contraceptive methods, such as foam, diaphragm, and condom, do not pose health risks, and still both male and female teenagers fail to use them. The larger questions here are how teenagers who are sexually active can be persuaded to use contraceptive methods and how males can be persuaded to share in the responsibility.

Of the almost 500 teenagers in the study above, 57 percent reported engaging in sexual intercourse without using some form of birth control. Although most teenagers in this study had knowledge of contraceptives, 57 percent did not always act on their knowledge. From our discussion of attitudes, we know that attitudes are generally based on knowledge or beliefs. However, we also know that general attitudes are only weakly related to behavior. Teenagers, as well as adults, may have a generally positive attitude about the value of birth control, but this does not necessarily mean they will use contraceptives. On the other hand, we know that attitudes toward specific behaviors, such as acquiring and regularly taking birth control pills, are more predictive of actual behaviors. In fact, a high correlation (.84) was found between attitudes toward the use of contraceptives and actual use in women (Davidson & Jaccard, 1975). These findings suggest that the use of contraceptives among teenagers might be increased if their attitudes toward specific birth control methods were made more positive.

Let's apply what we know about changing attitudes to the problem of encouraging sexually active teenagers to think and act positively about the use of contraceptives. One of the reasons for the success of the antismoking program for teenagers was its use of peer role models to present information. Peers might also be effective in changing beliefs and attitudes toward contraceptive use.

In changing the attitudes of males toward accepting more of the responsibility for contraceptive use, their partners need to convey the importance of using a contraceptive. The female's message to the male would be: "I know that you care about me; so I hope you will be concerned about using a contraceptive." Messages such as this help to create norms or standards that have been shown to be effective in influencing contraceptive behavior (McCarty, 1981). We also know that experiencing the fear of being pregnant, or actually being pregnant, should encourage the future use of contraceptives. This is because attitudes that result from direct experience have substantial influence on future behavior. Finally, we know that attitudes may change following counterattitudinal behavior. Having teenagers participate in open discussions about contraceptive use may result in their developing more positive attitudes toward using contraceptives when they become sexually active.

REVIEW

Like most other children, you grew up with many of the usual joys and pains. But suppose you had one that most children do not experience: your father was an alcoholic.

It was clear to you that getting drunk made your father's life miserable. The combination of your beliefs and negative feeling toward getting drunk is called an

(1) _____. This attitude predisposes you to

(2) _____ in a certain way to people, situations and events. In many situations, your attitudes

are closely related to and (3) _____ your behavior.

We want to predict whether you would drink alcohol at a party. Our prediction would not be very

accurate if it were based on your (4) _____ attitude toward alcohol. It would be more accurate if it were based on your attitude toward a specific behavior, such as drinking at a party. Our prediction would be more accurate if your attitude toward drinking at

parties developed from direct (5) _____ experience with the target behavior. Our prediction would also be more accurate if it were based on the knowledge that you value having your private beliefs match your public behavior, which means that you are

low in (6) _____ - _____.

When you first began to drink socially at parties, you felt uncomfortable. Leon Festinger would explain

your tension by using his theory of (7) _____

_____ . He would point to the need to be

(8) _____ in your beliefs, attitudes, and behaviors toward alcohol. Since you have a negative attitude toward drinking but drink socially at parties, you might experience dissonance as a result of this inconsistency. You could try to reduce your dissonance by changing one of your beliefs, such as your belief that drinking at parties means that you approve of getting drunk. You could add some new cognition, such

as the realization that many people drink socially and do not become alcoholics. Or you could reduce dissonance by changing the importance of one of your beliefs, such as deciding that social drinking isn't important for being liked.

You have been asked to speak to a group of students who have drinking problems. According to the

(9) _____ communication program on persuasion, there are a number of factors that you should consider in trying to change attitudes toward drinking. You are more likely to be persuasive if you,

as the speaker or (10) _____ of the message, are likable, trustworthy, and credible. Since you are delivering an antidrinking message to a group that

favors drinking, you should present a (11) _____ -sided message. You might use a (12) _____ -sided message if you are talking about alcohol to a group that already agrees with your position. If your message focused only on the physical dangers of drinking, you would be only moderately successful in changing the college drinkers' attitudes. This is because mes-

sages that use a (13) _____ - _____ approach are only moderately successful in changing attitudes.

You ask the students with drinking problems to discuss openly the kinds of problems alcohol creates and how they could lead happier lives without alcohol. By doing this, the students are engaging in what is

called (14) _____ behavior. Following their counterattitudinal behavior, the students may

show a more negative (15) _____ toward getting drunk. However, we do not know whether their change in attitude resulted from their trying to reduce cognitive dissonance, or from their wanting to create a

good public (16) _____ or maintain their

(17) _____ - _____.

Answers: (1) attitude; (2) behave; (3) influence, predict; (4) general; (5) behavioral; (6) self-monitoring; (7) cognitive dissonance; (8) consistent; (9) Yale; (10) source; (11) two; (12) one; (13) health-threat; (14) counterattitudinal; (15) attitude; (16) impression; (17) self-esteem.

GLOSSARY TERMS

| attitude (p. 548) | cognitive dissonance (p. 533) | consistency theory (p. 533) | counterattitudinal behavior (p. 554) |

18

Social Behaviors

Module 51 Aggression

For Ronald, everything seemed to go wrong.

He hated the first grade. School work was hard and his parents offered little help or encouragement. Ronald avoided doing his homework and turned to something he was better at—getting into fights. Besides fighting, Ronald liked watching TV westerns, especially those with plenty of violence.

By the sixth grade, Ronald was failing every subject. The teachers complained about his fighting and school bus drivers complained about his picking on younger kids. When the principal asked Ronald's parents to come and talk about discipline, they refused. His mother said that what Ronald did at school was the school's problem.

It was a different matter at home. If Ronald misbehaved or used foul language at home, his father spanked him hard and washed his mouth out with soap. Then Ronald would stalk out of the house and wander around the neighborhood, causing trouble and picking fights.

When Ronald was interviewed at the age of 19, he said that he had been arrested several times and was on probation for petty larceny. A year later, he was killed in a violent accident. For most of Ronald's short life, everything had indeed gone wrong (adapted from Eron, 1982).

We know about Ronald's life because he was part of a remarkable 22-year longitudinal study under the direction of Leonard Eron (1982, 1987). Eron and his colleagues interviewed children when they were about 8 years old, 19 years old, and, most recently, when they were in their thirties. The researchers' primary interest was the development of **aggressive behavior,** which they defined as an action intended to injure or irritate another person.

As was true for Ronald, the researchers found that aggressive behavior was very stable across 22 years (Eron et al., 1987; Huesmann et al., 1984). The correlation between a child being aggressive at age 8 and being aggressive at age 30 was .30 for girls and .50 for boys. This means that aggressive behaviors observed in grade school boys, such as hitting and fighting, were a relatively good predictor of aggressive behaviors observed in these same individuals 22 years later. Aggressive behaviors observed in adults included criminal activities, aggressiveness toward spouses, and severity in punishing their own children. But how does a young child learn to be aggressive and why does that behavior pattern persist into adulthood? Eron's research gives us several answers.

How does a child become a bully?

Once a child becomes a bully, there is a very good chance that if nothing is done, the child's aggressive behavior pattern will carry over into adulthood. (*Psychology Today,* February 1988, p. 52. Illustration by David Shannon)

ENVIRONMENTAL AND COGNITIVE INFLUENCES

Family Influences

What happens when parents don't care?

From family histories, Eron identified several parental behaviors that were associated with a young child's learning to be aggressive. Specifically, Eron found that the less accepting and less supportive parents are of a young boy's accomplishments, the more aggressive the child is likely to be in school. Also, the less a boy identifies with his father and the more the father physically punishes the boy's aggression at home, the greater the likelihood that the boy will behave aggressively at school. However, if a boy identifies with his father, punishment of the boy's aggressive behavior at home is effective in eliminating such behaviors. Apparently a boy's identification with his father encourages the boy to adopt the father's anti-aggressive values, which are clearly expressed when the father punishes aggressive behaviors.

However, if a boy does not identify with his father and the father punishes the boy's aggression, the boy becomes more aggressive. A likely explanation for why punishment made Ronald more aggressive comes from Albert Bandura's research on vicarious or observational learning (Modules 17 and 36). Bandura's research showed that children who observed a model's aggressive behaviors were likely to imitate these behaviors. In Ronald's case, his father spanked him for behaving aggressively. What Ronald's father did not understand was that by administering such harsh punishment he was serving as an aggressive role model for his son. When Ronald did not get his way or disagreed with his peers, he would imitate his father's behavior. Because Ronald's aggressive behaviors brought him attention and forced others to comply with his wishes, his aggression was *reinforced* and *maintained*. Besides vicarious learning, Eron identified several other factors, such as acquiring pro-aggressive beliefs, that encourage people like Ronald to remain combative.

what kids are most aggressive?

A father's yelling at his son will decrease the son's bad behavior only if the son identifies with the father. (Michael O'Brien/Archive)

Beliefs and Expectations

What do Ronald and other aggressive children learn that causes their aggressive behavior pattern to continue through adolescence and into adulthood?

Aggressive children acquire the *belief* that aggressive interactions will reduce their frustrations and their aggressive behaviors will be rewarded (Perry et al., 1986). For example, one of Ronald's pro-aggressive beliefs was that the best way to deal with frustration was by being aggressive. According to Leonard Berkowitz's (1982, 1983) **frustration-aggression hypothesis,** anger and aggression are common responses to frustration. However, Berkowitz adds that anger and aggression are only two of several reactions to frustration, since many people learn nonaggressive ways to deal with disappointment. Berkowitz emphasizes that our reaction to frustration depends upon how we interpret or process information about a frustrating situation. Once a child acquires the belief that frustration is best dealt with by being aggressive, this belief increases the likelihood that the child will persist in behaving aggressively in many different situations.

Aggressive children learn to get their way by disagreeing and arguing. This causes *conflicts* (Shantz, 1986). Once started, conflicts serve to increase and intensify aggressive interactions. Aggressive children learn to *perceive* their peers, not themselves, as acting more aggressively (Lochman, 1987). By blaming their peers, aggressive children are less likely to see their behavior as a problem and more likely to continue behaving aggressively. These studies confirm one of Eron's main points: If young children acquire pro-aggressive beliefs and expectations, they will process information in ways that lead to continued aggressive behavior through adolescence and adulthood.

What can be done to prevent a child from acquiring aggressive behaviors and expectations?

Prosocial Influences

Eron believes that there is a continuum, with aggression at one end and prosocial behaviors—which include helpfulness, friendliness, and other socially acceptable behaviors—at the other end. He found that children who showed prosocial behaviors at the age of 8 tended to show the same behaviors later in life. As adults, they also had lower rates of aggression and higher rates of social success and better mental health than children who showed aggressive behaviors as children. Eron thinks that children learn very early two different plans or strategies for dealing with situations. Some children learn a strategy that includes pro-aggressive behaviors, beliefs, and expectations. Others learn a strategy that includes prosocial behaviors, beliefs, and expectations. Eron emphasizes that one of the best ways to prevent a child from learning a pro-aggressive strategy is to teach that child a prosocial one. One such program is suggested later in this module. But first, let's examine one way a child's pro-aggressive strategy may be reinforced.

In the middle of a game, one baseball player takes a swing at another. Soon both teams become involved in the fight. According to the revised frustration-aggression theory, frustration can lead to aggression, depending upon how the person interprets the situation. (All, AP/Wide World Photos)

TELEVISION AND AGGRESSION

Ronald's pro-aggressive plan for dealing with frustrating situations may have been reinforced by his watching violent television programs. In most of these programs, actors and actresses take some aggressive action to solve their problems. Albert Bandura and his colleagues (1963) have shown that children will imitate a model's violent actions if the model was rewarded or suffered no consequences (Module 17). Based on Bandura's research as

Is there anything wrong with watching violent television programs?

Figure 18.1

TV violence and aggression. There is good evidence that watching violence on television is associated with more aggression in children. (Graph, adapted from Eron, 1982; photo, Mark Antman/The Image Works)

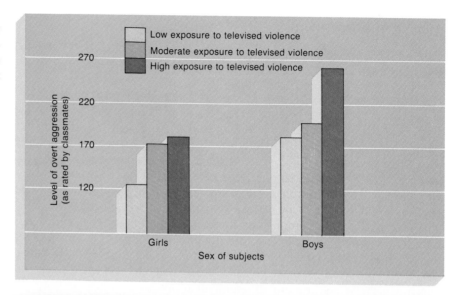

well as his own, Eron is convinced that watching violent television programs promotes the development of aggressive strategies to deal with situations (Figure 18.1). Does research back Eron's conviction?

The National Coalition on Television Violence found that a great many shows are dominated by aggression, much of it made to appear fun and exciting. For example, some prime-time programs have over 35 violent acts per hour (*San Diego Tribune*, November 15, 1982). By the time the average child is 18 years old, he or she will have spent nearly 40,000 hours watching television and will have witnessed hundreds of thousands of violent acts. How often do television programs show aggressive actions as being rewarded? This is an important question because Bandura found that children are more likely to imitate aggressive behaviors if the model's aggressive acts are rewarded. To answer this question, six different people watched and coded the top 100 television programs for both physical and verbal violence. They observed an average of 19 acts of aggression per hour, including physical assault, use of weapons, and verbal aggression. They also discovered that aggression was most often portrayed as a *solution* to conflict and was often the only solution tried (Williams et al., 1982). This means that children who watch aggressive acts on television are likely to see their pro-aggressive strategies reinforced and, therefore, to imitate aggressive behaviors.

But how much does watching television violence contribute to real-life aggression in children? After reviewing research in this area, Lynette Friedrich-Cofer and Aletha Huston (1986) concluded that watching violent television programs has a small but significant effect on causing aggression in children. They added that children who are aggressive may prefer to watch violent television programs, which in turn, reinforces their aggressive tendencies. Although there is some debate over the size of the effect, most agree that watching violent television programs may increase aggressive behavior in young viewers (Freedman, 1986). For example, both the American Psychological Association (1985) and the National Institute of Mental Health (Pearl et al., 1982) have reaffirmed the position that television violence has a causal effect on aggression in children and adolescents.

GENETIC AND HORMONAL INFLUENCES

The popular press misnamed these individuals "super males." Instead of the normal male chromosome pattern of XY, some are born with an XYY pattern—that is, they have an extra male or Y chromosome. Because reports indicate that criminals have a higher incidence of the XYY pattern, some researchers have suggested that the extra Y chromosome predisposes a man to be unusually aggressive (Witkin et al., 1976).

Although researchers discovered that XYY men have a relatively high likelihood of going to prison, they also have a lower than average level of intelligence. The reason that XYY males end up in prison so often is not because they are more aggressive but because their lower intellectual functioning causes them to be caught more easily after committing a crime (Witkin et al., 1976). Although there is good evidence that animals can be bred to be more or less aggressive, there is very little evidence that humans inherit a genetic predisposition to be aggressive.

Carefully consider the following findings: Young boys show more rough-and-tumble play than young girls; teenage boys show more antisocial and aggressive behavior than teenage girls; almost all of the violent crimes in our society are committed by adolescent or adult males; and men generally behave more aggressively than women (Eagly & Steffen, 1986). Is the fact that men generally behave more aggressively than women related to the presence of the male hormone, testosterone?

There is strong evidence that raising or lowering levels of testosterone in animals can increase or decrease levels of aggression (Adams, 1983). This means that testosterone levels greatly control the expression of aggressive behavior of rats, mice, and other animals. However, researchers generally report that levels of testosterone in humans are not associated with aggression (Sheard, 1979). For example, a study of prisoners showed that inmates who were involved in the most fights did not have higher testosterone levels than inmates who fought very little. In a few studies where a relationship was found between aggression and higher levels of testosterone, researchers have been unable to determine whether the testosterone caused the aggression, or whether increased aggression raised the levels of testosterone (Dabbs et al., 1987; Susman et al., 1987). In addition, we know that other factors, such as stress, alcohol, and various drugs, can affect testosterone levels.

All these studies point to a significant difference between animals and humans in how aggression is controlled. In animals, aggression is controlled primarily through a combination of genetic and hormonal factors, which interact with the social cues in the animals' environments. However, in

Can increased levels of male hormones lead to aggression?

human v. animal

genes v. env.

Unlike humans, animals inherit aggressive behavior patterns that are triggered by certain stimuli in the environment, such as the presence of another animal or some sort of threat. (Tom McHugh/Photo Researchers)

humans, aggression appears to be learned and controlled primarily through social-environmental factors (Bornstein et al., 1981). Working from the belief that human aggression is primarily learned, psychologists have developed a number of methods to reduce aggression.

APPLYING PSYCHOLOGY   Programs to Control Aggressive Behavior

Anger Control in Children

Ronald's bad temper often triggered his aggressive behavior. If he could learn to control his anger, he could curb his aggression. John Lochman and his associates (1981, 1984, 1986) have developed an Anger Control program to treat aggressive children, such as Ronald. The key to Lochman's program is the idea that aggressive children have social-cognitive deficits. For example, aggressive children do not know how to stop themselves from thinking in pro-aggressive ways or to overcome their belief that other children, not them, are acting aggressively. In Lochman's program, Ronald would learn to: (1) establish group rules, such as "no hitting," and receive reinforcement for obeying these rules; (2) use self-statements to inhibit his impulsive behavior, such as "think before acting"; (3) generate alternate, nonaggressive solutions to use when frustrated; (4) model those students who have recognized their anger and taken specific steps to control it; (5) make his own videotape of how these steps are used to solve frustrating problems. Lochman has shown this Anger Control program to be effective for reducing aggression. For example, after being in the program for 18 weeks, grade school children had significant reductions in parent-rated aggression and in disruptive and aggressive classroom behaviors, as well as increases in self-reported self-esteem.

Anger Control in Adults

What's wrong with getting angry?

Although Margaret is good at selling computer software, she becomes angry at clients and at herself if she loses a sale. She has developed a pattern of taking out her anger on her husband. As a result, their marriage is in trouble.

According to cognitive-social learning theory, one of the ways a child learns to be aggressive is from observing and imitating adult behavior. (Alan Carey/The Image Works)

Like Margaret, people whose quick tempers lead to problems were treated by Jerry Deffenbacher and his colleagues (1987). The researchers used a program that combined cognitive relaxation and social skills training (Hazaleus & Deffenbacher, 1986). During the first two weeks of this program, Margaret would practice progressive relaxation and monitor when, where, and why she became angry. During the next six sessions she would imagine events that made her angry, such as losing a sale, and then reduce her anger by relaxing. She would be told to continue monitoring events that made her angry outside the sessions, and to reduce her anger by relaxing rather than taking it out on her husband. In addition, she would be taught to minimize interpersonal anger by developing better listening and communications skills, such as how to ask questions, seek clarifications, and check for understanding. Deffenbacher found that five weeks after finishing this program, clients reported significant reductions both in suppressing and expressing anger and in coping better with potentially angering situations.

Although it may feel good to get angry and let off steam, these responses often lead to additional problems. By using an Anger Control program, you can avoid getting angry in the first place, avoid lashing out at others, and best of all, avoid more serious personal, job, or family problems.

RAPE AND SEXUAL AGGRESSION

Rape Myths

- Healthy women cannot be raped against their will.

- Women often falsely accuse men of rape.

- Rape is primarily a sex crime committed by sex-crazed maniacs.

- Only bad girls get raped.

- If a girl engages in necking or petting and she lets things get out of hand, it is her own fault if her partner forces sex on her.

How many people do you think believe the following statements?

These statements, called **rape myths,** are examples of the kinds of misinformed beliefs that many rapists and other individuals hold about women (Burt, 1980). Researchers have found that belief in rape myths is more common among men who had raped. However, rape myths are also held by college males. In a survey of male college students, David Giacopassi and Thomas Dull (1986) reported that from 17 to 75 percent of the students agreed with one or more of nine rape myths. The researchers hope that with continued education about sex, sexual aggression, and rape, men will be better informed and believe less in rape myths.

Kinds of Rapists

Although sex is a part of rape, most researchers agree that it is not the primary motivation. Based on interviews with rapists and their victims, A. Nicholas Groth (1979) concluded that the primary motivation for rape was to express power and anger. Gail Abarbanel, director of the Santa Monica Rape Treatment Center, describes four kinds of rapists (*Los Angeles Times*, February 24, 1984).

- The **power rapist,** who commits 70 percent of all rapes, is not out to hurt physically, but to possess. His acts are premeditated and often preceded by rape fantasies. He may carry a weapon not to hurt, but to overcome the victim. Many victims report suffering much guilt and self-blame for having given in out of fear.

- The **sadistic rapist** accounts for fewer than 5 percent of rapes, but he is the most dangerous because for him sexuality and aggression have become fused, and using physical force is arousing and exciting. Sadistic rapists often select women they regard as promiscuous and subject them to ritualistic bondage and torture and, in some cases, murder.

- For the **anger rapist**, rape is an impulsive, savage attack of uncontrolled physical violence. The act is of short duration, accompanied by abusive language, and the victim usually suffers extensive physical trauma, such as broken bones and bruises. The rapist's satisfaction comes from venting his hostility on his victim.

- The **acquaintance or date rapist** uses varying amounts of verbal and/or physical coercion to force his partner to engage in sexual activities.

Although the date rapist is clearly more motivated by sex than are the power, anger, and sadistic rapists, the date rapist still uses varying amounts of sexual aggression to achieve his goals. Recent surveys have shown that date rape and sexual aggression are relatively common. For example, Charlene Muehlenhard and Melaney Linton (1987) surveyed a sample of over 300 female and almost 300 male college students. Seventy-seven percent of the women reported being subjected to sexual aggression and about 15 percent reported being forced to have sexual intercourse. Among the men, 57 percent reported engaging in sexual aggression and 7 percent admitted to engaging in unwanted sexual intercourse. In a related national survey of approximately 3,000 male and 3,000 female college students, Mary Koss and her colleagues (1987) found that about 27 percent of the college females experienced either rape or attempted rape. About 8 percent of the college males reported committing or attempting rape.

Avoiding Date Rape and Sexual Aggression

According to Muehlenhard and Linton, one way to avoid sexual aggression is to know the risk factors. Factors that were associated with sexual aggression included the following: man's initiating the date, paying all the expenses, and driving; miscommunication about sex; heavy alcohol or drug use; "parking"; and men's acceptance of traditional sex roles, interpersonal violence, and rape myths. The length of time the partners knew each other was not a factor in date rape.

One of the problems in avoiding date rape is that men who are guilty of this act do not fit the stranger-in-the-dark-alley stereotype. Women are less likely to recognize what is happening and more likely to blame themselves or be blamed by others for arousing the man. To prevent sexual aggression, the researchers suggest that women avoid the risk factors associated with date rape, learn to recognize the cues very early, and clearly put a stop to unwanted sexual advances. The common method men use to obtain unwanted sex is to just do it, even if the woman has said "No." For this reason, Muehlenhard and Linton counsel women to use a strategy of increasing forcefulness, going from direct refusal to vehement verbal refusal and, if necessary, physical force. However, when women were presented with sexual situations and asked if they could refuse comfortably, only 60 percent said they could. This means that 40 percent of respondents would seem to be at risk for sexual aggression. The researchers suggest that women take assertiveness training if they foresee having a problem saying "No."

One of the ways to decrease the likelihood of date rape is to avoid high risk situations, such as "parking" or the heavy use of drugs.
(Steve Smith/Wheeler Pictures)

MAJOR CONCEPT Aggression

Please indicate which of the following statements are true (T) or false (F).

1. T/F The more accepting and supportive parents are, the less aggression a child is likely to show in school.

2. T/F If a father physically punishes his child for being aggressive, the physical punishment will increase the child's aggression away from home if the child identifies with the father.

3. T/F One of the reasons that an aggressive child persists in being aggressive through adulthood is that the child has learned to process information in a certain way, such as to react to frustration with aggression.

4. T/F According to the frustration-aggression hypothesis, a person will react to frustration by being aggressive if that person was punished for being aggressive as a child.

5. T/F One of the best strategies for teaching a child not to be aggressive is to teach the child prosocial behaviors.

6. T/F There is evidence that children may imitate and model some of the violent behaviors that they see on television.

7. T/F Research has shown that humans inherit a genetic predisposition to be aggressive.

8. T/F For most men, aggressive behaviors increase with increases in the level of the male hormone, testosterone.

9. T/F Of the four kinds of rapists, date rapists may be the most difficult to recognize since they do not fit the usual stereotype of a rapist.

Answers: 1 (T); 2 (F); 3 (T); 4 (F); 5 (T); 6 (T); 7 (F); 8 (T); 9 (T).

Victims' Reactions to Rape

During the first days and months after rape, the victims' lives are seriously disrupted. They report nightmares, headaches, nausea, exhaustion, fear, general anxiety, guilt, and self-blame. They find it difficult to function in social situations, at work, at school, or in the home. Many of these symptoms decrease with time. However, even one to two years after being raped, about 50 percent of the victims report problems of depression, fear of being alone, suspicion of others, and sexual problems. All these emotional difficulties indicate that the treatment of rape victims must deal with both short- and long-term effects, some of which may persist for years (Ellis et al., 1981; Nadelson et al., 1982).

REVIEW

Herman's father never gave him much support for anything he did and often spanked Herman for talking back and not minding his manners. Herman did not have many friends at school or around the neighborhood because Herman picked fights. Herman's fights would be an example of (1) _____ since he intended to injure or irritate his peers. Based on Herman's aggressive behavior as a child, there is a good chance that Herman will be aggressive as an (2) _____.

One of the reasons for Herman's aggressive behavior is his family environment. The less

(3) _____ the parents are at home, the more likely Herman will be aggressive at school. The

more the father physically (4) _____ Herman for talking back, the more likely it is that Herman will be aggressive. If Herman had gotten along and (5)

_____ with his father, Herman would have adopted his father's anti-aggressive values. Since Herman did not identify with his father, the father was a model for behaving aggressively and Herman

(6) _____ his father's aggressive behavior.

Once young Herman had learned to be aggressive, these behaviors were maintained by a number of factors, such as being rewarded by getting his own way. In addition, Herman acquired a number of pro-aggres-

sive (7) _____, such as thinking that aggressive behaviors paid off and that other people behaved more aggressively than he. These pro-aggressive

ideas resulted in Herman processing (8) _____ about situations in ways that often resulted in his behaving aggressively. For example, Herman's pro-aggressive beliefs would mean that when he is frustrated, he would most likely act according to the

(9) _____ - _____ hypothesis. According to this hypothesis, anger and aggression are common emotional responses to frustration but people

may show other, (10) _____ responses.

Eron believes that young children adopt one of two very different strategies for dealing with situations. Herman has adopted a pro-aggressive strategy. One way to teach Herman to adopt a nonaggressive strategy would be to reward Herman for performing helping or

(11) _____ behaviors. Children who perform these behaviors tend to become adults with low

rates of aggression and high levels of (12) _____

_____.

The pro-aggressive strategy that Herman learned as a young child may have been reinforced by watching violent television programs. In violent television programs, aggressive behaviors are often portrayed as the

solution to (13) _____, and thus aggressive behaviors appear to be rewarded. There is evidence that violent television programs contribute to (14) _____ in children and adolescents.

Although there is evidence that aggression in animals is under genetic control, there is little or no evidence that Herman has inherited a genetic

(15) _____ to be aggressive. In addition, despite the fact that aggression in animals is apparently influenced by levels of male hormones, there is little evidence that aggression in humans is influenced by

levels of the male hormone (16) _____.

Either as a child or adult, Herman could learn to reduce his anger, decrease his aggressive behaviors, and perhaps increase his self-esteem by taking part in an

(17) _____ control program.

Men who believe that women unconsciously want to be raped or only bad girls are raped are said to believe

in (18) _____ _____. Psychologists hope that continued information and education will undermine these myths.

One of Herman's buddies was arrested for attempted rape. There are four general types of rapists. The rapists who commit about 70 percent of all rapes and want to possess but not hurt are called

(19) _____ rapists. Those who want to hurt and become aroused by combining force and sex are

called (20) _____ rapists. Those who commit a savage attack of brief uncontrolled physical vio-

lence are called (21) _____ rapists. Those who use varying amounts of verbal or physical force to

get sex from an acquaintance are called (22) _____

rapists. There are a number of (23) _____ factors for date rape, such as "parking," miscommunication about sex, and heavy use of drugs. To avoid date rape, women should avoid the risks, learn to recognize the cues very early, and use increasing forcefulness in saying "No." Since many women feel uncomfortable in saying "No," they may need to take a

course in or practice (24) _____ training.

(1) aggression; (2) adult; (3) supportive or accepting; (4) punished, spanked; (5) identified; (6) imitated; (7) beliefs, expectations; (8) information; (9) frustration-aggression; (10) nonaggressive, emotional; (11) prosocial; (12) social success, mental health; (13) problems; (14) aggression; (15) predisposition; (16) testosterone; (17) anger; (18) rape myths; (19) power; (20) sadistic; (21) anger; (22) date; (23) risk; (24) assertiveness

GLOSSARY TERMS

acquaintance (date) rapist (p. 566)

aggressive behavior (p. 559)

anger rapist (p. 566)

frustration-aggression hypothesis (p. 561)

power rapist (p. 566)

prosocial behaviors (p. 561)

rape myths (p. 565)

sadistic rapist (p. 566)

Module 52 Conformity, Compliance, and Obedience

Former nurses, clerks, teachers, truck drivers, longshoremen, professionals, and students had followed the Reverend Jim Jones to the jungles of Guyana. Here Jones established Jonestown, a settlement for his over 900 followers. But reports leaked out that some of the Jonestown residents were being held against their will. To determine whether this was true, U.S. Congressman Leo D. Ryan from California, accompanied by journalists, went to Jonestown to investigate. Fearing that the investigators would destroy his socialistic commune, Jones had his police attack them as they were about to leave. Several were killed, but others escaped. After the attack, Jones set into motion a planned mass suicide. Over 900 adults and children were persuaded or forced to drink a cyanide-laced fruit punch. Jones told his followers that by taking their lives now, they would win peace in the hereafter. He walked among them, embracing them and saying that he'd see them in the next life. Tim Reiterman, a San Francisco newspaper reporter who was wounded with the Ryan party in Guyana, coauthored Raven, *a book on Jonestown. Reiterman concluded that what happened to the members of Jonestown could happen to almost anyone (adapted from the* Los Angeles Times, *November 18, 1983).*

How could a mass suicide/murder happen today?

Most of us are horrified that men, women, and children would obey an order to kill themselves. Although what happened at Jonestown is an extreme example, some of the reasons these people obeyed are similar to the reasons you obey people in authority and conform to group and social pressures. Let's look at some of these reasons, beginning with the causes of conformity.

CONFORMITY

Reverend Jones's followers conformed by sharing a set of religious beliefs and agreeing with the viewpoints of their leader. Students conform by wearing similar clothes on campus, believing in the importance of getting good grades, and complaining about all the work they must do. Business executives conform by wearing professional clothes, believing in the importance of making money, and complaining about paying taxes. **Conformity refers to any behavior you perform because of group pressure, even though that pressure involves no direct requests.** If you think you are too

At the command of Rev. James Jones, over 900 of his followers committed suicide. This is an extreme example of obedience, which is one form of compliance. (Philippe LeDru/Sygma)

independent to conform in most situations, you will probably be surprised at what research has shown.

Asch's Classic Experiment

What would you do in these situations?

- Most of the members of your fraternity get drunk at parties. Will you?

- Most of your co-workers needlessly complain about their jobs. Will you?

- Most of the members on the jury decide the suspect is guilty. Will you?

Many years ago, Solomon Asch (1958) attempted to answer questions like these. In a classic experiment, he studied the influence of group pressures to conform. How would you behave in Asch's study?

You have been told that you are taking part in a visual perception experiment, and you are seated at a round table with five others. The group is shown a straight line and then instructed to look at three more lines of different lengths and pick out the line equal in length to the original one. The three choices are different enough in length that it is not hard to pick out the correct one. Each person at the round table identifies his choice out loud, with you answering next to last. When you are ready to answer, you will have heard four others state their opinions. What you do not know is that these four other people are the experimenter's accomplices. On certain trials, they will answer correctly, making you feel your choice is right. On other trials they will deliberately answer incorrectly, much to your surprise. In these cases you will have heard four identical incorrect answers before it is your turn to answer. You will almost certainly feel some pressure to conform to the other's opinion. Will you conform? (adapted from Asch, 1958).

Out of 50 subjects in Asch's experiment 13 (25 percent) never conformed to the group pressure by giving an incorrect answer on any of the 12 critical trials. However, 22 subjects (44 percent) gave 1 to 5 conforming answers, and 15 subjects (30 percent) gave 6 to 11 conforming answers. (No one conformed on all 12 trials.) The data indicate that the desire to have your attitudes and behaviors match those of others in a group can be very powerful (Asch, 1958). One reason that Reverend Jones's followers conformed to his ideas was because of this kind of implicit group pressure. Let's look more closely at the motivation to conform and whether particular people are more likely to succumb to it.

The Motivation to Conform

Your task is to select the best solution to the following problem:

Geraldine and Lennie are college students who have been living together in an apartment near the campus. Lennie's allowance buys the food, and they are sharing the rent. Geraldine has told her parents she is rooming with another girl, and now her parents are coming to visit their daughter. They have never seen her apartment. Geraldine has asked Lennie to move out for the time that her parents are in town. Should he?

Would you conform to make yourself look better?

1. Yes. *His moving out will save a lot of trouble with her parents.*
2. No. *It would be hypocritical for them to pretend; Geraldine should tell her parents before they come.*

Because we are subjected to countless experiences when obedience is demanded, many of us develop a strong habit of obeying. (Thomas Hopker/Woodfin Camp & Associates)

3. Yes, *but Geraldine should pay for Lennie's new accommodations and food (adapted from Santee & Maslach, 1982).*

When students were asked individually to rate the solutions to this problem, they rated 1 and 2 as good and 3 as poor. However, social pressure can make students give different ratings.

Suppose you are in a situation in which you hear three other students give their opinions on solutions 1, 2, and 3. You hear all three students rate the third solution as a good one. Although you do not think this solution is very good, will you go along with the group? Like the subjects in Asch's original study, the subjects in this study tended to conform to the group opinion.

Those with low self-concepts were the most likely to conform. A low *self-concept* is related to being relatively less sure of your private beliefs, placing less value on being unique, and becoming more distressed than others when you disagree in public (Santee & Maslach, 1982). These data suggest that one reason for conforming to group pressure may be having a low self-concept and being very concerned about how you appear to others. These data also suggest that many of Reverend Jones's followers may have conformed to his viewpoints because they had low self-concepts.

Jones's followers, of course, did more than simply go along with group pressure. They also complied with their leader's direct requests, such as the request that they donate all their money to his church. **Compliance** refers to behavior performed under the added pressure of being directly asked to perform it. One kind of compliance is obedience. **Obedience** refers to behavior performed in response to an order given by someone in a position of authority. The 900 people of Jonestown will not be forgotten, because they obeyed the most extreme of all orders: they took their own lives. Let's consider what psychologists can tell us about the reasons for compliance and obedience.

COMPLIANCE

Why don't patients always follow doctor's orders?

As many as 50 percent and sometimes even 80 percent of patients do not do what their doctors tell them to do. Why do people consult a doctor and then fail to take the prescribed medication? Leventhal (1982) answers that some patients privately disagree with the doctor's diagnosis. These patients want to avoid arguing and challenging the doctor's authority, or they are afraid of looking foolish. They therefore say publicly that they will comply with what the doctor requests. In private, however, they show their disagreement by not taking their medicine or following the treatment program.

This example illustrates that public compliance does not always guarantee private compliance. How many of Reverend Jones's followers would have drunk the poison if they had been told to drink it in the privacy of their homes? One obvious way to increase compliance is to use group pressure. Another way is to use a technique you have probably experienced without even realizing it: the so-called foot-in-the-door technique.

Foot-in-the-Door Technique

A door-to-door salesperson soon learns that if she can get the customer to comply with her request to let her in the door, the customer is more likely to comply with a later request to buy the product. The **foot-in-the-door technique** refers to the increased probability of compliance to a second request if a person complies with a small, first request. In one of the first demonstrations of this phenomenon, housewives were asked to put up a

The person smoking at a no-smoking sign may be more likely to obey in the future if he can first be made to obey smaller requests. (Donald Getsug/Photo Researchers)

small sign in one of their windows or to sign a petition. Two weeks later, they were asked to put up a large, ugly sign on their front lawns. Results showed that significantly more women complied with the second request if they had been previously approached and had complied with the first request (Freedman & Fraser, 1966).

A review of fifteen years of research on the foot-in-the-door technique indicates that it is replicable and that it does occur often. However, since nearly half of the reviewed studies produced no effect or an opposite effect, it appears that the effect is small and that other unknown variables also contribute to increased compliance (Beaman et al., 1983). The authors of this review also question the most commonly accepted explanation for the foot-in-the-door finding—namely, self-perception. According to the self-perception explanation, your compliance with a first request may result in your thinking of yourself as a helpful person. Compliance with a subsequent second request is assumed to result from your desire to maintain this positive self-perception. The problem with the self-perception explanation is that it is not precise enough to predict many of the foot-in-the-door findings.

Jim Jones used the foot-in-the-door technique with his followers. When he was still in the United States, he slowly made more and more demands on the members of his church, such as attending services, giving money, and donating time. After the members agreed, he made larger requests, such as signing over their Social Security checks and ownership of their homes. Next, he asked them to move to the jungles of Guyana. Finally, he asked them to take their lives.

Should you ask someone for a small favor before you ask for a big favor?

OBEDIENCE

Milgram's Experiments

You have volunteered for a study on the effects of punishment on learning. After arriving in the laboratory at Yale University, you are selected to be the "teacher," and another volunteer is to be the "learner." Without your knowledge, you were deliberately chosen to be the teacher, while the learner is actually an accomplice in the experiment.

You watch as the learner is strapped into a chair and has electrodes placed on his wrists. The electrodes are attached to a shock generator in the next room. You and the researcher then leave the learner's room and go into an adjoining room.

The researcher gives you a list of questions to ask the learner over an intercom, and the learner is to signal his answer on a panel of lights before you. For each wrong answer, you are to shock the learner, and you are to increase the intensity of the shock by 15 volts. In front of you is the shock machine, with 30 separate switches. The first switch is marked 15 volts, Slight Shock, and the last switch is marked 450 volts, Danger: Severe Shock. You begin to ask the learner questions and as he misses them, you administer increasing intensities of shock.

After receiving 300 volts, the learner pounds on the wall. After 315 volts, he pounds again and then stops answering your questions. At this point you plead with the researcher to stop the experiment. The researcher tells you to continue asking questions and if the learner fails to respond, you should treat it as a wrong answer and deliver the next level of shock. Would you continue to follow the researcher's orders? How far would you go? (adapted from Milgram, 1963).

As Figure 18.2 shows, 65 percent of the "teachers" in this experiment by psychologist Stanley Milgram continued to deliver shocks until reaching the maximum of 450 volts (Milgram, 1963, 1974). An experiment similar to Milgram's was conducted some years later using children ages 6 to 16 as "teachers." This study found that 76 percent of the children delivered the maximum shock (Shanab & Yahya, 1977).

Figure 18.2
Data from the Milgram study. Subjects were told to deliver an increasingly strong shock each time the "learner" answered a question incorrectly. Even after the "learner" pounded on the wall and stopped answering questions, 65 percent of the subjects continued to deliver shocks, including the last shock labeled XXX, 450 volts. (Adapted from Milgram, 1963)

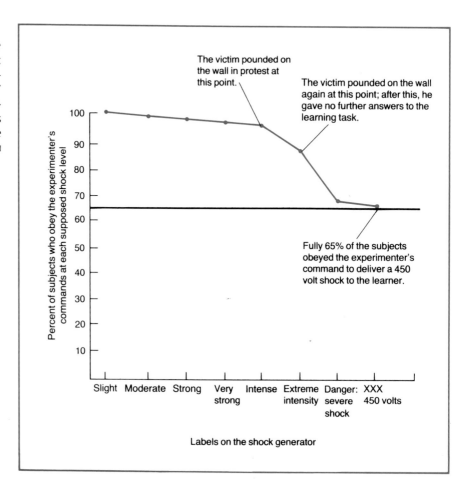

Performed in the early 1960s, the Milgram experiments are not forgotten. They are discussed in virtually every introductory psychology text, and for good reason. These experiments demonstrated what no one imagines could be true. Psychiatrists had been asked to predict how many people would deliver the full range of shocks, including the last 450 volts. They said that only 0.1 percent of the population would do so. The general public was asked the same question and predicted that only 2 percent would deliver the 450 volts. To the horror and dismay of many, including Milgram, 65 percent of the subjects delivered the full range of shocks. Milgram's experiments clearly demonstrated that a large percentage of people will obey orders that they know to be unreasonable.

MAJOR CONCEPT Conformity, Compliance, and Obedience

For each of the statements listed below, decide which of these three processes is being described.

	Conformity	Compliance	Obedience
1. Psychologist Stanley Milgram demonstrated this process in a controversial set of experiments.			X
2. If you find yourself criticizing people you really like because your friends are criticizing them, you are displaying this behavior.	X		
3. This behavior is actually a form of compliance.			X
4. Psychologist Solomon Asch demonstrated this process in a classic study many years ago.	X		
5. If you pull to the side of the road because you hear an ambulance siren, you are displaying this behavior.		X	
6. If you pull to the side of the road because a police officer orders you to, you are displaying this behavior.			X
7. The foot-in-the-door technique is one way to get you to show this behavior.		X	
8. One of the reasons why people show this behavior is their learned reactions to authority figures.			X

Answers: 1 obedience; 2 conformity; 3 obedience; 4 conformity; 5 compliance; 6 obedience; 7 compliance; 8 obedience

Why would people obey an
inhumane order?

Why Did Milgram's Subjects Obey?

Psychologists have suggested several reasons why so many subjects in Milgram's experiment obeyed to the end, even though they believed they were inflicting severe pain on someone else. One of the main reasons is that people obey because they have learned to follow the orders of *authority figures*, whether they are religious leaders, army commanders, doctors, scientists, or parents. In one of his follow-up studies, Milgram found that it is less difficult for people to defy an authority figure they do not have to deal with face to face.

In this variation of Milgram's original experiment, the researcher gave the subject the initial instructions and then left the room. If the subject hesitated at any point in the experiment, the researcher ordered him to continue over a telephone. In these circumstances, only 23 percent of the subjects complied throughout the experiment and gave the maximum shock (compared with 65 percent when the researcher was present in the same room). The physical presence of an authority figure, in other words, increases compliance. The fact that Reverend Jones walked among his followers and encouraged them to drink the poison probably increased their willingness to obey.

People also obey because they have learned to follow orders in their daily lives, whether it be in traffic, on the job, or in personal interactions. It is thought that obeying minor orders increases the probability of later obeying major ones. The followers of Reverend Jim Jones had a history of complying with his demands and never questioning them. In a famous trial after the Vietnam War, Lieutenant William Calley was accused of leading his men into a Vietnamese village and killing over 100 men, women, and children. When asked why, he said that his order to destroy a village was just another in a series of orders he had learned to obey. In a study of nurses, 95 percent were willing to administer an overdose of a drug a doctor had ordered because they were accustomed to obeying a doctor's orders (Hofling et al., 1966). In discussing the Milgram study, one author has suggested that the subjects' willingness to obey minor requests—delivery of small harmless shocks—contributed to their eventual willingness to deliver maximum shocks. This is similar to the foot-in-the-door technique, in which going along with small requests may result in compliance with subsequent, much larger requests (Gilbert, 1981).

RESEARCH ETHICS

Although the Milgram experiments provided important information about obedience, it is unlikely that they could be conducted today. This is because all experiments, especially those with the potential for causing psychological or physical harm, are now carefully screened by research committees, a practice that did not exist at the time of Milgram's research. These committees determine whether proposed experiments on animals or humans have the potential for psychological or physical *harm* and whether these potential damaging effects can be eliminated or counteracted. In the case of the Milgram experiments, there was an obvious potential for causing psychological harm to the subjects. The "teachers" would have to live with the knowledge that they had been willing to deliver maximum and potentially harmful shocks to another person. How could this damaging knowledge be counteracted?

How do researchers protect their
subjects?

When there is a possibility of an experiment causing psychological harm, the investigator must propose ways to eliminate or to counteract the potential harmful effects. Counteracting potential harmful effects is usually done by thoroughly debriefing the subjects. **Debriefing** includes explaining the purpose and method of the experiment, asking the subjects about their feelings of being in the experiment, and helping the subjects deal with possible doubts or guilt arising from their behaviors in the experiment. In the Milgram experiments, the subjects were told that, contrary to what they believed, no shock was actually delivered to the "learner." The subjects were also given the opportunity to discuss their feelings about the experiment and their own actions during it. In addition, some of the subjects were sent questionnaires or were interviewed a year later by a psychiatrist to determine whether there were any long-lasting harmful effects of having been a "teacher."

Based on the subjects' responses, Milgram concluded that they did not suffer any long-term harm from having been in his experiments. However, critics still question whether Milgram's experiments were justified, given the great immediate distress they caused subjects. They also wonder whether this distress could be erased merely through debriefing (Allen, 1978). Although scientists disagree over whether Milgram's experiments were justified, they agree that Milgram's findings dramatically changed our view about how much people will obey.

Behavior of Jury Members   **APPLYING PSYCHOLOGY**

Because it is not legal to observe or record the deliberations of a jury while it actually decides a case, psychologists create mock trials to study how jury members think, behave, and influence one another. For instance, is a jury of 12 members more likely to reach a just decision than a jury of six? Studies of mock juries have shown that a single dissenting person in a group of six is far more likely to conform to group pressure than are two dissenters in a group of twelve. Further, a single dissenter in a six-member jury is more likely to change his or her opinion because of a desire for social acceptance rather than because of persuasive evidence (Oskamp, 1984). These findings on jury size were cited by the U.S. Supreme Court when it ruled against juries composed of fewer than six persons.

Research on mock trials also suggests that juries' decisions should be based on unanimous agreement, rather than on agreement of two-thirds of the members. When only two-thirds need to agree, the jury deliberates for a shorter period and is less likely to be deadlocked by contradictory evidence. These findings indicate that innocent persons are less likely to be convicted in a system requiring unanimous decision. The Supreme Court has ruled that decisions must be unanimous in six-member juries, but has not deliberated the issue for twelve-member juries.

Should jury decisions be unanimous?

REVIEW

Mildred, who is Catholic, is faced with an important personal decision. In private discussions with her priest, she was ordered not to use birth control pills. Although she has not talked to her parents about the subject, she knows that they would not want her to use birth control pills either. However, Mildred's fiancé has requested that she begin taking the pills.

If Mildred follows the unspoken wishes of her par-

ents, she would be (1) _____, which means going along with the opinions and actions of others, even though they do not directly ask you to do so. If Mildred gives in to the wishes of her fiancé, she would be (2) _____, which means doing something because of a direct request. If Mildred follows her priest's direct order, she would be

(3) _____, which is one form of compliance.

Mildred attends a group discussion on birth control at her church. After listening to six of her peers speak out against using birth control pills, she is asked her opinion. Generalizing from Asch's studies on conformity, we can say that Mildred will feel pressure to

(4) _____ to the group's opinion. Besides conforming because of group pressure, Mildred might conform because of concern about how she appears to others.

The priest asks Mildred to attend group discussions on birth control for the next three weeks, and she agrees. Next the priest asks Mildred to lead a discussion on birth control techniques, and she agrees again. After agreeing to a small request to come to discussions, Mildred was more likely to agree to the larger request to lead them. This phenomenon is called the

(5) _____ - _____ - _____

- _____ technique: complying with a small

request increases the likelihood that a person will comply with a second, larger request.

In her social psychology class, Mildred watches a film on the Milgram obedience study. She is amazed that as many as (6) _____ percent of the subjects obeyed orders to deliver the maximum shock, which might have caused serious harm. Her professor tells the class that people tend to obey those in

(7) _____, such as a scientist, a police officer, or a priest. People also tend to obey because they have a well-established habit of obeying.

Mildred is relieved to learn from her professor that before experiments on animals or humans may be conducted, a research committee determines if the procedures involved have the potential for causing physical

or psychological (8) _____ to the subjects. In experiments with humans, researchers thoroughly

(9) _____ subjects to counteract any potential harmful effects.

Answers: (1) conforming; (2) complying; (3) obeying; (4) conform; (5) foot-in-the-door; (6) 65; (7) authority; (8) harm; (9) debrief

GLOSSARY TERMS

compliance (p. 572)	debriefing	foot-in-the-door	obedience
conformity (p. 569)	(p. 577)	technique (p. 572)	(p. 572)

Module 53 Behavior in Groups

HELPING

About 60 people had gathered around a serious car crash in a downtown area. They were talking about the accident and pointing at the victims, but no one was helping. One of the victims was a woman, obviously pregnant and unconscious. One person in the crowd was Ken Von. He came forward and tried to save the woman with cardiopulmonary and mouth-to-mouth resuscitation that he had learned by watching television. Many people in the crowd criticized Ken for helping. Ken kept the woman alive until paramedics arrived. Although the woman died later in the hospital, her unborn baby's life was saved because of Ken's help (adapted from the San Diego Tribune, *September 9, 1983).*

Ken's helping is an example of **prosocial behavior,** which is any behavior that benefits others or has positive social consequences. In this case, Ken's behavior saved the baby's life. One form of helping is called **altruism.** Altruism involves doing something, often at a cost or risk, for reasons other than the expectation of a material or social reward. Ken's helping may be described as altruistic, since he expected no external reward. As in Ken's case, helping may occur in emergency situations, such as aiding the victims of an accident or crime. Helping may also occur in nonemergency situations, such as giving someone directions or contributing to a charitable cause.

What motivates someone to help an accident victim?

From studies on helping behavior, we can say a great deal about Ken's motivation for helping the accident victim. Part of his motivation probably came from his identification with what the victim must be going through, called *empathy*. His motivation probably also came in part from his *personal distress*—that is, from feelings of fear, alarm, or disgust that arise upon seeing a victim in need. Another part of Ken's motivation probably came from his *norms and values*. For example, he may feel morally bound to help those in need, which is called a personal norm. He may also have adopted society's norm of social responsibility, which states that good persons help others who are in trouble. Had Ken been helping a friend, he might have been influenced by the *reciprocity norm*, which states that you should help those who have helped you in the past.

Explaining Decisions to Help

Almost all of those who watched the car crash probably experienced some of these motivations. Why was it that only Ken Von took action, while the others chose to watch (Figure 18.3)? To answer this question, we need to

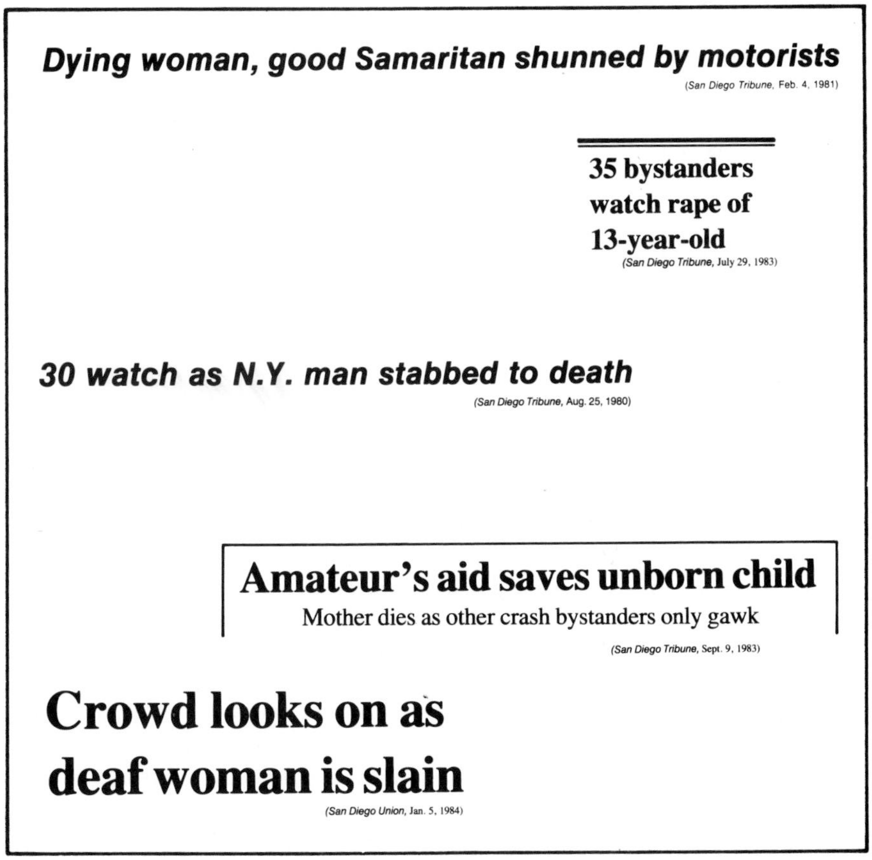

Dying woman, good Samaritan shunned by motorists
(San Diego Tribune, Feb. 4, 1981)

35 bystanders watch rape of 13-year-old
(San Diego Tribune, July 29, 1983)

30 watch as N.Y. man stabbed to death
(San Diego Tribune, Aug. 25, 1980)

Amateur's aid saves unborn child
Mother dies as other crash bystanders only gawk
(San Diego Tribune, Sept. 9, 1983)

Crowd looks on as deaf woman is slain
(San Diego Union, Jan. 5, 1984)

Figure 18.3
As these newspaper headlines indicate, people are often unwilling to help in emergencies. Why is this so?

consider how decisions are made in helping situations. Ken Von, for instance, had to process an enormous amount of information in a very short time: sounds of cars crashing, the sight of someone hurt, recognition that the victim was pregnant, concern about a possible gas tank explosion, shouts of onlookers to stand back. Let's examine two different models that explain how Ken made his decision to help.

Decision Stage Model.   According to the decision stage model of Bibb Latané and John Darley (1970), Ken went through five stages in deciding to help. First, he *noticed* the situation; second, he *interpreted* it as one in which help was needed; third, he assumed personal *responsibility*; fourth, he *chose* a form of assistance; and fifth, he *carried out* that assistance. Onlookers who did not help may have reached stage 3, deciding on personal responsibility, and decided at that point that it was not their responsibility. The advantage of this five-stage decision model is that it explains why people may fail to help even though they recognize the situation as an emergency.

Arousal-Cost-Reward Model.   According to a second model of making decisions to help (Piliavin et al., 1982), Ken calculated the costs and rewards of helping. More specifically, the accident caused him to feel an unpleasant emotional *arousal* which he wanted to reduce. In deciding how to reduce his unpleasant feelings, he calculated the *costs* and *rewards* of helping. Ken may have decided to help because the rewards of helping, such as living up to his own personal standards or maintaining his self-esteem, outweighed the costs, such as the potential danger to himself. Research indicates that Ken's self-esteem is an important factor in how he calculates the costs and rewards of helping (Fisher et al., 1982). Others may have decided not to help because they felt that the costs of helping, such as getting involved in a potentially dangerous situation, outweighed the rewards.

Both the arousal-cost-reward model and the decision stage model recognize the difficulty of explaining decisions to help or not to help. Some individuals, apparently acting on impulse, offer help in the face of enormous costs, even risking their own lives. There are also times when people fail to help even though they know help is needed and the cost of giving it is not very great. One reason for this failure to help is called the bystander effect.

The Bystander Effect

After visiting the zoo, a 13-year-old girl cooled off by wading into a large water fountain. While 35 people looked on, two older boys attacked and raped her in knee-deep water. The police reports indicated that the 35 people did nothing. Detective Harry Keeler said he did not understand the mentality of people who can just stand there and watch something like that. An 11-year-old passerby finally summoned help (adapted from the San Diego Tribune, *July 29, 1983).*

Are people less likely to help if others are present?

One reason that none of these onlookers helped is because they were part of a crowd. When the presence of others socially inhibits individuals from helping it is called the **bystander effect.** Data from over 50 studies indicate that 75 percent of people tested alone offer assistance in situations that require help, but fewer than 53 percent of those tested in a group do so (Latané & Nida, 1981). From these data we know that in an emergency situation, such as the rape of the 13-year-old girl, the presence of many people can actually make any one individual less likely to help.

Why does the presence of others inhibit helping?

How can we explain the bystander effect? What is it about the presence of 10, 20, 30 others that inhibits individuals from helping? If you had been one of the 35 witnesses to the attack of the 13-year-old girl, you might have

MAJOR CONCEPT   Prosocial Behavior

Indicate whether each statement is true (T) or false (F).

1. T/F   People who engage in prosocial behavior are often motivated by empathy, by personal distress at seeing others in need, and by various norms and values that encourage helping.

2. T/F   A person who fails to help in an emergency may have calculated that the costs of helping exceed the rewards in this situation.

3. T/F   People in a crowd who gather at the scene of an accident may fail to help because of diffusion of responsibility.

4. T/F   Witnesses to an emergency may hesitate to help until the behavior of others clearly confirms that the situation is serious.

5. T/F   Witnesses who offer help to the victims of an accident or crime generally do so because they have stronger humanitarian values than witnesses who merely watch.

Answers: 1 (T); 2 (T); 3 (T); 4 (T); 5 (F)

used the reactions of others to interpret the seriousness of the situation and the degree to which the girl needed help. If the other onlookers did not appear concerned and did not offer help, you might have assumed that the situation was not as serious as you first believed and that help was not needed (perhaps the three were friends and were only pretending to struggle). In other words, the failure of others to react may have caused you to misinterpret the situation.

In addition, if you were one of 35 onlookers, you might feel less personal responsibility for helping. Since others are present, it is not clear whose responsibility it is to take action. This is called **diffusion of responsibility,** meaning that in a group an individual may feel less responsibility to help than when alone (Latané, 1981).

Much of the research on the bystander effect has investigated the influence of group size, the seriousness of the emergency, and the physical traits of the victim. Social psychologists have been less concerned with developing practical ways for increasing bystander helping (Latané & Nida, 1981). However, if you are in an emergency situation, there are some measures you can take to decrease the bystander effect. You can increase the likelihood of others helping by signaling with your words or expression that the situation is an emergency, by telling those around you that it is your joint responsibility to help, and by initiating action that may provide the stimulus for others to help the victim (Latané & Nida, 1981).

Passers-by are less likely to stop and help a victim if others are present or if the situation is uncertain. For example, people would be more likely to stop and help if they knew for certain that this person was ill or in trouble, and not sleeping off a binge. (Dan Miller/Woodfin Camp)

Real Emergencies   **APPLYING PSYCHOLOGY**

You might suppose that Good Samaritans, or those who help in emergencies, would have different personality characteristics than nonhelpers. Generally, however, few personality characteristics predict helping (Deaux & Wrightsman, 1984). Why then do people sometimes risk great danger to help those in distress?

In one study, thirty-two individuals were interviewed because they had

Do helpers have special personalities?

Figure 18.4
Who helps in emergencies? People who help in emergencies do not differ in personality traits from nonhelpers. However, helpers are different in that they have had more first aid and lifesaving training than nonhelpers. (Adapted from Huston et al., 1981)

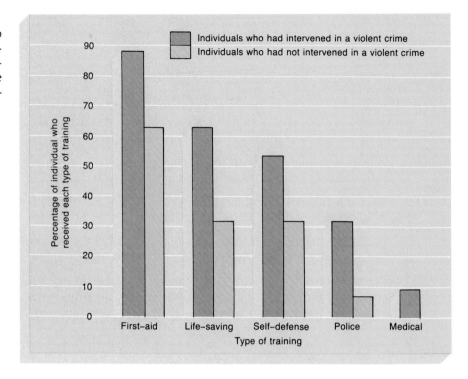

intervened in dangerous criminal episodes, such as street muggings, armed robberies, and bank holdups. During their interventions, 84 percent had received various injuries, indicating the dangerousness of the situations. Because of their intervention and help, these individuals had been given a monetary reward under California's Good Samaritan law. They were compared with a matched group who had no history of intervening in dangerous situations.

Contrary to what you might expect, and in agreement with previous studies, there were *no differences* in personality characteristics between the helpers and the nonhelpers. They did not differ in humanitarian beliefs, in anger reactions, or in feelings of social responsbility. However, compared with the nonhelpers, those who intervened in dangerous situations had themselves experienced two to three times as many crimes and had been victims of serious crimes twice as often. In addition, the most significant difference between the two groups was that interveners had had more training in first-aid, life-saving, and self-defense techniques (Figure 18.4). The authors concluded that these individuals risked their personal safety to help because they had a sense of being capable of helping, not because they held some strong humanitarian value (Huston et al., 1981). These data suggest that one way to increase the likelihood of people helping is to encourage training in first-aid, life-saving, and self-defense techniques. Apparently, possessing these skills makes people feel more capable and thus more likely to resist the bystander effect.

SOCIAL ROLES

Would you make a good prisoner?

Police picked up nine young men at their homes. After being spread-eagled, frisked, and handcuffed, the men were taken to a police station, booked, and put in jail. While in jail, they were referred to only as numbers, ate bland food, lined up three times a day to be counted, were assigned to work shifts, and were supervised when they went to the toilet. The three guards in charge of the prisoners seemed to enjoy their power and sometimes, for no particular reason, ordered the prisoners to do pushups or refused them permission to use the toilet. Over the course of a week, the prisoners began to feel more helpless and depressed and showed signs of physical and emotional distress (adapted from Haney et al., 1973).

These prisoners and guards were college students who had volunteered to participate in a two-week simulation of prison life. The prison was realistically constructed in the basement of the psychology building at Stanford University. The behavior of the prisoners and guards was closely monitored by the researchers. Although scheduled to last two weeks, the study was stopped after only six days because of the evident emotional distress of the prisoners. At the end of the study, the subjects were carefully debriefed, and the researchers maintained contact with each subject for a year to be sure that no harmful psychological effects persisted.

The behavior of these college students changed dramatically, depending upon their assigned *roles*. If assigned to the role of a guard, they began to enjoy their power and use it in arbitrary ways. If assigned to the role of a prisoner, they grew depressed and developed signs of emotional distress. The implications of this study are clear: Depending upon the situation, you assume different roles which, in turn, greatly affect your behavior. Let's look at how your social role and behavior might change, depending upon whether you are in a crowd or in a group, or on whether you are a leader or a follower.

Deindividuation in Crowds

A Puerto Rican handyman was perched on a narrow tenth-floor ledge for an hour. During that time a crowd of as many as 500 people gathered below. Some of the people shouted at the man in Spanish and English to jump. Even cries of "jump" or "Brinca" rang out; police pulled the man to safety (adapted from Mann, 1981).

Onlookers who were shouting for the man to jump would probably behave in a more responsible way if they were not in a **crowd,** a large group of

Would you behave differently in a crowd?

When people think they will not be recognized, they may perform antisocial behaviors like looting that they would never normally perform. (UPI/Bettmann Newsphotos)

persons most of whom are unacquainted. Because individuals cannot be identified easily in a crowd, they are more likely to take on an antisocial role, such as encouraging a potential suicide victim to jump. Using laboratory equivalents of crowd situations, many researchers have found similar results. Subjects are more likely to express verbal and physical hostility (delivering shocks) if there is less chance of being personally identified (Mann et al., 1982). This phenomenon is called **deindividuation.** One researcher thinks that it occurs because self-awareness, guilt, shame, or fear is reduced by the anonymity of being in a crowd (Zimbardo, 1970). According to this idea, if your guilt and self-awareness are reduced, you would be less controlled by internal standards and therefore more willing to take on a deviant or antisocial role (Prentice-Dunn & Rogers, 1982). But the effects of crowds are not always negative. Let's look at a situation in which a crowd may have a positive effect.

Social Facilitation in Crowds

Why do athletes break more records in front of large crowds?

If a mile runner is in great shape and has a history of successful competition, she may turn in a better performance in front of a large crowd. This increase in performance in the presence of a crowd is called **social facilitation.** On the other hand, if a mile runner is in poor shape or has a spotty history, she may turn in a worse performance in front of a large crowd, called **social inhibition.** Whether you show facilitation or inhibition depends partly on your previous experience in performing the particular task. For example, when above-average pool players played in front of an audience, they showed social facilitation by averaging a 10 percent improvement in accuracy. When below-average pool players played in front of an audience, they showed social inhibition by averaging a 10 percent decrease in accuracy (Michaels et al., 1982).

Roles Within Groups

When she is with her dozen computer friends, Sharon is very interested in sharing programming tips, finding out about new equipment, and helping others with problems. When she is with her basketball pals, she is very loud and aggressive and interested in "looking tough." Sharon's computer friends form one group, and her basketball friends form a different one. A **group** is composed of individuals who have similar goals and values and who share

Skilled athletes may break more records when performing in front of large crowds because of the phenomenon known as social facilitation. (Horst Schafer/Peter Arnold, Inc.)

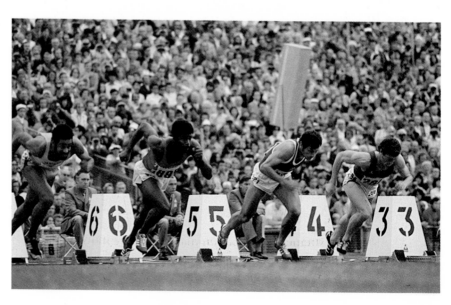

activities based on these goals and values. A group's *values* consist of the members' general ideas about what is good and bad, right and wrong, desirable and undesirable. Values hold the members together and give them motivation to share activities and help one another. Groups are also structured by formal or informal rules about how group members should behave. These rules are called *group norms*.

Sharon follows the norms of her computer group because she has the same values as the other members. In some groups, people follow the norms because they like or admire other members or because they are pressured to conform. When she is with her computer friends, Sharon's role is that of a cooperative problem solver. When she is with her basketball friends, her role becomes that of aggressive athlete. If her computer friends saw Sharon on the basketball court they would find her behavior hard to believe, and if her basketball friends saw her at her computer, they would also be very surprised. In a sense, Sharon becomes a different person, depending on the group she is in.

Among the advantages Sharon experiences from being a member of these two groups is support and encouragement for pursuing her goals and developing her skills. Among her computer friends she is encouraged to develop her professional skills, and among her basketball friends she is encouraged to develop her athletic skills. These and other groups will probably play a very important role in the direction of Sharon's life and may influence many of her major decisions. Now let's consider how groups function in decision making.

Group Decision Making

Suppose you are in a group of five people and your task is to decide which of two job offers a young lawyer named Shirley should accept. These are her choices:

The first offer is from a large, well-established law firm. It offers the most security, financial opportunities, and prestige. The partners in the firm have promised Shirley every opportunity to earn advancement. However, the firm has a poor record as an equal employer of women. Presently, it employs only one woman, who is in a relatively low-level position. The second firm is small, newly established, and offers little security or prestige. No one yet knows whether it will be financially successful, especially since it is competing with the more prestigious law firms. However, this firm has an excellent record in dealing with women and presently employs almost an equal number of women and men. Both women and men are found at all levels in the firm (author's files).

A group's discussion of this problem, in which you are forced to make a collective choice, often results in a shift of individual opinions. At one time it was thought that group discussion more often resulted in choosing the more risky of two alternatives—in this case, joining the newly established firm. This finding was initially labeled the *risky shift*. However, more recent research indicates that if a group is conservative to begin with, it may in fact make a more conservative choice, such as joining the established firm. These more recent findings indicate that group discussion on a forced-choice problem does tend to lead to more *polarization*—that is, to adopting a more extreme group opinion than any of the individuals would have taken alone (Isenberg, 1986). However, whether this polarization is in a risky or conservative direction depends on the initial leanings of the group.

LEADERSHIP ROLES

What do leaders have that makes
people follow them?

*Reverend Jim Jones led 900 of his followers to commit mass suicide. In
their minds Jones was an expert on all matters. They gave him all their
money, and he saw that their material needs were provided for. He
shaped their attitudes by constantly warning about the danger of the
outside world and the need for his protection. Everything that happened
at the Jonestown settlement was controlled by him, often through his
trusted aides. Reverend Jones insisted that his followers called him
"Dad," and that they were all his children. He reminded them that
children obey their parents. On the day that his 900 followers drank the
poisoned punch, he walked among them, reassuring them that he
would see them in the next life (adapted from Winfrey, 1979).*

Jim Jones had many of the traits and behaviors associated with a leader.
He had the ability to persuade his followers to work toward certain goals.
One of those goals was to form the new community of Jonestown; the last
goal was to commit mass suicide. As the group leader, Jones's functions
were to identify the group's goals, to motivate members to work toward
achieving those goals, and to build good relationships between the leader
and the group. Jones did this by controlling the group's finances, by frightening members about the dangers of the outside world, and by making
them assume the role of obedient children.

When Jones succeeded at setting up a new, financially secure and
independent community, he was performing a *task-oriented role*, one which
involves completing some specific task. When he succeeded in keeping his
followers happy with his leadership, he was performing an *interaction-
oriented role*, one which involves maintaining good relationships between
members and leader. Jones excelled at both roles, but this is not true of all
leaders. Some are successful in one role, but not necessarily in the other.

Why was Jim Jones so successful in fulfilling the roles of a leader?
Studies suggest that no single trait made him a good leader. Rather, a
number of traits are associated with successful leadership. These include
having a strong drive to complete a task, persisting to reach one's goals,
feeling great self-confidence, being able to manipulate followers, and knowing how to meet followers' needs (Barker et al., 1983; Heller & Van Til,
1982; Stogdill, 1974). One of the reasons that Jim Jones's followers took
their lives when he told them to do so was because he had so many of the
traits associated with being a leader.

One common stereotype is that leaders are usually men. However,
this stereotype is slowly changing as more and more women achieve roles
of power and leadership in government, business, and academia. Studies
on whether men or women make better leaders indicate that their effectiveness depends on their experience with being in a leadership role. For
example, when men and women were arbitrarily assigned to the role of
group leader, men were generally perceived as more effective, probably
because they had had more experience in being assertive and in demanding
and obtaining compliance. However, when men and women who had
actually held positions of leadership were compared, there were no differences in effectiveness (Hollander & Yoder, 1980). This is because both the
women and men had already learned the skills necessary for being an
effective leader.

Do you evaluate men and women
leaders in different ways?

Although actual effectiveness as a leader depends largely on experience, not on gender, *perceptions* of effectiveness are another matter. In one
study, researchers divided managerial students into 12 groups composed of
24 percent women and 76 percent men. Each member of a group was asked
to rate the other members in terms of two leadership styles: the *participation*

MAJOR CONCEPT Social Roles

Are these statements true (T) or false (F)?

1. T/F The harsh behavior that guards may display toward prison inmates is usually as much a product of their social role as it is a product of their personalities.

2. T/F Because individuals in a crowd cannot be identified easily, people in crowds are more likely to take on antisocial roles.

3. T/F When placed in the role of performing before a large audience, people almost always become nervous and fail to do their best.

4. T/F If you were part of a group asked to choose between two courses of action, your true feelings about the choice would not be altered by what the other group members said.

5. T/F Leadership is one major exception to the power of social roles. Effective leaders have inherent leadership qualities that are not in any way a product of the roles those people fill.

Answers: 1(T); 2(T); 3 (F); 4 (F); 5(F)

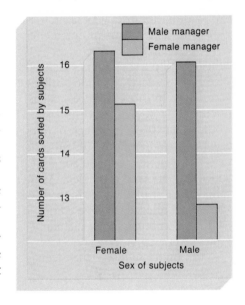

Figure 18.5
Worker productivity and sex of supervisor. Subjects worked harder when they thought they were working for a male manager than when they thought they were working for a female manager. Why do people often not follow a female leader the way they would a male? *(Adapted from Sanders & Schmidt, 1980)*

style, which means that the person reaches decisions after consulting with group members, and the *autocratic style*, which means that the person reaches decisions with very little feedback from the group.

Individuals, whether men or women, were given positive evaluations as leaders if they used the participative style. However, compared with men, women were given more negative evaluations if they used the autocratic style. These data suggest that some individuals were evaluated more negatively as leaders simply because they were women (Jago & Vroom, 1982). The autocratic women leaders may have been evaluated more negatively because people have less experience with a woman in an autocratic role than they do with a man in that same role. Another example of bias against women leaders is shown in Figure 18.5

REVIEW

Winston Moseley said he was looking for someone to rape, rob, and kill. He followed Kitty Genovese into her apartment building parking lot at 3:20 in the morning. Over the next 30 minutes, Winston raped and repeatedly stabbed her. Kitty Genovese's death made the national news not because of Winston Moseley's brutal behavior, but because of the behavior of witnesses. Thirty-eight residents in a neighboring apartment building had seen the attack or had heard Kitty Genovese's cries, but no one offered help or even called the police until it was far too late. Now, many years later, we understand why people may or may not help in such emergencies. As a social psychologist, you are asked to explain what happened in the Kitty Genovese case.

Thirty minutes after Winston began his attack on Kitty, one of the residents, who asked not be involved,

called the police. Since this resident had done something that aided Kitty or that had positive social con-

sequences, it would be called (1) _____ behavior. Since the resident who called the police expected no reward, it was a form of prosocial behavior

called (2) _____ .

According to Latané and Darley's (3) _____ stage model, the resident who called made five decisions. First, he noticed the situation. Second, he per-

ceived or (4) _____ the situation as need-

ing help. Third, he assumed personal (5) _____ for the situation. Fourth, he chose an action; and fifth, he actually carried out that action. Residents who failed to help made different decisions.

You could also explain the residents' behavior by using the (6) arousal- _____ - _____ model. According to this model, the resident who called the police calculated that the rewards of helping were greater than the costs. Residents who did not help calculated the opposite.

When questioned by police, some of the residents said they did not help because they assumed that others would. This is like the finding that an individual in a crowd is less likely to help a victim because of a phenomenon called (7) _____ of responsibility. Diffusion of responsibility means that a person in a crowd feels less personally responsible for helping a victim than the same person would alone. It is one explanation for the general reluctance of people in crowds to take action in emergencies, a phenomenon called the (8) _____ effect.

Just as social situations influence whether or not you will help in emergencies, social situations also influence the roles you play. As a social psychologist, how would you explain the different roles of these nine teenagers? As high school students, these teenagers were very responsible, received some of the highest grades, and were very well respected. As members of their so-called Legion of Doom group, these same nine teenagers were alleged to have committed 35 felonies, including bombing another student's car (*Los Angeles Times*, April 20, 1985).

In high school, the teenagers took on the (9) _____ of being very responsible, hardworking, and well-respected students. In their Legion of Doom group, which was dedicated to righting things they felt were wrong, they took on irresponsible roles. One reason for this role change is that as members of a group, they felt pressure to comply with the group's norms, goals, and values. By being in a group, these nine teenagers were able to help each other accomplish certain goals. Being in a group also changed some of their decisions. When they had a discussion about how to deal with an undesirable fellow student, their opinions would tend to be more (10) _____ than if they had decided individually. The Legion of Doom was considered a (11) _____ because the nine members had shared values and goals. If one of these members attended a football game, he would be considered part of a (12) _____, which is a collection of individuals who do not share many specific values.

Social psychology can explain not only helping and social roles; it can also explain some of the things that happen at a football game. As you watch a star player make some fantastic plays before a huge homecoming crowd, you might recognize this as an example of social (13) _____ . As you notice that less skilled players are playing especially badly, you might recognize this as an example of social (14) _____ . You also notice that some football fans shout and make obscene gestures, which they would not normally do. These fans seem to have lost their fear, guilt, and sense of responsibility, called (15) _____, by being nameless faces in a crowd. During halftime you listen to the coach talk to his players. The coach is considered a good leader because of a number of traits, such as completing tasks, pursuing goals, and having self-confidence. The coach is very good at motivating his team to win, which would be a (16) _____ -oriented role. He is not very good at establishing and maintaining social interactions between himself and the players, which would be an (17) _____ -oriented goal.

Answers: (1) helping or prosocial; (2) altruism; (3) decision; (4) interpreted; (5) responsibility; (6) cost-reward; (7) diffusion; (8) bystander; (9) role; (10) polarized; (11) group; (12) crowd; (13) facilitation; (14) inhibition (15) deindividuation; (16) task; (17) interaction

---

GLOSSARY TERMS

altruism (p. 579)
bystander effect (p. 580)
crowd (p. 583)

deindividuation (p. 584)
diffusion of responsibility (p. 581)

group (p. 584)
prosocial behavior (p. 579)

social facilitation (p. 584)
social inhibition (p. 584)

PERSONAL NOTE

When I was 8 years old I had to give a piano recital to an audience of parents. I walked on stage, sat down at the piano, and could not remember a single note. When I was 12 I had to take part in a spelling bee before an audience of parents and teachers. When my turn came, I stood up and misspelled "Tuesday." When I was 16 years old I had to give a speech before the school assembly. I walked to the lectern, faced the students, and could not speak a single word. For many years I could not explain why these things kept happening to me. Now I know: According to social psychologists, a person who is not very skilled at something tends to perform even worse in front of an audience. That is why I now play the piano, spell, and give speeches only in the privacy of my room.   —R.P.

Appendix

PREVIEW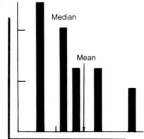

MODULE 1 Descriptive Statistics

Frequency Distributions
Measures of Central Tendency
Measures of Variability

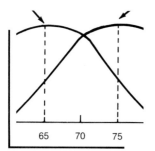

MODULE 2 Inferential Statistics

Chance and Reliability
Tests of Statistical Significance

Statistics in Psychology

Suppose you are curious about how many people are capable of being hypnotized. You read up on how to induce hypnosis and put together a list of five things that people under hypnosis have been known to do. These include feeling no pain when a finger is pricked, being unable to bend an arm when told that the arm will remain stiff, and acting like a young child when told to regress to infancy. You next persuade 20 people to participate in a little test. You attempt to bring them under hypnosis and then ask them to do each of the things on your list. Of your 20 subjects, 2 follow none of your suggestions, 4 follow only one, 7 go along with two suggestions, 4 go along with three, 2 go along with as many as four, and only 1 follows all five. The next day a friend asks you how your study worked out. How would you make generalizations about your findings?

Suppose you are an educational psychologist who has put together a special program to raise the IQ levels of children with learning disabilities. You expose one group of children with learning deficits to the special program and another group, with equal learning deficits, to the standard curriculum. At the end of a year you give all the subjects an IQ test. Those in the special program score an average of 10 points higher than those in the standard curriculum. Is this improved performance due to your program or simply to chance? Could the results have happened because, purely by luck, the children in the first group scored higher than those in the second one?

To answer such questions psychologists rely on statistics. Although you often hear that numbers "speak for themselves," this is not really true. Numbers must be sorted, organized, and presented in a meaningful fashion before they tell us much. Statistics, then, are the tools researchers use to analyze and summarize large amounts of data.

Module 1 Descriptive Statistics

If the very word "statistics" brings to mind complex formulas you think you could never master, you may be surprised how much you already use statistics in your everyday life. When you hear that a ball player has a batting average of 250 and you know this means he has gotten a hit 1 in every 4 times at the plate, you are using statistics. When you understand that a rise in the median income means that people, on average, are earning more money, you are understanding statistics. When you know that scoring in the 90th percentile on a final exam means you did better than 9 out of 10 of your classmates, you are showing a grasp of statistics. These are all examples of **descriptive statistics**—numbers used to present a collection of data in a brief yet meaningful form. One important part of descriptive statistics is presenting distributions of measurements and scores.

591

FREQUENCY DISTRIBUTIONS

Individual differences show up in everything that can be measured. There are no measurements—whether of height, heart rate, memory capability, shyness, or political opinion—that do not show individual variation. When we measure a sample of people regarding some trait, the range of scores we get and the frequency of each one is called the **frequency distribution**. Frequency distributions are often presented in graphic form so their patterns can be seen at a glance.

Normal Distributions

What makes a distribution "normal"?

For many traits in a large population the frequency distribution has a characteristic pattern. For instance, if you measured the height of 500 students chosen at random from your school, you would find a few very short and very tall people, with the majority falling in the middle. Height, like weight, IQ, years of education, and many other characteristics, has what is known as a **normal distribution**. When graphed, a normal distribution produces what is called a **normal curve**: the curve tapers off equally on either side of a central high point, as shown in Figure A.1. This characteristic "bell" shape shows that most of the measurements fall near the center, with as many falling to one side as to the other. When you measure a trait that is distributed normally throughout a population, your measurements should produce an approximately normal curve, provided that your sample is large enough.

Skewed Distributions

What does a lopsided curve show?

Not all traits are distributed normally, however. There are also **skewed distributions.** A skewed distribution means that more people fall toward one side of the scale than toward the other. When plotted on a graph, skewed distributions do not have a symmetrical shape. Instead, they have a "tail" on one end which shows that relatively fewer frequencies occur on that side of the horizontal scale. When the tail is on the right, as in Figure A.2, we say the distribution is skewed to the right (there are fewer frequencies at the higher end of the horizontal scale). When the tail is on the left, as in Figure A.3, we say the distribution is skewed to the left (there are fewer frequencies at the lower end of the horizontal scale).

The data you collected about susceptibility to hypnosis are a skewed distribution. If you plotted them on a graph, with score along the horizontal axis and number of people along the vertical one, the curve would be skewed to the right. This would say at a glance that more people in the sample fell at the low end of your hypnotic susceptibility scale than fell at the high end. In fact, your sample is fairly representative of the general population. About twice as many people are poor hypnotic subjects as are excellent ones. But note that in order to be assured

Figure A.1
A normal curve.

Number of Subjects

Measurements

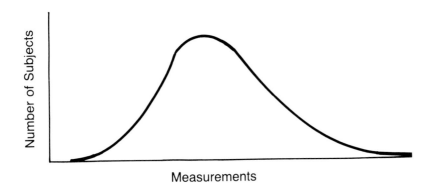

Figure A.2
A curve skewed to the right (also called a positive skew).

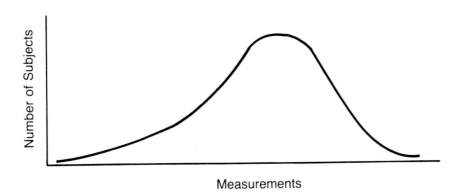

Figure A.3
A curve skewed to the left (also called a negative skew).

of obtaining the true distribution in a large population, you would usually have to test quite a large representative sample.

MEASURES OF CENTRAL TENDENCY

How would you define average?

Suppose you want to summarize in a few words the average height of people, the typical susceptibility to hypnosis, or the most common performance on an IQ test. For this you would need another kind of descriptive statistic, called a **measure of central tendency**. There are three measures of central tendency: the mean, the median, and the mode. Each is a slightly different way of describing what is "typical" within a given distribution.

The **mean** is the arithmetic average of all the individual measurements in a distribution. Suppose that ten students in a seminar take an exam. Their scores are 98, 96, 92, 88, 88, 86, 82, 80, 78, and 72. You find the mean by adding all the scores and dividing the sum by the total number of scores. In this case, the sum of all the scores is 860 and dividing this by 10 gives a mean of 86. The **median** is the score above and below which half the scores in the distribution fall. If you took our ten test results and arranged them in order from highest to lowest, the median would be the point right in the middle, between the fifth and sixth scores on the list. That would be 87. The **mode** is the most frequent measurement in a distribution, the one that occurs most often. In this group of scores, the mode is 88.

In the example just given, the mean, median, and mode are very close together, but this is not always true. In some distributions, particularly those that are strongly skewed, these three measures of central tendency may be quite far apart. In such cases, all three of the measures may be needed to give a complete understanding of what is "typical."

For instance, look at the graph in Figure A.4, which shows the distribution of income in an imaginary company. The mean income of its 50 employees is

Figure A.4
The distribution of income in an imaginary company. Note that this is not a normal distribution and the mean, median, and mode are not identical. Distributions of this kind (and of many other kinds) occur in psychology, but normal distributions are the most common.

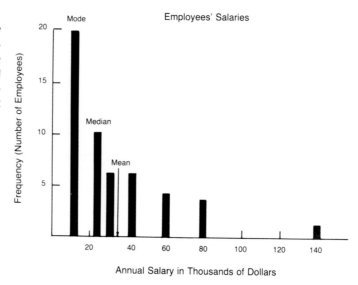

$30,600 a year, but look at the distribution. The president of the company earns $140,000, three other executives earn $80,000, and another four earn $60,000 a year. There are also six lower-level managers at $40,000, six salespeople at $30,000, and ten foremen at $25,000. The rest of the employees, the twenty people who keep the company records and run the machines, earn only $12,000 each. Thus, the mean of $30,600 does not really give a full indication of what is "typical" at this firm. A better measure of central tendency is probably the median, or $25,000. It tells us that half the people at the company earn no more than this amount. Also revealing is the mode, or most common salary; it is only $12,000 a year.

MEASURES OF VARIABILITY

Why does it matter how many other people got the same grade?

If you get an A in a course and are told that the grades range from A to F, you will feel a greater sense of accomplishment than if the grades ranged only from A to B. Why this difference in how you perceive a grade? The answer is that it is often important to take into account the extent to which scores in a distribution are spread out. In other words, it is often informative to have a **measure of variability,** an indication of how much scores vary from one another. On a graph, scores that vary greatly produce a wide, flat curve, while scores that vary little produce a curve that is narrow and steep. Figure A.5 illustrates these two patterns.

The **range,** or two most extreme scores at either end of a distribution, is one measure of variability. Another measure is called the **standard deviation.** The standard deviation takes into account all the scores in a distribution, not just the

Figure A.5
At left, a distribution with a great deal of variability. At right, a distribution with little variability.

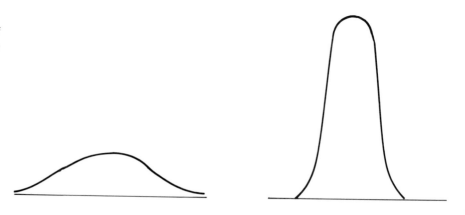

How to Find the Standard Deviation

Finding the standard deviation of a distribution is not difficult, although it is tedious without the aid of a calculator. To compute the standard deviation follow these five steps:

1. Determine the mean of all the measurements in the distribution.
2. Subtract the mean from each measurement and square the difference. (Squaring the difference eliminates the negative signs that result when dealing with measurements that fall below the mean.)
3. Add the squares together.
4. Divide the sum of the squares by the number of measurements.
5. Take the square root of the value you obtained in step 4. This figure is the standard deviation.

outermost extremes. It shows how widely these scores are scattered above and below the mean. If scores cluster closely around the mean, the standard deviation will be small; if scores are dispersed widely from the mean, the standard deviation will be large. Thus, the standard deviation is an indication of how representative the mean is. If the standard deviation is small, we know that the mean is very representative of most scores in the distribution. Conversely, if the standard deviation is large, we know that many scores are quite far from the mean. The box on this page gives the method for computing standard deviation.

Figure A.6 shows that the standard deviation divides a normal curve into several portions, each of which has a certain percentage of the total distribution. As you can see, 68.2 percent of all scores fall somewhere between the mean and one standard deviation to either side of it. If you move two standard deviations to either side of the mean, you will take in 95.4 percent of all the scores in the distribution. Finally, 99.8 percent of all the scores will fall between the mean and three standard deviations from it. Only a scant .2 percent fall beyond three standard deviations.

Knowing the mean and the standard deviation of any normal distribution allows you to determine just how "average" any given score is. For instance, suppose you take a difficult test consisting of 100 questions and receive a score of 80. How well did you perform? If you learn that the mean is 60 and the standard deviation is 8, you know that your score of 80 is very good indeed. The overwhelming majority of people—95.4 percent—scored no better than 76, or 2 standard deviations above the mean. Relative to what most others have done, an 80 is excellent. By the same token, a 40 is not very good at all; 95.4 percent of people scored 44 or higher on this test. Thus, if you received a 40 you are near the very bottom of the distribution and had better start studying much harder.

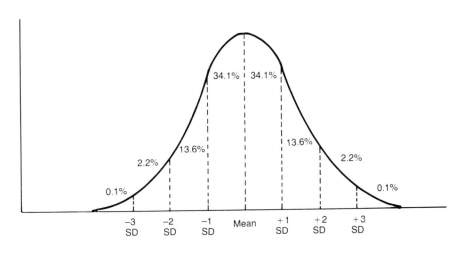

Figure A.6
A normal distribution showing the percentage of measurements that fall within 1, 2, or 3 standard deviations from the mean.

REVIEW

You are convinced you have a worse memory than almost anyone you know. To find out for sure, you randomly select 100 people from your college campus and ask them to take a simple memory test. You present your subjects with a string of 15 digits and then ask them to recall in order as many as they can. What you are collecting is data on the size of working memory. Once all this information is gathered, you must make sense of it. The tools that researchers use to analyze and summarize large amounts of data are called (1)

_____. You want to present your memory data in brief yet meaningful form. For this you need what are

called (2) _____ statistics.

You begin by making a list of all the scores received on your test, marking next to each one how frequently that particular score occurred. What you are laying out is called

a (3) _____ distribution. You discover that all of your subjects remembered somewhere between 5 and 9 of the digits on your list. This statistic, which states the two outermost extremes in a distribution, is called the

(4) _____. The range is one measure of

(5) _____, one indication of how much the scores in a distribution are spread out. A more sensitive

measure of variability is the (6) _____

_____ . It takes into account *all* the scores in a distribution, not just the outermost extremes.

When you plot your distribution on a graph you find it produces a steep, bell-shaped curve with an equal number of subjects falling on each side of the middle. Such a curve

is known as a (7) _____ _____ , and the distribution from which it is plotted is called a

(8) _____ _____ . If unwittingly you had included in your sample a large number of people who had taken a course in mnemonics (techniques for improving memory), there would have been relatively fewer scores at the low end of your scale and relatively more at the

high end. This is known as a (9) _____ distribution. When plotted it produces a curve with a "tail" on one end.

The graph of your data shows at a glance that 7 is the most frequently received score on your test—that is, most people recalled only 7 of the 15 digits. Another way of saying

this is that 7 is the (10) _____, or most frequently occurring score in the distribution. The mode is one

measure of (11) _____ _____, one indication of what is "typical" in a set of data. Two other measures of central tendency are the arithmetic average,

called the (12) _____, and the score above and below which half the scores fall, known as the

(13) _____. In your distribution the mean, median, and mode all equal 7. You find that when you take this test yourself, you too receive a score of 7. This tells you that your working memory is not nearly as bad as you thought.

Answers: (1) statistics; (2) descriptive; (3) frequency; (4) range; (5) variability; (6) standard deviation; (7) normal curve; (8) normal distribution; (9) skewed; (10) mode; (11) central tendency; (12) mean; (13) median

GLOSSARY TERMS

descriptive statistics (p. 591)
frequency distribution (p. 592)
mean (p. 593)

measure of central tendency (p. 593)
measure of variability (p. 594)
median (p. 593)

mode (p. 593)
normal curve (p. 592)
normal distribution (p. 592)
range (p. 594)

skewed distribution (p. 592)
standard deviation (p. 594)
statistics (p. 591)

Module 2 Inferential Statistics

In the mid-1970s many Americans were puzzled to learn that a distinguished panel of scientists could not determine with absolute certainty whether the artificial sweetener called cyclamate posed a risk of cancer. The scientists announced that based on months of research, costing millions of dollars, they could be only 95 percent sure that cyclamate was safe. Why this remaining margin of doubt? Why can't a team of highly skilled researchers, backed by government funds, manage to tell us absolutely if a substance is hazardous to our health?

Can scientists be 100 percent certain?

CHANCE AND RELIABILITY

The answer is that no one can totally eliminate the influence of chance on scientific findings. Even when you randomly select groups of subjects there is always the possibility that, just by chance, those groups will differ slightly in ways that affect your experiment. This is why scientists must rely on statistics to tell them the likelihood that a certain set of results could have happened purely by chance. If this likelihood is small—5 percent or less—the researchers are justified in rejecting the chance explanation and concluding instead that their findings are probably reliable. "Reliable" means that the investigators would probably obtain similar results if they repeated their study over and over with different groups of subjects.

Determining the reliability of experimental findings is a major way in which psychologists use **inferential statistics.** Inferential statistics are a set of procedures for determining what conclusions can be legitimately inferred from a set of data. These procedures include what are called **tests of statistical significance.** Tests of statistical significance were used to determine the 95 percent certainty of the finding that cyclamate is safe to eat. Different tests of statistical significance are needed for different kinds of data.

TESTS OF STATISTICAL SIGNIFICANCE

Let's return to one of the examples in the preview to this appendix—the educational psychologist who devised a special program for teaching children with learning disabilities. The psychologist's study produced two different mean IQs, with the experimental group's mean 10 points higher than that of the control group. Is this enough of a difference to reject the chance explanation and conclude that the program was a success? The most frequent procedure for answering questions like this is a test of statistical significance called the **t-test.**

Is this program successful?

The t-Test

Imagine that the results of the psychologist's experiment looked like the ones in Figure A.7. The mean IQs of the two groups differ by 10 points: 75 for the experimental subjects and 65 for the controls. But look at the variability in the two distributions; there is almost none. All the children in the experimental group received a score within 5 points of 75; all the children in the control group receive a score within 5 points of 65. It seems that some genuine effect is at work here. The IQ patterns in the two groups are so distinctly different. These are not the kinds of differences usually caused by chance.

Unfortunately, the results of most experiments are not this clear-cut. Far more often the distributions look more like those in Figure A.8. Here you can see that the mean difference in scores is still 10 points, but now there is a sizable amount of variability in the two groups. In fact, some of the experimental subjects are doing no better than some of the controls, while some of the controls are scoring

When is a mean difference reliable?

Figure A.7

Two possible distributions of IQ scores. The control group has a mean of 65, the experimental group a mean of 75. When distributions in a study show this little variability and no overlap between the two curves, they are not very likely to have happened purely by chance.

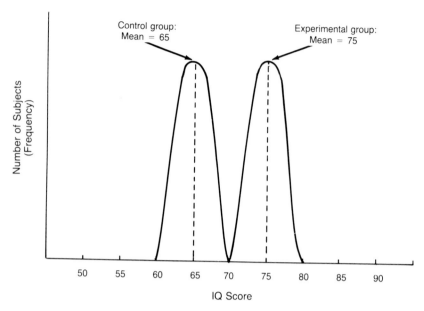

Figure A.8

A much more likely set of distributions than the one in Figure A.7. The mean is still 65 for the control group and 75 for the experimental group. But now the variability of the distributions is substantially greater. There is also substantial overlap between the two curves. Is the mean difference in this case statistically significant? A *t*-test can provide the answer.

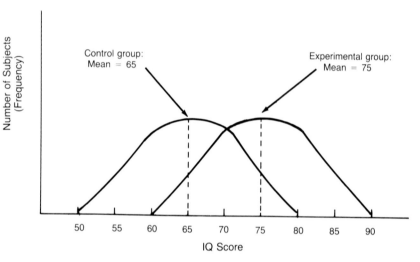

as high as some of those in the experimental program. Is a mean difference of 10 points in this case large enough to be considered reliable?

The *t*-test is an estimate of reliability that takes into account both the size of the mean difference and the variability in distributions. The *greater* the mean difference and the *less* the variability, the less the likelihood that the results happened purely by chance. The *t*-test also considers how many subjects are included in the study. You should not put much faith in a comparison of educational programs that tries out each approach on only two or three children. There is too much chance that such samples are not representative of the larger population from which they are drawn. Let's say that in the hypothetical experiment we have been describing the psychologist included 100 randomly selected children in each of the two groups. It is much less likely that samples of this size would be biased enough to distort the researcher's findings. If you want to know the steps involved in actually performing the *t*-test, read the box on the opposite page.

Analysis of Variance

What is an ANOVA?

Not all data lend themselves to a *t*-test, however. Often researchers want to compare the mean scores of more than two groups, or they want to make comparisons among groups that are classified in more than one way (for instance, does age or sex have an effect on how much children benefit from our special educational

How to Perform the *t*-Test

The *t*-test is an estimate of how reliable the difference between two means is. To determine the likelihood that the outcome occurred by chance, we first need to know the size of the mean difference (mean 1 minus mean 2). In general, the larger the mean difference the less the likelihood that it happened by chance alone. We also need a measure of the variability within the two distributions. This is called the *variance* within each group. In general, the less the variances, the less the likelihood that chance alone caused the results. Finally, we need to know how many subjects are in the random samples. In general, the larger the samples, the less the likelihood of a purely chance explanation. To calculate the *t*-test just follow these steps:

1. Determine the mean of the scores for each group and subtract one from the other.
2. Go back to the box on standard deviation and work through that calculation for each of your distributions, stopping at step 4. This gives you the variance of each distribution.
3. Add the two variances.
4. Add the total number of subjects minus 2 (in our example $200 - 2 = 198$).
5. Divide the summed variances by the number obtained in step 4 and take the square root.
6. Divide the mean difference between the two groups by the square root from step 5.

If the samples add up to more than 50 individuals, any value of *t* over 2 is statistically reliable more than 95 percent of the time.

program?). In such cases another test of statistical significance is needed. This test is called an **analysis of variance,** or **ANOVA** for short. An analysis of variance is rather like a more complex *t*-test. To learn more about the ANOVA technique, consult any introductory statistics text.

Chi-Square

Sometimes the data psychologists collect do not consist of sets of scores with group means or averages. Instead, the researchers have recorded who does what, or who falls into which of several categories. For instance, psychologists have found that chess players are more apt to be introverts than they are to be extroverts. Is this just a chance association? To answer such questions the **chi-square** is a frequent test of statistical significance.

Suppose you are a psychologist who wants to study the usefulness of fear tactics in changing people's behavior. You randomly select 200 habitual smokers who are willing to participate in an experiment. You expose half to a 20-minute talk on the known health hazards of smoking, complete with graphic illustrations of diseased lungs and hearts. You expose the rest to a 20-minute talk on the history of tobacco. After the talks, the members of each group are given the opportunity to sign up for a free "quit smoking" clinic. Some people from each group sign up for the clinic, while others do not. The easiest way to present their choices is with a 2 × 2 table, like the one set up in Table A.1.

Table A.2 shows how the distribution worked out in your study. Of the 100 subjects in your experimental group (the ones exposed to the fear tactic), 60 signed up for the quit-smoking clinic and 40 did not. Of the 100 subjects in the control group, 40 signed up for the free clinic and 60 did not. Is this difference in the distribution of choices statistically significant?

The chi-square estimates the reliability of such a difference by comparing it with the expected distribution if people had made their decisions purely by

Is it chance that chess players are more likely to be introverts?

TABLE A.1   The Format of a 2 × 2 Table

Talk heard	Signed up for clinic	Didn't sign up	Row total
Fear tactics			100
No fear tactics			100
Column totals			200 (Grand total)

TABLE A.2   Study Results in Our Example

Talk heard	Signed up for clinic	Didn't sign up	Row total
Fear tactics	60	40	100
No fear tactics	40	60	100
Column totals	100	100	200 (Grand total)

chance—for instance, by the toss of a coin. If chance had been the deciding factor, the same number of people would be expected to sign up for the clinic in each of the two groups. The accompanying box gives a step-by-step description of how to do the chi-square calculation.

How to Calculate Chi-Square

Chi-square (χ^2) is an estimate of how sure we can be that a distribution of events or of people did not happen just by chance. In our example, chi-square calculates the *expected* number of people that a chance distribution would place in each of the four cells in the table. This expected number is then compared with the actual *observed* number of people who fall into each cell (the data presented in Table A.2). If the difference between the expected and observed numbers is large enough, the distribution is not likely to have happened by chance alone. Here are the steps in making the chi-square calculation:

1. Figure out how many people, by chance alone, would be likely to fall into the upper-left cell. To do this, multiply the first row total by the first column total (100 × 100) and divide by the grand total (200). The expected number is 50.
2. Subtract the expected number (50) from the observed number in the upper-left cell (60). The difference is 10 (60 − 50 = 10). Square the difference to eliminate negative signs (10 × 10 = 100) and divide the result by the expected number: 100 ÷ 50 = 2.
3. Repeat steps 1 and 2 for each of the four cells. In this example the expected values are the same for each cell, but that won't always be true.
4. Sum the four values you get from calculating the difference between the expected and observed number for each cell. This is the chi-square.

The reliability of the chi-square value must be looked up in a table. In this example, the fear tactic subjects signed up for the clinic so much more often than the control subjects did that this distribution could have occurred by chance only two times in a hundred.

REVIEW

Your interest in human memory has been piqued by the study you conducted earlier. You begin to wonder whether working memory declines when a person grows older. You look back through your sample of 100 subjects and find two people over age 65. One received a score of 8 on your memory test and the other a score of 9. Their mean score of 8.5 is 1.5 points higher than the overall mean of 7. Can you conclude from this that working memory span generally increases with age? To answer this question, you would have to use procedures for determining what conclusions can be legitimately inferred from data. These procedures are known as (1) _____ statistics.

What you need is a test that estimates the probability of a set of data occurring by chance. This is called a test of (2) _____ _____. The specific test of statistical significance needed in your case is one that estimates how reliable the difference between two means is.

This is known as the (3) _____ - _____.

The *t*-test takes into account the size of the mean difference, the variability in the two distributions, and the number of subjects sampled. You quickly realize that your sample of only two older people is far too small to be reliable. It is quite likely that, just by chance, these two individuals have working memory capacities slightly larger than the overall mean.

Different tests of statistical significance are needed for different kinds of data. If you wanted to compare the mean scores of more than two groups, you could use what is called an (4) _____ of _____, or ANOVA for short. If you wanted to estimate the probability that a certain distribution of events or people didn't happen by chance, you could use a calculation known as the (5) _____ - _____. Whenever the probability of a chance explanation is quite low—only 5 times out of 100 or less—researchers are justified in concluding that their findings are very likely reliable.

Answers: (1) inferential; (2) statistical significance; (3) *t*-test; (4) analysis of variance; (5) chi-square

GLOSSARY TERMS

analysis of variance
   (ANOVA) (p. 599)
chi square (p. 599)

inferential statistics
   (p. 597)

t-test (p. 597)

tests of statistical
   significance (p. 597)

Glossary

absolute threshold The lowest level of stimulus energy needed in order for that stimulus to be perceived. Since this level varies depending upon the person and certain other conditions, an absolute threshold is often defined as the stimulus intensity a given individual can detect 50 percent of the time.

accommodation (1) In physiological psychology, accommodation is the process by which the muscles controlling the lens of each eye contract when you are viewing a very near object (thereby making the lenses rounder) and relax when you are viewing an object farther away (thereby making the lenses flatter). The brain uses the degree of accommodation as a cue to depth. (2) In Jean Piaget's theory of cognitive development, accommodation refers to modifying present strategies or concepts in response to some new environmental demand.

achievement motivation The motivation to perform well, reach high goals, and demonstrate competence. Sometimes also called *need for achievement*.

acquaintance rapist The rapist who is acquainted with his victim and who is often motivated more by sex than other rapists are.

acquired immune deficiency syndrome (AIDS) A virus, also known as HIV, that attacks the immune system which normally protects us from disease. HIV destroys many components and takes over cells of the immune system and uses them for its own reproduction. As HIV destroys the immune system, the AIDS sufferer becomes vulnerable to life-threatening diseases such as pneumonia. The majority of those infected in the United States have been homosexual and bisexual men, intravenous drug users, and prostitutes. At present there is no known cure for the disease.

action potential A sudden reversal in the polarity of a neuron's membrane, causing the inside of the membrane to be temporarily positive in charge relative to the outside.

activation-synthesis theory of dreaming The view that dreaming is caused by nothing more than random activity of neurons in the pons during REM sleep. The cortex then tries to make sense of these incoming signals, and the result is what we call a dream.

actor-observer effect The tendency to explain your own negative behaviors in terms of situational factors, but to explain negative behavior in others in terms of dispositional traits.

acupuncture A pain relief method in which small needles are inserted into various points on the body, often far removed from the site of the pain.

adaptation level theory A theory that explains why we eventually take new pleasures for granted. This theory has two principles, contrast and habituation. Because of the contrast principle, exceedingly good fortune makes ordinary things seem less pleasurable and thus takes away some of the happiness of the good fortune. Because of the habituation principle, we eventually take new pleasures for granted, and thus they contribute less and less to our level of happiness.

addiction A state of dependency in which a certain drug is needed for normal functioning. If the drug is suddenly stopped, an addicted person will experience withdrawal symptoms.

affective disorders Psychological disorders characterized by disturbances of mood or affect.

age regression Acting and thinking as if you were much younger than you are.

aggressive behavior An action intended to injure or irritate another person.

alarm stage The first stage in Selye's general adaptation syndrome, characterized by a state of physiological arousal.

alcoholic Usually defined as someone who has drunk heavily for a long period of time and has had problems in two or three major life areas, such as in social, personal, financial, medical, legal, or business matters.

alcohol-seeking behavior The behavior that begins in adolescence and early adulthood and contributes to developing alcoholism. An alcohol-seeking person tends to act impulsively, take risks, and engage in antisocial behaviors, such as getting into fights.

all-or-none law The fact that once a nerve impulse is started, it continues down the entire length of the neuron's axon, no matter how long the axon is.

alpha waves Low-amplitude, moderately slow-frequency brain waves (8–12 cycles per second) that occur in the EEG of a person who is relaxed, with eyes closed.

altered state of consciousness A pattern of mental awareness that diverges from what we experience when wide awake and alert.

altruism Doing something for others, often at a cost or risk to yourself, with no expectation of receiving a material or social reward.

amnesia A persistent total or partial forgetting of past experiences, often due to some kind of brain disorder, but occasionally caused simply by severe psychological stress.

amniocentesis The process of obtaining with a needle a

sample of cells sloughed off from a fetus as it develops inside the mother's uterus.

amplitude   The height of a wave, such as a sound wave or a brain wave.

anal stage   The second of Freud's stages of psychosexual development, during which toddlers focus their strivings for pleasure on sensations arising from movements of the bowels. Toilet training becomes a potential area of conflict during this time.

analgesia   Insensitivity to pain.

analysis of variance (ANOVA)   A test of statistical significance used when researchers want to compare the mean scores of more than two groups, or when they want to make comparisons among groups that are classified in more than one way.

androgyny   The idea that an individual may possess at the same time both "masculine" and "feminine" personality characteristics.

anger rapist   The rapist whose attack is characterized by impulsive and savage physical violence.

anorexia nervosa   A disorder characterized by deliberate and severe restriction of eating, excessive amounts of energy, a great desire to be very thin, and an intense fear of gaining weight.

anterograde amnesia   A form of amnesia that impairs memory only for events that happen *after* the disorder sets in.

antidepressant drugs   Drugs used to combat depression.

antipsychotics   Drugs used to reduce the bizarre hallucinations and delusions that mental health professionals label "psychotic."

antisocial personality disorder   A type of personality disorder characterized by flagrant disregard for obligations, unabashed lying, total lack of guilt or remorse, very impulsive, often reckless behavior, and failure to learn from experience.

anxiety   An unpleasant state which we associate with feelings of uneasiness and apprehension.

anxiously attached infant   A baby who is apparently insecure about the availability of the parents or other principal caregivers when comfort and reassurance are needed.

apparent motion   The illusion of motion created by presenting a rapid series of still images of movements. Apparent motion is distinguished from the actual motion that can be observed in real life.

approach-approach conflict   The conflict that arises when you must decide between two options, both of which are desirable.

approach-avoidance conflict   The conflict that arises when you must decide whether or not to do something that has both desirable and undesirable consequences.

assimilation   In Jean Piaget's theory of cognitive development, assimilation refers to incorporating some object or experience into present strategies or concepts.

association area   Area of the cortex that participates in higher-order mental processes.

associations   The relationship of one idea, perception, feeling, or event to another.

atmospheric perspective   A depth cue created by the presence of smog, dust, or mist which gives distant objects a hazy look and makes them appear farther away.

attentional processing   Encoding of information into long-term memory that involves deliberately paying attention and trying to store the data.

attitude   A positive or negative feeling toward some object or action.

attribution   The explanation we offer for why things happen as they do.

auditory fatigue   A temporary drop in the sensitivity of the auditory system after significant exposure to loud noise.

auditory nerve   A bundle of neural fibers that travels from the cochlea in each inner ear to the brain.

automatic encoding   Encoding of information into long-term memory that takes place very quickly without deliberate effort.

autonomic nervous system   See **autonomic pathways**.

autonomic pathways   Pathways in the peripheral nervous system that regulate involuntary actions of internal organs and glands, such as heartbeat, digestive processes, blood vessel contractions, and so forth. These pathways are collectively called the autonomic nervous system (ANS).

aversion training   Deliberately instilling an aversion to some unwanted behavior by repeatedly pairing it with an unpleasant stimulus, such as a drug that produces nausea or a mild electric shock.

avoidance-avoidance conflict   The conflict that arises when you must decide between two options, both of which are undesirable.

axon   A relatively long, single fiber extending away from the main body of a neuron and carrying information to a neighboring neuron, muscle, or gland.

babbling   The prespeech one-syllable utterances that babies make beginning at about 6 months of age.

Barnum principle   A strategy for appealing to the widest possible audience by phrasing something so generally that virtually everyone will think it applies to them. This technique is named after the famous circus owner P. T. Barnum.

basilar membrane   A membrane within the cochlea of the inner ear that contains the auditory receptors or hair cells.

behavior modification   See **behavior therapy**.

behavior therapy   A therapeutic approach that identifies a person's specific maladaptive behaviors and then applies learning principles in a deliberate effort to change them. Also called **behavior modification**.

behavioral intention   A plan to behave in some particular way.

behavioral perspective   An approach to understanding behavior that focuses on how specific stimuli in the environment elicit or encourage specific responses through learned associations.

behavioral rehearsal   A technique used in cognitive-behavior modification in which clients imagine performing some desired behavior so as to become aware of maladaptive thoughts that may be thwarting that behavior in everyday life.

behavioral theory of sleep   A theory that focuses on the biological factors underlying sleep: According to this theory, an animal's sleep patterns evolved because of the interaction between the animal's characteristics and its environment. Human ancestors slept at night because nighttime activity was dangerous. The human behavioral trait of sleeping at night thus developed because it helped humans to survive.

behaviorists   A school of psychologists who were interested in how individuals behave. They believed that the human mind could not be studied scientifically and that factors in the environment are probably the greatest influence on behavior. Originally behavioral psychologists studied only the external environment—what could be observed. Today, however, some behaviorists study the internal environment (beliefs, thoughts, feelings).

beliefs   Opinions or convictions that form the basis of a person's attitudes.

beta waves   Low-amplitude, fast-frequency brain waves (12 to 30 cycles per second) that predominate in the EEG of a person who is wide awake, with eyes open.

biofeedback   Any process that allows you to monitor a physiological response you would not normally be aware of, and which then involves trying to make that response more favorable.

biological marker A chemical or physiological factor in the body that can serve as an indicator that a particular disorder is present.

biological perspective An approach to understanding behavior that focuses on the workings of the brain, the nervous system, and the body's hormones.

bipolar disorder A type of affective disorder in which periods of depression are interspersed with periods of exaggerated elation or mania.

bisexual A person who is sexually attracted to members of both sexes.

brainstorming A group technique for encouraging divergent thinking in which group members are required not to criticize each other's suggestions, to generate as many ideas as possible, to attempt to be original, and to build on what others propose.

brightness constancy The perception of stable brightness even though actual brightness changes substantially.

Broca's area A region in the left frontal lobe of the brain's cortex that plays a vital role in the process of articulating speech sounds.

bulimia An eating disorder characterized by periodic gorging, often followed by self-induced vomiting or overuse of laxatives.

bystander effect When the presence of onlookers inhibits people from helping others.

catatonic schizophrenia A type of schizophrenia whose symptoms include periods of wild excitement and/or periods of rigid, prolonged immobility, with the person sometimes assuming the same frozen posture for hours.

catecholamine theory The theory that depression results when the levels of catecholamines in the brain are extremely low, and that mania results when catecholamine levels are extremely high.

catecholamines A type of neurotransmitter in the brain thought to be involved in affective disorders.

central nervous system All the many interconnected neurons contained in the brain and spinal cord.

cerebellum A region of the hindbrain that serves as a kind of coordination center for voluntary movements and balance.

chemical sense The senses of taste and smell, which both respond to the chemical structure of substances.

chi-square A test of statistical significance that is used when psychologists' data do not consist of sets of scores with group means or averages, but of recordings of who does what or who falls into which of several categories.

chromosomes Structures found within every cell of an organism's body and which carry that organism's genes.

chronological age A person's age in years and months.

chunking Grouping a number of items to be remembered into a unit, which is then processed as a whole.

circadian rhythm A naturally occurring daily cycle in the body, such as the sleep-wake cycle.

classical conditioning The process of pairing a neutral stimulus with some stimulus that elicits a reflex response, until the previously neutral stimulus itself elicits the reflex.

classical theory of concept formation The theory that people come to learn the meaning of a concept by becoming aware of the defining characteristics which instances of that concept share.

classical threshold theory An approach to studying perceptual thresholds dating back to the nineteenth century. It assumes that for any type of stimulus, such as light or sound, there is an absolute level below which a particular person can no longer perceive that stimulus.

clinical interview A personal interview that a mental health professional conducts in order to assess the condition of a person suspected to be suffering from a psychological disorder.

clinical psychologists Psychologists concerned with determining the causes of emotional problems, assessing personality, and developing treatment programs. They have completed Ph.D. programs and studied under the guidance of an experienced psychologist. Unlike psychiatrists, clinical psychologists do not assess the physical causes of mental problems or prescribe drugs.

closure The principle of perception that says we tend to fill in missing parts of a figure and see the figure as complete.

cochlea A set of spiral-shaped tubes in the inner ear, filled with fluid and containing the basilar membrane.

cochlear implant A treatment for certain cases of neural deafness in which a miniature electronic device is implanted in the ear and takes the place of damaged hair cells.

cognitive Pertaining to mental activities of any kind.

cognitive-behavior modification A therapeutic approach that identifies a person's maladaptive behaviors and negative, self-defeating thoughts, and then applies learning principles in an effort to eliminate these problems.

cognitive components approach An approach to understanding human intelligence that tries to explore the nature of the various mental processes different people use in thinking and reasoning.

cognitive dissonance A state of mental discord that arises when behavior is inconsistent with attitudes. According to Leon Festinger's theory of cognitive dissonance, people usually seek to reduce this unpleasant state by changing their cognitions in some way.

cognitive learning Learning that involves perceiving, processing, and manipulating new and remembered information.

cognitive perspective An approach to understanding behavior that focuses on individuals' mental activities, particularly on how they process, store, and use information.

cognitive schema See **schema**.

cognitive-social approach to personality An approach to understanding human personality that focuses on both a person's cognitive processes (how he or she perceives the world) and on environmental pressures the person experiences.

cognitive social psychology The study of how various cognitive processes influence how social information is interpreted.

cognitive theories Theories that explain human motivation by referring to what takes place in a person's mind, such as beliefs, expectations, and explanations.

cognitive theory of emotions The theory which holds that after you are physiologically aroused by a situation, you identify the emotion according to thoughts and environmental cues.

color constancy The perception of stable colors despite color changes due to differences in lighting.

compliance Behavior performed under the pressure of being directly asked to perform it.

compulsions Irresistible impulses to perform some act or ritual over and over.

concepts Mental constructs that enable a person to classify things by what those things have in common.

concrete operations stage In Jean Piaget's theory, this is the stage of cognitive development lasting from about ages 7 to 11 during which children become able to perform logical operations on concrete objects and events.

conditioned response A classical conditioning term referring to a new response elicited by a previously neutral stimulus due to the learning process.

conditioned stimulus A classical conditioning term referring to a stimulus that elicits a new response as a result of the learning process.

conduction deafness Deafness caused by injury to the eardrum or to the bones of the middle ear. The term comes from the fact that vibrations from sound waves weaken or die in the process of conduction to the oval window.

cones Photoreceptors in the eye's retina that allow us to see colors and fine details.

conformity Behavior performed because of group pressure, even though that pressure involves no direct requests.

consciousness An awareness of one's own mental processes.

consistency theory The theory that people try to maintain consistency among their beliefs, attitudes, and behaviors.

contingency management The process of giving and withdrawing rewards contingent upon performance of some desired behavior.

continuity A principle of perception that says we tend to perceive a series of points or lines along a smooth or continuous path.

continuous reinforcement schedule A schedule for delivering reinforcement in which every target behavior emitted is followed by a reinforcer.

control group In an experiment, a group of subjects that experience the same conditions as the experimental group *except* the key factor that the researcher is trying to assess. A control group thus provides an essential source of comparison.

conventional level of moral reasoning In Lawrence Kohlberg's theory of moral development, the stage at which rules are obeyed so as to do the "right" thing, to gain approval from others, or to maintain law and order. Most adolescents are presumably at this level.

convergence The tendency of the eyes to converge, or turn inward, in order to focus on a near object, that inward turning becoming greater the nearer the object is. The brain uses the degree of convergence as a cue to depth.

convergent thinking Thinking that involves focusing on a single approach or solution to a problem.

conversion disorder A type of somatoform disorder in which the bodily organs are healthy, but the person reports physical problems.

coping Trying to deal with stressful or disturbing situations through a variety of strategies.

cornea The transparent layer that covers the very front of the eye.

corpus callosum A band of nerve fibers that connects the two hemispheres of the forebrain.

correlation A relationship between two variables such that the occurrence of one can be used to predict to some extent the occurrence of the other.

correlation coefficient A statistical measure of the strength and direction of the relationship between two variables.

cortex A layer at the top of the forebrain that controls and co-ordinates an animal's most complex behaviors. In humans, the cortex provides impressive powers of thought and reasoning.

counterattitudinal behavior Public behavior that is counter to private attitudes.

creativity The ability to generate fresh approaches or to produce solutions that are highly original.

critical period A limited period of development during which a human or other animal is especially susceptible to acquiring a certain behavior.

cross-gender behaviors Behaviors deemed appropriate for the sex opposite to that to which a person belongs.

cross-sectional study A study in which a group of different-aged individuals are all studied at the same time.

crowd A large group of individuals, most of whom are not acquainted with one another.

cultural bias Bias toward the members of a particular social group.

culture-free test A test that is not unfairly influenced by the social and cultural backgrounds of those who take it.

date rapist See **acquaintance rapist**.

debriefing An interview with subjects held after an experiment is over in order to explain the study's purpose and method, to find out how subjects feel about their participation, and to dispel any possible misgivings or guilt subjects may have concerning the way they behaved.

deep structure A term proposed by the linguist Noam Chomsky to refer to a sentence's underlying meaning, which is represented in memory.

defense mechanisms In psychoanalytic theory, unconscious processes that reduce anxiety by causing a person to reinterpret or distort perceptions of the self and others.

defining characteristics Certain characteristics that are always present in an object. According to classical theory, we learn to identify objects because of these features.

deindividuation Losing a subjective sense of personal identity, including the sense of being accountable for your own actions. Deindividuation sometimes occurs when people are submerged in crowds and may increase the likelihood of antisocial acts.

delinquency A repetitive and persistent pattern of behaving so that the rights of others or of society are violated.

delta sleep The deepest stage of sleep, characterized by delta brain waves that are very slow in frequency and very high in amplitude.

dendrites The branchlike extensions of a neuron that receive information from the environment or from other neurons and carry it to the main body of the cell.

denial A defense mechanism in which we refuse to recognize some anxiety-provoking event or piece of information.

dependency (drug) The strong psychological need or desire to use a drug.

dependent variable An aspect of the behavior of an experimental subject that is expected to change as a result of a condition the researcher manipulates.

depressants Drugs that suppress normal activities in the central nervous system, causing slowed reactions, loss of physical coordination, and eventually unconsciousness. Alcohol is an example.

descriptive statistics Numbers used to present a collection of data in a brief yet meaningful form.

desensitization A behavior therapy technique for reducing anxiety or eliminating a phobia. Deliberate relaxation is practiced while threatening situations are presented in hierarchical order from least to most feared.

developmental (problems) Problems that occurred or began in childhood.

developmental psychologists Psychologists who study the physiological aspects of human behavior as well as how a person develops morally, personally, intellectually, and emotionally. They are concerned with the entire life cycle, from fetal development through old age.

dichromats People who have only two kinds of light-sensitive chemicals in the cones of the retina (instead of three), and who therefore have trouble distinguishing certain colors (usually red from green).

difficult babies Babies who are generally fussy, fearful of new situations, and tend to have relatively intense reactions to things.

diffusion of responsibility The tendency for people in a group to feel less personal responsibility for helping during an emergency because it is not clear who within the group should step forward and take action.

discrimination Unfair behaviors exhibited toward members of a particular group or category of people.

disease-prone personality A combination of traits associated with disease. The relationship between personality traits such as anxiety, depression, anger, and hostility and disease is comparable to that reported for other medical risk factors.

disorganized schizophrenia A type of schizophrenia characterized by very childish behavior, bizarre ideas, confused speech, great emotional swings, and often extreme neglect of personal appearance and hygiene.

displacement The redirecting of an emotion toward a safer, more acceptable target.

dispositional attribution Attributing someone's behavior to an internal factor such as personality, intelligence, or motivation.

dissociative disorder A psychological disorder in which part of a person's memory or personality is split off or dissociated.

divergent thinking Thinking that involves generating many possible approaches or solutions to a problem. Divergent thinking is often considered a measure of creativity.

DNA (deoxyribonucleic acid) The chemical substance of which genes are composed.

dominant gene A gene that will express itself whenever it is present, sometimes overriding the effects of another (recessive) gene.

dopamine theory The theory that the symptoms of schizophrenia are caused in part by increased activity in the system of brain cells that respond to the neurotransmitter dopamine.

double-blind technique Deliberately keeping both researchers and subjects in an experiment ignorant of who has experienced the experimental condition. This technique is intended to prevent participants in a study from turning the hypothesis being tested into a self-fulfilling prophecy.

double standard Two different sets of standards applied to two different groups of people. It is most commonly used in reference to sexual behavior, where expectations for males are more lenient than those for females.

Down's syndrome A developmental disorder that occurs when the mother's ovum, or sometimes the father's sperm, contains not one twenty-first chromosome, but two. Down's syndrome children have both abnormal physical traits and abnormal brain development, resulting in mental retardation.

dream analysis An important technique of psychoanalysis in which patients' dreams are examined for hidden meanings that may give clues to unconscious conflicts. Sigmund Freud believed that dreams often express the repressed feelings and wishes that are harbored in the unconscious.

drive An aroused state caused by some biological need, such as the need for food, water, oxygen, or avoidance of pain.

DSM-IIIR The abbreviation for the revised third edition of the *Diagnostic and Statistical Manual of Mental Disorders* published by the American Psychiatric Association. DSM-IIIR describes the symptoms of a variety of psychological disorders and provides mental health professionals with a system for diagnosing those disorders.

ear canal The short tunnel between the outer ear and the eardrum.

eardrum A thin membrane at the end of the ear canal that moves in and out in response to sound wave patterns.

easy babies Babies who are generally happy and quick to adapt to new situations.

eclectic Not following any one system, but selecting and using what are considered the best elements of various systems.

ECT See **electroconvulsive shock therapy**.

EEG See **electroencephalogram**.

ego In Freudian theory, a division of the mind that develops from the id and tries to find safe and socially acceptable ways of satisfying the id's desires.

egocentric Centered on the self and one's own feelings, thoughts, and perspectives. Egocentric individuals usually assume that others must feel and think the same way they do.

egocentrism See **egocentric**.

eidetic imagery Extremely clear and detailed visual images that persist for at least a few minutes after the stimulus that produced them has been removed. The ability to form eidetic imagery is most common in children under 12.

elaborative rehearsal The repeating of information and making new associations that will likely result in encoding the information into long-term memory.

electroconvulsive shock therapy (ECT) A treatment for severe and persistent depression in which a mild electrical current is passed through the brain, causing a seizure which for unknown reasons is therapeutic.

electroencephalogram (EEG) The printout produced by a machine that monitors brain wave activity.

emotional isolation The state of having the need for intimacy with someone special go unfulfilled.

encoding The act of attending to new information, perhaps using old information to analyze or manipulate the new, and then placing the result into long-term memory.

endorphins Naturally occurring chemicals in the body that act as hormones and neurotransmitters and that have essentially the same properties as morphine, a powerful painkiller.

enkephalins A class of natural body chemicals, related to the endorphins, which are believed to play a role in reactions to pain.

environmental factors Factors that explain why alcoholism runs in families. Environmental factors might include difficulties that children of alcoholics have in showing too much or too little trust and dependency in relationships and careers. Psychological problems may then lead to substance abuse by the adult children of alcoholic parents.

envy Wanting or coveting what someone else has and to which you have no claim.

episodic memories Memories that deal with distinct episodes you personally encounter.

equilibrium In Jean Piaget's theory of cognitive development, equilibrium is a state of cognitive harmony with the environment which is restored through the process of accommodation.

erectile dysfunction—organic The inability to have or maintain an erection because of some organic or physical problem. The disorder can result from alcoholism, diseases such as diabetes, and in rare cases, abnormally low levels of testosterone. It is also a side effect of some prescription drugs.

errors of overgeneralization Mistakes that involve applying a rule or concept in instances where it should not be applied.

ESP See **extrasensory perception**.

estrogen A female hormone produced by the ovaries.

excitement stage The first of four stages in Masters and Johnson's model of human sexual response. During the excitement stage, sexual stimuli arouse the body and begin to prepare it for sexual intercourse.

exhaustion stage The third and last stage in Selye's general adaptation syndrome, characterized by suppression of the immune system, greater susceptibility to infection, and possible breakdown of the body's internal organs.

expectations   Ideas about what is likely to happen.

experiment   A study conducted in accordance with the experimental method.

experimental group   A group of subjects in an experiment who experience some specific condition, the impact of which the researcher is trying to assess.

experimental method   A set of procedures for studying cause-and-effect relationships in which researchers carefully control conditions so as to rule out all other influences on their subjects' behavior except the factor being examined.

experimental psychologists   Psychologists who are concerned primarily with how we remember, think, and process information. In their research regarding sensation, perception, learning, motivation, and emotion, they have discovered principles that form the basis for teaching retarded children, developing weight-loss programs, and helping people overcome phobias.

extinction   The gradual weakening and eventual disappearance of a learned response.

extrasensory perception   Any perception that supposedly occurs outside normal sensory processes.

extroversion   The tendency to be outgoing and friendly, to seek out social activities and excitement, and to prefer to participate in events rather than merely to think about them.

facial feedback hypothesis   The idea that your brain's interpretation of muscle movements in your face as you adopt certain facial expressions is a primary cause of your subjective feelings of emotion.

fear of failure   The tendency to view the very thought of failure as highly threatening to self-esteem.

fertilization   The process by which a sperm cell penetrates an egg cell and starts the development of a new individual.

fetal alcohol syndrome (FAS)   A combination of physical and psychological symptoms found in babies whose mothers drank heavily during pregnancy.

figure and ground   A simple kind of perceptual organization in which part of what is perceived is made the center of attention (the figure), while the rest is considered less important (background).

first words   Words uttered at about 1 year of age. They usually refer to what can be seen, heard, and felt.

fixed-interval schedule of reinforcement   A partial reinforcement schedule in which a reinforcer is given following the first target behavior emitted after a fixed amount of time has passed.

fixed-ratio schedule of reinforcement   A partial reinforcement schedule in which a reinforcer is given after a fixed number of target behaviors have been emitted.

flashbulb memories   Vivid recollections we sometimes form of a dramatic incident.

flight-fight response   The body's physiological response to a physical or psychological threat, providing the increased energy needed to flee from the situation or to defend against it.

flooding   A behavior therapy technique for eliminating a phobia in which the client is immediately exposed to the feared situation and encouraged to experience an intense emotional reaction to it.

foot-in-the-door technique   Increasing the probability that a person will comply with a second request by getting that person to comply with a small, first request.

forebrain   The area of the brain which lies above the midbrain and is divided into two halves, or hemispheres. Its structures control many behaviors, such as emotions, motivations, sensations, perceptions, learning, remembering, and reasoning.

formal operations stage   In Jean Piaget's theory, this is the stage of cognitive development beginning at about age 12 and continuing on through adulthood, during which the person becomes able to reason abstractly and solve hypothetical problems.

fovea   An area near the center of the retina where cones are highly concentrated and which provides very sharp and detailed vision.

fraternal twins   Siblings produced from two separate fertilized egg cells that develop simultaneously within the mother's uterus.

free association   An important technique of psychoanalysis in which patients are encouraged to relax and say whatever comes to mind until eventually the free flow of ideas leads to thoughts that give clues to unconscious conflicts.

free nerve endings   Receptors embedded in the skin that are the start of most of our feeling sensations from the outside world.

frequency   (1) When measuring waves, such as sound waves or brain waves, frequency is the number of cycles occurring in a unit of time, usually in one second. (2) Used in a more general statistical sense, frequency refers to the number of times that any event occurs in a specified period.

frequency distribution   The range of scores we get and the frequency of each one when we measure a sample of people regarding some trait.

frequency theory of pitch   The theory that the brain perceives the pitch of lower-frequency sounds by receiving information about the frequencies at which groups of auditory neurons fire.

Freudian dream analysis   See **dream analysis**.

Freudian theory   See **psychoanalytic perspective**.

frontal lobes   Two lobes at the front of the cortex, one on each side of the brain. Their most forward regions (the prefrontal areas) play a major role in the abilities to plan actions and to show normal social and emotional behaviors. A region at the very back of the frontal lobes (the motor area) controls voluntary movements.

frustration   The feeling you have when your attempts to reach some goal are blocked.

frustration-aggression hypothesis   The theory that frustration may lead to anger and aggression.

fundamental attribution error   The common tendency when explaining another person's behavior to overestimate the importance of dispositional factors and underestimate the importance of situational ones.

gate control theory   The theory that the experience of pain depends on the relative activation of two types of nerves—large-diameter sensory nerves, which carry touch sensations, and small-diameter sensory nerves, which carry sensations of pain.

gender identity   A person's private or subjective feelings of being male or female.

gender-identity disorders   Disorders characterized by feelings of discomfort about one's anatomical sex and a persistent desire to be and live like the opposite sex.

general adaptation syndrome   A three-stage reaction the body goes through in responding to stress. These stages—alarm, resistance, and exhaustion—were proposed by the stress researcher Hans Selye.

generalized anxiety disorder   A psychological disorder characterized by a chronic and pervasive feeling of apprehension, worry about impending disasters, and extreme sensitivity to criticism. The person is generally nervous, restless, and irritable and often has physical symptoms of tension.

general problem solver A computer model of human problem solving that incorporates some of the general problem-solving strategies people use in approaching problems of all kinds.

genes The chemical blueprints for the development of an organism and the functioning of its cells.

genetic engineering Removing a gene from a cell and replacing it with another, thereby changing how the cell functions.

genetic factors Factors that affect the physiological, neurological, and psychological functioning of children of alcoholics. These factors indicate that there is an increased likelihood of children of alcoholics becoming alcoholics themselves.

genetic perspective An approach to understanding behavior that stresses the influences of biological inheritance carried in an individual's genes.

genital stage The fifth and last of Freud's stages of psychosexual development. It begins at puberty and lasts until sexual maturity; during this time the adolescent experiences sexual feelings toward others.

genotypes Genetic patterns carried inside cells, patterns that cannot normally be seen.

graded task assignment In behavior therapy or cognitive-behavior modification, these are increasingly difficult tasks set for the client so that he or she can gradually work up to the full-fledged desired response.

group A collection of people who have similar goals and values and who share activities based on those goals and values.

G-spot A small area on the upper wall of the vagina which when stimulated produces sexual arousal in some women. Also called the *Grafenberg spot*.

habituation The process of becoming so familiar with and accustomed to a certain stimulus that attention to it fades.

hair cells The auditory receptor cells of the inner ear, so named because of hairlike projections that bend and rub as the cochlear fluid moves, thus triggering a small electrical charge.

hallucinogens Drugs that produce vivid hallucinations, or sensory experiences that do not conform to reality. LSD, mescaline, and PCP are examples.

hammer, anvil, and stirrup The three tiny interconnected bones of the middle ear.

hardiness A cluster of traits that tend to be found in people who can experience a great deal of stress without becoming ill. These traits include commitment, active confrontation of challenges, and a belief in the ability to control what happens to oneself.

hassles The small, irritating, frustrating events of everyday life, such as noise, too much to do, misplacing things, and so forth.

heterosexual A person who is sexually attracted to members of the opposite sex.

heuristics Rules of thumb or cognitive strategies that serve as shortcuts in making decisions.

hidden observer phenomenon A phenomenon some think can be induced under hypnosis in which a person's consciousness seems to be split into two separate parts. One part is a hypnotized side that follows the hypnotist's suggestions. The other part is a "hidden" side, aware of normal sensations, which acts as an observer of the hypnotized half.

hierarchy construction An important step in the behavior

therapy technique called desensitization. The client makes a list of anxiety-arousing situations from least to most feared.

hierarchy of needs A theory of personality developed by Abraham Maslow in which all human needs develop in a sequence. According to this theory, we satisfy our needs in a certain order, and we cannot advance up the hierarchy of needs until we satisfy the needs lower in the hierarchy.

hindbrain The area at the base of the brain, above the spinal cord. The structures of the hindbrain control some very basic bodily functions such as breathing, heart rate, sleep-wake cycles, and the coordination of voluntary movements and balance.

homeostasis The tendency of the body to regulate its own internal environment and keep internal organs working at optimum levels.

homosexual A person who is sexually attracted to members of his or her own sex.

humanistic approach to personality An approach to understanding human personality that focuses on a person's own subjective experiences and what those experiences mean to that individual.

humanistic perspective An approach to understanding human behavior that stresses each individual's subjective feelings, personal freedom, intrinsic worth, and potential to strive for self-fulfillment.

hypnosis A state in which a person displays unusual openness to suggestion.

hypnotic susceptibility scales Standardized tests to determine how easily and deeply a particular person can be hypnotized.

hypothalamus A structure of the lower forebrain that influences many processes, including hunger, thirst, sexual arousal, emotional responses, and regulation of the body's internal temperature.

hypothesis An educated guess to explain a particular observation. When a number of related hypotheses are organized in a formal way, they become a more general theory.

id In Freudian theory, the collection of powerful biological drives a person is born with, expressed in the needs for food, water, and sexual gratification.

identical twins Siblings produced from a single fertilized egg cell that divides early in its development to yield two separate individuals. These twins are genetically identical.

identification The process by which children resolve the Oedipus complex—they repress sexual feelings toward the opposite-sex parent and try to become like the same-sex parent.

identity A subjective sense of who you are.

imprinting The set of responses by which an animal establishes social attachments early in life.

independent variable A condition in an experiment that the researcher deliberately manipulates.

industrial psychologists Psychologists who work as consultants to business, industry, and government. They study the employee, employer, and working conditions in order to decrease accidents, increase production, and improve employer-employee relations. They also try to make equipment more "user friendly" by analyzing how people respond to various machines.

inferential statistics A set of procedures for determining what conclusions can legitimately be inferred from a set of data.

inhibited sexual desire A sexual disorder characterized by an overall lack of interest in initiating or participating in sexual activity.

inner ear   The area of the ear on the inside of the oval window and containing the cochlea.

insomnia   Difficulty going to sleep or staying asleep for the night.

instinct   An innate biological force that predisposes someone to behave in a certain way when specific environmental conditions are present.

intelligence   Intelligence, according to Robert Sternberg, consists of those mental functions that you use intentionally when you adapt to, shape, and select the environment in which you live and function.

intelligence quotient (IQ)   A score that is the result of a test devised by French psychologist Alfred Binet. The test was revised and a formula was devised by Lewis Terman and associates at Stanford University. The IQ is arrived at by dividing a child's mental age by chronological age and multiplying by 100.

interactive images   Mental pictures in which the key elements involved are somehow actively related.

interference   A cause of forgetting in which old memories become blended with new ones similar in content.

interposition   A depth cue provided when the images of two objects overlap, suggesting that the one which partially covers the other must be closer to the viewer.

intervention   Any formal effort to intervene on behalf of people who suffer some disadvantage to help them to overcome their particular handicaps.

intrinsic motivation   The urge to perform a certain behavior because of an inner sense of satisfaction and accomplishment derived from doing so.

introversion   The tendency to be quiet and reserved with other people, to shun crowds and excitement, and to act on thoughtful consideration rather than impulse.

iodopsins   The three light-sensitive chemicals contained in the cones of the retina.

iris   A circular muscle surrounding the pupil of the eye and enabling the pupil to open and close. It is the pigment of the iris that gives the eyes their color.

James/Lange theory   The idea that subjective feelings of emotion arise from the brain's interpretation of the physiological changes evoked by particular situations.

jealousy   A combination of feelings, thoughts, and behaviors triggered by a real or perceived threat to a valued relationship or to one's happiness or self-esteem.

just noticeable difference   The increase or decrease in the intensity of a stimulus that a person can just manage to detect.

laboratory observation   The observational study of subjects in some specially created laboratory setting.

Lamaze method   A form of preparation for childbirth in which the woman is taught ways to control her pain during labor and to use her muscles to help in delivery.

latency stage   The fourth of Freud's stages of psychosexual development. The child enters this stage between the ages of 6 and 12. During this time, the child's sexual desires are on hold; children play mostly with other children of the same sex.

lateral hypothalamus (LH)   An area of the brain's hypothalamus involved in feelings of hunger and the motivation to eat.

LCU   See **life change units**.

learned helplessness   The learned tendency to stop trying to overcome some challenge because past failures have instilled a belief that this event cannot be controlled.

learned taste aversion   A learned aversion to a particular taste that in the past has been associated with severe nausea.

learning   Traditionally defined as a relatively permanent change in behavior resulting from experience.

lens   An almost transparent structure just inside the eye that helps to focus incoming light waves.

libido   Psychic energy derived from a person's sex drive.

life change units (LCU)   A test score that measures the amount of change a person has had to adjust to in a given period of time.

light and shadows   Depth cues provided by the way light and shadows are cast on an object, making it appear three-dimensional.

light waves   The oscillating patterns in which light travels.

limbic system   Structures connecting with the hypothalamus that form a ring in the forebrain and that are involved in memory and emotions. All the limbic structures are connected with and send their information to the top of the forebrain, the cortex.

linear perspective   A depth cue created by the seeming convergence of parallel lines as they extend away from the observer and into the distance.

lithium   A drug used to combat the mood swings found in bipolar depression, especially the periods of mania.

lobes   The major divisions of the forebrain's outer covering, or cortex.

locus of control   Where you think control over your life lies —within yourself (internal locus of control), or in outside forces (external locus of control).

longitudinal study   A study in which the same group of individuals is studied repeatedly across a period of many years.

long-term memory   The mental storage of information for a long period of time, accessible to working memory with the right retrieval cues.

loss-of-control behavior   Behavior that begins in late adulthood and contributes to developing alcoholism. The personality associated with this behavior tends to be emotionally dependent, rigid, introverted, and fearful and guilty about developing a dependency on alcohol. This personality is more characteristic of women and increases the risk of becoming an alcoholic three to four times.

maintenance rehearsal   The deliberate repetition of information held in working memory in an effort to keep it from being forgotten.

major depression   A type of affective disorder characterized by a sad or dejected mood, accompanied by a number of other symptoms such as poor appetite, difficulty sleeping, loss of interest in formerly pleasurable activities, and a negative self-concept.

maladaptive   Interfering with successful functioning or having adverse consequences for a person or society.

maladaptive behavior definition of abnormality   Defining abnormal behavior as that which interferes with a person's functioning or which poses a threat to the person or society.

mania   A type of affective disorder characterized by a hyper-elevated mood accompanied by a number of other symptoms, such as greatly increased activity, rapid-fire speech, overinflated self-esteem, and the tendency to make grandiose plans and impulsive, often disastrous decisions.

MAO (monoamine oxidase) inhibitors   A type of antidepressant drug that raises the levels of catecholamines in the brain.

maturation   An internally regulated process, largely programmed by a person's genes, which influences the emergence of many developmental skills and traits.

mean The arithmetic average of all the individual measurements in a distribution.

means-end analysis A problem-solving strategy that involves trying to find a way to close the gap between your current situation and one of your subgoals.

measure of central tendency Three measures—the mean, the median, and the mode—each a slightly different way of describing what is "typical" within a given distribution.

measure of variability The extent to which scores in a distribution are spread out, an indication of how much scores vary from one another.

median The score above and below which half the scores in a distribution fall.

medulla A region of the hindbrain that controls the vital processes of heart rate, respiration, and blood pressure.

melancholia A form of depression in which there appears to be no negative event that precipitates the dejected mood and in which the person suffers great physical lethargy along with the mental and emotional symptoms.

menarche The beginning of menstruation.

menstruation The process by which the lining of a woman's uterus, along with any unfertilized egg cells, is sloughed off every month in a naturally occurring cycle.

mental age A child's overall level of cognitive functioning as measured by a test that attempts to establish performance levels appropriate for children of different ages.

method of loci A mnemonic device that helps you remember a list in a certain order by associating each item on the list with one of a series of places already committed to memory.

midbrain The area of the brain that lies between the hindbrain and the forebrain.

middle ear An area of the ear containing three tiny bones that amplify the pressure sound waves exert on the eardrum.

Minnesota Multiphasic Personality Inventory (MMPI) A personality test used to identify abnormal patterns of behavior.

mixed schedules of reinforcement Any combination of ratio and interval schedules for delivering reinforcement.

mnemonic devices Memory techniques that help people store and retrieve information better by providing organization for encoding.

mode The most frequent measurement in a distribution, the one that occurs most often.

monochromats People who have only one kind of light-sensitive chemical in the cones of the retina (instead of three), and who therefore are totally color blind.

mood convergence The phenomenon whereby you are more likely to attend to, encode, and recall information and events that are consistent with your present mood.

mood-state-dependent memory A memory that cannot be retrieved unless you are in the same emotional state as you were when you originally stored the information.

morphemes The smallest combinations of speech sounds that convey meaning in a given language.

motivation A set of physiological and psychological forces that influences behavior by causing a change in activity level, directing actions toward particular goals and promoting responsiveness to certain goal-related stimuli.

motion parallax A depth cue created by the fact that near objects appear to move much more relative to far ones as an observer moves left and right or up and down.

motor area A part of the brain's cortex which lies at the back of the frontal lobes and regulates voluntary movements, such as moving an arm or a leg.

motor neurons Nerve cells that carry information from the brain and spinal cord to the muscles and glands.

multiple personality A type of dissociative disorder in which two or more distinct personalities coexist within one individual.

naturalistic observation The study of subjects in a natural environment without interference by the researcher, whose role is simply to keep careful records of what the subjects do or say.

need for achievement See **achievement motivation**.

negative cognitive set A generally negative way of looking at and interpreting the world. According to Aaron Beck, this is a major cause of depression.

negative reinforcer Any behavioral consequence that increases the probability of the behavior occurring again because it involves removal or avoidance of some unpleasant stimulus.

nerve impulse The transmission of information produced as an action potential moves down a neuron's axon from point to point.

neural deafness Deafness caused by injury to the hair cells of the inner ear or to the auditory nerve. In these cases, vibrations of the basilar membrane are never converted into nerve impulses, or nerve impulses, once started, never reach the brain.

neurons Cells of the nervous system that are specialized to receive and transmit information.

neurotic behaviors Maladaptive thoughts and actions that indicate anxiety over some repressed conflict.

neurotransmitters Chemicals that transmit information from one neuron to another, or from a neuron to a muscle or gland.

neutral stimulus A stimulus that does not elicit any distinctive reaction. In classical conditioning, a neutral stimulus is one that does not elicit a reaction similar to the unconditioned response.

node The term used to refer to each concept in a semantic network model of memory.

Non-Rapid-Eye-Movement (NREM) sleep All the stages of sleep that are not Rapid-Eye-Movement (REM) sleep. These NREM stages collectively consume about 80 percent of sleep time.

normal aging The gradual slowing of some physical and psychological processes.

normal curve The curve, with a characteristic bell shape, produced when a normal distribution is graphed. The curve tapers off equally on either side of a central point, and most of the measurements fall near the center.

normal distribution The characteristic pattern of the frequency distribution for many traits in a large population.

NREM sleep See **Non-Rapid-Eye-Movement sleep**.

obedience Behavior performed in response to an order given by someone in a position of authority.

object permanence In Jean Piaget's theory, an understanding of object permanence is a major cognitive development in the first two years of life. It is essentially the realization that objects are permanent and do not cease to exist when they are merely out of sight.

observational learning The process of learning various actions, beliefs, and feelings by observing the behavior of others.

obsession A persistent and recurring thought that a person is unable to control.

occipital lobes Two lobes at the back of the cortex, one on each side of the brain. They contain areas important to vision.

Oedipus complex The combination of unconscious sexual

desires and feelings of hatred and jealousy that occurs during the phallic stage of Freud's stages of psychosexual development.

olfactory bulbs　Structures at the forward base of the brain's hemispheres to which nerve impulses from the nose are first transmitted.

olfactory cells　Receptor cells in the nose that respond to molecules of odor-producing substances carried in the air.

operant conditioning　The process by which someone learns either to emit or to withhold a particular behavior because of its association with positive or negative consequences.

operations　In Jean Piaget's theory of cognitive development, operations is a term that refers to performing actions mentally or to rehearsing some sequence of events in your head.

opiates　Drugs such as heroin, morphine, and codeine which are derived from the opium poppy. They are used medically to kill pain and recreationally to achieve a euphoric feeling.

opponent process theory of color vision　The theory that color vision is produced by the actions of cells in the brain which respond in opposite ways (on or off) to the complementary colors red-green or blue-yellow.

optic nerve　The bundle of neural fibers that exits out of the back of each eye and goes to the brain.

oral stage　The first of Freud's stages of psychosexual development, during which babies focus their strivings for pleasure on sensations arising from the mouth, lips, and tongue. Feeding becomes a potential area of conflict at this time.

orgasm stage　The third of four stages in Masters and Johnson's model of human sexual response. During orgasm both males and females experience involuntary muscular contractions, greatly increased heart rate, blood pressure, and breathing, and intense feelings of pleasure. In males, orgasm is accompanied by ejaculation of semen.

outer ear　The part of the ear that is visible on the outside of the head.

oval window　A membrane that moves in and out in response to the movements of the bones in the middle ear, thus setting into motion the fluid of the inner ear.

overjustification effect　Decreased interest in and enjoyment of an activity after some unnecessary external reward has been received for engaging in it.

ovulation　The process by which one or more ova or egg cells is released from a female's ovaries.

panic disorder　A sudden and overwhelming state of terror and feeling of impending doom for no apparent reason. The panic is accompanied by physiological symptoms such as a pounding heart, dizziness, and difficulty breathing.

paranoid schizophrenia　A type of schizophrenia chiefly characterized by delusions. These are often delusions of being persecuted by others, although delusions of grandeur are also common.

paraphilias　Disorders characterized by sexual arousal to objects or situations that are not usually associated with sexual arousal and interfere in varying degrees with the capacity for affectionate sexual activity.

parasympathetic division　The division of the autonomic nervous system that slows heart rate, decreases blood pressure, and stimulates digestion, all of which calm the body and return it to a normal level of physiological functioning.

parietal lobes　Two lobes at the upper middle of the cortex, one on each side of the brain. They contain a region (the somatosensory area) where feeling sensations such as touch are processed.

partial reinforcement schedule　A schedule for delivering reinforcement in which only some of the target behaviors emitted are followed by reinforcers.

pathological aging　The process of aging in which an illness, such as Alzheimer's disease, destroys some part of the brain or body and results in serious physical and psychological deficits.

pegword system　A mnemonic device that helps you remember a list in a certain order by associating each item on the list with one of a series of number-word rhymes already committed to memory.

perception　The experience you have when you organize sensations into some meaningful pattern.

perceptual memories　Memories about the look, sound, smell, taste, and feel of things.

perceptual set　A frame of mind or set of expectations, based on past experiences, which influences future perceptions. A perceptual set can bias and distort what a person sees.

perceptual threshold　How intense a stimulus must be in order for it to be consciously perceived.

peripheral nervous system　The network of nerves located outside the brain and spinal cord. These nerves convey information from sensory receptors and transmit messages back to the muscles and glands.

personal constructs　In the humanistic theory of George Kelly, personal constructs are an individual's ways of looking at and interpreting the world.

personal fable　A subjective explanation, not based on reality.

personality　The collection of relatively stable and distinctive ways of thinking, behaving, and feeling that characterize how a particular person responds to other people and to situations.

personality assessment　A process that involves describing an individual's personality structure, making predictions about how that person is likely to behave, and identifying any psychological disorders from which the person may be suffering.

personality disorder　A psychological disorder characterized by inflexible, maladaptive personality traits that result in significantly impaired functioning or in personal distress.

personality inventories　Personality tests that typically include very specific or structured questions requiring very specific answers.

person-centered therapy　A form of psychotherapy, originated by Carl Rogers, in which the therapist communicates caring and respect for the client, as well as empathy for the client's feelings and viewpoints. Emphasis is placed on the client's own potential for change and self-fulfillment.

phallic stage　The third of Freud's stages of psychosexual development; lasts from the third to the sixth year. During this stage the child's primary source of satisfaction involves stimulation of the genitals. In addition, the child feels unconscious sexual desires for the opposite-sex parent and hatred and jealousy for the same-sex parent, who he views as a competitor and fears will punish him for his feelings.

phantom limb　The phenomenon of experiencing sensation in a limb that has been amputated.

phenothiazines　A family of drugs used to treat schizophrenia. One commonly used type is chlorpromazine.

phenotypes　Observable physical traits, such as eye color, height, and hair texture.

phenylketonuria (PKU)　A genetic disorder that results in lack of an enzyme needed to break down a protein found in milk and certain other foods. The accumulated protein acts as a toxic chemical on the brain, causing mental retardation.

phobia   An intense and irrational fear that is out of all proportion to the danger posed by a particular object or situation.

phonemes   The distinctive categories of sounds used in a given language to form words.

photographic memory   The ability to store detailed visual images in long-term memory and to recall those images at will even after a substantial time.

photoreceptors   Cells in the retina that generate small electrical charges when they absorb light.

physiological psychologists   Psychologists who are concerned with questions about the structure and function of the human brain and nervous system. They study how drugs affect learning and memory, what deficits appear when the brain is damaged, and how the body responds to stress.

physiological threshold   How intense a stimulus must be in order for it to excite sensory receptors and send nerve impulses to the brain. Note that this level of intensity may not be great enough for the stimulus to be consciously perceived.

pitch   The highness or lowness of a sound, determined by the frequency of the sound wave.

pituitary gland   A gland located at the base of the hypothalamus and regulated by it. Pituitary hormones affect secretions from other glands in the body, which is why the pituitary is often called the master gland.

placebo effect   A beneficial reaction that occurs merely because a person expects a pill recently taken to have a positive effect. In actual fact the pill taken was not a medicine at all; the person just *thought* it was.

placenta   An organ that develops in the uterus of a pregnant woman for the purpose of transferring oxygen and nutrients from her bloodstream to the bloodstream of her fetus.

place theory of pitch   The theory that the brain perceives the pitch of a sound by receiving information about which part of the basilar membrane a given sound wave vibrates the most.

plasticity of the brain   The ability of the brain's neurons to modify their structure and function depending on conditions.

plateau stage   The second of four stages in Masters and Johnson's model of human sexual response. During the plateau stage, sexual arousal intensifies and reaches a peak.

pleasure principle   In Freudian theory, the principle according to which the id functions—satisfying its needs immediately, without regard for reason, logic, or morality.

polygraph   A machine that records changes in heart rate, blood pressure, respiration, and activity of the sweat glands. It is commonly called a lie detector when used to try to determine if someone is telling the truth.

pons   A region of the hindbrain which, among other things, manufactures and distributes chemicals that regulate sleep.

positive regard   In the humanistic theory of Carl Rogers, positive regard includes love, sympathy, acceptance, and respect from those who are important to a person.

positive reinforcer   Any behavioral consequence that increases the probability of the behavior occurring again because it involves presentation of some pleasant stimulus.

postconventional level of moral reasoning   In Lawrence Kohlberg's theory of moral development, this is the stage at which rules are obeyed out of recognition that those rules are for the common welfare. Many but not all adults are presumably at this level.

posthypnotic amnesia   Forgetting what occurred when you were under hypnosis after coming out of the hypnotized state.

posthypnotic suggestion   A suggestion to act in a particular way after coming out of hypnosis.

power rapist   The rapist whose primary motivation is not to physically hurt, but rather to possess the victim.

preconventional level of moral reasoning   In Lawrence Kohlberg's theory of moral development, this is the stage at which rules are obeyed out of fear of being caught and punished. Most children under the age of 9 are presumably at this level.

prejudice   An unfair, biased, intolerant attitude toward a particular group or category of people.

premature ejaculation   A male sexual problem characterized by reaching orgasm so quickly that it interferes with the pleasure and gratification of the man's partner. Also called *rapid ejaculation*.

preoperational stage   In Jean Piaget's theory, this is the stage of cognitive development lasting from about ages 2 to 7, during which children become able to imagine and to use symbols, but are still very egocentric in their thinking.

prepared learning   Learning which occurs very easily because the nervous system is biologically prepared for this kind of learning.

previous-life regression   Claiming to be mentally transported back to a previous life.

primary auditory area   An area in each of the two temporal lobes of the cortex. The primary auditory area begins the sensation of "hearing" by processing tones of different pitches and volumes.

primary reinforcers   Stimuli such as food, water, shelter, and sex that satisfy basic needs.

primary orgasmic dysfunction   The condition in which a woman has never experienced an orgasm.

primary visual area   An area in each of the two occipital lobes of the cortex. The primary visual area begins the sensation of "seeing" by processing spots and lines of light, textures, and contours.

principle of bidirectionality   The finding that a child's behavior influences how the parents respond, while the parents' behavior, in turn, affects the child's reactions.

proactive interference   Forgetting that occurs when previously learned information acts forward upon and disrupts new information.

procedural memories   Memories of how to carry out various physical and mental procedures, such as riding a bicycle or dividing one number by another.

progesterone   A female hormone produced by the ovaries.

progressive relaxation   A psychotherapeutic procedure that involves tensing and relaxing various muscle groups in the body, beginning with the toes and working up to the head. It is designed to teach a person how to relax and eliminate physical tension.

projection   A defense mechanism in which we assign our own undesirable traits to other people.

projective tests   Personality tests that present people with ambiguous stimuli, such as inkblots or pictures, and ask them to report what each stimulus looks like or to compose a story about it. The underlying assumption is that the test taker will project unconscious or guarded feelings and motives onto the ambiguous stimuli.

prosocial behavior   Any behavior that benefits others or that has positive social consequences.

prosopagnosia   The sudden inability to recognize faces of familiar people; usually caused by a stroke.

prototype   A general concept of what something looks like. One's prototype of a dog, for example, is not any particular dog, but an abstract idea of what an average dog looks and sounds like.

prototype theory of concept formation   The theory that people come to learn the meaning of a concept by forming a general idea or prototype of that concept—essentially an image of the concept's "best" example.

proximity   A principle of perception that says that we tend to see as groups those objects that are physically close together.

psi phenomena   Another name for psychic phenomena that refer to various forms of extrasensory perception and the supposed ability to influence objects through thought.

psychiatrist   A mental health professional who has first been trained as a physician and then has completed a psychiatric residency which involves additional training in pharmacology, neurology, psychopathology, and psychotherapeutic techniques.

psychoanalysis   An approach to treating psychological problems, originally developed by Sigmund Freud, in which the analyst tries to uncover patients' unconscious conflicts by allowing them to talk freely about whatever they want until themes related to their conflicts emerge.

psychoanalyst   A mental health professional who has usually been trained as a psychiatrist and who has then received additional training in a psychoanalytic institute.

psychoanalytic perspective   An approach to understanding human behavior, begun by Sigmund Freud, in which therapists search for the roots of people's problems in guilt-producing drives and motivations that have become buried in the unconscious.

psychodynamic approach to personality   An approach to understanding human personality in which researchers look for unconscious drives, needs, and motives to explain individual behavior.

psychodynamic approach to psychotherapy   A form of therapy similar to traditional psychoanalysis in that it assumes that symptoms are signs of more basic underlying problems, that transference needs to be worked out, and that the primary role of the therapist is to interpret and clarify the patient's behaviors. But unlike in traditional psychoanalysis, the therapist takes an active role in interpreting, clarifying, and suggesting solutions.

psychodynamic perspective   The name given to the approach many contemporary psychoanalysts use. This perspective differs from Freud's traditional psychoanalytic theory in placing less emphasis on forbidden sexual urges and more emphasis on conscious motivations.

psychology   The systematic, scientific study of human and animal behavior, in which behavior refers to mental activities as well as to overt actions.

psychometric approach to intelligence   An approach to understanding human intelligence that tries to identify the various mental abilities that intelligence entails, to measure each of these abilities in people, and to determine an individual's overall IQ.

psychoneuroimmunology   The study of how psychosocial factors affect the brain and alter the body's immune system, making a person more or less susceptible to disease.

psychosexual dysfunctions   See **sexual dysfunctions**.

psychosexual stages   Sigmund Freud's stages of human development during which the child's central motivation is to gratify the drive for pleasure in a different part of the body.

psychosis   The loss of contact with reality.

psychosocial stages   Erik Erikson's stages of human development during which the person must somehow adapt to a different critical issue or challenge.

psychosomatic symptoms   Symptoms that occur primarily because of stress.

punisher   Any event or consequence that decreases the probability of a behavior occurring again.

pupil   An opening in the center of the eye that allows light to enter.

random assignment   Any method of assigning subjects to groups that gives each individual an equal chance of being placed in any one of the groups established.

range   A measure of variability that shows the two most extreme scores at either end of a distribution.

rape myths   False ideas about rape and the women who are victims of rape which a high percentage of rapists believe to be true.

rapid ejaculation   See **premature ejaculation**.

Rapid-Eye-Movement (REM) sleep   The stage of sleep in which the eyes move rapidly back and forth beneath closed eyelids, the sleeper shows signs of physiological arousal, and brain wave activity is very similar to that of a wide-awake person. REM sleep is also the time when dreams are most vivid and easily recalled.

rationalization   A defense mechanism in which a person makes up excuses for behaviors that cause anxiety.

reaction formation   A defense mechanism in which a person represses an unacceptable motive by enthusiastically endorsing the opposite one.

reaction range   The range within which a genetic influence can vary, depending on the effects of environment.

reality principle   In Freudian theory, the principle according to which the ego functions—finding appropriate and socially acceptable ways to fulfill the wishes of the id.

recall   A process of retrieving information from long-term memory that involves searching through memory stores and finding the desired piece of data.

recessive gene   A gene that will express itself only when it is paired with a similar recessive gene. In the presence of a dominant gene, the effects of a recessive gene are overridden.

recognition   A process of retrieving information from long-term memory that involves deciding whether a particular stimulus currently being considered "matches" what is stored in memory.

reflex arcs   Chains of neurons that link a sensory input to a response in the muscles or glands via the spinal cord. These responses occur automatically, without the conscious thought associated with the brain's involvement.

regenerate   The capacity of nerves in the peripheral nervous system to grow back together and regain their function after they are cut.

reinforcer   Any event or consequence that increases the probability of a behavior occurring again.

relative closeness to the horizon   A depth cue created by the fact that objects far away appear closer to the horizon than near objects do.

relative size   A depth cue created by the fact that an object looks smaller when it is farther away. When you know the actual size of an object, you can estimate its distance from you by how large it appears to be.

reliability   A characteristic possessed by a test if people receive approximately the same score after taking the test on a number of different occasions.

REM sleep   See **Rapid-Eye-Movement sleep**.

repression   A defense mechanism in which we push unacceptable feelings or impulses into the unconscious.

resilient children   Children who manage to cope successfully with stress.

resistance   In psychoanalysis, a patient's efforts to keep repressed thoughts and feelings from surfacing into consciousness.

resistance stage   The second stage in Selye's general adaptation syndrome, characterized by an apparent return to normal of physiological responses, but during which the body's energy stores continue to be depleted.

resolution stage The last of four stages in Masters and Johnson's model of human sexual response. During resolution, the body gradually returns to a nonaroused state.

responses The reactions a person has to a stimulus.

resting state The state in which a neuron is neither receiving nor transmitting information. In this state, the inside of the cell membrane is negatively charged relative to the outside.

restorative theory of sleep A theory proposing that activities during the day deplete key factors in the body which then require sleep to be replenished.

reticular formation A column of neurons at the base of the brain that plays a vital role in regulating consciousness. A person with a severely damaged reticular formation would lapse into a coma.

retina The light-sensitive inner surface of the eye.

retinal disparity The difference in image that each eye receives due to the fact that each is located on a different side of the face. The degree of retinal disparity varies depending on how near an object is, and the brain uses these variations as cues to depth.

retrieval cues Any thought, perception, feeling, or event that can help someone retrieve information stored in long-term memory.

retroactive interference Forgetting that occurs when new information acts backward upon and disrupts previously learned information.

retrograde amnesia A form of amnesia that impairs memory only for events that happened *before* the disorder set in.

rhodopsin The light-sensitive chemical contained in the rods of the retina.

risky shift A collective shift toward choosing the more risky of two alternatives after people have deliberated those alternatives within a group. Whether or not the risky shift occurs depends on the initial leanings of the group members.

rods Photoreceptors in the retina that allow us to see in dim light.

Rorschach Inkblot Test A projective personality test that presents a series of ambiguous inkblots and requires the test taker to say what they look like.

rules of phonology Rules that specify what speech sounds are acceptable in a particular language and how those speech sounds can be combined to form meaningful units of speech.

rules of semantics Rules that specify the meanings of words in various contexts.

rules of syntax Rules that specify the order in which words can be combined to form meaningful sentences.

sadistic rapist The rapist for whom physical force is eroticized and who derives pleasure from inflicting pain on the victim.

schema An organized network of information that develops from past experiences and that influences how a person perceives and reacts to people and events.

schizophrenia A very serious psychological disorder characterized by incoherent thought, difficulty focusing attention, hallucinations and delusions, blunted or inappropriate emotions, and sometimes abnormal motor behaviors.

secondary erectile dysfunction—psychological The inability to have or maintain an erection because of psychological factors such as tension, anxiety, stress, or depression.

secondary orgasmic dysfunction A condition in which a woman who previously had orgasms no longer has them or fails to have them in certain situations.

secondary reinforcers Stimuli that have come to provide reinforcement through their association with primary reinforcers.

secondary sexual characteristics Traits associated with being a male or a female that develop at puberty. Examples are breasts in females and facial hair in males.

second-order conditioning Classical conditioning in which a second conditioned stimulus is repeatedly paired with the first so that it eventually elicits by itself the conditioned response.

securely attached infant A baby who is apparently secure in the knowledge that the parents or other principal caregivers can be counted on to provide whatever comfort and reassurance the child may need.

selective attention The process of attending actively to only some of the information received by one of the senses. Without selective attention, we would soon be overwhelmed by sensory data.

self A person's characteristic thoughts, feelings, and physical traits taken together.

self-actualization A healthy psychological state that involves reaching your maximum potential as an individual, becoming the best person you can be.

self-centered thinking That inability to separate one's thoughts and feelings from those of others that is a characteristic of adolescence.

self-determination Being in control of what happens to you.

self-fulfilling prophecy When your expectations affect your behavior so that you unintentionally encourage the very outcomes you expect.

self-handicapping strategy The tendency to perceive reasons for your failures that are not your own fault and by so doing to preserve your self-esteem.

self-monitoring A technique used in behavior therapy or in cognitive-behavior modification in which clients keep track of their own actions or thoughts in various situations.

self-ratings Assessment a person makes about the self.

self-reinforcer Giving yourself a reward for performing a certain behavior, especially a mental reward such as feeling good about yourself.

self-selection bias The bias that affects the makeup of experimental groups and hence the outcome of the experiments. It occurs when researchers unintentionally select people who are likely to respond in the "right" way.

self-statements The various statements you make to yourself as you go about your daily activities.

self-theory A theory of personality developed by Carl Rogers. According to this theory, everyone has an inherent self-actualizing tendency, or push, for reaching a healthy psychological state and self-fulfillment. Only certain psychological climates, however, stimulate growth and promote self-actualization.

semantic memory A memory concerning the meaning of words and concepts.

semantic network model A model of how long-term memory is organized. In this model, concepts are intricately linked to one another via their known relationships.

sensate focus A procedure developed by Masters and Johnson to help couples become better aware and more appreciative of their bodily sensations, while at the same time overcoming the fears and performance pressures often associated with sexual dysfunctions.

sensation The process by which information about the world is registered by the senses and transmitted to the brain.

sensation-seeker Someone who tends to increase his or her arousal level by seeking out unusual and exciting experiences.

sensitive care A form of child care in which the parents show sensitivity to their child's needs by responding to them promptly and effectively.

sensorimotor stage In Jean Piaget's theory, this is a stage of cognitive development lasting from birth until about age 2, during which time children's knowledge of the world is limited to what they discover through direct sensory experiences and motor actions.

sensory adaptation A decrease in sensitivity to a constant stimulus after steady exposure to it. Sensory adaptation occurs in all our sensory systems, with the possible exception of pain.

sensory deprivation Greatly reducing or eliminating normal sensations in a specially created environment.

sensory memory The momentary lingering of sensory information after a stimulus has been removed.

sensory neurons Nerve cells that carry information from the sense organs to the spinal cord and brain.

separation anxiety Distress that infants tend to show when temporarily separated from the parents or other principal caregivers.

setpoint The ratio of fat to lean at which a particular person's body is biologically inclined to stabilize.

sex roles Cultural ideas about the behaviors, attitudes, feelings, and statuses deemed appropriate for males and females.

sexual dysfunction Sexual difficulties that are caused by poor sexual technique, psychological factors, or medical problems. The dysfunction is defined as **primary** if the person has never functioned successfully—for example, has never had an erection or orgasm. The dysfunction is defined as **secondary** if the person previously functioned successfully but no longer does or is able to function successfully in one situation and not another.

shape constancy The tendency to see an object as retaining its actual shape no matter what angle it is viewed from.

shaping An operant conditioning technique in which a subject is systematically reinforced for displaying closer and closer approximations of a target behavior.

short-term dynamic psychotherapy (STDP) An abbreviated version of psychodynamic therapy, limited to 25 or 30 sessions, in which the therapist takes a more active role than in traditional psychoanalysis while still focusing on resolving conflicts and working through transference.

short-term memory The process of attending to information in sensory memory or to conscious thoughts and perceptions at any given moment.

signal detection theory A contemporary approach to studying perceptual thresholds which assumes that thresholds depend on the interaction of three sets of factors: (1) the properties of the stimulus, or signal; (2) the characteristics of the subject (his or her acuity, motivation, alertness, and so forth); and (3) the presence of other stimuli (noise) in the environment.

similarity A principle of perception that says that we tend to group together elements that appear similar.

simplicity A principle of perception that says we tend to organize stimuli in the simplest way possible.

situational attribution Attributing someone's behavior to an external factor such as pressure from others, a difficult set of circumstances, or simply chance.

size constancy The tendency to perceive objects as the same size even when the images they project are continually growing and shrinking.

skewed distributions The range of scores when more people fall toward one side of the scale than toward the other. When plotted on a graph, these distributions do not have a symmetrical shape.

slow-to-warm-up babies Babies who tend to be more withdrawn than other infants and who take longer to adapt to new situations.

social attachments Strong affectional bonds that babies develop toward their parents or other principal caregivers.

social attributions The explanations we offer for behavior, either our own or that of others.

social-cognitive approach A theory of personality that views personality development as arising from the interaction among three factors—cognitive and personality factors, behavior, and the environment.

social facilitation Improved performance in the presence of others, especially for behaviors the person is already good at.

social inhibition Decreased performance in the presence of others, especially for behaviors the person is not very good at to begin with.

social isolation The state of being cut off or separated from other people to an unusual extent.

social norms definition of abnormality Defining abnormal behavior as that which falls outside the agreed-upon standards of a society.

social perception The way you perceive yourself or others.

social psychologists/personality psychologists Psychologists who study human behavior and how humans interact with one another, as well as how personality is formed and whether it can be changed.

social psychology The study of how an individual's thoughts and actions are influenced by other people and the characteristics they have.

social smiling Smiling directed toward other human beings that develops in a baby's first few months of life.

social support All the human relationships that have a lasting and positive impact on an individual's life. A strong social support network seems to be linked to more effective coping with stress.

sodium pump The structure that pushes back any stray sodium ions that manage to squeeze past the cell membrane into the neuron.

soma The main body of a neuron that furnishes the cell with nutrients and manufactures chemicals used in transmitting information.

somatic division Pathways in the peripheral nervous system that generally connect to the skeletal muscles, which are the muscles that move the bones of the body, such as those in the arms and legs. To a large extent, healthy people have conscious control over their somatic pathways.

somatic pathways Pathways in the peripheral nervous system that regulate voluntary movements of the skeletal muscles, such as those used to write or walk.

somatoform disorder A disorder characterized by some physical symptom caused by psychological distress.

somatosensory area A part of the cortex which lies at the front of the parietal lobes and registers feeling sensations such as touch and pressure.

sound waves Waves created when a vibrating object causes oscillations in pressure among air or water molecules.

split brain A brain in which the corpus callosum has been severed, thus severing the nerve fibers that connect the two hemispheres of the forebrain.

spontaneous recovery The sudden reappearance of a learned response that has undergone extinction.

sprouting New growth in the axons of healthy central nervous system neurons that lie near other neurons which have been destroyed. This growth actually promotes new connections among nerve cells and helps compensate for those that were lost.

squeeze technique   See **stop-start technique**.

standard deviation   A measure of variability that takes into account all the scores in a distribution, not just the extremes.

Stanford-Binet test   A widely used IQ test developed at Stanford University from an earlier test created by Alfred Binet.

states of consciousness   Noticeable variations in patterns and styles of mental awareness.

statistical definition of abnormality   Defining abnormal behavior as that which the minority of people display.

statistical frequency   How often a behavior occurs in the general population.

STDP   See **short-term dynamic psychotherapy**.

stereotype   A set of beliefs or traits that we tend to attribute uniformly to all members of a particular group or category of people. Stereotypes tend to be extreme and most often negative.

stimulants   Drugs that increase normal activities in the central nervous system, causing unusually high energy, arousal, and alertness. Amphetamine and cocaine are examples.

stimulus   Any change in energy someone is capable of processing through the senses and reacting to.

stimulus control   The fact that stimuli associated with the learning of some behavior often serve as cues that prompt the learned response. An example is a man who has learned to snack heavily at movies and who heads for the refreshment stand as soon as he enters a theater. In this case, the theater is a stimulus that exerts control over the man's behavior.

stimulus discrimination   When only a particular stimulus elicits a certain response, not stimuli that are merely similar to that particular one.

stimulus generalization   When a stimulus that is similar to, but not identical with, another stimulus comes to elicit a similar response.

stop-start technique   A treatment for premature ejaculation in which the man becomes more aware of the sensations immediately preceding orgasm and learns to postpone them. Also called the *squeeze technique*.

stress   The feeling we have when we interpret or appraise a situation as being threatening or challenging and when our personal resources are strained or outstripped by our dealings with the situation.

structuralist   A school of psychologists who defined psychology as the study of the conscious elements (beliefs, thoughts, feelings) of the normal human mind and who studied the structure of consciousness. They thought the workings of the mind could be studied scientifically.

subgoal analysis   A problem-solving strategy in which the overall problem is broken down into a series of smaller, more manageable subproblems, each involving a goal of its own.

sublimation   A defense mechanism in which we redirect threatening or forbidden desires to socially acceptable goals.

subliminal messages   Stimuli presented below the threshold for conscious awareness, but which the brain may nevertheless register to some degree.

superego   In Freudian theory, the part of the mind that contains the moral standards of parents and society and that judges behavior as being morally right or wrong.

surface structure   A term proposed by the linguist Noam Chomsky to refer to the actual words of a sentence.

survey   A method for assessing the opinions, characteristics, or behaviors of people in a particular population by asking appropriate questions of a representative sample.

symbol   An object, gesture, sound, or other stimulus that represents something other than itself.

sympathetic division   The division of the autonomic nervous system that increases heart rate, respiration, blood pressure, blood flow, release of sugar, and secretion of hormones, all of which cause physiological arousal.

synapse   The tiny space between the tip of a neuron's axon and the receptor sites on a neighboring neuron, muscle, or gland.

systematic desensitization   A three-part procedure, based on principles of classical conditioning, used to treat behavior established through classical conditioning. The subject is taught to put him or herself into a deeply relaxed state and to imagine a series of stressful situations while trying to remain relaxed. The point is to associate stressful situations with feelings of relaxation.

tardive dyskinesia   Slow, rhythmic, uncontrollable movements of the mouth and lips, as well as unusual movements of the limbs, arising as an effect of prolonged use of phenothiazines or related antipsychotic drugs.

target behavior   The behavior someone who is employing operant conditioning principles ultimately wants the subject to emit.

TAT   See **Thematic Apperception Test**.

telegraphic speech   A pattern of speech characteristic of toddlers in which sentences are limited mostly to concrete nouns and action verbs and are usually only two words in length.

temporal lobes   Two lobes at the sides of the cortex, one on each hemisphere. They contain areas important to hearing and to understanding speech.

terminal buttons   Structures at the very end of each axon. When a nerve impulse reaches the terminal button, it causes the vesicles to open and secrete their chemicals.

test anxiety   The distress caused by taking an exam that prevents some students from being able to remember material they have studied. It can be so severe that the student's mind "goes blank" during the test.

test of statistical significance   A procedure psychologists employ when they use inferential statistics that helps them determine if statistics are reliable.

testimonial   A statement in support of a particular viewpoint based on personal experience.

testosterone   A male hormone produced by the testes.

texture gradient   A depth cue provided by gradual changes in the seeming texture of objects as they move farther away.

thalamus   A structure of the lower forebrain that receives information from all the senses except smell. The thalamus organizes this incoming sensory data and relays it to higher brain areas.

Thematic Apperception Test (TAT)   A projective personality test that presents a series of ambiguous pictures and requires the person to make up stories about them.

theory   An organized set of assumptions about why things happen the way they do.

theta waves   Low-amplitude, slow-frequency brain waves (3 to 7 cycles per second) that appear in the EEG of a person who is in NREM stage 1 sleep.

thought-stopping procedure   Any mental procedure used in cognitive-behavior modification to help a person inhibit disturbing or maladaptive thoughts.

thought-substituting procedure   Any mental procedure used in cognitive-behavior modification to help a person substitute positive thoughts for disturbing, maladaptive ones.

time-out   A behavior therapy technique in which unwanted behavior is immediately followed by a period of time away from positive reinforcement.

tip-of-the-tongue phenomenon   The inability to retrieve a name or some information that we are sure we know because we have too few retrieval cues.

token economy A behavior therapy technique in which target behaviors are shaped and reinforced by tokens that can be exchanged for various desirable objects and activities.

tolerance Built-up resistance to a drug so that larger and larger doses are needed to produce the same effects.

trait In the study of personality, any enduring, relatively consistent characteristic that influences behavior and helps distinguish one person from another.

trait approach to personality An approach to understanding human personality in which researchers try to identify the relatively enduring personality characteristics a person possesses. These traits are assumed to influence behavior.

transcendental meditation (TM) A method of relaxation in which the person assumes a comfortable position, closes his or her eyes, and repeats a meaningless sound for about twenty minutes a day.

transference In psychoanalysis, the process of feeling toward the analyst all the conflict-ridden emotions felt toward someone important in the patient's childhood. Psychoanalysts believe that the emotions involved in transference must be worked out if the therapy is to be successful.

transformational rules Rules that allow us to convert a sentence's surface structure into deep structure, and deep structure back into surface structure.

transsexual A person with the gender identity of the opposite sex.

trichromatic theory of color vision The theory that color vision is produced by different relative activations of three types of light-sensitive chemicals in the cones—one sensitive to short-wave light, one sensitive to medium-wave light, and one sensitive to long-wave light.

tricyclics A type of antidepressant drug that raises the levels of catecholamines in the brain.

t-test A test of statistical significance and the most frequently used procedure for answering questions about the reliability of data in psychological experiments.

type A behavior A pattern of behavior found in people who lead a very fast-paced existence, are impatient with slowness, excessively competitive, and generally dissatisfied with life. Type A behavior is associated with a greater risk of heart attacks and vascular disease.

type B behavior A pattern of behavior found in people who are generally easygoing, calm, relaxed, and patient. Type B behavior is associated with a lower risk of heart attacks and vascular disease.

unconditional positive regard In the humanistic theory of Carl Rogers, unconditional positive regard means receiving love and acceptance from others even when you behave in some ways differently from what is generally expected.

unconditioned response A classical conditioning term referring to a response that is not learned, but that instead happens automatically—in other words, a reflex reaction.

unconditioned stimulus A classical conditioning term referring to a stimulus that elicits an unconditioned response, or reflex, without any form of training.

valid A characteristic possessed by a test if it measures what it was constructed to measure and if test results can be used to help predict behavior.

variable-interval schedule of reinforcement A partial reinforcement schedule in which a reinforcer is given following the first target behavior emitted after a variable amount of time has passed.

variable-ratio schedule of reinforcement A partial reinforcement schedule in which a reinforcer is given after a variable number of target behaviors have been emitted.

ventromedial hypothalamus (VMH) An area of the brain's hypothalamus involved in the feeling of fullness or satiation after eating and in the motivation to stop eating.

vesicles Swellings filled with tiny packets at the end of each axon that store chemicals. When a nerve impulse reaches the terminal button, it causes the vesicles to open and secrete their chemicals.

vestibular organs Structures of the inner ear that normally provide information about body motion. Under certain conditions they are involved in producing motion sickness.

vicarious learning Behaviors we acquire by observing other people.

visible spectrum A small portion of the total electromagnetic spectrum of energy—that portion to which the eyes are sensitive.

visual imagery Visual pictures and scenes created in a person's mind, not registered from objects in the external environment.

wavelength The distance between the crest of one wave and the crest of the next.

weapons effect The fact that the mere presence of a gun or other weapon can increase the likelihood of a person responding aggressively.

Weber's law The fact that the amount of increase in the intensity of a stimulus needed to produce a just noticeable difference grows as the intensity of the initial stimulus grows. This means that if you are playing a stereo very softly you can usually notice a very slight increase in volume, but if you are playing the stereo very loudly, a much larger increase in volume is needed in order for you to detect it.

Wechsler scales A widely used set of IQ tests developed by David Wechsler and his colleagues.

Wernicke's area A region in the left temporal lobe of the cortex involved in understanding the meaning of words and putting words together into meaningful sentences.

X chromosome One of two kinds of sex chromosomes. Normal females have two X chromosomes; normal males have only one.

Y chromosome One of two kinds of sex chromosomes. Normal males have one Y chromosome; normal females have none.

References

Abbey, A. (1982). Sex differences in attributions for friendly behavior: Do males misperceive females' friendliness? *Journal of Personality and Social Psychology, 42,* 830–838. [17]

Abelson, R. P. (1983). Whatever became of consistency theory? *Personality and Social Psychology Bulletin, 9,* 37–54. [17]

Abrams, D. B., & Wilson, G. T. (1983). Alcohol, sexual arousal, and self-control. *Journal of Personality and Social Psychology, 45,* 188–198. [5]

Abramson, L. Y., Seligman, M. E. P., & Teasdale, J. D. (1978). Learned helplessness in humans: Critique and reformulation. *Journal of Abnormal Psychology, 87,* 49–74. [6]

Adams, D. B. (1983). Hormone-brain interactions and their influence on agonistic behavior. In B. B. Svare (Ed.), *Hormones and aggressive behavior.* New York: Plenum. [18]

Addiego, F., Belzer, E. G., Jr., Comolli, J., Moger, W., Perry, J. D., & Whipple, B. (1981). Female ejaculation: A case study. *The Journal of Sex Research, 17,* 13–21. [10]

Ader, R. (Ed.). (1981). *Psychoneuroimmunology.* Orlando, FL: Academic Press. [14]

Ader, R., & Cohen, N. (1975). Behaviorally conditioned immunosuppression. *Psychosomatic Medicine, 37,* 333–340. [14]

Ader, R., & Cohen, N. (1981). Conditioned immunopharmacologic responses. In R. Ader (Ed.), *Psychoneuroimmunology.* Orlando, FL: Academic Press. [14]

Ainsworth, M. (1983). Patterns of infant-mother attachment as related to maternal care: Their early history and their contribution to continuity. In D. Magnusson & V. L. Allen (Eds.), *Human development: An interactional perspective.* Orlando, FL: Academic Press. [11]

Ajzen, I., & Fishbein, M. (1977). Attitude-behavior relations: A theoretical analysis and review of empirical research. *Psychological Bulletin, 84,* 888–918. [17]

Ajzen, I., Timko, C., & White, J. B. (1982). Self-monitoring and the attitude-behavior relation. *Journal of Personality and Social Psychology, 42,* 426–435. [17]

Alden, L., & Safran, J. (1978). Irrational beliefs and nonassertive behavior. *Cognitive Therapy and Research, 2,* 357–364. [16]

Allen, B. P. (1978). *Social behavior.* Chicago: Nelson Hall. [18]

Allman, W. F. (1986). Mindworks. *Science 86,* May. [8].

Alloy, L. (1982). The role of perceptions and attributions for response-outcome noncontingency in learned helplessness: A commentary and discussion. *Journal of Personality, 50,* 443–479. [6]

Allport, G. W. (1937). *Personality: A psychological interpretation.* New York: Holt. [13]

Alzate, H., & Hoch, Z. (1986). The "G Spot" and "female ejaculation": A current appraisal. *Journal of Sex & Marital Therapy, 12,* 211–220. [10]

Amabile, T. M. (1983). *The social psychology of creativity.* New York: Springer-Verlag. [8]

Amabile, T. M. (1985). Motivation and creativity: Effects of motivational orientation on creative writers. *Journal of Personality and Social Psychology, 48,* 393–399. [8]

Amabile, T. M., Hennessey, B. A., & Grossman, B. S. (1986). Social influences on creativity: The effects of contracted-for reward. *Journal of Personality and Social Psychology, 50,* 14–23. [8]

American Psychiatric Association. (1980). *Diagnostic and statistical manual of mental disorders.* 3rd ed. Washington, DC: APA.

American Psychiatric Association. (1987). *Diagnostic and statistical manual of mental disorders.* 3rd Edition—Revised (DSM-III-R). Washington, DC: American Psychiatric Association. [15]

American Psychological Association. (1985). *Violence on TV. A social issue release from the Board of Social and Ethical Responsibility for Psychology.* Washington, DC: Author. [18]

Anastasi, A. (1982). *Psychological testing.* 5th ed. New York: Macmillan. [8] [13]

Anastasi, A. (1988). *Psychological testing.* New York: Macmillan. [13]

Anders, T. F. (1982). Biological rhythms in development. *Psychosomatic Medicine, 44,* 61–72. [5]

Andersen, B. L. (1983). Primary orgasmic dysfunction: Diagnostic considerations and review of treatment. *Psychological Bulletin, 93,* 105–136. [10]

Anderson, A. (1982). How the mind heals. *Psychology Today,* December. [14]

Anderson, G. E. (1972). College schedule of recent experience. Master's thesis, North Dakota State University. [14]

Anderson, J. R. (1983). Retrieval of information from long-term memory. *Science, 220,* 25–30. [7]

Andreasen, N. C., Rice, J., Endicott, J., Coryell, W., Grove, W. M., & Reich, T. (1987). Familial rates of affective disorder. *Archives of General Psychiatry, 44,* 461–469. [15]

Andrews, L. B. (1984). Exhibit A: Language. *Psychology Today,* February. [8]

Andrykowski, M. A., & Redd, W. H. (1987). Longitudinal analysis of the development of anticipatory nausea. *Journal of Consulting and Clinical Psychology, 55,* 36–41. [6]

Aneshensel, C. S., & Stone, J. D. (1982). Stress and depression. *Archives of General Psychiatry, 39,* 1392–1396. [14]

Angier, N. (1984). Medical clues from babies' cries. *Discover,* September. [11]

Arlington-MacKinnon, D., & Troll, L. E. (1981). The adaptive function of the menopause: A devil's advocate position. *Journal of the American Geriatrics Society, 29,* 349–353. [10]

Asch, S. E. (1958). Effects of group pressure upon modification and distortion of judgments. In E. E. Maccoby, T. M. Newcomb, & E. L. Hartley (Eds.), *Reading in social psychology.* 3rd ed. New York: Holt, Rinehart and Winston. [18]

Atkinson, J. W. (1958). (Ed.). *Motives in fantasy, action and society.* Princeton, NJ: Van Nostrand Reinhold. [9]

Atkinson, J. W. (1964). *An introduction to motivation.* Princeton, NJ: Van Nostrand Reinhold. [9]

Atkinson, J. W., & Raynor, J. O. (1974). (Ed.). *Motivation and achievement.* Washington, DC: Winston. [9]

Attias, J., Gordon, C., Ribak, J., Binah, O., & Arnon, R. (1987). Efficacy of transdermal scopolamine against seasickness: A 3-day study at sea. *Aviation, Space and Environmental Medicine, 58,* 60–62. [3]

Axelsson, A., & Lindgren, F. (1982). Quoted in *Science News, 121,* 393. [3]

Azrin, N. H., & Foxx, R. M. (1974). *Toilet training in less than a day.* New York: Simon and Schuster. [6]

619

Bahrick, H. P. (1984). Semantic memory content in permastore: Fifty years of memory for Spanish learned in school. *Journal of Experimental Psychology: General, 113,* 1–29. [7]

Baker, R. A. (1982). The effect of suggestion on past-lives regression. *American Journal of Clinical Hypnosis, 25,* 71–76. [5]

Bandura, A. (1974). Behavior theory and the models of man. *American Psychologist, 29,* 859–869. [6]

Bandura, A. (1986). *Social foundations of thought and action: A social cognitive theory.* Englewood Cliffs, NJ: Prentice-Hall. [6, 9, 13, 14]

Bandura, A., Ross, D., & Ross, S. A. (1963). Vicarious reinforcement and imitative learning. *Journal of Abnormal and Social Psychology, 67,* 601–607. [18]

Barbach, L., & Flaherty, M. (1980). Group treatment of situationally orgasmic women. *Journal of Sex & Marital Therapy, 6,* 19–29. [10]

Barber, T. X. (1961). Antisocial and criminal acts induced by "hypnosis." *Archives of General Psychology, 5,* 301–312. [1]

Barber, T. X. (1965). Measuring "Hypnotic-like" suggestibility with and without "Hypnotic Induction": Psychometric properties, norms, and variables influencing responses to the Barber Suggestibility Scale (BSS). *Psychological Reports, 16,* 809–844. [5]

Barber, T. X. (1979). Suggested ("Hypnotic") behavior: The trance paradigm versus an alternative paradigm. In E. Fromm & D. E. Shor (Eds.), *Hypnosis: Developments in research and new perspectives.* New York: Aldine. [5]

Barker, L. L., Wahlers, K. J., Cegala, D. J., & Kibler, R. J. (1983). *Groups in process.* 2nd ed. Englewood Cliffs, NJ: Prentice-Hall. [18]

Barnes, D. M. (1987a). AIDS: Statistics but few answers. *Science, 236,* 1423–1425. [10]

Barnes, D. M. (1987b). Biological issues in schizophrenia. *Science, 235,* 430–433. [15]

Barnes, D. M. (1987c). Neural models yield data on learning. *Science, 236,* 1628–1629. [7]

Baron, M. (1986). Genetics of schizophrenia: II. Vulnerability traits and gene markers. *Biological Psychiatry, 21,* 1189–1211. [5]

Baron, R. A., & Byrne, D. (1984). *Social psychology.* 4th ed. Boston: Allyn and Bacon. [17]

Barron, F., & Harrington, D. M. (1981). Creativity, intelligence, and personality. *Annual Review of Psychology, 32,* 439–476. [8]

Bartus, R. T., Dean, R. L. III, Beer, B., & Lippa, A. S. (1982). The cholinergic hypothesis of geriatric memory dysfunction. *Science, 217,* 408–417. [7]

Baumeister, R. F. (1982). A self-presentational view of social phenomena. *Psychological Bulletin, 91,* 3–26. [17]

Baylis, G. C., Rolls, E. T., & Leonard, C. M. (1985). Selectivity between faces in the responses of a population of neurons in the cortex in the superior temporal sulcus of the monkey. *Brain Research, 342,* 91–102. [3]

Beaman, A. L., Cole, C. M., Preston, M., Lkentz, B., & Steblay, N. M. (1983). Fifteen years of foot-in-the-door research. *Personality and Social Psychology Bulletin, 9,* 181–196. [18]

Beck, A. T. (1976). *Cognitive therapy and the emotional disorders.* New York: International Universities Press. [16]

Beck, K. H., & Davis, C. M. (1980). Predicting smoking intentions and behaviors from attitudes, normative beliefs and emotional arousal. *Social Behavior and Personality, 8,* 185–192. [17]

Beck, K. H., & Lund, A. K. (1981). The effects of health threat seriousness and personal efficacy upon intentions and behavior. *Journal of Applied Social Psychology, 11,* 401–415. [17]

Bedrosian, R. C., & Beck, A. T. (1980). Principles of cognitive therapy. In M. J. Mahoney (Ed.), *Psychotherapy process.* New York: Plenum Press. [16]

Bee, H. L., & Mitchell, S. K. (1980). *The developing person.* New York: Harper & Row. [11]

Begg, I., & Sikich, D. (1984). Imagery and contextual organization. *Memory & Cognition, 12,* 52–59. [7]

Begleiter, H., Porjesz, B., Bihari, B., & Kissin, B. (1984). Event-related brain potentials in boys at risk for alcoholism. *Science, 225,* 1493–1496. [5]

Bekker, F. J. (1974). Personality development in XO-Turner's syndrome. In H. F. van Abeelen (Ed.), *The genetics of behaviour.* New York: American Elsevier. [10]

Bell, A. P., Weinberg, M. S., & Hammersmith, S. K. (1981). *Sexual preference: Its development in men and women.* Bloomington: Indiana University Press. [10]

Belsky, J., Gilstrap, B., & Rovine, M. (1984a). The Pennsylvania infant and family development project, I: Stability and change in mother-infant and father-infant interaction in a family setting at one, three and nine months. *Child Development, 55,* 692–705. [11]

Belsky, J., Rovine, M., & Taylor, D. G. (1984b). The Pennsylvania infant and family development project, III: The origins of individual differences in infant-mother attachment: Maternal and infant contributions. *Child Development, 55,* 718–728. [11]

Belzer, E. G., Jr. (1981). Orgasmic expulsions of women: A review and heuristic inquiry. *The Journal of Sex Research, 17,* 1–12. [10]

Bem, S. L. (1974). The measurement of psychological androgyny. *Journal of Consulting and Clinical Psychology, 42,* 155–162. [12]

Bem, S. L. (1976). Probing the promise of androgyny. In A. G. Kaplan & J. P. Bean (Eds.), *Beyond sex-role stereotypes.* Boston: Little, Brown. [12]

Bem, S. L. (1979). Theory and measurement of androgyny: A reply to the Pedhazur-Tetenbaum and Locksley-Colten critiques. *Journal of Personality and Social Psychology, 37,* 1047–1054. [12]

Benbow, C. (1987). Quoted in: Holden, C., Female math anxiety on the wane. *Science, 236,* 660–661. [11]

Benbow, C., & Stanley, J. (1980). Sex differences in mathematical ability: Fact or artifact. *Science, 210,* 1262–1264. [11]

Benderly, B. L. (1980). The great ape debate. *Science 80,* July–August. [8]

Bengtson, V. L., Cuellar, J. B., & Ragan, P. K. (1977). Stratum contrasts and similarities in attitudes toward death. *Journal of Gerontology, 32,* 76–88. [12]

Bennett, G. A., & Jones, S. E. (1986). Dropping out of treatment for obesity. *Journal of Psychosomatic Research, 30,* 567–573. [9]

Berg, J. H., & McQuinn, R. D. (1986). Attraction and exchange in continuing and noncontinuing dating relationships. *Journal of Personality and Social Psychology, 50,* 942–952. [12]

Berkowitz, L. (1982). Aversive conditions as stimuli to aggression. In L. Berkowitz (Ed.), *Advances in experimental social psychology.* Vol. 15. Orlando, FL.: Academic Press. [18]

Berkowitz, L. (1983). Aversively stimulated aggression. *American Psychologist, 38,* 1135–1144. [18]

Berman, R. A. (1983). On the study of first language acquisition. *Language Learning, 33,* 221–245. [8]

Bernstein, D. A., & Kleinknecht, R. A. (1982). Multiple approaches to the reduction of dental fear. *Journal of Behavior, Therapy and Experimental Psychiatry, 13,* 287–292. [6]

Bernstein, I. L. (1978). Learned taste aversion in children receiving chemotherapy. *Science, 200,* 1302–1303. [6]

Besag, F. (1987). Quoted in: Holden, C., Female math anxiety on the wane. *Science, 236,* 660–661. [11]

Billings, A. G., Cronkite, R. C., & Moos, R. H. (1983). Social-environmental factors in unipolar depression: Comparisons of depressed patients and nondepressed controls. *Journal of Abnormal Psychology, 92,* 119–133. [15]

Blackburn, J. A. (1984). The influence of personality, curriculum, and memory correlates on formal reasoning in young adults and elderly persons. *Journal of Gerontology, 39,* 207–209. [12]

Blackmore, S. (1987a). Where am I?: Perspectives in imagery and the out-of-body experience. *Journal of Mental Imagery, 11,* 53–66. [4]

Blackmore, S. (1987b). The elusive open mind: Ten years of negative research in parapsychology. *The Skeptical Inquirer, 11,* 244–255. [4]

Blackmore, S. J. (1985). Unrepeatability: Parapsychology's only finding. In B. Shapin & L. Coly (Eds.), *The repeatability problem in parapsychology.* New York: Parapsychology Foundation. [4]

Blakemore, C. (1977). Mechanics of the mind. London: Cambridge University Press. [1, 2]

Blanchard, E. B., Andrasik, F., Guarnieri, P., Neff, D. F., & Rodichok, L. D. (1987). Two-, three- and four-year follow-up on the self-regulatory treatment of chronic headache. *Journal of Consulting and Clinical Psychology, 55,* 257–259. [14]

Bland, R. C. (1982). Predicting the outcome in schizophrenia. *Canadian Journal of Psychiatry, 27,* 52–62. [15]

Blaney, P. H. (1986). Affect and memory: A review. *Psychological Bulletin, 99,* 229–246. [7]

Bohlen, J. (1986). Quoted in: Gallagher, W., The etiology of orgasm. *Discover,* 51–59. [10]

Bohlen, J. G., Held, J. P., Sanderson, M. O., & Ahlgren, A. (1982). The female orgasm: Pelvic contractions. *Archives of Sexual Behavior, 11,* 367–386. [10]

Boor, M. (1982). The multiple personality epidemic. *The Journal of Nervous and Mental Disease, 170,* 302–304. [15]

Booth-Kewley, S., & Friedman, H. S. (1987). Psychological predictors of heart disease: A quantitative review. *Psychological Bulletin, 101,* 343–362. [14]

Bootzin, R. R. (1982). A skill deficit approach to loneliness. In K. R. Blankstein & J. Polivy (Eds.), *Advances in the study of communication and affect.* Vol. 7. New York: Plenum Press. [13]

Bootzin, R. R., & Nicassio, P. N. (1978). Behavioral treatments for insomnia. In M. Hensen, R. M. Eisler, & P. M. Miller (Eds.), *Progress in behavior modification.* Vol. 6. Orlando, FL: Academic Press. [5]

Borkovec, T. D. (1982). Insomnia. *Journal of Counseling and Clinical Psychology, 50,* 880–895. [5]

Bornstein, P. H., Hamilton, S. B., & McFall, M. E. (1981). Modification of adult aggression: A critical review of theory, research and practice. In M. Hersen, R. M. Eisler, & P. M. Miller (Eds.), *Progress in behavior modification.* Vol. 12. Orlando, FL: Academic Press. [18]

Bouchard, C., & Tremblay, A. (1987). Quoted in: Kolata, G., Metabolic catch-22 of exercise regimens. *Science, 236,* 146–147. [9]

Bouchard, T. J., Jr. (1984). Twins reared together and apart: What they tell us about human diversity. In S. W. Fox (Ed.), *Individuality and determinism: Chemical and biological bases.* New York: Plenum Press. [13]

Bower, B. (1985). Getting into Einstein's brain. *Science News, 127,* 330. [1]

Bower, G. H. (1981). Mood and memory. *American Psychologist, 36,* 129–148. [7, 9]

Boy, A. V., & Pine, G. J. (1982). *Client-centered counseling: A renewal.* Boston: Allyn and Bacon. [16]

Boyd, T. L., & Lewis, D. J. (1983). Exposure is a necessary condition for fear-reduction: A reply to De Silva and Rachman. *Behavior Research and Therapy, 21,* 143–149. [15, 16]

Bradshaw, C. W., Jr. (1982). Validity of biorhythms for predicting death. *Journal of Psychology, 110,* 39–41. [1]

Brantner, J. P., & Doherty, M. A. (1983). A review of timeout: A conceptual and methodological analysis. In S. Axelrod & J. Apsche (Eds.), *The effects of punishment on human behavior.* Orlando, FL: Academic Press. [6]

Bray, G. (1986). Quoted in: Toufexis, A. Dieting: The losing game. *Time,* January 20, 54–60. [9]

Bregman, B. S., & Goldberger, M. E. (1982). Anatomical plasticity and sparing of function after spinal cord damage in neonatal cats. *Science, 217,* 553–554. [2]

Breskin, D. (1984). Dear mom and dad. *Rolling Stone,* November 8. [12]

Brickman, P., Coates, D., & Janoff-Bulman, R. (1978). Lottery winners and accident victims: Is happiness relative? *Journal of Personality and Social Psychology, 36,* 917–927. [9]

Broderick, J. E., Friedman, J. M., & Carr, E. G. (1981). Negotiation and contracting. In A. P. Goldstein, E. G. Carr, W. S. Davidson II, &

P. Wehr (Eds.), *In response to aggression.* New York: Pergamon Press. [12]

Broverman, I. K., Broverman, D. M., Clarkson, F. E., Rosenkrantz, P. S., & Vogel, S. R. (1970). Sex-role stereotypes and clinical judgments of mental health. *Journal of Consulting and Clinical Psychology, 34,* 1–7. [12]

Brown, G. W. (1981). Life events, psychiatric disorder and physical illness. *Journal of Psychosomatic Research, 25,* 461–473. [14]

Brown, J. (1987). A review of meta-analyses conducted on psychotherapy outcome research. *Clinical Psychology Review, 7,* 1–23. [16]

Brown, R., & Kulik, J. (1977). Flashbulb memories. *Cognition, 5,* 73–99. [7]

Brownell, K. D., & Venditti, E. M. (1982). The etiology and treatment of obesity. In W. E. Fann, I. Karacan, A. D. Pokorny, & R. L. Williams (Eds.), *Phenomenology and treatment of psychophysiological disorders.* New York: Spectrum. [9]

Bruch, H. (1981). Psychotherapy in anorexia nervosa. *International Journal of Eating Disorders, 1,* 3–14. [9]

Bruch, H. (1982). Anorexia nervosa: Therapy and theory. *American Journal of Psychiatry, 139,* 1531–1538. [9]

Buckout, R. (1980). Nearly 2,000 witnesses can be wrong. *Bulletin of the Psychonomic Society, 16,* 307–310. [7]

Burbach, J. P. H., Kovacs, G. L., Weid, D. D., van Nispen, J. W., & Greven, H. M. (1983). A major metabolite of arginine vasopressin in the brain is a highly potent neuropeptide. *Science, 221,* 1310–1312. [7]

Burch, G. E. (1983). Interesting aspects of the aging process. *Journal of the American Geriatrics Society, 31,* 766–779. [12]

Burisch, M. (1984). Approaches to personality inventory construction. *American Psychologist, 39,* 214–227. [13]

Burish, T. G., & Carey, M. P. (1986). Conditioned aversive responses in cancer chemotherapy patients: Theoretical and developmental analysis. *Journal of Consulting and Clinical Psychology, 54,* 593–600. [6]

Burt, M. R. (1980). Cultural myths and supports for rape. *Journal of Personality and Social Psychology, 38,* 217–230. [10, 18]

Buss, A. H., & Finn, S. E. (1987). Classification of personality traits. *Journal of Personality and Social Psychology, 52,* 432–444. [13]

Buss, D. M., & Barnes, M. (1986). Preferences in human mate selection. *Journal of Personality and Social Psychology, 50,* 559–570. [12]

Butters, N., & Albert, M. S. (1982). Process underlying failures to recall remote events. In L. S. Cermak (Ed.), *Human memory and amnesia.* Hillsdale, NJ: Lawrence Erlbaum. [7]

Cain, W. S. (1977). Differential sensitivity for smell: "Noise" at the nose. *Science, 195,* 796–798. [3]

Callero, P. L., & Piliavin, J. A. (1983). Developing a commitment to blood donation: The impact of one's first experience. *Journal of Applied Social Psychology, 13,* 1–16. [9]

Candee, D., & Kohlberg, L. (1987). Moral judgment and moral action: A reanalysis of Haan, Smith, and Block's (1968) Free Speech Movement Data. *Journal of Per-*

sonality and Social Psychology, 52, 554–564. [12]

Cantor, N. (1981). A cognitive-social approach to personality. In N. Cantor & J. F. Kihlstrom (Eds.), *Personality, cognition, and social interaction.* Hillsdale, NJ: Lawrence Erlbaum. [13]

Caplan, G. (1974). *Support systems and community mental health.* New York: Behavioral Publications. [14]

Caplan, G. (1981). Mastery of stress: Psychosocial aspects. *American Journal of Psychiatry, 138,* 413–419. [14]

Catchlove, R. F. H. (1983). Phantom pain following limb amputation in a paraplegic. *Psychotherapy and Psychosomatics, 39,* 89–93. [3]

Caton, C. L. M. (1982). Effect of length of inpatient treatment for chronic schizophrenia. *American Journal of Psychiatry, 139,* 856–861. [15]

Cattell, R. B. (1947). Confirmation and clarification of the primary personality factors. *Psychometrika, 12,* 197–220. [13]

Ceci, S. J., & Liker, J. K. (1986). A day at the races: A study of IQ, expertise, and cognitive complexity. *Journal of Experimental Psychology: General, 115,* 255–266. [8]

Ceci, S. J., Ross, D. F., & Toglia, M. P. (1987). Suggestibility of children's memory: Psycholegal implications. *Journal of Experimental Psychology: General, 116,* 38–49. [7]

Chafetz, M. E. (1979). Alcohol and alcoholism. *American Scientist, 67* (May–June), 293–299. [5]

Chance, P. (1986). Life after head injury. *Psychology Today,* October. [2]

Chance, P., & Fischman, J. (1987). The magic of childhood. *Psychology Today,* May. [11]

Chen, G., Li, S., & Jiang, C. (1986). Clinical studies on neurophysiological and biochemical basis of acupuncture analgesia. *American Journal of Chinese Medicine, 14,* 86–95. [3]

Chen, L. (1982). Topological structure in visual perception. *Science, 218,* 699–700. [4]

Chen, S., & Hillman, D. E. (1982). Plasticity of the parallel fiber-Purkinje cell synapse by spine takeover and new synapse formation in the adult rat. *Brain Research, 240,* 205–220. [2]

Chipman, S. F. (1987). Quoted in: Holden, C., Female math anxiety on the wane. *Science, 236,* 660–661. [11]

Chomsky, N. (1957). *Syntactic structures.* The Hague: Mouton. [8]

Chomsky, N. (1980). The linguistic approach. In M. Piatelli-Palmarini (Ed.), *Language and learning.* Cambridge, MA: Harvard University Press. [8]

Clark, M. S., & Fiske, S. T. (1982). *Affect and cognition.* Hillsdale, NJ: Lawrence Erlbaum. [9]

Clarke-Stewart, K. A., & Fein, G. G. (1983). Early childhood programs. In P. H. Mussen (Ed.), *Handbook of child psychology.* Vol. II. New York: Wiley. [11]

Clement, U. (1980). Sexual unresponsiveness and orgasmic dysfunction: An empirical comparison. *Journal of Sex & Marital Therapy, 6,* 274–281. [10]

Clifford, M. M. (1980). Effects of failure:

Alternative explanations and possible implications. In L. J. Fyans, Jr. (Ed.), *Achievement motivation*. New York: Plenum Press. [9]

Cloninger, C. R. (1987). Neurogenetic adaptive mechanisms in alcoholism. *Science, 236*, 410–416. [5]

Cloninger, C. R., Bohman, M., & Sigvardsson, S. (1981). Inheritance of alcohol abuse. *Archives of General Psychiatry, 38*, 861–868. [5]

Cochrane, G., & Friesen, J. (1986). Hypnotherapy in weight loss treatment. *Journal of Consulting and Clinical Psychology, 54*, 489–492. [5]

Cohen, B., & Murphy, G. L. (1984). Models of concepts. *Cognitive Science, 8*, 27–58. [8]

Cohen, D. B. (1979). *Sleep and dreaming: Origins, nature and functions*. New York: Pergamon Press. [5]

Cohen, N. J., & Squire, L. R. (1980). Preserved learning and retention of pattern-analyzing skill in amnesia: Dissociation of knowing how and knowing that. *Science, 210*, 207–210. [7]

Cohen, S. (1986). Marijuana research: Selected recent findings. *Drug Abuse & Alcoholism Newsletter*, January. [5]

Cohen, S., & Wills, T. A. (1985). Stress, social support, and the buffering hypothesis. *Psychological Bulletin, 98*, 310–357. [14]

Colby, A., Kohlberg, L., Gibbs, J., & Lieberman, M. (1983). A longitudinal study of moral judgment. Chicago: *Monograph of the Society for Research in Child Development, 48* (1–2, Serial No. 200). [12]

Coleman, R. M., Miles, L. E., Guilleminault, C. C., Zarcone, V. P., Jr., Van den Hoed, J., & Dement, W. C. (1981). Sleep-wake disorders in the elderly: A polysomnographic analysis. *Journal of the American Geriatrics Society, 29*, 289–296. [5]

Coleman, R. M., Roffwagg, H. P., Kennedy, S. J., Guilleminault, C., Cinque, J., Cohn, M. A., Karacan, I., Kupfer, D. J., Lemmi, H., Miles, L. E., Orr, W. C., Phillips, E. R., Roth, T., Sassin, J. F., Schmidt, H. S., Weitzman, E. D., Dement, W. C. (1982). Sleep-wake disorders based on a polysomnographic diagnosis. *Journal of the American Medical Association, 247*, 997–1003. [5]

Collins, R. L., Rothblum, E. D., & Wilson, G. T. (1986). The comparative efficacy of cognitive and behavioral approaches to the treatment of obesity. *Cognitive Therapy and Research, 10*, 299–318. [9]

Connery, D. S. (1982). *The inner source*. New York: Holt, Rinehart and Winston. [5]

Coons, P. M., Milstein, V., & Marley, C. (1982). EEG studies of two multiple personalities and a control. *Archives of General Psychiatry, 39*, 823–825. [15]

Cooper, H. M., & Good, T. L. (1983). *Pygmalion grows up*. New York: Longman. [1]

Coren, S., Porac, C., & Ward, L. M. (1984). *Sensation and perception*. 2d ed. Orlando, FL: Academic Press. [3, 4]

Corey, D. T., Etlin, D., & Miller, P. C. (1987). A home-based pain management and rehabilitation programme: An evaluation. *Pain, 29*, 219–229. [3]

Cornelius, S. W. (1984). Classic pattern of intellectual aging: Test familiarity, diffi-

culty and performance. *Journal of Gerontology, 39*, 201–206. [12]

Corsini, R. J. (Ed.). (1982). *Handbook of innovative psychotherapies*. New York: Wiley. [16]

Corteen, R. S., & Dunn, D. (1974). Shock-associated words in a nonattended message: A test for momentary awareness. *Journal of Experimental Psychology, 102*, 1143–1144. [4]

Corteen, R. S., & Wood, B. (1972). Autonomic responses to shock-associated words in an unattended channel. *Journal of Experimental Psychology, 94*, 308–313. [4]

Costa, P. T., McCrae, R. R., & Arenberg, D. (1983). Recent longitudinal research on personality and aging. In K. W. Schaie (Ed.), *Longitudinal studies of adult psychological development*. New York: Guilford Press. [13]

Cragoe, E. J., Gould, N. P., Woltersd, O. W., Ziegler, C., Bourke, R. S., Nelson, L. R., Kimelber, H. K., Waldman, J. B., Popp, A. J., & Sedransk, N. (1982). Agents for treatment of brain injury. *Journal of Medicinal Chemistry, 25*, 567–579. [2]

Craighead, L. W., Stunkard, A. J., & O'Brien. (1981). Behavior therapy and pharmacotherapy for obesity. *Archives of General Psychiatry, 38*, 763–768. [9]

Crane, M., & Markus, H. (1982). Gender identity: The benefits of a self-schema approach. *Journal of Personality and Social Psychology, 43*, 1195–1197. [17]

Crocker, J., Hannah, D. B., & Weber, R. (1983). Person memory and causal attributions. *Journal of Personality and Social Psychology, 44*, 55–66. [17]

Cromwell, R. L., Butterfield, E. C., Brayfield, F. M., & Curry, J. J. (1977). *Acute myocardial infarction*. St. Louis, MO: Mosby. [14]

Crook, T. H., & Miller, N. E. (1985). The challenge of Alzheimer's disease. *American Psychologist, 40*, 1245–1250. [2]

Crooks, R., & Baur, K. (1983). *Our sexuality*. 2nd ed. Menlo Park, CA: Benjamin Cummings. [10]

Crosby, F., Bromley, S., & Saxe, L. (1980). Recent unobtrusive studies of black and white discrimination and prejudice: A literature review. *Psychological Bulletin, 87*, 546–563. [17]

Crowley, C., Crowley, D., & Clodfelter, C. (1986). Effects of a self-coping cognitive treatment for test anxiety. *Journal of Counseling Psychology, 33*, 84–86. [7]

Csikszentmihalyi, M., & Figurski, T. J. (1982). Self-awareness and aversive experience in everyday life. *Journal of Personality, 50*, 15–28. [9]

Csikszentimihalyi, M., & Larson, R. (1984). *Being adolescent*. New York: Basic Books. [12]

Culp, R. E., Cook, A. S., & Housley, P. C. (1983). A comparison of observed and reported adult-infant interactions: Effects of perceived sex. *Sex Roles, 9*, 475–479. [11]

Cunningham, M. R. (1987). Measuring the physical in physical attractiveness: Quasi-experiments on the sociobiology of female facial beauty. *Journal of Personality and Social Psychology, 50*, 925–935. [17]

Curtiss, S. (1977). *Genie: A psycholinguistic study of a modern day "wild child."* Orlando, FL: Academic Press. [8]

Cutrona, C., Peplau, L. A., & Russell, D.

(1985). Quoted in: Meer, J., Loneliness. *Psychology Today*, July, 28–33. [13]

Cutrona, C. E. (1982). Transition to college: Loneliness and the process of social adjustment. In L. A. Peplau & D. Perlman (Eds.), *Loneliness*. New York: Wiley. [13]

Dabbs, J. M., Frady, R. L., Carr, T. S., & Besch, N. F. (1987). Saliva testosterone and criminal violence in young adult prison inmates. *Psychosomatic Medicine, 49*, 174–182. [18]

Damasio, A. R., Damasio, H., & Van Hoesen, G. W. (1982). Prosopagnosia: Anatomic basis and behavioral mechanisms. *Neurology, 32*, 331–341. [4]

Daniel, T. L., & Esser, J. K. (1980). Intrinsic motivation as influenced by rewards, task interest, and task structure. *Journal of Applied Psychology, 65*, 566–573. [9]

Darling, C. A., & Davidson, Sr., J. K. (1986). Coitally active university students: Sexual behaviors, concerns, and challenges. *Adolescence, 21*, 403–419. [10]

Davanloo, H. (1980a). A method of short-term dynamic psychotherapy. In H. Davanloo (Ed.), *Short-term dynamic psychotherapy*. New York: Jason Aronson. [16]

Davanloo, H. (Ed.). (1980b). *Short-term dynamic psychotherapy*. New York: Jason Aronson. [16]

Davidson, A. R., & Jaccard, J. (1975). Population psychology: A new look at an old problem. *Journal of Personality and Social Psychology, 31*, 1073–1082. [17]

Davidson, J. M., Camargo, C. A., & Smith, E. R. (1979). Effects of androgen on sexual behavior in hypogonàdal men. *Journal of Clinical Endocrinology and Metabolism, 48*, 955–958. [10]

Davidson, T. M., Jalowayski, A., Murphy, C., & Jacobs, R. D. (1987). Evaluation and treatment of smell dysfunction. *Western Journal of Medicine, 146*, 434–438. [3]

Davies, P., & Wolozin, B. L. (1987). Recent advances in the neurochemistry of Alzheimer's disease. *Journal of Clinical Psychiatry, 48*, 23–30. [2]

Davis, G. E., Blaker, S. N., Engvall, E., Varon, S., Manthorpe, M., & Gage, F. H. (1987). Human amnio membrane serves as a substratum for growing axons in vitro and in vivo. *Science, 236*, 1106–1116. [2]

Davis, J. M., & Janicak, P. G. (1982). Biological treatments. In J. E. Cavenar & H. K. H. Brodie (Eds.), *Critical problems in psychiatry*. Philadelphia: Lippincott. [15]

Davis, M. H., & Stephan, W. G. (1980). Attributions for exam performance. *Journal of Applied Social Psychology, 10*, 235–248. [9] [17]

Davison, G. C., & Neale, J. M. (1982). *Abnormal psychology*. 3rd ed. New York: Wiley. [15]

Deaux, K., & Wrightsman, L. S. (1984). *Social psychology in the 80s*. 4th ed. Monterey, CA: Brooks/Cole. [17, 18]

deCharms, R. (1980). The origins of competence and achievement motivation in personal causation. In L. J. Fyans, Jr. (Ed.), *Achievement motivation*. New York: Plenum Press. [9]

Deci, E. L., & Ryan, R. M. (1980). The empirical exploration of intrinsic motivational processes. In L. Berkowitz (Ed.), *Advances in experimental social psychology.* Vol. 13. Orlando, FL: Academic Press. [9]

Deffenbacher, J. L., Story, D. A., Stark, R. S., Hogg, J. A., Brandon, A. D. (1987). Cognitive-relaxation and social skills interventions in the treatment of general anger. *Journal of Counseling Psychology, 34,* 171–176. [18]

Deffenbacher, J. L., & Suinn, R. M. (1982). The self-control of anxiety. In P. Karoly & F. H. Kanfer (Eds.), *Self-management and behavior change.* New York: Pergamon Press. [16]

Dendato, K. M., & Diener, D. (1986). Effectiveness of cognitive/relaxation therapy and study-skills training in reducing self-reported anxiety and improving the academic performance of test-anxious students. *Journal of Counseling Psychology, 33,* 131–135. [7]

Denney, N. W. (1982). Aging and cognitive changes. In B. B. Wolman (Ed.), *Handbook of developmental psychology.* Englewood Cliffs, NJ: Prentice-Hall. [8]

Deregowski, J. B. (1980). *Illusions, patterns and pictures: A cross-cultural perspective.* Orlando, FL: Academic Press. [4]

Dermer, M. S., & Jacobsen, E. (1986). Some potential negative social consequences of cigarette smoking: Marketing research in reverse. *Journal of Applied Social Psychology, 16,* 702–725. [17]

Derry, P. A., & Kuiper, N. A. (1981). Schematic processing and self-reference in clinical depression. *Journal of Abnormal Psychology, 90,* 286–297. [15]

Detera-Wadleigh, S. D., Berrettini, W. H., Goldin, L. R., Boorman, D., Anderson, S., & Gershon, E. S. (1987). Close linkage of c-Harvey-ras-1 and the insulin gene to affective disorder is ruled out in three North American pedigrees. *Nature, 325,* 806–807. [15]

Dietz, W. (1986). Quoted in: Kolata, G., Obese children: A growing problem. *Science, 232,* 20–22. [9]

Digman, J. M., & Inouye, J. (1986). Further specification of the five robust factors of personality. *Journal of Personality and Social Psychology, 50,* 116–123. [13]

Digman, J. M., & Takemoto-Chock, N. K. (1981). Factors in the natural language of personality: Re-analysis and comparison of six major studies. *Multivariate Behavioral Research, 16,* 149–170. [13]

Dixon, N. F. (1981). *Preconscious processing.* New York: Wiley. [4]

Dobie, T. G., May, J. G., Elder, S. T., & Kubiyz, K. A. (1987). A comparison of two methods of training resistance to visually-induced motion sickness. *Aviation, Space and Environmental Medicine, 58,* A34–A41. [3]

Downing, F. L. (1986). *To see the promised land.* Macon, GA: Mercer University Press. [13]

Duncan, B. L. (1976). Differential social perception and attribution of intergroup violence: Testing the lower limits of stereotyping of blacks. *Journal of Personality and Social Psychology, 34,* 590–598. [17]

Eagly, A. H., Steffen, V. J. (1986). Gender and aggressive behavior: A meta-analytic review of the social psychological literature. *Psychological Bulletin, 100,* 309–330. [18]

Earle, J. R., & Perricone, P. J. (1986). Premarital sexuality: A ten-year study of attitudes and behavior on a small university campus. *The Journal of Sex Research, 22,* 304–310. [10]

Earn, B. M. (1982). Intrinsic motivation as a function of extrinsic financial rewards and subjects' locus of control. *Journal of Personality, 50,* 360–373. [9]

Eckenrode, J. (1984). Impact of chronic and acute stressors on daily reports of mood. *Journal of Personality and Social Psychology, 46,* 907–918. [14, 9]

Eden, D., & Shani, A. B. (1982). Pygmalion goes to boot camp: Expectancy, leadership, and trainee performance. *Journal of Applied Psychology, 67,* 194–199. [1]

Edwards, D. D. (1986). Nicotine: A drug of choice? *Science News, 129,* 44–45. [5]

Egeland, B., & Farber, E. A. (1984). Infant-mother attachment: Factors related to its development and changes over time. *Child Development, 55,* 753–771. [11]

Egeland, J. A., Gerhard, D. S., Pauls, D. L., Sussex, J. N., Kidd, K. K., Allen, C. R., Hostetter, A. M., & Housman, D. E. (1987). Bipolar affective disorders linked to DNA markers on chromosome 11. *Nature, 325,* 783–787. [15]

Ehrhardt, A. A., & Meyer-Bahlburg, H. F. L. (1981). Effects of prenatal sex hormones on gender-related behavior. *Science, 211,* 1312–1318. [10]

Eibl-Eibesfeldt, I. (1973). The expressive behavior of the deaf and blind-born. In M. von Cranach & I. Vine (Eds.), *Social communication and movement.* Orlando, FL: Academic Press. [9]

Eichorn, D. H., Clausen, J. A., Haan, N., Honzik, M. P., & Mussen, P. H. (Eds.). (1981). *Present and past in middle life.* Orlando, FL: Academic Press. [12]

Eijkman, E. G. J., Jongsma, H. J., & Vincent, J. (1981). Two-dimensional filtering oriented line detectors and figural aspects as determinants of visual illusions. *Perception & Psychophysics, 29,* 352–358. [4]

Einstein, G. O., Morris, J., & Smith, S. (1985). Note-taking, individual differences, and memory for lecture information. *Journal of Educational Psychology, 77,* 522–532. [1]

Ekman, P. (1984). Expression and the nature of emotion. In K. R. Scherer & P. Ekman (Eds.), *Approaches to emotion.* Hillsdale, NJ: Erlbaum. [9]

Ekman, P., & Friesen, W. V. (1975). *Unmasking the face.* Englewood Cliffs, NJ: Prentice-Hall. [9]

Ekman, P., Levenson, R. W., & Friesen, W. V. (1983). Autonomic nervous system activity distinguished among emotions. *Science, 361,* 1208–1210. [9]

Elkind, D. (1974). *Children and adolescents.* 2nd ed. New York: Oxford University Press. [12]

Ellis, A. (1962). *Reason and emotion in psychotherapy.* New York: Lyle Stuart. [16]

Ellis, A. (1970). *The essence of rational psychotherapy: A comprehensive approach to treatment.* New York: Institute for Rational Living. [16]

Ellis, L., & Ames, M. A. (1987). Neurohormonal functioning and sexual orientation: A theory of homosexuality-heterosexuality. *Psychological Bulletin, 101,* 233–258. [10]

Emmelkamp, P. M. G. (1979). The behavioral study of clinical phobias. In M. Hersen, R. M. Eisler, & P. M. Miller (Eds.), *Progress in behavior modification.* Vol. 8. Orlando, FL: Academic Press. [15]

Epstein, L. (1986). Quoted in: Kolata, G., Obese children: A growing problem. *Science, 232,* 20–21. [9]

Epstein, L. H., & Wing, R. R. (1987). Behavioral treatment of childhood obesity. *Psychological Bulletin, 101,* 331–342. [9]

Epstein, S., & O'Brien, E. J. (1985). The person-situation debate in historical and current perspective. *Psychological Bulletin, 98,* 513–537. [13]

Ericsson, K. A., Chase, W. G., & Faloon, S. (1980). Acquisition of a memory skill. *Science, 208,* 1181–1182. [7]

Erikson, E. H. (1968). *Identity, youth, and crisis.* New York: Norton. [12]

Erikson, E. H. (1982). *The life cycle completed: Review.* New York: Norton. [12]

Eron, L. D. (1982). Parent-child interaction, television violence and aggression of children. *American Psychologist, 37,* 197–211. [18]

Eron, L. D., Huesmann, L. R., Dubow, E., Romanoff, R., & Yarmel, P. W. (1987). Aggression and its correlates over 22 years. In D. H. Crowell, I. M. Evans, and C. R. O'Donnell (Eds.), *Childhood aggression and violence: Sources of influence, prevention, and control.* New York: Plenum Press. [18]

Evans, R. B., & Koelsch, W. A. (1985). Psychoanalysis arrives in America. *American Psychologist, 40,* 942–948. [1]

Evans, R. J., Rozelle, R. M., Maxwell, S. E., Raines, B. E., Dill, C. A., Guthrie, T. J., Henderson, A. H., & Hill, P. C. (1981). Social modeling films to deter smoking in adolescents: Results of a three-year field investigation. *Journal of Applied Psychology, 66,* 399–414. [17]

Eysenck, H. J. (1971). *The IQ argument: Race, intelligence, and education.* New York: Library Press. [8]

Eysenck, H. J. (1953). *The structure of human personality.* New York: Wiley. [13]

Fabes, R. A., & Laner, M. R. (1986). How the sexes perceive each other: Advantages and disadvantages. *Sex Roles, 15,* 129–143. [12]

Faraone, S. V., Tsuang, M. T. (1985). Quantitative models of the genetic transmission of schizophrenia. *Psychological Bulletin, 98,* 41–66. [15]

Fazio, R. H., Jeaw-mei, C., McDonel, E. C., & Sherman, S. J. (1982). Attitude accessibility, attitude-behavior consistency, and the strength of the object-evaluation association. *Journal of Experimental Social Psychology, 18,* 339–357. [17]

Fazio, R. H., & Zanna, M. P. (1981). Direct experience and attitude-behavior consistency. In L. Berkowitz (Ed.), *Advances in experimental social psychology.* Vol. 14. Orlando, FL: Academic Press. [17]

Featherstone, H. J., & Beitman, B. D. (1983). "Daily" common migraine: Psychosocial predictors of outcomes of medical therapy. *Headache, 23,* 110–112. [14]

Feier, C. D., & Leight, G. (1981). A communication-cognition program for elderly nursing home residents. *The Gerontologist, 21,* 408–415. [12]

Ferguson, T. J., Rule, B. G., & Carlson, D. (1983). Memory for personally relevant information. *Journal of Personality and Social Psychology, 44,* 251–261. [17]

Ferris, T. (1983). The other Einstein. *Science 83,* October. [1]

Festinger, L. A. (1957). *A theory of cognitive dissonance.* Palo Alto, CA: Stanford University Press. [17]

Festinger, L., & Carlsmith, J. M. (1959). Cognitive consequences of forced compliance. *Journal of Abnormal and Social Psychology, 58,* 203–210. [17]

Fhaner, G., & Hane, M. (1979). Seat belts: Opinion effects of law-induced use. *Journal of Applied Psychology, 64,* 205–212. [17]

Field, T. (1987). Quoted in: Trotter, R. J., The play's the thing. *Psychology Today,* January, 27–34. [11]

Field, T. M., Cohen, D., Garcia, R., & Greenberg, R. (1986). Mother-stranger face discrimination by the newborn. In S. Chess & A. Thomas (Eds.), *Annual progress in child psychiatry and child development,* 1985. New York: Brunner/Mazel. [11]

Field, T. M., Woodson, R., Greenberg, R., & Cohen, D. (1982). Discrimination and imitation of facial expression by neonates. *Science, 218,* 179–181. [11]

Fink, M. (1981). Random thoughts about ECT. *American Journal of Psychiatry, 138,* 484–485. [15]

Fisher, A. (1986). Waddeesay??? *Popular Science,* December 1986. [8]

Fisher, J. D., Nadler, A., & Whitcher-Alagna, S. (1982). Recipient reactions to aid. *Psychological Bulletin, 91,* 27–54. [18]

Fishman, S. M., & Sheehan, D. V. (1985). Anxiety and panic: Their cause and treatment. *Psychology Today,* April. [15]

Fisk, A. D., & Schneider, W. (1984). Memory as a function of attention, level of processing, and automatization. *Journal of Experimental Psychology: Learning, Memory, and Cognition, 10,* 181–197. [7]

Fiske, S. T., & Linville, P. W. (1980). What does the schema concept buy us? *Personality and Social Psychology Bulletin, 6,* 543–557. [17]

Flier, J. S., Cook, K. S., Usher, P., & Spiegelman, B. M. (1987). Severely impaired adipsin expression in genetic and acquired obesity. *Science, 237,* 405–408. [9]

Floody, D. R. (1981). Further systematic research with biorhythms. *Journal of Applied Psychology, 66,* 520–521. [1]

Florian, V., & Kravetz, S. (1983). Fear of personal death: Attribution, structure and relation to religious belief. *Journal of Personality and Social Psychology, 44,* 600–607. [12]

Flynn, J. R. (1987). Massive IQ gains in 14 nations: What IQ tests really measure. *Psychological Bulletin, 101,* 171–191. [8]

Foa, E. B., Grayson, J. B., Steketee, G. S., Doppelt, H. G., Turner, R. M., & Latimer, P. R. (1983). Success and failure in the behavioral treatment of obsessive-compulsives. *Journal of Consulting and Clinical Psychology, 51,* 287–297. [15]

Foenander, G., & Burrows, G. D. (1980). Phenomena of hypnosis: 1. Age regression. In G. D. Burrows & L. Dennerstein (Eds.), *Handbook of hypnosis and psychosomatic medicine.* New York: Elsevier/North-Holland. [5]

Folkman, S., Lazarus, R. S., Dunkel-Schetter, C., DeLongis, A., & Gruen, R. J. (1986). Dynamics of a stressful encounter: Cognitive appraisal, coping and encounter outcomes. *Journal of Personality and Social Psychology, 50,* 992–1003. [14]

Ford, M. R., & Lowery, C. R. (1986). Gender differences in moral reasoning: A comparison of the use of justice and care orientations. *Journal of Personality and Social Psychology, 50,* 777–783. [12]

Foulkes, D. (1983). Cognitive processes during sleep: Evolutionary aspects. In A. Mayes (Ed.), *Sleep mechanisms and functions.* Wokingham, Eng.: Van Nostrand Reinhold. [5]

Fowler, C. A. (1986). An operational definition of conscious awareness must be responsive to subjective experiences. *The Behavioral and Brain Sciences, 9,* 33–35. [4]

Francis, D. P., & Chin, J. (1987). The prevention of acquired immunodeficiency syndrome in the United States. *Journal of the American Medical Association, 257,* 1357–1366. [10]

Frank, S. J., McLaughlin, A. M., & Crusco, A. (1984). Sex role attributes, symptom distress, and defensive style among college men and women. *Journal of Personality and Social Psychology, 47,* 182–192. [12]

Frederiksen, N. (1986). Toward a broader conception of human intelligence. *American Psychologist, 41,* 445–452. [8]

Freed, W. J., Medinaceli, L., & Wyatt, R. J. (1985). Promoting functional plasticity in the damaged nervous system. *Science, 227,* 1544–1552. [2]

Freedman, D. X. (1984). Psychiatric epidemiology counts. *Archives of General Psychiatry, 41,* 931–933. [15]

Freedman, J. L. (1986). Television violence and aggression: A rejoinder. *Psychological Bulletin, 100,* 372–378. [18]

Freedman, J. L., & Fraser, S. C. (1966). Compliance without pressure: The foot-in-the-door technique. *Journal of Personality and Social Psychology, 4,* 195–202. [18]

Freeman, D. (1983). *Margaret Mead and Samoa.* Cambridge, MA: Harvard University Press. [1]

Fremont, J., & Craighead, L. W. (1987). Aerobic exercise and cognitive therapy in the treatment of dysphoric moods. *Cognitive Therapy and Research, 11,* 241–251. [15]

Freud, S. (1900). *The interpretation of dreams* (J. Strachey, Ed. and Trans.). New York: Avon, 1980. [5]

Freud, S. (1920). *Beyond the pleasure principle.* New York: Norton. [9]

Freud, S. (1955). *The interpretation of dreams.* New York: Basic Books (orig. 1900). [5]

Friedman, H. S., & Booth-Kewley, S. (1987). The "disease-prone personality." *American Psychologist, 42,* 539–555. [14]

Friedman, M., Thoresen, C. E., Gill, J. J., Powell, L. H., Ulmer, D., Thompson, L., Price, V. A., Rabin, D. D., Breall, W. S.,

Dixon, T., Levy, R., & Bourg, E. (1984). Alteration of Type A behavior and reduction in cardiac recurrences in postmyocardial infarction patients. *American Heart Journal, 108,* 237–248. [14]

Friedman, M. I., & Stricker, E. M. (1976). The physiological psychology of hunger: A physiological perspective. *Psychological Review, 83,* 409–431. [9]

Friedman, S., & Stevenson, M. (1980). Perception of movements in pictures. In M. Hagen (Ed.), *Perception of pictures. Vol. I: Alberti's window: The projective model of pictorial information.* Orlando, FL: Academic Press. [4]

Friedrich-Cofer, L., & Huston, A. C. (1986). Television violence and aggression: The debate continues. *Psychological Bulletin, 100,* 364–371. [18]

Fries, J. F., & Crapo, L. M. (1981). *Vitality and aging.* New York: W. H. Freeman. [12]

Funder, D. C., & Ozer, D. J. (1983). Behavior as a function of the situation. *Journal of Personality and Social Psychology, 44,* 107–112. [13]

Furumoto, L., & Scarborough, E. (1986). Placing women in the history of psychology. *American Psychologist, 41,* 35–42. [1]

Gagnon, J. H. (1987). Science and the politics of pathology. *The Journal of Sex Research, 23,* 106–129. [10]

Gallagher, W. (1986). The etiology of orgasm. *Discover,* February. [10]

Gallo, R. C. (1987). The AIDS virus. *Scientific American, 256,* 47–59. [10]

Gallois, C., & Callan, V. J. (1986). Decoding emotional messages: Influence of ethnicity, sex, message type and channel. *Journal of Personality and Social Psychology, 51,* 755–762. [9]

Garcia, J., Hankins, W. G., & Rusiniak, K. W. (1974). Behavioral regulation of the milieu interne in man and rat. *Science, 185,* 824–831. [6]

Gardner, B. T., & Gardner, R. A. (1975). Evidence for sentence constituents in the early utterances of child and chimpanzee. *Journal of Experimental Psychology: General, 104,* 244–267. [8]

Gardner, H. (1976). *The shattered mind.* New York: Vintage Books. [2]

Gardner, M. (1981). *Science: Good, bad, and bogus.* Buffalo, NY: Prometheus. [4]

Garelik, G., & Maranto, G. (1984). Multiple murderers. *Discover,* July. [13]

Garfield, S. L. (1980). *Psychotherapy: An eclectic approach.* New York: Wiley. [16]

Garfield, S. L. (1981a). Evaluating the psychotherapies. *Behavior Therapy, 12,* 295–307. [16]

Garfield, S. L. (1981b). Psychotherapy: A 40-year appraisal. *American Psychologist, 36,* 174–183. [16]

Garrow, D. J. (1986). *Bearing the cross.* New York: William Morrow. [13]

Gauquelin, M. (1982). Zodiac and personality: An empirical study. *The Skeptical Inquirer, 6,* 57–65. [13]

Gazzaniga, M. S. (1970). *The bisected brain.* New York: Appleton-Century-Crofts. [2]

Gazzaniga, M. S. (1983). Right hemisphere

language following brain bisection. *American Psychologist, 39,* 525–537. [2]

Gazzaniga, M. S. (1985). *The social brain.* New York: Basic Books. [2]

Gazzaniga, M. S., & LeDoux, J. E. (1978). *The integrated mind.* New York: Plenum. [2]

Gehringer, W. L., & Engel, E. (1986). Effect of ecological viewing conditions on the Ames' distorted room illusion. *Journal of Experimental Psychology: Human Perception and Performance, 12,* 181–185. [4]

Geiselman, R. E., Fisher, R. P., MacKinnon, D. P., & Holland, H. L. (1985). Eyewitness memory enhancement in the police interview: Cognitive retrieval mnemonics versus hypnosis. *Journal of Applied Psychology, 20,* 401–412. [7]

Geller, E. S., Russ, N. W., Altomari, M. G. (1986). Naturalistic observations of beer drinking among college students. *Journal of Applied Behavior Analysis, 19,* 391–396. [1]

Gelman, R., & Baillargeon, R. (1983). A review of some Piagetian concepts. In J. H. Flavell & E. M. Markman (Eds.), *Handbook of child psychology.* Vol. 3. New York: Wiley. [11]

George, S. G., & Jennings, L. B. (1975). Effect of subliminal stimuli on consumer behavior: Negative evidence. *Perceptual and Motor Skills, 41,* 847–854. [4]

Gerrard, M. (1987). Sex, sex guilt, and contraceptive use revisited: The 1980s. *Journal of Personality and Social Psychology, 52,* 975–980. [10]

Gfeller, J. D., Lynn, S. J., & Pribble, W. E. (1987). Enhancing hypnotic susceptibility: Interpersonal and rapport factors. *Journal of Personality and Social Psychology, 52,* 586–595. [5]

Ghosh, A., & Marks, I. M. (1987). Self-treatment of agoraphobia by exposure. *Behavior Therapy, 18,* 3–16. [15]

Giacopassi, D. J., & Dull, R. T. (1986). Gender and racial differences in the acceptance of rape myths within a college population. *Sex Roles, 15,* 63–75. [18]

Gibson, E. J., & Walk, R. D. (1960). The visual cliff. *Scientific American, 202,* 67–71. [4]

Gilbert, S. J. (1981). Another look at the Milgram obedience studies: The role of the graduated series of shocks. *Personality and Social Psychology Bulletin, 7,* 690–695. [18]

Gilligan, C. (1982). *In a different voice: Psychological theory and women's development.* Cambridge, MA: Harvard University Press. [12]

Ginsburg, H., & Opper, S. (1979). *Piaget's theory of intellectual development.* Englewood Cliffs, NJ: Prentice-Hall. [11]

Girden, E. (1978). Parapsychology. In E. C. Carterette & M. P. Friedman (Eds.), *Handbook of perception.* Orlando, FL: Academic Press. [4]

Glass, G. V., & Kliegl, R. M. (1983). An apology for research integration in the study of psychotherapy. *Journal of Consulting and Clinical Psychology, 31, 51,* 28–41. [16]

Glenberg, A. M., & Epstein, W. (1985). Calibration of comprehension. *Journal of Experimental Psychology: Learning, Memory and Cognition, 11,* 702–718. [1]

Glenberg, A. M., Sanocki, T., Epstein, W., & Morris, C. (1987). Enhancing calibration

of comprehension. *Journal of Experimental Psychology: General, 116,* 119–136. [1]

Goedert, J. J., Biggar, R. J., Weiss, S. H., Eyster, M. E., Melbye, M., Wilson, S., Ginzburg, H. M., Grossman, R. J., DiGioia, R. A., Sanchez, W. C., Giron, J. A., Ebbesen, P., Gallo, R. C., & Blattner, W. A. (1986). Three-year incidence of AIDS in five cohorts of HTLV-III-infected risk group members. *Science, 231,* 992–995. [10]

Goldberg, D. C., Whipple, B., Fishkin, R. E., Waxman, H., Fink, P. J., & Weisberg, M. (1983). The Grafenberg spot and female ejaculation: A review of initial hypotheses. *Journal of Sex & Marital Therapy, 9,* 27–37. [10]

Golden, C. J., Graber, B., Blose, I., Berg, R., Coffman, J., & Bloch, S. (1981). Difference in the brain densities between chronic alcoholic and normal control patients. *Science, 211,* 508–510. [5]

Goldfried, M. R. (1980). Toward the delineation of therapeutic change principles. *American Psychologist, 35,* 991–999. [16]

Goldfried, M. R. (1982). Resistance and clinical behavior therapy. In P. Wachtel (Ed.), *Resistance: Psychodynamic and behavioral approaches.* New York: Plenum Press. [16]

Goldfried, M. R., & Davison, G. C. (1976). *Clinical behavior therapy.* New York: Holt, Rinehart and Winston. [16]

Goldstein, A. P., Carr, E. G., Davidson, W. S. II, & Wehr, P. (1981). *In response to aggression.* New York: Pergamon Press. [6, 18]

Gonsiorek, J. C. (1982). Results of psychological testing on homosexual populations. In W. Paul, J. D. Weinrich, J. C. Gonsiorek, & M. E. Hotvedt (Eds.), *Homosexuality: Social, psychological, and biological issues.* Beverly Hills, CA: Sage Publications. [10]

Goodall, J. (1986). *The chimpanzees of Gombe.* Cambridge, MA: Harvard University Press. [1]

Gorenstein, E. E. (1984). Debating mental illness. *American Psychologist, 39,* 50–56. [15]

Gottesman, I., & Shields, J. (1976). A critical review of recent adoption, twin and family studies of schizophrenia: Behavioral genetics perspectives. *Schizophrenia Bulletin, 2,* 360–398. [15]

Gottschalk, L. A., Welch, W. D., & Weiss, J. (1983). Vulnerability and immune response. *Psychotherapy and Psychosomatics, 39,* 23–35. [14]

Gould, J. L., & Marler, P. (1987). Learning by instinct. *Scientific American, 256,* 74–85. [6]

Gould, S. J. (1981). *The mismeasure of man.* New York: Norton. [8]

Gove, W. R., Hughes, M., Style, C. B. (1983). Does marriage have positive effects on the psychological well-being of the individual? *Journal of Health and Social Behavior, 24,* 122–131. [14]

Grady, D. (1981). Overcoming brain damage. *Discover,* June. [2]

Grady, D. (1983). Boxing and the brain. *Discover,* January. [2] [7]

Graf, P., Squire, L. R., & Mandler, G. (1984). The information that amnesic patients do not forget. *Journal of Experimental Psychology: Learning, Memory and Cognition, 10,* 164–178. [7]

Graham, L. E. II, Taylor, C. B., Hovell, M. F., & Siegel, W. (1983). Five-year follow-up to a behavioral weight-loss program. *Journal of Consulting and Clinical Psychology, 51,* 322–323. [9]

Grant, I. (1987). Alcohol and the brain: Neuropsychological correlates. *Journal of Consulting and Clinical Psychology, 55,* 310–324. [5]

Grant, I., Yager, J., Sweetwood, H. L., & Olshen, R. (1982). Life events and symptoms. *Archives of General Psychiatry, 39,* 598–605. [14]

Green, B. (1987). *The "sissy boy syndrome" and the development of homosexuality.* New Haven, CT: Yale University. [10]

Greenberg, J. (1978). The Americanization of Roseto. *Science News, 113,* 378–382. [14]

Greenblatt, M., Becerra, R. M., & Serafetinides, E. A. (1982). Social networks and mental health: An overview. *American Journal of Psychiatry, 139,* 977–984. [14]

Greenwald, A. G., & Ronis, D. L. (1978). Twenty years of cognitive dissonance: Case study of the evolution of a theory. *Psychological Review, 85,* 53–57. [17]

Gregory, R. L. (1974). Recovery from early blindness: A case study. In R. L. Gregory (Ed.), *Concepts and mechanisms of perception.* London: Gerald Duckworth. [4]

Grellert, E. A., Newcomb, M. D., & Bentler, P. M. (1982). Childhood play activities of male and female homosexuals and heterosexuals. *Archives of Sexual Behavior, 11,* 451–478. [10]

Grinker, J. A. (1982). Physiological and behavioral basis of human obesity. In D. W. Pfaff (Ed.), *The physiological mechanisms of motivation.* New York: Springer-Verlag. [9]

Groth, A. N. (1979). *Men who rape.* New York: Plenum Press. [10, 18]

Guilford, J. P. (1967). *The nature of human intelligence.* New York: McGraw-Hill. [8]

Gulevich, G., Dement, W., & Johnson, L. (1966). Psychiatric and EEG observations on a case of prolonged (264 hours) wakefulness. *Archives of General Psychiatry, 15,* 29–35. [5]

Gwirtsman, H. E., Roy-Byrne, P., Yager, J., & Gerner, R. H. (1983). Neuroendocrine abnormalities in bulimia. *American Journal of Psychiatry, 140,* 559–563. [9]

Haan, N., Millsap, R., & Hartka, E. (1986). As time goes by: Change and stability in personality over fifty years. *Psychology and Aging, 1,* 220–232. [13]

Haber, N. R. (1980). Eidetic images are not just imaginary. *Psychology Today,* November. [7]

Hafner, R. J. (1983). Behaviour therapy for agoraphobic men. *Behavior Research and Therapy, 21,* 51–56. [15, 16]

Hagen, M., & Jones, R. (1978). Cultural effects on pictorial perception: How many words is one picture really worth? In R. Walk & H. Pick (Eds.), *Perception and experience.* New York: Plenum Press. [3, 4]

Hall, C. S., & Van de Castle, R. L. (1966). *The content analysis of dreams.* New York: Appleton-Century-Crofts. [5]

Hamilton, D. L. (1981). Stereotyping and intergroup behavior: Some thoughts on the cognitive approach. In D. L. Hamilton (Ed.), *Cognitive processes in stereotyping and intergroup behavior*. Hillsdale, NJ: Lawrence Erlbaum. [17]

Hamilton, D. L. (1983). Effects of bias on attribution and information processing: A cognitive-attributional analysis of stereotyping. In J. Murray & P. R. Abramson (Eds.), *Bias in psychotherapy*. New York: Praeger. [17]

Hamilton, D. L., & Rose, T. L. (1980). Illusory correlation and the maintenance of stereotypic beliefs. *Journal of Personality and Social Psychology, 39*, 832–845. [17]

Hammen, C. L., & Cochran, S. D. (1981). Cognitive correlates of life stress and depression in college students. *Journal of Abnormal Psychology, 90*, 23–27. [15]

Haney, C., Banks, C., & Zimbardo, P. (1973). Interpersonal dynamics in a simulated prison. *International Journal of Criminology and Penology, 1*, 69–97. [18]

Hardy, J. B., Welcher, D. W., Mellits, E. D., & Kagan, J. (1976). Pitfalls in the measurement of intelligence: Are standardized intelligence tests valid for measuring the intellectual potential of urban children? *Journal of Psychology, 94*, 43–51. [8]

Harris, M. (1983). The sleep-crawling question. *Psychology Today*, May. [1]

Harris, R. N., & Snyder, C. R. (1986). The role of uncertain self-esteem in self-handicapping. *Journal of Personality and Social Psychology, 51*, 451–458. [9]

Harry, J. (1983). Defeminization and adult psychological well-being among male homosexuals. *Archives of Sexual Behavior, 12*, 1–19. [10]

Hart, K. J., & Ollendick, T. H. (1985). Prevalence of bulimia in working and university women. *American Journal of Psychiatry, 142*, 851–854. [9]

Hart, S. N., & Brassard, M. R. (1987). A major threat to children's mental health: Psychological maltreatment. *American Psychologist, 42*, 160–165. [11]

Hartmann, E. L. (1973). Sleep requirement: Long sleepers, short sleepers, variable sleepers, and insomniacs. *Psychosomatic Medicine, 14*, 95–103. [5]

Harvey, S. M. (1987). Female sexual behavior: fluctuations during the menstrual cycle. *Journal of Psychosomatic Research, 31*, 101–110. [10]

Hassett, J. (1981). But that would be wrong. *Psychology Today*, November. [1]

Hastie, R. (1981). Schematic principles in human memory. In E. T. Higgins, C. P. Herman, & M. P. Zanna (Eds.), *Social cognition*. Hillsdale, NJ: Lawrence Erlbaum. [17]

Hauri, P. (1982). *The sleep disorders*. Kalamazoo, MI: Upjohn Company. [5]

Haviland, J. M., & Lelwica, M. (1987). The induced affect response: 10-week-old infants' responses to three emotion expressions. *Developmental Psychology, 23*, 97–104. [11]

Hayes, S. C., Munt, E. D., Korn, Z., Wulfert, E., Rosenfarb, I., & Zettle, R. D. (1986). The effect of feedback and self-reinforcement instructions on studying performance. *Psychological Record, 36*, 27–37. [1]

Hazaleus, S. L., & Deffenbacher, J. L. (1986). Relaxation and cognitive treatments of anger. *Journal of Consulting and Clinical Psychology, 54*, 222–226. [18]

Hebb, D. O. (1949). *The organization of behavior*. New York: Wiley. [4]

Hebb, D. O. (1978). On watching myself get old. *Psychology Today*, November. [12]

Hein, N., & Hursch, C. J. (1979). Castration for sex offenders: Treatment or punishment? A review and critique of recent European literature. *Archives of Sexual Behavior, 8*, 281–304. [10]

Heller, T., Van Til, J. (1982). Leadership and followership: Some summary propositions. *The Journal of Applied Behavioral Science, 18*, 405–414. [18]

Helzer, J. E., Robins, L. N., Taylor, J. R., Carey, K., Miller, R. H., Combs-Orme, T., & Farmer, A. (1985). The extent of long-term moderate drinking among alcoholics discharged from medical and psychiatric treatment facilities. *New England Journal of Medicine, 312*, 1678–1682. [5]

Henderson, S. (1981). Social relationships, adversity and neurosis: An analysis of prospective observations. *British Journal of Psychiatry, 138*, 391–398. [14]

Hendy, H. M. (1984). Effects of pets on the sociability and health activities of nursing home residents. In Robert K. Anderson, Benjamin J. Hart, & Lyne-te A. Hart (Eds.), *The pet connection*. Minneapolis: Center to Study Human–Animal Relationships and Environments, University of Minnesota. [12]

Heneson, N. (1984). The selling of PMS. *Science 84*, May. [1]

Herbert, W. (1982). An epidemic in the works. *Science News, 122*, 188–190. [15]

Herbert, W. (1982). Premenstrual changes. *Science News, 122*, 380–381. [1]

Herrera, M. G., Mora, J. O., Christiansen, N., Ortiz, N., Clement, J., Vuori, L., Waber, D., DeParedes, B., & Wagner, M. (1980). Effects of nutritional supplementation and early education on physical and cognitive development. In R. R. Turner & H. W. Reese (Eds.), *Life-span developmental psychology*. Orlando, FL: Academic Press. [11]

Hilgard, E. R. (1979). Divided consciousness in hypnosis: The implications of the hidden observer. In E. Fromm & R. E. Shor (Eds.), *Hypnosis: Developments in research and new perspectives*. 2nd ed. New York: Aldine. [5]

Hilgard, E. R., Macdonald, H., Morgan, A. H., & Johnson, L. S. (1978). The reality of hypnotic analgesia: A comparison of highly hypnotizables with simulators. *Journal of Abnormal Psychology, 87*, 239–246. [5]

Hirsch, H. V., & Spinelli, D. N. (1970). Visual experience modifies distribution of horizontally and vertically oriented receptive fields in cats. *Science, 168*, 869–871. [4]

Hirschfeld, R. M. A., & Cross, C. K. (1982). Epidemiology of affective disorders. *Archives of General Psychiatry, 39*, 35–46. [15]

Hobson, J. A., Lydic, R., & Baghdoyan, H. A. (1986). Evolving concepts of sleep cycle generation: From brain centers to neuronal populations. *The Behavioral and Brain Sciences, 9*, 371–448. [5]

Hobson, J. A., & McCarley, R. W. (1977). The brain as a dream state generator: An activation-synthesis hypothesis of the dream process. *American Journal of Psychiatry, 134*, 1335–1348. [5]

Hodgkinson, S., Sherrington, R., Gurling, H., Marchbanks, R., Reeders, S., Mallet, J., McInnis, M., Petursson, H., & Brynjolfsson, J. (1987). Molecular genetic evidence for heterogeneity in manic depression. *Nature, 325*, 805–806. [15]

Hoffman, R. S. (1982). Diagnostic errors in the evaluation of behavioral disorders. *Journal of the American Medical Association, 248*, 964–967. [15]

Hofling, C. K., Brotzman, E., Dalrymple, S., Graves, N., & Pierce, C. M. (1966). An experimental study in nurse-physician relationships. *Journal of Nervous and Mental Disease, 143*, 171–180. [18]

Hogan, D. B., & Cape, R. D. (1984). Marathoners over sixty years of age: Results of a survey. *Journal of the American Geriatrics Society, 32*, 121–123. [12]

Hogrebe, M. C. (1987). Gender differences in mathematics. *American Psychologist, 42*, 265–266. [11]

Hohmann, G. W. (1966). Some effects of spinal cord lesions on experienced emotional feelings. *Psychophysiology, 3*, 143–156. [9]

Holden, C. (1985). A guarded endorsement for shock therapy. *Science, 228*, 1510–1511. [15]

Holden, C. (1986). Depression research advances, treatment lags. *Science, 233*, 723–726. [5, 15]

Holden C. (1987). Is alcoholism treatment effective? *Science, 236*, 20–22. [5]

Holender, D. (1986). Semantic activation without conscious identification in dichotic listening, parafoveal vision, and visual masking: A survey and appraisal. *The Behavioral and Brain Sciences, 9*, 1–66. [4]

Hollander, E. P., & Yoder, J. (1980). Some issues in comparing women and men as leaders. *Basic and Applied Social Psychology, 1*, 267–280. [18]

Hollingworth, L. S. (1942). *Children above 180 IQ*. Yonkers, NY: World Book. [8]

Holmes, D. S. (1981). Existence of classical projection and the stress-reducing functions of attributive projection: A reply to Sherwood. *Psychological Bulletin, 90*, 460–466. [14]

Holmes, T. H., & Rahe, R. H. (1967). The social readjustment rating scale. *Journal of Psychosomatic Research, 11*, 213–218. [14]

Honorton, C. (1985). Meta-analysis of psi ganzfeld research: A response to Hyman. *Journal of Parapsychology, 49*, 51–91.

Hopson, J., & Rosenfeld, A. (1984). PMS: Puzzling monthly symptoms. *Psychology Today*, August 1984. [1]

Hopson, J. L. (1986). The unraveling of insomnia. *Psychology Today*, June. [5]

Houpt, K. A. (1982). Gastrointestinal factors in hunger and satiety. *Neuroscience & Biobehavioral Reviews, 6*, 145–164. [9]

Houston, J. P. (1976). *Fundamentals of learning*. New York: Academic Press. [6]

Howard, D. V. (1983). *Cognitive psychology*. New York: Macmillan. [7]

Hsu, L. K. G. (1980). Outcome of anorexia

nervosa. *Archives of General Psychiatry, 37,* 1041–1046. [9]

Hsu, L. K. G. (1986). The treatment of anorexia nervosa. *American Journal of Psychiatry, 143,* 573–581. [9]

Hubel, D., & Wiesel, T. (1979). Brain mechanisms of vision. *Scientific American, 82,* 84–97. [3]

Hubel, D. H., & Wiesel, T. N. (1962). Receptive fields, binocular interaction and functional architecture in the cat's visual cortex. *Journal of Physiology, 160,* 106–154. [3]

Hubel, D. H., & Wiesel, T. N. (1979). Brain mechanisms of vision. *Scientific American, 241,* 150–162. [4]

Huesmann, L. R., Eron, L. D., Lefkowitz, M. M., & Walder, L. O. (1984). The stability of aggression over time and generations. *Developmental Psychology, 20,* 1120–1134. [18]

Huesmann, L. R., Gruder, C. L., & Dorst, G. (1987). A process model of posthypnotic amnesia. *Cognitive Psychology, 19,* 33–62. [5]

Hume, K. I. (1983). The rhythmical nature of sleep. In A. Mayes (Ed.), *Sleep mechanisms and functions.* Wokingham, Eng.: Van Nostrand Reinhold. [5]

Humphrey, L. L., Apple, R. F., & Kirschenbaum, D. S. (1986). Differentiating bulimic-anorexic from normal families using interpersonal and behavioral observational systems. *Journal of Consulting and Clinical Psychology, 54,* 190–195. [9]

Hurd, P. D., Johnson, C. A., Pechacek, T., Bast, L. P., Jacobs, D. R., & Luepker, R. V. (1980). Prevention of cigarette smoking in seventh grade students. *Journal of Behavioral Medicine, 3,* 15–28. [17]

Huston, T. L., Ruggiero, M., Conner, R., & Geis, G. (1981). Bystander intervention into crime: A study based on naturally occurring episodes. *Social Psychology Quarterly, 44,* 14–23. [18]

Hyde, J. S. (1981). How large are cognitive gender differences? *American Psychologist, 36,* 892–901. [1]

Hyde, J. S. (1984). How large are gender differences in aggression? A developmental meta-analysis. *Developmental Psychology, 20,* 722–736. [11]

Hyman, R. (1985). The Ganzfeld psi experiment: A critical appraisal. *Journal of Parapsychology, 49,* 3–49. [4]

Hyman, R., & Honorton, C. (1986). A joint communique: The psi ganzfeld controversy. *Journal of Parapsychology, 50,* 351–364. [4]

Ingram, R. E., Smith, T. W., & Grehm, S. S. (1983). Depression and information processing: Self-schemata and the encoding of self-referent information. *Journal of Personality and Social Psychology, 45,* 412–420. [15]

Isaacs, C. D. (1982). Treatment of child abuse: A review of the behavioral interventions. *Journal of Applied Behavior Analysis, 15,* 273–294. [11]

Isen, A. M., & Hostorf, A. H. (1982). Some perspectives on cognitive social psychology. In A. H. Hostorf & A. M. Isen (Eds.), *Cognitive social psychology.* New York: Elsevier/North Holland. [17]

Isenberg, D. J. (1986). Group polarization: A critical review and meta-analysis. *Journal of Personality and Social Psychology, 50,* 1141–1151. [18]

Izard, C. (1977). *Human emotions.* New York: Plenum Press. [9]

Izard, C. (1987). Quoted in: Trotter, R. J., You've come a long way, baby. *Psychology Today,* May, 34–45. [11]

Izard, C. E. (1981). Differential emotions theory and the facial feedback hypothesis of emotion activation: Comments on Tourangeau and Ellsworth's "The role of facial response in the experience of emotion." *Journal of Personality and Social Psychology, 40,* 350–354. [9]

Izard, C. E., Hembree, E. A., & Huebner, R. R. (1987). Infants' emotional expressions to acute pain: Developmental change and stability of individual differences. *Developmental Psychology, 23,* 105–113. [11]

Jaccard, J., Hand, D., Ku, L., Richardson, K., & Abella, R. (1981). Attitudes toward male oral contraceptives: Implications for models of the relationship between beliefs and attitudes. *Journal of Applied Social Psychology, 11,* 181–191. [17]

Jackson, M., & Fiebert, M. S. (1980). Introversion-extroversion and astrology. *The Journal of Psychology, 105,* 155–156. [13]

Jacobson, J. L., & Wille, D. E. (1984). Influence of attachment and separation experience on separation distress at 18 months. *Developmental Psychology, 20,* 477–484. [11]

Jacobson, J. S., & Anderson, E. A. (1980). The effects of behavior rehearsal and feedback on the acquisition of problem-solving skills in distressed and nondistressed couples. *Behavior Research & Therapy, 18,* 25–36. [12]

Jacobson, N. S. (1979). Behavioral treatments for marital discord: A critical appraisal. In M. Hersen, R. M. Eisler, & P. M. Miller (Eds.), *Progress in behavior modification.* Vol. 8. Orlando, FL: Academic Press. [12]

Jacobson, N. S., Follette, W. C., & Waggoner McDonald, D. (1982). Reactivity to positive and negative behavior in distressed and nondistressed married couples. *Journal of Consulting and Clinical Psychology, 50,* 706–714. [12]

Jacoby, L. L. (1982). Knowing and remembering: Some parallels in the behavior of Korsakoff patients and normals. In L. S. Cermak (Ed.), *Human memory and amnesia.* Hillsdale, NJ: Lawrence Erlbaum. [7]

Jago, A. G., & Vroom, V. H. (1982). Sex differences in the incidence and evaluation of participative leader behavior. *Journal of Applied Psychology, 67,* 776–783. [18]

Janda, L. H., O'Grady, K. E., & Barnhart, S. A. (1981). Effects of sexual attitudes and physical attractiveness on person perception of men and women. *Sex Roles, 7,* 189–199. [17]

Jemmott, J. B. III, & Locke, S. E. (1984). Psychosocial factors, immunologic mediation, and human susceptibility to infectious diseases: How much do we know? *Psychological Bulletin, 95,* 78–108. [14]

Jenkins, F., & Davies, G. (1985). Contamination of facial memory through exposure to misleading composite pictures. *Journal of Applied Psychology, 70,* 164–176. [7]

Jensen, A. R. (1978). The nature of intelligence and its relation to learning. In *Melbourne studies in education.* Melbourne: University of Melbourne Press. [8]

Jensen, A. R. (1980). *Bias in mental testing.* New York: Free Press. [8]

Jeste, D. V., & Wyatt, R. J. (1982). Therapeutic strategies against tardive dyskinesia. *Archives of General Psychiatry, 39,* 803–816. [15]

Johnson, C. L., Stuckey, M. K., Lewis, L. D., & Schwartz, D. M. (1982). Bulimia: A descriptive survey of 316 cases. *International Journal of Eating Disorders, 2,* 3–15. [9]

Jones, D. J., Fox, M. M., Babigian, H. M., & Hutton, H. E. (1980). Epidemiology of anorexia nervosa in Monroe County, NY: 1960–1976. *Psychosomatic Medicine, 42,* 551–558. [9]

Jones, D. R., Levy, R. A., Gardner, L., Marsh, R. W., & Patterson, J. C. (1985). Self-control of psychophysiologic response to motion stress: Using biofeedback to treat airsickness. *Aviation, Space and Environmental Medicine, 56,* 1152–1157. [3]

Jones, E., & Berglas, S. (1978). Control of attributions about the self through self-handicapping strategies: The appeal of alcohol and the role of underachievement. *Personality and Social Psychology Bulletin, 4,* 200–206. [9]

Jones, H. S., & Oswald, I. (1968). Two cases of healthy insomnia. *Electroencephalography and Clinical Neurophysiology, 24,* 378–380. [5]

Jones, W. H., Freemon, J. E., & Goswick, R. A. (1981). The persistence of loneliness: Self and other determinants. *Journal of Personality, 49,* 27–48. [13]

Joyce, C. (1984). Lie detector. *Psychology Today,* February. [14]

Kagan, J. (1980). Perspectives on continuity. In O. G. Brim, Jr., & J. Kagan (Eds.), *Constancy and change in human development.* Cambridge, MA: Harvard University Press. [11]

Kagan, J. (1984). *The nature of the child.* New York: Basic Books. [11]

Kagan, J. (1987). Quoted in: Asher, J., Born to be shy? *Psychology Today,* April, 56–64. [11]

Kales, A., & Kales, J. (1973). Recent advances in the diagnosis and treatment of sleep disorders. In G. Usdin (Ed.), *Sleep research and clinical practice.* New York: Brunner/Mazel. [5]

Kandel, E. R., & Schwartz, J. H. (1982). Molecular biology of learning: Modulation of transmitter release. *Science, 218,* 433–443. [7]

Kanner, A. D., Coyne, J. C., Schaefer, C., & Lazarus, R. S. (1981). Comparison of two modes of stress measurement: Daily hassles and uplifts versus major life events. *Journal of Behavioral Medicine, 4,* 1–39. [14]

Kanzer, M. (1983). Reply to Dr. Lipton. *Contemporary Psychoanalysis, 19,* 46–52. [16]

Kaplan, H. (1974). *The new sex therapy.* New York: Brunner/Mazel. [10]

Kaplan, H. S. (1986). Quoted in: Gallagher, W.

The etiology of orgasm. *Discover*, February, 51–59. [10]

Kaplan, J. R., Manuck, S. B., Clarkson, T. B., Lusso, F. M., Taub, D. M., & Miller, E. W. (1983). Social stress and atherosclerosis in normocholesterolemic monkeys. *Science*, 220, 733–735. [14]

Kaplan, R. M., & Saccuzzo, D. P. (1982). *Psychological testing*. Monterey, CA: Brooks/Cole. [8]

Karacan, I., Aslan, C., & Hirshkowitz, M. (1983). Erectile mechanisms in man. *Science*, 220, 1080–1082. [10]

Karoly, P., & Kanfer, F. H. (Eds.). (1982). *Self-management and behavior change*. New York: Pergamon Press. [16]

Kastenbaum, R. (1981). *Death, society and human experience*. 2nd ed. St. Louis, MO: Mosby. [12]

Kaushall, P., Zetin, M., & Squire, L. R. (1982). A psychosocial study of chronic, circumscribed amnesia. *The Journal of Nervous and Mental Disease*, 169, 383–389. [7]

Keefe, F. J., & Gil, K. M. (1986). Behavioral concepts in the analysis of chronic pain syndromes. *Journal of Consulting and Clinical Psychology*, 54, 776–783. [3]

Kelly, E. L., & Conley, J. J. (1987). Personality and compatibility: A prospective analysis of marital stability and marital satisfaction. *Journal of Personality and Social Psychology*, 52, 27–40. [12]

Kempe, R. S., & Kempe, C. H. (1978). *Child abuse*. Cambridge, MA: Harvard University Press. [11]

Kendall, P., & Hollon, S. (Eds.). (1979). *Cognitive-behavioral interventions: Theory, research, and procedures*. Orlando, FL: Academic Press. [16]

Kendrick, K. M., & Baldwin, B. A. (1987). Cells in temporal cortex of conscious sheep can respond preferentially to the sight of faces. *Science*, 236, 448–450. [3]

Kiester, E., Jr. (1980). Images of the night. *Science 80*, May–June. [5]

Kihlstrom, J. F., & Harackiewicz, J. M. (1982). The earliest recollection: A new survey. *Journal of Personality*, 50, 134–148. [7]

Kilmann, P. R., & Auerbach, R. (1979). Treatments of premature ejaculation and psychogenic impotence: A critical review of the literature. *Archives of Sexual Behavior*, 8, 81–100. [10]

Kilmann, P. R., Mills, K. H., Bella, B., Caid, C., Davidson, E., Drose, G., & Wanlass, R. (1983). The effects of sex education on women with secondary orgasmic dysfunction. *Journal of Sex & Marital Therapy*, 9, 79–87. [10]

Klatzky, R. L. (1984). *Memory and awareness*. New York: W. H. Freeman. [7]

Klawans, H. (1988). Quoted in: Lewin, R., Cloud over Parkinson's therapy. *Science*, 240, 390. [2]

Klein, D. B., Zitrin, C. M., Woerner, M. G., & Ross, D. C. (1983). Treatment of phobias. *Archives of General Psychiatry*, 40, 139–145. [16]

Kleinke, C. L., Staneski, R. A., & Meeker, F. B. (1983). Attributions for smoking: Comparing smokers with nonsmokers and predicting smokers' cigarette consumption. *Journal of Research in Personality*, 17, 242–255. [17]

Klesges, R. C. (1983). An analysis of body image distortions in a nonpatient population. *International Journal of Eating Disorders*, 2, 37–41. [4, 9]

Klonoff, H., Fleetham, J., Taylor, R., & Clark, C. (1987). Treatment outcome of obstructive sleep apnea. *Journal of Nervous and Mental Disease*, 175, 208–212. [5]

Knight, L. J., & McKelvie, S. J. (1986). Effects of attendance, note-taking, and review on memory for a lecture: Encoding vs. external storage functions of notes. *Canadian Journal of Behavioral Science*, 18, 52–61. [1]

Knussmann, R., & Christiansen, K. (1986). Relations between sex hormone level and sexual behavior in men. *Archives of Sexual Behavior*, 15, 429–445. [10]

Kobasa, S. C. (1979). Stressful life events, personality, and health: An inquiry into hardiness. *Journal of Personality and Social Psychology*, 37, 1–11. [14]

Kobasa, S. C. (1982). Commitment and coping in stress resistance among lawyers. *Journal of Personality and Social Psychology*, 42, 707–717. [14]

Kobasa, S. C., Maddi, S. R., & Kahn, S. (1982a). Hardiness and health: A prospective study. *Journal of Personality and Social Psychology*, 42, 168–177. [14]

Kobasa, S. C., Maddi, S. R., & Puccetti, M. C. (1982b). Personality and exercise as buffers in the stress-illness relationship. *Journal of Behavioral Medicine*, 5, 391–404. [14]

Koger, L. J. (1980). Nursing home life satisfaction and activity participation. *Research on Aging*, 2, 61–72. [12]

Kohlberg, L. (1969). Stage and sequence: The cognitive-developmental approach to socialization. In D. A. Goslin (Ed.), *Handbook of socialization theory and research*. Chicago: Rand McNally. [12]

Kohlberg, L. (1981). *The philosophy of moral development: Essays on moral development*. Vol. I. San Francisco: Harper & Row. [12]

Kohlberg, L. (1984). *The psychology of moral development: Essays on moral development*. Vol. II. San Francisco: Harper & Row. [12]

Kohn, A. (1987). Art for art's sake. *Psychology Today*, September. [8]

Kolata, G. B. (1981b). Fetal alcohol advisory debated. *Science*, 214, 642–645. [11]

Kolata, G. (1986). Obese children: A growing problem. *Science*, 232, 20–21. [9]

Kolodny, R. C. (1981). Evaluating sex therapy: Process and outcome at the Masters & Johnson Institute. *The Journal of Sex Research*, 17, 301–318. [10]

Kopelman, M. D. (1986). The cholinergic neurotransmitter system in human memory and dementia: A review. *The Quarterly Journal of Experimental Psychology*, 38A, 535–573. [2]

Koren, P., Carlton, K., & Shaw, D. (1980). Marital conflict: Relations among behaviors, outcomes, and distress. *Journal of Consulting and Clinical Psychology*, 48, 460–468. [12]

Korsching, S. (1986). The role of nerve growth factor in the CNS. *Trends in Neuroscience*, 9, 510–515. [2]

Koss, M. P., Gidycz, C. A., & Wisniewski, N. (1987). The scope of rape: Incidence and prevalence of sexual aggression and victimization in a national sample of higher education students. *Journal of Consulting and Clinical Psychology*, 55, 162–170. [18]

Kovacs, A. L. (1982). Survival in the 1980s: On the theory and practice of brief psychotherapy. *Psychotherapy: Theory, Research and Practice*, 19, 142–159. [16]

Kovacs, M., Rush, A. J., Beck, A. T., & Hollon, S. D. (1981). Depressed outpatients treated with cognitive therapy or pharmacotherapy. *Archives of General Psychiatry*, 38, 33–39. [15, 16]

Kozel, N. J., & Adams, E. H. (1986). Epidemiology of drug abuse: An overview. *Science*, 234, 970–974. [5]

Krantz, S. E. (1983). Cognitive appraisals and problem-directed coping: A prospective study of stress. *Journal of Personality and Social Psychology*, 44, 638–643. [14]

Krasner, L. (1982). Behavior therapy: On roots, contexts, and growth. In G. T. Wilson & C. M. Franks (Eds.), *Contemporary behavior therapy*. New York: Guilford Press. [16]

Kraut, R. E., & Poe, D. (1980). Behavioral roots of person perception: The deception judgments of customs inspectors and laymen. *Journal of Personality and Social Psychology*, 38, 784–798. [17]

Kreitler, S., Kreitler, H., & Carasso, R. (1987). Cognitive orientation as predictor of pain relief following acupuncture. *Pain*, 28, 323–341. [3]

Kroll, N. E. A., Schepeler, E. M., & Angin, K. T. (1986). Bizarre imagery: The misremembered mnemonic. *Journal of Experimental Psychology: Learning, Memory and Cognition*, 12, 42–53. [7]

Kromer, L. F. (1987). Nerve growth factor treatment after brain injury prevents neuronal death. *Science*, 235, 214–216. [2]

Krueger, J. M., Pappenheimer, J. R., & Karnovsky, M. L. (1982). Sleep-promoting effects of muramyl peptides. *Proceedings of the National Academy of Science*, 79, 6102–6106. [5]

Kübler-Ross, E. (1969). *On death and dying*. New York: Macmillan. [12]

Kübler-Ross, E. (1970). The dying patient's point of view. In O. G. Brim, Jr., H. E. Freeman, S. Levine, & N. A. Scotch (Eds.), *The dying patient*. New York: Russell Sage Foundation. [12]

Kübler-Ross, E. (1974). *Questions and answers on death and dying*. New York: Macmillan. [12]

Kuhn, D. (1984). Cognitive development. In M. H. Bornstein & M. E. Lamb (Eds.), *Developmental psychology: An advanced textbook*. Hillsdale, NJ: Lawrence Erlbaum. [11]

Kuiper, N. A., Derry, P. A., & MacDonald, M. R. (1982a). Self-reference and person perception in depression: A social cognition perspective. In G. Weary & H. L. Mirels (Eds.), *Integrations of clinical and social psychology*. New York: Oxford University Press. [17]

Kuiper, N. A., & MacDonald, M. R. (1982b). Self and other perception in mild depressives. *Social Cognition*, 1, 223–239. [17]

Kurtines, W., & Greif, E. B. (1974). The development of moral thought: Review and evaluation of Kohlberg's approach. *Psychological Bulletin*, 81, 453–470. [12]

Labbe, R., Firl, A., Jr., Mufson, E. J., & Stein, D. S. (1983). Fetal brain transplants: Reduction of cognitive deficits in rats with frontal cortex lesions. *Science, 221,* 470–472. [2]

Lackner, J. R., & Graybiel, A. (1986). Head movements in non-terrestrial force environments elicit motion sickness: Implications for the etiology of space motion sickness. *Aviation, Space and Environmental Medicine, 57,* 443–448. [3]

Ladas, A. K., Whipple, B., & Perry, J. D. (1982). *The G-spot and other recent discoveries about human sexuality.* New York: Holt, Rinehart and Winston. [10]

Laird, J. D. (1974). Self-attribution of emotion: The effects of expressive behavior on the quality of emotional experience. *Journal of Personality and Social Psychology, 29,* 475–486. [9]

Lamb, M. E. (1984). Social and emotional development in infancy. In M. M. Bornstein & M. E. Lamb (Eds.), *Developmental psychology: An advanced textbook.* Hillsdale, NJ: Lawrence Erlbaum. [11]

Landl, S. D. (1982). Physiological and subjective measures of anxiety during flooding. *Behavior Research and Therapy, 20,* 81–88. [16]

Landman, J. T., & Dawes, R. M. (1982). Psychotherapy outcome: Smith and Glass' conclusions stand up under scrutiny. *American Psychologist, 37,* 504–516. [16]

Langer, E. J., & Rodin, J. (1976). The effects of choice and enhanced personal responsibility for the aged: A field experiment in an institutional setting. *Journal of Personality and Social Psychology, 34,* 191–198. [12]

Langone, J. (1981). Girth of a nation. *Discover,* February. [9]

Lanyon, R. I. (1984). Personality assessment. *Annual Review of Psychology, 35,* 57–58, 667–701. [13]

Lanzetta, J. T., Cartwright-Smith, J., & Kleck, R. E. (1976). Effects of nonverbal discrimination on emotional experience and autonomic arousal. *Journal of Personality and Social Psychology, 33,* 354–370. [9]

LaPlante, M. N., McCormick, N., & Brannigan, G. G. (1980). Living the sexual script: College students' views of influence in sexual encounters. *The Journal of Sex Research, 16,* 338–355. [10]

Larson, J., & Lynch, G. (1986). Induction of synaptic potentiation in hippocampus by patterned stimulation involves two events. *Science, 232,* 985–988. [7]

La Rue, A., & Jarvik, L. F. (1982). Old age and biobehavioral changes. In B. B. Wolman (Ed.), *Handbook of developmental psychology.* Englewood Cliffs, NJ: Prentice-Hall. [12]

Latané, B. (1981). The psychology of social impact. *American Psychologist, 36,* 343–356. [18]

Latané, B., & Darley, J. M. (1970). *The unresponsive bystander: Why doesn't he help?* New York: Appleton-Century-Crofts. [18]

Latané, B., & Nida, S. (1981). Ten years of research on group size and helping. *Psychological Bulletin, 89,* 308–324. [18]

Laudenslager, M. L., Ryan, S. M., Drugan, R. C., Hyson, R. L., & Maier, S. F. (1983). Coping and immunosuppression: Inescapable but not escapable shock suppresses

lymphocyte proliferation. *Science, 221,* 568–570. [14]

Lazar, B. S., & Dempster, C. R. (1981). Failures in hypnosis and hypnotherapy: A review. *The American Journal of Clinical Hypnosis, 24,* 48–54. [5]

Lazarus, R. S. (1984). On the primacy of cognition. *American Psychologist, 39,* 124–129. [9]

Lazarus, R. S., & Alfert, E. (1964). The short-circuiting of threat. *Journal of Abnormal and Social Psychology, 69,* 195–205. [14]

Lazarus, R. S., & Folkman, S. (1984). *Stress, appraisal, and coping.* New York: Springer. [14]

Lazarus, R. S., Opton, E. M., Nomikos, M. S., & Fankin, N. O. (1965). The principle of short-circuiting of threat: Further evidence. *Journal of Personality, 33,* 622–635. [14]

Leary, M. R., & Shepperd, J. A. (1986). Behavioral self-handicaps versus self-reported handicaps: A conceptual note. *Journal of Personality and Social Psychology, 51,* 1265–1268. [9]

Leckman, J. F., Sholomskas, D., Thompson, D., Belanger, A., & Weissman, M. M. (1982). Best estimate of lifetime psychiatric diagnosis. *Archives of General Psychiatry, 39,* 879–883. [15]

Lefcourt, H. M. (1982). *Locus of control.* 2nd ed. Hillsdale, NJ: Lawrence Erlbaum. [14]

Leventhal, H. (1982). Wrongheaded ideas about illness. *Psychology Today,* January. [18]

Levinson, D. (1986). A conception of adult development. *American Psychologist, 41,* 3–13. [12]

Levinson, D. J. (1978). *The seasons of a man's life.* New York: Knopf. [12]

Levy, J. (1983). Language, cognition and the right hemisphere. *American Psychologist, 39,* 538–541. [2]

Levy, J. (1985). Right brain, left brain: Fact and fiction. *Psychology Today,* May. [2]

Levy, J., & Trevarthen, C. (1976). Metacontrol of hemispheric function in human split-brain patients. *Journal of Experimental Psychology: Human Perception and Performance, 2,* 299–312. [2]

Levy, J., Trevarthen, C., & Sperry, R. W. (1972). Perception of bilateral chimeric figures following hemispheric deconnection. *Brain, 95,* 61–68. [2]

Lewin, R. (1987). Dramatic results with brain grafts. *Science, 237,* 245–247. [2]

Lewin, R. (1988). Cloud over Parkinson's therapy. *Science, 240,* 390–392. [2]

Lewis, D. (1983). The gynecologic consideration of the sexual act. *Journal of the American Medical Association, 250,* 222–227. [10]

Lewis, D. L. (1978). *King: A biography.* 2nd edition. Chicago: University of Illinois. [2]

Lewisohn, P. M., & Hoberman, H. M. (1984). Depression. In A. S. Bellack, M. Hersen, & A. E. Kazdin (Eds.), *International handbook of behavior modification and therapy.* New York: Plenum Press. [16]

Lewy, A. J., Wehr, T. A., Goodwin, F. K., Newsome, D. A., & Markey, S. P. (1980). Human sleep: Its duration and organization depend on its circadian phase. *Science, 210,* 1264–1268. [5]

Lhermitte, J., Chain, F., Escourolle, R., Ducarne, B., & Pillon, B. (1972). Etude

anatomo-clinique d'un cas de prosopagnosie. *Review Neurology* (Paris), *126,* 329–346. [4]

Lichstein, K. L., & Rosenthal, T. L. (1980). Insomniacs' perceptions of cognitive versus somatic determinants of sleep disturbance. *Journal of Abnormal Psychology, 89,* 105–107. [5]

Lichter, S., Haye, K., & Kammann, R. (1980). Increasing happiness through cognitive retraining. *New Zealand Psychologist, 9,* 57–64. [9]

Light, K. C. (1981). Cardiovascular responses to effortful active coping: Implications for the role of stress in hypertension development. *Psychophysiology, 18,* 216–225. [14]

Light, K. C., & Obrist, P. A. (1980). Cardiovascular reactivity to behavioral stress in young males with and without marginally elevated causal systolic pressure: A comparison of clinic, home and laboratory measures. *Hypertension, 2,* 802–808. [14]

Light, K. C., Koepke, J. P., Obrist, P. A., & Willis, P. W. IV. (1983). Psychological stress induces sodium and fluid retention in men at high risk for hypertension. *Science, 220,* 429–431. [14]

Light, L. L., & Anderson, P. A. (1983). Memory for scripts in young and older adults. *Memory & Cognition, 11,* 435–444. [12]

Lindsay, P. H., & Norman, D. A. (1977). *Human information processing.* 2nd ed. Orlando, FL: Academic Press. [4]

Linton, J. C., & Hirt, H. (1979). A comparison of predictions from peripheral and central theories of emotion. *British Journal of Medical Psychology, 52,* 11–15. [9]

Linton, M. (1978). I remember it well. *Psychology Today,* July, 81–86. [7]

Linton, M. (1982). Transformations of memory in everyday life. In Ulric Neisser (Ed.), *Memory observed.* New York: W. H. Freeman. [7]

Lipkowitz, M. H., & Idupuganti, S. (1983). Diagnosing schizophrenia in 1980: A survey of U.S. psychiatrists. *American Journal of Psychiatry, 140,* 52–55. [15]

Lipsitt, L. P. (1982). Infant learning. In T. M. Field, A. Huston, H. C. Quay, L. Troll, & G. E. Finley (Eds.), *Review of human development.* New York: Wiley. [11]

Lipsitt, L. P. (1987). Quoted in: Trotter, R. J., You've come a long way, baby. *Psychology Today,* May, 34–45. [11]

Lipton, S. D. (1983). A critique of so-called standard psychoanalytic technique. *Contemporary Psychoanalysis, 19,* 35–52. [16]

List, J. A. (1986). Age and schematic differences in the reliability of eyewitness testimony. *Developmental Psychology, 22,* 50–57. [7]

Litman, R. E. (1986). Quoted in: Holden, C., Youth suicide. New research focuses on a growing social problem. *Science, 233,* 839–841. [12]

Lochman, J. E. (1987). Self- and peer perceptions and attributional biases of aggressive and nonaggressive boys in dyadic interactions. *Journal of Consulting and Clinical Psychology, 55,* 404–410. [18]

Lochman, J. E., Burch, P. R., Curry, J. F., & Lampron, L. B. (1984). Treatment and generalization effects of cognitive behavioral and goal setting interventions with aggressive boys. *Journal of Consulting and Clinical Psychology, 52,* 915–916. [18]

Lochman, J. E., & Curry, J. F. (1986). Effects of social problem-solving training and self-instruction training with aggressive boys. *Journal of Clinical Child Psychology, 15,* 159–164. [18]

Lochman, J. E., Nelson, W. M., III, & Sims, J. P. (1981). A cognitive behavioral program for use with aggressive children. *Journal of Clinical Child Psychology, 10,* 146–148. [18]

Loftus, E. F. (1975). Leading questions and the eyewitness report. *Cognitive Psychology, 7,* 560–572. [7]

Loftus, E. F. (1979). *Eyewitness testimony.* Cambridge, MA: Harvard University Press. [7]

Loftus, E. F. (1984). Eyewitnesses: Essential but unreliable. *Psychology Today,* February. [7]

Logan, G. D. (1985). On the ability to inhibit simple thoughts and actions: II. Stop-signal studies on repetition priming. *Journal of Experimental Psychology: Learning, Memory, and Cognition, 11,* 675–691. [16]

Logue, A. W., Ophir, I., & Strauss, K. E. (1981). The acquisition of taste aversions in humans. *Behavior Research and Therapy, 19,* 319–335. [6]

Loken, B. (1982). Heavy smokers', light smokers', and nonsmokers' beliefs about cigarette smoking. *Journal of Applied Psychology, 67,* 616–622. [17]

Long, V. O. (1986). Relationship of masculinity to self-esteem and self-acceptance in female professionals, college students, clients, and victims of domestic violence. *Journal of Consulting and Clinical Psychology, 54,* 323–327. [12]

Loomis, T. (1982). The pharmacology of alcohol. In N. J. Estes & M. E. Heinemann (Eds.), *Alcoholism.* St. Louis, MO: Mosby. [5]

LoPiccolo, J. (1978). Direct treatment of sexual dysfunction. In J. LoPiccolo & L. LoPiccolo (Eds.), *Handbook of sex therapy.* New York: Plenum Press. [10]

LoPiccolo, J., & Stock, W. E. (1986). Treatment of sexual dysfunction. *Journal of Consulting and Clinical Psychology, 54,* 158–167. [10]

Lorsbach, T. C., & Simpson, G. B. (1984). Age differences in the rate of processing in short-term memory. *Journal of Gerontology, 39,* 315–321. [12]

Lovaas, O. I. (1981). *Teaching developmentally disabled children.* Baltimore: University Park Press. [6]

Lovaas, O. I. (1987). Behavioral treatment and normal educational and intellectual functioning in young autistic children. *Journal of Consulting and Clinical Psychology, 55,* 3–9. [6]

Lowenstein, J. M., & Zihlman, A. L. (1985). Human evolution and molecular biology. In E. D. Garber (Ed.), *Genetic perspectives in biology and medicine.* Chicago: University of Chicago Press. [8]

Lubinski, D., Tellegen, A., & Butcher, J. N. (1983). Masculinity, femininity, and androgyny viewed and assessed as distinct concepts. *Journal of Personality and Social Psychology, 44,* 428–439. [12]

Luria, A. R. (1968). *The mind of a mnemonist.* New York: Basic Books. [7]

Lykken, D. T. (1979). The detection of deception. *Psychological Bulletin, 86,* 47–53. [14]

Lykken, D. T. (1980). *A tremor in the blood: Uses and abuses of the lie detector.* New York: McGraw-Hill. [14]

Lytle, L. D. (1977). Control of eating behavior. In R. J. Wurtman & J. J. Wurtman (Eds.), *Nutrition and the brain.* Vol. 2. New York: Raven Press. [9]

Maccoby, E. (1987). Quoted in: Hall, E., All in the family. *Psychology Today,* 54–60. [11]

Maccoby, E. E. (1980). *Social development.* San Diego, CA: Harcourt Brace Jovanovich. [11]

Maccoby, E. E. (1984). Socialization and developmental change. *Child Development, 55,* 317–328. [11]

Maccoby, E. E., & Jacklin, C. N. (1974). *The psychology of sex differences.* Palo Alto, CA: Stanford University Press. [11]

Mackintosh, N. J. (1983). *Conditioning and associative learning.* Oxford: Clarendon Press. [6]

MacLusky, N. J., & Naftolin, F. (1981). Sexual differentiation of the central nervous system. *Science, 211,* 1294–1303. [10]

Maddi, S. R., Bartone, P. T., & Puccetti, M. C. (1987). Stressful events are indeed a factor in physical illness: Reply to Schroeder and Costa (1984). *Journal of Personality and Social Psychology, 52,* 833–843. [14]

Madrazo, I., Drucker-Colín, R., Díaz, V., Martinez-Mata, J., Torres, C., & Becerril, J. J. (1987). Open microsurgical autograft of adrenal medulla to the right caudate nucleus in two patients with intractable Parkinson's disease. *New England Journal of Medicine, 316,* 831–834. [2]

Magnusson, D., & Endler, N. S. (Eds.). (1977). *Personality at the crossroads: Current issues in interactional psychology.* Hillsdale, NJ: Lawrence Erlbaum. [13]

Maier, S. F., & Seligman, M. E. P. (1976). Learned helplessness: Theory and evidence. *Journal of Experimental Psychology: General, 103,* 3–46. [6]

Malan, D. H. (1980). The most important development since the discovery of the unconscious. In H. Davanloo (Ed.), *Short-term dynamic psychotherapy.* New York: Jason Aronson. [16]

Mann, L. (1981). The baiting crowd in episodes of threatened suicide. *Journal of Personality and Social Psychology, 41,* 703–709. [18]

Mann, L., Newton, J. W., & Innes, J. M. (1982). A test between deindividuation and emergent norm theories of crowd aggression. *Journal of Personality and Social Psychology, 42,* 260–272. [18]

Markman, H. J. (1981). Prediction of marital distress: A 5-year follow-up. *Journal of Consulting and Clinical Psychology, 49,* 760–762. [12]

Marks, D., & Kammann, R. (1980). *The psychology of the psychic.* Buffalo, NY: Prometheus. [4]

Marks, I. M. (1981a). Review of behavioral psychotherapy, I: Obsessive-compulsive disorders. *American Journal of Psychiatry, 138,* 584–592. [15]

Marks, I. M. (1981b). Review of behavioral psychotherapy, II: Sexual disorders. *American Journal of Psychiatry, 138,* 750–756. [10]

Marks, I. M., Gray, S., Cohen, D., Hill, R., Mawson, D., Ramm, E., & Stern, R. S. (1983). Imipramine and brief therapist-aided exposure in agoraphobics having self-exposure homework. *Archives of General Psychiatry, 40,* 153–162. [15, 16]

Markus, H., Crane, M., Bernstein, D. A., & Siladi, M. (1982). Self-schemas and gender. *Journal of Personality and Social Psychology, 42,* 38–50. [17]

Markus, H., Hamill, R., & Sentis, K. P. (1987). Thinking fat: Self-schemas for body weight and the processing of weight relevant information. *Journal of Applied Social Psychology, 17,* 50–71. [4]

Marlatt, G. A., & Parks, G. A. (1982). Self-management of addictive behaviors. In P. Karoly & F. H. Kanfer (Eds.), *Self-management and behavior change.* New York: Pergamon Press. [16]

Martin, G. L. (1982). Thought-stopping and stimulus control to decrease persistent disturbing thoughts. *Journal of Behavior Therapy and Experimental Psychiatry, 13,* 215–220. [16]

Maslow, A. H. (1968). *Toward a psychology of being.* 2nd ed. New York: Van Nostrand. [13]

Mason, J. W. (1975). Psychological stress and endocrine function. In E. J. Sachar (Ed.), *Topics in psychoendocrinology.* New York: Grune and Stratton. [14]

Masters, W. H., & Johnson, V. E. (1966). *Human sexual response.* Boston: Little, Brown. [10]

Masters, W. H., & Johnson, V. E. (1970). *Human sexual inadequacy.* Boston: Little, Brown. [10]

Masters, W. H., & Johnson, V.E. (1981). Sex and the aging process. *Journal of the American Geriatrics Society, 19,* 385–389. [12]

Masters, W. H., Johnson, V. E., & Kolodny, R. C. (1982). *Human sexuality.* Boston: Little, Brown, 386–387. [10]

Matsnev, E. I., Kuz'min, M. P., & Zakharova, L. N. (1987). Comparative assessment of vestibular, optokinetic, and optovestibular stimulation in the development of experimental motion sickness. *Aviation, Space and Environmental Medicine, 58,* 954–957. [3]

Matsumoto, D. (1987). The role of facial response in the experience of emotion: More methodological problems and a meta-analysis. *Journal of Personality and Social Psychology, 52,* 769–774. [9]

Matthews, K. A., & Haynes, S. G. (1986). Type A behavior pattern and coronary disease risk. *American Journal of Epidemiology, 123,* 923–960. [14]

Maugh, T. M. (1982). Sleep-promoting factor isolated. *Science, 216,* 1400. [5]

May, P. R. A., Tuma, A. H., & Dixon, W. J. (1981). Schizophrenia. *Archives of General Psychiatry, 38,* 776–784. [15]

Mayer, J. (1972). General discussion. *Advances, Psychosomatic Medicine, 7,* 322–336. [9]

Mayer, R. E. (1983). *Thinking, problem solving, cognition.* New York: W. H. Freeman. [8]

McCann, I. L., & Holmes, D. S. (1984). Influence of aerobic exercise on depression. *Journal of Personality and Social Psychology, 46*, 1142–1147. [15]

McCarthy, J. D., & Hoge, D. R. (1982). Analysis of age effects in longitudinal studies of adolescent self-esteem. *Developmental Psychology, 18*, 372–379. [12]

McCartney, K., Scarr, S., Phillips, D., & Grajek, S. (1985). Day care as intervention: Comparisons of varying quality programs. *Journal of Applied Developmental Psychology, 6*, 247–260. [11]

McCarty, D. (1981). Changing contraceptive usage intentions: A test of the Fishbein model of intention. *Journal of Applied Social Psychology, 11*, 192–211. [17]

McCarty, S. M., Siegler, I. C., & Logue, P. E. (1982). Cross-sectional and longitudinal patterns of three Wechsler Memory Scale subtests. *Journal of Gerontology, 37*, 169–175. [12]

McCaul, K. D., & Malott, J. M. (1984). Distraction and coping with pain. *Psychological Bulletin, 95*, 516–533. [3]

McClelland, D. C. (1955). Some social consequences of achievement motivation. In M. R. Jones (Ed.), *Nebraska Symposium on Motivation 1955*. Lincoln: University of Nebraska Press. [9]

McClelland, D. C. (1985). *Human motivation.* Glenview, IL: Scott Foresman. [9]

McClelland, D. C., Atkinson, J. W., Clark, R. W., & Lowell, E. L. (1953). *The achievement motive.* New York: Appleton-Century-Crofts. [9]

McConnell, M. V., Cutler, R. L., & McNeil, E. B. (1958). Subliminal stimulation: An overview. *American Psychologist, 13*, 229–242. [4]

McCrae, R. R. (1987). Creativity, divergent thinking, and openness to experience. *Journal of Personality and Social Psychology, 52*, 1258–1265. [8]

McCrae, R. R., & Costa, P. T., Jr. (1987). Validation of the five-factor model of personality across instruments and observers. *Journal of Personality and Social Psychology, 52*, 81–90. [13]

McDaniel, M. A., & Einstein, G. O. (1986). Bizarre imagery as an effective memory aid: The importance of distinctiveness. *Journal of Experimental Psychology: Learning, Memory and Cognition, 12*, 54–65. [7]

McDougall, W. (1908). *Social psychology.* New York: Putnam. [9]

McGaugh, J. L. (1983a). Hormonal influences on memory. *Annual Review of Psychology, 34*, 297–324. [7]

McGaugh, J. L. (1983b). Preserving the presence of the past. *American Psychologist, 38*, 161–174. [7]

McGuffin, P., Farmer, A., & Gottesman, I. I. (1987). Is there really a split in schizophrenia? The genetic evidence. *British Journal of Psychiatry, 150*, 581–592. [15]

McKay, H., Sinisterra, L., McKay, A., Gomez, H., & Lloreda, P. (1978). Improving cognitive ability in chronically deprived children. *Science, 200*, 270–277. [11]

McKean, K. (1982). A picture of Hinckley's brain. *Discover*, August. [15]

McKean, K. (1983b). Memory. *Discover*, November. [7]

McKean, K. (1985). Decisions, decisions. *Discover*, June. [8]

McWilliams, J. R., & Lynch, G. (1983). Rate of synaptic replacement in denervated rat hippocampus declines precipitously from the juvenile period to adulthood. *Science, 221*, 572–574. [2]

Mead, M. (1928). *Coming of age in Samoa.* New York: Morrow, 1961 (originally published in 1928). [1]

Meddis, R., Pearson, A. J. D., & Langford, G. (1973). An extreme case of healthy insomnia. *Electroencephalography and Clinical Neurophysiology, 35*, 391–394. [5]

Meichenbaum, D. (1977). *Cognitive behavior modification: An integrative approach.* New York: Plenum Press. [16]

Meichenbaum, D., & Cameron, R. (1982). Cognitive-behavior therapy. In G. T. Wilson & C. M. Franks (Eds.), *Contemporary behavior therapy.* New York: Guilford Press. [16]

Meltzoff, A. N., & Moore, M. K. (1977). Imitation of facial and manual gestures by human neonates. *Science, 198*, 75–78. [11]

Melzack, R., & Wall, P. D. (1965). Pain mechanisms: A new theory. *Science, 150*, 971–979. [3]

Mendels, J. (1987). Clinical experience with serotonin reuptake inhibiting antidepressants. *Journal of Clinical Psychiatry, 48*, 26–30. [15]

Meredith, D. (1986). Day-care: The nine-to-five dilemma. *Anthropology & Education Quarterly, 20*, 36–44. [11]

Merikle, P. M., & Cheesman, J. (1986). Consciousness is a "subjective" state. *The Biological and Brain Sciences, 9*, 42. [4]

Meyer, A. (1982). Do lie detectors lie? *Science 82*, June. [14]

Michaels, J. W., Blommel, J. M., Brocato, R. M., Linkous, R. A., & Rowe, J. S. (1982). Social facilitation and inhibition in a natural setting. *Replications in Social Psychology, 2*, 21–24. [18]

Milgram, S. (1963). Behavioral study of obedience. *Journal of Abnormal and Social Psychology, 67*, 371–378. [18]

Milgram, S. (1974). *Obedience to authority.* New York: Harper & Row. [18]

Millan, M. J. (1986). Multiple opioid systems and pain. *Pain, 27*, 303–347. [3]

Miller, M. W. (1986). Effects of alcohol on the generation and migration of cerebral cortical neurons. *Science, 233*, 1308–1311. [11]

Miller, N. (1980). Making school desegregation work. In W. G. Stephan & J. R. Feagin (Eds.), *School desegregation.* New York: Plenum Press. [17]

Miller, N. E. (1985). Rx: Biofeedback. *Psychology Today*, February. [14]

Miller, P. H. (1983). *Theories of developmental psychology.* New York: W. H. Freeman. [12]

Miller, R. C., & Berman, J. S. (1983). The efficacy of cognitive behavior therapies: A quantitative review of the research evidence. *Psychological Bulletin, 94*, 39–53. [16]

Millon, T. (1981). *Disorders of personality.* New York: Wiley. [15]

Milner, D. (1981). Racial prejudice. In J. C. Turner & H. Giles (Eds.), *Intergroup behavior.* Chicago: University of Chicago Press. [17]

Minor, T. R., & Lolordo, V. M. (1984). Escape deficits following inescapable shock: The role of contextual odor. *Journal of Experimental Psychology: Animal Behavior Processes, 10*, 168–181. [6]

Minter, R. E., & Kimball, C. P. (1980). Life events, personality traits and illness. In I. L. Kutash & L. B. Schlesinger (Eds.), *Handbook on stress and anxiety.* San Francisco: Jossey-Bass. [14]

Mischel, W. (1968). *Personality and assessment.* New York: Wiley. [13]

Mischel, W. (1981). *Introduction to personality.* 3rd ed. New York: Holt, Rinehart and Winston. [13]

Mischel, W. (1983). Alternatives in the pursuit of the predictability and consistency of persons: Stable data that yield unstable interpretations. *Journal of Personality, 51*, 578–604. [13]

Mischel, W. (1984). Convergences and challenges in the search for consistency. *American Psychologist, 39*, 351–364. [13]

Mischel, W., & Peake, P. K. (1982). Beyond déjà vu in the search for cross-situational consistency. *Psychological Review, 89*, 730–755. [13]

Mishkin, M., & Appenzeller, T. (1987). The anatomy of memory. *Scientific American, 256*, 80–89. [7]

Mitchell, D. (1980). The influence of early visual experience on visual perception. In C. Harris (Ed.), *Visual coding and adaptability.* Hillsdale, NJ: Lawrence Erlbaum. [4]

Money, J. (1975). Ablatiopenis: Normal male infant sex-reassigned as a girl. *Archives of Sexual Behavior, 4*, 65–72. [11]

Money, J. (1987). Sin, sickness or status? *American Psychologist, 42*, 384–399. [10]

Money, J., & Dalery, J. (1976). Iatrogenic homosexuality: Gender identity in seven 46,XX chromosomal females with hyperadrenocortical hermaphroditism born with a penis, three reared as boys, four reared as girls. *Journal of Homosexuality, 1*, 357–371. [10]

Money, J., & Ehrhardt, A. A. (1972). *Man & woman boy & girl.* Baltimore: Johns Hopkins University Press. [10]

Money, J., & Mathews, D. (1982). Prenatal exposure to virilizing progestins: Adult follow-up study of twelve women. *Archives of Sexual Behavior, 11*, 73–83. [10]

Money, J., Schwartz, M., & Lewis, V. G. (1984). Adult erotosexual status and fetal hormonal masculinization and demasculinization: 46,XX congenital virilizing adrenal hyperplasia and 46,XY androgen-insensitivity syndrome compared. *Psychoneuroendocrinology, 9*, 405–414. [10]

Moody, R. A. (1976). *Life after life.* Harrisburg, PA: Stackpole Books. [4]

Moore, T. E. (1985). Subliminal delusion. *Psychology Today*, July 1985. [4]

Moore-Ede, M. C., & Czeisler, C. A. (1984). *Mathematical models of the circadian sleep-wake cycle.* New York: Raven Press. [5]

Morgan, M. (1985). Self-monitoring of attained subgoals in private study. *Journal of Educational Psychology, 77*, 623–630. [1]

Morin, C. M., & Azrin, N. H. (1987). Stimulus control and imagery training in treating sleep-maintenance insomnia. *Journal of Consulting and Clinical Psychology, 55,* 260–262. [5]

Morokoff, P. J., & LoPiccolo, J. (1982). Self-management in the treatment of sexual dysfunction. In P. Karoly & F. H. Kanfer (Eds.), *Self-management and behavior change.* New York: Pergamon Press. [16]

Morris, N. M., Udry, J. R., Khan-Dawood, F., & Dawood, M. Y. (1987). Marital sex frequency and midcycle female testosterone. *Archives of Sexual Behavior, 16,* 27–37. [10]

Morrow, G. R. (1986). Effect of the cognitive hierarchy in the systematic desensitization treatment of anticipatory nausea in cancer patients: A component comparison with relaxation only, counseling and no treatment. *Cognitive Therapy and Research, 10,* 421–446. [6]

Mower, G. D., Christen, W. G., & Caplan, C. J. (1983). Very brief visual experience eliminates plasticity in the cat visual cortex. *Science, 221,* 178–180. [4]

Muehlenhard, C. L., & Linton, M. A. (1987). Date rape and sexual aggression in dating situations: Incidence and risk factors. *Journal of Counseling Psychology, 34,* 186–196. [18]

Munjack, D. J., Oziel, L. J., Kanno, P. H., Whipple, K., & Leonard, M. D. (1981). Psychological characteristics of males with secondary erectile failure. *Archives of Sexual Behavior, 10,* 123–131. [10]

Murray, J. B. (1986a). New psychoactive drugs. *Genetic, Social, and General Psychology Monographs, 111,* 429–453. [15]

Murray, J. B. (1986b). Psychological aspects of anorexia nervosa. *Genetic, Social and General Psychology Monographs, 112,* 5–40. [9]

Murray, J. B. (1986c). Successful treatment of obsessive-compulsive disorders. *Genetic, Social, and General Psychology Monographs, 112,* 173–199. [15]

Myers, D. G. (1981). The psychology of ESP. *Science Digest,* August. [4]

Myers, J. K., Weissman, M. M., Tischler, G. L., Holzer, C. E. III, Leaf, P. J., Orvaschel, H., Anthony, J. C., Boyd, J. H., Burke, J. D., Kramer, M., & Stoltzman, R. (1984). Six-month prevalence of psychiatric disorders in three communities. *Archives of General Psychiatry, 41,* 959–967. [15]

Nathan, P. E., & Skinstad, A. H. (1987). Outcome of treatment for alcohol problems: Current methods, problems and results. *Journal of Consulting and Clinical Psychology, 55,* 332–340. [5]

Nathans, J., Piantanida, T. P., Eddy, R. L., Shows, T. B., & Hogness, D. S. (1986a). Molecular genetics of inherited variation in human color vision. *Science, 232,* 203–210. [3]

Nathans, J., Thomas, D., & Hogness, D. S. (1986b). Molecular genetics of human color vision: The genes encoding blue, green, and red pigments. *Science, 232,* 193–202. [3]

Naitoh, P. (1976). Sleep deprivation in human subjects: A reappraisal. *Waking and Sleeping, 1,* 53–60. [5]

Neill, J. R., & Ludwig, A. M. (1980). Psychiatry and psychotherapy: Past and future. *American Journal of Psychotherapy, 34,* 39–50. [16]

Neisser, U. (1976). *Cognition and reality: Principles and implications of cognitive psychology.* New York: W. H. Freeman. [7]

Neisser, U. (Ed.). (1982). *Memory observed.* New York: W. H. Freeman. [7]

Neubuerger, O. W., Miller, S. I., Schmitz, R. E., Matarazzo, J. D., Pratt, H., & Hasha, N. (1982). Replicable abstinence rates in an alcoholism treatment program. *Journal of the American Medical Association, 248,* 960–963. [5]

Newell, A., & Simon, H. A. (1972). *Human problem solving.* Englewood Cliffs, NJ: Prentice-Hall. [8]

Newsom, C., Favell, J. E., & Rincover, A. (1983). The side effects of punishment. In S. Axelrod & J. Apsche (Eds.), *The effects of punishment on human behavior.* Orlando, FL: Academic Press. [6]

Nicassio, P., & Bootzin, R. (1974). A comparison of progressive relaxation and autogenic training as treatments for insomnia. *Journal of Abnormal Psychology, 83,* 253–260. [5]

Niles, W. J. (1986). Effects of a moral development discussion group on delinquent and predelinquent boys. *Journal of Counseling Psychology, 33,* 45–51. [12]

Nordstrom, G., & Berglund, M. (1987). Prospective study of successful long-term adjustment in alcohol dependence: Social drinking versus abstinence. *Journal of Studies on Alcohol, 48,* 95–103. [5]

Norman, D. A. (1982). *Learning and memory.* New York: Freeman. [7]

Noyes, R., Jr., Chaudry, D. R., & Domingo, D. V. (1986). Pharmacologic treatment of phobic disorders. *Journal of Clinical Psychiatry, 47,* 445–452. [15]

Noyes, R., Jr., Clancy, J., Hoenk, P. R., Slymen, D. J. (1980). The prognosis of anxiety neurosis. *Archives of General Psychiatry, 37,* 173–178. [15]

Nunes, E. V., Frank, K. A., & Kornfeld, D. S. (1987). Psychologic treatment for the type A behavior pattern and for coronary heart disease: A meta-analysis of the literature. *Psychosomatic Medicine, 48,* 159–173. [14]

Oakes, W. F. (1982). Learned helplessness and defensive strategies: A rejoinder. *Journal of Personality, 50,* 515–525. [6]

Oakes, W. F., & Curtis, N. (1982). Learned helplessness: Not dependent upon cognitions, attributions, or other such phenomenal experiences. *Journal of Personality, 50,* 387–408. [6]

Orne, M. T. (1959). The nature of hypnosis: Artifact and essence. *Journal of Abnormal and Social Psychology, 58,* 277–299. [5]

Orne, M. T. (1980). On the construct of hypnosis: How its definition affects research and its clinical application. In G. D. Burrows & L. Dennerstein (Eds.), *Handbook of hypnosis and psychosomatic medicine.* New York: Elsevier/North-Holland. [5]

Orne, M. T., & Evans, F. J. (1965). Social control in the psychological experiment: Antisocial behavior and hypnosis. *Journal of Personality and Social Psychology, 1,* 189–200. [1]

Osborn, A. F. (1963). *Applied imagination.* New York: Scribners. [8]

Oskamp, S. (1984). *Applied social psychology.* Englewood Cliffs, NJ: Prentice-Hall. [17, 18]

Overmier, J. B., & Seligman, M. E. P. (1967). Effects of inescapable shock upon subsequent escape and avoidance responding. *Journal of Comparative and Physiological Psychology, 63,* 28–33. [6]

Paivio, A. (1976). Imagery in recall and recognition. In J. Brown (Ed.), *Recall and recognition.* New York: Wiley. [7]

Parke, R. B., & Salby, R. G. (1983). Aggression: A multi-level analysis. In P. H. Mussen (Ed.), *Handbook of child psychology.* Vol. 4. New York: Wiley. [11]

Parker, F. L., Piotrkowski, C. S., & Peay, L. (1987). Head Start as a social support for mothers: The psychological benefits of involvement. *American Journal of Orthopsychiatry, 57,* 220–233. [8]

Parker, G. (1982). Re-searching the schizophrenogenic mother. *The Journal of Nervous and Mental Disease, 170,* 452–462. [15]

Parker, J. F., Haverfield, E., & Baker-Thomas, S. (1986). Eyewitness testimony of children. *Journal of Applied Social Psychology, 16,* 287–302. [7]

Parks, T. E., & Coss, R. G. (1986). Prime illusion. *Psychology Today,* October. [4]

Patterson, G. R. (1982). *Coercive family process.* Vol. 3. Eugene, OR: Castalia Publishing. [11]

Paul, S. M., Extein, I., Calil, H. M., Potter, W. Z., Chodoff, P., & Goodwin, F. K. (1981). Use of ECT with treatment-resistant depressed patients at the National Institute of Mental Health. *American Journal of Psychiatry, 138,* 486–489. [15]

Paul, W., Weinrich, J. D., Gonsiorek, J. C., & Hotvedt, M. E. (Eds.). (1982). *Homosexuality: Social, psychological, and biological issues.* Beverly Hills, CA: Sage Publications. [10]

Pearl, D., Bouthilet, L., & Lazar, J. (Eds.). (1982). *Television and behavior: Ten years of scientific progress and implications for the eighties.* Vols. 1 and 2. Washington, DC: U.S. Government Printing Office. [18]

Penfield, W., & Perot, P. (1963). The brain's record of auditory and visual experience. *Brain, 86,* 595–696. [8]

Peplau, L. A., & Perlman, D. (1982). Perspectives on loneliness. In L. A. Peplau & D. Perlman (Eds.), *Loneliness.* New York: Wiley. [13]

Perlmutter, M. (1978). What is memory aging the aging of? *Developmental Psychology, 14,* 330–345. [12]

Perlow, M. J., Freed, W. J., Hoffer, B. J., Seiger, A., Olson, L., & Wyatt, R. J. (1979). Brain grafts reduce motor abnormalities produced by destruction of nigrostriatal dopamine system. *Science, 204,* 643–646. [2]

Perrett, D. I., Rolls, E. T., & Caan, W. (1982). Visual neurones responsive to faces in the monkey temporal cortex. *Experimental Brain Research, 47,* 329–342. [3]

Perri, M. G., McAdoo, W. G., McAllister, D. A., Lauer, J. B., & Yancey, D. Z. (1986). Enhancing the efficacy of behavior therapy for obesity: Effects of aerobic exercise and a multicomponent maintenance program. *Journal of Consulting and Clinical Psychology, 54,* 670–675. [9]

Perry, D. G., Perry, L. C., & Rasmussen, P. (1986). Cognitive social learning mediators of aggression. *Child Development, 57,* 700–711. [18]

Perry, J. D., & Whipple, B. (1981). Pelvic muscle strength of female ejaculators: Evidence in support of a new theory of orgasm. *The Journal of Sex Research, 17,* 22–39. [10]

Persky, V. W., Kempthorne-Rawson, J., & Shekelle, R. B. (1987). Personality and risk of cancer: 20-year follow-up of the Western Electric study. *Psychosomatic Medicine, 49,* 435–449. [14]

Pervin, L. A. (1980). *Personality: Theory, assessment and research.* 3rd ed. New York: Wiley, 441. [13]

Pervin, L. A. (1983). The stasis and flow of behavior: Toward a theory of goals. In M. M. Page (Ed.), *Personality—Current theory and research.* Lincoln: University of Nebraska Press. [9]

Peterson, I. (1983). Playing chess bit by bit. *Science News, 124,* 236–237. [8]

Phillips, L. W. (1981). Roots and branches of behavioral and cognitive practice. *Journal of Behavior Therapy and Experimental Psychiatry, 12,* 5–17. [16]

Piaget, J. (1980). Language within cognition. In M. Piatelli-Palmarini (Ed.), *Language and learning.* Cambridge, MA: Harvard University Press. [8]

Piatelli-Palmarini, M. (1980). *Language and learning.* Cambridge, MA: Harvard University Press. [8]

Pierloot, R. (1981). Short-term dynamic psychotherapy: Progress, problems, perspectives. *Psychotherapy and Psychosomatics, 35,* 265–270. [16]

Piliavin, J. A., Dovidio, J. F., Gaertner, S. L., & Clark, R. D. III. (1982). Responsive bystanders: The process of intervention. In V. J. Derlega & J. Grzelak (Eds.), *Cooperation and helping behavior.* Orlando, FL: Academic Press. [18]

Pillemer, D. B. (1984). Flashbulb memories of the assassination attempt on President Reagan. *Cognition, 16,* 63–80. [7]

Pines, M. (1984). In the shadow of Huntington's. *Science 84, 5,* 32–39. [2]

Plomin, R. (1987). Quoted in: Hostetler, A. J., Scientists warn role of biology miscast in wake of Amish study. *APA Monitor, 18,* May, 16–17. [15]

Podlesny, J. A., & Raskin, D. C. (1977). Physiological measures and the detection of deception. *Psychological Bulletin, 84,* 782–799. [14]

Postman, L., & Egan, J. P. (1949). *Experimental psychology.* New York: Harper & Row. [3]

Prentice-Dunn, S., & Rogers, R. W. (1982). Effects of public and private self-awareness on deindividuation and aggression. *Journal of Personality and Social Psychology, 43,* 505–513. [18]

Pressley, M., Snyder, B. L., Levin, J. R., Murray, H. G., & Ghatala, E. S. (1987). Perceived readiness for examination performance (PREP) produced by initial reading of text and text containing adjunct ques-

tions. *Reading Research Quarterly, 22,* 219–236. [1]

Prioleau, L., Murdock, M., & Brody, N. (1983). An analysis of psychotherapy versus placebo. *The Behavioral and Brain Sciences, 8,* 275–285. [16]

Prochaska, J. O., & Norcross, J. C. (1983). Contemporary psychotherapists: A national survey of characteristics, practices, orientations, and attitudes. *Psychotherapy: Theory, Research and Practice, 20,* 161–173. [16]

Przewlocki, R., Lason, W., Konecka, A. M., Gramsch, C., Herz, A., & Reid, L. D. (1983). The opiod peptide dynorphin, circadian rhythms and starvation. *Science, 219,* 71–73. [5]

Putnam, F. W. (1982). Traces of Eve's faces. *Psychology Today,* October. [15]

Putnam, F. W., Guroff, J. J., Silberman, E. K., Barban, L., & Post, R. M. (1986). The clinical phenomenology of multiple personality disorder: Review of 100 recent cases. *Journal of Clinical Psychiatry, 47,* 285–293. [15]

Quasha, S. (1980). *Albert Einstein.* Larchmont, NY: Forest Publishing. [1]

Quinn, T. C., Mann, J. M., Curran, J. W., & Piot, P. (1986). AIDS in Africa: An epidemiologic paradigm. *Science, 234,* 955–963. [10]

Rabkin, S. W., Boyko, E., Shane, F., & Kaufert, J. (1984). A randomized trial comparing smoking cessation programs utilizing behavior modification, health education or hypnosis. *Addictive Behaviors, 9,* 157–173. [5]

Raloff, J. (1982). Childhood lead: Worrisome national levels. *Science News, 121,* 88. [11]

Ramachandran, V. S., & Anstis, S. M. (1986). The perception of apparent motion. *Scientific American, 254,* 102–109. [4]

Ramey, C. T., MacPhee, D., & Yeates, K. O. (1982). Preventing developmental retardation: A general system model. In D. K. Detterman & R. J. Sternberg (Eds.), *How and how much can intelligence be increased.* Norwood, NJ: Ablex Publishing. [8]

Rechtschaffen, A., Gilliland, M. A., Bergmann, B. M., & Winter, J. B. (1983). Physiological correlates of prolonged sleep deprivation in rats. *Science, 221,* 180–184. [5]

Reeder, G. D. (1982). Let's give the fundamental attribution error another chance. *Journal of Personality and Social Psychology, 43,* 341–344. [17]

Rehm, L. P. (1982). Self-management in depression. In P. Karoly & F. H. Kanfer (Eds.), *Self-management and behavior change.* New York: Pergamon Press. [15]

Reid, J. B., Taplin, P. S., & Lorber, R. (1981). A social interactional approach to the treatment of abusive families. In R. B. Stuart (Ed.), *Violent behavior: Social learning approaches to prediction, management and treatment.* New York: Brunner/Mazel. [11]

Reid, P. T. (1979). Racial stereotyping on television: A comparison of the behavior of both black and white television characters. *Journal of Applied Psychology, 64,* 465–471. [17]

Reiterman, T. (1982). *Raven.* New York: Dutton. [18]

Relman, A. S. (Ed.). (1982). *Marijuana and health.* Washington, DC: National Academy Press. [5]

Rescorla, R. A. (1966). Predictability and number of pairings in Pavlovian fear conditioning. *Psychonomics Science, 46,* 107–112. [6]

Restak, R. (1982). Islands of genius. *Science 82,* May. [8]

Rey, D. (1983). Concepts and stereotypes. *Cognition, 15,* 237–262. [8]

Reyneri, A. (1984). The nose knows, but science doesn't. *Science 84,* 26. [3]

Reynolds, A. G., & Flagg, P. W. (1983). *Cognitive psychology.* Boston: Little, Brown. [8]

Reznick, J. S., Kagan, J., Snidman, N., Gersten, M., Baak, K., & Rosenberg, A. (1986). Inhibited and uninhibited children: A follow-up study. *Child Development, 57,* 660–680. [11]

Rice, C. G., Hyley, J. B., Bartlett, B., Befored, W., Gregory, W., & Hallum, G. (1968). A pilot study on the effects of pop group music on hearing. Cited in K. D. Kryter (Ed.), *The effects of noise on man.* Orlando, FL: Academic Press, 1970. [3]

Rice, M. L. (1982). Child language. In T. M. Field, A. Huston, H. C. Quay, L. Troll, & G. E. Finely (Eds.), *Review of human development.* New York: Wiley. [8]

Richardson, P. H., & Vincent, C. A. (1986). Acupuncture for the treatment of pain: A review of evaluative research. *Pain, 24,* 15–40. [3]

Rimm, D. C., & Masters, J. C. (1979). *Behavior therapy.* Orlando, FL: Academic Press. [6]

Ring, K. (1980). Life at death: A scientific investigation of the near death experience. New York: Coward, McCann & Geoghegan. [4]

Ritter, R. C., Slusser, P. G., & Stone, S. (1981). Glucoreceptors controlling feeding and blood glucose: Location in the hindbrain. *Science, 213,* 451–453. [9]

Roberts, P., & Newton, P. M. (1987). Levinsonian studies of women's adult development. *Psychology and Aging, 2,* 154–163. [12]

Robbins, P. R., & Houshi, F. (1983). Some observations on recurrent dreams. *Bulletin of the Menninger Clinic, 47,* 262–265. [5]

Robins, L. N. (1966). *Deviant children grown up.* Baltimore: Williams and Wilkins. [15]

Robins, L. N., Helzer, J. E., Weissman, M. M., Orvaschel, H., Gruenberg, E., Burke, J. D., & Regier, D. A. (1984). Lifetime prevalence of specific psychiatric disorders in three sites. *Archives of General Psychiatry, 41,* 949–958. [15]

Robinson, E. A., & Price, M. G. (1980). Pleasurable behavior in marital interaction: An observational study. *Journal of Consulting and Clinical Psychology, 48,* 117–118. [12]

Roche, J. P. (1986). Premarital sex: Attitudes and behavior by dating stage. *Adolescence, 21,* 107–121. [10]

Rodgers, J. E. (1982). The malleable memory of eyewitnesses. *Science 82,* June. [7]

Rodin, J. (1978). Cognitive-behavioral strategies for the control of obesity. In D. Meichenbaum (Ed.), *Cognitive-behavior therapy.*

New York: BMA Audio Cassette Publications. [9]

Rodin, J. (1983). Behavioral medicine: Beneficial effects of self control training in aging. *International Review of Applied Psychology, 32*, 153–181. [12]

Rodin, J. (1984). Quoted in: Hall, E., A sense of control. *Psychology Today*, December, 38–45. [9]

Rodin, J. (1986). Aging and health: Effects of the sense of control. *Science, 233*, 1271–1276. [12]

Rogers, C. R. (1959). A theory of therapy, personality and interpersonal relationships, as developed in the client-centered framework. In S. Koch (Ed.), *Psychology: A study of a science*. Vol. 3. New York: McGraw-Hill. [13]

Rogers, C. R. (1980). *A way of being*. Boston: Houghton Mifflin. [13]

Rosch, E. (1978). Principles of categorization. In E. Rosch & B. B. Lloyd (Eds.), *Cognition and categorization*. Hillsdale, NJ: Lawrence Erlbaum. [8]

Rosen, G. M. (1976). The development and use of nonprescription behavior therapies. *American Psychologist, 31*, 139–141. [16]

Rosen, G. M. (1987). Self-help treatment books and the commercialization of psychotherapy. *American Psychologist, 42*, 46–51. [16]

Rosen, R. D. (1982). Self-help smorgasbord. *Psychology Today*, November. [16]

Rosenfeld, A. H. (1985). Depression: Dispelling despair. *Psychology Today*, June, 28–34. [15]

Rosenfield, D., Sheehan, D. S., Marcus, M. M., & Stephan, W. G. (1981). Classroom structure and prejudice in desegregated schools. *Journal of Educational Psychology, 73*, 17–26. [17]

Rosenman, R. H., & Chesney, M. A. (1985). Type A behavior pattern: Its relationship to coronary heart disease and its modification by behavioral and pharmacological approaches. In M. R. Zales (Ed.), *Stress in health and disease*. New York: Brunner/Mazel. [14]

Rosenthal, D. (1980). Genetic aspects of schizophrenia. In H. M. Van Praag (Ed.), *Handbook of biological psychiatry*. Part III. New York: Marcel Dekker. [15]

Rosenthal, R. (1983). Experimenter effects in laboratories, classrooms, and clinics. In J. Murray & P. R. Abramson (Eds.), *Bias in psychotherapy*. New York: Praeger. [1]

Rosenthal, R., & Fode, K. L. (1963). The effect of experimenter bias on the performance of the albino rat. *Behavioral Science, 8*, 183–189. [1]

Rosenthal, R., & Jacobson, L. (1968). *Pygmalion in the classroom: Teacher expectation and pupils' intellectual development*. New York: Holt, Rinehart and Winston. [1]

Rosenthal, R., & Rubin, D. B. (1978). Interpersonal expectancy effects: The first 345 studies. *Behavioral and Brain Sciences, 3*, 377–415. [1]

Rosenthal, T. L., & Zimmerman, B. J. (1978). *Social learning and cognition*. Orlando, FL: Academic Press. [8]

Roskies, E., & Avard, J. (1982). Teaching healthy managers to control their coronary-prone (Type A) behavior. In K. R. Blankstein & J. Polivy (Eds.), *Advances in the study of communication and affect*. Vol. 7. New York: Plenum Press. [14]

Rothbart, M. K., & Derryberry, D. (1981). Development of individual differences in temperament. In M. E. Lamb & A. L. Brown (Eds.), *Advances in developmental psychology*. Vol. 1. Hillsdale, NJ: Lawrence Erlbaum. [11]

Rotheram, M. J. (1987). Evaluation of imminent danger for suicide among youth. *American Journal of Orthopsychiatry, 57*, 102–110. [12]

Rotter, J. B. (1966). Generalized expectancies for internal versus external control of reinforcement. *Psychological Monographs, 80* (Whole No. 609). [14]

Rowe, J. W., & Kahn, R. L. (1987). Human aging: Usual and successful. *Science, 237*, 143–149. [12]

Rowland, L. W. (1939). Will hypnotized persons try to harm themselves or others? *Journal of Abnormal and Social Psychology, 34*, 114–117. [1]

Rowley, P. T. (1984). Genetic screening: Marvel or menace? *Science, 225*, 138–144. [11]

Roy, A. (1980). Hysteria. *Journal of Psychosomatic Research, 24*, 53–56. [15]

Rozin, P. (1986). One-trial acquired likes and dislikes in humans: Disgust as a US food predominance, and negative learning predominance. *Learning and Motivation, 17*, 180–189. [6]

Rubin, D. C. (1985). The subtle deceiver: Recalling our past. *Psychology Today*, September 1985. [7]

Rubin, D. C., & Kozin, M. (1984). Vivid memories. *Cognition, 16*, 81–95. [7]

Rubin, Z. J., Provenzano, F. J., & Luria, Z. (1974). The eye of the beholder: Parents' views on sex of newborns. *American Journal of Orthopsychiatry, 44*, 512–519. [11]

Rubinow, D. R., Roybyrne, P. L., Hoban, M. C., Gold, P. W., & Post, R. M. (1984). Prospective assessment of menstrually related mood disorders. *American Journal of Psychiatry, 141*, 684–686. [1]

Ruble, D. N. (1984). Sex-role development. In M. H. Bornstein & M. E. Lamb (Eds.), *Developmental psychology: An advanced textbook*. Hillsdale, NJ: Lawrence Erlbaum. [11]

Ruble, T. L. (1983). Sex stereotypes: Issues of change in the 1970s. *Sex Roles, 9*, 397–402. [12]

Ruderman, A. J. (1986). Bulimia and irrational beliefs. *Behavior Research and Therapy, 24*, 193–197. [9]

Rumbaugh, D. (1977). *Language learning by a chimpanzee: The Lana project*. New York: Academic Press. [8]

Rush, A. J., Beck, A. T., Kovacs, M., Weissenburger, J., & Hollon, S. D. (1982). Comparison of the effects of cognitive therapy and pharmacotherapy on hopelessness and self-concept. *American Journal of Psychiatry, 139*, 862–866. [15, 16]

Russell, J. A., & Bullock, M. (1986). Fuzzy concepts and the perception of emotion in facial expressions. *Social Cognition, 4*, 309–341. [9]

Russell, M., Dark, K. A., Cummins, R. W., Ellman, G., Callaway, E., & Peeke, H. V. S. (1984). Learned histamine release. *Science, 225*, 733–734. [14]

Sabom, M. D. (1982). Recollections of death: A medical investigation. New York: Harper & Row. [4]

Saklofske, D. H., Kelly, I. W., & McKerracher, D. W. (1982). An empirical study of personality and astrological factors. *The Journal of Psychology, 110*, 275–280. [13]

Salzman, L., & Thaler, F. H. (1981). Obsessive-compulsive disorders: A review of the literature. *American Journal of Psychiatry, 138*, 286–296. [15]

Sanders, G. S., & Simmons, W. L. (1983). Use of hypnosis to enhance eyewitness accuracy: Does it work? *Journal of Applied Psychology, 68*, 70–77. [7]

Sanders, R. E., Gonzalez, E. G., Murphy, M. D., Liddle, C. L., & Vitina, J. R. (1987). Frequency of occurrence and the criteria for automatic processing. *Journal of Experimental Psychology: Learning, Memory and Cognition, 13*, 241–250. [7]

Santee, R. T., & Maslach, C. (1982). To agree or not to agree: Personal dissent amid social pressure to conform. *Journal of Personality and Social Psychology, 42*, 690–700. [18]

Sarason, I. G., Johnson, J. H., & Siegel, J. M. (1979). Assessing the impact of life changes: Development of the life experiences survey. In I. G. Sarason & C. D. Spielberger (Eds.), *Stress and anxiety*. Vol. 6. New York: Halsted. [14]

Sarson, I. G., Potter III, E. H., & Sarason, B. R. (1986). Recording and recall of personal events: Effects on cognitions and behavior. *Journal of Personality and Social Psychology, 51*, 347–356. [9]

Sarason, I. G., Sarason, B. R., & Johnson, J. H. (1985). Stressful life events' measurement, moderators and adaptation. In S. R. Burchfield (Ed.), *Stress: Psychological and physiological interactions*. New York: Hemisphere. [14]

Sarbin, T. R., & Coe, W. C. (1972). *Hypnosis: A social psychological analysis of influence communication*. New York: Holt, Rinehart & Winston. [5]

Savage-Rumbaugh, S., McDonald, K., Sevcik, R. A., Hopkins, W. D., & Rubert, E. (1986). Spontaneous symbol acquisition and communicative use by pygmy chimpanzees (Pan paniscus). *Journal of Experimental Psychology: General, 115*, 211–235. [8]

Saxe, L., Dougherty, D., Esty, K., & Fine, H. (1983). *Health technology case study 22: The effectiveness and costs of alcoholism treatment*. Washington, DC: Congress of the United States, Office of Technology Assessment. [5]

Scarr, S. (1984). What's a parent to do? *Psychology Today*, May. [11]

Scarr, S., & Weinberg, R. A. (1976). IQ test performance of black children adopted by white families. *American Psychologist, 31*, 726–739. [8]

Schachter, S., & Rodin, J. (1974). *Obese humans and rats*. Washington, DC: Erlbaum/Halsted. [9]

Schachter, S., & Singer, J. (1962). Cognitive, social and physiological determinants of emotional state. *Psychological Review, 69,* 379–399. [9]

Schacter, D. L. (1983). Amnesia observed: Remembering and forgetting in a natural environment. *Journal of Abnormal Psychology, 92,* 236–242. [7]

Schiff, M., Duyme, M., Dumaret, A., & Tomkiewicz, S. (1982). How much could we boost scholastic achievement and IQ scores? A direct answer from a French adoption study. *Cognition, 12,* 165–196. [8]

Schimke, R. T., & Agniel, M. (1983). Biologic mechanisms in aging. *Journal of the American Geriatrics Society, 31,* 40–44. [12]

Schleifer, S. J., Keller, S. E., Camerino, M., Thornton, J. C., & Stein, M. (1983). Suppression of lymphocyte stimulation following bereavement. *Journal of the American Medical Association, 250,* 374–377. [14]

Schmitt, F. A., Murphy, M. D., & Sanders, R. E. (1981). Training older adult free recall rehearsal strategies. *Journal of Gerontology, 36,* 329–337. [12]

Schroeder, D. H., & Costa, P. T., Jr. (1984). Influence of life events stress on physical illness: Substantive effects or methodological flaws? *Journal of Personality and Social Psychology, 46,* 853–863. [14]

Schuckit, M. A. (1987). Biological vulnerability to alcoholism. *Journal of Consulting and Clinical Psychology, 55,* 301–309. [5]

Seeman, M. V. (1982). Gender differences in schizophrenia. *Canadian Journal of Psychiatry, 27,* 107–111. [15]

Seligman, M. E. P. (1975). *Helplessness: On depression, development and death.* New York: W. H. Freeman. [6]

Seligman, M. E. P., Maier, S. F., & Solomon, R. L. (1971). Unpredictable and uncontrollable aversive events. In F. R. Brush (Ed.), *Aversive conditioning and learning.* Orlando, FL: Academic Press. [6]

Selkoe, D. J. (1987). Deciphering Alzheimer's disease: The pace quickens. *Trends in Neuroscience, 10,* 181–184. [2]

Sewitch, D. E. (1987). Slow wave sleep deficiency insomnia: A problem in thermodownregulation at sleep onset. *Psychophysiology, 24,* 200–215. [5]

Selye, H. (1956). *The stress of life.* New York: McGraw-Hill. [14]

Serban, G. (1984). *Social and medical aspects of drug abuse.* New York: SP Medical & Scientific Books. [5]

Shaffer, D. (1986). Quoted in: Holden, C., Youth suicide. New research focuses on a growing social problem. *Science, 233,* 839–841. [12]

Shaffi, M. (1986). Quoted in: Holden, C., Youth suicide. New research focuses on a growing social problem. *Science, 233,* 839–841. [12]

Shaheen, S. J. (1984). Neuromaturation and behavior development: The case of childhood lead poisoning. *Developmental Psychology, 20,* 542–550. [11]

Shanab, M. E., & Yahya, K. A. (1977). A behavioral study of obedience in children. *Journal of Personality and Social Psychology, 35,* 530–536. [18]

Shantz, D. W. (1986). Conflict, aggression, and peer status: An observational study. *Child Development, 57,* 1322–1332. [18]

Shapiro, C. M. (1981). Growth hormone-sleep interaction: A review. *Research Communications in Psychology, Psychiatry and Behavior, 6,* 115–131. [5]

Shapiro, D. A., & Shapiro, D. (1982). Meta-analysis of comparative therapy outcome studies: A replication and refinement. *Psychological Bulletin, 92,* 581–604. [16]

Shapiro, D. H., Jr. (1985). Clinical use of meditation as a self-regulatory strategy: Comments on Holmes's conclusions and implications. *American Psychologist, 40,* 719–722. [14]

Shaver, P., Schwartz, J., Kirson, D., & O'Connor, C. (1987). Emotion knowledge: Further exploration of a prototype approach. *Journal of Personality and Social Psychology, 52,* 1061–1086. [9]

Shaw, L., & Ehrlich, A. (1987). Relaxation training as a treatment for chronic pain caused by ulcerative colitis. *Pain, 29,* 287–293. [3]

Sheard, M. H. (1979). Testosterone and aggression. In M. Sandler (Ed.), *Psychopharmacology of aggression.* New York: Raven Press. [18]

Sherwood, G. G. (1981). Self-serving biases in person perception: A reexamination of projection as a mechanism of defense. *Psychological Bulletin, 90,* 445–459. [14]

Shevrin, H. (1975). Does the average evoked response encode subliminal perception? Yes. A reply to Schwartz and Rem. *Psychophysiology, 12,* 395–398. [4]

Shevrin, H., & Fritzler, D. E. (1968). Visual evoked response correlates of unconscious mental processes. *Science, 161,* 295–298. [4]

Shevrin, H., Smith, W. H., & Fritzler, D. (1971). Average evoked response and verbal correlates of unconscious mental processes. *Psychophysiology, 8,* 149–162. [4]

Shukla, G. D., Sahu, S. C., Tripathi, R. P., & Gupta, D. K. (1982). Phantom limb: A phenomenological study. *British Journal of Psychiatry, 141,* 54–58. [3]

Sidtis, J. J., Volpe, B. T., Wilson, D. H., Rayport, M., & Gazzaniga, M. S. (1981). Variability in right hemisphere language function after callosal section: Evidence for a continuum of generative capacity. *Journal of Neuroscience, 1,* 323–331. [2]

Siegel, O. (1982). Personality development in adolescence. In B. B. Wolman (Ed.), *Handbook of developmental psychology.* Englewood Cliffs, NJ: Prentice-Hall. [12]

Sifneos, P. E. (1981). Short-term dynamic psychotherapy: Its history, its impact and its future. *Psychotherapy and Psychosomatics, 35,* 224–229. [16]

Silberner, J. (1986). Hypnotism under the knife. *Science News, 129,* 186–187. [5]

Silberner, J. (1987). What triggers AIDS? *Science News, 131,* 220–221. [10]

Simons, A. D., McGowan, C. R., Epstein, L. H., & Kupfer, D. J. (1985). Exercise as a treatment for depression: An update. *Clinical Psychology Review, 5,* 553–568. [15]

Simonton, D. K. (1984). *Genius, creativity, and leadership.* Cambridge, MA: Harvard University Press. [8]

Skakkebaek, N. E., Bancroft, J., Davidson, D. W., & Warner, P. (1981). Androgen replacement with oral testosterone un-decanoate in hypogonadal men: A double blind controlled study. *Clinical Endocrinology, 14,* 49–61. [10]

Skinner, B. F. (1957). *Verbal behavior.* New York: Appleton-Century-Crofts. [8]

Sklar, L. S., & Anisman, H. (1979). Stress and coping factors influence tumor growth. *Science, 205,* 513–515. [14]

Slater, W. H., Graves, M. F., & Piche, G. L. (1985). Effects of structural organizers on ninth-grade students' comprehension and recall of four patterns of expository text. *Reading Research Quarterly, 20,* 189–202. [1]

Small, G. W., & Nicholi, A. M. (1982). Mass hysteria among schoolchildren. *Archives of General Psychiatry, 39,* 721–724. [15]

Small, S. A., Feldin, S., & Savin-Williams, R. C. (1983). In search of personality traits: A multimethod analysis of naturally occurring prosocial and dominance behavior. *Journal of Personality, 51,* 1–16. [13]

Smith, C. A., & Ellsworth, P. C. (1987). Patterns of appraisal and emotion related to taking an exam. *Journal of Personality and Social Psychology, 52,* 475–488. [9]

Smith, D. (1982). Trends in counseling and psychotherapy. *American Psychologist, 37,* 802–809. [16]

Smith, E., & Medin, D. (1981). *Categories and concepts.* Cambridge, MA: Harvard University Press. [8]

Smith, J. C., & Seidel, J. M. (1982). The factor structure of self-reported physical stress reactions. *Biofeedback and Self-Regulation, 7,* 35–47. [14]

Smith, M. L., & Glass, G. V. (1977). Meta-analysis of psychotherapy outcome studies. *American Psychologist, 32,* 752–760. [16]

Smith, M. L., Glass, G. V., & Miller, T. I. (1980). *The benefits of psychotherapy.* Baltimore, MD: Johns Hopkins University Press. [16]

Smith, T. W. (1982). Irrational beliefs in the cause and treatment of emotional distress: A critical review of the rational emotive model. *Clinical Psychology Review, 2,* 505–522. [16]

Smith, T. W., Snyder, C. R., & Handelsman, M. H. (1982). On the self-serving function of an academic wooden leg: Test anxiety as a self-handicapping strategy. *Journal of Personality and Social Psychology, 42,* 314–321. [9]

Smith, T. W., Snyder, C. R., & Perkins, S. C. (1983). The self-serving function of hypochondriacal complaints: Physical symptoms as self-handicapping strategies. *Journal of Personality and Social Psychology, 44,* 787–797. [9]

Snarey, J. (1987). Cross-cultural universality of social-moral development: A critical review of Kohlbergian research. *Psychological Bulletin, 97,* 202–232. [12]

Snyder, C. R. (1974). Why horoscopes are true: The effects of specificity on acceptance of astrological interpretations. *Journal of Clinical Psychology, 30,* 577–580. [13]

Snyder, C. R., Shenkel, R. J., & Lowery, C. R. (1977). Acceptance of personality interpretations: The "Barnum effect" and beyond. *Journal of Consulting and Clinical Psychology, 45,* 104–114. [13]

Snyder, M. (1974). Self-monitoring of expressive behavior. *Journal of Personality and Social Psychology, 30,* 526–537. [17]

Snyder, M. (1981). On the self-perpetuating nature of social stereotypes. In D. L. Hamilton (Ed.), *Cognitive processes in stereotyping and intergroup behavior.* Hillsdale, NJ: Lawrence Erlbaum. [17]

Snyder, M. (1982a). Self-fulfilling stereotypes. *Psychology Today,* July. [17]

Snyder, M. (1982b). When believing means doing: Creating links between attitudes and behavior. In M. P. Zanna, E. T. Higgins, & C. P. Herman (Eds.), *Consistency in social behavior.* Vol. 2. Hillsdale, NJ: Lawrence Erlbaum. [17]

Snyder, M., Tanke, E. D., & Berscheid, E. (1977). Social perception and interpersonal behavior: On the self-fulfilling nature of social stereotypes. *Journal of Personality and Social Psychology, 35,* 656–666. [17]

Snyder, S. H. (1972). The true speed trip: Schizophrenia. *Psychology Today,* January. [5]

Snyder, S. H. (1980). *Biological aspects of mental disorder.* New York: Oxford University Press. [15]

Sosis, R. H., Strickland, B. R., & Haley, W. E. (1980). Perceived locus of control and beliefs about astrology. *The Journal of Psychology, 110,* 65–71. [13]

Sotile, W. M. (1979). The penile prosthesis: A review. *Journal of Sex & Marital Therapy, 5,* 90–102. [10]

Sotile, W. M., & Kilmann, P. R. (1977). Treatments of psychogenic female sexual dysfunctions. *Psychological Bulletin, 84,* 619–633. [10]

Spanos, N. P. (1982). Hypnotic behavior: A cognitive, social psychological perspective. *Research Communications in Psychology, Psychiatry and Behavior, 7,* 199–213. [5]

Spanos, N. P. (1986). Hypnotic behavior: A social-psychological interpretation of amnesia, analgesia, and the "trance logic." *Behavioral and Brain Sciences, 9,* 449–502. [5]

Spanos, N. P., Menary, E., Brett, P. J., Cross, W., & Ahmed, Q. (1987). Failure of posthypnotic responding to occur outside the experimental setting. *Journal of Abnormal Psychology, 96,* 52–57. [5]

Spanos, N. P., Robertson, L. A., Menary, E. P., Brett, P. J., & Smith, J. (1987). Effects of repeated baseline testing on cognitive-skill-training-induced increments in hypnotic susceptibility. *Journal of Personality and Social Psychology, 52,* 1230–1235. [5]

Spence, J. T. (1983). Comment on Lubinski, Tellegen, and Butcher's "Masculinity, femininity, and androgyny viewed and assessed as distinct concepts." *Journal of Personality and Social Psychology, 44,* 440–446. [12]

Spence, J. T. (1984). Masculinity, femininity and gender-related traits: A conceptual analysis and critique of current research. In B. A. Haher & W. B. Maher (Eds.), *Progress in experimental personality research.* Vol. 13. Orlando, FL: Academic Press. [12]

Sperry, R. (1982). Some effects of disconnecting the cerebral hemispheres. *Science, 217,* 1223–1226. [2]

Sperry, R. W. (1974). Lateral specialization in the surgically separated hemisphere. In

R. O. Schmitt and F. G. Worden (Eds.), *The neurosciences: Third study program.* Cambridge, MA: MIT Press. [2]

Spitz, H. H. (1986). *The raising of intelligence.* Hillsdale, NJ: Lawrence Erlbaum. [8]

Springer, K. J. (1981). Effectiveness of treatment of sexual dysfunction: Review and evaluation. *Journal of Sex Education and Therapy, 7,* 18–22. [10]

Springer, S. P., & Deutsch, G. (1985). *Left brain, right brain.* Rev. ed. New York: W. H. Freeman. [2, 3]

Squire, L. (1986). Mechanisms of memory. *Science, 232,* 1612–1619. [7]

Squire, L. R. (1982). The neuropsychology of human memory. *Annual Review of Neuroscience, 5,* 241–273. [7]

Squire, L. R., & Slater, P. C. (1983). Electroconvulsive therapy and complaints of memory dysfunction: A prospective three-year follow-up study. *British Journal of Psychiatry, 142,* 1–8. [15]

Squire, L. R., Slater, P. C., & Miller, P. L. (1981). Retrograde amnesia and bilateral electroconvulsive therapy. *Archives of General Psychiatry, 38,* 89–95. [15]

Sroufe, L. A., Fox, N. E., & Pancake, V. R. (1983). Attachment and dependency in developmental perspective. *Child Development, 54,* 1615–1627. [11]

Stanley, J. (1987). Quoted in: Holden, C., Female math anxiety on the wane. *Science, 236,* 660–661. [11]

Stark, E. (1984). Hypnosis on trial. *Psychology Today,* February. [7]

Stark, L. J., Collins, F. L., Osnes, P. G., & Stokes, T. F. (1986). Using reinforcement and cueing to increase healthy snack food choices in preschoolers. *Journal of Applied Behavior Analysis, 19,* 367–379. [6]

Stechler, G., & Halton, A. (1982). Prenatal influences on human development. In B. B. Wolman (Ed.), *Handbook of developmental psychology.* Englewood Cliffs, NJ: Prentice-Hall. [11]

Stein, B. S., Littlefield, J., Bransford, J. D., & Persampieri, M. (1984). Elaboration and knowledge acquisition. *Memory & Cognition, 12,* 522–529. [7]

Stein, M. I. (1975). *Stimulating creativity.* Vol. 1. New York: Academic Press. [8]

Steinman, D. L., Wincze, J. P., Sakheim, Barlow, D. H., & Mavissakalian, M. (1981). A comparison of male and female patterns of sexual arousal. *Archives of Sexual Behavior, 10,* 529–547. [10]

Steketee, G., Foa, E. B., & Grayson, J. B. (1982). Recent advances in the behavioral treatment of obsessive-compulsives. *Archives of General Psychiatry, 39,* 1365–1371. [15]

Stephan, W. G. (1983). Intergroup relations. In D. Perlman & P. C. Cozby (Eds.), *Social psychology.* New York: Holt, Rinehart and Winston. [17]

Stephan, W. G., & Feagin, J. R. (1980). *School desegregation.* New York: Plenum Press. [17]

Stern, G. S., McCants, T. R., & Pettine, P. W. (1982). Stress and illness: Controllable and uncontrollable life events' relative contributions. *Personality and Social Psychology Bulletin, 8,* 140–145. [14]

Stern, J. S. (1984). Is obesity a disease of

inactivity? In A. J. Stunkard & E. Stellar (Eds.), *Eating and its disorders.* New York: Raven Press. [9]

Sternberg, R. J. (1977). *Intelligence, information processing and analogical reasoning: The componential analysis of human abilities.* Hillsdale, NJ: Lawrence Erlbaum. [8]

Sternberg, R. J. (1983). Components of human intelligence. *Cognition, 15,* 1–48. [8]

Sternberg, R. J. (1985). Human intelligence: The model is the message. *Science, 230,* 1111–1118. [8]

Sternberg, R. J. (1986). A triangular theory of love. *Psychological Review, 93,* 119–135. [10]

Sternberg, R. J., & Davidson, J. E. (1982). The mind of the puzzler. *Psychology Today,* June. [8]

Sternberg, R. J., & Grajek, S. (1984). The nature of love. *Journal of Personality and Social Psychology, 47,* 312–329. [10]

Sternberg, R. J., & Wagner, R. K. (1986). *Practical intelligence.* New York: Cambridge University. [8]

Stevens, C. F. (1979). The neuron. *Scientific American, 241,* 55–65. [2]

Stevens-Long, J. (1984). *Adult life.* Palo Alto, CA: Mayfield. [12]

Stiles, W. B., Shapiro, D. A., & Elliott, R. (1986). Are all psychotherapies equivalent? *American Psychologist, 41,* 165–180. [16]

Stimson, A., Wase, J. F., & Stimson, J. (1981). Sexuality and self-esteem among the aged. *Research on Aging, 3,* 228–239. [12]

Stogdill, R. M. (1974). *Handbook of leadership: A survey of theory and research.* New York: Free Press. [18]

Stratton, G. M. (1917). The mnemonic feat of the "shass pollak." *Psychological Review, 24,* 244–247. [7]

Streissguth, A. P., Landesman-Dwyer, S., Martin, J. C., & Smith, D. W. (1980). Teratogenic effects of alcohol in humans and laboratory animals. *Science, 209,* 353–361. [11]

Streissguth, A. P., Martin, D. C., Barr, H. M., & Sandman, B. M. (1984). Intrauterine alcohol and nicotine exposure: Attention and reaction time in 4-year-old children. *Developmental Psychology, 20,* 533–541. [11]

Striegel-Moore, R. H., Silberstein, L. R., & Rodin, J. (1986). Toward an understanding of risk factors for bulimia. *American Psychologist, 41,* 246–263. [9]

Stromeyer, C. F. III. (1970). Eidetikers. *Psychology Today,* November. [7]

Strupp, H. H. (1980b). Success and failure in time-limited psychotherapy. *Archives of General Psychiatry, 37,* 595–603. [16]

Strupp, H. H., & Hadley, S. W. (1979). Specific and nonspecific factors in psychotherapy. *Archives of General Psychiatry, 36,* 1125–1136. [16]

Stuart, R. B., & Roper, B. L. (1979). Marital behavior therapy: A research reconnaissance. In P. O. Sjoden, S. Bates, & W. S. Dockens III (Eds.), *Trends in behavior therapy.* Orlando, FL: Academic Press. [12]

Stunkard, A. J. (1981). Adherence to medical treatment: Overview and lessons from behavioral weight control. *Journal of Psychosomatic Research, 25,* 187–197. [9]

Stunkard, A. J., & Penick, S. B. (1979). Behavior modification in the treatment of obesity: The problem of maintaining weight loss. *Archives of General Psychiatry, 36*, 801–806. [9]

Stunkard, A. J., Sorensen, T. I. A., Hanis, C., Teasdale, T. W., Chakraborty, R., Schull, W. J., & Schulsinger, F. (1986). An adoption study of human obesity. *New England Journal of Medicine, 314*, 193–198. [9]

Sugarman, S. (1983). Why talk? Comment on Savage-Rumbaugh et al. *Journal of Experimental Psychology: General, 112*, 493–497. [8]

Suls, J., & Mullen, B. (1981). Life changes and psychological distress: The role of perceived control and desirability. *Journal of Applied Social Psychology, 11*, 379–389. [14]

Sundberg, N. D., Taplin, J. R., & Tyler, L. E. (1983). *Introduction to clinical psychology.* Englewood Cliffs, NJ: Prentice-Hall. [15]

Susman, E. J., Inoff-Germain, G., Nottelmann, E. D., Loriaux, D. L., Cutler, G. B., Jr., & Chrousos, G. P. (1987). Hormones, emotional dispositions, and aggressive attributes in young adolescents. *Child Development, 58*, 1114–1134. [18]

Sweeney, P. D., Anderson, K., & Bailey, S. (1986). Attributional style in depression: A meta-analytic view. *Journal of Personality and Social Psychology, 50*, 974–991. [15]

Szmukler, G. I. (1985). The epidemiology of anorexia nervosa and bulimia. *Journal of Psychiatric Research, 19*, 143–153. [9]

Szyfelbein, S. K., Osgood, P. F., & Carr, D. B. (1985). The assessment of pain and plasma B-endorphin immunoactivity in burned children. *Pain, 22*, 173–182. [3]

Tanner, W. P., & Swets, J. A. (1954). A decision-making theory of visual detection. *Psychological Review, 61*, 401–409. [4]

Taylor, S. E., & Crocker, J. (1981). Schematic bases of social information processing. In E. T. Higgins, C. P. Herman, & M. P. Zanna (Eds.), *Social cognition.* Hillsdale, NJ: Lawrence Erlbaum. [17]

Teasdale, J. D., & Russell, M. L. (1983). Differential effects of induced mood on the recall of positive, negative and neutral words. *British Journal of Clinical Psychology, 22*, 163–171. [7]

Tedeschi, J. R., Schlenker, B. R., & Bonoma, T. V. (1971). Cognitive dissonance: Private ratiocination or public spectacle. *American Psychologist, 26*, 685–695. [17]

Tellegen, A., Lykken, D. T., Bouchard, T. J., Jr., Wilcox, K. J., & Segal, N. L. (1988). Personality similarity in twins reared apart and together. *Journal of Personality and Social Psychology, 54*, 1031–1039. [13]

Tempier, D. I., & Veleber, D. M. (1981). The decline of catatonic schizophrenia. *Orthomolecular Psychiatry, 10*, 156–158. [15]

Tennen, H., Drum, P. E., Gillen, R., & Stanton, A. (1982b). Learned helplessness and the detection of contingency: A direct test. *Journal of Personality, 50*, 426–442. [6]

Tennen, H., Gillen, R., & Drum, P. E. (1982a). The debilitating effect of exposure to noncontingent escape: A test of the learned helplessness model. *Journal of Personality, 50*, 409–425. [6]

Terman, L. M. (1916). *The measurement of intelligence.* Boston: Houghton Mifflin. [8]

Terman, L. M., & Oden, M. H. (1959). *The gifted group at mid-life.* Vol. 5. Stanford, CA: Stanford University Press. [8]

Terrace, H. S. (1981). A report to an academy, 1980. *Annals of the New York Academy of Sciences, 364*, 94–114. [8]

Thayer, R. E. (1987). Energy, tiredness, and tension effects of a sugar snack versus moderate exercise. *Journal of Personality and Social Psychology, 52*, 119–125. [9]

Thompson, R. F. (1986). The neurobiology of learning and memory. *Science, 233*, 941–947. [7]

Tobias, S. (1982). Sexist equations. *Psychology Today*, January. [11]

Toch, H. H., & Schulte, R. (1961). Readiness to perceive violence as a result of police training. *British Journal of Psychology, 52*, 389–393. [4]

Tomkins, S. S. (1981). The quest for primary motives: Biography and autobiography of an idea. *Journal of Personality and Social Psychology, 41*, 306–329. [9]

Tourangeau, R., & Ellsworth, P. C. (1979). The role of facial response in the experience of emotion. *Journal of Personality and Social Psychology, 37*, 1519–1531. [9]

Trotter, R. J. (1983). Baby face. *Psychology Today*, August. [11]

Trotter, R. J. (1986). Three heads are better than one. *Psychology Today*, August. [8]

Tsuang, M. T. (1982). Long-term outcome in schizophrenia. *Trends in Neuroscience, 5*, 202–207. [5, 15]

Tulving, E. (1972). Episodic and semantic memory. In E. Tulving and W. Donaldson (Eds.), *Organization of memory.* New York: Academic Press. [7]

Tulving, E. (1984). Precis of elements of episodic memory. *The Behavioral and Brain Sciences, 7*, 223–268. [7]

Turnbull, C. (1961). Some observations regarding the experiences and behavior of the Bambuti pygmies. *American Journal of Psychology, 74*, 304–308. [4]

Tversky, A., & Kahneman, D. (1974). Judgment under uncertainty: Heuristics and biases. *Science, 185*, 1124–1131. [8]

Tversky, A., & Kahneman, D. (1980). Causal schemas in judgments under uncertainty. In M. Fishbein (Ed.), *Progress in social psychology.* Hillsdale, NJ: Lawrence Erlbaum. [8]

Tversky, A., & Kahneman, D. (1983). Extensional versus intuitive reasoning: The conjunction fallacy in probability judgment. *Psychological Review, 90*, 293–315. [8]

Tversky, B., & Hemenway, K. (1984). Objects, parts and categories. *Journal of Experimental Psychology: General, 113*, 169–193. [8]

Valenstein, E. S. (1986). *Great and desperate cures.* New York: Basic Books. [2]

Vander Zanden, J. W. (1981). *Human development.* 2nd ed. New York: Knopf. [11]

Van Houten, R. (1983). Punishment: From the animal laboratory to the applied setting. In S. Axelrod & J. Apsche (Eds.), *The effects of punishment on human behavior.* Orlando, FL: Academic Press. [6]

Van Lancker, D. R., & Canter, G. J. (1982). Impairment of voice and face recognition in patients with hemispheric damage. *Brain and Cognition, 1*, 185–195. [2]

Van Voorhis, P. (1985). The utility of Kohlberg's theory of moral development among adult probationers in a restitution field setting. *Genetic, Social, and General Psychology Monographs, 111*, 101–126. [12]

Van Wyk, P. H. (1982). Relationship of time spent on masturbation assignments with orgasmic outcome in preorgasmic women's groups. *The Journal of Sex Research, 18*, 33–40. [10]

Veith-Flanigan, J., & Sandman, C. A. (1985). Neuroendocrine relationships with stress. In S. R. Burchfield (Ed.), *Stress.* New York: Hemisphere Publishing. [14]

Velten, E. (1968). A laboratory task for induction of mood states. *Behavior Research & Therapy, 6*, 473–482. [9]

Venn, J. (1986). Hypnosis and the reincarnation hypothesis: A critical review and intensive care study. *Journal of the American Society for Psychical Research, 80*, 408–425. [5]

Vitkus, J., & Horowitz, L. M. (1987). Poor social performance of lonely people: Lacking a skill or adopting a role? *Journal of Personality and Social Psychology, 52*, 1266–1273. [13]

Vokey, J. R., & Read, J. D. (1985). Subliminal messages. *American Psychologist, 40*, 1231–1239. [4]

Vonnegut, M. (1976). *The Eden express.* New York: Bantam. [15]

Vossel, G., & Froehlich, W. D. (1979). Life stress, job tension and subjective reports of task performance effectiveness: A cross-lagged correlational analysis. In I. G. Sarason & C. D. Spielberger (Eds.), *Stress and anxiety.* Vol. 6. New York: Halsted. [14]

Wachtel, P. L. (1982). What can dynamic therapies contribute to behavior therapy? *Behavior Therapy, 13*, 594–609. [16]

Wadden, T. A., & Anderton, C. H. (1982). The clinical use of hypnosis. *Psychological Bulletin, 91*, 215–243. [5]

Wadden, T. A., & Penrod, J. H. (1981). Hypnosis in the treatment of alcoholism: A review and appraisal. *The American Journal of Clinical Hypnosis, 24*, 41–47. [5]

Wagner, H. L., MacDonald, C. J., & Manstead, A. S. R. (1986). Communication of individual emotions by spontaneous facial expressions. *Journal of Personality and Social Psychology, 50*, 737–743. [9]

Waid, W. M., & Orne, M. T. (1981). Cognitive, social, and personality processes in the physiological detection of deception. In L. Berkowitz (Ed.), *Advances in experimental social psychology.* Vol. 14. Orlando, FL: Academic Press. [14]

Walker, D. W., Barnes, D. E., Zornetzer, S. F., Hunter, B. E., & Kubanis, P. (1980). Neuronal loss in hippocampus induced by prolonged ethanol consumption in rats. *Science, 209*, 711–713. [5]

Wallechinsky, D. (1986). *Midterm report.* New York: Viking. [12]

Warga, C. (1987). Pain's gatekeeper. *Psychology Today*, August. [3]

Warner, K. E. (1981). Cigarette smoking in the 1970s: The impact of the antismoking campaign on consumption. *Science, 211*, 729–731. [17]

Warnick, D. H., & Sanders, G. S. (1980). Why do eyewitnesses make so many mistakes. *Journal of Applied Social Psychology, 10,* 362–366. [7]

Warren, L. W., & McEachren, L. (1983). Psychosocial correlates of depressive symptomatology in adult women. *Journal of Abnormal Psychology, 92,* 151–160. [15]

Webb, W. B. (1983). Theories in modern sleep research. In A. Mayes (Ed.), *Sleep mechanisms and functions.* Wokingham, Eng.: Van Nostrand Reinhold. [5]

Webb, W. B., & Cartwright, R. D. (1978). Sleep and dreams. *Annual Review of Psychology, 29,* 223–252. [5]

Webb, W. B., & Friel, J. (1971). Sleep stage and personality characteristics of "natural" long and short sleepers. *Science, 171,* 587–588. [5]

Weinberg, H. I., Wadsworth, J., & Baron, R. S. (1983). Demand and the impact of leading questions on eyewitness testimony. *Memory and Cognition, 11,* 101–104. [7]

Weiner, B. (1986). *An attributional theory of motivation and emotion.* New York: Springer-Verlag. [9]

Weingarten, H. P. (1983). Conditioned clues elicit feeding in sated rats: A role for learning in meal initiation. *Science, 220,* 431–433. [9]

Weingartner, H., Grafman, J., Boutelle, W., Kaye, W., & Martin, P. R. (1983). Forms of memory failure. *Science, 221,* 380–382. [7]

Weinstock, C., & Bennett, R. (1971). From "waiting on the list" to becoming a "newcomer" and an "oldtimer" in a home for the aged: Two studies of socialization and its impact upon cognitive functioning. *Aging and Human Development, 2,* 45–58. [12]

Weisberg, R. W. (1980). *Memory, thought and behavior.* New York: Oxford University Press. [8]

Weitzman, E. D., Czeisler, C. A., Zimmerman, J. C., Ronda, J. M., & Knauer, R. S. (1982). Chronobiological disorders: Analytic and therapeutic techniques. In C. Guilleminault (Ed.), *Sleep and waking disorders.* Reading, MA: Addison-Wesley. [5]

Werner, E. E., Bierman, J. M., & French, F. E. (1971). *The children of Kauai.* Honolulu: University of Hawaii Press. [11]

Werner, E. E., & Smith, R. S. (1977). *Kauai's children come of age.* Honolulu: University of Hawaii Press. [11]

Werner, E. E., & Smith, R. S. (1982). *Vulnerable but invincible.* New York: McGraw-Hill. [11]

West, S. G. (1983). Personality and prediction: An introduction. *Journal of Personality, 51,* 275–285. [13]

Whitam, F. L. (1980). Childhood predictors of adult homosexuality. *Journal of Sex Education and Therapy, 6,* 11–16. [10]

White, W. A. (1932). *Outlines of psychiatry.* 13th ed. New York: Nervous and Mental Disease Publishing Company. [15]

Wieder, G. B., & Weiss, R. L. (1980). Generalizability theory and the coding of marital interactions. *Journal of Consulting and Clinical Psychology, 48,* 469–477. [12]

Williams, J. G., & Solano, C. H. (1983). The social reality of feeling lonely. *Personality and Social Psychology Bulletin, 9,* 237–242. [13]

Williams, T. M., Zabrack, M. L., & Joy, L. A. (1982). The portrayal of aggression on North American television. *Journal of Applied Social Psychology, 12,* 360–380. [18]

Williamson, D. A., Kelley, M. L., Davis, C. J., Ruggiero, L., & Blouin, D. S. (1985). Psychopathology of eating disorders: A controlled comparison of bulimic, obese, and normal subjects. *Journal of Consulting and Clinical Psychology, 53,* 161–166. [4]

Wilson, G. D. (1978). Introversion/extroversion. In H. London & J. E. Exner (Eds.), *Dimensions in personality.* New York: Wiley. [13]

Wilson, G. T. (1982). Adult disorders. In G. T. Wilson & C. M. Franks (Eds.), *Contemporary behavior therapy.* New York: Guilford Press. [16]

Wilson, G. T., Rossiter, E., Klefield, E. I., & Lindholm, L. (1986). Cognitive-behavioral treatment of bulimia nervosa: A controlled evaluation. *Behavior Research and Therapy, 24,* 277–288. [9]

Wilson, T. D., & Linville, P. W. (1982). Improving the academic performance of college freshmen: Attribution therapy revisited. *Journal of Personality and Social Psychology, 42,* 367–376. [17]

Winfrey, C. (1979). Why 900 died. *New York Times Magazine,* February 25. [18]

Wingerson, L. (1982). Training the mind to heal. *Discover,* May. [14]

Winograd, E., & Soloway, R. M. (1986). On forgetting the locations of things stored in special places. *Journal of Experimental Psychology: General, 115,* 366–372. [7]

Winton, W. M. (1986). The role of facial response in self-reports of emotion: A critique of Laird. *Journal of Personality and Social Psychology, 50,* 808–812. [9]

Wise, E., & Rafferty, J. (1982). Sex bias and language. *Sex Roles, 8,* 1189–1196. [12]

Witkin, H. A., Mednick, S. A., Schulsinger, F., Bakkestrom, E., Christiansen, K. O., Goodenough, D. R., Hirschhorn, K., Lundsteen, C., Owen, D. R., Philip, J., Rubin, D. B., & Stocking, M. (1976). Criminality in XYY and XXY men. *Science, 193,* 547–555. [18]

Wong, D. F., Wagner, H. N., Jr., Tune, L. E., Dannals, R. F., Pearlson, G. D., Links, J. M., Tamminga, C. A., Broussolle, E. P., Ravert, H. T., Wilson, A. A., Toung, J. K. T., Malat, J., Williams, J. A., O'Tuama, L. A., Snyder, S. H., Kuhar, M. J., & Gjedde, A. (1986). Positron emission tomography reveals elevated D2 dopamine receptors in drug-naive schizophrenics. *Science, 234,* 1558–1563. [15]

Wood, W. (1982). Retrieval of attitude-relevant information from memory: Effects on susceptibility to persuasion and on intrinsic motivation. *Journal of Personality and Social Psychology, 42,* 798–810. [17]

Woods, B. T., Schoene, W., & Knisley, L. (1982). Are hippocampal lesions sufficient to cause lasting amnesia? *Journal of Neurology, Neurosurgery and Psychiatry, 45,* 243–247. [7]

Woolfolk, R. L., & McNulty, T. E. (1983). Relaxation treatment for insomnia: A component analysis. *Journal of Consulting and Clinical Psychology, 51,* 495–503. [5]

Wurtman, R. J. (1985). Alzheimer's disease. *Scientific American, 252,* 62–74. [2]

Wyer, R. S., Jr., & Martin, L. L. (1986). Person memory: The role of traits group stereotypes, and specific behaviors in the cognitive representation of persons. *Journal of Personality and Social Psychology, 50,* 661–675. [17]

Wynne, L. C. (1981). Current concepts about schizophrenics and family relationships. *The Journal of Nervous and Mental Disease, 169,* 82–89. [15]

Yeo, E. A., Turkheimer, E., Faz, N., & Bigler, E. D. (1987). Volumetric asymmetries of the human brain: Intellectual correlates. *Brain and Cognition, 6,* 15–23. [8]

Young, J. (1985). Quoted in: Meer, J., Loneliness. *Psychology Today,* July, 28–33. [13]

Yule, W., & Fernando, P. (1980). Blood phobia—beware. *Behavior Research and Therapy, 18,* 587–590. [16]

Yulevich, L., & Axelrod, S. (1983). Punishment: A concept that is no longer necessary. In M. Hersen, R. M. Eisler, & P. M. Miller (Eds.), *Progress in behavior modification.* Vol. 14. Orlando, FL: Academic Press. [6]

Zagury, D., Bernard, J., Leonard, R., Cheynier, R., Feldman, M., Sarin, P. S., & Gallo, R. C. (1986). Long-term cultures of HTLV-III-infected T cells: A model of cytopathology of T-cell depletion in AIDS. *Science, 231,* 850–853. [10]

Zahn, T. P., & Rapoport, J. L. (1987). Autonomic nervous system effects of acute doses of caffeine in caffeine users and abstainers. *International Journal of Psychophysiology, 5,* 33–41. [5]

Zaidel, E. (1983). A response to Gazzaniga. *American Psychologist, 39,* 542–546. [2]

Zajonc, R. B. (1980). Feeling and thinking. *American Psychologist, 35,* 151–175. [9]

Zajonc, R. B. (1984). On the primacy of affect. *American Psychologist, 39,* 117–123. [9]

Zaleski, C. (1987). *Otherworld journeys.* New York: Oxford University. [4]

Zechmeister, E. G., & Nyberg, S. E. (1982). *Human memory.* Monterey, CA: Brooks/Cole. [7]

Zigler, E. (1986). Quoted in: Meredith, D., The nine-to-five dilemma. *Psychology Today,* February, 36–44. [11]

Zigler, E., & Seitz, V. (1982). Social policy and intelligence. In R. J. Sternberg (Ed.), *Handbook of human intelligence.* Cambridge: Cambridge University Press. [8]

Zilbergeld, B. (1978). *Male sexuality: A guide to sexual fulfillment.* Boston: Little, Brown. [10]

Zilbergeld, B., & Evans, M. (1980). The inadequacy of Masters and Johnson. *Psychology Today,* August. [10]

Zimbardo, P. G. (1970). The human choice: Individuation, reason and order versus deindividuation, impulse and chaos. In W. J. Arnold & D. Levine (Eds.), *Nebraska Symposium on motivation.* Lincoln: University of Nebraska Press. [18]

Zitrin, C. M., Klein, D. F., Woerner, M. G., & Ross, D. C. (1983). Treatment of phobias. I. Comparison of imipramine hydrochloride and placebo. *Archives of General Psychiatry, 40,* 125–138. [15]

Zucker, R. A., & Gomberg, E. S. (1986). Etiology of alcoholism reconsidered. *American Psychologist, 41,* 783–793. [5]

Zuckerman, M. (1979). *Sensation seeking: Beyond the optimal level of arousal.* Hillsdale, NJ: Lawrence Erlbaum. [9]

Zuckerman, M., Klorman, R., Larrance, D. T., & Speigel, N. H. (1981). Facial, autonomic, and subjective components of emotion: The facial feedback hypothesis versus the externalizer-internalizer distinction. *Journal of Personality and Social Psychology, 41,* 929–944. [9]

Credits and Acknowledgments

CHAPTER 1

Figure 1.2 From Louis Harris, *Inside America*. New York: Vintage Books, May 1987.
Figure 1.3 Adapted from E. S. Geller, N. W. Russ, and M. G. Altomari, "Naturalistic Observation of Beer Drinking College Students," *Journal of Applied Behavior Analysis*, 1986, *19*, 391–396. Reprinted by permission of the Society for the Experimental Analysis of Behavior, Inc.
Figure 1.4 From D. Eden and A. B. Shani, "Pygmalion Goes to Boot Camp: Expectancy, Leadership, and Trainee Performance," *Journal of Applied Psychology*, 1982, *67*, 194–199. Copyright © 1982 by the American Psychological Association. Reprinted by permission of the authors.

CHAPTER 2

Figure 2.3 From R. Plotnik and S. Mollenauer, *Brain and Behavior*, 1978. Reprinted by permission of Harper & Row, Publishers, Inc.
Figure 2.4 From R. Plotnik and S. Mollenauer, *Brain and Behavior*, 1978. Reprinted by permission of Harper & Row, Publishers, Inc.
Figure 2.7 Copyright © 1981 by Torstar Books, Inc.
Figure 2.9 From D. H. Hubel, "The Brain," copyright © 1979 by Scientific American, Inc. All rights reserved.
Figure 2.14 Adapted from C. Wortman and E. Loftus, *Psychology*, 2nd ed. Copyright © 1985, 1981 by Alfred A. Knopf, Inc.
Figure 2.15 Adapted from J. Levy, C. Trevarthen, and R. W. Sperry, "Perception of Bilateral Chimeric Figures Following Hemispheric Disconnection," *Brain 95*, 1972, 68, Fig. 4.
Figure 2.16 From S. Scarr and J. Vander Zanden, *Understanding Psychology*, 4th ed. Copyright © 1974, 1977, 1980, 1984 by Random House, Inc.

CHAPTER 3

Figure 3.5 From J. P. Frisby, *Seeing: Illusion, brain and mind*. New York: Oxford University Press, 1980. Fig. 51 (Plate 4), p. 68.
Figure 3.11 Copyright 1984 Time Inc. All rights reserved. Reprinted by permission from *Time*.

CHAPTER 4

Figure 4.28 Reprinted by permission from *Nature*, 1973, 228, 477–478. Copyright © 1973 by Macmillan Journals Limited.
Figure 4.29 From H. H. Toch and R. Schulte, "Readiness to Perceive Violence as a Result of Police Training," *British Journal of Psychology*, 1961, 52, 389–393. Reprinted by permission.

CHAPTER 5

Figures 5.2–5.8 From P. Hauri, *The Sleep Disorders*, copyright © 1982 by The Upjohn Company.
Figure 5.9 Bar graph based on R. L. Woolfolk and T. F. McNulty, "Relaxation Treatment for Insomnia: A Component Analysis," *Journal of Consulting and Clinical Psychology*, 1983, 51, 495–503. Copyright © 1983 by the American Psychological Association. Adapted by permission of the authors.
Figure 5.10 From a Roper Poll as reported in the *San Diego Tribune*, 1984.
Figure 5.12 Adapted from R. A. Baker, "The Effect of Suggestion on Past-Lives Regression," *American Journal of Clinical Hypnosis*, 1982, 25, 71–76. Reprinted by permission of the American Society of Clinical Hypnotists.
Figure 5.13 Based on S. W. Rabkin et al., "A Randomized Trial Comparing Smoking Cessation Programs Utilizing Behavior Modification, Health Education or Hypnosis," *Addictive Behaviors*, 1984, 9, 157–173. Copyright © 1984 by Pergamon Press, Inc. Reprinted by permission of the author and Pergamon Press, Inc.
Figure 5.14 Chart for *Psychology Today* by Karen Karlsson.
Figure 5.16 Drawing after Tom Arna, © 1985 DISCOVER PUBLICATIONS.
Figure 5.19 Data from 1986 Gallup Poll. Reprinted with permission of the Gallup Organization.
Table 5.1 From S. Scarr and J. Vander Zanden, *Understanding Psychology*, 4th ed. Copyright © 1974, 1977, 1980, 1984 by Random House, Inc.

CHAPTER 6

Figure 6.3 From L. J. Stark, F. L. Collins, P. G. Osnes, and T. F. Stokes, "Using Reinforcement and Cueing to Increase Healthy Snack Food Choices in Preschoolers," *Journal of Applied Behavior Analysis*, 1986, *19*, 371. Reprinted by permission of the Society for the Experimental Analysis of Behavior, Inc.
Figure 6.4 From *Operant Learning*, by J. L. Williams. Copyright © 1973 by Wadsworth Publishing Co., Inc. Reprinted by permission of Brooks/Cole Publishing Co., Pacific Grove, California 93950.
Figure 6.5 From the *San Diego Tribune*, Nov. 29, 1982.
Figure 6.6 Graph based on T. R. Minor and V. M. LoLordo, "Escape Deficits Following Inescapable Shock," *Journal of Experimental Psychology: Animal Behavior Processes*, 1984, *10*, 168–181. Copyright © 1984 by the American Psychological Association. Adapted by permission of the authors.

CHAPTER 7

Figure 7.1 Based on P. Graf et al., The Information That Amnesic Patients Do Not Forget," *Journal of Experimental Psychology: Learning, Memory and Cognition*, 1984, *10*, 164–178. Copyright © 1984 by the American Psychological Association. Adapted by permission of the authors.
Figure 7.3 Reprinted by *Psychology Today* Magazine. Copyright © 1985 American Psychological Association.
Figure 7.4 Based on H. P. Bahrick, "Semantic Memory Content in Permastore," *Journal of Experimental Psychology: General*, 1984, *113*, 11. Copyright © 1984 by the American Psychological Association. Adapted by permission of the author.
Figure 7.5 Adapted from *Learning and Memory* by Donald A. Norman. Copyright 1982 W. H. Freeman and Company. Reprinted with permission.
Figure 7.7 From S. J. Ceci, D. F. Ross, and M. P. Toglia, "Suggestibility of Children's Memory: Psychological Implications," *Journal of Experimental Psychology: General*, 1987, *116*, 41. Copyright © 1987 by the American Psychological Association. Reprinted by permission of the author.
Figure 7.8 From M. Mishkin and T. Appenzeller, "The Anatomy of Memory," copyright © 1987 by Scientific American, Inc. All rights reserved.
Figure 7.9 By Paul Gioni. Copyright © 1983, DISCOVER PUBLICATIONS.

CHAPTER 8

Figure 8.2 Wechsler Intelligence Scale for Children. Copyright © 1949 by The Psychological Corporation. Reproduced by permission. All rights reserved.
Figure 8.4 From L. J. Schweinhart and D. P. Weikart, Young children grow up: The effects of the Perry Preschool Program on Youth through age 15. *Monographs of the High/Scope Educational Research Foundation*, 1980, No. 7. Courtesy of Dr. Schweinhart.
Figure 8.6 From W. F. Allman, "Mindworks," *Science 86*, 1986, 26. Reprinted with permission of the American Association for the Advancement of Science.
Figure 8.7 From *Parade* magazine. Copyright 1987, Patrick McDonnell.
Figure 8.8 a & b From *Science 86*, 1986, 27. Reprinted with permission of the American Association for the Advancement of Science.
Figure 8.9 From C. Wortman and E. Loftus, *Psychology*, 2nd ed. Copyright © 1985 by Alfred A. Knopf, Inc.
Figure 8.12 From W. F. Allman, "Mindworks," *Science 86*, 1986, 24–25. Reprinted with permission of the American Association for the Advancement of Science.
Figure 8.13 Drawing by Chon Day; © 1975 The New Yorker Magazine, Inc.
Figure 8.14 Illustrations Copyright Saul Mandel 1986. All Rights Reserved.

CHAPTER 9

Figure 9.1 Based on H. P. Weingarten, "Conditioned Clues Elicit Feeding in Sated Rats," *Science*, 1983, 220, 431–433. Copyright © 1983 by the American Association for the Advancement of Science.
Table 9.1 Courtesy *Statistical Bulletin*, Metropolitan Life Insurance Company.

Figure 9.2 Adapted from R. E. Thayer, "Energy, Tiredness and Tension Effects of a Sugar Snack versus Moderate Exercise," *Journal of Personality and Social Psychology*, 1987, *52*, 122. Copyright 1987 by the American Psychological Association. Adapted by permission of the author.

Figure 9.3 Based on T. W. Smith et al., "The Self-Serving Function of Hypochondriacal Complaints: Physical Symptoms as Self-Handicapping Strategies," *Journal of Personality and Social Psychology*, 1983, *44*, 787–797. Copyright © 1983 by the American Psychological Association. Adapted by permission of the authors.

Figure 9.4 Adapted from P. Shaver, J. Schwartz, D. Kirson, and C. O'Connor, *Journal of Personality and Psychology*, 1987, *52*, 1067. Copyright 1987 by the American Psychological Association. Adapted by permission of the author.

Figure 9.6 From C. J. Patrick, K. D. Craig, and K. M. Prkachin, "Observer Judgments of Acute Pain: Facial Action Determinants," *Journal of Personality and Social Psychology*, 986, *50*, 1297. Copyright 1986 by the American Psychological Association. Reprinted by permission of the author.

Figure 9.7 Adapted from P. Shaver, J. Schwartz, D. Kirson, and C. O'Connor, "Emotion Knowledge: Further Exploration of a Prototype Approach," *Journal of Personality and Social Psychology*, 1987, *52*, 1080. Copyright 1987 by the American Psychological Association. Adapted by permission of the author.

CHAPTER 10

Figure 10.5 Reprinted from *Psychology Today* Magazine. Copyright © 1986 American Psychological Association.

Figure 10.6 From *Psychology Today* Magazine, 1983. Adapted by permission of National Image Makers.

Figure 10.7 Reprinted from *Psychology Today* Magazine. Copyright © 1983 American Psychological Association.

CHAPTER 11

Figure 11.1 By Bergman Hake Design, Inc. Copyright © 1983, DISCOVER PUBLICATIONS.

Figure 11.4 From J. Raloff, "Childhood Lead: Worrisome National Levels," *Science News*, 1982, *121*, 88. Used by permission of Vantage Art, Inc.

Figure 11.6 Based on L. A. Sroufe, N. E. Fox, and V. R. Pancake, *Child Development*, 1983, *54*, 1615–1627. Copyright © 1983 The Society for Research in Child Development, Inc.

Figure 11.7 Reprinted from *Psychology Today* Magazine. Copyright © 1983 American Psychological Association.

CHAPTER 12

Figure 12.1 Reprinted by permission of *Daedalus*, Journal of the American Academy of Arts and Sciences, "Adulthood," Vol. 105, No. 2, Spring 1976, Cambridge, Massachusetts.

Figure 12.2 Data reprinted with permission of American Enterprise Institute for Public Policy Research.

Figure 12.3 Reprinted from *Psychology Today* Magazine. Copyright © 1983 American Psychological Association.

Figure 12.4 Copyright © 1985 by Newsweek, Inc. All rights reserved. Reprinted by permission.

Figure 12.6 Copyright 1987 *USA Today*. Reprinted with permission.

CHAPTER 13

Figure 13.1 "Self Actualizing People," from *Motivation and Personality*, 2/e by Abraham H. Maslow. Copyright 1954 by Harper & Row, Publishers, Inc. Copyright © 1970 by Abraham H. Maslow. Reprinted by permission of Harper & Row, Publishers, Inc.

Figure 13.2 From R. I. Lanyon and L. D. Goodstein, *Personality Assessment*, copyright © 1971 by John Wiley & Sons, Inc. Reprinted by permission of John Wiley & Sons, Inc.

CHAPTER 14

Figure 14.1 Copyright 1987 *USA Today*. Excerpted with permission.
Figure 14.2 Reprinted with permission from *The San Diego Union*.
Figure 14.3 Diagram from David Raskin, University of Utah.

Figure 14.4 Adapted from K. C. Light and P. A. Obrist, "Cardiovascular Reactivity to Behavioral Stress in Young Males with and without Marginally Elevated Causal Systolic Pressure," *Hypertension*, 1980, *2*, 802–808. Reprinted by permission of the American Heart Association, Inc.

Figure 14.5 Adapted from M. Russell et al., "Learned Histamine Release," *Science*, 1984, *225*, 733–734. Copyright © 1984 by the American Association for the Advancement of Science.

Figure 14.6 From G. S. Stern, T. R. McCants, and P. W. Pettine, "Stress and Illness," *Personality and Social Psychology Bulletin*, 1982, *8*, 140–145. Copyright © 1982 by the Society for Personality and Social Psychology, Inc. Reprinted by permission of Sage Publications, Inc.

Figure 14.7 Diagram adapted from M. Friedman et al., "Alteration of Type A Behavior and Reduction in Cardiac Recurrences in Post-myocardial Infarction Patients," *American Heart Journal*, 1984, *108*, 237–248. Reprinted by permission of The C. V. Mosby Company.

CHAPTER 15

Figure 15.2 Adapted from L. N. Robins et al., "Lifetime Prevalence of Specific Psychiatric Disorders in Three Sites," *Archives of General Psychiatry*, 1984, *41*, 949–958. Reprinted by permission of the American Medical Association.

Figure 15.6 Adapted from I. I. Gottesman and J. Shields, "A Critical Review of Recent Adoption, Twin and Family Studies of Schizophrenia: Behavioral Genetics Perspectives," *Schizophrenia Bulletin*, 1976, *2*, 360–398. Reprinted by permission of the authors.

Table 15.1 Adapted from G. C. Davison and J. M. Neale, *Abnormal Psychology*, 3rd ed., pp. 70–72. Copyright © 1982 by John Wiley & Sons, Inc. Used by permission.

CHAPTER 16

Figure 16.2 From D. Smith, "Trends in Counseling and Psychotherapy," *American Psychologist*, 1982, *37*, 802–809. Copyright © 1982 by the American Psychological Association. Reprinted by permission of the author.

Figure 16.3 From G. V. Glass, "Effectiveness of Different Psychotherapies," *Journal of Consulting and Clinical Psychology*, 1983, *31*, 28–41. Copyright © 1983 by the American Psychological Association. Adapted by permission of the authors.

Figure 16.8 Adapted from R. J. Hafner, "Behavior Therapy for Agoraphobic Men," *Behavior Research and Therapy*, 1983, *21*, 51–56. Copyright © 1983 by Pergamon Press, Inc. Reprinted by permission of the author and Pergamon Press, Inc.

Figure 16.11 Adapted from M. Kovacs et al., "Depressed Outpatients Treated with Cognitive Therapy or Pharmacotherapy," *Archives of General Psychiatry*, 1981, *38*, 33–39. Copyright 1981, American Medical Association.

CHAPTER 17

Figure 17.1 Adapted from N. A. Kuiper and M. R. MacDonald, "Self and Other Perception in Mild Depressives," *Social Cognition*, 1982, *1*, 223–239. Published by The Guilford Press. Reprinted by permission.

Figure 17.2 Adapted from T. D. Wilson and P. W. Linville, "Improving the Academic Performance of College Freshmen," *Journal of Personality and Social Psychology*, 1982, *42*, 367–376. Copyright © 1982 by the American Psychological Association. Adapted by permission of the authors.

Figure 17.3 From R. A. Baron and D. Byrne, *Social Psychology: Understanding Human Interaction*, 4th ed. Copyright © 1984 by Allyn and Bacon, Inc. Reprinted with permission.

Figure 17.4 Adapted from P. D. Hurd et al., "Prevention of Cigarette Smoking in Seventh Grade Students," *Journal of Behavioral Medicine*, 1980, *3*, 15–18. Reprinted by permission of Plenum Publishing Corp.

CHAPTER 18

Figure 18.2 From R. A. Baron and D. Byrne, *Social Psychology: Understanding Human Interaction*, 4th ed. Copyright © 1984 by Allyn and Bacon, Inc. Reprinted with permission.

Name Index

643

Subject Index

Child Development - modules 29, 30, 20

CHROMOSOMES (23 pair in every cell, except gametes which have 23)
DNA (the substance of which chromosomes are composed)
GENE (the portion of the CHROMOSOME that determines one characteristic or trait)
GAMETES (either sperm or ova (egg) cells)
ZYGOTE (an ovum that has been fertilized by a sperm)
EMBRYO (a human between the 2nd and 8th week after conception)
FETUS (a human from the 3rd month to birth)

DEVELOPMENT = HEREDITY × ENVIRONMENT × TIME

· **GENOTYPE:** one's inherited or genetic makeup; characteristics that are fixed by heredity; both dominant and recessive traits.

· **PHENOTYPE:** the characteristics that actually appear in a person's development.

How can we study the difference? With twins.

Identical {monozygotic, one-egg} twins; the same genetically.
Fraternal {dizygotic, two-egg} twins; different genetically.

WHAT DOES ONE INHERIT?

1) Basic body build and physical features (eye, hair, skin color)
2) Personality traits, temperament?
3) Developmental timetable for

a) **MATURATION:** the genetically determined process of physical change that continues the biological development of the organism to complete adulthood. It is independent of learning, but may be hampered by a subnormal environment.

ability test 4-6 mo. → (swimming, walking, toilet training, talking, reading, puberty) 3 yrs.

9-16 mo. → not day up to 2.5 yr. → not night up to 4 yrs.

THE POINT OF READINESS is when a certain physical system (muscles, nerves, organs, etc.) has developed enough so that learning is possible.

b) **IMPRINTING:** in some species of birds and perhaps other animals the development of a strong irreversible attachment to some moving stimulus. Usually, the mother, experienced during a critical period shortly after birth or hatching. (*Konrad Lorenz*)

4) **NEEDS or DRIVES** (internal bodily states that stimulate behavior)

5) **REFLEXES** (a simple, automatic, involuntary, unlearned response of a particular part of the body to a particular stimulus)

5) **INSTINCTS** (a drive followed by a complex inborn and unlearned sequence of programmed activity appropriate to satisfy the drive and fixed in all members of a species)
No instincts in humans.
eg. spider making certain web, bird making certain nest.
(DRIVE PLUS COMPLEX UNLEARNED GENETICALLY PROGRAMMED BEHAVIOR)

7) **INTELLECTUAL POTENTIAL**

Identical twins:	.88	correlation of intelligence
Fraternal twins:	.63	
Siblings:	.53	

Erik Erikson

PSYCHOSOCIAL DEVELOPMENT STAGES

Test on Tues., 11/17
Richard Schmidt

Age		
0-1	Infancy	Trust v. Mistrust
1-3	Early Ch.	Autonomy v. Shame & doubt
3-5	Play Age	Initiative v. Guilt
5-P	School Age	Industry v. Inferiority
P-	Adolescence	Identity v. Identity Confusion
	Young Adult	Intimacy v. Isolation
	Adulthood	Generativity v. Self-absorption
	Mature Age	Integrity v. Disgust & despair

Kohlberg's Levels of Moral Development - pp. 316-317

PSYCHOLOGICAL TESTING

STANDARDIZATION: Every test is first given to a large standardization group or groups. These results serve as a reference to which one may later compare an individual's scores.

VALIDITY: A test is valid if it measures what it purports to measure.

RELIABILITY: A test is reliable if it measures whatever it measures consistently.

INTELLIGENCE TESTS

1904 French government hired Alfred Binet to develop a test to screen slow learners.

1905 Alfred Binet and Theodore Simon introduced their test.

1908 The Binet-Simon tests were revised and standardized to classify children according to their mental age.

W.W.I To screen poor learners, the U.S. Army developed two group tests; the Army Alpha Test (for readers) and the Army Beta Test (for non-readers).

1916 An American, Terman, at Stanford University revised the Binet-Simon Test and called it the Stanford-Binet Intelligence Scale. Terman converted mental age to an intelligence quotient using this formula:

$$I.Q. = \frac{MA}{CA} \times 100$$

The Stanford-Binet was revised in 1937 and a number of times since then.

1939 David Wechsler introduced the Wechsler-Bellevue Intelligence Scale which did not use mental age and was therefore more suited for adults.

1949 Wechsler Intelligence Scale for Children (WISC) for ages 6-15 uses 6 verbal and 5 performance (non-verbal) subtests.

1955 Wechsler Adult Intelligence Scale (WAIS) for age 16 and older uses both verbal and performance subtests.

Wechsler Primary and Preschool Scale of Intelligence (WPPSI).

WHAT DOES AN INTELLIGENCE TEST MEASURE?

{1} Innate capacity?
{2} Acquired knowledge or ability?
{3} Communication skills?

The electroencephalograph (EEG) consists of scalp electrodes, amplifiers, and recording pens. It measures the cumulative voltage fluctuations of millions of neurons beneath each electrode.

BRAIN WAVE STAGES:

Stage	Frequency	Amplitude	Explanation	Level of Consciousness
Beta	13-30 Hz	Low	More random firing	Alert or paradoxical sleep or hypnosis
Alpha	8-12 Hz	Low	Synchronized bursts	Relaxed or meditation or hypnosis
Theta	4-7 Hertz	Higher	Increased synchronization	Sleep
Delta	1-3 Hertz	Highest		Deep sleep

CHARACTERISTICS OF PARADOXICAL SLEEP:

(1) Also called REM-1 sleep.
(2) Occurs approximately every 90 minutes.
(3) Beta brain waves.
(4) Rapid eye movements (REM).
(5) Clear dreaming.
(6) Skeletal muscles are relaxed (therefore no sleepwalking).
(7) Autonomic nervous system aroused (e.g., increased heart rate, stomach acids, sexual arousal).
(8) Adults spend 20-25% of the night in REM-1 sleep; babies 50-60%.
(9) When prevented from REM-1 sleep for several nights, adults will spend 60% of the following night in REM-1 sleep. (Called REM REBOUND.)

SLEEP PHENOMENA

Stage 1	Stage 4
REM	NREM
Clear dreams	Sleepwalking
Nightmares	Night terrors } infrequent
Beta	Delta

THEORIES OF DREAMING

FREUD: Dreams are the fantasy fulfillments of hidden repressed desires (that is, dreams are sexual wish fulfillments).

JUNG: Dreams are fantasy compensations for deficiencies we experience in our lives.

ACTIVATION-SYNTHESIS THEORY: Dreams are perceptions caused by the random activity of brain neurons, and therefore dreams cannot be logically interpreted.

OTHER CURRENT THEORISTS: Dreams are merely a consolidation process where the brain processes the large amount of daily stimulation. Dreams are like information processing by the brain while one sleeps.

HYPNOSIS AS A THERAPEUTIC METHOD IS ACCREDITED BY THE:

[1] American Medical Association
[2] American Psychiatric Association
[3] American Dental Association
[4] American Psychological Association

Do you get your "facts" about hypnosis from the professional research or from Hollywood?

HYPNOSIS IS NOT:

[1] Sleep.
[2] Giving up your will.
[3] Being under the "power" of the hypnotist.

HYPNOSIS IS:

[1] A normal altered state everyone experiences periodically.
[2] Something you do to yourself or consent to.
[3] Focused attention.
[4] Heightened suggestibility.

EVERYONE IS SUGGESTIBLE:

[1] It is a God-created inborn attribute.
[2] It is the fundamental mechanism which produces socialization, identification, and enculturation.
[3] Self-concept and language dialect are two products of our suggestibility.
[4] Our suggestibility can be used for good or for evil.

OUR SUGGESTIBILITY IS OFTEN HEIGHTENED IN THESE EVERYDAY STATES INDUCED BY:

[1] Charismatic leaders, such as Hitler, Jim Jones.
[2] Driving monotony ("highway hypnosis").
[3] Some movies.
[4] Some television programs, such as soaps, etc.
[5] Some music rhythms.
[6] Pre-sleep reverie.

HYPNOSIS CONSISTS OF TWO ELEMENTS:

[1] The induction.
[2] The suggestions given while in the state.

(handwritten notes, left margin:)

Stage 1 NREM
Theta begins

Stage 1 — Theta
Beta

Soma is Greek for body.

ABNORMAL BEHAVIOR

PERSONALITY DISORDERS are certain inflexible, maladaptive personality traits. They refer to persons with long-standing, inflexible, maladaptive ways of relating to self and others.
Example: antisocial personality.

NEUROSIS, NEUROTIC DISORDERS. The term has been discontinued since 1980. It originally referred to a group of disorders (a) caused by anxiety, (b) marked by dramatic emotional, physical or behavioral symptoms, (c) unaccompanied by gross personality deterioration, distortion of reality, and inability to cope with everyday activities.

PSYCHOSIS, PSYCHOTIC DISORDERS are a group of disorders in which the person is dominated by dramatic emotional or physical or behavioral symptoms, accompanied by gross personality deterioration, or distortion of reality, or the inability to cope with everyday activities. Psychoses may be either caused by brain destruction (organic psychoses) or may be psychogenic (functional psychoses).

ANXIETY DISORDERS
phobic disorder: a persistent and irrational fear of a specific object, activity, or situation that results in a compelling desire to avoid the dreaded object, activity, or situation.
social phobia: a phobia of a situation where a person might be exposed to scrutiny or might act in a way that might be embarrassing.
agoraphobia: a phobia of being alone or in public places where escape might be difficult or help not available if incapacitated.

Anxiety state: a chronic vague sense of apprehension and uneasiness, accompanied by muscle tension and autonomic hyperactivity, the cause of which is unknown or unrecognized.
Panic disorder: an overwhelming, acute attack of intense apprehension, anxiety or terror in a situation.
Obsessive-compulsive disorder: recurrent, persistent unwanted thoughts or impulses, and repetitive stereotyped behavior.

DISSOCIATIVE DISORDERS
Psychogenic amnesia: psychogenic extensive loss of memory. — *massive repression*
Psychogenic fugue: psychogenic loss of memory in which the person travels to another locale and assumes a new identity.
Multiple personality: the existence within the individual of two or more distinct personalities, each dominant at a particular time. This is bizarre, but not considered a psychosis because the personalities can function adequately in reality.

SOMATOFORM DISORDERS (include physical symptoms for which there are no organic findings.)
Somatization disorder: recurrent and multiple (over 14) bodily complaints of several years duration.
Conversion disorder: a loss of physical function (usually sensory or motor) which is psychogenic and without any organic disease, e.g., blindness, deafness, anesthesia, paralysis.
Hypochondriasis: preoccupation with the fear or belief of having a serious illness.
(cf. Psychosomatic disorder: an actual organic illness that is caused by or notably influenced by the emotional state of the person.)

In hypochondriasis, there are physical complaints but no loss or distortion of bodily function, and no physical disease.
In conversion disorder, there is a loss or distortion of sensory, motor or visceral function, but no underlying physical disease.
In psychosomatic disorder, there is a physical disease.
All three of these disorders are psychogenic (psychologically caused).

AFFECTIVE DISORDERS (MOOD DISORDERS)
Dysthymic disorder (formerly neurotic depression)
Major depression (formerly psychotic depression)

Normal depression	Dysthymic disorder	Major (psychotic) depression
is related to a specific event, such as a loss; is controllable; can be deep.	tends to be prolonged depression, in which there is a strong element of guilt or self-blame, and worth- lessness. 2 year period.	is marked by a loss of control, an overall feeling of worthlessness and hope- lessness, and an inability to function adequately at daily tasks. 2 year period.

● Treatment: tricyclic antidepressants
ECT
Prozac (anti-depressant)

Bipolar disorder (formerly manic-depression) is characterized by mood swings from manic and depressive episodes every few days. A manic episode is a period of excessive euphoria, excitement and hyperactivity. A depressive episode is characterized by a mood of excessive sadness, hopelessness and despondency. ● Treatment: lithium

Cyclothymic disorder is a personality characterized by mood swings from highs to lows, which are not as extreme as in the bipolar disorder.

HALLUCINATION is where a person experiences a sight, sound or other sensation (sensory impression) without there being any real stimulus in the environ-ment to cause the sensation.

DELUSION is a strong irrational belief about reality, that is, however, opposed to reality and that is maintained in spite of logical evidence to the contrary. Delusions are usually associated with paranoid states.
Delusion of grandeur: thinking you are Jesus or Napoleon or famous.
Delusion of persecution: persons or groups are out to get you.
Delusion of reference: people are always talking about you.

PARANOID DISORDERS are characterized by strong delusionary beliefs about oneself or one's culture or world view.

SCHIZOPHRENIC DISORDERS
Simple (undifferentiated) type is a psychosis marked by personality disorganization, detachment from reality and meaningful interpersonal relationships, disturbed thought processes (perhaps hallucinations or delusions), and emotional blunting.
Disorganized schizophrenia is marked by the above plus shallow and inappropriate emotion, unpredictable giggling and silly mannerisms.
Paranoid schizophrenia may include some of the symptoms of simple schizo-phrenia plus paranoid delusions of the types mentioned above. These delusions are personal and fragmented compared with the paranoid state which delusions may include a complete world view.
Catatonic schizophrenia may be marked by symptoms of the simple type plus disturbances of motor activity. The person may become physically rigid and immobile in ordinarily awkward positions. Sometimes catatonic schizophrenia may include rapid irrational motor activity such as walking.
Process schizophrenia is long-standing (perhaps from teen years) and gradual in its onset, whereas reactive schizophrenia is rapid in its onset, without any history, and is more curable.

Treatment: phenothiazines
(but: tardive dyskinesia)

Labels (handwritten): FEELING, MOTOR, THINKING, CHRONIC

Richard Schmidt
Intro to Psych

20 questions are diagnosis - type

I want to wash
my more
my more

COPING WITH STRESS

Stress, an engineering term, was first applied to humans in the 1930s by a Montreal researcher, Hans Selye, who became the world's leading authority on stress. Selye defined stress as "the body's nonspecific response to any demand placed upon it, whether that demand is pleasant or unpleasant." Stress has a profound effect on the sympathetic nervous system, the endocrine glands (pituitary, adrenal), and the entire immune system. Death is due to the cumulative effect of stress over a lifetime.

TYPES OF STRESSORS:

Hans Selye (1956)

Physical stressors:
   temperature, fatigue, strenuous activity, microorganisms, etc.
Chemical stressors:
   tobacco, alcohol, drugs, caffeine, air and water pollutants, lack of nutrients.
Psychological stressors:
   threat or fear, failure, frustration (having a path to a goal blocked), conflict (types), anger, tension, purposelessness, overwork, time pressure, etc.
Social stressors:
   criticism, conflict, unhappiness in relations with family, friends, and colleagues at work, etc.

Holmes and Rahe (1967)

Life changes (43) measured on the Social Readjustment Rating Scale.

Organizational Sources of Work Stress

work overload, underutilization, job uncertainty, lack of control, lack of meaningfulness, change, interpersonal relations.

EFFECTS OF STRESS:

GENERAL ADAPTATION SYNDROME (Hans Selye)

(1) The alarm reaction
(2) The stage of resistance (sympathetic and endocrine responses)
(3) The stage of exhaustion (resistance capabilities decrease)

SPECIFIC EFFECTS OF STRESS

(1) Psychosomatic illness (an actual physical, organic illness with emotional or stress-related causes). Examples: hypertension, peptic ulcers, headaches, backaches, etc.

(2) Physical illness (Holmes and Rahe, 1967, Social Readjustment Rating Scale). [What causes disease? Microorganisms or one's decreased resistance or immunity? Immunity is affected by genetic weakness and stress factors.] Examples: coronary heart disease, etc.

(3) Psychological, emotional and behavioral problems.
   (a) tension, anxiety, irritability, depression, low self-esteem, fatigue, resentment;
   (b) neurotic and psychotic behaviors.

(4) Burnout stages:
   (a) emotional exhaustion
   (b) cynicism (and lack of sensitivity)
   (c) futility

INDIVIDUAL WAYS OF HANDLING STRESS:

(1) Eliminate stressors

(2) Increase one's stress tolerance:

   (a) Modify personality from Type A towards Type B.

   (b) General relaxation training:
      i. meditation
      ii. progressive relaxation
      iii. biofeedback training
      iv. taking time for aesthetics

(3) Develop cognitive reappraisal strategies. [Lazarus & Folkman define stress (with a cognitive emphasis) as the feeling we get when we interpret or appraise a situation as being threatening or challenging and when our personal resources are strained or outstripped.] Cognitive appraisal is our evaluation of how threatening or challenging events are to our personal resources.

   (a) Cultivate hardiness [a sense of having an internal locus of control, commitment, and sense of challenge].

   (b) Cultivate positive attitudes [adopting the right attitude can convert negative stress (distress) into positive stress (eustress).]

(4) Develop coping skills that are problem-focused rather than emotion-focused. Substitute action for anxiety.

(5) Develop social support.

(6) Develop good nutrition and exercise programs.

An American psychologist, trained and taught at Harvard University. The leading American behaviorist today.

(Operant behavior is behavior emitted by an organism which does not seem to have an observable preceding stimulus causing it.)

(Operant level (rate), the rate at which a response occurs normally and naturally without reinforcement.

Three possibilities with behavior:
1) Increase behavior.
2) Decrease behavior.
3) Create new behavior.

(1) Procedures to increase behavior:

REINFORCER: Any event which follows a response and <u>increases its likelihood of occurrence</u> (strengthens it).

TYPES OF REINFORCERS:

(a) MATERIAL REINFORCERS: Tangible items such as food, jewelry, clothes, toys, books, etc.
(b) ACTIVITY REINFORCERS: Things a person likes to do, such as skating, television, recess, activity center, playing, reading, etc.
(c) SOCIAL REINFORCERS: Recognition, attention, approval, praise, feedback, etc.
(d) TOKEN REINFORCERS: Anything given which can be exchanged for material, activity, or social reinforcers.

(2) Procedures for creating new behavior:

(a) <u>Shaping</u>: molding an organisms responses by reinforcing successive approximations of the desired response until only the desired response is made and reinforced.

(b) <u>Modeling</u>: demonstrating (presenting an example of) the exact behavior to be performed.

(c) <u>Prompting</u>: using words, gestures, signs, or physical assistance to make it more likely a new behavior will be performed correctly.

(3) Procedures for decreasing behavior:

(a) Withhold reinforcer of the behavior (including attention, etc.) to get extinction. (Temporary spontaneous recovery may occur.)

(b) Countercondition. Decrease a response by reinforcing a response that is opposite to or incompatible with the unwanted response. For example, condition a child to share (if he has previously been fighting).

(c) Give punishment. This may not eliminate the learning, only suppress performance. A child may imitate the aggressive behavior if physical punishment is used.

TIME-OUT is a punishment procedure for decreasing behavior. It is defined as the temporary removal of an individual from reinforcing events or situations for a brief, specified period of time, and to a specified place, every time a specified inappropriate behavior occurs.

RESPONSE COST is a punishment procedure for decreasing behavior by taking away a reward, tokens, or privilege when the behavior occurs.

A Russian physiologist and pharmacologist, he became world renowned for his research on blood circulation and the digestive glands. In 1904 he was awarded the Nobel Prize for his work on the physiology of digestion. In 1902 Pavlov set forth a theory of conditioning which was discovered as he researched saliva output in dogs. He discovered techniques for causing experimental neuroses in dogs, and during the latter part of his life (1928-36), he concentrated on applying conditioning techniques in psychiatric clinics.

Classical (respondent, reflex) conditioning

According to _____ Pavlov, our repertory of responses at birth are reflex responses and any new behaviors that are learned are learned through reflex conditioning. All learned behaviors are conditioned reflexes. All human behavior is either reflex or conditioned reflex, and all learning can be explained through classical conditioning. This still tends to be the Soviet explanation for learning, but in the United States other theoretical explanation of learning have been preferred.

In an <u>inborn reflex</u>, an unconditioned stimulus elicit the unconditioned response.
In the process of <u>reflex conditioning</u>, a neutral stimulus is repeatedly presented immediately prior to the unconditioned stimulus (and thus they become associated as a result of this contiguity and repetition).
In a <u>conditioned reflex</u>, the neutral stimulus has become a <u>conditioned stimulus</u> which can elicit the reflex response (now called the <u>conditioned response</u>.

When a neutral stimulus is paired with an unconditioned stimulus a number of times, it gains the ability to elicit the same response as the unconditioned stimulus.

INBORN REFLEX:	US {meat}	→ UR {salivation}
REFLEX CONDITIONING:	NS (bell) + US {meat}	→ UR {salivation}
CONDITIONED REFLEX:	CS (bell)	→ CR {salivation}

<u>Experimental extinction</u> is the gradual disappearance of a CR when the CS is repeated without being reinforced occasionally by the US.

<u>Spontaneous recovery</u>: After extinction and after a number of hours has elapsed, the CS may again temporarily elicit a CR.

<u>Reinforcement</u>: The process of following the CS by the US occasionally to strengthen the elicitation of the CR (i.e., to prevent extinction).

<u>Stimulus generalization</u>: when other stimuli similar to the CS also elicit the CR.

<u>Discrimination</u>: When other stimuli, perhaps similar to the CS, do not elicit the CR, i.e., when the organism responds differentially to two different (although perhaps similar) stimuli.

JOHN WATSON (1878-1958)

An American psychologist, born in Greenville, S.C. He graduated from the University of Chicago with his Ph.D. in 1903; founded "behaviorism" in 1913.

Watson adopted the classical conditioning ideas of Pavlov as his basic explanation for learning. All learning is human emotional responses. One of Watson's prime areas of interest was human emotional responses. We felt that we are born with three <u>unconditioned emotional reflex responses</u> (innately).
(a) <u>fear</u> of loud noises or falling.
(b) <u>anger</u> when our movements are frustrated or we are hungry and not fed, and
(c) <u>love</u> when we are caressed or petted.

All other emotional reactions, and reactions to stimuli different from the above, are conditioned. He demonstrated this with a 9-month old fearless baby named Albert.

PARTS OF THE BRAIN

THALAMUS (L: little room, attic)

A body of millions of neurons. The relay station for ascending sensory fibers, and also descending motor fibers.

BRAIN STEM

Ascending and descending fibers connected to the spinal cord. Reflex centers for heart, respiration, and peristalsis. (Karen Ann Quinlan)—*Brain dead, lived w/o life support.*

LIMBIC SYSTEM

Numerous bodies beneath the cerebrum that work together as a system. The seat of motivation, emotion, and values.

HYPOTHALMUS (L: below the little room)

Part of the limbic system. Regulates metabolism (*define*), and drives such as hunger, thirst, temperature, sex. Manufactures at least three hormones that are stored in the pituitary gland. Controls the pituitary gland.

PITUITARY GLAND

The master gland of the body. It releases 9+ hormones into the bloodstream which control other glands.

CEREBELLUM (L: little cerebrum)

Controls balance, posture, muscular coordination, and muscle tone. Smooths out movements which originate in the cerebral cortex. (Example: a cat without a cerebellum.)

CEREBRUM (L: brain)   (Sometimes cortex or neocortex.)

The largest part of the brain. It has 6 strata (levels) of neurons from the surface to the center.

CEREBRAL CORTEX (Cortex L: bark, outer layer)

Consists mainly of projection areas for sense perception, and motor control.

ASSOCIATION AREAS

The five inner levels of neurons in the cerebrum. The center of learning, remembering, thinking, etc.

RETICULAR ACTIVATING SYSTEM

Neural fibers from the brain stem that spread to all areas of the cerebrum, and through their general stimulation, control the level of arousal or consciousness of the cerebrum.

CEREBRAL HEMIPHERIC SPECIALIZATION

LEFT HEMISPHERE

Language dominant in 97% of adults:
(a) Right-handers who write normal
(b) Left-handers who write hooked

Right body motor control
Right body sensations

ANALYTIC INFORMATION PROCESSING

Language abilities (Broca's & Wernicke's areas)
Mathematical calculations
Logical, sequential reasoning
Using symbols

RIGHT HEMISPHERE

Language dominant in 3% of adults:
(a) Right-handers who write hooked
(b) Left-handers who write normal

Left body motor control
Left body sensations

HOLISTIC INFORMATION PROCESSING

Visual processing
Spatial relations (depth, distance judgments)
Pattern recognition (faces, body image, etc.)
Intuitive thinking

CORPUS
CALLOSUM
FIBERS

Sperry
Split-brain surgery for epilepsy

THE MELZACK-WALL "SPINAL GATE" THEORY OF PAIN

Touch nerve fibers and pain nerve fibers from a certain portion of the body or surface of the skin (dermatome) enter into the same spinal cord segment.

Intensely stimulated touch fibers are faster and appear to block the activity or firing of the slower pain fibers just as they enter the spinal cord.

Both sets of fibers must enter the same spinal cord segment (that is, they must be from the same dermatome.)

NERVOUS SYSTEM CONCEPTS

Ricky Schmidt

CENTRAL

PERIPHERAL

I. ORGANIZATION OF THE NERVOUS SYSTEM

    A. Central Nervous System   Brain and spinal cord.

    B. Peripheral Nervous System   Nerves connecting the CNS to the effec-
                                    tors (muscles, glands) and receptors.

        Body
      1) Somatic Nervous System   Nerves servicing external receptors and
                                    skeletal muscles.

       Visceral
      2) Autonomic Nervous System   Nerves regulating internal activity of
       ↳*Self-regulating*   the body (organs, glands, blood vessels)

        a) Parasympathetic Division Normal regulatory functions.

        b) Sympathetic Division   Emergency regulatory functions.

II. BASIC UNITS OF THE NERVOUS SYSTEM

    A. Anatomy of the Neuron: cell body, nucleus, dendrites, axon, axon end-
       ings (synaptic knobs), synapse, motor end plate, myelin sheath, node
       of Ranvier; multiple sclerosis.

    B. Types of Nerves: afferent or sensory, efferent or motor, and associ-
       ation neurons.

    C. The Spinal Reflex (Sensory-Motor Reflex Arc).

    D. Supporting Cells, e.g., glial cells, myelin sheath.

    E. Neuronal (Axonal) Transmission

      (1) electrical in nature;
      (2) all-or-none principle (a nerve fiber does not fire unless the   *— like a rifle*
          intensity of stimulation is above a certain threshold, then it *(trigger pressure*
          fires full strength);   *doesn't matter)*
      (3) threshold (the minimum stimulation necessary to cause a neuron to
         fire);
      (4) action potential (the electrical discharge of neuron when firing); *the voltage*
      (5) absolute refractory period (the period immediately after firing
         when a neuron cannot fire again); *can only fire 1,000 x's sec.* *Normally transmits fires 100 x's/sec.*
      (6) relative refractory period (the period following the absolute
         refractory period when only strong stimulation can cause a
         neuron to fire). *NEURO-TRANSMITTER SUBSTANCES (≈ 20 different chemicals)*

    F. Synaptic Transmission

      (1) chemical discharge;
      (2) more-or-less principle, summation (the chemical secreted across the
         synapse can vary according to the number of stimulated presynap-
         tic neurons converging on the postsynaptic neuron).

III. BRAIN STRUCTURE

    A. Central core
      (a) medulla, brain stem
      (b) thalamus (*"little room"*)
      (c) cerebellum
      (d) reticular activating system
    B. Limbic system
      (a) hypothalamus
      (b) pituitary gland
      (c) hippocampus
    C. Cerebrum
      (a) lobes (frontal, parietal, occipital, temporal);
      (b) outer layer (cerebral cortex): sensory (touch, vision, hearing) and
         motor projection areas;
      (c) inner layers: association areas for learning and memory;
      (d) hemispheres: specializations, corpus callosum, split-brain, Sperry,
         epilepsy, Broca's language area;
      (e) brain waves.

IV. OTHER CONCEPTS

    homeostasis

PRINCIPLE DEBATES: What should psychology investigate?
What methods should be used?
What are humans like in their basic nature?

CONTEMPORARY SCHOOLS   **HISTORICAL SCHOOLS**

SCHOOL OF THOUGHT WITHIN PSYCHOLOGY	PRINCIPLE PERSON(S)	AREA OF INTEREST AND STUDY
Structuralism	Wundt 1879 (1875) (Germany)	THE STUDY OF THE CONTENTS (ELEMENTS) OF THE CONSCIOUS MIND (SPECIFICALLY, SENSATIONS, FEELINGS, AND IMAGES) THROUGH INTROSPECTIVE ANALYSIS.
Gestaltism	ca. 1912 (Germany)	THE STUDY OF THE GESTALTS' (ORGANIZED PATTERNS OR WHOLES) OF PERCEPTION. [CONSCIOUSNESS CANNOT BE ANALYZED, OR IT LACKS MEANING. "THE WHOLE IS GREATER THAN THE SUM OF THE PARTS."] *more important*
Functionalism	Wm. James 1875 (U.S.A.)	THE USEFULNESS OF OUR MENTAL PROCESSES. HOW THE MIND AND BEHAVIOR ENABLES ONE TO COPE WITH THE ENVIRONMENT.
Psychoanalysis	Sigmund Freud ca. 1900 (Austria)	ABNORMAL BEHAVIOR AND THE UNCONSCIOUS MIND. *-said adult personality formed by age of 5. felt basic drive: animal nature, bad*
Behaviorism	John Watson 1913 (U.S.A.)	THE STUDY OF OBSERVABLE, MEASURABLE BEHAVIOR, NOT CONSCIOUSNESS. THE STUDY OF... *felt human nature was neutral. bad/good depends on learning*
Cognitive Psychology	(U.S.A.)	THE STUDY OF COGNITIVE PROCESSES (THINKING, KNOWLEDGE, IDEAS, MEMORY, LEARNING, ETC.) THAT LIE BEHIND BEHAVIOR.
Humanistic Psychology	1930's Carl Rogers Abraham Maslow (U.S.A.)	THE STUDY OF PERSONALITY AND THERAPY AND THE INBORN POTENTIALS FOR GROWTH OF PERSONS. *felt people were good by birth; basic drive: self-actualization*

Takes best from **ECLECTIC**

A PSYCHIATRIST
- has an M.D. in Medicine plus 3 years of psychiatric internship in a hospital (does not have a Psychology degree)
- diagnoses and treats emotional & personality problems
- relies heavily on pharmaceuticals, with some psychotherapy, and hospitalization, and perhaps shock treatment

A CLINICAL PSYCHOLOGIST
- has a Ph.D. or Psy.D. in Psychology plus 2 years of supervision in a clinical setting
- diagnoses and treats emotional & personality problems
- uses counseling, psychotherapy, behavior modification, and psychological testing

A PSYCHOANALYST
is a psychiatrist or psychologist with 3 additional years of training at a Psychoanalytic Institute

THE EXPERIMENTAL METHOD
—MUST READ TEXT—
(esp. bold)

A hypothesis: a suspected or predicted relationship between two variables or events, usually between a stimulus and behavior.

A stimulus: anything that influences behavior.

THE STIMULUS VARIABLE (INDEPENDENT VARIABLE) → THE RESULTING BEHAVIOR (DEPENDENT VARIABLE)

Experiment: testing a hypothesis under carefully controlled conditions.

Variables involved in an experiment:
Independent variable: the factor whose effects are being examined in an experiment. It is changed in some systematic and predetermined manner while other variables are controlled. ("the experimental treatment" is the ind. var.)

Dependent variable: In an experiment, the factor which the hypothesis predicts will change with changes in the independent variable.

2/1